America COOKS

The General Federation
of Women's Clubs
COOK BOOK

The General Federation
of Women's Clubs
COOK BOOK

America COOKS

Edited by Ann Seranne

G. P. PUTNAM'S SONS, NEW YORK

Foreword

Founded in 1890, the General Federation of Women's Clubs, the oldest and largest women's service organization in existence, has been dedicated to the task of uniting women's clubs for consolidated efforts to improve the communities of this nation and of the world. In the many decades that have passed since the Federation came into being, it has energetically engaged in numerous programs to achieve this goal. Among these programs is one that centers on home life, and *America Cooks: The General Federation of Women's Clubs Cook Book* is a project that drew its impetus from the manifold interests and activities of the GFWC's Home Life Department.

Launching a completely new, major, all-purpose cook book is an enormous undertaking under any circumstances. However, *America Cooks*, which sought not only to achieve perfection as a basic cook book but also to establish a new modern standard in American cuisine as it exists today in every area of the country, presented formidable problems of a special nature. These problems could not have been met and overcome without the unstinting cooperation of the national officers of the GFWC and the state chairmen of the Home Life Department who made it possible to reach the women of America and invite them to contribute their favorite treasured recipes as candidates for inclusion in this unprecedented cook book.

As a result of announcements in the national bulletin of the GFWC and special announcements by the Home Life Department in each state, more than a million individual tested recipes and cooking hints were received. From this mass of material the editor selected the best recipes, organized them in sections and chapters, arranged them in systematic order and edited them for ease of preparation and consistency. In addition, the recipes were checked and rechecked by special consultants who assisted the editor in making the final selections.

The choice of which recipes to include and which to omit was neither easy nor simple. Many recipes were exact duplications or merely offered minor variations in ingredients. In these cases priority was given to those recipes which were received first, and on occasion the factor determining selection was the necessity to provide broader regional representation so that no area of the country would be overlooked. Some excellent recipes had to be bypassed because they called for the use of unusual ingredients that were not available outside a small local area.

Every recipe in the book is attributed to the woman who submitted it and her club or, when the recipes were not individually signed, to the club itself. Recipes signed *A. S.* have been contributed by the editor. In any undertaking so vast as this cook book, which has been in preparation for many years, it is impossible to keep abreast of changes that took place in the final months before publication. Although every effort was made to check current club titles of contributors, their latest place of residence, marital status, etc., we are aware of the fact that some changes have undoubtedly occurred. Needless to say, all errors of this nature will be corrected in subsequent editions of *America Cooks*, and it is our hope, too, that in the years to come many more recipes will be added to the already huge compendium of recipes now contained in this volume.

We wish to take this opportunity to thank the president and honorary presidents of the GFWC as well as all the national officers and the state chairmen of the Home Life Department for their interest in this volume and for the considerable assistance they have provided at every stage of its production. At the same time we wish to express our appreciation and gratitude for the cooperation of the thousands upon thousands of women—whether or not it proved feasible to include their contributions in these pages—who were instrumental in turning this long-nurtured dream of a truly modern national American cook book into reality.

THE PUBLISHERS

Contents

Foreword 5

Introduction 11

KITCHEN HINTS 15

Essential Information for Every Cook ... 15
  General Hints 15
  Baking Hints 15
  Beverage Hints 16
  Bread Hints 16
  Economy Hints 16
  Egg Hints 16
  Frosting and Topping Hints 17
  Fruit Hints 17
  Meat, Poultry and Fish Hints 17
  Pudding Hints 18
  Salad Hints 18
  Sauce and Gravy Hints 18
  Soup and Stew Hints 19
  Storing Hints 19
  Vegetable Hints 19
Substitutions 20
What Makes What? 21
Table of Measurements 22
How to Measure 22
Food for Fifty 23
Simple Rules of Cooking 24
Meal Planning 25
Nutrition—A Part of Menu Planning ... 25
Nutrients of Familiar Foods 26
Calorie Chart 26
Pot and Pan Dimensions 34
Commercial Can Sizes 34
Servings and Pounds 34
Herbs, Seeds and Spices 36
Wine and Spirits in Cooking 37
Wine Cookery Chart 37
Oven Temperature Chart 38
Baking Chart 38
Pressure Cooking 39
Canning 39
Home Freezing 41
Glossary of Cooking Terms 42

1. APPETIZERS 47

First-Course Appetizers 47
  Fruit and Vegetable Juices 47
  Fruit Cocktails 49
  Seafood Cocktails 50
  Seafood Cocktail Sauces 52
Cocktail Snacks and Wafers 53
Hors d'Oeuvres 57
  Cold Hors d'Oeuvres 57
  Hot Hors d'Oeuvres 65
Dips 71
Canapés and Party Sandwiches 77
  Cold Canapés and Party Sandwiches ... 77
  Hot Canapés 86

2. HEARTY SANDWICHES 91

  Cold Sandwiches 93
  Hot Sandwiches 96
  Beef Burgers 102
  Other Burgers 105
  Frankfurter Specials 106

3. QUICK BREADS 108

  Loaves 108
  Biscuits 119
  Muffins and Popovers 125
  Pancakes and Waffles 131
  Doughnuts and Fried Cakes 138

4. YEAST BREADS 143

  Breads 144
  Coffee Cakes 150
  Rolls and Biscuits 154
  Pancakes, Waffles and Doughnuts
  Ready-Made Breads and Toasts 167

5. SOUPS 170

  Stocks and Consommés 170
  Clear Meat, Chicken and Vegetable
    Soups 171
  Bean, Pea and Lentil Soups 177
  Gumbos, Chowders and Fish Stews ... 180
  Cream Soups and Bisques 185
  Cold Soups 191
  Quick Soups 193
  Soup Garnishes 195

6. EGGS AND EGG DISHES 197

  Eggs—A Variety of Dishes 197
  Hard-Cooked Egg Dishes 201
  Omelets 205
  Soufflés 207

7. CHEESE AND CHEESE DISHES 210

8. FISH, SHELLFISH AND OTHER
FOODS PREPARED LIKE FISH 217

Fish 217
  All About Fish 217
  Methods of Cooking Fish 218
Shellfish 237
  Abalone 237
  Clams 238
  Conches 239
  Crabs 240
  Crayfish 244
  Lobsters 244
  Mussels 248
  Oysters 248
  Scallops 251
  Shrimp 252

Mixed Seafood Dishes   257
Frogs' Legs   258
Snails   258
Terrapin and Turtle   259

9. POULTRY AND GAME BIRDS   260
All About Chicken and Other Poultry 260
Timetable for Roasting Stuffed
    Poultry   261
How to Carve a Bird   261
Chicken   262
    Basic Methods of Cooking Chicken 262
    Baked Chicken   264
    Braised Chicken   271
    Stewed Chicken   275
    Chicken Breasts   280
    Cooked Chicken Dishes   284
Chicken Livers   290
Rock Cornish Game Hen   291
Guinea Fowl   292
Squab   292
Turkey   293
Goose   294
Duck   295
Game Birds   296
    Dove   296
    Grouse   296
    Partridge   296
    Pheasant   297
    Quail   297
    Wild Duck   298
    Wild Goose   299

10. MEAT   300
All About Meat   300
Meat Cuts and Their Preparation
    (Charts)   302
Beef   301
    How to Carve Beef Roasts   301
    How to Carve a Steak   301
    Timetable for Cooking Beef   306
    Large Cuts of Beef   307
    Steaks   308
    Pot Roasts   312
    Corned Beef   315
    Dried Beef   316
    Braised Steaks   317
    Beef Goulashes, Stews and Pies 320
    Hamburgers, Meat Balls and Meat
        Loaves   324
    Ground Beef Dishes   330
    Cooked Beef Dishes   338
    Frankfurters   339
Pork   340
    Timetable for Cooking Pork   341
    Pork Roasts   341
    Pork Chops   343
    A Variety of Pork Dishes   346
    Spareribs   348
    Ham   350
    How to Carve a Ham   350
    Sausage   356
Veal   358
    Timetable for Cooking Veal   358
Lamb   364
    Timetable for Cooking Lamb   365
    How to Carve Lamb Roasts   365
    Roast Lamb   365
    Lamb Steaks and Chops   367
    Lamb Shanks   368
    Lamb Casseroles and Stews   369

Ground Lamb Dishes   371
Cooked Lamb Dishes   372
Specialty Meats   373
    Brains   373
    Kidneys   373
    Liver   374
    Sweetbreads   376
    Tongue   377
Game   378

11. VEGETABLES   383
    Frying Batter for Vegetables   383
Artichokes   383
Jerusalem Artichokes   384
Asparagus   385
Avocado   386
Bananas   387
Beans   387
Snap or String Beans   387
Lima or Butter Beans   391
Beets   392
Broccoli   394
Brussels Sprouts   395
Cabbage   396
Red Cabbage   397
Cabbage Palm   398
Chinese Cabbage   398
Carrots   398
Cauliflower   400
Celery   402
Celery Root (Celeriac)   403
Chard (Swiss Chard)   403
Chayote (Mexican Squash)   403
Chestnuts   403
Corn   404
Cucumbers   407
Dasheen   407
Eggplant   407
Endive   411
Fennel   411
Greens (Turnip, Mustard, Beet, Kale, 411
    etc.)
Kale   411
Kohlrabi (Turnip Cabbage)   411
Leeks   411
Lentils   411
Lettuce   411
Mushrooms   412
Okra   413
Onions   414
Oyster Plant (Salsify)   416
Parsnips   416
Peas   416
Peppers, Green and Red   418
Potatoes   418
    Basic Ways to Cook Potatoes   419
    Baked Potatoes   420
    Fried Potatoes   421
    Potato Pancakes   422
    Raw Potato Dishes   422
    Cooked Potato Dishes   424
    Mashed Potato Dishes   425
Sweet Potatoes   426
Radish   429
Sauerkraut   429
Spinach   430
Squash   432
Tomatoes   434
Turnips   436
Water Chestnuts   437

Zucchini 437
Mixed Vegetable Dishes 438

12. SAUCES FOR FISH, POULTRY, MEAT AND VEGETABLES 441

13. STUFFINGS AND GARNISHES FOR FISH, POULTRY, MEAT AND VEGETABLES 452

Stuffings 452
Garnishes 456

14. DUMPLINGS AND OTHER STARCH SUBSTITUTES 460

Dumplings 460
Cereals 463
  Corn Meal 464
  Farina (Cream of Wheat) 465
  Hominy 466
  Barley 467
  Bulgur (Cracked Wheat) 467
  Kasha (Buckwheat Groats) 468
Dried Beans, Peas and Lentils 468

15. RICE AND RICE DISHES 473

Rice—A Variety of Dishes 473
Fried Rice 476
Baked Rice Dishes 478
Rice Dishes with Fish or Seafood 480
Rice Dishes with Poultry 482
Rice Dishes with Meat 485
Wild Rice 487

16. PASTA DISHES AND SAUCES FOR PASTA 490

Noodles 490
Filled Pasta Dishes 496
Macaroni 498
Spaghetti 502
Sauces for Pasta 505

17. SALADS AND SALAD DRESSINGS 508

Tossed Green Salads 508
Bean and Vegetable Salads Vinaigrette 509
Bean and Vegetable Salads with Cream or Mayonnaise 512
Macaroni, Potato and Rice Salads 515
Fish and Shellfish Salads 518
Chicken and Meat Salads 520
Fruit Salads 522
Frozen Salads 525
Molded Salads 526
Aspics 537
Savory Mousses 540
Salad Dressings 541

18. PIES AND PASTRIES 547

Equipment for Pie Baking 547
Baking Temperatures for Pies 547
Common Causes of Failure in Making Pies 547
How to Make a 2-Crust Pie 547
How to Make a 1-Crust Pie 547
How to Make a Pie Shell 547
How to Make a Lattice-Topped Pie 548
Piecrusts 548
2-Crust Pies 553
1-Crust Pies 555

Pie Fillings for Baked Pie Shells and Crumb Crusts 563
Crustless Pies 576
Tarts, Turnovers and Small Pastries 577

19. CAKES 583

How to Make Good Cakes 583
Frosting the Cake 583
Freezing Cakes 584
Storing Cakes 584
Simplified Chart for High-Altitude Cake Baking 584
Cake Pan Substitutes 584
White Cakes 585
Yellow Cakes 586
Chocolate Cakes 590
Butterscotch and Caramel Cakes 594
Fruit-Flavored Cakes 596
Spice Cakes 601
Poundcakes 603
Coffee Cakes 604
Upside-Down Cakes 608
Angel, Chiffon and Sponge Cakes 609
Fruitcakes 612
Cheesecakes 615
Tortes 616
Cupcakes 619

20. FROSTINGS AND FILLINGS 622

Sugar Frostings 622
Creamy Frostings 623
Cooked Frostings 625
Glazes and Toppings 629
Soft Cooked Fillings 630

21. COOKIES 633

Rolled Cookies 634
Drop Cookies 637
Molded or Pressed Cookies 645
Refrigerator Cookies 650
Pan Cookies 652
No-Bake Cookies 659

22. DESSERTS 663

Baked and Steamed Puddings 664
Creamy Desserts and Custards 676
Gelatin Desserts 679
Crumb and Cake Desserts 683
Frozen Desserts 687
Fruit Desserts 694
Meringue Desserts 696
Dessert Pancakes and Fritters 697
Sweet Omelets and Soufflés 698

23. DESSERT SAUCES 700

24. CANDY 704

Rules for Candy Making 704
Cooking Syrups 704
Degrees and Stages of Boiling Syrups 704
Cold-Water Tests 704
Pulling Taffy 704
Chocolate Dipping 704
Coloring Sugar 705
Candied Fruit 705
Fudge, Penuche, Creams, Fondant and Pralines 705
Caramels 709
Divinities, Taffies and Nougat 710

Butterscotch and Toffees   711
Brittles and Hard Candies   712
Uncooked Confections   713

25. PRESERVES   716

Types of Preserves   716
Rules for Successful Preserving   716
Out-of-Season Jams, Jellies and
    Conserves   716
Test for Pectin   716
Test for Acid   717
Jelly-Making Properties of Fruit   717
How Much Sugar?   717
Test for Jellying Stage   717
Sterilizing Jars   717

Sealing with Paraffin   717
Jams and Jellies   717
*Preserves, Conserves, Marmalades
    and Chutneys*   720
Pickles, Relishes and Condiments   723

26. BEVERAGES   732

The Service of Wine   732
General Guide to the Service of
    Wine   732
Tea   732
Coffee   733
Hot Beverages   733
Cold Beverages   737

INDEX   743

Introduction

The recipes in *America Cooks: The General Federation of Women's Clubs Cook Book* come from every state in the Union—from rural areas and small towns and from great city complexes—and among them are the favorites of Mrs. Lyndon B. Johnson, Mrs. Jacqueline Kennedy, Mrs. Hubert Humphrey, Senator Margaret Chase Smith, Mrs. Harry Truman, Mrs. Dwight Eisenhower, to mention only a few, set side by side with recipes contributed by thousands of women in every walk of life who share the same avid interest in cooking well for their own pleasure and for the pleasure and health of their families.

All the recipes are tested favorites of the women of America. Although many are family secrets—handed down, in some cases, for generations—they all reflect how the American homemaker cooks today, not how Grandmother used to cook. This book shows how to prepare an almost infinite variety of delicious simple dishes, as well as gourmet dishes, which the American homemaker daily sets on her table or proudly presents to guests on special occasions.

No longer are there any state lines or international boundaries in cooking, for American homemakers have borrowed recipes from every state in the Union, from every country in the world. Here we find hush puppies from Utah, Texas chili from Minnesota and Boston baked beans from California; sukiyaki from Ohio, sweet and sour spareribs from North Dakota and enchiladas from Tennessee. The influence of Mexican, Chinese, French, Italian, German, Hungarian, Swedish and many other cultures is widespread in the land and is strongly reflected in the recipes in this book. All the recipes, however, have been adapted to American tastes and have been tested in the most important testing ground of all—the American kitchen. Short cuts are often applied to classic methods that kept our grandmothers in the kitchen all day, and imaginative substitutions have been made for obscure ingredients; but the original flavors remain unsurpassed and superb.

No longer is American cooking based on poultry, steaks and chops, as delicious and nourishing as these may be. American cooks have learned to be creative with fish, with vegetables, with the lesser cuts of meat, and have become proficient in the preparation of gourmet sauces. Exotic spices and herbs have become staples in every American kitchen and are used with a knowing hand. Today the food eaten in American homes is an interesting blend of textures and flavors in keeping with the economy and vitality of our time.

America Cooks is the new twentieth-century basic all-purpose cook book, written by the best cooks in the country, representing the finest cooking in the United States. As such, it not only sets the standard for an up-to-date modern American cuisine, but makes a valuable contribution to international cuisine as well.

ANN SERANNE

America COOKS

The General Federation
of Women's Clubs
COOK BOOK

Kitchen Hints

Essential Information for Every Cook

GENERAL HINTS

- A shaker of mixed salt and pepper kept near the stove is very useful. Use ¾ parts salt to ¼ part pepper.
- When food is scorched, set the pan immediately in cold water to eliminate the burned taste from the food that was not scorched.
- A peeled potato or two simmered in oversalted soup for a little while will absorb excess salt. Discard the potato.
- To save washing extra cups and spoons, first measure dry ingredients; put them on waxed paper; then use the same cup or spoon for measuring liquids or fats.
- Dinner for one? Save TV dinner trays. Put leftovers in compartments, and freeze or refrigerate. There's a whole dinner ready in a jiffy.
- Chewing gum while peeling onions helps prevent tears.
- To keep the kitchen cool, use a covered electric skillet for cooking a small roast or meat loaf or for baking a few potatoes.
- A few unshelled pecans in the saucepan used to cook collards, kale, etc., will help keep odor down.
- Boil several cloves in a cup of water to rid the house of objectionable food odors, especially seafood.
- When cooking onions or cabbage, boil a little vinegar in a saucepan; it will remove the odor of the cooking vegetables.
- When boiling cauliflower, add a piece of white bread to eliminate odor.
- When doubling a recipe, don't double the seasonings until you taste the dish.
- If you need a lot of ice cubes for a party, remove them from trays and store them in plastic bags in freezer.
- If you have trouble cleaning a grater after grating cheese, rub raw potato over it before washing.
- A few drops of ammonia dropped into greasy pans before hot water is poured in will make them much easier to clean.
- To cool a hot dish in a hurry, place it in a pan of salted cold water. It will cool more rapidly than in plain cold water.
- To keep milk from sticking to a pan, first rub a little butter in the pan bottom.
- Lightly oil gelatin molds before filling. It makes for easier unmolding.
- Raw rice added to the salt shaker will keep salt free-flowing.
- After peeling onions, wash hands in cold water; then rub them with salt.

BAKING HINTS

- To make a fine-textured cake, add a few drops of boiling water to butter and sugar when creaming.
- When a custard pie shrinks from the crust, it has been baked in too hot an oven.
- When cutting cream pies, dip the knife in warm water, so none of the filling will stick to it.
- If a bread or cake browns too quickly before it is done, place a pan of warm water on the rack above it in the oven.
- Dredge dried fruits and nuts with some of the flour called for in a cake recipe to prevent them from sinking to the bottom of the pan during baking.
- For a rich piecrust, substitute light cream or sour cream for the liquid in a packaged pastry mix.
- Shredded coconut added to unbaked pastry for a shell is great for a cream-style pie filling.
- Crisp and freshen cookies which have become soft by placing them in a very low oven for 5 minutes.
- Instead of using grease on a griddle when frying pancakes, try sprinkling it with a little salt. Pancakes will brown nicely and will not stick.
- For the best baked biscuits on meat pie, have the meat bubbling hot before the biscuits are placed on top. The biscuits will bake faster, and be lighter, and the bottoms will not get soggy. Use the same trick for fruit cobblers.

- A few drops of vinegar added to ice water when making pastry will make it flakier.
- When baking meringue kisses or shells, line the baking sheet with brown paper bag cut to fit.
- Keep a jar of vanilla sugar on hand for baking. Bury a piece of vanilla bean in an airtight jar of granulated sugar for several days before using.
- Black walnuts put through the meat grinder or ground in a blender and added to pumpkin pies greatly improve flavor.
- To prevent a cake from falling after putting the batter in a pan, lift up the pan, and drop it suddenly to the table to release air bubbles.
- Warming a pan before putting in the undercrust of a pie will keep the crust from becoming soft and soggy during baking.
- When carrying a meringue-topped pie any distance, insert four or more cocktail picks around the center. Then cover the pie with waxed paper. The picks will prevent the paper from coming in contact with the meringue.
- Roll out pastry between two sheets of waxed paper; when the top sheet is pulled off, the pastry can be turned into a pie plate with little effort.
- Coat pastry shells with egg white before baking to prevent a soggy crust.
- To melt chocolate over hot water, fit a piece of waxed paper in the top of a double saucepan, and place the chocolate on it. When the chocolate has melted, remove the paper, and transfer the chocolate with scraper to a mixing bowl. No pan to clean!
- A tablespoon of maple syrup added to pancake batter will improve the flavor.
- A teaspoon of wine added to the batter will prevent waffles from sticking to the waffle iron.

BEVERAGE HINTS

- Iced tea or coffee is greatly improved if the ice cubes are made of coffee or tea instead of water.
- You can avoid cloudiness in iced tea by letting freshly brewed tea cool to room temperature before refrigerating it. If the tea becomes cloudy, pour a little boiling water into it until it clears.
- For a new taste in tea, add a small bit of dried orange peel to the teapot.
- When making lemonade, put the lemons through a meat grinder. The juice will go twice as far and have a better flavor.
- For better iced fruit drinks, make a syrup with equal parts of sugar and water, and boil it for 8 minutes. Store it in the refrigerator.
- A dash of salt added to coffee that has been overcooked or reheated will freshen the taste.

BREAD HINTS

- To freshen French or Italian bread, hard rolls and so on, sprinkle the crust with cold water, and place it in a preheated 350° F. oven for 10 minutes.
- To make cutouts from bread slices, first freeze the bread to give it clean, sharp edges.
- Don't waste leftover sandwiches. Brush them with melted butter, and sauté. They are delicious and taste fresh.
- Dipping the knife in hot water before using it will make a fresh loaf of bread easier to slice.
- Fresh bread will keep its shape if cut with a hot knife.

ECONOMY HINTS

- Don't discard the rinds of grapefruits, oranges, or lemons. Grate them; put in tightly covered jars; store in refrigerator. They make excellent flavorings for cakes and frostings.
- To use the last bit of catsup from a bottle, pour in some oil and vinegar, and shake. It makes a delicious salad dressing.
- Green leaves on the outside of lettuce contain more vitamins than the inside leaves, so don't throw away any more than necessary.
- Don't throw away a stale loaf of bread. Wrap it in a damp cloth for about 1 minute. Then place it in preheated 350° F. oven for about 20 minutes. Serve warm.

EGG HINTS

- To prevent an egg from cracking while cooking in simmering water, pierce both ends with a needle before putting it in water.
- When poaching eggs, add a dash of vinegar or lemon juice to the water to keep the white from spreading.
- To cut hard-cooked eggs without breaking the yolks, dip the knife in water.
- Use a potato masher or pastry blender to chop hard-cooked eggs.
- When frying eggs, sprinkle a little flour into the fat to prevent splattering.

- A teaspoon of cold water added to egg whites while beating will almost double the quantity of stiffly beaten egg whites.
- To keep an omelet from collapsing, add a pinch of cornstarch and a pinch of confectioners' sugar to the yolks before folding in the whites.
- When hard-cooking eggs, add a tablespoon of salt to the water. This loosens the shells, and they come off easily.
- Before poaching eggs, rub the bottom of the pan with butter to prevent them from sticking and breaking. It also makes the pan easier to wash.
- To keep egg yolks, cover them with cold water; store in refrigerator.

FROSTING AND TOPPING HINTS

- To make a good quick frosting, boil a small potato until soft. Mash potato; then beat in confectioners' sugar and vanilla.
- Glaze the tops of rolls before baking with 1 egg white beaten lightly with 1 tablespoon milk.
- To keep boiled icing from getting hard, add ⅓ teaspoon vinegar during the cooking.
- A little flour or cornstarch sprinkled over the tops of cakes, will prevent the icing from running off.
- When melting chocolate to use in a frosting, add 1 teaspoon butter to every ounce of chocolate.
- In a meringue pie topping, never add more than 2 tablespoons sugar for each egg white. Spread the meringue right to pastry rim. Cool the baked pie slowly and away from drafts.
- When frosting cakes, dip the knife or spatula into cold water frequently.
- To glaze cakes and pastries, use 1 tablespoon milk in which a little brown sugar has been dissolved.
- To 1 cup heavy cream, whipped, add 2 teaspoons sugar and ½ teaspoon vanilla. For puddings and pies, add cinnamon or nutmeg.
- When cream won't whip, add a little lemon juice.
- For an attractive glazed top on a 2-crust pie, brush the pastry with light cream and sprinkle it with sugar before baking.
- Before putting meringue on a pie filling, make sure the filling is cool.
- A teaspoon of honey added to whipped cream sweetens it and gives a delicious flavor.
- A dash of salt added to cream during the whipping makes it whip very quickly.

FRUIT HINTS

- When thawing a frozen fruit, leave it in the unopened package. Exposure to air robs the fruit of some of its flavor and color.
- To ripen fruit, put it in a paper bag in a dark place for a few days.
- For full flavor, always cook dried fruit in same water in which it was soaked.
- Cut apples into quarters before peeling and coring, and the job will go much faster.
- When cooking fruit for jam or jelly, add a small piece of butter, and there will be no foam to skim off the top.
- If jelly does not set, place glasses in a drip pan half full of cold water, and bake it in moderate oven for 30 minutes.
- If citrus fruits are warmed in the oven for a few minutes, they will give much more juice.
- Lemons and limes will not wilt and shrink if stored in water and kept in the refrigerator. Place a small plate or saucer on the lemons to keep them underwater.
- To prevent apples and bananas used in salads from turning dark, sprinkle them with lemon juice.
- To plump raisins which have become too dry, wash them, and place them in a shallow dish. Bake them, covered, in a preheated 350° F. oven until they puff.
- Chopped dates mixed with apples in a pie or baked pudding offer a pleasant surprise.
- To ripen avocados quickly, tuck them in a wool sock, and put in a dark place.
- Ripe olives are made more delicious by soaking them overnight in olive oil to which a clove of garlic has been added.
- Pimientos keep longer in the refrigerator if a little vinegar is added to the juice.
- A simple dressing for fruit salad is grated orange rind and orange juice stirred into sour cream.
- Add sliced unpeeled orange to applesauce in the last few minutes of cooking.

MEAT, POULTRY AND FISH HINTS

- To flour meat, poultry or fish for frying, shake it in a brown paper bag containing flour and seasonings.
- If possible, always cut meat across instead of with the grain for easier eating and better appearance.
- Add a bit of rosemary to a ham loaf mixture for a complementary flavor.

- When baking a ham, slit the rind lengthwise on the underside before it is placed in the roasting pan. As it bakes, the rind will pull away and can be removed easily without lifting the ham from the pan.
- Don't salt roast beef or steak until it is three-fourths cooked in order to retain juices and flavor.
- For a delicious juicy hamburger steak, mix ¼ cup milk into each pound of ground beef.
- When boiling tough meat, add a little vinegar to make it tender.
- When frying bacon, sprinkle the slices with a little flour to keep them from curling.
- Rolling sausages in flour before frying will prevent their shrinking.
- Try baking a meat loaf mixture in greased muffin pans. It bakes faster and is attractive for individual servings.
- Add some ground salami to ground beef for a change of flavor in meat loaf.
- Quick-cooking oats make an excellent substitute for bread crumbs in a meat loaf or as a coating.
- A few slices of lemon added to stewing chicken will make it more tender and delicious.
- The easiest way to singe a fowl is to saturate a wad of cotton the size of a walnut with rubbing alcohol. Stick it onto end of a short wire, and light it. This never leaves any black marks.
- To stuff poultry quickly, use salad tongs to insert stuffing.
- When cooking venison or other game or game birds, put a few grapes in the pan to give a special flavor.
- Chopped toasted almonds add a pleasant crunchiness and make an attractive garnish for fish.
- The flavor of canned shrimp is improved if the can is soaked in ice water for 1 hour before it is opened.
- To clean shrimp, hold it under a slow stream of cold water, and run the tip of an icepick up the back of the shrimp. The shrimp is cleaned and remains whole.
- When frying fish, sprinkle the bottom of the skillet with salt to keep the fish from sticking.
- Pour boiling water over clams, and they will open more easily.
- A little grated onion added to butter in which fish is sautéed improves the flavor.

PUDDING HINTS

- For a flaming pudding, soak sugar cubes in orange or lemon extract. Place them on the pudding and ignite.
- To prevent skin from forming on a pudding, cover it with waxed paper while still hot.
- If a boiled custard curdles, remove it from heat, and beat it vigorously with a whisk.

SALAD HINTS

- Use sweet pickle juice instead of vinegar when making dressing for coleslaw.
- To make lettuce or salad greens crisp, add 1 tablespoon vinegar to a pan of water, and let the vegetables soak in it for 15 minutes.
- Salt crisp salad greens only before serving; otherwise salt will wilt the greens.
- Potato salad may be made more quickly and easily if the potatoes are peeled and diced or sliced before they are cooked.
- For a colorful touch when serving salad greens, fill a small bowl with water, and sprinkle paprika on the surface. Revolve the greens in the water. The leaves will be fringed with paprika.
- Celery stalks will be crisp and delicious if soaked in cold water containing 1 teaspoon sugar for about 1 hour.
- Parsley keeps fresher longer if stored in a tightly closed jar in the refrigerator.
- Sprinkle salads with grated Parmesan cheese after they are tossed in dressing.
- For a different coleslaw, add 1 cup seedless grapes to 4 cups shredded cabbage. Use a sour cream dressing.
- A little soy sauce and curry powder added to mayonnaise for turkey or chicken salad adds zest for those who like a spicy salad.

SAUCE AND GRAVY HINTS

- A pinch of salt added to flour before it is mixed with a liquid helps keep gravy from becoming lumpy.
- If a gravy does not brown, add a little coffee. There is no risk of the gravy taking on a coffee flavor.
- When making a meat gravy, try thinning it with the liquid in which vegetables have been cooked for added flavor.
- A dash of nutmeg in any white sauce works wonders.

- To remove excess fat from gravy or stew, wrap an ice cube in a piece of cheesecloth, and pull it back and forth over the surface. The fat will harden and stick to the cloth as it comes in contact with the ice.
- A tablespoon of cold water beaten into Hollandaise which has curdled will often bring it back to a smooth texture.

SOUP AND STEW HINTS

- Never let a soup or stew boil. It should barely simmer.
- A little oatmeal or quick-cooking oats add flavor and thickening to stew.
- Rub a bowl with garlic; then toss in freshly popped corn in melted butter. Serve on tomato soup.
- A touch of curry powder added to canned cream of chicken soup makes it a gourmet dish.
- Brown slices of frankfurter in butter, and add them to hot cream of pea soup.
- Grate a potato into a stew for a good thickener.
- To give canned soups a distinctive taste, add nutmeg to chicken or mushroom soup, curry to chicken soup with rice, orégano to tomato soup, chili powder to black bean soup and thyme to clam chowder. Heat tomato soup with a bay leaf.
- Garnish soups with paprika, finely cut chives or dill, grated cheese and slivers of ham or chicken. Slices of avocado are excellent for consommé, green pea or tomato soup.
- Store the liquid from canned vegetables, mushrooms, etc., in a large container in the freezer. It is a valuable addition to soup stock.

STORING HINTS

- To keep brown sugar soft, transfer it from the package to an airtight container. Store it in the refrigerator.
- Dampen a cloth; sprinkle it with vinegar and wrap it around cheese to keep it from hardening.
- Stick a garlic clove on a wooden pick before dropping it into a stew. This permits quick removal of the garlic.
- To keep cookies fresh and crisp, place a crumpled tissue in the bottom of the jar.
- To preserve the flavor of coffee after it has been ground, store it in refrigerator.
- To keep crisp cookies crisp and soft cookies soft, place only one kind in a jar.
- A cake will keep fresh longer if half an apple is put in the cake box.
- Before putting ground beef into the freezer, form the meat into patties; place each patty on a square of waxed paper; wrap each in freezer paper. Seasonings may be added before or during cooking.

VEGETABLE HINTS

- When cooking corn on the cob, add a little milk and dash of sugar to the cooking water.
- Use chili sauce, prepared mustard, Worcestershire, soy sauce or sour cream to season vegetables. This saves making a special sauce.
- Fried potatoes will be deliciously golden brown if sprinkled lightly with flour before frying.
- Most vegetables are improved by adding a dash of sugar to the cooking water.
- Sprinkling salt into water in which you are washing fresh vegetables will draw worms or insects to the surface.
- Rice grains will stay separated and white if 1 teaspoon lemon juice is added to each quart of water.
- Never salt turnips while they are cooking; it extracts the sweetness.
- Before cooking cauliflower, soak it, head down, for about 30 minutes in salted water to remove grit and insects.
- To clean spinach quickly, wash it in fairly warm water.
- A little cream poured over cooked vegetables makes them especially good.
- Herbs add a taste treat to buttered vegetables.
- Add chopped walnuts or pecans to wild rice during the last few minutes of cooking for a delicious flavor and aroma.
- Hot milk added to potatoes during the mashing will keep them from becoming soggy or heavy.
- For a crisp outer crust rub skins of baking potatoes with butter before baking.
- Bake potatoes in a muffin pan. The potatoes will not roll around and will be easy to remove from its oven.
- Before baking potatoes, soak them in salted water for 20 minutes or in hot water for 15 minutes, and they will bake more rapidly.
- As soon as potatoes are baked, prick them with a fork to release steam, so that they will not get soggy.
- Fresh tomatoes keep longer if stored with the stems down.
- A sherry-flavored mushroom sauce turns baked whole tomatoes into an unusual treat.

- When cooking fresh peas, add a few pods to the water to improve the flavor and color.
- Bake tomatoes, stuffed green peppers or apples in well-greased muffin pans. They will keep their shape better and be more attractive when served.
- Add a teaspoon of baking powder to potatoes when mashing; then beat them vigorously to make them light and creamy.
- A piece of butter about the size of a nutmeg added to water in which any greens are cooking will prevent them from boiling over. No stirring is needed.

Substitutions

IF YOU DON'T HAVE THIS	YOU CAN USE THIS
1 tablespoon cornstarch	2 tablespoons flour
1 cup presifted flour	1 cup plus 2 tablespoons sifted cake flour
1 teaspoon baking powder	1 teaspoon cream of tartar plus 1 teaspoon baking soda
1 cup sour milk or buttermilk	1 cup sweet milk plus 1 tablespoon vinegar
1 square (1 ounce) chocolate	3 tablespoons cocoa powder plus 1 tablespoon shortening
⅔ cup honey	1 cup sugar plus ⅓ cup water
1½ cups corn syrup	1 cup sugar plus ½ cup water
1 whole egg	2 egg yolks plus 1 tablespoon water
1 cup canned tomatoes	1⅓ cups chopped fresh tomatoes simmered for 10 minutes
1 teaspoon orégano	1 teaspoon marjoram
½ cup catsup or chili sauce	½ cup tomato sauce plus 2 tablespoons sugar, 1 tablespoon vinegar, ⅛ teaspoon ground cloves
Few drops Tabasco	Dash of cayenne or red pepper
1 teaspoon Worcestershire	1 teaspoon bottled steak sauce
½ cup tartar sauce	6 tablespoons mayonnaise plus 2 tablespoons chopped pickle relish
1 cup tomato juice	½ cup tomato sauce plus ½ cup water
1 cup canned beef bouillon	1 beef bouillon cube or 1 envelope instant beef broth or 1 teaspoon beef extract dissolved in 1 cup boliing water
1 cup canned chicken broth	1 chicken bouillon cube or 1 envelope instant chicken broth dissolved in 1 cup boiling water
1 cup Chicken or Beef Stock	1 cup canned chicken or beef broth
½ pound mushrooms	4-ounce can mushroom caps
3-ounce can Chinese noodles	2 2¼-ounce cans potato sticks
10-ounce package frozen strawberries	1 cup sliced fresh strawberry plus ⅓ cup sugar
½ cup seedless raisins	½ cup cut dried prunes
1 pound shrimp, shelled, deveined and cooked	5-ounce can shrimp
½ pound ground pork	½ pound sausage meat
1½ cups diced cooked ham	12-ounce can pork luncheon meat, diced
1 teaspoon Italian seasoning	¼ teaspoon each orégano, basil, thyme and rosemary plus dash of cayenne
1 teaspoon pumpkin pie spice	½ teaspoon cinnamon, ¼ teaspoon ginger, ⅛ teaspoon each ground nutmeg and cloves
¼ cup cinnamon sugar	¼ cup granulated sugar plus 1 teaspoon cinnamon
1 teaspoon allspice	½ teaspoon cinnamon plus ⅛ teaspoon ground cloves

What Makes What?

Foods change their measurements when cooked, crumbed, grated or chopped. Questions pop up every day: How many crackers in a cup of crumbs? How many fresh cherries will fill a pie when pitted? Will a pound of cranberries make enough sauce for 8?

To answer these questions, the following table was prepared by Jessie Prother, Twentieth Century Club, Waynesburg, Pa.

BEFORE PREPARATION	AFTER PREPARATION
Cereals and Pasta	
1 cup quick-cooking oats	1¾ cups cooked
1 cup macaroni	2 cups cooked
1 cup noodles or spaghetti	2 cups cooked
1 cup rice	3 cups cooked
1 cup corn meal	4 cups cooked
Crackers and Bread	
18 small crackers	1 cup coarsely crushed
21 small crackers	1 cup finely crushed
9 graham cracker squares	1 cup coarsely crumbed
11 to 12 graham cracker squares	1 cup finely crumbed
26 to 30 vanilla wafers	1 cup finely crumbed
9 slices zwieback	1 cup finely crumbed
1 slice bread	½ cup finely crumbed
1 cup potato chips, firmly packed	½ cup potato chip crumbs
12 thin pretzels	½ cup pretzel crumbs
Dried Fruits	
1 pound prunes (2¾ cups)	4 cups cooked
1 pound apricots (3 to 3¾ cups)	4½ cups cooked
1 pound peaches (3⅔ cups)	4½ cups cooked
1 pound figs (2¼ cups)	4½ cups cooked
1 pound pears (2⅔ cups)	5⅓ cups cooked
1 pound raisins (3 to 3¼ cups)	4 cups plumped
1 pound unpitted dates (2½ cups)	1¾ cups pitted
Fresh Fruits	
1 pound apples (3 medium)	3 cups pared and diced
1 quart red cherries	2 cups pitted
1 pound Tokay grapes	2¾ cups seeded
1 average lemon	3 to 4 tablespoons juice
	1½ teaspoons grated rind
1 average orange	½ cup juice
	1 cup diced pulp
	1 tablespoon grated rind
1 pound cranberries (4¾ cups)	3 to 3½ cups sauce
Nuts	
1 pound soft shell almonds	2 cups shelled
1 pound hard shell almonds	1 cup shelled
1 pound walnuts in shell	2½ cups shelled
¼ pound walnut meats	1 cup chopped nut meats
Dried Vegetables	
1 cup Lima beans	2½ cups cooked
1 cup red beans	2 cups cooked
1 cup white beans	3 cups cooked
Fresh Vegetables	
1 pound Lima beans in pod	⅔ cup shelled
1 pound peas in pod	1 cup shelled
1 pound beets (4 medium)	2 cups diced
1 pound cabbage	4 cups shredded
1 pound carrots (7 to 8 medium)	4 cups diced
1 pound celery (2 small bunches)	4 cups diced
12 ears corn	3 cups cut kernels
1 pound potatoes (4 medium)	2½ cups diced
Cream, Cheese and Eggs	
1 cup heavy cream	2 cups whipped
1 pound Cheddar cheese	4 cups shredded
12 hard-cooked eggs	3½ cups chopped

Table of Measurements

THIS MEASUREMENT	EQUALS THIS MEASUREMENT
3 teaspoons	1 tablespoon
2 tablespoons liquid	1 ounce
6 tablespoons	⅜ cup
4 tablespoons	¼ cup
5⅓ tablespoons	⅓ cup
8 tablespoons	½ cup
16 tablespoons	1 cup
1 cup	8 ounces or ½ pint
2 cups	1 pint
4 cups	1 quart
2 pints	1 quart
4 quarts	1 gallon
8 quarts	1 peck
4 pecks	1 bushel
2 tablespoons fat or butter	1 ounce
Butter, size of egg	2 ounces or 4 tablespoons
1 stick butter	½ cup
½ pound butter or lard	1 cup
1 pound granulated sugar	2 cups
1 pound brown sugar	3 cups
1 pound confectioners' sugar	3½ cups
1 pound flour	4 cups
1 pound rice	2 cups
1 pound ground coffee	3½ cups
1 pound pitted dates	2 cups
1 square chocolate	1 ounce
16 marshmallows	¼ pound
1 pound quick-cooking oats	5⅓ cups
1 pound corn meal	2⅔ cups
1 pound cornstarch	3 cups
1 pound diced cooked chicken	3 cups
1 pound cranberries	4 cups
1 pound chopped onions	3 cups
1 pound ground beef	2 cups
1 cup egg whites	8 to 12
1 cup egg yolks	13 to 14
1 cup whole eggs	5
1 cup lemon juice	4 to 6 lemons
1 pound bananas	3 medium
1 pound potatoes	3 to 4 medium
1 cup bread crumbs	2¾ ounces
½ pound candied fruit or rind	1½ cups chopped
1 pound shredded coconut	5 cups

How to Measure

Granulated sugar needs sifting only if it is lumpy. Spoon the sugar lightly into dry measuring cup, and level off with the straight edge of a knife or spatula.

Confectioners' sugar should be sifted if it is lumpy or if the recipe specifies *sifted* confectioners' sugar. Spoon it lightly into a dry measuring cup, and level off.

Brown sugar should be sifted or pulverized in an electric blender if it is lumpy. Large moist lumps may be crushed with a rolling pin. Unless the recipe specifies otherwise, brown sugar should always be first packed into a dry measuring cup and leveled off. When brown sugar is firmly packed, it will hold its shape when turned out of the cup.

Flour should be spooned lightly into a dry measuring cup to overflowing and leveled off. Most all-purpose or enriched flours today are presifted and need no further sifting. When a recipe specifies presifted flour, it means all-purpose or enriched flour that states on the packages "needs no sifting" or "presifted," otherwise, flour should be sifted before it is measured. Cake flours usually need sifting.

Spices, salt and baking powder: Fill the spoon to overflowing, and level off.

Solid shortening may be packed into a dry measuring cup and leveled off in the same way as brown sugar. If less than ¼ cup is required, measuring spoons should be used. Remove the shortening from the cup or spoon with a rubber spatula. Solid shortening may also be measured by the *water-replacement method:* Use a liquid measuring cup;

subtract the amount of shortening called for in recipe from 1 cup; put that amount of cold water in the cup. For example, if you need ¼ cup shortening, fill the cup with water to the ¾-cup level; then add solid shortening until the water reaches the 1-cup level; be sure all the shortening is completely covered with water; drain off the water; remove the shortening.

Butter or margarine may be measured in the same way as solid shortening. If stick butter or margarine is used, measurements may be made by the following amounts:

¼ stick	equals	2 tablespoons
½ stick	equals	4 tablespoons or ¼ cup
1 stick	equals	½ cup or ¼ pound
4 sticks	equals	2 cups or 1 pound

Melted fat may be measured before or after melting. It doesn't matter, for the amount will be the same. Fat is easier to measure after it has been melted, however. Measure melted fat or salad oil just as you would any other liquid.

Molasses: Use a graduated dry measuring cup. The molasses will round up and should therefore be leveled off with the straight edge of a spatula or knife. Remove it from the cup with a spatula. It will be easier to remove if the cup is lightly greased before molasses is measured.

Milk or water: Use a liquid measuring cup. Place the cup on a level surface. Slowly pour the liquid into the cup to the desired measurement. Raise the cup to eye level to check if quantity is correct.

Grated cheese: Pack lightly into a dry measuring cup until it is level with the top.

Dried fruit: Pack lightly into a dry measuring cup until it is level with the top.

Food for Fifty

MEAT

Fresh ham	25 pounds
Canned ham	12 pounds
Fried chicken	35 pounds
Baked chicken	25 to 30 pounds
Creamed chicken	15 to 18 pounds
Chicken stew	4 hens, each about 5 pounds
Chicken croquettes	12 pounds
Roast beef	20 pounds
Hamburger	16 to 18 pounds
Meat loaf	12 to 15 pounds
Frankfurters	12½ pounds
Turkey, dressed and drawn	22 to 25 pounds
Sausages	16 pounds

VEGETABLES

Cabbage for slaw	10 pounds
Lettuce for salad	12 large heads
Tomatoes, sliced	12 pounds
Peas or green beans	14 1-pound 4-ounce cans
Creamed whole potatoes	16 pounds
Buttered whole potatoes	20 pounds
Au gratin potatoes	1 pound cheese, 4 cups Medium White Sauce, 15 pounds potatoes
Sweet potato soufflé	16 pounds
Sweet potatoes, candied	18 to 20 pounds
Turnips	12 pounds

SALADS

Potato salad	6½ quarts potatoes, 18 hard-cooked eggs, 2 bunches celery, pickles, 4 green peppers, mayonnaise and seasonings
Vegetable salad	8 quarts
Fruit salad	8 quarts
Molded salad	4 quarts

BEVERAGES

Ground coffee	1½ pounds
Coffee, tea, cocoa	12 quarts
Lemonade	60 lemons
Juice for cocktail	6½ quarts
Tea bags	50

Food for Fifty (Cont.)

BREAD AND ROLLS
Bread	8 1-pound loaves
Rolls	14 dozen small

DAIRY PRODUCTS
Coffee cream	1½ quarts
Butter	2 pounds
Ice cream	2 gallons

CEREALS
Rice	3 pounds
Grits	2½ pounds

MISCELLANEOUS
Granulated sugar for coffee	1½ pounds
French dressing	1½ quarts
Pies	10
Apples for pies	18 pounds
Olives	2 quarts
Sandwiches	100
Salted nuts	2½ pounds
Soup	2½ gallons
Jelly for bread or rolls	6 8-ounce glasses

QUANTITY COOKING
Bread	1 sandwich loaf makes 20 sandwiches
Cakes	1 8- or 9-inch square cake serves 16
Butter	1 pound makes 50 sandwiches
Coffee	½ pound makes 20 cups
Ice cream	1 gallon serves 25
Meat	35 pounds serves 100
Potatoes	1 peck mashed serves 50
	1 peck creamed or au gratin serves 70
Salad	1 gallon serves 40
Vegetables	1 gallon serves 36 to 40
Meat loaf	12 to 15 pounds chopped meat serves 50

Simple Rules of Cooking

READ THE RECIPE: Make sure that you understand every step of the recipe. Look up unfamiliar terms in the Glossary of Cooking Terms (p. 42). Check to see that you have all the ingredients needed.

ASSEMBLE INGREDIENTS: Don't begin to make a recipe until you have set out all the ingredients you are going to need.

ROUND UP UTENSILS: All the utensils you will need—measuring spoons, spatula, mixing bowl, baking pan—should be within easy reach.

MEASURING METICULOUSLY: Measure all ingredients accurately according to the recipe. Only the most experienced cook who has tried a recipe several times is able to use the "pinch of this and speck of that" method successfully.

FOLLOWING DIRECTIONS: A recipe is a guide to a good dish. Follow it step by step.

MEASURING MUSTS: Always use standard measuring cups and spoons. Unless a recipe states otherwise, all measurements should be level. There are two kinds of measuring cups—those for dry ingredients and those for liquid ingredients. *Dry measuring cups* are made straight across the top, so that ingredients can be leveled off with the straight edge of a spatula or knife. They may be purchased in a set of graduated sizes which include ¼, ⅓, ½ and 1 cup measures. *Liquid measuring cups* are usually made of glass or plastic. They have a rim that extends above the top measurement mark to prevent liquids from spilling when being measured. Liquid measuring cups also have an extended lip to make pouring easier. They can be purchased in 1-cup, 2-cup and 1 quart sizes with ounce and cup levels indicated on the side.

Measuring spoons come in sets with ¼-teaspoon, ½-teaspoon, 1-teaspoon and 1-tablespoon sizes. They are used for both dry and liquid ingredients for less than ¼-cup measure. See the Table of Measurements (p. 22).

Meal Planning

One of the most difficult tasks for a new homemaker is the planning of menus that are not too difficult, time-consuming or expensive, yet that provide variety and flavor contrasts of foods that are popular with the family.

Fortunately, today, the emphasis is on wholesome simplicity, and homemakers have broadened their concepts of cooking to include many new flavors that not so long ago would have been considered too far out for family enjoyment. Imagination has also entered American cookery, as exemplified throughout this book, and what were formerly considered exotic foods—such as soy bean sprouts, bamboo shoots and water chestnuts—are used daily in a variety of simple dishes to add a distinctively glamorous touch. There are so many wonderfully easy-to-prepare and different recipes in AMERICA COOKS that no homemaker can possibly get into the rut of serving the same dish too often. By trying several new recipes each week, a homemaker can develop a repertoire of tried-and-true dishes to suit any occasion.

Menus should be planned in advance to ensure adequate nutrition, to have appealing flavor and to provide interesting contrasts of color and texture. The same basic food should not be repeated in two or more courses of the same meal. For example, if there is cream in the sauce for the meat or chicken, there should be no cream in the soup or dessert. If the soup contains tomatoes, stewed or broiled tomatoes should not be served as a vegetable, and sliced tomatoes should be omitted from the salad.

These few simple basic considerations offer no handicap even to the novice cook. As a result, menu planning can be fun, and cooking can be an exciting adventure, rather than a daily chore.

Nutrition—A Part of Menu Planning

The principles of good nutrition cannot be overlooked in meal planning, for the proteins, minerals and vitamins provided in our daily foods are essential to health. They build and restore tissues—bones, muscles, nerves, blood, vital organs, skin, hair and fingernails—regulate body processes to keep them functioning at their best, and supply energy for every conscious and unconscious action.

Protein ranks first as a body builder. The best sources of protein are animals and animal products—meat, poultry, fish, eggs, cheese and milk. Beans, peas and nuts are also excellent sources of protein. The most important minerals for health are calcium and iron. By eating foods rich in these minerals, one will also absorb the secondary minerals, for they are generally found in the same foods.

Calcium is important for healthy nerves, muscle tissue and strong bones and teeth. It is present in generous quantities in milk, cheese and cream.

Iron is needed to build red blood cells and enables the blood to carry oxygen from the lungs to the body cells. Liver is the best source of iron, but other foods rich in iron are lean meats, fish and poultry, egg yolks, beans and green leafy vegetables.

Vitamins. There are some twenty vitamins important to good nutrition, but if you concentrate on watching your A, B, C and D's, you will not have to worry.

Vitamin A is important in preventing eye disorders, maintaining healthy skin, promoting growth, and resisting infection. Milk, cream, butter, ice cream, cheeses made from whole milk, egg yolks, liver, green and yellow vegetables and sweet potatoes are good sources of this vitamin.

Vitamin B complex. The most important elements in this complex are thiamine, riboflavin, niacin and vitamins B_6 and B_{12}. They combat fatigue, promote growth, aid digestion and improve vitality. Food rich in the B complex are milk, fish, poultry, meats—especially internal organs—eggs, beans, peanuts, whole grain breads and cereals.

Vitamin C, so indispensable to good nutrition, is found in a limited number of foods. It helps form and maintain strong teeth, bones, blood vessels and muscles and helps heal of wounds more quickly. The best sources of this vitamin are citrus fruits and tomatoes, but it is also found in potatoes and cabbage.

Vitamin D—the "sunshine" vitamin—must be present in the body to aid in the absorption of minerals to build bones and teeth. The prime source of this vitamin is direct sunshine, but fish oils and Vitamin D milk can supply the additional amount needed by people who spend most of their time indoors.

Carbohydrates and fats are the chief sources of energy in the diet and are essential foods to relieve fatigue and improve vitality. All foods supply some energy, but those that contain sugar, starch or fat give the most energy—or calories. A calorie is the unit which measures the amount of energy the body gets from a given amount of food. An excellent guide to good meal planning is first to choose foods that supply proteins, minerals and vitamins and then to add carbohydrates and fats.

Nutrients of Familiar Foods

The following ratings are based on daily allowances of nutrients for a moderately active man as recommended by the National Research Council. Some foods within a group have more of a nutrient than others, but in a varied diet, which is common in this country, a group is likely to average as shown.

Kind of Food	Size of Serving	Protein	Calcium	Iron	Vitamin A Value	Thiamine	Riboflavin	Niacin	Vitamin C (ascorbic acid)
Leafy, green, yellow vegetables	½ cup			★	★★★★				★★
Tomatoes, tomato products	½ cup			★	★★★			★	★★★
Potatoes	1 medium			★		★		★	★
Sweet potatoes	1 medium			★	★★★★★	★		★	★★★
Other vegetables	½ cup								★
Citrus fruits	½ cup								★★★★★
Other fruits	½ cup				★				★
Milk, cheese, ice cream	1 cup milk	★	★★★		★	★	★★		
Meat, poultry, fish	4 ounces	★★		★★	★	★★	★	★★★	
Eggs	1 egg	★		★	★				
Dried beans and peas, nuts	¾ cup beans cooked	★★	★	★★★		★★	★	★★	
Baked goods, flour, cereals	2 slices bread	★		★		★	★	★	
Butter, fortified margarine	1 pat				★				
Other fats (includes bacon, salt pork)	2 tablespoons								
Sugar, all kinds	2 teaspoons								
Molasses, syrups, preserves	2 tablespoons			★					

★★★★★ More than 50 percent of daily   ★★★ About 30 percent of daily need.
          need.   ★★ About 20 percent of daily need.
★★★★ About 40 percent of daily need.   ★ About 10 percent of daily need.

Woman's Club, Palmdale, Calif.

Calorie Chart*

	Amount	Calories
Almonds, dried, unblanched	1 cup	848
Apple juice, fresh or canned	1 cup	124
Apple, raw	1 medium	76
	1 cup, cubed	83
Applesauce:		
Unsweetened, canned	1 cup	100
Sweetened, canned	1 cup	184
Apricots:		
Raw	3	54
Canned, water pack	1 cup halves with liquid	77
Canned, syrup pack	1 cup halves with liquid	205
Dried, uncooked	28 large halves or 1 cup	423
Dried, cooked, unsweetened	1 cup	242
Dried, cooked sweetened	1 cup with syrup	400
Asparagus:		
Cooked	1 cup cut spears	36
Canned	1 cup cut spears with liquid	42
	6 spears with 2 tablespoons liquid	22
Avocados, raw	1 cup cubed	372
	½, peeled	279
Bacon, medium fat, broil or fried and drained	2 slices	97
Bacon, Canadian, raw	4 ounces	262

Calorie Chart (Cont.)

	Amount	Calories
Banana, raw	1 medium	88
	1 cup slices	136
Barley, dry, pearl	1 cup	708
Beans:		
Red kidney, canned or cooked	1 cup	230
Others, including navy, pea,		
marrow, raw	1 cup	642
Canned with pork and molasses	1 cup	325
Canned with pork and tomato sauce	1 cup	295
Beans, Lima:		
Cooked	1 cup	152
Canned	1 cup with liquid	176
	1 cup, drained	152
Beans, snap, cooked or canned	1 cup, drained	27
Beef, cooked, without bone:		
Chuck	3 ounces	265
Flank	3 ounces	270
Hamburger	3 ounces	316
Porterhouse	3 ounces	293
Rib roast	3 ounces	266
Round	3 ounces	197
Rump	3 ounces	320
Sirloin	3 ounces	257
Beef, corned hash, canned	3 ounces	120
Beef, dried or chipped	2 ounces	115
Beef and vegetable stew	1 cup	252
Beet greens, cooked	1 cup	39
Beets, cooked or canned	1 cup, drained	68
Blueberries:		
Raw	1 cup	85
Canned, water pack	1 cup with liquid	90
Canned, syrup pack	1 cup with syrup	245
Bouillon cube	1	2
Brains, all kinds, raw	3 ounces	106
Bran cereals	1 cup	145
Bran flakes	1 cup	117
Bran, raisin	1 cup	149
Brazil nuts, shelled	1 cup	394
Breads:		
Boston brown made with corn meal	1 slice	105
Cracked wheat (bulgur)	1 slice	60
Rye	1 slice	57
White, enriched	1 slice	64
Whole wheat	1 slice	55
Bread crumbs, dry	1 cup	339
Broccoli, cooked	1 cup	44
Brussels sprouts, cooked	1 cup	60
Butter	1 tablespoon	100
Buttermilk	1 cup	86
Cabbage:		
Raw	1 cup shredded	24
Cooked	1 cup	40
Cabbage, Chinese:		
Raw	1 cup	14
Cooked	1 cup	27
Cakes:		
Angel food	2-inch section	108
Fruit, dark	2 x 2 x ½-inch piece	106
Plain, without icing	3 x 2 x 1½-inch piece	180
Cupcake	2¾-inch in diameter	131
Plain, iced, layer	2-inch segment	322
Cupcake	2¾-inch in diameter	161
Pound	2¾ x 3 x ⅝-inch slice	130
Sponge	2-inch section	117
Candy:		
Butterscotch or caramel	1 ounce	118
Chocolate, sweetened milk	1 ounce	143

Calorie Chart (Cont.)

	Amount	Calories
Chocolate, sweetened milk, with almonds	1 ounce	151
Chocolate creams	1 ounce	110
Fudge, plain	1 ounce	116
Marshmallows	1 ounce	92
Peanut brittle	1 ounce	125
Cantaloupe, raw	½ melon	37
	1 cup diced	30
Carrots:		
Raw	1 medium	21
	1 cup grated	45
Cooked or canned	1 cup diced and drained	44
Cauliflower:		
Raw	1 cup flower buds	25
Cooked	1 cup flower buds	30
Celery:		
Raw	3 small inner stalks	9
	1 large outer stalk	7
	1 cup diced	18
Cooked	1 cup diced	24
Chard:		
Leaves and stalks, cooked	1 cup	30
Leaves, cooked	1 cup	47
Cheese:		
Blue veined, domestic	1 ounce	104
Camembert	1 ounce	85
Cheddar	1 ounce (1-inch cube)	113
	1 cup grated	446
Cheddar, processed	1 ounce	105
Cottage, from skim milk	1 cup	215
Cream	1 ounce	106
Parmesan	1 ounce	112
Swiss	1 ounce	105
Cherries:		
Raw, sour or sweet	1 cup pitted	94
Canned, red, sour, pitted	1 cup	122
Chicken, raw:		
Broilers	½ bird (8 ounces without bone)	332
Roasters	4 ounces without bone	227
Fryers	1 breast (8 ounces without bone)	210
	1 leg (5 ounces without bone)	159
Canned, boned	3 ounces	169
Chili con carne without beans, canned	⅛ cup	170
Chili sauce	1 tablespoon	17
Chocolate:		
Bitter or unsweetened	1 ounce	142
Plain sweetened	1 ounce	133
Chocolate beverage, made with milk	1 cup	239
Chocolate syrup	1 tablespoon	42
Clams:		
Raw, meat only	4 ounces	92
Canned, solids and liquid	3 ounces	44
Cocoa, breakfast, plain dry powder	1 tablespoon	21
Cocoa beverage, made with milk	1 cup	236
Coconut:		
Fresh meat	1 cup shredded	349
Dried, shredded and sweetened	4-ounce package	629
Milk only	1 cup	60
Cod:		
Raw	4 ounces	84
Dried	1 ounce	106
Coleslaw	1 cup	102
Cookies, plain and assorted	3 inches in diameter, ½ inch thick	109
Corn, sweet, white or yellow:		
Cooked	1 ear	84
Canned	1 cup drained	140
Corn bread or muffins	1 muffin, 2¾ inches in diameter	106

Calorie Chart (Cont.)

	Amount	Calories
Cornflakes	1 cup	96
Corn flour	1 cup sifted	406
Corn meal, white or yellow:		
Dry bolted	1 cup	459
Cooked	1 cup	119
Crabs, hard-shell, canned or cooked	3 ounces meat	89
Crackers:		
Graham	4 small	55
Saltines	2 (2-inch squares)	34
Soda, plain	2 (2½-inch squares)	47
Oyster	1 cup	119
Cranberries, raw	1 cup	54
Cranberry sauce, sweetened, canned		
or cooked	1 cup	549
Cream:		
Light, table or coffee	1 tablespoon	30
Heavy or whipping	1 tablespoon	49
Cress, garden, raw	1 pound	186
Cress, water, leaves and stems, raw	1 pound	84
Cucumbers, raw	1 medium	25
Currants, red, raw	1 cup	60
Dates	1 cup pitted	505
Doughnuts, cake type	1	136
Eggs:		
Raw	1 whole	77
	1 white	15
	1 yolk	61
Hard-cooked	1	77
Omelet	1 egg	106
Poached	1	77
Scrambled	1	106
Endives, raw	1 pound	90
Farina, cooked	1 cup	104
Fats, cooking (vegetable)	1 tablespoon	110
Figs:		
Raw	3 small	90
Dried	1 cup cut	453
Fig bars	1 small	56
Flounder, raw	4 ounces	78
Fruit cocktail, canned	1 cup fruit with syrup	179
Gelatin:		
Dry plain	1 tablespoon	34
Dessert powder	3-ounce package	324
Dessert, ready to serve, plain	1 cup	155
Dessert, ready to serve, with fruit	1 cup	172
Grapefruit:		
Raw	½ medium	75
	1 cup sections	77
Canned	1 cup fruit with syrup	181
Grapefruit juice:		
Fresh	1 cup	87
Canned unsweetened	1 cup	92
Canned sweetened	1 cup	131
Frozen concentrate	1 can (6 ounces)	197
Grapefruit–orange juice blend:		
Canned unsweetened	1 cup	99
Sweetened	1 cup	132
Frozen concentrate	1 can (6 ounces)	297
Grape juice, bottled commercial	1 cup	170
Grapes, raw:		
Slip skins	1 cup with skins and seeds	84
Adherent skins	1 cup	102
Haddock, cooked or fried	1 fillet (4 x 3 x ½ inches)	158
Halibut, cooked or broiled	1 steak (4 x 3 x ½ inches)	228
Ham: See Pork		
Hamburger: See Beef		
Heart, raw:		
Beef, lean	3 ounces	92

Calorie Chart (Cont.)

	Amount	Calories
Chicken	3 ounces	134
Pork	3 ounces	100
Herring:		
Atlantic, raw	4 ounces	217
Lake, raw	4 ounces	159
Pacific, raw	4 ounces	106
Smoked, kippered	3 ounces	180
Honey, strained	1 tablespoon	62
Honeydew melon, raw	1 wedge (2 x 7 inches)	49
Ice cream, plain	8 ounces (1 cup)	294
Jams, marmalades, preserves	1 tablespoon	55
Jellies	1 tablespoon	50
Kale, cooked	1 cup	45
Kidneys, raw:		
Beef	3 ounces	120
Pork	3 ounces	97
Sheep	3 ounces	89
Kohlrabi:		
Raw	1 cup diced	41
Cooked	1 cup	47
Lamb, cooked:		
Rib chop	3 ounces without bone	356
Shoulder roast	3 ounces without bone	293'
Leg roast	3 ounces without bone	230
Lard	1 tablespoon	126
Lemon juice, fresh or canned unsweetened	1 tablespoon	4
Lemons	1 medium	20
Lettuce	1 head, loose leaf	32
	1 head, compact	68
	2 large or 4 small leaves	7
Lime juice, fresh	1 cup	58
Limes	1 medium	19
Liver:		
Beef, cooked or fried	2 ounces	118
Calf, raw	3 ounces	120
Chicken, raw	3 ounces	120
Pork, raw	3 ounces	114
Sheep or lamb, raw	3 ounces	116
Lobster, canned	3 ounces	78
Macaroni:		
Dry	1 cup elbow type	463
	1 cup (2-inch pieces)	324
Cooked	1 cup	209
Macaroni and cheese, baked	1 cup	464
Mackerel, canned	3 ounces with liquids	155
Margarine	1 tablespoon	101
Mayonnaise: See Salad dressings		
Marmalades: See Jams		
Milk:		
Whole	1 cup	166
Nonfat (skim)	1 cup	87
Canned, evaporated	1 cup	346
Canned, sweetened condensed	1 cup	981
Dried whole	1 tablespoon	39
Nonfat solids	1 tablespoon	28
Malted dry powder	1 ounce	115
Malted beverage	1 cup	281
Malted beverage chocolate-flavored	1 cup	185
Half and half	1 cup	330
Molasses, cane:		
First extraction	1 tablespoon	50
Second extraction	1 tablespoon	46
Third extraction (blackstrap)	1 tablespoon	43
Muffins	1 (2¾ inches in diameter)	134
Mushrooms, canned	1 cup with liquid	28
Mustard greens, cooked	1 cup	31

Calorie Chart (Cont.)

	Amount	Calories
Noodles:		
Dry	1 cup	278
Cooked	1 cup	107
Oat cereal, ready-to-eat	1 cup	100
Oils, salad or cooking	1 tablespoon	124
Okra, cooked	8 pods	28
Olives:		
Green	10 mammoth	72
Ripe, Mission	10	106
Onions:		
Raw	1 medium	49
Cooked	1 cup	79
Young green	6 small without tops	23
Orange juice:		
Fresh	1 cup	108
Canned unsweetened	1 cup	109
Canned sweetened	1 cup	135
Frozen concentrate	1 can (6 ounces)	300
Oranges	1 large	106
	1 cup sections	87
Oysters, raw, shucked	1 cup	200
Pancake mix, dry, self-rising	1 cup	471
Pancakes	1 (4 inches in diameter)	59
Parsley	1 tablespoon chopped	1
Parsnips, cooked	1 cup	94
Peaches:		
Raw	1 medium	46
Canned, water pack	1 cup with liquid	66
Canned, syrup pack	1 cup with syrup	174
Frozen	4 ounces	89
Peanut butter	1 tablespoon	92
Peanuts, shelled roasted	1 cup	805
Pears:		
Raw	1 medium	95
Canned, water pack	1 cup with liquid	75
Canned, syrup pack	1 cup syrup	174
Peas, green:		
Cooked	1 cup	111
Canned	1 cup with liquid	145
Split, dry	1 cup	689
Pecans	1 cup halves	752
Peppers, green	1 medium	16
Pickles:		
Dill, cucumber	1 large	15
Bread and butter type, cucumber	1 cup	118
Sour, cucumber	1 large	15
Sweet, cucumber or mixed	1 (2¾ inches long)	22
	1 cup chopped	225
Pies:		
Apple	4-inch wedge	331
Blueberry	4-inch wedge	291
Cherry	4-inch wedge	340
Coconut custard	4-inch wedge	266
Custard	4-inch wedge	266
Lemon meringue	4-inch wedge	302
Mince	4-inch wedge	341
Pumpkin	4-inch wedge	263
Pimientos, canned	1 medium	10
Pineapple:		
Raw	1 cup diced	74
Canned, syrup pack	1 cup crushed with syrup	204
	1 large slice plus 2 tablespoons syrup	95
Frozen	4 ounces	97
Pineapple juice, canned	1 cup	121
Plums (all except prunes), raw	1 medium	29
Plums (Italian prunes), canned, syrup pack	1 cup with syrup	186

Calorie Chart (Cont.)

	Amount	Calories
Popcorn, popped	1 cup	54
Pork, fresh:		
Ham	3 ounces without bone	338
Loin or chops	3 ounces without bone	284
Pork, cured:		
Ham, smoked, cooked	3 ounces without bone	339
Luncheon meat, canned spiced	2 ounces	164
Sausage: See Sausage		
Potato chips	7 large	108
Potatoes:		
Baked	1 medium	97
Boiled, peeled	1 medium	105
French-fried	8 pieces	157
Hashed brown	1 cup	470
Mashed	1 cup	159
Canned	3 to 4 small	118
Pretzels	5 small sticks	18
Prunes, dried:		
Uncooked	4 large	94
Cooked, no sugar	1 cup with ⅓ cup liquid	310
Cooked, sugar added	1 cup with liquid	483
Prune juice, canned	1 cup	170
Pumpkin, canned	1 cup	76
Radishes, raw	4 small	4
Raisins, seedless:		
Dried	1 cup	429
Cooked, sugar added	1 cup	572
Raspberries:		
Black, raw	1 cup	100
Red, raw	1 cup	70
Red, frozen	3 ounces	84
Rhubarb, cooked, sugar added	1 cup	383
Rice, cooked	1 cup	204
Rolls:		
Plain	1	176
Sweet	1	178
Rutabagas, cooked	1 cup cubed	50
Rye wafers	2	43
Salad dressings:		
Commercial (mayonnaise type)	1 tablespoon	58
French	1 tablespoon	59
Home-cooked, boiled	1 tablespoon	28
Mayonnaise	1 tablespoon	92
Salmon, cooked:		
Steak	1 (4 x 3 x ½ inches)	204
Canned, Sockeye or Red	3 ounces with liquid	147
Sardines:		
Canned in oil	3 ounces drained	182
Canned in tomato sauce	3 ounces with liquid	184
Sauerkraut	1 cup with liquid	39
Sausage:		
Bologna	1 piece (1 x 1½ inches)	467
Frankfurter, cooked	1	124
Liverwurst	2 ounces	150
Pork links or bulk, raw	4 ounces	510
Vienna, canned	4 ounces	244
Scallops, raw edible muscle	4 ounces	89
Shad, raw	4 ounces	191
Sherbet	½ cup	118
Shrimp, canned	3 ounces with liquid	76
Soups, canned ready-to-serve:		
Bean	1 cup	191
Beef	1 cup	100
Bouillon, broth and consommé	1 cup	9
Chicken	1 cup	75
Clam chowder	1 cup	86
Cream soups	1 cup	201

Calorie Chart (Cont.)

	Amount	Calories
Noodle, rice or barley	1 cup	117
Pea	1 cup	141
Tomato	1 cup	90
Vegetable	1 cup	82
Spaghetti, cooked	1 cup	218
Spinach, cooked	1 cup	46
Squash:		
Summer, cooked	1 cup diced	34
Winter, baked	1 cup mashed	97
Starch, arrowroot, corn, etc.	1 tablespoon	29
Strawberries:		
Raw	1 cup	54
Frozen	3 ounces	90
Sugar:		
Granulated	1 tablespoon	48
	1 lump (1⅛ x ⅝ inches)	27
Powdered	1 tablespoon	31
Brown	1 tablespoon	51
Maple	1 piece (1¾ x 1¼ x ½ inches)	104
Sweet potatoes:		
Baked	1 (5 x 2 inches)	183
Boiled	1 (5 x 2½ inches)	252
Candied	1 small	314
Canned, solid pack	1 cup	233
Swordfish, cooked or broiled	1 steak (3 x 3 x ½ inches)	223
Syrup, corn	1 tablespoon	57
Tangerine juice, unsweetened, fresh		
or canned	1 cup	95
Tangerines	1 medium	35
Tapioca, dry	1 cup	547
Tomato juice, canned	1 cup	50
Tomato catsup	1 tablespoon	17
Tomatoes:		
Raw	1 medium	30
Canned or cooked	1 cup	46
Tomato purée, canned	1 cup	90
Tongue, beef, raw	4 ounces	235
Tuna fish, canned	3 ounces with liquid	247
Turkey, medium fat, raw	4 ounces	304
Turnip greens, cooked	1 cup	43
Turnips, cooked	1 cup diced	42
Veal, cooked:		
Cutlet	3 ounces without bone	184
Shoulder roast	3 ounces without bone	193
Stew meat	3 ounces without bone	252
Vinegar	1 tablespoon	2
Waffles, baked	1	216
Walnuts	1 cup halves	654
Watermelons	½ slice (¾ x 10 inches)	45
Wheat flours:		
Self-rising	1 cup sifted	385
All-purpose	1 cup sifted	401
Cake or pastry flour	1 cup sifted	364
Wheat products:		
Bran flakes	1 cup	125
Puffed	1 cup	43
Shredded	1 large (4 x 2¼ inches)	102
White sauce, Medium	1 cup	429
Wild rice, raw	1 cup	593
Yeast:		
Compressed	1 ounce	24
Dried	1 tablespoon	24
Yogurt, plain	1 cup	168

Pot and Pan Dimensions

Baking or Cake Pans:

Oblong   10 x 6 x 1½ inches
11 x 7 x 1½ inches
11½ x 7⅜ x 1½ inches
13 x 9½ x 2 inches
13¼ x 8¾ x 1¾ inches

Round   8 x 1½ inches
8⅜ x 1¼ inches
9 x 1½ inches
10 x 1½ inches

Square   8 x 8 x 2 inches
9 x 9 x 1¾ inches
10 x 10 x 1½ inches

Tube   9 x 3½ inches
10 x 4 inches

Casseroles, or covered utensils in which food may be baked and served:

10 ounces
1 quart
1½ quarts
2 quarts
3 quarts

Baking or cooky sheets, or flat, rectangular pans which may be open on one, two or three sides, especially designed for baking cookies and biscuits:

14 x 10 inches
15½ x 12 inches
17 x 14 inches

Custard cups, or small, deep, individual, bowl-shaped utensils, specially desigend for oven use:

5 ounces
5½ ounces
6¾ ounces

Jelly roll pan, or a shallow, rectangular sheet, usually 1 inch deep:

15½ x 10½ x 1 inches

Loaf pans, or deep, narrow, rectangular pans with slightly flared sides, designed for oven use:

7⅜ x 3⅝ x 2¼ inches
8 x 4 x 3 inches
8½ x 4½ x 2½ inches
9½ x 5¼ x 2¾ inches
10 x 5 x 3 inches

Muffin or cupcake pan, or traylike utensils containing a number of suspended individual cups, almost straight-sided, and which are integral parts of the pan. The cups measure:

2½ x 1¼ inches
3 x 1½ inches

Pie pans or plates, or round, open utensils with flared sides, specially designed for pies:

4¼ x 1⅛ inches
5 x 1 inches
5½ x ¾ inches
6¾ x 1⅛ inches
7½ x 1¼ inches
8 x 1¼ inches
8½ x 1¼ inches

Roasters, or covered or uncovered pans, with or without a rack, specially designed for roasting meat and poultry. The size is designated by the weight of the roast it will hold: 7, 12, 18 or 23 pounds.

Commercial Can Sizes

Size	Weight	Approximate Amount in Cups
6 ounce	6 fluid ounces	¾ cup
8 ounce	7¾ fluid ounces	1 cup
No. 1	10½ ounces	1¼ cups
	9½ fluid ounces	1⅔ cups
No. 303 or 1½	1 pound	2 cups
No. 2	20 ounces	2½ cups
No. 2½	28 ounces	3½ cups
No. 3	33 ounces	4 cups
46 ounce	1 quart 14 fluid ounces	5¾ cups
No. 10	106 ounces	12 to 13 cups

Servings and Pounds

How much meat to buy for dinner? How many servings in a pound of fresh beans? The wise homemaker learns to buy carefully and in quantities she can use without waste. The following chart can help you estimate how much you actually need.

The amount of meat, poultry or fish per serving varies with the amount of bone and fat and the way it is prepared. It also varies with the amount of extenders—such as stuffing, potatoes or rice—served with the meat. The size of serving for fruits and vegetables is given for whichever way they are commonly served—cooked or uncooked. The size of serving for dried beans, peas, oats, rice, oatmeal, grits and pasta products is given for the cooked product.

MEAT, POULTRY, FISH

Meat	*Amount to Buy Per Serving*
Much bone or gristle	½ to 1 pound
Medium amounts of bone	⅓ to ½ pound
Little bone	¼ to ⅓ pound
No bone	⅕ to ¼ pound

Poultry, Dressed Weight	
Chicken, broiling	¼ to ½ bird
Chicken, frying or roasting	¾ to 1 pound
Chicken, stewing	⅓ to ¾ pound
Ducks	1 to 1¼ pounds
Geese	¾ to 1 pound
Turkey	⅔ to ¾ pound

Fish	
Whole	1 pound
Dressed, large	½ pound
Steaks, fillets	¼ pound

VEGETABLES AND FRUITS

Fresh Vegetables	*Size of Serving*	*Servings per Pound as Purchased*
Asparagus, cut	½ cup	4
Asparagus, spears	4 to 5	4
Beans, Lima	½ cup	2 (in pod)
Beans, snap	½ cup	6
Beets, diced	½ cup	4
Broccoli	2 stalks	3 to 4
Brussels sprouts	½ cup	5 to 6
Cabbage, raw shredded	½ cup	7 to 8
Cabbage, cooked	½ cup	4 to 5
Carrots, raw shredded	½ cup	8
Carrots, cooked	½ cup	5
Cauliflower	½ cup	3
Celery, cooked	½ cup	3 to 4
Collards	½ cup	2
Corn, cut	½ cup	2 (in husks)
Eggplant	½ cup	4
Onions, cooked	½ cup	4
Parsnips	½ cup	4
Peas	½ cup	2 (in pod)
Potatoes	½ cup	4 to 5
Spinach	½ cup	3 to 4
Sweet potatoes	½ cup	3 to 4
Turnips	½ cup	4

Fresh Fruits		
Apples	1 medium	3
Apricots	2 medium	5 to 6
Bananas	1 medium	3
Berries, raw	½ cup	4 to 5
Cherries, pitted, cooked	½ cup	2
Oranges	1 medium	3
Peaches	1 medium	4
Pears	1 medium	3
Plums	2 large	4
Rhubarb, cooked	½ cup	4

Legumes		
Dried beans, cooked	¾ cup	9
Dried peas, lentils, cooked	¾ cup	7

Canned Vegetables or Fruits		
8-ounce can	½ cup	2 per can
No. 2 can (1 pound 4 ounces)	½ cup	4 to 5 per can
No. 2½ can (1 pound 12 ounces)	½ cup	6 to 7 per can

Servings and Pounds (Cont.)

Fresh Vegetables	Size of Serving	Servings per Pound as Purchased
No. 303 can (1 pound)	½ cup	4 per can
46-ounce cylinder	½ cup	11 to 12 per can
Frozen Vegetables or Fruits		
10-ounce package	½ cup	3 to 4 per package
Juices, concentrated, 6-ounce can		6 per can

CEREALS AND PASTA

Flaked corn cereals	1 cup	18 to 24
Other flaked cereals	¾ cup	21
Puffed cereals	1 cup	32 to 38
Corn meal, cooked	¾ cup	16
Wheat cereals, coarse	¾ cup	12
Wheat cereals, fine	¾ cup	16 to 22
Oatmeal	¾ cup	13
Hominy grits	½ cup	20
Macaroni and noodles	¾ cup	12
Rice	½ cup	16
Spaghetti	¾ cup	13

Herbs, Seeds and Spices

COMMON HERBS	USE IN OR WITH
Basil	Eggs, fish, cheese, meat loaf and stews. Especially good with venison, duck, tomatoes and spaghetti sauce.
Bay leaf	Meat pies, stews, soups, tomato juice, sauces and salads.
Chervil	Fresh in green salads or chopped as a soup garnish.
Chives	Cottage cheese or cream cheese, fish and egg dishs or any dish that is improved by the delicate onion flavor. Delicious on new potatoes, peas or carrots.
Dill	Fish sauces, cheese dishes, salads, on sliced tomatoes, with buttered vegetables. Extensively used in making pickles.
Marjoram	Pork, lamb, meat loaf, meat pies and stews. Especially good in poultry stuffing.
Mint	Lamb or any lamb dish. Fresh in beverages. Especially good with buttered new peas or potatoes.
Orégano	Spaghetti sauces, tomato sauces, vegetable soups. Good in green salads and salad dressings. A must on pizza.
Parsley	Fresh all year. The perfect colorful garnish for eggs, meat, fish, salad or any dish. Nice finely chopped with cottage or cream cheese.
Rosemary	Chicken, fish, lamb, pork and stews.
Sage	Sausage or pork dishes and poultry stuffing.
Savory	Omelets, salads, soups, stews and poultry stuffings. A nice touch to buttered green beans.
Tarragon	Eggs, fish, chicken, veal and vegetables. Also delicious in salads or salad dressings and in consommés.
Thyme	Fish, chowder, meat loaf and stews. Especially good with chicken, turkey and salads.

COMMON SEEDS AND SPICES	USE IN OR WITH
Allspice	Cakes, cookies, fruit pies and compotes, mincemeat and steamed puddings.
Aniseeds	Cookies, cakes, sweet breads. Excellent addition to fruit pies, puddings, compotes and beverages. Try with buttered carrots.
Caraway seeds	Cookies, breads and coffeecakes. Excellent in sauerkraut and coleslaw. Try with cottage or cream cheese.
Cardamon, ground or whole	Cakes, cookies and pastries.
Celery seed	Salads, sauces, vegetables, pickles, stocks and soups.

Herbs, Seeds and Spices (Cont.)

COMMON SEEDS AND SPICES (Cont.)	USE IN OR WITH
Cinnamon, ground or stick	Cakes, cookies, baked and steamed puddings, coffee beverages, nogs and punches.
Cloves, whole or ground	Cakes, cookies, pastries, soups and stocks, sauces, ham, cooked squash or sweet potatoes.
Cumin, whole or ground	Meat dishes, especially chilis, and with rice. Good with cheese, sausages, pickles and soups.
Curry powder	All kinds of meat, poultry, fish and vegetables. Try a little in soups, sauces, mayonnaise and salad dressings. Delicious with sautéed green pepper or corn.
Fennel seeds	Pies, baked fruits, sauces, stews and pickles. Nice topping for baked bread or rolls.
Ginger	Gingerbread, cakes and cookies, baked and steamed puddings, pies, soups and sauces. Good with boiled tongue, chicken or beef stock. Excellent with roast lamb.
Mace	Poundcake, fruit pies, baked puddings. Especially good addition to fish dishes and fruit salad dressings.
Mustard	Cheese rarebits and soufflés; scalloped, stuffed and creamed fish dishes; deviled eggs and other deviled dishes; cream sauces for fish and vegetables; salad dressings.
Mustard seeds	Coleslaw and cooked cabbage, pickles, sauces and stews.
Nutmeg	Chicken, mushrooms, spinach, cakes, cookies, stewed or baked fruits and pies, sauces and cooked vegetables, especially spinach.
Paprika	Meat, chicken, vegetable salads. As a garnish for potatoes, cream cheese, eggs.
Poppy seeds	Topping for bread and rolls. In butter sauces for fish, noodles and vegetables.
Saffron	Rice, chicken and fish stews.
Sesame seeds	Toasted in breads, cakes and pastries. On buttered noodles and in salads. Good in apple pie.
Turmeric	Pickles and curried dishes.

Wine and Spirits in Cooking

Use wine in cooking with discretion. It should improve the flavor of ingredients but not dominate them.

TYPE OF WINE OR SPIRIT	USE IN OR WITH
Sherry	Soups and sauces. Particularly delicious with seafood, chicken dishes and many desserts.
White wine	Fish and chicken dishes.
Red wines	Meat stews, braised meats, gravies and sauces. Used to marinate meat and game.
Dessert wines (sweet)	Fruit compotes and sweet sauces.
Brandy	Adds richness to many meat and chicken dishes. For pudding sauces, custards, and with fruit compotes.
Rum	Fruit cups or desserts containing pineapple, sweet sauces for puddings.

Wine Cookery Chart

FOOD	AMOUNT	WINES
Meat and vegetable soups	1 tablespoon per cup	Burgundy or sherry
Cream soups	1 tablespoon per cup	Sauterne or sherry
Cream sauce	1 tablespoon per cup	Sherry or sauterne
Brown or tomato sauce	1 tablespoon per cup	Sherry or burgundy
Cheese sauce	1 tablespoon per cup	Sherry or sauterne
Dessert sauce	1 tablespoon per cup	Port or muscatel or madeira

Wine Cooking Chart (Cont.)

FOOD	AMOUNT	WINES
Pot roast	¼ cup per pound	Burgundy
Gravy for roasts	2 tablespoon per cup	Burgundy, sherry or sauterne
Stew, lamb or veal	¼ cup per pound	Sauterne
Stew, beef	¼ cup per pound	Burgundy
Ham, baked	2 cups for basting	Port or muscatel
Liver, braised	¼ cup per pound	Burgundy or sauterne
Tongue, boiled	½ cup per pound	Burgundy
Fish, broiled, baked or poached	½ cup per pound	Dry white wine or sauterne
Chicken	¼ cup per pound	Dry white wine, sauterne or burgundy
Gravy for roast fowl	2 tablespoons per cup	Sauterne, burgundy or sherry
Duck, roast	¼ cup per pound	Burgundy
Venison	¼ cup per pound	Burgundy
Pheasant or game birds	¼ cup per pound	Sauterne, burgundy or sherry
Fruit cups, compotes, syrups, juices	2 tablespoons per cup	Port, muscatel, sherry, rosé, sauterne or burgundy
Drained fruits	2 tablespoons per cup	Champagne or other sparkling wine

Woman's Club, Lake Hopatcong, N.J.

Oven Temperature Chart

Slow oven	250° to 325° F.	Hot oven	400° to 450° F.
Moderate oven	325° to 375° F.	Very hot oven	450° to 500° F.
Moderately hot oven	375° to 400° F.		

Baking Chart

	MINUTES	TEMPERATURE
YEAST BREADS		
Loaves	50 to 60	400° F.
Rolls	20 to 30	400° F.
QUICK BREADS		
Biscuits	12 to 15	450° F.
Corn bread	25 to 30	400° F.
Gingerbread	30 to 40	325° F.
Muffins	20 to 25	400° F.
Nut bread	50 to 60	350 °F.
Popovers	30 to 40	425° F.
PASTRY		
Pastry shell	12 to 15	450° F.
2-crust with cooked filling	25 to 35	425° F.
2-crust with uncooked filling	30 to 45	400° F.
Custard type or pumpkin	35	400° F.
Meringue shell	10 to 15	350° F.
COOKIES		
Drop	10 to 15	400° F.
Rolled	8 to 12	400° F.
Refrigerator	8 to 12	400° F.
Pan	25 to 30	350° F.
Molasses	10 to 15	350° F.

Baking Chart (Cont.)

CAKES	MINUTES	TEMPERATURE
Angel	60	325° F.
Sponge	60	325° F.
Fruit	2 to 4 hours	250° to 275° F.
Cakes with shortening:		
Cupcakes	20 to 25	350° F.
Layers	25 to 30	375° F.
Loaf	45 to 60	350° F.
Sheet	15 to 30	375° F.
PUDDINGS		
Custard	25 to 30	325° F.
Bread	40 to 50	350° F.
Rice	60	300° F.
MEAT		
Beef, rare	18 to 20 per pound	300° F.
Beef, medium	22 to 25 per pound	300° F.
Beef, well done	27 to 30 per pound	300° F.
Lamb, pink	15 per pound	325° F.
Lamb, well done	30 per pound	300° F.
Pork	40 per pound	350° F.
Ham, smoked	30 per pound	300° F.
Veal	30 per pound	325° F.
All rolled roasts	Add 10 to15 minute per pound	
Chicken	25 per pound	350° F.
Duck	25 per pound	350° F.
Turkey, small	25 per pound	300° F.
Turkey, large	20 per pound	275° F.
Fish	20 per pound	375° F.

Pressure Cooking

A couple of decades ago there was a great rage for pressure cooker cookery, but over the years the popularity of this time-reducing method of cooking has decreased. A pressure cooker must be used carefully and intelligently. Be sure to read the manufacturer's instructions, and follow them meticulously.

Canning

With the exception of remote areas of the country—such as Alaska, where the season for fresh fruits and vegetables is short and where imported canned foods are limited and expensive—relatively little home canning is done in American kitchen today. Most busy homemakers do not feel they can spare the time to process foods, especially when our supermarkets are filled with a fabulous selection of every conceivable canned product from snails to pork and beans. Commercial processing is conducted under strict supervision, the produce used is generally at the peak of perfection and the finished product is less expensive than if it were canned in small batches in the home. Home freezing is a simpler and much safer method of preserving fresh foods, and in great part, it has taken the place of home canning in the United States.

Of course, there are still many homemakers who on occasion like to cold-pack some garden tomatoes or to can some home-grown peaches in syrup. Fruits are the safest type of food to can, and little is needed other than a few widemouthed jars with new vacuum-seal metal covers and a large kettle. The home canning of vegetables is not recommended because of the deadly toxin produced by the botulinus organisms which can develop in jars that are not properly sterilized or are not processed under pressure at a sufficiently high temperature for the prescribed length of time.

CANNING FRUITS OTHER THAN TOMATOES

1. Select only perfect, fully ripe fruits. Prepare them acording to the instruction in the Canning Chart below. They may be canned whole, halved or cut into specific shapes. If cut, the pieces should be uniform in size.

2. Use widemouthed jars with new vacuum-seal metal covers. Make sure the jars have been sterilized.

3. Some fruits are best simmered briefly in syrup before being packed in the jars; others should be packed as tightly as possible without crushing as soon as they are prepared. Syrup is then added to within ½ inch of the top of the jar. In either case, slip a knife down the side of the jar and around the fruit to release any air bubbles. Wipe off the rim of the jar carefully.

4. Dip the cover into hot water, and set it on the jar. Put on the screw band, and screw it gently but firmly into place. Do not force the cover.

5. Set the jars on the rack in a preserving pan, or set them on a folded kitchen towel in the bottom of a large pot, leaving a ½-inch space between the jars for the water to circulate. Fill the pot with boiling water to within 1 inch of the tops of the jars. Bring the water to a full rolling boil, and keep it boiling steadily during the processing time specified in the Canning Chart below.

SYRUPS FOR CANNING FRUIT

Thin Syrup	*Medium Syrup*	*Heavy Syrup*
1 cup sugar	1 cup sugar	1 cup sugar
3 cups water	2 cups water	1 cup water

Combine sugar and water in saucepan. Bring to boil; simmer until sugar dissolves. Keep boiling hot.

Canning Chart

NOTE: To keep apples or peaches from darkening as they are prepared for canning, drop the pieces immediately into water containing 1 tablespoon each of salt and vinegar for each 2 quarts of water.

Fruit	Amount Needed for Each Quart	Preparation	Processing Time in Minutes
APPLES	2½ to 3 pounds	Pare; core; cut into uniform pieces. Simmer in Thin Syrup for 5 minutes.	Pints: 15 Quarts: 20
APPLESAUCE		Prepare according to recipe (p. 457). Heat until simmering. Pack into jars to within ¼ inch of top.	Pints or quarts: 10
APRICOTS	2 to 3 pounds	Peel, halve; remove pits. Simmer in syrup until tender.	Pints: 20 Quarts: 25
BLUEBERRIES	1½ quarts	Wash; stem. Blanch in boiling water for 15 seconds; plunge into cold water. Drain. Pack with syrup.	Pints: 16 Quarts: 21
CHERRIES	2½ pounds	Stem; remove pits if desired. Pack with syrup.	Pints: 20 Quarts: 25
PEACHES	2 to 3 pounds	Dip into boiling water. Strip off skins; halve; remove pits; slice, if desired. Heat in hot syrup. Pack with syrup.	Pints: 20 Quarts: 25
PEARS	2 to 3 pounds	Peel; core; halve or leave whole with stems on. Heat in hot syrup. Pack with syrup.	Pints: 20 Quarts: 25

Canning Chart (Cont.)

Fruit	Amount Needed for Each Quart	Preparation	Processing Time in Minutes
PINEAPPLE	2 pounds	Slice ½ inch thick; pare; remove core. Simmer in syrup for 10 minutes. Pack with syrup.	Pints or quarts: 20
PLUMS	2 to 2½ pounds	Prick skins with fork if processing whole; or halve and remove pits if freestone. Heat to boiling in syrup. Pack with syrup.	Pints: 20 Quarts: 25
RASPBERRIES	1½ quarts	Wash; remove caps and stems. Pack with syrup.	Pints: 10 Quarts: 15
STRAWBERRIES	do not can well	Make into jams or preserves.	

CANNING TOMATOES

Tomatoes need no liquid other than their own. Count on 3 pounds tomatoes per quart jar, or 1 bushel for 18 quarts. Use ripe tomatoes free of blemishes. Dip into boiling water; then plunge into cold. Strip off skins. Cut out stems and white cores. Press tightly into jars. Add 1 teaspoon salt for each quart. Processing time: pints, 35 minutes; quarts, 45 minutes.

TOMATO JUICE

Cook tomatoes in saucepan until soft. Rub through food mill or press through colander to remove skins and cores. Season to taste with salt, pepper, celery salt, cayenne, Tabasco, Worcestershire, onion or garlic salt. Fill jars with the seasoned liquid. Processing time for pints or quarts: 5 minutes.

Home Freezing

Home freezing is a safe and simple method of preserving foods but, better still, it permits the homemaker to prepare favorite dishes in advance for use when her time for cooking is short or for entertaining easily without fuss and muss. Freezer emphasis today is definitely on prepared foods, rather than on the storage of large quantities of uncooked meat, poultry, fish, fruits and vegetables.

FREEZING TIPS

1. Freeze the foods your family likes best. Freeze the most popular in the greatest quantity. Make a well-balanced selection according to the size of your freezer.
2. Freeze fruits and vegetables at the peak of flavor, and only quality meats, poultry and fish. Since you get nothing better out of your freezer than you put in, don't waste valuable space with inferior foods.
3. Prepare fresh or raw foods carefully, and work quickly. Process only small quantities at a time, and don't burden your freezer with too many unfrozen package at one time.
4. Package meal-size portions that best fit your family needs.
5. Package carefully in moistureproof and vaporproof materials, whether paper sheets or containers.
6. Label clearly with the type of food, the weight or number of servings and the date of freezing.
7. Freeze packaged foods immediately. Store all food of one kind together.
8. Keep an inventory, and plan a constant turnover of the contents of your freezer. No food improves with long storage. Most uncooked foods will keep well for 3 to 6 months, but cooked dishes are best stored no longer than 1 month.

NOTE: The freezing compartment of your refrigerator is not a freezer. It will keep frozen foods and ice cream for several days, but it should not be used for longer periods of storage. Foods must be frozen quickly, as soon as possible after they are prepared, and must be stored at 0° F. or below.

Glossary of Cooking Terms

ALLEMANDE A thickened sauce made from meat, chicken or fish stock and containing egg yolks and lemon juice.

ALLUMETTE Cut into thin matchlike strips.

ANGLAISE, À L' A plain dish, roast or boiled, in a style typical of England.

ASPIC A savory jelly made from stock or tomato juice, containing sufficient gelatin to hold its shape when cold.

BABA A light yeast cake usually containing currants.

BAIN-MARIE Similar to a double saucepan in which foods are kept hot without coming into contact with direct heat.

BARQUETTE A boat-shaped pastry.

BASTE To moisten with liquid or food juices while cooking.

BAVAROISE A cold creamy custard set with gelatin.

BÉARNAISE A rich egg sauce flavored with wine and herbs.

BÉCHAMEL A foundation white sauce.

BEIGNETS Anything dipped in batter and fried in deep fat, such as a fritter.

BEURRE, AU Tossed or sautéed in butter.

BEURRE NOIR Cooked in browned butter.

BEURRE NOISETTE Tossed or dressed with butter heated until it turns nut brown.

BIGARADE Originally a bitter or sour orange, now a term used for foods cooked in orange juice.

BISQUE A creamy soup usually made of shellfish.

BLANC, AU Poached or simmered and served with a white sauce.

BLANCH To cook in boiling water for a short time; then to plunge into cold water to chill quickly.

BLANQUETTE A stew usually of chicken or veal served with a white sauce enriched with egg yolks or cream.

BLEND To mix well.

BLINI A pancake made with buckwheat flour and served with caviar.

BOEUF EN DAUBE A spicy top round of beef.

BOIL To cook in water at a temperature of 212° F. at sea level.

BOMBE An ice cream dessert, usually frozen in a mold.

BONNE FEMME Housewife style.

BORDELAISE A basic brown sauce using Bordeaux wine for part of the liquid.

BOUCHÉE A small patty made of puff paste.

BOUILLABAISSE A stew containing several varieties of fish and shellfish.

BOUILLON A clear soup or strong broth.

BOUQUET GARNI A small bunch of fresh herbs or dried herbs tied in cheesecloth and used to flavor stocks and stews; usually consisting of parsley, thyme, tarragon, bay leaf, marjoram and chervil.

BOUQUETIÈRE, À LA Garnished with a variety of cooked vegetables.

BOURGUIGNONNE Food cooked in a rich sauce containing burgundy wine, braised onions and often mushrooms.

BRAISE To brown, then to cook, tightly covered, in a slow oven with a small amount of liquid.

BRIOCHE A light yeast bread enriched with eggs.

BROCHETTE, EN Cooked or served on a skewer.

BROIL To cook under direct heat.

BROTH Beef or chicken stock or bouillon.

BRUNOISE With finely diced vegetables.

CAFÉ Coffee.

CAFÉ DOUBLE Double-strength coffee.

CAFÉ AU LAIT Equal parts of hot coffee and hot milk.

CAFÉ NOIR Black coffee.

CAMEMBERT A cheese made in this district of France.

CANAPÉ A savory appetizer on a base of bread, toast or crisp cracker.

CAPERS The unopened flower buds of the caper plant preserved in vinegar.

CAPON An emasculated male chicken.

CARAMEL Sugar cooked almost to the burning point or to a deep brown syrup.

CARDINAL   Served with a wine sauce containing shrimp or lobster.

CASSOLETTE   A small casserole dish for individual servings.

CHAPON   A crust of bread rubbed with garlic.

CHARLOTTE   A dish of custard.

CHARLOTTE RUSSE   A cream containing gelatin molded in a mold lined with cake.

CHASSEUR   Hunter's style or with a robust tomato, garlic and mushroom sauce, often containing red wine.

CHATEAUBRIAND   A thick fillet of beef.

CHAUD-FROID   Chicken, fish or game masked with a white sauce, usually garnished with aspic and served cold.

CHEMISE, EN   Vegetables served with their skins on; also small pieces of food wrapped in a thin layer of dough and baked.

CHIFFONADE   Shredded vegetables or meats used as a garnish in soups; also served with French dressing.

CHILL   To refrigerate food until cold, not frozen.

CHOP   To cut foods into small pieces with a knife or meat grinder.

CHORIZO   A highly seasoned pork sausage.

CLOCHE, SOUS   Food served under a glass bell.

COAT   To roll, shake or sprinkle foods until well covered with flour, meal or bread crumbs.

COMPOTE   Fruits stewed in a light syrup.

CONDIMENTS   Spiced and highly flavored relishes or sauces.

CONSOMMÉ   A clear soup made from meat or poultry and vegetables.

COQUILLE   A scallop or shell; also a dish cooked and served in shells.

CORNETS   A slice of meat or bread or a square of thin pastry or cooky dough rolled into a cone.

COUPE   Fruit served in a glass dish, often topped with ice cream.

COURT BOUILLON   Liquid in which fish is cooked, usually containing water, white wine, vegetables, herbs, salt and peppercorns.

CREAM   To mix shortening until light and fluffy.

CRÉCY   A dish containing puréed carrots.

CRÊPES   Thin French pancakes.

CROISSANT   Rich pastry or puff paste in the form of a crescent.

CROQUETTES   Minced meat, poultry, fish or vegetables bound with a thick sauce, breaded and usually deep-fried.

CROUSTADES   Various shapes of fried bread used for serving meat, poultry or fish entrees.

CROÛTE   A thick piece of fried bread.

CROÛTE, EN   Encrusted or wrapped in pastry before cooking.

CROUTONS   Small cubes of fried bread used to garnish soups and other dishes.

CUBE   To cut into regularly shaped dice.

CUMBERLAND   A wine sauce flavored with red currant jelly.

CUT AND FOLD   To cut down through a mixture with spoon or spatula and to turn the mixture from the bottom up to the top.

DAUBE   Braised meat or poultry.

DEMITASSE   A small cup or half a glass of black coffee or bouillon.

DIABLE   Deviled; usually grilled or broiled foods seasoned with a hot spiced sauce.

DICE   To cut into small cubes.

DUCHESSE   Mashed with cream and enriched with egg yolk and pressed out through a pastry tube; usually applies to potatoes.

ÉCLAIR   A French pastry filled with cream or custard.

ÉMINCÉ   Meat or poultry in thin slices.

ENTREE   A light dish served between other courses at dinner; also a dish generally served with a sauce as the main course.

ESPAGNOLE   A rich brown sauce containing tomato purée.

FARCI   Stuffed; usually refers to bread, rice or other savory stuffing.

FETA   A Greek cheese made from goat's milk.

FILÉ   A powder made from ground tender leaves of sassafras, added to a stew or gumbo just before serving.

FILLET   The tenderloin of meat; also a slice of fish without bones.

FINES HERBES   A mixture of finely chopped fresh herbs for omelets, soups, salads and sauces, usually consisting of tarragon, dill, chives, chervil and parsley. Dried herbs are often substituted.

FINNAN HADDIE   Smoked haddock.

FLAMANDE   Flemish style.

FLAMBÉ   To set afire and allow to blaze until flame burns out; often performed at the table in front of guests.

FLAN   An open custard or fruit tart.

FLORENTINE   Food served with or on a bed of spinach, often creamed.

FOIE GRAS   Fat goose liver.

FONDANT   A creamy mixture, such as an icing or small candy, that melts readily.

FRAPPÉ   With finely crushed ice or partially frozen.

FRICASSEE   A stew of chicken, rabbit or veal in a white sauce.
FRITTER   A food dipped in batter or in a beaten egg and crumbs and fried.
FROMAGE, AU   With cheese.
FRY   To cook, uncovered, in fat or shortening.
GARNISH   To decorate a serving plate or platter attractively.
GÂTEAU   A rich cake usually made of beaten eggs, butter and sugar.
GAUFRETTE   A thin wafflelike wafer.
GELÉE, EN   Food molded in jelly or glazed with aspic.
GIGOT   Leg of lamb.
GLAZE   Icing or glossing over, such as meats covered with aspic or custards covered with a layer of caramel.
GNOCCHI   Light dumplings made of flour or potatoes and eggs.
GRATIN, AU   Baked with a browned crusty topping of crackers or bread crumbs, sometimes with cheese.
GRILL   *See* BROIL.
GRUYÈRE   A cheese named for the village and valley in Switzerland where it is made.
GUISADO   A Spanish stew of meat and potatoes.
GUMBO   Okra or a stew containing okra.
HACHÉ   Hashed or minced.
HARICOT   Bean; also used to describe a thick meat stew.
HOLLANDAISE   Dutch style; also the name of a rich egg and butter sauce.
HONGROISE   Hungarian style.
INDIENNE, À L'   Indian style; generally applied to dishes containing curry.
ITALIENNE, À L'   Italian style; usually a dish containing macaroni or noodles and tomato sauce, served with grated Parmesan cheese.
JARDINIÈRE, À LA   Prepared or garnished with young vegetables.
JULIENNE   Food cut into thin, narrow, lengthwise strips.
JUS, AU   Meat served with its natural pan juices, seasoned but not thickened with flour.
KEDGEREE   An Indian dish of curried fish and rice.
KING, À LA   Food served in a rich cream sauce.
KIRSCHWASSER   A spirit distilled from cherries.
KNEAD   To place dough on a flat surface and to work it by pressing down with the knuckles, folding over and repeating the action as often as needed.
LARD   To insert strips of fat bacon into lean meat; also to cover with bacon or salt pork.
MACÉDOINE   A mixture of various vegetables or fruits of a uniform size.
MAIGRE, AU   Prepared without meat.
MAÎTRE D'HÔTEL   A plainly cooked meat served with a butter or white sauce whose predominate flavor is parsley.
MARINADE   A savory mixture in which food is soaked.
MARINATE   To soak in a savory marinade of wine, vinegar and spices.
MARMITE   A heavy kettle or earthenware pot used to make stocks.
MARRONS GLACÉS   Candied or glazed cooked chestnuts.
MATELOTE   A rich fish stew.
MAYONNAISE   A thick oil and egg sauce.
MÉLANGE   A mixture; usually applied to fruit.
MERINGUE   A sweet cake or cooky made of beaten egg whites and sugar; also a topping for pies and pastries.
MEUNIÈRE, À LA   Sautéed foods, usually fish, served with butter-lemon sauce.
MINCE   To chop very finely.
MIREPOIX   A mixture of chopped vegetables and herbs used in the braising of meats.
MODE, À LA   A dessert, usually pie or cake, served with ice cream; also beef marinated and stewed with vegetables.
MORNAY   A rich sauce containing melted cheese.
MOUSSE   A light frothy mixture containing either whipped cream or beaten egg whites; may be sweet or savory.
NATUREL, AU   Uncooked or cooked in a very simple manner.
NAVARIN   A kind of lamb or mutton stew.
NESSELRODE   A dessert flavored with cooked chestnuts.
NEUFCHÂTEL   A creamy Swiss cheese.
NOISETTE   Hazelnut; also a small, round piece of lean meat.
PANADA   A thick binding sauce containing bread crumbs or flour.
PAN-BROIL   To cook, uncovered, in an ungreased hot skillet.
PAN-FRY   To cook in a small amount of hot fat in a skillet.
PAPILLOTE, EN   Wrapped in parchment or aluminum foil, cooked and served in the parchment or foil.
PARBOIL   To cook briefly in boiling water or seasoned liquid.
PARMENTIER   A dish including potatoes in some form.
PARMESAN   A hard Italian cheese, usually grated and served with pasta.
PASTA   Any one of the many forms of macaroni or noodle products.
PÂTE   A paste, dough or frying batter.
PÂTÉ   A savory pie or pasty.

PÂTÉ DE FOIE GRAS A paste made from the livers of fattened geese.

PAUPIETTES Slices of meat rolled around a filling or stuffing.

PETITE MARMITE A French soup containing beef and chicken broth.

PETITS FOURS Small cakes or rich cookies, usually frosted and decorated.

PILAU or **PILAF** A rice dish flavored with saffron or turmeric, often containing meat, poultry or fish.

PIQUANT A sharp flavor.

PLÄTTAR A small thin pancake baked in a special skillet containing shallow, round indentations.

POACH To cook in liquid that is barely simmering.

POIVRADE A dish flavored strongly with pepper.

POLONAISE, À LA Polish style; often containing red cabbage or sour cream.

PORT DE SALUT A fine French cheese.

PORTUGAISE Portuguese style; usually containing tomato in some form.

POTAGE A thick soup.

POT-AU-FEU Literally "pot on the fire"; a rich broth in which beef and vegetables were cooked.

PRALINE Flavored with browned almonds, usually browned in syrup.

PRINTANIER Served or garnished with early spring vegetables.

PROVENÇALE, À LA Dishes originating in the region of France known as Provence and containing garlic and olive oil.

PROFITEROLE A small pastry or fritter made of puff paste.

PURÉE A mixture which has been pressed through a sieve or strainer or blended in an electric blender until smooth.

QUENELLES Finely ground raw meat or fish mixed with eggs, shaped into ovals and poached.

RAGOUT A rich brown stew containing meat and vegetables.

RAMEKIN A small individual serving dish.

RAVIGOTE A rich sauce containing herbs, garlic and vinegar.

RÉCHAUD A chafing dish or other vessel which keeps foods hot for serving.

RÉMOULADE A cold sauce flavored with herbs and mustard.

RIS DE VEAU Calf's sweetbreads.

RISOTTO An Italian dish of rice, usually containing tomato and saffron.

RISSOLÉ Browned by frying or baking, often covered with crumbs.

ROAST To cook in an oven by dry heat; originally to cook on a spit over a fire.

ROQUEFORT A blue-veined cheese made from sheep's milk.

ROULADE Meat roll.

ROUX A mixture of flour and shortening used to thicken soups and gravies.

ROYAL An egg custard used to garnish soups.

SABAYON A frothy dessert made of eggs, sugar and wine.

SALMAGUNDI An ancient English dish made of chopped meat, hard-cooked eggs, beets and pickles.

SAUTÉ To cook in a small amount of fat over high heat; also a quick-cooking process.

SCALD To heat to just below boiling, or 196° F.

SCALLOP A shellfish; also to bake in layers in a sauce.

SCHNITZEL A thin slice of meat, usually veal.

SCORE To make cuts in an edge or surface.

SEAR To brown quickly over high heat.

SET Until firm enough to hold its shape; usually applied to gelatin dishes.

SHASHLIK Cubes of seasoned meat cooked on a skewer.

SHRED To cut into small, thin pieces.

SHORTENING Cooking fat or oil.

SIMMER To cook in liquid below the boiling point.

SINGE To remove or burn off small down from a plucked bird by holding and turning it over a flame.

SLIVER To cut into very thin slices.

SOAK To submerge in water.

SORBET A partially frozen water ice with fruit and liqueur flavoring.

SOUBISE Strongly flavored with onion or a purée of onion.

SOUFFLÉ A light puffed mixture containing eggs, which may be sweet or savory.

SPATULA A flat utensil of wood, steel or rubber used for spreading soft mixtures.

STEAM To cook on a rack above boiling water in a tightly closed container; also to cook in a double saucepan.

STEW To cook in liquid over low heat.

STIR To blend with a circular motion.

SUISSE, À LA Swiss style.

SUPREME The most delicate; thus, the choice piece of chicken or meat or a cream sauce enriched with egg yolks.

SYLLABUB A type of frothy milk punch.

TARTARE A cold sauce of mayonnaise, mustard, capers and pickles.

TIMBALE A mold of some savory preparation.

TORTE   An open pie or rich cake.

TORTILLA   Thin Mexican bread made from corn.

TOURNEDOS   Fillets of beef thin enough to cook "before you turn around."

TRUFFLE   A fungus, similar to a mushroom, which grows under the roots of young oak trees.

VELOUTÉ   A rich velvety sauce made with cream and either fish or chicken stock.

VERT, AU   Served in or with a green sauce.

VINAIGRETTE   A sauce of vinegar, oil, salt, pepper and herbs.

VOL-AU-VENT   A case made of puff pastry, filled with creamed mixtures of chicken, sweetbreads, meat, or fish.

ZEST   The oil from the outer thin yellow or orange rind of citrus fruits.

1. Appetizers

First-Course Appetizers

Most dinners, even simple, casual ones, begin with an appetizing food before the main course is served. This pleasant custom should not be neglected in the rush and turmoil of our time. The first-course appetizer need not be elaborate; a glass of cool fruit juice or tomato juice, half a grapefruit or a slice of ripe melon is sufficient to let one relax for a few minutes, to clear the palate and stimulate the appetite before you settle down to the meat and potatoes. On more formal occasions you may choose to serve a mixed fruit cup; a shrimp, clam or oyster cocktail; half an avocado with a savory dressing, herring marinated in sour cream; liver pâté in aspic; or a plate of mixed hors d'oeuvres, known in Italy as antipasto and in Sweden as smorgasbord.

This section includes only those appetizers that are best served at the table rather than cocktail accompaniments, but in the sections that follow there are many savory recipes from every state in the Union, which are suitable for or can easily be adapted to serving as a first course before the rest of the meal. Any hot or cold hors d'oeuvres and many canapés, especially the hot ones, may be used to begin a menu. To serve canapés at table, make the individual servings larger, rather than bite size for passing on trays; these should, of course, be eaten with a fork.

Fruit and Vegetable Juices

Any fruit juice—fresh, canned or defrosted, alone or in combination with other fruit juices, well chilled and sweetened or seasoned to taste—makes a refreshing beginning to a meal. In addition to tomato juice and citrus juice cocktails and combinations of these, the fine selection of frozen fruit concentrates available today makes possible innumerable flavors. There are also the bottled and canned juices, such as cranberry; apple; grape and prune; and apricot, peach and pear nectars.

Take a moment to garnish the glass attractively with a sprig of mint, a fresh herb or a rose geranium leaf. For special occasions, serve first-course beverages in unusual containers, such as coupe glasses, champagne glasses or large brandy snifters.

Garnish with a long cocktail or wooden pick studded with alternated melon balls, strawberries and orange or tangerine sections. Frost the rim of the glass by dipping it first in lemon juice, then in confectioners' sugar. Chill the glass in the freezer or refrigerator for half an hour before serving.

The increasing number of electric vegetable juicers in American kitchens makes it possible to serve fresh vegetable juice cocktails and combinations of vegetable and fruit juices. One of the most delicious is half orange juice and half fresh carrot juice. Fresh pineapple and carrot juice are also excellent. Fresh cucumber juice or equal parts of cucumber and water cress juice flavored with a little lime are very refreshing. Canned sauerkraut juice is enjoyable as an appetizing drink and blends well with celery and other vegetable juices. Serve fresh vegetable juices over cracked ice as soon as possible after they are juiced.

CHILLED JUICES

Fill cocktail glasses with crushed ice; pour one of the following chilled juice combinations over the ice:

1. Two parts tomato juice and one part sauerkraut juice.
2. Grapefruit juice with mint garnish.
3. Equal parts pineapple and orange juice with a lime wedge.
4. One part grape juice and two parts unsweetened pineapple juice.
5. Equal parts pineapple and grapefruit juice.
6. Equal parts pineapple or orange juice and prune juice.

Community Service Club Cook Book,
Ferriday, La.

FRESH CRANBERRY JUICE COCKTAIL

Serves 6

    2 cups cranberries
    3 cups water
    ½ cup sugar
        Lemon juice, ginger ale or unsweetened pineapple juice to taste

1. Cook cranberries in water until skins pop; strain through cheesecloth.
2. Cook cranberry liquid with sugar for 2 minutes, or until dissolved.
3. Chill. Serve with lemon juice, ginger ale or pineapple juice.

Community Service Club Cook Book,
Ferriday, La.

SPICED CRANBERRY JUICE COCKTAIL

Serves 6

    2 cups cranberries
    1 slice lemon
    4 cloves
    1-inch cinnamon stick
    3 cups water
    ⅓ cup sugar

1. Put all ingredients except sugar in saucepan. Cover. Cook over high heat until steaming; reduce heat; cook for 20 minutes, or until tender.
2. Strain through cheesecloth.
3. Add sugar to hot liquid; stir until dissolved. Chill before serving.

Mrs. H. G. Hearnsberger, Sesame Club, Fordyce, Ark.

MINTED PINEAPPLE JUICE COCKTAIL

Serves 6

    ¼ cup chopped mint leaves
    ½ cup fine sugar
    2 cups pineapple juice
    ¼ cup lime or lemon juice
    3 cups ice water

1. Bruise mint leaves and sugar together. Add remaining ingredients. Chill for 1 hour.
2. Strain into cocktail glasses with crushed ice.

Mrs. E. F. Clay, Woman's Club, Eustis, Fla.

PINEAPPLE WATER CRESS COCKTAIL

Serves 6

Although an electric blender cannot extract juice from vegetables, it makes one of the finest vegetable–fruit juice combinations.

    2 cups pineapple juice
    2 cups water cress leaves
    ½ cup lemon juice
    2 teaspoons honey
    1 cup cracked ice

1. Put all ingredients in container of electric blender.
2. Blend on high speed for 20 seconds.

A. S.

SAUERKRAUT JUICE COCKTAIL

Serves 6

    2 cups sauerkraut juice
    2 tablespoons lemon juice
    ½ cup finely diced apple
    ¼ teaspoon caraway seeds

1. Combine all ingredients.
2. Serve cold in cocktail glasses.

Woman's Club, Newnan, Ga.

TOMATO JUICE COCKTAIL

Serves 8

    1 quart tomato juice
    8 teaspoons sugar
    4 teaspoons grated onion
    ¼ cup lemon juice
    ¼ cup vinegar
    1 bay leaf
    4 stalks celery, bruised

1. Combine all ingredients. Let stand for 15 minutes.
2. Strain through cheesecloth. Chill before serving.

Mrs. Ella Weihing McKee, Woman's Club, Murray, Ky.

TOMATO–ORANGE JUICE COCKTAIL

Serves 8

    1 quart tomato juice
    Juice of 2 oranges
    Juice of 1 lemon
    1 teaspoon Worcestershire
    Salt and pepper to taste

Combine all ingredients. Chill before serving.

VARIATIONS: Curry powder, cloves, cinnamon, tarragon or parsley may be added and allowed to soak in juice. Strain before serving.

Mrs. C. C. Crowdis, Cosmos Club, Vandalia, Mo.

Fruit Cocktails

Perhaps one of the most popular first courses is a fruit cocktail, made preferably with fresh fruits and berries, but, when necessary, mixed with canned or frozen ingredients.

The best combinations include a sweet and a sour fruit. They should be served thoroughly chilled and garnished with a mint sprig, flower leaf, fresh strawberry or maraschino cherry. If desired, top with a scoop of orange or lemon ice.

Here are a few suggested combinations from a book, *Open Sesame to Tasty Treasures*, compiled by the Sesame Club of Fordyce, Arkansas:

1. Cantaloupe or watermelon balls, berries and mint sprigs.
2. Diced pineapple, halved strawberries, shredded coconut and pineapple juice.
3. Sliced oranges, bananas and seedless grapes.
4. Watermelon, cantaloupe and honeydew melon balls chilled in ginger ale.
5. A scoop of mint ice in center of 4 or 5 grapefruit sections. Garnish with mint leaves and maraschino cherries.

FRUIT COCKTAIL SUGGESTIONS

1. Roll orange and grapefruit sections in confectioners' sugar. Arrange like a spoke on a chilled plate. Fill center with berries or cubed melon.
2. Fill a ½-inch pared ring of cantaloupe or honeydew melon with choice berries, seedless grapes or canned fruit cocktail.
3. Remove centers and seeds from grapefruit halves. Cut around each section. Fill center with combination of ground cranberries and ground whole oranges, sweetened to taste with sugar.
4. Pour cold ginger ale over chilled canned fruit cocktail in sherbet glasses.

Community Service Club Cook Book, Ferriday, La.

FRUIT CUP
Serves 4

1-pound can fruit cocktail or
2 cups fresh fruits
3 tablespoons frozen orange juice
  concentrate
3 tablespoons maraschino cherry juice
  Sugar to taste
2 bananas, sliced

1. Combine fruit cocktail or fresh fruits, orange juice concentrate and cherry juice. Add sugar. Chill.
2. Arrange in fruit cocktail glasses. Top with bananas just before serving.

Amy McKibbin, Junior Woman's Club,
Glastonbury, Conn.

FRUIT COCKTAIL WITH SHERRY
Serves 4

4 large oranges
1 pineapple
4 tablespoons fine sugar
2 tablespoons finely chopped mint
1 tablespoon lemon juice
1 tablespoon pineapple juice
½ cup sherry
4 maraschino cherries
  Mint sprigs

1. Cut away rind and all white bitter skin from oranges. Cut into ¼-inch-thick slices.
2. Peel, core and cut pineapple into cubes.
3. Combine oranges with equal quantity of pineapple. Sprinkle with sugar.
4. Add chopped mint, lemon juice, pineapple juice and sherry.
5. Serve in cocktail cups garnished with cherries and mint sprigs.

Woman's Club Cook Book, Eustis, Fla.

TO REMOVE SECTIONS FROM AN ORANGE OR A GRAPEFRUIT: With a sharp knife, remove skin and all white membrane, leaving fruit exposed. Insert knife deep into center of fruit on each side of membrane covering each section. Remove sections. Squeeze juice remaining in membrane and center core over the sections.

Or you may cut fruit in half and scoop out sections with a grapefruit knife or spoon.

AVOCADO COCKTAIL
Serves 6

2 large ripe avocados
½ cup catsup
1 teaspoon horseradish
1 teaspoon Worcestershire
2 tablespoons, lemon juice
¼ teaspoon salt
  Dash of Tabasco

1. Cut avocados in half lengthwise; remove pits; peel. Cut pulp into cubes. Spoon into sherbet glasses.
2. Combine remaining ingredients. Mix well. Spoon evenly over each serving. Refrigerate for 30 minutes, or until well chilled.

Mrs. W. H. Hasebroock, Honorary President,
General Federation of Women's Clubs,
West Point, Neb.

CHERRY PINEAPPLE COCKTAIL
Serves 6

2 cups sweet cherries, halved
  and pitted
1 cup cubed pineapple
½ cup pineapple juice
  Juice of ½ lime
  Minted Sugar

1. Combine fruits; pour juices over them; chill thoroughly.
2. Spoon into fruit cocktail glasses. Sprinkle with Minted Sugar.

MINTED SUGAR: Mash finely chopped mint leaves in granulated sugar.

Cook's Book, Woman's Club, Panama City, Fla.

GRAPEFRUIT OR ORANGE COCKTAIL
Serves 6

3 large oranges or grapefruit
3 tablespoons fine sugar
6 tablespoons sherry
12 maraschino cherries

1. Use ½ orange or grapefruit per serving. Discard seeds. Scoop out sections, reserve juice. Put sections and juice in fruit cocktail glass.
2. Sprinkle each serving with ½ tablespoon sugar and 1 tablespoon sherry.
3. Garnish with 2 of the maraschino cherries. Refrigerate until very cold.

Woman's Club Cook Book, Eustis, Fla.

HOT BRANDIED GRAPEFRUIT
Serves 2

1 grapefruit
4 tablespoons dark brown sugar
2 teaspoons butter
2 tablespoons brandy

1. Cut grapefruit in half. Loosen sections. Put 2 tablespoons of the sugar, 1 teaspoon of the butter and 1 tablespoon of the brandy on each half.
2. Broil under low heat until topping bubbles and grapefruit is heated through. Serve piping hot.

Mrs. Herbie Burnette, Junior Woman's Club,
Bristol, Tenn.-Va.

BROILED GRAPEFRUIT
Serves 2

1 grapefruit, halved
2 tablespoons brown sugar
  Red wine or maraschino cherry juice
2 maraschino cherries

1. Cut around grapefruit halves to loosen pulp from rind. Loosen sections. Cover with sugar. Pour wine or juice over sugar. Top with cherry.
2. Broil for 15 to 30 minutes. Serve hot.

Mrs. Albert Macias, Junior Woman's Club,
Benson, Ariz.

MELON BALL COCKTAIL

Watermelon or cantaloupe
1 lemon
Mint sprigs

1. Scoop out balls from watermelon or cantaloupe with melon ball cutter.
2. Arrange in fruit cocktail glasses. Squeeze juice of lemon over melon. Chill thoroughly.
3. Garnish each serving with mint sprig.

Woman's Club, Murray, Ky.

ORANGE MINT COCKTAIL

Serves 6

6 small sour oranges
Confectioners' sugar
3 tablespoons lemon or pineapple juice
2 tablespoons granulated sugar
Mint sprigs

1. Separate oranges into sections. Discard thin membranes. Chill thoroughly; arrange in fruit cocktail glasses. Sprinkle with confectioners' sugar.
2. Combine juice and granulated sugar. Spoon a little over oranges in each glass. Garnish with mint sprig.

Mrs. Joe T. Parker, Woman's Club, Murray, Ky.

PAPAYA APPETIZER COCKTAIL

Arrange balls of ripe papaya in fruit cocktail glasses. Moisten with a dressing made of lime juice, a little sugar and salt. Garnish with mint sprig.

Mrs. N. P. Sloan, Woman's Club, Naples, Fla.

FLOWER COCKTAIL

Pineapple wedges
Sugar Syrup (p. 737)
Green food coloring
Pears, cut into thin lengthwise slices
Red food coloring
Cantaloupe balls
Ginger ale
Mint sprig

1. Simmer pineapple in Sugar Syrup tinted with green food coloring. Simmer pears in Sugar Syrup tinted with red food coloring. Chill.
2. Arrange cantaloupe in fruit cocktail glass for the center of flower. Arrange pears and pineapples for petals and leaves.
3. Moisten with ginger ale. Garnish with mint sprig.

Mrs. W. C. Malone, Woman's Club,
Greenville, Ky.

STRAWBERRY ORANGE CUP

Serves 2

1 cup sliced strawberries
½ cup sugar
1 cup orange juice
1 tablespoon lemon juice

1. Sprinkle strawberries with sugar. Let stand for 2 hours.
2. Add juices. Chill well before serving.

Mrs. Peter J. O'Neil, Sr., Junior Woman's Club,
Thibodaux, La.

WATERMELON COCKTAIL

Watermelon
Sugar Syrup (p. 737)
Sherry
Finely chopped mint

1. Scoop out balls from watermelon with melon ball cutter.
2. Moisten balls with a little thin Sugar Syrup. Chill.
3. When ready to serve, arrange in sherbet glasses. Pour 1 tablespoon sherry over each serving. Sprinkle with mint.

Woman's Club Cook Book, Eustis, Fla.

Seafood Cocktails

High on the list of favorite appetizers in this country are oyster, clam or shrimp cocktails served with wedges of lemon and a spicy tomato sauce. Freshly opened clams and oysters served on a bed of crushed ice are hard to beat. All the varieties of oysters along the Eastern seaboard and the tiny Olympias on the West Coast, although differing in size and flavor, are delicious; the tiniest clams—the little necks—and the slightly larger cherrystones are truly tender morsels from the sea.

Not to be forgotten in the list of seafood cocktails are fresh or frozen crab meat and lobster and the tiny bay scallops or the larger sea scallops, which are best quartered or sliced for an appetizer. Although usually poached in a little white wine or simmered for a moment in a cream sauce, fresh scallops are wonderful served raw. All they need is a grating of fresh pepper and a lime wedge. They may also be served with cocktail sauce if preferred.

SEAFOOD COCKTAIL

Serves 6

1 cup chili sauce
1 tablespoon lemon juice
1 teaspoon horseradish
½ teaspoon grated onion
Few drops Tabasco
1 pound cooked flaked crab meat, whole shrimp, oysters, or flaked fish
Chopped celery (optional)
Lemon wedges

1. Combine chili sauce, lemon juice horseradish, onion and Tabasco.
2. Put seafood in cocktail cups. Add sauce. Add celery, if desired. Serve with lemon wedges.

Elizabeth Davidson, Century Club,
Coraopolis, Pa.

MIXED SEAFOOD COCKTAIL

Use 1 pound mixed cooked lobster, shrimp and crab meat in recipe above.

FRESH CRAB MEAT COCKTAIL
Serves 4

1 pound cooked crab meat
1 cup minced celery
Lettuce
¾ cup chili sauce
¼ cup lemon juice
1½ tablespoons horseradish
1 tablespoon Worcestershire
¼ teaspoon grated onion
½ teaspoon salt
Dash of Tabasco

1. Mix crab meat and celery. Arrange in lettuce-lined cocktail cups. Chill.
2. Combine remaining ingredients. Chill thoroughly.
3. Spoon sauce over crab meat. Serve very cold.

Gulf Coast Gourmet, Woman's Club, Foley, Ala.

FRESH LOBSTER COCKTAIL
Use cooked lobster in place of crab meat in recipe above.

CANNED CRAB MEAT COCKTAIL
Serves 2

6½-ounce can crab meat, drained
1 cup finely chopped celery
Lettuce
Crab Meat Cocktail Sauce (p. 52)

1. Flake crab meat, removing all cartilage.
2. Combine crab meat and celery. Chill well.
3. Serve in lettuce-lined cocktail cups.
4. Serve with Crab Meat Cocktail Sauce.

Mrs. J. S. Morris, Community Service Club, Ferriday, La.

CANNED LOBSTER COCKTAIL
Use 1 cup flaked canned lobster in place of crab meat in recipe above.

HAWAIIAN FISH COCKTAIL
Serves 4

This is really raw fish, but it is "cooked" by cold lime juice in the refrigerator. The juice turns each tidbit white and tender. Any delicate white-fleshed fish may be used. Frozen fillets of ocean perch make a particularly attractive dish because of the rosy-flecked skin. Prepared in this way, inexpensive fish takes on all the elegance and savor of shrimp, crab meat or lobster.

1-pound package frozen fillets of ocean perch
Salt to taste
1 cup lime or lemon juice (reserve shells)
1 tablespoon chopped parsley
Cocktail sauce

1. Thaw fillets just enough to handle. Cut into thin strips about the size of small shrimp. Discard coarse skin.
2. Sprinkle with salt. Add juice. (If there is not enough juice to cover fish completely, add a little ice water.)

3. Sprinkle with parsley. Refrigerate for about 4 hours.
4. Drain. Serve with cocktail sauce in lemon or lime shells.

Mrs. E. W. Lander, Woman's Club, Roswell, N.M.

OYSTER COCKTAIL I
Serves 2

Serve with salted crackers or wafers.

12 small oysters
2 tablespoons lemon juice
Pinch of salt
Dash of paprika
2 tablespoons catsup
1 teaspoon horseradish
2 drops Tabasco

1. Divide 6 small oysters into 2 long-stemmed cocktail glasses.
2. Combine remaining ingredients. Pour over oysters. Chill.

Woman's Club Cook Book, Eustis, Fla.

OYSTER COCKTAIL II
Serves 6

1½ pints oysters, freshly shucked
Lettuce
Lemon wedges
1 cup catsup or chili sauce
2 tablespoons wine vinegar
1 tablespoon horseradish
1 tablespoon minced celery
1 tablespoon minced onion
½ teaspoon salt
1 teaspoon Worcestershire
2 dashes of Tabasco

1. Drain oysters. Divide into lettuce-lined cocktail cups (about 6 oysters per serving). Garnish with lemon. Chill.
2. Combine remaining ingredients. Chill.
3. Spoon sauce over oysters, or serve small container of sauce at each place.

Gulf Coast Gourmet, Woman's Club, Foley, Ala.

OYSTER COCKTAIL IN TOMATO CUPS
Serves 1

1 ripe small tomato
4 small oysters
1 teaspoon horseradish
1 tablespoon lemon juice
1 teaspoon cider vinegar
1 teaspoon Worcestershire
2 drops Tabasco
Salt, pepper and paprika to taste

1. Scald, peel and chill tomato.
2. Hollow out tomato deeply. Chop pulp finely.
3. Put oysters in tomato.
4. Combine tomato pulp with remaining ingredients. Spoon over oysters. Chill until ready to serve.

Mrs. J. S. Morris, Community Service Club, Ferriday, La.

PARTY OYSTERS ON THE HALF SHELL

Serves 4

½ pound sliced bacon
24 freshly shucked oysters on half shell
2 tablespoons lemon juice
2 teaspoons seasoned salt
1½ cups tomato purée
¾ cup grated Swiss cheese
Freshly ground pepper
1 bunch parsley

1. About 30 minutes before serving, sauté bacon until partially cooked. Drain.
2. Preheat oven to 450° F.
3. Arrange oysters in single layer in large shallow roasting pan. Top each with about ¼ teaspoon of the lemon juice, a little of the seasoned salt, then about 1 tablespoon of the tomato purée. Top each with ½ slice of the bacon. Sprinkle each with about ½ tablespoon cheese. Dust with pepper.
4. Bake in preheated oven for 10 minutes.
5. Serve on a bed of parsley on large tray.

Mrs. Edward Baker, Junior Civic Woman's Club, Parkersburg, W. Va.

TO COOK SHRIMP FOR SHRIMP COCKTAIL

Serve in cocktail glasses lined with shredded lettuce. Serve with favorite cocktail sauce.

Serves 4

1½ pounds shrimp
1 quart boiling water
2 tablespoons salt
¼ cup shrimp-and-crab boil or mixed pickling spices tied in bag

1. Peel shrimp. Make a shallow cut lengthwise down back of each shrimp. Rinse out sand vein.
2. Put shrimp in water. Add salt and shrimp-and-crab boil or pickling spices. Bring back to boil, cover; simmer over low heat for 5 minutes.
3. Drain. Cool quickly. Chill.

Gulf Coast Gourmet, Woman's Club, Foley, Ala.

SHRIMP COCKTAIL

Serves 6

3 dozen medium to large shrimp or
2 10-ounce packages frozen shrimp
1 quart water
2 tablespoons salt
1 tablespoon prepared shrimp spices or mixed pickling spices
Shrimp or Oyster Cocktail Sauce (p. 53)
Lemon wedges

1. Bring water to boil in large kettle. Add salt, spices (tied in cheesecloth) and shrimp.
2. Cook for 5 to 8 minutes. (Cook frozen shrimp according to package directions, adding spices.) Drain. Shell and devein shrimp. Chill.
3. Arrange shrimp in individual serving dishes or on a bed of crushed ice. Serve

with Shrimp or Oyster Cocktail Sauce and lemon wedges.

Mrs. W. H. Hasebroock, Honorary President, General Federation of Women's Clubs, West Point, Neb.

SHRIMP AVOCADO APPETIZER COCKTAIL

Serves 2

½ pound shrimp, shelled, deveined, cooked and diced
1 avocado, diced
2 tablespoons mayonnaise
2 tablespoons catsup
1 tablespoon finely chopped ripe tomato
1 tablespoon finely chopped green pepper
1 tablespoon chili sauce

1. Combine equal portions of shrimp and avocado.
2. Prepare sauce: Stir together remaining ingredients.
3. Chill thoroughly before serving shrimp with sauces.

Mrs. N. P. Sloan, Woman's Club, Naples, Fla.

Seafood Cocktail Sauces

CHILI SAUCE COCKTAIL SAUCE

Makes About 1½ Cups

1½ cups chili sauce or 1⅛ cups catsup
3 tablespoons lemon juice
1 tablespoon Worcestershire
½ teaspoon salt
2 teaspoons grated onion
4 dashes of Tabasco
1 or 2 tablespoons horseradish

Combine all ingredients. Chill.

Phil Karam, Junior Woman's Club, Glastonbury, Conn.

CRAB MEAT COCKTAIL SAUCE

Makes About ½ Cup

6 tablespoons catsup
2 tablespoons lemon juice
1 tablespoon horseradish
½ teaspoon grated onion
1 teaspoon Worcestershire
3 drops Tabasco
Salt to taste

Blend all ingredients well. Chill thoroughly.

Mrs. J. S. Morris, Community Service Club, Ferriday, La.

SEAFOOD COCKTAIL SAUCE

Makes About 1 Cup

Excellent with shrimp, lobster or crab meat chunks or a mixture of all three.

1 cup catsup
2 tablespoons vinegar
¼ teaspoon Tabasco
1 teaspoon lemon juice
1 teaspoon horseradish
2 teaspoons mayonnaise
1 teaspoon Worcestershire

1. Combine all ingredients. Mix well.
2. Store in covered container. Chill until serving time.

Mrs. J. C. Youngblood, Zeta Chi Club,
Atwood, Kan.

SHRIMP OR OYSTER COCKTAIL SAUCE
Makes About 1¼ Cups

1 cup catsup or chili sauce
¼ teaspoon Tabasco
2 tablespoons lemon juice
¼ teaspoon salt
1 tablespoon horseradish
2 tablespoons minced celery

1. Blend together catsup or chili sauce and Tabasco. Stir in remaining ingredients.
2. Chill thoroughly.

Mrs. W. H. Hasebroock, Honorary President,
General Federation of Women's Clubs,
West Point, Neb.

Cocktail Snacks and Wafers

Often, especially before a heavy meal, a selection of hors d'oeuvres or a tray of assorted canapés is both unnecessary and apt to dull the appetite for the dinner to follow. Yet with a preprandial beverage, you should offer some snack, such as a bowl of olives or mixed nuts, a plate of crisp cheese sticks or wafers or assorted raw vegetables with some coarse salt on the side for dipping. Here is a selection of America's favorite nibble foods.

KUMQUAT TIDBITS

Preserved kumquats
Cottage cheese
Salted pecans, chopped

Cut kumquats in half; remove seeds. Top each half with a spoonful of cottage cheese. Sprinkle with pecans.

Woman's Club, Boynton Beach, Fla.

FRENCH-FRIED PEANUTS

3 pounds large raw peanuts
Fat for deep frying
Salt

1. Day before, shell peanuts. Put in bowl. Pour boiling water over them; let stand for a few minutes; then slip off skins without taking peanuts from water. Spread peanuts on absorbent paper to dry overnight.
2. Next day, heat fat to 365° F. in small deep pot.
4. Put peanuts in large strainer. Submerge in fat. Fry until golden brown.
5. Drain. Spread on absorbent paper. Sprinkle liberally with salt.
6. When cool, store in airtight container.

Mrs. W. B. Sewell, Woman's Club, Starke, Fla.

CURRIED NUTS

2 cups mixed nuts
½ teaspoon curry powder

1. Preheat oven to 400° F.
2. Arrange nuts in shallow baking dish. Sprinkle with curry powder.
3. Roast for 5 to 10 minutes in preheated oven, stirring occasionally.

Mrs. W. H. Hasebroock, Honorary President,
General Federation of Women's Clubs,
West Point, Neb.

SPICED NUTS

¾ cup confectioners' sugar
2 tablespoons cinnamon
½ teaspoon cloves
½ teaspoon nutmeg
1 teaspoon salt
2 tablespoons cooking oil
2 cups shelled nuts

1. Combine sugar and spices. Put 3 tablespoons of mixture in skillet with salt and oil. Add nuts. Cook over medium heat, stirring constantly.
2. When nuts are lightly toasted, drain off excess liquid.
3. Spread half the remaining sugar in shallow pan; sprinkle nuts on top; cover with remaining sugar.
4. When cool, store in airtight container.

Mrs. B. G. Hickey, Sesame Club, Fordyce, Ark.

ROQUEFORT PECANS OR WALNUTS
Makes 60 to 72

3-ounce package Roquefort or blue cheese
3-ounce package cream cheese
¾ pound pecan or walnut halves

1. Crumble Roquefort or blue cheese. Beat into cream cheese until fluffy.
2. Spread on flat side of a nut half; put flat side of another nut on top. Press together. Chill.

Rosemary Surgi, Gentilly Woods Woman's Club,
New Orleans, La.

COCKTAIL NIBBLES
Makes 4 Quarts

6 ounces thin pretzel sticks
1 pound salted peanuts
1 quart bite-size rice cereal
1 quart bite-size oat cereal
1 quart bite-size wheat cereal
1½ cups butter or margarine
1¼ cups Worcestershire
1 tablespoon garlic salt
1 tablespoon onion salt
1 tablespoon celery salt

1. Preheat oven to 225° F.
2. Combine pretzels, peanuts and cereals in large roasting pan.
3. Melt butter or margarine. Stir in remaining ingredients. Pour over cereals. Mix thoroughly.
4. Cover. Bake in preheated oven for 1 hour. Remove cover; bake for 1 hour longer, stirring occasionally.
5. When cool, store in airtight container.

G. Mulholland, Woman's Club, Linbrook, N.J.

HOT NUT CRACKERS

Makes 48

½ cup butter
1 cup presifted flour
½ pound mild Cheddar cheese, shredded
¼ teaspoon salt
½ teaspoon red pepper
4 tablespoons ice water
Pecan halves

1. Cream butter until fluffy. Combine flour, cheese, salt and pepper. Mix along with water into butter, to make a firm dough. Chill.
2. Preheat oven to 350° F. Grease baking sheet.
3. Roll out dough thinly on lightly floured board. Cut into rounds with small biscuit cutter. Place pecan half on each round; fold over like tiny turnover; and seal edge with fork.
4. Bake in preheated oven for 15 minutes, or until crisp.

Our Heritage Cook Book, Pontotoc, Miss.

GARLIC RIPE OLIVES

Makes About 1 Cup

9-ounce can ripe olives
Olive oil
2 cloves garlic, halved
½ cup cracked ice

1. Drain olives. Put in bowl. Cover with oil to depth of ¼ inch. Stir in garlic and ice.
2. Cover. Let stand at room temperature for 2 or 3 hours. Drain before serving.

Mrs. Charles Davis, Junior Woman's Club, Benson, Ariz.

CURRIED RIPE OLIVES

Makes About 1 Cup

9-ounce can ripe olives
½ teaspoon curry powder
1 teaspoon Worcestershire

1. Day before, drain liquid from olives into small saucepan. Add curry powder and Worcestershire. Bring to boil. Remove from heat.
2. Put olives in small container. Pour liquid over them. Cover. Refrigerate for at least 1 day before serving.

Carliene Jacques, El Camino Real Junior Woman's Club, Capistrano Beach, Calif.

CURRIED STUFFED OLIVES

Makes 1½ Cups

1 tablespoon instant minced onion or ¼ cup minced fresh onions
2 tablespoons lemon juice
1 tablespoon curry powder
½ cup cooking oil
1½ cups drained stuffed green olives

1. At least 3 days before, in bowl of electric mixer combine onion, lemon juice and curry powder. Slowly beat in oil.
2. Put olives in pint jar; pour mixture over them; cover.

3. Refrigerate for at least 3 days before serving.

Fran Runyon, Junior Woman's Club, Jacksonville, Fla.

OLIVE PUFFS

Makes 48

2 cups grated sharp American cheese
¼ pound butter
1 cup presifted flour
48 small stuffed olives

1. Thoroughly cream cheese and butter. Add flour. Mix well.
2. Coat olives with cheese mixture. Freeze.
3. Preheat oven to 400° F.
4. Arrange olives on baking sheet. Bake in preheated oven for 20 minutes. Serve hot.

Grace B. Moran, Junior Woman's Club, Glastonbury, Conn.

OLIVES IN FLAKY PASTRY

Makes 60

These may be prepared in advance and kept in refrigerator until ready to be baked.

2 cups presifted flour
1 teaspoon salt
1 cup shortening
¼ cup water
60 medium stuffed olives

1. Preheat oven to 450° F.
2. In mixing bowl combine flour and salt.
3. Cut in shortening until broken into small particles.
4. Sprinkle water over mixture, a tablespoon at a time. Mix with fork until all flour is moistened.
5. Gather dough into ball. Cut in half. Roll out one half at a time ⅛ inch thick on lightly floured board. Cut into 2-inch squares.
6. Place 1 of the olives in center of each square. Fold pastry around it. Roll lightly between palms of hands to form balls.
7. Arrange on baking sheet. Bake in preheated oven for 15 minutes, or until crisp and delicately browned.

Mrs. Ray F. Lucas, Junior Woman's Club, Thibodaux, La.

BLACK ROSEBUDS

Makes 50

These may be made the day before and refrigerated. They are nice stuck on one end of a cocktail pick, with the other end of the pick stuck into a head of green cabbage.

3-ounce package cream cheese
1 ounce blue cheese
2 tablespoons lemon juice
3 to 4 tablespoons brandy
4 tablespoons chopped black walnuts
50 large pitted ripe olives
2 hard-cooked egg yolks, sieved
Paprika

1. Divide cream cheese in half. Put each half in small bowl.

2. To one half, add blue cheese, 1 tablespoon of the lemon juice and 1½ to 2 tablespoons of the brandy. Mix well. Set aside.

3. To other half, add remaining lemon juice and brandy and walnuts. Mix well.

4. Drain olives well. Fill half with blue cheese mixture and half with nut mixture. Sprinkle those with blue cheese filling with sieved egg yolk and the others with paprika.

Mrs. John Selden, Coco Plum Woman's Club,
Coral Gables, Fla.

BUTTERED POPCORN
Makes 1½ Quarts
½ cup corn oil or peanut oil
½ cup or ½ 10-ounce package
   popcorn kernels
6 tablespoons butter, melted
Salt to taste

1. Heat oil in 1½-quart saucepan until it just begins to smoke.

2. Add popcorn; cover tightly; cook over high heat until corn begins to pop actively. Turn heat to very low. Cook until popping stops, shaking pan vigorously several times.

3. Turn into serving bowl; add butter and salt; toss lightly.

A. S.

HERB BUTTER POPCORN
Makes 4 Quarts
½ cup butter or margarine
2 tablespoons minced chives
1 teaspoon basil
¼ teaspoon thyme
¼ teaspoon marjoram
1 teaspoon salt
4 quarts freshly popped popcorn

1. Melt butter or margarine in large saucepan.

2. Add chives, basil, thyme, marjoram and salt. Simmer over very low heat for 5 minutes.

3. Add popcorn. Toss lightly and evenly.

Mrs. Bill Andrews, Junior Woman's Club,
Greenville, Miss.

ROAST PUMPKIN SEEDS
2 cups pumpkin seeds
1½ tablespoons melted butter or cooking oil
1¼ teaspoons salt

1. Preheat oven to 250° F.

2. Combine pumpkin seeds, butter or oil and salt. Mix well. Spread in shallow pan.

3. Roast in preheated oven for 30 to 40 minutes, or until browned and crisp, stirring often to brown evenly.

Shirley Martin, Junior Women's Club,
Vernon, Conn.

CHEESE GARLIC BREAD STICKS
Makes About 64

If wrapped in waxed paper and sealed in a tightly closed container, these will stay crisp for several days.

¾ cup olive oil
3 cloves garlic
1 loaf day-old sliced bread
   Grated imported Romano or Parmesan cheese

1. Preheat oven to 300° F.

2. Pour oil into shallow bowl. Squeeze garlic through garlic press. Add to oil. Mix well.

3. Trim crusts from bread; discard. Cut each slice into 4 rectangular strips. Dip both sides of strips in garlic oil; then dip into cheese, coating both sides. Place on baking sheet.

4. Bake in preheated oven until golden brown, turning sticks once to brown on both sides.

Ora Reddell, Gentilly Woods Woman's Club,
New Orleans, La.

BASIC CHEESE STICKS
Makes 72
1½ cups presifted flour
1 teaspoon salt
½ cup shortening
1¾ cups shredded sharp cheese
1 tablespoon water

1. Preheat oven to 425° F.

2. Combine flour and salt. Cut in shortening and cheese.

3. Stir in water with pastry blender or fork.

4. Gather dough into a ball. Roll out about the thickness of piecrust on lightly floured pastry canvas. Cut into strips ½ inch wide and 4 inches long.

5. Arrange on baking sheet. Bake in preheated oven for 8 to 10 minutes, or until lightly browned.

Study Club, Balsam Lake, Wis.

ROQUEFORT CHEESE STICKS
Makes 24

If stored in airtight container, they will keep for three weeks.

9-ounce package pastry mix
3 ounces Roquefort cheese
¼ cup chopped parsley
2 tablespoons ice water

1. Preheat oven to 400° F.

2. Put pastry mix and cheese in mixing bowl. Crumble in cheese; stir to mix.

3. Add parsley and ice water. Blend until moist.

4. Roll out dough about ¼ inch thick on lightly floured board. Cut into 3-inch strips.

5. Place on baking sheet. Bake in preheated oven for 15 minutes, or until lightly browned.

6. Cool on wire rack.

Jean Shields, Finneytown Junior Women's Club,
Cincinnati, Ohio

CHEESE MOONS
Makes 24
1 cup presifted flour
¼ teaspoon salt
1 cup shredded sharp cheese
¼ teaspoon Worcestershire
½ teaspoon prepared mustard
½ cup butter or margarine
　　Paprika

1. Preheat oven to 350° F.
2. In mixing bowl combine flour, salt and cheese. Add Worcestershire and mustard. Cut in butter or margarine. Knead lightly to form a soft dough.
3. Roll a teaspoonful at a time into marble-size ball. Place 2 inches apart on baking sheet.
4. Bake in preheated oven for 15 minutes, or until golden brown. Leave some balls plain; sprinkle others lightly with paprika.

Mrs. N. A. Herren, Woman's Club, Naples, Fla.

BARBECUE WAFERS
Makes About 48
¼ pound butter
1 pound sharp cheese, shredded
¾ package onion soup mix, pulverized
2 cups presifted flour
½ teaspoon chili powder
½ teaspoon water

1. Mix butter and cheese well. Work in remaining ingredients. Form into rolls; wrap in waxed paper; refrigerate for 3 to 4 hours.
2. Preheat oven to 400° F.
3. Slice rolls; arrange on baking sheet; bake in preheated oven for 10 to 12 minutes.

Mrs. A. A. Sappington, Jr., Woman's Club, Gainesville, Fla.

DOUBLE CHEESE CRESCENTS
Makes About 24
½ cup butter or margarine
　　Dash of red pepper
3-ounce package cream cheese
¼ teaspoon salt
1 cup sifted cake flour
2 ounces mild cheese slices

1. Cream butter or margarine, red pepper and cream cheese until smooth. Add salt. Gradually work in flour, blending until smooth. Chill well.
2. Roll out dough ⅛ inch thick on lightly floured board; cut into 2-inch rounds. On half of each round, place a bit of mild cheese; fold over; press edges together, forming crescent. Chill.
3. Preheat oven to 450° F.
4. Arrange crescents on baking sheet. Bake in preheated oven for 8 to 10 minutes, or until lightly browned and slightly puffed. Serve hot.

Mrs. A. M. Ellison, Woman's Club, Williamsburg, Ky.

NIPPY CHEESE BALLS
Makes 48
Baked and cooled cheese balls may be wrapped in aluminum foil or freezer paper and frozen. To serve, remove from freezer, place on baking sheet and bake in preheated 375° F. oven for 10 minutes.

½ cup butter or margarine
1 cup shredded sharp cheese
⅛ teaspoon salt
1 teaspoon Worcestershire
½ teaspoon prepared mustard
1¼ cups presifted flour

1. Cream butter or margarine until soft. Blend in cheese, salt, Worcestershire and mustard.
2. With fingers, work in flour to make a smooth dough. Shape into ball. Pinch off small pieces of dough; shape into balls ¾ inch in diameter.
3. Place balls on baking sheet. Refrigerate for 30 minutes.
4. Preheat oven to 400° F.
5. Bake in preheated oven for 15 to 20 minutes, or until lightly browned. Serve warm.

Mrs. Warren Whitmore, Woman's Club, South Jacksonville, Fla.

CHEESE PUFFS
Makes About 12
¼ cup butter
1 cup shredded sharp cheese
¾ cup presifted flour
¼ teaspoon celery seed
　　Dash of salt

1. Preheat oven to 450° F.
2. Cream butter and cheese. (Use electric mixer if available.)
3. Stir in remaining ingredients.
4. Form into small balls; flatten with fork; place on baking sheet about ½ inch apart.
5. Bake in preheated oven for 10 minutes. Serve hot.

Mrs. James Hughy, Modern Culture Club, Tuscaloosa, Ala.

BOHEMIAN SAUERKRAUT SNACKS
Makes About 24
1 cup presifted flour
½ teaspoon baking powder
½ teaspoon salt
4 tablespoons butter
1 cup chopped sauerkraut
1 tablespoon milk

1. Preheat oven to 400° F.
2. Sift together flour, baking powder and salt into mixing bowl. Cut in butter. Add sauerkraut and milk. Mix well.
3. Roll out dough ¼ inch thick on lightly floured board. Cut into small rounds with floured biscuit cutter. Place on baking sheet.
4. Bake in preheated oven for 20 minutes.

Mrs. John Molnar, Golfview Hills Woman's Club, Hinsdale, Ill.

CORN MEAL CRACKERS

Makes About 48

2 cups packaged corn meal mix
½ cup grated Parmesan cheese
4 to 5 tablespoons water
Poppy seeds or sesame seeds

1. Preheat oven to 350° F.
2. Put corn meal mix and cheese in mixing bowl.
3. Stir in water, mixing only until dry ingredients are moistened.
4. Turn onto lightly floured board. Knead gently a few times.
5. Roll out dough 1/16 inch thick.
6. Cut into rectangles. Arrange on baking sheets. Prick with fork. Sprinkle with seeds.
7. Bake in preheated oven for 10 to 12 minutes, or until just golden.

Louise W. Carmichael, Junior and Senior Woman's Clubs, Grundy, Va.

Hors d'Oeuvres

Hors d'oeuvres may be some savory food as simple as a stalk of crisp celery stuffed with a flavorful mixture or as elaborate as a mold of foie gras in aspic, garnished with tiny cutouts of black truffle. Most hors d'oeuvres are suitable for serving as a first-course appetizer at the table. Accompanied by some sliced cold meats, assorted cheeses and hot French bread, sliced and buttered whole wheat bread or pumpernickel, or assorted crackers, they are also excellent for party buffet suppers.

The buffet table may concentrate on cold hors d'oeuvres or may combine hot and cold. Usually the cold foods are placed at one end of the table and the hot foods at the other. Sometimes, however, the cold selection is served first, followed by the hot selection.

Hors d'oeuvres, meaning outside the work, are frequently called antipasto, meaning before the pasta. They should be highly seasoned, piquant and appetizing. For best effect, they should be attractively served and garnished.

HORS D'OEUVRES SUGGESTIONS

1. Cut stuffed olives in half. Spear on cocktail picks with a tiny cube of cheese between each half.
2. Spear cooked shrimp on cocktail picks; serve with well-seasoned cocktail sauce in a notched lemon cup.
3. Spear any of the following on cocktail picks, and arrange attractively on a plate: sweet pickle and cube of cooked meat, such as salami, bologna, liver sausage or frankfurter; lightly browned mushroom and stuffed olive; cheese cube, a stuffed olive half and a pickled onion; browned cocktail sausages.

Community Service Club Cook Book, Ferriday, La.

HORS D'OEUVRES SUGGESTIONS

1. Marinate chunks of canned, frozen or fresh pineapple in French dressing; then roll in chopped mint or finely grated coconut. Spear with cocktail picks.
2. Cut sliced salami into ½-inch cubes. Spear with cocktail picks. Serve with Clam Dip (p. 74) or cocktail sauce.
3. Scoop out center of radishes, cooked tiny beets or small Italian tomatoes. Stuff center with Roquefort or blue cheese. Spear with cocktail picks.
4. Remove pimiento from stuffed olives. Press Roquefort or blue cheese into cavity.
5. Marinate banana slices, cut about ¼ inch thick, in pineapple juice. Drain just before serving. Top generously with crisp bacon bits. Spear with cocktail picks.

Mrs. S. A. Cebula, Junior Woman's Club, Forest Park, Ga.

HORS D'OEUVRES SUGGESTIONS

1. Stuff crisp celery stalks with cheese or anchovy paste.
2. Form cream cheese into balls. Roll in minced chipped beef or caviar.
3. Serve deviled hard-cooked egg halves in water cress nests.

Mrs. Fred Block, Junior Woman's Club, Thibodaux, La.

Cold Hors d'Oeuvres

ANCHOVY RADISHES

Slice tops off crisp round radishes. Drain rolled anchovies. Put one on each radish. Spear with cocktail picks to hold together and to handle easily.

Mrs. Al Porche, Junior Woman's Club, Thibodaux, La.

ANTIPASTO

On a platter arrange Italian salami, Deviled Eggs (p. 60), sardines, tuna, prosciutto, Eggplant Marinara (p. 61), Garlic Ripe Olives (p. 54), Italian Raw Mushrooms (p. 63), Marinated Artichokes (p. 58), pimientos, celery stalks and so on. The combinations of flavors and textures are endless. Almost any cold hors d'oeuvre has its rightful place on the antipasto platter; just try not to repeat flavors or colors. Serve with hot Italian bread.

Mrs. Charles Davis, Junior Woman's Club, Benson, Ariz.

APPLE PINCUSHION

Salami
Pickled onions
1 apple

Cut salami into ½-inch cubes. Spear a cube of salami and an onion on cocktail pick. Insert end of the pick into apple, pincushion-style. Continue until apple is studded with hors d'oeuvres. Place apple on plate. Let guests help themselves.

Helen Beatty, Woman's Club, Boynton Beach, Fla.

MARINATED ARTICHOKES
Serves 6
2 packages frozen artichoke hearts
2 drops Tabasco
1½ cups French dressing
12 anchovies

1. Cook artichokes according to package directions. Drain. Cut each artichoke in half.
2. Mix Tabasco and dressing. Pour over artichokes. Marinate in refrigerator for 2 to 3 hours. Serve topped with anchovies.

Mrs. Charles Davis, Junior Woman's Club, Benson, Ariz.

ARTICHOKES IN LEMON
Serves 4 to 6
13-ounce jar artichoke hearts
3 tablespoons lemon juice
2 tablespoons olive oil
1 clove garlic, crushed
¼ teaspoon salt
⅛ teaspoon pepper

1. Chill artichokes.
2. Combine remaining ingredients. Pour over artichokes. Let stand until ready to serve.

Mrs. Donald Turner, Junior Woman's Club, Benson, Ariz.

CHEESE CAVIAR MOLD
Makes 4 Cups
2 cups creamed cottage cheese
⅛ teaspoon Tabasco
½ teaspoon salt
1 clove garlic, minced
2 teaspoons Worcestershire
2 cups sour cream
4 teaspoons gelatin
6 tablespoons sherry
Juice of ½ lemon
4 ounces red caviar

1. In bowl of electric mixer combine cottage cheese, Tabasco, salt, garlic, Worcestershire and sour cream. Beat at high speed until lumps disappear.
2. In custard cup soak gelatin in sherry to soften; set cup in hot water; stir until gelatin is dissolved. Add to cheese mixture. Beat until light.
3. Pour into oiled 1-quart mold. Chill for 12 hours.
4. Unmold onto serving plate.
5. Combine lemon juice and caviar. Spread on mold.

Mrs. M. J. Soule, Jr., Woman's Club, Gainesville, Fla.

STUFFINGS FOR CELERY
(2-Inch Pieces)
1. Cream cheese and drained crushed pineapple.
2. Flaked crab meat and lemon-flavored mayonnaise.
3. Mashed avocado seasoned with lemon juice, salt and grated onion.
4. Pimiento cheese and chopped ripe olives.

Averil McKechnie, Woman's Literary Union, Portland, Me.

STUFFED CELERY RINGS
1 medium bunch celery
Tangy cheese, creamed aged Cheddar or Roquefort spread

1. Cut top off celery. Wash and dry each stalk.
2. Fill smallest stalk with cheese; then fill next smallest stalk; press firmly into first. Continue filling and pressing stalks together until all celery is formed into bunch. Tie with string. Chill.
3. To serve, cut crosswise into ½-inch-thick slices.

Peg Ludwig, Woman's Club, Fern Creek, Ky.

CELERY STUFFED WITH CREAM CHEESE
1 bunch celery
3-ounce package cream cheese
¼ teaspoon salt
⅛ teaspoon pepper
Paprika
2 or 3 drops Worcestershire
Mayonnaise

1. Wash celery; separate stalks; use tender inner ones. Chill.
2. Mash cheese. Mix with salt, pepper, ⅛ teaspoon of the paprika and Worcestershire. Beat in enough mayonnaise to make a smooth paste of spreading consistency.
3. Fill stalks with cheese mixture. Sprinkle with paprika. Arrange on platter. Chill before serving.

Woman's Club, Murray, Ky.

CELERY CURLS
Cut stalks of celery into 3- or 4-inch pieces. With sharp knife, make 5 or 6 incisions down stalk, stopping within 1½ inches of end. Drop pieces into water. Refrigerate for several hours. Split ends will curl back along stalk, making attractive garnish for platters of canapés or hors d'oeuvres.

Woman's Club, Murray, Ky.

CELERY STUFFED WITH CREAM CHEESE AND PEANUT BUTTER
Makes About ¾ Cup Stuffing
3-ounce package cream cheese
1 teaspoon onion juice
2 teaspoons chili sauce
3 tablespoons peanut butter
5 olives, chopped
12 stalks celery

1. Let cheese soften at room temperature.
2. Mix cheese, onion juice, chili sauce, peanut butter and olives.
3. Fill celery stalks. Chill before serving.

Mrs. Edna Hamilton, Woman's Club, Hapeville, Ga.

BAGUETTES DE BERNE (Swiss Sticks)
Makes About 48
⅓ cup Roquefort cheese
1 cup butter
8 ounces Swiss cheese slices
Bunch of water cress

1. Mix Roquefort cheese and butter until smooth.
2. Spread on Swiss cheese. Chill until Roquefort mixture is firm.
3. Cut into thin sticks. Arrange on bed of water cress.

Woman's Club, Palisade, N.J.

CHEESE APPLES
Makes 12
8-ounce package mild cheese
½ cup chopped nut
12 pickled small onions, chopped
Paprika
Cloves

1. Mash and soften cheese with fork.
2. Stir in nuts and onions.
3. Form into small balls. Roll one side of each ball in paprika.
4. Insert a clove in each ball.

Culinary Favorites, Study Club,
Lake Wilson, Minn.

ROSY CHEESE BALL
Makes One 3-Inch Ball
½ pound Cheddar cheese, shredded
3-ounce package cream cheese, softened
3 tablespoons sherry
¼ cup coarsely chopped pitted ripe olives
½ teaspoon Worcestershire
Dash of onion salt
Dash of garlic salt
Dash of celery salt
½ cup coarsely snipped dried beef

1. With elecrtic mixer at medium speed, blend all ingredients except beef. When thoroughly blended, shape into ball. Wrap in aluminum foil. Chill.
2. About 30 minutes before serving, remove foil. Reshape ball; roll in beef.

Mrs. George Newell, Women's Club,
Barrington, R.I.

CHEESE BALLS
Makes One 3-Inch Ball
8-ounce package cream cheese
Mayonnaise
8-ounce package Cheddar cheese, shredded
Garlic salt, Tabasco, grated onion, Worcestershire, red pepper and seasoned salt to taste
Paprika
Curry powder

1. Beat cream cheese with a little mayonnaise until smooth and fluffy.
2. Beat in Cheddar cheese. Season with garlic salt, Tabasco, grated onion, Worcestershire, red pepper and seasoned salt. Knead well. Form into marble-size balls.
3. Roll balls in an equal amount of paprika and curry powder, mixed. Refrigerate or freeze.

Mrs. T. Wade Harrison, Woman's Club,
Gainesville, Fla.

MINT BOUQUET
Serves 4
8-ounce package cream cheese
2 tablespoons minced mint
½ teaspoon salt
3 tablespoons brandy
Finely chopped toasted almonds
Mint leaves

1. Blend cream cheese, minced mint, salt and brandy.
2. Form mixture into balls. Roll in almonds.
3. Circle serving plate with mint leaves.

Something to Crow About Cook Book,
Junior Woman's Club, Simsbury, Conn.

ROQUEFORT BALL
Makes One 4-Inch Ball
or Two 2-Inch Balls
6 ounces Roquefort cheese
2 4-ounce jars sharp cheese
12 ounces cream cheese
1 tablespoon Worcestershire
1 teaspoon monosodium glutamate
2 tablespoons grated onion
¼ cup minced parsley
½ cup ground nuts

1. Day before, leave cheeses at room temperature to soften. Then combine and blend with Worcestershire, monosodium glutamate and onion. Refrigerate for 24 hours.
2. Next day, form into 1 large ball or 2 small balls; roll in parsley, mixed with nuts.

Jean Turman, Junior Woman's Club,
Greeley, Colo.

CHEESE CAVIAR IN TOMATO CUP
Serves 4
Serve at room temperature with crackers.
1 tablespoons caviar
Dash of lemon juice
8-ounce package cream cheese
1 large tomato

1. Mix caviar, lemon juice and cheese.
2. Scoop out tomato. Drain to use as serving container.
3. Pile cheese mixture into tomato cup. Top with additional caviar, if desired.

Helen Pyles, Junior Civic Woman's Club,
Parkersburg, W.Va.

CHEESE ROLLS
Makes 2
½ pound mild Cheddar cheese, diced
½ pound sharp Cheddar cheese, diced
½ pound pimiento cheese, diced
2 cloves garlic
3-ounce package cream cheese
1 tablespoon Worcestershire
¼ teaspoon cayenne
Parsley flakes
Paprika

1. Day before, let cheeses soften at room temperature; then put Cheddar and pimiento cheeses and garlic through fine blade of meat grinder. Turn into mixing bowl.

2. Add cream cheese, Worcestershire and cayenne. Work with hands until well mixed.

3. Divide in half. Shape each half into roll.

4. Coat one roll with parsley flakes and the other with paprika.

5. Wrap in waxed paper. Refrigerate overnight.

6. Next day, remove from refrigerator about 1 hour before serving.

Submitted to Woman's Club, Kankakee, Ill., by Mrs. Everett McKinley Dirkson, Washington, D.C.

CHICKEN LIVER PÂTÉ
Makes About 2 Cups

2 tablespoons butter or margarine
½ pound chicken livers
3-ounce can mushrooms, drained
2 tablespoons chopped chives
¼ cup chopped parsley
½ cup mayonnaise
Salt and pepper to taste

1. Melt butter or margarine; in skillet sauté livers over medium heat, turning frequently, until pink color disappears.

2. Put livers and mushrooms through medium blade of meat grinder.

3. Turn into bowl. Stir in chives, parsley and mayonnaise.

4. Season with salt and pepper. Mix well. Chill.

Mrs. R. C. Richardson, Woman's Club, Lovell, Wyo.

CHICKEN LIVER AND MUSHROOM PÂTÉ
Makes About 2 Cups

¼ cup butter
½ pound chicken livers
2 tablespoons chopped onion
¼ pound mushrooms
2 tablespoons dry sherry
⅛ teaspoon salt
Dash of pepper

1. Melt butter in skillet; sauté livers, onion and mushrooms until livers are lightly browned on all sides.

2. Empty into container of electric blender. Add sherry, salt and pepper. Blend until smooth. Chill.

Betty Scott, Women's Club, Barrington, R.I.

CHIPPED BEEF PECAN LOG
Makes 2 Cups

8-ounce package cream cheese
1 teaspoon grated onion
1 to 2 teaspoons horseradish
2 drops Tabasco
½ cup finely cut chipped beef
½ cup finely chopped salted pecans
Minced parsley

1. Combine cheese, onion, horseradish and Tabasco. Beat until fluffy. Beat in beef and pecans.

2. Form into a log about 1½ inches in diameter. Roll in parsley. Chill.

3. Cut into thin slices to serve.

Our Heritage Cook Book, Pontotoc, Miss.

CUCUMBER CHEESE SLICES
Serves 4

1 medium cucumber
Salt to taste
2 6-ounce packages cream cheese
2 tablespoons chopped onion
¼ cup chopped green pepper
Paprika
Pepper and Worcestershire to taste

1. Halve cucumber crosswise. Pare. Remove seeds, leaving center hollow. Sprinkle with salt. Let drain.

2. Combine cheese, onion, green pepper and enough paprika to make filling red. Season with salt, pepper and Worcestershire.

3. Dry cucumber halves; pack firmly with cheese mixture; press halves back together. Chill.

4. To serve, cut crosswise into ¼-inch-thick slices.

Mrs. Ed Keating, Junior Woman's Club, Pompano Beach, Fla.

DEVILED EGGS
Makes 12 Halves

6 eggs, hard-cooked
1 tablespoon lemon juice or vinegar
¼ cup melted butter
¼ teaspoon salt
⅛ teaspoon pepper
½ teaspoon celery salt
½ teaspoon dry mustard
1 teaspoon grated onion
Paprika

1. Halve eggs lengthwise. Press yolks through sieve. Reserve whites.

2. Blend yolks, lemon juice or vinegar, butter, seasonings, mustard and onion.

3. Spoon filling into egg white halves. Sprinkle with paprika.

4. Chill until ready to serve.

Study Club, Balsam Lake, Wis.

PICKLED EGGS
Makes 18

2 cups white vinegar
2 tablespoons sugar
1 teaspoon salt
½ teaspoon mixed pickling spices
1 medium onion, sliced
18 eggs, hard-cooked

1. Day before, in saucepan combine vinegar, sugar, salt, spices and onion. Bring to boil. Simmer over low heat for 5 minutes.

2. Put eggs in 2-quart heatproof jar. Cover with hot mixture.

3. Cover; cool; then refrigerate at least overnight before serving.

Mrs. Orrin W. Gilbert, Woman's Club, Anchorage, Alaska

EGGPLANT MARINARA

Serves 6

1 unpeeled eggplant, cut into
1-inch cubes
½ cup white wine vinegar
1 teaspoon salt
½ teaspoon white pepper
1 clove garlic, minced
1 teaspoon orégano
½ teaspoon basil
¾ cup olive oil

1. Day before, cook eggplant in water to cover for 8 to 10 minutes, or until cubes are soft but retain their shape. Drain.
2. Combine vinegar, salt, pepper, garlic, orégano and basil. Mix with eggplant. Refrigerate overnight.
3. Before serving, add oil. Mix well.

Mrs. Charles Davis, Junior Woman's Club,
Benson, Ariz.

POOR MAN'S CAVIAR

Serves 12

1 large or 2 small unpeeled
eggplants, cubed
2 medium onions, finely chopped
¼ cup olive oil
2 cloves garlic, minced
1 green pepper, seeded and
chopped (optional)
4 to 6 tomatoes, peeled and cubed,
or 2 cups canned tomatoes; or
1 cup tomato sauce
1 tablespoon sugar
2 tablespoons vinegar
Salt and pepper to taste
2 tablespoons Worcestershire

1. Day before, cook eggplant in boiling water to cover for about 25 minutes, or until tender. Drain. When cool enough to handle, remove skin. Chop finely.
2. Heat oil; sauté onions, garlic and green pepper until tender but not browned. Add eggplant, tomatoes or tomato sauce, sugar, vinegar, salt and pepper. Simmer over low heat for about 1½ hours, stirring occasionally.
3. Add Worcestershire; mix well. Continue to cook until thick and beginning to get dry.
4. Remove from heat; beat well; pack into jars. Cool. Let ripen in refrigerator for at least 24 hours before serving.

Mrs. John Bach, Woman's Club, Williamsburg, Ky.

SEVICHE (Fish in Lime Juice)

Serves 6

1 pound frozen fillets of sole or
haddock, partially defrosted
10 golf-ball size Bermuda onions
2½-ounce bottle capers
½ cup cider vinegar
1 cup lime juice
1½ teaspoons red pepper flakes
4 to 6 drops Tabasco
2 tablespoons sugar

1. 48 hours before, dice fish. Cut onions into very thin slices.
2. Put fish and onions in shallow dish. Add remaining ingredients.
3. Refrigerate for at least 48 hours, stirring occasionally.

Mrs. George King, Woman's Club,
McLean, Va.

APPETIZER HAM BALL

Makes 4-Inch Ball

2 4½-ounce cans deviled ham
3 tablespoons chopped stuffed
green olives
1 tablespoon prepared mustard
Tabasco to taste
12-ounce package cream cheese
2 teaspoons milk
Parsley

1. Combine ham, olives, mustard and Tabasco. Form into ball on serving dish. Chill.
2. Soften cheese. Beat in milk until fluffy. Frost ball with cheese. Chill.
3. Remove from refrigerator 15 minutes before serving. Garnish with parsley.

Barbara Waddle, Woman's Club,
Warner Robins, Ga.

CRANBERRY HAM ROLLUPS

Makes 12

1 cup jellied cranberry sauce
1 teaspoon grated onion
¼ cup finely chopped celery
1 cup coarsely crushed crisp salted
crackers
12 slices boiled ham

1. Combine cranberry sauce, onion, celery and crackers. Mix well.
2. Spread about 1 tablespoon of cranberry mixture on each ham slice, keeping it 1 inch from edge. Roll up. Chill.

Mrs. Harry F. Schieman, Thursday Morning Club,
Madison, N.J.

SPICED PINEAPPLE AND
HAM KEBABS

Serves 8

1-pound can pineapple chunks
¾ cup vinegar
1¾ cups sugar
6 cloves
4-inch cinnamon stick
1 pound cooked ham, cubed

1. Drain syrup from pineapple into measuring cup; reserve ¾ cup.
2. In saucepan combine reserved syrup, vinegar, sugar, cloves and cinnamon. Bring to boil. Simmer over low heat for 10 minutes.
3. Add pineapple; cool in syrup. Cover. Refrigerate.
4. To serve, spear chunks of pineapple and cubes of ham on cocktail picks.

Wanda Roper, Junior Study Club,
San Augustine, Tex.

HAM AND VEAL PÂTÉ

Makes 1 Loaf

Serve with dark bread or melba toast.

½ pound chicken meat
½ pound lean veal
2 teaspoons seasoned salt
2 eggs, lightly beaten
½ pound sliced.bacon
2 small bay leaves
1 sprig thyme
½ pound thinly sliced ham
¾ pound thinly sliced veal cutlets
½ cup pistachio nuts
　　Salt to taste
3 tablespoons brandy
½ cup beef consommé

1. Preheat oven to 300° F.
2. Grind together chicken and veal. Beat in seasoned salt and eggs. Set aside.
3. Line sides and bottom of 8-inch loaf pan with bacon, reserving a few strips for top of pâté. Place bay leaves and thyme on bacon.
4. Trim ham and veal cutlets to fit pan.
5. Place slice of ham on bacon in bottom of pan. Spread with layer of ground meat. Sprinkle with ¼ cup of the nuts. Cover with slice of veal cutlet. Sprinkle with a little salt.
6. Repeat Step 5 until all sliced meat is used, ending with veal. Sprinkle top layer with brandy.
7. Top with reserved bacon. Cover pan with aluminum foil.
8. Bake in preheated oven for 2¾ hours. Remove foil; pour consommé into pan; re-cover; bake for 15 minutes longer.
9. Remove pâté from oven, place heavy weight on top; let stand until cool.
10. Remove foil. Chill.
11. Cut into thin slices.

*Mrs. William Bell, Woman's Club,
Morristown, N.J.*

CIGARETTES DE BAYONNE

Makes 32

2 ounces pâté de foie gras
¾ cup butter
16 thin slices boiled ham
2 tablespoons finely chopped truffles

1. Blend pâté and ½ cup of the butter until soft and creamy.
2. Spread on slices of ham. Roll up each slice like a jelly roll.
3. Refrigerate for 1 hour. Cut each roll in half.
4. Spread remaining butter on ends of rolls. Sprinkle with truffles.
5. Chill before serving.

Woman's Club, Palisade, N.J.

MARINATED HERRING IN SOUR CREAM

Serves 6

1 cup sour cream
3 tablespoons lemon juice
1 tablespoon peppercorns
1 teaspoon salt
¼ teaspoon monosodium glutamate
1 large onion, thinly sliced
1-pound jar fillets of herring
　　Lemon slices (optional)

1. In mixing bowl blend sour cream, lemon juice, peppercorns, salt and mono-sodium glutamate.
2. Add onion; mix well.
3. Add herring; stir carefully to coat pieces evenly.
4. Cover. Chill for at least 2 hours be-fore serving.
5. Arrange in serving dish. Garnish with lemon, if desired.

*Mrs. Michael Halliday, Civic League,
Greenville, Pa.*

PICKLED SALTED HERRING

Serves 6

3 large salted herrings
1 cup white vinegar
½ cup sugar
½ cup chopped onions or onion rings
3 bay leaves
12 peppercorns
　　Chopped dill or chives

1. Remove heads from herrings. Clean fish. Soak in water to cover for 8 to 12 hours. Drain; bone; fillet. Cut fillets cross-wise into thin strips.
2. Combine vinegar, sugar, onion, bay leaves and peppercorns.
3. Arrange herring in serving dish, re-forming slices into shape of fillets. Pour vinegar mixture over fish. Marinate in re-frigerator for several hours.
4. Before serving, sprinkle with dill or chives.

*Mrs. Ralph Larson, Woman's Club,
Stromsburg, Neb.*

STUFFED LETTUCE

Serves 8

1 firm head lettuce
8-ounce package cream cheese
2 tablespoons grated carrot
2 tablespoons finely cut tomato
2 tablespoons Roquefort cheese
1 tablespoon minced green pepper
1 tablespoon onion juice
　　Salt to taste

1. Hollow out head of lettuce. Keep re-moved lettuce for another use.
2. Combine remaining ingredients. Stuff lettuce.
3. Wrap in waxed paper. Chill until ready to serve.
4. To serve, slice into pieces of desired thickness.

*Grace Rethmeier, South Side Woman's Club,
Denver, Colo.*

ASPIC OF FOIE GRAS

Serves 6 to 8

10½-ounce can condensed beef
consommé
1 envelope gelatin
2 4½-ounce cans liver pâté
½ teaspoon Worcestershire
⅛ teaspoon Tabasco
2 tablespoons chopped parsley
Olives
Water cress
Radish roses

1. Pour consommé into small saucepan. Sprinkle gelatin on top to soften. Stir over low heat until gelatin is completely dissolved.
2. Pour consommé into 2-cup bowl. Chill for 1 to 2 hours, or until set.
3. Meanwhile, mix liver pâté with Worcestershire, Tabasco and parsley.
4. When consommé is completely set, scoop out center portion with spoon, leaving a lining about ½ inch thick on bottom and sides of bowl. Reserve removed center portion. Pack pâté carefully into scooped-out hole. Smooth top.
5. Melt reserved consommé over low heat. Pour over pâté. Chill until firm.
6. To serve, set bowl briefly in warm water to loosen. Place serving plate over bowl. Invert both plate and bowl. Garnish with olives, water cress and radish roses.

Jo Dunning, Woman's Club, Warner Robins, Ga.

ITALIAN RAW MUSHROOMS

Serves 4 to 6

½ pound small mushrooms
¼ teaspoon salt
¼ teaspoon pepper
½ teaspoon orégano
3 tablespoons lemon juice
½ cup olive oil

1. Day before, remove stems from mushrooms. Wash mushroom cups. Dry with absorbent paper.
2. Combine remaining ingredients. Toss with mushroom cups. Marinate in refrigerator overnight.

*Mrs. Charles Davis, Junior Woman's Club,
Benson, Ariz.*

TIPSY MUSHROOMS

Makes About 1 Pint

⅔ cup tarragon vinegar
½ cup olive oil
1 clove garlic
1 tablespoon sugar
1½ teaspoons salt
Dash of pepper
2 tablespoons water
Dash of Tabasco
1 pound button mushrooms, washed
and skinned, or 2 8-ounce cans
button mushrooms, drained
1 medium onion, sliced and separated
into rings

1. In mixing bowl combine vinegar, oil, garlic, sugar, salt pepper, water and Tabasco. Stir until well blended.

2. Add mushrooms and onion. Toss lightly.
3. Cover. Refrigerate for at least 8 hours, stirring occasionally.
4. Drain. Serve as hors d'oeuvres on cocktail picks or as relish.

*Marge Leiner, Junior Woman's Club,
Lombard, Ill.*

RULLEPOLZE (Spiced Meat)

Serves 8 to 10

This is an Old World recipe from Scandinavia adapted as a present-day appetizer.

9 x 7-inch flank steak
½ pound veal, cut into 1-inch cubes
½ pound pork, cut into 1-inch cubes
Salt and pepper
2 teaspoons ginger
1 cup grated onions
¼ cup sugar

1. 2 or 3 days before, spread steak on board. Cover with veal and pork.
2. Sprinkle generously with salt and pepper, then with ginger and onions.
3. Roll up steak like a jelly roll. Sew up ends to keep filling secure.
4. In Dutch oven or large saucepan combine ½ pound salt, sugar and 2 quarts water. Bring to boil. Boil for 5 minutes. Cool.
5. Arrange steak in large container (not metal). Cover with cooled solution. Marinate for 2 to 3 days.
6. When ready to use, remove steak from marinade; roll in piece of cheesecloth; sew up cheesecloth.
7. In Dutch oven or heavy saucepan bring 2 quarts water and 2 teaspoons salt to boil.
8. Add steak roll; cover; simmer over low heat for 2 hours, or until tender.
9. Remove steak from liquid; remove cheesecloth; place meat in large container. Top with wooden board and heavy weight to weigh down meat. Chill for 2 to 3 hours.
10. To serve, cut into very thin slices.

Mrs. Donald Ness, Woman's Club, Lovell, Wyo.

CORNETS DE SAUMON FUMÉ
(Smoked Salmon Cones)

Makes About 36

2 cups flaked cooked codfish
½ cup mayonnaise
Salt and pepper to taste
8 thin slices smoked salmon
¼ cup finely chopped parsley

1. Combine codfish and mayonnaise. Season with salt and pepper.
2. Cut salmon slices into triangles, making about 4 triangles from each slices, depending on size of slice.
3. Roll up each triangle to form a cone; secure at base with cocktail pick; fill cones with codfish mixture.
4. Sprinkle parsley on edges of cones. Arrange on serving dish. Chill for at least 1 hour.

Woman's Club, Palisade, N.J.

SHRIMP BALLS

Makes 24 to 36

1 pound shrimp, shelled, deveined,
   cooked and chopped
8-ounce package cream cheese
1 small onion, minced
   Dash of Worcestershire
   Salt to taste
   Minced parsley

1. Combine shrimp, cheese, onion,
Worcestershire and salt.

2. Roll into small balls; roll in parsley.

3. Insert cocktail pick into each ball.
Serve at room temperature.

Mrs. James L. Parsons, Junior Woman's Club,
College Park, Md.

MARINATED SHRIMP

Serves 3 or 4

1 pound shrimp, shelled, deveined
   and cooked
2 tablespoons lemon juice
1 teaspoon salt
⅛ teaspoon pepper
¼ cup cooking oil
2 tablespoons vinegar
¼ teaspoon paprika
½ teaspoon garlic powder
3 tablespoons horseradish
1 small onion, minced
   Minced parsley

1. Put shrimp in bowl. Add remaining
ingredients. Toss to mix. Refrigerate for
several hours, tossing shrimp in marinade
occasionally.

2. Serve on cocktail picks.

Helen Fagone, Woman's Literary Union,
Portland, Me.

SHRIMP IN BEER

Serves 6

2 12-ounce cans beer
2 bay leaves
2 tablespoons mustard seed
1 tablespoon celery seed
½ teaspoon crushed red peppers
½ teaspoon freshly ground pepper
1½ pounds shrimp, shelled and
   deveined
3 tablespoons wine vinegar
1 clove garlic

1. In saucepan combine beer, bay leaves
and seasonings. Bring to boil. Boil for 5
minutes.

2. Add shrimp. Simmer over low heat
for 10 minutes.

3. Remove from heat. Add vinegar and
garlic. Let stand for at least 20 minutes.
Drain. Chill shrimp.

Mrs. Richard Miller, Women's Club,
Arvin, Calif.

MOLDED SHRIMP PÂTÉ

Makes 4 Cups

3 12-ounce packages frozen deveined
   shrimp
¾ cup softened butter
½ cup mayonnaise

1 tablespoon Worcestershire
1 tablespoon lemon juice
½ teaspoon salt
¼ teaspoon pepper
¼ teaspoon Tabasco
   Dash of cayenne
   Dash of curry powder
   Water cress or parsley

1. Cook shrimp according to package
directions. Drain; cool. Set aside 12 shrimp
for garnish. Put remaining shrimp through
coarse blade of meat grinder.

2. In large bowl combine ground shrimp
with all remaining ingredients except water
cress or parsley. With wooden spoon beat
mixture to smooth paste. Press mixture,
one-third at a time, into 1-quart mold.
Cover. Refrigerate for 8 hours or overnight.

3. Loosen edge of mold with spatula.
Stand bottom of mold in hot water for
½ minute; shake gently to release pâté
from mold; turn onto serving platter.

4. Garnish with reserved shrimp and
water cress or parsley.

Fran Runyon, Junior Women's Club,
Jacksonville, Fla.

TORRID SHRIMP

Serves 6

1 pound fresh or frozen shrimp
3 cloves garlic, crushed
½ cup lemon juice
1 teaspoon salt
3 hot red peppers

1. Cook shrimp in boiling water for
5 minutes. Drain. Plunge into ice water.

2. Shell and devein shrimp. Put in deep
bowl.

3. In another bowl blend remaining
ingredients. Pour over shrimp. Let stand
for 4 to 5 hours.

4. Drain shrimp. Serve on cocktail picks.

Lillian T. de Canais, President,
Puerto Rico Federation of Women's Clubs

TONGUE AND CHEESE HORS
D'OEUVRES

3-ounce package cream cheese,
   softened
   Salt, Worcestershire and paprika
   to taste
5 paper-thin slices tongue

1. Season cheese with salt, Worcestershire and paprika; spread on slices of
tongue.

2. Stack slices one on top of the other.
Chill until firm.

3. Cut into small squares. Serve on cocktail picks.

VARIATION: Use bologna, liver sausage,
cooked ham or other sliced luncheon meat
in place of tongue.

Mrs. Richard Evans, Woman's Club,
Gainesville, Fla.

Hot Hors d'Oeuvres

CHUTNEY BACON BALLS
Serves 10

12-ounce bottle imported chutney
12 hard-cooked egg yolks
½ pound sliced bacon

1. Preheat oven to 350° F.
2. Drain syrup from chutney. (Reserve for some other purpose—excellent mixed with cream cheese for tea sandwiches.) Chop chutney finely. Mix with egg yolks to make a paste; roll into balls. Wrap each ball in half a slice of bacon. Secure with wooden picks. Arrange on baking sheet.
3. Bake in preheated oven for 10 minutes, or until bacon is crisp.

Woman's Club, Greenville, Ky.

STUFFED CHEESE BALLS

1 cup grated sharp cheese
3 tablespoons butter or margarine
½ cup presifted flour
½ teaspoon salt
Cayenne to taste
Stuffed olives, Vienna sausage, cooked shrimp or tiny pickled mushrooms
Paprika

1. Preheat oven to 400° F.
2. Combine cheese, butter or margarine, flour, salt and cayenne. Mix thoroughly.
3. Shape into small balls around olives, pieces of Vienna sausage, shrimp or mushrooms.
4. Sprinkle with paprika. Arrange in baking sheet. Bake in preheated oven for 15 minutes, or until golden brown.

Leonore Kirchem, Gentilly Woods Woman's Club, New Orleans, La.

QUICHE TARTLETS
Makes 24 Tartlets

Pastry for a 2-Crust Pie (p. 548)
6 slices bacon
2 ounces natural Swiss cheese
2 eggs
1 cup heavy cream
Pinch of nutmeg
½ teaspoon salt
1 teaspoon sugar
Pinch of cayenne
Pinch of pepper
Butter or margarine

1. Roll out Pastry for a 2-Crust Pie thinly on lightly floured board. Cut into fluted rounds slightly larger than muffin cups. Use 2 muffin pans, each with 12 cups measuring 1¾ x ¾ inches. Fit a pastry round into each cup, pricking well with fork. Cover with aluminum foil. Chill for several hours.
2. Preheat oven to 400° F.
3. Fry bacon until crisp. Drain well. Crumble.
4. Shred cheese finely.
5. Combine eggs, cream, nutmeg, salt, sugar, cayenne and pepper. Beat well to blend.

6. Spread a little butter or margarine over pastry in each muffin cup; sprinkle with a little bacon and cheese. Fill each cup to just below top with egg mixture. Sprinkle with additional nutmeg, if desired.
7. Bake in preheated oven for 15 minutes; reduce temperature to 300° F.; bake for 15 minutes longer, or until pastry is golden brown and filling is puffy.
8. Let cool slightly before removing carefully from pans. Serve warm.

Hazell A. Swindell, Women's Club, Barrington, R.I.

PARTY CHICKEN LIVERS
Makes 36

1 pound chicken livers
Seasoned salt to taste
½ cup margarine
Cornflake crumbs

1. Preheat oven to 350° F.
2. Cut each liver into 4 pieces. Season well with salt.
3. Melt margarine in shallow pan large enough to hold all the livers in one layer. Roll livers in margarine, then in crumbs. Return to pan.
4. Bake in preheated oven for 45 minutes.
5. Serve on cocktail picks.

Mrs. Warren Whitmore, Woman's Club of South Jacksonville, Jacksonville, Fla.

CHOPPED CHICKEN LIVERS
Makes 1½ Cups

Serve in lettuce-lined cups or as a spread for crackers or bread.

¼ cup chicken fat
½ pound chicken livers, quartered
1 medium onion, diced
2 eggs, hard-cooked and chopped
½ teaspoon salt
¼ teaspoon pepper
Pinch of thyme

1. Melt fat in skillet; sauté livers and onion for about 8 minutes, or until livers are cooked and onion is golden. Cool. Chop livers; mix with onion and fat.
2. Combine liver mixture with eggs; stir in salt, pepper and thyme.
3. Chill.

A. S.

RUMAKI (Oriental Chicken Liver Appetizers)
Makes 30

2 tablespoons soy sauce
¾ teaspoon salt
½ teaspoon monosodium glutamate
½ teaspoon garlic salt
¼ teaspoon pepper
½ pound chicken livers
5-ounce can water chestnuts
½ pound sliced bacon

1. Combine soy sauce, salt, monosodium glutamate, garlic salt and pepper. Cut livers and water chestnuts in half. Let them soak in savory mixture, preferably overnight.

2. Preheat oven to 450° F.

3. Cut bacon slices in half crosswise. Hold a piece of liver on one end of bacon slice; fold bacon over; add half a water chestnut; again fold bacon over. Secure with wooden pick. Place on baking sheet.

4. Bake in preheated oven for 10 minutes. Turn. Bake for 10 minutes longer.

Mrs. Raymond Stewart, Pioneer Woman's Club
Dunbar, W. Va.

GROSTINI (Chicken Livers and Capers in Tomato Sauce)

Makes About 1½ Pints

3¼-ounce jar capers
   Vinegar
2 tablespoons olive oil
¼ cup grated onions
1 clove garlic, crushed
¼ cup chopped parsley
1 pound fresh or frozen chicken
   livers, finely chopped
8-ounce can tomatoes, drained
1 teaspoon salt
¼ teaspoon pepper
   Dash of Tabasco
1½-ounce can anchovies, drained and
   finely chopped
2 tablespoons butter or margarine

1. Day before, drain brine from capers; leave capers in jar. Fill jar with vinegar. Let stand overnight.

2. Next day, heat oil in large skillet; sauté onions until transparent.

3. Stir in garlic, parsley and livers. Simmer, stirring occasionally, until livers change color.

4. Drain capers. Add capers and tomatoes to liver mixture, mashing tomatoes with fork.

5. Add salt, pepper and Tabasco. Simmer for 5 minutes.

6. Cool. Refrigerate.

7. When ready to serve, return to skillet. Heat to serving temperature, stirring occasionally.

8. Stir in anchovies and butter or margarine. Simmer for 1 minute.

Lauline Trimarco, Woman's Club,
Dundee, Ill.

CHILES RELLENOS CON QUESO
(Stuffed Chili Peppers)

Serves 6

6 fresh long green or large can
   chili peppers jalapeña
½ pound Mexican or other semi-soft
   cheese (Monterey Jack or Bel
   Paese)
3 eggs, separated
1 tablespoon flour
   Fat for deep frying
   Salt and black pepper to taste

1. If chili peppers are fresh, roast in preheated 450° F. oven for 10 minutes; wrap in towel for few minutes to let steam: then skin, slit and remove seeds, but leave stems on. If chilis are canned, remove seeds.

2. Fill each chili with long strip of cheese.

3. Beat egg whites until stiff. Set aside.

4. Beat egg yolks until thick and pale. Stir in flour. Fold in egg whites.

5. Dip chilis in egg batter. Fry in deep fat heated to 365° F. until golden brown. Drain on absorbent paper. Sprinkle with salt and pepper.

Erma Trent, Gentilly Woods Woman's Club,
New Orleans, La.

DEEP FRIED CORNED BEEF AND SAUERKRAUT APPETIZERS

Makes 60 Balls

These may be made ahead, refrigerated or frozen, then reheated in a 400° F. oven for 10 minutes.

14-ounce can sauerkraut, drained
1½ cups water
12-ounce can corned beef
1 small onion, quartered
¼ cup margarine
   Flour
¼ teaspoon dry mustard
1 teaspoon horseradish
¾ cup milk
   Fine bread crumbs
2 eggs, beaten
   Fat for deep frying

1. Simmer sauerkraut in water for 15 minutes. Drain.

2. Put sauerkraut, corned beef and onion through medium blade of meat grinder.

3. Melt margarine in saucepan. Stir in ¼ cup flour, mustard and horseradish. Gradually stir in milk. Cook, stirring constantly, until thickened and smooth.

4. Add ground mixture. Stir in ½ cup crumbs. Cook for a few minutes longer. Chill.

5. Form chilled mixture into 1-inch balls. Roll in flour; dip in egg; roll in crumbs.

6. Fry in deep fat heated to 365° F. until golden brown. Drain on absorbent paper.

Mrs. Don Henkel, Study Club,
Hatton, N.D.

CRAB CREAM PUFFS

Makes 24

1 cup hot Medium White Sauce
   (p. 441)
6½-ounce can crab meat, drained
   and flaked
   Dash of cayenne
24 Cream Puffs (p. 552), baked

1. Combine Medium White Sauce, crab meat and cayenne.

2. Split each Cream Puff down side with sharp knife. Fill with crab mixture. Serve immediately.

Madelyn Lamb, Woman's Club, Murray, Ky.

COCK KEBABS

Serve with cocktail sauce.

   Cheese Pastry (p. 549)
   Tiny stuffed olives
1-inch cubes Vienna sausage,
   salami or bologna

1. Preheat oven to 475° F. Cover baking sheet with aluminum foil.

2. Roll out Cheese Pastry ⅛ inch thick on lightly floured cloth-covered board. Cut into 1-inch rounds.

3. Alternate rounds of pastry with olives and sausage cubes on wooden picks, kabob-style. Place on baking sheet.

4. Bake in preheated oven for 10 to 15 minutes, or until lightly browned.

Nana Miller, Junior Woman's Club, Corning, N.Y.

EGG ROLLS

Makes 8

¾ cup finely chopped celery
1 cup shredded cabbage
½ cup water
   Peanut oil
½ cup diced cooked shrimp
½ cup diced cooked pork, ham, veal, beef or chicken
¾ cup finely chopped water chestnuts
4 finely chopped scallions
8 Pancake Skins for Egg Rolls (p. 136)
1 tablespoon flour
2 tablespoons chicken broth

1. In small saucepan combine celery, cabbage and water. Bring to boil; drain well.

2. Heat 2 tablespoons oil in skillet. Add shrimp and meat. Stir over medium heat for 3 minutes.

3. Add celery mixture, water chestnuts and scallions. Cook over medium heat, stirring constantly, until delicately brown. Remove from heat. Cool.

4. Place about 4 tablespoons filling on each egg roll skin. In small bowl, blend flour and broth to a paste; use to brush edges of skins. Fold in 2 sides of skins; roll up; press lightly to seal.

5. Heat sufficient oil in large skillet to come 1 inch up side. Fry egg rolls, turning frequently, until golden on all sides.

6. Drain on absorbent paper. Serve at once.

Woman's Club, Palisade, N.J.

PRONTO-PUPPY HORS D'OEUVRES

Serves 4

These may be made ahead and reheated in a preheated 400° F. oven for about 5 minutes.

   Fat for deep frying
1 egg
½ cup milk
1 cup self-rising flour
2 tablespoons yellow corn meal
¼ teaspoon paprika
½ teaspoon dry mustard
⅛ teaspoon cayenne
1 pound miniature frankfurters

1. Heat fat to 365° F.

2. Combine egg and milk. Stir in dry ingredients to make batter.

3. Dip frankfurters in batter. Fry in fat for 2 to 3 minutes, or until lightly browned.

4. Serve on cocktail picks.

Mrs. Gordon McBride, Junior Woman's Club, Joliet, Ill.

SPICY APPETIZER FRANKFURTERS

Serves 4 to 8

Serve on cocktail picks or with crackers or chunks of French bread.

1½-ounce package spaghetti sauce mix
8-ounce can tomato sauce
1½ cups water
2 tablespoons cooking oil
1 to 2 pounds frankfurters

1. Combine spaghetti sauce mix, tomato sauce, water and oil.

2. Cut frankfurters into 1-inch pieces.

3. Chill sauce and franks until serving time.

4. Heat franks in sauce in casserole over candle warmer or in chafing dish.

Mary Jo. Jenkins, Junior Women's Club, Miamisburg, Ohio

GOUGÈRE (Cheese Puff)

Serves 12

Serve this hot in wedges for an hors d'oeuvre; it is also excellent served with soups or hearty salads. If you like bite-size d'oeuvres, the gougère paste may be made into tiny cheesy cream puffs.

2 cups water
1 cup butter
2 cups presifted flour
⅛ teaspoon cayenne
⅛ teaspoon freshly ground black pepper
¼ teaspoon salt
¼ teaspoon dry mustard
¼ teaspoon paprika
9 medium or large eggs
1½ cups crumbled Gruyère cheese
¼ cup freshly grated Parmesan cheese
1 tablespoon cream

1. In deep saucepan combine water and butter. Bring slowly to boil over medium heat.

2. Combine flour and all seasonings. Dump all at once into water-butter mixture. Stir rapidly until ball forms in center.

3. Remove from heat. Beat in 8 of the eggs, one at a time, beating well after each addition.

4. Combine cheeses; fold into egg mixture. Refrigerate until paste stands in stiff peak when tested with spoon.

5. Preheat oven to 375° F. Grease 2 baking sheets.

6. Form paste into 2 rings, each 9 inches round, 2 inches wide and 1 inch high, on baking sheets.

7. Beat remaining egg lightly with cream; use to brush rings. Sprinkle with additional paprika.

8. Bake in preheated oven for 1 hour. Pierce in several places with wooden pick to release steam; reduce temperature to 300° F.; bake for 10 to 15 minutes longer.

Mrs. S. J. Radzwiller, Woman's Club, Morristown, N.J.

STUFFED GRAPE LEAVES
Makes 50

Grape leaves packed in brine can be purchased at stores selling Middle Eastern foods; rinse the leaves thoroughly in cold water, squeeze out the moisture and separate the leaves carefully. Grape leaves picked from the vine should be washed in cold water and soaked in hot water for about 15 minutes to soften; then squeeze out moisture, and cut out stem from each leaf.

1 cup rice, rinsed in water
1 pound lamb or beef, finely chopped
Salt
Pepper to taste
Dash of allspice
50 grape leaves
Lamb bones or chicken wings or necks
Juice of 2 lemons

1. Prepare stuffing: Combine rice, meat, salt to taste, pepper and allspice.
2. Place 1 tablespoon stuffing across each grape leaf. Fold end and sides of leaf over stuffing like an envelope. Roll up away from you.
3. Place lamb bones or chicken pieces in pan. As leaves are stuffed, arrange in rows over bones. Alternate direction of each row, as well as each layer. Sprinkle with 1 teaspoon salt. Place heavy plate or inverted lid on rolls. Add water to reach edge of plate.
4. Cover. Cook over low heat for 35 to 40 minutes, or until leaves are tender. During last 10 minutes of cooking, add lemon juice.
5. Serve hot or cold.

Mrs. Michael Shalhoup, Junior Women's Club, Nashua, N.H.

HAM CHEESE BALLS
Makes About 16

½ pound ground cooked smoked ham
¾ cup grated Cheddar cheese
2 tablespoons grated onion
1 egg
¼ cup cracker crumbs
½ cup milk
1 cup crushed cornflakes
Fat for deep frying

1. Put ham, cheese, onion, egg and crumbs in mixing bowl.
2. Mix well. Shape into 1½-inch balls.
3. Dip balls into milk. Coat with cornflakes.
4. Fry in deep fat heated to 365° F. for 4 minutes, or until golden.
5. Drain on absorbent paper. Serve at once.

Mrs. Jack Fletcher, Junior Woman's Club, Conover, N.C.

CHINESE MEAT BALLS
Makes About 24

1 pound ground beef
¾ cup minced celery
¼ cup finely chopped almonds
1 clove garlic, crushed
1 teaspoon salt
½ cup bread crumbs
1 tablespoon soy sauce
½ teaspoon monosodium glutamate
2 eggs, beaten
Cornstarch
3 tablespoons cooking oil
Pineapple Sauce (p. 448)

1. Combine beef, celery, almonds, garlic and salt; mix well. Add crumbs, soy sauce, monosodium glutamate and eggs; mix well.
2. Shape into balls the size of walnuts. Roll in cornstarch.
3. Heat oil in large skillet. Brown meat balls on all sides.
4. Simmer for 15 minutes, turning occasionally.
5. Spear meat balls with cocktail picks. Serve with Pineapple Sauce.

Mrs. Frederick Ziesenheim, Woman's Club, Forest Hills, Pa.

COCKTAIL MEAT BALLS
Makes About 72

3 pounds ground beef
1 egg
¼ cup bread crumbs
Worcestershire
2½ teaspoons salt
¼ teaspoon pepper
1 tablespoon parsley
2 tablespoons shortening
½ cup chopped onions
½ teaspoon paprika
Few grains cayenne
½ teaspoon dry mustard
2½ cups chili sauce
5 tablespoons vinegar
4 tablespoons brown sugar
½ cup lemon juice

1. Combine beef, egg, crumbs, 2 teaspoons Worcestershire, 1½ teaspoons of the salt, pepper and parsley.
2. Roll into tiny balls. Melt shortening in skillet; brown meat balls quickly on all sides.
3. In saucepan combine remaining ingredients. Bring to boil. Simmer for 30 minutes. Add meat balls. Simmer for 10 minutes longer.
4. Place meat balls and sauce in chafing dish. Serve with cocktail picks.

Marion Stevens, Woman's Club, East Concord, N.H.

CHAFING DISH SWEET AND SOUR MEAT BALLS
Makes 50 to 60

2 pounds ground beef
1 egg, beaten
1 large onion, grated
Salt and pepper to taste
12-ounce bottle chili sauce
Juice of ½ lemon
¾ cup grape jelly

1. Combine beef, egg, onion, salt and pepper.
2. Shape into small balls.

3. In saucepan combine remaining ingredients. Bring to boil. Add meat balls. Simmer for 30 minutes.

4. Serve in chafing dish with cocktail picks.

Jet Christopher, Woman's Club,
Warner Robins, Ga.

CHILI MEAT BALLS

Makes About 25

1 pound ground beef
¾ teaspoon Tabasco
2 tablespoons minced onion
2 tablespoons chili sauce
1 tablespoon plus 1 teaspoon salt
¼ teaspoon orégano
2 tablespoons butter
2 tablespoons flour
1 cup water
1 tablespoon horseradish
½ teaspoon celery salt or celery seed
1 tablespoon prepared mustard

1. Combine beef, ¼ teaspoon of the Tabasco, onion, chili sauce, 1 tablespoon of the salt and orégano.

2. Shape into small balls. Melt butter in skillet; brown meat balls on all sides.

3. Remove meat balls from skillet. Stir flour into fat remaining in skillet. Gradually stir in water. Cook, stirring constantly, until sauce is thickened and smooth. Stir in remaining ingredients.

4. Return meat balls to sauce; bring to boil; simmer for 15 minutes.

5. Serve on cocktail picks.

Mrs. T. L. Aldrich, Glendale Estates Woman's
Club, Decatur, Ga.

WINE MEAT BALLS

Makes About 50

Mrs. Ahlgren writes: "In Panama, as a guest of the United States embassy, I tasted the most delectable meat balls imaginable. Mrs. Joseph S. Farland, wife of our ambassador, gave me the recipe."

1 pound lean pork
1 clove garlic
2 small onions
Parsley
¾ teaspoon nutmeg
¼ teaspoon cinnamon
¼ teaspoon allspice
1 teaspoon salt
¼ teaspoon black pepper
¾ cup sherry
¾ cup water
Cinnamon stick
2 cloves
½ cup brown sugar

1. Put pork, garlic, onions and 1 sprig of the parsley through meat grinder.

2. Mix ground meat, nutmeg, ¼ teaspoon cinnamon, allspice, salt, pepper and 1 tablespoon of the sherry. Let stand for 2 hours.

3. Roll 1 level teaspoon of mixture in palms of hands into ball the size of marble. Continue until all meat mixture is formed into balls.

4. Put water, cinnamon stick, cloves and sugar in heavy frying pan. Bring to boil.

5. Drop meat balls into boiling mixture. Add remaining sherry. Cook over low heat until meat balls have turned dark brown and most of liquid has evaporated.

6. Remove meat balls. Attach a bit of parsley to each one with cocktail pick.

Mrs. Oscar A. Ahlgren, Honorary President,
General Federation of Women's Clubs,
Washington, D.C.

BAKED MUSHROOMS STUFFED WITH CHEESE

Serves 4 to 6

1 pound mushrooms
2 tablespoons margarine
6 tablespoons crumbled blue cheese
2 tablespoons sour cream

1. Wash mushrooms. Separate stems from caps; reserve caps; chop stems finely.

2. Melt margarine in skillet; sauté chopped stems for 5 minutes.

3. Preheat oven to 350° F.

4. Combine cheese, cream and stems.

5. Stuff reserved caps with cheese mixture.

6. Arrange caps on baking sheet. Bake in preheated oven for 15 minutes.

Mrs. John R. Hiebel, Junior Woman's Club,
Pompano Beach, Fla.

MUSHROOMS STUFFED WITH CRAB MEAT

Makes 24

24 large mushroom caps
½ cup melted butter or margarine
1½ cups flaked crab meat
2 eggs, lightly beaten
3 tablespoons mayonnaise
½ cup grated onions
2 teaspoons lemon juice
½ cup fresh bread crumbs
½ cup grated Parmesan cheese

1. Preheat oven to 375° F. Grease baking sheet.

2. Wash and dry mushroom caps. Dip in butter or margarine. Arrange on baking sheet, cap side up.

3. In mixing bowl combine crab meat, eggs, mayonnaise, onion, lemon juice and crumbs; mix lightly.

4. Fill mushroom caps with crab meat mixture. Sprinkle with cheese.

5. Bake in preheated oven for 15 minutes.

Penny Katsafanas, North Hills Junior Woman's
Club, Glenshaw, Pa.

OYSTER PATTIES

Makes 48 to 60

½ cup margarine
4 tablespoons flour
6 scallions, minced
36 oysters, freshly shucked, drained and chopped (reserve liquor)
¼ cup minced parsley
¼ teaspoon thyme
8 green olives, minced
Salt and pepper to taste
48 to 60 tiny cocktail patties

1. Melt margarine in saucepan. Add flour. Cook, stirring, until smooth.

2. Add onions and oysters. Mix well. Add parsley, thyme and olives.

3. Slowly stir in reserved oyster liquor. Cook for 30 minutes, stirring frequently. (Add a little water, if necessary, for mixture should have puddinglike consistency.) Season with salt and pepper.

4. Fill cocktail patties to serve.

Gloria Taylor, Gentilly Woods Woman's Club,
New Orleans, La.

PIGS IN BLANKETS
Makes 12

12 large oysters, freshly shucked
　and drained
½ teaspoon salt
　Pepper
　Cayenne
1 pimiento, cut into 12 strips
12 slices bacon

1. Preheat broiler.

2. Season oysters with salt, pepper and cayenne.

3. Place 1 pimiento strip on each oyster. Wrap in 1 bacon slice.

4. Secure with wooden pick. Arrange on broiler pan.

5. Broil 4 to 5 inches from heat for 5 minutes, or until bacon is crisp and brown.

Woman's Club, Wahoo, Neb.

PINEAPPLE WRAPPED IN BACON
Makes 12

4 slices bacon
12 pineapple chunks

1. Preheat broiler.

2. Cut each bacon slice crosswise into thirds. Wrap each piece around 1 pineapple chunk. Fasten with wooden pick.

3. Broil 4 inches from heat, turning until well cooked on all sides.

Mrs. W. H. Hasebroock, Honorary President,
General Federation of Women's Clubs,
West Point, Neb.

COCKTAIL POTATO PUFFS
Makes 18

½ cup presifted flour
1½ teaspoons baking powder
¼ teaspoon salt
1 cup mashed potatoes
2 eggs, beaten
　Fat for deep frying

1. Combine all ingredients.

2. Form into small balls. Fry in deep fat heated to 365° F. until golden brown.

3. Drain on absorbent paper. Serve on cocktail picks.

Pat Paull, Service League, Lombard, Ill.

SAUSAGE ROLL
Makes About 18

2 cups baking powder biscuit mix
1 pound sausage meat

1. Making baking powder biscuit dough according to package directions. Divide into 4 equal portions.

2. Roll out each portion about ¼ inch thick on lightly floured board. Spread with sausage meat. Roll in waxed paper. Freeze.

3. Preheat oven to 450° F.

4. Cut rolls into thin slices; place on baking sheet; bake in preheated oven for 12 to 15 minutes.

VARIATION: Use ground ham mixed with mustard instead of sausage meat.

Mrs. Charles Evans, Woman's Club,
Gainesville, Fla.

BARBECUED SHRIMP
Serves 4 to 6

1 pound medium shrimp
1 envelope Italian salad dressing
　mix
2 tablespoons minced green pepper
¼ cup minced onions
½ teaspoon minced garlic
⅔ cup dry white wine
⅔ cup cooking oil
2 tablespoons lemon juice

1. Shell and devein shrimp. Cut each shrimp deeply along vein line. Flatten, butterfly-fashion.

2. In baking dish combine remaining ingredients. Add shrimp, making sure all are covered with marinade. Cover. Chill for 2 hours.

3. Preheat broiler. Line broiler pan with heavy-duty aluminum foil.

4. Arrange shrimp on foil. Broil 4 inches from heat for 2 to 3 minutes. Turn; baste with marinade; broil for 2 to 3 minutes longer.

5. Serve shrimp plain or accompanied by heated marinade as a dip.

Pat Grady, Women's Club, Addison, Ill.

BUTTERFLY SHRIMP
Serves 8 to 12

2 pounds shrimp, shelled and
　deveined (leave tails on)
1 cup presifted flour
½ teaspoon salt
1½ teaspoons baking powder
⅔ cup water
2 tablespoons lemon juice
1 egg, well beaten
1 tablespoon cooking oil
　Fat for deep frying
　Tartar Sauce for Fish (p. 450)

1. Split shrimp partway down middle.

2. In mixing bowl combine flour, salt and baking powder. Stir in water and lemon juice.

3. Combine egg and oil. Stir slowly into batter.

4. Drop 4 or 5 shrimp into batter at a time. Drain 1 shrimp at a time; drop into deep fat heated to 365° F. Fry until golden brown.

5. Serve with Tartar Sauce for Fish.

Gulf Coast Gourmet, Woman's Club, Foley, Ala

SHRIMP BALLS WITH SOUR CREAM CAPER SAUCE

Serves 6

1 pound shrimp, shelled, deveined, cooked and finely chopped
½ teaspoon salt
1 cup mashed potatoes
1 tablespoon grated onion
1 tablespoon minced parsley
¼ teaspoon Worcestershire
Dash of pepper
2 teaspoons horseradish
2 egg yolks
Cracker crumbs
Fat for deep frying
Sour Cream Caper Sauce (p. 450)

1. Combine all ingredients except crumbs, fat and caper sauce. Roll into balls the size of marbles.
2. Roll shrimp balls in crumbs. Fry in deep fat heated to 365° F. until golden brown.
3. Drain on absorbent paper. Serve on cocktail picks with Sour Cream Caper Sauce.

Mrs. Norman Herren, Woman's Club, Naples, Fla.

STUFFED SHRIMP

Serves 12

¼ cup butter
1 tablespoon minced onion
1 tablespoon minced green pepper
1 teaspoon minced celery
6 slices bread, crumbled
½ cup milk
¾ cup flaked cooked crab meat
Dash of cayenne
Salt and pepper to taste
36 large shrimp, shelled and deveined (leave tails on)
Flour
2 to 3 eggs
Cracker meal
Fat for deep frying
Cocktail sauce

1. Melt butter in skillet; sauté onion, green pepper and celery until tender.
2. Soak bread in milk.
3. Combine sautéed vegetables, bread and crab meat. Mix thoroughly. Season with cayenne, salt and pepper.
4. Split shrimp almost in half. Stuff with crab meat mixture. Press halves together.
5. Dip shrimp in flour; then in beaten egg (beat 1 egg at a time). Roll shrimp in cracker meal. Chill until ready to fry.
6. Fry a few shrimp at a time in deep fat heated to 365° F. until golden brown.
7. Serve with cocktail sauce.

Gulf Coast Gourmet, Woman's Club, Foley, Ala.

FRIED WONTONS

Makes 50

Wonton pastry may be purchased fresh or frozen at Chinese food shops. Or see p. 196 for Wontons recipe.

1 tablespoon bacon drippings
3 scallions, chopped
1 medium onion, chopped
1½ pounds coarsely ground pork
2 cups coarsely chopped mushrooms
7 shrimp, shelled, deveined and chopped
Salt and pepper to taste
¼ teaspoon monosodium glutamate
1 pound wonton pastry
1 egg, beaten
Fat for deep frying
Hot mustard

1. Heat bacon drippings in heavy skillet; sauté scallions and unions until tender.
2. Add pork and mushrooms. Sauté, stirring occasionally, for 10 minutes, or until well browned.
3. Add shrimp, salt, pepper and monosodium glutamate. Continue to cook until shrimp turn pink.
4. Place 1 teaspoon of the filling in middle of each wonton pastry. Moisten edges of wontons with egg. Bring ends to center to enclose filling. Press to seal.
5. Fry wontons, 4 or 5 at a time, in deep fat heated to 365° F. until golden. Drain on absorbent paper. Keep warm in low oven.
6. Serve accompanied by mustard.

Rita Ong, Woman's Club, Elroy, Ariz.

Dips

Not hors d'oeuvres and not truly canapés, dips have found a permanent and happy place in modern America's culinary life. Dips became popular after World War II. Before that time it would have been hard to find a recipe for one in any cook book, but today's cook books contain many recipes for this category of party foods for casual entertaining. Following is a selection of the best dips created by American homemakers. Serve any one or several, for taste variety, with a bowl of potato chips, corn chips, pretzel sticks, raw vegetables (such as cucumber, cauliflowerets, carrots, etc.) or assorted crackers.

ANCHOVY CREAM CHEESE DIP

Makes About 1 Cup

8-ounce package cream cheese
Dash of paprika
½ teaspoon celery seed
2 tablespoons minced onion
1 tablespoon lemon juice
2 teaspoons anchovy paste
2 tablespoons cream

Soften cream cheese. Add other ingredients. Beat until smooth.

Mrs. James Griparis, Junior Woman's Club, Joliet, Ill.

ANCHOVY SOUR CREAM DIP

Makes About 1 Cup

1 cup sour cream
2 teaspoons anchovy paste
1 teaspoon horseradish
2 teaspoons sweet pickle juice
1 teaspoon sugar
1 tablespoon mayonnaise

Combine all ingredients. Chill for 30 minutes before serving.

Virginia Millitzer, Woman's Club, Apopka, Fla.

AVOCADO DIP

Makes About 1½ Cups

2 ripe avocados
2 teaspoons lemon juice
1 teaspoon onion salt
½ teaspoon salt
Dash of Worcestershire

Mash avocados. Mix with remaining ingredients. Cover. Keep cold until ready to serve.

*Virginia Ancell, Pine River Pow Wow,
Bayfield, Colo.*

AVOCADO SOUR CREAM DIP

Makes About 2 Cups

1 avocado
3-ounce package cream cheese
1 cup sour cream
1 clove garlic, minced
1 tablespoon grated onion
1 teaspoon salt
1 tablespoon Worcestershire

Peel and mash avocado. Add other ingredients; mix well. Chill.

*Mrs. Harding Dawahare, Woman's Club,
Pikeville, Ga.*

GUACAMOLE

Makes About 2 Cups

Mexicans like guacamole very hot, but it is wise to experiment with the amount of green chilis or Tabasco before it is served to family or guests either as a dip or spread on toasted tortillas.

1 medium tomato, peeled
2 ripe avocados
1 small onion, minced
3 tablespoons finely chopped canned green chili peppers or a few drops Tabasco
Few drops lemon juice
Salt to taste

1. Mash avocado and tomato with fork until creamy.
2. Add remaining ingredients. Mix well.
3. Cover. Keep cold until ready to serve.

*Virginia Leslie, Junior Woman's Club,
Sandy Springs, Ga.*

HOT BEAN DIP

Makes About 2½ Cups

1-pound can refried beans
3 canned jalapeña chili peppers, chopped
1 teaspoon jalapeña juice from can
1 medium onion, minced
1 clove garlic, minced
2 tablespoons butter or margarine
¼ pound sharp Cheddar cheese, shredded

In top of double saucepan combine all ingredients. Heat over simmering water, stirring constantly, until cheese is melted and mixture is hot.

*Mrs. Hal Marshall, Pueblo Junior Woman's Club,
Tucson, Ariz.*

DARK MYSTERY DIP

Makes 2 Cups

10½-ounce can condensed black bean soup
2 3-ounce packages cream cheese
4 drops Tabasco
1 teaspoon Worcestershire
½ teaspoon salt
¼ teaspoon powdered garlic or 1 clove garlic, minced

Combine soup and cream cheese. Mix well. Season Texas-style (that means hot) with Tabasco and Worcestershire. Stir in salt and garlic.

*Mrs. Hugh Gingras, Coco Plum Woman's Club,
Coral Gables, Fla.*

CHILI BEEF DIP

Makes About 3 Cups

10½-ounce can condensed chili-beef soup
1 cup sour cream
¾ cup canned condensed beef consommé
½ teaspoon Worcestershire
¼ teaspoon chili powder
Pinch of hickory-smoked salt

Combine all ingredients. Cover. Chill for 2 to 3 hours to blend flavors.

*Mary Missoni, Junior Woman's Club,
Corning, N.Y.*

RED CAVIAR DIP

Makes 2¾ Cups

2 cups sour cream
Dash of lemon juice
6-ounce jar red caviar

Combine sour cream and juice. Turn into serving bowl. Empty caviar in center.

*Mrs. R. E. Greene, Jr., Marshall County
Woman's Club, Holly Springs, Miss.*

BLUE CHEESE FLUFF

Makes 1½ Cups

2 3-ounce packages cream cheese
½ cup crumbled blue cheese
¼ teaspoon garlic salt
3 tablespoons milk
Minced parsley

Soften cream cheese. Beat in blue cheese, garlic salt and milk. Mound in serving bowl. Sprinkle with parsley.

*Barbara Waddle, Woman's Club,
Warner Robins, Ga.*

BLUE CHEESE AND SOUR CREAM DIP

Makes About 1½ Cups

1½-ounce package blue cheese
3-ounce package cream cheese
1 cup sour cream
1 tablespoon minced onion
1 clove garlic, minced
3 or 4 drops Tabasco
¼ teaspoon Worcestershire

Let cheeses soften at room temperature; then mash. Mix well with other ingredients, using electric or rotary beater.

*Shirley Martin, Junior Women's Club,
Vernon, Conn.*

DOUBLE GOOD BLUE CHEESE DIP
Makes About 1½ Cups

3 ounces blue cheese
3-ounce package cream cheese
2 tablespoons chopped ripe olives
1 teaspoon grated onion
1 tablespoon chopped parsley
½ cup chopped nuts
Sour cream

1. Let cheeses soften at room temperature; then blend thoroughly.
2. Stir in olives, onion, parsley and nuts.
3. Beat in enough sour cream to give desired consistency.

*Rae West, Woman's Literary Union,
Portland, Me.*

CHEESE AND GREEN PEPPER DIP
Makes About 1 Cup

2 3-ounce packages cream cheese
1½-ounce triangle Roquefort cheese
1 tablespoon minced green pepper
1 tablespoon chopped pimiento
2 tablespoons minced onion
2 tablespoons minced celery
Dash of Tabasco
Dash of Worcestershire
Mayonnaise

1. Let cheeses soften at room temperature; then mash.
2. Blend with other ingredients.
3. Moisten with mayonnaise to give dip desired consistency. Chill.

Nita Hansen, Woman's Club, Jacksonville, Fla.

DIP FOR CHIPS
Makes About 1¼ Cups

¾ cup cottage cheese
½ cup mayonnaise
½ teaspoon dry mustard
½ teaspoon garlic salt
½ teaspoon Tabasco
1 teaspoon anchovy paste
1 teaspoon chili sauce
½ teaspoon curry powder

Combine all ingredients. Chill well.

*Betty Anderson, Women's Club,
Barrington, R.I.*

CREAM CHEESE DIP
Makes About 1¼ Cups

½ pound cream cheese
½ teaspoon celery seed
2 teaspoons onion juice
1 teaspoon lemon juice
Dash of paprika
2 to 3 tablespoons cream

Blend all ingredients until smooth.

*Mrs. James Grace, Junior Woman's Club,
Joliet, Ill.*

CREAM CHEESE–HORSERADISH DIP FOR VEGETABLES
Makes About 1 Cup

Serve with any or all of the following: carrot sticks, cucumber sticks, cauliflowerets, radishes, cherry tomatoes, celery sticks.

3-ounce package cream cheese
½ cup French dressing
1 teaspoon horseradish
Few drops Worcestershire
1 teaspoon chopped parsley
Dash of garlic powder

1. Cream the cheese well. Beat in dressing.
2. Add other ingredients.

Nancy Scrofani, Woman's Club, Linbrook, N.J.

CREAM CHEESE AND OLIVE DIP
Makes About 2 Cups

2 3-ounce packages cream cheese
1 small onion, minced
½ cup chopped stuffed olives
1 egg, hard-cooked and chopped
¼ cup chopped pecans
Mayonnaise
Salt to taste

1. Mash cheese. Combine with onion, olives, egg and pecans.
2. Stir in enough mayonnaise to make either a spread or a dip. Season with salt.

*Mrs. L. E. Schoonmaker, Woman's Club,
Gainesville, Fla.*

SMOKY CHEESE-OLIVE DIP
Makes About 1½ Cups

⅓ cup pineapple juice
1 tablespoon lemon juice
¼ teaspoon Tabasco
2 3-ounce packages cream cheese, quartered
6-ounce roll smoky cheese, sliced
1 small clove garlic
⅓ cup chopped stuffed olives

1. Put all ingredients except olives in container of electric blender (or use electric mixer). Blend until smooth.
2. Stir in olives. Keep cold until ready to serve.

*Mrs. W. A. Robinson, Junior Civic Woman's Club,
Parkersburg, W. Va.*

MEXICAN BEAN DIP
Makes About 5 Cups

2 1-pound cans pork and beans
½ cup grated sharp Cheddar cheese
1 teaspoon garlic salt
1 teaspoon chili powder
½ teaspoon salt
Dash of cayenne
1 teaspoon Tabasco
2 teaspoons vinegar
2 teaspoons Worcestershire
½ teaspoon liquid hickory smoke flavoring
8 slices bacon, cooked and crumbled

1. Put pork and beans in container of electric blender. Blend until smooth.
2. Turn into top of chafing dish or double saucepan.
3. Add all remaining ingredients except bacon.
4. Mix well. Heat to serving temperature, stirring constantly.
5. Sprinkle with bacon.

*Mrs. Frederick Ziesenheim, Woman's Club,
Forest Hills, Pa.*

MEXICAN DIP
Makes About 6 Cups
Serve this with crisp small tortillas.

1-pound 12-ounce can tomatoes, undrained
4-ounce can green chili peppers, drained and chopped
1 onion, chopped
1 pound Cheddar cheese, shredded

1. In saucepan combine tomatoes, chilis and onion. Bring to boil. Simmer until thick, stirring occasionally.
2. Add cheese; stir over low heat until melted.
3. Serve in chafing dish.

Mrs. Hal Marshall, Pueblo Junior Woman's Club,
Tucson, Ariz.

CHILE CON QUESO DIP
(Cheese and Hot Peppers Dip)
Makes About 4 Cups
¾ to 1 cup milk
2 pounds mild yellow cheese, cut into squares
2 4-ounce cans green chili peppers, drained and chopped
1 teaspoon garlic salt
4-ounce can pimientos, drained and finely chopped

1. Heat milk in top of double saucepan. Add remaining ingredients.
2. Heat, stirring occasionally, until cheese melts.
3. Serve in chafing dish.

Mrs. William J. Van Essen, President,
Woman's Club, Albuquerque, N.M.

HOT CHEESE DIP
Makes About 4 Cups
Serve in chafing dish as a dip for cubes of French bread and cooked ham.

1 pound mild yellow cheese
1 cup condensed milk
1 tomato, finely chopped
1 tablespoon chopped onion
2 tablespoons chopped pimiento
2 tablespoons chopped green chili pepper
2 teaspoons prepared mustard
1 teaspoon Worcestershire

Heat cheese and milk in top of double saucepan over simmering water until smooth, stirring frequently. Add remaining ingredients. Heat.

Geneva Ryan, Pine River Pow Wow,
Bayfield, Colo.

SALSA DIP (Saucy Dip)
Makes About 3 Cups
6-ounce can stewed tomatoes, drained
2 cups cream-style cottage cheese
½ to 1 4-ounce can green chili peppers, drained and chopped
Chili powder, salt and pepper to taste

1. Combine tomatoes, cheese and chilis.
2. Stir in chili powder, salt and pepper.

Marilyn Duckworth, Junior Woman's Club,
Scottsdale, Ariz.

CLAM DIP
Makes About 2 Cups
2 3-ounce packages cream cheese, softened
1 teaspoon lemon juice
1 tablespoon Worcestershire
Paprika
7½-ounce can minced clams, drained
1 tablespoon clam broth
½ teaspoon grated onion or to taste
Parsley

1. Combine cheese, lemon juice, Worcestershire, dash of paprika, clams, broth and onion. Mix well.
2. Pile into serving bowl. Sprinkle with paprika. Garnish with parsley.

Mrs. Clarence Miller, Woman's Club,
Sylvester, Ga.

FAVORITE CRAB DIP
Makes 2 Cups
3-ounce package cream cheese
½ cup mayonnaise
⅔ cup canned condensed tomato soup
½ pound cooked or 6½-ounce can crab meat, flaked
1 clove garlic, minced
Salt and pepper to taste
6 drops Tabasco

1. Soften cheese. Blend with mayonnaise and soup.
2. Stir in remaining ingredients.

Mrs. Howard G. Fahy, President,
Mount Diablo Women's Club, Concord, Calif.

ROQUEFORT CRAB DIP
Makes 1½ Cups
⅓ cup Roquefort cheese
⅓ cup cream cheese
2 tablespoons mayonnaise
½ teaspoon Worcestershire
1 tablespoon grated onion
1 teaspoon lemon juice
¼ teaspoon Tabasco
½ cup flaked cooked crab meat

1. Combine cheeses. Beat until soft and fluffy.
2. Beat in remaining ingredients in order given.

Mrs. Joseph St. Clair, Thursday Morning Club,
Madison, N.J.

PARTY CRAB MEAT DIP
Makes About 4 Cups
Serve hot with small pieces of garlic-buttered rye toast.

2 8-ounce packages cream cheese
⅓ cup mayonnaise
1½ teaspoons prepared mustard
3 tablespoons sauterne
4 teaspoons confectioners' sugar
½ teaspoon salt
¼ teaspoon garlic salt
½ teaspoon onion juice
2 6½-ounce cans crab meat, drained and flaked

1. In top of double saucepan combine all ingredients except crab meat. Heat over simmering water until well blended, stirring occasionally.

2. Stir in crab meat. Heat thoroughly.

Mrs. Eugene Braun, Women's Club,
Barrington, R.I.

SOUR CREAM CRAB MEAT CAPER DIP

Makes 2 Cups

1 cup sour cream
6½-ounce can crab meat, drained and flaked
1 tablespoon grated onion
¼ cup mayonnaise
1 tablespoon chopped capers
1 tablespoon lemon juice
Salt and pepper to taste

Combine all ingredients. Chill.

Mrs. Augustus H. Mueller, Woman's Club,
Clearwater, Fla.

DIPPING SAUCE FOR COOKED CRAB MEAT, LOBSTER, SHRIMP OR COLD CRISP VEGETABLES

Makes 2 Cups

½ cup mayonnaise
½ cup sour cream
2 tablespoons wine vinegar
½ teaspoon dry mustard
1 teaspoon Worcestershire
2 tablespoons grated onion
1 clove garlic, minced
3 eggs, hard-cooked and chopped
3 tablespoons chopped olives

Blend all ingredients. Chill for 2 hours before serving.

Mrs. Benjamin Schreiber,
Woman's Literary Union, Portland, Me.

CUCUMBER CREAM CHEESE DIP

Makes 1½ Cups

8-ounce package cream cheese
½ cup finely shredded unpeeled cucumber
½ teaspoon Worcestershire
Dash of garlic salt

Combine all ingredients. Blend well.

Peg Johnson, Woman's Club, Linbrook, N.J.

CUCUMBER SOUR CREAM DIP

Makes 1 Cup

1 large cucumber, unpeeled
½ small onion, grated
3 tablespoons sour cream
½ teaspoon salt
¼ teaspoon pepper
½ teaspoon paprika
2 teaspoons chopped parsley
2 teaspoons lemon juice
1 to 2 teaspoons chopped fresh dill or ¼ teaspoon dill seed
Pinch of sugar (optional)

1. Grate cucumber. Add onion. Drain thoroughly in strainer for at least 1 hour.

2. Put cucumber and onion in bowl. Add remaining ingredients. Stir to mix. Chill for at least 30 minutes for flavors to blend.

Anice Dittmar, Junior Woman's Club,
Jacksonville, Fla.

CURRY DIP

Makes 1 Cup

Serve with crisp cauliflowerets, broccoli, or celery.

1 cup mayonnaise
1 teaspoon grated onion
1 teaspoon horseradish
1 teaspoon tarragon vinegar
¼ teaspoon curry powder

Combine all ingredients. Blend well. Chill.

Diane Scoville, Junior Woman's Club,
Glastonbury, Conn.

EGG AND CHIVE CREAM CHEESE DIP

Makes About 1½ Cups

6-ounce package chive cream cheese
½ teaspoon salt
2 eggs, hard-cooked and sieved
½ teaspoon Worcestershire
2 tablespoons mayonnaise
1 teaspoon dry mustard
⅛ teaspoon pepper
3 tablespoons milk

Combine all ingredients. Beat with electric mixer at low speed until well mixed. Chill for at least 1 hour.

Mrs. Ray V. Moseley, Woman's Club,
Gainesville, Fla.

EGG AND DEVILED HAM DIP

Makes 1⅓ Cups

2 3-ounce cans deviled ham
2 eggs, hard-cooked and finely chopped
1 teaspoon horseradish
2 tablespoons finely chopped sweet pickle

Combine all ingredients. Mix well. Keep cold until ready to serve.

Virginia Ancell, Pine River Pow Wow,
Bayfield, Colo.

RED DIP

Makes About 3 Cups

Place this in a bowl in the middle of a serving tray. Surround it with Vienna sausages or boiled shrimp, as desired.

1-pound can small beets, drained
3 small onions
1 dill pickle
3 eggs, hard-cooked
Red pepper, celery salt and garlic salt to taste

1. Put beets, onions, pickle and eggs through meat grinder.

2. Season with red pepper, celery salt and garlic salt.

Mrs. Wayne Chastain, State Federation of
Women's Organizations, Spokane, Wash.

DEVILED HAM DIP
Makes 1½ Cups
5-ounce jar pimiento cheese spread
2½-ounce can deviled ham
½ cup mayonnaise or salad dressing
2 tablespoons minced parsley
1 tablespoon minced onion
Dash of monosodium glutamate
4 drops Tabasco

Beat all ingredients with electric mixer until well blended. Keep cold until ready to serve.

Junior Women's Club, Edgewood, R.I.

ONION DIP
Makes About 1¼ Cups
1 cup sour cream
¼ cup finely diced onion
1 tablespoon drained horseradish
1 teaspoon sugar
1 teaspoon mayonnaise
Pinch of salt
1 tablespoon vinegar from jar of sweet pickles

Combine all ingredients. Chill for 30 minutes before serving.

Virginia Millitzer, Woman's Club, Apopka, Fla.

CREAMY SHRIMP DIP
Makes About 2 Cups
⅓ cup cream
2 teaspoons lemon juice
½ teaspoon onion juice
Dash of Worcestershire
8-ounce package cream cheese
¾ cup chopped cooked shrimp

1. Gradually work cream, lemon juice, onion juice and Worcestershire into cheese.
2. Add shrimp. Mix well. Keep cold until ready to serve.

Betty Kirkland, Woman's Club, Leonia, N.J.

SHRIMP SOUP DIP
Makes About 2¼ Cups
10-ounce can frozen shrimp soup
8-ounce package cream cheese
1 teaspoon Worcestershire
1 teaspoon onion juice

1. Let soup defrost at room temperature.
2. Mix soup and cheese, beating well. Stir in Worcestershire and onion juice. Chill until ready to serve.

Sue Peck, Junior Woman's Club, Corning, N.Y.

SHRIMP COCKTAIL DIP
Makes About 1¼ Cups
Serve as a dip for cooked shrimp or as a shrimp cocktail sauce.
1 cup tomato sauce
1 teaspoon prepared mustard
1 teaspoon mayonnaise
1 tablespoon lemon juice
2 tablespoons horseradish
Salt and freshly ground pepper to taste

Combine all ingredients. Keep cold until ready to serve.

Carol Alston, Culture Club, Columbiana, Ala.

HOT SHRIMP DIP
Makes About 2 Cups
¼ cup butter
1 small onion, chopped
¼ cup chopped green pepper
2 5-ounce cans shrimp, drained and broken into small pieces
½ cup shredded yellow cheese
¼ cup cocktail sauce

1. Melt butter in top of double saucepan; sauté onion and green pepper for about 10 minutes, or until tender but not browned.
2. Add remaining ingredients. Cook over simmering water until cheese melts, stirring often.

Mrs. Vernon Carlson, Study Club, Washburn, N.D.

QUICK DIP 'N' DUNK
Makes 1½ Cups
1½ cups sour cream
2 tablespoons chopped chives
2 tablespoons lemon juice
Few dashes of Tabasco
1 teaspoon onion juice

1. Combine all ingredients. Chill.
2. Serve in bowl surrounded by cracked ice.

Mrs. John R. Hiebel, Woman's Club, Pompano Beach, Fla.

SOUR CREAM HORSERADISH DIP
Makes About 1½ Cups
1 cup sour cream
⅓ to ½ cup drained horseradish
½ teaspoon salt
½ teaspoon celery seed
1 teaspoon Worcestershire
¼ teaspoon paprika

Combine all ingredients. Chill.

Mrs. C. Lee Olin, Junior Woman's Club, Joliet, Ill.

KIM CHEE PARTY DIP
Makes About 1 Cup
⅓ cup finely chopped Kim Chee (p. 727) with juice to cover
3-ounce package cream cheese
Cream

Blend Kim Chee into cheese. Beat in enough cream for desired consistency.

Mrs. R. J. Winans, Woman's Club, Hilo, Hawaii

PINK DEVIL DIP
Makes 3 Cups
Also delicious as a salad dressing on mixed greens.
2 cups sour cream
6-ounce can deviled ham
¼ cup catsup
1 teaspoon grated onion
Dash of horseradish (optional)

Combine all ingredients. Chill for 1 hour before serving.

Mrs. John T. Loche, Women's Club, Ashland, Mass.

Canapés and Party Sandwiches

Although canapés belong to the overall category of hors d'oeuvres and appetizers, they are specifically savory, bite-size mouthfuls on a base of bread, toast, crackers or rich pastry. Some are served hot and others cold.

Plain bread, cut into small rounds, squares, diamonds, half-moons, rectangles or triangles, is sometimes used, but more frequently the bread is toasted. Slices may be toasted in a toaster, then trimmed and cut, or the trimmed and cut pieces may be arranged on a baking sheet and toasted in the oven or under the broiler. Sautéed bread is especially good as a base for canapés.

SAUTÉED CANAPÉ BASES

Trim and cut bread into different shapes. Melt a little butter or margarine in skillet until light brown; sauté bread, a few pieces at a time, until golden on one side; turn and brown other side. Drain on absorbent paper. Add butter or margarine as needed.

OVEN CANAPÉ BASES

Spread bread pieces with softened butter; arrange on baking sheet. For crisp toast, bake in preheated 275° F. oven until golden; turn; spread other side with butter; continue to bake until lightly browned. For soft toast, place under broiler for 2 to 3 minutes, or until butter sizzles and bread browns; turn; butter other side; continue to broil until golden. Watch carefully to be sure bread does not burn.

MELBA TOAST CANAPÉ BASES

Arrange thinly sliced bread pieces between two nested shallow baking pans. Bake in preheated 300° F. oven for 30 minutes. Flip pans over. Bake for 30 minutes longer.

COCKTAIL PASTRY BOATS

Makes 16

Fill with Seafood Salad Spread (p. 85), Crab Meat Spread (p. 82) or any other savory mixture, hot or cold.

Pastry for a 2-Crust Pie (p. 548)

1. Preheat oven to 425° F.
2. Divide Pastry for a 2-Crust Pie in half. With lightly floured cloth-covered rolling pin, roll out each half ⅛ inch thick on heavy-duty aluminum foil.
3. Cut foil and pastry into 5 x 2-inch rectangles. Prick pastry well with fork. Moisten narrow ends with water. Fold in half lengthwise, foil side out; pinch ends together firmly.
4. Place on baking sheet. Spread sides out like a canoe so that each boat balances and stands by itself.
5. Bake pastry boats in preheated oven for 10 to 12 minutes. Cool. Remove foil.

Nana Miller, Junior Woman's Club, Corning, N.Y.

Cold Canapés and Party Sandwiches

SAVORY BUTTERS FOR COLD CANAPÉS AND SANDWICHES

Canapé bases may be spread with savory butters before adding other spreads, although many of these butter spreads are delicious enough to require no further embellishment. Savory butters are also suitable for tiny party or tea sandwiches.

Combine ¼ pound butter with any one of the following ingredients or mixtures to make a smooth paste:

ALMOND: ¼ cup finely chopped blanched almonds.

ANCHOVY: 6 anchovies and a few drops lemon juice.

ANCHOVY EGG: ¼ cup minced anchovies or anchovy pates, 2 sieved hard-cooked egg yolks and 1 teaspoon lemon juice.

ARTICHOKE: 6 small artichoke hearts, cooked and sieved, and 1 teaspoon lemon juice.

CAPER: 2 tablespoons minced capers.

CHEESE: ¼ cup grated Parmesan cheese (or 3 tablespoons crumbled Roquefort or blue cheese) and ½ cup shredded Cheddar cheese.

CHIVE: ¼ cup chopped chives.

CHUTNEY: 2 tablespoons minced chutney.

CRAB MEAT: ½ cup flaked cooked crab meat.

EGG: 4 sieved hard-cooked egg yolks and pinch of cayenne.

GARLIC: 1 teaspoon minced garlic.

HAM AND EGG: ½ cup ground cooked ham and 2 sieved hard-cooked egg yolks.

HONEY: 2 tablespoons honey or honey butter.

HORSERADISH: ¼ cup grated fresh or drained horseradish.

JAM: 2 tablespoons jam.

LEMON: 2 teaspoons grated lemon rind and 1½ tablespoons lemon juice.

LIVER: ½ cup liver pâté, 1 tablespoon minced truffles and 1 tablespoon cognac.

LOBSTER: ½ cup minced cooked lobster meat.

MARMALADE: 2 tablespoons marmalade.

MUSTARD: 2 tablespoons prepared mustard.

NUT: ¼ cup finely chopped walnuts, pecans, cashews or peanuts.

OLIVE: ¼ cup ground stuffed olives.

ORANGE: 2 tablespoons grated orange rind and 1½ tablespoons orange juice.

PARSLEY: ¼ cup minced parsley.

PIMIENTO: ¼ cup mashed pimientos.

SARDINE: ½ cup mashed sardines.

SHRIMP: ½ cup minced cooked shrimp.

SPICE: ½ teaspoon nutmeg or cinnamon or 1 teaspoon crushed poppy or caraway seeds.

WATER CRESS: ½ cup minced water cress.

GARNISHES FOR CANAPÉS

Select a garnish that is colorful, yet complements the flavor of the filling. Here are a few suggestions:

Eggs, hard-cooked, then finely chopped, sieved or sliced.

Small stuffed, olives, whole, chopped or sliced; chopped green or ripe olives.

Onions, minced; tiny cocktail pickled onions.

Tomatoes, thinly sliced or chopped; whole tiny cherry tomatoes.

Anchovy, fillets or rolled.

Cucumbers, thinly sliced or minced.

Pickles, sliced or chopped.

Capers, drained and left whole or chopped.

Truffles, thinly sliced and cut into fancy shapes.

Green pepper, minced or cut into thin strips.

Pimiento, cut into strips or tiny fancy cutouts, or strips rolled into rosettes.

Radishes, sliced or roses.

Mayonnaise, softened cream cheese or mashed egg yolk and butter, pressed through a tiny fluted pastry tube.

HOW TO KEEP CANAPÉS AND SANDWICHES FRESH

Wrap snugly in transparent film, sandwich bags or aluminum foil. Refrigerate until ready to serve.

PARTY SANDWICHES

When you make sandwiches for a party or for the tea tray, use fresh or day-old bread. Use a variety of breads for flavor and color; cut sandwiches into different shapes and sizes. Crusts are usually trimmed from small party or tea sandwiches.

When spreading bread with filling, line up matching slices; spread evenly right to edge. If using thinly sliced turkey, beef, cheese, smoked salmon, sturgeon, etc., trim slices to fit bread base.

RIBBON SANDWICHES

Put 4 trimmed slices of bread together with filling between, alternating white slice with whole wheat slice; press slices together firmly; wrap the stacks; refrigerate. To serve, slice down across layers, making thin sandwiches.

CHECKERBOARD SANDWICHES

Make Ribbon Sandwiches. Chill for several hours. Unwrap. Cut stack into ½-inch slices. Spread cut sides with more filling and mayonnaise or butter. Pile 4 slices on top of one another with strips of bread all running in same direction, but with whole wheat strips over white, and white over whole wheat. Again press stacks together firmly; wrap; chill. To serve, cut each stack into thin slices.

FINGER SANDWICHES

Put trimmed slices of bread together with filling between. Cut each sandwich into 4 rectangles.

PINWHEELS

Trim sliced bread. Arrange 3 slices in a band on a damp towel, one slice slightly overlapping the other. Flatten with rolling pin. Spread with filling. Roll up, beginning at one narrow end. Chill. To serve, cut each roll into 6 slices. If desired, arrange a row of stuffed olives along narrow edge of bread before rolling.

LILIES

Trim bread slices. Flatten with rolling pin. Spread with filling. Roll into cone shape, one end closed and opposite end open. Secure with cocktail pick. Insert strips of carrot or green pepper into open end to make "stamen" of lily.

MOSAIC SANDWICHES

Cut thinly sliced white and whole wheat bread into small rounds. Spread half the rounds with a savory butter or sandwich spread. Cut a smaller round from center of remaining rounds. Insert a whole wheat cutout into a ring of white, and vice versa. Top spread rounds with two-toned rounds. Shapes may be varied, such as heart shapes, diamonds, squares, and stars.

FIESTA RIBBON SANDWICHES
Makes 68 Sandwiches

1 loaf unsliced whole wheat bread
1 loaf unsliced white bread
Deviled Ham Filling (p. 79)
Cream Cheese and Green Pepper Filling (p. 79)
Egg Salad Filling (p. 79)

1. Trim crusts from bread. From each loaf, cut 4 lengthwise slices, each ½ inch thick. Cover with transparent film to keep moist.

2. To make first loaf, spread whole wheat slice with half the Deviled Ham Filling; top with white slice. Spread with half the Cream Cheese and Green Pepper Filling; top with whole wheat slice. Spread with remaining ham filling; cover with white slice.

3. To make second loaf, spread white slice with half the Egg Salad Filling; top with whole wheat slice. Spread with remaining cream cheese filling; top with white slice. Spread with remaining egg salad filling; cover with whole wheat slice.

4. Wrap loaves in transparent film. Refrigerate for at least 3 hours.

5. To serve, cut each loaf into 17 slices and each slice in half crosswise.

Mrs. Lyle Clark, Woman's Club, Azusa, Calif.

FIESTA RIBBON SANDWICH FILLINGS

DEVILED HAM FILLING

2 4½-ounce cans deviled ham
1 tablespoon chili sauce
1 teaspoon grated onion
¼ teaspoon Worcestershire

Combine all ingredients.

CREAM CHEESE AND GREEN PEPPER FILLING

1½ ounces cream cheese, softened
4 teaspoons mayonnaise
⅔ cup finely chopped green pepper
¼ cup sweet pickle relish, drained

1. Mix cheese and mayonnaise until smooth.
2. Stir in green pepper and relish.

EGG SALAD FILLING

12 eggs, hard-cooked and coarsely chopped
1 teaspoon salt
1 tablespoon cider vinegar
⅔ cup mayonnaise

Combine all ingredients.

Mrs. Lyle Clark, Woman's Club, Azusa, Calif.

POINSETTIA SANDWICH LOAF

Makes 16 Slices

2-pound loaf unsliced bread, crusts removed
Butter, softened
Walnut Cheese Filling (below)
Tuna Filling (opposite)
Egg Filling (opposite)
8-ounce package cream cheese
⅓ cup milk
4-ounce can pimientos, drained
Green pepper

1. Slice loaf lengthwise into 4 equal slices.
2. Butter slices. Put 2 together with Walnut Cheese Filling.
3. Cover top slice with Tuna Filling. Place third slice on top.
4. Spread third slice with Egg Filling. Cover with fourth slice.
5. Press slices together firmly; wrap in waxed paper; refrigerate.
6. Soften cream cheese. Beat in milk. Spread top and sides of loaf with cheese mixture.
7. Garnish with pimientos in the form of poinsettia with stems made of green pepper. Chill. Slice into 16 slices.

Ruth Johnson, Woman's Club, Orem, Utah

POINSETTIA SANDWICH LOAF FILLINGS

WALNUT CHEESE FILLING

¼ cup chopped walnuts
⅓ cup cheese spread
½ teaspoon Worcestershire
⅓ cup mayonnaise

Combine all ingredients. Chill.

TUNA FILLING

½ cup flaked tuna fish
¼ cup chopped olives
¼ cup mayonnaise
½ teaspoon lemon juice

Combine all ingredients. Chill.

EGG FILLING

3 eggs, hard-cooked and chopped
2 tablespoons lemon juice
2 tablespoons mayonnaise
⅛ teaspoon salt
⅛ teaspoon dry mustard

Combine all ingredients. Chill.

Ruth Johnson, Woman's Club, Orem, Utah

A CANAPÉ TRAY

For canapé bases, cut bread into small shapes of your choice. Toast only one side. (Small round crackers may be substituted.) Spread untoasted side of bread with a savory mixture.

Slice an orange or any other citrus fruit in half. Place half, cut side down, in center of large tray. Insert cocktail picks in skin of fruit. Place stuffed olives, pickled onions, bits of Vienna sausages, black Bing cherries stuffed with softened cream cheese, etc., on exposed ends of picks. Place canapés (all of one kind together) around centerpiece of fruit half.

What's Cookin?, Woman's Club, Apopka, Fla.

SUGGESTIONS FOR CANAPÉ SPREADS

CHEESE BACON BUTTER

With electric mixer beat ½ cup shredded Cheddar cheese and 2 tablespoons softened butter until well blended. Stir in 2 slices of bacon, crisply fried and crumbled.

CREAM CHEESE AND OLIVE SPREAD

Combine softened cream cheese with chopped stuffed olives.

CREAM CHEESE AND SHRIMP SPREAD

Combine softened cream cheese, minced onion, minced cooked shrimp and lemon juice to taste.

GARLIC AND PARSLEY BUTTER

With electric mixer beat ½ cup butter until very light and fluffy. Beat in 2 tablespoons light cream, ¼ teaspoon garlic powder, ¼ teaspoon salt and ¼ cup finely minced parsley.

HAM SPREAD

Mix deviled ham with hard-cooked eggs and horseradish.

HORSERADISH BUTTER

With electric mixer beat ½ cup butter until very light and fluffy. Gradually beat in 2 tablespoons light cream, 3 tablespoons horseradish and ½ teaspoon salt.

LOBSTER SPREAD

Chop cooked lobster meat finely. Mix with mayonnaise. Season with salt, pepper and lemon juice.

PIMIENTO BUTTER

With electric mixer beat ½ cup butter until very light and fluffy. Gradually beat in ¼ cup sieved canned pimientos, ¼ teaspoon celery salt, ¼ teaspoon onion salt and ¼ teaspoon salt.

SARDINE SPREAD

Mash sardines. Mix with lemon juice, salt and Worcestershire.

La Fourchette, Junior Woman's Club,
Thibodaux, La.

CANAPÉ SUGGESTIONS

COTTAGE CHEESE WITH OLIVES AND PICKLES

Mix cottage cheese, finely chopped stuffed olives, finely chopped sweet pickles and a little celery seed. Spread on crackers.

ROQUEFORT AND CREAM CHEESE SPREAD

Mix equal parts of Roquefort and cream cheese. Spread on wafers.

SARDINE CANAPES

Place 2 small sardines on strip of toasted bread. Sprinkle lightly with lemon juice and a few drops Tabasco. Top with a bit of cream cheese mixed with chopped pickle.

STRAWBERRY NUT SPREAD

Mix strawberry jam and chopped nut meats. Spread on toast rounds.

Open Sesame to Tasty Treasures,
Sesame Club, Fordyce, Ark.

FINGER SANDWICH FILLINGS

To make finger sandwiches, see pp. 77.

CARROT PEANUT FILLING

Fills 20 Sandwiches

Combine 1 cup grated carrots, 3 teaspoons piccalilli, ⅓ cup finely chopped salted peanuts and ¼ cup mayonnaise.

OLIVE CHEESE FILLING

Fills 16 Sandwiches

Combine 1 cup shredded sharp cheese, ⅓ cup chopped ripe olives, ¼ teaspoon minced onion, ¼ teaspoon salt, ⅓ cup mayonnaise and a dash of Tabasco.

Round Table Club, Goodland, Kan.

ANCHOVY CANAPÉS

Makes 12

1 can anchovy fillets preserved in oil
1 tablespoon cold butter
1 tablespoon lemon juice
½ teaspoon cayenne
12 ¼-inch-thick, 1½-inch-wide and 3-inch-long strips stale bread
4 tablespoons melted butter
2 eggs, hard-cooked

1. Put 4 of the anchovy fillets in mortar. Add cold butter, lemon juice and cayenne. Pound to a smooth paste.
2. Sauté bread in melted butter until golden on both sides. Cool. Spread with anchovy paste.
3. Cut remaining anchovy fillets into thin strips. Arrange 2 anchovy strips near edge of each strip of toast.
4. Chop egg whites finely. Press egg yolks through coarse sieve. Alternate little mounds of egg whites and yolks in space between anchovy strips.

Mrs. Stanley Porche, Junior Woman's Club,
Thibodaux, La.

AVOCADO SPREAD

Makes About 1 Cup

Prepare just before serving, if possible, or keep tightly covered so avocado will not turn dark. Use as sandwich filling, or spread on chunks of lettuce or tomato wedges for a cold hors d'oeuvre.

1 ripe avocado
1 teaspoon lemon juice
½ teaspoon mayonnaise
Bit of minced onion (optional)
Dash of salt and pepper

Peel avocado. Cut into pieces. Mash with work. Mix with remaining ingredients.

Mrs. David R. Tweet, Woman's Club,
Williamsburg, Ky.

BACON, TOMATO AND PEANUT BUTTER SQUARES

Sliced white bread
Peanut butter
Small tomatoes, sliced very thinly
Salt
Tabasco
Crisp bacon, crumbled

1. Trim bread slices; cut into squares. Place on baking sheet. Toast in oven until crisp and browned.
2. Spread each square with peanut butter. Top with tomato slice. Sprinkle with salt and Tabasco.
3. Sprinkle with bacon.

Mrs. Ethel Gallup, Women's Club of Wilton
Manors, Fort Lauderdale, Fla.

CAVIAR AND SMOKED SALMON CANAPÉS

Small jar caviar
Little grated onion
Lemon juice
Smoked salmon
Toast squares or square crackers

1. Mix a small jar of caviar with onion and lemon juice.
2. Place strip of smoked salmon across center of toast or cracker. Spoon a little caviar on each side of salmon strip.

Mrs. Stanley Porche, Junior Woman's Club,
Thibodaux, La.

CHEDDAR CHEESE AND CHUTNEY SPREAD

Makes About 3 Cups

This keeps well in a covered crock in refrigerator. Serve on dark pumpernickel bread.

1 pound soft Cheddar cheese
5-ounce can pecans, chopped
10-ounce jar stuffed olives, drained and chopped
6 tablespoons chutney

Soften cheese. Mix with other ingredients. Chill.

Mrs. M. C. Chaillet, Jr., Woman's Club,
Morristown, N.J.

DANISH CREAM VEGETABLE SPREAD

Makes About 4 Cups

Spread on rounds or other shapes of dark Danish or German bread.

3 large cucumbers
Salt
1 bunch radishes, thinly sliced
8 stalks celery, finely chopped
2 8-ounce packages cream cheese
¼ cup minced chives

1. Peel and seed cucumbers; cut lengthwise; sprinkle with salt. Set aside to drain for 4 hours. Then dice; drain for 30 minutes longer.
2. Combine all vegetables in towel; squeeze gently to remove excess moisture.
3. Beat cheese until soft and fluffy. Stir in vegetables and chives.

Mrs. Joseph Seltzer, Woman's Club,
Morristown, N.J.

GARLIC CHEESE NUT CANAPÉS

Makes About 4 Cups

1 pound Cheddar cheese
1 cup nuts
1 large clove garlic
2 3-ounce packages cream cheese
Paprika
Melba toast rounds or round crackers

1. Put Cheddar cheese, nuts and garlic through meat grinder. Mix well with cream cheese. Shape into 1 large or 2 small rolls. Roll in paprika. Wrap in waxed paper. Chill for several hours.
2. To serve, slice thinly. Place each slice on toast rounds or crackers.

Mrs. Victor F. Pettit, Woman's Club,
Williamsburg, Ky.

PIMIENTO CHEESE SPREAD

Makes About 2½ Cups

½ pound Cheddar cheese, shredded
8-ounce can pimientos, drained and chopped
4 tablespoons vinegar
1 tablespoon flour
2 tablespoons sugar
1 teaspoon salt
1 egg, lightly beaten

1. In saucepan combine all ingredients except egg. Cook over low heat, stirring, until creamy and bubbling. Stir in egg. Bring almost to boil, stirring rapidly.
2. Remove from heat. Cool before spreading.

Mrs. George Owens, Woman's Club,
Pontotoc, Miss.

CREAM CHEESE AND EGG SPREAD

Makes About 1 Cup

Serve on crackers, or use as a sandwich filling.

3-ounce package creame cheese
1 teaspoon minced onion
1 tablespoon mayonnaise
1 egg, hard-cooked and mashed
12 stuffed olives, chopped
Salt and pepper to taste

Combine all ingredients. Chill for a few hours to blend flavors.

Carolyn Yorio, Junior Woman's Club,
Corning, N.Y.

CHEESE NUT CANAPÉS

Makes 48 to 64

1 pound sharp cheese, shredded
8-ounce package cream cheese
1½ ounces Roquefort cheese
1 pound mild Cheddar cheese, shredded
1 cup cottage cheese
2 ounces blue cheese
1 cup chopped pecans
Dash of Worcestershire
2 cloves garlic, pressed
Chili powder, minced parsley or finely chopped nuts
Toast rounds or crackers

1. Blend together cheeses, pecans, Worcestershire and garlic. Form into 6 or 8 rolls.
2. Roll in chili powder, parsley or nuts.
3. Wrap in waxed paper or transparent film. Store in refrigerator (where they will keep up to a month).
4. To serve, slice and place on toast rounds or crackers.

Sue Phillips, Culture Club, Columbiana, Ala.

CHICKEN SPREAD

Makes About 1½ Cups

1 cup minced cooked chicken
2 tablespoons chopped apple
2 slices bacon, crisply cooked and crumbled
¼ cup mayonnaise
Salt and pepper to taste

Combine all ingredients. Chill.

Katie Hinton, Woman's Club, Pikeville, Ky.

CHICKEN SALAD SPREAD

Makes 36

Use as a sandwich filling, spread on canapés or fill tiny cocktail puffs.

5-pound stewing chicken
1 cup finely chopped celery
1 small onion, minced
1 cup ground pecans
½ cup sweet relish
4 eggs, hard-cooked and mashed
Dash of Tabasco
Salt and pepper to taste
Mayonnaise to moisten

1. Simmer chicken in salted water to cover for 1½ hours, or until tender. Cool. Remove meat from bones. Discard skin. Cut meat finely.
2. Combine chicken with remaining ingredients.

Jeannette Kincaid, Woman's Club, Starke, Fla.

CHICKEN LIVER SPREAD
Makes About 1½ Cups

Spread on crackers or toast squares.

½ cup butter
1 cup chopped onions
1 pound chicken livers
2 hard-cooked egg yolks
1½ teaspoons salt
⅛ teaspoon pepper
1 teaspoon lemon juice

1. Melt ¼ cup of the butter in large skillet; sauté onions over medium heat, stirring frequently, until transparent. Remove from skillet. Set aside.
2. Add remaining butter to skillet. Melt; sauté livers over medium heat, stirring frequently, for 10 minutes, or until tender. Remove from heat. Cool slightly.
3. Press onions, livers and egg yolks through sieve or food mill, or put through meat grinder.
4. Stir in remaining ingredients. Mix well. Chill.

Sandy Deckenback, Woman's Club, Lake Hiawatha, N.J.

COCONUT TROPICAL DREAM SPREAD
Makes 1 Cup

Spread on whole wheat bread squares or rounds.

½ cup diced peeled coconut meat
½ cup minced pimientos
¼ cup horseradish
Salt and pepper to taste
Mayonnaise

1. Put coconut through meat grinder.
2. Mix coconut, pimientos, horseradish, salt and pepper.
3. Bind with a little mayonnaise.
4. Chill.

Mrs. C. Johnston, Woman's Club, Morristown, N.J.

CORNED BEEF EGG SPREAD
Makes About 4 Cups

12-ounce can corned beef
6 large sweet pickles
4 or 5 eggs, hard-cooked
½ cup mayonnaise
3 teaspoons Worcestershire
3 tablespoons prepared mustard

1. Put beef, pickles and eggs through meat grinder.
2. Mix ground ingredients with remaining ingredients. Chill.

I. Victoria Harris, Woman's Literary Union, Portland, Me.

ZIPPY CORNED BEEF SPREAD
Makes About 2½ Cups

Serve on party rye, spread with mayonnaise and topped with a dash of paprika.

12-ounce can corned beef
½ cup sour cream
½ cup mayonnaise
3 teaspoons horseradish
2 tablespoons chopped chives
¾ teaspoon garlic salt

1. Flake or shred corned beef. Add remaining ingredients. Blend well, mashing any lumps of meat. Cover tightly. Refrigerate for at least 45 minutes before using. (It is even better if made a day before.)
2. Remove from refrigerator to soften before spreading.

Mrs. Guy Seashole, Jr., Woman's Club of South Jacksonville, Jacksonville, Fla.

CRAB MEAT SPREAD
Makes About 1 Cup

Spread on crackers or toast rounds or between slices of buttered bread. This may also be served hot; pile it into Cocktail Pastry Boats (p. 77); top with strip of cheese; broil about 5 inches from heat until cheese melts.

6½-ounce can crab meat, drained and flaked
½ teaspoon salt
¼ cup minced celery
¼ cup mayonnaise
1 teaspoon Worcestershire
½ teaspoon dry minced onion
1 dill pickle, minced

Combine all ingredients. Chill.

Nana Miller, Junior Woman's Club, Corning, N.Y.

CUCUMBER CANAPÉS
Makes About 16

½ cup butter
1 teaspoon lemon juice
2 tablespoons horseradish
Sliced bread
Minced parsley
Cucumber, thinly cut and scored
Stuffed olives, sliced
Tiny parsley sprigs

1. With electric mixer at high speed, beat butter and lemon juice just until fluffy. Beat in horseradish.
2. Cut bread slices into diamond shapes. Toast.
3. For each canapé, spread with the lemon butter; then dip two of parallel edges into minced parsley.
4. Twist a cucumber slice. Place in center of each diamond.

5. Garnish with olives and parsley sprigs tucked into cucumber twist.

Our Heritage Cook Book, Pontotoc, Miss.

CUCUMBER SANDWICHES

Cucumbers
Butter
Thinly sliced bread
Mayonnaise

1. Peel cucumbers; slice thinly; soak in salted water until ready to use.
2. Butter thin slices of bread.
3. Drain and dry cucumber slices; roll in mayonnaise; place between buttered bread slices. Trim; cut into squares.

Harriet Hawthorn, Woman's Club,
Hawthorne, Fla.

DATE NUT SANDWICH FILLING
Makes About 6 Cups
8-ounce can crushed pineapple, undrained
3 tablespoons orange juice
1 tablespoon lemon juice
30 marshmallows
2 8-ounce packages pitted dates, chopped
1 cup chopped nuts
1 cup mayonnaise

1. Turn pineapple into small saucepan. Add juices and marshmallows. Stir over low heat until marshmallows are melted. Stir in dates. Remove from heat. Cool.
2. Stir in nuts and mayonnaise.

Jet Christopher, Woman's Club
Warner Robins, Ga.

DRIED BEEF CANAPÉS
Makes About ¾ Cup
1 tablespoon butter
1 teaspoon minced onion
2½-ounce package dried beef, finely chopped
3-ounce package cream cheese
Bread rounds or crackers

1. Melt butter in skillet; sauté onion until tender but not browned. Add beef; cook until slightly crisp.
2. Add beef mixture to cheese. Mix well.
3. Spread on bread rounds or crackers.

Janet Blattner, Study Club, Balsam Lake, Wis.

MÉLANGE D'OEUFS (Egg, Bacon and Mushroom Spread)
Makes About 4 Cups

Serve on rounds or other shapes of dark bread.

12 eggs, hard-cooked and chopped
1 pound bacon, crisply cooked and crumbled
8-ounce can sautéed chopped mushrooms, drained
Mayonnaise

Combine eggs, bacon and mushrooms. Bind with a little mayonnaise. Chill.

Mrs. R. J. Gibbons, Woman's Club,
Morristown, N.J.

FRENCH ROLL CANAPÉS
Makes 32
1 large green pepper, chopped
1 firm ripe tomato, chopped
1 teaspoon salt
2 teaspoons grated onion
2 tablespoons softened butter
3 3-ounce packages cream cheese
4 French rolls

1. Day before, combine green pepper, tomato, salt and onion. Cream butter and cheese; mix with vegetables. Hollow out French rolls; pack with cheese mixture. Wrap in aluminum foil. Refrigerate overnight.
2. Next day, slice thinly just before serving.

VARIATION: Use anchovy paste and chopped canned pimientos in place of green pepper and tomato.

Mrs. John H. Rudd, Jr., Woman's Club,
West Palm Beach, Fla.

HAM PINWHEELS
Makes About 42
4 ounces Roquefort or blue cheese
3-ounce package cream cheese
¼ cup butter or margarine
Boiled ham slices
Buttered bread rounds or round crackers

1. Day or so before, blend cheeses and butter or margarine until smooth; Spread on ham slices. Roll up each like a jelly roll. Wrap in freezer paper. Freeze.
2. When ready to use, slice thinly. Place each slice on bread round or cracker.

Elaine Jones, Finneytown Junior Women's Club,
Cincinnati, Ohio

HAM CANAPÉS
Makes 6
6 rounds dark bread
2 tablespoons butter
½ teaspoon prepared mustard
1 cup minced ham
¼ cup India relish
Stuffed olives, sliced

1. Toast rounds only on one side. Cream butter and mustard; use to spread untoasted side.
2. Combine ham and relish; spread on rounds. Garnish with olives. Chill before serving.

Our Heritage Cook Book, Pontotoc, Miss.

GOOBER HAM SPREAD
Makes About 3 Cups

Serve on rounds or other shapes of dark bread.

2 cups ground smoked ham
6 tablespoons minced green pepper
¼ cup grated peanuts
¼ teaspoon dry mustard
2 tablespoons beer
1 tablespoon grated onion
6 tablespoons mayonnaise

1. Combine ham, green pepper and peanuts. Mix mustard and beer. Add to ham mixture. Stir in onion and mayonnaise.
2. Chill for several hours before using.

Mrs. F. Ensminger, Woman's Club,
Morristown, N.J.

LIVER CHEESE

Makes About 3 Cups

A wonderful spread for dark bread.

1 pound liver
2 slices bacon
1 medium onion
1 tablespoon flour
1 cup light cream
2 eggs, beaten
1 tablespoon melted butter
Salt, pepper and pinch of ginger
to taste

1. Put liver, bacon and onion through meat grinder.
2. Preheat oven to 350° F. Grease 1-quart casserole.
3. Mix ground ingredients with remaining ingredients.
4. Turn into casserole; set casserole in shallow pan containing 1 inch hot water; bake in preheated oven for 1 hour. Cool. Refrigerate.

Wilma Iverson, Woman's Literary Union,
Portland, Me.

LIVER PÂTÉ SPREAD WITH TRUFFLES

Makes About 5 Cups

Serve on small crackers or toast squares.

½ pound calf's liver
1 pound fillet of pork
1 pound leaf lard
1 teaspoon salt
1 teaspoon black pepper
½-ounce can truffles, drained and thinly sliced
Worcestershire, Tabasco and grated onion to taste

1. Put liver, pork and leaf lard through medium blade of meat grinder.
2. Turn into skillet. Cook over moderate heat for 5 minutes, or until partially cooked, stirring frequently.
3. Drain through collander; reserve juice and fat. Put meat through finest blade of grinder.
4. Return to heat with reserved juice and fat; Add salt and pepper; cook for 15 minutes, stirring constantly. Stir in truffles; cook for 5 minutes longer.
5. Pour into hot clean jars. Seal. Store in cool place.
6. When ready to serve, remove lard from surface, season pâté with Worcestershire, Tabasco and onion.

Mrs. Lawrence Levert, Junior Woman's Club,
Thibodaux, La.

OYSTER SANDWICH SPREAD

Makes 2 Cups

1 pint oysters, freshly shucked
Salt and pepper to taste
1 tablespoon butter
3 tablespoons bread crumbs
Mayonnaise

1. Chop oysters finely. Sprinkle with salt and pepper.
2. Melt butter in skillet. Add crumbs and oysters. Cook for 5 minutes, stirring frequently.
3. Cool. Moisten with mayonnaise.

Harriet Hawthorn, Woman's Club, Hawthorne, Fla.

PICKLE CANAPÉS

Serves 8

1 large dill pickle
2 slices liverwurst
Mayonnaise
Toasted buttered crackers or toast

1. Cut ends off pickle. Hollow out center.
2. Mash liverwurst and mayonnaise to smooth paste. Use to stuff center of pickle. Chill.
3. Slice thinly. Serve on crackers or toast.

Mrs. John Gavin, Woman's Club, Gainesville, Fla.

PINEAPPLE NUT SANDWICH SPREAD

Makes About 4 Cups

2 cups crushed pineapple, drained
1 cup sugar
1 cup chopped nuts
8-ounce package cream cheese
Milk or mayonnaise

1. In saucepan combine pineapple and sugar. Bring to boil. Cook until thick, stirring constantly. Cool.
2. Stir in nuts.
3. Soften and mash cheese with enough milk or mayonnaise to make a good spreading consistencey. Combine with pineapple-nut mixture.

Julianne Mathews, Woman's Club,
Warner Robins, Ga.

SALMON AVOCADO HALF-AND-HALF CANAPÉS

Makes 8

½ cup flaked cooked salmon
2 tablespoons mayonnaise
1½ tablespoons lemon juice
¼ teaspoon salt
Dash of pepper
½ cup mashed avocado
8 toast rounds
Softened butter
Pimiento strips

1. Combine salmon, mayonnaise, ½ tablespoon of the lemon juice, salt and pepper.
2. Combine avocado and remaining lemon juice.
3. Spread toast rounds with butter. Spread half of each round with salmon

mixture. Spread other half with avocado mixture.

4. Mark division with pimiento strip.

Madeline Knudsen, Woman's Literary Union, Portland, Me.

SALMON SPREAD

Makes 1 Cup

1 cup flaked cooked salmon
2 tablespoons lemon juice
1 tablespoon horseradish
4 tablespoons mayonnaise
Salt and pepper to taste

Combine all ingredients. Chill.

Katie Hinton, Woman's Club, Pikeville, Ky.

CURRIED SMOKED SALMON SPREAD

Makes About 2 Cups

Serve on rounds or squares of heavy dark bread.

1 pound smoked Nova Scotia salmon
1 medium onion
½ teaspoon curry powder
½ teaspoon grated orange rind
¼ cup sour cream
1 tablespoon mayonnaise

1. Put salmon and onion through finest blade of meat grinder.
2. Mix salmon and onion with remaining ingredients.
3. Chill for at least 1 hour.

Mrs. T. Barabutes, Woman's Club, Morristown, N.J.

SARDINE OLIVE CANAPÉS

Makes About 32

½ tablespoon lemon juice
1½ tablespoons mayonnaise
½ cup mashed sardines
1 tablespoon minced pimientos
3 tablespoons chopped olives
2-inch toast squares or crackers
Sliced stuffed olives

1. Combine lemon juice and mayonnaise. Mix with sardines, pimientos and chopped olives.
2. Spread on toast or crackers; garnish each with a slice of stuffed olive.

Mrs. E. A. Doolan, Woman's Club, Lombard, Ill.

SEAFOOD SALAD SPREAD

Makes 2 Cups

Serve on crackers or toast rounds, between slices of buttered bread or in Cocktail Pastry Boats (p. 77).

1 cup chopped cooked lobster, crab meat or shrimp
1 teaspoon minced onion
1 cup diced celery
1 teaspoon lemon juice
Salt and paprika to taste
Mayonnaise to bind

Combine all ingredients lightly. Chill.

Nana Miller, Junior Woman's Club, Corning, N.Y.

SHRIMP BUTTER

Makes About 2½ Cups

Serve on crackers.

1 cup minced cooked shrimp
¾ pound butter
2 tablespoons minced onion
2 tablespoons lemon juice
2 tablespoons mayonnaise
⅛ teaspoon salt

1. Cream shrimp and butter until light and fluffy.
2. Stir in remaining ingredients.
3. Chill for a few hours.

Mrs. Edward C. Holt, Woman's Club, Casselton, N.D.

SHRIMP CARNATIONS

When these are placed on a serving tray, they look like flowers.

Sliced white bread
Mayonnaise
Parsley clusters
Jumbo shrimp

1. With biscuit cutter, cut bread into small rounds.
2. Spread rounds with mayonnaise. Top each with a shrimp. Between ends of shrimp place small cluster of parsley with stem protruding.

Mrs. H. A. Johnston, Women's Club of Wilton Manor, Fort Lauderdale, Fla.

SHRIMP CANAPÉS

Makes 36 Canapés

1 pound ground cooked shrimp
4 to 5 drops Tabasco
¼ teaspoon salt
1 tablespoon grated onion
2 teaspoons lemon juice
About ⅔ cup mayonnaise
1 teaspoon minced celery
1 teaspoon grated lemon rind
Pepper and Worcestershire to taste
Buttered bread rounds or squares

Combine all ingredients except bread. Spread on bread.

Julianne Mathews, Woman's Club, Warner Robins, Ga.

HORSERADISH TUNA SPREAD

Makes About 2 Cups

Use as a spread for crackers or rye bread.

7-ounce can tuna, drained and broken into small pieces
½ cup horseradish
3-ounce package cream cheese
3 tablespoons lemon juice
Mayonnaise to moisten

Mix all ingredients to desired consistency.

VARIATIONS:

1. Use shrimp or crab meat instead of tuna.
2. Use ground ham instead of tuna.

Mrs. Mary Howell, Sesame Club, Fordyce, Ark.

Hot Canapés

COCKTAIL TEASERS

Makes 36

Wrapping the teasers is time-consuming and should be done far ahead of serving time. After wrapping, the teasers may be frozen; if not frozen, refrigerate until ready to bake.

    1 cup baking powder biscuit mix
    ¼ cup softened butter
    3 tablespoons boiling water
    Canned button mushrooms, stuffed
      olives or cocktail sausages
    Celery or poppy seeds

1. Put biscuit mix and butter in mixing bowl. Add water. Stir with fork until dough forms and comes cleanly away from sides of bowl.
2. Roll out dough ¼ inch thick on lightly floured board. Cut into strips.
3. Drain mushrooms or olives well, or use cocktail sausages or assortment of all three. Wrap dough around foods just to cover; seal ends; dip rolls in celery or poppy seeds. Freeze or refrigerate.
4. To bake, preheat oven to 450° F. Arrange teasers on baking sheet. Bake in preheated oven for 8 to 10 minutes.

Lee Said, Junior Woman's Club, Corning, N.Y.

COCKTAIL TWIRLUPS

Makes About 24

    1 envelope active dry yeast
    ½ cup lukewarm water
    ⅓ cup melted shortening
    2 teaspoons sugar
    1 teaspoon salt
    1 egg, beaten
    2¼ cups presifted flour
    Favorite sandwich spread

1. Grease baking sheet.
2. Soften yeast in water. Stir in shortening, sugar, salt and egg. Gradually stir in flour to make a soft, well-blended dough.
3. Divide dough into 3 portions. On lightly floured board, roll out each portion into rectangle ⅛ inch thick.
4. Spread rectangles with sandwich spread. Roll up as for a jelly roll.
5. Cut rolls into slices ½ inch thick. Arrange on baking sheet. Flatten slightly. Let rise in warm place for about 45 minutes.
6. Preheat oven to 425° F.
7. Bake in preheated oven for 15 minutes.

Margaret Riddle, Woman's Club, Fern Creek, Ky.

COCKTAIL DREAMS

Makes 30

    1 can buttermilk refrigerator biscuits
    30 cooked canned cocktail sausages
    Olive oil
    Poppy seeds
    Salt and pepper to taste

1. Preheat oven to 425° F.
2. Cut each biscuit into 3 strips.
3. Pull each strip slightly lengthwise.

Wrap around 1 of the cocktail sausages. Secure with wooden pick.
4. Arrange on baking sheet. Brush with oil. Sprinkle with poppy seeds, salt and pepper.
5. Bake in preheated oven for about 10 minutes, or until golden brown.

Jo Dunning, Woman's Club, Warner Robins, Ga.

ANCHOVY CANAPÉS

Makes 6

    2 2-ounce cans anchovy fillets,
      (p. 119)
    2 cloves garlic, crushed
    1 tablespoon olive oil
    1 teaspoon lemon juice
    3 slices bread

1. Preheat broiler.
2. Put anchovy fillets and garlic in bowl. Mash until smooth. Add oil and lemon juice. Mix well.
3. Trim crusts from bread. Cut each slice in half lengthwise. Spread anchovy mixture on bread. Place on broiler pan. Broil for 3 to 4 minutes.

Orptec Club, Aberdeen, S.D.

BACON BISCUITS

Makes About 24

    Basic Baking Powder Biscuits
      (p. 119)
    ¼ teaspoon crushed sage
    Coarsely crushed black pepper
    Bacon drippings

1. Follow directions for Basic Baking Powder Biscuits, adding sage and ¼ teaspoon of the pepper to flour mixture and substituting bacon drippings for shortening. Roll out thinly, as for crisp biscuits. Cut with small biscuit cutter. Place on baking sheet. Dust with pepper. Bake according to recipe directions.
2. For bake-ahead biscuits, bake at 350° F. until cooked but not browned. Cool. Store in covered container in refrigerator. Before serving, bake at 350° F. for 5 to 7 minutes.

VARIATION: Follow directions for Basic Baking Powder Biscuits, substituting sausage drippings for shortening. If sausage is mild, season with cayenne; if sausage is hot, sprinkle tops of uncooked biscuits with mild paprika.

Dot Montgomery, Woman's Club, Crawford, Ga.

BACON 'N' EGG CANAPÉS

Makes About 12

    3 slices bacon, diced
    2 eggs, hard-cooked and finely
      chopped
    4 teaspoons cream
    1 teaspoon tarragon vinegar
    ½ teaspoon crushed chervil leaves
    ¼ teaspoon crushed rosemary
    White or rye bread
    Mayonnaise
    Slivered green pepper or tomato

1. Cook bacon until crisp; drain on absorbent paper; crumble.

2. Mix bacon, eggs, cream, vinegar, chervil and rosemary.

3. Cut bread into 1½-inch rounds. Toast one side. Spread untoasted side with 1 teaspoon of bacon-egg mixture. Top with thin layer of mayonnaise.

4. Broil about 2 inches from heat for about 1 minute, or until golden brown.

5. Garnish with green pepper or tomato.

Our Heritage Cook Book, Pontotoc, Miss.

BAMBINOS

Serves 24

⅔ cup milk
2 cups baking powder biscuit mix
6-ounce can tomato paste
1 teaspoon garlic salt
¼ teaspoon orégano
¼ pound Mozzarella cheese
⅛ pound sliced peperoni

1. Pour milk all at once into biscuit mix. Stir to make a stiff dough. Roll out dough ¼ inch thick on lighly floured board. Cut into small rounds with biscuit cutter. Place on baking sheet.

2. Preheat oven to 450° F.

3. Combine tomato paste, garlic salt and orégano. Spread top of biscuits with mixture. Top each with 1 slice cheese and 2 slices peperoni.

4. Bake in preheated oven for 10 to 15 minutes.

Mrs. Charles Davis, Junior Woman's Club, Benson, Ariz.

COCKTAIL PIZZAS

Makes 24

12 English muffins, halved
8-ounce can pizza sauce
About 4 ounces Mozzarella cheese, thinly sliced
About 4 ounces pizza cheese, thinly sliced
Grated Parmesan cheese
Orégano
Thinly sliced peperoni or sliced mushrooms

1. Preheat oven to 350° F.

2. Spread each muffin half with 1 level teaspoon pizza sauce. Top with 1 slice Mozzarella and 1 slice pizza cheese. Top with dab of pizza sauce. Sprinkle with a little Parmesan cheese and orégano. Top each pizza with 2 slices peperoni or mushrooms.

3. Bake in preheated oven for 15 to 30 minutes, or until cheese is melted.

TOPPING VARIATIONS: Anchovies, shrimp, oysters, hot sausages.

Leonore Kirchem, Gentilly Woods Woman's Club, New Orleans, La.

CHEESE DATE ROUNDS

Makes 92

These keep almost indefinitely under refrigeration. Heat before serving.

8-ounce package dates
1 cup butter or margarine
1 pound sharp American cheese, shredded

4 cups presifted flour
1 teaspoon salt
¾ to 1 teaspoon red pepper

1. Cut dates into thirds.

2. Preheat oven to 400° F.

3. Cream butter or margarine and cheese. Work in flour, salt and pepper.

4. Turn dough onto lightly floured board. Roll out ¼ inch thick.

5. Cut dough into small rounds with floured biscuit cutter. Place a piece of date on each round; fold over; seal edges. Place turnovers on baking sheet.

6. Bake in preheated oven for 5 minutes. Reduce temperature to 300° F. Bake for 10 minutes longer, or until lightly browned.

Mrs. Ira L. Price, Inter Se Circle, Marion, Ala.

BROILED CHEESE ROLLS

Makes 20 to 24

2 3-ounce packages sharp cheese
¼ cup chili sauce
2 teaspoons grated onion
Thinly sliced bread
Melted butter

1. Bring cheese to room temperature; then mash.

2. Blend in chili sauce and onion.

3. Trim crusts from bread. Spread with cheese mixture. Roll up like small jelly rolls. Fasten with wooden picks.

4. Arrange rolls, seam side down, on damp towel. Store in refrigerator.

5. When ready to use, preheat broiler. Place rolls on baking sheet. Brush with butter.

6. Toast under broiler until golden brown.

May Anderson, Woman's Literary Union, Portland, Me.

BLUE CHEESE COCKTAIL BISCUITS

Makes 40

1 can refrigerator biscuits
½ cup butter
4 ounces blue cheese

1. Preheat oven to 400° F.

2. Cut each biscuit into quarters. Arrange in shallow baking pan.

3. Melt butter and cheese over low heat. Spoon over biscuits.

4. Bake in preheated oven for 15 minutes.

Mrs. Luke Blatt, Woman's Club, Lavalette, W. Va.

HOT CHEESE CANAPÉS

Makes About 36

½ pound sharp Cheddar cheese, grated
3-ounce package cream cheese
1 egg yolk
1 tablespoon chopped chives or scallion tops
½ teaspoon dry mustard
Salt to taste
Butter
About 36 rounds or squares of trimmed bread

1. Beat cheeses, egg yolk, chives or scallion tops, mustard and salt with electric mixer until well blended.
2. Melt a little butter in skillet; sauté one side of bread.
3. Spread untoasted side of bread with cheese mixture. Place on rack in shallow baking pan.
4. Broil until delicately browned.

Mrs. W. E. Arrington, Quest Club,
Bowling Green, Mo.

CHEDDAR CHEESE PUFFS
Makes 48

½ cup grated Cheddar cheese
1½ cups mayonnaise
  Melba rye rounds
1 small onion, thinly sliced

1. Combine cheese and mayonnaise.
2. Top each melba round with onion slice. Top with spoonful of cheese mixture.
3. Arrange on baking sheet. Broil for about 1 minute, or until cheese puffs and is slightly browned.

Mrs. Donna Kuhn, Juniors of Eastchester
Woman's Club, Eastchester, N.Y.

BROILED OLIVE, CHEESE AND BACON CANAPÉS
Makes 24

6 slices white bread
1 cup shredded sharp cheese
½ cup chopped stuffed green olives
2 egg whites, stiffly beaten
2 slices bacon, cooked and crumbled

1. Trim crusts from bread; cut into quarters; toast on only one side.
2. Combine remaining ingredients.
3. Spread on untoasted side of bread.
4. Arrange on baking sheet. Broil until cheese melts.

Mrs. Wallace Thurston, Thursday Morning Club,
Madison, N.J.

ENGLISH RAREBIT CANAPÉS
Makes 24

6 slices bread, trimmed
2 to 3 tablespoons butter
1 cup shredded sharp American cheese
⅛ teaspoon black pepper
¼ teaspoon dry mustard
4 teaspoons dry sherry
  Dried parsley flakes

1. Cut bread slices into quarters. Melt butter in skillet; sauté one side of bread. Toast other side of bread under broiler.
2. Combine cheese, pepper, mustard and sherry. Spread on sautéed side of bread.
3. Arrange on baking sheet. Broil for ½ to 1 minute, or until cheese is melted and lightly browned.
4. Sprinkle with parsley.

Ann Nelson, Junior Woman's Club, Joliet, Ill.

CHEESE TURNOVERS
Makes 12

1 cup presifted flour
½ teaspoon salt

½ cup butter
3-ounce package cream cheese
  Anchovy paste or deviled ham

1. Preheat oven to 400° F.
2. In mixing bowl combine flour and salt.
3. Combine butter and cheese. Blend with flour.
4. Roll out very thinly on lightly floured board. Cut into 2-inch rounds with floured biscuit cutter.
5. Spread with anchovy paste or ham. Fold in half. Arrange on baking sheet.
6. Bake in preheated oven for about 10 minutes.

Mrs. Jack Stubbs, Marshall County Woman's
Club, Holly Springs, Miss.

ROQUEFORT CREAM CHEESE ROLLS
Makes 12

¼ pound Roquefort cheese
3-ounce package cream cheese
2 tablespoons mayonnaise
  Dash of red pepper
12 slices bread, trimmed

1. Mix all ingredients except bread until smooth. Spread on bread. Roll up each slice like a jelly roll. Secure with wooden picks. Chill.
2. Preheat oven to 275° F.
3. Arrange rolls on baking sheet. Toast in oven until golden.

Mrs. A. B. Banks, Sesame Club, Fordyce, Ark.

NOCHE SPECIALS (Evening Cheese Snacks)
Makes 24

6 Tortillas (p. 136) or canned tortillas
  Fat for deep frying
½ cup grated Cheddar cheese
6-ounce can jalapeña chili peppers, drained and sliced

1. Preheat oven to 425° F. Grease baking sheet.
2. Cut Tortillas into quarters. Fry in deep fat heated to 365° F. for about 3 minutes, or until browned and crisp.
3. Drain on absorbent paper. Arrange on baking sheet.
4. Top each quarter with 1 teaspoon of the cheese and 1 slice of the chilis.
5. Bake in preheated oven for 5 minutes, or until cheese is melted.

Junior Study Club, San Augustine, Tex.

CLAM PUFFS
Makes About 24

8-ounce can minced clams, drained
3-ounce package cream cheese
  Dash of Worcestershire
1 teaspoon finely grated onion
1 egg white, well beaten
  About 24 crisp crackers

1. Combine clams and cheese. Add Worcestershire and onion. Fold in egg white.
2. Drop by teaspoons on crackers.
3. Arrange on baking sheet. Broil until puffy and golden brown.

VARIATIONS:
1. Add horseradish to taste.
2. Omit egg white. Spread clam mixture thickly on toast squares. Sprinkle with shredded American cheese. Broil until lightly browned.

Mrs. John H. Rudd, Jr., Woman's Club,
West Palm Beach, Fla.

HOT CLAM ROLLS
Makes 24

8-ounce can minced clams
1 tablespoon butter
2 tablespoons chopped onion
1½ tablespoons flour
¼ teaspoon Worcestershire
Dash of garlic powder
12 thin slices bread, trimmed
Melted butter

1. Drain clams; reserve liquid.
2. Melt butter in skillet; sauté onion until tender. Remove from heat. Stir in flour, Worcestershire, garlic powder and reserved clam liquid.
3. Return to low heat. Bring to boil, stirring constantly. Stir in clams. Cool.
4. Preheat oven to 425° F. Grease baking sheet.
5. Flatten each slice of bread with rolling pin. Spread each with clam mixture; roll up; cut each roll in half; fasten with wooden pick.
6. Arrange on baking sheet. Brush with melted butter. Bake in preheated oven for 8 to 10 minutes.

Joan Rohde, Junior Woman's Club,
Glastonbury, Conn.

CRAB MEAT CANAPÉS
Makes About 12

6½-ounce can crab meat, drained
and flaked
2 3-ounce packages cream cheese
½ teaspoon mayonnaise
½ teaspoon Worcestershire
Dash of seasoned salt
Bread rounds
Paprika

1. Combine crab meat, cheese, mayonnaise, Worcestershire and seasoned salt.
2. Toast bread rounds on both sides. Spread with crab meat mixture. Sprinkle with paprika.
3. Arrange on baking sheet. Brown under broiler.

Mrs. William Suter, Coco Plum Woman's Club,
Coral Gables, Fla.

DEVILED HAM PUFFS
Makes 24

8-ounce package cream cheese
1 teaspoon grated onion and juice
½ teaspoon baking powder
1 egg yolk
Seasoned salt to taste
24 small bread rounds, toasted
on one side
2 2½-ounce cans deviled ham

1. Combine cheese, onion and juice, baking powder, egg yolk and seasoned salt.

2. Spread untoasted sides of bread rounds with ham. Cover each with mound of cheese mixture. Arrange on baking sheet. Chill.
3. Preheat oven to 400° F.
4. Bake in preheated oven for 10 to 12 minutes.

Carole Holsinger, Service League, Lombard, Ill.

HAWAIIAN SANDWICHES

Toast
Mayonnaise
Sliced pineapple
Mild cheese slices
Sliced bacon, partially cooked

1. Spread toast with mayonnaise. Top with pineapple slices, cheese slices and bacon slices. Arrange on baking sheet.
2. Broil until cheese melts and bacon is crisp.

Patty Graham, Woman's Club,
Lavalette, W. Va.

MUSHROOM CANAPÉS
Makes 8

8 large mushrooms
Butter
16-ounce can lobster or crab meat,
drained
1 tablespoon chili sauce
1 tablespoon lemon juice
1 tablespoon melted butter
8 2½-inch toast rounds
1 hard-cooked egg yolk, grated
Parsley sprigs

1. Peel mushrooms; remove stems. Place, cup side up, on baking sheet; dot each with butter; broil for 4 to 5 minutes.
2. Shred lobster or crab meat. Mix with chili sauce, lemon juice and melted butter. Fill mushrooms with mixture.
3. Sprinkle toast rounds with egg yolk. Return mushrooms to broiler. Cook until sizzling hot. Place each on toast round. Garnish each with parsley sprig.

Mrs. Elmer D. Hall, Woman's Club,
Williamsburg, Ky.

MUSHROOM ROLLS
Makes 48

3 4-ounce cans mushrooms, drained
1 medium onion
2 tablespoons butter or margarine
Salt and pepper to taste
1 loaf thin-sliced bread
Melted butter
Finely chopped walnuts or pecans

1. Prepare filling: put mushrooms and onion through medium blade of meat grinder. Melt butter or margarine in small skillet; sauté mushrooms and onion for 5 minutes. Season with salt and pepper. Cool.
2. Trim crusts from bread. With rolling pin flatten each slice in middle of damp cloth as thin as possible.
3. Spread filling on each bread slice. Roll up like a jelly roll. Dip in melted butter.

4. Roll in walnuts or pecans. Chill, covered, for 3 hours, or freeze until needed.

5. Preheat oven to 325° F.

6. Cut rolls into thirds. Place on baking sheet.

7. Bake in preheated oven for 5 minutes, or until hot.

Mrs. Bertrand H. Reynolds, Outlook Club,
Falmouth, Mass.

SARDINE AND BACON CANAPÉS
Makes 8

8 sardines
Lemon juice
Paprika
8 thin slices bacon
Prepared mustard
8 slices buttered toast

1. Preheat oven to 450° F.

2. Sprinkle sardines with lemon juice and paprika.

3. Spread bacon with mustard; roll a slice around each sardine; secure with wooden pick. Arrange on baking sheet.

4. Bake in preheated oven for 7 minutes, or until bacon is crisp. Serve on toast.

Woman's Club, Murray, Ky.

SAUSAGE BITES
Makes 24

1 loaf thin-sliced bread
2 tablespoons prepared mustard
Horseradish to taste
1 package brown-and-serve sausages
Melted butter

1. Trim crusts from bread. Cut each slice in half. Flatten with rolling pin.

2. Preheat oven to 400° F.

3. Combine mustard and horseradish.

4. Spread each piece of bread with a little of mustard mixture.

5. Cut each sausage in half. Place a sausage half on each piece of bread; roll up; arrange in baking pan.

6. Brush with butter. Bake in preheated oven for 20 minutes, or until nicely browned.

Mrs. Benjamin Schreiber, Woman's Literary
Union, Portland, Me.

SAUSAGE ROLLS
Makes 24

2 cups baking powder biscuit mix
1 cup milk
1 pound hot or mild sausage meat

1. Combine biscuit mix and milk. Divide dough in half.

2. Roll out each half on lightly floured board. Spread with half the sausage meat. Roll up like a jelly roll. Refrigerate.

3. Preheat oven to 450° F.

4. Slice rolls thinly. Place slices on baking sheet. Bake in preheated oven for 10 minutes.

Mrs. A. L. Coffey, Coco Plum Woman's Club,
Coral Gables, Fla.

HOT TUNA CRAB CANAPÉS
Makes 36

7-ounce can tuna, drained
7-ounce can crab meat, flaked
1 teaspoon lemon juice
½ cup chili sauce
1 teaspoon Worcestershire
½ cup mayonnaise
French bread
Butter

1. Combine tuna, crab meat, lemon juice, chili sauce, Worcestershire and mayonnaise.

2. Slice bread. Butter both sides. Arrange on baking sheet.

3. Toast in broiler on one side. Turn. Cover with fish mixture. Broil for 1 to 2 minutes longer.

Mrs. W. C. Wyatt, Junior Women's Club,
Miamisburg, Ohio

TUNA OLIVE BITES
Makes 150

10-ounce package corn bread mix
1 tablespoon instant minced onion
7-ounce can tuna, drained
¾ cup sliced stuffed olives

1. Preheat oven to 400° F. Grease jelly roll pan.

2. In mixing bowl combine corn bread mix, onion and tuna. Mix according to package directions. Stir in olives.

3. Spread batter in jelly roll pan. Bake in preheated oven for 15 to 20 minutes.

4. Cut into tiny squares.

Gloria Keller, Woman's Club, Pikeville, Ky.

2. Hearty Sandwiches

In addition to the sandwich fillings and suggestions in the section in Chapter 1 on Canapés and Party Sandwiches (which may also be used separately or in combination to create delicious sandwiches for hearty appetites), there are many other full-bodied sandwiches to suit every occasion. In this chapter you will find America's favorite luncheon and supper sandwiches, sandwiches for the lunch box and for picnics and a variety of intriguing recipes for beef and other burgers, frankfurter specials and pizzas.

SANDWICHES—A GENERAL NOTE

Because they are easy to make and easy to serve, besides offering valuable nourishment in a single dish, sandwiches, with their wide variety of content, occupy a steady position of importance in meal planning.

Although numerous suggestions and combinations are given in this chapter, the ingenious and imaginative cook will be able to create an almost limitless number of variations, matching the proper sandwich filling with the need at hand.

Whether the sandwiches are for plate service, lunch boxes for school or work, a picnic, a barbecue or an impromptu supper, they should be served as fresh as possible. Sandwiches for lunch boxes should be wrapped in aluminum foil or in plastic sandwich bags and tightly closed. Sandwiches that are to be kept overnight should be placed in the refrigerator. Butter or margarine should be spread on both slices of bread to prevent soft fillings from soaking into the bread, as well as to give added flavor to the filling.

Any sandwich filling is complemented by the selection of the right kind of bread, which includes white bread, whole wheat or rye bread, nut, date or fruit bread, pumpernickel or whole grain dark bread, cheese or garlic bread, corn bread and many types of rolls. Whether or not to trim off crusts is a matter of individual taste.

Lettuce leaves, tomato slices, pickle or bacon should be added just before serving. Colorful garnishes which can be picked up with the fingers include radishes, crisp lettuce hearts, olives, pickles and celery sticks.

Snack-Time Symphony, County Women's Club, Hopewell, Pa.

SANDWICH SUGGESTIONS

AMERICAN CHEESE OPEN FACE

American cheese slices, crushed pineapple, bacon slices, prepared mustard, toast. Broil open face.

BLUE CHEESE OR ROQUEFORT

Blue cheese or roquefort, finely chopped almonds, grated onion. Mix with bottled meat sauce.

BOLOGNA

Bologna pieces, horseradish, grated onion, chopped green pepper, chopped hard-cooked eggs. Mix with mayonnaise.

CHEDDAR BEEF

Grated sharp cheese, dried beef pieces, horseradish, prepared mustard. Mix with mayonnaise.

CHEESE AND EGG

Shredded American cheese; chopped pimiento, pickle, onion and hard-cooked egg; seasoning. Mix with mayonnaise.

CHEESE AND OLIVE

Shredded American cheese, crisp bacon pieces, chopped pickles, olives, Worcestershire. Mix with mayonnaise.

CHICKEN

Diced cooked chicken and celery, seasoning. Mix with mayonnaise.

CHICKEN AND GRAPE

Diced cooked chicken, seeded Tokay grape halves, finely chopped celery, seasoning. Mix with mayonnaise.

CHICKEN AND PINEAPPLE

Chopped cooked chicken, broken nuts, drained crushed pineapple. Mix with mayonnaise.

CORNED BEEF

Chopped corned beef, grated onion, chopped kosher pickle, diced celery. Mix with tomato purée.

COTTAGE CHEESE AND BACON

Cottage cheese, crisp bacon pieces, horseradish, seasonings. Mix with mayonnaise.

COTTAGE CHEESE AND NUTS

Cottage cheese creamed with mayonnaise, chopped nuts, diced celery, onion salt. Mix with mayonnaise.

CREAM CHEESE AND APPLE

Cream cheese mixed with cinnamon apple butter. Very good spread on buttered gingerbread slices.

CREAM CHEESE AND APRICOT

Cream cheese, apricot juice. Mix with a little mayonnaise. Serve on whole wheat bread.

CREAM CHEESE AND CUCUMBER

Cream cheese, finely shredded cucumber, minced onion tops. Spread on raisin bread.

CREAM CHEESE AND DATE

Cream cheese, chopped dates and nuts, dash of lemon juice, drained crushed pineapple. Mix with mayonnaise.

CREAM CHEESE AND DRIED BEEF

Cream cheese, dried beef pieces, grated onion, diced celery. Soften with cream.

CREAM CHEESE AND PINEAPPLE

Mashed cream cheese, drained crushed pineapple. Mix with mayonnaise and pineapple juice.

CREAM CHEESE AND RASPBERRY

Cream cheese mixed with raspberry jelly or jam. Serve on whole wheat bread.

CUCUMBER

Minced pimientos, cucumbers, onion, chives. Mix with mayonnaise. Serve on whole wheat bread.

EGG AND OLIVE

Chopped hard-cooked eggs, chopped stuffed olives, chopped celery, seasonings. Mix with mayonnaise.

FISH

Tuna, salmon or sardines; diced celery; seasonings; dash of onion juice. Mix with mayonnaise.

FRANKFURTER

Sliced cooked frankfurters, chopped scallion, salt. Mix with prepared mustard.

HAM

Chopped cooked ham, chopped hard-cooked eggs, diced sweet pickle, seasonings. Mix with mayonnaise.

HAMBURGER

Two thin hamburger patties. Sandwich together with tomato and onion slices between. Broil or pan-fry.

LIVERWURST

Liverwurst, chopped stuffed olives, chopped celery. Mix with mayonnaise. Serve on rye bread.

MEAT

Any chopped cooked meat, chili sauce, minced celery, minced water cress, seasonings. Mix with prepared mustard.

MEAT LOAF

Sliced cooked meat loaf, catsup or prepared mustard, celery salt or onion salt. Serve on whole wheat bread.

MUSHROOM

Sautéed mushrooms, Worcestershire, chopped almonds, seasonings. Chopped cooked meat, if desired.

ORANGE PEANUT BUTTER

Peanut butter, shredded coconut, honey, orange juice, grated orange rind. Serve on rye bread.

PÂTÉ

Mashed liverwurst, horseradish, mustard, mayonnaise, Worcestershire, minced celery, salt.

PEANUT BUTTER AND MAYONNAISE

Peanut butter creamed with mayonnaise, banana slices. Serve on whole wheat bread.

PEANUT BUTTER AND PICKLE

Peanut butter, minced raisins, chopped sweet pickle. Mix with mayonnaise. Serve on whole wheat bread.

PEANUT BUTTER AND PRUNE

Chopped cooked prunes, peanut butter, salt. Mix with mayonnaise.

PORK AND BEANS

Cold sliced pork with beans, shredded cheese, pickle relish, chili sauce, seasonings.

Snack-Time Symphony, County Women's Club,
Hopewell, Pa.

SANDWICH SUGGESTIONS

With a few exceptions, sandwiches, sandwich fillings or spreads can be frozen for later use. It is best not to freeze jelly, mayonnaise or salad dressing when the filling is used as a spread. They soak into the bread, making it soggy. Lettuce, celery, tomatoes, raw carrots and hard-cooked eggs do not freeze well.

CHICKEN

Ground cooked chicken (preferably white meat), chopped celery, chopped parsley. Mix with Thick White Sauce (p. 441) or Chicken Sauce (p. 441). Season to taste.

CRAB OR SHRIMP

Flaked cooked crab meat or chopped cooked shrimp, chopped celery, chopped onion. Mix with mayonnaise.

EGG

Chopped hard-cooked egg; finely minced celery, onion, parsley and green pepper;

salt and pepper to taste. Mix with mayonnaise. Crumbled crisp bacon is a nice addition.

TUNA OR SALMON

Tuna or salmon; finely chopped celery, onion and parsley. Mix with mayonnaise.

RAISIN AND CARROT

Chopped seedless raisins, shredded carrots, lemon juice, salt. Mix with mayonnaise.

SARDINES

Mashed sardines, grated onion, vinegar, prepared mustard. Mix with mayonnaise. Serve on rye bread.

TOMATO OPEN FACE

Toast spread with mayonnaise, topped with tomato slices, cheese slice, bacon slices. Broil open face.

Century Club Cook Book, Coraopolis, Pa.

Cold Sandwiches

OPEN-FACE BEEF SANDWICHES
Makes 4

⅓ cup mayonnaise
2 teaspoons horseradish
4 slices white bread
4 slices roast beef
8 slices bacon, cripsly cooked
3½-ounce can French-fried onion rings

1. Blend mayonnaise and horseradish. Spread on bread.
2. Top each with 1 slice of the roast beef and 2 slices of the bacon.
3. Arrange onion rings on top.

Junior Service League, Statesville, N.C.

HE-MAN SANDWICHES
Makes 4

For real he-man appetites, use additional slices of meat and cheese for each sandwich.

4 thin slices roast beef
8 slices buttered rye bread
4 slices cheese
Prepared mustard
Lettuce leaves (optional)

1. Place 1 slice of the roast beef on each of 4 slices of the rye bread.
2. Add 1 slice of the cheese; brush with mustard; cover with lettuce leaf, if desired.
3. Top with remaining rye bread.

VARIATIONS: Thin slices of cooked ham, pastrami, salami, capocollo or other sliced luncheon meats may be used in place of beef.

Woman's Literary Union, Portland, Me.

HEROES
Makes 2

2 large hard rolls
¼ cup softened butter
¼ pound sliced boiled ham
1 tomato, thinly sliced
¼ pound sliced Swiss cheese
Prepared mustard
¼ pound sliced pork roll
Lettuce leaves
Salt and pepper to taste

1. Split rolls. Spread cut sides with butter.
2. On bottom halves, arrange ham, tomato and cheese slices. Spread cheese with mustard.
3. Add pork slices and lettuce leaves. Sprinkle with salt and pepper.
4. Top with upper halves of rolls.

VARIATIONS:
1. Use mayonnaise or sour cream instead of butter.
2. Use sliced provolone or Cheddar cheese in place of Swiss cheese.

A. S.

HERO FOR SIX
Makes 6 Large Servings

1 20-inch loaf French bread
Mayonnaise
Sliced Cheddar cheese
Green pepper rings
Sliced pickles
Sliced sweet onion
Stuffed olives
Sliced Swiss cheese
Sliced cooked ham
Sliced liverwurst

1. Split bread lengthwise. Spread cut sides with mayonnaise.
2. On bottom half, arrange one layer of Cheddar cheese slices, then a layer of green pepper rings, pickles, sweet onion and olives.
3. Top with slices of Swiss cheese, ham and liverwurst. Cover with top half of loaf.
4. Cut into 6 servings.

A. S.

BOBETTE SANDWICHES
Makes 6

2 medium green peppers
1 cup blanched almonds
1 apple, quartered and cored
12 ripe olives, pitted
⅛ teaspoon curry powder
½ teaspoon salt
1 teaspoon lemon juice
½ cup mayonnaise
1 cup finely chopped lettuce
12 slices buttered bread

1. Put green peppers, almonds, apple and olives through medium blade of meat grinder.
2. Turn into mixing bowl. Add curry powder, salt, lemon juice, mayonnaise and lettuce. Mix well.
3. Spread filling on 6 slices of bread. Top each with remaining bread slices.

Mrs. G. Otto, Woman's Club,
Menomonee Falls, Wis.

CAVIAR OPEN-FACE SANDWICHES
Makes 4

½ cup caviar
1 tablespoon grated onion
2 teaspoons lemon juice
4 slices toast
1 egg, hard-cooked

1. In small bowl lightly mix caviar, onion and lemon juice.
2. Trim toast. Spread with caviar.
3. Separate egg white and yolk. Finely chop white; arrange around edge of each sandwich.
4. Press egg yolk through sieve; arrange in center of each sandwich.

Woman's Club, Monticello, Fla.

CHICKEN SANDWICHES
Makes 4

1 cup finely chopped cooked chicken
¼ cup chopped olives
¼ cup chopped pimientos
½ cup mayonnaise
8 slices buttered bread

1. In mixing bowl combine chicken, olives, pimientos and mayonnaise. Mix well.
2. Spread on 4 slices of the bread. Top with remaining bread slices.

Woman's Club, Monticello, Fla.

CHICKEN DELIGHT SANDWICHES
Makes 4

1 cup shredded lettuce
½ cup finely chopped tomato
¼ cup grated onion
¼ cup sweet pickle relish
Salt and pepper to taste
1 ripe large avocado
8 slices toast
8 slices roast chicken

1. Prepare lettuce filling: Put lettuce, tomato, onion and pickle relish in mixing bowl. Season with salt and pepper. Mix well.
2. Peel and pit avocado; then mash.
3. Spread toast with avocado. Sprinkle with salt.
4. Arrange chicken on 4 slices of toast. Top with lettuce filling.
5. Cover with remaining toast slices.

Myrt Finch, Woman's Club, Cupertino, Calif.

COTTAGE CHEESE SANDWICHES
Makes 4

1 cup cream-style cottage cheese
3 tablespoons minced green pepper
3 tablespoons minced scallions
½ teaspoon salt
½ teaspoon paprika
8 slices buttered whole wheat bread

1. In mixing bowl blend cheese, green pepper, scallions, salt and paprika.
2. Spread on 4 slices of the bread. Top with remaining bread slices.

Study Club, Lake Wilson, Minn.

CUCUMBER SANDWICHES
Makes 4

1 medium cucumber, peeled
1 teaspoon salt
½ cup mayonaise
8 thin slices buttered bread

1. Slice cucumber thinly into medium bowl. Sprinkle with salt. Add cold water just to cover. Let stand until ready to prepare sandwiches.
2. Drain cucumbers well. Return to bowl.
3. Add mayonnaise. Mix well.
4. Arrange cucumber slices on 4 slices of the bread. Top with remaining bread slices.

Harriet Hawthorn, Woman's Club, Hawthorne, Fla.

EGG AND CHEESE SANDWICHES
Makes 4

2 eggs, hard-cooked
½ small onion
½ cup stuffed olives
3-ounce package cream cheese
½ teaspoon salt
Dash of cayenne
1 teaspoon Worcestershire
1 tablespoon softened butter
8 slices white bread

1. Put eggs, onion and olives through medium blade of meat grinder.
2. In mixing bowl beat cheese, salt, cayenne, Worcestershire and butter until blended.
3. Add egg mixture. Mix well.
4. Spread on 4 slices of bread. Top with remaining bread slices.

Alma Kellogg, Woman's Club, Patten, Mass.

FIG SANDWICHES
Makes 8

½ pound finely chopped figs
⅓ cup sugar
½ cup boiling water
2 tablespoons lemon juice
16 slices buttered whole wheat bread

1. In top of double saucepan combine figs, sugar, water and lemon juice.
2. Cook over hot water, stirring frequently, for about 20 minutes, or until thickened. Remove from heat. Cool.
3. Spread filling on 8 slices of the bread. Top with remaining bread slices. Trim crusts. Cut in half.

Mrs. Grace Cochrane, Women's Club, Monroe, Ia.

FRESH FRUIT SANDWICHES
Makes 2

2 ripe bananas
1 teaspoon cream
1 teaspoon sugar
4 thin slices well-buttered whole wheat bread

1. Crush bananas with fork. Mix in cream and sugar.
2. Spread between slices of bread.

VARIATION: Use strawberries or any other fresh fruit in place of bananas.

Mrs. J. L. Garnett, Woman's Club, Boynton Beach, Fla.

DEVILED HAM SANDWICHES
Makes 4

4½-ounce can deviled ham
3 eggs, hard-cooked and finely chopped
2 teaspoons horseradish
⅓ cup mayonnaise
8 slices buttered whole wheat bread

1. Blend ham, eggs, horseradish and mayonnaise.
2. Spread on 4 slices of the bread. Top with remaining bread slices.

Woman's Club, Clarkton, N.C.

LIVER SANDWICHES
Makes 4

4½-ounce can liver spread
¼ cup mayonnaise
¼ cup finely chopped stuffed olives
1 teaspoon Worcestershire
8 slices buttered pumpernickel

1. Blend liver spread and mayonnaise.
2. Add olives and Worcestershire. Mix well.
3. Spread on 4 slices of the bread. Top with remaining bread slices.

Lolita Eshom, Woman's Club, Guernsey, Wyo.

LIVERWURST SANDWICHES
Makes 4

¼ pound liverwurst
6 stuffed olives
1 small onion
½ cup shredded lettuce
⅓ cup mayonnaise
8 slices buttered bread

1. Put liverwurst, olives and onion through medium blade of meat grinder.
2. Combine liverwurst mixture, lettuce and mayonnaise.
3. Spread on 4 slices of the bread. Top with remaining bread slices.

Study Club, Lake Wilson, Minn.

LIVERWURST, CHEESE AND EGG SANDWICHES
Makes 12

½ pound liverwurst
¼ pound Swiss cheese
4 eggs, hard-cooked
¼ pound salami
1 medium onion
3 drops Tabasco
¼ cup mayonnaise
Salt and pepper to taste
24 slices buttered rye bread

1. Put liverwurst, cheese, eggs, salami and onion through large blade of meat grinder.
2. Add Tabasco and mayonnaise. Season with salt and pepper.
3. Mix well. Spread on 12 slices of the bread. Top with remaining bread slices.

Mrs. D. D. Jones, Woman's Club, Meadows, Ida.

MARMALADE SANDWICHES
Makes 4

3-ounce package cream cheese
¼ cup orange marmalade
½ teaspoon ginger
8 slices whole wheat bread

1. In mixing bowl blend cream cheese, marmalade and ginger.
2. Spread on 4 slices of the bread. Top with remaining bread slices. Trim crusts. Cut into quarters, if desired.

B. Little, Woman's Literary Club, Bar Harbor, Me.

NUT AND PIMIENTO SANDWICHES
Makes 4

1 cup finely chopped pecans
4-ounce can pimientos, drained and finely chopped
3-ounce package cream cheese
½ cup mayonnaise
8 slices buttered bread

1. In medium bowl combine pecans, pimientos, cheese and mayonnaise.
2. Beat until well blended.
3. Spread on 4 slices of the bread. Top with remaining bread slices.

Woman's Club, Monticello, Fla.

PINEAPPLE AND PECAN SANDWICHES
Makes 4

9-ounce can crushed pineapple, drained
1 cup finely chopped pecans
⅓ cup mayonnaise
8 slices buttered bread

1. In medium bowl combine pineapple, pecans and mayonnaise; mix well.
2. Spread on 4 slices of the bread. Top with remaining bread slices.

Woman's Club, Monticello, Fla.

OPEN-FACE SARDINE SANDWICHES
Makes 4

4 slices buttered white bread
1 teaspoon curry powder
1½-ounce can sardines, drained
2 eggs, hard-cooked and sliced
4 small strips pimiento

1. Sprinkle bread with curry powder.
2. Mash sardines. Spread on bread.
3. Arrange egg slices on sardines. Garnish each sandwich with pimiento strip.

Junior Service League, Statesville, N.C.

OPEN-FACE SHRIMP SANDWICHES
Makes 4

4 slices dark pumpernickel
½ cup Tartar Sauce for Fish (p. 450)
2 4½-ounce cans small shrimp, drained
Parsley sprigs

1. Trim crusts from bread. Spread with Tartar Sauce for Fish.
2. Arrange shrimp on bread. Garnish with parsley.

Junior Service League, Statesville, N.C.

OPEN-FACE TONGUE SANDWICHES
Makes 4

1 cup cooked mixed vegetables
¼ cup mayonnaise
4 slices buttered whole wheat bread
8 small slices smoked tongue
2 teaspoons capers

1. In small bowl blend vegetables and mayonnaise.
2. Arrange tongue on bread slices. Spread with vegetable mixture.
3. Top with capers.

Junior Service League, Statesville, N.C.

Hot Sandwiches

GRILLED APPLESAUCE AND BACON SANDWICHES
Makes 4

8 slices bacon
4 slices toast
½ cup applesauce
4 slices American cheese

1. Preheat broiler.
2. Cook bacon in skillet until it starts to brown. Drain on absorbent paper.
3. Arrange toast on broiler pan. Spread with applesauce.
4. Top each slice of toast with 1 slice of the cheese and 2 slices bacon.
5. Broil about 4 inches from heat for 2 minutes, or until bacon is crisp and cheese is melted.

Lucy Schoff, Junior Woman's Club,
St. Clouds, Fla.

BUN-IES
Makes 6

6 hamburger buns
Olive oil
6 eggs
Salt and pepper to taste
½ cup buttered bread crumbs
6 slices American cheese

1. Preheat oven to 325° F. Grease baking sheet.
2. Cut circles from top of each bun. Scoop out 1-inch holes. Brush outside and inside of buns with oil.
3. Arrange on baking sheet. Break 1 egg into center of each bun. Season with salt and pepper. Sprinkle with crumbs.
4. Bake in preheated oven for 20 minutes.
5. Remove baking sheet from oven. Put 1 slice of cheese on each bun.
6. Bake for 5 minutes longer, or until cheese puffs.

Pauline Sanville, Woman's Club, Sunland, Calif.

BAKED CHEESE SANDWICHES
Makes 6

12 slices whole bread
6 slices Swiss cheese, cut in half
4 eggs, beaten
2 cups milk
1 teaspoon salt
Dash of cayenne

1 tablespoon Worcestershire
2 cups grated Cheddar cheese
Paprika
6 tomato slices

1. Preheat oven to 375° F. Grease 13 x 9½ x 2-inch baking pan.
2. Arrange 6 slices of the bread in pan. Top each with ½ slice of the Swiss cheese. Top with remaining bread slices, then with remaining Swiss cheese.
3. In medium bowl blend eggs, milk, salt, cayenne and Worcestershire. Pour over sandwiches. Sprinkle with Cheddar cheese and paprika.
4. Bake in preheated oven for 20 minutes, or until sandwiches puff.
5. Top each sandwich with 1 tomato slice. Bake for 5 minutes longer.

Joan North, Adams-Arapahoe Women's Club,
Aurora, Colo.

OPEN-FACE CHEESE SANDWICH
Makes 4

1 cup grated mild Cheddar cheese
½ cup diced cucumber
1 tablespoon grated onion
¼ cup sour cream
⅛ teaspoon pepper
½ teaspoon chili powder
4 slices white bread

1. Preheat oven to 375° F. Line baking sheet with aluminum foil.
2. In mixing bowl blend cheese, cucumber, onion, sour cream, pepper and chili powder.
3. Spread on bread slices. Arrange on baking sheet.
4. Bake in preheated oven for 12 minutes, or until cheese is melted.

Mrs. Jay Montgomery, Junior Women's Club,
Steubenville, Ohio

DEVONSHIRE SANDWICH
Makes 6

18 slices bacon
1¼ cups presifted flour
2 quarts hot milk
1 tablespoon salt
1 teaspoon dry mustard
½ teaspoon poultry seasoning
1 teaspoon monosodium glutamate
½ pound sharp Cheddar cheese, diced
6 slices bread
1½ pounds sliced cooked chicken
or turkey
2 tablespoons grated Parmesan cheese
1 teaspoon paprika

1. Cook bacon slowly in skillet until crisp. Drain on absorbent paper.
2. Stir flour into fat remaining in skillet; blend to a smooth paste. Gradually stir in milk. Cook until sauce is thickened and smooth, stirring constantly.
3. Cook over low heat for 10 minutes, stirring frequently.
4. Add salt, mustard, poultry seasoning and Cheddar cheese. Stir until cheese is melted.
5. Preheat oven to 350° F.

6. Toast bread on both sides. Trim crusts, if desired.

7. Arrange toast on heatproof platter or plate. Place 3 bacon slices on each slice of toast. Arrange chicken on bacon. Cover completely with sauce.

8. Combine Parmesan cheese and paprika. Sprinkle over top. Bake in preheated oven for 10 minutes.

Ange Weisner, Century Club, Coraopolis, Pa.

HOT COMBINATION SANDWICH FOR A PARTY

Makes 30

2 cups cubed American cheese
1 pound shaved ham, cubed
¾ cup mayonnaise
½ cup chili sauce
4 medium onions, finely chopped
12 eggs, hard-cooked and chopped
30 hamburger buns

1. Preheat oven to 425° F. Cut 30 squares of aluminum foil.
2. In mixing bowl combine cheese, ham, mayonnaise, chili sauce, onions and eggs. Mix well.
3. Split hamburger buns. Spread with ham mixture. Wrap each in foil. Arrange foil-wrapped buns on baking sheets.
4. Bake in preheated oven for 12 to 15 minutes.

Lucille Peckman, Junior Woman's Club,
Turtle Creek, Pa.

ITALIAN OPEN SANDWICHES

Makes 8

1 pound sharp Cheddar cheese, grated
1 cup chopped ripe olives
1 medium green pepper, finely chopped
½ teaspoon garlic salt
8-ounce can tomato sauce
2 tablespoons olive oil
8 round hard-crusted rolls

1. Preheat oven to 400° F. Grease baking sheet.
2. In mixing bowl combine all ingredients except rolls.
3. Split rolls. Spread filling on roll halves.
4. Arrange on baking sheet. Bake in preheated oven for 10 minutes.

Woman's Club, Van Nuys, Calif.

LULLABY SPECIAL

Makes 6

½ cup mayonnaise
2 tablespoons chopped sweet pickle
2 tablespoons chopped stuffed olives
1 small onion, grated
3 eggs, hard-cooked and chopped
8-ounce package American cheese, cubed
1 cup diced boiled ham
6 hamburger buns or hard rolls

1. Preheat oven to 375° F. Cut 6 squares of aluminum foil; arrange on baking sheet.
2. In mixing bowl combine mayonnaise, pickles, olives and onion.
3. Add eggs, cheese and ham. Mix well.

4. Split rolls. Fill with ham mixture. Wrap each in foil; place on baking sheet.
5. Bake in preheated oven for 20 minutes.

Lullaby Club, Canton, Ohio

TOASTED CHICKEN SANDWICHES

Makes 8

3 cups diced cooked chicken
1½ cups finely chopped celery
1 cup grated Cheddar cheese
¼ cup finely chopped stuffed olives
½ cup finely chopped walnuts
1½ teaspoons salt
¼ teaspoon pepper
1 cup mayonnaise
8 slices bread

1. Preheat broiler.
2. In mixing bowl combine chicken, celery, cheese, olives and walnuts. Add salt, pepper and mayonnaise. Mix well.
3. Arrange bread on broiler pan. Spread with chicken mixture.
4. Broil 5 inches from heat for 8 minutes, or until golden.

Olive Mann, Woman's Club, Hinckley, Ill.

CORNED BEEF SANDWICHES

Makes 6

12-ounce can corned beef
1 cup diced Cheddar cheese
½ cup chopped olives
½ cup catsup
¼ cup grated onion
2 tablespoons Worcestershire
6 frankfurter rolls, split

1. Preheat oven to 375° F. Cut 6 pieces of aluminum foil; place on baking sheet.
2. Mash corned beef lightly.
3. Add cheese, olives, catsup, onion and Worcestershire. Mix well.
4. Pile filling into rolls. Wrap each in foil. Place on baking sheet.
5. Bake in preheated oven for 20 minutes.

Marty Marken, Woman's Club,
Slippery Rock, Pa.

HOT CRAB SANDWICHES

Makes 6

3-ounce package cream cheese
½ cup grated Parmesan cheese
1 teaspoon prepared mustard
1 egg
½ teaspoon Worcestershire
6 slices white bread
¼ cup mayonnaise
1 cup flaked cooked crab meat

1. Preheat broiler.
2. Blend cheeses, mustard, egg and Worcestershire.
3. Place bread slices on broiler pan. Toast on one side.
4. Turn. Spread with mayonnaise.
5. Arrange crab meat on mayonnaise. Cover with cheese mixture.
6. Broil 3 to 4 inches from heat for 5 minutes, or until bubbling and golden.

Mrs. Frank Vrana, Junior Woman's Club,
College Park, Md.

TOASTED CRAB AND EGG SANDWICHES

Makes 6

1 cup flaked cooked crab meat
3 eggs, hard-cooked and chopped
1 tablespoon grated onion
1 teaspoon Worcestershire
¼ cup mayonnaise
½ teaspoon salt
⅛ teaspoon pepper
6 slices bread
¼ cup grated Cheddar cheese

1. Preheat broiler. Line broiler pan with aluminum foil.
2. In mixing bowl blend crab meat, eggs, onion, Worcestershire, mayonnaise, salt and pepper to a paste.
3. Toast bread slices on one side. Spread untoasted side with crab mixture.
4. Sprinkle with cheese. Place on broiler pan.
5. Broil 4 inches from heat for 5 minutes, or until bubbling and browned.

G. Musinoff, Woman's Club, East Hartford, Conn.

OPEN-FACE KING CRAB SANDWICHES

Makes 4

6½-ounce can king crab meat, flaked
4 eggs, hard-cooked and chopped
¼ teaspoon onion salt
Coarsely ground pepper to taste
2 tablespoons mayonnaise
4 slices bread, toasted on only one side
4 slices American cheese

1. Preheat oven to 325° F.
2. Combine crab meat, eggs, onion salt, pepper and mayonnaise. Cook over low heat until hot.
3. Heap crab mixture on untoasted side of each bread slice; top with 1 slice cheese. Place on baking sheet.
4. Bake in preheated oven until cheese is melted.

Mrs. Ken C. Johnson, Woman's Club,
Anchorage, Alaska

HOT EGG SANDWICH

Makes 1

Hamburger bun
Deviled ham
2 thin slices onion
1 egg, scrambled
Shredded American cheese

1. Split bun. Spread each side with deviled ham; top with onion.
2. Spoon egg on onion slices. Sprinkle with a layer of cheese.
3. Broil until cheese is melted.

Ginnie Carey, Woman's Club,
Warner Robins, Ga.

BAR-B-Q SANDWICHES

Makes 12

1 pound lean pork shoulder, cut into 2-inch cubes
1 pound lean beef, cut into 2-inch cubes
2 large onions, quartered

1 medium green pepper, sliced
Bouquet garni (see Glossary)
2 cups water
1½ cups catsup
2 tablespoons brown sugar
2 tablespoons dry mustard
1 tablespoon salt
12 hamburger buns, split

1. Put pork, beef, onions, green pepper, bouquet garni and water in Dutch oven or heavy saucepan.
2. Bring to boil. Cover. Simmer for 40 minutes.
3. Drain; reserve liquid. Discard bouquet garni.
4. Put meats, onions and green pepper through large blade of meat grinder. Return ground ingredients to pan.
5. Stir in reserved liquid, catsup, sugar, mustard and salt.
6. Bring to boil. Then simmer, uncovered, stirring occasionally, for 30 minutes, or until thick.
7. Spoon mixture on bottom halves of buns. Top with upper halves.

Hattie Listenberger, Friendly Hour Home
Demonstration Club, Bremen, Ind.

BARBECUED HAM SANDWICHES

Makes 8

1 onion, minced
2 tablespoons vinegar
1 tablespoon flour
1½ tablespoons Worcestershire
2 tablespoons hot water
Pinch of red pepper
¼ teaspoon black pepper
1 teaspoon paprika
1 teaspoon dry or prepared mustard
½ cup catsup
2 tablespoons brown sugar
1 pound shaved ham
8 hamburger buns, split

1. Preheat oven to 350° F.
2. Combine all ingredients except buns in 1-quart baking dish, adding ham last.
3. Cover. Bake in preheated oven for 1 hour.
4. Spoon mixture generously on bottom halves. Top with upper halves.

Dottie Lucas, Woman's Civic Club,
Cumberland, Md.

HOT HAM AND CHEESE BUNS

Makes 6

¼ cup prepared mustard
¼ cup finely chopped onions
½ cup softened butter or margarine
6 hamburger buns
6 slices Swiss cheese
6 slices baked ham

1. Preheat oven to 350° F. Line baking sheet with aluminum foil.
2. In medium bowl blend mustard, onion and butter or margarine.
3. Split buns; spread both halves with mustard mixture.
4. Put cheese slice and ham slice between halves of each bun. Place on baking sheet.

5. Bake in preheated oven for 15 minutes.

Dorothy Fill, Woman's Club,
Prospect Heights, Ill.

HOT FRENCH ROLL SANDWICHES
Makes 24

1½ pounds ham or corned beef,
    ground
1 pound Cheddar cheese, shredded
2 medium onions, grated or ground
4 medium carrots, grated or ground
4 tablespoons sweet pickle relish
4 tablespoons chili sauce
½ cup sour cream
3 tablespoons mayonnaise
3 tablespoons prepared mustard
1 teaspoon garlic salt
1 teaspoon celery salt
1 teaspoon black pepper
1 teaspoon sugar
    Dash of cayenne or Tabasco
24 French rolls

1. Combine all ingredients except rolls.
2. Slice rolls lengthwise; scoop out centers; fill with mixture.
3. Replace tops of rolls. Wrap in aluminum foil. (Freeze, if desired.)
4. When ready to serve, preheat oven to 400° F.
5. Bake foil-wrapped rolls in preheated oven for 20 minutes.

Reba Robertson, El Camino Women's Club,
Ventura, Calif.

GRILLED HEROINE
Makes 6

1 long loaf French or Italian bread
    Garlic butter
6 slices Cheddar cheese
6 slices cooked ham
6 slices luncheon loaf

1. Slice bread into 1-inch pieces, without cutting through bottom crust.
2. Spread garlic butter generously between each slice.
3. Between each slice insert 1 slice each Cheddar cheese, ham and luncheon loaf.
4. Brush crust with garlic butter. Wrap in foil. Heat for 20 to 25 minutes on grill.

A. S.

SLUMGULLION SANDWICHES
Makes 12

½ pound cooked ham
¼ pound Cheddar cheese
1 small onion
1 small green pepper
½ cup stuffed olives
½ cup pickle relish or pickles
½ cup mayonnaise
½ cup catsup
6 hamburger buns, split

1. Preheat broiler.
2. Put ham, cheese, onion, green pepper, olives and pickle relish or pickles through medium blade of meat grinder. Stir in mayonnaise and catsup. Spread on split side of buns.

3. Broil, open face, until hot and bubbling.

Mary Walter, Junior Women's Club,
Papillion, Neb.

HAM SOUFFLÉ SANDWICHES
Makes 4

4 slices baked ham
4 slices toast
10-ounce package frozen asparagus
    spears, cooked and drained
⅔ cup mayonnaise
¼ cup grated sharp Cheddar cheese
¼ cup sliced stuffed olives
¼ teaspoon salt
2 tablespoons finely chopped green
    pepper
2 egg whites

1. Preheat broiler. Line broiler pan with aluminum foil.
2. Place 1 slice of ham on each slice of toast. Arrange on broiler pan. Put 2 or 3 asparagus spears on each slice of ham.
3. Blend mayonnaise, cheese, olives, salt and green pepper.
4. In mixing bowl beat egg whites until stiff but not dry. Fold into mayonnaise mixture.
5. Spread over asparagus and ham.
6. Broil 4 to 5 inches from heat for 5 to 6 minutes, or until golden brown.

Lorraine Gillespie, Woman's Club,
Prospect Heights, Ill.

BABY SUBMARINE SANDWICHES
Makes 6

½ pound shaved ham
½ pound sharp Cheddar cheese, cut
    into ¼-inch cubes
⅓ cup chopped onions
2 eggs, hard-cooked and chopped
½ cup chopped olives
3 tablespoons mayonnaise
½ cup chili sauce
6 frankfurter rolls

1. Preheat oven to 400° F. Cut 6 squares of aluminum foil.
2. In mixing bowl combine all ingredients except rolls. Mix well.
3. Split rolls. Fill with ham mixture. Wrap each roll in foil. Place on baking sheet.
4. Bake in preheated oven for 15 minutes.

Betty Harvey, Woman's Club, Clearfield, Pa.

MONTE CRISTO SANDWICHES
Makes 4

2 eggs
2 tablespoons flour
½ cup milk
1 teaspoon salt
¼ teaspoon pepper
8 slices buttered bread
4 slices boiled ham
4 thin slices roast chicken
4 slices American cheese
⅓ cup butter or margarine
    Sour cream
    Strawberry jam

1. In shallow dish blend eggs, flour, milk, salt and pepper.

2. On each of 4 slices of the bread arrange 1 slice each of ham, chicken and cheese.

3. Cover with remaining bread slices.

4. Dip into egg mixture, coating both sides well.

5. Melt butter or margarine in large skillet. Brown sandwiches on both sides.

6. Serve at once topped with sour cream and strawberry jam.

Marlita Rich, Woman's Club, La Habra, Calif.

PIZZA ITALIAN STYLE

Serves 6 to 8

1 envelope active dry yeast
2 tablespoons lukewarm water
1 cup boiling water
1 tablespoon shortening
1 teaspoon salt
½ teaspoon sugar
3 cups presifted flour
6-ounce package provolone cheese, sliced
1½ cups drained canned tomatoes
½ cup finely chopped onions
½ teaspoon basil
½ teaspoon orégano
   Pepper
½ cup spaghetti sauce
½ cup sliced peperoni
2-ounce can anchovies, drained

1. Preheat oven to 425° F. Grease 14-inch pizza pan or similar flat round pan.

2. Soften yeast in lukewarm water in small bowl. Let stand for 5 minutes. Then stir until dissolved.

3. Pour boiling water over shortening in mixing bowl. Add salt and sugar. Stir until smooth. Cool to lukewarm. Stir in yeast.

4. Gradually add flour, beating well to make a soft dough. Knead on lightly floured board until smooth.

5. Roll out dough ¼ inch thick. Pat into shape in pan. Cover with cloth. Let rise in warm place for 15 minutes.

6. Arrange cheese slices across dough. Top with tomatoes. Sprinkle with onions. Sprinkle with basil, orégano and pepper.

7. Spread spaghetti sauce evenly on top. Garnish with peperoni slices and anchovies.

8. Bake in preheated oven for 25 minutes, or until crust is golden brown. Cut into wedges.

Mrs. Troy Lambert, Beau Jour Club, Batesville, Miss.

ARMENIAN PIZZA

Makes 12 Individual Pizzas

1 envelope active dry yeast
¾ cup lukewarm water
½ teaspoon sugar
½ teaspoon salt
¼ cup melted shortening
3¼ cups presifted flour
1 pound ground beef
2 cups finely chopped onions

½ cup finely chopped green pepper
¼ cup chopped parsley
1 clove garlic, crushed
6-ounce can tomato paste
1-pound can whole tomatoes, well drained
   Salt and pepper to taste

1. Soften yeast in ½ cup of the water in mixing bowl. Add remaining water; stir until dissolved.

2. Stir in sugar, ½ teaspoon salt, shortening and flour; beat until smooth and softer than pie crust dough.

3. Turn onto lightly floured board. Knead for 5 minutes. Return to bowl. Cover with cloth. Let rise in warm place for 2 hours, or until doubled in bulk.

4. Meanwhile, in large skillet combine beef, onions and green pepper. Cook over medium heat, stirring frequently, until meat is browned. Stir in remaining ingredients. Simmer for 15 minutes, stirring occasionally.

5. When dough has doubled in bulk, heat oven to 450° F., and grease baking sheets.

6. Divide dough into 12 pieces. Roll each piece into a ball. Let stand for 10 minutes.

7. Roll out each ball to 8-inch circle. Place on baking sheets. Spread with meat mixture.

8. Bake in preheated oven for 15 minutes.

Mary Bogoian, Woman's Junior Club Newington, Conn.

JUMBO PIZZA SANDWICH

Serves 4 to 6

½ pound ground beef
¼ cup chopped ripe olives
2 tablespoons grated onion
¾ teaspoon salt
⅛ teaspoon pepper
¼ teaspoon orégano
6-ounce can tomato paste
¼ cup grated Parmesan cheese
1 loaf French or Italian bread
14 thin slices tomato
8-ounce package mild cheese slices

1. Preheat oven to 400° F.

2. Brown beef in large skillet, stirring occasionally.

3. Remove from heat. Stir in olives, onion, salt, pepper, orégano, tomato paste and Parmesan cheese. Mix well.

4. Cut bread in half lengthwise. Arrange on baking sheet, cut sides up. Spread meat mixture on each half. Top with tomato.

5. Bake in preheated oven for 15 minutes.

6. Cut cheese slices in half diagonally. Arrange on tomato.

7. Bake in preheated oven for 5 minutes longer.

Bev Higgins, Junior Women's Club, Papillion, Neb.

QUICK PIZZAS

Makes 4 Individual Pizzas

2 cups biscuit mix
⅔ cup milk
8-ounce can tomato sauce
½ pound sharp Cheddar cheese, diced
1 cup chopped salami
⅛ teaspoon pepper
½ teaspoon garlic salt
2 tablespoons olive oil
1 tablespoon grated onion

1. Preheat oven to 425° F. Grease baking sheet.
2. Put biscuit mix in mixing bowl. Add milk. Mix with fork until blended.
3. Turn onto lightly floured board. Knead gently 10 times. Divide into quarters. Roll out each quarter to 5½-inch circle.
4. Arrange circles on baking sheet. Crimp edges slightly to make small rims. Arrange cheese and salami on circles, dividing evenly. Sprinkle with pepper, garlic salt, oil and onion.
5. Bake in preheated oven for 20 minutes, or until cheese is bubbling.

Dorothy Robertson, Senior Woman's Club,
Highland Springs, Va.

OPEN PORK AND BEAN SANDWICHES

Makes 6

1-pound can pork and beans
6 slices buttered bread
6 slices mild Cheddar cheese
12 slices bacon

1. Preheat broiler.
2. Arrange pork and beans equally on bread slices. Top with cheese. Arrange 2 slices of bacon on each cheese slice.
3. Broil until bacon is crisp.

Nordessa McCants, 20th Century Club,
Clayton, N.M.

POW-WOW SANDWICHES

Makes 6

½ pound sliced bacon
2½ ounces shreded dried beef
¾ cup chili sauce
⅓ cup sweet pickle relish
6 hamburger buns, split and buttered
6 slices American cheese

1. Preheat oven to 375° F. Cut 6 slices of aluminum foil; place on baking sheet.
2. Cook bacon in large skillet until crisp. Drain on absorbent paper. Crumble. Turn into mixing bowl.
3. Add beef, chili sauce and pickle relish. Mix well.
4. Spread filling on bottoms of buns; place on center of foil. Top each sandwich with a slice of cheese; top with upper half of bun. Wrap in foil. Place on baking sheet.
5. Bake in preheated oven for 20 minutes.

Anne Carter, Woman's Club, Sunland, Calif.

SALMON GRILLED CHEESE SANDWICHES

Makes 4

7½-ounce can salmon, drained, boned and flaked
2 tablespoons finely chopped green pepper
2 tablespoons mayonnaise
½ teaspoon salt
¼ teaspoon pepper
1 tablespoon vinegar
1 egg, hard-cooked and finely chopped
2 tablespoons sweet pickle relish
Dash of Tabasco
1½ cups shredded Cheddar cheese
4 slices bread

1. Preheat broiler. Line broiler pan with aluminum foil.
2. In mixing bowl combine all ingredients except cheese and bread.
3. Add cheese. Blend well.
4. Spread on bread. Arrange on pan.
5. Broil 4 to 5 inches from heat for 7 to 10 minutes, or until bubbling and golden.

Pat Kellingworth, Junior Women's Club,
Renton, Wash.

HOT SANDWICH LOAF

Serves 10

4 eggs, hard-cooked and chopped
8-ounce can ripe olives, drained and chopped
7-ounce can tuna, drained and flaked
2 tablespoons finely chopped onion
2 tablespoons chopped parsley
½ cup mayonnaise
2 10½-ounce cans condensed cream of mushroom soup
1 large loaf unsliced white bread
8 ounces cheese spread
½ cup butter or margarine

1. Day before, in mixing bowl combine eggs, olives, tuna, onion, parsley, mayonnaise and ½ can soup for filling. Mix well. Set aside. Refrigerate remaining ½ can soup.
2. Trim crusts from bread. Cut loaf lengthwise into 3 slices. Spread filling between slices. Reassemble into loaf shape.
3. In mixing bowl beat cheese and butter or margarine until blended. Spread over top and sides of loaf. Place on large piece of aluminum foil; fold up sides and ends of foil to cover loaf completely.
4. Refrigerate overnight.
5. Next day, preheat oven to 350° F. Place foil-wrapped loaf on baking sheet. Bake in preheated oven for 40 minutes.
6. Meanwhile, prepare sauce: Place remaining soup in saucepan. Heat to serving temperature over low heat, stirring occasionally.
7. Serve sauce over cut slices of loaf.

Mrs. Harry Christian, Fargo Chapter of Pioneer
Daughters, Fargo, N.D.

TACOS (Mexican Sandwiches)

Tortillas (p. 136) or canned tortillas
Any sliced cooked meat or cheese
Fat
Shredded lettuce and sliced tomatoes

1. Put a slice of meat or cheese on a Tortilla. Roll up; fasten with wooden pick.
2. Fry in deep fat heated to 365° F., or brown in a little hot fat in skillet.
3. Serve with lettuce and tomatoes.

Felicitas Alarid, 20th Century Club,
Clayton, N.M.

SWEDISH TAMALES (Stuffed Rolls)

Makes 12

6 eggs, hard-cooked
1 small onion
5 ripe olives, pitted
7-ounce can tuna, drained
½ green pepper
Few springs parsley
½ cup diced cheese
⅓ cup mayonaise
Salt and pepper to taste
½ teaspoon paprika
12 frankfurther rolls
Butter

1. Put eggs, onion, olives, tuna, green pepper, parsley and cheese through meat grinder. Mix well.
2. Stir in mayonnaise, salt, pepper and paprika.
3. Hollow out rolls. Spread lightly with butter. Fill with ground mixture. Wrap in aluminum foil, twisting ends tightly. Chill.
4. When ready to use, preheat oven to 350° F. Arrange in shallow baking pan.
5. Bake in preheated oven for 30 minutes. Serve in foil.

Betty Abrahamson, North Long Beach Women's
Club, Long Beach, Calif.

BAKED TUNA SANDWICHES

Makes 4

8-ounce package refrigerator biscuits
7-ounce can tuna, drained and flaked
½ cup grated sharp Cheddar cheese
3 tablespoons mayonnaise
1 tablespoon melted butter

1. Preheat oven to 425° F. Grease baking sheet.
2. Separate biscuits onto lightly floured board. Roll out each to 4-inch circle.
3. In mixing bowl blend tuna, cheese and mayonnaise.
4. Arrange half the biscuit circles on baking sheet.
5. Top with tuna mixture. Arrange remaining biscuits on top. Press edges together with fork tines. Brush with butter.
6. Bake in preheated oven for 15 to 20 minutes, or until golden.

Mrs. Ed Carter, Federated Civic Club,
Mount Vernon, Ill.

DE LUXE TUNA SANDWICH

Makes 5

Butter
15 slices bread
7-ounce can tuna, drained and flaked
4 eggs, hard-cooked and chopped
3-ounce can mushroom pieces, drained
½ cup chopped ripe olives
¼ cup grated onion
¼ cup mayonnaise
10½-ounce can condensed cream of chicken soup
1 cup sour cream

1. Preheat oven to 350° F. Grease baking sheet.
2. Spread butter on both sides of bread.
3. In mixing bowl combine tuna, eggs, mushrooms, olives, onion and mayonnaise. Mix well.
4. Use 3 slices of bread for each sandwich. Put slices together with filling between. Secure with wooden picks. Place on baking sheet.
5. Bake in preheated oven for 20 minutes.
6. Meanwhile, prepare Chicken Soup Sauce: In top of double saucepan blend soup with sour cream. Heat over hot water to serving temperature, stirring frequently.
7. Pour sauce over sandwiches. Serve at once.

Ann McMillin, Progressive Woman's Club,
Fresno, Calif.

Beef Burgers

BEEF 'N' CHEESE BAR-B-QUE

Makes 8

2 tablespoons butter
¼ cup minced onion
¾ pound ground beef
2 tablespoons flour
1 tablespoon sugar
⅛ teaspoon ground cloves
¼ teaspoon dry mustard
Dash of pepper
1 teaspoon Worcestershire
2 tablespoons water
1 cup shredded cheese
4 hamburger buns, split, buttered and toasted

1. Melt butter in skillet; sauté onion and beef until onion is tender and beef is browned.
2. Stir in flour, sugar, cloves, mustard and pepper.
3. Add Worcestershire, water and cheese. Heat, stirring constantly, until mixture is slightly thickened and cheese is melted.
4. Serve on bun halves.

Stella Hunt, Altruistic Club, Carlisle, Ark.

BEEF-WICHES

Makes 10

1½ pounds ground beef
1 small onion, minced
1 teaspoon salt
¼ teaspoon pepper
½ teaspoon sage
1 egg, lightly beaten
½ cup milk
1 cup bread crumbs
10 thin slices onion
1½ cups grated American cheese
10 thin slices ripe tomato
10 hamburger buns, split

1. Preheat broiler.
2. Combine beef, minced onion, seasonings, egg, milk and crumbs. Shape into 20 very thin patties.
3. Place onion slices on 10 patties; sprinkle with cheese; cover with tomato. Top with remaining patties.
4. Broil for 7 minutes; turn carefully; broil for 7 minutes longer.
5. Serve between bun halves.

Mary Lunden, Carmichaels and Cumberland Township Civic Club, Carmichaels, Pa.

IRISH SWEEP STEAK

Serves 12

1 pound ground beef
1 teaspoon garlic salt
1 teaspoon dry mustard
½ teaspoon paprika
1 pound cheese, shredded
1 egg, lightly beaten
Milk
12 hamburger buns, split
12 carrot slices
12 radishes

1. Combine beef, garlic salt, mustard and paprika. Cook in skillet until meat loses all red color. Cool.
2. Preheat oven to 400° F.
3. Mix cooled meat, cheese and egg. Moisten to spreading consistency with milk. Spread bottom half of each bun with mixture. Arrange on baking sheet.
4. Bake in preheated oven for about 5 minutes, or until cheese is melted.
5. In center of each, insert wooden pick garnished with carrot slice and radish.
6. Serve as open sandwich with top of bun on side.

Flo Bonheimer, North Phoenix Woman's Club, Phoenix, Ariz.

MAID RITES

Makes 8

2 tablespoons cooking oil
3 medium onions, chopped
1 pound ground beef
1½ teaspoons chili powder
1 tablespoon ground cumin
1 cup catsup
½ teaspoon salt
8 hamburger buns, split

1. Heat oil in skillet; brown onions. Add beef; cook until browned, stirring occasionally.

2. Add chili powder, cumin, catsup and salt. Cover. Simmer for 1 hour, stirring frequently.
3. Serve between bun halves.

Mary Jameson, Anna Day Club, Troy, Mo.

PIZZA BURGERS

Makes 6

1 pound ground beef
1½ cup chopped onions
6-ounce can tomato paste
1 teaspoon crushed orégano
¼ teaspoon garlic powder
6 hamburger buns, split, toasted
and buttered
Onion rings or sliced Mozzarella
cheese (optional)

1. Cook beef and onions in skillet until beef loses red color and onions are transparent.
2. Add tomato paste and seasonings. Bring to boil. Simmer for 15 minutes.
3. Spoon mixture between or over bun halves. If desired, slip an onion ring or cheese slice into each bun.

Mrs. Robert Maier, Pueblo Junior Woman's Club, Tucson, Ariz.

SARAH'S HULAMAGUSHA

Makes 6

1 pound ground beef
1 teaspoon salt
⅛ teaspoon pepper
½ teaspoon chili powder
⅛ teaspoon orégano
⅛ teaspoon tarragon
⅛ teaspoon thyme
⅛ teaspoon basil
⅛ teaspoon marjoram
½ cup chopped green pepper
½ cup chopped onions
10½-ounce can condensed tomato soup
6 hamburger buns, split

1. Cook beef gently in skillet until light brown.
2. Add salt, pepper, chili powder, herbs, green pepper and onions. Simmer until tender.
3. Add soup. Cook until well mixed and slightly thickened.
4. Spoon over bun halves.

Marvel Porter, Mothers Club, Osborne, Kans.

SOUTHERN BURGERS

Makes 6

1 tablespoon fat
1 pound ground beef
1 medium onion, diced
3 tablespoons catsup
3 tablespoons prepared mustard
10½-ounce can condensed chicken
gumbo soup
6 hamburger buns, split and toasted

1. Heat fat in skillet; brown beef and onion. Stir in catsup, mustard and soup.
2. Simmer for about 15 minutes, or until slightly thickened.
3. Spoon over bun halves.

Mrs. C. A. Sheldrake, Thursday Morning Club, Madison, N.J.

SLOPPY JOE HAMBURGERS
Makes 8 to 10

2 pounds ground beef
2 teaspoons salt
¼ teaspoon pepper
2 tablespoons shortening
2 tablespoons horseradish
2 tablespoons Worcestershire
¼ teaspoon Tabasco
1 cup chili sauce
1½ cups catsup
1 medium green pepper, finely chopped
1 large onion, finely chopped
1 cup celery, finely chopped
8 to 10 hamburger buns, split and toasted

1. Preheat oven to 225° F. Grease 3-quart casserole.
2. In mixing bowl blend beef, salt and pepper.
3. Melt shortening in large skillet. Brown beef, stirring frequently. Drain on absorbent paper to remove all fat.
4. Meanwhile, in large saucepan combine all remaining ingredients except buns. Bring to boil. Simmer for 5 minutes.
5. Pack meat into casserole. Top with sauce.
6. Cover. Bake in preheated oven for 2 hours.
7. Spoon over bun halves.

Mrs. John House, Woman's Club,
Batesville, Miss.

SLOPPY JOES
Makes 12

3 tablespoons shortening
2 large onions, finely chopped
1 medium green pepper, finely chopped
3 pounds ground beef
½ cup presifted flour
2 teaspoons salt
½ teaspoon pepper
2 8-ounce cans tomato sauce
1 cup catsup
2 teaspoons Worcestershire
12 hamburger buns, split

1. Melt shortening in large skillet. Add onions and green pepper. Sauté for 5 minutes.
2. Stir in beef. Cook until browned.
3. Stir in all remaining ingredients except buns. Mix well. Simmer, uncovered, for 15 minutes.
4. Spoon over bun halves.

Mrs. Edwin T. Love, Junior Women's Club,
Nashua, N.H.

STROGANOFF BUNS
Makes 8

¼ cup butter or margarine
½ cup finely chopped onions
1 clove garlic, crushed
1 pound ground beef
2 tablespoons flour
1 teaspoon salt
¼ teaspoon monosodium glutamate
¼ teaspoon pepper
¼ teaspoon paprika

1-pound can mushrooms, drained
10½-ounce can condensed cream of chicken soup
8 hamburger buns
1 cup sour cream
Chopped parsley

1. Melt butter in skillet; sauté onions for 5 minutes.
2. Add garlic and beef. Cook, stirring frequently, until beef is browned.
3. Sprinkle with flour, salt, monosodium glutamate, pepper, and paprika. Add mushrooms and soup. Bring to boil. Simmer for 15 minutes.
4. Meanwhile, make 2-inch circle in top of each bun with sharp knife. Hollow out buns. Place on serving dish.
5. Stir sour cream into beef mixture. Heat to serving temperature.
6. Fill buns with beef mixture. Sprinkle with parsley.

Betty Meyer, Service League, Lombard, Ill.

SUPER HAMBURGERS
Makes 6

1 pound ground beef
½ pound liver sausage
½ pound ground lean pork
1½ tablespoons finely chopped onion
1½ tablespoons finely chopped green celery leaves
1½ tablespoons finely chopped parsley
1½ tablespoons finely chopped green pepper
1½ tablespoons finely chopped pimiento
1½ teaspoons salt
½ teaspoon paprika
⅓ cup bread crumbs
½ cup water
1 clove garlic, finely chopped
6 hamburger buns, split and toasted

1. Combine all ingredients except buns.
2. Form into 6 patties. Broil over charcoal or in broiler.
3. Serve between bun halves.

Favorite Recipes, Woman's Club,
Las Vegas, N.M.

TEXAS BAR-B-QUE BURGERS
Makes 6

2 pounds ground beef
1 small onion, chopped
1½ teaspoons dry mustard
2 teaspoons chili powder
1 cup catsup
½ cup vinegar or lemon juice
1 teaspoon sugar
1 teaspoon Worcestershire
½ cup water
Salt to taste
6 hamburger buns, split and toasted

1. Cook beef in skillet until it loses red color. Pour off excess fat.
2. Add all remaining ingredients except buns. Simmer for 45 minutes.
3. Spoon over bun halves.

Mrs. H. H. Lines, Woman's Aladdin Club,
Canutillo, Tex.

WIMPIES

Makes 6

1 pound ground beef
½ cup finely chopped onions
¾ cup chili sauce
1 teaspoon prepared mustard
1 teaspoon salt
¼ teaspoon pepper
6 hamburger buns, split

1. Preheat broiler.
2. Combine all ingredients except buns. Mix well.
3. Spread meat mixture on cut side of each half bun. Place on broiler pan.
4. Broil 4 to 5 inches from heat for about 8 minutes, or until meat is cooked.

Mrs. William Frey, Jr., Woman's Club, Covington, Ky.

Other Burgers

CHICKEN BURGERS

Makes 8

3 cups soft bread crumbs
2 cups chopped cooked chicken
½ teaspoon salt
⅛ teaspoon pepper
1 teaspoon minced onion
2 teaspoons minced green pepper
1½ tablespoons minced celery
½ cup milk
½ teaspoon Worcestershire
2 eggs, lightly beaten
8 hamburger buns, split and buttered

1. Combine crumbs, chicken, salt, pepper, onion, green pepper and celery.
2. Combine milk, Worcestershire and eggs. Stir into chicken mixture. Form into 8 patties.
3. Cook on well-greased griddle until browned on both sides.
4. Serve between bun halves.

Mrs. John F. Nelles, Thursday Morning Club, Madison, N.J.

CRAB BURGERS

Makes 6

1 cup flaked cooked crab meat
½ cup diced celery
½ cup mayonnaise
2 tablespoons chopped onion
½ cup shredded sharp Cheddar cheese
6 hamburger buns, split and buttered

1. Combine crab meat, celery, mayonnaise, onion and cheese.
2. Spread on cut side of each bun half.
3. Place on broiler pan. Broil until bubbling.

Mrs. Roy E. Tomlinson, Women's Club, Richland, Wash.

AVOCADO CRAB BURGERS

Makes 8

3 tablespoons butter
2 tablespoons flour

1½ cups half-and-half
Salt and pepper to taste
Pinch of cayenne
½ cup shredded Cheddar cheese
2 tablespoons grated Parmesan cheese
2 6½-ounce cans crab meat, drained and flaked
8 hamburger buns, split and toasted
8 slices Cheddar cheese
8 slices avocado

1. Melt butter in saucepan. Stir in flour. Gradually stir in half-and-half. Cook, stirring, until sauce is thickened and smooth.
2. Add seasonings, shredded Cheddar cheese and Parmesan cheese. Cook, stirring, until melted.
3. Put spoonful of sauce over bottom half of each bun. Top with crab meat. Top with 1 slice of Cheddar cheese and 1 slice of avocado. Spoon more sauce on top.
4. Arrange sauced buns on baking sheet. Brown under broiler.
5. Top with upper halves of buns.

Bettie Peck, Woman's Club, Anchorage, Alaska

BARBECUED HAM BURGERS

Makes 16

12-ounce bottle catsup
1 cup brown sugar
2 teaspoons dry mustard
¼ teaspoon chili powder
¼ cup vinegar
⅛ teaspoon ground cloves
2 pounds boiled or spiced ham
16 hamburger buns, split and toasted

1. In heavy saucepan blend all ingredients except ham and buns. Bring to boil. Cover. Simmer for 20 minutes, stirring occasionally.
2. Meanwhile, shred ham. Stir into sauce. Heat to serving temperature.
3. Spoon over bottom halves of buns. Cover with tops.

Marion Maloney, Woman's Club, Prospect Heights, Ill.

BARBECUED PORK BURGERS

Makes 8

1 tablespoon cooking oil
¼ cup chopped onion
8-ounce can tomato sauce
¼ cup bottled steak sauce
2 tablespoons brown sugar
Dash of salt
2 cups thinly sliced roast pork
8 hamburger buns, split and toasted

1. Heat oil in skillet; sauté onion until tender.
2. Stir in tomato sauce, steak sauce, sugar and salt. Bring to boil.
3. Add pork. Cover. Simmer for 10 minutes.
4. Spoon over bun halves.

Woman's Culture Club, West Point, Miss.

SEA BURGERS

Makes 8

7-ounce can tuna, salmon, crab
   meat or lobster
8-ounce package sharp American
   cheese, cubed
¼ cup grated onion
¼ cup sweet pickle relish
½ cup catsup
¼ cup mayonnaise
1 cup finely chopped celery
1½ teaspoons salt
½ teaspoon pepper
2 tablespoons finely chopped
   pimiento
8 hamburger buns, split

1. Preheat oven to 350° F. Cut 8 squares of aluminum foil.
2. Drain and flake fish. Turn into mixing bowl.
3. Add all remaining ingredients except buns. Mix well. Fill buns.
4. Wrap each bun in foil. Place on baking sheet.
5. Bake in preheated oven for 20 minutes.

Helen R. Hogan, Service League, Lombard, Ill.

SHRIMP BOAT BURGERS

Makes 6

6 frankfurter rolls, partially split
Butter
¼ clove garlic, minced
½ cup sour cream
¾ teaspoon dry mustard
½ teaspoon salt
1 tablespoon lemon juice
¼ tablespoon chopped olive
10½-ounce can frozen shrimp soup
¼ cup chopped mushrooms

1. Preheat broiler.
2. Press rolls open to lie flat. Spread with butter.
3. Combine remaining ingredients. Spread on rolls. Place on broiler pan.
4. Broil 2 to 3 inches from heat until browned and bubbling.

Mrs. Leland Pietsch, Cynosure Women's Club,
Casselton, N.D.

TUNA BURGERS

Makes 4

7-ounce can tuna, drained and
   flaked
¼ cup chopped celery
¼ cup chopped green pepper
½ cup mayonnaise
Dash of salt
¼ teaspoon pepper
½ teaspoon paprika
Dash of cayenne
4 hamburger buns, split and
   buttered

1. Preheat broiler.
2. In mixing bowl combine all ingredients except buns. Mix well.
3. Spread on bottom halves of buns. Place on broiler pan.

4. Broil 3 to 4 inches from heat for 5 minutes, or until golden.
5. Top with upper halves of buns.

Betty Holcomb Allen, Zeta Chi Club,
Attwood, Kans.

BUMSTEADS

Makes 6

7-ounce can tuna, drained and
   flaked
1 cup grated Cheddar cheese
2 tablespoons grated onion
2 tablespoons sweet pickle relish
2 tablespoons chopped ripe olives
3 eggs, hard-cooked and chopped
½ cup mayonnaise
6 frankfurter rolls, partially split

1. Preheat oven to 350° F. Cut 6 pieces of aluminum foil. Place on baking sheet.
2. In mixing bowl combine all ingredients except rolls; mix well.
3. Fill rolls.
4. Wrap rolls in foil. Place on baking sheet.
5. Bake in preheated oven for 25 minutes.

Mrs. Leona DeLeon, Woman's Club,
Clearfield, Pa.

Frankfurter Specials

CREOLE WIENERS

Makes 10

8 slices bacon, cut into ½-inch
   squares
3 cups chopped onions
1 green pepper, chopped
1 cup chopped celery
2½ cups canned tomatoes
¾ teaspoon salt
⅛ teaspoon pepper
⅛ teaspoon cayenne
10 frankfurters
10 frankfurter rolls, split and
   buttered

1. Cook bacon in heavy skillet until crisp. Drain on absorbent paper. Crumble; set aside. Pour off all but 2 tablespoons of rendered fat.
2. Prepare Creole Sauce: Add onions, green pepper and celery to fat remaining in skillet. Sauté for 10 minutes, or until tender. Add tomatoes, salt, pepper and cayenne.
3. Place frankfurters on top. Cover. Simmer for 1 hour, stirring occasionally. Remove cover. Boil hard for 5 to 10 minutes to evaporate excess liquid.
4. Put a frankfurter and a spoonful of Creole Sauce in each roll. Sprinkle with bacon.

Mrs. T. L. Hoff, North Phoenix Woman's Club,
Phoenix, Ariz.

HOT DOG SURPRISE

Makes 8

2 cups finely chopped frankfurters
⅓ cup grated sharp American cheese
2 eggs, hard-cooked and chopped
3 tablespoons chili sauce
2 tablespoons pickle relish
1 teaspoon prepared mustard
½ teaspoon garlic salt
8 frankfurter rolls, partially split

1. Preheat oven to 375° F. Cut 8 pieces of aluminum foil; place on baking sheet.
2. Combine all ingredients except rolls.
3. Open rolls; hollow out soft centers; fill with frankfurter mixture.
4. Close rolls. Wrap each in a piece of foil, sealing securely. Arrange on baking sheet.
5. Bake in preheated oven for 10 to 12 minutes.

Mrs. Paul Pumphrey, President,
Woman's Club, Ovid, Colo.

RED HOT SANDWICHES

Makes 8

1 pound frankfurters, diced
¾ pound Cheddar cheese, diced
3 tablespoons grated onion
⅓ cup chopped olives
3 eggs, hard-cooked and chopped
¼ cup chili sauce
3 tablespoons mayonnaise
8 frankfurter rolls, partially split

1. Preheat oven to 375° F. Cut 8 pieces of alumnium foil; place on baking sheet.
2. Combine all ingredients except rolls; mix well. Fill rolls.
3. Wrap each roll in piece of foil. Arrange on baking sheet.
4. Bake in preheated oven for 20 minutes.

Marty Marken, Woman's Club, Slippery Rock, Pa.

SESAME DOGS

Makes 8

1 pound skinless frankfurters
3-ounce jar Cheddar cheese spread
8-ounce package refrigerator biscuits
Melted butter
Sesame seeds

1. Preheat oven to 425° F. Grease baking sheet.
2. Split frankfurters almost through. Spread inside with cheese.
3. On lightly floured board, roll out biscuits to thin circles. Wrap thin circle of dough around each frankfurter, covering as much as possible.
4. Dip in butter. Roll in sesame seeds. Arrange on baking sheet.
5. Bake in preheated oven for 12 minutes, or until golden.

North Jacksonville Woman's Club,
Jacksonville, Fla.

3. Quick Breads

There is no category of food that takes less time to make, yet offers more eating pleasure, than freshly baked quick breads. They are versatile, too, contributing to the breakfast table, adding to a lunch or supper or standing alone as tempting accompaniments to an afternoon cup of coffee or tea.

Quick breads are those leavened with baking powder or baking soda or a combination of both. No kneading is needed, nor should the batter be beaten unless specified. The general method of making quick breads is to add the combined dry ingredients to the moist ones and to stir only enough to dampen the flour. (In some recipes this procedure is reversed, but the batter is usually still stirred only until the flour is moistened.)

Bake a quick bread according to recipe time and temperature. It is done when lightly browned or when a cake tester inserted into the center comes out clean. When it is done, remove from oven. Let stand for 5 minutes; then run a spatula or knife around loaf or muffin to loosen it from pan; lift out or invert pan so that bread comes away from pan. Place upright on wire rack to cool.

Almost any fruit purée adds flavor to a quick bread, and nuts and raisins are frequently added for texture and taste. Most quick breads are delicious when thinly sliced and toasted.

Loaves

APPLESAUCE NUT BREAD

Makes 1 Loaf

2 cups presifted flour
¾ cup sugar
3 teaspoons baking powder
½ teaspoon baking soda
1 teaspoon salt
½ teaspoon cinnamon
1 egg, lightly beaten
1 cup applesauce
2 tablespoons melted shortening
1 cup chopped nuts

1. Preheat oven to 350° F. Grease 8½-inch loaf pan.
2. Into mixing bowl sift together dry ingredients.
3. Add egg, applesauce and shortening. Mix until dry ingredients are moistened.

4. Fold in nuts.
5. Turn batter into pan. Bake in preheated oven for 50 minutes.

Mrs. Eddie Rasmussen, Study Club, Balsam Lake, Wis.

APRICOT BREAD

Makes 1 Loaf

1 cup dried apricots
1 cup sugar
2 tablespoons margarine
1 egg
¼ cup pineapple juice
½ cup orange juice
2 cups presifted flour
2 teaspoons baking powder
¼ teaspoon baking soda
1 teaspoon salt
½ cup chopped nuts

1. Grease and flour 9½-inch loaf pan.
2. Soak apricots in warm water to cover for 30 minutes. Drain and chop apricots.
3. In mixing bowl cream sugar, margarine and egg. Stir in fruit juices.
4. Combine dry ingredients. Stir into sugar mixture.
5. Stir in nuts and chopped apricots.
6. Turn batter into pan. Let stand for 30 minutes.
7. Preheat oven to 350° F.
8. Bake in preheated oven for 55 to 65 minutes.

Mrs. G. C. Hilman, Cosmos Club, Ruston, La.

BANANA NUT BREAD

Makes 1 Loaf

1½ cups sugar
⅔ cup shortening
2 eggs, separated
1 cup mashed ripe bananas
4 tablespoons sour milk or
  buttermilk
1 teaspoon vinegar
1 teaspoon baking soda
1 tablespoon warm water
½ cup chopped nuts
1½ cups presifted flour
1 teaspoon vanilla
  Pinch of salt

1. Preheat oven to 325° F. Grease 9½-inch loaf pan.
2. In mixing bowl beat sugar and shortening until thoroughly blended. Beat in egg yolks and bananas.
3. Combine sour milk or buttermilk and vinegar. Stir into banana mixture.

4. Dissolve baking soda in water. Stir into batter.

5. Stir in nuts, flour, vanilla and salt.

6. Beat egg whites until stiff but not dry. Fold into batter.

7. Turn batter into pan. Bake in preheated oven for 1 hour.

Mrs. William Huntington, Junior Woman's Club,
Diamond Bar, Calif.

SOUR CREAM BANANA BREAD
Makes 1 Loaf

½ cup shortening
1 cup sugar
½ teaspoon salt
2 eggs, well beaten
1 cup mashed ripe bananas
½ cup sour cream
1 teaspoon baking soda
2 cups presifted flour

1. Preheat oven to 350° F. Grease 8-inch loaf pan.

2. In mixing bowl beat shortening and sugar until smooth and creamy. Add salt, eggs, bananas, sour cream and baking soda.

3. Stir in flour.

4. Turn batter into pan. Bake in preheated oven for 45 minutes to 1 hour.

Mrs. Ray L. Buck, Cosmos Club,
St. John, N.D.

BANANA PEANUT BUTTER BREAD
Makes 1 Loaf

½ cup shortening
1 cup sugar
2 eggs
1 teaspoon baking soda
2 cups presifted flour
1 cup mashed ripe bananas
1 tablespoon crunchy peanut
    butter

1. Preheat oven to 325° F. Grease and flour 8-inch loaf pan.

2. In mixing bowl cream shortening and sugar.

3. Beat in eggs.

4. Sift together baking soda and flour. Stir into egg mixture.

5. Stir in bananas and peanut butter.

6. Turn batter into pan. Bake in preheated oven for 1 hour.

Mrs. T. J. Shelnutt, President,
Magazine Club, Roanoke, Ala.

BANANA DATE BREAD
Makes 1 Loaf

½ cup shortening
1 cup sugar
2 eggs
2 large or 3 small ripe bananas,
    sliced
2¼ cups presifted flour
1 teaspoon salt
1 teaspoon baking soda
¼ cup chopped nuts
½ cup cut dates

1. Preheat oven to 350° F. Grease 8-inch loaf pan.

2. In mixing bowl cream shortening and sugar.

3. Beat in eggs.

4. Add bananas. Beat well.

5. Combine dry ingredients. Stir into egg mixture.

6. Stir in nuts and dates.

7. Turn batter into pan. Bake in preheated oven for about 1 hour.

Irene Holmberg, Study Club, Balsam Lake, Wis.

BISHOP'S BREAD
Makes 1 Oblong Loaf

2⅔ cups presifted flour
3 teaspoons baking powder
1 teaspoon salt
1 cup brown sugar
½ cup softened butter or margarine
2 eggs
1 cup milk
½ cup granulated sugar
½ cup presifted flour
¼ cup butter or margarine
1 teaspoon cinnamon

1. Preheat oven to 375° F. Grease 13¼ x 8¾ x 1¾-inch baking pan.

2. Sift together 2⅔ cups flour, baking powder and salt.

3. In large mixing bowl cream brown sugar and ½ cup butter or margarine. Add eggs. Beat until light and fluffy.

4. Stir in milk. Add flour mixture. Beat just until all ingredients are combined.

5. Turn batter into pan.

6. Combine granulated sugar, ½ cup flour, ¼ cup butter or margarine and cinnamon to make crumbs. Sprinkle over batter.

7. Bake in preheated oven for 25 minutes.

Mrs. Joanne Teppen, Junior Woman's Club,
Port Washington, Wis.

SOUR MILK BISHOP'S BREAD
Makes 1 Square Loaf

2 cups brown sugar
½ cup melted butter or margarine
1 egg
2½ cups presifted flour
2 teaspoons baking powder
1 teaspoon cinnamon
½ teaspoon salt
¾ cup sour milk or buttermilk
1 cup chopped dates
    Granulated sugar mixed with
    cinnamon (optional)

1. Preheat oven to 375° F. Grease 9-inch square baking pan.

2. In mixing bowl cream sugar and butter or margarine. Add egg; beat until smooth.

3. Sift together dry ingredients. Add to creamed mixture, alternately with sour milk or buttermilk.

4. Fold in dates.

5. Pour batter into pan. Bake in preheated oven for 35 to 40 minutes. If desired, sprinkle top with sugar-cinnamon mixture.

Mrs. Paul Clements, Pierien Study Club,
Vivian, La.

BAKED BROWN BREAD
Makes 1 Loaf

1 egg
⅔ cup sour milk or buttermilk
1 cup molasses
1 cup presifted flour
1 cup whole wheat flour
1 teaspoon baking soda
½ teaspoon salt
2 to 4 tablespoons sugar
½ cup seedless raisins

1. Preheat oven to 350° F. Grease 9½-inch loaf pan.
2. In mixing bowl beat egg lightly. Stir in sour milk or buttermilk and molasses.
3. Add remaining ingredients, stirring only enough to mix well.
4. Turn batter into pan. Bake in preheated oven for about 1 hour.

Mrs. J. H. Middleton, Quest Club, Bowling Green, Mo.

HEIRLOOM BOSTON BROWN BREAD
Makes 2 Loaves

2 cups buttermilk
½ cup molasses
2 cups graham or whole wheat flour
½ cup presifted flour
2 teaspoons baking soda
1 teaspoon salt
1 cup seedless raisins

1. Grease 2 1-pound coffee cans or other cans of same size.
2. Combine buttermilk and molasses.
3. Into mixing bowl sift together dry ingredients. Stir in raisins. Stir in buttermilk mixture.
4. Spoon batter into cans. Let stand for 30 minutes.
5. Preheat oven to 350° F.
6. Bake in preheated oven for 40 to 50 minutes, or until cake tester comes out clean.
7. Remove bread from cans to cool on wire rack.

Mrs. Roy F. Lincoln, Home and Country Study Club, Fayette, Mo.

STEAMED BROWN BREAD
Makes 3 Loaves

This recipe was bought by a pioneer North Dakota grandmother from New York State first to Iowa in 1849 and then to the Dakota Territory in 1882.

3 cups graham flour
1 teaspoon salt
1½ cups buttermilk
½ cup sugar
½ cup molasses
3 teaspoons baking soda
2 tablespoons hot water

1. Grease 3 1-pound coffee cans.
2. In mixing bowl combine flour and salt. Stir in buttermilk.
3. Stir in sugar and molasses.
4. Dissolve baking soda in water. Stir into batter.

5. Fill cans two-thirds full. Cover with waxed paper or aluminum foil.
6. Place on rack in steamer. Steam for 2 hours.

Mrs. Robert A. Ritterbush, Pioneer Daughter Club, Bismarck, N.D.

BROWN SUGAR NUT BREAD
Makes 1 Loaf

2 cups presifted flour
2½ teaspoons baking powder
¾ teaspoon salt
1 cup brown sugar
1 cup milk
1 cup chopped nuts
1 cup seedless raisins

1. Preheat oven to 325° F. Grease 9½-inch loaf pan.
2. In mixing bowl combine dry ingredients.
3. Stir in milk, nuts, and raisins.
4. Turn batter into pan. Bake in preheated oven for about 1 hour.

Mrs. Victor Hellstrom, Woman's Club, Lombard, Ill.

BUTTERSCOTCH NUT BREAD
Makes 1 Large or 2 Small Loaves

1 cup brown sugar
1 tablespoon melted shortening
1 egg, lightly beaten
2 cups presifted flour
¾ teaspoon baking soda
½ teaspoon baking powder
¼ teaspoon salt
1 cup buttermilk
1 cup chopped nuts

1. Preheat oven to 325° F. Grease 1 large or 2 small loaf pans.
2. In mixing bowl combine sugar, shortening and egg.
3. Sift together dry ingredients. Add to sugar mixture alternately with buttermilk.
4. Stir in nuts.
5. Turn batter into pan or pans. Bake in preheated oven for about 1 hour.

MayBelle Binkley, Study Club, Balsam Lake, Wis.

CARROT BREAD
Makes 1 Loaf

This bread is delicious when toasted and spread with softened cream cheese.

1 cup sugar
¾ cup cooking oil
2 eggs
1½ cups presifted flour
3 teaspoons baking powder
1 teaspoon salt
1 teaspoon cinnamon
1 cup grated carrots
½ cup chopped nuts
1 teaspoon vanilla

1. Preheat oven to 350° F. Grease 9½-inch loaf pan.
2. In mixing bowl blend sugar and oil.
3. Add eggs, one at a time, beating well after each addition.
4. Stir in dry ingredients.
5. Stir in carrots, nuts and vanilla.

6. Turn batter into pan. Bake in preheated oven for about 50 minutes.

Mrs. Willis C. Wasson, Woman's Literary Union,
Portland, Me.

CARROT CORN BREAD
Makes 1 Loaf

1 cup grated carrots
1 cup yellow corn meal
2 tablespoons cooking oil
1 tablespoon honey
¾ cup boiling water
2 eggs, separated
2 tablespoons cold water

1. Preheat oven to 400° F. Warm and grease 9-inch square baking pan.
2. In mixing bowl combine carrots, corn meal, oil and honey. Stir in boiling water.
3. Beat egg yolks and cold water. Stir into corn meal mixture.
4. Beat egg whites until stiff but not dry. Fold into batter.
5. Pour batter into pan. Bake in preheated oven for 25 to 30 minutes.

Mrs. William R. Thompson, Woman's Club,
Holtville, Calif.

CHEESE BREAD
Makes 1 Loaf

2 cups presifted flour
3 teaspoons baking powder
¾ teaspoon salt
1½ teaspoons sugar
1 cup grated American cheese
½ cup chopped pecans
1 egg, lightly beaten
¾ cup milk
2 tablespoons melted butter

1. Grease 8-inch loaf pan.
2. Into mixing bowl sift together dry ingredients.
3. Add cheese and pecans.
4. Combine egg, milk and butter.
5. Pour liquid into dry ingredients. Stir only until dry ingredients are moistened. (Batter should not be smooth.)
6. Turn batter into pan. Let stand for 15 minutes.
7. Preheat oven to 350° F.
8. Bake in preheated oven for 1 hour.

Villa Guy McCune, Woman's Club,
Vandalia, Mo.

CORN BREAD
Makes 1 Square Loaf
1½ cups yellow corn meal
½ cup presifted flour
1 tablespoon baking powder
1 teaspoon salt
1 tablespoon sugar
1 egg
¼ cup melted butter or margarine
1 cup milk

1. Preheat oven to 425° F. Grease 8-inch square baking pan.
2. Into mixing bowl sift together dry ingredients.

3. In small bowl blend egg, butter or margarine and milk.
4. Add to dry ingredients. Stir only until dry ingredients are moistened.
5. Turn batter into pan. Bake in preheated oven for 20 to 25 minutes, or until golden brown.

Carrie Mae Champagne, Study Club,
Hull and Daisetta, Tex.

BEST YET CORN BREAD
Makes 1 Square Loaf or 10 to 12
Sticks or Muffins
⅓ cup presifted flour
1 tablespoon sugar
1 teaspoon baking powder
½ teaspoon baking soda
½ teaspoon salt
1⅓ cups white corn meal
1 egg, lightly beaten
1 cup sour cream
2 tablespoons cooking oil or melted shortening

1. Preheat oven to 400° F.
2. Into mixing bowl sift together flour, sugar, baking powder, baking soda and salt.
3. Stir in corn meal.
4. Combine egg, sour cream and oil or shortening. Add to dry ingredients. Stir only until dry ingredients are moistened.
5. Preheat 8-inch square baking pan, corn stick pan or muffin tin in oven; then grease generously.
6. Turn batter into pans or tin. Bake in preheated oven for 25 minutes.

Mrs. William Corbin, Woman's Club,
St. Mary's, W. Va.

NORTH DAKOTA BUTTERMILK CORN BREAD
Makes 1 Square Loaf
1 cup yellow corn meal
1 cup presifted flour
2 teaspoons baking powder
2 tablespoons sugar
1 teaspoon salt
¼ cup mixed butter and lard
1 cup buttermilk
2 eggs, separated
¼ teaspoon baking soda
1 tablespoon water

1. Preheat oven to 400° F. Grease 9-inch square baking pan.
2. In mixing bowl combine dry ingredients.
3. Cut in butter and lard.
4. Combine buttermilk and egg yolks. Add to dry ingredients. Stir only until dry ingredients are moistened.
5. Dissolve baking soda in water. Stir into batter.
6. Beat egg whites until stiff but not dry. Fold into batter.
7. Spread batter in pan. Bake in preheated oven for 20 to 30 minutes.

Ione Roberts, Friday Club, Barlow, N.D.

PROUTS NECK CORN CAKE
Makes 1 Square Loaf

1 cup presifted flour
½ cup corn meal
½ cup sugar
1 teaspoon cream of tartar
½ teaspoon baking soda
1 teaspoon salt
1 egg, beaten
¾ cup milk
1 tablespoon melted shortening

1. Preheat oven to 450° F. Grease 8- or 9-inch square baking pan.
2. Into mixing bowl sift together dry ingredients.
3. Combine egg and milk. Add to dry ingredients. Stir only until dry ingredients are moistened.
4. Stir in shortening.
5. Spoon into pan. Bake in preheated oven for about 30 minutes.

Mrs. Rollin C. Clark, Woman's Literary Union,
Portland, Me.

CORN MEAL SKILLET BREAD
Makes 1 Round Loaf

To make this bread, two skillets of the same size and proportion are required.

1 egg
5 tablespoons sifted corn meal
1 teaspoon salt
1 cup milk
1 tablespoon melted shortening
1 teaspoon baking powder

1. In mixing bowl beat egg. Stir in corn meal, salt and milk.
2. Stir in shortening and baking powder.
3. Pour into hot greased skillet. Cover with inverted greased duplicate pan. Cook over low heat for 20 minutes, or until brown on underside.
4. Invert pans so that bread falls, unbrowned side down, into upper pan. With upper pan over heat, cook for 20 minutes longer.

Mrs. Alfred S. Holcomb, Woman's Club,
Panama City, Fla.

CUSTARDY CORN BREAD
Serves 4

¾ cup corn meal
¼ cup presifted flour
½ tablespoon sugar
½ teaspoon salt
1 teaspoon baking powder
1½ cups plus 1 tablespoon milk
1 egg, lightly beaten
2 tablespoons butter

1. Preheat oven to 400° F.
2. In mixing bowl combine dry ingredients. Stir in 1 cup plus 1 tablespoon of the milk. Stir in egg.
3. Melt butter in 8-inch square baking pan. When butter is hot, pour batter into pan. Pour remaining milk over top, but *do not stir.*
4. Bake in preheated oven for 30 minutes.

Mrs. James A. Chustz, Maids & Matrons Club,
Jackson, Miss.

JALAPEÑA BUTTERMILK CORN BREAD
Serves 6 to 8

Especially good with fried fish.

1 cup corn meal
½ cup presifted flour
½ teaspoon baking soda
1 teaspoon salt
½ teaspoon sugar
1 cup cream-style corn
1 medium onion, chopped
2 or more (to taste) jalapeña chili peppers, chopped
¼ pound grated Cheddar cheese
½ cup olive oil
2 eggs, lightly beaten
1 cup buttermilk

1. Preheat oven to 450° F. Grease 8-inch skillet.
2. In mixing bowl combine dry ingredients.
3. Stir in corn, onion, chilis and cheese.
4. Combine oil, eggs and buttermilk. Add to dry ingredients. Stir only until dry ingredients are moistened.
5. Turn into skillet. Bake in preheated oven for 20 to 25 minutes, or until lightly browned.

Billie Le Bleu, Aggressive Study Club,
De Quincy, La.

SPANISH CORN BREAD
Serves 8 to 10

1 cup buttermilk
1 cup yellow corn meal
1 cup presifted flour
3 teaspoons sugar
1 teaspoon salt
1 teaspoon baking powder
½ teaspoon baking soda
1 egg, lightly beaten
¼ cup melted shortening
8-ounce can whole-kernel corn, drained
4-ounce can roasted green peppers, drained and chopped
4-ounce can pimientos, drained and chopped
2 cups grated Cheddar cheese

1. In small mixing bowl combine buttermilk and corn meal. Let stand for 30 minutes.
2. Preheat oven to 375° F. Grease 13 x 9½ x 2-inch baking pan.
3. Into large mixing bowl sift together dry ingredients.
4. Add egg, shortening and corn meal mixture. Stir well.
5. Add corn, green peppers and pimientos. Stir well.
6. Add cheese. Mix well.
7. Turn batter into pan. Bake in preheated oven for 30 minutes. Serve warm.

Mrs. H. P. C. Evers, Pierian Study Club,
San Saba, Tex.

CRACKLING BREAD
Makes 1 Square Loaf

Cracklings are made from the browned rind of roast pork or baked ham. They can also be made from diced pork fat by cooking it in a heavy vessel on top of the stove or in a slow oven, pouring off the liquid fat every few minutes, until only the browned crisp cracklings remain.

1 cup cracklings
1½ cups corn meal
¾ cup presifted flour
½ teaspoon baking soda
¼ teaspoon salt
1 cup sour milk or buttermilk

1. Preheat oven to 400° F. Grease 8-inch square baking pan.
2. In mixing bowl combine cracklings and dry ingredients.
3. Add sour milk or buttermilk. Stir until dry ingredients are moistened.
4. Turn batter into pan. Bake in preheated oven for 30 minutes.

Mrs. E. C. Riall, Kuwot Study Club, Mooringsport, La.

CRANBERRY BANANA BREAD
Makes 1 Large or 2 Small Loaves

¼ cup butter or margarine
1 cup sugar
1 egg
2 cups presifted flour
3 teaspoons baking powder
½ teaspoon salt
½ teaspoon cinnamon
Grated rind of 1 orange
1 cup mashed ripe bananas
½ cup milk
1 cup cranberries, ground and drained
1 cup broken pecans

1. Preheat oven to 350° F. Grease 9½-inch loaf pan or 2 smaller loaf pans.
2. In mixing bowl cream butter or margarine and sugar. Beat in egg.
3. Sift together dry ingredients.
4. Combine orange rind, bananas and milk.
5. Add dry ingredients to sugar mixture alternately with banana mixture, mixing until smooth after each addition.
6. Stir in cranberries and pecans.
7. Turn batter into pan. Bake in preheated oven for 1 hour and 15 minutes. If 2 smaller pans are used, bake about 1 hour.

Blanche W. Miller, Woman's Club, Crystal Lake, Ill.

CRANBERRY JELLY BANANA BREAD
Makes 1 Square Loaf

1½ cups presifted flour
2 teaspoons baking powder
½ teaspoon baking soda
¾ teaspoon salt
¾ cup sugar
½ cup chopped nuts
1 cup mashed ripe bananas
1 egg, lightly beaten
½ cup melted shortening

4 ¼-inch-thick slices canned jellied cranberry sauce
16 pecan halves

1. Preheat oven to 400° F. Grease 8-inch square baking pan.
2. Into mixing bowl sift together flour, baking powder, baking soda, salt and ½ cup of the sugar.
3. Add chopped nuts. Mix well.
4. Combine bananas, egg and shortening. Stir into dry ingredients. Mix until smooth.
5. Pour batter into pan.
6. Cut cranberry slices into quarters. Arrange pieces evenly on batter. Put pecan half on each piece of cranberry. Sprinkle with remaining sugar.
7. Bake in preheated oven for 30 minutes.

Kathryn Harrison, Culture Club, Columbiana, Ala.

CRANBERRY ORANGE BREAD
Makes 1 Loaf

2 cups presifted flour
½ teaspoon salt
1½ teaspoons baking powder
½ teaspoon baking soda
1 cup sugar
1 egg, lightly beaten
Juice and grated rind of 1 orange
2 tablespoons shortening
1 cup chopped walnuts
1 cup quartered cranberries

1. Preheat oven to 375° F. Grease 8½-inch loaf pan.
2. Into mixing bowl sift together dry ingredients.
3. Add egg.
4. Put orange juice and rind and shortening in 1-cup measure. Add enough hot water to total ¾ cup. Stir until shortening is melted.
5. Add orange mixture to batter. Stir until blended.
6. Stir in walnuts and cranberries.
7. Turn batter into pan. Bake in preheated oven for 60 minutes; raise temperature to 375° F.; bake for 15 minutes longer.

Dorothy Olson, Washington Junior Woman's Club, Phoenix, Ariz.

DATE NUT BREAD
Makes 3 Loaves

2¼ cups chopped nuts
3 cups cut dates
4¼ teaspoons baking soda
1½ teaspoons salt
½ cup butter or margarine
2¼ cups boiling water
6 eggs
1 tablespoon vanilla
3 cups sugar
4¼ cups presifted flour

1. In mixing bowl combine nuts, dates, baking soda, salt and butter or margarine. Add water. Let stand for 20 minutes.
2. Preheat oven to 350° F. Grease 3 9½-inch loaf pans.

3. In large mixing bowl beat eggs with fork. Add vanilla. Stir in sugar and flour.

4. Add date-nut mixture to flour mixture. Mix only until flour is moistened.

5. Turn batter into pans. Bake in preheated oven for 1 hour and 15 minutes.

Avis Mabry, Study Club, Balsam Lake, Wis.

DATE NUT–BROWN SUGAR BREAD
Makes 1 Loaf

1 cup boiling water
1 cup cut dates
1 teaspoon baking soda
4 tablespoons shortening
¾ cup brown sugar
1 egg
1½ cups presifted flour
½ teaspoon salt
1 cup chopped walnuts

1. Preheat oven to 300° F. Line 9½-inch loaf pan with waxed paper.

2. In mixing bowl pour water over dates. Stir in baking soda. Let stand for 5 minutes.

3. In mixing bowl cream shortening and sugar. Beat in egg.

4. Stir in flour, salt and walnuts.

5. Stir in date mixture. Mix well.

6. Turn batter into pan. Bake in preheated oven for 45 to 60 minutes.

Lucile Lukens, Mutual Improvement Club, Sterling, Kans.

GINGERBREAD
Makes 24 Squares

¾ cup melted shortening, margarine or lard
¾ cup brown sugar
2 eggs, lightly beaten
¾ cup dark molasses
2½ cups presifted flour
2 teaspoons ginger
½ teaspoon ground cloves
2 teaspoons baking soda
½ teaspoon baking powder
½ teaspoon nutmeg
1½ teaspoons cinnamon
1 cup boiling water

1. Preheat oven to 350° F. Grease 13 x 9½ x 2-inch baking pan.

2. In mixing bowl cream shortening, margarine or lard and sugar. Add eggs. Mix well. Stir in molasses.

3. Into another mixing bowl, twice sift together dry ingredients. Stir into egg mixture.

4. Stir in water.

5. Turn batter into pan. Bake in preheated oven for 30 to 40 minutes.

Jennette McGregor, Clio Woman's Club, Columbus, Kans.

ELECTION DAY GINGERBREAD
Makes 24 Squares

This gingerbread was sold at the polls on Election Day and may still be in evidence in small towns in New Hampshire.

1 cup molasses
½ cup softened butter
1 teaspoon ground ginger
1 egg, lightly beaten
1 teaspoon baking soda
1 tablespoon boiling water
About 3¼ cups presifted flour
1 teaspoon milk, mixed with
1 teaspoon molasses

1. Preheat oven to 350° F. Grease shallow pan or baking sheet.

2. In mixing bowl combine molasses, butter, ginger and egg.

3. Dissolve baking soda in water. Add to molasses.

4. Work in enough flour to make dough that is a little sticky.

5. With back of spoon, press dough into pan or onto sheet, keeping it about ¼ inch thick.

6. Bake in preheated oven for 20 minutes.

7. Remove from oven. While still hot, brush with milk mixture.

Frances L. Whitman, Woman's Club, West Concord, N.H.

SMALL-FAMILY GINGERBREAD
Makes 1 Loaf

1¼ cups presifted flour
¾ teaspoon baking soda
½ teaspoon cinnamon
½ teaspoon ginger
¼ teaspoon ground cloves
¼ teaspoon salt
¼ cup sugar
½ cup molasses
1 egg
¼ cup melted shortening
½ cup hot water

1. Preheat oven to 350° F. Grease 8-inch loaf pan.

2. Onto piece of waxed paper sift together flour, baking soda, cinnamon, ginger, cloves and salt.

3. In mixing bowl beat together sugar, molasses and egg until blended. Add shortening. Beat well.

4. Add flour mixture and water alternately, beating well after each addition.

5. Turn batter into pan. Bake in preheated oven for 45 minutes.

Mrs. Arline Rozelle, New Idea Woman's Club, Milo, Me.

SOFT GINGERBREAD
Makes 1 Square Loaf

½ cup shortening
½ cup brown sugar
1 cup molasses
1 egg
½ teaspoon ginger
1 teaspoon cinnamon
½ teaspoon salt
1½ cups presifted flour
1 teaspoon baking soda
1 cup boiling water

1. Preheat oven to 350° F. Grease 8-inch square baking pan.

2. In mixing bowl cream shortening and sugar.

3. Beat in molasses and egg.

4. Into mixing bowl sift together seasonings and flour.

5. Dissolve soda in water.

6. Stir seasoned flour into molasses.

7. Stir in soda water. (Batter will be very thin, but it is thinness that makes gingerbread soft.)

8. Pour batter into pan. Bake in preheated oven for about 40 minutes.

Kate Walker, Priscilla Club, Butler, Mo.

GRAPE-NUT QUICK BREAD
Makes 2 Loaves

1 cup grape-nut cereal
2 cups sour milk or buttermilk
1 egg, well beaten
1 cup sugar
4 cups presifted flour
4 teaspoons baking powder
1 teaspoon salt
1 teaspoon baking soda

1. Combine grape-nut cereal and milk. Let soak for 20 minutes.

2. Preheat oven to 350° F. Grease 2 8½-inch loaf pans.

3. Stir egg and sugar into grape-nut mixture.

4. Into mixing bowl sift together remaining ingredients.

5. Stir in grape-nut mixture.

6. Pour batter into pans. Bake in preheated oven for 60 minutes.

*Mrs. Lydia O. Jackson, Riverside Woman's Club
& Sigma Rho Club, Grafton, N.D.*

HOBO BREAD
Makes 6 Loaves

2 cups boiling water
3 cups seedless raisins
4 teaspoons baking soda
¼ cup shortening
2 cups sugar
2 eggs
Dash of salt
4 cups presifted flour
1 cup chopped walnuts

1. Preheat oven to 350° F. Grease 6 1-pound 4-ounce cans.

2. Pour water into mixing bowl. Stir in raisins and baking soda. Let stand until cool.

3. In another mixing bowl beat shortening, sugar and eggs until smooth.

4. Stir in salt, flour and raisin mixture. Blend well.

5. Stir in walnuts.

6. Pour batter into cans until half full (mixture will rise to top when baked). Bake in preheated oven for 45 to 60 minutes.

*Clara D. Wilson, Woman's Club,
West Frankfort, Ill.*

STEAMED INDIAN BREAD
Serves 6

1 cup presifted flour
1 cup corn meal
½ teaspoon baking soda
½ teaspoon baking powder
¼ teaspoon salt
½ cup molasses
1 cup milk

1. Grease 1-quart mold.

2. Into mixing bowl sift together dry ingredients.

3. Add molasses and milk. Beat until smooth.

4. Turn batter into mold. Cover.

5. Put mold in saucepan. Add sufficient boiling water to come halfway up side of mold. Steam for 2 hours, adding water as necessary. Unmold. Slice.

Mrs. Lee Austin, Seminar Club, Cuba, Mo.

IRISH SODA BREAD
Makes 1 Loaf

Originally the daily bread was made with just caraway seeds. For Sundays, raisins were added and the loaf was iced.

3½ cups presifted flour
⅔ cup sugar
1 teaspoon salt
1 tablespoon baking powder
1 teaspoon baking soda
1½ cups seedless raisins
1 tablespoon caraway seeds
2 eggs, lightly beaten
1½ cups buttermilk
2 tablespoons melted butter

1. Preheat oven to 375° F. Grease 8½-inch loaf pan.

2. Into mixing bowl sift together dry ingredients.

3. Add raisins and caraway seeds.

4. Combine eggs, buttermilk and butter. Add to dry ingredients. Mix lightly only until dry ingredients are moistened.

5. Turn batter into pan. Bake in preheated oven for about 1 hour.

*Alice McHugh, Woman's Club of Baldwin
Borough, Pittsburgh, Pa.*

LEMON BREAD
Makes 1 Loaf

⅓ cup shortening
1⅓ cups sugar
2 eggs
1½ cups presifted flour
1½ teaspoons baking powder
¼ teaspoon salt
½ cup milk
Grated rind and juice of 1 lemon

1. Preheat oven to 350° F. Grease 8½-inch loaf pan.

2. In mixing bowl beat together shortening and 1 cup of the sugar until light and fluffy.

3. Add eggs, one at a time, beating well after each addition.

4. Onto piece of waxed paper sift together dry ingredients.

5. Add dry ingredients and milk alternately to sugar mixture, beating well after each addition.

6. Stir in lemon rind.

7. Turn batter into pan. Bake in preheated oven for 50 to 60 minutes.

8. Meanwhile, blend remaining sugar and lemon juice. Pour over bread as soon as it comes from oven.

*Mrs. Julian Whitney, Junior Century Club,
Manchester, Conn.*

LITTLE BREADS

Makes 6

2 cups water
1 cup seedless raisins
2 teaspoons baking soda
¼ pound margarine
2 cups sugar
2 eggs
1 teaspoon vanilla
4 cups presifted flour

1. In saucepan combine water, raisins and baking soda. Bring to boil. Cook, stirring, for 2 minutes. Cool.
2. Preheat oven to 350° F. Grease 6 10½-ounce soup cans.
3. In mixing bowl cream margarine and sugar. Add eggs and vanilla.
4. Stir in flour alternately with raisin mixture. Mix well.
5. Pour batter into cans about two-thirds full. Place on baking sheet.
6. Bake in preheated oven for 1 hour.

Anne B. Kuebner, Junior Woman's Club,
Eustis, Fla.

MARMALADE BREAD

Makes 1 Loaf

3 cups presifted flour
3 teaspoons baking powder
1 teaspoon salt
¼ teaspoon baking soda
1-pound jar orange marmalade
1 egg, lightly beaten
¾ cup orange juice
¼ cup cooking oil
1 cup chopped walnuts

1. Preheat oven to 350° F. Grease 9½-inch loaf pan.
2. Into mixing bowl sift together dry ingredients.
3. In large measuring cup blend 1¼ cups of the marmalade, egg, orange juice and oil.
4. Add to dry ingredients. Stir just until moistened.
5. Stir in walnuts.
6. Turn batter into pan. Bake in preheated oven for 1 hour.
7. Remove loaf from pan to baking sheet. Spread top with remaining marmalade.
8. Return to oven for 1 minute, or until top is glazed.

Pat Martin, Woman's Club,
New Johnsonville, Tenn.

NUT BREAD WITH LEMON FILLING

Makes 2 Loaves

4 cups presifted flour
1 teaspoon salt
6 teaspoons baking powder
½ cup sugar
1 cup chopped nuts
1 egg, lightly beaten
2 cups milk
2 tablespoons melted butter
Lemon Filling (p. 631)

1. Preheat oven to 350° F. Grease 2 8½-inch loaf pans.

2. Into mixing bowl sift together dry ingredients. Add nuts.
3. Combine egg and milk. Add to dry ingredients; stir only until moistened.
4. Turn batter into pans. Let stand for 45 minutes.
5. Bake in preheated oven for 50 to 60 minutes.
6. Remove loaves from pans. Brush tops with butter.
7. When cold, slice thinly. Spread one slice with Lemon Filling; cover with another slice, sandwich-fashion.

Mrs. William H. Ramey, Woman's Club,
Lombard, Ill.

SOUR CREAM NUT BREAD

Makes 2 Loaves

2 cups brown sugar
3¼ cups presifted flour
2 teaspoons baking soda
½ teaspoon salt
2 eggs, lightly beaten
2 cups sour cream
½ cup chopped nuts
1 cup seedless raisins (optional)

1. Preheat oven to 325° F. Grease only bottoms of 2 8½-inch loaf pans.
2. In mixing bowl combine dry ingredients. Stir in eggs and sour cream. Fold in nuts and raisins, if desired.
3. Turn batter into pans. Bake in preheated oven for 1 hour.

Mrs. Del DeForest, Junior Woman's Club,
Diamond Bar, Calif.

WHITE NUT BREAD

Makes 2 Loaves

4 cups presifted flour
6 teaspoons baking powder
1 cup sugar
1 teaspoon salt
1 cup chopped nuts
1 cup white raisins
2 eggs
2 cups milk

1. Grease 2 8½-inch loaf pans.
2. Into mixing bowl sift together dry ingredients.
3. Stir in nuts and raisins.
4. Combine eggs and milk. Add to dry ingredients, mix only until moistened.
5. Turn batter into pans. Let stand for 20 minutes.
6. Preheat oven to 350° F.
7. Bake in preheated oven for 55 minutes.

American Home Department, Woman's Club,
Middletown, N.J.

WHOLE WHEAT NUT BREAD

Makes 1 Loaf

1½ cups whole wheat flour
1½ cups presifted flour
6 teaspoons baking powder
¼ teaspoon baking soda
1 teaspoon salt
½ cup sugar
1 egg
1 cup sour milk or buttermilk
1 cup chopped nuts

1. Grease 8½-inch loaf pan.
2. In mixing bowl combine dry ingredients.
3. Combine egg and milk. Add to dry ingredients. Mix until blended.
4. Stir in nuts.
5. Turn batter into pan. Let stand for 15 minutes.
6. Preheat oven to 350° F.
7. Bake in preheated oven for 45 to 50 minutes.

Mrs. L. S. McLarry, Woman's Club,
Panama City, Fla.

ONION CHEESE BREAD
Makes 1 Square Loaf
1 tablespoon shortening
½ cup chopped onions
1 egg, lightly beaten
½ cup milk
1½ cups baking powder biscuit mix
1 cup grated Cheddar cheese
1 tablespoon poppy seeds
2 tablespoons melted butter

1. Preheat oven to 400° F. Grease 8-inch square baking pan.
2. Melt shortening in skillet; sauté onions until transparent. Set aside.
3. Combine egg and milk. Add to biscuit mix; stir until moistened.
4. Stir in onion and ½ cup of the cheese.
5. Spread dough in pan. Sprinkle with remaining cheese, poppy seeds and butter.
6. Bake in preheated oven for 20 to 25 minutes.

Mrs. Charles Davis, Junior Woman's Club,
Benson, Ariz.

ORANGE DATE LOAF
Makes 1 Loaf
1 cup dates
Rind of 1 orange
Juice of 2 medium oranges
1 cup sugar
2 tablespoons melted butter
1 egg, lightly beaten
1 teaspoon vanilla
2 cups presifted flour
1 teaspoon baking soda
1 teaspoon baking powder
¼ teaspoon salt
½ cup chopped nuts

1. Preheat oven to 357° F. Grease 8½-inch loaf pan.
2. Put dates and orange rind through meat grinder.
3. Pour orange juice into measuring cup. Fill with enough hot water to total 1 cup.
4. In mixing bowl combine sugar, butter, egg, vanilla and orange juice.
5. Combine dry ingredients. Stir quickly into orange mixture. Stir in date mixture and nuts.
6. Spoon batter into pan. Bake in preheated oven for 45 minutes.

Mrs. H. William Garbe, Thursday Morning Club,
Madison, N.J.

ORANGE DATE–BROWN SUGAR BREAD
Makes 1 Loaf
½ cup boiling water
1 cup cut dates
½ cup orange juice
1 tablespoon soft shortening
¾ cup brown sugar
1 egg
1⅞ cups presifted flour
3 teaspoons baking powder
½ teaspoon salt
1 cup chopped nuts
¼ cup grated orange rind

1. In mixing bowl pour water over dates. Cool slightly.
2. Grease 9-inch loaf pan.
3. Add orange juice, shortening, sugar and egg to dates. Beat well.
4. Combine dry ingredients. Stir into date mixture.
5. Stir in nuts and orange rind.
6. Pour batter into pan. Let stand for 20 minutes.
7. Preheat oven to 350° F.
8. Bake in preheated oven for 55 to 60 minutes.

Mrs. Beckurth C. Stephenson,
Cassadaga–Lake Helen Woman's Club,
Cassadaga, Fla.

PAIN D'ÉPICE (Honey Bread)
Makes 1 Oblong Loaf
This recipe, the result of the collaboration of Adrienne Radzwiller and Audrey Bell, duplicates the famous pain d'épice served as a special teatime bread in Parisian homes. Serve it with sweet butter or cream cheese.

4 cups presifted flour
1⅛ cups sugar
2½ teaspoons baking soda
1 teaspoon powdered anise
2 teaspoons cinnamon
¼ teaspoon ginger
Dash of ground cloves
Dash of salt
1¼ cups boiling water
¾ cup honey
3 tablespoons rum or coffee

1. Day before, into mixing bowl sift together dry ingredients; add water; beat with wooden spoon until smooth. Cover; let stand at room temperature overnight.
2. Next day, preheat oven to 400° F. Grease 10 x 6 x 1½-inch baking pan.
3. Add honey and rum or coffee to batter. Mix well.
4. Turn batter into pan.
5. Cover pan with aluminum foil. Bake in preheated oven for 15 minutes.
6. Reduce temperature to 350°F. Bake for 45 minutes longer.
7. Remove pan from oven. Let stand for 10 minutes.
8. Place heavy weight on foil-covered bread. Cool. Cut into paper-thin slices.

Mrs. William Bell, Woman's Club,
Morristown, N.J.

PEANUT BUTTER BREAD
Makes 1 Loaf

2 cups presifted flour
½ cup sugar
3 teaspoons baking powder
1 teaspoon salt
¾ cup peanut butter
1 egg
1 cup milk

1. Preheat oven to 350° F. Grease 9½-inch loaf pan.
2. Into mixing bowl sift together dry ingredients.
3. Cut in peanut butter.
4. Beat egg and milk. Add to dry ingredients. Stir until well blended.
5. Turn batter into pan. Bake in preheated oven for 1 hour.

Mrs. John Rego, Women's Club,
Ashland, Mass.

PINEAPPLE NUT BREAD
Makes 1 Loaf

1⅓ cups presifted flour
2 teaspoons baking powder
½ teaspoon salt
¼ teaspoon baking soda
¾ cup sugar
3 tablespoons butter
2 eggs
¾ cup chopped nuts
8½-ounce can or 1 cup crushed
  pineapple, undrained
2 tablespoons sugar
½ teaspoon cinnamon

1. Preheat oven to 350° F. Grease 9½-inch loaf pan.
2. Combine flour, baking powder, salt and baking soda.
3. In mixing bowl gradually beat ¾ cup sugar into butter.
4. Add eggs, one at a time, beating after each addition until smooth.
5. Sift in about half the flour mixture. Stir (do not beat) just until dry ingredients are moistened.
6. Add pineapple. Then stir in remaining flour mixture.
7. Spoon batter into pan.
8. Combine 2 tablespoons sugar and cinnamon. Sprinkle over batter.
9. Bake in preheated oven for 60 to 70 minutes.

Mrs. Roberta Berthiaume,
Junior Woman's Club, Port Washington, Wis.

POPPY SEED BREAD
Makes 2 Loaves

4 ounces poppy seeds
⅔ cup evaporated milk
4 eggs
2 cups sugar
1½ cups cooking oil
1 teaspoon vanilla
3 cups presifted flour
1½ teaspoons baking powder
1 teaspoon salt

1. Day before, put poppy seeds in milk. Let stand overnight.
2. Next day, preheat oven to 350° F. Grease 2 8½-inch loaf pans.
3. Beat eggs and sugar until thick and pale.
4. Stir in oil, vanilla and poppy seed mixture.
5. Into large mixing bowl sift together dry ingredients. Gradually stir in poppy seed mixture.
6. Turn batter into pans. Bake in preheated oven for 45 minutes.

Mrs. Harry Clark, Priscilla Club, Butler, Mo.

PUMPKIN BREAD
Makes 2 Loaves

1½ cups sugar
⅓ cup shortening
2 eggs
1⅔ cups presifted flour
¼ teaspoon baking powder
1 teaspoon baking soda
¾ teaspoon salt
½ teaspoon cinnamon
¼ teaspoon ground cloves
⅓ cup water
1 cup canned pumpkin purée
½ cup chopped walnuts

1. Preheat oven to 350° F. Grease 2 7⅝-inch loaf pans.
2. In mixing bowl cream sugar and shortening. Add eggs, one at a time, beating well after each addition.
3. Stir in dry ingredients.
4. Stir in water, pumpkin and walnuts.
5. Turn batter into pans. Bake in preheated oven for 1 hour.

Nancy Bramhall, Anna Day Club, Troy, Mo.

PUMPKIN RAISIN NUT BREAD
Makes 3 Loaves

1 cup cooking oil
4 eggs, lightly beaten
⅔ cup water
2 cups mashed cooked pumpkin
3⅓ cups presifted flour
3⅓ teaspoons salt
1 teaspoon nutmeg
2 teaspoons baking soda
1 teaspoon cinnamon
3 cups sugar
½ cup chopped pecans
½ cup seedless raisins

1. Preheat oven to 350° F. Grease and flour 3 8½-inch loaf pans.
2. Combine oil, eggs, water and pumpkin.
3. Into mixing bowl sift together dry ingredients. Make a well in center. Add pumpkin mixture. Blend just until dry ingredients are moistened.
4. Stir in pecans and raisins.
5. Turn batter into pans. Bake in preheated oven for about 1 hour.

Mrs. Jeanne Walstra, Junior Woman's Club,
Port Washington, Wis.

TOMATO BREAD

Makes 1 Loaf

1⅓ cups milk
⅔ cup grape-nut cereal
2¼ cups presifted flour
¾ cup sugar
3 teaspoons baking powder
1½ teaspoons salt
¼ cup soft shortening, melted
2 eggs, well beaten
1 cup chopped tomatoes

1. Day before, in small saucepan heat milk just until bubbles form around edge; remove from heat. Pour over cereal in medium bowl. Let cool.
2. Preheat oven to 375° F. Grease 9½-inch loaf pan.
3. Into large mixing bowl sift together dry ingredients.
4. Stir shortening, eggs, and tomato into cereal mixture. Add to dry ingredients, stirring just until moistened.
5. Turn batter into pan. Bake in preheated oven for about 1 hour.
6. Wrap cooled bread in waxed paper or transparent film. Refrigerate overnight.
7. When ready to serve, cut into thin slices.

Mrs. Philip P. LeBlanc, President,
Hillsborough County Federation of Women's
Clubs, Tampa, Fla.

WALNUT HONEY LOAF

Makes 1 Loaf

1 cup honey
½ cup sugar
1 cup milk
2½ cups presifted flour
1 teaspoon baking soda
1 teaspoon salt
½ cup chopped walnuts
¼ cup melted shortening
2 egg yolks

1. Preheat oven to 325° F. Grease and lightly flour 9½-inch loaf pan.
2. In 3-quart saucepan combine honey, sugar and milk. Stir over moderate heat until mixture is lukewarm and sugar is dissolved. Cool.
3. Sift together dry ingredients. Add to honey mixture along with walnuts, shortening and egg yolks. Beat for 2 minutes, or about 300 strokes, until well blended.
4. Turn batter into pan. Bake in preheated oven from 75 to 90 minutes.

Mrs. Frank Morrison, Woman's Club,
Waterloo, Neb.

Biscuits

Biscuits may be leavened with either baking powder or baking soda. The shortening is blended into the dry ingredients with either a pastry blender or two knives, one in each hand, used with a cross cutting motion until the mixture of flour and shortening resembles coarse corn meal. Then the cold liquid is added, all at once, and is mixed in quickly and lightly until the dough gathers together and cleans the bowl. The resulting dough should be kneaded very lightly with floured fingers on a lightly floured board for about 30 seconds, or 12 kneading strokes. The dough is then rolled and cut.

If the biscuits are placed apart on a baking sheet, they will be golden brown on both the tops and the sides; if placed close together in a baking pan, only the tops will be browned and crusty, while the sides will remain soft. Biscuits are usually baked in a hot oven for 12 to 20 minutes, depending on size.

COMMON CAUSES OF FAILURE IN BISCUITS

1. Rough biscuits are caused by insufficient mixing.
2. Dry biscuits are caused by baking in too slow an oven and by handling the dough too much.
3. Uneven browning of biscuits is caused by cooking in a dark-surfaced pan (use a cooky sheet or shallow bright-finish pan), by too high a temperature and by rolling the dough too thinly.

Anniversary Cook Book, Woman's Club,
Ashland, Mass.

STANDARD BISCUITS

Makes 14 to 16

2 cups presifted flour
½ teaspoon salt
3 teaspoons baking powder
3 to 4 tablespoons shortening
¾ cup milk

1. Preheat oven to 425° F.
2. In mixing bowl combine dry ingredients.
3. With pastry blender or two knives, cut in shortening until mixture resembles fine crumbs.
4. Add milk. Stir gently with fork until dough holds together. Gather dough into a ball. Turn out onto lightly floured board. Knead gently with floured fingers, about 12 kneading strokes.
5. Roll out dough ½ inch thick. Cut with floured biscuit cutter.
6. Arrange biscuits about 1 inch apart on baking sheet. Bake in preheated oven for 12 to 15 minutes.

Mrs. J. S. Allred, Community Service Club,
Ferriday, La.

BASIC BAKING POWDER BISCUITS

Makes 16

2 cups presifted flour
½ teaspoon salt
4 teaspoons baking powder
½ teaspoon cream of tartar
2 teaspoons sugar
½ cup shortening
⅔ cup milk

1. Preheat oven to 425° F.
2. In mixing bowl combine dry ingredients.

3. With pastry blender or two knives, cut in shortening until mixture resembles fine crumbs.

4. Add milk. Stir gently with fork until dough holds together. Gather dough into a ball. Turn out onto lightly floured board. Knead gently with floured fingers, about 12 kneading strokes.

5. Roll out dough ½ inch thick. Cut with floured biscuit cutter.

6. Arrange biscuits about 1 inch apart on baking sheet. Bake in preheated oven for 12 to 15 minutes.

DROP BISCUITS: Increase milk in recipe above to make a dough that is sticky but light enough to drop from a spoon into muffin cups or onto baking sheet.

Mrs. Paul L. McBride, Community Service Club, Ferriday, La.

BISCUIT VARIATIONS

CHEESE BISCUITS: Add ¾ cup shredded American cheese to shortening-flour mixture before adding liquid.

ORANGE BISCUITS: Add 3 tablespoons grated orange rind to shortening-flour mixture before adding liquid.

PARSLEY BISCUITS: Add 3 tablespoons chopped parsley to shortening-flour mixture before adding liquid. Especially nice when used to top meat pies.

PEANUT BUTTER BISCUITS: Use 2 tablespoons peanut butter in place of 2 tablespoons of the shortening in biscuit recipe.

SOUR MILK BISCUITS: Use sour milk or buttermilk in place of milk, but reduce baking powder by 1 teaspoon and add ½ teaspoon baking soda.

Mrs. W. T. McGowin, Woman's Club, Panama City, Fla.

REFRIGERATOR SODA BISCUITS
Makes 36

5 cups presifted flour
1 teaspoon salt
1 teaspoon baking soda
8 teaspoons baking powder
¾ cup shortening
Buttermilk

1. Preheat oven to 425° F. Grease baking sheet.
2. In mixing bowl combine dry ingredients.
3. Cut in shortening until it resembles very fine crumbs.
4. Stir in buttermilk with fork to make a soft dough. Turn out on lightly floured board. Knead gently with floured fingers, about 12 kneading strokes.
5. Roll out half the dough ½ inch thick. Cut with floured biscuit cutter. Arrange on baking sheet. Bake in preheated oven for 12 to 15 minutes, or until golden.
6. Mound up remaining dough. Wrap in waxed paper. Store in refrigerator, where it will keep for several days.

Mrs. Albert Clayton, Study Club, Collinsville, Ala.

MASTER MIX FOR BISCUITS, PANCAKES, WAFFLES, ETC.

If lard or any other perishable shortening is used, store in refrigerator; otherwise, store in a covered container in a cool dry place. When ready to use, measure 2 cups of the mix into bowl. Add milk to make either a dough for biscuits or batter for pancakes or waffles.

9 cups presifted flour
⅓ cup baking powder
4 teaspoons salt
2½ teaspoons cream of tartar
2 cups shortening

1. Into mixing bowl sift together dry ingredients.
2. Cut in shortening until mixture resembles fine crumbs.

Irene Holmberg, Study Club, Balsam Lake, Wis.

BACON BISCUITS
Makes 16

2 cups presifted flour
2½ teaspoons baking powder
1 teaspoon salt
1 teaspoon coarsely ground black pepper
⅓ cup bacon drippings
⅔ cup milk

1. Preheat oven to 425° F.
2. Into mixing bowl sift together flour, baking powder, salt and ¼ teaspoon of the pepper.
3. Add drippings and milk. Stir gently with fork.
4. Turn dough onto lightly floured board. Knead gently with floured fingers, about 12 kneading strokes.
5. Roll out dough ½ inch thick. Cut with floured 2-inch biscuit cutter.
6. Arrange biscuits on baking sheet. Sprinkle with remaining pepper.
7. Bake in preheated oven for 12 to 15 minutes.

SAUSAGE BISCUITS: Follow directions for Bacon Biscuits, but substitute sausage drippings for bacon drippings and omit pepper. Add a dash of cayenne. Dust tops with paprika for color.

Dot Montgomery, Woman's Club, Crawford, Ga.

BEATEN BISCUITS
Makes About 48

This recipe was handed down from Mrs. Howe's great-grandmother, Sarah Whitaker Standeford Weeks, of Shelbyville, Ky.

6 cups cake flour
2 tablespoons sugar
1 teaspoon salt
1 teaspoon baking powder
½ cup lard
1 cup water

1. Preheat oven to 425° F.
2. In mixing bowl combine dry ingredients.
3. Cut in lard until mixture resembles fine crumbs.

4. Add water. Mix well.

5. Turn dough onto lightly floured board. Knead gently with floured fingers for 5 minutes.

6. Beat with iron mallet on chopping board for 20 minutes.

7. Cut with floured 2-inch biscuit cutter. Place on baking sheets.

8. Bake in preheated oven for 12 minutes.

Katharine Howe, Women's Club, Durham, N.Y.

BUTTER DIPS

Makes 32

⅓ cup butter
1½ cups presifted flour
1 tablespoon sugar
3½ teaspoons baking powder
1½ teaspoons salt
1 cup milk

1. Heat oven to 450° F.

2. Melt but do not brown butter in 13 x 9½ x 2-inch baking pan.

3. In mixing bowl combine dry ingredients. Add milk. Stir with fork just until dough clings together.

4. Turn dough onto well-floured board; roll over to coat with flour; then knead lightly with floured fingers, about 10 kneading strokes.

5. Roll out dough ½ inch thick into 12 x 8-inch rectangle.

6. With floured knife, cut dough lengthwise in half, then crosswise into 16 strips.

7. With both hands pick up strips, one at a time. Dip both sides in butter in pan.

8. Arrange strips close together in 2 rows in pan.

9. Bake in preheated oven for 15 to 20 minutes, or until golden brown.

VARIATIONS (especially good when served with Italian dishes and spicy crisp salads):

CHEESE DIPS: Add ½ cup shredded American cheese to dry ingredients.

GARLIC DIPS: Add ½ clove garlic, minced, to butter before melting.

GREEN DIPS: Add ¼ cup minced chives or parsley to dry ingredients.

SAVORY DIPS: Sprinkle paprika, celery seed or garlic salt over strips before baking.

Mrs. Grace Hulbert, Junior Woman's Club, Port Washington, Wis.

BUTTERMILK BISCUITS

Makes 16

2 cups presifted flour
2 teaspoons salt
2 teaspoons baking powder
⅓ teaspoon baking soda
⅓ cup shortening
¾ cup buttermilk

1. Preheat oven to 425° F.

2. In mixing bowl combine dry ingredients.

3. Cut in shortening until mixture resembles fine crumbs.

4. Add buttermilk. Stir gently with fork until dough holds together. Gather dough into a ball. Turn onto lightly floured

board. Knead gently with floured fingers, about 12 kneading strokes.

5. Roll out dough ½ inch thick. Cut with floured biscuit cutter.

6. Arrange about 1 inch apart on baking sheet. Bake in preheated oven for 12 to 15 minutes.

NOTE: For richer biscuits, increase shortening to ½ cup.

Community Service Club Cook Book, Ferriday, La.

CHEESE BISCUITS

Makes 30

1¼ cups presifted flour
1½ teaspoons baking powder
½ teaspoon salt
⅛ teaspoon cayenne
½ cup butter or margarine
1 cup grated Cheddar cheese
½ cup milk

1. Preheat oven to 425° F. Lightly grease baking sheet.

2. Into mixing bowl sift together dry ingredients.

3. Cut in butter or margarine until mixture resembles fine crumbs.

4. Stir in cheese.

5. Add milk. Stir gently with fork until dough holds together.

6. With floured fingers knead gently on floured board. Roll out dough ½ inch thick. Cut with floured 2-inch biscuit cutter.

7. Arrange on baking sheet. Bake in preheated oven for 12 to 15 minutes.

Mrs. W. Stewart Carter, Buechel Woman's Club, Louisville, Ky.

CHEESE ROLLS

Makes 12

2 cups presifted flour
4 teaspoons baking powder
1 teaspoon salt
3 tablespoons shortening
⅔ cup milk
2 tablespoons melted butter
4-ounce package pimiento cheese spread
3 tablespoons olive oil

1. Preheat oven to 400° F. Grease 12 muffin cups.

2. Into mixing bowl sit together dry ingredients.

3. Cut in shortening until mixture resembles fine crumbs.

4. Add milk. Mix to a dough.

5. Knead gently with floured fingers 4 or 5 times. Roll out dough on lightly floured board into 12-inch square.

6. Brush with butter. Roll up like a jelly roll.

7. Cut into 1-inch slices. Arrange in muffin cups.

8. In small bowl blend cheese spread with oil. Spread on rolls.

9. Bake in preheated oven for 12 to 15 minutes.

Mrs. Francis Mayfield, Butte, Montana, Federation of Colored Women's Clubs, Great Falls, Mont.

CHEESE SWIRLS
Makes 24

2 cups presifted flour
2½ teaspoons baking powder
1 teaspoon salt
⅓ cup shortening
⅔ cup milk
2 cups grated sharp Cheddar
cheese
1 teaspoon dry mustard
⅛ teaspoon cayenne

1. Preheat oven to 425° F.
2. Into mixing bowl sift together flour, baking powder and salt.
3. Cut in shortening until mixture resembles fine crumbs.
4. Add milk. Mix with fork until dough holds together.
5. Place dough on lightly floured board. Knead gently with floured fingers, about 12 kneading strokes.
6. Roll out dough into 12-inch square.
7. In medium bowl lightly toss cheese, mustard and cayenne.
8. Sprinkle on dough.
9. Roll up like a jelly roll. Cut into ½-inch slices.
10. Place on baking sheet. Bake in preheated oven for 12 to 15 minutes, or until golden.

*Mrs. Ruth Anne Ceder, Woman's Club,
Blandinsville, Ill.*

CINNAMON APPLE BISCUITS
Makes 16

2 cups presifted flour
3 teaspoons baking powder
1 teaspoon salt
¼ cup shortening
¾ cup milk
3 tablespoons softened butter
1 to 3 apples, finely cut
¼ cup sugar
1 teaspoon cinnamon

1. Preheat oven to 425° F. Grease baking sheet or muffin cups.
2. Into mixing bowl sift together flour, baking powder and salt.
3. Cut in shortening until mixture resembles coarse crumbs.
4. Add milk. Stir until dough gathers into a ball.
5. Turn dough onto lightly floured board. Knead gently with floured fingers, about 10 kneading strokes.
6. Roll out dough about ½ inch thick into rectangle.
7. Spread surface of dough with butter; sprinkle with apples, sugar and cinnamon. Roll up like a jelly roll.
8. Cut roll into 1-inch-thick slices. Arrange on baking sheet or in muffin cups.
9. Bake in preheated oven for about 15 minutes. Remove biscuits from sheet or cups immediately.

*May Anderson, Woman's Literary Union,
Portland, Me.*

CLOUD BISCUITS
Makes About 24

2 cups presifted flour
1 tablespoon sugar
4 teaspoons baking powder
½ teaspoon salt
½ cup shortening
1 egg, lightly beaten
⅔ cup milk

1. Preheat oven to 450° F.
2. Into mixing bowl sift together dry ingredients.
3. Cut in shortening until mixture resembles coarse crumbs.
4. Add egg and milk. Stir only until dry ingredients are moistened.
5. Turn onto lightly floured board. With floured fingers, knead lightly a few times.
6. Roll out dough ¾ inch thick. Cut with floured 2-inch biscuit cutter.
7. Arrange biscuits on baking sheets. Bake in preheated oven for 10 to 14 minutes, or until golden brown.

*Mrs. Pearl McDonald, Woman's Club,
Osage, Wyo.*

CORN MEAL BISCUITS
Makes 24

¾ cup milk
½ cup yellow corn meal
1½ cups presifted flour
4 teaspoons baking powder
1 teaspoon salt
4 tablespoons melted shortening
Melted butter

1. Preheat oven to 425° F.
2. Scald milk. Remove from heat. Stir in corn meal.
3. In mixing bowl combine dry ingredients.
4. Stir in shortening and corn meal mixture.
5. Turn onto lightly floured board. Knead gently with floured fingers until smooth.
6. Roll out dough ¼ inch thick. Cut with floured biscuit cutter. Score biscuits slightly off center with back of knife. Brush with butter. Fold over pocketbook style.
7. Arrange on baking sheet. Bake in preheated oven for about 15 minutes.

Julia L. Tompos, Woman's Club, Elroy, Ariz.

OVEN-BUTTERED CORN FINGERS
Makes 24

⅓ cup butter
2¼ cups presifted flour
2 tablespoons sugar
4 teaspoons baking powder
2 teaspoons salt
¼ cup milk
1 cup cream-style corn

1. Preheat oven to 450° F. Melt butter in 13 x 9½ x 2-inch baking pan.
2. Into mixing bowl sift together dry ingredients. Stir in milk and corn to make a firm dough.
3. Turn dough onto lightly floured board. Knead gently with floured fingers, about 15 kneading strokes.

4. Roll out dough ½ inch thick into rectangle. Cut into 1-inch strips.

5. Roll strips in butter. Arrange in pan.

6. Bake in preheated oven for 20 minutes.

*Nancy Winkelmann, Junior Woman's Club,
Wisner, Neb.*

DATE BUTTERSCOTCH PINWHEELS
Makes 60

1 pound pitted dates
2½ cups brown sugar
1 cup water
½ cup broken nuts
½ cup shortening
2 eggs, well beaten
1 teaspoon vanilla
3½ cups presifted flour
½ teaspoon salt
1 teaspoon baking soda
1 teaspoon cream of tartar

1. Day before, in saucepan combine dates, ½ cup of the sugar and water. Bring to boil. Cook for 10 minutes, or until thick, stirring occasionally. Add nuts. Cool.

2. In mixing bowl cream shortening and remaining sugar. Stir in eggs and vanilla. Combine remaining ingredients. Beat into shortening mixture, adding flour if necessary to make a soft dough.

3. Divide dough into 3 portions. On lightly floured board, roll out one portion at a time thinly. Spread with date filling. Roll up like a jelly roll. Wrap in waxed paper. Refrigerate overnight.

4. Next day, preheat oven to 350° F. Grease baking sheet.

5. Slice rolls ¼ inch thick. Arrange on baking sheet. Bake in preheated oven for 10 minutes, or until lightly browned.

*Mrs. C. W. Hatcher, Sr., Junior Woman's Club,
Bristol, Tenn.-Va.*

EMPANADAS (Biscuit Turnovers)
Makes 12

2 cups presifted flour
2 tablespoons sugar
2 teaspoons baking powder
½ teaspoon salt
½ cup shortening or lard
⅓ cup ice water
Mincemeat

1. Into mixing bowl sift together dry ingredients.

2. Cut in shortening or lard until mixture resembles crumbs.

3. Add water. Stir with fork just until dough holds together.

4. Preheat oven to 375° F.

5. Roll out dough thinly on lightly floured board. Cut into rounds 3 or 4 inches in diameter.

6. Place spoonful of mincemeat on half of each round. Wet edge with water; fold over; press edges together to seal.

7. Arrange on baking sheet. Prick with fork. Bake in preheated oven for 15 minutes, or until golden brown.

*Mrs. J. A. Ikard, Woman's Aladdin Club,
Canutillo, Tex.*

JELLY BISCUITS

Basic Baking Powder
Biscuits dough (p. 119)
Jelly

1. Preheat oven to 450° F.

2. Prepare Basic Baking Powder Biscuits dough. Roll out ½ inch thick on lightly floured board.

3. Cut half the dough with floured small biscuit cutter; cut other half with floured small doughnut cutter.

4. Place biscuit rounds on baking sheet. Top each round with a tiny doughnut. Fill hole with jelly.

5. Bake in preheated oven for about 12 minutes.

*Mrs. Stanley Porche, Junior Woman's Club,
Thibodaux, La.*

MILE-HIGH BISCUITS
Makes 24

3 cups presifted flour
4½ teaspoons baking powder
¾ teaspoon cream of tartar
2½ tablespoons sugar
¾ teaspoon salt
¾ cup shortening
1 egg
1 cup milk

1. Preheat oven to 450° F. Grease baking sheet.

2. Into mixing bowl sift together dry ingredients.

3. Cut in shortening until mixture resembles coarse crumbs.

4. Beat egg lightly; add to milk. Add to dry ingredients. Mix with fork until dough holds together.

5. Turn dough onto lightly floured board. Knead lightly with floured fingers.

6. Roll out dough 1 inch thick. Cut with floured biscuit cutter.

7. Arrange on baking sheet. Bake in preheated oven for 12 minutes.

*Mrs. John Foreman, President, Woman's Club,
Fort Collins, Colo.*

ONION BISCUITS
Makes 16

Basic Baking Powder
Biscuits dough (p. 119)
2 tablespoons butter or margarine
2¼ cups sliced onions
Dash of salt
1 egg
½ cup sour cream

1. Preheat oven to 450° F. Grease 8-inch square baking pan.

2. Prepare Basic Baking Powder Biscuits dough. Roll out into 8-inch square.

3. Pat dough into bottom of pan.

4. Melt butter or margarine in skillet; sauté onions over medium heat until golden.

5. Add salt. Cool.

6. Beat egg until frothy. Stir in sour cream.

7. Arrange onions on dough in pan. Spread sour cream on top.

8. Bake in preheated oven for 20 minutes.

9. To serve, cut into 2-inch squares.

*Mrs. James Foster, Golfview Hills Woman's Club,
Hinsdale, Ill.*

UPSIDE-DOWN ORANGE BISCUITS
Makes 12

¼ cup butter
½ cup orange juice
¾ cup sugar
2 teaspoons grated orange rind
Basic Baking Powder
Biscuits dough (p. 119)
½ teaspoon cinnamon

1. In saucepan combine butter, orange juice, ½ cup of the sugar and orange rind. Bring to boil. Simmer for 2 minutes. Pour into 12 muffin cups.
2. Prepare Basic Baking Powder Biscuits dough.
3. Preheat oven to 425° F.
4. Roll out dough ¼ inch thick into rectangle. Sprinkle with remaining sugar and cinnamon. Roll up like a jelly roll. Cut into 1-inch-thick slices.
5. Place slices in muffin cups. Bake in preheated oven for 20 minutes.

*Mrs. Charles W. Cameron, Norumbega Club,
Bangor, Me.*

SWEET POTATO BISCUITS
Makes About 18

1¾ cups presifted flour
3 teaspoons baking powder
2 tablespoons sugar
1 teaspoon salt
⅓ cup melted shortening or cooking oil
1 cup mashed cooked sweet potatoes
¾ cup milk

1. Preheat oven to 450° F.
2. Into mixing bowl sift together dry ingredients.
3. Stir shortening or oil into sweet potatoes. Combine with milk.
4. Add sweet potato mixture to dry ingredients. Mix lightly with fork just until dry ingredients are moistened.
5. Turn dough onto lightly floured board. Knead gently with floured fingers, about 5 or 6 kneading strokes.
6. Pat or roll out dough ½ inch thick. Cut with floured 2-inch biscuit cutter.
7. Arrange on baking sheet. Bake in preheated oven for 18 to 22 minutes.

*What's Cookin' in Hapeville?, Woman's Club,
Hapeville, Ga.*

TOMATO CHEESE WHIRLS
Makes 18

2 cups presifted flour
½ teaspoon baking soda
1 teaspoon salt
¼ cup shortening
¾ cup tomato juice
3 tablespoons softened butter or margarine
1 cup grated Cheddar cheese
1 teaspoon paprika

1. Preheat oven to 425° F. Grease baking sheet.
2. Into mixing bowl sift together flour, baking soda and salt.
3. Cut in shortening until mixture resembles fine crumbs.
4. Add tomato juice. Mix only until dry ingredients are moistened.
5. Turn dough onto lightly floured board. Roll out ¼ inch thick into rectangle.
6. Spread dough with butter or margarine. Sprinkle with cheese and paprika.
7. Roll up like a jelly roll, starting from longer side.
8. Cut into ½-inch slices. Place, cut side down, on baking sheet.
9. Bake in preheated oven for 20 minutes.

*Mrs. C. J. Campbell, Woman's Club,
Lincoln, Neb.*

ROYAL RUSKS
Makes About 48

2 cups sugar
1 cup butter
2 eggs
1 cup sour cream
About 5 cups presifted flour
1 teaspoon baking soda
Pinch of salt
1 cup ground almonds
1 teaspoon almond extract

1. Preheat oven to 350° F.
2. In mixing bowl cream sugar and butter.
3. Beat in eggs. Stir in sour cream.
4. Combine dry ingredients. Stir into butter mixture, adding flour, if necessary, to make a stiff dough.
5. Work in almonds and almond extract.
6. Roll out dough into long rolls 1 inch thick. Place on baking sheet.
7. Bake in preheated oven for 30 minutes, or until lightly browned.
8. While warm, cut on bias into ½-inch-thick slices. Arrange, cut side up, on baking sheet. Dry in 250° F. oven until golden, turning once to dry and brown both sides.

*Mrs. Wilmer Anderson, Woman's Club,
Stromsburg, Neb.*

BREAKFAST SCONES
Makes 12 to 16

2 cups presifted flour
3 teaspoons baking powder
1 teaspoon salt
2 tablespoons sugar
2 tablespoons butter
2 eggs, lightly beaten
Ice water
Milk
Sugar

1. Preheat oven to 450° F.
2. In mixing bowl combine dry ingredients.
3. Cut in butter.
4. Stir in eggs and enough water to make a soft dough.
5. Turn dough onto lightly floured board. Knead gently with floured fingers, about 12 kneading strokes.

6. Roll out dough ½ inch thick. Cut into rounds or squares.

7. Arrange on baking sheet. Brush with milk. Sprinkle with sugar.

8. Bake in preheated oven for 10 to 15 minutes.

Mrs. E. T. Gardner, Woman's Club,
Panama City, Fla.

POTATO GRIDDLE SCONES
Makes 16

2 cups presifted flour
1 teaspoon salt
3 teaspoons baking powder
⅓ cup shortening
1 cup cold mashed potatoes
1 egg, lightly beaten
⅓ cup milk

1. Into mixing bowl sift together dry ingredients.

2. Cut in 3 tablespoons of the shortening until mixture resembles fine crumbs.

3. In measuring cup blend potatoes, egg and milk.

4. Add potato mixture to flour mixture. Work together until smooth.

5. Turn onto lightly floured board. Cut in half.

6. With floured fingers lightly knead each half for few seconds; then roll out ½ inch thick to a circle.

7. Cut each circle into 8 pie-shaped wedges.

8. Lightly grease hot griddle or large skillet with some of remaining shortening.

9. Put scones on griddle. Cook for about 15 minutes, turning occasionally, until golden on both sides and dry. (To determine this, press down slightly in center of scone; no batter should ooze at sides.)

Mrs. Lloyd Smith, Woman's Club,
Cornelia, Ga.

Muffins and Popovers

Muffins and popovers are perhaps the easiest of all quick breads to make. In basic muffin recipes all the liquid ingredients are combined with all the dry ingredients. This is known as the muffin method. A few quick stirs—12 to 14—are all it takes to moisten the flour-sugar mixture. Care should be taken *not* to overblend. Muffin cups should be well greased, or aluminum or paper liners should be used, and the cups should be filled about two-thirds full.

Muffins are baked in a fairly hot, 375° to 400° F., oven for 20 to 30 minutes, depending on their size, or until a wooden pick inserted in the center of a muffin comes out clean. Unless a recipe specifies removing muffins immediately from pans, let them stand for 5 minutes; then turn them onto wire racks to cool. Better still,

serve them piping hot with marmalade, jam or sweet butter.

The batter for popovers is thinner than that for muffins and is usually mixed until smooth. Popovers can be baked in muffin cups, in individual custard cups set on a baking sheet or in special heavy iron popover pans. Follow directions for time and temperature.

COMMON CAUSES OF FAILURE IN MUFFINS

1. Coarse texture is caused by insufficient stirring and by baking at too low a temperature.

2. Tunnels in muffins, peaks in center and a soggy texture are caused by overmixing.

Anniversary Cook Book, Women's Club,
Ashland, Mass.

PERFECT BREAKFAST MUFFINS
Makes 12

2 cups presifted flour
3 teaspoons baking powder
½ teaspoon salt
2 eggs, lightly beaten
1 cup milk
2 tablespoons melted shortening

1. Preheat oven to 400° F. Grease muffin cups.

2. In mixing bowl combine dry ingredients.

3. Beat together eggs, milk and shortening. Add to dry ingredients; stir gently just until moistened.

4. Spoon batter into muffin cups, filling them two-thirds full. Bake in preheated oven for 20 to 25 minutes.

VARIATIONS:

BUTTERMILK MUFFINS: Use only 2 teaspoons baking powder; add ½ teaspoon baking soda; use buttermilk or sour milk in place of milk.

SWEET MUFFINS: Add 2 to 4 tablespoons sugar to dry ingredients.

VERY SWEET MUFFINS: Add ½ cup sugar to dry ingredients.

BACON MUFFINS: Add ½ cup crumbled crisply cooked bacon to dry ingredients.

CHEESE MUFFINS: Add ½ cup shredded American cheese to dry ingredients.

CRANBERRY MUFFINS: Fold 1 cup halved fresh or frozen cranberries into Very Sweet Muffins batter just before putting batter into muffin cups.

NUT MUFFINS: Add ½ cup chopped pecans or walnuts to dry ingredients.

Mrs. Ira Hutchison, Woman's Club,
Panama City, Fla.

APPLE MUFFINS

Makes 12

1 egg
½ cup milk
¼ cup melted shortening
1 cup coarsely chopped unpeeled
    apples
1½ cups presifted flour
2 teaspoons baking powder
½ teaspoon salt
½ cup sugar
½ teaspoon cinnamon
Sugar

1. Preheat oven to 400° F. Grease muffin cups.
2. In mixing bowl beat egg. Stir in milk, shortening and apples.
3. Combine flour, baking powder, salt, ½ cup sugar and cinnamon.
4. Add dry ingredients all at once to liquid ingredients. Stir only enough to moisten.
5. Spoon batter into muffin cups, filling them two-thirds full. Sprinkle sugar liberally over each.
6. Bake in preheated oven for 20 minutes.

Mrs. Donald McKay, Past President, Our Neighborhood Club, Maine Federation of Women's Clubs, Old Town, Me.

APPLE PECAN MUFFINS

Makes 12

2 cups presifted flour
½ cup sugar
¾ teaspoon salt
2 teaspoons baking powder
1 egg, lightly beaten
1 cup milk
½ cup melted butter
1 cup chopped apples
1 cup chopped pecans
2 tablespoons sugar
Dash of mace
½ teaspoon cinnamon
¼ teaspoon nutmeg

1. Preheat oven to 375° F. Grease muffin cups.
2. Into mixing bowl sift together flour, ½ cup sugar, salt and baking powder.
3. Combine egg, milk and ¼ cup of butter. Add to flour mixture along with apples and pecans. Stir only enough to moisten dry ingredients.
4. Spoon batter into muffin cups, filling them two-thirds full.
5. Combine remaining butter, 2 tablespoons sugar, mace, cinnamon and nutmeg.
6. Brush tops of muffins with spiced butter. Bake in preheated oven for 30 minutes.

Mrs. George Doll, Thursday Morning Club, Madison, N.J.

UPSIDE-DOWN APRICOT MUFFINS

Makes 12

2 cups presifted flour
½ cup granulated sugar
3 teaspoons baking powder
½ teaspoon salt
¼ cup melted shortening
2 eggs
1 cup milk
¼ cup melted butter or margarine
¼ cup brown sugar
12 cooked apricot halves

1. Preheat oven to 375° F. Grease muffin cups.
2. Into mixing bowl sift together flour, granulated sugar, baking powder and salt.
3. Add shortening, eggs and milk. Beat until smooth.
4. In small bowl blend butter or margarine with brown sugar.
5. Turn brown sugar mixture into muffin cups.
6. Place apricot half, cup side up, in bottom of each cup.
7. Spoon batter into cups, filling them two-thirds full. Bake in preheated oven for 25 minutes.
8. Cool for 5 minutes. Then turn upside-down onto rack.

Wilmot Freeman, Twentieth Century Club, Waynesburg, Pa.

BANANA MUFFINS

Makes 12

½ cup shortening
1 cup less 1 tablespoon sugar
2 eggs
1 cup mashed ripe bananas
2 cups presifted flour
2 teaspoons baking powder
1 teaspoon baking soda
½ teaspoon salt
3 tablespoons milk

1. Preheat oven to 400° F. Grease muffin cups.
2. In mixing bowl cream shortening and sugar.
3. Beat in eggs.
4. Add bananas. Beat thoroughly.
5. Combine dry ingredients. Stir into banana mixture alternately with milk.
6. Spoon batter into muffin cups, filling them two-thirds full. Bake in preheated oven for 20 to 25 minutes.

Ruth S. White, Woman's Club, Panama City, Fla.

BLUEBERRY MUFFINS

Makes 12

¼ cup sugar
¼ cup shortening
1 egg
2 cups presifted flour
4 teaspoons baking powder
½ teaspoon salt
1 cup milk
½ to 1 cup fresh or defrosted
    frozen blueberries

1. Preheat oven to 400° F. Grease muffin cups.
2. In mixing bowl cream sugar and shortening.
3. Beat in egg.
4. Combine dry ingredients. Stir into shortening mixture alternately with milk.
5. Stir in berries.

6. Spoon butter into muffin cups, filling them two-thirds full. Bake in preheated oven for 20 to 25 minutes.

Mrs. R. E. Walker, Woman's Club,
Lombard, Ill.

MAINE BLUEBERRY MUFFINS
Makes 9 to 12

1½ cups presifted flour
½ teaspoon salt
3 tablespoons sugar
3 tablespoons baking powder
1 egg, lightly beaten
¾ cup milk
1½ cups blueberries, washed and
    thoroughly drained
3 tablespoons melted shortening

1. Preheat oven to 400° F. Grease muffin cups.
2. Into mixing bowl sift together dry ingredients.
3. Combine egg and milk. Add to dry ingredients; mix only until moistened.
4. Fold in blueberries and shortening.
5. Spoon batter into muffin cups, filling them two-thirds full. Bake in preheated oven for 20 minutes.

Margaret Chase Smith, Woman's Literary Union,
Portland, Me.

BRAN MUFFINS
Makes 12

¾ cup milk
1 cup 100% bran
1½ cups presifted flour
3½ teaspoons baking powder
1 teaspoon salt
¼ cup cooking oil
½ cup sugar
1 egg

1. Preheat oven to 375° F. Grease muffin cups.
2. Mix milk and bran.
3. In large bowl combine flour, baking powder and salt. Make a well in middle. Put oil, sugar and egg into well.
4. Add bran mixture. Stir just until dry ingredients are moistened. Spoon batter into muffin cups, filling them two-thirds full. Bake in preheated oven for 25 minutes.

Mrs. C. F. Hoffman, Junior Woman's Club,
Thibodaux, La.

ALL-BRAN MOLASSES MUFFINS
Makes 12

1 cup all-bran
1½ cups milk
½ cup molasses
1 egg, lightly beaten
1 cup presifted flour
½ teaspoon salt
1 teaspoon baking soda

1. Put bran in mixing bowl. Stir in milk and molasses. Let soak for 15 minutes.
2. Preheat oven to 400° F. Grease muffin cups.
3. Add egg to bran mixture. Beat well.
4. Into mixing bowl sift together remaining ingredients. Add to bran mixture. Stir until dry ingredients are moistened.

5. Spoon batter into muffin cups, filling them two-thirds full. Bake in preheated oven for 20 minutes.

VARIATION: Add 2 tablespoons seedless raisins to batter; sprinkle tops of unbaked muffins with a little bran for extra crunchiness.

Annie E. Brown, Woman's Literary Union,
Portland, Me.

BRAN MUFFINS BY THE PAILFUL
Makes About 48

4 cups all-bran
2 cups 100% bran cereal
1 teaspoon salt
2 cups boiling water
1 quart buttermilk
3 cups sugar
1 cup shortening
4 eggs
5 cups presifted flour
5 teaspoons baking soda

1. Combine all-bran, 100% bran cereal and salt. Stir in water and buttermilk. Cool to lukewarm.
2. In mixing bowl cream sugar and shortening. Add eggs, one at a time, beating well after each addition. Stir into bran mixture.
3. Combine flour and baking soda. Add to bran mixture. Stir just enough to moisten dry ingredients.
4. Store batter in refrigerator, where it will keep for 4 weeks.
5. When ready to use, preheat oven to 375° F. Grease muffin cups.
6. Spoon batter into muffin cups, filling them two-thirds full. Bake in preheated oven for 20 to 25 minutes.

Mrs. Frank Hoehn, Junior Woman's Club,
Port Washington, Wis.

RAISIN NUT BRAN MUFFINS
Makes 12

¾ cup presifted flour
4 teaspoons baking powder
2 tablespoons sugar
¼ teaspoon salt
1¼ cups bran flakes
3 tablespoons melted shortening
1 egg, lightly beaten
1 cup milk
½ cup seedless raisins
⅓ cup chopped walnuts

1. Preheat oven to 400° F. Grease muffin cups.
2. Into mixing bowl sift together flour, baking powder, sugar and salt.
3. Add bran flakes. Mix.
4. Add shortening, egg and milk. Beat until well blended.
5. Stir in raisins and walnuts.
6. Spoon batter into muffin cups, filling them two-thirds full. Bake in preheated oven for 20 minutes.

Ellen Drury, Twentieth Century Club,
Waynesburg, Pa.

CINNAMON HONEY MUFFINS
Makes 12

¼ cup honey
2 cups presifted flour
3 teaspoons baking powder
½ teaspoon salt
1 teaspoon cinnamon
¼ cup melted shortening
1 egg, well beaten
1 cup milk

1. Preheat oven to 400° F. Grease muffin cups.
2. Put 1 teaspoon of the honey in each cup.
3. Into mixing bowl sift together dry ingredients.
4. Add remaining ingredients. Stir only until dry ingredients are moistened.
5. Spoon batter into muffin cups, filling them two-thirds full. Bake in preheated oven for 20 to 25 minutes.

Mrs. S. P. Griffin, Woman's Club,
Lombard, Ill.

SOUR CREAM CORN STICKS OR MUFFINS
Makes 10 to 12

⅓ cup presifted flour
½ teaspoon salt
1 teaspoon baking powder
½ teaspoon baking soda
1 tablespoon sugar
1 egg
1 cup sour cream
1⅓ cups yellow corn meal
2 tablespoons shortening

1. Preheat oven to 400° F.
2. Onto piece of waxed paper sift together flour, salt, baking powder, baking soda and sugar.
3. In mixing bowl beat egg until frothy.
4. Add sour cream. Blend well.
5. Stir in corn meal and flour mixture. Mix only until dry ingredients are moistened.
6. Put shortening in corn stick pans or muffin cups. Heat in preheated oven. Remove from oven.
7. Spoon batter into pans or cups, filling them two-thirds full. Bake in preheated oven for 25 minutes.

Mrs. T. A. Thompson, Woman's Club,
Williston, Fla.

KENTUCKY CORN STICKS OR MUFFINS
Makes 24

2 cups milk
¼ teaspoon baking soda
½ teaspoon salt
2 teaspoons baking powder
2 tablespoons sugar
1 cup presifted flour
2 cups corn meal
1 egg, lightly beaten

1. Preheat oven to 450° F. Grease corn stick pans or muffin cups.
2. In mixing bowl combine milk, baking soda, salt, baking powder and sugar. Stir until sugar is dissolved.

3. Add flour and corn meal. Stir until smooth.
4. Add egg. Beat well.
5. Spoon batter into pans or cups, filling them about three-fourths full. Bake in preheated oven for 20 minutes.

Mrs. R. A. Sims, Young Business Woman's Club,
Bradenburg, Ky.

CREAM MUFFINS
Makes 12

1 egg
1½ cups heavy cream
½ cup milk
2½ cups presifted flour
2½ teaspoons baking powder
Pinch of salt
5 teaspoons sugar

1. Preheat oven to 400° F. Grease muffin cups.
2. Beat egg lightly. Stir in cream and milk.
3. Into mixing bowl sift together dry ingredients. Gradually stir in cream mixture. Beat briskly until smooth.
4. Spoon batter into muffin cups, filling them two-thirds full. Bake in preheated oven for 20 to 25 minutes.

Nettie Stetson, Woman's Club, Western, Neb.

LUNCHEON DATE MUFFINS
Makes 12

2 cups presifted flour
¼ cup sugar
3 teaspoons baking powder
½ teaspoon baking soda
1 teaspoon salt
1 large egg, lightly beaten
1 cup buttermilk
⅓ cup melted butter
1½ teaspoons grated lemon rind
1 cup chopped dates

1. Preheat oven to 400° F. Grease muffin cups.
2. Into mixing bowl sift together dry ingredients.
3. Combine egg, buttermilk and butter.
4. Add lemon rind and dates to dry ingredients. Add liquid ingredients. Stir just until dry ingredients are moistened.
5. Spoon batter into muffin cups, filling them two-thirds full. Bake in preheated oven for 20 minutes.

Mrs. Hollis E. Suits, Fortnightly Club,
Kirkwood, Mo.

FRENCH BREAKFAST PUFFS
Makes 12

⅓ cup shortening
1 cup sugar
1 egg
1½ cups presifted flour
1½ teaspoons baking powder
½ teaspoon salt
¼ teaspoon nutmeg
½ cup milk
⅓ cup melted butter or margarine
1 teaspoon cinnamon

1. Preheat oven to 375° F. Grease muffin cups.
2. In mixing bowl beat shortening, ½ cup of the sugar and egg until light.
3. Onto piece of waxed paper sift together flour, baking powder, salt and nutmeg.
4. Add flour mixture and milk alternately to creamed mixture, beating well after each addition.
5. Spoon batter into muffin cups, filling them two-thirds full. Bake in preheated oven for 20 to 25 minutes.
6. Remove puffs from cups. Immediately roll in butter or margarine.
7. Blend remaining sugar with cinnamon. Roll puffs in sugar mixture.

Lucy Solomon, Woman's Junior Chilhowee Club, Maryville, Tenn.

REFRIGERATOR GINGER MUFFINS
Makes 48

1¼ cups shortening
1 cup sugar
4 eggs
1 cup molasses
4 cups cake flour
1 teaspoon salt
2 teaspoons baking soda
2 teaspoons ginger
¼ teaspoon cinnamon
¼ teaspoon allspice
1 cup buttermilk

1. In mixing bowl cream shortening and sugar.
2. Add eggs, one at a time, beating well after each addition.
3. Add molasses. Beat well.
4. Into another mixing bowl sift together dry ingredients. Add to molasses mixture alternately with buttermilk, mixing well after each addition.
5. Store in refrigerator until ready to bake.
6. When ready to use, preheat oven to 400° F. Grease muffin cups.
7. Spoon batter into muffin cups, filling them two-thirds full. Bake in preheated oven for 20 minutes.

Mrs. James O'Dell, Woman's Club, Wildwood, Fla.

MARMALADE MUFFINS
Makes 12

½ cup plus 1 tablespoon sugar
2 eggs, lightly beaten
1 cup milk
2 cups presifted flour
3½ teaspoons baking powder
¼ teaspoon salt
¼ teaspoon allspice
¼ teaspoon nutmeg
1/16 teaspoon pepper
1/16 teaspoon ground cloves
2 tablespoons orange marmalade

1. Preheat oven to 400° F. Grease muffin cups.
2. In mixing bowl combine sugar, eggs and ¼ cup of the milk.

3. Into another mixing bowl sift together dry ingredients. Add to egg mixture alternately with remaining milk.
4. Stir in marmalade.
5. Spoon batter into muffin cups, filling them two-thirds full. Bake in preheated oven for about 20 minutes.

Edith M. Kaler, Woman's Literary Union, Portland, Me.

OATMEAL MUFFINS
Makes 12

1 egg, well beaten
1 cup sour milk or buttermilk
1 cup oatmeal
½ cup brown sugar
1 cup presifted flour
1 teaspoon baking powder
1 teaspoon salt
½ teaspoon baking soda
⅓ cup shortening, melted and cooled

1. Preheat oven to 375° F. Grease muffin cups.
2. In mixing bowl combine egg, sour milk or buttermilk, oatmeal and sugar.
3. Into another mixing bowl sift together dry ingredients. Stir into egg mixture.
4. Stir in shortening.
5. Spoon batter into muffin cups, filling them two-thirds full. Bake in preheated oven for 20 minutes.

Doris Neerland, Study Club, Balsam Lake, Wis.

ONION CORN GEMS
Makes 12

½ cup corn meal
3 teaspoons sugar
¼ cup presifted flour
2 teaspoons baking powder
¼ teaspoon salt
1 egg
½ cup milk
1 tablespoon melted butter
1 small onion, minced

1. Preheat oven to 375° F. Grease muffin cups.
2. In mixing bowl combine dry ingredients.
3. Combine egg and milk. Add to dry ingredients; mix only until moistened.
4. Stir in butter and onion.
5. Spoon batter into muffin cups, filling them two-thirds full. Bake in preheated oven for about 20 minutes.

Mrs. Isaac Byrd, Woman's Club, Panama City, Fla.

ORANGE MUFFINS
Makes 12

2 cups presifted flour
3 teaspoons baking powder
½ cup sugar
¾ teaspoon salt
4 to 6 tablespoons lard or shortening
2 tablespoons grated orange rind
1 egg, lightly beaten
½ cup orange juice

1. Preheat oven to 425° F. Grease muffin cups.

2. Into mixing bowl sift together dry ingredients.

3. Cut in lard or shortening until mixture resembles fine crumbs.

4. Add orange rind.

5. Combine egg and orange juice. Add to dry ingredients; stir only until moistened.

6. Spoon batter into muffin cups, filling them two-thirds full. Bake in preheated oven for 15 to 20 minutes.

Mary Holland, Woman's Club, Arlington, Ore.

ORANGE BUTTERMILK MUFFINS
Makes 12

½ cup shortening
1 cup sugar
1 egg
2 cups presifted flour
1 teaspoon baking soda
Pinch of salt
1 cup buttermilk
1 cup ground seedless raisins
1 orange with rind, seeded and
     ground

1. Preheat oven to 375° F. Grease muffin cups.

2. In mixing bowl cream shortening and sugar. Beat in egg.

3. Combine dry ingredients; stir into egg mixture alternately with buttermilk.

4. Stir in raisins and orange.

5. Spoon batter into muffin cups, filling them two-thirds full. Bake in preheated oven for 20 to 25 minutes.

Sandy Iacino, Junior Woman's Club,
Simsbury, Conn.

ORANGE PECAN SOUR CREAM MUFFINS
Makes 12

1⅓ cups presifted flour
1 teaspoon baking powder
½ teaspoon baking soda
½ teaspoon salt
3 tablespoons sugar
1 tablespoon butter
1 tablespoon grated orange rind
1 egg
1 cup sour cream
½ cup chopped pecans

1. Preheat oven to 375° F. Grease muffin cups.

2. Into mixing bowl sift together dry ingredients except sugar.

3. In another mixing bowl beat together sugar, butter, orange rind and egg.

4. Stir in sour cream, dry ingredients and pecans.

5. Spoon batter into muffin cups, filling them two-thirds full. Bake in preheated oven for 25 to 30 minutes.

Study Club, Balsam Lake, Wis.

PEACH GEMS
Makes 18

3 tablespoons melted butter or
     margarine
¼ cup brown sugar
36 peach slices
18 pecan halves

2½ cups cake flour
2½ teaspoons baking powder
⅓ cup granulated sugar
1 egg
1¼ cups milk
⅓ cup cooking oil

1. Preheat oven to 400° F. Grease muffin cups.

2. In small bowl mix butter or margarine and brown sugar; place a little of mixture in each cup.

3. Arrange 2 peach slices separated by pecan half in each cup.

4. Into mixing bowl sift together flour, baking powder and granulated sugar.

5. Add egg, milk and oil. Stir only until dry ingredients are moistened.

6. Spoon batter into muffin cups, filling them two-thirds full. Bake in preheated oven for 25 minutes.

Peggy Eidson, Woman's Junior Chilhowee Club,
Maryville, Tenn.

PRUNE RYE MUFFINS
Makes 12 Large or 18 Small Muffins

1 cup sifted rye flour
1 cup presifted flour
3 teaspoons baking powder
½ teaspoon salt
⅓ cup cooked prunes, cut into small
     pieces
½ cup prune juice
½ cup milk
¼ cup melted shortening
2 tablespoons molasses
2 eggs, well beaten

1. Preheat oven to 400° F. Grease muffin cups.

2. Into mixing bowl sift together dry ingredients.

3. Add remaining ingredients, mixing just until dry ingredients are moistened.

4. Spoon batter into muffin cups, filling them two-thirds full. Bake in preheated oven for 20 minutes.

Edith M. Kaler, Woman's Literary Union,
Portland, Me.

RICE MUFFINS
Makes 12

1½ cups presifted flour
½ teaspoon salt
3 teaspoons baking powder
2 tablespoons sugar
1 cup cold cooked rice
2 eggs, well beaten
1 cup milk
4 tablespoons melted shortening

1. Preheat oven to 400° F. Grease muffin cups.

2. Into mixing bowl sift together dry ingredients.

3. Combine remaining ingredients. Add to dry ingredients; stir gently only until moistened.

4. Spoon batter into muffin cups, filling them two-thirds full. Bake in preheated oven for 20 to 25 minutes.

Mrs. Collins Bird, Woman's Club,
Panama City, Fla.

BASIC POPOVERS

Makes 12

2 eggs, well beaten
Pinch of salt
1 cup presifted flour
½ cup water
½ cup milk

1. Preheat oven to 425° F. Grease popover pan. Put in oven to heat while preparing batter.
2. In mixing bowl combine eggs and salt.
3. Stir in flour.
4. Gradually beat in water. Beat vigorously with wire whisk.
5. Add milk. Continue to beat until bubbling and smooth.
6. Pour batter into smoking-hot popover cups, filling them three-fourths full. Bake in preheated oven for 30 to 40 minutes.

Mrs. Collins Bird, Woman's Club,
Panama City, Fla.

VARIATIONS:

BACON POPOVERS: Add ¼ cup crumbled crisply cooked bacon to batter.

CHEESE POPOVERS: Drop ½-inch cube Cheddar or Swiss cheese into center of each cup just before baking.

HERB POPOVERS: Stir ½ teaspoon of any favorite dried herb into batter before filling cups.

POPOVERS

Makes 8

1 cup presifted flour
¼ teaspoon salt
2 eggs
1 tablespoon shortening
1 cup milk

1. Preheat oven to 350° F. Grease custard cups.
2. Into mixing bowl sift together flour and salt.
3. Make a well in center of flour. Break eggs into it.
4. Add shortening and milk. Stir with wooden spoon until smooth.
5. Pour batter into custard cups filling them three-fourths full.
6. Bake in preheated oven for 20 minutes. Raise temperature to 450° F.; bake for 10 minutes longer. Reduce temperature to 350° F.; bake for 10 minutes longer. (Regulation of temperature is very important.)

Louise Hanson, Study Club,
Balsam Lake, Wis.

NO-BEAT POPOVERS

Makes 8

The secret of these popovers is starting with a cold oven and not peeking during the 30-minute baking time.

2 eggs
1 cup milk
1 cup presifted flour
½ teaspoon salt

1. Grease muffin cups.
2. Break eggs into mixing bowl. Add remaining ingredients.
3. Mix well with spoon, disregarding lumps.
4. Spoon batter into cups, filling them three-fourths full.
5. Set oven at 450° F. Immediately put cups in oven.
6. Bake for 30 minutes.

Mrs. Lowell Ellison, Jr.,
Federation of Women's Clubs, Vt.

YORKSHIRE PUDDING

Serves 6 to 8

Although traditionally served with roast beef in England either with or instead of potatoes, Yorkshire Pudding is nothing more than a large popover.

¾ cup presifted flour
½ teaspoon salt
3 eggs
½ cup milk
¼ cup water
½ cup roast beef drippings

1. Preheat oven to 450° F.
2. Onto piece of waxed paper sift together flour and salt.
3. In mixing bowl beat eggs, milk and water. Gradually beat in flour; beat until entire surface bubbles.
4. Pour beef drippings into 8-inch square baking pan; keep in oven until fat starts to smoke.
5. Pour batter into pan. Bake for 20 minutes, or until puffed and golden.
6. Cut into squares.

Ruth Patton, Woman's Club,
Prospect Heights, Ill.

Pancakes and Waffles

Pancakes, or griddle cakes, are baked on a hot griddle, usually lightly greased, until the batter is bubbling and the cakes are golden brown on one side. They are then turned to allow the other side to brown. To test the temperature of the griddle, flick a drop of water on the hot surface. The water should dance around on the griddle for a moment before it evaporates. If the water disappears immediately, the griddle is too hot. If it flattens out and sizzles, the griddle is not hot enough.

Very thin pancakes, known as crêpes, are cooked in a small skillet in which ½ teaspoon butter or margarine is heated to the point where it just begins to turn brown. A couple of tablespoons of the batter are poured into the pan, and the pan is immediately tipped and rotated to spread the batter evenly in a very thin layer over the bottom of the skillet. Crêpes are turned to brown on both sides, but the thin pancakes or skins used for blintzes are cooked on only one side. For dessert crêpes and blintzes, see Index.

The batter for waffles is similar to a pancake batter. To bake, follow the directions supplied with your make of waffle iron.

BASIC PANCAKES OR GRIDDLE CAKES

Makes 6

½ cup milk
1 egg
2 tablespoons melted butter
1 cup presifted flour
2 teaspoons baking powder
1 tablespoon sugar
½ teaspoon salt
    Melted butter and maple syrup or honey

1. In mixing bowl lightly beat together milk, egg and butter.
2. Into another mixing bowl sift together remaining ingredients. Add to milk mixture all at once. Stir just until dry ingredients are moistened.
3. Transfer batter to large measuring cup or pitcher.
4. For each pancake pour about ¼ cup batter onto hot greased griddle. Cook until cake is full of bubbles and underside is nicely browned. Turn with pancake turner or spatula. Cook until brown on other side.
5. Serve immediately with butter and maple syrup or honey.

VARIATIONS:

WHOLE WHEAT PANCAKES: Follow recipe above, but use ⅓ cup whole wheat flour and ⅔ cup presifted white flour in place of 1 cup presifted flour. Sweeten with molasses instead of sugar.

BUCKWHEAT PANCAKES: Follow recipe above, but use ½ cup buckwheat flour and ½ cup presifted white flour in place of 1 cup presifted flour.

APPLE PANCAKES: Follow recipe above. Stir 1 apple, peeled and thinly sliced, into batter.

BLUEBERRY PANCAKES: Follow recipe above. Stir ½ cup fresh or drained canned blueberries into batter.

CHEESE PANCAKES: Follow recipe above. Stir ½ cup shredded Cheddar cheese into batter.

PANCAKE DE LUXE MIX

Makes About 7 Cups

3 cups whole wheat flour
1 cup buckwheat flour
1 cup corn meal
1 cup wheat germ
2 teaspoons salt
4 teaspoons baking powder
2½ teaspoons baking soda
3 tablespoons sugar

1. In mixing bowl blend all ingredients.
2. Store in covered container in refrigerator. Use as desired.

Rona Horn Rose, Woman's Club,
La Crescenta, Calif.

PANCAKES DE LUXE

Makes 8

Serve warm with syrup, if desired.

1 cup Pancake De Luxe Mix (opposite)
1 cup milk
1 egg
2 tablespoons melted shortening

1. In mixing bowl combine all ingredients. Blend only until dry ingredients are moistened.
2. Use ¼ cup batter for each pancake. Drop batter onto hot greased griddle or into large skillet.
3. Cook until bubbles form on surface and edges become dry.
4. Turn pancakes. Cook for 2 minutes longer, or until browned on underside.

Rona Horn Rose, Woman's Club,
La Crescenta, Calif.

BANANA PANCAKES WITH SWEET AND SOUR SAUCE

Makes 12

2 eggs, separated
2 tablespoons flour
2 tablespoons cream
2 ripe bananas, mashed
    Butter
2 cups water
1 cup sugar
2 teaspoons cornstarch
2 tablespoons vinegar

1. Beat egg yolks, flour and cream.
2. Beat egg whites until stiff but not dry. Fold into egg yolk mixture.
3. Fold in bananas.
4. Melt a little butter in skillet. Swirl to coat bottom. For each pancake, spoon about 2 tablespoons batter into skillet. Cook, turning once, until browned on both sides.
5. In saucepan combine water, sugar, cornstarch, 1 tablespoon butter and vinegar. Bring to boil. Boil until sauce is reduced by half. Serve sauce over pancakes.

Melba Jenkins, Beta Study Club, Shreveport, La.

SUPER DUPER BUTTERMILK PANCAKES

Makes 8

1 cup presifted flour
2 teaspoons sugar
¾ teaspoon baking powder
¼ teaspoon salt
1¼ cups buttermilk
½ teaspoon baking soda
2 egg yolks, lightly beaten
2 tablespoons softened butter
2 egg whites, stiffly beaten

1. Into mixing bowl sift together flour, sugar, baking powder and salt.
2. Combine buttermilk, baking soda and egg yolks. Add to dry ingredients. Mix until smooth.
3. Stir in butter.
4. Fold in egg whites.
5. Cook on hot greased griddle, turning once, until cakes are browned on both sides.

LaVerne Dykins, Woman's Club, Elroy, Ariz.

BUTTERMILK PANCAKES WITH WHEAT GERM

Makes 8

1 egg
2 tablespoons corn oil
1 cup buttermilk
¼ teaspoon salt
½ teaspoon baking soda
2 heaping tablespoons wheat germ
plus enough presifted flour to
total 1 cup

1. Beat egg lightly. Stir in oil and buttermilk.
2. Add dry ingredients. Mix until blended.
3. Cook on hot lightly oiled griddle, turning once, until cakes are browned on both sides.

Mrs. J. R. Cudworth, Quest Club, Tuscaloosa, Ala.

CARROT PANCAKES

Makes About 8

5 medium carrots
⅓ cup yellow corn meal
½ cup whole wheat flour
½ cup presifted flour
1 teaspoon salt
2 teaspoons baking powder
1 tablespoon brown sugar
2 eggs
1½ cups milk

1. Grate carrots.
2. Into mixing bowl sift together dry ingredients. Make a deep well in center of mixture; put eggs and carrots in it. Add milk. Stir until well blended. (If too thick, add milk.)
3. Cook on hot greased griddle, turning once, until cakes are browned on both sides.

Mrs. William R. Thompson, Woman's Club, Holtville, Calif.

CORN GRIDDLE CAKES

Makes 8

½ cup presifted flour
4 teaspoons baking powder
½ teaspoon salt
1 teaspoon sugar
1 cup yellow corn meal
1½ cups milk
1 egg
2 tablespoons melted butter or margarine

1. Into mixing bowl sift together flour, baking powder, salt and sugar.
2. Stir in corn meal.
3. In large measuring cup combine remaining ingredients.
4. Add milk mixture to flour mixture, blend only until moistened.
5. Using ¼ cup batter for each cake, cook on hot greased griddle until bubbles form on surface and edges become dry.
6. Turn cakes. Cook until underside is browned.

Alma J. Sphar, Clover Leaf Sewing Club, Charleroi, Pa.

CRISP CORN DOLLARS

Makes 16

1 cup corn meal (waterground if possible)
1 teaspoon salt
¼ teaspoon sugar
Boiling water

1. Preheat oven to 450° F. Grease baking sheet generously.
2. Put corn meal, salt and sugar in 4-cup measuring pitcher.
3. Gradually add a little water at a time, stirring constantly until mixture is consistency of waffle batter.
4. Drop batter by teaspoons a few inches apart onto baking sheet. Bake in preheated oven for 15 minutes.

Mrs. Gilbert Fisher, Magazine Club, Union Springs, Ala.

CORN MEAL—MOLASSES GRIDDLE CAKES

Makes About 46

1½ cups corn meal
6 tablespoons shortening
3 cups boiling water
2½ cups milk
6 eggs, lightly beaten
3 tablespoons molasses
3 cups presifted flour
1 tablespoon salt
1 tablespoon baking powder

1. Put corn meal in mixing bowl; cut in shortening until mixture resembles fine crumbs.
2. Pour in water; mix; let stand for 5 minutes.
3. Stir in milk. Cool.
4. Add eggs and molasses. Mix.
5. Into mixing bowl sift together remaining ingredients. Add to corn meal mixture. Beat until smooth.
6. Using about ¼ cup batter for each cake, drop batter onto hot greased griddle.
7. Cook over medium heat until bubbles form on surface and edges become dry. (These should cook a little more slowly than regular griddle cakes.)
8. Turn cakes. Cook until underside is browned.

Mrs. Julian Oneto, Woman's Club, Manteo, N.C.

COTTAGE CHEESE PANCAKES

Makes 8

6 eggs
½ cup melted butter
6 tablespoons baking powder biscuit mix
1 cup cream-style cottage cheese
Dash of salt

1. In mixing bowl beat eggs until foamy.
2. Stir in remaining ingredients. Mix until blended.
3. Using about ¼ cup batter for each cake, drop batter onto hot greased griddle.
4. Cook for about 4 minutes, or until underside is golden.

5. Turn cakes. Cook until other side is browned.

Phyllis Bauer, Bay Area Zenith Club,
North Bend, Ore.

DUTCH PANCAKE

Serves 6

Serve with favorite syrup.

1 cup presifted flour
1 tablespoon sugar
1 teaspoon salt
6 eggs
1 cup milk
1 tablespoon butter

1. Preheat oven to 425° F.
2. Onto piece of waxed paper sift together dry ingredients.
3. In mixing bowl beat eggs until frothy.
4. Add milk. Beat well.
5. Gradually stir in flour mixture. Beat until smooth.
6. Melt butter in 10-inch skillet.
7. Quickly pour batter into skillet. Cook over medium heat for 2 to 3 minutes.
8. Bake in preheated oven for 10 minutes, or until cake is golden brown and top springs back when lightly touched in center.

Terri Avers, Junior Women's Club, Elmore, Ohio

HAM PANCAKE OMELET

Serves 4

Serve hot with applesauce.

1 cup pancake mix
3 eggs, separated
¾ cup milk
2 cups diced cooked ham
1 teaspoon butter

1. Preheat broiler.
2. Put pancake mix in mixing bowl.
3. Beat egg yolks. Stir in milk. Add liquid all at once to pancake mix. Stir until fairly smooth.
4. Beat egg whites until stiff but not dry. Fold into yolk mixture. Fold in ham.
5. Melt butter in 9- or 10-inch skillet.
6. Pour batter into skillet. Cook over direct heat for about 3 minutes, or until underside is golden brown.
7. Place in broiler 3 inches from heat. Cook until top is delicately browned.

Mrs. Ben A. Steinhaus, Woman's Club,
Ashley, N.D.

KRAPSUA (Oven Pancake)

Serves 4 to 6

Serve with maple syrup.

¼ cup butter
2 eggs
2 cups milk
1 cup presifted flour
½ teaspoon salt
3 tablespoons sugar

1. Preheat oven to 450° F.

2. Put butter in 10 x 6 x 1½-inch baking pan. Place in oven until melted.
3. Meanwhile, beat eggs in mixing bowl.
4. Add milk and flour alternately, beating well after each addition.
5. Stir in salt and sugar.
6. Pour batter into pan. Stir well.
7. Bake in preheated oven for 30 to 40 minutes, or until brown and set.
8. Cut into squares.

Mrs. Harold Kauppila, Women's Club,
Negaunee, Mich.

ORANGE CRÊPES

Makes 12

2 cups presifted flour
¼ teaspoon salt
4 eggs, lightly beaten
2 cups milk
1 tablespoon orange juice
1 tablespoon melted butter
Butter
Currant jelly
Confectioners' sugar

1. Into mixing bowl sift together flour and salt.
2. Stir eggs and milk into flour mixture. Continue stirring until smooth. Batter should just coat spoon; if too thick, stir in a little milk.
3. Stir in orange juice and butter.
4. Let stand for 2 hours to improve texture of cakes.
5. To cook crêpes, heat 5- or 6-inch skillet until very hot. Add about ½ teaspoon butter. Swirl to coat bottom and sides.
6. Pour in about 2 tablespoons batter. Tilt pan in circular motion to spread batter evenly and thinly to edge. This must be done quickly before batter has chance to set.
7. Cook for about 1 minute, or until set and browned on one side. Turn. Brown other side.
8. Spread with currant jelly. Roll up. Sprinkle with confectioners' sugar.

Mrs. George Ward, Woman's Club of Mount
Washington, Baltimore, Md.

PAPER-THIN PANCAKES OR CRÊPES

Makes 12

2 large eggs
½ cup presifted flour
Pinch of salt
1 cup milk
Jelly, syrup or jam

1. Break eggs into small mixing bowl. Add flour. Beat very slowly but thoroughly.
2. Add salt. Gradually beat in milk, beating slowly to prevent mixture from getting frothy.
3. Put medium skillet on high heat. Grease bottom well. Let get hot.

4. Pour in about ¼ cup batter. Quickly swirl pan to coat bottom evenly with thin layer. Be ready to loosen it almost immediately. Turn over. Cook for a few seconds longer, or until other side is browned.

5. Turn onto a warm plate. Spread with jelly, syrup or jam. Roll up.

Mrs. Wayne Chastain, President, State Federation of Women's Organizations, Spokane, Wash.

POTATO PANCAKES: See p. 422.

RICE PANCAKES

Makes 12

2½ cups presifted flour
4 teaspoons baking powder
2 teaspoons salt
2 teaspoons sugar
1 cup cold cooked rice
¼ cup melted shortening
2 eggs, lightly beaten
2 cups milk

1. Into mixing bowl sift together dry ingredients.
2. Stir in rice. Mix well.
3. Add remaining ingredients. Mix just until combined.
4. Using about ¼ cup batter for each pancake, drop batter onto hot greased griddle.
5. Cook for about 2 minutes, or until bubbles form on surface and edges become dry.
6. Turn cakes. Cook until underside is browned.

Mrs. M. W. Peck, Woman's Club, Sparta, Ga.

SOUR MILK GRIDDLE CAKES

Makes 24

2 cups presifted flour
1 teaspoon baking soda
1 teaspoon salt
1 tablespoon sugar
1 egg, lightly beaten
2½ cups sour milk
1 tablespoon melted shortening

1. Into mixing bowl sift together dry ingredients.
2. Blend remaining ingredients.
3. Add egg mixture to dry ingredients. Stir only until smooth.
4. Drop batter by spoonfuls onto hot greased griddle.
5. Cook for 2 to 3 minutes on each side, or until golden.

Friendship Club, La Monte, Mo.

MRS. SHEPARD'S SWEDISH HOT CAKES

Makes About 60

3 eggs
Pinch of salt
6 tablespoons sugar
1 quart milk
1 cup presifted flour
1 cup melted butter

1. In large mixing bowl beat together eggs, salt and sugar.

2. Gradually add about ¾ cup of the milk to thin. Add flour a little at a time, to avoid lumping. Continue to add flour alternately with remaining milk.
3. Stir in butter.
4. Pour 2 tablespoons batter into medium-hot 6-inch skillet. Tilt pan to spread batter paper-thin over bottom. Lightly brown one side. Turn. Brown other side.

FOR BREAKFAST: Serve with butter and sugar or syrup or jam.

FOR DESSERT: Spread with butter. Sprinkle with confectioners' sugar and lemon juice. Roll up. Sprinkle again with confectioners' sugar.

Norma Jamar, El Camina Women's Club, Ventura, Calif.

PLÄTTAR (Swedish Pancakes)

Makes About 40

Serve with syrup, jam or lingenberries.

¾ cup presifted flour
½ teaspoon salt
3 tablespoons sugar
3 eggs
2 cups milk
3 tablespoons melted shortening

1. Onto piece of waxed paper sift together dry ingredients.
2. In mixing bowl beat eggs until frothy.
3. Add flour mixture and milk alternately to eggs, beating well after each addition.
4. Add shortening. Beat until smooth and blended.
5. Grease and heat plätt iron. (This may be purchased in specialty houseware stores; if not available, use large skillet.)
6. Drop batter into indentations in plätt iron (or drop 1 teaspoon batter at a time into skillet). Pancakes should be about the size of silver dollar and very thin.
7. Cook until golden on both sides.

Mrs. George E. West, Sr., Woman's Club, Abington, Mass.

RHODE ISLAND JOHNNY CAKES

Makes 8

1 cup Rhode Island white johnny cake meal (corn meal)
Dash of salt
A little sugar
Boiling water
1 egg
Milk
Shortening

1. Put johnny cake meal into mixing bowl. Add salt and sugar.
2. Make a well in center of meal. Pour in water to scald mixture. Let stand for a few minutes.
3. Beat in egg.
4. Thin batter to right consistency by adding milk and beating well.
5. Drop by spoons in hot shortening on griddle. Cook thoroughly on one side be-

fore turning. Do not cook too fast, or inside will not be done.

Pawtucket Woman's Club Cook Book, Pawtucket, R.I.

TORTILLAS

Makes 6

1 cup boiling salted water
1 cup white corn meal
1 teaspoon bacon drippings

1. Combine all ingredients.
2. Pat into very thin flat cakes about as large as salad plates.
3. Cook on griddle until brown on both sides.
4. Serve very hot, or keep and use for Tacos (p. 102) or Enchiladas (p. 215).

Teresitia Gonzales, 20th Century Club, Clayton, N.M.

PANCAKE SKINS FOR EGG ROLLS

Makes 8

½ cup presifted flour
2 teaspoons cornstarch
¼ teaspoon salt
1 egg, lightly beaten
Dash of sugar
1 cup water
¼ cup peanut oil
Egg Roll filling (p. 67)

1. Into mixing bowl sift together flour, cornstarch and salt.
2. Add egg and sugar. Beat well.
3. Add water. Beat until smooth.
4. Heat a few drops of the oil in 6-inch skillet.
5. Pour 3 tablespoons batter into hot skillet. Tilt pan to spread batter evenly over bottom.
6. Place skillet over medium heat. Cook until batter shrinks from sides of pan.
7. Turn. Cook for 1 to 2 minutes longer.
8. Remove from pan. Cool. Repeat with remaining batter.
9. Fill with Egg Rolls filling and fry. (Or stack with 2 pieces of waxed paper between each skin, freezer-wrap, and freeze for future use.)

Woman's Club, Palisades, N.J.

BASIC VELVET WAFFLES

Makes 7 or 8

Serve with butter and syrup or confectioners' sugar.

2 cups presifted flour
3 teaspoons baking powder
¾ teaspoon salt
2 tablespoons sugar (optional)
3 eggs, separated
1¾ cups milk
¼ cup cooking oil or melted butter

1. Preheat waffle iron.
2. Sift together dry ingredients three times, the last time into mixing bowl.
3. Beat egg whites until stiff enough to stand in peaks but not dry.

4. Beat egg yolks. Combine with milk and oil or butter. Add to dry ingredients. Beat with rotary beater until smooth.
5. Fold in egg whites lightly but thoroughly.
6. Pour ½ cup batter for each waffle into preheated waffle iron. Cook according to manufacturer's directions.
7. Allow waffle to remain in iron a few seconds longer for added crispness.

VARIATIONS:

NUT WAFFLES: Sprinkle 1 tablespoon chopped nuts over each waffle before baking.

COCOA WAFFLES: Add ¼ cup cocoa and 1 additional tablespoon sugar to dry ingredients. Increase milk by 2 tablespoons. Serve with ice cream, sweetened whipped cream or Hard Sauce (p. 702).

HAM WAFFLES: Stir 1 cup chopped cooked ham into batter.

CORN WAFFLES: Stir 1 cup cooked corn kernels into batter.

SOUR CREAM WAFFLES: Use 2 cups sour cream in place of milk. Add ½ teaspoon baking soda to dry ingredients. Use only 3 tablespoons oil or butter.

GINGERBREAD WAFFLES: Stir 1 teaspoon ginger into batter. Use molasses in place of sugar.

What's Cookin' in Hapeville?, Woman's Club, Hapeville, Ga.

CHOCOLATE WAFFLES

Serves 4

1½ cups cake flour
1½ teaspoons baking powder
½ teaspoon salt
2 eggs, separated
½ cup milk
½ cup melted butter or margarine
2 ounces unsweetened chocolate, melted
¾ cup sugar
½ teaspoon vanilla
Marmalade, jelly or whipped cream

1. Preheat waffle iron.
2. Into mixing bowl sift together flour, baking powder and salt.
3. Beat egg yolks with milk, melted butter and chocolate.
4. Stir flour mixture into chocolate mixture and beat until smooth.
5. In mixing bowl beat egg whites until stiff but not dry. Fold beaten egg whites into batter.
6. Pour about ½ cup batter for each waffle into preheated waffle iron and cook according to manufacturer's directions.
7. Serve with marmalade, jelly or whipped cream, as desired.

Lela Olson, Civic Club, Sandpoint, Ida.

SPICED CHOCOLATE WAFFLES
Serves 4

Serve hot with ice cream.

1½ cups sifted cake flour
2½ teaspoons baking powder
¼ teaspoon salt
¼ teaspoon cinnamon
¼ teaspoon nutmeg
½ cup butter or margarine
2 eggs
1 teaspoon vanilla
2 ounces semi-sweet chocolate, melted
½ cup milk

1. Preheat waffle iron.
2. Combine dry ingredients.
3. In mixing bowl cream butter or margarine. Add eggs, one at a time, beating well after each addition. Stir in vanilla and chocolate.
4. Stir dry ingredients alternately with milk into butter mixture.
5. Bake in preheated waffle iron according to manufacturer's directions.

*Mrs. John D. Robinson, Junior Woman's Club,
Bristol, Tenn.*

COCONUT WAFFLES
Serves 4

1½ cups presifted flour
3 teaspoons baking powder
½ teaspoons salt
3 eggs, separated
1 cup milk
3 tablespoons melted butter
¾ cup shredded coconut

1. Preheat waffle iron.
2. Into mixing bowl sift together dry ingredients.
3. Beat egg yolks. Combine with milk and butter.
4. Stir liquid ingredients into dry ingredients.
5. Beat egg whites until stiff but not dry. Fold into batter. Fold in coconut.
6. Bake in preheated waffle iron according to manufacturer's directions.

VARIATION: Use drained crushed pineapple, chopped ham, diced bacon or diced cheese in place of coconut.

*Mrs. Ivan Sharp, Monday Study Club,
Poplar Bluffs, Mo.*

CORN MEAL WAFFLES
Serves 6

¾ cup water
¼ cup corn meal
¾ cup sour milk
1 cup presifted flour
2 tablespoons sugar
½ teaspoon salt
½ teaspoon baking powder
¼ teaspoon baking soda
1 egg, separated
1 tablespoon melted butter

1. Preheat waffle iron.
2. Bring water to boil. Stir in corn meal. Cook for 5 minutes, stirring occasionally. Remove from heat. Stir in milk.
3. Into mixing bowl sift together dry ingredients.
4. Stir in corn meal mixture, egg yolk and butter.
5. Beat egg white until stiff but not dry. Fold into batter.
6. Bake in preheated waffle iron according to manufacturer's directions.

A. S.

HONEY WAFFLES
Serves 4

Serve hot with additional honey, if desired.

2 cups presifted flour
2 teaspoons baking powder
½ teaspoon salt
3 eggs
¼ cup honey
⅓ cup melted shortening
1⅓ cups milk

1. Preheat waffle iron.
2. Onto piece of waxed paper sift together dry ingredients.
3. In mixing bowl beat eggs and honey until blended.
4. Add shortening and milk. Beat until blended.
5. Gradually add dry ingredients, beating until smooth.
6. Pour about ⅓ cup batter into preheated waffle iron. Cook according to manufacturer's directions.

*Mrs. Howard Potter, President, Woman's Club,
Ithaca, Mich.*

JAMES RIVER BUTTERMILK WAFFLES
Serves 4

3 eggs, separated
2 cups buttermilk
2 cups presifted flour
1 teaspoon baking soda
2 teaspoons baking powder
½ teaspoon salt
6 tablespoons melted butter or shortening

1. Preheat waffle iron.
2. Beat egg yolks until light. Stir in 1 cup of the buttermilk.
3. Combine dry ingredients. Add to egg yolk mixture. Beat well. Stir in remaining buttermilk. Beat again.
4. Stir in butter or shortening.
5. Beat egg whites until stiff but not dry. Fold into egg yolk mixture; do *not* beat.
6. Cook in preheated waffle iron according to manufacturer's directions.

*Mrs. W. J. Payne, Publicity Chairman,
Woman's Club, Clayton, N.C.*

SUNDAY NITE WAFFLES
Serves 4 to 6

Serve with applesauce or honey and sausage cakes, as desired.

    3 eggs, separated
    1½ cups milk
    ⅓ cup cooking oil
    2 cups presifted flour
    ½ teaspoon salt
    4 teaspoons baking powder
    2 cups grated Cheddar cheese
    8-ounce can crushed pineapple,
        drained

1. Preheat waffle iron.
2. In mixing bowl beat egg yolks until thick.
3. Stir in milk and oil. Beat until blended.
4. Into mixing bowl sift together dry ingredients. Beat until smooth.
5. Add cheese and pineapple. Mix well.
6. In another mixing bowl beat egg whites until stiff but not dry. Fold into flour mixture.
7. Pour about ½ cup batter into preheated waffle iron. Cook according to manufacturer's directions.

Sarah T. Tucker, Woman's Club,
Vero Beach, Fla.

WHOLE WHEAT BUTTERMILK WAFFLES
Serves 6 to 8

    3 cups whole wheat flour
    1½ teaspoons baking soda
    1 teaspoon salt
    3 cups buttermilk
    2 eggs, beaten
    2 tablespoons melted shortening

1. Preheat waffle iron.
2. In mixing bowl combine dry ingredients.
3. Beat buttermilk, eggs and shortening.
4. Add egg mixture to dry ingredients; stir only until moistened.
5. Pour about ½ cup batter into preheated waffle iron. Cook according to manufacturer's directions.

Mrs. Fred Kirsch, Menifee County Woman's Club,
Frenchburg, Ky.

Doughnuts and Fried Cakes

Doughnuts are fried in deep oil, fat or shortening heated to 365° F. Test the frying temperature before frying a few doughnuts at a time. The best way to check the temperature is with a frying thermometer; otherwise, drop a 1-inch square of bread into the hot shortening. If it browns in 60 seconds, the temperature is right (365° F.).

As soon as a doughnut rises to the surface and shows a little color, turn it over. Turn again when the underside is browned. When it is golden brown all over, remove with a slotted spoon to absorbent paper to drain.

In making doughnut dough, be careful not to add too much flour, or the doughnuts will be tough. The softer the dough, the more delicate and tender the texture of the doughnuts. The dough should be sticky; chill it thoroughly until it can be handled, rolled and cut. Roll out about ⅓ inch thick. Cut with doughnut cutter dipped in flour. If no doughnut cutter is available, use two plain round cooky cutters, one about 1 inch larger in diameter than the other. Use the smaller cutter for the hole.

BASIC DOUGHNUTS WITH SWEET MILK
Makes 36 to 48

    2 eggs
    1 cup sugar
    1 cup milk
    4 cups presifted flour
    ⅓ teaspoon baking soda
    4 teaspoons baking powder
    ⅓ teaspoon nutmeg
    ½ teaspoon lemon juice
    4 tablespoons melted butter
    Fat for deep frying

1. In mixing bowl beat eggs until light. Stir in sugar and milk.
2. Into another mixing bowl sift together dry ingredients.
3. Stir half the dry ingredients into egg mixture. Then stir in lemon juice and butter.
4. Stir in remaining flour mixture to make a light dough. Chill.
5. Roll out dough on lightly floured board. Cut with floured doughnut cutter.
6. Fry a few at a time in deep fat heated to 365° F. until golden brown. Drain on absorbent paper.

VARIATIONS:

SUGAR DOUGHNUTS: Put fine granulated or confectioners' sugar in a paper bag. Add doughnuts, two or three at a time. Shake bag gently until doughnuts are well coated.

JELLY DOUGHNUTS: Cut dough into rounds with cooky cutter. Do not cut out hole. Put 1 teaspoon jam or jelly on half the rounds. Brush edges with lightly beaten egg. Cover with other rounds. Press edges together. Fry.

Mrs. Vaemond Crane, Study Club,
Balsam Lake, Wis.

BASIC BUTTERMILK DOUGHNUTS
Makes 60 to 72

    3 large eggs, well beaten
    2 cups sugar
    1½ cups buttermilk
    5¼ cups presifted flour
    2 teaspoons baking soda
    2 teaspoons baking powder
    1½ teaspoons salt
    ¼ teaspoon ginger
    ½ teaspoon nutmeg
    4 tablespoons melted butter
    Additional flour for rolling
    Fat for deep frying

1. In mixing bowl combine eggs, sugar and buttermilk.
2. Into another mixing bowl sift together dry ingredients.
3. Add to egg mixture. Stir until well blended.
4. Stir in butter. Chill. (Dough will keep for 3 to 4 days in refrigerator.)
5. When ready to fry, work in enough additional flour to make a soft dough.
6. Roll out dough on lightly floured board. Cut with floured doughnut cutter.
7. Fry a few at a time in deep fat heated to 365° F. until golden brown. Drain on absorbent paper.

Mrs. Helen La Chapelle, Woman's Club, Altoona, Wis.

CREAM DOUGHNUTS
Makes 36

3 eggs, lightly beaten
1 cup sugar
¾ cup heavy cream
¼ cup half-and-half
3 teaspoons baking powder
½ teaspoon nutmeg
½ teaspoon salt
Flour
Fat for deep frying

1. In mixing bowl combine eggs, sugar, cream and half-and-half.
2. Stir in baking powder, nutmeg and salt.
3. Stir in enough flour to make a soft dough.
4. Roll out dough on lightly floured board. Cut with floured doughnut cutter.
5. Fry a few at a time in deep fat heated to 365° F. until golden brown. Drain on absorbent paper.

Audrey Jennings, Study Club, Balsam Lake, Wis.

BANANA DOUGHNUTS
Makes About 48

¼ cup butter
1 cup sugar
3 eggs, beaten
1 cup mashed ripe bananas
½ cup sour milk or buttermilk
5 cups presifted flour
4 teaspoons baking powder
1 teaspoon baking soda
1 teaspoon nutmeg
½ teaspoon cinnamon
2 teaspoons salt
Fat for deep frying

1. Cream butter and sugar.
2. Stir in eggs, bananas and milk.
3. Stir in dry ingredients. Chill.
4. Roll out dough on lightly floured board. Cut with floured doughnut cutter.
5. Fry a few at a time in deep fat heated to 365° F. until golden brown. Drain on absorbent paper.

Mrs. Kloid Skibstad, Flaherty Flat Homemakers Club, Columbus, Mont.

TARRY-HI BANANA FRITTERS
Makes 16
Serve dusted with confectioners' sugar or plain with maple syrup or corn syrup.

2 cups presifted flour
4 teaspoons baking powder
½ cup sugar
½ teaspoon salt
2 eggs, lightly beaten
1 cup mashed ripe bananas (about 3 or 4)
1½ tablespoons lemon juice
Fat for deep frying

1. Into mixing bowl sift together dry ingredients. Add eggs.
2. Combine bananas and lemon juice. Stir into dry ingredients.
3. Drop by teaspoons into deep fat heated to 365° F. Fry until golden brown. Drain on absorbent paper.

Mrs. W. B. Sewell, Woman's Club, Starke, Fla.

CINNAMON DOUGHNUTS
Makes 18 to 24

4 eggs, lightly beaten
⅔ cup sugar
⅓ cup milk
⅓ cup shortening, melted and cooled
3½ cups presifted flour
3 teaspoons baking powder
¾ teaspoon salt
1 teaspoon cinnamon
½ teaspoon nutmeg
Fat for deep frying
½ cup sugar
1 to 2 teaspoons cinnamon

1. In mixing bowl beat together eggs and ⅔ cup sugar until light and fluffy. Stir in milk and shortening.
2. Into another mixing bowl sift together dry ingredients. Stir into egg mixture. Chill thoroughly.
3. Roll out dough ⅜ inch thick on lightly floured board. Cut with floured doughnut cutter. Let stand for 15 minutes.
4. Fry a few at a time in deep fat heated to 365° F. until golden brown. Drain on absorbent paper.
5. While warm, shake in paper bag containing ½ cup sugar and 1 to 2 teaspoons cinnamon.

Mrs. Gayce Ellard, Sr., Book Lovers Club, Kosciusko, Miss.

ORANGE DOUGHNUTS
Makes 36 to 48

1 cup sugar
2 eggs
¼ teaspoon cinnamon
¼ teaspoon nutmeg
3 tablespoons softened butter
Grated rind of 1 orange
1 teaspoon salt
3 tablespoons baking powder
1 cup milk
Presifted flour
Fat for deep frying
Sugar

1. In mixing bowl beat together 1 cup sugar and eggs until thick and pale.
2. Add cinnamon, nutmeg, butter, orange rind, salt and baking powder.
3. Stir in milk. Gradually stir in enough flour to make a soft dough.
4. Roll out on lightly floured board. Cut with floured doughnut cutter.
5. Fry a few at a time in deep fat heated to 365° F. until golden brown. Drain on absorbent paper. Roll in sugar.

VARIATION: Use lemon rind in place of orange rind.

Round Table, Goodland, Kans.

POTATO DOUGHNUTS
Makes About 24

3¾ cups presifted flour
4 teaspoons baking powder
1 teaspoon salt
1 teaspoon nutmeg
⅓ cup shortening
½ teaspoon vanilla
1 cup sugar
2 eggs
¾ cup cold mashed potatoes
¾ cup milk
Fat for deep frying

1. Onto piece of waxed paper sift together flour, baking powder, salt and nutmeg.
2. In mixing bowl beat shortening until fluffy.
3. Add vanilla and sugar. Beat until light and fluffy.
4. Add eggs. Blend well.
5. Add potatoes. Blend until smooth.
6. Add flour mixture and milk alternately, beating well after each addition. Chill for 1 hour.
7. Roll out half of dough at a time ½ inch thick on lightly floured board. Cut with floured doughnut cutter. Let stand for 10 minutes.
8. Fry a few at a time in deep fat heated to 365° F. until golden brown. Drain on absorbent paper.

Iris L. Cushing, President, Hancock County Republican Woman's Club, Bucksport, Me.

EIROHRLI (Swiss Fried Squares)
Makes About 36

2 cups presifted flour
½ teaspoon salt
3 eggs
¼ cup heavy cream
1 tablespoon brandy
Fat for deep frying
Confectioners' sugar

1. Into mixing bowl sift together flour and salt.
2. Add eggs, cream and brandy. Work together to a smooth dough. Chill if necessary.
3. Roll out dough 1/16 inch thick on lightly floured board. Cut into 3-inch squares.
4. Drop a few squares at a time into deep fat heated to 365° F.

5. Stroke squares with fork as they fry so that they ruffle. Fry for about 4 minutes, or until light golden.
6. Drain on absorbent paper. Sprinkle with confectioners' sugar.

Federation of Women's Clubs, Berks County, Pa.

FIOCCHI OR GUANTI
Makes About 48

Bowknots or gloves—whatever you want to call them—they take their name from whatever shape people give them when they are cut for deep frying.

4 eggs
6 tablespoons granulated sugar
3 tablespoons cooking oil
½ cup milk
4 cups presifted flour
1 teaspoon baking powder
1 teaspoon lemon flavoring
Fat for deep frying
Confectioners' sugar
Honey
Chopped walnuts

1. In mixing bowl beat eggs and granulated sugar until thick and lemon-colored.
2. Add oil. Beat well.
3. Gradually add milk, flour, baking powder and lemon flavoring. Blend to a soft dough. Chill if necessary.
4. Turn onto lightly floured board. Cover with mixing bowl. Let stand for about ½ hour.
5. For bowknots, divide dough in quarters. Roll out each quarter ⅛ inch thick.
6. Cut into 1 x 8-inch strips. Gently tie each strip into bow.
7. Drop a few at a time into deep fat heated to 365° F. Fry for 2 to 3 minutes, or until golden brown.
8. Drain on absorbent paper. Sprinkle with confectioners' sugar.
9. Drizzle lightly with honey. Sprinkle with walnuts.

Woman's Club, Monessen, Pa.

SOPAPILLAS (Mexican Fritters)
Serves 6 to 8

2 cups presifted flour
3 teaspoons baking powder
⅛ teaspoon salt
1 tablespoon shortening
Milk
Fat for deep frying
Honey

1. In mixing bowl combine dry ingredients.
2. Cut in shortening until mixture resembles fine crumbs.
3. Add about 1 cup milk to make a firm dough.
4. With floured fingers, mix and knead dough on lightly floured board until smooth and elastic.
5. Return to bowl. Let stand for 30 minutes.
6. Roll out dough on floured board, using as little flour as possible, until very, very thin.

7. Cut into 1½-inch squares.

8. Fry in deep fat heated to 365° F. for about 2 miuntes, or until golden brown.

9. Drain on absorbent paper. Serve at once with honey.

Mrs. Nancy Witters, Junior Women's Club, Cheyenne, Wyo.

DROP DOUGHNUTS

Makes About 36

2 eggs
½ cup sugar
1 tablespoon melted shortening
1 cup milk
1 teaspoon vanilla
3½ cups presifted flour
2 teaspoons baking powder
⅛ teaspoon salt
    Fat for deep frying
    Confectioners' sugar

1. In mixing bowl beat eggs until light. Beat in sugar, shortening, milk and vanilla.

2. Into another mixing bowl sift together dry ingredients. Stir into egg mixture to make a soft dough.

3. Drop by teaspoons into deep fat heated to 365° F. Fry until doughnuts turn themselves over and are golden brown on all sides. Drain on absorbent paper.

4. Dust with confectioners' sugar before serving.

Mrs. Albert Clayton, Study Club, Collinsville, Ala.

AFTERNOON TEA DOUGHNUTS

Makes About 24

2 eggs
7 tablespoons sugar
¼ teaspoon nutmeg
¾ teaspoon salt
2 tablespoons melted shortening
6 tablespoons milk
2 cups presifted flour
3 teaspoons baking powder
    Fat for deep frying
    Confectioners' sugar

1. In mixing bowl beat eggs until very light.

2. Stir in sugar, nutmeg, salt, shortening and milk.

3. Combine flour and baking powder. Stir into egg mixture. Mix well.

4. Drop by teaspoons into deep fat heated to 365° F. Fry until doughnuts turn themselves over and are golden brown on all sides.

5. Drain on absorbent paper. When cool, sprinkle with confectioners' sugar.

Mary Lincoln, Woman's Club, Leonia, N.J.

POTATO POPOVERS

Makes About 12

1 cup mashed potatoes
1 egg
2 teaspoons baking powder
1 cup presifted flour
½ teaspoon salt
    Fat for deep frying

1. Put potatoes, egg, baking powder, flour and salt in mixing bowl.

2. Mix until blended.

3. Drop by tablespoons into deep fat heated to 365° F. Fry for 4 to 5 minutes, or until golden. Drain on absorbent paper. Serve hot.

Mrs. Neil Epler, Woman's Club, Topton, Pa.

INDIAN FRIED BREAD

Makes 6 Cakes

All ethnic and religious groups have foods that are associated with them, and this bread is associated with the Pima Indians. It would be hard to tell exactly why or where or how it was first made. It is by no means their basic diet or the only bread they eat. To some of them it is a special treat, and there are only a few who really know how to make and pat the bread as it should be. The members of the Maricopa Girl Scout Troop have learned this skill in appreciation of Pima history and culture.

3 cups presifted flour
2 teaspoons baking powder
1 teaspoon salt
    Lard or shortening
    Warm water or milk
    Fat for deep frying

1. In mixing bowl combine dry ingredients. Cut in 1 tablespoon lard or shortening.

2. Add enough water or milk to make a dough that is easy to handle.

3. With floured fingers, knead dough until very smooth. (This is important. You must knead dough until soft, yet elastic. Don't use a lot of extra flour while working dough.)

4. Divide dough into balls about the size of lemons. Melt some lard or shortening; use to brush dough. Let stand for 30 to 45 minutes.

5. Pat out each ball with hands until it is a round, flat shape about 5 to 6 inches in diameter and about ¼ inch or less thick. (Because this requires much practice and skill, you may not be able to pat out dough by hand, and you may have to use a rolling pin to roll out balls of dough.)

6. Fry in deep fat heated to 365° F. Dough should rise to top of fat immediately. Cook until brown on one side: turn; brown other side. Be careful not to pierce crust of bread in turning. Drain on absorbent paper.

Maricopa Girl Scout Council, Junior Woman's Club, Scottsdale, Ariz.

NAVAJO FRIED BREAD

Makes 8 Cakes

4 cups presifted flour
4 teaspoons baking powder
1½ teaspoons salt
1⅔ cups water
    Fat for deep frying

1. In mixing bowl combine dry ingredients. Add water. Mix to a dough.

2. Turn dough onto lightly floured board. With floured fingers, knead for at

least 5 minutes, or until smooth and elastic. Cover with cloth or pan. Let stand for 10 minutes or longer. The longer dough stands, the better the bread.

3. Divide dough into 8 parts. Roll out each part into ¼-inch-thick round.

4. Fry in deep fat heated to 365° F. until golden brown. Drain on absorbent paper. Serve hot.

Eula F. Haley, Woman's Club, Seligman, Ariz.

HUSH PUPPIES

Makes 8

¼ cup presifted flour
2 teaspoons baking powder
½ teaspoon salt
¾ cup corn meal
1 small onion, finally chopped
1 egg
½ cup milk
Fat for deep frying

1. Into mixing bowl sift together flour, baking powder and salt.

2. Add corn meal. Mix.

3. Add onion, egg and milk. Stir just until dry ingredients are moistened.

4. Drop by tablespoons into deep fat heated to 365° F. Fry for 5 to 6 minutes or until golden and crisp on both sides. Drain on absorbent paper. Serve hot.

Mrs. S. Joy McDuffie, Woman's Club, Nettleton, Miss.

GEORGIA HUSH PUPPIES

Makes 24

2 cups corn meal
1 cup presifted flour
1½ tablespoons baking powder
1 tablespoon salt
1 medium onion, chopped
1 medium green pepper, chopped
1½ cups buttermilk
Fat for deep frying

1. Into mixing bowl sift together dry ingredients.

2. Add onion and green pepper.

3. Add buttermilk. Stir with fork until dry ingredients are moistened.

4. Drop by spoons into deep fat heated to 365° F. Fry until golden brown. Drain on absorbent paper. Serve hot.

What's Cookin' in Hapeville?, Woman's Club, Hapeville, Ga.

4. Yeast Breads

Nothing smells quite so wonderful as homemade bread in the baking. And nothing tastes quite so delicious as a substantial loaf, hot from the oven, the slices spread with a dollop of fresh sweet butter or homemade jam. It's an experience that no one should miss.

Fortunately the American homemaker is still a baker at heart, and it was gratifying to receive literally thousands of recipes for yeast breads, sweet rolls, rich coffee cakes and yeast-raised pastries. Only a representative number could be included in this book, but they will serve to inspire the reader to get out the mixing bowl and set a batch of dough to rising.

The making of yeast breads is by no means difficult or time-consuming. True, one must be around the house (but not necessarily in the kitchen all the time) to punch down the dough when it is ready and to mold it into loaves, rolls or cakes. Many yeast doughs may be set in the evening and allowed to rise during the night. Others may be stored in the refrigerator and used as needed.

YEAST in active dry or compressed form may be used. One envelope of active dry yeast is equal to one cake of compressed yeast.

Compressed yeast is perishable and should be kept refrigerated and used within a week. When fresh, it is moist and practically odorless. If it is dry and sour-smelling, it should not be used.

Dry yeast will keep for many weeks on the pantry shelf and does not become activated until the dormant yeast cells are moistened in water.

To use yeast: Before being used in a recipe, both dry and compressed yeast should be softened in warm water for at least 5 minutes, then stirred to blend yeast and liquid thoroughly. The water for compressed yeast should be only lukewarm (85° F.), but for dry yeast it can be quite hot to the hand (110° F.)

FLOUR is the chief ingredient in all breads. It is the gluten in the flour that enables the dough to stretch and hold the leavening gas produced by yeast. There are two kinds of wheat flour:

Soft wheat flour, or cake flour, makes a fine-grained bread.

Hard wheat flour, or bread flour, makes a more porous bread and requires a little more liquid than soft wheat flour to make a workable dough.

All-purpose flour is a blend of hard and soft wheat flours. Almost all the all-purpose flours available today are presifted or enriched.

SUGAR, in addition to adding flavor to bread, is quick food or energy for yeast and is partly responsible for producing a good golden crust. The standard amount of sugar for plain bread is 1 tablespoon for each 2 cups flour.

SHORTENING lubricates the meshwork of gluten in the dough so that it can expand easily. It also makes the bread rich and tender, increases the keeping quality of the baked loaf and aids in the browning of the crust. The minimum amount of vegetable shortening, margarine, lard, butter or cooking oil for plain bread and rolls is 1 teaspoon for each 2 cups flour.

SALT gives flavor to bread, helps the dough expand smoothly and tends to stabilize the fermentation process.

EGGS make a richly flavored bread with a delicate texture and a flaky crust.

KNEADING develops the gluten and makes a bread dough elastic so that it can capture and hold the gas manufactured by the yeast. It is a three-step rhythm that quickly becomes automatic. On a floured pastry cloth or board, fold dough over on itself toward you, and press down and away from you with the heels of the hands. Give the dough a quarter turn, and repeat. Not all yeast doughs require kneading. Some may be thoroughly mixed by beating.

THE DOUGH MUST RISE. After kneading, when the dough is smooth and elastic, shape it into a smooth ball, and place it in a lightly greased warm bowl. Either brush the surface of the dough lightly with melted shortening or oil, or turn the ball of dough in the bowl so that all its surfaces are lightly greased. The shortening keeps the surface of the dough from drying so that it can stretch as the dough rises. Don't cover dough tightly, since yeast—a living plant organism—needs air and moisture, in addition to warmth and the nutriment supplied by the dough, in order to grow. Cover the bowl lightly with a towel, and put it in a *warm* place to rise until it is doubled in bulk. To determine when the dough has risen sufficiently, plunge two fingers deep into the center. If deep holes remain, the dough is ready to be shaped into loaves on rolls.

TO PUNCH DOUGH DOWN: Plunge a fist into the center of the raised dough. As the dough sinks, pull the edges from the sides of bowl into the center. Some recipes specify that the dough be shaped immediately into loaves or rolls; others that it be allowed to rise a second time. In general, yeast doughs made from soft wheat or all-purpose (presifted) flour may be shaped after one rising; those made from hard wheat flour should be allowed to rise a second time. However, a second rising will not spoil any dough, no matter what kind of flour is used. After a second rising, a gentle finger test which leaves a slight indentation will indicate that the dough is ready to shape.

TO SHAPE A LOAF: With the palms of the hands, flatten a ball of dough into a rectangle. Fold it lengthwise, and flatten it again. Stretch the dough gently to elongate it, overlap the ends at the center and press together firmly. Now, with the hands, roll the dough lengthwise, and seal the edges. Place the molded loaf in a greased bread or loaf pan, the sealed edge down. The exact size of the pan is not critical. If too large a pan is used, the bread will conform to shape of pan; if too small a pan is used, the bread will rise high above edges.

Breads

COMMON CAUSES OF FAILURE IN BREAD MAKING

1. Porous yeast bread is caused by over-rising or cooking at too low a temperature.
2. A crust that is dark and blisters is caused by under-rising.
3. A yeast dough that does not rise is caused by over-kneading, by old yeast or softening the yeast in water that is too hot, thus killing it.
4. Streaked bread is caused by under-kneading and by not kneading evenly.
5. Uneven baking is caused by using old dark pans, by putting too much dough in the pan, by crowding the oven shelf or by cooking at too high a temperature.

Anniversary Cook Book, Women's Club, Ashland, Mass.

HOW TO MAKE PERFECT WHITE BREAD

Makes 3 Loaves
or 36 Rolls

2 cups milk
4 tablespoons sugar
4 teaspoons salt
5 tablespoons shortening
2 cups water

2 yeast cakes or 2 envelopes active dry yeast
12 cups presifted flour
Melted shortening

1. Heat but don't boil milk until top has puckery film.
2. Stir in sugar, salt and 5 tablespoons shortening until dissolved. Cool to luke-warm.
3. Heat water only to lukewarm. Add yeast; stir for about 10 minutes, or until thoroughly dissolved.
4. Add yeast to milk mixture. Stir in 6 cups of the flour. Beat until smooth.
5. Add remaining flour. Work it in well with hand or spoon.
6. Turn slightly lumpy, slightly sticky dough onto lightly floured board. Knead hard with heels of hands to mix all ingredients thoroughly and to work and stretch dough to give bread an even texture. While kneading, sprinkle a little flour on board to keep dough from sticking (go easy because too much flour will make bread coarse and heavy). Keep kneading until dough looks smooth, satiny and springy.
7. Put dough in greased bowl. Brush or wipe top with melted shortening. Cover with clean towel. Let stand in warm place away from drafts or direct heat for 1½ to 2 hours, or until dough doubles in size or indentations remain when two fingers are poked into dough and drawn out fast.
8. Grease 3 8½-inch loaf pans.
9. Collapse dough by punching center with fist. Then pull edges from sides of bowl; knead into center of dough.
10. Again turn dough onto lightly floured board. Cut into 3 portions. Shape warm, light, responsive dough into 3 loaves. Put each portion in loaf pan. Cover with towel. Let stand in warm place for about 1 hour, or until doubled in bulk.
11. Preheat oven to 400° F.
12. Bake in preheated oven for about 50 minutes, or until bread is golden brown. If bread slips out of pan easily when pan is tipped and if loaf sounds hollow when tapped on bottom or sides with knuckles, bread is perfectly baked. Invert pans Place bread on top to cool.

NOTE: This recipe may also be used for making variously shaped rolls (see section on Rolls and Biscuits).

Favorite Recipes, Junior Women's Club, Edgewood, R.I.

BASIC WHITE BREAD

Makes 2 Loaves

1 cup milk
2 tablespoons sugar
2 teaspoons salt
2 tablespoons shortening or cooking oil
1 cup cold water
1 yeast cake or 1 envelope active dry yeast
1 cup lukewarm water
6 cups presifted flour

1. Scald milk. Remove from heat. Add sugar, salt and shortening or oil. Stir until sugar is dissolved. Add cold water. Cool to lukewarm.

2. Soften yeast in lukewarm water. Add to milk mixture.

3. Gradually work in flour, mixing to a smooth dough.

4. Turn onto lightly floured board. Knead for 10 minutes, or until smooth and satiny.

5. Shape dough into ball. Place in greased bowl; cover; let rise for 1 hour, or until doubled in bulk. Punch down. Let rise again for 1 hour, or until doubled in bulk.

6. Grease 2 loaf pans.

7. Knead dough down. Divide in half. Mold each half into loaf. Place in pan; cover; let rise for about 45 minutes, or until doubled in bulk.

8. Preheat oven to 400° F.

9. Bake in preheated oven for 15 minutes. Reduce temperature to 350° F. Bake for 30 minutes longer. Tap crust; if there is a hollow sound, bread is done.

Irma Arndt, Junior Woman's Club,
Port Washington, Wis.

BUTTERMILK BREAD

Makes 2 Loaves

1 envelope active dry yeast
¼ cup lukewarm water
2 cups warm buttermilk
¼ cup sugar
1½ teaspoons salt
¾ teaspoon baking soda
6 cups presifted flour
¼ cup melted butter

1. Soften yeast in water.

2. Add buttermilk, sugar, salt and baking soda. Mix.

3. Add 3 cups of the flour. Beat until smooth.

4. Stir in butter.

5. Add remaining flour to make a light dough. Turn onto lightly floured board. Knead for about 8 minutes, or until smooth and elastic.

6. Place dough in greased bowl, turning dough to grease all surfaces; cover; let rise for about 1½ hours, or until doubled in bulk.

7. Grease 2 9½-inch loaf pans.

8. Punch dough down. Divide in half. Shape each half into loaf. Put in loaf pan; cover; let rise for about 45 minutes, or until doubled in bulk.

9. Preheat oven to 400° F.

10. Bake in preheated oven for 30 to 35 minutes. Cover tops with aluminum foil if loaves brown too fast.

Mrs. Charles Puckett, Junior Woman's Club,
Port Washington, Wis.

WHITE WATER BREAD

Makes 2 Large Loaves

2¼ cups warm water
2 tablespoons sugar
2 enevlopes active dry yeast

1 tablespoon salt
2 tablespoons soft shortening
6 to 6½ cups presifted flour

1. In mixing bowl combine water, sugar, yeast, salt and shortening.

2. Gradually work in enough flour to make a soft dough that leaves sides of bowl and does not stick to hands.

3. Turn onto lightly floured board. Knead until smooth and elastic.

4. Place dough in greased bowl; cover; let rise for about 1½ hours, or until doubled in bulk.

5. Punch dough down; let rise again for about 1 hour. Punch down; form into loaves.

6. Grease 2 loaf pans. Put loaves in pans; cover; let rise until dough rounds over tops of pans.

7. Preheat oven to 425° F.

8. Bake in preheated oven for 30 minutes.

Mrs. Leo Burdette, Study Club,
Balsam Lake, Wis.

FRENCH BREAD

Makes 2 Loaves

2½ cups warm water
2 envelopes active dry yeast
1 tablespoon salt
1 tablespoon melted margarine
7 cups presifted flour
About 1 cup corn meal
1 egg white, mixed with 1 tablespoon cold water

1. Put water in warm large bowl. Sprinkle in yeast. Stir until dissolved.

2. Add salt and margarine. Gradually stir in flour to make a sticky dough.

3. Place dough in greased bowl, turning dough to grease all surfaces; cover; let rise for about 1 hour, or until doubled in bulk.

4. Grease baking sheet.

5. Punch dough down. Turn onto lightly floured board. Divide in half. Roll each half into an oblong 15 x 10 inches. Beginning at wide side, roll up tightly toward you. Pinch edges to seal. Taper ends by gently rolling back and forth.

6. Place loaves on baking sheet. Sprinkle with corn meal. Let rise, uncovered, until doubled in bulk.

7. With sharp knife, make 4 diagonal cuts on top of each loaf.

8. Preheat oven to 450° F.

9. Bake in preheated oven for 25 minutes. Remove from oven. Brush loaves with egg white mixture. Return to oven. Bake for 5 minutes longer.

Mrs. John K. Bradstreet, Jr., Women's Club,
Ashland, Mass.

CRUSTY FRENCH BREAD

Makes 2 Small Loaves

1 envelope active dry yeast
2 cups lukewarm water
1 tablespoon sugar
4 cups presifted flour
2 teaspoons salt

1. Soften yeast in water. Stir in sugar.
2. Combine flour and salt. Add all at one time to yeast mixture. Stir until dough leaves sides of bowl.
3. Let rise for 2 hours, or until doubled in bulk.
4. Punch dough down. Knead on lightly floured board until smooth. Dough will be very sticky.
5. Grease 2 1-quart glass casseroles.
6. Divide dough in half. Shape each half into round loaf. Put each loaf in casserole. Let rise for about 45 minutes, or until dough is gently rounded over tops of casseroles.
7. Preheat oven to 400° F.
8. Bake in preheated oven for 45 minutes. Turn immediately onto wire racks to cool.

Mrs. Alan Cree, Thursday Morning Club, Madison, N.J.

ANADAMA BREAD

Makes 3 Loaves

    3 cups milk
    ¾ cup yellow corn meal
    ¾ cup molasses
    2 tablespoons butter
    2 teaspoons salt
    2 envelopes active dry yeast
    ¾ cup warm water
    8 cups presifted flour
      Melted butter

1. Heat milk to scalding. Remove from heat. Gradually stir in corn meal, stirring constantly until thick and smooth.
2. Stir in molasses, 2 tablespoons butter and salt. Cool to lukewarm.
3. Soften yeast in water. Add to corn meal mixture. Gradually stir in 5 cups of the flour. Beat until very smooth. Stir in remaining flour to make a soft dough.
4. Turn onto well-floured board. Let stand for 10 minutes. Then knead for 6 to 8 minutes. Place dough in greased large bowl. Brush top with melted butter. Cover; let rise for about 2 hours, or until doubled in bulk.
5. Grease 3 loaf pans.
6. Punch dough down. Divide into 3 parts. Flatten one part at a time into rectangle about 8 x 15 inches. Starting at narrow end, roll up dough. Pinch at ends to seal. Place, seam edge down, in loaf pan.
7. Brush tops of loaves with melted butter; cover; let rise for about 1 hour, or until doubled in bulk.
8. Preheat oven to 350° F.
9. Bake in preheated oven for 50 to 60 minutes.

Mary Lou Leone, Anna Day Club, Troy, Mo.

MINNESOTA CENTENNIAL SALT-RISING BREAD

Makes 2 Loaves

An old pioneer recipe. Salt-rising bread depends on yeast spores in the air to start fermentation. Salt-rising bread is not as light as regular yeast bread, but it is moist and crumbly.

    1 cup milk
    2 tablespoons corn meal
    2 tablespoons sugar
    2 teaspoons salt
    1 cup lukewarm water
      About 5 cups presifted flour
    1 teaspoon melted butter

1. Scald milk in small saucepan. Cool to lukewarm.
2. Turn into large mixing bowl. Stir in corn meal, 1 tablespoon of the sugar and 1 teaspoon of the salt. Cover; place in pan of hot water (120° F.); let stand for 6 to 7 hours until signs of fermentation, or bubbles, appear.
3. Add remaining sugar and salt, water and 2 cups of the flour. Beat thoroughly. Cover; let rise for 2 to 3 hours, or until doubled in bulk and very light.
4. Grease 2 9½-inch loaf pans.
5. Gradually add remaining flour to batter, mixing well. Add more flour, if necessary, so that dough is stiff enough to be kneaded.
6. Turn onto lightly floured board. Knead for 10 to 15 minutes.
7. Shape into 2 loaves. Place in loaf pans. Brush tops with butter. Cover.
8. Let rise until very light and more than doubled in size.
9. Preheat oven to 375° F.
10. Bake in preheated oven for 10 minutes. Reduce temperature to 350° F. Bake for 25 to 30 minutes longer.

Gertrude Cross, Civic Club, Brewster, Minn.

MIXED BREAD

Makes 2 Loaves

    1 envelope active dry yeast
    2 cups lukewarm water
    2 tablespoons lard
    2 tablespoons sugar
    2 teaspoons salt
    2 cups cooked hominy
      Flour

1. Soften yeast in water.
2. Add lard, sugar, salt and hominy.
3. Gradually beat and work in enough flour to make a stiff dough.
4. Let dough rise for 1½ hours, or until doubled in bulk.
5. Grease 2 loaf pans.
6. Punch dough down. Shape into 2 loaves. Place in pans; cover; let rise again for about 1 hour, or until doubled in bulk.
7. Preheat oven to 425° F.
8. Bake in preheated oven for 40 minutes.

Gladys Corley, President, Athena Club, Lexington, S.C.

OATMEAL BREAD

Makes 1 Large or 2 Small Loaves

2 cups boiling water
1 cup quick-cooking oats
1 envelope active dry yeast
½ cup sugar
½ cup warm water
6 cups presifted flour
1 tablespoon salt
2 tablespoons melted shortening

1. Day before, pour boiling water over oats in large mixing bowl. Stir well. Cool.
2. Sprinkle yeast into small bowl. Add ¼ cup of the sugar, warm water and ½ cup of the flour. Stir until blended. Let stand for 10 minutes.
3. Add salt and remaining sugar to oat mixture.
4. Stir in yeast mixture and shortening.
5. Gradually work in enough remaining flour to make a dough that does not stick to hands.
6. Turn onto lightly floured surface. Knead until smooth and elastic.
7. Place dough in greased bowl; cover; let rise overnight (or for at least 3 to 4 hours), until doubled in bulk.
8. Next day, grease 1 large or 2 small loaf pans.
9. Punch dough down. Knead again.
10. Shape into loaf or loaves. Place in pans; cover; let rise for 1 to 2 hours, or until doubled in bulk.
11. Preheat oven to 375° F.
12. Bake in preheated oven for 15 minutes. Reduce temperature to 350° F. Bake for 20 minutes longer for small loaves; 30 minutes longer for large loaf.

Mrs. William B. Davenport, Jr., President,
Mid-Nassau Woman's Club, Rockville Centre, N.Y.

OATMEAL MOLASSES RAISIN BREAD

Makes 3 Loaves

3 cups quick-cooking oats
2 teaspoons salt
2 tablespoons shortening
1 cup seedless raisins
1 quart boiling water
1 cup molasses
2 envelopes active dry yeast
½ cup lukewarm water
6 to 7 cups presifted flour

1. In large mixing bowl combine oats, salt, shortening, raisins and boiling water.
2. Add molasses. Beat well. Cool.
3. Soften yeast in lukewarm water. Stir into oats mixture. Stir in enough flour to make a stiff dough that is easy to handle.
4. Place dough in greased bowl; cover; let rise for about 1½ hours, or until doubled in bulk.
5. Grease 3 loaf pans.
6. Punch dough down. Cut into 3 equal portions. Form each portion into loaf; put in pan; cover; let rise for about 1 hour, or until very light.
7. Preheat oven to 350° F.

8. Bake in preheated oven for about 45 minutes.

Mrs. Raye Tompkins, Woman's Literary Club,
Pingree, N.D.

BONNIE BLUESTONE BREAD

Makes 3 9-inch Loaves

2 cups quick-cooking oats
2 tablespoons shortening
1½ teaspoons salt
3 cups boiling water
2 tablespoons lukewarm water
2 envelopes active dry yeast
1 cup molasses
6 cups presifted flour
Melted butter

1. In saucepan combine oats, shortening, salt and boiling water.
2. Cook over medium heat, stirring frequently, for 5 minutes.
3. Turn into mixing bowl. Cool to lukewarm.
4. In small bowl blend lukewarm water and yeast. Let stand for 5 minutes. Then stir until yeast is dissolved.
5. Stir yeast and molasses into oats mixture.
6. Gradually add flour. Mix well until blended. Dough should be soft but not sticky; if necessary, add flour to obtain correct consistency.
7. Sprinkle top with butter. Cover; let rise for 2 hours, or until doubled in bulk.
8. Grease 3 9-inch loaf pans.
9. Grease hands. Remove dough from bowl. Shape into 3 loaves.
10. Place dough in pans; cover; let rise for about 30 minutes, or until doubled in bulk.
11. Preheat oven to 350° F.
12. Bake in preheated oven for 1 hour. Remove loaves from pans. Brush tops with butter.

Clarice Lux, South Parkersburg Woman's Club,
Parkersburg, W. Va.

MILWAUKEE RYE BREAD

Makes 2 Loaves

6 cups sifted rye flour
2 cups presifted flour
¾ cup white or yellow corn meal
1½ cups cold water
1½ cups boiling water
4 teaspoons salt
1 tablespoon sugar
½ tablespoon shortening
2 teaspoons caraway seeds (optional)
1 envelope active dry yeast
¼ cup lukewarm water
2 cups mashed potatoes
1 tablespoon corn meal

1. Combine rye and presifted flours.
2. Put ¾ cup corn meal in saucepan. Gradually stir in cold water, keeping mixture smooth. Stir in boiling water. Bring to boil. Simmer for 2 minutes, stirring constantly.
3. Add salt, sugar, shortening and caraway seeds to corn meal mixture; mix; let stand until lukewarm.

4. Soften yeast in lukewarm water for 10 minutes. Add to corn meal mixture. Add potatoes. Stir in flour mixture to make a firm dough.

5. Turn onto lightly floured board; cover with bowl; let stand for 10 minutes. Then knead dough for about 10 minutes, or until smooth and elastic.

6. Place dough in lightly greased bowl; grease surface; cover; let rise for about 1½ hours, or until doubled in bulk.

7. Punch dough down. Turn onto lightly floured board. Cut in half; round up each half; cover with bowls; let stand for 10 minutes.

8. Grease baking sheet.

9. Shape each half of dough into loaf about 14 inches long. Place loaves on baking sheet; sprinkle with 1 tablespoon corn meal; cover; let rise for about 1 hour, or until doubled in bulk.

10. Preheat oven to 375° F.

11. Bake in preheated oven for 50 to 60 minutes.

Mrs. Clyde Connors, Study Club,
Balsam Lake, Wis.

SWEDISH LIMPA (Rye Bread)
Makes 6 Loaves

2 envelopes active dry yeast
½ cup warm water
1 teaspoon granulated sugar
3 tablespoons shortening
⅔ cup brown sugar
2 teaspoons salt
½ cup molasses
2 cups cold water
1 teaspoon baking soda
4 cups buttermilk
6 cups rye flour
6 cups presifted flour

1. Soften yeast in warm water with granulated sugar.

2. In saucepan combine shortening, brown sugar, salt, molasses and cold water. Bring to boil, stirring until shortening is dissolved. Turn into large mixing bowl.

3. Stir baking soda into buttermilk. Stir into hot liquid.

4. Add rye flour. Mix well. Cool to lukewarm.

5. Stir in yeast. Work in enough presifted flour to make a dough that does not stick to hands. Knead thoroughly.

6. Place dough in greased bowl; cover; let rise for about 2 hours, or until doubled in bulk.

7. Turn onto lightly floured board. Knead and shape into loaves.

8. Grease 6 loaf pans.

9. Place loaves in pans; cover; let rise for 1 hour, or until almost doubled in bulk.

10. Preheat oven to 350° F.

11. Bake in preheated oven for 1 hour.

VARIATION: ¼ cup caraway seeds or aniseed or grated lemon rind may be added along with rye flour.

Mrs. Lillian Edwards, Merry Aces, Loretta, Wis.

SHREDDED WHEAT BREAD
Makes 3 Loaves

4 shredded wheat biscuits
2 cups boiling water
3 cups milk, scalded
½ cup molasses
½ cup brown sugar
2 tablespoons salt
2 envelopes active dry yeast
½ cup lukewarm water
½ cup melted shortening
6 to 8 cups presifted flour

1. Grease 3 9½-inch loaf pans.

2. In mixing bowl soak shredded wheat in boiling water for 1 hour.

3. Put milk in another mixing bowl. Stir in molasses, sugar and salt. Cool to lukewarm.

4. In small bowl soften yeast in lukewarm water. Stir until dissolved.

5. Stir shredded wheat, yeast, and shortening into milk mixture.

6. Add 1 cup flour at a time to mixture, blending well to make soft dough.

7. Turn onto lightly floured board. Knead until smooth.

8. Place dough in greased bowl; cover; let rise until doubled in bulk.

9. Cut dough into thirds. Shape into loaves.

10. Put loaves in pans; cover; let rise until doubled in bulk.

11. Preheat oven to 375° F.

12. Bake in preheated oven for 40 to 45 minutes.

Iris L. Cushing, President, Hancock County
Republican Woman's Club, Bucksport, Me.

WHOLE WHEAT BREAD
Makes 2 Loaves

4 cups warm milk
1 cup brown sugar
1 tablespoon salt
4 tablespoons shortening
2 envelopes active dry yeast
½ cup warm water
4 cups presifted flour
8 cups whole wheat flour

1. In mixing bowl combine milk, sugar, salt and shortening.

2. Soften yeast in water for 10 minutes. Then stir into milk mixture.

3. Stir in flours to make dough that does not stick to hands.

4. Turn onto lightly floured board. Knead until smooth and elastic.

5. Place dough in greased bowl; grease top of dough; cover; let rise for about 2 hours, or until doubled in bulk.

6. Punch dough down; cover; let rise again for about 1½ hours, or until doubled in bulk.

7. Grease baking sheet.

8. Cut dough in half. Shape into 2 loaves.

9. Place on baking sheet; cover; let rise until doubled in bulk.

10. Preheat oven to 400° F.

11. Bake in preheated oven for 50 to 60 minutes.

Mrs. Lloyd Anderson, Study Club,
Balsam Lake, Wis.

CASEROLE BREAD
Makes 2 Loaves

1 envelope active dry yeast
1 cup warm water
4 cups presifted flour or sifted
  unbleached flour
1 tablespoon sugar
2 teaspoons salt
¼ to ½ cup cold water
  Melted butter

1. Soften yeast in warm water.
2. Put flour in mixing bowl. Mix with sugar and salt. Add yeast mixture. Blend. Add enough cold water to make soft dough. Cover; let rise for 2 hours, or until doubled in bulk.
3. Generously grease 2 1-quart round glass casseroles.
4. Punch dough down. Divide in half. Put in casseroles; cover; let rise again for about 1 hour, or until doubled in bulk.
5. Preheat oven to 400° F.
6. Bake in preheated oven for 40 minutes. Remove loaves from casseroles while hot. Brush crusts with butter.

Ginnie Swope, Suburban Newark Women's Club,
Newark, Del.

ONION CASEROLE BREAD
Makes 1 Loaf

1 cup milk, scalded
3 tablespoons sugar
1½ tablespoons butter
2 envelopes active dry yeast
¾ cup warm water
1 envelope onion soup mix
4 cups presifted flour

1. In mixing bowl combine milk, sugar and butter. Cool to lukewarm.
2. Add yeast to water. Stir until dissolved.
3. Add to milk mixture.
4. Stir in onion soup mix and flour to make a soft dough. Stir and blend for about 2 minutes. Cover; let rise for about 45 minutes, or until doubled in bulk.
5. Grease 1½-quart casserole.
6. Stir dough down. Beat vigorously for ½ minute.
7. Turn into casserole; cover; let rise until doubled in bulk.
8. Preheat oven to 375° F.
9. Bake in preheated oven for 1 hour.

Mrs. Ethel Nunn, Fortnightly Club,
Dawson, N.D.

SESAME EGG BRAIDS
Makes 2 Loaves

½ cup warm water
2 envelopes active dry yeast
1½ cups milk, scalded and cooled
¼ cup sugar
⅓ cup softened butter
1 teaspoon salt
3 eggs, lightly beaten

7 to 7½ cups presifted flour
  Cooking oil or soft shortening
1 egg yolk
1 tablespoon water
2 tablespoons sesame seeds

1. Put warm water in large mixing bowl. Sprinkle in yeast. Stir until thoroughly dissolved.
2. Add milk, sugar, butter, salt and eggs.
3. Beat in about 4 cups flour. Then work in enough remaining flour to make dough that is easy to handle.
4. Turn onto lightly floured board. Knead for about 5 minutes, or until smooth and elastic.
5. Place in greased bowl. Brush top with oil or shortening. Cover with damp cloth; let rise for about 1½ hours, or until doubled in bulk.
6. Punch dough down; cover; let rise again for about 30 minutes, or until almost doubled in bulk.
7. Grease baking sheet.
8. Turn dough onto lightly floured board. Knead down. Divide in half. Cut each half into 3 equal pices. Roll each piece into strip about 15 inches long. Place 3 strips on baking sheet. Braid, fastening strips securely at both ends.
9. Repeat with second half of dough.
10. Cover; let rise for about 1 hour, or until doubled in bulk.
11. Preheat oven to 385° F.
12. Mix egg yolk and water. Brush top and sides of braids. Sprinkle with sesame seeds.
13. Bake in preheated oven for 30 to 35 minutes.

Lou Wright, Gentilly Woods Woman's Club,
New Orleans, La.

HERB BREAD
Makes 2 Loaves

2 cups milk
¼ cup sugar
¾ teaspoon salt
1 envelope active dry yeast
2 eggs, well beaten
1 teaspoon nutmeg
2 teaspoons crumbled sage leaves
4 teaspoons caraway seeds
7½ to 8 cups presifted flour
¼ cup melted butter

1. Scald milk. Stir in sugar and salt. Cool to lukewarm.
2. Add yeast. Stir until thoroughly dissolved.
3. Add eggs, nutmeg, sage, caraway seeds and 4 cups of the flour. Beat until smooth.
4. Add butter and enough remaining flour to make a soft dough that is easy to handle.
5. Turn onto lightly floured board. Knead until smooth and elastic.
6. Place dough in greased bowl; cover; let rise for about 2 hours, or until doubled in bulk.
7. Grease 2 loaf pans.

8. Punch dough down. Divide in half. Shape each half into loaf.

9. Place loaves in pans; cover; let rise for about 1 hour, or until doubled in bulk.

10. Preheat oven to 425° F.

11. Bake in preheated oven for 15 minutes. Reduce temperature to 375° F. Bake for 35 minutes longer.

Mrs. E. A. Doolan, Woman's Club, Lombard, Ill.

IRISH MOLLY BREAD

Makes 3 Loaves

2 cups mashed potatoes
2 cups boiling water
2 envelopes active dry yeast
½ cup warm water
    Sugar
¼ cup shortening
2 tablespoons salt
    About 8 cups presifted flour
    Melted shortening

1. Combine potatoes and boiling water. Mix until smooth. Cool to lukewarm.

2. Soften yeast in warm water with 1 teaspoon sugar for 10 minutes.

3. Beat ¼ cup sugar, ¼ cup shortening and salt into potato mixture. Gradually add about 4 cups of the flour. Beat thoroughly.

4. Stir in yeast.

5. Work in enough remaining flour to make dough that does not stick to hands.

6. Turn onto lightly floured board. Knead until smooth and elastic.

7. Cover; let rise for about 2 hours, or until doubled in bulk.

8. Punch dough down; cover; let rise again for about 1½ hours, or until doubled in bulk.

9. Grease baking sheet.

10. Shape dough into 3 loaves. Place on baking sheet; cover; let rise for about 1 hour, or until doubled in bulk.

11. Preheat oven to 375° F.

12. Brush loaves with melted shortening. Bake in preheated oven for 45 minutes. Remove bread from oven. Again brush with shortening.

Betty Dernell, Study Club, Balsam Lake, Wis.

PINEAPPLE BREAD

Makes 4 Loaves

4 cups presifted flour
3 tablespoons sugar
1 teaspoon salt
1 cup shortening
1 envelope active dry yeast
¼ cup warm water
1 cup milk, scalded and cooled
4 egg yolks, beaten
    Drained crushed pineapple

1. In mixing bowl combine dry ingredients. Cut in shortening.

2. Soften yeast in water for 5 minutes.

3. Combine yeast, milk and egg yolks. Add to dry ingredients. Mix to a soft dough.

4. Turn onto lightly floured board. Knead until smooth and satiny. Chill for 1 hour.

5. Divide dough into quarters. Roll out each quarter to ¼-inch-thick rectangle. Spread surface of each rectangle with pineapple. For each loaf, fold one-third of dough over onto itself; then fold over remaining third.

6. Grease 2 baking sheets.

7. Place loaves on baking sheets; cover; let rise until doubled in bulk.

8. Preheat oven to 350° F.

9. Bake in preheated oven for about 30 minutes.

Roberta Berthiaume, Junior Woman's Club, Port Washington, Wis.

RAISIN BREAD

Makes 2 Loaves

1 cup warm water
1 cup warm milk
1 envelope active dry yeast
¾ cup sugar
½ cup butter or margarine
4 eggs
6 to 7 cups presifted flour
1 cup seedless raisins
    Cinnamon to taste
    Confectioners' Sugar Icing (p. 622)

1. In large mixing bowl combine water, milk, yeast, sugar, butter or margarine and eggs. Cover; let stand until foamy.

2. Add 3 cups of the flour. Beat well.

3. Shake raisins in a bag with ½ cup of the flour. Add along with cinnamon to dough. Beat until smooth and elastic.

4. Add enough remaining flour to make a dough that is easy to handle.

5. Turn onto lightly floured board. Knead well, adding flour as needed to make a slightly sticky but easily shaped dough.

6. Put in greased bowl; cover; let rise for 2 hours, or until doubled in bulk.

7. Punch dough down. Cover; let rise again for 1 hour.

8. Grease 2 loaf pans.

9. Divide dough in half. Shape each half into loaf.

10. Place in pans; cover; let rise for 1 hour, or until doubled in bulk.

11. Preheat oven to 375° F.

12. Bake in preheated oven for 1 hour. When cool, frost with Confectioners' Sugar Icing.

Mrs. John W. Thompson, Women's Club, Ashland, Mass.

Coffee Cakes

There are two types of coffee cakes: those made with yeast, and those made with baking powder or baking soda. The ones in this section are raised with yeast and made in the same way as yeast bread.

They are sweet loaves, often enriched with large quantities of eggs or egg yolks, and frequently include spices, fruits and nuts.

For the cake type of coffee cake, see Chapter 19.

BUBBLE LOAF

Makes 1 Loaf

1 cup milk
½ cup cooking oil
1½ cups sugar
1 teaspoon salt
2 yeast cakes or 2 envelopes active dry yeast
2 eggs, lightly beaten
4½ cups presifted flour
½ cup butter
1 tablespoon cinnamon
½ cup chopped nuts
1 cup seedless raisins

1. Scald milk. Remove from heat. Add oil, ½ cup of the sugar and salt. Cool to lukewarm.

2. Add yeast to lukewarm milk. Stir until well blended.

3. Add eggs. Beat in enough flour to make a soft dough.

4. Turn onto lightly floured board. Knead until smooth and elastic. Place in greased bowl; cover with damp cloth; let rise for 1½ hours, or until doubled in bulk.

5. Punch dough down. Let stand for 10 minutes.

6. Melt butter in small saucepan.

7. In small bowl combine remaining sugar, cinnamon, nuts and raisins.

8. Form dough into small balls about the size of walnuts or smaller. Roll each ball in butter, then in sugar-nut mixture.

9. Grease angel cake tube pan.

10. Arrange balls in layers in pan, staggering rows, until all dough is used.

11. Cover; let rise for about 1 hour, or until doubled in bulk.

12. Preheat oven to 350° F.

13. Bake in preheated oven for 45 minutes. Turn onto board or wire rack to cool.

Olive May, Every Other Friday Club, Jesup, Ia.

COFFEE KRINGLE

Makes 1 Cake

¼ cup milk
2 cups presifted flour
¼ cup sugar
½ teaspoon salt
¼ cup margarine
½ cup warm water
2 envelopes active dry yeast
1 egg, lightly beaten
1½ cups chopped stewed prunes
3 tablespoons sugar
3 tablespoons lemon juice
½ teaspoon grated lemon rind
Confectioners' Sugar Icing (p. 622)

1. Scald milk; cool to lukewarm.

2. In mixing bowl combine flour, ¼ cup sugar and salt. Cut margarine in well.

3. Put water in warm large bowl. Sprinkle in yeast; stir until dissolved. Stir in milk, egg and flour mixture.

4. Put dough in greased bowl; turn to grease all surfaces; cover; let rise for 1 hour, or until doubled in bulk.

5. Meanwhile, combine prunes, 3 tablespoons sugar, lemon juice and rind.

6. Grease 15½ x 10½ x 1-inch jelly roll pan.

7. Punch dough down. Turn onto well-floured board. Divide in half. Roll out each half into rectangle about 16 x 12 inches. Place one rectangle in pan. Spread with prune mixture. Cover with second rectangle of dough. Seal edges well.

8. Cover; let rise for about ½ hour, or until doubled in bulk.

9. Preheat oven to 350° F.

10. Bake in preheated oven for 20 minutes. Remove from oven. Turn out of pan immediately. When cool, frost with Confectioners' Sugar Icing.

Mrs. Clark Tousely, Woman's Club, Scobey, Mont.

DANISH COFFEE CAKE

Makes 2 Cakes

4 cups presifted flour
5 tablespoons sugar
1 teaspoon salt
1 cup butter
1 envelope active dry yeast
1 cup cold milk
3 eggs, separated
½ teaspoon cinnamon
½ cup chopped nuts
Confectioners' Sugar Icing (p. 622)

1. In mixing bowl combine flour, 2 tablespoons of the sugar and salt.

2. Cut in butter until mixture resembles crumbs.

3. Soften yeast in milk.

4. Beat egg yolks. Stir into milk mixture. Add to flour mixture. Mix well. Refrigerate for several hours or overnight.

5. Cut dough in half. Turn onto lightly floured board. Roll out each half to thin rectangle.

6. Preheat oven to 375° F. Grease baking sheet.

7. Beat egg whites until stiff but not dry. Gradually beat in remaining sugar. Continue to beat until meringue is glossy. Stir in cinnamon and nuts.

8. Spread meringue over dough. Roll up each rectangle lengthwise like a jelly roll. Shape each into crescent. Place on baking sheet.

9. Bake in preheated oven for 30 to 35 minutes. While hot, spread with Confectioners' Sugar Icing.

Mrs. Robert Meyer, Woman's Club, Altoona, Ill.

OVERNIGHT GERMAN REFRIGERATOR COFFEE KUCHEN
Makes 1 Kuchen

3 cups presifted flour
1 teaspoon salt
1 teaspoon mace or nutmeg
¼ pound butter
3 egg yolks
3 tablespoons granulated sugar
1 cup heavy cream
1 envelope active dry yeast
¼ cup warm milk
¼ cup melted butter
4 to 6 apples, peeled and chopped
½ cup seedless raisins
¼ cup chopped nuts
   Brown sugar
   Cinnamon
   Confectioners' Sugar Icing (p. 622)
   Nuts for garnish

1. Day before, in mixing bowl combine flour, salt and mace or nutmeg. Cut in butter until mixture resembles coarse crumbs.
2. Beat together egg yolks and granulated sugar. Add to flour mixture.
3. Stir in cream.
4. Soften yeast in milk for 5 minutes. Add to dough. Mix well.
5. Refrigerate in covered greased bowl overnight.
6. Next day, roll out on lightly floured board into large rectangle.
7. Brush surface with butter. Sprinkle with apples, raisins and nuts. Sprinkle with brown sugar and cinnamon to taste. Roll up like a jelly roll. Place on greased baking sheet.
8. Cover; let rise for about 2 hours, or until doubled in bulk.
9. Preheat oven to 350° F.
10. Bake in preheated oven for 30 to 40 minutes. When cool, frost with Confectioners' Sugar Icing. Decorate with nuts.

Mrs. William Sommerfeldt, Sr., Study Club, Balsam Lake, Wis.

KUGELHOPF
Makes 1 Loaf

½ cup sugar
½ teaspoon salt
¼ cup butter
½ cup hot milk
1 envelope active dry yeast
½ cup warm water
2 eggs, beaten
2½ cups presifted flour
   Fine bread crumbs
14 or 15 blanched almonds
½ cup seedless raisins
1 teaspoon grated lemon rind

1. In mixing bowl combine sugar, salt, butter and milk. Cool to lukewarm.
2. Soften yeast in water. Add to milk mixture.

3. Add eggs and flour. Beat well. Cover; let rise for about 1½ hours, or until doubled in bulk.
4. Generously grease 1½-quart casserole or fancy mold. Sprinkle with crumbs. Arrange almonds attractively in bottom.
5. Stir dough down. Beat in raisins and lemon rind.
6. Turn into casserole or mold; cover; let rise for 1 hour.
7. Preheat oven to 350° F.
8. Bake in preheated oven for 50 minutes.

Mrs. Keith Kuehn, Merry Aces, Loretta, Wis.

POTECA (Polish Coffee Bread)
Makes 1 Loaf

1 envelope active dry yeast
¼ cup warm water
¾ cup lukewarm milk
¼ cup granulated sugar
1 teaspoon salt
2 eggs
¼ cup soft shortening
3½ to 3¾ cups presifted flour
¼ cup softened butter
½ cup brown sugar
¼ cup cold milk
½ teaspoon vanilla
½ teaspoon lemon extract
2 cups finely ground walnuts

1. In mixing bowl soften yeast in water. Stir in lukewarm milk, granulated sugar, salt, 1 of the eggs and shortening.
2. Mix in flour until dough is soft but does not stick to fingers.
3. Turn onto lightly floured board. Let stand for 10 minutes. Then knead until smooth and elastic.
4. Form dough into a ball; put in greased bowl; turn in bowl to bring greased side up. Cover with damp cloth; let rise for about 2 hours, or until doubled in bulk.
5. Punch dough down; turn onto lightly floured board; cover; let stand for 15 minutes.
6. Meanwhile, make filling: Combine butter, brown sugar and remaining egg; mix well. Stir in cold milk, vanilla and lemon extract. Stir in walnuts.
7. Grease baking sheet.
8. Roll out dough almost paper-thin into rectangle 20 x 30 inches. Spread filling on dough.
9. Starting at wide side of rectangle, lift cloth; roll up dough like a jelly roll. Pinch edge of roll into dough to seal.
10. Place on baking sheet. Form into snail shape. Cover; let rise for about 1 hour, or until deep impression remains when finger is pressed lightly into dough.
11. Preheat oven to 375° F.
12. Bake in preheated oven for 30 to 35 minutes, or until lightly browned.

Mrs. Robert Bicknell, Junior Women's Club, Nashua, N.H.

SAFFRON CROWN
Makes 2 Crowns

¾ cup milk
¼ cup margarine
½ cup granulated sugar
¼ teaspoon salt
Pinch of crushed saffron
1 envelope active dry yeast
¼ cup warm water
2 eggs, lightly beaten
4½ cups presifted flour
1 teaspoon grated lemon rind
Chopped candied pineapple and cherries (optional)
Soft shortening
3 tablespoons confectioners' sugar
½ teaspoon cold water
Red and green candied cherries

1. In small saucepan heat milk, margarine, granulated sugar and salt until milk is hot and margarine is melted. Stir in saffron. Cool to lukewarm.
2. In large bowl soften yeast in warm water.
3. Stir in milk mixture and eggs.
4. Stir in half the flour. Beat until smooth.
5. Stir in remaining flour, lemon rind and candied pineapple and cherries, if desired, mixing until dough forms a soft ball that leaves sides of bowl.
6. Turn onto lightly floured board. Knead until smooth and elastic, adding a little flour, if necessary, to keep dough from sticking. Return to bowl. Brush top with shortening. Cover; let rise for about 1 hour, or until doubled in bulk.
7. Grease baking sheet.
8. Punch dough down. Turn onto lightly floured board. Divide in half; then divide each half into thirds. Shape each third into roll about 25 inches long. Braid 3 rolls together, sealing ends. Place each braid on baking sheet; form into circle, pinching ends to seal. Cover; let rise for 45 minutes, or until doubled in bulk.
9. Preheat oven to 375° F.
10. Bake in preheated oven for 30 to 35 minutes. Cool on wire rack.
11. Combine confectioners' sugar and cold water to make a soft icing. Spread icing on crowns. Decorate with bits of cherries, held in place with icing.

Irene Leavelle, Suburban Women's Club,
Newark, Del.

SWEDISH COFFEE BRAIDS
Makes 2 Braids

1 cup milk
½ cup granulated sugar
½ teaspoon salt
1½ teaspoons ground or crushed cardamom seeds
2 envelopes active dry yeast
¼ cup warm water
3½ to 4¼ cups presifted flour
⅓ cup softened butter
1 egg, lightly beaten
⅓ cup chopped blanched almonds
⅓ cup crushed loaf sugar

1. Scald milk; add to granulated sugar, salt and cardamom seeds in large mixing bowl. Cool to lukewarm.
2. Soften yeast in water. Add to milk mixture. Stir in half the flour. Beat until smooth.
3. Stir in butter, then enough remaining flour to make a soft dough.
4. Turn onto lightly floured board. Knead until smooth and elastic. Put in greased bowl; cover; let rise for 50 to 60 minutes, or until impression remains when finger is pressed deep into side of dough.
5. Punch dough down. Let rise again for 15 minutes.
6. Grease baking sheet or 2 round baking pans.
7. Turn dough onto lightly floured board. Divide in half, then divide each half into thirds. Roll each third into rope-like strip about 1 inch in diameter and 12 inches long. Place 3 strips 1 inch apart; braid, beginning in middle and working toward each end; seal ends well. Repeat with remaining strips. Arrange on baking sheet, or curve in baking pans. Cover; let rise for 30 minutes.
8. Preheat oven to 350° F.
9. Brush braids with egg. Sprinkle with almonds and loaf sugar.
10. Bake in preheated oven for 25 to 30 minutes.

Mrs. Gerrit J. Van Westenbrugge, Women's Club,
Ashland, Mass.

SWEETHEART COFFEE CAKE
Makes 2 Large Cakes

2 envelopes active dry yeast
½ cup lukewarm water
⅓ cup butter or shortening
1⅓ cups sugar
2 teaspoons salt
⅔ cup milk, scalded
2 eggs
4½ to 5 cups presifted flour
1 cup chopped nuts
2 teaspoons cinnamon
¼ cup melted butter
Confectioners' Sugar Icing (p. 622)

1. Soften yeast in water.
2. In mixing bowl combine butter or shortening, ⅓ cup of the sugar, salt and milk. Stir until butter or shortening is melted. Cool to lukewarm.
3. Stir in eggs and yeast.
4. Gradually stir in enough flour to make a stiff dough. Turn onto lightly floured board. Knead until smooth and satiny. Place in greased bowl; cover; let rise for about 1½ hours, or until doubled in bulk.
5. Combine nuts, remaining sugar and cinnamon.
6. Grease baking sheet.
7. Punch dough down. Divide in half. Roll out each half on lightly floured board into rectangle 15 x 10 inches. Brush each rectangle with melted butter; sprinkle with half the nuts mixture.

8. Roll each rectangle lengthwise like a jelly roll. Place on baking sheet. Fold half of each roll on top of other half. Seal ends.

9. Starting at folded end, cut with scissors or knife down center of roll to within 1 inch of other end; turn cut pieces of dough flat on side, cut side up, to form a heart. Repeat with remaining dough. Cover; let rise for about 45 minutes.

10. Preheat oven to 350° F.

11. Bake in preheated oven for 25 to 30 minutes. While still hot, drizzle with Confectioners' Sugar Icing.

Mrs. Marie Brown, Woman's Club, Altoona, Wis.

Rolls and Biscuits

Yeast breads may be shaped into a great variety of small breads. Make the yeast bread dough, and let it rise according to recipe directions. Roll, cut and shape according to recipe directions or as outlined below. Arrange rolls in greased pan or on greased baking sheet. For crusty rolls, leave 2 inches between each roll; for soft-sided rolls, place close together. Brush with butter, cover and let rise until doubled in bulk. Bake basic bread rolls in a preheated 425° F. oven for 12 to 20 minutes, depending on size or according to recipe directions.

HOW TO SHAPE ROLLS AND BISCUITS

CLOVERLEAF ROLLS: Shape pieces of dough into 1-inch balls. Place three balls close together in greased muffin cups.

PARKER HOUSE ROLLS: Roll out dough ¼ inch thick. Cut with floured round biscuit cutter. Let dough stand for 10 minutes; then score just off center with floured back of knife. Brush with melted butter. Fold in half along score line.

STICKS: Shape pieces of dough into thin sticks.

BOWKNOTS AND TWISTS: Tie sticks loosely into knots, or twist.

FANTANS: Roll out dough ¼ inch thick. Cut into regular strips. Spread with melted butter. Stack 4 or 5 strips evenly into a pile. Slice across stack at intervals of about 1 inch.

PINWHEELS: Roll out dough thinly; brush with melted butter. Roll up like a jelly roll. Slice across roll at ¾- to 1-inch intervals.

CRESCENTS: Roll out dough into 12-inch circles about ¼ inch thick or less. Cut each circle into 12 pie-shaped wedges. Roll each wedge, beginning with outer edge. Place on greased baking sheet. Bend ends to form crescents.

BISCUITS: Roll out dough ⅓ to ½ inch thick. Cut with floured plain or fluted biscuit cutter.

CLOVERLEAF ROLLS

Makes 24

1 envelope active dry yeast
¼ cup lukewarm water
¼ cup shortening
1 teaspoon salt
2 tablespoons sugar
1 cup boiling water
2 eggs, beaten
3½ cups presifted flour
2 tablespoons melted butter

1. Soften yeast in lukewarm water. Grease muffin cups.

2. Add shortening, salt and sugar to boiling water in mixing bowl. Cool to lukewarm.

3. Stir in yeast and eggs. Stir in enough flour to make soft dough that does not stick to hands. Turn onto lightly floured board; knead until smooth.

4. Put dough in greased bowl; cover; refrigerate for 2 hours or overnight.

5. Pinch off small portions of dough. Form into balls. Arrange 3 balls in each muffin cup.

6. Brush tops of balls with butter. Cover; let rise for 2 hours.

7. Preheat oven to 400° F.

8. Bake in preheated oven for 15 to 20 minutes.

Mrs. Grace Woodington, Woman's Club, Altoona, Wis.

PARKER HOUSE ROLLS

Makes 24

1 cup milk, scalded
2 tablespoons shortening
2 tablespoons sugar
1 teaspoon salt
1 envelope active dry yeast
¼ cup lukewarm water
1 egg, well beaten
3½ cups presifted flour
Melted shortening

1. In mixing bowl combine milk, 2 tablespoons shortening, sugar and salt. Stir until shortening is melted. Cool to lukewarm.

2. Soften yeast in water. Add to milk mixture. Add egg. Gradually stir in flour to make a soft dough. Beat vigorously. Cover; let rise for about 2 hours, or until doubled in bulk.

3. Punch dough down. Roll out ¼ inch thick on lightly floured board. Cut into rounds with floured biscuit cutter.

4. Brush each round with melted shortening. Make crease with back of knife across each round, just off center. Fold smaller half over larger half. Pinch ends together.

5. Grease baking sheet. Arrange rolls close together on sheet. Brush with more melted shortening. Cover; let rise for about 1 hour, or until doubled in bulk.

6. Preheat oven to 400° F.

7. Bake in preheated oven for about 15 minutes, or until lightly browned.

Mrs. Grace Hulbert, Junior Woman's Club, Port Washington, Wis.

LOW-CALORIE PARTY ROLLS

Makes 40 (50 Calories per Roll)

¾ cup plus 2 tablespoons warm water
1 envelope active dry yeast
1 cup nonfat dry milk solids
1 tablespoon sugar
½ cup wheat germ
1 tablespoon cooking oil
1 teaspoon salt
2 eggs, lightly beaten
2¾ to 3 cups presifted flour
Melted margarine

1. Put ½ cup of the water in mixing bowl. Add yeast. Let soften for 5 minutes.
2. Add milk solids, remaining water, sugar, wheat germ, oil, salt and eggs. Beat with electric beater until smooth.
3. Stir in enough flour to make a soft dough.
4. Turn onto lightly floured board. Knead for 3 to 5 minutes.
5. Place dough in greased bowl. Brush with oil; cover with damp towel; let rise for 2 hours.
6. Grease baking sheet.
7. Punch dough down; knead briefly. Divide into 5 portions. Roll out each portion into circle about 9 inches in diameter. Cut each circle into 8 pie-shaped wedges. Roll up each wedge, starting at wide side of wedge; place on baking sheet; shape into crescent.
8. Brush crescents with margarine. Cover; let rise for 35 to 40 minutes.
9. Preheat oven to 400° F.
10. Bake in preheated oven for 10 to 15 minutes.

Jerry Winston, Junior Solitic Club, Crowley, La.

BARBECUE BUNS

Makes 20

2 cups warm water
1 envelope active dry yeast
⅓ cup nonfat dry milk solids
¼ cup sugar
1 tablespoon salt
6 to 6½ cups presifted flour
⅓ cup melted butter
Melted butter for brushing

1. Put water in mixing bowl. Sprinkle in yeast; stir until dissolved. Add milk solids, sugar, salt and 3 cups of the flour. Beat until smooth.
2. Stir in ⅓ cup butter and enough remaining flour to make a soft dough.
3. Turn onto lightly floured board. Knead until smooth and elastic.
4. Place dough in greased bowl; turn once to grease all sides; cover; let rise for about 1 hour, or until doubled in bulk.
5. Punch dough down; cover; let rise again for about 45 minutes, until doubled in bulk.
6. Grease baking sheet.
7. Divide dough in half. Cut each half into 10 portions. Shape each portion into a round ball. Place on baking sheet; cover; let rise for about 1 hour, or until doubled in bulk.

8. Preheat oven to 375° F.
9. Bake in preheated oven for about 20 minutes, or until browned. Remove from oven. Brush with melted butter.

Mrs. Dale Melstrom, Study Club,
Balsam Lake, Wis.

FRENCH PETIT DÉJEUNER ROLLS

Makes 24

2 tablespoons sugar
½ teaspoon salt
½ cup milk, scalded
1 envelope active dry yeast
2 tablespoons lukewarm water
2 cups presifted flour
2 tablespoons melted shortening
1 egg, lightly beaten
¼ cup melted butter

1. Put sugar and salt into large bowl. Add milk. Cool to lukewarm.
2. Soften yeast in water for 5 minutes. Stir into milk mixture.
3. Add ¾ cup of the flour. Beat well. Cover; let rise for about 1 hour, or until foamy.
4. Stir in shortening and egg. Work in enough remaining flour to make a light dough that does not stick to hands.
5. Turn onto lightly floured board. Knead lightly. Cover; let rise for about 1 hour, or until doubled in bulk.
6. Punch dough down. Pinch off tiny rounds. Form into rolls. Roll in butter. Arrange about 1 inch apart in baking pan. Cover; let rise for 30 minutes, or until doubled in bulk.
7. Preheat oven to 400° F.
8. Bake in preheated oven for 20 minutes, or until browned.

POPPY SEED ROLLS: Follow recipe above, but do not roll in butter. Let rise. Just before baking, beat 1 egg yolk with 2 tablespoons water; use to brush rolls. Sprinkle with poppy seeds.

Mrs. F. A. Shippey, Thursday Morning Club,
Madison, N.J.

ITALIAN BREAD STICKS

Makes 48

1 envelope active dry yeast
⅔ cup warm water
2 tablespoons cooking oil
2 tablespoons olive oil
1 teaspoon salt
1 tablespoon sugar
About 2¼ cups presifted flour
1 egg, lightly beaten
Poppy or sesame seeds

1. Soften yeast in water. Add oils, salt, sugar and 1 cup of the flour. Beat until smooth. Work in enough remaining flour to make stiff dough.
2. Turn onto lightly floured board. Knead for about 5 minutes, or until smooth. Shape into ball. Place in greased bowl; cover; let rise for about 1 hour, or until doubled in bulk.
3. Grease baking sheet.
4. Punch dough down. Divide in half. Cut each half into 24 pieces. Roll each

piece into pencil-thick strip from 6 to 8 inches long. Place strips about ½ inch apart in parallel rows on baking sheet. Brush with egg. Sprinkle with seeds. Let rise, uncovered, until nearly doubled in bulk.

5. Preheat oven to 325° F.

6. Bake in preheated oven for 30 minutes. Cool thoroughly before storing.

Almira Littleford, Woman's Club,
West Concord, N.H.

BUTTERMILK ROLLS

Makes 24

    1 envelope active dry yeast
    ¼ cup warm water
    1½ cups lukewarm buttermilk
    3 tablespoons sugar
    ½ cup melted shortening
    4½ cups presifted flour
    ½ teaspoon baking soda
    1 teaspoon salt

1. In mixing bowl soften yeast in water.

2. Add buttermilk, sugar and shortening.

3. Into another mixing bowl sift together dry ingredients. Stir into buttermilk mixture.

4. Beat until smooth. Let stand for 10 minutes.

5. Grease baking sheet.

6. Roll out dough. Shape into rolls; arrange on baking sheet. Cover; let rise for about 30 minutes.

7. Preheat oven to 400° F.

8. Bake in preheated oven for 15 to 20 minutes.

Mrs. E. T. Lee, Woman's Club, Marion, Ala.

BATTER ROLLS

Makes 12

    ¾ cup milk
    ¼ cup sugar
    1 teaspoon salt
    ¼ cup margarine
    ½ cup warm water
    2 envelopes active dry yeast
    1 egg, lightly beaten
    3½ cups presifted flour

1. Scald milk. Stir in sugar, salt and margarine. Cool to lukewarm.

2. Put water in mixing bowl; add yeast; stir until softened.

3. Stir in lukewarm milk mixture, egg and 2 cups of the flour. Beat until smooth. Stir in enough remaining flour to make a soft dough. Cover; let rise for about 30 minutes, or until doubled in bulk.

4. Grease baking sheet.

5. Punch dough down. Shape into rolls. Place on baking sheet; cover; let rise for about 30 minutes, or until doubled in bulk.

6. Preheat oven to 400° F.

7. Bake in preheated oven for about 15 minutes.

Mrs. Shirley Frazier, Veritas Club,
Greenboro, Ala.

HALF-TIME SPOON ROLLS

Makes 12

    1 envelope active dry yeast
    ¼ cup lukewarm water
    ⅓ cup shortening
    1 teaspoon salt
    ¾ cup milk, scalded
    ½ cup cold water
    2 eggs or egg whites
    3½ cups presifted flour

1. Soften yeast in lukewarm water.

2. In mixing bowl combine shortening, salt and milk.

3. Cool to lukewarm by adding cold water. Beat in eggs or egg whites and yeast.

4. Stir in flour. Mix until well blended. Turn dough into greased bowl. Cover; let stand until doubled in bulk.

5. Grease muffin cups well.

6. Stir dough down. Spoon into cups, filling them half full. Let rise until dough reaches edge of cups.

7. Preheat oven to 400° F.

8. Bake in preheated oven for 15 to 20 minutes.

Thelma Stevens, Woman's Club, Lavalette, W. Va.

BRIOCHES

Makes 16

    1 envelope active dry yeast
    ¼ cup lukewarm water
    3 cups presifted flour
    4 eggs
    1 teaspoon salt
    1 tablespoon sugar
    1 cup butter

1. Day before, in small bowl add yeast to water. Let stand for 5 minutes. Then stir until dissolved.

2. Stir in ½ cup of the flour. Mix to a ball. Place in small bowl. Cover with lukewarm water.

3. Cover with clean towel. Let stand for 1 hour, or until ball floats.

4. Meanwhile, put remaining flour in mixing bowl. Beat in 3 of the eggs, salt and sugar. Add butter. Beat until smooth.

5. Remove yeast ball from water; add to flour mixture; blend well.

6. Cover; let stand for 3 to 4 hours, or until doubled in bulk.

7. Knead on lightly floured board. Return to clean bowl. Cover; let stand in cool place overnight.

8. Next day, preheat oven to 450° F. Grease baking sheet.

9. Turn dough onto lightly floured board. Cut into 16 pieces. Cut off about ¼ of each piece; roll each into a smooth ball; set aside as topknots.

10. Shape each remaining piece of dough to a smooth ball; place about 2 inches apart on baking sheet.

11. With moistened finger, make indentation in top of each ball. Press a reserved topknot into indentation.

12. Cover; let rise for about 1 hour, or until doubled in bulk.

13. In small bowl beat remaining egg. Brush over brioches.

14. Bake in preheated oven for about 20 minutes.

Mrs. William Bell, Woman's Club, Morristown, N.J.

BUTTER SEMMELS

Makes About 72

For a morning kaffeeklatsch, sprinkle baked semmels generously with confectioners' sugar, and serve piping hot; for luncheon or dinner, top with sesame or poppy seeds.

1 envelope active dry yeast
¼ cup lukewarm water
½ cup mashed potatoes
1 cup sugar
½ cup butter or margarine
1½ teaspoons salt
2 cups milk, scalded
8 to 8½ cups presifted flour
2 eggs, lightly beaten
Melted butter
Sesame or poppy seeds (optional)

1. In mixing bowl soften yeast in water. Let stand for 5 minutes. Then stir until dissolved.

2. Stir in potatoes and ½ cup of the sugar. Mix well. Cover with towel; let stand until doubled in bulk.

3. In large mixing bowl put remaining sugar, butter or margarine and salt. Stir in milk. Cool.

4. Gradually add 1 cup of the flour. Beat until smooth.

5. Beat in eggs. Then stir in yeast mixture.

6. Gradually add enough remaining flour to form a soft dough. Turn onto lightly floured board. Knead until smooth.

7. Place dough in greased bowl; cover with towel; let rise until doubled in bulk.

8. Punch dough down. Using about ¼ of dough at a time, place on lightly floured board.

9. Grease baking sheets.

10. Form dough into desired shape:

BRAIDS: Roll portion of dough ¼ inch thick. Cut into 3 x ¾-inch-thick strips. With hands, roll and stretch each strip. Braid 3 strips together; tuck ends under; place on baking sheets.

SNAILS: Make strips as for braids. Hold one end of strip down on baking sheet. Wind strip around and around. Tuck end firmly underneath.

CRESCENTS: Roll dough into 10-inch circle ¼ inch thick. Cut into 8 pie-shaped wedges. Stretch wide end of triangle a little; roll dough toward small end. Shape into crescent. Place on baking sheets.

TWISTS: Roll dough into an oblong about ¼ inch thick. Brush surface with melted butter. Fold in half lengthwise. With sharp knife, cut crosswise into strips ¾ inch wide. Take hold of each end of strip; twist in opposite directions; seal ends firmly. Place on baking sheets.

11. Cover with towel; let rise until doubled in bulk.

12. Preheat oven to 400° F.

13. If using sesame or poppy seeds, brush with melted butter, and sprinkle with seeds.

14. Bake in preheated oven for 8 to 10 minutes, or until golden brown.

Mae Arndt, Women's Mid-Week Club, Centralia, Mo.

CROISSANTS

Makes 32

2 envelopes active dry yeast
¼ cup lukewarm water
4 cups presifted flour
½ teaspoon salt
1 tablespoon sugar
1½ cups milk
1½ cups butter
1 egg yolk, beaten with 2 tablespoons milk

1. In mixing bowl soften yeast in water. Let stand for 5 minutes. Then stir until dissolved.

2. Add about 1 cup of the flour. Mix to a smooth dough.

3. Form into ball in bowl; cover; let stand for 1 hour, or until doubled in bulk.

4. Into another mixing bowl sift together remaining flour, salt and sugar. Add milk. Work to a smooth dough. Add ball of raised dough. Knead together until smooth. Cover; let stand for 15 minutes.

5. Meanwhile, wash butter; press in cloth to remove excess moisture.

6. Turn dough onto lightly floured board. Roll out into rectangle ½ inch thick, making length of dough three times the width.

7. Spread butter on dough. Fold third of dough over center third; fold remaining third on top, making three layers.

8. Give dough a quarter turn in order to face open end. Again roll out, fold and turn dough. Refrigerate for several hours or overnight.

9. When ready to use, roll, fold and turn dough two more times.

10. Preheat oven to 400° F. Grease baking sheets.

11. Cut dough in half. Roll out each half ¼ inch thick into circle. Cut each circle into 16 triangles. Starting with broad end of triangle, roll up each like a jelly roll. Turn ends in toward each other to form crescent. Place on baking sheets; cover; let stand for 1 hour, or until doubled in bulk.

12. Brush with egg yolk mixture.

13. Bake in preheated oven for 5 minutes. Reduce temperature to 350° F. Bake for 15 minutes longer.

Mrs. F. D. Gassmere, President, Chicago Lawn Woman's Club, Chicago, Ill.

RAISED BISCUITS
Makes 24

3½ cups presifted flour
¼ teaspoon salt
4 tablespoons dry milk solids
4 teaspoons baking powder
6 tablespoons shortening
1 envelope active dry yeast
¾ cup lukewarm water
⅔ cup buttermilk

1. In mixing bowl combine dry ingredients.
2. Cut in shortening until mixture resembles coarse crumbs.
3. Soften yeast in water. Add along with buttermilk to dry ingredients. Mix with fork until dough holds together.
4. Turn onto lightly floured board. Knead for about 4 minutes.
5. Pat dough out. Cut with floured biscuit cutter.
6. Preheat oven to 375° F. Grease baking sheet.
7. Arrange biscuits on baking sheet. Let stand for about 8 minutes.
8. Bake in preheated oven for 15 minutes.

Mrs. Ersel Meriwether, Woman's Club,
Azusa, Calif.

SQUASH BISCUITS
Makes About 48

½ envelope active dry yeast
2 cups warm sieved cooked yellow squash
⅞ cup sugar
½ cup shortening
1 teaspoon baking soda
1 teaspoon salt
½ cup water
About 6 cups presifted flour

1. Day before, in mixing bowl soften yeast in squash. Beat in sugar, shortening, baking soda and salt.
2. Stir in water. Work in enough flour to make a stiff dough.
3. Turn dough onto lightly floured board. Knead until smooth.
4. Put dough in greased bowl; cover; let rise overnight.
5. Next day, punch dough down. Cut with floured biscuit cutter. Arrange on baking sheet. Cover; let rise for about 1 hour, or until doubled in bulk.
6. Preheat oven to 350° F.
7. Bake in preheated oven for 30 to 40 minutes.

Mrs. W. S. Eager, Tuesday Club, Berlin, Mass.

REFRIGERATOR ROLLS
Makes 24 Medium Rolls

1 envelope active dry yeast
2 tablespoons warm water
1 teaspoon salt
¼ cup sugar
6 tablespoons shortening
1 cup boiling water
1 egg, well beaten
3½ cups presifted flour

1. Soften yeast in warm water; cover; let stand.
2. In mixing bowl combine salt, sugar, shortening and boiling water. Cool to lukewarm.
3. Stir in yeast, egg and flour. Beat well. Refrigerate until ready to use.
4. About 1½ hours before baking, grease baking sheet.
5. Roll out dough on lightly floured board. Shape into rolls. Place on baking sheet. Cover; let rise until doubled in bulk.
6. Preheat oven to 425° F.
7. Bake in preheated oven for about 10 minutes.

Mrs. Wells Turner, Three Arts Club,
Monroeville, Ala.

REFRIGERATOR POTATO ROLLS
Makes 36

1 envelope active dry yeast
½ cup lukewarm water
1 teaspoon sugar
1 cup hot mashed potatoes
½ cup sugar
1 teaspoon salt
⅔ cup butter or shortening
2 eggs, lightly beaten
1 cup lukewarm milk
About 6½ cups presifted flour
Melted butter

1. Soften yeast in water with 1 teaspoon sugar.
2. In mixing bowl combine potatoes, ½ cup sugar, salt, butter or shortening and eggs. Beat well.
3. Beat in yeast mixture and milk.
4. Stir in enough flour to make a soft dough. Cover; let rise for about 3 hours, or until doubled in bulk.
5. Punch dough down; brush top generously with melted butter; refrigerate until ready to use.
6. About 2 hours before baking, grease muffin cups.
7. Form dough into small balls. Place in cups. Cover; let rise for 2 hours.
8. Preheat oven to 400° F.
9. Bake in preheated oven for 20 minutes.

Mrs. Lloyd Powell, Jr., Young Business Woman's
Club, Bradenburg, Ky.

SOUR CREAM CRESCENTS
Makes 48

1 cup sour cream
1½ envelopes active dry yeast
⅓ cup warm water
1 cup butter or margarine, softened
½ cup sugar
½ teaspoon salt
4 cups presifted flour
2 eggs, well beaten

1. Heat sour cream in top of double saucepan over simmering water until slightly yellow around edges (separation of cream will not affect product).
2. Meanwhile, soften yeast in water; let stand for 5 to 10 minutes.

3. Put butter or margarine, sugar and salt in large bowl. Immediately pour sour cream over them. Stir until butter or margarine is melted. Cool to lukewarm.

4. Blend 1 cup of the flour into sour cream mixture, beating until smooth. Stir yeast; add to sour cream mixture, mixing well. Add 1 cup of remaining flour; beat until smooth.

5. Thoroughly beat in eggs, then remaining flour. Cover bowl. Refrigerate for 6 hours or overnight.

6. When ready to bake, grease baking sheets.

7. Divide dough into fourths. On a lightly floured board roll each fourth into a round ¼ inch thick. Cut each round into 12 pie-shaped wedges. Roll up, beginning at wide end.

8. Place on baking sheets with points underneath. Curve into crescents. Let stand, uncovered, in warm place for about 1 hour, or until light.

9. Preheat oven to 375° F.

10. Bake in preheated oven for 15 minutes.

Mrs. John N. Nelson, Book and Thimble Club, Portland, N.D.

BASIC RICH SWEET DOUGH
Makes 36 Sweet Rolls or 3 Coffee Cakes

1½ cups milk, scalded
1 cup sugar
2 envelopes active dry yeast
About 6 cups presifted flour
4 eggs, lightly beaten
1 teaspoon salt
1 cup melted butter or margarine
Cooking oil

1. Pour milk over sugar in large bowl. Cool to lukewarm.

2. Add yeast to milk mixture; let stand for 5 minutes; then stir to blend.

3. Stir in 3 cups of the flour; mix well. Cover; let rise for about 45 minutes, or until bubbly.

4. Add eggs, salt and butter or margarine. Mix well.

5. Gradually work in enough remaining flour to make a soft dough. Cover; let rise for about 1½ hours, or until doubled in bulk.

6. Punch down; spread with oil; cover. Store until ready to use in refrigerator, where it will keep for 4 to 5 days.

Mimi Seiler, Cutler Ridge Woman's Club, Miami, Fla.

SWEET ROLLS
Makes 12 to 24

1 envelope active dry yeast
¼ cup warm water
¾ cup milk, scalded and cooled
¼ cup sugar
1 teaspoon salt
1 egg, lightly beaten
¼ cup soft shortening
3½ to 3¾ cups presifted flour

1. In mixing bowl soften yeast in water. Stir in milk, sugar, salt, egg, shortening and half the flour. Mix and beat until smooth.

2. Work in enough remaining flour to make a soft dough that does not stick to hands. Cover; let rise for 1½ hours, or until doubled in bulk. Punch dough down. Cover; let rise again for 1 hour, or until doubled in bulk.

3. Shape dough into rolls. Cover; let rise for 45 minutes, or until doubled in bulk.

4. Preheat oven to 400° F.

5. Bake in preheated oven for 12 to 15 minutes.

Connie Hill, Study Club, Balsam Lake, Wis.

LITTLE BABAS (French Yeast Cakes)
Makes 8

1 envelope active dry yeast
¼ cup lukewarm water
1½ cups presifted flour
1 tablespoon sugar
½ teaspoon salt
2 large or 3 small eggs
¼ cup milk
⅔ cup butter or margarine, softened
1 tablespoon seedless raisins
1 tablespoon currants
Apricot Sauce (see below)

1. In small bowl soften yeast in water for 5 minutes; then stir until blended.

2. In large mixing bowl combine flour, sugar and salt.

3. Stir in yeast, eggs, milk and butter or margarine. Beat until smooth.

4. Stir in raisins and currants.

5. Grease 8 baba molds or custard cups.

6. Spoon batter into molds or cups, filling them half full.

7. Let batter rise for about 1 hour, or until it is rounded over rim of molds or cups.

8. Preheat oven to 400° F.

9. Bake in preheated oven for 12 to 15 minutes.

10. Unmold babas. Drop them into saucepan of Apricot Sauce.

APRICOT SAUCE: In saucepan combine ¾ cup sugar and 1½ cups apricot juice. Bring to boil; boil rapidly for 5 minutes. Remove from heat. Stir in 2 teaspoons lemon juice.

VARIATIONS:

APRICOT RUM SAUCE: Stir ½ cup dark rum into Apricot Sauce.

FLAMING BABAS: Drop hot babas into Apricot Rum Sauce. When ready to serve, put babas and sauce in flameproof dish or chafing dish. Sprinkle with 2 tablespoons sugar. Then pour ¼ cup warm rum over all; set aflame. Serve when flame dies out.

Mrs. Frank Battista, Woman's Club, Ebensburg, Pa.

BROWN BUNS
Makes About 50
½ cup corn meal
½ cup molasses
1 teaspoon salt
½ cup oatmeal
½ cup shortening
3 teaspoons brown sugar
3 cups boiling water
2 envelopes active dry yeast
About 7 cups presifted flour

1. In mixing bowl combine corn meal, molasses, salt, oatmeal, shortening and sugar.
2. Pour water over mixture. Stir until shortening is melted. Cool to lukewarm.
3. Add yeast; stir until dissolved.
4. Gradually work in enough flour to make a soft dough. Cover; let rise for 1½ to 2 hours, or until doubled in bulk.
5. Grease baking sheets.
6. Punch dough down. Form into buns. Arrange on baking sheets. Cover; let rise for about 1 hour, or until doubled in bulk.
7. Preheat oven to 400° F.
8. Bake in preheated oven for 15 minutes.

Mrs. Elmer Melby, Study Club, Washburn, N.D.

BUTTER HORNS
Makes 48
4 cups presifted flour
½ cup sugar
½ teaspoon salt
1 cup shortening
1 envelope active dry yeast
1 cup milk, scalded and cooled
   to lukewarm
2 eggs, lightly beaten
Confectioners' Sugar Icing (p. 622)

1. Day before, put flour, sugar and salt in mixing bowl. Cut in shortening.
2. Soften yeast in milk.
3. Add yeast and eggs to dry ingredients. Mix to a soft dough.
4. Pour dough into greased casserole. Refrigerate overnight.
5. Next day, grease baking sheet.
6. Cut dough into 6 portions. Roll out each portion into a round about ¼ inch thick. Cut each round into 8 pie-shaped wedges. Roll up each wedge like a fat jelly roll. Place on baking sheet. Cover; let rise until very light and more than doubled in bulk.
7. Preheat oven to 350° F.
8. Bake in preheated oven for 15 minutes, watching carefully, since rolls burn easily.
9. Remove from oven. While warm, frost with Confectioners' Sugar Icing.

Mrs. Herbert Peters, Junior Woman's Club,
Port Washington, Wis.

QUICK CINNAMON ROLLS
Makes About 24
½ cup hot milk
3 tablespoons shortening
3 tablespoons granulated sugar
1½ teaspoons salt
1 envelope active dry yeast
½ cup warm water
1 egg, lightly beaten
3¼ cups presifted flour
   Softened butter, brown sugar
   and cinnamon

1. In mixing bowl combine milk, shortening, granulated sugar and salt.
2. Soften yeast in water. Add to milk mixture.
3. Add egg. Stir in flour to make a soft dough.
4. Turn onto lightly floured board. Knead lightly until smooth.
5. Grease 13 x 9½ x 2-inch baking pan.
6. Roll out dough into rectangle. Spread with butter; sprinkle with brown sugar and cinnamon. Roll up lengthwise like a jelly roll. Cut into 1-inch-thick slices. Arrange in pan. Let rise for about 1 hour.
7. Preheat oven to 350° F.
8. Bake in preheated oven for about 30 minutes.

La Veta Dunn, Study Club, Balsam Lake, Wis.

DAKOTA BUTTERSCOTCH ROLLS
Makes 24
1 envelope active dry yeast
¼ cup warm water
1 cup milk, scalded
3 tablespoons shortening
3 tablespoons granulated sugar
1 teaspoon salt
1 egg, well beaten
3½ cups presifted flour
2 tablespoons melted butter
1¼ cups brown sugar
2 tablespoons light corn syrup
1 tablespoon butter

1. Soften yeast in water; stir; let stand for 5 minutes.
2. Combine milk, shortening, granulated sugar and salt. Cool to lukewarm.
3. Add yeast and egg.
4. Gradually stir in flour to form a soft dough. Beat vigorously. Cover with greased waxed paper and towel. Let rise for about 2 hours, or until doubled in bulk.
5. Turn onto lightly floured board. Roll out ¼ inch thick into rectangle 8 x 16 inches. Brush with melted butter; sprinkle with ¼ cup of the brown sugar. Roll lengthwise like a jelly roll.
6. In shallow pan combine remaining brown sugar, corn syrup and 1 tablespoon butter. Heat slowly until butter is melted and sugar is dissolved.
7. Cut roll into slices 1 inch thick. Arrange, cut side down, on top of brown sugar mixture. Cover; let rise for 30 minutes, or until doubled in bulk.
8. Preheat oven to 375° F.
9. Bake in preheated oven for 25 minutes. Remove from pan immediately. Cool, bottom side up, on wire rack.

Mrs. Harry Christian, Pioneer Daughters Club,
Fargo, N.D.

DANISH PASTRIES
Makes 24

½ cup sugar
1½ teaspoons salt
1¾ cups butter
¾ cup hot milk
2 envelopes active dry yeast
½ cup warm water
2 eggs, separated
1½ teaspoons grated lemon rind
3½ cups unsifted flour
2 tablespoons cornstarch
Jelly
1 tablespoon cold water
Sugar for sprinkling

1. Day before, add sugar, salt and ¼ cup of the butter to milk in mixing bowl. Cool to lukewarm.
2. Soften yeast in warm water. Stir into milk mixture.
3. Beat egg yolks and 1 of the egg whites (reserve second white). Add to yeast mixture.
4. Stir in lemon rind and 1 cup of the flour. Mix well.
5. Combine cornstarch and remaining flour. Stir into dough just until mixed. Chill thoroughly.
6. Spread remaining butter on waxed paper to form rectangle 10 x 12 inches.
7. Roll chilled dough into rectangle 12 x 16 inches.
8. Turn butter rectangle onto two-thirds of dough; fold remaining third over center section; cover with remaining third. Give dough a quarter turn. Roll out again into rectangle 12 x 16 inches. Repeat. Chill.
9. Repeat Step 8 two more times. Refrigerate overnight.
10. Next day, divide dough in half; refrigerate half until ready to shape. Roll out thinly. Cut into 3-inch squares. Put ½ tablespoon jelly in center of each square; fold in half, forming triangle; seal edges. Arrange on baking sheet. Chill for 1 hour.
11. Preheat oven to 375° F.
12. Combine reserved egg white with cold water; use to brush surface of triangles. Sprinkle lightly with sugar.
13. Bake in preheated oven for 15 to 20 minutes.

Mrs. Merrill Paulson, Study Club, Balsam Lake, Wis.

HUNGARIAN PASTRIES
Makes 60 to 72

4 cups presifted flour
½ teaspoon salt
2 envelopes active dry yeast
¾ pound butter
1 cup sour cream
1 teaspoon vanilla
3 eggs, separated
1 cup granulated sugar
Shaved chocolate or chopped nuts
Confectioners' sugar

1. In mixing bowl combine flour, salt and yeast.
2. Cut in butter.

3. Combine sour cream, vanilla and egg yolks. Add to flour mixture. Stir with fork until dough holds together.
4. Divide dough into 6 portions. Wrap each portion in waxed paper. Chill.
5. Beat egg whites until stiff but not dry. Gradually beat in granulated sugar. Continue to beat until meringue is glossy, but not too thick.
6. Preheat oven to 400° F.
7. On lightly floured board, roll out dough, one portion at a time, into circle.
8. Spread thinly with meringue; sprinkle with chocolate or nuts or a little of both. Cut into 10 or 12 pie-shaped wedges. Roll up each wedge from wide end to point; place on baking sheet; curve into crescent.
9. Bake in preheated oven for 12 to 15 minutes, or until lightly browned. Remove from oven. Sprinkle with confectioners' sugar.

Mrs. Thomas J. Sinner, Woman's Club, Casselton, N.D.

HOT CROSS BUNS
Makes About 24

1 envelope active dry yeast
1 teaspoon sugar
2 tablespoons lukewarm water
1 cup milk
¼ cup shortening
⅓ cup sugar
1 teaspoon salt
1 egg
1 teaspoon cinnamon
¼ teaspoon allspice
3½ to 4 cups presifted flour
½ cup seedless raisins
1 egg white
Confectioners' Sugar Icing (p. 622)

1. In small bowl soften yeast with 1 teaspoon sugar and water. Let stand for 5 minutes.
2. Meanwhile, scald milk. Add shortening and ⅓ cup sugar. Let stand until lukewarm.
3. Blend milk mixture with yeast. Stir until dissolved. Turn into mixing bowl.
4. Add salt, egg, cinnamon, allspice and 1 cup of the flour. Beat until smooth.
5. Gradually add enough remaining flour, a cup at a time, to make a soft dough, beating after each addition.
6. Add raisins. Mix well.
7. Turn onto lightly floured board. Knead until smooth.
8. Return dough to clean bowl; cover; let rise for about 1½ hours, or until doubled in bulk.
9. Grease baking sheets.
10. Form dough into 1½-inch balls. Place 2 inches apart on baking sheets.
11. Brush with egg white; cover; let stand for 30 minutes, or until doubled in bulk.
12. Preheat oven to 400° F.
13. Snip a cross in top of each bun with scissors.

14. Bake in preheated oven for 15 to 20 minutes. Remove. Cool on wire rack.

15. Fill crosses on tops of buns with Confectioners' Sugar Icing.

Mildred M. Dicker, Order of the Eastern Star, Waukomis, Okla.

CZECHOSLOVAKIAN KOLACHKY
Makes 48

2 cups milk, scalded
½ cup half shortening and half butter
½ cup sugar
2 teaspoons salt
2 envelopes active dry yeast
¼ cup lukewarm water
2 eggs, lightly beaten
5 to 6 cups presifted flour
Kolachky Filling (below)
Softened butter

1. In mixing bowl pour milk over shortening, sugar and salt. Cool to lukewarm.
2. Soften yeast in water. Add to milk mixture. Stir in eggs.
3. Gradually stir in flour, beating well after each addition until smooth.
4. Turn dough into greased bowl; cover; let rise for about 1½ hours, or until doubled in bulk.
5. Punch dough down. Shape into balls 1 inch in diameter. Place on lightly floured board; cover; let rise for 30 minutes.
6. Grease baking sheets.
7. Flatten each ball to a round about 3 inches in diameter. Put Kolachky Filling in center; fold edges to center. Arrange on baking sheets. Spread top of each with a little softened butter. Cover; let rise for about 1 hour, or until doubled in bulk.
8. Preheat oven to 400° F.
9. Bake in preheated oven for 20 minutes.

KOLACHKY FILLINGS:

PRUNE FILLING: Soak and cook 2 pounds prunes. Cool. Pit; then chop finely. Sweeten to taste with about 1½ cups sugar. Add pinch of salt, ¼ teaspoon each cinnamon, ground cloves and allspice, 1 teaspoon lemon juice and 2 tablespoons melted butter. Mix well.

APRICOT FILLING: Soak and cook 1 pound dried apricots. Cool. Chop finely. Stir in 2 cups sugar and ¼ teaspoon each cinnamon and mace.

CHEESE FILLING: Put 2 cups dry cottage cheese through food chopper. Mix with 1 egg, 1 egg yolk, some seedless raisins, 1 tablespoon butter, ½ cup sugar. Cook in top of double saucepan over simmering water until thick, stirring frequently. Remove from heat. Stir in either 1 teaspoon lemon flavoring or grated nutmeg.

POPPY SEED FILLING: Combine 1 cup poppy seeds, ½ cup white or yellow cake crumbs, and 1 cup cooky crumbs. Moisten with a little water, if necessary.

Mrs. John Dill, Woman's Club, Mound, Minn.

KRISPIE ROLLS
Makes 12

1 envelope active dry yeast
¼ cup lukewarm water
½ cup milk, scalded and cooled
1 egg, lightly beaten
½ teaspoon salt
2¼ cups presifted flour
½ cup softened butter or margarine
¼ cup chopped nuts
1 teaspoon cinnamon
1 cup sugar
2 tablespoons melted butter

1. In mixing bowl soften yeast in water.
2. Stir in milk, egg, salt and 2 cups of the flour.
3. Turn onto lightly floured board. Sprinkle with remaining flour. Roll out ¼ inch thick. Spread dough with butter or margarine.
4. Fold dough over; roll out again. Repeat folding and rolling three times.
5. Combine nuts, cinnamon and sugar.
6. Roll out dough into rectangle 13 x 15 inches. Brush with melted butter; and sprinkle with one-fourth of sugar mixture. Roll lengthwise like a jelly roll.
7. Grease baking sheet.
8. Cut roll into slices 1 inch thick. Place, cut sides down, on baking sheet. Chill for 30 minutes.
9. Spread remaining sugar mixture on waxed paper. Place each slice of dough on sugar mixture. Roll out ¼ inch thick. Arrange, sugar side up, on baking sheet. Cover; let rise for 45 minutes.
10. Preheat oven to 375° F.
11. Bake in preheated oven for 15 minutes. Remove from baking sheet immediately to cool on wire rack.

Mrs. Paul Pumphrey, President, Woman's Club, Ovid, Colo.

LEMON NUT ROLLS
Makes 16

1 envelope active dry yeast
¼ cup lukewarm water
1 cup granulated sugar
⅓ cup shortening
½ cup mashed potatoes
1 teaspoon salt
½ cup milk, scalded
1 egg
4 teaspoons grated lemon rind
2 tablespoons lemon juice
3½ to 4 cups presifted flour
½ cup chopped pecans
2 tablespoons melted butter
½ cup sifted confectioners' sugar

1. In small bowl soften yeast in water for 5 minutes; then stir until dissolved.
2. In mixing bowl combine ¼ cup of the granulated sugar, shortening, potatoes, salt and milk. Stir until well blended.
3. Cool to lukewarm. Stir in egg, 1 teaspoon of the lemon rind, 1 tablespoon of the lemon juice and yeast.
4. Gradually add flour, beating well after each addition, to form a stiff dough.

5. Cover; let rise for about 1 hour, or until doubled in bulk.

6. Grease 2 8-inch layer cake pans.

7. Combine remaining granulated sugar, 2 teaspoons of remaining lemon rind and pecans.

8. Roll out dough on lightly floured board into 16 x 12-inch rectangle.

9. Brush with melted butter. Sprinkle with pecan mixture.

10. Roll up dough like a jelly roll, starting with 16-inch side. Cut into 16 1-inch slices. Arrange, cut side down, in pans.

11. Cover; let rise for about 30 minutes.

12. Preheat oven to 375° F.

13. Bake in preheated oven for 25 minutes.

14. While rolls are baking, prepare glaze: Blend remaining lemon rind, remaining lemon juice and confectioners' sugar. Stir until smooth. Drizzle over warm rolls.

Mrs. Ernest McCann, Women's Club, New Meadows, Ida.

MAGYAR VAJAS TESZTA OR KNIFLI (Hungarian Nut Rolls)

Makes 24

2 envelopes active dry yeast
½ cup warm milk
Granulated sugar
4½ cups presifted flour
½ teaspoon salt
1 pound butter
2 teaspoons cream
3 eggs, separated
1 to 2 cups ground nuts
⅛ teaspoon almond extract
Confectioners' sugar

1. Day before, add yeast to milk. Stir in 3 teaspoons of the granulated sugar. Let stand for 20 minutes, or until bubbling.

2. Put flour, salt and 3 teaspoons of the granulated sugar in mixing bowl.

3. Cut in butter until mixture resembles fine crumbs.

4. Stir in 1 egg and 2 of the egg yolks. (Reserve 2 egg whites for filling.) Stir in yeast mixture.

5. Turn dough onto lightly floured board. Knead until smooth, adding a little flour, if necessary. Refrigerate dough and reserved egg whites overnight.

6. Next day, combine nuts, granulated sugar to taste and almond extract with enough of reserved egg whites to make a paste.

7. Preheat oven to 350° F.

8. Cut dough in half. On lightly floured board, roll out half at a time until thinner than pie dough.

9. Spread surface of dough with nut paste. Cut into squares. Roll up square like tiny jelly rolls. Place on baking sheet.

10. Bake in preheated oven for 20 to 25 minutes. Remove from oven. Sprinkle with confectioners' sugar while still warm.

Mrs. L. P. Whiting, Crafts and Hobbies Club, St. Louis, Mo.

ORANGE YEAST ROLLS

Makes 36

1 cup milk
½ cup shortening
⅓ cup sugar
1½ envelopes active dry yeast
¼ cup lukewarm water
1 teaspoon salt
¼ cup orange juice
3 tablespoons grated orange rind
2 eggs, lightly beaten
About 5 cups presifted flour
Orange Icing (optional) (p. 622)

1. Scald milk. Add shortening and sugar. Cool to lukewarm.

2. In mixing bowl soften yeast in water. Add milk mixture. Add salt, orange juice and rind. Stir in eggs. Add 2 cups of the flour; beat until smooth. Work in enough remaining flour to make a stiff dough.

3. Turn onto lightly floured board. Knead until smooth. Form into a ball; put in greased bowl; cover; let rise for about 1½ hours, or until doubled in bulk.

4. Grease baking sheet.

5. Punch dough down. Again knead until smooth. Cut dough into 6 parts. Cut each into 6 pieces. Form each piece into a roll. Place on baking sheet. Cover; let rise until doubled in bulk.

6. Preheat oven to 400° F.

7. Bake in preheated oven for 10 to 12 minutes.

8. If desired, frost with Orange Icing.

Dorothy Buckminster, Woman's Club, West Concord, N.H.

PECAN ROLLS

Makes 3 Large or 24 Small

⅓ cup melted shortening
2½ cups granulated sugar
1¼ teaspoons salt
1⅓ cups boiling water
2 envelopes active dry yeast
3 eggs, lightly beaten
6 cups presifted flour
3 tablespoons nonfat dry milk solids
½ cup melted butter
1 tablespoon cinnamon
½ cup brown sugar
¼ cup dark corn syrup
1 cup chopped pecans

1. In mixing bowl combine shortening, ½ cup of the granulated sugar, salt and ⅔ cup of the water. Stir to blend. Cool to lukewarm.

2. In small bowl put remaining water. Cool to lukewarm. Stir in yeast; let stand for 5 minutes; then stir until dissolved.

3. Add sugar mixture.

4. Add eggs; beat to blend. Sift in 1 cup of the flour and milk solids; stir to mix. Add 2 cups of the flour; beat until smooth. Gradually add enough remaining flour to make a soft dough. Beat until smooth.

5. Turn onto lightly floured board. Knead for 5 minutes.

6. Clean bowl; grease lightly; place dough in bowl. Cover; let stand for about 1 hour, or until doubled in bulk.

7. Preheat oven to 425° F. Grease 13 x 9½ x 2-inch baking pan.

8. Punch dough down. Turn onto lightly floured board.

9. Divide dough in thirds. Roll each into rectangle 14 x 8 inches. Brush with butter.

10. In small bowl combine remaining granulated sugar and cinnamon. Sprinkle over rectangles. Roll up each rectangle like a jelly roll, along 14-inch side.

11. Place remaining butter in small saucepan. Stir in brown sugar and corn syrup. Cook over low heat, stirring frequently, only until sugar is dissolved. Remove from heat. Stir in pecans. Spread on bottom of pan.

12. Place rolls in pan. Cover; let stand for 15 minutes, or until doubled in bulk.

13. Bake in preheated oven for 20 minutes. Let stand for 5 minutes; then turn rolls upside down on wire rack to cool.

Vera Powell, Progressive Study Club,
Bryan, Ohio

PINEAPPLE ROLLS

Makes 36

2 envelopes active dry yeast
2 cups milk, scalded and cooled
    to lukewarm
2 cups sugar
¾ cup melted butter
2 eggs, lightly beaten
3 egg yolks, lightly beaten
1¼ teaspoons salt
½ teaspoon grated lemon rind
¼ teaspoon mace
6 cups presifted flour
2 cups crushed pineapple

1. Soften yeast in ½ cup of the milk with 2 tablespoons of the sugar for 3 minutes.

2. In mixing bowl combine remaining milk, ½ cup of the sugar, butter, eggs, egg yolks, salt, lemon rind and mace.

4. Add 2 cups of the flour. Beat until smooth.

5. Add yeast and 2 cups of the flour. Again beat until smooth.

6. Work in enough remaining flour to make a soft dough. Cover; let rise for about 1½ hours, or until doubled in bulk. Punch dough down. Let rise for 45 minutes.

7. Grease baking sheet.

8. Turn dough onto lightly floured board. Form into small rounds. Place 1½ inches apart on baking sheet. Let rise until doubled in bulk.

9. In saucepan combine pineapple and remaining sugar. Cook until filling is slightly thickened. Cool.

10. Press center of each roll with thumb, making deep depression. Fill center with 1 teaspoon filling. Let rolls rise for 30 minutes longer.

11. Preheat oven to 375° F.

12. Bake in preheated oven for 20 to 30 minutes.

Fay Clark, Woman's Club, Salem, Ia.

RUM ROLLS

Makes 12

1 tablespoon rum
½ recipe for Basic Rich Sweet
    Dough (p. 159)
2 tablespoons melted butter
¼ cup sugar
    Nutmeg or cinnamon
2 tablespoons softened butter
    Chocolate Rum Frosting (p. 623)

1. Work rum into Basic Rich Sweet Dough.

2. Roll out thinly on lightly floured board into rectangle.

3. Brush rectangle with melted butter; sprinkle with sugar. Dust lightly with nutmeg or cinnamon.

4. Roll up dough lengthwise like a jelly roll. Pinch ends together.

5. Grease 9-inch square baking pan with softened butter.

6. Cut roll into slices 1 inch thick. Arrange side by side in pan. With palm of hand, mash slices flat to spread dough to cover bottom.

7. Cover; let rise for about 1 hour.

8. Preheat oven to 450° F.

9. Bake in preheated oven for 20 minutes.

10. Turn onto plate. Frost immediately with Chocolate Rum Frosting.

Mrs. Murray Snoddy, Magazine Club,
Roanoke, Ala.

SAFFRON BUNS

Makes 24

This recipe was brought over by English immigrants. The buns are as typical of the Copper Country as they were of England.

1 tablespoon saffron
½ cup boiling water
¾ cup milk
1 envelope active dry yeast
1 teaspoon sugar
⅓ cup cold water
4½ cups presifted flour
¾ cup sugar
1 teaspoon salt
1 teaspoon nutmeg
1 tablespoon lemon extract (optional)
½ cup part shortening and part lard
1 cup seedless raisins or currants
    Chopped candied lemon peel or
    citron (optional)

1. Day before, put saffron in boiling water. Soak overnight.

2. Next day, scald milk. Cool to lukewarm. Add yeast; stir until dissolved. Pour into mixing bowl.

3. Add 1 teaspoon sugar, cold water and 1½ cups of the flour. Add saffron with liquid. Beat until smooth.

4. Cover; let rise for about 1 hour.

5. Stir in remaining ingredients.

6. Beat and work in remaining flour. Knead until smooth and elastic.

7. Cover; let rise until doubled in bulk.

8. Shape into buns. Place on baking sheet. Let rise for about 30 minutes, or until doubled in bulk.

9. Preheat oven to 350° F.

10. Bake in preheated oven for 25 to 30 minutes.

Mrs. John J. Burke, President, Woman's Club,
Calumet, Mich.

Pancakes, Waffles and Doughnuts

Pancakes, waffles and doughnuts are often leavened with yeast instead of baking powder or baking soda. Thin yeast batters for waffles and pancakes are usually allowed to rise for several hours or overnight at room temperature. The batter is then stirred down, eggs are added to enrich it, and it is ready to bake. For pancakes, see baking instructions, p. 131. For waffles, follow manufacturer's directions.

Doughnut doughs are allowed to rise like bread. Actually any plain or sweet bread dough may be fried into doughnuts. After the dough has risen, punch it down, and roll out ½ inch thick on lightly floured board. Cut it into strips, squares or diamond-shaped pieces; cover for 10 to 15 minutes; fry. Or you can simply pull off irregular chunks of dough and drop them into hot fat. These are known as Doughboys. To fry doughnuts, see p. 166.

RAISED PANCAKES OR WAFFLES
Makes 8

½ cup lukewarm water
1 envelope active dry yeast
2 cups lukewarm milk
½ cup melted butter
1 teaspoon salt
1 tablespoon sugar
2 cups presifted flour
2 eggs, lightly beaten
Pinch of baking soda

1. Day before, in mixing bowl combine water and yeast; let stand for 5 minutes.

2. Stir in milk, butter, salt and sugar.

3. Beat in flour. Cover; let stand overnight.

4. Next day, stir in eggs and baking soda. Batter will be thin.

5. Bake in cakes on hot griddle, using about ¼ cup batter per cake, until browned on both sides, turning once, or bake in preheated waffle iron according to manufacturer's directions.

A. S.

BLINIS (Small Russian Pancakes)
Makes 24

1 envelope active dry yeast
3 cups lukewarm milk
3 cups buckwheat flour
½ cup melted butter
3 eggs, separated
½ teaspoon salt

1. In mixing bowl soften yeast in 1 cup of the milk. Let stand for 5 minutes.

2. Add remaining milk. Beat in 2 cups of the flour and butter; let stand at room temperature for 2 to 3 hours.

3. Stir in egg yolks, remaining flour and salt. Mix thoroughly.

4. Beat egg whites until stiff, but not dry. Fold into batter. Let stand for 30 minutes before baking.

5. Bake in small cakes on hot greased griddle until browned on both sides, turning once.

A. S.

OLD-FASHIONED BUCKWHEAT CAKES
Makes 12

⅓ cup bread crumbs
2 cups milk
½ teaspoon salt
¼ envelope active dry yeast
½ cup lukewarm water
1½ cups buckwheat flour
1 tablespoon molasses
2 tablespoons melted shortening
½ teaspoon baking soda
¼ cup warm water

1. Day before, soak crumbs in milk for 30 minutes. Add salt.

2. Soften yeast in lukewarm water. Add to crumb mixture.

3. Stir in flour; cover; let rise overnight.

4. Next day, stir in molasses, shortening and baking soda mixed with warm water.

5. Bake on hot griddle, using about ¼ cup batter per cake, until browned on both sides, turning once.

Mrs. Opal Burfield, Junior Civic Woman's Club,
Parkersburg, W. Va.

SOURDOUGH PANCAKES

Many people in Mrs. Gapen's area have starters which have been kept going for a great many years, even before Wyoming became a state in 1890. Men on hunting trips often take along a starter to make pancakes for a hearty breakfast before they begin a strenuous day.

STARTER

1 cup grated raw potatoes
1 tablespoon presifted flour
1 tablespoon sugar
1 tablespoon salt
1 quart water
1 envelope active dry yeast

PANCAKES

2 cups warm water
¼ cup sugar
Presifted flour
2 eggs, well beaten
2 tablespoons sugar
Salt to taste
1 teaspoon baking soda
1 tablespoon cold water

1. 2 days before, prepare starter: In saucepan combine potatoes, flour, sugar,

salt and water. Bring to boil. Boil until clear, being careful it does not burn. Cool; then stir in yeast. Cover lightly. Let stand for 24 hours before using.

2. Next day, prepare pancakes: Pour starter into mixing bowl. Stir in warm water. Stir in ¼ cup sugar and enough flour to make a stiff batter. Let stand overnight.

3. Next day, set aside 1 quart of mixture for new starter.

4. Add eggs, 2 tablespoons sugar and salt to remaining mixture. Mix well.

5. Dissolve baking soda in cold water. Fold into batter.

6. Bake in cakes on hot griddle, using about ¼ cup batter per cake, until browned on both sides, turning once.

Mrs. Clarke Gapen, President,
Wyoming Federation of Women's Clubs,
Basin, Wyo.

ENGLISH MUFFINS

Makes 12

½ envelope active dry yeast
1½ cups milk, scalded and cooled
1 tablespoon sugar
1 teaspoon salt
3 cups presifted flour
1 egg, well beaten
⅛ teaspoon baking soda

1. Soften yeast in milk. Stir in sugar and salt.

2. Beat in enough flour to make a drop batter. Beat well.

3. Let batter rise for about 2 hours, or until light and doubled in bulk.

4. Stir down. Add egg and baking soda. Beat again thoroughly.

5. Drop in cakes on hot greased griddle, using about ¼ cup batter per muffin. Bake slowly until browned on both sides, turning once.

Mrs. L. S. McLarry, Woman's Club,
Panama City, Fla.

OLD-FASHIONED DOUGHNUTS

Makes 36 to 48

1 cup milk
2 tablespoons shortening
½ cup sugar
1 teaspoon salt
1 envelope active dry yeast
¼ cup lukewarm water
3½ to 3¾ cups presifted flour
1 egg
½ teaspoon nutmeg
Fat for deep frying

1. Scald milk. Pour into mixing bowl. Add shortening, sugar and salt. Stir until shortening is melted. Cool to lukewarm.

2. Soften yeast in water. Stir into milk mixture.

3. Add ½ cup of the flour. Beat until smooth.

4. Beat in egg and nutmeg.

5. Work in enough remaining flour to make a stiff dough. Knead until smooth and elastic. Cover; let rise for about 2 hours, or until doubled in bulk.

6. Punch dough down. Roll out ½ inch thick on lightly floured board. Cut with floured doughnut cutter.

7. Fry in deep fat heated to 365° F. until golden brown.

8. Drain on absorbent paper.

Mrs. Guy Motz, Study Club, Balsam Lake, Wis.

LONG JOHNS

Makes 60

½ cup shortening
1 cup boiling water
1 cup evaporated milk
3 envelopes active dry yeast
½ cup warm water
2 eggs, well beaten
½ teaspoon nutmeg
½ cup sugar
2 teaspoons salt
8½ to 9 cups presifted flour
Fat for deep frying
Brown Sugar Icing (p. 627)

1. In mixing bowl add shortening to boiling water; stir until melted. Cool to lukewarm. Add milk.

2. Soften yeast in warm water.

3. Add eggs, nutmeg, sugar and salt; stir well. Stir into milk mixture.

4. Add 4 cups of the flour. Beat until smooth.

5. Work in enough remaining flour to make a soft dough.

6. Turn onto lightly floured board. Knead for 5 minutes. Let stand for 10 minutes.

7. Roll out dough ¼ inch thick. Cut into strips 1 x 6 inches.

8. Place strips on waxed paper; cover; let rise until doubled in bulk.

9. Drop a few at a time into deep fat heated to 365° F. Fry until golden brown.

10. Drain on absorbent paper. When cool, frost with Brown Sugar Icing.

Lena Burkley, Woman's Club, Salem, Ia.

REFRIGERATOR YEAST DOUGHNUTS

Makes 48

4 cups presifted flour
5 tablespoons sugar
1 teaspoon salt
½ cup butter
1 envelope active dry yeast
¼ cup lukewarm water
1 teaspoon sugar
3 egg yolks
1 cup warm milk
Fat for deep frying

1. Day before, into mixing bowl sift together flour, 5 tablespoons sugar and salt.

2. Cut in butter.

3. Soften yeast in water with 1 teaspoon sugar.

4. Add egg yolks to milk. Beat well.

5. Combine all ingredients. Refrigerate overnight.

6. Next day, roll out on lightly floured board. Cut with floured doughnut cutter.

Fry in deep fat heated to 365° F. until golden brown.

Mrs. A. E. Schulz, Woman's Club, Altoona, Wis.

Ready-Made Breads and Toasts

Toast has a sweeter, nuttier flavor than plain bread. For soft toast, toast fresh bread in a toaster, in a hot oven or under the broiler. Frozen bread slices may be toasted in the same manner but need a little extra toasting time.

To make a crisp buttery toast, spread bread slices on one side with softened butter, and arrange on baking sheet. Bake in a slow (250° F.) oven until lightly browned. Remove, turn and butter other side. Return to the slow oven to crisp and brown the other side.

Stale bread should never be thrown out, unless it is to the birds! Put it in a 250° F. oven until very dry and crisp; then grind it through the medium blade of a meat grinder or in an electric blender.

MELBA TOAST

Arrange thin slices of bread between two nested shallow baking pans. Bake in a preheated 300° F. oven for 30 minutes. Flip pans over. Bake for 30 minutes longer.

GARLIC TOAST

Slice French bread thinly. Arrange on baking sheet. Spread with Garlic Butter (p. 77). Bake in 400° F. oven for 10 minutes, or toast under broiler.

CINNAMON TOAST

    Sliced bread
    Sugar
    Cinnamon
    Softened butter

1. Trim crusts from bread. Toast bread. Cut into strips or triangles.
2. Stir ½ teaspoon cinnamon into each ¼ cup sugar.
3. Spread toast with butter; sprinkle with sugar mixture. Put under broiler or in hot oven until sugar melts.

Mrs. Ira A. Hutchison, Woman's Club, Panama City, Fla.

BUTTERSCOTCH TOAST

    ½ cup softened butter
    4 tablespoons brown sugar
    2 teaspoons cinnamon
    Toasted bread

1. Combine butter, sugar and cinnamon.
2. Spread fairly thick on bread. Broil for a few seconds, or until sugar melts.

Virginia Morefield, Woman's Club, Palmdale, Calif.

FRENCH TOAST

Serves 3

Serve hot, with marmalade, jelly or maple syrup and crisp bacon, as desired.

    2 eggs
    ⅛ teaspoon salt
    1 tablespoon granulated sugar
    ¼ cup milk
    6 slices bread
    4 tablespoons butter
    Confectioners' sugar

1. Combine eggs, salt, sugar and milk. Pour into shallow pan.
2. Dip bread into mixture, turning to coat both sides.
3. Melt butter in skillet; brown bread until golden on both sides.
4. Sprinkle with confectioners' sugar.

Mrs. Emmett Smith, Study Club, Collinsville, Ala.

BACON-FLAVORED FRENCH TOAST

Serves 3 or 4

    2 eggs
    ½ teaspoon salt
    ½ cup milk
    6 slices bread
    ¼ cup bacon drippings

1. In mixing bowl beat eggs, salt and milk.
2. Dip bread into egg mixture. Coat well on both sides.
3. Melt bacon drippings in large skillet; sauté bread slices until golden on both sides.

Mrs. C. G. Poindexter, Woman's Club, North Wilkesboro, N.C.

SPICED BREAKFAST FRENCH TOAST

Serves 4

Serve this hot with pats of butter, syrup and crisp bacon, as desired.

    3 eggs
    ¼ teaspoon salt
    2 tablespoons sugar
    ⅛ teaspoon cinnamon
    ⅛ teaspoon nutmeg
    1 cup milk
    Butter
    8 slices white bread, halved

1. Beat eggs in shallow pan until light and fluffy. Stir in salt, sugar, cinnamon, nutmeg and milk.
2. Melt butter in large skillet.
3. Dip bread slices, one at a time, into egg mixture. Sauté until golden brown on both sides, adding butter as needed.

Mrs. Tom Kerrigan, Town and Country League, Cheyenne, Wyo.

OVEN FRENCH TOAST

Serves 4 to 6

    3 eggs, lightly beaten
    ½ teaspoon salt
    ½ teaspoon almond extract
    2 tablespoons sugar
    ¾ cup milk
    12 slices white bread
    Whipped butter

1. Preheat oven to 450° F. Grease baking sheet.

2. In shallow dish beat eggs, salt, almond extract and sugar.

3. Add milk. Beat until blended.

4. Dip bread into egg mixture, coating both sides. Arrange on baking sheet.

5. Bake in preheated oven for 7 minutes.

6. Turn slices. Bake for 7 minutes longer, or until golden.

7. Serve at once with whipped butter.

Doris Miser, Woman's Club, Sunland, Calif.

EASY TOAST PATTY SHELLS FOR CREAMED FOODS

Makes 6

Fill as desired with creamed chicken, turkey or seafood.

12 slices bread
½ cup melted butter or margarine

1. Preheat oven to 375° F. Grease 6 muffin cups.

2. Remove crusts from bread.

3. Press a slice of bread into each cup so that one corner covers bottom of cup and opposite corner sticks up.

4. Press another slice of bread in same manner, placing corners that stick up opposite each other. Press bread well against sides of cup.

5. Brush insides of bread cups with butter or margarine.

6. Bake in preheated oven for 10 minutes, or until golden and crisp.

Myrtle C. MacIntosh, Trirosis Club,
Canton, Ohio

HOT FRENCH BREAD WITH SEASONED BUTTER

1 loaf French bread
Chive or Garlic Butter (below)

1. Preheat oven to 400° F.

2. Cut bread into thick slices, but do not cut through bottom crust.

3. Spread one side of each slice with Chive or Garlic Butter. Place loaf in brown paper bag. Fold over end of bag to seal.

4. Heat in preheated oven for 10 minutes.

CHIVE OR GARLIC BUTTER:

4 tablespoons butter
2 tablespoons chopped chives or
½ teaspoon grated garlic

1. Beat butter until soft.

2. Gradually stir in chives or garlic.

Study Club, Balsam Lake, Wis.

GARLIC BREAD

½ cup butter
1 teaspoon garlic salt
½ teaspoon garlic powder
1 loaf French bread, sliced

1. Preheat broiler.

2. Melt butter over low heat. Add garlic salt and powder. Stir until thoroughly mixed.

3. Arrange bread on baking sheet. Brush generously with butter mixture.

4. Broil for 3 to 4 minutes, or until brown and bubbling.

Gen Di Gristina, Woman's Club, Addison, Ill.

ROMAN GARLIC BREAD

½ cup softened butter
½ teaspoon garlic salt
3 teaspoons chopped parsley
½ teaspoon orégano
2 tablespoons grated Parmesan cheese
4 tablespoons sour cream
1 loaf French or Italian bread

1. Combine all ingredients except bread. Let stand for 20 to 30 minutes for flavors to blend.

2. Preheat oven to 400° F.

3. Slice bread not quite through bottom crust. Spread cut sides with seasoned butter.

4. Bake in preheated oven for 10 to 15 minutes, or until hot and crusty.

Mrs. Paul Bryant, Northside Junior Woman's
Club, Atlanta, Ga.

GARLIC BREAD STICKS

Makes 16

1 loaf of unsliced bread
½ cup butter, melted
2 tablespoons garlic salt
¼ cup sesame seeds

1. Preheat oven to 400° F.

2. Cut loaf in half crosswise, then in half lengthwise. Cut each piece crosswise into 4 sticks, 1¼ inches thick.

3. Combine butter and garlic salt. Brush on all sides of sticks.

4. Arrange in 13 x 9½ x 2-inch baking pan so that sticks do not touch one another. Sprinkle with sesame seeds.

5. Bake in preheated oven for about 10 minutes, or until golden brown.

Mrs. Harry K. Jeanneret, Woman's Club,
Clarkton, N.C.

TOASTED HERB LOAF

¾ cup butter
¼ teaspoon salt
¼ teaspoon paprika
Dash of cayenne
¼ teaspoon dried savory
½ teaspoon dried thyme
1 loaf day-old unsliced bread

1. Soften butter. Blend with salt, paprika, cayenne and herbs.

2. Preheat oven to 375° F.

3. Cut crusts from bottom and sides of loaf. Peel off top crust. Cut bread in half lengthwise (not quite all the way through); then cut diagonally 2 inches apart in both directions.

4. Spread top of bread, sides and all cuts with herb butter mixture.

5. Place on baking sheet. Bake in preheated oven for 30 minutes, or until nicely browned.

Dee Dunn, Junior Woman's Club,
Simsbury, Conn.

PEANUT STICKS

Makes About 49

These are better if made in advance and stored in airtight container.

 7 slices white bread
 ⅓ cup cooking oil
 ½ cup cream-style peanut butter

1. Preheat oven to 250° F.
2. Remove crusts from bread. Cut each slice into 7 sticks.
3. Place sticks and crusts on baking sheet.
4. Bake in preheated oven for 1 hour, or until light golden.
5. Cool sticks. Crush crusts to make crumbs.
6. Beat oil and peanut butter until smooth and creamy.
7. Dip sticks in peanut butter mixture. Roll in crumbs.

Mrs. A. M. Furr, Castalian Club, Tupelo, Miss.

5. Soups

~~~~~~

Stock is the basis of most soups, stews and chowders. The richer the stock, the more flavorful the soup.

Although canned soups, bouillons, consommés and broths are popularly accepted in America, there are still many people who refuse to forgo the pleasures of a really good homemade soup.

In general, there are three kinds of stock which serve as bases for soups (it should be noted that the words "stock," "broth" and "bouillon" may be used interchangeably). These are:

White or chicken stock, made with chicken, veal bones and vegetables.

Brown or beef stock, made with beef, bones and vegetables.

Fish stock, made with the bones and trimmings of white fish and vegetables.

Fish stock requires a relatively short cooking time, whereas white and brown stock need long simmering over very low heat to extract all the flavor from the meat, bones and vegetables.

Consommés begin with a basic stock which is resimmered with additional meat and vegetables to make a richer, more concentrated soup.

Milk soups use mostly milk for liquid, but often combine stock and milk, plus a little cream.

Cream soups begin with a thin white sauce made with butter, flour and milk or a combination of stock and milk. To this are added puréed vegetables and meat or fish. Usually a little cream and often an egg yolk are used for additional richness.

Chowders are soups with a milk or stock base made thick with lots of fish or meat and diced vegetables.

Bean, lentil or split pea soups are made by simmering presoaked dried beans, lentils or peas in water or stock. Often the broth is flavored with a ham bone or salt pork.

Stocks and Consommés

CHICKEN STOCK OR BOUILLON (WHITE STOCK)

Makes 3 Quarts Lightly Salted Stock

5-pound stewing chicken, ready
   to cook

1 pound veal knuckle bones
2 carrots
1 onion, stuck with 2 cloves
1 stalk celery with leaves
3 sprigs parsley
1 bay leaf
¼ teaspoon thyme
¼ teaspoon peppercorns
2 teaspoons salt
5 quarts water

1. Put all ingredients into heavy kettle.
2. Bring to boil, skimming off scum as it rises to surface.
3. Reduce heat. Simmer for 3 hours.
4. Strain stock through sieve lined with cheesecloth.
5. Cool. Skim fat from surface.

NOTE: Many recipes in this book call for chicken broth. In every case, this homemade Chicken Stock may be used; indeed, many cooks would use nothing else. However, canned chicken broth may be substituted.

A. S.

BEEF STOCK OR BOUILLON (BROWN STOCK)

Makes 3 Quarts Lightly Salted Stock

2 pounds beef shin, cubed
3 pounds veal knuckle, cubed
¼ pound lean ham, diced
2 tablespoons cooking oil
3 carrots, sliced
2 onions, sliced
2 stalks celery with leaves, chopped
1 clove garlic (optional)
5 quarts water
3 sprigs parsley
½ teaspoon peppercorns
2 teaspoons salt
2 bay leaves
½ teaspoon thyme

1. Preheat oven to 425° F.
2. Spread meat and bones in shallow baking pan. Sprinkle with oil. Bake in preheated oven for about 1 hour, or until well browned, stirring occasionally.
3. Sprinkle meat and bones with carrots, onions, celery and garlic. Bake for 15 minutes longer.
4. Transfer meat and vegetables to heavy kettle.
5. Add remaining ingredients. Bring to boil, skimming off scum as it rises to surface.

6. Reduce heat. Simmer for 3 hours.

7. Strain stock through sieve lined with cheesecloth.

8. Cool. Skim fat from surface.

NOTE: Many recipes in this book call for beef broth. In every case, this homemade Beef Stock may be used; indeed, many cooks would use nothing else. However, canned beef broth may be substituted.

A. S.

FISH STOCK

Makes About 2 Quarts

2 pounds bones and trimmings of
  any white fish
2 onions, sliced
3 sprigs parsley
6 peppercorns
1 teaspoon salt
  Juice of ½ lemon
2½ quarts water

1. Put all ingredients in heavy kettle.

2. Bring to boil, skimming off scum as it rises to surface.

3. Reduce heat. Simmer for 30 minutes.

4. Strain stock through sieve lined with cheesecloth.

5. Cool quickly.

A. S.

VEAL STOCK

Makes 2 Quarts

Recommended for delicate soups.

6 pounds veal knuckle, chopped
4 quarts water
1 tablespoon salt
6 peppercorns
½ teaspoon celery seed
1 onion

1. Wipe veal with damp cloth. Put in heavy kettle with water. Bring to boil, skimming off scum as it rises to surface.

2. Add remaining ingredients. Simmer until meat falls from bones and liquid is reduced by half.

3. Strain stock. Cool. Remove fat from surface. Refrigerate until ready to use.

Woman's Club Cook Book, Eustis, Fla.

HOT CONSOMMÉ MADRILENE

Serves 6

3 cups beef or chicken consommé or
  Chicken Stock (p. 170)
2 cups tomato juice
2 or 3 cloves
¼ teaspoon saltless celery seasoning
¼ teaspoon pepper
¼ teaspoon onion powder
  Lemon slices
  Chopped parsley

1. In saucepan combine consommé or Chicken Stock, tomato juice, cloves, celery, seasoning, pepper and onion powder. Bring to boil. Simmer for 20 minutes. Strain.

2. Serve hot with a lemon slice and parsley in each serving.

Mrs. Cecil Brake, Pioneer Woman's Club,
Dunbar, W. Va.

Clear Meat, Chicken and Vegetable Soups

MURIEL HUMPHREY'S BEEF SOUP

Serves 6

Mrs. Humphrey writes: "The recipe that sustains the Vice-President's vim, vigor and vitality. My father used to love to make this. It is now famous because my husband loves it and has proclaimed it all over the United States. Low in calories but high in food value, it is especially good for a light supper with fruit salad, a glass of milk, lots of crackers, and dessert."

1½ pounds stewing beef or chuck
  steak
1-pound soup bone
1 teaspoon salt
½ teaspoon pepper
2 bay leaves
1 cup chopped celery
½ cup chopped onions
4 to 5 medium carrots, sliced
1 cup chopped cabbage
1-pound 4-ounce can Italian-style
  tomatoes
1 tablespoon Worcestershire
1 beef bouillon cube
  Pinch of orégano or any other
  herb you prefer

1. Cover meat with water in 3-quart heavy kettle. Add salt, pepper and bay leaves. Heat water to bubbling while preparing vegetables.

2. Turn heat to low. Add celery, onions, carrots and cabbage. Simmer for at least 2½ hours, or until meat is very tender. Skim; remove bone and bay leaves; cut meat into bite-size pieces. Return meat to soup.

3. Add tomatoes, Worcestershire, bouillon cube and herb. Simmer for 30 minutes longer before serving.

Mrs. Hubert H. Humphrey

ALBONDIGAS (Beef Ball Soup)

Serves 8

2 tablespoons cooking oil
4 green onions, chopped
1 clove garlic, chopped
2 green peppers, diced
2 cups canned tomatoes
3 quarts water
1½ pounds ground beef
1 cup quick-cooking rice
1 egg, lightly beaten
  Salt and pepper to taste

1. Heat oil in large saucepan. Simmer onions, garlic, green peppers and tomatoes for about 5 minutes. Add water. Bring to boil. Simmer for 30 minutes.

2. Combine beef, rice, egg, salt and pepper. Form into small balls; drop into boiling mixture. Cook over low heat for 30 minutes longer, or until meat is done.

3. Serve beef balls with broth in soup bowls.

Ruth Flores, Woman's Club, Elroy, Ariz.

AUTUMN BEEF-TOMATO SOUP
Serves 6

1 pound ground beef
1 tablespoon hot fat
1 cup chopped onions
1 quart hot water
1 cup chopped carrots
1 cup sliced celery
1 cup diced potatoes
2 teaspoons salt
½ teaspoon pepper
1 teaspoon meat extract
1 bay leaf
Pinch of basil
6 tomatoes, stemmed

1. In soup kettle brown beef slowly in fat. Add onions. Sauté for 5 minutes.
2. Loosen meat from bottom of kettle. Add all remaining ingredients except tomatoes. Bring to boil; cover; simmer for 20 minutes.
3. Add tomatoes. Simmer for 10 minutes longer.
4. Serve with a whole tomato in each serving.

Mrs. Delores Hecathorn, Junior Women's Club, Miamisburg, Ohio

BEEF VEGETABLE SOUP
Serves 6

Soup bone
1 pound stewing beef, cubed
2 quarts water
1 large onion, chopped
3 stalks celery, chopped
1 tablespoon celery salt
½ teaspoon salt
½ teaspoon pepper
2 tablespoons parsley flakes
1 bay leaf
1-pound 12-ounce can tomatoes
¼ cup rice
1 large potato, sliced
3 carrots, diced
8-ounce can whole-kernel corn

1. Day before, in soup kettle combine soup bone, beef, water, onion, celery, celery salt, salt, pepper, parsley flakes and bay leaf. Bring to boil; skim surface; cover; simmer for 2 hours. Discard bay leaf and bone. Refrigerate overnight.
2. Next day, remove most of fat from surface. Add remaining ingredients. Bring to boil. Simmer for 2 hours. Correct seasoning.

M. W. Emmel, D.V.M., Woman's Club, Murray, Ky.

MENUDO (Mexican Tripe Soup)
Serves 12

The proper way to serve this soup is with minced scallions and minced mint leaves.

2 calf's feet
6 quarts water
5 pounds beef tripe
3 cups hominy
3 onions, minced
4 cloves garlic, minced
1 tablespoon orégano
2 teaspoons dried or 2 sprays fresh cilantro (coriander leaves)
Salt and pepper to taste

1. Wash calf's feet. Put in large kettle with water. Bring to boil. Simmer for 1 hour.
2. Wash tripe. Cut into pieces about 1 x 2 inches. Add to kettle.
3. Add hominy, onions and garlic.
4. Tie orégano and cilantro in cheesecloth bag. Add to soup. Add salt and pepper. Cover. Simmer for 6 to 7 hours.

Mrs. Albert Macias, Junior Woman's Club, Benson, Ariz.

SCOTCH BROTH
Serves 4 to 6

2 pounds mutton
1 slice turnip, finely chopped
2 carrots, finely chopped
1 onion, finely chopped
1 stalk celery, finely chopped
½ cup barley
2 quarts water
1 tablespoon flour
1 tablespoon butter
1 teaspoon chopped parsley
Salt and pepper to taste

1. Cut meat from bones. Remove all fat. Cut meat into small pieces.
2. Put meat, vegetables, barley and 6 cups of the water in soup kettle. Bring to boil. Cover. Simmer for 2 hours.
3. Put bones and remaining water in saucepan. Bring to boil. Cover; simmer for 2 hours. Strain broth from bones into kettle.
4. Combine flour and butter. Gradually stir into soup. Cook until slightly thickened.
5. Add parsley. Season with salt and pepper.

Cook Book, Ladies of Enosburg, Enosburg, Vt.

OXTAIL SOUP
Serves 6

2½-pound oxtail, cut into 1½-inch pieces
½ cup presifted flour
2 tablespoons shortening
2 quarts water
1 tablespoon salt
½ teaspoon pepper
1 cup sliced onions
1-pound can tomatoes, undrained
2 tablespoons Worcestershire
1 tablespoon sugar
3 teaspoons celery salt
3 cloves
2 bay leaves
4 carrots, sliced
1-pound can green beans, drained
4 medium potatoes, peeled and diced
⅓ cup barley

1. Roll oxtail pieces in flour.
2. Heat shortening in Dutch oven or large saucepan; brown oxtail well on all sides.

3. Add water, salt, pepper, onions, tomatoes, Worcestershire, sugar, celery salt, cloves and bay leaves. Bring to boil; cover; simmer for 2 hours.

4. Add remaining ingredients; cover; simmer for 1 hour longer.

Kari Morlock, Junior Woman's Club, Lansing, Ill.

PEPPER POT SOUP

Serves 6

4 tablespoons butter
¾ cup chopped green pepper
¼ cup chopped celery
⅓ cup sliced onions
3½ tablespoons flour
5 cups hot Veal Stock (p. 171) or chicken broth
½ pound honeycomb tripe, cubed
1½ cups cubed potatoes
½ teaspoon pounded peppercorns
1 teaspoon salt
½ cup heavy cream
Celery salt to taste (optional)

1. Melt 3 tablespoons of the butter in heavy saucepan. Add green pepper, celery and onions. Cook slowly for 15 minutes.

2. Stir in flour. Mix well.

3. Gradually stir in Veal Stock or chicken broth.

4. Stir in tripe, potatoes, peppercorns and salt. Bring to boil. Cover tightly; simmer for 1 hour.

5. Just before serving, stir in cream, remaining butter and celery salt.

*Mrs. Frieda Hart, Women's Civic Club,
Richardson Park, Wilmington, Del.*

POT-AU-FEU

Serves 6

If you want to make this in the real French style, use a rabbit instead of beef.

4 pounds beef (brisket, rump, shin, plate, chuck or round) with bone
3 quarts cold water
1 tablespoon salt
Bouquet garni (see Glossary)
2 cups chopped mixed vegetables (onions, carrots, celery, white turnips, parsnips)
6 leeks (white parts only)
3 carrots, quartered
6 cabbage wedges
6 potatoes, quartered

1. Put beef with bones in Dutch oven or heavy saucepan. Add water, salt and boquet garni. Bring to boil, skimming frequently.

2. Cover; simmer for 4 hours, or until meat is almost tender.

3. Add vegetables. Cover; simmer for 45 minutes longer, or until vegetables are tender. Discard bouquet garni.

4. Remove meat to serving dish; surround with vegetables; serve for main course after soup is served.

*Anne Lambert, Federated Women's Club,
Levittown, Pa.*

CHICKEN NOODLE SOUP

Serves 6

3½-pound stewing chicken, cut up
5 cups water
2½ teaspoons salt
⅛ teaspoon pepper
¼ teaspoon basil
1 bay leaf
4 medium carrots
½ pound small white onions
1 cup fine noodles
1 tablespoon chopped parsley

1. Wash chicken. Put in soup kettle with water. Add seasonings and herbs. Bring to boil; cover; simmer for 1½ hours, or until chicken is tender.

2. Meanwhile, wash and peel carrots; cut into 1-inch chunks. Wash and peel onions.

3. When chicken is tender, remove it, along with bay leaf, from stock. Skim stock.

4. Add carrots and onions. Bring to boil; cover; simmer for 45 minutes longer.

5. Meanwhile, remove skin and bones from chicken, leaving chicken meat in large pieces.

6. Ten minutes before vegetables are tender, add noodles and chicken pieces.

7. Ladle into soup plates. Sprinkle each serving with parsley.

Grete Heims, Women's Club, Addison, Ill.

EASY CHICKEN NOODLE SOUP

Serves 6

2 chicken breasts
3 medium carrots, diced
1 quart chicken broth
2 cups water
½ teaspoon salt
⅛ teaspoon basil
⅛ teaspoon pepper
1 cup fine noodles
½ cup canned tiny onions
2 tablespoons chopped parsley

1. Skin chicken breasts. Remove excess fat.

2. Put chicken, carrots, broth, water, salt, basil and pepper in heavy saucepan. Bring to boil; cover; simmer for 30 minutes.

3. Remove chicken from pan. Cool. Bone chicken; cut meat into thin strips; return to pan. Add noodles. Cover; simmer for 10 minutes, or until noodles are cooked.

4. Add onions and parsley. Simmer for 5 minutes, stirring occasionally. Correct seasoning before serving.

*Barbara Koempel, North Hills Junior Woman's
Club, Glenshaw, Pa.*

LE WATERZOIE (Belgian Chicken Soup)

Serves 6

4-pound stewing chicken, ready-
to-cook
½ lemon
4 cloves
2 large onions
½ cup chopped celery
3 leeks, minced
½ cup diced carrots
1 tablespoon chopped parsley
Pinch of thyme
1 bay leaf
2 cups dry white wine
Salt and pepper to taste
Parsley (optional)

1. Rub chicken with lemon. Put in heavy saucepan. Add sufficient water to half-cover chicken. Bring to boil. Skim surface.
2. Insert two cloves into each onion drop into saucepan. Add remaining ingredients. Cover; simmer for about 1½ hours, or until chicken is tender.
3. To serve, remove chicken from broth; carve. Place chicken in soup tureen; cover with broth. Sprinkle with parsley, if desired.

Mrs. Oswald Mick, Woman's Club,
Breton Woods, N.J.

EGG DROP SOUP

Serves 2

2 cups boiling water
2 chicken bouillon cubes
1 egg
2 tablespoons chopped scallions

1. Put water and bouillon cubes in medium saucepan. Simmer until cubes are dissolved.
2. Meanwhile, in small bowl beat egg. Slowly pour into broth, stirring constantly. Simmer for 1 minute.
3. Serve topped with scallions.

Nipser Mackey, Crest Century Club,
Wilmington, Del.

CHINESE EGG PETAL SOUP

Serves 4 to 6

¼ pound lean pork, shredded
1½ teaspoons sherry
1½ teaspoons soy sauce
1½ teaspoons cornstarch
2 tablespoons cooking oil
1½ quarts chicken broth
1 scallion, sliced
1 cucumber, sliced
¼ teaspoon monosodium glutamate
Salt and pepper to taste
1 egg, lightly beaten

1. Combine pork, sherry, soy sauce and cornstarch.
2. Heat oil in heavy kettle; brown pork mixture quickly. Add broth; bring to boil; simmer for 10 minutes.
3. Add onion, cucumber and monosodium glutamate. Season with salt and pepper. Simmer for 5 minutes longer.

4. Bring to fast boil. Slowly add egg, stirring constantly. Turn off heat at once to ensure that egg will form petals.

Eleanor Brazell, Junior Woman's Club,
Sandy Springs, Ga.

WONTON SOUP

Serves 4 to 6

1½ quarts chicken broth
20 cooked Wontons (p. 196) or frozen wontons
2 tablespoons chopped scallions
2 tablespoons soy sauce

1. In saucepan bring broth to boil. Then simmer for 3 minutes.
2. Arrange Wontons in each soup bowl. Sprinkle with scallions and soy sauce.
3. Pour broth into bowl. Serve at once.

Woman's Club, Palisades, N.J.

AVGOLEMONO (Greek Lemon Soup)

Serves 6

6 cups chicken broth
⅓ cup rice
3 eggs
Juice of 1 lemon

1. Bring broth to boil.
2. Add rice. Simmer for 20 minutes.
3. Beat eggs, lemon juice and 1 cup of broth. Gradually add to rest of broth, beating vigorously. Do not let boil.
4. Serve immediately.

A. S.

TURTLE SOUP

Serves 6

2 pounds turtle meat
Salt
Pepper
3 tablespoons cooking oil
3 tablespoons flour
2 large onions, chopped
1 cup chopped celery
½ cup chopped green pepper
2 cloves garlic, chopped
1 cup tomato sauce
½ lemon, sliced
4 medium bay leaves
1 tablespoon chopped parsley
¼ cup dry sherry
1 tablespoon Worcestershire
3 eggs, hard-cooked and sliced
Paprika

1. Clean turtle meat. Cut into small pieces. Sprinkle with ½ teaspoon salt and ¼ teaspoon pepper.
2. Heat oil in saucepan. Sauté turtle meat until lightly browned. Remove turtle meat.
3. Add flour to fat remaining in pan; stir; cook, stirring occasionally, until golden brown.
4. Add onions, celery, green pepper and garlic. Cook for 10 minutes, or until tender.
5. Return turtle meat to vegetable mixture. Add tomato sauce and 1 cup water. Simmer for 30 minutes.
6. Add lemon, bay leaves and 2 quarts water. Simmer for 1 hour. Discard bay leaves.

7. Add parsley, sherry, Worcestershire and salt and pepper to taste. Pour soup into large soup plates; garnish with egg; sprinkle with paprika.

Mrs. Edward Hebert, Jr., Junior Woman's Club, Thibodaux, La.

MOCK TURTLE SOUP

A quick soup which has a remarkable turtle flavor is made by heating equal parts of chicken and beef consommé and flavoring it with sherry or light rum.

A. S.

VEGETABLE SOUP

Serves 6

4- to 5-pound soup bone with meat
3 quarts water
1 cup diced carrots
1 cup diced turnips
2 large onions, chopped
2 large potatoes, diced
1 cup chopped celery
1 large green pepper, chopped
1 small head cabbage, shredded
1-pound 12-ounce can tomatoes
1 tablespoon sugar
Salt and pepper to taste

1. Put bone in soup kettle with water. Bring to boil; skim surface; cover; simmer for 1 hour.
2. Add remaining ingredients; cover; simmer for 4 to 5 hours.
3. Cut meat from bone into small pieces; discard bone; return meat to soup.

Mrs. C. P. Summerall, Woman's Club, Eustis, Fla.

VEGETABLE BARLEY SOUP

Serves 6

2-pound soup bone, cracked
½ pound beef, cubed
2 tablespoons fat or shortening
2½ quarts water
1½ teaspoons salt
¼ teaspoon pepper
Piece of hot red pepper
2 tablespoons minced parsley
¼ cup barley
1 cup diced carrots
2 cups cooked tomatoes
¼ cup chopped onion
½ cup chopped celery
1 cup peas
1 cup cubed potatoes
½ cup chopped cabbage

1. Put soup bone in large kettle.
2. Brown beef lightly in fat or shortening. Add to kettle. Add water, salt, pepper, red pepper and parsley. Bring to boil; cover; cook for 1 hour, skimming surface occasionally.
3. Add barley. Cook for 1 hour longer.
4. Add carrots, tomatoes, onions and celery; cover; simmer for 45 minutes.
5. Add remaining ingredients. Cook for 15 minutes longer.

Club House Cook Book, Woman's Club, Greenville, Ky.

BORSCHT

Serves 4

A traditional Russian soup. Serve with sour cream, if desired.

1 bunch beets
1 cup fresh or undrained canned tomatoes
1 quart water
1 small onion, chopped
½ to 1 pound breast of beef, cut into small pieces
1 tablespoon lemon juice
¼ cup sugar
¼ teaspoon salt
4 eggs

1. Peel beets; cut into long strips. Put in soup kettle.
2. Press tomatoes through sieve over beets, not letting any seeds through. Add water, onion and beef. Bring to boil; cover; simmer for 30 minutes.
3. Add lemon juice, sugar and salt; cover; simmer for 30 minutes longer.
4. Beat eggs with a little hot soup. Gradually stir into rest of soup, being careful that eggs do not curdle.

Mrs. Clyde Case, Woman's Club, Mound, Minn.

SWEET AND SOUR CABBAGE SOUP

Serves 6

2 tablespoons cooking oil
1 pound beef, cubed
2 quarts water
Salt and pepper to taste
1 head cabbage
Juice of 2 lemons
½ cup seedless raisins
About ¾ cup brown sugar according to taste
Croutons (p. 195)

1. Heat oil in soup kettle; sauté beef until browned on all sides. Add water, salt and pepper. Bring to boil; cover; simmer for 1 hour.
2. Shred cabbage. Add to kettle. Add lemon juice, raisins and sugar. Cover; simmer for 1 hour longer.
3. Serve with Croutons.

Virginia O'Rourke, Woman's Club, West Palm Beach, Fla.

CORN SOUP

Serves 6 to 8

12 ears corn
4 hard-cooked egg yolks
1 tablespoon flour
1 teaspoon salt
½ cup melted butter
1 tablespoon chopped parsley

1. Cut kernels from 6 of the ears of corn. Grate kernels from remaining ears of corn. Place in saucepan.
2. Add sufficient cold water to cover. Bring to boil. Stir in whole corn.
3. In small bowl mash egg yolks. Blend in flour, salt and butter.

4. Stir egg yolk mixture into corn. Simmer for 10 minutes, stirring frequently.

5. Sprinkle with parsley.

Rene Kiso, Woman's Club, Morton Grove, Ill.

MINESTRONE

Serves 6

½ pound beef shin with bone
1¾ quarts water
1 tablespoon salt
¼ teaspoon pepper
2 teaspoons olive oil
1 clove garlic
¼ cup chopped onion
¼ cup chopped parsley
½ cup cooked kidney beans
½ cup green beans
½ cup peas
1 cup shredded cabbage
2 tablespoons tomato paste
¼ cup spaghetti, broken into small
  pieces
Grated Parmesan cheese

1. Put beef, water, salt and pepper in large heavy saucepan. Bring to boil; cover; simmer for 1 hour.

2. Remove cover; skim off fat. Cover; simmer for 3 hours longer.

3. Remove meat and bone; discard bone. Cut meat into bite-size pieces; set aside. Leave stock in pan.

4. Heat oil in medium skillet; sauté garlic until golden. Discard garlic. Add onion and parsley to fat remaining in skillet; sauté for 5 minutes.

5. Put onion and parsley in pan with stock. Add kidney beans, green beans, peas, cabbage and tomato paste. Bring to boil; cover; simmer for 30 minutes.

6. Stir in spaghetti and meat; cover; simmer for 10 minutes longer.

7. Serve with cheese.

*Nancy Butler, Woman's Club
Montgomery, Ohio*

MEATLESS MINESTRONE

Serves 10 to 12

¼ cup cooking oil
1 clove garlic, minced
1 cup chopped onions
1 cup chopped celery
2 6-ounce cans tomato paste
12-ounce can vegetable juice
2½ quarts water
10-ounce package frozen peas and
  carrots
Salt to taste
¼ teaspoon pepper
½ teaspoon Italian seasoning
1-pound can kidney beans, undrained
1 cup small elbow macaroni
10-ounce package frozen chopped
  spinach

1. Heat oil in large kettle; cook garlic, onions and celery for 5 minutes, or until onions are transparent. Stir in tomato paste, vegetable juice, water, peas and carrots, salt, pepper and Italian seasoning. Bring to boil; cover; simmer for 1 hour.

2. Add remaining ingredients; cook for 15 minutes longer.

*Kathy Baker, Junior Woman's Club,
Corning, N.J.*

MUSHROOM POTATO SOUP

Serves 6

1 cup dried mushrooms
½ cup small barley
2 quarts water
1 tablespoon cooking oil
1 medium onion, chopped
3 or 4 medium potatoes, diced
2 or 3 medium carrots, diced
2 bouillon cubes
Salt and pepper to taste
2 tablespoons butter

1. Break mushrooms into small pieces. Wash well.

2. Wash barley. Put in soup kettle with water and mushrooms. Bring to boil; cover; simmer for 45 minutes.

3. Heat oil in saucepan; sauté onion until lightly browned; add to soup.

4. Add remaining ingredients; cover; simmer for 20 minutes longer, or until carrots and potatoes are tender.

*Mrs. Milton J. Stipek, Woman's Club,
Cicero, Ill.*

FRENCH ONION SOUP

Serves 12

1 pound butter
16 to 18 large onions, thinly sliced
8 10½-ounce cans condensed beef
  consommé
2 soup cans water
Toasted French bread
Grated Parmesan cheese

1. Melt butter in saucepan; cook onions and 1 can of the consommé until tender but not browned; stir frequently.

2. In oven heat at least 4-quart casserole.

3. In another saucepan bring remaining consommé and water to boil.

4. Turn onions into casserole. Pour consommé over onions. Arrange bread on top. Sprinkle generously with cheese.

5. Place under broiler heat until cheese is lightly browned.

*Mrs. Charles Davis, Junior Woman's Club,
Benson, Ariz.*

CLEAR TOMATO SOUP

Serves 3

1 tablespoon butter
1 tablespoon minced onion
1 tablespoon minced green pepper
12-ounce can tomato juice
½ 10½-ounce can condensed beef
  consommé
½ soup can water
2 tablespoons dry red wine or
  sherry
¾ teaspoon salt
Pinch of orégano
Dash of pepper

1. Melt butter in saucepan; sauté onion and green pepper until onion is golden.

2. Add remaining ingredients. Bring to boil. Simmer for 8 to 10 minutes. Strain.

Mrs. Shannon Johnson, Woman's Club,
Ponca City, Okla.

Bean, Pea and Lentil Soups

BEAN SOUP

Serves 12

1 pound dried navy, kidney or
   Lima beans, washed
4 quarts water
½ pound salt pork
1 large onion, coarsely cut
4 stalks celery, coarsely cut
1 tablespoon flour
2 tablespoons water
   Salt and pepper to taste
2 tablespoons chopped parsley
   Lemon slices
   Hard-cooked egg slices (optional)

1. Day before, put beans in 2 quarts of the water. Soak overnight.
2. Next day, add remaining 2 quarts water, pork, onion and celery. Bring to boil; cover; simmer for 1½ hours, or until beans are soft.
3. Remove pork. Cut into small pieces.
4. Press bean mixture through sieve. Return to heat. Add pork.
5. Combine flour and 2 tablespoons water. Stir into soup. Season with salt and pepper. Stir in parsley.
6. Serve with lemon slice on each portion. Egg may also be used for garnish, if desired.

La Fourchette, Recipes from Bayou Lafourche,
Compiled by Junior Woman's Club,
Thibodaux, La.

BEAN SOUP WITH POTATOES

Serves 12

1 pound dried navy beans,
   washed
3 quarts water
1 ham bone with meat
1 large onion, chopped
1 bay leaf
1 clove garlic, crushed
1 cup mashed potatoes
1 cup chopped celery
1 cup diced carrots
   Salt and pepper to taste
½ cup light cream

1. Day before, put beans and water in large heavy saucepan; soak overnight. (Or put over high heat, bring to boil and boil rapidly for 2 minutes; then remove from heat; cover and let stand for 1 hour.)
2. Next day, add ham bone, onion, bay leaf and garlic. Cover; simmer for 2 hours, or until beans are almost tender.
3. Add potatoes, celery, carrots, salt and pepper. Cover; simmer for 1 hour longer.
4. Remove ham bone from soup. Cut off meat; dice it. Return meat to soup. Reheat just to boiling.

5. Stir in cream just before serving.

Mrs. Charles Lanier, Jr., Junior Woman's Club,
Fort Myers, Fla.

SOUP OF THE INNER SANCTUM
(Senate Restaurant Bean Soup)

Serves 8

Delicious served with corn sticks and butter.

1½ pounds dried pea, navy or Lima
   beans, washed
2 tablespoons butter
4 large yellow onions, chopped
1 large clove garlic, chopped
6 sprigs parsley
¾ teaspoon thyme
1½ large bay leaves
1 carrot, chopped
½ lemon, sliced
1 pound smoked ham hock or
   shank end of smoked ham
   Freshly ground pepper
1 tablespoon salt

1. Day before, put beans in large bowl; cover with water to depth of 4 to 5 inches; let soak overnight.
2. Next day, drain beans; rinse well under hot water. Put in heavy kettle. Add 3 quarts water.
3. Melt butter in saucepan; sauté onions and garlic for about 5 minutes, or until transparent. Add to kettle.
4. Tie parsley, thyme, bay leaves, carrot and lemon in cheesecloth; add to kettle. Add ham. Bring to boil; cover; cook over low heat for 3 hours, or until liquid is reduced by half and beans are cooked.
5. Discard cheesecloth bag. Remove ham; let cool. Remove 2 cups beans with a little liquid; purée through sieve or in electric blender; return to soup.
6. Cut ham into small pieces; add to soup. Add pepper and salt.
7. Reheat carefully.

Mrs. D. D. Fuller, Alkaid Club, Lindsborg, Kans.

CALIFORNIA PEA BEAN SOUP

Serves 4

1 cup dried pea beans, washed
1 carrot, sliced
2 onions, sliced
¼ cup chopped celery
2 tablespoons chopped parsley
1 cup tomatoes
¼ cup olive oil
   Salt and pepper to taste

1. Day before, put beans in water to cover; soak overnight.
2. Next day, drain beans put in soup kettle with 1½ quarts water. Bring to boil; cover; simmer for 1½ hours, or until soft.
3. Add carrot, onions, celery and parsley; simmer for 30 minutes longer.
4. Stir in tomatoes and oil. Cook for 10 to 15 minutes longer. Season with salt and pepper.

Mrs. Nicholas Colovos, Woman's Club,
Durham, N.H.

BEAN CHOWDER

Serves 8 to 10

1 cup dried beans, washed
1 ham bone
¾ cup diced carrots
8-ounce can tomatoes
1 large onion, finely chopped
⅓ cup finely chopped green pepper
½ teaspoon salt
Dash of pepper
1 tablespoon flour
1½ cups milk

1. Day before, put beans in water to cover. Soak overnight.

2. Next day, put ham bone in large saucepan. Add 2 quarts water. Bring to boil; skim surface; cover; simmer for 2 hours.

3. Remove bone; shred any meat; return meat to pan.

4. Drain beans; add to chowder. Cover; simmer for 1 hour.

5. Add carrots, tomatoes, onion, green pepper, salt and pepper. Cover; simmer for 20 minutes.

6. Combine flour and ¼ cup water. Stir into chowder. Cook, stirring, for 5 minutes.

7. Add milk. Heat to serving temperature.

Virginia Eastham, Younger Woman's Club,
Somerset, Ky.

HAMBURGER BEAN POT SOUP

Serves 8

1 cup dried marrow beans, washed
3 quarts water
1-pound 4-ounce can tomatoes
1 cup diced celery
1 carrot, cubed
1 medium potato, cubed
¼ cup rice
⅓ cup chopped onions
1 beef bouillon cube
1 teaspoon salt
½ teaspoon pepper
1 tablespoon shortening
½ pound ground beef

1. Put beans in large saucepan. Add water. Bring to boil. Boil for 2 minutes. Remove from heat. Let stand for 1 hour.

2. Return beans to low heat; cover; simmer for 20 minutes.

3. Stir in vegetables, rice, bouillon cube, salt and pepper. Bring to boil.

4. Meanwhile, melt shortening in medium skillet; brown beef well.

5. Add beef to soup; cover; simmer for 1 hour.

Mary Jane Boutwell, Junior Woman's Club,
Cheshire, Conn.

BAKED BEAN SOUP

Serves 8

1 tablespoon bacon drippings
1 medium onion, chopped
1 clove garlic, crushed
1 medium green pepper, chopped
1 cup chopped drained tomatoes
2 cups beef consommé
1-pound can baked beans (not in tomato sauce)
1 bay leaf
1 stalk celery, diced
1 tablespoon chopped parsley
Salt and pepper to taste
½ cup red wine

1. Melt bacon drippings in medium in medium saucepan. Add onion, garlic and green pepper; sauté for 5 minutes.

2. Stir in all remaining ingredients except wine. Bring to boil; cover; simmer for 30 minutes.

3. Press mixture through sieve, or blend in electric blender. Return to saucepan. If too thick, stir in a little consommé. Heat to serving temperature, stirring frequently.

4. Just before serving, stir in wine.

Norma Anderson, Junior Alpha Club,
Lompoc, Calif.

LIMA BEAN AND MACARONI SOUP

Serves 6

1 pound dried Lima beans, washed
1 large ham bone with meat
1 large onion, chopped
1-pound 12-ounce can tomatoes
2 medium potatoes, diced
½ cup elbow macaroni
Salt and pepper to taste

1. Day before, put beans in water to cover generously. Soak overnight.

2. Next day, drain beans; add ham bone, onion and 2 quarts water. Bring to boil; cover; simmer for 1 hour.

3. Add tomatoes; simmer for 30 minutes longer.

4. Add potatoes and macaroni. Cook for 30 minutes longer. Season with salt and pepper.

Mrs. Cecil C. Bidwell, Woman's Club,
Tampa, Fla.

SPANISH BEAN SOUP WITH CHORIZO

Serves 6

½ pound dried garbanzos (chickpeas), washed
2 tablespoons salt
1 beef bone
1 ham bone
4 tablespoons cooking oil
¼ pound bacon, diced
1 onion, chopped
1 pound potatoes, diced
Pinch of saffron
1 chorizo (sausage), cut into small pieces

1. Day before, put garbanzos and 1 tablespoon of the salt in water to cover well. Soak overnight.

2. Next day, drain beans. Put in soup kettle with bones and 2 quarts water. Bring to boil; cover; simmer for 45 minutes.

3. Heat oil in skillet; sauté bacon and onion until bacon is crisp and onion is golden. Add to kettle. Add potatoes, saffron and remaining salt. Simmer for 20 minutes, or until potatoes are tender.

4. Remove from heat. Add chorizo.

North Jacksonville's Woman's Club,
Jacksonville, Fla.

SPLIT PEA OR LENTIL SOUP

Serves 6

1 pound dried split peas or lentils, washed
½ pound chunk bacon, cut into small cubes
1 large onion, diced
½ pound butter
3 tablespoons brown sugar or to taste
Salt and pepper to taste

1. Day before, put peas or lentils in water to cover generously. Soak overnight.

2. Next morning, drain peas or lentils; rinse several times. Add fresh water to cover generously. Add bacon and onion. Bring to boil. Cover; cook briskly for 4 hours, adding water, when needed, to keep peas or lentils well moistened. Reduce heat. Cover; simmer for about 4 hours longer.

3. Add remaining ingredients; cover; cook over low heat for 30 minutes longer.

Merril W. Doolittle, Junior Woman's Club,
Thibodaux, La.

GREEN SPLIT PEA SOUP

Serves 6

1 ham bone with meat
2 to 3 quarts water
1 pound green split peas, washed
1 carrot, diced
1 small onion, diced
Salt and pepper to taste

1. Put ham bone in kettle with water. Bring to boil; cover; simmer for 1½ hours, or until meat falls off bone.

2. Discard bone. Add peas. Simmer for 1 hour longer, or until peas are cooked to purée, stirring occasionally.

3. Add carrot and onion. Cook for 20 minutes, or until tender.

4. Just before serving, season with salt and pepper. (Use salt sparingly because ham is salty.)

Mrs. Ellen Krause, Junior of Eastchester
Woman's Club, Eastchester, N.Y.

BLACK BEAN SOUP: Follow recipe above, using black beans in place of split peas. Add 1 clove garlic and 2 stalks celery, chopped, if desired. Just before serving, add 3 tablespoons butter. Serve with thin slices of lemon and hard-cooked eggs.

COUNTRY PEA SOUP

Serves 8

1 pound green split peas, washed
2 quarts water
4 cups canned tomato juice
1 ham bone or meaty ham hock
1½ cups diced potatoes
1 cup diced celery
1 cup diced onions
1 cup diced carrots
1 bay leaf
1 teaspoon salt
¼ teaspoon pepper
1 egg, lightly beaten
2 tablespoons chopped parsley
1 tablespoon flour
Herbed Bread Chunks (p. 195)

1. In soup kettle combine peas, water, tomato juice, ham bone or hock, potatoes, celery, onions, carrots, bay leaf, salt and pepper. Bring to boil; cover; simmer, stirring occasionally, for 1½ hours, or until peas are mushy-tender.

2. Remove ham bone or hock. Cut off lean meat; grind for ham balls.

3. Combine 1 cup ground ham, egg, parsley and flour. Mix well. Form into tiny balls.

4. About 10 minutes before serving, drop balls into soup.

5. Serve in big bowls with Herbed Bread Chunks.

Colette Wirshing, Junior Woman's Club,
Pompano Beach, Fla.

SAUSAGE AND PEA WITH EGG DUMPLINGS

Serves 8

½ pound green split peas, washed
1 large onion, quartered
3 stalks celery, quartered
1 teaspoon celery salt
2 teaspoons salt
½ teaspoon pepper
1 pound smoked sausage
Egg Dumplings (p. 460)
Fried or Toasted Croutons (p. 195)

1. Day before, put peas in large saucepan; cover with water. Cover; soak overnight.

2. Next day, add onion, celery, and seasonings. Bring to boil; cover; simmer for 1½ hours, or until peas are tender.

3. Press peas and liquid through sieve. Return to saucepan. Add water, if necessary, to correct consistency.

4. Add sausage. Cover; simmer for 1 hour.

5. Add Egg Dumplings, dropped by teaspoons. Cover; simmer for 30 minutes.

6. Remove sausage; cut into thin slices; return to soup. Serve with Fried or Toasted Croutons.

Mrs. Michael Gray, Golfview Hills Woman's Club,
Hinsdale, Ill.

LENTIL SOUP

Serves 4

1 cup lentils
½ pound link sausages, cut into
    bite-size pieces
½ cup presifted flour
Salt to taste

1. Day before, put lentils in water to cover; soak lentils overnight.
2. Next day, drain lentils. Put in soup kettle. Add 1 quart water. Bring to boil; cover; simmer for 1 hour.
3. Add sausages. Simmer for 1 hour longer.
4. Put flour in skillet. Stir over medium heat until golden brown. Add ½ cup water; combine. Stir into soup. Cook, stirring, until thickened. Season with salt.

Mrs. J. R. Beckenbach, Woman's Club,
Murray, Ky.

Gumbos, Chowders and Fish Stews

Gumbos, chowders and fish stews are hearty soups that often may be considered a meal in themselves. Served in large chowder bowls, with hot bread or crackers, they need little else to round out a meal except a simple dessert.

Most gumbos and chowders are improved if made one day and served the next. Fish stews, however, should be enjoyed the moment they are ready to serve.

FILÉ

Filé (pronounced fee-lay) is made from young sassafras leaves that have been dried and pounded to a powder. It was originated by the Choctaw Indians of Louisiana. It gives a spicy flavor to gumbo but is seldom used while the soup is on the heat. Nor should the soup be reheated once filé has been added, for it then becomes unpleasantly ropy. Most Louisianans prefer to put filé on their individual servings. However, there are as many ideas on this subject as there are ways to make gumbo. Gumbo without filé may be refrigerated and reheated the next day. When okra is used in a gumbo, no filé is necessary.

CHICKEN GUMBO

Serves 4 to 6

⅓ cup presifted flour
⅓ cup shortening
3 quarts water
1 chicken, cut up
Salt and pepper to taste
Dash of cayenne
1 small onion, finely chopped
Snipped tops of scallions
Chopped parsley

Hot cooked rice
Filé

1. In heavy kettle combine flour and shortening. Cook, stirring constantly, until mixture (called roux) is almost black. Roux must be very brown for gumbo.
2. Immediately add water. Bring to low boil.
3. Add chicken, seasonings, onion, scallion tops and parsley. Cover; simmer for 1½ hours, or until tender, keeping chicken always covered with liquid; add water as necessary.
4. Serve in bowl of rice. Sprinkle with filé.

Marie Treme, Aggressive Study Club,
De Quincy, La.

FRENCH GUMBO FILÉ

Serves 6

2 tablespoons lard
2 tablespoons flour
1 large onion, finely chopped
2 cloves garlic, minced
2 sprigs parsley, minced
1 bay leaf
Salt and pepper to taste
2 quarts water
½ hen or 1 frying chicken, cut into
    small portions
1 slice cooked ham, diced
12 freshly shucked oysters with liquor
1 teaspoon filé

1. Heat lard in soup kettle. Add flour. Cook, stirring, until dark brown.
2. Add onion, garlic, parsley, bay leaf, salt and pepper. Cook until onion is wilted.
3. Add water, chicken and ham. Bring to boil; cover; simmer for 1½ hours, or until chicken is tender, adding water if needed.
4. Add oysters. Cook for 15 minutes longer.
5. Remove from heat. Stir in filé before serving.

Mrs. George C. Poret, Woman's Club,
Murray, Ky.

CRAB GUMBO

Serves 8

24 hard-shell crabs
4 tablespoons butter
1 tablespoon flour
1 medium onion, minced
6 cups chicken broth
3 bay leaves
1 tablespoon chopped green onion
Salt and pepper to taste
¼ teaspoon thyme
1 tablespoon filé
Cooked rice

1. Scald and clean crabs (p. 240). Sauté crabs in half the butter for about 10 minutes.

2. Melt remaining butter in heavy kettle. Stir in flour. Cook until lightly browned.

3. Add onion. Cook slowly, stirring constantly, until onion is golden brown.

4. Add broth, crabs, and all remaining ingredients except filé and rice. Bring to boil; cover; simmer for about 40 minutes.

5. Slowly stir in filé. Bring to boil only once. Serve with rice.

Gulf Coast Gourmet, Woman's Club, Foley, Ala.

CREOLE GUMBO
Serves 6

2 tablespoons bacon drippings
3 tablespoons flour
2 quarts chicken broth
3 slices bacon, diced
2 large onions, finely chopped
2 cloves garlic, crushed
1 small green pepper, minced
3 cups chopped okra
1-pound can peeled tomatoes, drained (reserve liquid)
4 bay leaves
1 teaspoon salt
1 teaspoon pepper
Dash of Tabasco
Dash of cayenne
Dash of Worcestershire
2 pounds shrimp, shelled and deveined
1 pound crab meat or 6 crabs, cleaned
1 pint oysters, freshly shucked
Cooked rice

1. Heat bacon drippings in heavy saucepan. Stir in flour; cook until lightly browned. Gradually stir in broth. Set aside.

2. Sauté bacon in soup kettle until crisp. Add onions, garlic, green pepper, okra and tomatoes. Cover; cook, stirring occasionally, until onions are golden.

3. Stir broth into vegetable mixture. Add reserved tomato liquid and all seasonings. Bring to boil; cover; simmer for 2 hours.

4. About 30 minutes before serving, add seafood and salt if necessary. Cook slowly.

5. Serve on a mound of rice.

Gulf Coast Gourmet, Woman's Club, Foley, Ala.

OYSTER GUMBO FILÉ
Serves 4 to 6

½ cup bacon drippings
¼ cup flour
1 quart water
1 cup diced celery
½ cup chopped green pepper
1 cup chopped onions
Salt and pepper to taste
36 freshly shucked or frozen oysters with liquor
1 teaspoon filé
Cooked rice

1. Melt bacon drippings in Dutch oven or large heavy saucepan. Stir in flour;

sauté over medium heat, stirring frequently, until brown. Gradually stir in water. Cook over medium heat, stirring constantly, until thickened and smooth.

2. Add celery, green pepper, onions, salt and pepper. Cover; simmer over low heat for 15 minutes.

3. Stir in oysters. Simmer over low heat just until edges of oysters begin to curl.

4. Remove from heat. Stir in filé. Serve on rice.

Mabel Kirby, Pierian Study Club, Vivian, La.

SEAFOOD GUMBO WITH CHICKEN
Serves 12 to 15

Some people like whole dressed crabs in gumbo. If so, about 6 to 8, added along with crabmeat, will give a stronger crab flavor. When oysters are in season, a pint of oysters may also be added. This gumbo can be frozen and kept for six weeks to 2 months. Filé should not be added until gumbo is reheated for serving.

4- to 5-pound hen or 2 frying chickens
1-pound 12-ounce can tomatoes
6 tablespoons bacon drippings
6 tablespoons flour
4 medium onions, finely chopped
2 or 3 green peppers, finely chopped
½ medium stalk celery, finely chopped
1½ quarts boiling water
Salt, black pepper, Worcestershire and cayenne to taste
1 pound crab meat
1 pound shrimp, shelled and deveined
1½ pounds okra, cut
Filé
Cooked rice (optional)

1. Simmer chickens in water to cover until tender. Remove to cool.

2. Mash meaty parts of tomatoes; add tomatoes and liquid to chicken stock.

3. Heat bacon drippings in skillet. Stir in flour; cook until lightly browned. Add onions, green peppers and celery. Continue to cook until dark brown. Add boiling water. Simmer for 10 minutes.

4. Stir vegetable mixture gradually into chicken stock. Season with salt and pepper, a little Worcestershire and dash of cayenne.

5. Add seafood and okra; cover; simmer for 2 hours, stirring occasionally.

6. Add enough filé to thicken and add flavor. Simmer for 30 minutes longer. If desired, serve on rice.

Louise C. Stamps, Arts Club, Aliceville, Ala.

BOUILLABAISSE

Serves 6

3 tablespoons olive oil
3 onions, thickly sliced
3 cloves garlic, crushed
1 shallot or scallion, minced
2 10½-ounce cans condensed
   consommé
2 teaspoons salt
½ teaspoon pepper
   Good dash of cayenne
1 bay leaf
¾ teaspoon basil
¾ teaspoon marjoram
1 pound red snapper, cut into
   2-inch squares
1 pound shrimp, shelled and
   deveined
2 cups cooked quartered potatoes
⅓ cup dry red wine
½ cup minced parsley
2 tomatoes, cut into wedges
1 loaf French bread

1. Heat oil in Dutch oven or heavy kettle. Sauté onions, garlic and shallot or green onion for about 10 minutes, or until tender but not browned.
2. Add consommé, salt, pepper, cayenne, bay leaf, basil and marjoram. Cover; bring to boil.
3. Add red snapper, shrimp and potatoes. Cover; simmer for about 20 minutes. Add wine, parsley and tomatoes. Stir gently. Keep warm until ready to serve.
4. Slice and toast bread. Spoon bouillabaisse over toasted bread in soup bowls.

Gulf Coast Gourmet, Woman's Club,
Foley, Ala.

CIOPPINO

Serves 8

½ cup olive oil
2 cloves garlic, finely chopped
1 small onion, minced
1-pound 12-ounce can solid-pack
   tomatoes
2 8-ounce cans tomato sauce
1½ cups water
1 teaspoon monosodium glutamate
1 cup sherry
½ teaspoon basil
½ teaspoon marjoram
   Salt and pepper to taste
1½ pounds halibut or combination of
   rock cod, sea bass and sole, cut
   into bite-size pieces
1 pound prawns or shrimp, shelled
   and deveined
2 cups cooked crab meat
2 pounds clams in shell, well
   scrubbed

1. Day before, prepare sauce so that seasonings will blend: Heat oil in kettle; lightly brown garlic and onion. Add tomatoes, tomato sauce, water, monosodium glutamate, sherry, basil, marjoram, salt and pepper. Bring to boil; cover; simmer for 1½ hours. Cool; then refrigerate.
2. Next day, reheat sauce to simmering.

3. Add fish and prawns or shrimp. Cover; cook over low heat for 20 minutes, do not stir.
4. Add crab meat and clams. Cover; cook for 10 minutes longer, or until clams have opened. Serve in soup plates.

Mrs. Stuart Watson, Woman's Civic Club,
Visalia, Calif.

CLAM CHOWDER

Serves 6 to 8

½ peck clams in shell
4 or 5 medium potatoes, diced
3 slices salt pork, diced
3 onions, sliced
   Salt and pepper to taste
1 quart milk
2 tablespoons butter

1. Wash clams well. After washing, leave in water for a few minutes; if any are dead, they will rise to surface. Discard badly broken and dead clams.
2. Put clams in large kettle over high heat for about 20 minutes, or until shells are well opened (do not add any water). Remove shells; reserve liquor. Discard coarse covering from clams; cut off black necks with scissors.
3. Put potatoes in soup kettle with enough water to cover. Bring to boil; simmer.
4. Sauté salt pork in skillet until pork is crisp and fat is rendered. Remove bits of pork; reserve. Sauté onions in fat in skillet until lightly browned.
5. Add onions to potatoes. Strain and add reserved liquor. Season with salt and pepper. Simmer for 10 minutes, or until vegetables are tender.
6. Add clams and milk. Heat thoroughly, but do not boil.
7. Add butter and reserved pork.

Bertha G. Simpson, Woman's Club,
Durham, N.H.

MANHATTAN CLAM CHOWDER: Follow recipe above, but use 1 quart stewed fresh or canned tomatoes in place of milk.

RHODE ISLAND QUAHOG
CHOWDER

Serves 6

½ pound salt pork, diced
3 to 4 onions, chopped
6 potatoes, diced
   Salt and pepper to taste
1 quart freshly shucked quahogs
   with liquor
   About 2 tablespoons tomato soup
   or purée

1. Cook salt pork in soup kettle until browned and crisp. Remove with slotted spoon to absorbent paper to drain.
2. Add onions to fat remaining in kettle; sauté until lightly browned. Add potatoes; sprinkle with salt and pepper; sauté until lightly browned.
3. Drain liquor from quahogs; measure and add equal quantity of water. Add

liquor mixture to kettle; bring to boil; simmer for 20 minutes.

4. Chop and add quahogs; simmer for a few minutes longer.

5. Just before serving, stir in enough soup or purée to add a little color.

Woman's Club, Pawtucket, R.I.

RED FISH COURT BOUILLON

Serves 10

½ cup olive oil
1 cup chopped onions
3 cloves garlic, crushed
¾ cup presifted flour
1 quart water
2 6-ounce cans tomato paste
½ cup finely chopped celery
1 medium green pepper, finely chopped
2 bay leaves
4 pounds fillets of red snapper, cut into 3-inch squares
1 tablespoon lemon juice
Salt to taste
⅛ teaspoon cayenne
1 tablespoon Worcestershire
¼ cup chopped parsley
Cooked rice

1. Heat oil in Dutch oven or large heavy saucepan; sauté onions and garlic over medium heat for 5 minutes.

2. Stir in flour. Cook, stirring constantly, until browned.

3. Gradually stir in water. Cook over medium heat, stirring constantly, until thickened and smooth.

4. Add tomato paste, celery, green pepper and bay leaves. Bring to boil. Cover; simmer for 15 minutes.

5. Add fish; cover; simmer for 20 minutes.

6. Stir in lemon juice; season with salt. Stir in cayenne, Worcestershire and parsley. Remove from heat. Let stand, covered, for 5 minutes. Serve with rice.

Junior Woman's Club, Thibodaux, La.

CRAB MEAT CHOWDER

Serves 4

3 tablespoons butter
1 slice onion, finely chopped
7¼-ounce can crab meat, drained and flaked
⅓ cup cracker crumbs
1 quart hot milk
2 cups cooked diced potatoes
¾ teaspoon salt
Dash of cayenne

1. Melt butter in saucepan. Sauté onion for 2 minutes, stirring constantly. Add crab meat. Cook over low heat for 10 minutes.

2. Add crumbs and milk. Add potatoes and salt. Heat thoroughly. Just before serving, season with cayenne.

Mrs. E. G. Ritzman, Woman's Club, Durham, N.H.

NEW ENGLAND FISH CHOWDER

Serves 6

2 pounds haddock
2 cups water
2 ounces diced salt pork
2 onions, sliced
4 large potatoes, diced
1 cup chopped celery
1 bay leaf, crumbled
1 teaspoon salt
Freshly ground black pepper
1 quart milk
2 tablespoons butter

1. Simmer haddock in water for 15 minutes. Drain; reserve broth. Flake fish, discarding bones and skin.

2. Cook pork in heavy kettle until crisp and golden. Remove pork; reserve.

3. Add onions to fat remaining in kettle; sauté until golden brown. Add fish, potatoes, celery, bay leaf, salt and pepper.

4. Add enough boiling water to reserved broth to total 3 cups. Add to saucepan; simmer for 30 minutes.

5. Add milk and butter; simmer for 5 minutes.

6. Ladle into soup bowls. Sprinkle each serving with a little reserved pork.

Mrs. John F. Kennedy, Junior Woman's Club, Concord, Calif.

LIVE LOBSTER STEW

Serves 4

1½-pound lobster
½ cup butter
1 quart milk

1. Plunge lobster into boiling water. Simmer for 15 minutes. Drain. Split lobster; discard intestinal vein and sac in back of head; remove meat immediately from shell. Reserve tomalley (liver), coral and thick white substance from inside shell.

2. In heavy saucepan simmer tomalley, coral and white substance in butter for 5 minutes.

3. Add lobster meat; cover; simmer for 10 minutes.

4. Remove from heat. Very gradually trickle in milk, stirring constantly.

5. Let stand for 5 to 6 hours. Reheat before serving.

Muriel Hubbard, Woman's Literary Union, Portland, Me.

LOBSTER STEW

Serves 4

1½ pounds cooked lobster meat
4 tablespoons butter
1 quart milk
Salt and pepper to taste

1. Cut lobster meat into medium pieces. Melt butter in top of double saucepan; sauté lobster for 5 to 6 minutes.

2. Add milk. Cook very slowly over simmering water until hot. The longer the stew blends, the better the flavor.

3. Season with salt and pepper.

Mrs. Tilford D. Miller, Women's Club, Glen Ridge, N.J.

OYSTER STEW
Serves 4 to 6
1 quart freshly shucked oysters
  with liquor
2 cups water
2 teaspoons salt
2 tablespoons butter
⅛ teaspoon pepper
2 cups milk
¼ cup fine cracker crumbs

1. Pick over oysters, removing any bits of shell and seaweed.

2. Put oysters and water in saucepan. Bring to boil. Cook over low heat for about 5 minutes, or until oysters are plump and edges curl.

3. With slotted spoon remove oysters immediately. Put in soup tureen. Add salt, butter and pepper.

4. Heat milk to scalding. Add oyster liquid. Strain over oysters.

5. Serve sprinkled with crumbs.

What's Cookin' in Boynton Beach, Woman's Club,
Boynton Beach, Fla.

OYSTER SOUP
Serves 6
½ cup butter
1 cup thinly sliced onions
3 large cloves garlic, chopped
3 tablespoons flour
1½ quarts water
  Salt and cayenne to taste
4 tablespoons minced parsley
½ teaspoon thyme
3 bay leaves
1 quart freshly shucked oysters
  with liquor
1 cup hot milk
1 cup hot cream

1. Melt butter in soup kettle; sauté onions and garlic until onions are transparent. Stir in flour. Gradually stir in water. Bring to boil, stirring constantly.

2. Add seasonings and oysters. Cover; simmer for 3 hours.

3. Just before serving, add milk and cream. Do not let boil after milk and cream have been added.

Mrs. Frank Becker, Woman's Club, Murray, Ky.

SALMON CHOWDER
Serves 6
1-pound can salmon, undrained
1-pound can whole-kernel corn,
  undrained
1 cup rice
10½-ounce can condensed tomato
  soup
1 quart water
2 teaspoons salt
⅛ teaspoon pepper
1 bay leaf
  Dash of Tabasco
1 cup milk
¼ cup chopped celery leaves

1. Put all ingredients except milk and celery leaves in large heavy saucepan.

2. Mix well. Bring to boil; cover; simmer for 30 minutes, stirring occasionally.

3. Stir in milk and celery leaves; cover; simmer for 15 minutes longer.

Jeanette McCormick, Mendocino Study Club,
Little River, Calif.

SCALLOP STEW
Serves 4
3 cups milk
1 cup heavy cream
2 tablespoons butter
1 teaspoon bottled steak sauce
1 teaspoon salt
1 pound scallops (cut up if large)
  Paprika
  Chopped parsley

1. In saucepan combine milk, cream, butter, steak sauce and salt. Heat to scalding.

2. Add scallops. Poach for 5 minutes (do not boil).

3. Ladle into soup bowls. Sprinkle each serving with paprika and parsley.

Mrs. Wallace A. Price, Woman's Literary Union,
Portland, Me.

SHRIMP CHOWDER
Makes About 2 Quarts
The longer this chowder cooks, the better the blend of flavors. Water may be added as needed. Leftover chowder may be frozen.

1 cup diced potatoes
1 cup diced celery
1-pound 12-ounce can tomatoes
2 pounds shrimp, shelled and
  deveined
1 cup cut corn kernels
¼ teaspoon garlic salt
2 tablespoons butter
½ cup sliced carrots
1 cup diced onions
2 teaspoons salt
12 peppercorns
1 quart water
½ cup diced green pepper
¼ teaspoon crushed red pepper
  flakes
1 teaspoon garlic juice

Combine all ingredients in soup kettle. Bring to boil; cover; cook over low heat until vegetables are tender.

Mrs. Peyton I. Lingle, Woman's Club,
Avondale, Ga.

OLD-FASHIONED NEW ENGLAND BACON AND CORN CHOWDER
Serves 8
6 slices bacon, cut into thin
  crosswise strips with scissors
1 medium onion, thinly sliced
4 cups cooked potatoes, cut into
  ¼-inch-thick slices
2 cups boiling water
1-pound can cream-style corn
1 quart milk
  Salt and pepper to taste
  Dash of Worcestershire

10½-ounce can condensed Manhattan
    clam chowder
1 soup can cold water
8 green pepper rings

1. Cook bacon in saucepan until crisp
and golden.
2. Add onion. Cook for 5 minutes, stirring frequently.
3. Add potatoes, boiling water, corn and
milk. Bring to boil.
4. Season with salt and pepper. Add
Worcestershire.
5. Combine clam chowder with cold
water; stir into soup. Return to boil; simmer for 5 minutes.
6. Garnish each serving with a green
pepper ring.

Woman's Club, Plainville, Conn.

CORN CHOWDER

Serves 6

3 medium potatoes, diced
1 small onion, grated
1 cup water
¼ cup butter
1-pound can whole-kernel corn,
    undrained
3 cups milk
Salt and freshly ground pepper
    to taste
Chopped chives (optional)

1. In saucepan combine potatoes, onion,
water and butter. Bring to boil; cover;
simmer for 10 to 15 minutes, or until
potatoes are tender.
2. Add corn and milk. Simmer for 15
minutes longer. Be careful chowder does
not boil.
3. Season with salt and pepper. If desired, garnish each serving with chives.

Mrs. N. B. Tomlinson, Jr., Thursday Morning
Club, Madison, N.J.

HEARTY CORN AND CRAB MEAT CHOWDER

Serves 6

2 cups diced potatoes
¾ cup thinly sliced onions
1 teaspoon salt
1½ cups hot water
2½ cups milk
7½-ounce can crab meat, drained
    and flaked
1-pound can cream-style corn
1 tablespoon minced parsley

1. In soup kettle combine potatoes,
onions, salt and water. Bring to boil; cover;
simmer for 10 minutes.
2. Add milk, crab meat and corn. Heat
to just below boiling point.
3. Serve sprinkled with parsley.

Ruth A. Prentiss, Woman's Club, Orange, Mass.

Cream Soups and Bisques

Cream soups and bisques make delicious luncheon fare. When they are the
first course of a dinner, the rest of the meal
should be fairly simple, and no other dish
containing milk or cream should be served.

The word "bisque" means a rich cream
soup containing fish or seafood, but it is
sometimes used to describe a soup with
special flavor appeal.

FOUNDATION WHITE SAUCE FOR CREAM SOUPS

Makes About 2 cups

3 tablespoons butter
4 tablespoons flour
½ teaspoon salt
⅛ teaspoon pepper
2 cups hot milk

1. Melt butter in saucepan. Stir in flour,
salt and pepper. Add milk. Cook, stirring,
until thickened and smooth.
2. Use immediately, or cool and then
store in covered container in refrigerator.

CREAM OF CORN SOUP

Serves 4

To 2 cups Foundation White Sauce, add
2 cups cooked corn kernels and 1 onion,
thinly sliced; heat; season to taste. Serve
with popcorn, dash of paprika and strips of
pimiento.

CREAM OF PEA OR ASPARAGUS SOUP

Serves 4

To 2 cups Foundation White Sauce, add
2½ cups pea or asparagus purée and 1
teaspoon grated onion; heat; season to
taste.

CREAM OF POTATO SOUP

Serves 4

To 2 cups Foundation White Sauce, add
2 cups cooked potatoes, 1 cup potato water
and 1 tablespoon grated onion; heat; season to taste.

CREAM OF SPINACH OR CAULIFLOWER SOUP

Serves 4

To 2 cups Foundation White Sauce, add
1½ cups spinach or cauliflower purée and
½ teaspoon sugar; heat; season to taste.
Serve with Toasted Croutons (p. 195).

CREAM OF TOMATO SOUP

Serves 4

To 2 cups Foundation White Sauce, add
2½ cups tomato purée, pinch of baking
soda and 1 teaspoon grated onion; heat;
season to taste. Serve topped with whipped
cream.

Woman's Club, Murray, Ky.

CREAM OF ALMOND SOUP

Serves 6

3 cups chicken broth
3 tablespoons chopped onion
2 cups finely chopped celery
2 cups milk
1 cup heavy cream
3 tablespoons butter or margarine
3 tablespoons flour
1 teaspoon salt
⅛ teaspoon pepper
Dash of Tabasco
½ teaspoon almond extract
⅓ cup chopped toasted almonds

1. Put broth, onion and celery in medium saucepan. Bring to boil; cover; simmer for 20 minutes.
2. Press through sieve or blend in electric blender until smooth.
3. Stir in milk and cream.
4. Melt butter or margarine in another medium saucepan; stir in flour, salt and pepper. Gradually stir in broth mixture. Cook over medium heat, stirring constantly, until thickened and smooth.
5. Remove from heat. Stir in Tabasco and almond extract.
6. Serve in bowls. Sprinkle with almonds.

Virginia Peet, Woman's Club,
La Crescenta, Calif.

AVOCADO SOUP

Serves 6

3 tablespoons butter
1 medium onion, minced
¼ cup celery leaves
3 tablespoons flour
2 cups milk
3 cups chicken broth
1 ripe avocado
½ teaspoon salt
½ teaspoon white pepper
6 slices avocado

1. Melt butter in saucepan; sauté onion and celery leaves until onion is tender but not browned.
2. Stir in flour. Gradually add milk and broth. Cook, stirring, until slightly thickened.
3. Peel and seed avocado. Slice flesh; press through fine sieve, or blend with 1 cup soup in electric blender. Stir into soup. Bring to boil. Add salt and pepper.
4. Pour into soup cups. Garnish each serving with avocado.

Mrs. Eugene Parker, Woman's Club, Naples, Fla.

CREAM OF CARROT SOUP

Serves 6

2 cups chopped carrots
2 cups water
¼ cup rice
2 cups hot milk
¼ cup butter
1 small onion, sliced
2 tablespoons flour

Salt and pepper to taste
½ cup hot cream
Minced parsley

1. Cook carrots in water for 20 minutes, or until tender. Drain; reserve liquid. Press carrots through sieve, or blend with liquid in electric blender until well puréed. Set aside.
2. Combine rice and milk. Cook in top of double saucepan over simmering water for 30 minutes, or until rice is tender.
3. Melt butter in saucepan; sauté onion until tender and golden brown. Stir in flour. Add rice mixture. Cook, stirring, until thickened. Stir in carrot purée and reserved liquid.
4. Season with salt and pepper. Bring to boil. Stir in cream.
5. Serve sprinkled with parsley.

Mrs. H. J. Allen, Woman's Club, Largo, Fla.

POTAGE CRÉCY

Serves 6

When serving, pass the pepper mill.

1 bunch carrots, pared
2 large Idaho potatoes, peeled
3 bunches leeks (white parts only)
6 tablespoons butter
Milk or milk and light cream
Salt, pepper and nutmeg to taste

1. Dice carrots and potatoes; slice leeks ⅛ inch thick. Cover with boiling salted water; bring to boil; cover; boil until tender. Cool.
2. Press vegetables with liquid through sieve, or blend in electric blender until puréed.
3. Add butter. Bring to boil.
4. Gradually add enough milk or milk and cream to achieve desired consistency. Do not let boil, or soup will curdle.
5. Just before serving, add seasonings.

Hildreth Dexter, Century Club, Coraopolis, Pa.

ENGLISH SOUP

Serves 6

3 tablespoons butter
1 pound ground beef
¼ cup minced onion
1 cup water
3 cups tomato juice
2 10½-ounce cans condensed cream of celery soup
¼ teaspoon pepper
⅛ teaspoon marjoram
1 bay leaf
¼ teaspoon garlic salt
1 teaspoon sugar
2 cups shredded carrots

1. Melt butter in deep kettle; cook beef and onion until onion is well browned and meat has lost all red color.
2. Combine water, tomato juice and soup. Stir into meat.
3. Add remaining ingredients; cover; simmer for 1 hour.

Nell Fletcher, Literary Club, Moab, Utah

ELEGANT CHEESE SOUP

Serves 8 to 10

½ cup butter or margarine
1 small green pepper, finely chopped
4 small carrots, finely chopped
4 stalks celery with leaves, finely
chopped
1 teaspoon salt
¼ teaspoon pepper
1½ quarts chicken broth
4 cups Medium White Sauce (p. 441)
1 pound grated sharp Cheddar
cheese

1. Melt butter or margarine in medium saucepan; sauté green pepper, carrots and celery for 5 minutes.
2. Stir in salt, pepper and broth. Bring to boil; cover; simmer for 15 minutes.
3. Meanwhile, prepare Medium White Sauce; leave in saucepan. Stir in cheese; cook over low heat, stirring frequently, until melted.
4. Stir vegetable mixture into cheese mixture. Blend well.
5. Correct seasoning. Simmer for 2 minutes.

Betty Bohstedt, Woman's Club,
Prospect Heights, Ill.

DUCHESS SOUP

Serves 4

1 quart milk
2 tablespoons quick-cooking
tapioca
1 teaspoon salt
1 tablespoon grated onion
2 tablespoons butter
¼ cup grated cheese
½ teaspoon Worcestershire
1 egg yolk, beaten
2 tablespoons chopped parsley
Whipped cream
Paprika

1. Put milk, tapioca, salt and onion in top of double saucepan. Cook over simmering water until tapioca is clear and soup is slightly thickened.
2. Add butter, cheese and Worcestershire.
3. Beat egg yolk with a little of soup. Stir into rest of soup.
4. Add parsley. Top each serving with 1 teaspoon whipped cream; sprinkle with paprika.

Mrs. William Bonanno, Thursday Morning Club,
Madison, N.J.

CHICKEN BISQUE

Serves 8

3-pound stewing hen
4 quarts water
3 tablespoons salt
4 stalks celery, chopped
4 carrots, cut
2 onions, sliced
½ cup butter
1 cup presifted flour
½ cup chopped pimientos
½ cup chopped green pepper,
partially cooked

1 teaspoon monosodium glutamate
½ teaspoon pepper
Yellow food coloring (optional)

1. In covered soup kettle simmer hen, water, salt, celery, carrots and onions until vegetables are tender and meat falls off bones.
2. Strain 8 cups broth into saucepan. Set aside 1½ cups chopped chicken meat from hen.
3. Melt butter in small saucepan. Stir in flour.
4. Bring broth to very low boil. Slowly stir in the butter-flour mixture; simmer for 15 minutes.
5. Add pimientos, reserved chicken, green pepper, monosodium glutamate and pepper. Cook for 5 minutes longer, stirring constantly.
6. Add a few drops food coloring, if desired.

Mrs. Raymond W. Sears, Woman's Club,
McLean, Va.

CREAM OF FRESH CORN SOUP

Serves 6

6 ears corn
1 quart water
2 cups milk
1 slice onion
2 teaspoons flour
2 teaspoons butter
1 teaspoon salt
Whipped cream
Paprika

1. Score corn kernels; press out pulp. Put pulp and cobs in saucepan; add water. Bring to boil; cover; simmer for 20 minutes.
2. Discard cobs. Strain corn through sieve. Return to low heat.
3. Bring milk and onion to scalding point. Discard onion. Stir milk into corn mixture.
4. Combine flour and butter to smooth paste. Gradually stir into soup. Add salt.
5. Serve with a topping of whipped cream sprinkled with paprika.

Lillian A. Scobey, Woman's Club, Eustis, Fla.

CRAWFISH BISQUE

Serves 10 to 12

These freshwater shellfish resembling tiny lobsters are abundant in Louisiana. Although the correct term is crayfish (*écrevisse* on French menus), they are generally called crawfish in the South and elsewhere in the United States.

8 cups crawfish
½ cup olive oil
5 tablespoons flour
2 cloves garlic, crushed
2 large onions, chopped
½ cup chopped celery
¼ cup chopped green pepper
Salt and pepper to taste
4 eggs, hard-cooked and finely
chopped
2 cups fresh bread crumbs

1. Remove heads from crawfish; wash well; set aside. Clean crawfish; cook half of them in boiling salted water for 10 minutes, or until tender; drain; chop meat finely; set aside.
2. Heat ¼ cup of the oil in large skillet. Add 2 tablespoons of the flour; cook, stirring, over low heat until browned. Stir in half the garlic, half the onions, half the celery and half the green pepper.
3. Cook over low heat for 5 minutes. Remove from heat. Season with salt and pepper. Add cooked crawfish, eggs and crumbs; mix well.
4. Preheat oven to 375° F.
5. Fill crawfish heads with stuffing. Place on baking sheet. Bake heads in preheated oven for 10 minutes, or until browned. Set aside.
6. Heat remaining oil in Dutch oven or large heavy saucepan. Add rest of garlic, onion, celery and green pepper. Sauté over medium heat for 5 minutes.
7. Stir in remaining flour. Cook over medium heat for 2 minutes, or until flour starts to brown.
8. Gradually stir in 1 quart water. Cook over medium heat, stirring constantly, until thickened and smooth.
9. Season with salt and pepper; cover; cook over low heat for 15 minutes.
10. Stir in uncooked crawfish; cover; simmer over low heat for 15 minutes, or until cooked.
11. Turn into serving dish. Garnish with stuffed heads.

Mrs. Jennie Alexandry, Junior Woman's Club, Thibodaux, La.

CREAM OF CUCUMBER SOUP
Serves 6 to 8
2 medium cucumbers, unpeeled
4 tablespoons butter
3 tablespoons flour
1 quart milk
1 cup chicken broth
Salt and pepper to taste
Pinch of dried dill
Whipped cream
Chopped chives or parsley

1. Wash cucumbers. Grate on coarse grater.
2. Melt 2 tablespoons of the butter in saucepan; stew cucumbers until tender.
3. Press through sieve or blend in electric blender until puréed. Set aside.
4. Add remaining butter to pan. Stir in flour. Gradually stir in milk, broth, salt and pepper. Cook, stirring, until thickened and smooth. Add cucumber purée and dill. Bring to boil.
5. Serve topped with whipped cream and chives or parsley.

Mrs. Harry J. Sommerkamp, Women's Club, Glen Ridge, N.J.

LOBSTER, SHRIMP OR CRAB BISQUE
Serves 6
2 tablespoons butter
1 teaspoon minced onion

2 tablespoons flour
1 tablespoon tomato paste
2 cups hot chicken broth
1½ cups minced cooked lobster, shrimp or crab meat
1 cup milk
1 cup cream
Salt and cayenne to taste

1. Melt butter in saucepan; sauté onion until soft and golden.
2. Stir in flour and tomato paste.
3. Stir in broth. Cook, stirring, until slightly thickened.
4. Add lobster, shrimp or crab meat. Cook over low heat for 10 minutes.
5. Stir in milk and cream. Heat to serving temperature, but do not boil.
6. Season with salt and cayenne before serving.

A. S.

MULLIGATAWNY SOUP
Serves 8
2 quarts beef broth
1 tablespoon curry powder
2 medium onions, diced
1 stalk celery, diced
1 large tomato, diced
1 carrot, diced
2 tablespoons flour
½ cup milk
1 tablespoon butter
Salt to taste

1. In large saucepan combine broth, curry powder and vegetables. Bring to boil; cover; simmer for 2 hours.
2. Strain. Return to clean pan.
3. In small bowl mix flour and milk to a smooth paste; add with butter to soup. Bring to boil, stirring constantly. Season with salt; cover; simmer over low heat for 5 minutes.

Woman's Club, Monticello, Fla.

CREAM OF MUSHROOM SOUP
Serves 6
3 tablespoons butter
1 medium onion, chopped
½ pound mushrooms, sliced
3 tablespoons flour
2 cups chicken broth
1 cup milk
1 cup cream
Salt and pepper to taste
Pinch of celery seed
Paprika

1. Melt butter in saucepan; sauté onion for 10 minutes, or until tender. Add mushrooms. Cook for 1 minute.
2. Stir in flour.
3. Gradually stir in broth, milk and cream. Cook, stirring, until slightly thickened and hot. Season with salt, pepper and celery seed.
4. Top each serving with a sprinkling of paprika.

Mrs. Harry J. Sommerkamp, Women's Club, Glen Ridge, N.J.

CREAM OF ONION SOUP

Serves 6

3 large onions, sliced
3 cups water or chicken broth
2 potatoes, sliced
1½ tablespoons butter
1 onion, chopped
1 tablespoon flour
1 cup cream
  Salt and pepper to taste
  Toasted Croutons (p. 195)

1. Cook sliced onions in water or broth for 20 minutes. Add potatoes; cook for 20 minutes longer, or until potatoes are tender.
2. Press vegetables through sieve.
3. Melt ½ tablespoon of the butter in skillet; sauté chopped onion until lightly browned; add to soup. Bring to boil. Blend flour and remaining butter to a paste; stir into soup.
4. Add cream, salt and pepper.
5. Sprinkle a few Toasted Croutons in each serving.

Woman's Club Cook Book, Woman's Club,
Eustis, Fla.

OLD-FASHIONED PEANUT SOUP

Serves 10

½ cup butter
1 small onion, diced
2 stalks celery, diced
3 tablespoons flour
2 quarts hot chicken broth
2 cups peanut butter
⅓ teaspoon celery salt
1 teaspoon salt
1 tablespoon lemon juice
½ cup ground peanuts

1. Melt butter in saucepan; cook onion and celery over low heat for 5 minutes.
2. Stir in flour. Add broth. Bring to boil, stirring; cover; simmer for 30 minutes. Remove from heat; strain.
3. Stir in peanut butter, celery salt, salt and lemon juice. Heat, but do not boil.
4. Just before serving, stir in peanuts.

Mrs. Lilly M. Rank, Masonic Service Association,
Washington, D.C.

GOLDEN POTATO SOUP

Serves 4

4 large potatoes, sliced
1 onion, sliced
1 quart hot milk
1 tablespoon minced parsley
2 egg yolks, lightly beaten
  Salt and white pepper to taste
  Toasted Croutons (p. 195)

1. Put potatoes and onion in saucepan with water to cover. Bring to boil; cover; cook for 20 minutes, or until tender. Drain; reserve liquid.
2. Mash potatoes and onions; press through sieve. Stir in milk and parsley.

Add enough reserved potato liquid to make soup of desired consistency. Heat to simmering.
3. Pour soup gradually into egg yolks, beating constantly. Season with salt and pepper.
4. Serve with a sprinkling of Toasted Croutons.

Edith L. Smith, Woman's Club, Eustis, Fla.

POTATO AND LEEK SOUP

Serves 4

4 large potatoes, thinly sliced
1 bunch leeks (white parts only),
  thinly sliced
1 small stalk celery, thinly sliced
1 onion, thinly sliced
1 cup water
  Salt and pepper to taste
1½ cups beef broth or 13¼-ounce
  can chicken broth
1 cup cream
  Finely chopped chives
  Finely shredded cooked carrots

1. Put potatoes, leeks, celery and onion in saucepan with water. Season with salt and pepper. Bring to boil; cover; simmer until vegetables are mushy.
2. Add broth. Bring to boil.
3. Strain soup; press vegetables through sieve. Stir in cream.
4. Heat. Serve with chives and carrots.

Mrs. John Scott Miller, Woman's Club,
Pikeville, Ky.

FRENCH PEASANT POTATO SOUP

Serves 6 to 8

3 medium potatoes, cut into
  small pieces
1 onion, sliced
1 stalk celery, sliced
1 teaspoon salt
  Dash of pepper
2 cups boiling water
3 tablespoons butter
3 tablespoons flour
3 cups milk
  Toasted Croutons (p. 195)
  Chopped parsley or chives

1. In saucepan combine potatoes, onion, celery, salt, pepper and water. Bring to boil; cover; cook for 15 to 20 minutes, or until tender. Strain; reserve 1 cup of liquid. Press vegetables through sieve; combine with reserved liquid; set aside.
2. Melt butter in saucepan. Stir in flour. Slowly stir in milk. Cook, stirring, until thickened and smooth. Correct seasoning.
3. Stir in vegetable purée. Heat to serving temperature.
4. Garnish each serving with Toasted Croutons and parsley or chives.

Pat Hagedorn, Woman's Club,
Lake Hopatcong, N.J.

SOUR CREAM POTATO SOUP
Serves 6

4 tablespoons butter
1 medium onion, chopped
1½ quarts water
1 stalk celery
1 medium carrot
6 stalks parsley
3 pounds potatoes, peeled and
    diced
Salt and pepper
1 egg
½ cup presifted flour
1 cup sour cream

1. Melt butter in large saucepan; sauté onion until golden.
2. Add water. Bring to boil.
3. Tie together celery, carrot and parsley; add to liquid. Add potatoes and salt and pepper to taste. Simmer for 15 minutes. Discard tied vegetables.
4. Meanwhile, blend egg, flour and pinch of salt into a firm dough; grate over large holes of grater. Add to soup; simmer for 10 minutes longer.
5. Reduce heat to very low. Gradually stir in sour cream by spoonfuls.

*Mrs. George Sabo, President, Woman's Club,
Garfield, N.J.*

SEAFOOD BISQUE
Serves 8

¼ cup butter or margarine
¼ cup chopped onion
⅓ cup chopped scallions
2 cups chicken broth
1 cup chopped celery
3 carrots, chopped
1 tablespoon salt
¼ teaspoon thyme
⅓ teaspoon black pepper
2 bay leaves
½ pound frozen haddock, thawed
    and diced
3 cups milk
⅓ cup presifted flour
1 cup cream
6-ounce package frozen cooked crab
    meat, defrosted
7½-ounce can minced clams, drained
Parsley

1. Heat butter or margarine in saucepan; sauté onion and scallions until tender. Add broth, celery, carrots, seasonings and haddock. Bring to boil; cover; simmer for 30 minutes, or until vegetables are tender.
2. Combine 1 cup of the milk and flour. Stir into soup. Cook, stirring, until thickened. Stir in remaining milk and cream. Bring to boil. Stir in crabmeat and clams. Heat.
3. Discard bay leaves. Serve in soup bowls garnished with parsley.

*Mrs. Winston W. Little, Woman's Club,
Murray, Ky.*

EASY CREAM OF SPINACH SOUP
Serves 4

⅓ cup butter
2 tablespoons flour
Salt and freshly ground black
    pepper to taste
2 cups hot milk
1 cup hot cream
10-ounce package frozen chopped
    spinach, defrosted
1 small onion

1. Melt butter in saucepan. Stir in flour, salt and pepper. Add milk and cream. Cook, stirring, until slightly thickened and smooth. Cook over low heat for 8 minutes.
2. Put spinach and onion through fine blade of meat grinder. Add to sauce. Cook for 5 minutes longer, stirring constantly.

*Mrs. Duncan Hines, Woman's Club,
Williamsburg, Ky.*

GARDEN CREAM OF TOMATO SOUP
Serves 4

8 firm ripe tomatoes, halved
1 small onion, quartered
2 tablespoons sugar
1 bay leaf
2 vegetable bouillon cubes
¼ teaspoon cinnamon
⅛ teaspoon ground cloves
½ teaspoon salt
¼ teaspoon pepper
½ cup Thick White Sauce (p. 441)
1 cup light cream
Toasted Croutons (p. 195)
    (optional)

1. In saucepan combine tomatoes, onion, sugar, bay leaf, bouillon cubes, cinnamon, cloves, salt and pepper. Bring to boil; cover; simmer over low heat for 1 hour.
2. Strain through cheesecloth-lined sieve.
3. In another saucepan combine Thick White Sauce and cream. Cook over low heat, stirring constantly, until simmering and smooth.
4. Slowly stir in tomato mixture. Correct seasoning. Heat to serving temperature, stirring constantly.
5. Serve with Toasted Croutons, if desired.

*Dorothy Geering, Woman's Club,
Paramus, N.J.*

CREAM OF TOMATO BISQUE
Serves 8

2 1-pound 4-ounce cans tomatoes,
    undrained
1 medium onion, sliced
1 teaspoon salt
1 teaspoon sugar
¼ teaspoon pepper
2 tablespoons butter or margarine
2 tablespoons flour
1 quart milk
1 teaspoon baking soda
Toasted Croutons (p. 195)

1. In large saucepan combine tomatoes, onion, salt, sugar and pepper. Bring to boil; cover; simmer over low heat for 20 minutes.

2. Press mixture through sieve until puréed. Return to clean pan. Keep warm.

3. Meanwhile, in another saucepan melt butter or margarine; blend in flour. Gradually stir in milk. Cook over low heat, stirring constantly, until thickened and smooth.

4. At serving time, add baking soda to purée. Bring to boil.

5. Remove from heat. Stir in thickened milk.

6. Serve at once with Toasted Croutons.

Woman's Club, Monticello, Fla.

TOMATO RICE SOUP

Serves 6

3½ cups diced ripe tomatoes
3 sprigs parsley
6 cloves
1 bay leaf
¼ teaspoon pepper
2 slices onion
1 teaspoon sugar
1¾ teaspoons salt
2½ tablespoons butter
2½ tablespoons flour
2½ cups milk
1 cup cooked rice

1. In saucepan combine tomatoes, parsley, cloves, bay leaf, pepper, onion, sugar and ¾ teaspoon of the salt. Bring to boil; cover; simmer for 5 minutes, or until tomatoes are mushy. Press through sieve until purée totals 2 cups. (If not enough, add boiling water.)

2. Melt butter in another saucepan. Stir in flour and remaining salt. Gradually stir in milk. Cook, stirring, until thickened.

3. Add rice to purée.

4. When ready to serve, stir purée slowly into sauce. (This prevents curdling.)

*Mrs. W. H. Pond, Woman's Club,
Lombard, Ill.*

CALAMITY JANE CREAM OF TURNIP SOUP

Serves 6

1 quart milk
1 onion, halved
1 tablespoon flour
2 tablespoons melted butter or
  margarine
2 cups grated white turnips
1 teaspoon salt
Chopped parsley

1. In top of double saucepan heat milk and onion over simmering water.

2. Combine flour and butter or margarine. Stir into milk, bit by bit. Cook, stirring, until thickened.

3. Add turnips and salt. Cook for about 10 minutes longer, or until turnips are tender.

4. Discard onion.

5. Sprinkle individual serving dishes with parsley. Pour in soup.

*Snack-Time Symphony, Hopewell Township
Women's Club, Hopewell, Pa.*

VELVET SOUP

Serves 6 to 8

1 quart chicken broth
1½ cups cream
  Salt and pepper to taste
4 egg yolks

1. In saucepan combine broth and 1 cup of the cream. Bring to boil. Season with salt and pepper.

2. Beat egg yolks with remaining cream. Gradually pour soup into egg mixture, stirring rapidly. Reheat, but do not boil.

3. Serve in bouillon cups.

*Woman's Club Cook Book, Woman's Club,
Eustis, Fla.*

Cold Soups

When serving a cold soup, be sure that it is *really* cold. The perfect way to serve cold soups is in bouillon cups, each set in an attractive container filled with cracked ice.

ICED AVOCADO SOUP

Serve very cold with tostados, which are tortillas fried crisp in deep fat.

Jellied Consommé (p. 192) or
bouillon
Ripe avocado, sieved
Sour cream
Salt
Dash of chili powder
Onion juice to taste
Lemon juice to taste

Combine equal parts of Jellied Consommé or bouillon (canned will do nicely), avocado and sour cream. Season well with salt, chili powder, onion juice and lemon juice.

Mrs. Dean Rusk, Washington, D.C.

CREAM OF BORSCHT

Serves 6

1 cup sour cream
1 cup cooked sliced or diced beets
1 cup beet liquid
½ very small onion
½ teaspoon salt
1-inch-thick slice of lemon, peeled
  Sour cream for garnish
  Chopped chives (optional)

1. Put all ingredients except sour cream for garnish, in container of electric blender.

2. Cover. Blend on high speed for 15 seconds, or until very smooth. Chill.

3. Serve with a dab of sour cream in each cup. If desired, sprinkle with chives.

A. S.

JELLIED CONSOMMÉ

Serves 6

1-pound 2-ounce can tomatoes
1 cup water
½ teaspoon pickling spices
Salt to taste
2 10½-ounce cans condensed
   consommé or bouillon
2 envelopes gelatin
Juice of ½ lemon or to taste
Sliced lemon
Parsley sprigs

1. In saucepan combine tomatoes, ½ cup of the water, pickling spices and salt. Bring to boil; cover; simmer for 10 minutes.
2. Add consommé or bouillon; bring to boil.
3. Soften gelatin in remaining water. Add to soup. Stir until thoroughly dissolved.
4. Remove from heat. Stir in lemon juice. Strain; cool; then chill until set.
5. To serve, beat consommé lightly with fork. Pile into consommé cups. Serve with lemon slice and parsley sprig in each cup.

Mrs. George Campbell Lewis, Woman's Club,
Williamsburg, Ky.

BREAKFAST FRUIT SOUP

Serves 4 to 6

3 tablespoons quick-cooking
   tapioca
2 tablespoons sugar
Dash of salt
2½ cups water
6-ounce can frozen orange juice
   concentrate
1 banana, sliced
2 peaches, sliced
1 orange, peeled and sectioned
½ cup sliced strawberries
1 tablespoon lemon juice

1. In saucepan combine tapioca, sugar, salt and 1 cup of the water. Bring to full rolling boil, stirring occasionally.
2. Pour into bowl. Stir in orange juice concentrate and remaining water. Cool for 15 minutes. Then stir; cover; chill.
3. When soup is slightly thickened, stir in fruits and lemon juice.
4. Serve in cups or dessert bowls.

Corrine Hedlund, Junior Woman's Club,
Greeley, Colo.

NORWEGIAN FRUIT SOUP

Serves 4

3 tablespoons quick-cooking tapioca
3 cups water
4 tablespoons sugar
⅛ teaspoon salt
½ cup cooked seedless raisins
½ cup cooked pitted prunes
3 tablespoons lemon juice

1. In top of double saucepan combine tapioca and water. Bring to boil: Cook over simmering water until clear.
2. Add remaining ingredients. Cook for 5 minutes longer.
3. Serve cold or hot.

VARIATION: Use 1 cup crushed lingenberries, strawberries, gooseberries or currants in place of raisins and prunes. Omit lemon juice if currants or gooseberries are used.

Mary Louise Stolz, Woman's Club,
Fern Creek, Ky.

ICED TOMATO SOUP

Serves 6

6 large tomatoes, diced
1 large onion, chopped
¼ cup water
½ teaspoon salt
2 tablespoons tomato paste
2 tablespoons flour
2 cups chicken broth
1 cup heavy cream

1. Put tomatoes, onion, water and salt in saucepan. Bring to boil; cover; simmer for 10 minutes.
2. In small bowl blend tomato paste and flour. Stir into tomato mixture.
3. Add broth. Cook over medium heat, stirring constantly, until thickened. Simmer for 5 minutes.
4. Remove from heat. Press through sieve. Chill.
5. Just before serving, stir in cream.

Mrs. James Saxon, Junior Woman's Club,
Elyria, Ohio

TROPICAL GAZPACHO

Serves 4

6 slices bread
1 cup water
½ cup tomato sauce
¼ cup cider vinegar
1 cucumber, peeled and seeded
¼ cup olive oil
1 teaspoon garlic salt
1 teaspoon grated onion
8 ice cubes
Garnishes:
   2 eggs, hard-cooked and diced
   1 medium green pepper, diced
   1 large tomato, diced
   1 cup croutons, sautéed
      in 1 tablespoon olive oil

1. Tear bread into container of electric blender. Add water. Cover; turn blender on low speed.
2. Remove cover. Gradually add tomato sauce, vinegar, cucumber, oil, garlic salt and onion. Cover; blend on low speed for 3 minutes.
3. Turn into soup tureen. Add ice cubes. Chill until serving time. If too thick, stir in some ice water.
4. When served, pass garnishes, each in a separate dish.

Lillian T. de Canais, President, Puerto Rico
Federation of Women's Clubs

VEGETABLE SALAD SOUP

Serves 6

2½ cups tomato juice
3 ripe tomatoes, finely diced
½ tablespoon chopped chives
½ cucumber, peeled and finely diced

½ cup finely diced celery
1 tablespoon lemon juice
½ teaspoon salt
Dash of pepper
Sour cream

1. In mixing bowl combine tomato juice, tomatoes, chives, cucumber and celery. Season with lemon juice, salt and pepper. Cover. Refrigerate for 2 to 3 hours.
2. Top each serving with a dollop of sour cream.

Mrs. Gordon A. Barker, Pueblo Junior Woman's Club, Tucson, Ariz.

SENEGALESE SOUP WITH FRESH PINEAPPLE

Serves 6

2 cups chicken broth
3 egg yolks, slightly beaten
2 cups half-and-half
2 cups finely chopped cooked chicken
¾ teaspoon curry powder
Salt
1 cup finely diced pineapple
1 cup heavy cream

1. Heat broth to simmering. Mix a little with egg yolks; stir into broth. Continue to cook, stirring constantly, until slightly thickened, but do not let boil. Remove from heat. Cool.
2. Add half-and-half, chicken, curry powder and salt to taste. Refrigerate for several hours or overnight.
3. Just before serving, stir in pineapple. Whip cream with ¼ teaspoon salt; top each serving with a large spoonful.

Mrs. William H. Hasebroock, Honorary President, General Federation of Women's Clubs, West Point, Neb.

VICHYSSOISE

Serves 6 to 8

2 tablespoons butter
4 leeks (white parts only), finely sliced
3 stalks celery, chopped
1 small onion, sliced
5 medium potatoes, thickly sliced
1 quart chicken broth
2 cups hot milk
2 cups heavy cream
Salt, pepper and cayenne to taste
Finely chopped chives

1. Melt butter in saucepan; sauté leeks, celery and onion over low heat until tender but not browned.
2. Add potatoes and broth. Bring to boil; cover; simmer for 30 minutes. Put first through food mill then through fine sieve, or blend in electric blender until well puréed.
3. Add milk and 1 cup of the cream. Season with salt, pepper and cayenne. Bring just to boil. Remove from heat; cool, then refrigerate.

4. Just before serving, stir in remaining cream.
5. Serve sprinkled with chives.

Mrs. J. B. Gatliff, Jr., Woman's Club, Williamsburg, Ky.

Quick Soups

QUICK CANNED SOUP COMBINATIONS

Zippy flavors are easily obtained by combining two or more canned soups for appetizing variations. Follow directions on cans. Then blend, heat and serve hot in bowls, mugs or cups with crisp crackers, toast or seasoned bread sticks. Savory party-time garnishes include ice-cold celery sticks, carrot sticks and pickles; tart olives, lemon slices, scallions, green pepper strips, radishes, nippy cheese, sliced frankfurters, popcorn, corn chips, potato chips and hard rolls.

COMBINE (follow directions on cans, diluting condensed soups as specified):

Chicken bouillon and onion soup
Chicken noodle soup and chicken bouillon
Chicken soup and celery or tomato soup
Clam chowder and chicken gumbo
Corn chowder and chicken soup
Corn chowder and cream of tomato
Cream of asparagus and chicken gumbo
Cream of celery and chicken noodle soup
Cream of celery and onion soup
Cream of mushroom and cream of pea
Cream of oyster and corn chowder
Cream of oyster and cream of mushroom
Cream of spinach and cream of celery
Cream of tomato and cream of spinach
Tomato soup and cream of pea
Vegetable soup and chicken noodle soup

Snack-Time Symphony, Hopewell Township Women's Club, Hopewell, Pa.

QUICK PARISIAN BEEF SOUP

Serves 6

10½-ounce can condensed beef noodle soup
10½-ounce can condensed vegetable soup
2 4-ounce cans sliced mushrooms
¼ cup dry red wine

1. Prepare soups according to directions on cans.
2. Combine soups.
3. Add mushrooms and wine. Heat to serving temperature.

Helen Fagone, Woman's Literary Union, Portland, Me.

QUICK CEBOLLA-FRIJOLES SOUP

Serves 10

1 envelope onion soup mix
1 large can refried beans

1. Make soup according to package directions.
2. Add beans. Simmer for 10 minutes.

Mrs. Ben Rutherford, Junior Woman's Club, Benson, Ariz.

CLARET SOUP

Serves 8

4 10½-ounce cans condensed
   beef bouillon
   Cinnamon stick
1½ tablespoons sugar
2 cups claret or dry red wine

1. In saucepan combine bouillon, cinnamon and sugar.
2. Heat to just below boiling point.
3. Stir in wine. Heat to serving temperature, but do not boil.

Sara Cotten, Junior Alpha Club,
Lompoc, Calif.

QUICK CRAB BISQUE

Serves 6 to 8

10½-ounce can condensed cream
   of asparagus soup
10½-ounce can condensed cream
   of mushroom soup
2½ cups milk
1 cup light cream
6½-ounce can crab meat, drained
   and flaked
¼ cup dry sherry

1. In saucepan combine soups.
2. Add milk and cream. Stir until smooth.
3. Bring to boil over low heat, stirring frequently.
4. Add crab meat. Simmer for 5 minutes.
5. Remove from heat. Stir in sherry.

Annette O'Brien, Junior Woman's Club,
Floral Park, N.Y.

QUICK SENEGALESE SOUP

Serves 4

2 10½-ounce cans condensed
   cream of chicken soup
1 soup can milk
2 teaspoons curry powder
2 tablespoons water
   Juice of 1 lemon
   Chopped chives

1. In saucepan combine soup and milk. Heat to simmering.
2. Combine curry powder and water; stir into soup. Simmer gently for 10 minutes to blend flavors.
3. Remove from heat. Stir in lemon juice.
4. Serve hot or cold with chives.

Mrs. Claude S. Nunn, Woman's Club,
Glen Ridge, N.J.

QUICK LENTEN SOUP

Serves 6

10½-ounce can condensed pepper
   pot soup
10½-ounce can condensed cream
   of mushroom soup
1 cup flaked crab meat
1 cup tomato soup
14-ounce can evaporated milk
½ teaspoon curry powder

Combine all ingredients in saucepan. Stir over moderate heat to serving temperature.

Sally Blair, Junior Woman's Club,
Greeley, Colo.

QUICK PEANUT BUTTER AND TOMATO SOUP

Serves 4

10½-ounce can condensed
   tomato soup
½ cup catsup
1 cup cream
8-ounce jar peanut butter

1. In saucepan combine soup, catsup and cream. Heat slowly.
2. Add peanut butter. Cook over very low heat, stirring constantly, until melted.

Mrs. D. W. Christian, Woman's Club,
Greenville, Ky.

QUICK CURRIED PEA SOUP

Serves 2

10½-ounce can condensed pea soup
½ soup can milk
¼ teaspoon curry powder
1 cup shaved carrots
½ cup heavy cream, whipped

1. In saucepan combine soup, milk and curry powder. Heat.
2. Serve garnished with carrots and whipped cream.

Meal on Wheels, Woman's Club,
Greenwich, Conn.

QUICK POTAGE ST. GERMAIN

Serves 4

10½-ounce can condensed pea soup
½ cup tomato juice
3 tablespoons tomato paste
1 cup cream
   Salt and pepper to taste
   Chopped scallions

1. Blend soup, tomato juice and tomato paste well, or combine in electric blender. Turn into saucepan. Bring to boil.
2. Stir in cream, salt and pepper.
3. Garnish each serving with scallions.

Mrs. Arthur Totton, Thursday Morning Club,
Madison, N.J.

PURÉE MONGOLE

Serves 6

10½-ounce can condensed tomato soup
10½-ounce can condensed green pea
   soup
1 soup can milk
1 soup can water
   Dash of curry powder (optional)

1. Mix soups well.
2. Gradually stir in milk and water. Heat, but do not boil.

Jean Welch, Woman's Club,
Thompson Falls, Mont.

QUICK TOMATO ASPARAGUS SOUP

Serves 4 to 6

10½-ounce can condensed tomato
    soup
10½-ounce can condensed asparagus
    soup
2 soup cans milk
Salt and pepper to taste
Potato chips
Chopped chives or parsley

1. Combine soups and milk. Heat to simmering. Season with salt and pepper.
2. Ladle into soup plate. Float a few potato chips in each serving.
3. Sprinkle with chives or parsley.

*What's Cookin' in Boynton Beach,
Woman's Club, Boynton Beach, Fla.*

QUICK TOMATO MUSHROOM BISQUE

Serves 4 to 6

10½-ounce can condensed tomato
    soup
10½-ounce can condensed mushroom
    soup
2 cups milk
2 tablespoons grated onion
½ teaspoon garlic salt (optional)

1. Combine soups and milk.
2. Add onion and garlic salt, if desired. Bring to boil; simmer for 10 minutes, stirring occasionally.

*May Anderson, Woman's Literary Club,
Portland, Me.*

Soup Garnishes

Most soups are improved with a garnish, which may be as simple as a sprinkling of paprika; some chopped parsley, celery leaves, chives or dill; dab of sour cream, or a few of the special soup garnishes which follow. Other garnishes suitable for soups will be found in section on dumplings in Chapter 14. Even leftover thin pancakes, cut into fine strips, are excellent when added to clear soups. See recipe for Crêpes (p. 134).

HERBED BREAD CHUNKS

These are also good with salads.

1 long loaf French bread
½ cup softened butter
2 tablespoons grated Parmesan
    cheese
½ teaspoon mixed salad herbs

1. Preheat oven to 500° F.
2. Cut bread in half crosswise; split each half to make 4 pieces. Slash pieces about 1 inch apart, but do not cut through crusts.
3. Spread generously with butter. Sprinkle lightly with cheese and salad herbs.

4. Place on baking sheet. Bake in preheated oven for about 5 minutes, or until golden and crisp. Serve piping-hot.

*Colette Wirshing, Junior Woman's Club,
Pompano Beach, Fla.*

CRACKER MEAL BALLS

Makes About ½ Cup

1 cup cracker meal
1 egg, lightly beaten
⅓ cup water
½ teaspoon salt
Hot soup

1. Mix all ingredients. Form into small balls.
2. Drop balls into hot soup; cover; simmer for 10 minutes.

*Mrs. C. W. Coulter, Woman's Club,
Durham, N.H.*

CRACKER BALLS

Makes About ½ Cup

2 eggs, lightly beaten
10 crackers, rolled into fine crumbs
1 teaspoon minced parsley
1 teaspoon baking powder
1 tablespoon chicken fat
1 egg white, beaten until stiff
    but not dry
Boiling chicken broth or any clear
    soup

1. Combine all ingredients except egg white. Fold in egg white.
2. Form into balls about 1½ inches in diameter. Chill for 15 minutes or longer.
3. Drop into broth or soup; cover; simmer for 10 minutes.

*Mrs. R. E. Daniels, Woman's Club,
Greenville, Ky.*

FRIED CROUTONS

Cut day-old bread into ½-inch cubes; put in wire basket; fry in deep fat heated to 365° F. until golden. Drain on absorbent paper. Sprinkle with salt to taste.

TOASTED CROUTONS

Butter day-old slices of bread; cut into ½-inch cubes. Place on baking sheet. Bake in preheated 400° F. oven for 6 minutes, or until browned.

*Woman's Club Cook Book, Woman's Club,
Eustis, Fla.*

GARLIC CROUTONS

1 cup bread cubes
2 tablespoons olive oil
1 clove garlic, crushed

1. Heat oil in saucepan; add garlic; brown bread cubes.
2. Discard garlic. Drain on absorbent paper.

A. S.

EGG DROPS

1 egg
½ cup presifted flour
Pinch of salt
Boiling clear soup

1. Beat egg. Stir in flour and salt.

2. Add a little water to make very soft batter which will fall off tip of spoon by drops. Drop slowly into soup so that each drop cooks separately.

Mrs. G. A. Peters, Woman's Club, Lombard, Ill.

RIVELS

Serves 8

2 cups presifted flour
½ teaspoon salt
1 egg, well beaten
Boiling soup

1. Blend all ingredients until crumbly.

2. Add to soup; cover; simmer for 10 minutes. Rivels will look like boiled rice when cooked.

Mrs. E. A. Doolan, Woman's Club, Lombard, Ill.

ITALIAN SPONGES

Serves 12

1 cup presifted flour
1½ teaspoons baking powder
12 eggs, lightly beaten
1 cup grated Romano or
  Parmesan cheese

1. Preheat oven to 375° F. Grease 15½ x 10½ x 1-inch jelly roll pan.

2. Into mixing bowl sift together flour and baking powder.

3. Add eggs. Beat until smooth.

4. Stir in cheese. Pour into pan.

5. Bake in preheated oven for 12 minutes, or until set and browned.

6. Cut into small squares.

Mrs. Mary Jane Donato, Civic League,
Greenville, Pa.

WONTONS

Makes 20

2 cups presifted flour
1½ teaspoons salt
2 eggs
1 pound finely ground cooked
  pork
1 tablespoon soy sauce
¼ teaspoon pepper

1. To prepare Wonton Pastry: Into mixing bowl sift together flour and 1 teaspoon of the salt. Add 1 of the eggs and ⅓ cup water, adding water a few drops at a time; mix to a smooth dough.

2. Turn onto lightly floured board. Knead until smooth. Cover; let stand for 20 minutes.

3. Roll out dough until paper-thin. Cut into 2-inch squares.

4. To prepare filling: combine remaining salt, remaining egg, pork, soy sauce and pepper. Work together until smooth.

5. Put a little filling in center of each square of dough. Fold over each square to make triangle; press edges together, but leave point of triangle open.

6. Drop wontons a few at a time into boiling salted water. Cook until they rise to surface. Remove with slotted spoon. Drain on absorbent paper.

Woman's Club, Palisade, N.J.

6. Eggs and Egg Dishes

There are more ways than one to scramble an egg, but there is one infallible rule in egg cookery: "never boil an egg, unless it is in the shell."

A scrambled egg is simply an egg that has been curdled by the heat of a pan. The best scrambled eggs are those cooked slowly over very low heat with constant stirring, until they are creamy, are just beginning to set, but are still moist.

The only time direct high heat should be used in egg cookery is for a French omelet. Here the brevity of cooking is the secret. There is a saying that if it takes longer than 1 minute to make an omelet, it is not worth eating.

Perhaps the most difficult cooking assignments for the inexperienced homemaker are making egg sauces (Chapter 12) and custards (Chapter 22). But if she remembers the infallible rule—never let sauce or custard boil—she has nothing to worry about.

TO SEPARATE AN EGG: You need 2 bowls. Tap the center of the side of an egg lightly but sharply on the edge of one of the bowls. Then, with both hands, carefully open the egg, and holding the egg, cracked side up, over a bowl, let the yolk slip into half of the shell. As this is done, some of the egg white will slip into the bowl. Slip the yolk back and forth from one of the half shells to the other until no white remains in the shells. Should the yolk break and a bit slip into the egg white, pick it out with a clean piece of broken shell, for if even the slightest speck of egg yolk remains, the white will not whip. Drop the yolk into the other bowl.

Eggs—A Variety of Dishes

SOFT-COOKED EGG

1. Slip egg gently from a spoon into rapidly boiling water to cover.
2. Lower heat to keep water just simmering. Cook for desired length of time: 3; 3½, 4, 4¼ or 5 minutes.
3. Remove egg. Serve at once.

SIX-MINUTE "BOILED" EGG
(*Oeuf Mollet*)

1. Follow directions for Soft-Cooked Egg, but cook egg for 5½ to 6 minutes.
2. Remove egg; plunge into cold water. Immediately crack and peel away shell. White will be set and firm, but yolk will still be creamy.

HARD-COOKED EGG

1. Follow directions for Soft-Cooked Egg, but simmer egg for 10 minutes from time water resumes slow boil.
2. Drain; cover with running cold water. Peel as soon as egg is cool enough to handle.

CODDLED EGG

1. Slip an egg into boiling water. Cover saucepan with tight-fitting lid. Remove from heat.
2. Let egg cool in water for 10 to 15 minutes. White will remain creamy and is believed to be more digestible than white cooked at simmering point.

POACHED EGG

1. Break egg into cup or saucer; slip into boiling salted water.
2. Cook over low heat, without letting water boil again, until white has enveloped yolk and may be touched without breaking.
3. Remove egg with slotted spoon or perforated spatula.

A. S.

POACHED EGGS, COUNTRY STYLE
Serves 4

1 tablespoon butter
1 cup light cream
4 eggs
Salt and pepper to taste
2 tablespoons crushed cornflakes
4 slices buttered hot toast

1. Melt butter in skillet. Add cream. Heat until just bubbling.
2. Add eggs, one at a time. Cook over low heat until whites become firm around edges.
3. Sprinkle with salt, pepper and cornflakes.

4. Cover; cook over low heat until eggs are done to taste.

5. Place each egg on slice of toast. Spoon cream over it.

Maxine Stetzel, Woman's Club, Casey, Ia.

EGGS BENEDICT
Makes 1 Per Person
Thinly sliced ham
Toasted English muffins
Poached egg
Hollandaise Sauce (p. 444)

1. Place ham slice on muffin.
2. Top with egg.
3. Spoon Hollandaise Sauce over all.

Elizabeth Davidson, Century Club,
Coraopolis, Pa.

SCRAMBLED EGGS
Serves 2
4 eggs
Salt to taste
Dash of white pepper
Butter
Heavy cream (optional)

1. Break eggs into bowl. Add salt and a dash of white pepper. Beat quickly but lightly with rotary beater or fork.
2. Melt 1 tablespoon butter in skillet. Tip skillet so butter coats bottom and sides. Give one last beat to eggs; just before butter begins to sizzle, pour into skillet.
3. Stir constantly with wooden spoon, scraping bottom and sides of pan to prevent eggs from sticking, until mixture has soft, creamy consistency.
4. Remove from heat. Stir in small piece of butter or a little cream, if desired.

A. S.

SCRAMBLED BREAKFAST EGGS
Serves 6 to 8
6 slices bacon
1 cup fresh bread crumbs
½ cup milk
6 eggs, lightly beaten
Salt and pepper to taste

1. Cook bacon in skillet until crisp. Set aside in warm place.
2. Add crumbs to fat remaining in skillet; cook until browned and crisp. Set aside.
3. Beat milk into eggs. Stir into fat remaining in skillet. Scramble eggs until nearly set.
4. Stir in crumbs and bacon. Continue to cook until eggs reach desired firmness. Season with salt and pepper.

Mrs. Charles E. Weber, Woman's Club,
Vero Beach, Fla.

SCRAMBLED EGGS AND PEPPERS
Serves 2 or 3
4 tablespoons olive oil
2 large green peppers, chopped
6 eggs
6 tablespoons milk
Salt and pepper to taste

1. Heat oil in skillet. Sauté green peppers until tender.
2. Beat together remaining ingredients.
3. Add to peppers. Cook, stirring constantly, until eggs are creamy.

Lucile Miller, Woman's Civic Club,
Cumberland, Md.

SCRAMBLED EGGS AND ZUCCHINI
Serves 4
2 tablespoons cooking oil
1 cup diced zucchini
1 tablespoon chopped green pepper
2 tablespoons finely chopped onion
4 eggs
1 teaspoon salt
¼ teaspoon pepper
Dash of cayenne

1. Heat oil in medium skillet; sauté zucchini, green pepper and onion over low heat for 10 minutes, stirring occasionally.
2. Meanwhile, in bowl beat eggs and seasonings.
3. Add eggs to skillet. Cook, stirring frequently, until eggs reach desired firmness.

Joan Horton, Junior Women's Club,
Renton, Wash.

MEXICAN SCRAMBLED EGGS
Serves 4
2 tablespoons olive oil
1 small onion, finely chopped
½ clove garlic, crushed
1 small green pepper, finely chopped
½ cup chopped drained canned tomatoes
1 teaspoon salt
½ teaspoon pepper
6 eggs, lightly beaten

1. Heat oil in large skillet; sauté onion, garlic and green pepper over medium heat for 5 minutes.
2. Stir in tomatoes, salt and pepper. Simmer for 5 minutes.
3. Stir in eggs. Cook, stirring occasionally, until eggs reach desired firmness.

M. W. Emmel, Woman's Club, Jainesville, Fla.

STZUDDLA BROD
Serves 1
This fine Pennsylvania Dutch breakfast is best when 1 serving is made at a time.

1 tablespoon butter
2 slices bread, broken into large pieces
1 egg, lightly beaten

1. Melt butter in small skillet. Add bread; toss constantly with fork until slightly browned.
2. Add egg. Continue to toss until bread is well coated with egg and egg is cooked.

Berks County Federation of Women's Clubs,
Berks County, Pa.

FLUFFY EGGS

Serves 2

3 eggs, separated
1 cup milk
1 teaspoon salt
Crisp bacon (optional)
Parsley (optional)

1. Grease and flour top of double saucepan.
2. In mixing bowl beat egg yolks until light and lemon-colored. Stir in milk and salt.
3. In another mixing bowl beat egg whites until stiff but not dry. Fold into egg yolk mixture. Turn into top of double saucepan.
4. Cover; cook over hot water for 15 minutes. Do not remove cover during cooking.
5. Turn onto hot serving dish. Garnish with bacon and parsley, if desired.

*Malva Duttera, Woman's Community Club,
Littlestown, Pa.*

BAKED OR SHIRRED EGGS

Serves 1

1 tablespoon butter
2 eggs
Salt to taste

1. Preheat oven to 350° F.
2. Melt butter in individual casserole. Carefully break eggs into butter. Sprinkle with salt. Cook over low heat for 1 minute.
3. Spoon a little of melted butter over yolk. Cook in preheated oven for about 15 minutes, or until whites are set but still creamy.

A. S.

EGG IN NEST

Serves 1

1 egg
1 slice buttered toast
Salt and pepper to taste

1. Preheat oven to 350° F., or preheat broiler.
2. Separate egg white from yolk.
3. Beat white until stiff but not dry. Pile onto toast; make nest in center. Drop yolk into nest. Season with salt and pepper.
4. Bake in preheated oven or broil until yolk is partially cooked and white is toasted golden brown.

Mrs. Minnie Tinsley, Woman's Club, Elroy, Ariz.

BAKED EGG-CHEESE DISH

Serves 3 to 6

6 slices Cheddar cheese
1 teaspoon dry mustard
½ teaspoon salt
Dash of cayenne
¾ cup light cream
6 eggs

1. Preheat oven to 350° F. Grease 8-inch pie plate.
2. Arrange cheese around sides and bottom of pie plate.

3. In small bowl mix mustard, salt, cayenne and cream. Pour half on cheese.
4. Carefully break eggs into pie plate. Top with remaining cream mixture.
5. Bake in preheated oven for 10 to 15 minutes, or until eggs are done to taste.

*Mrs. Edson D. Fuller, Woman's Club,
Mount Dora, Fla.*

BELGIAN EGG CASSEROLE

Serves 6

12 pork sausages
2 tablespoons flour
1-pound 4-ounce can tomatoes, drained
1 teaspoon salt
½ teaspoon pepper
Dash of basil
6 eggs
1½ cups fresh bread crumbs
¼ cup butter or margarine

1. Preheat oven to 350° F. Grease 10 x 6 x 1½-inch baking pan.
2. Fry sausages in large skillet according to package directions. Remove from skillet. Set aside.
3. Drain all but 2 tablespoons fat from skillet. Stir flour into fat remaining in skillet. Stir in tomatoes. Cook over low heat, stirring constantly, until bubbling.
4. Remove from heat. Stir in salt, pepper and basil. Spread in pan.
5. Arrange sausages on sauce. Break eggs between sausages. Sprinkle with crumbs. Dot with butter or margarine.
6. Bake in preheated oven for 15 minutes, or until eggs reach desired firmness.

*Anna Dahlstrom, Woman's Club,
Sebastian, Fla.*

BAKED HUEVOS RANCHEROS

Serves 6

3 tablespoons butter or margarine
1 large onion, chopped
1 cup chopped green pepper
1 clove garlic, stuck on wooden pick
1 tablespoon flour
1-pound 13-ounce can tomatoes, drained
1 teaspoon salt
¼ teaspoon pepper
½ teaspoon orégano
6 eggs
½ cup grated sharp Cheddar cheese
½ cup sliced pitted ripe olives

1. Preheat oven to 350° F. Grease 10-inch pie plate or other shallow baking dish.
2. Melt butter or margarine in skillet; sauté onion, green pepper and garlic over medium heat for 5 minutes. Stir in flour. Add tomatoes, salt, pepper and orégano. Simmer for 5 minutes. Discard garlic. Turn vegetables into pie plate or baking dish.
3. Break one egg at a time on vegetables.
4. Arrange cheese and olives around eggs.

5. Bake in preheated oven for 15 minutes, or until eggs reach desired firmness.

Evelyn Jackman, Progress Club, South Bend, Ind.

EGGS À LA JUNKIN

Serves 3

½ cup diced bacon
2 eggs, well beaten
1 cup milk
½ teaspoon salt
⅛ teaspoon pepper
2 slices bread, diced
Orange marmalade

1. Preheat oven to 350° F.
2. Cook bacon in skillet until crisp and golden. Drain off fat.
3. Beat eggs, milk, salt and pepper. Stir in bacon.
4. Put bread in shallow baking dish. Pour egg mixture over it.
5. Bake in preheated oven for 20 minutes.
6. Serve hot with orange marmalade.

Mrs. K. W. Woodward, Woman's Club, Durham, N.H.

EGGS AND TOMATOES

Serves 6

6 firm large tomatoes
6 eggs
1 cup fresh bread crumbs
1 teaspoon salt
¼ teaspoon pepper
¼ cup melted butter

1. Preheat oven to 350° F. Grease 10 x 6 x 1½-inch baking pan.
2. Cut slice from top of each tomato; scoop out some pulp. Place tomatoes, cut side up, in pan.
3. Slip egg into each toamto.
4. In small bowl combine crumbs, salt, pepper and butter. Sprinkle over eggs.
5. Add ¼ inch water to pan. Bake in preheated oven for 20 minutes.

F. E. Hartshorn, Woman's Club, Harvard, Mass.

PAN-FRIED OR SAUTÉED EGGS

Serves 1 or 2

1 tablespoon butter or bacon drippings
2 eggs
Salt to taste

1. Melt butter or bacon drippings in skillet.
2. Carefully break eggs into saucer; slip into skillet. Cook over low heat, basting eggs with some of hot fat, until white is no longer transparent and yolk is set. Season with salt.

A. S.

COUNTRY BREAKFAST

Serves 6

6 slices bacon, diced
4 cups cooked cubed potatoes
½ cup chopped green pepper
2 tablespoons chopped onion
Salt and pepper to taste

6 eggs
1 cup shredded sharp Cheddar cheese

1. Cook bacon in skillet until crisp. Remove from skillet. Pour off excess fat.
2. Add potatoes, green pepper and onion to fat remaining in skillet. Cook until lightly browned. Season with salt and pepper.
3. Break eggs over potato mixture; cover; cook until eggs reach desired firmness.
4. Sprinkle with cheese and bacon. Cover; heat until cheese is melted.

Carolyn Talbert, Woman's Club, Warner Robins, Ga.

EGGS FOO YOUNG

Serves 4

4 eggs
About 1½ cups chopped cooked chicken, pork, shrimp or crab meat
8-ounce can button mushrooms
1-pound can bean sprouts, drained
1 scallion, chopped
½ stalk celery, chopped
Salt and pepper to taste
1 tablespoon cornstarch
1 teaspoon soy sauce
1½ cups chicken broth
¼ teaspoon sugar
Cooking oil

1. In mixing bowl beat eggs lightly. Stir in chicken, meat or seafood, mushrooms, bean sprouts, onion, celery, salt and pepper. Set aside.
2. In saucepan combine cornstarch, soy sauce, broth, sugar, salt and pepper. Bring to boil. Cook over medium heat, stirring, until thickened. Keep warm.
3. Cover bottom of 6-inch skillet with oil; heat. Pour in about one-fourth of egg mixture. Cook over low heat until browned on one side. Turn carefully. Cook until browned on other side.
4. Serve on hot dish with sauce.

VARIATION: Use sliced water chestnuts in place of mushrooms.

Mrs. Abe H. Stewart, Woman's Club, St. Mary's, W. Va.

SHRIMP EGGS FOO YOUNG

Serves 4

Cooking oil
½ cup chopped celery
¼ cup chopped scallions
½ pound shrimp, shelled, deveined and diced
1-pound can bean sprouts, drained
6 eggs
½ teaspoon ginger
1 tablespoon dry sherry
1 tablespoon soy sauce
1 tablespoon flour
1 teaspoon salt
¼ teaspoon pepper
½ teaspoon monosodium glutamate

1. Heat 2 tablespoons oil in medium skillet. Add celery and scallions. Sauté for 5 minutes.

2. Stir in shrimp and bean sprouts. Simmer, stirring frequently, for 8 minutes, or until shrimp are cooked. Remove from heat. Cool.

3. Beat eggs in mixing bowl until foamy. Stir in remaining ingredients and shrimp mixture.

4. Heat thin layer of oil in large skillet; drop batter by tablespoons. Cook for 2 to 3 minutes on each side, or until golden.

Mary Wolfson, Junior Woman's Club, Newington, Conn.

DEEP-FRIED EGGS

This is a popular method of cooking raw or hard-cooked eggs in Mexico and South America. Sometimes the hard-cooked eggs are stuffed, re-formed and coated with bread crumbs before being fried in deep fat heated to 365° F.

FRIED RAW EGGS

Cooking oil or shortening
Eggs

1. Heat oil or shortening to 365° F. in heavy pan or skillet, making sure oil or shortening, when melted, is about 1 inch deep.

2. Break eggs into saucer; slip them, one at a time, into oil or shortening. Fry for 1 or 2 minutes, or until white is crisp and browned and yolk is set.

3. Drain on absorbent paper.

DEEP-FRIED HARD-COOKED EGGS: Fry as above, but use enough oil or shortening to cover eggs completely.

A. S.

Hard-Cooked Egg Dishes

EGGS À LA GOLDENROD
Serves 4
1 cup Medium White Sauce (p. 441)
Salt and pepper to taste
3 eggs, hard-cooked
4 slices toast
Parsley sprigs

1. Put Medium White Sauce in small saucepan. Season with salt and pepper.

2. Separate egg yolks from whites. Chop whites finely.

3. Add whites to sauce. Simmer for 2 minutes, stirring occasionally.

4. Arrange toast on serving dish. Pour sauce over all slices.

5. Press egg yolks through sieve; sprinkle on top of sauce.

6. Garnish with parsley.

Elsie Hermann, Woman's Club, Menomonee Falls, Wis.

EGGS CONTINENTAL
Serves 4
½ cup fresh bread crumbs
5 eggs, hard-cooked and sliced
5 slices bacon, diced

1 cup sour cream
2 tablespoons chopped parsley
2 tablespoons chopped chives
¼ teaspoon salt
Paprika
½ cup grated sharp Cheddar cheese

1. Preheat oven to 375° F. Grease 4 individual ramekins or casseroles.

2. Sprinkle bottoms of ramekins or casseroles with crumbs. Top with egg slices.

3. Cook bacon in skillet until crisp. Drain on absorbent paper. Put in mixing bowl.

4. Add sour cream, parsley, chives, salt and ¼ teaspoon paprika; mix well.

5. Spoon over eggs. Sprinkle with cheese and additional paprika.

6. Bake in preheated oven for 20 minutes, or until bubbling and golden.

Mrs. George Peterson, Golfview Hills Woman's Club, Hinsdale, Ill.

SCALLOPED EGGS
Serves 4
2 cups Medium White Sauce (p. 441)
Salt and pepper to taste
Dash of cayenne
¼ teaspoon dry mustard
6 eggs, hard-cooked and sliced
1 cup fresh bread crumbs
2 tablespoons butter

1. Preheat oven to 350° F. Grease 1-quart casserole.

2. Season Medium White Sauce with salt and pepper. Stir in cayenne and mustard.

3. In casserole arrange alternate layers of sauce, eggs and crumbs. Dot with butter.

4. Bake in preheated oven for 25 minutes.

Cordius Dean, Pathfinder Club, Compton, Calif.

EGGS 'N' CHIPS
Serves 5 or 6
10½-ounce can condensed cream
   of mushroom soup
½ cup milk
2 tablespoons minced onion
2 cups crushed potato chips
6 eggs, hard-cooked and sliced
Salt and pepper to taste

1. Preheat oven to 400° F. Grease 1-quart casserole.

2. Combine soup, milk and onion.

3. In casserole make a layer of 1 cup of the chips. Top with eggs. Sprinkle with salt and pepper. Add soup mixture. Top with remaining potato chips.

4. Bake in preheated oven for 25 minutes, or until bubbling.

Eddie Wilson, Woman's Club, Palmdale, Calif.

BAKED EGGS IN MUSHROOM SAUCE

Serves 4 to 6

½ cup butter or margarine
½ pound mushrooms, sliced
¼ cup presifted flour
3 cups milk
1 teaspoon salt
¼ teaspoon pepper
8-ounces mild Cheddar cheese, grated
6 eggs, hard-cooked and sliced
½ cup buttered bread crumbs

1. Preheat oven to 350° F. Grease 1½-quart casserole.
2. Melt butter or margarine in medium saucepan; sauté mushrooms over medium heat for 5 minutes.
3. Stir in flour. Gradually add milk. Cook over medium heat, stirring constantly, until thickened and smooth.
4. Stir in salt, pepper and cheese. Cook, stirring frequently, until cheese is melted.
5. Stir in eggs. Turn into casserole. Sprinkle with crumbs.
6. Bake in preheated oven for 25 minutes, or until golden.

Phyllis H. Turner, Woman's Club,
Shell Beach, Calif.

CASSEROLE CORONADO

Serves 6

2 tablespoons butter
2 tablespoons flour
1 cup milk
10½-ounce can condensed cream of mushroom soup
⅔ cup chopped ripe olives
¼ cup chopped pimientos
2 tablespoons chopped parsley
⅔ cup crushed potato chips
6 eggs, hard-cooked and sliced
Pepper to taste

1. Preheat oven to 325° F. Grease 1½-quart casserole.
2. Melt butter in saucepan. Blend in flour. Gradually stir in milk. Cook, stirring, until thickened and smooth.
3. Stir in soup, olives, pimientos, parsley, half the potato chips, eggs and pepper.
4. Pour into casserole. Top with remaining potato chips.
5. Bake in preheated oven for 20 minutes.

Mrs. Ewing Dunlap, Woman's Club,
Wynnburg, Tenn.

EASTER MONDAY EGGS AND DEVILED HAM

Serves 4

1½ cups Medium White Sauce (p. 441)
Salt and pepper to taste
4 eggs, hard-cooked
¾ cup thinly sliced celery
4 slices toast
3-ounce can deviled ham
1 tablespoon chopped parsley

1. Heat Medium White Sauce. Season with salt and pepper.

2. Dice 3 of the eggs; add to sauce. Add celery. Simmer for 3 minutes.
3. Meanwhile, spread toast with ham. Arrange on serving dish.
4. Pour sauce over toast. Garnish with remaining egg, sliced. Sprinkle with parsley.

Mrs. W. William Graham, Athenaeum Club,
Kansas City, Mo.

EGGS TETRAZZINI

Serves 4

8-ounce package thin spaghetti
4-ounce can sliced mushrooms
2 tablespoons butter or margarine
2 tablespoons flour
1 cup light cream
10½-ounce can condensed cream of mushroom soup
¼ teaspoon salt
1 tablespoon prepared mustard
6 eggs, hard-cooked and quartered
¼ cup grated Parmesan cheese

1. Preheat oven to 400° F. Grease 2-quart casserole.
2. Cook spaghetti in boiling salted water according to package directions; drain.
3. Drain mushrooms; reserve liquid.
4. Melt butter or margarine in saucepan. Blend in flour. Gradually add reserved mushroom liquid, cream and soup. Cook over low heat, stirring constantly, until thickened and smooth.
5. Remove from heat. Stir in salt, mustard, mushrooms and eggs.
6. Arrange half the spaghetti in casserole. Cover with half the egg mixture. Top with remaining spaghetti. Cover with remaining egg mixture. Sprinkle with cheese.
7. Bake in preheated oven for 20 minutes, or until browned.

Mrs. P. J. Smith, Senior Woman's Club,
Nazareth, Pa.

COUNTRY CLUB EGGS

Serves 4

2 tablespoons fat
½ cup chopped onions
2 tablespoons flour
1½ cups milk
Salt and pepper to taste
2 tablespoons minced parsley
2 tablespoons chopped pimiento
2 tablespoons lemon juice
½ cup shredded American cheese
6 eggs, hard-cooked and sliced
4 slices butter toast
Paprika

1. Heat fat in saucepan; sauté onions until soft and yellow. Stir in flour. Gradually stir in milk. Cook, stirring, until thickened and smooth.
2. Stir in salt, pepper, parsley, pimiento and lemon juice. Add cheese; cook, stirring, until melted.
3. Arrange eggs on toast. Top with cheese sauce. Sprinkle with paprika.

Favorite Recipes, Woman's Club,
Las Vegas, N.M.

SCOTCH WOODCOCK

Serves 4

1 cup milk
1½ cups bread crumbs
1½ tablespoons butter
Salt and pepper to taste
1 tablespoon anchovy paste
3 eggs, hard-cooked and sliced
Buttered toast

1. Heat milk in saucepan. Add crumbs. Cook over low heat, stirring, until smooth.
2. Stir in butter, salt, pepper and anchovy paste.
3. Fold in eggs. Heat to serving temperature.
4. Serve on toast.

Ruth M. Cann, New Century Club,
Wilmington, Del.

EGGS AND ASPARAGUS AU GRATIN

Serves 4 to 6

1 cup Medium White Sauce (p. 441)
1 cup grated Cheddar cheese
1 cup fresh bread crumbs
¼ cup melted butter
4 eggs, hard-cooked and sliced
15-ounce can asparagus, drained
2 canned piminetos, cut into strips

1. Preheat oven to 350° F. Grease 1½-quart casserole.
2. Combine Medium White Sauce and cheese.
3. Combine crumbs and butter; spread half in casserole.
4. Arrange alternate layers of eggs, asparagus, pimientos and cheese sauce in casserole. Top with remaining crumbs.
5. Bake in preheated oven for 15 minutes, or until top is golden and bubbling.

Mrs. Robb Gover, Woman's Club,
Charleston, W. Va.

BELGIAN EGGS

Serves 6

1 tablespoon melted butter or
margarine
1 tablespoon chopped parsley
½ teaspoon dry mustard
1 teaspoon salt
1½ teaspoons paprika
1½ cups heavy cream
1 cup grated Cheddar cheese
6 eggs, hard-cooked and chopped
3 cups chopped cooked shrimp
or lobster

1. Preheat oven to 375° F. Grease 2-quart casserole.
2. In mixing bowl blend butter or margarine, parsley, mustard, salt and paprika. Stir in cream and cheese. Mix well.
3. Add eggs and seafood. Stir well. Turn into casserole.
4. Bake in preheated oven for 20 minutes, or until top is browned.

Mrs. Clarence W. Adams, Woman's Club,
South Pasadena, Calif.

CREOLE EGGS

Serves 4

2 tablespoons fat
2 tablespoons flour
1 cup milk
Salt and pepper to taste
2 tablespoons butter
2 tablespoons chopped onion
2 tablespoons chopped green pepper
1-pound can tomatoes, drained
1 clove garlic, minced
¼ teaspoon chili powder
4 eggs, hard-cooked and sliced
½ cup shredded cheese
½ cup soft bread crumbs
Hot crisp toast

1. Preheat oven to 350° F. Grease 1½-quart casserole.
2. Melt fat in saucepan. Stir in flour. Gradually stir in milk. Cook, stirring, until sauce is thickened and smooth. Season with salt and pepper.
3. Melt butter in another saucepan; sauté onion and green pepper until soft. Add tomatoes, garlic and chili powder. Bring to boil. Cook over low heat for about 20 minutes, or until thick. Stir into sauce.
4. Arrange alternate layers of sauce and eggs in casserole. Top with cheese and crumbs.
5. Bake in preheated oven for 15 to 20 minutes. Serve on toast.

Mrs. Gerald Stabler, Arts Club, Aliceville, Ala.

SPANISH EGG CASSEROLE

Serves 6 to 8

6-ounce package medium noodles
3 tablespoons shortening
½ cup chopped onions
½ cup chopped green pepper
1-pound 4-ounce can tomatoes,
undrained
1 cup grated Cheddar chese
¼ cup butter or margarine
¼ cup presifted flour
½ teaspoon salt
6 eggs, hard-cooked and sliced

1. Preheat oven to 350° F. Grease 2-quart casserole.
2. Cook noodles in boiling salted water according to package directions; drain.
3. Melt shortening in skillet; sauté onions and green pepper for 10 minutes. Stir in tomatoes. Simmer for 10 minutes. Stir in cheese.
4. Melt butter or margarine in saucepan. Blend in flour and salt. Gradually stir in tomato mixture. Cook over medium heat, stirring constantly, until thickened.
5. Arrange half the noodles in casserole. Top with half the eggs. Cover with half the tomato mixture. Repeat layers, finishing with layer of tomatoes.
6. Bake in preheated oven for 30 minutes.

Mrs. Harold Beamer, Jr., Senior Woman's Club,
Wytheville, Va.

BAKED STUFFED EGGS

Serves 6

6 eggs, hard-cooked
½ cup ground cooked ham
3 scallions, minced
⅓ teaspoon prepared mustard
½ teaspoon Worcestershire
¼ cup softened butter
2 cups Medium White Sauce (p. 441)
½ cup shredded cheese

1. Preheat oven to 350° F. Grease shallow casserole.
2. Cut eggs in half lengthwise. Remove yolks.
3. Mix yolks, ham, onions, mustard, Worcestershire and butter. Stuff eggs. Press halves together, re-forming eggs.
4. Arrange eggs in casserole. Pour Medium White Sauce over eggs. Sprinkle with cheese.
5. Bake in preheated oven for 30 minutes.

Bettie Bonnewitz, North Long Beach Women's Club, Long Beach, Calif.

CREAMED STUFFED EGGS

Serves 6

6 eggs, hard-cooked
1 teaspoon prepared mustard
1 teaspoon sweet pickle relish
2 slices bacon, cooked and crumbled
½ teaspoon salt
⅛ teaspoon pepper
¼ teaspoon paprika
2 cups cooked asparagus, cut into
1-inch pieces
2 cups Medium White Sauce (p. 441)
1 cup grated Cheddar cheese
½ cup buttered bread crumbs

1. Preheat oven to 375° F. Grease 10 x 6 x 1½-inch baking pan.
2. Cut eggs in half lengthwise. Remove yolks; mash. Add mustard, pickle relish, bacon, salt, pepper and paprika; mix well.
3. Fill egg white halves with yolk mixture.
4. Arrange asparagus in pan. Top with egg halves.
5. Blend Medium White Sauce and cheese. Pour over eggs in pan. Sprinkle with crumbs.
6. Bake in preheated oven for 30 minutes.

Morgan Park Woman's Club, Chicago, Ill.

CURRIED EGGS IN SHRIMP SAUCE

Serves 6 to 8

8 eggs, hard-cooked
½ cup mayonnaise
½ teaspoon salt
1 teaspoon curry powder
½ teaspoon paprika
¼ teaspoon dry mustard
4 tablespoons butter
2 tablespoons flour
10½-ounce can frozen condensed
cream of shrimp soup, defrosted
1¼ cups milk

1 cup grated sharp Cheddar cheese
1 cup fresh bread crumbs

1. Preheat oven to 350° F. Grease 10 x 6 x 1½-inch baking pan.
2. Cut eggs in half lengthwise. Remove yolks; put in medium bowl. Add mayonnaise, salt, curry powder, paprika and mustard; mash until smooth.
3. Fill egg whites with yolk mixture. Arrange in pan.
4. Melt 2 tablespoons of the butter in medium saucepan. Stir in flour. Gradually stir in soup and milk. Cook over low heat, stirring constantly, until sauce is thickened and smooth. Add cheese; stir over low heat until melted.
5. Cover eggs with sauce.
6. Melt remaining butter in small pan. Stir into crumbs; sprinkle onto sauce.
7. Bake in preheated oven for 20 minutes, or until browned.

Nancy Morss, Junior Woman's Club, Simsbury, Conn.

EGG LUNCHEON DISH

Serves 4

6 eggs, hard-cooked
1 egg, lightly beaten with
2 tablespoons milk
1 cup cracker crumbs
⅓ cup butter or margarine

1. Cut eggs in half lengthwise.
2. Dip each half in beaten egg. Coat with crumbs.
3. Melt butter or margarine in large skillet; sauté egg halves until golden on both sides.

Woman's Club, Chandlerville, Ill.

FRIED STUFFED EGGS

Serves 3 to 6

6 eggs, hard-cooked
1 tablespoon finely chopped pecans
1 tablespoon mayonnaise
1 teaspoon salt
½ teaspoon black pepper
1 teaspoon prepared mustard
½ teaspoon celery seed
Cracker crumbs
Fat for deep frying

1. Cut eggs in half lengthwise. Remove yolks. Reserve whites.
2. Press yolks through fine sieve. Mix with pecans, mayonnaise and seasonings.
3. Fill egg whites. Press two halves together to reshape eggs.
4. Roll in crumbs. Fry in deep fat heated to 365° F. until golden brown. Drain on absorbent paper. Serve hot.

Mrs. E. C. Riall, Kuwot Study Club, Mooringsport, La.

EGG AND CHEESE CROQUETTES

Serves 8

½ pound sharp cheese, shredded
1 cup Cream Sauce (p. 441)
6 tablespoons diced pimiento
12 eggs, hard-cooked and diced
Cracker crumbs

Fat for deep frying
Mushroom Sauce (p. 447)

1. Add cheese to Cream Sauce. Cook over low heat, stirring, until melted.

2. Stir in pimiento and eggs. Cool to room temperature. Then form into croquettes. Roll in crumbs.

3. Fry in deep fat heated to 365° F. for about 3 minutes, or until golden brown.

4. Drain on absorbent paper. Serve with Mushroom Sauce.

Kathryn Oshsenhirt, Century Club,
Coraopolis, Pa.

BAKED EGG CROQUETTES

Serves 6

3 tablespoons shortening
1 tablespoon grated onion
¼ cup finely chopped celery
⅓ cup presifted flour
1½ cups milk
2 cups cooked elbow macaroni
6 eggs, hard-cooked and chopped
1 tablespoon chopped parsley
¼ teaspoon poultry seasoning
Salt and pepper to taste
2 cups bread crumbs

1. Melt shortening in saucepan; sauté onion and celery until golden.

2. Stir in flour. Gradually stir in milk. Cook over medium heat, stirring constantly, until thickened.

3. Remove from heat. Stir in macaroni, eggs, parsley and poultry seasoning. Season with salt and pepper. Spread in shallow pan. Chill for 30 minutes.

4. Preheat oven to 375° F. Grease baking sheet.

5. Shape mixture into croquettes. Roll in crumbs. Place on baking sheet.

6. Bake in preheated oven for 15 minutes. Turn croquettes. Bake for 15 minutes longer, or until golden.

Mrs. William Cummings, Homemakers,
Meade County, Ky.

EGG CURRY RING

Serves 6

2 cups chicken broth
1 tablespoon curry powder
2 envelopes gelatin
¼ cup water
1½ cups mayonnaise
4 eggs, hard-cooked and finely chopped
Salt and pepper to taste
Stuffed olive slices
Lettuce

1. In saucepan bring broth to boil. Remove from heat. Stir in curry powder.

2. In small bowl soften gelatin in water. Add to broth. Stir until dissolved. Chill until slightly thickened.

3. Blend in mayonnaise and eggs. Season with salt and pepper.

4. Turn into 8-inch ring mold. Chill until firm.

5. Unmold onto serving dish. Garnish sides with olive slices. Fill center with lettuce.

Vilma Paananen, Woman's Club, Lantana, Fla.

Omelets

FRENCH OMELET

There are many ways to make an omelet, but this is the classic method.

The Omelet Pan: Reserve a heavy 9- or 10-inch skillet for omelet making only. If it is new or if it has been used for other purposes, it will generally need tempering. This is done by covering the bottom with cooking oil. Heat oil almost to smoking-hot. Remove from heat; let stand overnight. Next day, pour out oil; wipe skillet clean with absorbent paper.

3 eggs
1 tablespoon water
¼ teaspoon salt
1 tablespoon butter
Desired filling

1. Break eggs into bowl. Add water and salt. Beat with fork until thoroughly blended but not frothy.

2. In omelet pan heat butter over moderately high heat until it sizzles and gives off characteristic nutty aroma. Swirl pan to coat bottom evenly.

3. Give final beat to eggs; pour into pan. Immediately stir briskly with fork, letting flat of fork touch flat of pan without scraping. At same time shake pan briskly back and forth over heat to prevent omelet from sticking.

4. When eggs are set on bottom but still moist on top, quickly add desired filling.

5. Immediately roll up: Raise pan to 45° angle; with fork, roll omelet from top of pan downward.

6. Grasp handle, palm turned up. Holding pan over warm serving plate, invert omelet onto plate.

SUGGESTED FILLINGS:

Creamed cooked chicken, turkey, fish or ham.
Chopped cooked chicken livers, lobster, shrimp or crab meat.
Creamed or sautéed mushrooms.
Creamed spinach.
Chopped or stewed tomatoes.

CHEESE OMELET

Follow directions for French Omelet, but stir ¼ cup shredded Cheddar or Swiss cheese into eggs before cooking. Omit filling.

FINES HERBES OMELETTE

Follow directions for French Omelet, but before cooking, stir into eggs 1 teaspoon each finely chopped fresh parsley and chives and ½ teaspoon chopped fresh tarragon, dill or chervil. Omit filling.

A. S.

LOBSTER OMELET

Serves 4

5 eggs, separated
¼ teaspoon sugar
¾ teaspoon salt
3¼ cups light cream
¼ cup butter
¼ cup presifted flour
    Dash of pepper
1 cup flaked cooked lobster

1. Preheat oven to 350° F. Grease shallow 12-inch baking dish.
2. Combine egg yolks, sugar, ¼ teaspoon salt and 1¼ cups cream; beat until smooth.
3. Beat egg whites until stiff but not dry. Fold into egg yolk mixture. Pour into baking dish.
4. Bake in preheated oven for 15 to 20 minutes, or until puffed and golden.
5. Meanwhile, prepare Lobster Sauce: Melt butter in saucepan. Blend in flour. Gradually stir in remaining cream. Cook over low heat, stirring constantly, until thickened and smooth. Season with remaining salt and pepper. Stir in lobster. Simmer for 5 minutes, stirring constantly.
6. Arrange omelet on serving dish. Top with sauce.

Mrs. Percy Scofield, Woman's Club,
Newark, Ill.

MEXICAN OMELET

Serves 3 or 4

6 eggs
½ teaspoon salt
20 ripe olives, chopped
1 tablespoon capers
2 small green chili peppers,
    finely chopped
1 tablespoon butter

1. In mixing bowl beat eggs and salt. Stir in olives, capers and chilis.
2. Melt butter in medium skillet until it just begins to brown. Pour in egg mixture. Stir rapidly with fork until it begins to set. Smooth surface of eggs. Cook until just set.
3. Roll up. Turn onto hot serving dish.

Mrs. J. P. Proctor, W.I.A., Las Cruces, N.M.

MIDNIGHT OMELET SCRAMBLE

Serves 4

4 slices bacon, diced
¼ cup finely chopped onions
4-ounce can mushroom pieces,
    drained
6 eggs
½ cup light cream
    Salt and pepper to taste
    Toast points or chopped parsley
    (optional)

1. Put bacon and onions in large skillet. Cook over medium heat until bacon starts to become crisp.
2. Add mushrooms. Cook for 5 minutes longer.

3. In mixing bowl beat eggs and cream. Season with salt and pepper.
4. Stir egg mixture into bacon mixture. Cook over low heat until eggs reach desired firmness.
5. Turn onto serving dish. Garnish with toast points or parsley, if desired.

Berks County Federation of Women's Clubs,
Berks County, Pa.

NORMANDY OMELET

Serves 2

3 eggs, separated
2 tablespoons milk
¼ teaspoon salt
1 tablespoon butter

1. In mixing bowl beat egg whites until stiff but not dry.
2. In small bowl beat egg yolks, milk and salt.
3. Melt butter in medium skillet. Swirl pan to coat bottom and sides well.
4. Spread egg whites in skillet. Cook over low heat until golden.
5. Carefully turn egg white mixture; at same time pour egg yolk mixture into bottom of pan, so it is under egg whites.
6. Cook over low heat for 2 to 3 minutes, or until yolks are set.
7. Remove from skillet.

Anna T. Peck, Woman's Club, Paxton, Mass.

SOUR CREAM SOUFFLÉ OMELET

Serves 4

5 eggs, separated
1 cup sour cream
1 teaspoon salt
2 tablespoons butter or margarine
    Cherry preserves

1. Preheat oven to 325° F.
2. Put egg yolks in mixing bowl. Beat until thick and lemon-colored. Beat in ½ cup of the sour cream and salt.
3. In another mixing bowl beat egg whites until stiff but not dry. Fold into yolk mixture.
4. Heat butter or margarine in 10-inch skillet. Pour in omelet mixture, leveling gently. Cook over low heat for about 5 minutes, or until lightly browned.
5. Place in preheated oven. Bake for about 15 minutes, or until browned.
6. Top with remaining sour cream and cherry preserves.

Betty Gainey and Norma Schindeldecker,
Woman's Club, Prospect Heights, Ill.

SPANISH OMELET

Serves 4

1 cup cooked or canned tomatoes
1 small green pepper, chopped
½ onion, chopped
1 tablespoon chopped parsley
½ cup chopped celery
8 to 10 stuffed olives, diced
4 eggs, separated
½ teaspoon salt
⅛ teaspoon pepper
1 tablespoon fat

1. In saucepan combine tomatoes, green pepper, onion, parsley, celery and olives. Bring to boil. Simmer for 15 minutes, or until liquid is reduced to few tablespoons.
2. Preheat oven to 350° F.
3. In small bowl beat egg yolks until thick and pale. Stir in salt.
4. In medium bowl beat egg whites until stiff but not dry. Fold into yolks.
5. Fold in vegetable mixture and pepper.
6. Heat fat in skillet. Pour omelet mixture into fat. Cook until lightly browned on bottom.
7. Transfer to preheated oven. Bake for 10 to 15 minutes, or until puffed and browned.
8. Crease omelet through center; fold over; turn onto warm serving platter.

*Mrs. Willard H. McDowell, New Century Club,
Wilmington, Del.*

TOP O' THE RANGE OMELET
Serves 4

4 eggs, separated
½ teaspoon salt
¼ cup water
    Dash of pepper
2 tablespoons flour
2 tablespoons shortening
    Parsley
    Cheese Sauce (p. 442)

1. Put egg whites, salt and water in mixing bowl. Beat until stiff but not dry.
2. Put egg yolks in another mixing bowl. Add pepper and flour. Beat until light and thick.
3. Carefully fold egg whites into yolk mixture.
4. Melt shortening in 10-inch skillet. Pour egg mixture into center of skillet. Reduce heat; cover. Cook slowly for 5 to 8 minutes, or until puffed and golden.
5. Remove cover. Cook for 20 minutes longer, or until knife inserted in center comes out clean.
6. Fold in half. Turn onto serving dish. Garnish with parsley. Serve with Cheese Sauce.

*Jessie Powers, Woman's Club,
Monterey Park, Calif.*

Soufflés

It's not difficult to make perfect soufflés, and they are great for using up leftovers, because they can be made with cooked poultry, fish, seafood, meat, cheese or vegetables.

The basis of any savory soufflé is a thick sauce, usually made with milk but sometimes made with Chicken Stock (p. 170) or Beef Stock (p. 170). (Canned chicken or beef broth may be substituted.)

Separate the eggs. Beat the yolks until thick and pale. Then stir the beaten yolks thoroughly into the hot sauce along with the main ingredient. Allow the mixture to cool before adding the egg whites.

When possible, use 1 or 2 additional egg whites to give extra lightness and height to the soufflé. Beat the egg whites until they are very thick but by no means dry. The greatest volume is obtained by whisking them with a large balloon whisk, but perhaps this is asking too much of the busy homemaker whose kitchen is filled with electric appliances. When using an electric beater, beat on low speed until the egg whites are very frothy; then increase to medium speed, and continue to beat until they are thick and creamy.

Add half the egg whites to the egg yolk mixture; fold in very thoroughly to keep the particles of fish, meat or vegetables in suspension. Then add the remaining egg whites; fold in lightly.

Bake soufflés according to recipe directions. Serve them immediately.

HOW TO MAKE A BASIC
SAVORY SOUFFLÉ
Serves 4

1. Make 1 cup foundation sauce, which is usually a White Sauce (p. 441) or Sauce Velouté (p. 441). Cool slightly.
2. Beat 4 egg yolks until thick and pale. Stir into sauce.
3. Stir in 1 cup of main ingredient, such as ground cooked ham, chicken or lobster, shredded cheese, or puréed cooked spinach or other vegetable. Cool.
4. Preheat oven to 400° F. Grease 1½-quart soufflé dish.
5. Beat 5 or 6 egg whites until stiff but not dry. Fold half the egg whites thoroughly into yolk mixture. Add remaining egg whites; fold in lightly and quickly.
6. Pour into dish. Put into preheated oven. Immediately reduce temperature to 375° F. Bake soufflé for 40 to 50 minutes.
7. Serve immediately.

NOTE: Many soufflés and soufflé types of casseroles will be found elsewhere in this book. The following are a few classics. For others, see the Index.

A. S.

CHEDDAR CHEESE SOUFFLÉ
Serves 4

¼ cup butter or margarine
¼ cup flour
½ teaspoon salt
    Dash of paprika
1 cup milk
1 cup grated Cheddar cheese
4 eggs, separated

1. Preheat oven to 450° F. Grease 1-quart soufflé dish or casserole.
2. Melt butter or margarine in medium saucepan. Stir in flour, salt and paprika. Gradually stir in milk. Cook over low heat, stirring constantly, until thickened and smooth.
3. Add cheese. Cook over low heat, stirring frequently, until melted.
4. Remove from heat. Cool slightly. Then beat in egg yolks. Cool.

5. Meanwhile, in mixing bowl beat egg whites until stiff but not dry. Carefully fold into cheese mixture. Turn into dish.

6. Place dish in pan of hot water. Bake in preheated oven for 10 minutes.

7. Reduce temperature to 350° F. Bake for 25 minutes longer.

Mrs. Frank Wilson, Woman's Club, Essex, Conn.

CHEESE SOUFFLÉ WITH BREAD
Serves 2 or 3

1½ cups milk
2 cups bread crumbs
1½ cups shredded cheese
½ teaspoon salt
⅛ teaspoon paprika
3 eggs, separated

1. Pour milk over crumbs. Let stand until soft.

2. Preheat oven to 350° F. Grease 1-quart casserole.

3. Add cheese, salt, paprika and egg yolks to crumb mixture. Mix well.

4. Beat egg whites until stiff but not dry. Fold into yolk mixture.

5. Turn into casserole. Bake in preheated oven for 30 minutes.

Winnie B. Moody, Arts Club, Aliceville, Ala.

CHEESE OMELET SOUFFLÉ
Serves 2 or 3

2 cups milk
8 ounces cheese, cut into small pieces
2 tablespoons butter
Salt to taste
1 cup soft bread crumbs
2 eggs, separated

1. Preheat oven to 350° F. Grease 1½-quart soufflé dish.

2. Heat milk in saucepan. Add cheese; cook over low heat, stirring constantly, until melted. Stir in butter, salt and crumbs.

3. Remove from heat. Beat in egg yolks.

4. Beat egg whites until stiff but not dry. Fold into cheese mixture.

5. Turn into dish. Bake in preheated oven for 20 minutes, or until set.

Mrs. Ira Burns, New Century Club, Wilmington, Del.

CHEESE AND MUSHROOM SOUFFLÉ
Serves 4

3 slices bacon, diced
10½-ounce can condensed cream of mushroom soup
3 eggs, separated
½ cup grated sharp Cheddar cheese

1. Preheat oven to 350° F. Grease 1½-quart casserole.

2. Cook bacon in skillet until crisp. Drain on absorbent paper.

3. Blend soup, egg yolks and cheese.

4. In mixing bowl beat egg whites until stiff but not dry. Fold into soup mixture. Turn into casserole. Sprinkle with bacon.

5. Bake in preheated oven for 50 minutes.

Shurley Whittaker, Junior Woman's Club, Lansdale, Pa.

CHICKEN SOUFFLÉ
Serves 4

2 tablespoons butter
2 tablespoons flour
1 teaspoon salt
⅛ teaspoon pepper
2 cups hot milk
½ cup soft bread crumbs
2 cups finely chopped cooked chicken
3 eggs, separated
1 tablespoon minced parsley
Mushroom Sauce (p. 447)

1. Preheat oven to 350° F. Grease 2-quart casserole.

2. Melt butter in saucepan. Stir in flour. Cook, stirring, until bubbling. Stir in salt and pepper. Add milk. Stir vigorously until thickened and smooth. Stir in crumbs. Cook for 2 minutes.

3. Remove from heat. Stir in chicken. Beat egg yolks; add. Stir in parsley.

4. Beat egg whites until stiff but not dry. Fold into chicken mixture.

5. Turn into casserole. Bake in preheated oven for 35 minutes. Serve with Mushroom Sauce.

Joan Roberts, Junior Woman's Club, Cathedral City, Calif.

HOT CRAB SOUFFLÉ SANDWICH
Serves 8 to 10

8 slices bread
2 cups flaked crab meat
½ cup mayonnaise
1 medium onion, finely chopped
1 medium green pepper, finely chopped
1 cup finely chopped celery
4 eggs
3 cups milk
10½-ounce can condensed cream of mushroom soup
½ cup grated Cheddar cheese
Paprika

1. Grease 11 x 7 x 1½-inch baking pan.

2. Dice 4 slices of the bread. Spread in pan.

3. In mixing bowl combine crab meat, mayonnaise, onion, green pepper and celery. Spread over bread in pan.

4. Remove crusts from remaining bread slices. Arrange on crab mixture.

5. Beat eggs and milk until blended. Pour over mixture in pan. Refrigerate for 3 hours.

6. Preheat oven to 325° F.

7. Bake in preheated oven for 15 minutes. Spoon soup over top; sprinkle with cheese and paprika. Bake in preheated oven for 1 hour longer.

Mrs. Harvey Coleman, Woman's Club, Yakima, Wash.

HAM AND CHEESE SOUFFLÉ
Serves 8

4 slices white bread, cubed
2 cups grated Cheddar cheese
2⅔ cups hot milk
2 tablespoons butter
1 pound ground ham
2 teaspoons grated onion
4 eggs, separated
½ teaspoon paprika
2 teaspoons chopped parsley

1. Preheat oven to 325° F. Grease 2½-quart casserole.
2. Place bread and cheese in mixing bowl. Toss lightly. Add milk and 1 tablespoon of the butter. Let stand for 20 minutes.
3. Meanwhile, melt remaining butter in skillet; sauté ham and onion until lightly browned. Place in casserole.
4. Beat egg yolks and paprika. Stir into bread mixture along with parsley.
5. In mixing bowl beat egg whites until stiff but not dry; fold into yolk mixture. Stir a little into ham in casserole. Pour rest of egg mixture on top.
6. Bake in preheated oven for 40 to 60 minutes, or until risen and set.

S. Madsen, Women's Club, Porterville, Calif.

SPINACH SOUFFLÉ
Serves 4 to 6

¼ cup butter or margarine
1 tablespoon grated onion
5 tablespoons flour
1 cup milk
1 cup grated Cheddar cheese
1 cup cooked chopped spinach
1 teaspoon salt
⅛ teaspoon pepper
3 eggs, separated

1. Preheat oven to 350° F. Grease 1½-quart casserole.
2. Melt butter or margarine in saucepan; sauté onion for 5 minutes. Blend in flour. Gradually stir in milk. Cook over medium heat, stirring constantly, until thickened and smooth.
3. Remove from heat. Stir in cheese, spinach, salt and pepper.
4. In mixing bowl beat egg yolks until thick and lemon-colored.
5. In another mixing bowl beat egg whites until stiff but not dry. Carefully fold into cheese mixture along with yolks.
6. Turn into casserole. Bake in preheated oven for 45 minutes.

M. Shannon, Junior Woman's Club,
Pacific Beach, Calif.

7. Cheese and Cheese Dishes

There are hundreds of recipes in this book that use cheese. This chapter contains only a small selection of dishes in which cheese is a main ingredient and which do not fall logically into other chapters. You will find cheese appetizers and sandwiches in Chapters 1 and 2, cheese soup in Chapter 5, cheese soufflés in Chapter 6, cheese rolls and biscuits in Chapter 3 and 4 and many pies, cakes and desserts using cheese in Chapters 18, 19 and 22. They all are listed in the Index under Cheese.

The United States is a cheese-loving nation, and many cities have specialty stores that carry a great variety of both imported and domestic cheeses. Although France, Italy, Switzerland, The Netherlands, Great Britain, and Denmark all are leading cheese-producing countries, America does not take a back seat with its famous Cheddars, its California Monterey Jack, its own Liederkranz and American made Brie, Camembert, ricotta, and cottage and cream cheeses, all of excellent quality and flavor.

All table cheeses should be served at room temperature.

TYPES OF CHEESE AND HOW TO USE THEM

Cheeses fall naturally into six main categories:

1. *The hard grating cheeses* used primarily over pasta dishes, as additions to soups, such as onion soup and minestrone, and as toppings for creamed baked dishes and casseroles. They may be added in small quantity to cheese soufflés and sauces for a slightly sharper flavor. The most widely used hard cheeses are:

> Parmesan from Italy
> Romano from Italy
> Sapsago from Switzerland

2. *The firm or semi-hard cheeses,* used for sandwiches, soufflés, cheese sauces, for melting in rarebits and fondues or for serving with crusty bread after the main course, are:

> American cheese (usually a kind of mild Cheddar)
> Cheddar made in America or imported from Britain
> Cheshire from Britain
> Edam from The Netherlands
> Gouda from The Netherlands
> Gruyère from Switezrland
> Samsoe from Denmark
> Swiss or Emmantaler from Switzerland

3. *The semi-soft cheeses,* excellent for sandwiches, for cooking and for serving after the main course with crusty bread or with fruit for dessert, are:

> Bel Paese from Italy
> Feta from Greece
> Fontina from Italy
> Limburger from Germany and Belgium
> Monterey Jack only from America
> Mozzarella from Italy but also made in America
> Muenster from Germany but also made in America
> Oka or Trappist from Canada
> Pont l'Évêque from France
> Port du Salut from France
> Provolone from Italy
> Reblochon from France
> Tilsit from Germany and Denmark

4. *The soft-ripening cheeses,* served after the main course with crusty bread and salad or with fruit for dessert, are:

> Brie from France
> Camembert from France
> Certosino from Italy
> Liederkranz made only in America

5. *The blue-veined cheeses,* for salads and salad dressings or for serving after the main course with crusty bread or with fruit for dessert, are:

> Bleu or blue from Denmark and France
> Gorgonzola from Italy
> Roquefort from France
> Stilton from England

6. *The soft cheeses,* served in salads and used in baked dishes and in many desserts (the soft cream type of cheeses are perfect with berries), are:

> Cottage cheese made in America
> Cream cheese made in America
> Crema Danica from Denmark
> Crème Chantilly from France
> Neufchâtel from France

Petite Suisse from France
Ricotta from Italy but also made in America
Triple Crème from France

CHEESE BLINTZES
Serves About 12

¾ pound cottage cheese
1 egg
Salt and pepper to taste or
2 teaspoons sugar and cinnamon
2 eggs, well beaten
1 cup milk
1 cup presifted flour
Butter
Sugar and cinnamon or sour cream

1. Press cheese through colander. Beat in 1 egg; season with salt and pepper or with 2 teaspoons sugar and cinnamon.
2. Prepare blintz batter: Combine well-beaten eggs, 1 teaspoon salt and milk. Gradually stir into flour, stirring until smooth.
3. Heat well-greased 5- or 6-inch iron frying pan. Pour in only enough batter to make very thin pancake; swirl pan to coat bottom. Cook on one side only until pancake blisters. Shake, cooked side down, onto kitchen towel. Continue until all batter is used.
4. Put spoonful of cheese mixture on center of each pancake. Fold over from both sides; then fold over top to form 3-inch square.
5. Fry in butter until golden brown on both sides.
6. Serve hot. If sweet, serve with sugar and cinnamon. If not, serve with sour cream.

Mrs. David Kaufman, Women's Civic Club, Wilmington, Del.

SWISS FONDUE
Serves 3

1½ tablespoons flour
2 cups grated Swiss cheese
1 clove garlic
¾ cup Chablis or dry white wine
¼ teaspoon salt
Dash of pepper
Dash of nutmeg
2 tablespoons kirschwasser
French bread, cut into chunks

1. Toss flour and cheese. Set aside.
2. Rub chafing dish with garlic; discard garlic. Pour wine into chafing dish. Heat over low flame until just below boiling point.
3. Add cheese; stir until melted and smooth. Stir in seasonings and kirschwasser.
4. When bubbling, serve with bread.

Pat Chabert, Junior Woman's Club, Floral Park, N.Y.

SWISS FONDUE WITH SAUTERNE

In place of a fondue cooker, this recipe may be prepared in a saucepan on stove and poured into a chafing dish for serving.
Serves 8

3 cups Swiss cheese, cut into strips
1 tablespoon flour
1 clove garlic, halved
1¼ cups sauterne
Dash of pepper
Dash of nutmeg
3 tablespoons sherry
French bread, cubed

1. Toss cheese and flour.
2. Rub inside of fondue cooker with garlic. Add sauterne; warm until bubbles begin to rise. Add cheese, a handful at a time, stirring constantly.
3. When all cheese is blended, stir in seasoning and sherry.
4. Spear cubes of bread on long-handled forks; dunk.

Mrs. Robert L. Scheuermann, Thursday Morning Club, Madison, N.J.

WELSH RAREBIT
Serves 2 or 3

1 tablespoon flour
¼ teaspoon dry mustard
½ teaspoon salt
1 cup milk
1 egg
1 cup shredded Cheddar cheese
Dash of cayenne
1 tablespoon butter
Hot toasted crackers

1. Combine flour, mustard, salt and 2 tablespoons of the milk. Beat in egg.
2. Heat remaining milk to just below boiling point. Gradually stir in egg mixture. Cook over low heat, stirring, until thickened and smooth.
3. Add cheese; cook, stirring, until melted. Stir in cayenne and butter.
4. Serve on crackers.

May Drake, Woman's Club, Carpinteria, Calif.

WELSH RAREBIT WITH BEER
Serves 4 to 6

4 cups shredded Cheddar cheese
½ teaspoon salt
½ teaspoon dry mustard
Dash of cayenne
1 teaspoon Worcestershire
½ cup beer
2 eggs, lightly beaten
Toast or crackers

1. Put cheese, salt, mustard, cayenne and Worcestershire in top of double saucepan. Cook over hot water, stirring frequently, until cheese is melted and smooth.
2. Slowly stir in beer and eggs. Cook over hot water, stirring constantly, until thickened and smooth.
3. Serve on toast or crackers.

Dale Carstens, Junior Woman's Club, Glastonbury, Conn.

CHEESE MONKEY

Serves 4

1 cup fresh bread crumbs
1 cup milk
1 tablespoon butter
1 cup grated Cheddar cheese
1 egg
½ teaspoon salt
Dash of cayenne
4 slices buttered toast

1. Put crumbs in medium bowl. Add milk. Let stand for 15 minutes.
2. Melt butter in top of double saucepan. Stir in crumb mixture, cheese, egg, salt and cayenne. Cook over hot water, stirring constantly, until thickened and smooth.
3. Serve on toast.

Mrs. J. S. Zimmerman, Woman's Club,
North Wilkesboro, N.C.

EASY RAREBIT

Serves 2

10½-ounce can condensed cream of
    mushroom soup
½ cup milk
1 cup grated Cheddar cheese
½ teaspoon Worcestershire
Paprika
Toast strips

1. Blend soup and milk in saucepan. Bring to boil, stirring frequently.
2. Stir in cheese and Worcestershire; heat, stirring frequently, until melted.
3. Pour into preheated individual casseroles. Sprinkle with paprika. Serve with toast.

Lottie Campbell, Woman's Club,
Red Bank, N.J.

RED DEVIL

Serves 6

2 cups cream of tomato soup
1 pound Cheddar cheese, shredded
1 egg, lightly beaten
¼ teaspoon dry mustard
    Worcestershire to taste
    Salt and pepper to taste
    Buttered toast

1. Heat soup. Add cheese; cook, stirring, until melted.
2. Combine egg, mustard, Worcestershire and a little of cheese mixture. Stir into rest of cheese mixture. Cook over low heat, stirring, for 2 minutes.
3. Season with salt and pepper. Serve on toast.

Woman's Club Cook Book, Hancock, N.H.

RINKTUM DIDDIE

Serves 4

2 tablespoons butter
2 tablespoons flour
¾ cup cream
1½ cups tomatoes
⅛ teaspoon baking soda
1 teaspoon salt
    Dash of paprika
    Dash of cayenne

Pinch of nutmeg
2 cups finely cut Cheddar cheese
2 eggs, lightly beaten
    Buttered salted crackers

1. Melt butter in saucepan. Add flour; stir until smooth. Gradually stir in cream, tomatoes, baking soda and seasonings. Cook over moderate heat, stirring constantly, until thickened.
2. Add cheese; stir over very low heat until melted. Turn off heat. Stir in eggs.
3. Serve on crackers.

Mrs. James W. Lattomus, New Century Club,
Wilmington, Del.

SPANISH RAREBIT

Serves 6

1 pound mild Cheddar cheese
8-ounce can cream-style corn
½ cup chopped canned green
    chili peppers
1 tablespoon Worcestershire
1 teaspoon salt
    Dash of pepper
2 eggs, lightly beaten
1 cup chopped drained canned
    tomatoes
    Crisp toast

1. Put cheese in top of double saucepan. Cook over hot water, stirring occasionally, until melted and smooth. Stir in corn, chilis and seasonings. Simmer over hot water for 5 minutes.
2. Stir in eggs. Cook over hot water, stirring frequently, until thickened and creamy. Stir in tomatoes. Remove from heat.
3. Serve on toast.

Pearl Griggers, Pathfinder Club, Compton, Calif.

WINKUM

Serves 4

1 tablespoon butter
¼ pound Cheddar cheese, diced
10½-ounce can condensed tomato
    soup
    Pinch of baking soda
6½-ounce can crab meat, drained
    and flaked
¾ cup evaporated milk
1 egg, lightly beaten
    Toast or crackers

1. Melt butter in top of double saucepan. Add cheese; cook over simmering water until melted. Combine soup and baking soda; add to cheese. Stir in crab meat and milk. Cook for 10 minutes, stirring occasionally.
2. Remove from heat. Stir in egg.
3. Serve on toast or crackers.

Esther E. Peterson, Women's Club,
Barrington, R.I.

MUSHROOM RAREBIT

Serves 12

4 tablespoons butter
1 cup finely cut celery
1 pound mushrooms, sliced
4 tablespoons flour
2 cups milk

½ teaspoon salt
8 ounces mild Cheddar cheese, diced
10½-ounce can condensed cream of mushroom soup
½ cup finely cut pimientos
4 eggs, hard-cooked and sliced
Dash of paprika
Toast or Chinese noodles

1. Melt butter in saucepan or large skillet; sauté celery and mushrooms for about 5 minutes, or until tender.
2. Stir in flour. Gradually stir in milk. Cook, stirring, until thickened and smooth.
3. Add salt.
4. Stir in cheese and soup; cook, stirring, until melted. Stir in remaining ingredients.
5. Serve on toast or Chinese noodles, as desired.

Sara Lindsay, Woman's Civic Club,
Cumberland, Md.

OYSTER RAREBIT

Serves 6

1 cup freshly shucked oysters with liquor
2 tablespoons butter
½ pound Cheddar cheese, shredded
¼ teaspoon salt
Pinch of cayenne
2 eggs
6 slices toast

1. Poach oysters until edges curl. Drain; reserve liquor.
2. Melt butter in saucepan. Add cheese, salt and cayenne; cook over low heat, stirring, until melted.
3. Beat eggs with reserved liquor. Gradually stir into cheese mixture. Add oysters. Heat to serving temperature, but do not boil.
4. Serve on toast.

Pauline M. Osgood, Woman's Club,
Medway, Mass.

CHEESE STRATA

Serves 10 to 12

12 slices white bread
¾ pound sharp Cheddar cheese, sliced
10-ounce package frozen broccoli, cooked and drained
2½ cups finely diced ham
6 eggs, lightly beaten
2 tablespoons instant minced onion
½ teaspoon salt
¼ teaspoon dry mustard

1. Grease 13 x 9½ x 2-inch baking pan.
2. Remove crusts from bread. Cut 12 doughnuts and holes from center of each slice. Place bread scraps in pan.
3. Arrange cheese on bread scraps. Top with a layer of broccoli, then a layer of ham. Arrange bread doughnuts and holes on ham.
4. In mixing bowl combine remaining ingredients. Pour over ingredients in pan; cover; refrigerate for 6 hours or overnight.

5. When ready to use, preheat oven to 325° F.
6. Place pan, uncovered, in preheated oven. Bake for 55 minutes, or until custard is set. Remove from oven. Let stand for 10 minutes to firm before serving.

Gretchen Skilton, Women's Club,
Porterville, Calif.

CHEESE BAKE

Serves 6

12 slices stale bread, trimmed
8 ounces American cheese, sliced
4 eggs
2½ cups milk
½ teaspoon dry mustard
1 tablespoon minced onion
Salt and pepper to taste

1. Grease casserole or baking pan. Arrange 6 slices of the bread. Cover with cheese. Top with remaining bread slices.
2. Combine remaining ingredients. Pour over bread and cheese. Let stand for 1 hour.
3. Preheat oven to 325° F.
4. Bake in preheated oven for 1 hour, or until custard is set.

Mance Kallenberger, Woman's Club,
Buckeye, Ariz.

OVERNIGHT CHEESE STRATA

Serves 8

½ pound sharp Cheddar cheese
½ cup butter
12 slices bread, cubed
4 eggs
2 cups milk

1. Day before grease 2-quart casserole.
2. Melt cheese and butter in top of double saucepan over simmering water, stirring occasionally, until smooth.
3. Put 6 slices of the bread in casserole; cover with half the cheese mixture. Top with remaining bread.
4. Beat eggs well; stir in milk. Pour into casserole; cover; refrigerate overnight.
5. Next day, preheat oven to 325° F.
6. Set casserole in pan containing about 1 inch water. Bake in preheated oven for 1 hour. Reduce temperature to 225° F. Bake for 1 hour longer.

Mrs. William Klumb, Junior Woman's Club,
Wauwatosa, Wis.

CHEESE PUDDING

Serves 4

1 cup soft bread crumbs
1 cup milk
1 cup shredded sharp cheese
2 eggs, lightly beaten
2 tablespoons melted butter
Salt and red pepper to taste

1. Preheat oven to 350° F. Grease 1-quart casserole.
2. Soak crumbs in milk. Add cheese. Stir in eggs and butter. Season with salt and red pepper.

3. Pour into casserole. Bake in preheated oven for 30 minutes, or until custard is set.

Mrs. Ig Brown, Woman's Club, Livingston, Mont.

CHEESE PUFF

Serves 4
2 tablespoons butter or margarine
2 tablespoons flour
1½ cups milk
1 cup grated Cheddar cheese
¾ teaspoon salt
⅛ teaspoon pepper
¼ teaspoon paprika
1 cup cooked rice
3 eggs, separated

1. Preheat oven to 350° F. Grease 1½-quart casserole.
2. Melt butter or margarine in saucepan. Stir in flour. Gradually stir in milk. Cook over low heat, stirring constantly, until thickened and smooth.
3. Remove from heat. Stir in cheese, seasonings and rice; mix well.
4. Stir in egg yolks. Beat until well blended.
5. In mixing bowl beat egg whites until stiff but not dry. Fold into cheese mixture. Turn into casserole.
6. Place casserole in pan of hot water. Bake in preheated oven for 1 hour.

Margaret Colton, Woman's Club,
East Hartford, Conn.

CHEESE CASSEROLE

Serves 4
1¼ cups fresh bread crumbs
1 cup light cream
3 eggs, separated
¼ cup melted butter or margarine
1 tablespoon chopped parsley
1 teaspoon onion juice
1 teaspoon salt
1 cup grated Cheddar cheese
2 cups cooked elbow macaroni, chopped

1. Preheat oven to 325° F. Grease 1½-quart casserole.
2. Put crumbs in mixing bowl. Stir in cream. Add all remaining ingredients except egg whites; mix well.
3. In another mixing bowl beat egg whites until stiff but not dry. Fold into macaroni mixture. Turn into casserole.
4. Place casserole in pan of hot water. Bake in preheated oven for 45 minutes, or until set.

Mrs. James Duff, Woman's Club, Blacksburg, Va.

QUICHE LORRAINE

Serves 6 to 8
Pastry for a 1-Crust Pie (p. 548)
6 slices bacon
6 thin slices (about 2 x 3 inches) Swiss cheese
4 eggs
2 cups light cream
1 tablespoon flour
1 teaspoon nutmeg
½ teaspoon salt

Freshly ground black pepper
Few grains of cayenne

1. Line 9-inch pie plate with Pastry for a 1-Crust Pie.
2. Preheat oven to 400° F.
3. In skillet cook bacon until crisp. Drain well; crumble. Sprinkle in pie shell. Arrange cheese over bacon.
4. In mixing bowl combine remaining ingredients. Beat briskly with wire whisk or rotary beater for at least 1 minute. Pour into pie shell.
5. Bake on lowest rack of oven for 15 minutes. Reduce temperature to 325° F. Bake for about 30 minutes longer, or until knife gently inserted into center comes out clean. Pie will be slightly puffed and golden brown.
6. Cut into wedges. Serve hot or cold.

Mrs. W. H. Hasebroock, Honorary President,
General Federation of Women's Clubs,
West Point, Neb.

SWISS CHEESE PIE

Serves 6 to 8
Pastry for a 1-Crust Pie (p. 548)
1 tablespoon butter
1 small onion, finely chopped
5 eggs
1½ teaspoons salt
2½ cups milk
1½ teaspoons Worcestershire
Dash of pepper
4 cups grated Swiss cheese
2-ounce can anchovies, drained

1. Line 9-inch pie plate with Pastry for a 1-Crust Pie.
2. Preheat oven to 425° F.
3. Melt butter in small skillet; sauté onion over low heat until transparent.
4. Beat eggs in mixing bowl. Stir in onion, salt, milk, Worcestershire and pepper. Add cheese. Mix well.
5. Pour into pie shell. Bake in preheated oven for 10 minutes. Reduce temperature to 325° F. Bake for 40 minutes longer, or until set.
6. Remove from oven. Garnish with anchovies.

Mrs. A. Robert Swanson, Book & Needle Club,
Oradell, N.J.

CHEESE CROQUETTES

Serves 4
½ cup Thick White Sauce (p. 441)
2 egg yolks
1 cup grated Cheddar cheese
¼ teaspoon salt
Dash of pepper
Dash of Tabasco
1 egg
2 tablespoons milk
1 cup bread crumbs
Fat for deep frying

1. Combine Thick White Sauce, egg yolks, cheese, salt, pepper and Tabasco. Chill for 30 minutes.
2. Beat 1 egg and milk. Put in shallow bowl.

3. Shape cheese mixture into 2 x 1-inch cones. Roll in crumbs; dip in egg mixture; roll again in crumbs. Reshape if necessary.

4. Fry in deep fat heated to 365° F. for 4 minutes, or until golden. Drain on absorbent paper.

Lucy J. Barker, Woman's Club, Bellows Falls, Vt.

ENCHILADAS
Makes 12

Olive oil
12 Tortillas (p. 136) or canned tortillas
1 cup hot red chili sauce
2 cups grated sharp Cheddar cheese
1 cup chopped scallions
⅓ cup chopped ripe olives

1. Preheat oven to 350° F.
2. Heat oil in skillet. Fry Tortillas lightly on both sides. Drain.
3. Dip each tortilla in chili sauce.
4. In small bowl mix 1 cup of the cheese, scallions and olives.
5. Spoon 2 to 3 tablespoons of cheese filling down center of each tortilla. Roll each tortilla around filling. Turn, seam side down, into 13 x 9½ x 2-inch baking pan.
6. Pour remaining chili sauce over tortillas. Sprinkle with remaining cheese.
7. Bake in preheated oven for 15 minutes.

Mrs. Joseph Glider, Women's Improvement Club, Blythe, Calif.

GREEN ENCHILADA CASSEROLE
Serves 4 to 6

¼ cup cooking oil
12 Tortillas (p. 136) or canned tortillas
½ cup finely chopped onions
1 cup grated Cheddar cheese
10½-ounce can condensed cream of chicken soup
¾ cup light cream
4-ounce can green chili peppers, drained and chopped

1. Preheat oven to 350° F. Grease 2½-quart casserole.
2. Heat oil in skillet. Fry Tortillas until crisp on both sides.
3. In casserole arrange alternate layers of tortillas, onions and cheese, finishing with tortillas.
4. Blend soup, cream and chilis. Pour into casserole.
5. Bake in preheated oven for 35 minutes.

Mrs. William J. Van Essen, President, Woman's Club, Albuquerque, N.M.

CHILI CON QUESO ON TORTILLAS
Serves 4

1 tablespoon olive oil
4 chili peppers, finely chopped
1 small tomato, finely chopped
½ small green pepper, finely chopped
1 clove garlic, minced, or 2 teaspoons minced onion

Salt to taste
½ pound mild Cheddar cheese, shredded
Fat for frying
Tortillas (p. 136) or canned tortillas

1. Heat oil in saucepan; sauté chilis, tomato, green pepper and garlic or onion until limp. Season with salt. Add cheese. Remove from heat. Mix well.
2. Heat fat well in skillet. Fry Tortillas for a few seconds on each side. Drain on absorbent paper.
3. Preheat broiler.
4. Spread Tortillas with chili mixture. Broil until cheese is melted.

Leonore Kirchem, Gentilly Woods Woman's Club, New Orleans, La.

SWEDISH OSTRAKA
(Cheese Custard)
Serves 6

This may be used as a dessert or as a substitute for mashed potatoes or rice with chicken or turkey.

4 eggs
¾ cup sugar
¼ cup presifted flour
3 cups cream-style cottage cheese
⅛ teaspoon salt

1. Preheat oven to 400° F. Grease 1½-quart casserole.
2. In mixing bowl beat eggs until foamy. Add sugar. Beat until thickened.
3. In another mixing bowl blend flour and cheese. Stir in salt. Stir cheese into eggs. Pour into casserole.
4. Place casserole in pan of hot water. Bake in preheated oven for 30 minutes. Reduce temperature to 300° F. Bake for 30 minutes longer.

Dorothy Silkenson, Pathfinder Club, Compton, Calif.

ARMENIAN CHEESE-FILLED BORAKS (Turnovers)
Makes 14

Delicious as a substitute for bread or other starchy food. Or they may be served as a main course for supper or luncheon.

2 cups presifted flour
1 teaspoon baking powder
1½ teaspoons salt
½ cup milk
1 egg
¼ cup melted butter
1 tablespoon butter
½ cup thinly sliced scallion tops
½ cup minced parsley
1 pound Monterey Jack cheese, shredded
Fat for deep frying

1. Into mixing bowl sift together flour, baking powder and 1 teaspoon of the salt. Combine milk and egg; add to dry ingredients. Stir with fork until thoroughly mixed; then stir in melted butter, a tablespoon at a time.

2. Turn dough onto lightly floured board. Knead for 3 to 4 minutes, or until smooth. Shape into ball; cover with bowl; and let stand for 30 minutes.

3. Melt 1 tablespoon butter; sauté scallion tops and parsley for about 10 minutes, or until tender. Stir in remaining salt. Remove from heat. Stir in cheese.

4. Roll out dough ⅛ inch thick on lightly floured board. Cut into 14 rounds, using 1-pound coffee can as cutter.

5. Spoon equal amounts of cheese mixture onto center of each round. Pack down

slightly. Moisten edge of dough with water; fold in half over cheese filling; press edges together, forcing out any air pockets. Press edges with fork to seal.

6. In large skillet heat to 365° F. enough fat to measure about 1 inch deep. Fry boraks until golden on each side. Drain on absorbent paper.

7. Serve immediately, or refrigerate, and reheat in preheated 350° F. oven for 10 to 15 minutes.

Mrs. Lee Krikorian, Woman's Club,
McFarland, Calif.

8. Fish, Shellfish and Other Foods Prepared Like Fish

⚜⚜⚜⚜⚜⚜⚜⚜⚜⚜⚜⚜⚜⚜⚜⚜⚜⚜⚜⚜⚜⚜⚜

Fish

The majority of fresh fish and shellfish recipes in this chapter have come from coastal areas—as is to be expected—but a tremendous number of recipes for excellent quick and easy casseroles, loaves and other dishes made from convenience fish foods, canned or frozen, have also come from every state in the country, indicating that today's homemaker understands the importance of fish in menu planning for health, for low calorie content and for economy.

All About Fish

SMOKED AND SALTED FISH

In addition to canned and frozen fish and shellfish, a variety of salted and smoked fish is available in most markets. Some, such as smoked salmon, whitefish, mullet and eel, are excellent served cold as appetizers with a wedge of lemon and a sprinkling of freshly ground pepper. Sometimes capers are served on the side, and thinly sliced pumpernickel is an appropriate accompaniment. Other smoked fish, such as herring (kippers), smoked haddock and finnan haddie, are delicious treats, especially for breakfast—with or without scrambled eggs—dotted with butter and broiled or baked, then served hot, again with lemon and freshly ground pepper and with buttered toast.

Smoked fish may also be steamed or poached for 10 to 15 minutes in a small quantity of milk, then flaked and added to Cream Sauce (p. 441).

Salted fish, such as herring, should be soaked for several hours or overnight, depending on the degree of saltiness, which can be determined only by tasting the fish and changing the water several times until most of the salt has been removed. It is then ready to be fried, broiled or poached.

SELECTING FRESH FISH

Anyone who has tasted freshly caught fish realizes the importance of selecting only the freshest in the fish market. Choose a fish with eyes that are clear and protruding, not shriveled or sunken. The flesh should be firm, not soft or flabby; the gills should be red or pink, not gray or brown; and there should be no unpleasant fishy odor.

STORING FISH

Fish deteriorates rapidly and should be cleaned and cooked as soon as possible after it is caught or purchased. If it is necessary to keep it for a short time, wrap it in heavy paper, or place it in a covered dish, and then store it in the coldest part of the refrigerator. If it is necessary to keep it longer than a few hours, it is best to freeze it. In fact, even though you plan to cook a freshly caught fish the next day, it is better to clean it and place it in the freezer immediately rather than keep it overnight in the refrigerator. The sudden impact of the very low freezer temperature drops the temperature of the fish so fast that little or no decomposition can take place.

TO FREEZE A WHOLE FISH

Dip the cleaned fish in cold water, and place it, unwrapped, in the freezer. As soon as it is frozen solid, remove it; dip it again in cold water; wrap it in freezer paper. Return it to the freezer for storage, but do not store it for too long. The sooner it is eaten, the better.

CLEANING AND DRESSING FISH

If you live in a city, your fresh fish will be cleaned or partially cleaned and scaled when you buy it, but it should be checked as soon as you arrive home. Make sure there are no blood clots along the backbone; if there are, scrape and rinse them out. Remove the gills, and run your hand over the skin to make sure all the scales have been rubbed off.

If you are fortunate enough to live near a source of freshly caught fish, you should know how to deal with them:

TO SCALE A FISH

Place the fish on a sheet of heavy paper.

217

Hold the head firmly with one hand. With the other hand, scrape off the scales, working from the tail to the head; use a strong knife or fish scaler. Rinse well in running cold water.

TO CLEAN A FISH

With a sharp knife, slit the stomach skin from the head to the vent, and remove the entrails. Scrape and rinse out the blood-clots in the abdominal cavity close to the backbone. Remove the head, if desired, by cutting above the collarbone. If you wish to cook the fish with the head on or if you are using the head to make Fish Stock (p. 171), the gills should be removed.

To remove the backbone, use a sharp knife to cut deeply into the flesh of the fish along both sides of the back fin; grasp the fin at the widest point, and pull out both the fin and the bony structure underneath. Then cut around the pectoral fins (those near the head on both sides), and pull them out. Do the same with the pelvic fins (near the head on the underside).

Finally, wash the fish inside and out in running cold water, and dry it thoroughly with paper towels.

TO FILLET A FISH

Place the fish on its side on a flat surface with the head toward you. Hold the tail in the left hand, using a cloth if needed, and draw a very sharp strong knife under the skin and flesh close to the rib bones on the upper side, beginning at the tail and drawing the knife toward the head. Remove the entire fillet in one piece. Turn the fish over, and repeat on the other side.

TO SKIN A FISH FILLET

Place the fillet, skin side down, on a flat surface. Hold the tail end tightly, and cut down through the flesh to the skin about half an inch from the end of the tail. Flatten the knife against the skin, and draw it from the tail to the head section under the fleshy part but just over the skin.

TO CLEAN AND BONE A WHOLE FISH, SUCH AS RED SNAPPER AND BASS, WITHOUT SLITTING THE BELLY

Scale the fish thoroughly, and cut out the pelvic and pectoral fins. Then slit the skin down the back on both sides of the back fin, using a very sharp knife, such as a boning knife. Cut the flesh away from both sides of the rib bones, exposing the backbone with the ribs attached. Cut through the backbone at the head and tail, and pull out the entire bone structure. Discard the entrails, and rinse out the abdominal cavity. The fish may now be stuffed and skewered or sewed closed along the back.

TO CLEAN AND BONE A FLAT FISH, SUCH AS FLUKE AND FLOUNDER

Scale the fish, and cut off the fins close to the body with kitchen scissors. Place the fish, white skin side up, on a cutting board.

With a sharp knife, slit the skin from the head to the tail down the backbone. Using the knife, carefully cut away the flesh from each side, exposing the bone. Cut through the bone at the head and at the tail end. With kitchen scissors, cut through all the fine rib bones on both sides as close as possible to the edge of the fish. Lift up one end of the backbone; again use the knife to strip the flesh away from the underside of the bone, being careful not to cut through the dark skin below. Discard the entrails from the pouch directly under the mouth of the fish, and wash the fish inside and out. There is now a large pocket in the fish, free of bones, which can be stuffed.

TO PREPARE FISH STEAKS

Fish steaks are crosswise slices cut from a large fish. Each steak contains a piece of the backbone.

Methods of Cooking Fish

There is no such thing as a tough fish, so the first and most important rule of fish cookery is not to overcook. A fish is cooked to develop flavor, and as soon as the flesh loses its translucency and flakes easily, it is done.

TO TEST FOR DONENESS

Insert a fork into the thickest part of the flesh, close to the backbone. Separate the meat. If the flesh is no longer translucent, but is white and still moist, the fish is done.

POACHING A LARGE WHOLE FISH, SUCH AS SALMON

Use a fish kettle large enough to accommodate the fish easily. If there is no rack in the fish kettle, tie the fish in cheesecloth or a kitchen towel so that it may be easily removed when cooked. Put sufficient water or enough part water and part white wine in the kettle to cover the fish. Add salt; peppercorns; 1 bay leaf; 1 onion, ½ carrot and 1 stalk celery with leaves, all coarsely chopped; and 1 slice lemon. Bring to boil. Simmer for 15 to 20 minutes to extract the flavors from the vegetables; then lower the fish gently into the water. Cover; cook over low heat, keeping the water just below the boiling point, until the flesh flakes easily. The cooking time varies according to the size of the fish, but in general 8 to 10 minutes per pound is sufficient.

POACHING FILLETS OR SMALL FISH

A large skillet with a tight lid is good for poaching fillets or small fish. It should be large enough to hold all the fish without overlapping. They may be cooked either over direct heat or in a preheated 350° F. oven. Use only sufficient liquid to cover the fish, and cook, covered, for 8 to 10 minutes. To conserve space, fillets may be rolled and secured with wooden picks before being poached.

Sauces: Serve hot poached fish with Butter Sauce (p. 442), Beurre Noir (p. 442), or Egg and Caper Sauce (p. 441). Serve cold poached fish with Sauce Verte (p. 445), Cucumber Mayonnaise (p. 445), Sauce à la Ritz (p. 446) or any savory mayonnaise sauce.

BAKING FISH

Whole fish, stuffed or unstuffed, steaks and fillets may be baked. Arrange fish in greased baking pan. An excellent precaution to prevent fish from sticking to the pan is to put a few outer leaves of lettuce in the bottom of the pan. Use moderate heat—from 325° to 350° F. Fish 1 inch thick will take about 20 minutes; 2 inches thick, about 30 minutes; 3 inches thick, from 40 to 45 minutes. If a whole fish is stuffed, it may require a slightly longer cooking time.

Stuffings: Bread (p. 452), Oyster (p. 454), Mushroom (p. 453 and Crab Meat (p. 241) Stuffings are excellent.

Sauces: If stuffed, such sauces as Five-Minute Tomato (p. 450) and Creole (p. 443) are excellent. If unstuffed, Lemon Butter (p. 444) and Lemon Caper Butter (p. 445) are perfect. Also good are Egg Cream Sauce (p. 441), Horseradish Sauce for Fish (p. 444) and Curry Sauce (p. 441).

BROILING FISH

Small whole fish, split fish, fish steaks and fillets may be broiled in the oven or over charcoal, but care should be taken not to overcook and let the fish dry out.

Charcoal Broiling: Use a hinged grill, and brush it well with oil. Heat well over the fire. It should be hot enough to score the fish when placed in it. Broil until the flesh flakes easily when tested with a fork, basting several times with butter, oil or marinade during the cooking. A whole fish may take about 6 minutes per side; a steak, such as salmon and swordfish, about 4 minutes per side; a fillet, a *total* of 5 to 6 minutes.

Oven Broiling: Preheat the broiler for about 10 minutes. Grease the broiling pan well; arrange fish on it. Fillets and split fish do not need to be turned, but steaks and whole fish should be turned halfway through the cooking. Broil until the flesh flakes easily, basting several times with butter, oil or a mixture of wine or lemon juice and butter. Broil whole fish about 6 inches from heat for 4 to 5 minutes on one side; turn; cook for 6 to 8 minutes longer. Broil steaks or split fish 2 to 3 inches from heat for 6 to 10 minutes. Broil fillets 2 inches from heat for 5 to 8 minutes. Season broiled fish after it has been cooked.

Sauces: Serve with Sauce Tartare (p. 446), Sauce Gribiche (p. 446), Sauce Ravigote (p. 446), Sauce Rémoulade (p. 446), or Cucumber Mayonnaise (p. 445), Hollandaise Sauce (p. 444) or Béarnaise Sauce (p. 444).

SAUTÉING FISH

Small whole fish, split fish steaks, and fillets may be cooked by this method. If desired, the fish may be dipped in milk and coated with flour. Melt enough butter in skillet just to coat the bottom. When it is foaming, arrange the fish in the pan, and cook over low heat until it is nicely browned on one side. Turn, and brown the other side. Transfer to a hot plate, and sprinkle with salt, pepper and minced parsley. Serve with a wedge of lemon and a little melted butter.

Sauces: Served with Almond Butter Sauce (p. 442), Mushroom Sauce (p. 447), Hollandaise Sauce (p. 444) or Wine Butter Sauce (p. 442).

BREADING AND PAN-FRYING FISH

This is a popular method of cooking small whole fish, such as perch, smelt or trout, fish steaks and fillets.

For each 2 pounds of fish, beat 1 egg and 2 tablespoons milk or water. Roll the fish in flour; dip it in the egg mixture, and finally coat it with bread crumbs or corn meal. Heat enough oil or fat in a skillet to coat the bottom generously. Arrange the fish in the hot fat, and cook over brisk heat until nicely browned on one side. Turn; brown the other side. Transfer to a hot plate, and sprinkle with salt and pepper. Serve with a wedge of lemon.

Sauces: The usual sauce served with pan-fried fish is Sauce Tartare (p. 446), but any other favorite sauce may be used. Horseradish Cream Sauce (p. 442) is particularly good.

DEEP-FRYING FISH

Deep-fried fish are usually coated to protect the tender flesh from the intense heat of the frying oil. Dip the fish in flour; bread it as above, or dip it in Frying Batter (p. 223).

In a deep skillet or heavy pan heat to 365° F. enough oil or shortening to cover the fish completely. Fry the fish for 3 to 5 minutes, or until the coating is golden brown. Drain on absorbent paper, and sprinkle with salt and pepper before serving.

Sauces: Serve with Sauce Tartare (p. 446), Five-Minute Tomato (p. 450) or Creole Sauce (p. 443) or with soy sauce and hot mustard.

Garnishes for Fish: water cress, parsley, sliced tomato or cucumber, sliced or chopped hard-cooked eggs, pickles or pickled beets, French-fried potatoes or onion rings.

BAKED FISH

Serves 6 to 8

½ cup butter
1 cup water
1½ teaspoons paprika
¾ teaspoon dry mustard
1 teaspoon Worcestershire
1 teaspoon pepper
1 teaspoon sugar
1 teaspoon salt
1 teaspoon chili powder
2 tablespoons vinegar
1 clove garlic, crushed
1 medium onion, finely chopped
⅛ teaspoon Tabasco
5- or 6-pound striped bass or
   bluefish, dressed

1. Preheat oven to 350° F. Line shallow roasting pan with aluminum foil.
2. In saucepan combine all ingredients except fish. Bring to boil. Cook over low heat for 20 minutes.
3. Arrange fish in pan. Pour sauce over it.
4. Bake in preheated oven, basting frequently with sauce, for about 1 hour, or until fish flakes easily.

Mrs. James E. Staples, Sorosis Woman's Club, Orlando, Fla.

BAKED FISH FLORIDA

Serves 4 to 6

2- to 4-pound whole red snapper,
   trout or other fish, dressed
1 medium onion, thinly sliced
¼ cup melted butter or margarine
1 teaspoon salt
Dash of pepper
3 tablespoons orange juice
   concentrate
1 tablespoon soy sauce

1. Preheat oven to 350° F. Grease 13 x 9½ x 2-inch baking pan.
2. Arrange fish in pan. Make several slashes in skin. Insert onion slices into slashes.
3. In small bowl blend remaining ingredients. Pour over fish.
4. Bake in preheated oven for 20 to 30 minutes, or until fish flakes easily. Baste frequently with juices during cooking.

Jeanne Gotcher, Junior Woman's Club, Cocoa, Fla.

BAKED FISH WITH OYSTER STUFFING

Serves 6

3- to 4-pound cod or haddock
Salt and pepper to taste
Lemon juice to taste
1 pint freshly shucked oysters
   with liquor
1 onion, minced
1 cup prepared bread crumb
   stuffing
3 tablespoons melted butter
1 egg, lightly beaten
Milk

1 onion, sliced
4 thin slices salt pork
Hollandaise Sauce (p. 444)

1. Clean fish well; remove head and skin. Cut out fins and backbone. Sprinkle fish inside and out with salt, pepper and lemon juice.
2. Prepare Oyster Stuffing: Drain oysters; reserve liquor. Chop oysters; mix with minced onion, crumb stuffing, butter, egg, reserved liquor and enough milk to moisten. Season with salt and pepper. Stuff fish. Skewer or sew opening.
3. Preheat oven to 350° F.
4. Place sliced onion in baking pan. Put fish on top. Arrange salt pork on fish.
5. Bake in preheated oven for 1 hour, or until fish flakes easily.
6. Serve with Hollandaise Sauce.

Louisa M. Graeber, Woman's Club, Eustis, Fla.

MARINATED STUFFED FISH

Serves 5 or 6

3- to 5-pound fish, dressed and
   backbone removed
1 bay leaf
1 teaspoon salt
1 teaspoon peppercorns
1 teaspoon marjoram
3 tablespoons cider vinegar
2 tablespoons lemon juice
2 tablespoons slivered lemon peel
2 tablespoons grated onion
2 tablespoons water
1 clove garlic, crushed
⅓ cup olive oil
Bread (p. 452) or Rice Stuffing
   (p. 455)

1. Day before, put fish in close-fitting dish.
2. Prepare marinade: Combine in saucepan all remaining ingredients except stuffing. Bring to boil. Pour over fish.
3. Cool; cover tightly; refrigerate for 24 hours.
4. Next day, preheat oven to 350° F. Grease shallow roasting pan.
5. Remove fish from marinade; wipe dry. Reserve marinade.
6. Stuff fish with Bread or Rice Stuffing. Sew or skewer opening.
7. Place fish in pan. Strain marinade over it.
8. Bake in preheated oven for 40 minutes, or until fish flakes easily. Baste frequently during cooking.

Mrs. Emerone Froelich, Plum Lake Woman's Club, Star Lake, Wis.

SIZZLING FISH–VEGETABLE PLATTER BAKE

Serves 6 to 8

3- or 4-pound haddock, bluefish,
   snapper, pompano, sea trout,
   bass or whitefish, dressed
Salt
Olive oil
2 lemons, thinly sliced
6 medium potatoes, peeled and
   sliced

6 medium onions, thinly sliced
3 large tomatoes, halved
2 medium green peppers, seeded
   and cut into strips
   Parsley
   Pimiento strips

1. Preheat oven to 400° F. Grease large stainless-steel or aluminum platter.
2. Rub fish with salt. Arrange on platter.
3. Make deep slices on diagonal about 1 inch apart in fish; arrange lemon slices in slits. Brush fish with oil.
4. Arrange potatoes, onions, tomatoes and green peppers around fish. Brush vegetables with oil; sprinkle with salt.
5. Bake in preheated oven for 10 minutes. Reduce temperature to 350° F. Bake for 45 minutes longer, or until fish flakes easily.
6. Garnish with parsley and pimiento.

Virginia Snyder, Eastmont Junior Women's Club,
East Wenatchee, Wash.

BARBECUED WHOLE FISH

Use flounder, perch or sea trout, and cook on outdoor grill or over open fire.

   1 cup catsup
   2 tablespoons brown sugar
   ¼ cup vinegar
   ½ teaspoon dry mustard
   ½ cup cooking oil
   2 tablespoons Worcestershire
   1 slice onion, chopped
   Salt
   Whole small fish, dressed
   Garlic salt or minced garlic
   Pepper to taste
   Butter
   Large onion slices
   Tomato slices

1. Prepare Barbecue Sauce: In saucepan combine catsup, sugar, vinegar, mustard, oil, Worcestershire, chopped onion and ½ teaspoon salt. Heat to simmering. Keep hot.
2. Sprinkle fish with garlic salt or minced garlic, salt and pepper. Place pat of butter on each fish. Cook over glowing coals for 10 minutes, turning once.
3. At same time, grill onion slices with a slice of tomato on each.
4. Dip fish in sauce. Serve with grilled onion and tomato and with additional sauce on side.

Amy Loomis, Women's Club,
Arroyo Grande, Calif.

BAKED FISH FILLETS

Serves 4

   4 fillets of sole or haddock
   Salt and pepper to taste
   1 egg, lightly beaten
   ⅔ cup cracker crumbs
   ½ cup butter

1. Preheat oven to 400° F.
2. Season fillets with salt and pepper; dip in egg; coat with crumbs.

3. Put butter in 10 x 6 x 1½-inch baking pan. Place pan in preheated oven until butter is melted and browned.
4. Dip fillets in butter, coating them on both sides. Arrange in pan.
5. Bake in preheated oven for 15 minutes, or until fish flake easily, basting frequently with butter.
6. Remove pan; continue to baste with butter until all the butter is absorbed.

Mrs. John W. Stiles, Sorosis Woman's Club,
Orlando, Fla.

STUFFED FILLETS OF FISH

Serves 6

   ½ cup butter
   2 tablespoons chopped onion
   ¼ cup finely chopped celery
   1½ teaspoons salt
   Pepper
   ½ teaspoon sage
   2 cups fresh bread crumbs
   2 1-pound fillets of halibut or
   haddock

1. Preheat oven to 350° F. Grease 10 x 6 x 1½-inch baking pan.
2. Prepare Bread Stuffing: Melt ¼ cup of the butter in skillet; sauté onion and celery for 5 minutes. Remove from heat. Stir in ½ teaspoon of the salt, dash of pepper, sage and crumbs; mix well.
3. Season fillets with remaining salt and dash of pepper. Arrange 1 fillet in pan. Spread with stuffing. Arrange other fillet on stuffing; secure with wooden picks. Dot with remaining butter.
4. Bake in preheated oven for 35 minutes, or until fish flakes easily.

Jane Daddario, Junior Woman's Club,
Glastonbury, Conn.

FISH CHEESE PUFF

Serves 6

   2 pounds fillets of haddock or
   halibut
   ½ cup sour cream
   ½ cup grated sharp Cheddar cheese
   2 eggs, separated
   2 tablespoons chopped stuffed
   olives
   1 tablespoon grated onion
   ½ teaspoon salt

1. Preheat oven to 350° F. Grease 13 x 9½ x 2-inch baking pan.
2. Wipe fillets. Arrange in single layer in pan.
3. In mixing bowl blend all remaining ingredients except egg whites.
4. Beat egg whites until stiff but not dry; fold into sour cream mixture; spread on fish. Bake in preheated oven for 30 minutes, or until fish flakes easily.

Mrs. Eugene Nicholson, Carlisle County
Homemakers Association, Bauville, Ky.

ROLLED STUFFED FILLETS

Serves 6

1 cup fresh bread crumbs
1 small onion, grated
1 cup flaked cooked crab meat
1 egg, lightly beaten
½ teaspoon salt
Dash of cayenne
6 fillets of flounder or halibut
2 tablespoons melted butter or
margarine
Parsley sprigs

1. Preheat oven to 350° F. Grease 10 x 6 x 1½-inch baking pan.
2. Prepare Crab Meat Stuffing: Combine crumbs, onion, crab meat, egg, salt and cayenne; mix well.
3. Spread stuffing on fillets; roll up each fillet like a jelly roll. Secure with wooden picks; arrange in pan. Brush fillets with butter or margarine.
4. Bake in preheated oven for 25 minutes.
5. Arrange fillets on serving dish; remove wooden picks; garnish with parsley.

Gloria Martino, Whitfield Woman's Club, Reading, Pa.

FILLETS WITH MUSTARD SOUR CREAM SAUCE

Serves 4

1 pound fillets of a white fish
Flour
1 medium onion, minced
1 tablespoon chopped parsley
1 cup sour cream
1¼ teaspoons dry mustard
1 teaspoon salt
½ teaspoon sugar

1. Preheat oven to 400° F. Grease shallow baking pan large enough to hold fillets without overlapping.
2. Dust fillets with flour. Arrange in pan. Sprinkle with onion and parsley.
3. Prepare Mustard Sour Cream Sauce: Combine sour cream, mustard, salt and sugar. Spread evenly on fish.
4. Bake in preheated oven for 15 minutes, or until fish flakes easily.

Mrs. Walter Vreeland, Pueblo Junior Woman's Club, Tucson, Ariz.

FILLETS WITH SHRIMP SAUCE

Serves 4

1 pound fillets of perch or haddock, skinned, or frozen fillets, defrosted
10-ounce can frozen shrimp soup, defrosted
2 tablespoons milk
¼ cup fresh bread crumbs
2 tablespoons butter
Paprika

1. Preheat oven to 350° F. Grease 1½-quart casserole or shallow baking dish.
2. Arrange fillets in casserole or dish. Mix soup and milk; pour over fish. Sprinkle with crumbs; dot with butter; sprinkle with paprika.

3. Bake in preheated oven for 30 minutes, or until fish flakes easily.

Mrs. Frederick W. Marriner, President, Woman's Club, Watertown, Mass.

FILLETS BAKED IN TOMATO SAUCE

Serves 3

¼ cup salad oil
1 cup sliced onions
1 clove garlic, minced
10½-ounce can condensed tomato soup
⅛ teaspoon crushed dried basil
½ teaspoon salt
⅛ teaspoon pepper
1 pound fillets of cod or haddock
½ cup grated Swiss cheese

1. Preheat oven to 350° F. Grease baking dish.
2. Prepare Skillet Tomato Sauce: Heat oil in skillet; sauté onions and garlic for 5 minutes, or until onions are transparent. Add soup and seasonings. Bring to boil; simmer for 10 minutes.
3. Arrange fillets in baking dish. Pour sauce over fish. Bake in preheated oven for 15 minutes.
4. Sprinkle with cheese. Bake for 15 minutes longer, or until fish flakes easily.

Mrs. Earl A. Reynolds, Probieren Club, Weatherford, Okla.

BROILED OR BAKED FISH WITH GREEN SAUCE

Serves 8

Use speckled trout, Spanish mackerel or a similar fish that is large enough to fillet nicely. Fillets should be free of bone and skin.

3 to 4 pounds fillets of fish
Salt
1 cup finely chopped onions
1 cup finely chopped green pepper
1 cup minced parsley
1 clove garlic, minced
1 teaspoon Worcestershire
Several dashes of Tabasco
1 cup melted butter
Bread crumbs (preferably made from French bread)

1. Preheat broiler or oven to 450° F.
2. Place fillets in broiling pan. Sprinkle with salt.
3. Prepare Green Sauce: Combine onions, green pepper, parsley, garlic, Worcestershire, Tabasco and butter. Spoon evenly over fish.
4. Put under broiler or in preheated oven for 10 to 15 minutes; do not let brown.
5. Remove from heat. Sprinkle fish with enough crumbs to absorb butter and make a crust. Return to broiler or oven for about 5 minutes longer, or until lightly browned.

Mrs. Phil A. Boykin, Woman's Club, Hapeville, Ga.

PAN-BROILED FISH

Serves 4

¼ cup butter or margarine
1½ pounds fillets of mullet, large
   trout or other large fish
¼ cup lemon juice
1 small onion, chopped
½ small green pepper, chopped
¼ cup water
1½ teaspoons salt
¼ teaspoon pepper

1. Melt butter or margarine in large skillet; brown fillets quickly on both sides.
2. Reduce heat. Sprinkle fish with remaining ingredients. Cover; simmer over low heat for 8 to 10 minutes.

Mrs. Robert Wight, Woman's Club, Cairo, Ga.

FRIED FILLET ROLLS

Serves 6

2 pounds fillets of flounder, sole
   or haddock
1½ teaspoons salt
2½ teaspoons paprika
1 egg
1 tablespoon water
1 cup crushed cornflakes or sifted
   bread crumbs
Fat for deep frying
Quick Tomato Sauce (p. 451)

1. Cut fillets into serving portions. Combine salt and paprika; coat fish on both sides with mixture. Roll up fillets; fasten with wooden picks.
2. Beat egg and water. Dip fish in egg mixture; then roll in cornflakes or crumbs.
3. Fry rolls in deep fat heated to 365° F. for about 4 minutes, or until golden brown. Drain on absorbent paper.
4. Serve with Quick Tomato Sauce.

Marion Weeks, Women's Club, Portsmouth, N.H.

GEFULLTE FISH

Makes About 36 Fish Balls

4 pounds whitefish, carp or pike
   or mixed whitefish, carp or pike
   with skin, heads and bones
3 medium onions, quartered
3 carrots, coarsely cut
1 stalk celery with leaves, coarsely
   cut
4 teaspoons salt
2 eggs
¼ teaspoon white pepper
¼ cup matzo meal

1. Fillet fish. Reserve heads, bones and skins. Dice fish; set aside for fish balls. It should measure about 3 cups.
2. Prepare fish stock, put fish heads, bones and skins in large saucepan. Add 2 of the onions, 2 of the carrots, celery, 2 teaspoons of the salt and 2 quarts water. Bring to boil; cover; and simmer for 30 minutes.
3. Meanwhile, put diced fish, remaining onion and remaining carrot through fine blade of meat grinder. Mix with remaining salt, eggs, ½ cup water and pepper. Stir in matzo meal; mix thoroughly. Chill for 30 minutes.

4. With moist hands, shape mixture into small balls, using about 1 tablespoon for each. Carefully lower balls into fish stock; cover; simmer for 1 to 1½ hours.
5. Remove fish balls from stock with slotted spoon. Strain stock over fish balls. Refrigerate until liquid is slightly set.

BLENDER METHOD FOR FISH BALLS: Fillet fish and make stock as in Steps 1 and 2 above. In container of electric blender combine 1 of the eggs, ¼ cup water, remaining salt, pepper and half the remaining onion. Cover; turn on high speed. Leaving motor on, remove cover; gradually add half the fish and half the remaining carrot. Blend for 1 minute longer, or until smooth, stopping to stir down if necessary. Turn into mixing bowl. Repeat with remaining egg, ¼ cup water, onion, fish and carrot. Stir matzo meal into fish mixtures. Refrigerate for 20 minutes. Shape, cook and finish the gefullte fish as in Steps 4 and 5 above.

A. S.

SWEET SOUR PINEAPPLE FISH BALLS

Serves 6

1 pound fresh or defrosted frozen
   fillets of sole or halibut
5-ounce can water chestnuts,
   drained
⅔ cup almonds
1 tablespoon finely chopped
   preserved ginger
2 tablespoons cornstarch
2 tablespoons soy sauce
⅔ cup peanut oil
Sweet Sour Pineapple Sauce
   (p. 450)

1. Put fillets, water chestnuts and almonds through fine blade of meat grinder.
2. Add ginger, cornstarch and soy sauce; mix well; form into 1-inch balls.
3. Heat oil in large skillet, cook fish balls over low heat, turning occasionally, until browned on all sides. Drain on absorbent paper.
4. Heat Sweet Sour Pineapple Sauce to serving temperature. Add fish balls. Simmer for 2 minutes.

Valene Klamt, Woman's Club, St. Anthony, Ida.

DEEP-FRIED FISH

Serves 3 or 4

2 eggs
1 teaspoon prepared mustard
2 tablespoons water
1 teaspoon salt
¼ teaspoon pepper
1 pound fillets of sole or haddock
Flour
¾ cup bread crumbs
Fat for deep frying
Lemon wedges

1. Prepare Frying Batter: In flat dish beat eggs, mustard, water, salt and pepper.
2. Cut fillets into small pieces. Dip in flour. Dip in batter. Coat with crumbs.

3. Fry in deep fat heated to 365° F. for 5 to 7 minutes, or until golden on both sides.

4. Drain on absorbent paper. Serve with lemon wedges.

Mrs. Don Hanson, Woman's Club, Sebring, Fla.

BAKED FISH STEAKS

Serves 6

6 6-ounce cod or salmon steaks
½ teaspoon salt
½ teaspoon paprika
⅛ teaspoon pepper
10½-ounce can condensed cream of celery soup
½ cup milk
1 tablespoon dry mustard
2 tablespoons melted butter or margarine
1 cup buttered bread crumbs
2 tablespoons chopped parsley

1. Preheat oven to 350° F. Grease 10 x 6 x 1½-inch baking pan.

2. Arrange steaks in pan. Sprinkle with salt, paprika and pepper.

3. Blend soup, milk, mustard and butter or margarine. Pour over steaks. Sprinkle with crumbs and parsley.

4. Bake in preheated oven for 35 minutes, or until fish flakes easily.

Carolyn Wanner, Junior Woman's Club, Muhlenberg, Pa.

HERB BROILED FISH

Serves 4

⅓ cup melted butter
1 tablespoon grated onion
3 tablespoons lemon juice
1 teaspoon salt
¼ teaspoon pepper
½ teaspoon marjoram
1 tablespoon chives
2 tablespoons chopped parsley
4 6-ounce halibut, salmon, cod or swordfish steaks

1. Preheat broiler. Grease broiler pan.

2. Prepare Herb Sauce: In small bowl blend all ingredients except fish. Spread half the mixture on steaks.

3. Broil 5 to 6 inches from heat for 6 minutes. Turn steaks; spread with remaining sauce. Broil for 8 minutes longer, or until fish flakes easily.

Esther Bartlett, Junior Woman's Club, Simsbury, Conn.

FISH SOUFFLÉ WITH PECAN SAUCE

Serves 4 to 6

1 cup fresh bread crumbs
1-pound fillets of halibut or flounder, cooked and flaked
1 teaspoon salt
¼ teaspoon pepper
½ cup milk
½ cup heavy cream
4 egg whites
Pecan Sauce (p. 449)

1. Preheat oven to 350° F. Grease 1½-quart casserole.

2. In top of double saucepan combine crumbs, fish, salt, pepper, milk and cream. Cook over hot water, stirring frequently, until creamy. Cool slightly.

3. Beat egg whites until stiff but not dry. Fold into fish mixture. Turn into casserole.

4. Place casserole in shallow pan containing 1 inch of hot water. Bake in preheated oven for 45 minutes.

5. Cut into slices. Serve with Pecan Sauce.

Mrs. William Sager, Junior Women's Club, Orange, N.J.

BAKED BLUEFISH IN SOUR CREAM

Serves 6

2 tablespoons butter
2 medium onions, thinly sliced
1 medium green pepper, cut into thin rings
6 fillets of bluefish
Salt and pepper to taste
2 cups sour cream

1. Preheat oven to 375° F.

2. Melt butter in large ovenproof skillet. Sauté onions and green pepper over low heat for 5 minutes, but do not let brown. Remove vegetables from skillet.

3. Season fillets liberally with salt and pepper. Arrange in skillet. Add vegetables. Cover fish with sour cream. Sprinkle lightly with salt and pepper.

4. Bake in preheated oven for 15 to 20 minutes, or until fish flakes easily.

5. Serve directly from skillet, since fish will break if you try to transfer it to serving dish.

Junior Women's Club, Riverside, N.J.

BROILED BLUEFISH

Serves 2

About 1½-pound bluefish, filleted
2 tablespoons olive oil
1 tablespoon lemon juice
Salt and pepper to taste
Lemon Butter (p. 444)

1. Preheat broiler.

2. Rub both sides of fish with oil and lemon juice. Sprinkle with salt and pepper.

3. Place, skin side up, on broiler pan. Broil about 5 inches from heat for 5 minutes. Turn fish; broil for 10 minutes longer, or until fish flakes easily.

4. Serve with Lemon Butter.

Mrs. Harvey Brooks, Woman's Club, Essex, Conn.

CODFISH CAKES

Serves 4

Very good served with crisp slices of salt pork around the edge of platter and with hot tomato sauce or tomato salad.

1 cup finely diced salt codfish
2 cups finely diced potatoes
½ cup boiling salted water

1 tablespoon butter
Dash of pepper
1 egg
¼ cup bacon drippings

1. Put fish, potatoes and water in saucepan. Cover; simmer for 20 minutes. Drain; turn into mixing bowl.
2. Add butter and pepper. Mash until smooth. Stir in egg; mix well. Shape into 4 flat cakes.
3. Heat bacon drippings in skillet. Sauté cakes on both sides until golden.

Mrs. Thomas Smith, Vermont Federation of Women's Clubs

CODFISH BALLS

Serves 4

1 cup salt codfish
4 medium potatoes
1 tablespoon butter
¼ teaspoon pepper
Salt (optional)
½ cup cracker crumbs
1 egg, well beaten
Fat for deep frying

1. Shred codfish. Peel and quarter potatoes.
2. Put fish and potatoes in saucepan. Cover with boiling water. Boil for 25 minutes, or until potatoes are soft.
3. Drain. Mash, then beat mixture until light. Beat in butter, pepper and salt, if desired.
4. Shape into balls. Roll in crumbs; dip in egg; roll again in crumbs.
5. Fry in deep fat heated to 365° F. until golden brown.
6. Drain on absorbent paper.

Doris Goodhope, Senior and Junior Club, Bellevue, Neb.

CODFISH TIMBALES

Serves 6

½ pound salt codfish
2 eggs
2 cups tomato juice
2 tablespoons grated onion
Dash of pepper

1. Soak codfish in cold water for 2 hours. Drain. Cut into small pieces; put in saucepan. Cover with water; bring to boil; simmer for 15 minutes. Drain and flake fish.
2. Preheat oven to 350° F. Grease 6 individual baking dishes.
3. In mixing bowl beat eggs. Stir in remaining ingredients and fish.
4. Turn into baking dishes; set dishes in shallow pan containing 1 inch of hot water; bake in preheated oven for 1 hour, or until knife inserted in center comes out clean.
5. Serve in baking dishes, or unmold.

Mrs. Earl Wood, Jr., Women's Club, Arroyo Grande, Calif.

CODFISH PAMPLONA

Serves 4 to 6

This codfish dish was discovered by Ernest Hemingway and his wife in 1926 in Marcelino's Café in Pamplona, Spain.

1 pound salt codfish
2 tablespoons cooking oil
2 cloves garlic, minced
2 tomatoes, sliced
1 large onion, thinly sliced
1 green pepper, thinly sliced
2 tablespoons chili sauce
2 bay leaves
½ teaspoon sugar
¼ teaspoon cumin seeds
¼ teaspoon orégano
¼ teaspoon marjoram
Black pepper to taste
½ cup white wine
6½-ounce can crab meat, drained and flaked
1 cup shelled deveined shrimp
4-ounce can whole mushrooms, drained
Cooked black beans
Cooked rice

1. Day before, cover codfish with cold water; let stand for 20 minutes; then drain. Cut fish into pieces. Add cold water to cover; soak overnight.
2. Next day, bring fish in soaking water to boil. Simmer for 45 minutes. Taste; if too salty, rinse in warm water. Drain thoroughly.
3. Meanwhile, heat oil in large skillet. Add garlic, tomatoes, onion, green pepper, chili sauce, bay leaves, sugar, seasonings and wine. Bring to boil; cover; simmer over low heat for 30 minutes.
4. Add codfish; simmer for 20 minutes longer.
5. Add crab meat, shrimp and mushrooms; simmer for 10 minutes longer. Fish will absorb liquid.
6. Serve with black beans and rice.

Mrs. Albert Bakker, Tuesday Study Club of Fairhope, Battles Wharf, Ala.

EEL

Eel are excellent grilled or sautéed and served with Lemon Butter (p. 444) or Sauce Tartare (p. 446). They also make delicious stews and casseroles. If purchased at a fish market, the eel will be skinned and cleaned. If the eel is freshly caught, it may be necessary to do this yourself: With a sharp knife, cut around the skin just back of the head. Turn back the skin, and strip it off from head to tail, turning it inside out as it pulls away from the flesh. Discard the head and entrails. Cut the flesh into 3-inch pieces, and wash thoroughly in salted water.

BAKED EEL

Serves 4 to 6

2-pound eel, skinned and cut into sections
Salt and pepper to taste
¼ cup olive oil
1 clove garlic, minced
Pinch of thyme
Juice of ½ lemon
Chopped parsley

1. Preheat oven to 375° F.
2. Sprinkle eel with salt and pepper.
3. Heat oil in small casserole. Add garlic, eel, thyme and lemon juice.
4. Bake in preheated oven for 30 minutes. Sprinkle with parsley before serving.

A. S.

BAKED FLOUNDER SUPREME

Serves 5

1½ pounds fillets of flounder
  1 cup cracker crumbs
  1 teaspoon salt
  ½ teaspoon pepper
  1 egg, beaten with 2 tablespoons
    water
6½-ounce can crab meat, drained
    and flaked
    Paprika
    Butter or margarine

1. Preheat oven to 425° F. Line 5 custard cups with aluminum foil; set on baking sheet.
2. Cut fillets into long strips.
3. On piece of waxed paper combine crumbs, salt and pepper. Coat fish with crumbs; dip in egg mixture; again coat with crumbs. Lay flat on table.
4. Spread fish with crab meat. Roll up each strip like a jelly roll. Secure with wooden picks.
5. Place pat of butter or margarine in each cup. Place fish roll on top. Sprinkle with paprika; dot with butter or margarine.
6. Bake in preheated oven for 20 minutes.

Mrs. Dolores Gayton, Woman's Club,
Brooklawn, N.J.

BROILED FLOUNDER

Serves 1 or 2

¼ cup butter
2 tablespoons lemon juice
  Salt
  Dash of Worcestershire
⅛ teaspoon minced garlic
1 medium flounder
  Pepper to taste

1. Prepare Lemon Butter: Melt butter in small saucepan. Add lemon juice, ⅛ teaspoon salt, Worcestershire and garlic. Keep hot over low heat.
2. Preheat broiler.
3. Rub fish with salt, pepper and 1 tablespoon of Lemon Butter.
4. Place on broiler rack. Broil until fish flakes easily, basting once or twice with Lemon Butter.
5. Transfer to hot serving plate. Pour remaining Lemon Butter over fish.

Gulf Coast Gourmet, Woman's Club,
Foley, Ala.

HADDOCK FILLETS PROVENÇALE IN TOMATO SAUCE

Serves 4

2 tablespoons butter
1 pound fillets of haddock
½ cup dry white wine

1 small onion, halved
½ clove garlic
⅓ cup parsley sprigs
¼ teaspoon thyme
1 teaspoon salt
¼ teaspoon pepper
1-pound can tomatoes, undrained
2 tablespoons flour
4-ounce can mushrooms, drained
  Cooked rice or toast

1. Melt butter in large skillet; sauté fillets for 2 minutes. Add wine; cover; simmer for 5 minutes.
2. Meanwhile, prepare Blender Tomato Sauce: Put onion, garlic, seasonings, tomatoes and flour into container of electric blender. Cover; blend on high speed for 5 seconds, or until smooth.
3. Pour over fish in skillet. Stir in mushrooms. Cook over low heat, stirring constantly, until sauce comes to boil. Cover; cook over low heat for 10 minutes.
4. Serve on rice or toast.

Edwina Curtis, Junior Woman's Club,
Glastonbury, Conn.

SCALLOPED HADDOCK

Serves 6

3 pounds haddock, cooked and
    flaked
2 cups Medium White Sauce
    (p. 441)
    Salt and pepper to taste
2 eggs, hard-cooked and chopped
8-ounce can peas, drained
¼ cup chopped pimientos
1 cup fresh bread crumbs
¼ cup melted butter or margarine

1. Preheat oven to 375° F. Grease 2-quart casserole.
2. Stir fish into Medium White Sauce. Season with salt and pepper.
3. Stir in eggs, peas and pimientos. Turn into casserole.
4. In small bowl blend crumbs with butter or margarine. Sprinkle over mixture.
5. Bake in preheated oven for 25 minutes.

Mrs. Waldo H. Nason, Woman's Club,
Norwood, Mass.

HADDOCK CRUMB PIE

Serves 8

½ cup melted butter or margarine
4 cups fresh bread crumbs
2 tablespoons grated onion
1¼ teaspoons salt
¼ teaspoon pepper
¾ teaspoon celery salt
¼ teaspoon sage
⅓ cup shortening
⅓ cup presifted flour
2 cups milk
2 cups flaked cooked haddock
1 cup buttered bread crumbs

1. Preheat oven to 375° F. Grease 2½-quart casserole.
2. Prepare Bread Crumb Crust: In mixing bowl combine butter or margarine, fresh crumbs, onion, 1 teaspoon of the salt,

⅛ teaspoon of the pepper, ½ teaspoon of the celery salt and sage; mix well.

3. Press mixture onto bottom and sides of casserole.

4. Bake in preheated oven for 25 minutes. Turn temperature up to 425° F.

5. Melt shortening in skillet. Blend in flour. Gradually stir in milk. Cook over medium heat, stirring constantly, until thickened and smooth.

6. Remove from heat. Stir in remaining seasonings and fish. Turn onto crust. Top with buttered crumbs.

7. Bake for 20 minutes, or until browned.

Mrs. S. Haraden, Women's Literary Club,
Bellevue, Neb.

FINNAN HADDIE À LA KING
Serves 4

1 pound smoked haddock
¼ cup butter or margarine
2 tablespoons finely chopped green pepper
2 tablespoons chopped pimiento
1 cup sliced mushrooms
2 tablespoons flour
1 cup milk
1 cup light cream
3 eggs, hard-cooked
Salt and pepper to taste

1. Put haddock in saucepan; cover with warm water. Let stand for 20 minutes; then drain.

2. Cover with cold water. Bring to boil; cover; simmer over low heat for 30 minutes. Drain and flake fish.

3. Melt butter or margarine in saucepan; sauté green pepper, pimiento and mushrooms for 5 minutes. Sprinkle with flour. Gradually stir in milk and cream. Cook over medium heat, stirring constantly, until sauce is thickened and smooth.

4. Separate egg whites from yolks. Press yolks through sieve into sauce.

5. Add fish. Season with salt and pepper. Simmer for 5 minutes, stirring occasionally.

6. Chop egg whites.

7. Arrange fish in serving dish. Sprinkle with egg whites.

Mrs. Gerald Hannay, Woman's Club,
Orange, N.J.

HALIBUT BAKED IN MILK
Serves 4

2 1-pound halibut steaks
Salt
Flour
¼ cup butter
Onion, sliced
1½ cups milk
Parsley
Lemon wedges

1. Preheat oven to 425° F.

2. Sprinkle steaks with salt. Roll in flour.

3. Melt butter in baking dish; arrange steaks in dish.

4. Put several slices of onion on steaks; add milk.

5. Bake in preheated oven for about 20 minutes, or until fish flakes easily and most of milk is absorbed.

6. Garnish with parsley. Serve with lemon wedges.

Mrs. E. S. Griffith, Woman's Club,
Azusa, Calif.

HALIBUT STEAK CREOLE
Serves 4 to 6

¼ cup melted margarine
2-pound halibut steak
2 teaspoons salt
¼ teaspoon pepper
½ cup sliced onions
1 cup chopped drained canned tomatoes

1. Preheat oven to 400° F. Brush baking dish with a little of the margarine.

2. Put halibut in dish. Brush with remaining margarine.

3. Sprinkle fish with salt and pepper. Arrange onions on top; cover with tomatoes.

4. Bake in preheated oven for 30 minutes, or until fish flakes easily.

Millie Kessinger, Woman's Club,
Temple City, Calif.

HERB BROILED HALIBUT
Serves 4 to 6

2 pounds fresh or frozen 1-inch-thick halibut steaks
⅓ cup butter or margarine
2 tablespoons minced onion
1 clove garlic, minced
½ teaspoon salt
¼ teaspoon coarsely ground black pepper
¼ teaspoon dried thyme
⅛ teaspoon dried tarragon
¼ teaspoon dried basil
¼ teaspoon dried parsley
1 tablespoon lemon juice

1. If halibut is frozen, let stand for 30 minutes at room temperature.

2. Preheat broiler. Line broiler pan with aluminum foil.

3. Arrange steaks in pan.

4. Cream butter or margarine, onion, garlic, seasonings and herbs. Gradually beat in lemon juice.

5. Spread half the herb butter over fish. Broil 2 inches from heat for 3 minutes if fresh halibut; for 5 minutes if partially thawed halibut.

6. Carefully turn fish with pancake turner. Spread with remaining herb butter. Broil for 3 to 5 minutes longer, or until fish flakes easily.

7. Place steaks on warm serving platter. Spoon sauce in broiler pan over them.

Favorite Recipes, Woman's Club, Erwin, Tenn.

BAKED SPANISH MACKEREL
Serves 6

6 slices bacon
1 small onion, finely chopped
1 tablespoon chopped green
    pepper
½ teaspoon salt
Dash of pepper
2 cups fresh bread crumbs
4- to 5-pound mackerel, dressed
Lemon wedges

1. Preheat oven to 400° F.
2. Prepare stuffing: dice 3 slices of the bacon in skillet; cook with onion and green pepper over medium heat for 5 minutes. Remove from heat. Stir in salt, pepper and crumbs; mix lightly.
3. Arrange mackerel on rack in shallow roasting pan. Fill cavity with stuffing. Sew up or skewer opening. Place remaining bacon on fish.
4. Bake in preheated oven for 30 minutes, or until fish flakes easily, basting frequently during cooking with pan juices.
5. Arrange fish on serving dish. Garnish with lemon wedges.

Mrs. J. L. Walthall, Jeffersonville Woman's Club,
Tazewell, Va.

BARBECUED MULLET
Serves 8 to 10

1 cup butter or margarine
1 cup chili sauce
1 cup French dressing
1 cup catsup
1 cup vinegar
2 tablespoons lemon juice
½ teaspoon pepper
1 tablespoon salt
6- to 8-pound mullet

1. Prepare sauce; melt butter in saucepan. Stir in all remaining ingredients except mullet. Bring to boil. Simmer for 10 minutes. Set aside.
2. Remove head from mullet. Clean inside of fish, but do not scale. Slit up center so fish will lie flat.
3. Heat charcoal fire.
4. When ready to cook, arrange fish, skin side up, on grill. Cover fish with aluminum foil. Grill for 20 minutes. Remove foil. Turn fish so that skin side is down.
5. Brush inside of fish generously with sauce. Cover fish with foil. Grill for 15 minutes longer, or until fish flakes easily, opening foil to baste frequently with sauce.
6. Heat remaining sauce. Serve with fish.

Mrs. L. P. Creech, Woman's Club,
Pine Level, N.C.

BAKED OCEAN PERCH
Serves 4 or 5

1 lemon, thinly sliced
1 medium onion, thinly sliced
Salt and pepper
1½ pounds fillets of ocean perch
1 cup sour cream
1 teaspoon prepared mustard
1 teaspoon paprika

1. Preheat oven to 400° F. Grease 10 x 6 x 1½-inch baking pan.
2. Arrange lemon and onion slices in pan. Sprinkle lightly with salt and pepper.
3. Top with fillets. Season lightly with salt and pepper. Cover with aluminum foil. Bake in preheated oven for 20 minutes.
4. Remove foil. Turn temperature to Broil.
5. In small bowl blend sour cream, mustard, paprika, ¼ teaspoon salt and a dash of pepper. Spread on fish.
6. Broil 3 inches from heat for 5 minutes, or until browned.

Tennessee Federation of Women's Clubs

PERCH MAÎTRE D'HÔTEL
Serves 8

½ cup olive oil
1 tablespoon lemon juice
1 small onion, finely chopped
1 tablespoon finely chopped celery
1 tablespoon finely chopped
    parsley
1 tablespoon salt
½ teaspoon pepper
¼ teaspoon cayenne
8 medium perch, dressed
Hollandaise Sauce (p. 444)

1. Prepare marinade: In bowl blend all ingredients except perch and Hollandaise Sauce.
2. Arrange perch in large shallow dish. Sprinkle with marinade. Marinate for at least 1 hour.
3. Preheat broiler. Line broiler pan with aluminum foil.
4. Remove fish from marinade; arrange on foil. Broil 4 to 5 inches from heat for 8 minutes on each side, or until fish flakes easily.
5. Serve with Hollandaise Sauce.

Mrs. Ed Deramee, Junior Woman's Club,
Thibodaux, La.

BAKED NORTHERN PIKE
Serves 8 to 10

6- to 8-pound pike, dressed
Salt and pepper to taste
3 cups Bread Stuffing (p. 452)
6 slices bacon
1 large tomato, thinly sliced
¼ cup water

1. Preheat oven to 375° F. Grease large shallow roasting pan.
2. Sprinkle cavity of pike with salt and pepper. Fill cavity with Bread Stuffing. Sew or skewer opening.
3. Arrange pike in pan. Top with bacon slices, then with tomato slices. Pour water over all.
4. Bake in preheated oven for 1¼ hours, or until fish flakes easily.

Mrs. George Erdman, Plum Lake Woman's Club,
Star Lake, Wis.

POMPANO EN PAPILLOTE

Serves 8

8 fillets of pompano
¼ cup butter
3 tablespoons finely chopped scallions
3 teaspoons minced parsley
¼ cup finely chopped mushrooms
Freshly ground pepper
Salt to taste
Juice of 1 large lemon or lime
½ cup dry white wine
1 cup fresh crab meat or shelled
deveined shrimp, finely chopped
2 tablespoons butter
½ cup heavy cream
3 egg yolks

1. Preheat oven to 450° F. Grease shallow baking dish.
2. Arrange fillets in baking dish, side by side; do not overlap. Dot with ¼ cup butter; sprinkle with onions, parsley, mushrooms, pepper, salt and lemon or lime juice.
3. Bake in preheated oven for 5 minutes.
4. Add wine; cover; bake for 10 minutes longer. Remove from oven.
5. Cut squares of parchment or aluminum foil large enough to enclose fillets. Place a fillet on each square; pin or seal 3 sides. Arrange on baking sheet.
6. Put seafood and 2 tablespoons butter in saucepan. Cook over moderate heat for 5 minutes, tossing constantly. Add to dish in which fillets were baked.
7. Combine cream and egg yolks. Stir into seafood. Cook over low heat, stirring constantly, until sauce is thickened.
8. Divide sauce over fillets in parchment or foil; seal fourth side.
9. Bake in preheated oven for 15 minutes.
10. Serve in packages—1 per person.

Gulf Coast Gourmet, Woman's Club, Foley, Ala.

BROILED FILLETS OF POMPANO OR MULLET

Serves 4

1½ pounds fillets of pompano or
mullet
Salt and pepper to taste
¼ cup lemon juice
¼ cup olive oil
Chopped parsley
Butter Sauce (p. 442) (optional)

1. Preheat broiler. Line broiler pan with aluminum foil.
2. Arrange fillets on foil. Sprinkle with salt, pepper and lemon juice.
3. Brush well with oil. Broil 4 to 5 inches from heat for about 15 minutes. Turn fillets; brush with oil; broil for 5 minutes longer, or until fish flakes easily.
4. Garnished with parsley. Serve with Butter Sauce, if desired.

Woman's Club, Cairo, Ga.

BAKED RED SNAPPER IN WINE SAUCE

Serves 8

4-pound red snapper
½ cup olive oil
½ cup lemon juice
2 carrots, sliced
2 medium onions, sliced
Small bunch parsley
2 bay leaves
3 cloves garlic
2 teaspoons salt
¼ teaspoon peppercorns
⅓ cup butter
2 cups dry white wine
Dash of cayenne
Lemon wedges, parsley sprigs and
capers (optional)

1. Clean and scale red snapper. Place in shallow pan (not metal).
2. Pour oil and lemon juice over fish. Top with carrots, onions, parsley, bay leaves, garlic, salt and peppercorns. Marinate for 30 minutes.
3. Preheat oven to 350° F. Grease roasting pan.
4. Remove fish from marinade; place in roasting pan. Reserve marinade. Dot fish with butter. Add wine.
5. Bake in preheated oven for 45 minutes, or until fish flakes easily. Baste frequently with wine.
6. Place fish on serving dish; keep in warm place.
7. Add marinade to wine in roasting pan; simmer for 10 minutes. Correct seasoning; add cayenne. Strain; pour over fish.
8. Garnish with lemon wedges, parsley sprigs and capers, if desired.

Mrs. Paul Campbell, Woman's Club, Sebring, Fla.

PICKLED SPICED SALMON

Serves 12

2 cups dry white wine
1 quart water
1 carrot, quartered
1 large onion, quartered
1 stick celery, quartered
1 tablespoon salt
7- to 8-pound salmon, dressed
3 cups white vinegar
12 cloves
12 blades sliced nutmeg
1 teaspoon whole allspice
1 teaspoon peppercorns
2 tablespoons butter

1. Prepare Wine Stock: In large fish kettle or roasting pan large enough to take whole fish combine wine, water, carrot, onion, celery and salt. Bring to boil; add salmon. Cover; simmer for 1 hour and 10 minutes.
2. Cool salmon in stock.
3. Remove fish; pat dry; set aside.
4. Strain stock. Cook over high heat until reduced to about 3 cups. Add vinegar and spices. Return to boil.
5. Remove from heat. Skim surface; stir in butter.

6. Place fish in large shallow dish (not metal); pour liquid over it. Chill until ready to use.

Mrs. Olive Milam, Woman's Club,
Monterey Park, Calif.

STUFFED BAKED SALMON

Serves 12

6-pound shoulder cut of salmon
Salt to taste
Celery leaves
Parsley sprigs
Butter
¼ cup finely chopped celery
¼ cup finely chopped onion
1-pound can sliced mushrooms, drained
2 cups crushed salted crackers
1 tablespoon minced parsley

1. Rinse salmon in cold water. Dry thoroughly. Season inside with salt. Set aside.
2. Preheat oven to 400° F. Grease baking pan. Cover bottom with a few celery leaves and parsley sprigs.
3. Prepare Mushroom Stuffing: Melt 4 tablespoons butter in saucepan; sauté celery and onion until lightly browned. Add mushrooms; simmer for 2 to 3 minutes. Stir in crackers and minced parsley.
4. Fill salmon lightly with stuffing; tie with string. Gash top of salmon; insert bits of butter.
5. Arrange fish in pan. Bake in preheated oven for 1½ hours.

Mrs. Earl W. Wood, Jr., Women's Club,
Arroyo Grande, Calif.

RICE-STUFFED BAKED SALMON

Serves 8 to 10

½ cup butter
¼ cup finely chopped onion
¼ cup finely chopped celery
¼ cup finely chopped green pepper
½ pound mushrooms, finely chopped
Salt and pepper
1½ cups cooked rice
¼ teaspoon orégano
¼ teaspoon paprika
1 teaspoon chopped parsley
4- to 6-pound salmon, dressed
Lemon wedges and water cress (optional)

1. Preheat oven to 400° F. Grease shallow roasting pan.
2. Prepare Rice Stuffing: Melt ¼ cup of the butter in large skillet; sauté onion, celery and green pepper for 5 minutes. Stir in mushrooms; sauté for 5 minutes longer, stirring occasionally. Season with 1 teaspoon salt and ¼ teaspoon pepper.
3. Remove from heat. Stir in rice, orégano, paprika and parsley.
4. Sprinkle inside of salmon with salt and pepper. Fill cavity with stuffing. Secure with skewers. Place in pan.
5. Melt remaining butter in small saucepan. Brush salmon with it.
6. Bake in preheated oven for 1 hour, or until fish flakes easily. Allow 10 to 15

minutes per pound. Baste frequently with melted butter during cooking.
7. Arrange salmon on serving dish. Remove skewers. Garnish with lemon wedges and water cress, if desired.

Florence Willis, Mendocino Study Club,
Little River, Calif.

ALASKA BAKED SALMON FILLETS WITH DRESSING

Serves 6

6 tablespoons butter or margarine
¾ cup finely chopped celery
4 cups fresh bread crumbs
4 teaspoons minced onion
Salt and pepper
Catsup
6 fillets of salmon
Butter

1. Preheat oven to 350° F. Line baking dish with aluminum foil. Grease foil.
2. Prepare Bread Dressing: Melt butter or margarine in skillet; sauté celery for 10 minutes, or until tender. Combine with crumbs, onion, 1 teaspoon salt and ½ teaspoon pepper. Moisten with enough catsup to hold together.
3. Sprinkle fillets on both sides with salt and pepper. Arrange largest fillets in baking dish. Cover with dressing. Arrange smaller fillets over dressing. Dot with butter.
4. Cover; bake in preheated oven for 25 to 30 minutes, or until fish flakes easily.

Bettie Peck, Woman's Club, Anchorage, Alaska

SALMON STEAKS WITH BLUE CHEESE SAUCE

Serves 4

4 salmon steaks
Olive oil
Salt and pepper to taste
½ cup butter
2 egg yolks, lightly beaten
2 tablespoons lemon juice
½ teaspoon horseradish
¼ cup crumbled blue cheese
2 tablespoons chopped cucumber
1 teaspoon grated onion
⅛ teaspoon freshly ground pepper

1. Brush steaks with oil; sprinkle with salt and pepper. Set aside.
2. Prepare Blue Cheese Sauce: Melt butter in top of double saucepan over hot water. Add egg yolks, lemon juice and horseradish. Cook, stirring constantly, until thickened. Add remaining ingredients; mix well.
3. Preheat broiler for 5 minutes.
4. Brush broiler pan with oil. Arrange steaks on it. Broil, turning each steak once, until fish flakes easily.
5. Serve with hot sauce.

Mrs. Paul Kaatz, Woman's Club,
Anchorage, Alaska

SALMON BOX

2 cups Thin White Sauce (p. 441)
2 tablespoons chopped green pepper

¼ teaspoon Worcestershire
1-pound can salmon, drained,
  boned and flaked
2 cups cooked rice
¾ cup buttered bread crumbs

1. Preheat oven to 350° F. Grease 1½-quart casserole.
2. Combine Thin White Sauce, green pepper and Worcestershire.
3. In casserole arrange alternate layers of salmon, rice and sauce. Top with crumbs.
4. Bake in preheated oven for 20 minutes.

Mrs. W. C. Thatcher, President,
Women's Club, Fort Dodge, Ia.

SPRING SALMON CASSEROLE

Serves 6 to 8

2 1-pound cans green beans
½ cup butter or margarine
6 tablespoons flour
2 cups milk
¾ teaspoon salt
¼ teaspoon pepper
2 1-pound cans salmon, drained,
  boned and flaked
¼ cup sweet pickle relish
1 cup fresh bread crumbs

1. Preheat oven to 350° F. Grease 2½-quart casserole.
2. Drain beans; reserve 1 cup liquid.
3. Melt 6 tablespoons of the butter or margarine in medium saucepan. Stir in flour. Gradually stir in milk and reserved liquid. Cook over low heat, stirring constantly, until sauce is thickened and smooth. Stir in salt and pepper.
4. In casserole arrange alternate layers of beans, salmon and pickle relish. Pour sauce over layers.
5. Melt remaining butter in small pan; mix with crumbs. Sprinkle over sauce.
6. Bake in preheated oven for 30 minutes, or until top is golden brown.

Clara Null, Woman's Club, Blandinsville, Ill.

DEEP-DISH SALMON PIE

Serves 6

1½ cups Medium White Sauce (p. 441)
1½ cups whole-kernel corn
1-pound can salmon, drained,
  boned and flaked
Dash of Tabasco
Pastry for a 1-Crust Pie (p. 548)
Pastry leaves (optional)
1 egg yolk, lightly beaten

1. Preheat oven to 425° F. Grease 9-inch pie plate.
2. Combine Medium White Sauce, corn, salmon and Tabasco; turn into pie plate.
3. Roll out Pastry for a 1-Crust Pie into 10-inch circle. Cut ½-inch edging from circumference. Moisten rim of pie plate; press edging over rim. Moisten edging; cover pie with pastry circle. Press edges to seal and to flute. Make 2 slits in center to allow steam to escape.

4. Decorate top of pie with pastry leaves, if desired.
5. Brush with egg yolk.
6. Bake in preheated oven for 10 minutes. Reduce temperature to 350° F. Bake for 30 minutes longer, or until flaky and golden.

Jeanne Hollenbeck, Leroy Fidelis Club,
Crown Point, Ind.

SALMON TETRAZZINI

Serves 4

1-pound can salmon
2-ounce can sliced mushrooms
2 tablespoons cooking oil
2 tablespoons flour
½ teaspoon salt
Dash of Tabasco
8-ounce can tomato sauce
2 cups cooked spaghetti
¼ cup grated Parmesan cheese

1. Preheat oven to 350° F. Grease 2-quart casserole.
2. Drain liquid from salmon and mushrooms into measuring cup, add enough water to total 1 cup; reserve. Set mushrooms aside.
3. Bone and flake salmon; set aside.
4. Heat oil in saucepan. Stir in flour, salt and Tabasco. Gradually stir in reserved liquid and tomato sauce. Cook, stirring, until thickened and smooth.
5. Mix half the sauce with spaghetti and mushrooms; put in casserole. Mix remaining sauce with salmon; place in center of spaghetti. Sprinkle with cheese.
6. Bake in preheated oven for 30 minutes.

Mrs. S. E. Hargadine, Quest Club,
Bowling Green, Mo.

SALMON CROQUETTES

Serves 4

1 cup Thick White Sauce (p. 441)
½ teaspoon salt
⅛ teaspoon pepper
1 cup fresh bread crumbs
1-pound can salmon, drained,
  boned and flaked
Flour
1 egg, beaten with 2 tablespoons
  milk
1¼ cups dry bread crumbs
⅓ cup shortening
Tartar Sauce for Fish (p. 450)

1. In mixing bowl combine Thick White Sauce, salt, pepper, fresh crumbs and salmon. Chill for 2 hours.
2. Shape salmon mixture into croquettes; dredge in flour.
3. Dip in egg mixture; coat with dry crumbs. Reshape if necessary.
4. Melt shortening in skillet. Fry croquettes over medium heat until golden.
5. Drain on absorbent paper. Serve with Tartar Sauce for Fish.

Perk Rosienski, Junior Woman's Club,
Simsbury, Conn.

ALASKAN NUGGETS

Serves 4

1-pound can salmon, drained and
  boned
½ cup mashed potatoes
1 tablespoon butter
1 tablespoon minced celery
1 tablespoon minced onion
½ teaspoon salt
¼ teaspoon pepper
1 teaspoon Worcestershire
½ pound sharp Cheddar cheese,
  cut into ½-inch cubes
1 egg, lightly beaten
1 cup cornflake crumbs
Fat for deep frying
Cheese Sauce (p. 442)

1. Flake salmon; mash and mix with
potatoes.
2. Melt butter in skillet; sauté celery
and onion for 5 minutes, or until tender.
Mix with salmon. Add seasonings.
3. Shape into balls the size of walnuts.
Press cube of cheese into center of each
ball; reshape.
4. Roll balls in egg, then in crumbs.
5. Fry in fat deep enough to cover and
heated to 365° F. until golden brown on all
sides.
6. Drain well on absorbent paper. Serve
with Cheese Sauce.

Mrs. M. Carlson, Woman's Club,
Anchorage, Alaska

SALMON LOAF

Serves 6

1-pound can salmon
  Milk
2 tablespoons butter
2 tablespoons flour
½ teaspoon salt
¼ teaspoon white pepper
2 eggs, lightly beaten
1 tablespoon lemon juice
1 tablespoon Worcestershire
1 tablespoon grated onion
2 cups soft bread crumbs
8 large stuffed olives, sliced
3 eggs, hard-cooked

1. Drain liquid from salmon into measuring cup. Flake and bone salmon; set
aside.
2. Add enough milk to salmon liquid
to total 1 cup. Pour into small saucepan.
Heat to simmering.
3. Preheat oven to 350° F. Grease 8½-
inch loaf pan.
4. Melt butter in another saucepan. Stir
in flour, salt and pepper. Add salmon
liquid. Cook over moderate heat, stirring
rapidly, until sauce is thickened and
smooth. Gradually pour into beaten eggs,
stirring rapidly.
5. Combine salmon and sauce. Stir in
lemon juice, Worcestershire, onion and
crumbs.
6. Cover bottom of loaf pan with olives.
Spoon in half the salmon mixture; spread
evenly to edges; press in hard-cooked eggs

lengthwise. Cover with remaining salmon
mixture.
7. Bake in preheated oven for 45 minutes. Turn onto warm serving dish.

Margaret E. Sparks, Woman's Club,
Anchorage, Alaska

STEAMED SALMON LOAF

Serves 4

1-pound can salmon, undrained
1 cup cracker crumbs
2 eggs, lightly beaten
1 cup milk
2 tablespoons melted butter
1 tablespoon grated onion
  Salt and pepper to taste

1. Grease top of double saucepan.
2. Put all ingredients in mixing bowl.
Mix well. Turn into top of saucepan.
3. Cover. Steam over hot water for 1
hour.

Mrs. Robert L. Woolfolk, Homemakers,
Meade County, Ky.

SALMON LOAF WITH SHRIMP SAUCE

Serves 8

2 1-pound cans salmon
  Milk
¼ cup finely chopped onion
¼ cup chopped parsley
2 cups cracker crumbs
¼ cup lemon juice
½ teaspoon salt
½ teaspoon pepper
½ teaspoon thyme
4 eggs, lightly beaten
¼ cup melted butter
  Quick Shrimp Sauce (p. 449)

1. Preheat oven to 350° F. Grease 9-
inch loaf pan well.
2. Drain liquid from salmon into measuring cup. Add enough milk to total 1
cup; reserve.
3. Flake salmon in mixing bowl; add
onion, parsley, crumbs, lemon juice and
seasonings; mix well.
4. Add reserved liquid, eggs and butter;
mix well. Turn into pan.
5. Bake in preheated oven for 1 hour,
or until set in center.
6. Let stand for 5 minutes; then unmold
onto serving dish. Serve with Quick Shrimp
Sauce.

Mrs. H. Powell, New Century Club,
Parkside, Pa.

SARDINE PADDIES

Serves 4

4 eggs
¼ teaspoon paprika
1 tablespoon Worcestershire
12 large sardines, skinned and boned
½ cup milk
1½ cups bread crumbs
1½ cups heavy cream
Fat for deep frying
Cheese Sauce (p. 442)

1. In top of double saucepan beat eggs until fluffy.
2. Add paprika, Worcestershire, sardines and milk; mix well. Cook over hot water for 5 minutes, stirring frequently. Remove from heat; stir in ½ cup of the crumbs.
3. Cool slightly. Shape into 1-inch balls. Roll in remaining crumbs; dip into cream; roll again in crumbs. Reshape if necessary.
4. Fry in deep fat heated to 365° F. for 4 minutes, or until golden.
5. Drain on absorbent paper. Serve with Cheese Sauce.

Mrs. Dalton Wheeler, Woman's Club, Basin, Wyo.

BAKED CELERY-STUFFED SHAD
Serves 6 to 8

4½- to 5-pound shad, dressed
    Salt
    Celery Dressing (p. 453)
    Lemon wedges
    Parsley sprigs

1. Preheat oven to 550° F. Grease shallow roasting pan.
2. Sprinkle cavity of shad with salt. Fill loosely with Celery Dressing. Sew or skewer opening. Arrange in pan, in form of letter S.
3. Bake in preheated oven for 10 minutes. Reduce temperature to 425° F. Bake for 10 minutes longer, or until fish flakes easily. (Allow 10 minutes per pound.)
4. Arrange fish on serving dish. Remove stitches or skewers. Garnish with lemon wedges and parsley.

Mrs. Henry Bourne, Junior Wednesday Club,
Danville, Va.

SHAD ROE

Shad roe may be broiled and served with crisp bacon, sautéed in butter or baked in aluminum foil with a little white wine. Whatever method is used, care should be taken not to overcook it, or it will become dry and tasteless.

SHAD ROE POACHED IN BUTTER
Serves 1

1 small pair or 1 large half shad roe
2 tablespoons buttter
    Salt and freshly ground pepper
    to taste
2 tablespoons chopped parsley
    Lemon wedges

1. Melt butter in skillet over low heat until foamy but not browned. Carefully add roe. Sprinkle with salt and pepper.
2. Cover. Poach over low heat for 5 minutes.
3. Turn roe; sprinkle with parsley; cook, uncovered, for 5 minutes longer. Serve with lemon wedges.

A. S.

SHAD ROE BAKED IN FOIL
Serves 2

1 large pair shad roe
    Salt and freshly ground pepper
    to taste

2 tablespoons butter
2 tablespoons chopped parsley
2 tablespoons dry white wine
    Lemon wedges

1. Preheat oven to 350° F.
2. Sprinkle roe on both sides with salt and pepper.
3. Cut piece of aluminum foil large enough to enclose roe. Spread center of foil with half the butter; place roe on butter.
4. Sprinkle with parsley and white wine. Dot with remaining butter. Seal foil.
5. Bake in preheated oven for 20 minutes. Serve with lemon wedges.

A. S.

FILLETS OF SOLE AMANDINE
Serves 6

6 large fillets of sole
⅓ cup chopped scallions
¼ teaspoon rosemary
½ cup chopped mushrooms
½ cup dry white wine
1 tablespoon butter or margarine
½ cup heavy cream
½ cup chopped almonds

1. Arrange fillets in large skillet. Sprinkle with scallions, rosemary, mushrooms and wine. Cover; marinate for 2 hours.
2. Preheat broiler. Grease 10 x 6 x 1½-inch baking pan.
3. Bring liquid in skillet to boil; then simmer for 8 minutes, or until fish flakes easily.
4. Carefully transfer fillets to baking pan.
5. Cook liquid in skillet over high heat until reduced by half. Stir in butter or margarine and cream. Bring to boil. Pour over fish. Sprinkle with almonds.
6. Broil about 8 inches from heat for 7 to 10 minutes, or until browned.

Mrs. Charles Allen, Jr., Junior Woman's Club,
Coronado, Calif.

FILETS DE SOLE AU RAISINS BLANCS
Serves 4

¼ cup butter
1 pound small fillets of Dover sole
½ teaspoon salt
1 tablespoon lemon juice
    Dash of cayenne
½ cup dry white wine or brandy
¼ teaspoon monosodium glutamate
    Paprika
½ cup seedless white grapes, halved
⅛ teaspoon grated lemon peel
1 teaspoon chopped chervil or
    parsley

1. Melt butter in heavy skillet; cook fillets for about 5 minutes, or until lightly browned.
2. Turn carefully with spatula. Sprinkle with salt, lemon juice and cayenne.
3. Combine wine or brandy and monosodium glutamate. Pour over fish. Cook for about 5 minutes.

4. With spatula, transfer fillets to heated platter. Sprinkle with paprika.

5. Add remaining ingredients to pan. Bring to boil; then simmer for a few minutes, or until grapes are hot. Pour over fillets.

Lucille Porter, Quest Club, Bowling Green, Mo.

FILLETS OF SOLE MARGUERY
Serves 8

From the cuisine of the famed Café Marguery, Paris, where one of America's great restaurateurs, George Rector, served his apprenticeship and later introduced this succulent dish to the United States.

  1 quart water
  Fish bones and trimmings
  Salt
  Bouquet garni (see Glossary)
  ½ pound small shrimp
  1 small lobster
  2 tablespoons finely chopped
    shallots or onion
  8 fillets of sole
  6 tablespoons butter or margarine
  Paprika
  Cayenne
  ½ cup dry white wine
  3 tablespoons flour
  ½ cup light cream
  1 egg yolk
  ¼ cup grated Parmesan cheese

1. Prepare court bouillon: In large saucepan put water, fish bones and trimmings, 1 teaspoon salt and bouquet garni. Bring to boil; simmer for 10 minutes.

2. Add shrimp. Simmer for 8 minutes. Remove shrimp; shell and devein; set aside in warm place.

3. Add lobster to court bouillon; bring back to boil; cook over medium heat for 10 minutes. Remove lobster; crack shells; remove meat; cut into large pieces. Set aside in warm place with shrimp.

4. Preheat oven to 350° F. Grease 10 x 6 x 1½-inch baking pan. Cut piece of waxed paper 10 x 6 inches; grease.

5. Sprinkle shallots or onion in pan. Arrange fillets in pan. Dot with 3 tablespoons of the butter or margarine. Sprinkle with salt, paprika and a little cayenne. Pour wine on top. Cover with greased waxed paper.

6. Bake in preheated oven for 15 minutes, or until flesh has turned white.

7. Transfer fillets to heatproof serving dish. Garnish with shrimp and lobster. Keep covered, in warm place.

8. Prepare wine sauce: Add liquid from baking pan to court bouillon. Bring to boil; boil rapidly until liquid is reduced to about 1½ cup. Strain liquid; reserve.

9. In clean saucepan melt remaining butter or margarine; blend in flour. Gradually stir in reserved liquid. Cook over low heat, stirring constantly, until sauce is thickened and smooth. Season with salt and dash of cayenne.

10. In small bowl blend cream and egg yolk; stir into sauce. Cook over low heat, stirring constantly, until just below boiling point.

11. Remove from heat. Pour sauce over fish; sprinkle with cheese.

12. Place under broiler for 3 to 4 minutes, or until browned and bubbling.

Junior Woman's Club, Thibodaux, La.

BAKED SOLE IN FOIL
Serves 6

  ¼ cup butter or margarine
  ½ pound mushrooms, sliced
  6 large fillets of sole
  6½-ounce can crab meat, drained
    and flaked
  36 tiny shrimp, shelled and deveined
  1 cup sour cream
  2 tablespoons chopped chives
  1 tablespoon lemon juice
  ½ teaspoon rosemary
  1 teaspoon salt
  ¼ teaspoon pepper
  ¼ cup chopped parsley

1. Preheat oven to 350° F. Cut 6 squares of heavy aluminum foil.

2. Melt butter or margarine in medium skillet; sauté mushrooms for 5 minutes. Arrange a fillet in center of each square of foil. Top with mushrooms, crab meat and shrimp.

3. In small bowl blend sour cream with remaining ingredients. Spoon onto fish.

4. Seal each square of foil like a package; place on baking sheet.

5. Bake in preheated oven for 25 minutes.

*Alice Rabitte, Mendocino Study Club,
Little River, Calif.*

SQUID

Not a true fish, but a mollusk, the squid or cuttlefish, first cousin to the octopus, may be cooked in many ways. It is frequently served with a highly spiced tomato sauce, but the simplest and possibly most delicious way to cook squid is to sauté it in olive oil.

SAUTÉED SQUID
Serves 2

  2 medium or 4 small squid
  Flour
  ¼ teaspoon salt
  ⅛ teaspoon white pepper
  6 tablespoons olive oil
  Lemon wedges

1. Pull head from body of each squid; discard transparent "spine" inside body. Cut tentacles from head; reserve. Discard head with "innards" attached. Cut each body in half or quarters.

2. Flour bodies and tentacles lightly; sprinkle with salt and pepper.

3. Heat oil in skillet; sauté squid for about 8 minutes on each side, or until golden. Reduce heat. Cook for about 10 minutes longer. Serve with lemon wedges.

A. S.

CHARCOAL-GRILLED SWORDFISH STEAK

Serves 4

½ cup soy sauce
2 cloves garlic, chopped
4 tablespoons tomato sauce
2 tablespoons lemon juice
¼ cup chopped parsley
1 teaspoon finely powdered orégano
½ cup orange juice
1 teaspoon freshly ground pepper
4 individual servings swordfish
    steaks

1. Combine all ingredients except swordfish. Pour over steaks. Marinate for at least 2 hours.
2. Have charcoal fire burning well, because marinade tends to put out fire. Grill steaks, turning once and basting frequently with marinade during grilling, for about 20 minutes, or until fish flakes easily.

Mrs. Nelson Schaenen, Jr.
Thursday Morning Club, Madison, N.J.

BAKED TROUT

Serves 6 to 8

4-pound trout, dressed
½ lemon
    Salt and pepper to taste
1-pound 4-ounce can tomatoes
1 medium onion, finely chopped
⅓ cup finely chopped celery
2 tablespoons butter or margarine
1 egg yolk
½ cup heavy cream
2 teaspoons Worcestershire

1. Preheat oven to 375° F. Grease shallow roasting pan.
2. Rub trout inside and out with lemon. Arrange in pan; sprinkle with salt and pepper.
3. Combine tomatoes, onion, and celery. Pour over fish; dot with butter or margarine.
4. Bake in preheated oven for 45 minutes, or until fish flakes easily.
5. Arrange fish on serving dish; keep warm.
6. Strain liquids from roasting pan into saucepan. Blend egg yolk, cream and Worcestershire; gradually stir into pan liquids. Cook over low heat for 3 minutes, stirring constantly. Pour over fish.

Sesame Club, Marshall, Tex.

BROILED TROUT

Serves 4

¼ cup butter
1 tablespoon lemon juice
2 teaspoons salt
1 teaspoon monosodium glutamate
½ teaspoon paprika
¼ teaspoon pepper
4 10-ounce trout, dressed
    Parsley
    Lemon wedges

1. Preheat broiler. Line broiler pan with aluminum foil.

2. Melt butter in small saucepan. Stir in lemon juice, salt, monosodium glutamate, paprika and pepper. Simmer for 1 minute. Remove from heat.
3. Arrange trout on pan. Brush with half the butter mixture.
4. Broil trout 3 inches from heat for 6 minutes. Turn; brush with remaining butter mixture; broil for 7 minutes longer, or until fish flakes easily.
5. Arrange on serving dish. Garnish with parsley and lemon wedges.

Ruth A. Sharp, Woman's Club,
Lake Hopatcong, N.J.

SAUTÉED RAINBOW TROUT

Serves 2

2 rainbow trout
    Salt and pepper to taste
⅓ cup milk
⅓ cup presifted flour
1 egg, beaten with 1 tablespoon
    milk
½ cup bread crumbs
2 tablespoons olive oil
2 tablespoons butter
2 slices tomato
    Lemon wedges
    Parsley

1. With sharp knife, cut away backbone from trout's flesh on each side of body cavity. Cut backbone behind head and in front of tail. Pull out backbone and bones already cut away from flesh.
2. Open fish flat. Season with salt and pepper.
3. Dip fish in milk; coat with flour. Dip in egg; roll in crumbs.
4. Melt and heat oil and butter in skillet. Add fish; cook over medium heat until browned on both sides.
5. Arrange fish on serving dish; keep in warm place.
6. Dip tomato slices in remaining flour; fry in fat remaining in skillet until browned on both sides.
7. Place tomato slice on each fish. Garnish with lemon wedges and parsley.

Peggy Bussard, Leota Club, Englewood, Colo.

TROUT GULF COAST

Serves 6

1 pound fillets of trout
1 pound shrimp, shelled, deveined
    and cooked
1 tablespoon butter
1 onion, minced
1 tablespoon flour
1 cup cream
    Salt and pepper to taste
1 teaspoon chopped parsley
1 teaspoon chopped bay leaf
4-ounce can chopped mushrooms,
    drained
2 eggs, hard-cooked and chopped
1 cup shredded American cheese

1. Preheat oven to 400° F. Grease 2-quart casserole.
2. Put fillets in saucepan with water to cover. Bring to boil. Set aside to cool.

3. When cool, cut fillets and shrimp into small pieces.

4. Melt butter in saucepan; sauté onion for 5 minutes, or until soft but not browned. Add flour; stir until well blended. Gradually stir in cream; cook, stirring constantly, until thickened and smooth. Add salt, pepper, parsley and bay leaf. Add mushrooms, fish and eggs. Turn into casserole. Sprinkle with cheese.

5. Bake in preheated oven for 15 minutes, or until cheese is melted and slightly browned.

Gulf Coast Gourmet, Woman's Club,
Foley, Ala.

LUNCHEON YUM YUMS

Serves 4

7-ounce can tuna, drained and flaked
1½ cups mayonnaise
Dash of Tabasco
1 teaspoon Worcestershire
1 teaspoon lemon juice
¼ teaspoon pepper
4 slices bread
¼ cup butter or margarine
4 large slices tomato
2 eggs, hard-cooked and halved
  lengthwise

1. In bowl blend tuna, ½ cup of the mayonnaise, Tabasco, Worcestershire, lemon juice and pepper. Set aside.

2. Preheat broiler. Line broiler pan with aluminum foil.

3. Cut large circle from each slice of bread.

4. Melt butter or margarine in skillet; fry bread circles until golden on both sides.

5. Arrange fried bread in broiler pan. Top each with tomato slice, then half an egg. Mound tuna mixture on egg halves; cover completely with remaining mayonnaise.

6. Place in broiler 4 to 5 inches from heat. Broil for 7 to 8 minutes, until puffed and golden.

Mrs. A. W. Engstrom, Coco Plum Woman's Club,
Coral Gables, Fla.

TUNA FRITTERS

2 cups baking powder biscuit mix
1 teaspoon seasoned salt
1 egg, lightly beaten
⅔ cup evaporated milk
1 tablespoon lemon juice
1½ cups flaked tuna
2 tablespoons finely chopped onion
2 tablespoons finely chopped
  green pepper
2 tablespoons chopped parsley
½ cup finely chopped celery
Fat for deep frying
Cheese Sauce (p. 442)

1. Combine biscuit mix, salt, egg, milk and lemon juice.

2. Add tuna and vegetables; mix well.

3. Drop by teaspoons into deep fat heated to 365° F. Fry for 1½ to 2 minutes.

Turn; fry until golden brown all over. Drain on absorbent paper.

4. Serve with Cheese Sauce.

Mrs. Jack D. McCrea, Woman's Club,
Azusa, Calif.

TUNA TERRAPIN

Serves 6

3 tablespoons butter
3 eggs, hard-cooked
3 tablespoons flour
¾ teaspoon prepared mustard
1 teaspoon salt
2 cups milk
2 7-ounce cans tuna, drained
  and flaked
1 pimiento, diced
1 tablespoon chopped green
  pepper
4 ripe olives, diced
1 tablespoon lemon juice
Patty shells or toast cups

1. Melt butter in skillet over medium heat.

2. Separate egg yolks from whites. Set whites aside. Mash yolks.

3. Add yolks, flour, mustard and salt to butter; mix well. Gradually stir in milk. Cook, stirring constantly, until sauce thickens.

4. Dice egg whites. Add along with remaining ingredients to sauce. Cook over low heat until heated through.

5. Serve in patty shells or toast cups.

Geneva Masterson, El Camino Women's Club,
Ventura, Calif.

TUNA BAKE WITH CHEESE SWIRLS

Serves 6 to 8

3 tablespoons shortening
⅓ cup chopped green pepper
¼ chopped onion
1 teaspoon salt
⅓ cup presifted flour
1½ cups milk
10½-ounce can condensed chicken
  with rice soup
7-ounce can tuna, drained and flaked
1 tablespoon lemon juice
1 recipe for Cheese Swirls (p. 122),
  unbaked

1. Preheat oven to 425° F. Grease 10 x 6 x 1½-inch baking pan.

2. Melt shortening in saucepan; sauté green pepper and onion for 5 minutes. Stir in salt and flour; gradually stir in milk. Cook over low heat, stirring constantly, until thickened and smooth.

3. Stir in soup, tuna and lemon juice.

4. Turn into pan. Top with Cheese Swirls.

5. Bake in preheated oven for 30 minutes.

Mrs. Ruth Anne Ceder, Woman's Club,
Blandinsville, Ill.

TUNA CASSEROLE

Serves 4

2 cups cooked macaroni
2 7-ounce cans tuna, drained and
  flaked
1 cup sour cream
½ cup ripe olives, sliced
¾ cup chopped mushrooms
¼ cup diced green pepper
¼ cup chopped cashew nuts
¼ teaspoon orégano

1. Preheat oven to 350° F. Grease 1½-quart casserole.
2. Combine all ingredients; mix well. Turn into casserole.
3. Bake in preheated oven for 25 to 30 minutes.

Mrs. William Mason, American Home and Garden Department, Woman's Club, Silvis, Ill.

TUNA NOODLE CASSEROLE

Serves 4

1½ cups broken noodles
10½-ounce can condensed cream
  of mushroom soup
½ cup milk
7-ounce can tuna, drained and
  flaked
1 cup grated Cheddar cheese
⅓ cup finely chopped onion
½ cup broken potato chips
Paprika

1. Preheat oven to 425° F. Grease 1½-quart casserole.
2. Cook noodles according to package directions. Drain. Turn into mixing bowl.
3. Stir in soup, milk, tuna, cheese and onion. Mix well; turn into casserole.
4. Sprinkle with potato chips and paprika.
5. Bake in preheated oven for 15 minutes, or until bubbling.

Mrs. R. H. Hobbs, North Jacksonville Woman's Club, Jacksonville, Fla.

TUNA POLYNESIAN

Serves 4

¼ cup shortening
1 onion, chopped
1 cup rice
8-ounce can crushed pineapple,
  undrained
1 cup water
10½-ounce can condensed cream
  of mushroom soup
2 7-ounce cans tuna, drained and
  flaked
½ cup toasted almonds
1 teaspoon salt
Pepper to taste

1. Melt shortening in saucepan; brown onion and rice lightly.
2. Add pineapple and water. Bring to rapid boil.
3. Stir in remaining ingredients. Cover tightly. Cook over low heat for 20 minutes.

Mrs. Cecil C. Bidwell, Woman's Club, Tampa, Fla.

TUNA OR SALMON BISCUIT LOAF

Serves 6 to 8

1 cup flaked tuna or 1½ cups
  flaked cooked or canned salmon
¼ cup chopped onion
1 cup well-drained cooked Lima
  or green beans or peas
1½ teaspoons salt
¼ teaspoon pepper
1 cup diced American cheese
2 cups presifted flour
3 teaspoons baking powder
⅓ cup cooking oil
⅔ cup milk
10½-ounce can condensed cream
  of mushroom soup
Tabasco
Worcestershire

1. Combine tuna or salmon, onion, beans or peas, ½ teaspoon of the salt, pepper and cheese.
2. Preheat oven to 425° F.
3. In mixing bowl combine flour, baking powder and remaining salt. Stir in oil and milk to make a firm dough. Turn onto lightly floured board; knead, about 10 kneading strokes.
4. Roll out dough into rectangle; transfer to baking sheet. Spoon cheese mixture down center of rectangle in a band about 4 inches wide. Slash dough on each side at intervals of about 1 inch. Then lace one side, then the other, up and over cheese mixture.
5. Bake in preheated oven for about 20 to 25 minutes.
6. Meanwhile, heat soup flavored with a little Tabasco and Worcestershire. Serve as sauce.

Mrs. Ray Remster, Woman's Club, Devil's Lake, N.D.

Shellfish

Abalone

Abalone is indigenous to California waters, and no fresh abalone can be bought outside the state. Abalone is the foot of a large sea mollusk with a single spiral-like shell and is therefore muscular and tough. Usually it has been tenderized when purchased at the fish market; otherwise, it must be cut into thin slices, which must be well pounded on both sides with a heavy mallet. Abalone may be sautéed in butter, breaded and pan-fried, or dipped in frying batter and deep-fried. Sauté or fry it very briefly, or it will be tough no matter how much it was tenderized. Canned tenderized abalone may be obtained in specialty food stores. A pound of abalone will serve 3 or 4.

SAUTÉED ABALONE

Serves 6

1 cup presifted flour
2 teaspoons paprika
Dash of garlic salt
Dash of onion salt
½ teaspoon salt
¼ teaspoon monosodium glutamate
Dash of pepper
Peanut oil
2 to 3 pounds abalone, sliced
    and pounded

1. An hour before cooking, combine all ingredients except oil and abalone. Dust abalone well with seasoned flour; cover with aluminum foil; refrigerate.
2. Heat ½ inch oil in large frying pan. When a small piece of bread browns very quickly, oil is hot enough. Fry no more than 2 slices of abalone at a time. Cook for 15 seconds on one side. Turn; cook for 15 seconds longer. Do not overcook.

Mrs. Richard Miller, Women's Club,
Arvin, Calif.

Clams

There are two main species of clam found in Atlantic and Pacific waters: soft-shell and hard-shell. Soft-shell clams are usually steamed and served with melted butter and a cup of the clam broth. Hard-shell clams are divided into categories according to size. Although they all are technically quahogs or quahaugs, only the largest are purchased by this name. The smallest ones are known as little necks; those slightly larger are known as cherrystones. Little necks and cherrystones are generally eaten raw on the half shell, but they may be cooked in any manner suited to oysters. The large hard-shell clams are usually minced or ground for use in soups, casseroles and chowders.
Along the Pacific coast there are varieties of clams known as razor clams, pismo clams and the largest member of the family, the gweduc or goeduck.

TO SHUCK, OR OPEN, SOFT-SHELL CLAMS
These shells are easily opened. Wash each clam thoroughly. Insert a strong knife blade between the shells, and pry open. Cut clam away from shells, working over a bowl to save the juices. Pull off and discard the skin from the siphon, or neck. This is easy if you first slit the skin with a sharp knife or kitchen scissors. The clam is now ready to cook in chowders or casserole dishes, creamed, scalloped or deviled.

STEAMED CLAMS

Serves 2

2 quarts unshucked soft-shell clams
Melted butter

1. Scrub clams thoroughly. Put in large kettle with ½ inch water in bottom. Cover tightly. Cook over high heat for 6 to 10

minutes from the time water begins to boil rapidly, or until clams open. Discard clams that do not open.
2. Serve in soup plates with a bowl of melted butter for dipping and a cup of hot broth from clams for sipping.

A. S.

TO SHUCK, OR OPEN, HARD-SHELL CLAMS
OR OYSTERS
There are various clam-opening gadgets on the market, but the best is a clam knife and a strong wrist. Wash each clam thoroughly in running cold water. If you look at the edge where the two shells come together, you will find a small dark spot near the most bulbous end of the clam. This is a soft spot and the easiest place to start. Insert the clam knife deeply between the shells; then twist the knife along the inside of the upper shell to cut the upper muscle that holds the shells together. Discard the upper shell, keeping the lower shell horizontal to save the valuable juices, and run the knife under the clam to sever the lower muscle.

CLAMS ON THE HALF SHELL

Little neck or cherrystone clams
Lemon wedges, freshly ground
    pepper, fresh horseradish or
    favorite cocktail sauce

1. Shuck clams as directed above. Keep clams in lower half of shell; refrigerate until ready to serve.
2. Serve 6, 8 or 12 per person on a bed of crushed ice, with lemon wedges, pepper, horseradish or cocktail sauce.

A. S.

CLAMBAKE FOR TEN

Serves 10

Recommended only for hearty appetites. It is best to use a large washboiler kept expressly for this purpose; if possible, one with a spigot at the lower part, to draw off broth.

Large quantities of seaweed,
    washed free of sand
12 large hard-shell clams
 5 2-pound broiling chickens, split
    Salt and pepper to taste
10 sweet potatoes
10 ears of corn
10 baby lobsters
10 medium white potatoes
120 soft-shell clams, washed free
    of sand
 4 quarts water
    Babcock Sauce (p. 442)

1. Put a thick layer of seaweed into boiler. Add hard-shell clams; cover with layer of seaweed.
2. Season chickens with salt and pepper; wrap each half in cheesecloth. Arrange chicken on seaweed in boiler; surround with sweet potatoes and corn. Cover with layer of seaweed.

3. Arrange lobsters on seaweed in boiler; surround with white potatoes.

4. Cover with another layer of seaweed. Top with soft-shell clams.

5. Pour in water. Cover with a final layer of seaweed.

6. Clamp on cover. Bring to boil. This is best done outdoors, on either a fire or a gasoline stove of suitable size. Cook for about 1½ hours from time boiling starts. It will take considerable time to start boiling.

7. When ready to serve, open boiler. Discard first layer of seaweed. Serve clams with Babcock Sauce and cups of hot clam broth drained from spigot of boiler.

8. Discard next layer of seaweed; serve next course. Follow through, serving each course in turn.

Betty Cook, Woman's Club, Breton Woods, N.J.

STUFFED QUAHOGS

Serves 5

5 large quahogs
1 medium onion, quartered
¼ teaspoon salt
Dash of pepper
½ teaspoon orégano
1 cup fresh bread crumbs
2 tablespoons butter or margarine

1. Preheat oven to 400°.

2. Shuck quahogs; remove meat; reserve shells.

3. Put meat and onion through medium blade of meat grinder: reserve liquid. Combine ground mixture and liquid, salt, pepper, orégano and crumbs. Fill reserved shells.

4. Place on baking sheet. Dot with butter or margarine.

5. Bake in preheated oven for 20 minutes.

Alberta Terry, Tuesday Club, Assonet, Mass.

BAKED CLAMS AU GRATIN

Serves 4

3 slices bacon, diced
¼ cup butter or margarine
½ cup finely chopped celery
½ cup finely chopped green pepper
½ cup finely chopped onions
3 tablespoons flour
2 cups milk
1 teaspoon salt
¼ teaspoon pepper
1 cup grated Cheddar cheese
2 eggs, lightly beaten
2 cups finely chopped clams

1. Preheat oven to 350° F. Grease 1½-quart casserole.

2. Put bacon and butter or margarine in saucepan. Cook over low heat for 3 minutes. Stir in celery, green pepper and onions; sauté for 5 minutes. Blend in flour. Gradually stir in milk. Cook over low heat, stirring constantly, until thickened and smooth.

3. Remove from heat. Stir in salt, pepper, ½ cup of the cheese, eggs and clams.

4. Pour into casserole. Sprinkle with remaining cheese.

5. Bake in preheated oven for 25 minutes, or until golden and bubbling.

*Ruth Curtzwiler, Woman's Club,
Shell Beach, Calif.*

KENNEBUNKPORT CLAM PIE

Serves 4

Pastry for a 1-Crust Pie (p. 548)
2 slices salt pork
1 medium onion, finely chopped
3 potatoes, peeled and cubed
Salt and pepper to taste
1 cup chopped clams

1. Prepare Pastry for a 1-Crust Pie. Preheat oven to 400° F.

2. Fry out pork in skillet; sauté onion until lightly browned.

3. Add potatoes, salt, pepper and a little water. Cover; simmer for about 15 minutes, or until potatoes are cooked. Add water, if necessary, to prevent burning. Stir in clams. Pour into 6-inch pie plate.

4. Cover with layer of pastry. Flute edges. Slash top in 2 places to allow steam to escape.

5. Bake in preheated oven for 25 minutes, or until crust is golden.

Viola Smith, Woman's Club, Durham, N.H.

CORN CLAM CASSEROLE

Serves 6

10½-ounce can minced clams
Milk
1-pound 4-ounce can cream-style
corn
2 eggs, lightly beaten
1 cup cracker crumbs
¼ cup finely chopped onion
1 teaspoon salt
¼ teaspoon pepper
2 teaspoons Worcestershire
¼ cup finely chopped green pepper
2 tablespoons butter or margarine

1. Preheat oven to 350° F. Grease 1-quart casserole.

2. Drain liquid from clams into measuring cup. Add sufficient milk to total ¾ cup; reserve.

3. Put clams in mixing bowl. Add reserved liquid, corn, eggs, crumbs, onion, seasonings and green pepper; mix well. Turn into casserole. Dot with butter or margarine.

4. Bake in preheated oven for 30 to 45 minutes, or until set.

*Mrs. Charles Selheimer, Civic League,
Starkville, Miss.*

Conches

Like the California abalone, the conch must be pounded with a heavy mallet or the edge of a plate to tenderize it before it is cooked. Then it may be sliced, dipped in Frying Batter (p. 223) and deep-fried. If ground for fritters, it needs no tenderizing.

Crabs

There are many types of crab, two of which are becoming increasingly popular—the Pacific coast Dungeness crab and the giant Alaska king crab. Only a small quantity of frozen Dungeness crab is shipped to the East, but the king crab in canned and frozen form is widely distributed.

The best-known crab on the Atlantic coast is the blue crab, which has either a hard or a soft shell, depending on when it is caught. In the process of maturing, the blue crab sheds its hard shell frequently. Under the hard shell is a very soft shell—so soft, in fact, that it can be eaten along with the tender sweet meat underneath. If the crab is caught before the soft shell has had a chance to become hard, usually in the early spring, the blue crab is known as the soft-shell crab.

The hard-shell blue crab yields several grades of crab meat, fresh, frozen or canned. The choicest is the fresh lump crab meat. Canned crab may be substituted in any recipe calling for fresh lump crab meat. Count on 1 pound to serve 4.

TO COOK LIVE HARD-SHELL CRABS

Crabs
Hot Lemon Butter (p. 444) or
Blender Mayonnaise (p. 445)

1. Allow 2 crabs per person. Wash them in several changes of cold water. Then drop them headfirst into rapidly boiling sea water or salted water. Boil rapidly for 5 minutes; then simmer for 10 to 15 minutes, or until shells turn red.
2. Drain. When cool enough to handle, break off the apron, or tail; then pull the upper and lower shells apart. Discard spongy parts at side of body and any substance sticking to upper shell. Edible meat lies in claws and in two compact masses on lower shell.
3. Crack claws. Serve hot or cold with Lemon Butter or Blender Mayonnaise.

NOTE: The meat may be used in cocktails, in creamed dishes or casseroles or in any recipe calling for crab meat.

TO CLEAN CRAB SHELLS
Reserve upper shells if you wish to use them for Deviled Crab (p. 241). Wash and scrub them thoroughly with stiff brush. Then drop them into large kettle of rapidly boiling water to which 1 teaspoon baking soda has been added. Boil for 20 minutes. Drain and dry.

FRIED SOFT-SHELL CRABS

Serves 6

12 soft-shell crabs
2 teaspoons salt
½ teaspoon pepper
Milk
¾ cup presifted flour
2 eggs, lightly beaten
¾ cup cracker meal
Fat for deep frying
Parsley
Lemon wedges
Sauce Tartare (p. 446) (optional)

1. Wash crabs carefully in cold water. (Hot water damages delicate flavor.) Remove feathery substances under side points and sand bags from under shell, between eyes. Discard apron (tail).
2. Wipe dry with absorbent paper. Sprinkle with salt and pepper. Soak in milk to cover for about 30 minutes.
3. Drain crabs. Roll in flour. Dip in eggs. Roll in cracker meal.
4. Fry in deep fat heated to 365° F. until golden and crisp. Drain on absorbent paper.
5. Garnish with parsley and lemon wedges. Serve with Sauce Tartare, if desired.

Gulf Coast Gourmet, Woman's Club, Foley, Ala.

STUFFED CRABS À LA CREOLE

Serves 6

18 hard-shell crabs
½ cup butter
1 clove garlic, crushed
2 tablespoons grated onion
2 tablespoons finely chopped celery
2 tablespoons chopped scallions
1½ cups fresh bread crumbs
2 tablespoons chopped parsley
Dash of cayenne
½ teaspoon salt
1 cup dry bread crumbs

1. Scald crabs. Remove meat; set aside. Boil shells in water; clean with stiff brush.
2. Preheat oven to 400° F. Arrange shells on baking sheet.
3. Melt butter in medium skillet; sauté garlic, onion, celery and scallions over medium heat for 5 minutes.
4. Remove from heat. Stir in crab meat, fresh crumbs, parsley, cayenne and salt. Arrange mixture in crab shells. Sprinkle with dry crumbs.
5. Bake in preheated oven for 20 minutes, or until tops are golden.

Mrs. H. L. Alston, Contact Study Club, De Quincy, La.

MARYLAND CRAB CAKES

Serves 6

1 tablespoon chopped parsley
2 tablespoons mayonnaise
½ teaspoon prepared mustard
¼ teaspoon cayenne
½ teaspoon salt
1 tablespoon Worcestershire
1 cup fresh bread crumbs
1 egg, lightly beaten
1 pound crab meat, flaked
½ cup butter or margarine

1. In mixing bowl combine parsley, mayonnaise, mustard, cayenne, salt and Worcestershire; mix well. Stir in crumbs and egg. Add crab meat; mix well. Shape into 6 flat patties. Refrigerate for 1 hour.

2. Melt butter or margarine in skillet; sauté cakes until golden on both sides.

Mrs. Charles O. Middlekauf, Chairman, Credentials Committee, General Federation of Women's Clubs, Washington, D.C.

SAUTÉED CRAB CUTLETS

Serves 6

1 cup Thick White Sauce (p. 441)
½ teaspoon salt
¼ teaspoon pepper
1 egg
  Dash of celery salt
1 tablespoon grated onion
2 cups crab meat, flaked
  Flour
⅓ cup mayonnaise
¾ cup bread crumbs
½ cup butter or margarine
  Cheese Sauce (p. 442) (optional)
  Lemon wedges (optional)

1. In medium saucepan blend Thick White Sauce, salt, pepper, egg, celery salt and onion. Bring to boil over low heat, stirring constantly. Simmer for 2 minutes.
2. Remove from heat. Stir in crab meat. Spread on large plate. Refrigerate until cool.
3. Divide cooled mixture into 6 parts. Shape each like a cutlet or round cake. Coat with flour; spread completely with mayonnaise. Dip in crumbs; press in crumbs with blade of knife. Reshape, if necessary.
4. Melt butter or margarine in large skillet; sauté cakes for about 10 minutes, or until golden on both sides.
5. Arrange on serving dish. Serve with Cheese Sauce and lemon wedges, if desired.

Kitty Evans, Gardens Century Club, Wilmington, Del.

DEVILED CRAB

Serves 6

2 pounds fresh lump crab meat
2 cups thick Cream Sauce (p. 441)
1 teaspoon dry mustard
  Juice of ½ lemon
¼ cup sherry
¼ cup chopped chives
3 eggs, hard-cooked and chopped
  Bread crumbs
  Paprika
  Butter

1. Preheat oven to 450° F. Grease 6 crab shells or 2-quart casserole.
2. Combine crab meat and thick Cream Sauce. Stir in mustard, lemon juice, sherry, chives and eggs. Fill shells or casserole. Sprinkle with crumbs. Sprinkle with paprika; dot with butter.
3. Bake in preheated oven for 15 minutes, or until lightly browned.

Greta M. Jeffs, Woman's Club, Anchorage, Alaska

FLORIDA DEVILED CRAB

Serves 4

4 slices buttered toast, diced
½ cup hot water
1 pound crab meat, flaked
1 medium onion, grated
2 eggs, lightly beaten
1 tablespoon Worcestershire
1 tablespoon catsup
  Salt and pepper to taste
2 tablespoons butter

1. Preheat oven to 350° F. Grease 4 crab shells or individual casseroles.
2. Place toast in mixing bowl; soften with water.
3. Stir in crab meat, onion, eggs, Worcestershire and catsup; season with salt and pepper; mix well. Pack into shells or casseroles. Dot with butter.
4. Bake in preheated oven for 30 minutes.

Mrs. Vincent J. Welp, Woman's Club, West Palm Beach, Fla.

MARYLAND DEVILED CRAB

Serves 6

¼ cup butter
2 tablespoons flour
1 teaspoon dry mustard
1 teaspoon salt
¼ teaspoon pepper
1 tablespoon chopped parsley
1 cup milk
1 pound crab meat, flaked
2 eggs, hard-cooked and chopped
2 teaspoons lemon juice
½ cup cracker crumbs
2 tablespoons melted butter

1. Preheat oven to 425° F. Grease 6 crab shells.
2. Melt ¼ cup butter in medium saucepan. Stir in flour, mustard, salt, pepper and parsley. Gradually stir in milk. Cook over low heat, stirring constantly, until thickened and smooth. Stir in crab meat and eggs. Heat to serving temperature. Remove from heat. Stir in lemon juice.
3. Turn into shells. Sprinkle with crumbs and melted butter.
4. Bake in preheated oven for 15 minutes, or until browned.

Audrey Smith, Dulaney Valley Woman's Club, Inc., Towson, Md.

DEVILED CRAB MEAT OR STUFFING FOR CRAYFISH OR LOBSTER

Serves 4 to 6

This is an excellent dish served on toast points or as a stuffing for cooked lobster or crayfish. If used as a stuffing, for crayfish or lobster, fill the tails with the crab meat mixture, and place under a broiler for about 10 minutes, but not too close to heat, or it will burn before the crayfish or lobster is heated through. Serve with melted butter and lemon wedges.

1 egg yolk
½ cup heavy cream
2 cups Medium White Sauce (p. 441)
2 6½-ounce cans Alaska king crab
　　meat
4-ounce can pimientos, drained
　　and diced
¼ cup finely chopped green pepper
¼ cup finely chopped onion
½ teaspoon salt
¼ teaspoon pepper
1 teaspoon Worcestershire
Dash of cayenne
1 tablespoon prepared mustard
1 tablespoon dry sherry
Toast points

1. In small bowl blend egg yolk and cream.

2. Put Medium White Sauce in saucepan. Stir in cream mixture. Cook over low heat, stirring constantly, just to boiling point. Stir in crab meat, pimientos, green pepper, onion and seasonings. Cook over low heat to serving temperature.

3. Remove from heat. Stir in sherry. Serve on toast points, or use as a stuffing for crayfish or lobster, described above.

Mrs. E. F. Shilts, Woman's Club,
Clearwater, Fla.

BAKED CRAB CASSEROLE

Serves 4

1 pound crab meat, flaked
4-ounce can pimientos, drained
　　and chopped
3 tablespoons finely chopped green
　　pepper
2 tablespoons prepared mustard
1 teaspoon Worcestershire
1 teaspoon salt
1 egg, lightly beaten
¼ cup cracker crumbs
2 tablespoons milk
1 cup mayonnaise
2 egg yolks

1. Preheat oven to 425° F. Grease 1½-quart casserole.

2. In mixing bowl combine all ingredients except mayonnaise and egg yolks. Mix well. Turn into casserole.

3. In small bowl blend mayonnaise and egg yolks. Spread on crab mixture.

4. Bake in preheated oven for 15 minutes, or until golden brown.

Norma Schindeldecker, Woman's Club,
Prospect Heights, Ill.

BAKED CRAB AND EGG SALAD

Serves 8

1 cup crab meat, flaked
1 cup fresh bread crumbs
1 cup light cream
1½ cups mayonnaise
6 eggs, hard-cooked and diced
1 tablespoon grated onion
½ teaspoon salt
¼ teaspoon pepper
½ cup buttered bread crumbs

1. Preheat oven to 350° F. Grease 8 crab shells or individual casseroles.

2. In mixing bowl combine all ingredients except buttered crumbs; mix well. Turn into shells or casseroles. Sprinkle with buttered crumbs.

3. Bake in preheated oven for 20 minutes, or until golden.

Mrs. Henry A. Simen, Woman's Club,
Vero Beach, Fla.

SUPERB CRAB MEAT CASSEROLE

Serves 8

2½ cups Medium White Sauce (p. 441)
Salt and pepper to taste
2 6½-ounce cans crab meat,
　　drained and flaked
2 4-ounce cans mushroom stems and
　　pieces, drained
½ cup finely chopped green pepper
2 pimientos diced
½ cup slivered almonds
4 eggs, hard-cooked and diced
2 teaspoons lemon juice
1 cup grated Cheddar cheese
½ cup buttered bread crumbs

1. Preheat oven to 350° F. Grease 2-quart casserole.

2. Put Medium White Sauce into mixing bowl. Season with salt and pepper. Stir in all remaining ingredients except cheese and crumbs; toss lightly.

3. Turn into casserole. Sprinkle with cheese and crumbs.

4. Bake in preheated oven for 45 minutes.

Carol Hilton, Junior Woman's Club,
Glastonbury, Conn.

IMPERIAL CRAB À LA MARYLAND

Serves 6

½ cup Medium White Sauce (p. 441)
1 egg, separated
2 tablespoons mayonnaise
2 teaspoons Worcestershire
1 teaspoon dry mustard
¼ teaspoon red pepper
1 teaspoon salt
1 pound fresh lump crab meat, flaked
1 egg, lightly beaten
Bread crumbs
Butter

1. Preheat oven to 500° F. Grease 6 crab shells or ramekins.

2. Combine Medium White Sauce, egg yolk, mayonnaise, Worcestershire, mustard, red pepper and salt.

3. Combine crab meat and beaten egg; stir into sauce.

4. Beat egg white until stiff but not dry; fold into crab mixture. Divide into shells or ramekins. Sprinkle with crumbs; dot with butter.

5. Bake in preheated oven for 15 minutes.

Mrs. Louis B. Eten, Thursday Morning Club,
Madison, N.J.

CASEROLE OF CRAB IMPERIAL

Serves 4 to 6

2 cups Medium White Sauce (p. 441)
1 teaspoon salt
⅛ teaspoon pepper
½ teaspoon celery salt
Dash of cayenne
1 egg yolk
2 tablespoons dry sherry
2 cups crab meat, flaked
1 cup fresh bread crumbs
1 tablespoon chopped parsley
1 tablespoon grated onion
3 tablespoons melted butter
Paprika

1. Preheat oven to 400° F. Grease 1½-quart casserole.
2. Prepare Imperial Sauce: Put Medium White Sauce in saucepan. Stir in salt, pepper, celery salt, cayenne and egg yolk. Cook over medium heat, stirring constantly, until hot.
3. Remove from heat. Stir in sherry, crab meat, ¾ cup of the crumbs, parsley and onion; mix well. Turn into casserole.
4. Combine remaining crumbs and butter; sprinkle onto casserole. Dust with paprika.
5. Bake in preheated oven for 20 minutes, or until browned.

M. Rebecca Wallaston, Gardens Century Club, Wilmington, Del.

CRAB MONZA

Serves 6

3 tablespoons butter
1 cup sliced mushrooms
2 tablespoons flour
½ cup dry sherry
1 cup light cream
Dash of paprika
1 tablespoon chopped parsley
½ teaspoon salt
2 6½-ounce cans crab meat, drained and flaked
¼ cup chopped pitted ripe olives
¼ cup drained canned pimientos, chopped
6 hot biscuits
½ cup grated Cheddar cheese

1. Melt butter in top of double saucepan. Add mushrooms; cook over simmering water for 10 minutes. Blend in flour. Gradually stir in sherry and cream. Cook over hot water, stirring constantly, until thickened and smooth.
2. Stir in paprika, parsley, salt, crab meat, olives and pimientos. Cook over hot water, stirring frequently, to serving temperature.
3. Serve on biscuits; sprinkle with cheese.

Evelyn Harford, Pathfinder Club, Compton, Calif.

CRAB MEAT MORNAY

Serves 6 to 8

2 cups crab meat, flaked
2 tablespoons lemon juice
1 cup fresh bread crumbs

2 cups Pat's Mornay Sauce (p. 446)
1 tablespoon butter

1. Preheat oven to 400° F. Grease 1½-quart casserole.
2. Arrange crab meat in casserole. Sprinkle with lemon juice. Sprinkle with crumbs; top with Pat's Mornay Sauce. Dot with butter.
3. Bake in preheated oven for 12 minutes, or until golden.

Pat Pollard, Suburban Women's Club, Newark, Del.

CRAB MEAT AND MUSHROOMS IN WINE SAUCE

Serves 4

1 pound fresh lump crab meat or
2 8-ounce cans crab meat, drained
¼ cup butter
¼ pound mushrooms, sliced
2 tablespoons flour
½ cup milk
½ cup dry white wine
½ teaspoon dry mustard
¼ teaspoon tarragon
½ teaspoon salt
⅛ teaspoon pepper
½ cup bread crumbs

1. Preheat oven to 350° F. Grease 4 individual casseroles.
2. Flake crab meat; remove membranes. Set aside.
3. Melt butter in saucepan; sauté mushrooms for 5 minutes. Stir in flour. Gradually stir in milk and wine. Cook over low heat, stirring constantly, until thickened and smooth. Stir in mustard, tarragon, salt, pepper and crab meat. Simmer for 2 minutes.
4. Turn into casseroles. Sprinkle with crumbs.
5. Bake in preheated oven for 30 minutes.

Shirley H. Pilipski, Junior Woman's Club, Cheshire, Conn.

CRAB NEWBURG

Serves 6

1 pound fresh lump crab meat
½ cup butter
3 tablespoons flour
½ teaspoon salt
½ teaspoon paprika
Dash of cayenne
2 tablespoons grated onion
2 cups cream
3 egg yolks lightly beaten with
2 tablespoons sherry
6 slices buttered toast

1. Remove any shell or cartilage from crab meat, being careful not to break meat into too small pieces.
2. Melt butter in saucepan. Stir in flour, seasonings and onion. Gradually stir in cream. Cook, stirring, until thickened and smooth.
3. Add crab meat; heat to serving temperature.

4. Remove from heat. Stir in egg yolks.
5. Serve on toast.

Gulf Coast Gourmet, Woman's Club, Foley, Ala.

SCALLOPED CRAB MEAT
Serves 4

This recipe is easily doubled; half may be put in the freezer for use at some later date. When doubling the recipe, 1 can of shrimp may be substituted for 1 can of crab meat.

1 tablespoon butter or margarine
1 tablespoon flour
½ cup milk
10½-ounce can condensed cream of
   mushroom soup
¼ cup dry sherry (optional)
   Salt and pepper to taste
1 cup grated Cheddar cheese
7½-ounce can crab meat, drained
   and flaked
2 cups cubed fresh bread

1. Preheat oven to 375° F. Grease 2-quart casserole.
2. Prepare Mushroom Sauce: Melt butter or margarine in saucepan. Stir in flour. Gradually stir in milk. Cook over medium heat, stirring constantly, until sauce is thickened and smooth. Stir in soup.
3. Remove from heat. Stir in sherry, salt, pepper, ¾ cup of the cheese, crab meat and bread.
4. Turn into casserole. Sprinkle with remaining cheese.
5. Bake in preheated oven for 45 minutes.

Mrs. Donald Bridge, President, Heptorean and Somerville Woman's Club, Somerville, Mass.

EASY CRAB PIE
Serves 4 to 6

1½ cups herb-seasoned packaged
   bread stuffing
¾ cup melted butter or margarine
3 tablespoons finely chopped green
   part of scallions
¼ cup presifted flour
1½ cups milk
1½ cups crab meat, flaked
2 tablespoons chopped pimientos
¼ teaspoon dry mustard
   Salt and pepper to taste
½ cup sour cream
   Finely chopped parsley

1. Preheat oven to 425° F. Grease 8-inch pie plate.
2. Crush stuffing with rolling pin; turn into mixing bowl. Stir in ½ cup of the butter or margarine. Press mixture on bottom and sides of pie plate.
3. Melt remaining butter or margarine in saucepan; sauté scallions. Sprinkle with flour; gradually stir in milk; cook over medium heat, stirring constantly, until thickened and smooth. Stir in crab meat, pimientos and mustard; season with salt and pepper.
4. Remove from heat. Stir in sour cream. Turn into pie plate.

5. Bake in preheated oven for 10 minutes.
6. Sprinkle with parsley just before serving.

Armelia Bachman, Civic Woman's Club, Cumberland, Md.

CRAB MEAT POTATO SOUFFLÉ
Serves 4 to 6

4-serving package instant mashed
   potatoes
   Salt
4 eggs, separated
6-ounce can crab meat, drained
   and flaked
⅛ teaspoon cayenne
   Piquant Sauce (p. 449)

1. Preheat oven to 350° F. Grease 1½-quart soufflé dish or casserole.
2. Prepare potatoes according to package directions, increasing amount of salt to 1½ teaspoons.
3. Blend in egg yolks, crab meat and cayenne.
4. Beat egg whites until stiff but not dry. Fold into potato mixture.
5. Turn into soufflé dish or casserole. To make "high hat," cut through mixture with spatula, making circle 1 inch from edge of dish or casserole.
6. Bake in preheated oven for 50 to 60 minutes, or until deep golden brown.
7. Serve with Piquant Sauce.

Mrs. Paul Willingham, Woman's Club, Wynnburg, Tenn.

Crayfish

Crayfish, or crawfish, are found in fresh-water lakes and streams; they resemble miniature lobsters. Count on at least 12 per serving, depending on the size. After a thorough washing, the tiny crayfish are cooked in a spicy court bouillon (p. 183) for no more than 5 minutes. They are served cold in the shell, or the meat is removed from the tail and served cold, with Sauce Rémoulade (p. 446) or any other mayonnaise sauce, or hot, in Cream Sauce (p. 441) or Wine Sauce (p. 451).

Lobsters

Two species of lobster abound in American waters. The one found in northern waters, the homard, with the claws, is considered the more delicious, but the clawless rock or spiny lobster found in warm waters is also a great delicacy. The easiest method of cooking the lobster is to boil and serve it, 1 medium lobster per person, hot, with melted butter and lemon juice, or cold, with good homemade Blender Mayonnaise (p. 445).

BOILED LOBSTER

Bring large kettle of sea water or salted water to rapid boil. Plunge live lobster into boiling water headfirst. Cover; simmer for 10 minutes for 1-pound lobster; 12 minutes for 1½ pound lobster; 15 minutes for 2-pound lobster.

Remove lobster from water with tongs; place on its back on chopping board. With heavy knife, split in half from head to tail. Spread open the two halves; discard intestinal vein and sac at back of head. Do not discard tomalley (green liver) or red roe, found only in female lobsters; both are flavorful dividends to sweet meat. Crack claws before serving.

BROILED LOBSTER

Use 1½- to 2-pound lobsters, 1 for each person. Have dealer split and clean lobsters if you wish. To do it yourself, kill each lobster by inserting sharp knife deeply into its back at point where head joins body to sever spinal cord. Turn lobster over on back; split it from head to tail, cutting right through back shell. Discard intestinal vein and sac at back of head. Leave tomalley (green liver) and red roe, if you are lucky to have some.

Preheat broiler. Arrange lobster halves on broiler rack, flesh side to heat. Broil for 12 to 15 minutes, basting occasionally with melted butter. Place on hot plate; sprinkle with salt. Serve with additional melted butter and lemon wedges.

BROILED LOBSTER TAILS

Serves 6

½ cup dry white wine
1 cup olive oil
3 cloves garlic, crushed
1 teaspoon salt
¼ teaspoon pepper
6 lobster tails
Melted butter (optional)
Lemon wedges (optional)

1. Prepare marinade: Blend wine, oil, garlic, salt and pepper in medium bowl.
2. Clean lobster tails. Cut feelers and membrane from underside. Pull out sand vein. Split tail without cracking shell. Place in marinade. Cover; refrigerate for 4 to 6 hours.
3. Preheat broiler or prepare charcoal fire.
4. Remove lobster tails from marinade. Place on rack, shell side toward heat. Grill or broil in oven or over charcoal for 15 minutes, basting frequently with marinade.
5. Serve with melted butter and lemon wedges, if desired.

Mrs. Harold White, Coco Plum Woman's Club,
Coral Gables, Fla.

BAKED LOBSTER

Serves 2

2 live 1½-pound lobsters
1 cup bread crumbs
Melted butter
1 tablespoon chopped parsley
½ teaspoon salt
⅛ teaspoon pepper
Lemon wedges

1. Insert point of sharp knife through back of each lobster at point where head joins body to sever spinal cord. Turn lobster on its back; split it through just to back shell, leaving shell intact. Wash lobsters; remove intestinal vein and sac in head section. Drain, shell side up, for 30 minutes.
2. Preheat oven to 425° F. Grease baking sheet.
3. Prepare crumb dressing: Combine crumbs, 3 tablespoons melted butter, parsley, salt and pepper.
4. Arrange lobsters, cut side down, on baking sheet. Bake in preheated oven for 12 to 15 minutes. Reduce temperature to 350° F.
5. Turn lobsters; fill with crumb dressing. Bake for 10 minutes longer, or until browned.
6. Serve with melted butter and lemon wedges.

Lois Gensler, Junior Woman's Club,
Simsbury, Conn.

LOBSTER CARDINALE

Serves 6

6 live 1½-pound lobsters
2 quarts boiling salted water
½ cup butter
¼ cup presifted flour
1½ teaspoons salt
2 tablespoons dry white wine
¼ cup finely chopped cooked mushrooms
2 tablespoons grated Parmesan cheese

1. Drop lobsters into water. When water returns to boil, cook for 15 minutes; remove; cool.
2. Boil water rapidly until reduced to 2 cups; reserve.
3. Place each lobster on its back. With sharp knife, split lobster in half from head to tail. Remove and discard intestinal vein and sac at back of head.
4. Remove meat from claws and body; cut into 1-inch pieces.
5. Place shells in 13 x 9½ x 2-inch baking pan.
6. Preheat broiler.
7. Prepare Cardinale Sauce: Melt ¼ cup of the butter in medium saucepan. Stir in flour. Gradually stir in reserved liquid. Cook over low heat, stirring constantly, until sauce is thickened and smooth. Simmer, stirring frequently, for 10 minutes. Stir in salt, wine, mushrooms and remaining butter.
8. Spread a little sauce in each shell; top with lobster meat. Spoon remaining sauce over lobster. Sprinkle with cheese.
9. Broil 3 to 4 inches from heat for about 5 minutes, or until hot and browned.

Mrs. John F. Kennedy, Jr., Woman's Club,
Pompano Beach, Fla.

LOBSTER THERMIDOR

Serves 2

2 live 1½-pound lobsters
½ cup butter
1 cup chopped mushrooms
3 tablespoons flour
½ teaspoon salt
⅛ teaspoon dry mustard
    Dash of cayenne
1 cup light cream
1 tablespoon chopped parsley
1 tablespoon chopped pimiento
2 tablespoons dry sherry
1 tablespoon brandy
¼ cup grated Parmesan cheese
    Paprika

1. Cook and clean lobsters. Remove meat; dice. Rinse shells; reserve.
2. Preheat oven to 350° F. Grease 10 x 6 x 1½-inch baking pan.
3. Prepare Thermidor Sauce: Melt ¼ cup of the butter in skillet; sauté mushrooms for 5 minutes. Sprinkle in flour, salt, mustard and cayenne. Gradually stir in cream. Cook over low heat, stirring constantly, until thickened and smooth.
4. Remove from heat. Stir in parsley, pimiento, sherry, brandy and lobster.
5. Spoon into reserved shells; place in pan. Sprinkle with cheese; dust with paprika.
6. Bake in preheated oven for 15 minutes.

Marge Wroble, Woman's Club,
Prospect Heights, Ill.

STUFFED LOBSTER TAILS

Serves 12

12 frozen 5-ounce rock lobster tails
1 medium onion, quartered
1 clove garlic, crushed
2 cups Medium White Sauce (p. 441)
2 cups grated Cheddar cheese
1 cup buttered bread crumbs
    Melted butter
    Lemon slices
    Cooked brown rice

1. In large saucepan cover lobster tails with boiling salted water. Add onion and garlic. Cover; simmer for about 25 minutes. Drain. Carefully remove meat from tails; reserve shells. Cut meat into bite-size pieces.
2. Preheat oven to 400° F. Lightly grease 13 x 9½ x 2-inch baking pan.
3. Put Medium White Sauce in mixing bowl. Stir in cheese and lobster meat.
4. Fill shells with lobster mixture; arrange in pan. Top with crumbs. Bake in preheated oven for 15 minutes, or until browned.
5. Remove from oven. Immediately pour ¼ cup melted butter over stuffed lobster shells.
6. Serve with large bowl of melted butter, lemon slices and rice.

Tyna K. Stone, Women's Club, Negaunee, Mich.

LOBSTER CANTONESE

Serves 4

2 frozen rock lobster tails, defrosted
2 tablespoons cooking oil
1 clove garlic, minced
1 onion, minced
½ pound lean pork, ground
3 tablespoons soy sauce
1 teaspoon sugar
1 teaspoon salt
1 teaspoon pepper
1½ cups hot chicken broth
1 tablespoon cornstarch
¼ cup water
1 egg, lightly beaten
    Cooked rice

1. Remove lobster meat from tails. Cut into 1-inch cubes. Set aside.
2. Heat oil in saucepan; brown garlic and onion lightly. Add pork; cook, stirring, until browned.
3. Combine soy sauce, sugar, salt, pepper and broth. Stir into pork mixture. Add lobster. Cover; simmer for 10 minutes.
4. Combine cornstarch and water; stir into lobster mixture. Cook, stirring constantly, until slightly thickened.
5. Turn off heat. Quickly stir in egg.
6. Serve on cooked rice.

Mrs. Joe Huneycutt, Woman's Club,
Albemarle, N.C.

LOBSTER CASSEROLE WITH WILD RICE

Serves 6

2 tablespoons butter
1 cup chopped onions
1 carrot, chopped
1 tablespoon chopped parsley
2 10½-ounce cans condensed consommé
2 cups water
1½ cups wild rice
2½ cups cooked lobster meat
1½ cups frozen cream of shrimp soup, defrosted
2 tablespoons dry sherry
2 tablespoons melted butter
2 tablespoons grated Parmesan cheese
½ teaspoon salt
¼ teaspoon pepper

1. Melt 2 tablespoons butter in saucepan. Add onions, carrot, parsley, consommé, water and rice. Bring to boil; cover; simmer for 40 minutes, or until liquid is absorbed.
2. Preheat oven to 375° F. Grease 2-quart casserole.
3. Arrange lobster in casserole. Combine remaining ingredients; pour over lobster. Spread rice mixture on top.
4. Cover. Bake in preheated oven for 30 minutes.

Mrs. Paul T. Rotter, Thursday Morning Club,
Madison, N.J.

LOBSTER FRA DIAVOLO

Serves 6

½ cup olive oil
2 cloves garlic, crushed
1-pound 13-ounce can tomatoes,
  undrained
1¼ teaspoons salt
⅛ teaspoon pepper
1 tablespoon chopped parsley
1 teaspoon orégano
2 live lobsters or 6 frozen lobster
  tails
½ cup red wine
Dash of cayenne
Cooked spaghetti or rice

1. Prepare Marinara Sauce: Heat oil in
large skillet; sauté garlic over medium
heat until golden. Stir in tomatoes, salt,
pepper, parsley and orégano. Bring to boil.
Cook over medium heat for 15 minutes, or
until sauce is thickened, stirring occasionally.
2. Meanwhile, cook and clean lobsters,
or cook lobster tails according to package
directions. Remove meat from lobsters; cut
into large chunks.
3. When sauce is thickened, stir in wine,
cayenne and lobster. Simmer for 2 minutes.
4. Serve on spaghetti or rice.

Mrs. George L. Moore, Junior New Century Club,
West Chester, Pa.

LOBSTER NEWBURG

Serves 2

1 medium lobster, cooked
1 cup heavy cream
1 cup Thick White Sauce (p. 441)
⅛ teaspoon pepper
½ teaspoon paprika
3 tablespoons dry sherry
1 tablespoon butter
Toast points or patty shells

1. Remove meat from lobster; cut into
small pieces.
2. Put lobster in large skillet; add cream.
Cover; simmer for 25 minutes. Stir in Thick
White Sauce, pepper and paprika. Simmer,
stirring frequently, for 20 minutes. Add
sherry; simmer for 10 minutes longer.
3. Remove from heat. Beat in butter.
4. Serve on toast points or in patty
shells.

VARIATION: Clams, crab meat and shrimp
may be used together with the lobster
meat (about 1 cup altogether) for Seafood
Newburg.

Jinx Stearns, Woman's Club, Annandale, Pa.

CAPE COD LOBSTER PIE

Serves 4

This recipe may be doubled and a can
of shrimp or crab meat added.

5 tablespoons butter
¼ cup sherry
1 cup lobster meat
1 tablespoon flour
¾ cup light cream
2 egg yolks

¼ cup cracker meal
¼ teaspoon paprika
1 tablespoon finely crushed potato
  chips
1½ tablespoons grated Parmesan
  cheese
1½ tablespoons melted butter
2 to 4 tablespoons sherry to taste

1. Preheat oven to 300° F. Grease
shallow casserole or pie plate.
2. Melt 2 tablespoons of the butter in
saucepan. Add ¼ cup sherry. Bring to boil;
simmer for 1 minute. Add lobster. Set aside.
3. In another saucepan melt 3 tablespoons butter. Add flour. Cook, stirring,
for 1 minute. Remove from heat. Gradually
stir in cream and sherry drained from
lobster.
4. Mix egg yolks with a little sauce;
gradually stir into rest of sauce. Cook
over hot, not boiling, water, stirring constantly, for about 3 minutes, or until
thickened and smooth. Add lobster. Turn
into casserole or pie plate.
5. Combine remaining ingredients.
Sprinkle over lobster.
6. Bake in preheated oven for 10 minutes.

Woman's Club Cook Book, Woman's Club,
Pawtucket, R.I.

ROCK LOBSTER TETRAZZINI

Serves 6

6 frozen rock lobster tails
8-ounce package thin spaghetti
10½-ounce can condensed cream of
  mushroom soup
1 cup milk
1 teaspoon salt
1 teaspoon paprika
1 teaspoon aromatic bitters
½ cup shredded sharp Cheddar cheese

1. Drop lobster tails into large pan of
boiling salted water. When water comes
back to boil, cook according to package
directions.
2. Remove tails. Break spaghetti into
boiling lobster water. Cook according to
package directions. Drain; rinse.
3. Cool lobster tails under running cold
water. Remove meat from shells; dice.
4. Combine soup and milk, heat, stirring, until smooth. Stir in salt, paprika and
bitters.
5. Combine half the sauce with lobster
meat and half with spaghetti.
6. Preheat oven to 450° F. Grease 6 individual casseroles.
7. Fill casseroles with spaghetti mixture.
Make deep nest in center of each; fill with
lobster mixture. Sprinkle with cheese.
8. Bake in preheated oven for 10 minutes.

Mrs. R. E. Bailey, North Carolina Federation of
Women's Clubs, Inc., Winston-Salem, N.C.

Mussels

Mussels, the black shelled bivalve mollusks, abundant on both coasts, are among the most delicious of all shellfish. They may be steamed in a little water or white wine, the plump, flavorful yellow or orange flesh may be dipped in Lemon Butter (p. 444), added to Cream Sauce (p. 441), or Wine Butter Sauce (p. 451) or baked in casseroles. Mussels are frequently used as a garnish for fillet of sole dishes. In Portugal they are a popular appetizer. Guests sit around a chafing dish of simmering red wine and poach the raw mussels a few at a time, in the wine, just until the shells open; they are eaten hot with melted garlic butter. In France and in French restaurants the most popular method of cooking them is mariner's style, or *marinière*.

MOULES MARINIÈRE

Serves 4

2 quarts mussels
6 tablespoons butter
1 small onion, chopped, or 4 shallots, minced
1 clove garlic, minced
1 bay leaf
Pinch of thyme
Coarsely ground black pepper
1 cup dry white wine
2 tablespoons chopped parsley
Hot French bread

1. Discard any mussels that feel extraordinarily heavy, for they are usually empty shells filled with sand, called clinkers. Wash and scrub mussels thoroughly with stiff brush. With heavy knife or clam knife, scrape off any seaweed or barnacles adhering to them; pull out the beard, a little tuft by which mussel attached itself to rock or wharf.
2. Melt 3 tablespoons of the butter in large heavy kettle. Add onion or shallots and garlic. Simmer for 10 minutes, or until onion or shallots are transparent.
3. Add mussels, bay leaf, thyme, pepper and wine. Cover tightly. Cook over high heat until shells have opened. Discard any mussels that do not open.
4. Divide mussels into 4 soup plates.
5. Add remaining butter and parsley to wine and mussel liquor in kettle. Cook over moderate heat until butter is melted. Pour over mussels.
6. Serve with plenty of bread for dunking. Servings should be accompanied by small fork or cocktail pick to remove mussels from shells and by soup spoon for broth.

VARIATION: Add 1 cup heavy cream to mussel liquor along with butter and parsley.

A. S.

Oysters

Many varieties of oyster are found off both the Atlantic and the Pacific coasts. They range in size from the tiny Olympia oyster of the Pacific to the Atlantic blue points. Some are plump, and some are thin. Some are salty; others have a palate-pleasing alkaline flavor. All are delicious served raw on the half shell (p. 238) or cooked in numerous ways.

TO SHUCK, OR OPEN, OYSTERS: See p. 238.

OYSTER SCALD

Serves 12 to 15

2 cups catsup
1 cup vinegar
1 teaspoon salt
¼ teaspoon pepper
2 tablespoons horseradish
1 bushel oysters in shells

1. Bring large kettle of water to boil.
2. Prepare Dip for Oysters: In bowl blend catsup, vinegar, salt, pepper and horseradish; mix well.
3. Put oysters in wire basket; lower into kettle. Leave in water only long enough for oysters to open slightly.
4. Remove oysters. Serve with dip and a cup of oyster liquor on the side.

Hazel Madsen, President, Woman's Club,
St. Mary's County, Md.

BAKED OYSTERS HOMESTEAD

Serves 6

24 freshly shucked oysters with liquor
2 tablespoons butter
2 medium green peppers, diced
4 medium mushrooms, diced
1 cup hot Cream Sauce (p. 441)
1 egg yolk
4 drops yellow food coloring
Salt and pepper to taste
1 tablespoon whipped cream
¼ pound fresh lump crab meat, flaked
½ cup grated Parmesan cheese

1. Put oysters in saucepan. Bring to boil. Remove from heat. Pinch off hard muscle from each oyster. Arrange 4 oysters in each of 6 scallop or clam shells.
2. Melt butter in skillet; cook green peppers and mushrooms over low heat for 10 minutes, or until peppers are tender but not browned.
3. Preheat oven to 450° F.
4. Combine Cream Sauce, egg yolk, food coloring, salt and pepper. Fold in whipped cream.
5. Combine sauce, vegetables and crab meat. Spoon over oysters. Sprinkle with cheese.
6. Bake in preheated oven for 10 minutes, or until sauce is bubbling and cheese is browned.

Mrs. Richard Humphery, Woman's Club,
Naples, Fla.

ROASTED OYSTERS

Serves 4

24 large oysters in shells
  Salt and pepper to taste
½ cup melted butter

1. Preheat oven to 450° F. Grease 2 baking sheets.
2. Clean outsides of oysters. Place on baking sheets.
3. Bake in preheated oven for 5 minutes, or until shells are easily separated.
4. Remove flat shell. Sprinkle oysters with salt, pepper and butter.
5. Serve in shells.

*Junior Woman's Club,
Thibodaux, La.*

BROILED OYSTERS

Serves 4

¾ cup sifted bread crumbs
½ teaspoon dry mustard
  Dash of cayenne
¼ teaspoon paprika
½ teaspoon salt
24 oysters, freshly shucked and
  drained
¼ cup melted butter
  Lemon wedges

1. Preheat broiler. Grease shallow baking pan.
2. Combine crumbs, mustard, cayenne, paprika and salt. Roll oysters in crumb mixture. Arrange in pan in a single layer. Sprinkle with half the butter. Broil until lightly browned.
3. Turn oysters; sprinkle with remaining butter; broil until browned.
4. Serve with lemon wedges.

*Mrs. Alton J. Smith, New Century Club,
Wilmington, Del.*

ALABAMA FRIED OYSTERS

Serves 6

1 quart oysters, freshly shucked
  and drained
2 eggs, well beaten
2 tablespoons cream
1 teaspoon salt
⅛ teaspoon pepper
1 cup cracker or yellow corn meal
  Fat for frying
  Tartar Sauce for Fish (p. 450)
  Lemon wedges

1. Dry oysters on absorbent paper.
2. Combine eggs and cream. Season with salt and pepper.
3. Dip oysters in egg mixture; gently roll in meal.
4. Fry in skillet containing about 1 inch oil heated to 365° F. until golden brown on both sides, turning once.
5. Drain on absorbent paper. Serve with Tartar Sauce for Fish and lemon wedges.

VARIATION: This recipe is also excellent when clams are substituted for oysters.

Gulf Coast Gourmet, Woman's Club, Foley, Ala.

MARYLAND OYSTERS

Serves 4

1-pound ham slice
1 pint freshly shucked oysters with
  liquor
1 tablespoon flour
1 tablespoon softened butter

1. Brown ham well on both sides in skillet. Transfer to warm serving platter; keep warm.
2. Drain oysters; reserve liquor.
3. Add oysters to juices remaining in skillet. Cook, stirring in brown bits from bottom and sides of pan.
4. When edges of oysters curl, gradually stir in liquor.
5. Blend flour and butter to a smooth paste. Stir into oyster liquor, bit by bit, until sauce is slightly thickened.
6. Pour oysters and sauce over ham.

*Elsie O. Huber, New Century Club,
Wilmington, Del.*

OYSTERS BIENVILLE

Serves 6

2 tablespoons bacon drippings
2 tablespoons butter
½ cup minced shallots or scallions
4 tablespoons flour
1 tablespoon fresh bread crumbs
1¼ cups light cream
  Liquid from 4-ounce can sliced
  mushrooms
1½ teaspoons salt
2 dashes of black pepper
¼ teaspoon Tabasco
4 drops garlic juice
¼ cup finely chopped mushrooms
12 shrimp, shelled, deveined, cooked
  and minced
2 tablespoons minced pimientos
6 freshly shucked oysters with liquor
¼ cup lemon juice
2 tablespoons sherry
36 oysters on half shell
  Rock salt
¾ cup dry bread crumbs

1. Melt bacon drippings and butter in skillet; cook shallots or scallions until golden.
2. Stir in flour and fresh crumbs. Gradually stir in cream. Cook, stirring constantly, until sauce is smooth. Add mushroom liquid, salt, pepper, Tabasco, garlic juice, mushrooms, shrimp and pimientos. Heat.
3. Put oysters with liquor in small skillet; cover; cook over low heat for 2 minutes. Remove oysters; mince; stir into sauce.
4. Remove sauce from heat. Stir in lemon juice and sherry. Let stand for 30 minutes.
5. Preheat oven to 450° F.
6. Arrange oysters on half shell on shallow bed of rock salt. Put 1 tablespoon sauce on each oyster. Sprinkle with dry crumbs.
7. Bake in preheated oven for 15 minutes.

Gulf Coast Gourmet, Woman's Club, Foley, Ala.

CREAMED OYSTERS

Serves 2

½ cup butter
½ cup chopped scallions
1 pint oysters, freshly shucked and
drained
1 tablespoon flour
Salt and pepper to taste
Pinch of thyme
Toast

1. Set aside 1 tablespoon of the butter.
2. Heat remaining butter in saucepan until it just begins to turn golden; sauté scallions for 3 minutes, or until tender. Add oysters. Cook over very low heat.
3. Combine reserved butter and flour. As oysters begin to emit juices, gradually stir in butter-flour mixture. Season with salt, pepper and thyme.
4. As soon as edges of oysters curl, serve on toast.

Loee S. Sonnier, Modern Study Club, Mobile, Ala.

CURRIED OYSTERS

Serves 4

2 tablespoons butter
1 onion, minced
½ green pepper, minced
1 clove garlic, minced
½ teaspoon curry powder or to taste
2 tablespoons flour
½ cup cream
1 pint freshly shucked oysters with
liquor
Hot cooked rice
Indian chutney

1. Melt butter in saucepan; sauté onion, green pepper and garlic for 10 minutes, or until tender.
2. Combine curry powder, flour and cream. Stir into vegetable mixture. Cook, stirring, until thickened.
3. Drain oysters; reserve liquor. Drop oysters into hot mixture; cook only until edges curl. Stir in liquor, cook, stirring, until hot.
4. Make a ring of rice on warm platter. Pour curried oysters into center. Serve with chutney.

Helen Urbany, Carmichaels and Cumberland Township Civic Club, Carmichaels, Pa.

OYSTERS ROCKEFELLER

Serves 6

2 pounds spinach, ready to cook,
or 2 10-ounce packages frozen
spinach, defrosted
6 scallions
4 tablespoons parsley clusters
2 stalks celery
Butter
½ cup toasted bread crumbs
Salt to taste
Cayenne to taste
Juice of 1 large lemon
2 tablespoons Worcestershire
2 tablespoons Pernod
36 oysters on half shell
Rock salt

½ cup grated Parmesan cheese
½ cup cracker crumbs

1. Put spinach, scallions, parsley and celery through meat grinder. Chop in ½ cup butter. Add bread crumbs. Season with salt, cayenne, lemon juice, Worcestershire and Pernod.
2. Preheat oven to 400° F.
3. Arrange oysters in shallow pan on bed of rock salt. Cover oysters with vegetable mixture. Sprinkle lightly with cheese and cracker crumbs. Dot with butter.
4. Bake in preheated oven for about 10 minutes, or until lightly browned.

Gulf Coast Gourmet, Woman's Club, Foley, Ala.

SCALLOPED OYSTERS

Serves 6

½ cup butter
2 tablespoons chopped onion
1 teaspoon celery salt
⅛ teaspoon pepper
1 tablespoon lemon juice
1 teaspoon Worcestershire
1½ cups fine cracker crumbs
1 pint oysters, freshly shucked and
drained
½ cup light cream

1. Preheat oven to 350° F. Grease 1½-quart casserole.
2. Melt butter in skillet; sauté onion for 5 minutes.
3. Remove from heat. Stir in celery salt, pepper, lemon juice, Worcestershire and crumbs; mix well.
4. Arrange about one-third of crumb mixture in casserole; top with half the oysters. Add another layer of crumbs; top with remaining oysters. Sprinkle with remaining crumbs. Pour cream over top.
5. Bake in preheated oven for 30 minutes, or until browned.

Bernice Fogg, Woman's Club, Durham, N.H.

SCALLOPED CORN AND OYSTERS

Serves 4

8-ounce can oysters
1-pound can corn cream-style corn
10 soda crackers, crushed
Salt and pepper to taste
1 medium onion, finely chopped
1 medium green pepper, finely
chopped
¼ cup diced pimientos
1 cup grated Cheddar cheese

1. Preheat oven to 350° F. Grease 1½-quart casserole.
2. Drain oysters; reserve liquid in measuring cup.
3. Put half the corn in casserole. Top with a layer of half the crackers and half the oysters. Season with salt and pepper. Top with a layer of half the onion, green pepper and pimientos. Repeat layers in same order.
4. Add sufficient water to reserved liquid to total 1 cup. Pour over top layer in casserole. Sprinkle with cheese.

5. Bake in preheated oven for 45 minutes.

Mrs. Jim Widrig, Delphian Junior Woman's Club, Beloit, Kans.

GRATIN OF OYSTERS AND MUSHROOMS

Serves 8

½ cup butter
1 medium green pepper, finely chopped
1 medium onion, thinly sliced
8-ounce can sliced mushrooms, drained
¼ cup presifted flour
1½ cups heavy cream
1 cup light cream
¼ cup grated Parmesan cheese
Dash of nutmeg
Paprika
Dash of Tabasco
Salt and pepper to taste
⅓ cup dry white wine
2 cups freshly shucked oysters, drained
1 cup fresh bread crumbs

1. Melt ¼ cup of the butter in skillet; sauté green pepper, onion and mushrooms until tender.
2. Melt remaining butter in top of double saucepan over hot water. Stir in flour. Gradually stir in heavy and light cream. Cook over hot water, stirring constantly, until sauce is thickened and smooth.
3. Preheat broiler. Grease 10 x 6 x 1½-inch baking pan.
4. Add 2 tablespoons of the cheese, nutmeg, dash of paprika and Tabasco to sauce in top of double saucepan. Season lightly with salt and pepper. Stir in sautéed vegetables.
5. Sprinkle wine over oysters; add to sauce. Stir; pour into pan. Sprinkle with crumbs, remaining cheese and paprika.
6. Broil 4 to 5 inches from heat for 5 minutes, or until golden and bubbling.

Mrs. J. D. Vance, Woman's Club, Batesville, Miss.

OYSTER PIE

Serves 4

3 tablespoons butter or margarine
1 cup sliced mushrooms
2 cups Medium White Sauce (p. 441)
½ teaspoon salt
⅛ teaspoon pepper
½ teaspoon celery salt
1 pint oysters, freshly shucked and drained
Pastry for a 1-Crust Pie (p. 548)

1. Preheat oven to 425° F. Grease 8-inch pie plate.
2. Melt butter or margarine in medium skillet; sauté mushrooms for 5 minutes. Stir in Medium White Sauce and seasonings. Cook over medium heat, stirring constantly, until bubbling.
3. Remove from heat. Stir in oysters. Pour into pie plate.

4. Roll out Pastry for a 1-Crust Pie on lightly floured board ⅛ inch thick and about 1 inch larger than pie plate.
5. Place pastry over pie plate; trim edges; flute. Cut 2 slits in center to allow steam to escape.
6. Bake in preheated oven for 30 minutes, or until golden.

Blanche Holston, Gardens Century Club, Wilmington, Del.

Scallops

Two types of scallop are sold in fish markets—the tiny, delicate bay scallop and the large, coarser-fleshed, but delicious sea scallop. The edible part of a scallop is the thick muscle that opens and shuts the pretty fluted shell to propel the scallop through the water. The shells are easy to open by inserting a clam knife between the shells and cutting the muscle away, first from one shell, then from the other. The rest of the meat is washed away from the muscle and discarded. A pound of scallops will make 2 large or 3 average portions.

Scallops may be dipped in Frying Batter (p. 223) and fried in deep fat, but they are much more succulent sautéed in butter.

SAUTÉED SCALLOPS

Scallops
Flour
Egg, lightly beaten with 1 tablespoon water
Bread crumbs or corn meal
Butter
Salt and pepper to taste
Lemon wedges

1. Dry scallops well on absorbent paper.
2. Roll in flour; dip in egg.
3. Roll in crumbs or corn meal.
4. Melt a little butter in skillet; sauté scallops until golden brown on both sides. Do not overcook.
5. Sprinkle with salt and pepper. Serve with lemon wedges.

A. S.

BROILED SCALLOPS

Serves 4

2 tablespoons olive oil
1½ cups bay scallops
½ cup French Dressing (p. 541)
1½ cups bread crumbs
Favorite sauce

1. Preheat broiler. Line broiler pan with aluminum foil; brush foil with oil.
2. Dip scallops in French Dressing; roll in crumbs.
3. Heat broiler pan for 2 minutes.
4. Arrange scallops on pan. Broil 2 inches from heat for 5 minutes on each side, or until golden brown, resembling toasted marshmallows.
5. Serve with favorite sauce.

Evelyn Morse, Junior Woman's Club, New Bedford, Mass.

SCALLOPS BAKED IN CREAM

Serves 4

1 cup cracker crumbs
1½ teaspoons salt
¼ teaspoon pepper
½ teaspoon basil
½ teaspoon orégano
1 tablespoon finely chopped parsley
2 pounds scallops
1 cup heavy cream

1. Preheat oven to 375° F. Butter 11 x 7 x 1½-inch baking pan.
2. On piece of waxed paper combine crumbs, salt, pepper, basil, orégano and parsley. Use to coat scallops. Arrange in pan. Pour cream over scallops.
3. Bake in preheated oven for 25 minutes, or until bubbling and lightly browned.

Mrs. John I. Vail, Blair Woman's Club, Blairstown, N.J.

SCALLOPS BAKED IN SHELLS

Serves 8

To serve 16, increase measurements by ½ and add 1 pound chopped cooked shrimp.

2 pounds scallops
2 cups dry white wine
½ teaspoon salt
½ pound mushrooms, chopped
  Butter
2 tablespoons water
1 tablespoon chopped parsley
1 teaspoon lemon juice
1 small onion, minced
4 tablespoons softened butter
4 tablespoons flour
2 egg yolks
4 tablespoons heavy cream
  Fine bread crumbs

1. Put scallops, wine and salt in saucepan. Bring to boil. Simmer for 10 minutes. Drain; reserve broth. Cut scallops into small pieces.
2. In clean saucepan combine mushrooms, 2 tablespoons butter, water, parsley, lemon juice and onion. Bring to boil; cover; simmer for 10 minutes. Drain, adding liquid to reserved broth.
3. In another saucepan combine softened butter and flour. Gradually stir in reserved liquid. Cook, stirring constantly, until sauce is thickened and smooth. Remove from heat. Beat egg yolks with cream; stir into sauce. Stir in scallops and mushrooms.
4. Preheat broiler.
5. Fill 8 scallop shells or ramekins with mixture, piling high in center. Dust with crumbs; dot with butter.
6. Broil until browned.

Barbara Hetlage, Anna Day Club, Troy, Mo.

COQUILLES ST. JACQUES

Serves 6

1½ pounds scallops
1 onion, sliced
1 scallion, crushed
  Dry white wine

4 tablespoons butter
2 tablespoons flour
2 egg yolks
½ cup cream
  Salt and white pepper to taste
¼ pound mushrooms, finely chopped
  Grated Gruyère cheese

1. Put scallops, onion and scallion in shallow baking dish. Add wine to cover. Bring to boil. Poach over low heat for 8 minutes. Strain broth; reserve. Discard onions.
2. Melt 2 tablespoons of the butter in saucepan. Stir in flour. Stir in reserved broth. Cook, stirring, until sauce is thickened and smooth.
3. Combine egg yolks and cream; stir into sauce. Season with salt and pepper.
4. Preheat oven to 450° F.
5. Melt remaining butter in skillet; sauté mushrooms. Spoon over scallops. Pour sauce over scallops. Sprinkle with cheese.
6. Bake in preheated oven for 10 to 12 minutes.

Mrs. William Huntington, Junior Woman's Club, Diamond Bar, Calif.

SCALLOPS IN WHITE WINE SAUCE

Serves 3 or 4

1½ pounds bay scallops
¾ cup dry white wine
3 tablespoons butter
2 tablespoons flour
½ cup heavy cream
  Salt and pepper to taste

1. Put scallops and wine in skillet. Bring to boil. Then simmer for 2 to 3 minutes, or until tender. Drain; reserve liquid. Set scallops aside.
2. Melt butter in saucepan. Stir in flour. Gradually stir in reserved liquid. Cook over low heat, stirring constantly, until thickened and smooth. Stir in cream and scallops. Heat to serving temperature. Remove from heat. Season with salt and pepper.

Mrs. Olga Wilson, Woman's Club, Essex, Conn.

Shrimp

Quick-frozen shrimp, either raw or cooked, are available throughout the country. Shrimp in the shell range in size from the giant prawns, which average 8 to 10 to the pound, to the medium, averaging 12 to 16 per pound, to the small, about 24 per pound. Count on from ⅓ to ½ pound per serving, depending on whether they are served as an entree or a first course and whether they are served plain or sauced.

Freshly cooked shrimp are sometimes sold shelled and deveined; raw shrimp are usually decapitated and sold in the shell. They may be poached in the shells, then shelled and deveined, but the flavor is considered more delicate if the shrimp are shelled and cleaned before they are cooked.

TO SHELL AND DEVEIN, OR CLEAN, SHRIMP

Remove the small legs from the underside of the body, and peel off the shell. For some methods of cooking, the tail shell is left on. With a sharp knife, slit along the curve of the back, and wash out the black vein.

TO BUTTERFLY SHRIMP

Cut deeply along the curve of the back so that the shrimp is almost halved. Place on waxed paper, and flatten with the palm of the hand.

POACHED SHRIMP

Serves 6 to 8

2 cups water
1 cup vinegar
2 bay leaves
1 tablespoon salt
2 tablespoons dry mustard
2 tablespoons mustard seed
2 tablespoons celery seed
1 teaspoon pepper
2 pounds shrimp, shelled and deveined

1. Prepare court bouillon: In saucepan combine water, vinegar, bay leaves, salt, mustard, mustard seed, celery seed and pepper. Bring to boil. Simmer for 10 minutes.
2. Add shrimp; cover; simmer for 5 to 7 minutes, stirring occasionally. Drain. Serve hot or cold.

Mrs. Blanche Seiter, Woman's Club, DeBary, Fla.

PICKLED SHRIMP

Serves 6 to 8

This should be made at least 24 hours before serving time.

Salt
15 whole allspice
1 teaspoon peppercorns
⅛ teaspoon thyme
¼ teaspoon hot red pepper
Juice and rind of ½ lemon
6 cloves garlic, sliced
3 small onions, quartered
2 stalks celery, sliced
½-ounce box bay leaves
Few sprigs parsley
⅓ cup Worcestershire
2½ pounds shrimp
1¼ cups olive oil
¾ cup white vinegar
2½ teaspoons celery seed
2½ teaspoons capers with juice
1 tablespoon prepared mustard
4 medium onions, thinly sliced

1. Prepare court bouillon: In large saucepan combine 3 tablespoons salt, allspice, peppercorns, thyme, red pepper, lemon juice and rind, garlic, quartered onions, celery, 2 of the bay leaves, parsley and 1 tablespoon of the Worcestershire. Bring to boil. Simmer for 20 minutes.
2. Add shrimp. Bring back to boil. Simmer for 12 to 15 minutes; cool.

3. Drain shrimp. Shell and devein. Set aside.
4. Prepare marinade: Blend 1½ teaspoons salt, remaining Worcestershire, oil, vinegar, celery seed, capers and mustard.
5. In large bowl arrange alternate layers of shrimp, sliced onions, and remaining bay leaves, pouring marinade over each layer. Cover bowl. Marinate for at least 24 hours.

Trixie Urie, President, Jaycettes, Gulfport, Miss.

SHRIMP CREOLE

Serves 4

⅓ cup olive oil
½ cup chopped onions
½ cup chopped green pepper
½ cup chopped celery
1 clove garlic, crushed
2 tablespoons flour
1 teaspoon salt
¼ teaspoon pepper
Dash of cayenne
1 bay leaf, crushed
1-pound 4-ounce can tomatoes
1½ pounds shrimp, shelled and deveined
1 teaspoon sugar
¼ cup chopped parsley
Cooked rice

1. Heat oil in large skillet; sauté onions, green pepper, celery and garlic for 5 minutes. Stir in flour, salt, pepper, cayenne, bay leaf and tomatoes. Bring to boil; cover; simmer for 20 minutes.
2. Stir in shrimp, sugar and parsley. Cover; simmer for 15 minutes, or until shrimp are cooked.
3. Serve on rice.

Mrs. Bill Eaker, Book Club, Tallulah, La.

SHRIMP MARENGO

Serves 8

7 slices bacon
¼ teaspoon garlic powder
3½ pounds shrimp, shelled, deveined and cooked
1 cup chopped onions
1 pound mushrooms, sliced
2-pound 3-ounce can Italian tomatoes
6-ounces can tomato paste
10½-ounce can condensed consommé
1 teaspoon monosodium glutamate
1 teaspoon orégano
1 teaspoon basil
1½ teaspoons salt
⅛ teaspoon pepper
1 tablespoon sugar
1 tablespoon prepared mustard
¼ cup presifted flour
½ cup water
Cooked rice
Chopped parsley

1. Cook bacon in large skillet until crisp. Drain on absorbent paper; crumble.
2. Sprinkle fat remaining in skillet with garlic powder; sauté shrimp for 3 minutes. Add onions and mushrooms; sauté for a few minutes longer. Add tomatoes, tomato paste, consommé, seasonings, sugar, mus-

tard and bacon. Simmer for 10 minutes, stirring frequently.

3. Combine flour and water. Stir into sauce. Boil for 1 minute longer. Correct seasoning.

4. Serve on rice. Sprinkle with parsley.

Mrs. Roswell Newton Hait, Thursday Morning Club, Madison, N.J.

SHRIMP ROYALE

Serves 4

2 tablespoons cooking oil
1 large onion, chopped
3 stalks celery with leaves, chopped
4-ounce can sliced mushrooms
2 tablespoons soy sauce
1 pound shrimp, shelled and deveined
1 tablespoon cornstarch, mixed with
2 tablespoons water
Cooked rice

1. Heat oil in saucepan; sauté onion and celery until onion is transparent. Add mushrooms and soy sauce; simmer for 20 minutes.

2. Add shrimp. Stir in cornstarch. Simmer for 10 minutes longer.

3. Serve on rice.

Mildred O. Felton, Woman's Club, Key West, Fla.

SHRIMP ITALIANO OR SCAMPI

Serves 6

1 cup olive oil
½ cup dry white wine
½ teaspoon orégano
2 cloves garlic, crushed
2 pounds large shrimp, shelled and deveined

1. Prepare marinade: In mixing bowl blend oil, wine, orégano and garlic. Add shrimp. Cover. Refrigerate for 4 to 6 hours; stir occasionally.

2. Preheat broiler. Line broiler pan with aluminum foil.

3. Place shrimp and marinade on broiler pan. Broil 4 to 5 inches from heat for 7 minutes. Turn shrimp; broil for 10 minutes longer.

4. Serve shrimp with marinade.

Mrs. Harold White, Coco Plum Woman's Club, Coral Gables, Fla.

SHRIMP DI SCIULLE

Serves 4

2 pounds large shrimp, shelled and deveined
Salt and pepper to taste
Flour
2 large eggs, lightly beaten
¾ cup butter
2 cups sliced mushrooms
¼ cup dry white wine

1. Rinse shrimp in cold water; drain on absorbent paper.

2. Season with salt and pepper; coat with flour. Dip in eggs.

3. Melt ½ cup of the butter in large skillet; sauté shrimp over medium heat, turning frequently, until golden.

4. Meanwhile, melt remaining butter in another large skillet; sauté mushrooms for 5 minutes.

5. When shrimp are golden, stir in mushrooms; sprinkle with wine. Cook over high heat, stirring frequently, until wine has evaporated.

Mrs. Ruby White, Island Woman's Club, Anna Maria, Fla.

FRIED SHRIMP

Serves 6

2 pounds shrimp, shelled and deveined
Salt
2 eggs
2 tablespoons water
¾ cup cracker crumbs
Fat for deep frying
Lemon wedges

1. Drain shrimp on absorbent paper. Sprinkle with salt.

2. In small bowl beat eggs and water.

3. Dip shrimp in eggs; coat completely. Dip in crumbs, coating well.

4. Fry shrimp in deep fat heated to 365° F. for about 5 minutes, or until golden. Drain on absorbent paper. Serve with lemon wedges.

Mrs. Henry Bailey, Woman's Club, Sebring, Fla.

BUTTERFLY SHRIMP

Serves 3

Large shrimp
Salt and pepper to taste
Cornstarch
2 eggs, well beaten
Sweet Sour Pineapple Sauce
(p. 450) (optional)

1. Shell shrimp, leaving last joint of shell and tail on. Devein; wash; drain.

2. Season shrimp with salt and pepper; roll in cornstarch.

3. Make a batter by combining ¾ cup cornstarch and eggs. Holding shrimp by tail, dip in batter.

4. Fry in deep fat heated to 365° F. for about 3 minutes.

5. If desired, serve with Sweet Sour Pineapple Sauce. *These must be eaten hot.*

Mrs. Leonore Kirchem, Gentilly Woods Woman's Club, New Orleans, La.

SHRIMP TEMPURA

Serves 4

1 pound shrimp
1 cup presifted flour
1 teaspoon baking powder
Pinch of salt
Pinch of sugar
¼ cup white corn meal
2 tablespoons shortening
2 eggs
1 cup milk
Fat for deep frying

1. Remove shells from shrimp, leaving tails intact. With sharp knife, slit shrimp deeply down back without cutting all the way through; devein.

2. Wash shrimp; spread open on towel. Cover with another towel.

3. In mixing bowl sift together dry ingredients. Cut in shortening until mixture resembles fine crumbs. Stir in eggs and milk; mix until blended and fairly thick.

4. Dip shrimp in batter. Fry a few at a time in deep fat heated to 365° F. for about 3 minutes, or until golden brown. Drain on absorbent paper.

Mrs. Gladys Robinson, Woman's Club, DeBary, Fla.

STUFFED FRIED SHRIMP

Serves 6

2 tablespoons shortening
1 large onion, finely chopped
½ cup finely chopped celery
1 clove garlic, crushed
¼ cup finely chopped green pepper
2 cups crab meat, flaked
2 tablespoons finely chopped scallions
2 tablespoons finely chopped parsley
4 eggs
¼ cup presifted flour
½ teaspoon salt
⅛ teaspoon cayenne
⅛ teaspoon pepper
24 large shrimp
1 cup cracker crumbs
Fat for deep frying

1. Prepare Crab Meat Stuffing: Melt shortening in large skillet; sauté onion, celery, garlic and green pepper over low heat for 5 minutes. Stir in crab meat, scallions, parsley, 2 of the eggs, flour, salt, cayenne and pepper. Cook over low heat, stirring constantly, until thickened and bound together. Remove from heat. Cool.

2. Shell and devein shrimp. Cut deeply down back but not quite through shrimp.

3. Press about 1 tablespoon stuffing into each shrimp. Roll in crumbs.

4. Beat remaining eggs; dip shrimp first in eggs, then in crumbs.

5. Fry in deep fat heated to 365° F. for 4 minutes, or until golden. Drain on absorbent paper.

Mrs. William P. Gilbert, Junior Woman's Club, Thibodaux, La.

SHRIMP MANHATTAN

Serves 4

1 cup Medium White Sauce (p. 441)
1 cup grated Cheddar cheese
1-pound can tomatoes, well drained
1 cup diced cooked shrimp
Salt and pepper to taste
½ teaspoon paprika
4 slices toast

1. Put Medium White Sauce in saucepan. Add cheese, tomatoes and shrimp. Season with salt and pepper; add paprika.

2. Cook over medium heat, stirring constantly, until cheese is melted and sauce bubbles.

3. Serve on toast.

Doris Pare, Bay Area Zenith Club, North Bend, Ore.

SHRIMP CURRY

Serves 8 to 10

This is better if made a day ahead. Add the cream just before serving.

½ cup butter or margarine
2 large carrots, chopped
1 medium green pepper, chopped
2 medium onions, chopped
3 stalks celery, chopped
1 clove garlic, crushed
3 tablespoons curry powder or to taste
5 tablespoons flour
3 cups chicken broth
Salt and pepper to taste
5 pounds shrimp, shelled, deveined and cooked
½ cup heavy cream
Cooked rice

1. Melt butter or margarine in large skillet. Add carrots, green pepper, onions, celery and garlic; sauté for 5 minutes.

2. Stir in curry powder and flour; sauté for a few moments. Stir in broth; cook over low heat, stirring constantly, until thickened. Season with salt and pepper. Cover; simmer for 20 minutes.

3. Stir in shrimp; cook for 5 minutes. Stir in cream; cook for 2 to 3 minutes.

4. Serve on rice.

Lois Merritt, Woman's Club, Flemington, N.J.

SHRIMP NEWBURG STYLE

Serves 6

4 tablespoons butter
2½ tablespoons flour
2 cups cream
6 tablespoons catsup
1½ tablespoons Worcestershire
2 pounds shrimp, shelled, deveined and cooked
Salt, paprika and cayenne to taste
4 tablespoons sherry
Toast points, rice or grits

1. Melt butter in saucepan. Stir in flour. Slowly stir in cream. Cook, stirring constantly, until thickened and smooth.

2. Stir in catsup and Worcestershire. Add shrimp. Heat well. Season with salt, paprika and cayenne.

3. Just before serving, stir in sherry.

4. Serve on toast points or on rice or grits, as desired.

Mrs. Louis B. Eten, Thursday Morning Club, Madison, N.J.

SHRIMP DE JONGHE

Serves 8

2 quarts plus 1 cup water
2 tablespoons salt
4 pounds fresh or frozen shrimp
1 cup butter
2 cloves garlic, minced
⅔ cup chopped parsley
½ teaspoon paprika
Dash of cayenne
½ cup sweet sherry
2 cups fresh bread crumbs

1. Preheat oven to 325° F. Grease 11 x 7 x 1½-inch baking pan.
2. In large saucepan bring water and salt to boil. Add shrimp; cover. Bring back to boil; then simmer gently for about 10 minutes, or until shrimp turn pink. Drain. Cool in cold water.
3. Shell and devein shrimp. Turn into baking pan.
4. Melt butter in saucepan. Remove from heat. Stir in garlic, half the parsley, paprika, cayenne and sherry. Add crumbs; toss lightly. Spoon crumb mixture over shrimp.
5. Bake in preheated oven for 20 to 25 minutes, or until browned. Sprinkle with remaining parsley before serving.

Betty Lee Smith, Woman's Club, Canterbury, N.H.

ADLAI'S DELIGHT SHRIMP CASSEROLE

Serves 3

2½ cups artichoke hearts
¾ pound shrimp, shelled, deveined and cooked
2 tablespoon butter
¼ pound mushrooms, sliced
1 tablespoon Worcestershire
¼ cup dry sherry
1½ cups medium Cream Sauce (p. 441)
¼ cup grated Parmesan cheese
Paprika
Parsley

1. Preheat oven to 375° F. Grease 1½-quart casserole.
2. Arrange artichokes in casserole. Spread shrimp on them.
3. Melt butter in skillet; sauté mushrooms for 6 minutes. Add to casserole.
4. Combine Worcestershire, sherry and medium Cream Sauce. Pour into casserole. Sprinkle with cheese and paprika.
5. Bake in preheated oven for 30 to 40 minutes.
6. Garnish with parsley before serving.

Mrs. James Humphrey, Juniors, Saratoga, Fla.

SHRIMP CHOW MEIN

Serves 6 to 8

¼ cup cooking oil
1 cup sliced celery
1 cup chopped green pepper
1 cup chopped onions
2 teaspoons cornstarch
¾ cup water
10½-ounce can condensed cream of mushroom soup
¼ cup soy sauce
2 pounds shrimp, shelled, deveined and cooked
5-ounce can water chestnuts, drained and sliced
1-pound can bean sprouts, drained
4-ounce can sliced mushrooms, drained
Chinese noodles

1. Heat oil in large skillet; sauté celery, green pepper and onions for 3 minutes.
2. In small bowl blend cornstarch and water; stir into vegetables.

3. Stir in soup and soy sauce. Cook over low heat, stirring constantly, until thickened and smooth.
4. Stir in shrimp, water chestnuts, bean sprouts and mushrooms. Heat to serving temperature, stirring occasionally.
5. Serve on Chinese noodles.

Ellen Roisman, Junior Woman's Club, Simsbury, Conn.

SHRIMP FIESTA

Serves 6

2 tablespoons butter or margarine
¼ cup chopped onion
3 tablespoons chopped green pepper
10½-ounce can condensed cream of mushroom soup
¼ cup milk
1 pound shrimp, shelled, deveined, cooked and chopped
½ cup chopped pimientos
1 teaspoon Worcestershire
Basic Baking Powder Biscuits dough (p. 119)
½ cup grated Cheddar cheese

1. Preheat oven to 400° F. Grease 2-quart casserole.
2. Melt butter or margarine in skillet; sauté onion and green pepper until tender. Stir in soup, milk, shrimp, 2 tablespoons of the pimientos and Worcestershire; mix well. Turn into casserole.
3. Roll out Basic Baking Powder Biscuits dough on lightly floured board to 12 x 7-inch rectangle. Sprinkle with remaining pimientos and cheese. Roll up like a jelly roll, starting from 12-inch side. Cut into 1-inch slices. Place on mixture in casserole.
4. Bake in preheated oven for 25 minutes.

Mrs. George Merrill, Junior Women's Club, Kennewick, Wash.

SHRIMP TETRAZZINI

Serves 4

2 tablespoons butter
½ pound mushrooms, sliced
½ pound spaghetti, cooked
1 pound shrimp, shelled, deveined and cooked
2 10½-ounce cans condensed cream of mushroom soup
½ cup light cream
2 tablespoons sherry
⅓ cup grated Parmesan cheese

1. Preheat oven to 375° F. Grease 1½-quart casserole.
2. Melt butter in saucepan; sauté mushrooms for 5 minutes. Add spaghetti, shrimp, soup, cream and sherry. Turn into casserole. Sprinkle with cheese.
3. Bake in preheated oven for 25 minutes. If necessary, place under broiler for a few moments to brown top.

Eleanor Stroner, Woman's Club, Crystal Lake, Ill.

SHRIMP THERMIDOR

Serves 6

1 pound shrimp, shelled, deveined and cooked

½ cup butter
½ cup sliced mushrooms
¼ cup presifted flour
1 teaspoon salt
½ teaspoon dry mustard
Dash of cayenne
2 cups milk
Grated Parmesan cheese
Paprika

1. Preheat oven to 400° F. Grease 6 individual baking shells or 6-ounce ramekins.
2. Cut shrimp in half lengthwise.
3. Melt butter in saucepan; sauté mushrooms for 5 minutes. Stir in flour, salt, mustard and cayenne. Gradually stir in milk. Cook, stirring constantly, until thickened and smooth. Stir in shrimp.
4. Divide into shells or ramekins. Sprinkle with cheese and paprika.
5. Bake in preheated oven for 10 minutes, or until cheese is browned.

Gulf Coast Gourmet, Woman's Club, Foley, Ala.

Mixed Seafood Dishes

ARTICHOKE AND SEAFOOD CASSEROLE

Serves 6

12 artichoke hearts, cooked
1 cup cooked rice
6½-ounce can lobster, flaked
6½-ounce can crab meat, flaked
10½-ounce can condensed cream of mushroom soup
⅓ cup dry sherry or dry vermouth
4 slices American cheese, cut into triangles
2 tablespoons chopped parsley
Paprika

1. Preheat oven to 375° F. Grease 2-quart casserole.
2. Arrange artichokes in casserole; top with rice, then with lobster and crab.
3. In medium bowl blend soup and wine until smooth. Pour over mixture in casserole; top with triangles of cheese. Sprinkle with parsley; dust with paprika.
4. Bake in preheated oven for 30 minutes.

Mary Schimpf, Woman's Club, Redwood City, Calif.

EASY DOWN EAST SEAFOOD CASSEROLE

Serves 6 to 8

Available substitutes may be used for the seafood in this recipe, with the exception of the fresh lobster.

3 medium lobsters, cooked and shelled
½ pound scallops, cooked
½ pound shrimp, shelled, deveined and cooked
1 tablespoon lemon juice
½ pound haddock or halibut, cooked

1 teaspoon salt
¼ teaspoon pepper
¼ teaspoon paprika
1 teaspoon dry mustard
2 teaspoons Worcestershire
2 tablespoons dry sherry
3 cups light cream
4-ounce can sliced mushrooms, drained
2 cups fresh bread crumbs
¼ cup melted butter

1. Preheat oven to 350° F. Grease 2½-quart casserole.
2. Cut lobster meat into bite-size pieces. Sprinkle lobster, scallops and shrimp with lemon juice.
3. In mixing bowl flake haddock or halibut; add seasonings and sherry; mix well. Stir in cream and mushrooms.
4. Combine crumbs and butter.
5. In casserole arrange alternate layers of lobster, scallops, shrimp, fish mixture and crumbs, finishing with layer of crumbs.
6. Bake in preheated oven for 30 minutes, or until bubbling.

Mrs. Elmer M. Sewall, Woman's Club, Orono, N.C.

SEAFOOD AND EGG CASSEROLE

Serves 6 to 8

3 eggs, hard-cooked and sliced
6½-ounce can tuna, drained
⅔ cup shrimp, shelled, deveined and cooked
1 cup crab meat, flaked
1 cup sliced mushrooms
1 cup diced Cheddar cheese
2 cups Medium White Sauce (p. 441)
1 cup fresh bread crumbs
¼ cup melted butter

1. Preheat oven to 350° F. Grease 2-quart casserole.
2. Arrange eggs in casserole. Top with tuna, shrimp, crab meat, mushrooms and cheese.
3. Pour Medium White Sauce over mixture.
4. Mix crumbs and butter together; sprinkle over sauce.
5. Bake in preheated oven for 35 minutes.

Margaret Meech, Masonic Service Association, Washington, D.C.

SEAFOOD-STUFFED EGGPLANT

Serves 4

2 medium eggplants
¼ cup butter or margarine
½ cup finely chopped onions
½ cup finely chopped celery
4 cloves garlic, crushed
2 hamburger buns, crumbled
2 eggs, lightly beaten
1 pound shrimp, shelled, deveined, cooked and chopped
½ pound crab meat, flaked
¼ cup chopped scallions
¼ cup chopped parsley
½ teaspoon salt
Dash of pepper
1 teaspoon Worcestershire

1. Preheat broiler. Line broiler pan with aluminum foil.

2. Cut eggplants in half lengthwise; scoop out centers, leaving ½-inch shell. Arrange halves, cut side up, on broiler pan. Broil for 10 minutes, or until tender. Reduce temperature to 350° F.

3. Arrange halves, cut side up, in 13 x 9½ x 2-inch baking pan; set aside.

4. Chop scooped-out eggplant pulp. Melt butter or margarine in large skillet. Add chopped eggplant, onions, celery and garlic. Sauté over medium heat for 10 minutes, stirring frequently.

5. Meanwhile, combine hamburger buns and eggs; set aside.

6. Stir eggplant mixture and remaining ingredients into bun mixture. Mix well. Pile into eggplant halves.

7. Bake in preheated oven for 20 minutes.

Mrs. Gus W. Dyer, Jr., Junior Wednesday Club, Danville, Va.

SHRIMP AND CRAB MEAT LOAF

Serves 6

1 pimiento, chopped
1 medium green pepper, chopped
¼ medium onion, minced
1 cup chopped celery
6½-ounce can crab meat, flaked
5¾-ounce can shrimp, drained
½ teaspoon salt
⅛ teaspoon pepper
1 teaspoon Worcestershire
1 cup mayonnaise
1 cup buttered bread crumbs

1. Preheat oven to 350° F.

2. Combine all ingredients except crumbs.

3. Turn into loaf pan or six individual baking shells or ramekins. Sprinkle with crumbs.

4. Bake in preheated oven for 30 minutes for loaf; 15 to 20 minutes for individual shells or ramekins.

Margaret E. Hodgdon, Women's Club, Dedham, Mass.

SHELLFISH DELIGHT

Serves 6

¾ cup butter
¾ cup presifted flour
3 cups hot milk
10 ounces Swiss cheese
¼ teaspoon garlic powder
3 teaspoons salt
½ teaspoon monosodium glutamate
¼ teaspoon dry mustard
2 teaspoons tomato paste
2 teaspoons lemon juice
½ pound scallops
½ cup water or white wine
1 pound shrimp, shelled and deveined
2 tablespoons butter
½ pound mushrooms, sliced
2 tablespoons chopped green pepper
½ teaspoon nutmeg
Cooked rice or noodles

1. Melt ¾ cup butter in saucepan. Stir in flour; cook, stirring, until smooth. Add milk; cook over moderate heat, beating vigorously, until sauce is thickened and smooth. Add cheese, garlic powder, salt, monosodium glutamate, mustard, tomato paste and lemon juice; cook, stirring, until cheese is melted.

2. Poach scallops in water or wine for 7 minutes. Drain; reserve ½ cup broth.

3. Poach shrimp in water to cover for 7 minutes. Drain.

4. Add scallops, reserved broth and shrimp to sauce.

5. Melt 2 tablespoons butter in skillet; sauté mushrooms and green pepper for 5 minutes, or until tender. Add to sauce. Stir in nutmeg. Heat.

6. Serve on rice or noodles.

Mrs. Toni Vogelaar, Juniors, Saratoga, Fla.

Frogs' Legs

Ready-to-cook frogs' legs, either fresh or frozen, are available in most localities. They come in a variety of sizes, but the small ones are preferred by lovers of this delicate-fleshed amphibian. Count on about 6 small legs per serving.

FROGS' LEGS SAUTÉS

Frogs' legs
Milk
Flour
Butter
Olive oil (optional)
Salt and pepper to taste
Lemon wedges

1. Soak frogs' legs in milk to cover for about 1 hour.

2. Dry well on absorbent paper; then roll in flour.

3. Melt enough butter mixed with oil, if desired, to cover bottom of skillet. Sauté frogs' legs very quickly until lightly browned on one side. Turn carefully with spatula; sauté until browned on other side.

4. Season with salt and pepper. Serve with lemon wedges.

A. S.

FROGS' LEGS PROVENÇALE

Cook frogs' legs as in preceding recipe; keep warm. For each serving, put 2 tablespoons butter; 1 clove garlic, minced; and 1 tablespoon chopped parsley in pan. Swirl pan over heat until butter foams. Pour over frogs' legs.

Snails

Almost all the snails prepared and eaten in this country come from a can. When you buy the can, a bag of shells comes with it so that the snails may be served in the traditional way, which is:

SNAILS BOURGUIGNONNE
Serves 4

1 cup butter
3 cloves garlic, minced
½ cup minced parsley
½ teaspoon salt
Freshly ground black pepper
24 canned snails
24 snail shells
Hot French bread

1. Prepare snail butter: Cream butter thoroughly. Work garlic, parsley, salt and pepper into butter.
2. Put a dab of snail butter in each shell. Put a snail in each shell; pack entrance of shell with more snail butter.
3. Arrange snails on baking sheet or in individual snail pans. Let stand at room temperature for about 1 hour.
4. Preheat oven to 450° F.
5. Bake in preheated oven for about 10 minutes, or until sizzling hot.
6. Serve with bread to dip in snail butter.

VARIATION: Cream butter with ¼ cup dry white wine before adding garlic, parsley, salt and pepper.

A. S.

Terrapin and Turtle

Both the small Southern terrapin and the larger snapping or soft-shell turtles are considered great delicacies and are relished by gourmets throughout the country.

HOW TO PREPARE DIAMOND-BACK TERRAPIN

1 terrapin
1 small carrot, sliced
1 small onion, sliced
1 stalk celery, quartered
1 teaspoon salt

1. Bring large saucepan of water to boil. Plunge terrapin into water; boil for 5 minutes. Drain terrapin. Remove skin by rubbing with towel. Draw out head with skewer to get skin from neck.
2. Cut under shell; remove upper shell; then carefully remove and discard gallbladder, sand bag and thick heavy intestines.
3. Liver, small intestines and eggs are used with meat; put these back in pan; cover with boiling water. Add remaining ingredients. Cover; simmer for 30 to 40 minutes, or until meat is tender.
4. Remove meat from stock; use as desired or in recipe below for Terrapin à la Maryland. Strain stock; use to make soup.

Hazel Madsen, President, Woman's Club,
St. Mary's County, Md.

TERRAPIN À LA MARYLAND
Serves 3 or 4

Prepared terrapin meat (opposite)
1 tablespoon butter
1 tablespoon flour
½ cup light cream
2 egg yolks
1 teaspoon lemon juice
1 tablespoon dry sherry
1 egg, hard-cooked and sliced
Lemon wedges
Parsley sprigs

1. Cut terrapin meat into small pieces. Chop liver and small intestines; mix with terrapin eggs and terrapin meat.
2. Melt butter in saucepan; stir in flour. Gradually stir in cream. Cook over low heat, stirring constantly, until sauce is thickened and smooth.
3. Beat egg yolks in small bowl; stir in a little sauce. Return to rest of sauce. Cook over low heat, stirring constantly, until mixture begins to simmer. Stir in terrapin mixture, lemon juice and sherry. Heat to serving temperature.
4. Pour into serving dish, or use terrapin shell.
5. Garnish with egg slices, lemon wedges and parsley sprigs.

Hazel Madsen, President, Woman's Club,
St. Mary's County, Md.

TURTLE WITH SAUCE PIQUANT
Serves 6 to 8

⅓ cup olive oil
⅓ cup presifted flour
1-pound can tomatoes
8-ounce can tomato sauce
3 cloves garlic, minced
1 large onion, chopped
1 cup chopped celery
1 cup chopped green pepper
1 quart water
2 teaspoons Tabasco
2 bay leaves
Salt and pepper to taste
3 pounds turtle meat, diced
¼ cup chopped parsley
¼ cup chopped scallions
1 cup dry sherry

1. Heat oil in large heavy saucepan or Dutch oven. Add flour; stir over medium heat until browned. Stir in tomatoes, tomato sauce, garlic, onion, celery, green pepper and water. Bring to boil, stirring constantly. Add Tabasco, bay leaves, salt and pepper. Cover; simmer for 10 minutes.
2. Add turtle meat; cover; simmer until tender. Add parsley and scallions; simmer for 5 minutes.
3. Just before serving, remove from heat; stir in sherry.

Junior Woman's Club, Thibodaux, La.

9. Poultry and Game Birds

Poultry is available at all times of the year. It's always a good buy, and American homemakers love to cook and serve it. Cook books and recipes submitted by members of organizations affiliated with the General Federation of Women's Clubs clearly demonstrate that homemakers have contributed more imaginative touches to poultry dishes than to almost any other category of food, borrowing from Italy, China, Hawaii, Spain and other countries to create new and interesting dishes.

All About Chicken and Other Poultry

SELECTING POULRTY

Poultry is one of the most carefully controlled foods we eat. Every step in the processing, including water and equipment, is rigidly inspected by officials of the U.S. Department of Agriculture to ensure that birds are strictly fresh.

Whether you buy fresh poultry, drawn to order, ready-to-cook, or plastic wrapped poultry, fresh or frozen, look for the government inspection stamp on wing or wrapper. If it is not there, make sure that the wooden crate in which the birds were shipped to market carried the stamp of government approval.

HOW MUCH TO BUY

Count on ¾ pound of chicken per serving. You will need 2 1½-pound broiling chickens, split; a 3-pound frying chicken or 3 pounds of chicken parts to serve 4 persons with average appetites. If you have one or more potential football players in the family, you may have to allow considerably more.

HOW TO STORE

Store fresh chicken or chicken parts in the coldest part of the refrigerator, where it will keep for several days. If the bird is wrapped in plastic, slit the plastic at one end, and leave it in the wrapper. If it is wrapped in butcher paper, remove the paper, and wrap it loosely in aluminum foil or transparent film.

Keep frozen chicken at 0° F. until 24 hours before cooking. Slit the freezer wrapping to allow the bird to "breathe," and let it defrost in the refrigerator overnight. For rapid defrosting, unwrap the poultry, and soak it in cold water for about 2 hours for a chicken, longer for a capon or turkey.

TYPES OF CHICKENS

Roasting chicken is a tender chicken, about twelve weeks old, weighing from 3½ to 5 pounds.

Frying chicken is a tender young chicken weighing from 3 to 3½ pounds.

Broiling chicken is about nine weeks old, very tender, and ranges in weight from 1½ to 3½ pounds.

Stewing chicken or fowl is a mature bird, less tender than a roasting chicken.

Capon is a desexed male bird, weighing from 5 to 8 pounds. It is very tender with plump breasts.

TO DRAW A BIRD

All commercially produced poultry is sold oven-ready or ready to cook. The birds have been plucked, singed, drawn and thoroughly cleaned inside, and the giblets, cleaned and wrapped, are tucked inside the body cavity.

Should it ever be necessary to draw your own bird, however, here is how to do it:

1. Slit neck skin down center back to shoulders, and sever neck at this point. Remove neck; reserve for making stock.

2. Loosen crop, which is attached to skin near base of neck, and the windpipe and esophagus, which are attached to neck skin, by inserting fingers into neck opening and moving them around cavity as far down as possible. Pull crop, windpipe, and esophagus out as far as possible; cut off at a point where they enter body; discard.

3. Place bird on its back. Make incision in abdomen, starting 3 inches above vent. Continue incision toward tail, and encircle vent, cutting all around about ¾ inch from center of vent.

4. Remove viscera by inserting forefinger into opening and circling it around intestines. Hold carcass firmly with one hand, and insert other hand through opening. Lo-

cate gizzard near center of viscera. Grasp gizzard firmly, and draw entrails completely out of cavity.

5. Remove lungs, which are located in two sections, one on each side of backbone over ribs. This is important, since they contain blood.

6. Make sure heart has been removed. It is found just under wishbone.

7. Rinse out body cavity with cold water. Drain thoroughly, or wipe with damp cloth.

8. Detach heart, liver and gizzard from other entrails.

9. Discard heart sac; cut off blood vessels; wash heart to remove blood.

10. Cut gallbladder away from liver, being very careful not to break it, and discard any part of liver that might be stained green by contact with gallbladder. Should gallbladder break, you will have to discard not only the liver but also any part of chicken it might have touched.

11. Make slit in one side of gizzard, being careful not to cut inner sac. Force slit open with thumbs. Pull gizzard gently but firmly away from sac. Discard sac with intestines and remaining viscera.

12. Wash giblets in cold water. Drain well.

TO STUFF AND TRUSS A BIRD

1. Place bird on large square of aluminum foil.

2. Fill cavity loosely with stuffing, bearing in mind that the stuffing expands as bird cooks. Also, stuff cavity in neck, filling out V at breastbone. Fold surplus neck skin over filling and down back of bird.

3. Tuck wings close to body, and twist wing tips behind bird, over neck skin.

4. Sew opening, or close by means of small metal skewers with string, crisscross fashion.

5. Tie ends of legs together over opening in center with long piece of heavy string. Turn bird breast down. Bring string around tail, and tie securely. Bring each end of string up back of bird, around main joint of wing and over wing tips, tying securely at center back.

TO BONE A BIRD

If you have a really sharp knife or professional boning knife, which you may be able to buy from your butcher, it is a simple job to bone a bird, and the larger the bird, the easier it is to do.

1. Cut off wing tips and first wing joint of bird.

2. Slit skin of bird down back, and use knife to scrape away skin and flesh from both sides, revealing shoulder and thigh joints. Cut through these joints, and continue cutting away skin and flesh around and over breast.

3. Lift out and discard entire carcass.

4. Scrape away skin and flesh from wing bones; remove bones.

5. Scrape away skin and flesh from thigh bones, revealing knee joints. Cut through knee joints, and remove thigh bones.

6. Continue scraping flesh and skin away from leg bones, and remove leg bones. Bird is now boneless, with meat and skin intact.

TO BONE CHICKEN BREASTS

1. Split whole chicken breast down through center.

2. Place halves on flat surface, and pull off skin, which comes off quite easily

3. With sharp knife, make small incision between breastbone and meat, and use knife and fingers to scrape and pull meat carefully away from bones.

BONED CHICKEN BREASTS FRENCH STYLE

Ask butcher to leave main wing bones attached to breast. These are not removed when breastbone is cut away.

How to Carve a Bird

Place bird on platter; legs should be to carver's right. Insert carving fork in arc formed by breastbone, with tines straddling the backbone. With blunt edge of carving knife, pull thigh and leg away from body. With point of knife, cut through joint; place on auxiliary plate.

Cut through leg-thigh joint. Hold thigh with fork, and cut meat into thick slices. Hold leg with hand, and cut meat into long, thin slices.

Pull wing away from body of bird, and work knife through joint. The socket lies farther under the bird than the leg socket. Twist wing from body, and transfer to auxiliary plate.

Carve breast in slices about ⅛ inch thick —not too thick or paper-thin. Make first slice from top of breastbone over entire length of one side of breast.

Cut slices parallel to breastbone from

Timetable for Roasting Stuffed Poultry at 325° F.

Type of Bird	Ready-to-Cook Weight	Approximate Roasting Time
Chickens, capons or ducks	4 to 5 pounds	20 to 25 minutes per pound
Chickens	Over 5 pounds	35 to 40 minutes per pound, or 2½ hours
Turkeys or capons	6 to 10 pounds	20 to 25 minutes per pound
Turkeys	10 to 16 pounds	18 to 20 minutes per pound
Turkeys	18 to 25 pounds	15 to 18 minutes per pound
Geese—same as turkeys of similar weight		

top to bottom. Slices will increase in size, and angle of knife must change a little toward rear of bird with each slice. Each slice should have a layer of crisp brown skin on top. If possible, carve only one side, leaving other side intact for second helpings.

Chicken

Basic Methods of Cooking Chicken

ROAST CHICKEN WITH PAN GRAVY

Serves 6

    4- to 5-pound roasting chicken
    Rice and Mushroom Stuffing
      (p. 455)
    Melted fat or shortening
    Butter or margarine
    4 tablespoons flour
    3 cups stock made by simmering
      neck and giblets in water
    Salt and pepper to taste

1. Wipe chicken with damp cloth. Fill neck opening with stuffing. Fold skin of neck over back; hold in place with skewer or wooden pick; then fold wing tips flat against back. Finish stuffing chicken. Place skewers across opening; lace with string. Tie legs together; then fasten to tail.
2. Preheat oven to 325° F.
3. Place chicken, breast up, on rack in roasting pan. Brush with fat or shortening. Cover with cheesecloth soaked in fat or shortening.
4. Roast in preheated oven, basting with a little fat every half hour, for 3 to 3½ hours. Chicken is done when it is brown and drumstick meat feels soft. Place on serving platter. Remove string and skewers.
5. Put pan drippings in saucepan; add enough butter or margarine to total 4 tablespoons. Stir in flour; stir over low heat until thick and bubbling. Gradually stir in stock. Cook, stirring constantly, until thickened and smooth. Season with salt and pepper. Simmer for a few minutes.

Mrs. Stanley Thomson, Woman's Club, Anchorage, Alaska

ROAST CHICKEN IN FOIL WITH OYSTER CRACKER STUFFING

Serves 4 or 5

    5-pound roasting chicken
    1 cup water
    ½ cup chopped green pepper
    ½ cup chopped scallions
    2 cups soda cracker crumbs
    1 tablespoon chopped parsley
    2 cloves garlic, crushed
    1 teaspoon salt
    ¼ teaspoon pepper
    1 cup oysters, freshly shucked and
      drained
    ½ cup melted butter

1. In small saucepan boil giblets in water until tender; drain; reserve ½ cup

liquid. Chop giblets finely; put in mixing bowl.
2. Preheat oven to 350° F. Line roasting pan with large square of heavy aluminum foil.
3. Prepare Oyster Cracker Stuffing: Add green pepper, scallions, crumbs, parsley, garlic, salt, pepper and oysters to giblets. Toss lightly. Add reserved liquid and ¼ cup of the butter; mix well.
4. Loosely fill neck and body cavity of chicken with stuffing.
5. Place chicken on foil in pan; brush with remaining butter. Fold up foil to form package.
6. Roast in preheated oven for 2 hours. Open foil. Roast for 30 minutes longer, or until tender.

Mrs. Merlyn Castiglia, President, Dixie H. D. C., Long Beach, Miss.

ROAST WHOLE BONELESS CHICKEN WITH WILD RICE AND FOIE GRAS STUFFING AND SAUCE VERONICA

Serves 4

    2 2½-pound broiling chickens, boned
    Wild Rice and Foie Gras Stuffing
      (p. 456)
    ¼ cup melted butter
    Sauce Veronica (p. 451)

1. Preheat oven to 325° F.
2. Stuff chickens with Wild Rice and Foie Gras Stuffing. Sew or skewer opening. Place on rack in shallow roasting pan. Brush chickens generously with butter.
3. Roast in preheated oven, basting frequently with pan drippings, for 1¼ hours, or until tender.
4. Arrange chickens on serving dish. Coat with Sauce Veronica.

Mrs. Alan Grubbs, Junior Woman's Club, Spartansburg, Pa.

BROILED CHICKEN WESTERN STYLE

Serves 4

    ½ cup cooking oil
    ¾ cup white wine
    1 tablespoon lemon juice
    ½ teaspoon rosemary
    ½ teaspoon marjoram
    2½- to 3-pound broiling chicken, cut
      into serving pieces
    1 cup water
    Salt and pepper to taste

1. Day before or early in day, combine oil, wine, lemon juice and herbs. Put chicken in bowl. Pour wine mixture over chicken; cover; refrigerate.
2. Simmer neck and giblets in water until tender. Cool. Chop giblets; return to broth; cover; refrigerate.
3. About 45 minutes before serving, preheat broiler.
4. Arrange chicken, skin side down, in shallow pan. Season with salt and pepper. Pour wine mixture over chicken. Broil

slowly, turning and basting, for 30 to 45 minutes, or until well browned.

5. Make gravy, using giblets and broth.

*Mrs. J. Frank Honold, Thursday Morning Club,
Madison, N.J.*

BROILED CHICKEN CALYPSO

Serves 6

3 small broiling chickens, split
1 tablespoon sugar
1 teaspoon dry mustard
1 teaspoon ginger
½ cup pineapple juice
⅓ cup soy sauce
¼ cup lemon juice
Cooking oil

1. Day before, arrange chicken in shallow pan.

2. In bowl blend all remaining ingredients except oil. Pour over chicken. Marinate in refrigerator overnight or for several hours, turning chicken frequently.

3. Next day, drain chicken; reserve marinade.

4. Preheat broiler.

5. Arrange chicken on broiler pan; brush well with oil. Broil about 6 to 8 inches from heat for 30 minutes, or until tender, turning chicken frequently and basting with reserved marinade every few minutes.

Elizabeth Hallock, Home Club, Cromwell, Conn.

BUTTERMILK FRIED CHICKEN

Serves 4

3-pound frying chicken, cut into
    serving pieces
1 quart buttermilk
½ cup presifted flour
1 teaspoon salt
¼ teaspoon pepper
¼ teaspoon paprika
2 tablespoons butter or margarine
2 tablespoons olive oil

1. Arrange chicken in large container; cover with buttermilk. Let stand for 1 hour. Remove chicken from buttermilk; place on absorbent paper for 5 minutes, to allow buttermilk to dry slightly.

2. Combine flour and seasonings in paper bag; add chicken; shake well to coat.

3. Heat butter or margarine and oil in large skillet; brown chicken well on all sides.

4. Cover; simmer for 45 minutes, or until tender.

5. Remove cover; heat for 5 minutes, to allow chicken to become slightly crisp.

*Mrs. I. Wilbur Bays, Woman's Club,
Beckley, W. Va.*

GEORGIA FRIED CHICKEN WITH CREAM GRAVY

Serves 4

2 pounds shortening
1 cup presifted flour
2 teaspoons salt
⅛ teaspoon black pepper
1 teaspoon paprika

2 frying chickens, cut into serving
    pieces and chilled
2 tablespoons butter
1 cup milk
1 cup hot water
Cooked rice
Sliced tomatoes

1. Heat shortening in deep heavy frying pan to just below smoking point.

2. Combine flour, salt, pepper and paprika in paper bag. Add a few pieces of chicken at a time; shake well to coat. Reserve 4 tablespoons of remaining flour.

3. Place largest pieces of chicken in center of frying pan; surround with smaller pieces. When pan is full, reduce heat slightly. When chicken begins to brown on underside, cover for about 4 minutes. When brown on underside, turn (once only); cook until golden brown all over. Total cooking time is about 30 minutes.

4. Drain on absorbent paper.

5. Prepare gravy: Pour off all but 2 tablespoons of fat in pan. Remove from heat. Stir in butter and reserved flour. Cook, stirring, over low heat until slightly browned. Quickly add milk and water. Bring to rolling boil. Correct seasoning.

6. Serve with rice and tomatoes.

*Evelyn D. Adamson, New Century Club,
Wilmington, Del.*

DIXIE DEVILED CHICKEN

Serves 4

1 cup chili sauce
2 tablespoons cooking oil
2 eggs, lightly beaten
1½ teaspoons monosodium glutamate
½ teaspoon pepper
¼ teaspoon Tabasco
2 broiling chickens, skinned and
    cut into serving pieces
1 cup presifted flour
2 teaspoons salt
4 teaspoons paprika
½ teaspoon cayenne
2 teaspoons dry mustard
2 teaspoons garlic salt
4 tablespoons grated Parmesan
    cheese
Fat for deep frying

1. Beat chili sauce, oil, eggs, monosodium glutamate, pepper and Tabasco. Marinate chicken in sauce for several hours or overnight, turning occasionally. Remove from marinade. Drain on absorbent paper.

2. Combine all remaining ingredients except fat in paper bag. Put a few pieces of chicken at a time in bag; shake well to coat.

3. In deep skillet heat fat to a depth of 1 to 1½ inches. Lower chicken pieces into fat; cook for about 8 minutes on each side. Drain well on absorbent paper.

4. Serve immediately, or cool and wrap in aluminum foil to take on picnic.

*Mrs. Wiley Stanford, Jr., New Century Club,
Pine Apple, Ala.*

MISSOURI DEEP-FRIED CHICKEN
Serves 2 or 3

    1 egg yolk
    ½ cup milk
    ½ cup presifted flour
    2 teaspoons salt
    1 teaspoon paprika
    2- to 2½ pound frying chicken, cut
      into serving pieces
    1 cup soft bread crumbs
    Fat for deep frying

1. Combine egg yolk, milk, flour, salt and paprika. Dip chicken in egg mixture, then in crumbs. Place on rack to dry for a few minutes.

2. Fry a few pieces of chicken at a time, in deep fat heated to 365° F. for 10 to 15 minutes, or until golden brown and tender. Drain on absorbent paper. Keep warm in low oven until ready to serve.

Mrs. Jack Hinchey, Monday Study Club, Poplar Bluffs, Mo.

CHICKEN NEW ORLEANS
Serves 4

    1½ cups packaged pancake mix
    1 cup milk
    1 egg
    3-pound frying chicken, cut into
      serving pieces
    Fat for deep frying

1. Preheat oven to 350° F. Grease 11 x 7 x 1½-inch baking pan.

2. In mixing bowl blend pancake mix, milk and egg just until dry ingredients are moistened. Dip chicken in batter; coat completely.

3. Fry in deep fat heated to 365° F. for 5 minutes, or until golden. Remove from fat. Place in pan.

4. Bake in preheated oven for 40 minutes.

Lee Carl, Junior Woman's Club, Owensboro, Ky.

POULE AU POT
(Poached Chicken in the Pot)
Serves 6

    5-pound roasting chicken
    1 tablespoon salt
    ½ teaspoon peppercorns
    1 beef shin
    3 or 4 carrots
    2 turnips
    3 leeks
    Small bunch parsley
    ¼ teaspoon thyme
    1 bay leaf

1. Truss chicken; put in heavy kettle with water to barely cover. Add remaining ingredients. Bring to boil; then simmer for 15 minutes, skimming off sediment that rises to surface of liquid. Cover; cook over low heat for about 2 hours, or until very tender.

2. Strain liquid; serve as soup. Serve chicken with vegetables.

POULE AU POT HENRI IV: Poach chicken as above; keep hot in liquid. In small saucepan combine 1 tablespoon butter and 1 tablespoon flour. Strain 2 cups chicken liquid; add to saucepan. Cook, stirring constantly, until sauce is slightly thickened and smooth. Beat 1 egg yolk, ½ cup warm cream and juice of ½ lemon; add to sauce. Cook over low heat for 3 minutes, stirring constantly, but do not boil. Serve sauce in sauceboat with chicken and vegetables.

A. S.

Baked Chicken

BAKED CHICKEN
Serves 6

    2 2½-pound frying chickens, cut
      into serving pieces
    ½ cup butter
    1⅓ cups cornflake crumbs
    Salt, pepper and paprika to taste

1. Split each breast. Each chicken makes 6 good meaty pieces. Reserve necks and backs for use in cooking soup.

2. Preheat oven to 350° F.

3. Put butter in shallow casserole; place in oven to melt.

4. Wash chicken; pat dry. Roll each piece in butter; roll in crumbs. Arrange, skin side up, in casserole.

5. Season with salt, pepper and paprika. Bake, uncovered, in preheated oven for 50 minutes. It is not necessary to turn chicken.

Mrs. Doris Durden, Junior Woman's Club, Forest Park, Ga.

BUTTER-CRUSTED BAKED CHICKEN
Serves 8

    2 3½-pound frying chickens,
      quartered
    ½ cup butter or margarine
    ⅓ cup presifted flour
    1 teaspoon salt
    1 teaspoon paprika

1. Preheat oven to 425° F. Lightly grease 13 x 9½ x 2-inch baking pan.

2. Wipe chicken with damp cloth; place, skin side up, in pan.

3. In small bowl cream remaining ingredients until light and fluffy. Spread on skin side of chicken.

4. Bake in preheated oven for 20 minutes. Reduce temperature to 300° F. Bake for 1 hour longer.

Ethel D. Mixon, Culture Club, Hueytown, Ala.

CORN-CRISPED CHICKEN
Serves 4

    1½ cups cornflake crumbs
    1 teaspoon monosodium glutamate
    1 teaspoon salt
    ¼ teaspoon pepper
    2½-pound frying chicken, cut into
      serving pieces
    ½ cup evaporated milk

1. Preheat oven to 350° F. Line shallow baking pan with aluminum foil.

2. Combine crumbs and seasonings.

3. Dip chicken in milk; roll in crumbs. Place on foil in baking pan.

4. Bake in preheated oven for about 1 hour.

Mrs. Vincent DiGiorgio, Women's Club, Arvin, Calif.

SESAME BAKED CHICKEN

Serves 4

¼ cup sesame seeds
⅔ cup fine cracker crumbs
2½- to 3-pound frying chicken, cut into serving pieces
⅓ cup evaporated milk
½ cup melted margarine
Salt and pepper to taste

1. Preheat oven to 350° F.
2. Sprinkle sesame seeds in baking pan; bake in preheated oven for 10 minutes, stirring once or twice. Combine seeds and crumbs.
3. Dip chicken in milk; roll in crumb mixture. Arrange chicken in 11½ x 7⅜ x 1½-inch baking dish. Pour margarine over chicken. Season with salt and pepper.
4. Bake in preheated oven for 1½ hours.

Marie Anderson, Woman's Club, McFarland, Calif.

PARMESAN OVEN-FRIED CHICKEN

Serves 6

1 cup presifted flour
¼ teaspoon pepper
2 teaspoons salt
2 teaspoons paprika
2 eggs
3 tablespoons milk
⅓ cup fine bread crumbs
⅔ cup grated Parmesan cheese
6 to 8 pieces frying chicken
2 tablespoons fat or shortening

1. Preheat oven to 400° F.
2. Combine flour, pepper, salt and paprika.
3. Beat eggs and milk lightly.
4. Combine crumbs and cheese.
5. Coat chicken with flour mixture; dip in egg mixture; roll in crumb mixture. Let stand for 5 to 10 minutes.
6. Melt fat or shortening in shallow baking pan in preheated oven.
7. Place chicken, skin side down, in pan. Bake for 30 minutes. Turn. Bake for 30 minutes longer.

Mrs. E. H. Thach, Twentieth Century Club, Eudora, Ark.

OVEN-FRIED CHICKEN

Serves 4

2½- to 3-pound broiler-fryer, cut into serving pieces
½ cup presifted flour
1 teaspoon salt
⅓ teaspoon pepper
½ teaspoon poultry seasoning
½ cup melted butter or margarine

1. Preheat oven to 400° F.
2. Wipe chicken well with damp towel.

3. Combine flour and seasonings in paper bag. Put a few chicken pieces at a time in bag; shake to coat well.
4. Arrange in shallow roasting pan; brush with butter or margarine; cover with aluminum foil.
5. Bake in preheated oven for 30 minutes.
6. Remove foil. Increase temperature to 450° F. Bake for 15 to 20 minutes longer, or until golden brown.

Mrs. Retie Short, Sorosis Club, Salem, Ark.

SUNDAY CHICKEN

Serves 4

½ cup presifted flour
1½ teaspoons salt
1 teaspoon paprika
1 tablespoon dehydrated onion flakes
3-pound frying chicken, cut into serving pieces
2 tablespoons lemon juice
½ cup butter or margarine

1. Preheat oven to 325° F. Grease 10 x 6 x 1½-inch baking pan.
2. On piece of waxed paper mix flour, salt, paprika and onion flakes; use to coat chicken well. Arrange in pan. Sprinkle with lemon juice; dot with butter or margarine.
3. Cover pan with aluminum foil. Bake in preheated oven for 1 hour. Remove foil. Bake for 30 minutes longer, or until golden.

Mrs. Lillian Godwin, Woman's Club, Pine Level, N.C.

BAKED FROZEN CHICKEN

Serves 4

NOTE: Do not preheat oven!

1 package frozen chicken, defrosted and cut into serving pieces
2 10½-ounce cans condensed cream of chicken soup
2 teaspoons poultry seasoning
½ cup bread crumbs

1. Arrange chicken in 13 x 9½ x 2-inch baking pan.
2. Cover with soup; sprinkle with poultry seasoning. Sprinkle with crumbs.
3. Place pan in oven. Turn oven to 300° F. Bake for 1½ hours.

Mrs. B. D. Kaiser, Progress Club, South Bend, Ind.

BARBECUED CHICKEN

Serves 4

3 tablespoons catsup
2 tablespoons vinegar
1 tablespoon lemon juice
4 tablespoons water
3 tablespoons brown sugar
2 tablespoons Worcestershire
2 tablespoons butter
1 teaspoon salt
1 teaspoon dry mustard
1 teaspoon chili powder
1 teaspoon paprika
½ teaspoon red pepper (optional)
3-pound chicken, cut into serving pieces

1. In saucepan combine all ingredients except chicken. Heat, stirring, to simmering.

2. Preheat oven to 500° F.

3. Dip chicken in sauce; arrange in baking dish. Pour remaining sauce over chicken.

4. Cover; bake in preheated oven for 15 minutes. Reduce temperature to 350° F. Bake for 1 hour and 15 minutes longer. Do not disturb during baking.

Jeanne Pendrake, by Alice Summerville,
Arts Club, Aliceville, Ala.

SOUTH CAROLINA BARBECUED CHICKEN

Serves 4

3 tablespoons catsup
2 tablespoons vinegar
1 tablespoon lemon juice
2 tablespoons Worcestershire
2 tablespoons hot water
¼ teaspoon Tabasco
3-pound broiler-fryer, quartered
1 teaspoon salt
2 tablespoons melted butter

1. Preheat oven to 300° F. Grease 13 x 9½ x 2-inch baking pan.

2. Prepare barbecue sauce: In small bowl combine catsup, vinegar, lemon juice, Worcestershire, water and Tabasco.

3. Rub chicken with salt; brush with butter. Put chicken, skin side up, in pan. Cook under broiler for 5 minutes.

4. Turn chicken; top with half the sauce.

5. Bake in preheated oven for 1 hour. Turn chicken; top with remaining sauce. Bake for 1 hour longer.

Sara McColl, Woman's Club, McColl, S.C.

CALIFORNIA BAKED CHICKEN

Serves 4

3- to 4-pound frying chicken, cut into serving pieces
Salt and pepper to taste
1 envelope onion soup mix
3 slices bacon, diced
¼ cup water
¼ cup sherry

1. Preheat oven to 350° F.

2. Arrange chicken skin side up, in single layer, in shallow pan. Pieces should fit snugly.

3. Sprinkle with salt, pepper, onion soup mix and bacon. Add water and sherry.

4. Cover; bake in preheated oven for 30 minutes. Remove cover; bake for 30 minutes longer.

Mrs. Robert Bittourna, Junior Woman's Club,
Diamond Bar, Calif.

PARTY PERFECT GLAZED CHICKEN

Serves 6 to 8

6 slices bacon, diced
1 medium onion, finely chopped
½ cup presifted flour
1 tablespoon curry powder

1 tablespoon sugar
10½-ounce can condensed beef broth
2 tablespoons flaked coconut
2 tablespoons applesauce
2 tablespoons catsup
2 tablespoons lemon juice
1½ teaspoons salt
1 teaspoon ginger
2 3-pound broiling chickens, cut into serving pieces
½ cup melted butter or margarine
Cooked rice
Chutney (optional)

1. Preheat oven to 400° F. Grease 13 x 9½ x 2-inch baking pan.

2. Cook bacon in saucepan for 5 minutes. Add onion; sauté for 5 minutes, stirring frequently. Stir in 2 tablespoons of the flour, curry powder and sugar. Gradually add broth. Cook over low heat, stirring constantly, until glaze is thickened and smooth.

3. Stir in coconut, applesauce, catsup and lemon juice. Simmer, uncovered, for 15 minutes.

4. Meanwhile, on piece of waxed paper combine remaining flour, salt and ginger. Dredge chicken in flour mixture; dip in butter or margarine to coat completely. Arrange chicken, skin side up, in pan.

5. Bake in preheated oven for 20 minutes. Spoon half the glaze over chicken; bake for 20 minutes. Spoon remaining glaze over chicken; bake for 20 minutes longer.

6. Serve on bed of rice, with lemon cups filled with chutney, if desired.

Mrs. Carl Sanders, Junior Woman's Club,
Sylvester, Ga.

CHICKEN BAKED IN HONEY

Serves 4

¼ cup honey
¼ cup prepared mustard
1 tablespoon lemon juice
3 tablespoons melted butter or margarine
2½-pound broiling chicken, quartered
Salt and pepper to taste

1. Preheat oven to 350° F.

2. Combine honey, mustard and lemon juice.

3. Put butter or margarine in 9-inch square baking pan. Add chicken. Season with salt and pepper. Top with honey mixture.

4. Bake in preheated oven for 30 minutes. Turn; bake for 30 minutes longer.

Mrs. A. P. Webb, Jr., 20th Century Club,
Atmore, Ala.

OVEN LEMON CHICKEN

Serves 4

½ cup presifted flour
1½ teaspoons salt
2 teaspoons paprika
3-pound frying chicken, cut into serving pieces
⅓ cup butter or margarine
¼ cup lemon juice

1 tablespoon olive oil
2 tablespoons grated onion
1 small clove garlic, crushed
½ teaspoon pepper
½ teaspoon thyme

1. Preheat oven to 375° F.
2. On piece of waxed paper combine flour, 1 teaspoon of the salt and paprika. Coat chicken generously with flour mixture.
3. Melt butter or margarine in 10 x 6 x 1½-inch baking pan over low heat. Remove from heat; add chicken; coat with butter on all sides. Place chicken, skin side down, in a single layer in pan.
4. Bake in preheated oven for 30 minutes.
5. Meanwhile, in small bowl blend remaining salt and all remaining ingredients.
6. Turn chicken; pour lemon mixture over chicken. Bake for 30 minutes longer, or until brown.

Mrs. Raymond Faubion, Junior Woman's Club,
Fort Myers, Fla.

CHICKEN LEONE
Serves 6

½ cup chopped celery leaves
2 medium onions, finely chopped
2 tablespoons chopped parsley
1 teaspoon orégano
3 2½-pound broiling chickens, split
Salt and pepper to taste
2 oranges
1 cup dry white wine

1. Preheat oven to 400° F. Grease 13 x 9½ x 2-inch baking pan.
2. In pan combine celery leaves, onions and parsley. Sprinkle evenly with orégano. Arrange chicken, skin side up, in pan. Season with salt and pepper.
3. Cut oranges in half. Squeeze out juice; sprinkle over chicken. Place orange halves in pan. Sprinkle chicken with wine. Cover pan with aluminum foil.
4. Bake in preheated oven for 1 hour. Remove foil. Bake for 15 minutes longer. Discard orange halves.

Mrs. Mildred Walker, Woman's Club,
McLean, Va.

LITTLE RED CHICK
Serves 4

2½-pound broiling chicken, quartered
½ cup sliced onions
½ cup sliced green pepper
½ clove garlic, minced
1 bay leaf
2 sprigs parsley
½ teaspoon orégano
1¾ cups tomato purée
2 tablespoons brown sugar
2 tablespoons prepared mustard
1 teaspoon salt
¼ teaspoon pepper
¼ cup vinegar
1 tablespoon Worcestershire
¼ teaspoon cayenne

6-ounce can mushrooms
1 chicken bouillon cube

1. Preheat oven to 350° F.
2. Arrange chicken in casserole.
3. Combine all remaining ingredients except mushrooms and bouillon cube. Mix well. Pour evenly over chicken.
4. Bake, uncovered, in preheated oven for 1½ hours.
5. Drain liquid from mushrooms; bring to boil. Add bouillon cube; stir until dissolved. Add mushrooms. Pour over chicken.
6. Bake for 30 minutes longer.

Mrs. Alven Fossceco, Woman's Club, Rye, Colo.

CHICKEN BAKED IN SOUR CREAM
Serves 4

1 teaspoon garlic salt
1 teaspoon celery seed
1 cup sour cream
1 cup melted butter or margarine
3½-pound frying chicken, quartered
1 cup bread crumbs

1. Preheat oven to 325° F. Arrange 4 12-inch squares of aluminum foil on baking sheet.
2. In small bowl blend garlic salt, celery seed and sour cream.
3. Dip chicken in butter or margarine, then in sour cream; coat with crumbs.
4. Arrange each quarter in center of each piece of foil; sprinkle with remaining butter or margarine. Fold foil to form a sealed package.
5. Bake in preheated oven for 1 hour and 15 minutes. Open foil packages. Bake for 15 minutes longer, or until chicken is browned.

Mrs. Leon Adams, Glendale Estates Woman's
Club, Decatur, Ga.

CHICKEN TERIYAKI
Serves 4

⅔ cup soy sauce
¼ cup dry white wine
1 medium onion, sliced
½ cup sugar
½ teaspoon ginger
1 clove garlic, crushed
3½-pound frying chicken, cut into
bite-size pieces

1. Prepare Teriyaki Sauce: In bowl blend soy sauce, wine, onion, sugar, ginger and garlic.
2. Add chicken; marinate for at least 1 hour.
3. Preheat oven to 325° F. Grease 10 x 6 x 1½-inch baking pan.
4. Remove chicken from sauce; place in pan.
5. Bake in preheated oven for 1 hour, basting occasionally with sauce.

Mrs. Frank O'Hashi, Junior Women's Club,
Cheyenne, Wyo.

CHICKEN ALFRED

Serves 4

½ cup butter or margarine
2 2½-pound frying chickens, split
2 large onions, grated
1 pound mushrooms, sliced
2 tablespoons chopped parsley
1 cup sweet sherry
Salt and pepper to taste

1. Preheat broiler. Line broiler pan with aluminum foil.
2. Melt butter or margarine in large skillet. Arrange chicken on broiler pan; brush well with butter or margarine.
3. Broil chicken about 5 inches from heat for 8 minutes on each side.
4. Turn temperature to 350° F. Grease 11 x 7 x 1½-inch baking pan. Arrange chicken in pan; set aside.
5. Add onions to fat remaining in skillet; sauté over medium heat for 5 minutes. Add mushrooms; cover; simmer for 10 minutes.
6. Remove from heat. Stir in parsley and sherry; season with salt and pepper. Pour over chicken.
7. Bake in preheated oven for 40 minutes, basting frequently with sauce.

Edith Meeker, Woman's Club,
Redwood City, Calif.

BAKED CHICKEN BARBECUE

Serves 6

1 teaspoon salt
½ teaspoon pepper
1 tablespoon paprika
1 tablespoon sugar
½ clove garlic, minced, or
  ½ teaspoon garlic salt
1 cup catsup
1 medium onion, finely chopped
½ cup water
⅓ cup lemon juice or vinegar
1 tablespoon Worcestershire
¼ cup butter or margarine
5 pounds chicken parts
Seasoned flour
Fat for frying

1. Prepare Barbecue Sauce: In saucepan blend salt, pepper, paprika and sugar. Stir in garlic, catsup, onion, water, lemon juice or vinegar, Worcestershire and butter or margarine. Bring to boil. (Makes 2½ cups.)
2. Preheat oven to 325° F.
3. Coat chicken with seasoned flour.
4. In skillet heat enough fat to depth of at least ½ inch; brown chicken on all sides.
5. Arrange chicken, one layer deep, in shallow baking pan. Spoon Barbecue Sauce over chicken.
6. Bake in preheated oven for 45 to 60 minutes.

Mrs. Vincent Youngren, Woman's Club,
Hugoton, Kans.

DOROTHY'S EASY BAKED CHICKEN

Serves 4

2 tablespoons butter
1 tablespoon cooking oil
2½-pound frying chicken, cut
  into serving pieces
1 medium onion, finely chopped
8-ounce can tomato sauce
½ cup water
1 teaspoon salt
¼ teaspoon pepper
Dash of rosemary
1 bay leaf
Dash of orégano
¼ cup dry red wine
Cooked rice

1. Preheat oven to 300° F.
2. Heat butter and oil in large skillet; brown chicken on all sides. Arrange in roasting pan.
3. Prepare Tomato Sauce: In small bowl mix onion, tomato sauce, water, salt, pepper, rosemary, bay leaf and orégano.
4. Pour sauce over chicken. Bake in preheated oven for 1 hour. Add wine. Bake for 30 minutes longer.
5. Serve with rice.

Mrs. S. James Bessolo, President, Michigan State
Federation of Women's Clubs, Negaunee, Mich.

BAKED CHICKEN CACCIATORE

Serves 4

1 frying chicken, cut into pieces,
  or 4 to 6 chicken parts
Salt and paprika to taste
Flour
¼ cup olive oil
¼ cup chopped onion
1 or 2 cloves garlic, chopped
¼ cup chopped celery
1 teaspoon mixed dried herbs
1 cup tomato juice
2-ounce can chopped mushrooms,
  drained
Cooked rice
Grated Parmesan cheese

1. Season chicken with salt and paprika. Roll in flour.
2. Heat oil in skillet; sauté chicken until golden on all sides. Transfer to casserole.
3. Preheat oven to 325° F.
4. Sauté onion and garlic in oil remaining in skillet until onion is golden. Add celery, herbs and tomato juice. Bring to boil. Pour over chicken. Cover; bake in preheated oven for 1 hour.
5. Sprinkle with mushrooms. Bake for 5 minutes longer.
6. Serve with rice and cheese.

Mrs. Richard A. Queen, Junior Woman's Club,
Forest Park, Ga.

CHICKEN CHA-CHA-CHA

Serves 8 to 10

4-pound frying chicken, cut into
  serving pieces
1 tablespoon salt

½ teaspoon black pepper
¼ teaspoon cayenne
2 tablespoons olive oil
2 tablespoons bacon drippings
   or shortening
1 large onion, chopped
1 medium green pepper, chopped
1-pound can tomatoes
2 cups water
3 chicken bouillon cubes
4-ounce can mushroom stems
   and pieces
3 cups rice
¼ cup chopped parsley
1 clove garlic, crushed
¾ cup diced cooked ham
1 cup sweet white wine
¼ cup chopped scallions

1. Preheat oven to 375° F.
2. Season chicken with salt, pepper and cayenne.
3. Heat oil, bacon drippings or shortening in Dutch oven or large heavy ovenproof pan; brown a few pieces of chicken at a time well on all sides. Remove from pan; set aside.
4. Add onion and green pepper to fat remaining in pan; sauté for 5 minutes. Stir in tomatoes, water and bouillon cubes. Bring to boil; simmer for 10 minutes.
5. Stir in remaining ingredients. Return chicken to pan. Cover; bake in preheated oven for 1 hour. Reduce temperature to 350° F. Bake for 45 minutes longer.

Mrs. S. L. Wright II, Attakapas Study Club,
Crowley, La.

BAKED CHICKEN IN CURRANT SAUCE

Serves 6

4-pound roasting chicken, cut into
   serving pieces
6 tablespoons flour
¼ cup bacon drippings
2 cups chicken broth
2 tablespoons finely chopped green
   pepper
2 tablespoons grated orange rind
½ cup currant jelly
1½ teaspoons salt
¼ teaspoon pepper

1. Preheat oven to 300° F. Grease 3-quart casserole.
2. Dip chicken in water; then coat with 4 tablespoons of the flour.
3. Melt bacon drippings in large skillet; brown chicken well on all sides. Arrange in casserole.
4. Stir remaining flour into fat remaining in skillet. Gradually stir in broth. Cook over low heat, stirring constantly, until thickened and smooth. Add remaining ingredients. Cook for 5 minutes, stirring frequently. Pour over chicken.

5. Bake in preheated oven for 2 hours, basting occasionally with pan juices.

Marcia Lines, Junior Woman's Club,
Sunland, Calif.

BAKED CHICKEN EPICURE

Serves 4

2-pound frying chicken, cut into
   serving pieces
¼ cup presifted flour
½ cup shortening
2 medium onions, chopped
1 green pepper, chopped
1 clove garlic, minced
3 tomatoes, peeled and quartered
8-ounce can tomato purée
¾ cup beer
¼ teaspoon pepper
1 tablespoon paprika
2½ teaspoons salt
¼ teaspoon thyme

1. Preheat oven to 350° F.
2. Coat chicken with flour. Melt shortening in large skillet; brown chicken well on all sides. Arrange in 2-quart casserole.
3. Sauté onions, green pepper and garlic in fat remaining in skillet until lightly browned. Remove from heat. Add remaining ingredients; pour over chicken.
4. Cover tightly. Bake in preheated oven for at least 1 hour.

Martha Bradley, Woman's Club, Sunapee, N.H.

CHICKEN BAKED WITH ORANGE

Serves 4

⅓ cup presifted flour
1 teaspoon salt
¼ teaspoon pepper
3-pound frying chicken, cut into
   serving pieces
⅓ cup shortening
½ cup sliced onions
½ teaspoon celery seed
¾ cup orange juice
1 large orange, unpeeled

1. Preheat oven to 350° F. Grease 2-quart casserole.
2. On piece of waxed paper combine flour, salt and pepper. Dip chicken in flour mixture.
3. Melt shortening in large skillet; brown chicken on all sides. Arrange in casserole.
4. Sauté onions in fat remaining in skillet for 2 minutes. Stir in celery seed and orange juice. Bring to boil. Remove from heat.
5. Cut orange into slices; arrange on chicken. Pour orange juice mixture over orange slices and chicken.
6. Cover; bake in preheated oven for 1 hour.

Marylou Shuttleworth, Junior Woman's Club,
Glastonbury, Conn.

BAKED CHICKEN WITH SOUR CREAM WINE SAUCE

Serves 4

½ cup shortening
3½-pound chicken, cut into
    serving pieces
1 apple, finely chopped
⅓ cup minced celery
1 small onion, minced
1 tablespoon flour
1 cup sour cream
1 cup white wine or water
Salt and pepper to taste

1. Melt shortening in skillet; brown chicken on all sides. Arrange in casserole. Sprinkle with apple, celery and onion.
2. Preheat oven to 300° F.
3. Pour off all but 1 tablespoon shortening from skillet. Stir in flour. Gradually stir in sour cream and wine or water. Cook over low heat, stirring constantly, until slightly thickened. Season with salt and pepper. Pour over chicken.
4. Bake in preheated oven for 1½ hours.

NOTE: This recipe is also excellent if pheasant is substituted for chicken.

Nancy Bramhall, Anna Day Club, Troy, Mo.

CHICKEN SUPREME

Serves 8

1 cup presifted flour
1 teaspoon salt
¼ teaspoon pepper
1 teaspoon paprika
½ teaspoon dry mustard
2 frying chickens, cut into serving
    pieces
8 slices bacon, diced
1 medium onion, chopped
1 medium green pepper, chopped
2 10½-ounce cans condensed
    cream of chicken soup

1. Preheat oven to 350° F. Grease 2½-quart casserole.
2. In bowl combine flour, salt, pepper, paprika and mustard; coat chicken with flour mixture; set aside.
3. Cook bacon in large skillet until crisp. Drain on absorbent paper; crumble.
4. Brown chicken well on all sides in fat remaining in skillet; arrange in casserole. Sprinkle with bacon.
5. Add onion and green pepper to fat remaining in skillet; sauté for 5 minutes, scraping in all brown bits. Stir in soup. Bring to boil.
6. Pour soup mixture over chicken. Bake in preheated oven for 45 minutes.

Mrs. William J. Van Essen, President,
Woman's Club, Albuquerque, N.M.

COUNTRY CAPTAIN

Serves 4

3 tablespoons butter or margarine
2 2½-pound frying chickens, split
3 medium green peppers, chopped
3 large onions, chopped
2 cloves garlic, crushed
1-pound 4-ounce can tomatoes
1½ cups seedless raisins

1 teaspoon curry powder
1 teaspoon thyme
Salt and pepper to taste
½ cup finely chopped toasted
    almonds
Cooked rice

1. Preheat oven to 300° F. Grease roasting pan.
2. Melt butter or margarine in large skillet; brown chicken on both sides over medium heat.
3. Arrange in roasting pan.
4. Sauté green peppers, onions and garlic in fat remaining in skillet for 5 minutes. Stir in tomatoes, raisins, curry powder, thyme, salt and pepper. Bring to boil. Pour over chicken.
5. Cover. Bake in preheated oven for 3½ hours.
6. Just before serving, stir in almonds. Serve with rice.

Mrs. Carl P. Bernet, President, Town and
Country Garden Club, Greenwood, Miss.

COQ AU VIN

Serves 6

2 3-pound frying chickens, cut
    into serving pieces
Salt and pepper to taste
Flour
¾ cup butter
3 cups red wine
2 large onions, minced
1 clove garlic, minced
2 carrots, sliced
1 tablespoon chopped parsley
2 bay leaves
½ pound mushrooms, sliced
18 stuffed olives, sliced

1. Rub chicken with salt, pepper and flour. Melt ½ cup of the butter in large skillet; brown chicken well on all sides. Arrange in casserole.
2. Preheat oven to 350° F.
3. Add 2 tablespoons flour to fat remaining in skillet; cook, stirring in all brown bits from bottom and sides. Gradually stir in wine. Cook, stirring constantly, until slightly thickened and smooth. Add onions, garlic, carrots, parsley and bay leaves. Pour over cihcken. Cover; bake in preheated oven for 1 hour.
4. Meanwhile, melt remaining butter in clean skillet; sauté mushrooms for 5 minutes. Add with olives to casserole. Bake for 30 minutes longer.

Mrs. James Mitchell, III, Overlook Hills
Women's Club, Abington, Pa.

CHICKEN FILIPINO

Serves 4

⅓ cup soy sauce
2 tablespoons lemon juice
1 teaspoon poultry seasoning
1½ teaspoons salt
½ teaspoon pepper
1 teaspoon ginger
3-pound frying chicken, cut into
    serving pieces
Flour

¼ cup shortening
2 medium onions, sliced
1 cup boiling water

1. Combine soy sauce, lemon juice, poultry seasoning, salt, pepper and ginger in shallow pan; mix well. Add chicken; marinate for at least 30 minutes, turning occasionally.
2. Preheat oven to 350° F. Grease 2-quart casserole.
3. Remove chicken from marinade; roll in flour. Reserve marinade.
4. Melt shortening in large skillet; brown chicken well on all sides. Arrange in casserole.
5. Add onions to fat remaining in skillet; sauté over medium heat for 5 minutes. Stir in reserved marinade and water. Bring to boil. Pour over chicken.
6. Bake in preheated oven for 45 minutes.

Mrs. R. E. Charette, Junior Woman's Club,
Spartanburg, S.C.

CHICKEN MONTEREY WITH PECAN PILAF

Serves 8

¾ cup presifted flour
2 teaspoons seasoned salt
¾ teaspoon dry tarragon
2 3½-pound frying chickens, cut into serving pieces
6 tablespoons butter
1 pound mushrooms, sliced
3 cups chicken broth
1 chicken bouillon cube
1 tablespoon Curaçao
6 cups hot cooked rice
1 cup coarsely chopped pecans
Salt and pepper to taste
Mandarin orange segments
Cluster of seedless green grapes

1. Combine flour, 1 teaspoon of the seasoned salt and tarragon; use to coat chicken; let dry for a few minutes. Reserve flour mixture.
2. Melt 3 tablespoons of the butter in large skillet; sauté a few pieces of chicken at a time until golden on all sides. Arrange in baking pan.
3. Preheat oven to 325° F.
4. Add mushrooms to butter remaining in skillet; sauté for 5 minutes, or until lightly browned. Spoon over chicken.
5. Add remaining butter to skillet. Stir in ¼ cup of reserved flour mixture. Gradually stir in broth. Cook, stirring constantly, until sauce is thickened and smooth. Stir in bouillon cube and Curaçao. Pour over chicken. Cover tightly with aluminum foil. Bake in preheated oven for 1 hour.
6. Prepare Pecan Pilaf: Toss rice with pecans; season with salt and pepper.
7. Arrange chicken on bed of pilaf. Spoon a little sauce over all; serve remaining sauce separately. Garnish with orange segments and grapes.

Mrs. Charles Beattie, Juniors, Saratoga, Fla.

CHICKEN TCHAKHOKHBELLI
(in Paprika Sauce)

Serves 4

¼ pound butter
3-pound frying chicken, cut into serving pieces
1 large onion, sliced
½ cup tomato juice
½ cup sherry
1 teaspoon paprika
1 teaspoon salt
Pepper to taste
1 cup water

1. Preheat oven to 400° F.
2. Melt butter in skillet; brown chicken lightly on all sides. Arrange in shallow baking pan so each piece lies flat without overlapping.
3. Add onion to butter remaining in skillet; sauté until transparent but not browned. Add remaining ingredients. Bring to boil. Pour over chicken.
4. Bake in preheated oven for 30 minutes. Turn chicken. Bake for ½ hour longer.

Jayne Pulliam, Woman's Club,
Lemon Grove, Calif.

Braised Chicken

CHICKEN IN ALMOND-ORANGE SAUCE

Serves 4 to 6

¼ cup butter or margarine
2½-pound frying chicken, cut into serving pieces
2 tablespoons flour
⅛ teaspoon cinnamon
Dash of ginger
1 teaspoon salt
1½ cups orange juice
½ cup slivered almonds
½ cup seedless raisins
1 cup orange sections
4 cups cooked rice

1. Melt butter or margarine in large skillet; brown chicken well on all sides over medium heat. Remove chicken; set aside.
2. Stir flour, cinnamon, ginger and salt into fat remaining in skillet. Gradually stir in orange juice. Cook over low heat, stirring constantly, until thickened and smooth.
3. Return chicken to skillet; stir in almonds and raisins. Cover; simmer for 45 minutes.
4. Add orange sections; simmer for 2 minutes.
5. Serve chicken and sauce on rice.

Mrs. Louis Parsons, Junior Woman's Club,
Fort Myers, Fla.

CHICKEN CACCIATORE
Serves 8 to 10
½ cup cooking oil
3 2-pound frying chickens, cut
　　into serving pieces
1 cup minced green pepper
1½ cups minced onions
3 1-pound cans tomatoes
3 6-ounce cans tomato sauce
2 4-ounce cans mushroom pieces and
　　stems
1½ tablespoons salt
¾ teaspoon pepper
1½ bay leaves
⅜ teaspoon thyme
¾ teaspoon marjoram
½ teaspoon ground allspice
Cooked spaghetti

1. Heat oil in electric skillet or large
skillet; brown chicken evenly on all sides.
Remove chicken; set aside.
2. Sauté green pepper and onions in oil
remaining in skillet until onions are transparent. Add all remaining ingredients except spaghetti. Bring to simmer.
3. Meanwhile, remove bones from
chicken, leaving fairly large pieces of meat.
Return to sauce. Simmer, uncovered, for 30
to 40 minutes.
4. Serve with spaghetti.

Suzanne Inlow, Three Arts Club, Marion, Ala.

CEYLON CHICKEN
Serves 6
2 tablespoons butter
1 medium onion, finely chopped
2 green peppers, chopped
1 clove garlic
1 banana, sliced
3 slices pineapple, crushed
2 tablespoons flour
2 tablespoons curry powder
1 quart hot milk or coconut milk
½ cup Indian chutney
2 frying chickens, cut into serving
　　pieces
Salt and pepper to taste
Flour
1¼ cups shortening
Cooked rice

1. Melt butter in saucepan; sauté onion,
green peppers and garlic until onion is
transparent. Add banana and pineapple.
Stir in flour and curry powder; cook, stirring, for 3 minutes. Gradually stir in milk.
Cook, stirring constantly, until thickened.
Stir in chutney. Cook over low heat for 30
minutes.
2. Meanwhile, season chicken with salt
and pepper; roll in flour.
3. Melt shortening in skillet; brown
chicken on all sides.
4. Blend curry sauce in electric blender
or force through sieve until puréed; pour
over chicken. Cover; simmer for 30 minutes.
5. Serve with rice.

Mrs. A. E. Hancock, Women's Club,
San Bernardino, Calif.

CRANBERRY-BRAISED CHICKEN
Serves 6
¼ cup butter or margarine
4-pound frying chicken, cut into
　　serving pieces
¼ cup presifted flour
1½ teaspoons salt
1 cup burgundy
1-pound can whole cranberry sauce
Cooked rice

1. Melt butter or margarine in large
skillet; brown chicken well on all sides.
Remove chicken; set aside.
2. Stir flour into fat remaining in skillet;
stir in salt, burgundy and cranberry sauce.
Cook over medium heat, stirring constantly,
until sauce comes to boil and thickens.
3. Return chicken to skillet. Cover; simmer for 30 minutes.
4. Serve on rice.

Pat Rose, Ginter Park Junior Woman's Club,
Richmond, Va.

HAWAIIAN CHICKEN
Serves 4
¼ cup presifted flour
1 tablespoon salt
¼ teaspoon pepper
3½-pound frying chicken, cut into
　　serving pieces
2 tablespoons shortening
9-ounce can pineapple chunks
2 tablespoons brown sugar
2 tablespoons vinegar
¼ cup catsup
1 small onion, quartered
1 medium green pepper, seeded and
　　cut into 1-inch squares

1. Combine flour, salt and pepper in
paper bag. Add chicken; shake well to
coat.
2. Melt shortening in skillet; brown
chicken on all sides.
3. Drain syrup from pineapple into 2-
cup measure. Add enough water to total
1¼ cups. Stir in sugar, vinegar and catsup.
Pour over chicken. Add onion. Bring to
boil; cover; simmer for 1¼ hours.
4. Add green pepper and pineapple
chunks. Simmer for 5 minutes.

Jane Culbertson, El Camino Women's Club,
Ventura, Calif.

CHICKEN HONDURAS
Serves 4
¼ cup olive oil
2 cloves garlic
3½-pound frying chicken, cut into
　　serving pieces
2 large tomatoes, cut into thin
　　wedges
4-ounce can pimientos, drained
　　and sliced
2 tablespoons capers
12 stuffed olives, halved
½ teaspoon salt
½ teaspoon pepper
¼ cup tomato juice
Cooked rice

1. Heat oil in large skillet; sauté garlic until golden. Discard garlic. Add chicken; brown well on all sides.

2. Add all remaining ingredients except rice. Bring to boil; cover; simmer for 1 hour.

3. Serve with rice.

Arlene Williams, Progressive Home Club,
Fresno, Calif.

JAPANESE CHICKEN CASSEROLE
Serves 4

¼ cup presifted flour
1 teaspoon ginger
2½-pound frying chicken, cut into
   serving pieces
¼ cup butter or margarine
¼ cup soy sauce
½ cup water
2 tablespoons red wine vinegar
¼ cup brown sugar
1-pound 4-ounce can crushed
   pineapple, drained

1. Combine flour and ginger. Use to coat chicken.

2. Melt butter or margarine in electric skillet or large skillet until bubbling; brown chicken well on all sides. Drain off excess butter or margarine.

3. Blend soy sauce, water, vinegar and sugar. Pour over chicken. Top with pineapple. Cover; simmer for 50 minutes.

Ann Gardner, Woman's Club, Spencer, Wis.

CHICKEN MARGO
Serves 6

¾ cup olive oil
6 links pork sausage
3½-pound frying chicken cut into
   serving pieces
1¼ cups rice
2 cups chicken or beef broth, well
   salted
1 bay leaf
1 pound shrimp, shelled, deveined
   and cooked
½ teaspoon saffron
4-ounce can pimientos, drained and
   finely cut
Additional broth, if needed
10-ounce package frozen peas

1. Heat oil in heavy kettle; brown sausage. Drain on absorbent paper.

2. In oil remaining in kettle brown chicken well on all sides. Remove; keep warm.

3. Add rice to kettle; cook, stirring, for about 5 minutes. Add chicken and sausage. Add broth. Bring to boil; then simmer for 5 minutes.

4. Add bay leaf and shrimp; simmer for 5 minutes longer. Add saffron, pimientos and broth, if needed, to prevent rice from burning. Add peas; simmer for 5 minutes longer.

5. Cover; cook over low heat for about 30 minutes, or until chicken is tender.

Mrs. Charles Bloodworth, Monday Study Club,
Poplar Bluffs, Mo.

CHICKEN À LA MARYLAND
Serves 6

4-pound frying chicken, cut into
   serving pieces
Salt and pepper to taste
1 egg
2½ cups milk
1½ cups fine cracker crumbs
½ cup butter

1. Season chicken with salt and pepper.

2. Combine egg and ½ cup of the milk. Dip chicken in egg mixture; coat well with crumbs.

3. Melt butter in large skillet; brown chicken well on all sides.

4. Meanwhile, heat remaining milk to just below boiling point.

5. Add milk to browned chicken. Cover; simmer for 40 minutes.

Mrs. J. J. Pickford, Simi Valley Woman's Club,
Simi, Calif.

CHICKEN PAPRIKA
Serves 8

2 2½-pound quartered broiler-
   fryers
½ cup butter or margarine
1½ cups chopped onions
1 cup chicken broth
2 teaspoons salt
¼ teaspoon Tabasco
2 to 3 tablespoons paprika
¼ cup presifted flour
2 cups sour cream
Favorite dumplings

1. Wipe chicken with damp cloth.

2. Melt butter or margarine in large skillet; sauté onions until tender but not browned. Arrange chicken on onions; sauté for about 12 minutes. Turn chicken.

3. Stir in broth, salt and Tabasco. Cover; cook for about 25 minutes, or until chicken is tender. Place chicken on serving dish; cover; keep in warm place.

4. Stir paprika into liquid remaining in skillet. Blend flour and sour cream; slowly stir into skillet. Cook over low heat, stirring constantly, until sauce is thickened, but do not boil.

5. Pour sauce over chicken. Serve with dumplings.

Mrs. William S. Shary, President,
Second District Formers, New York State
Federation of Women's Clubs, and Formers
New York State Federation of Women's Clubs

CHICKEN AND RICE POLYNESIAN
Serves 8

¼ cup presifted flour
1 teaspoon garlic salt
1 teaspoon paprika
2 2½-pound frying chickens, cut
   into serving pieces
½ cup olive oil
1 cup finely chopped onions
1 clove garlic, crushed
½ cup finely chopped green pepper
1 teaspoon chili powder
2 cups rice
3½ cups chicken broth
1 teaspoon salt
½ teaspoon pepper

1. Preheat oven to 375° F. Grease 13 x 9½ x 2-inch baking pan.

2. Mix flour, garlic salt and paprika in paper bag. Add chicken; toss to coat thoroughly.

3. Heat oil in large skillet; brown chicken well on all sides. Transfer chicken to baking pan.

4. Add onions, garlic, green pepper and chili powder to oil remaining in skillet. Sauté over medium heat for 5 minutes, stirring frequently.

5. Stir in rice; sauté over medium heat for 5 minutes, stirring frequently. Add broth, salt and pepper; bring to boil. Pour over chicken; cover pan with aluminum foil.

6. Bake in preheated oven for 1 hour, or until chicken is tender and all liquid has been absorbed.

Mrs. Joe Tom Nelson, Junior Forum, Seymour, Tex.

CHICKEN SAUTÉ SEC

Serves 3 or 4

¼ cup presifted flour
1½ teaspoons salt
¼ teaspoon pepper
3-pound frying chicken, cut into serving pieces
¼ cup butter or margarine
2 shallots, finely chopped
2 tablespoons chopped parsley
½ teaspoon basil
¼ teaspoon thyme
½ cup dry white wine
4-ounce can sliced mushrooms, drained

1. Combine flour, salt and pepper in paper bag. Add chicken; shake to coat well.

2. Melt butter or margarine in large skillet; brown chicken well on all sides.

3. Sprinkle chicken with shallots, parsley, basil, thyme and wine. Cover; simmer for 30 minutes.

4. Add mushrooms; cover; simmer for 15 minutes longer.

Dorothy Geering, Woman's Club, Paramus, N.J.

SHERRIED CHICKEN

Serves 4

3-pound broiling chicken, cut into serving pieces
1½ teaspoons salt
¼ teaspoon pepper
¼ cup butter or margarine
1 cup chopped onions
1 cup chopped celery
2 tablespoons flour
1 teaspoon poultry seasoning
1½ cups water
½ cup sweet sherry
½ pound mushrooms, sliced
½ cup chopped parsley

1. Season chicken with salt and pepper. Melt butter in large skillet; sauté chicken until golden on all sides. Remove chicken; set aside.

2. Stir onions and celery to fat remaining in skillet; sauté for 5 minutes. Stir in flour and poultry seasoning. Gradually stir in water. Cook over low heat, stirring constantly, until thickened and smooth. Stir in sherry and mushrooms. Bring to boil.

3. Return chicken to skillet. Sprinkle with parsley. Cover; simmer for 1 hour.

Mrs. W. L. Rountree, Book Club, Tallulah, La.

POPPY SEED SMOTHERED CHICKEN

Serves 4

2 tablespoons butter or margarine
3-pound frying chicken, cut into serving pieces
2 tablespoons flour
1 cup sour cream
2 teaspoons seasoned salt
½ teaspoon pepper
2 tablespoons chopped parsley
1 tablespoon poppy seeds
2 cups water
1 tablespoon lemon juice

1. Melt butter or margarine in large skillet; brown chicken well on all sides. Remove chicken.

2. Stir flour into fat remaining in skillet; cook, stirring in all brown bits adhering to bottom and sides. Stir in all remaining ingredients except lemon juice. Bring to boil, stirring constantly.

3. Return chicken to skillet; cover; simmer for 45 minutes.

4. Just before serving, stir in lemon juice.

Mrs. Vernon Beloat, Woman's Club, Buckeye, Ariz.

GRACE MOORE'S SPANISH CHICKEN

Serves 4

2 frying chickens, cut into serving pieces
Salt and pepper to taste
6 tablespoons butter
1 onion, finely chopped
2 cloves garlic, minced
8 canned pimientos, rubbed through sieve
4 tablespoons flour

1. Sprinkle chicken lightly with salt and pepper.

2. Melt 3 tablespoons of the butter in skillet; sauté chicken until golden brown on all sides.

3. Add onion, garlic and pimiento purée. Add boiling water just to cover chicken. Bring to boil; cover; cook over low heat for 30 minutes. Place chicken on serving dish.

4. Combine remaining butter and flour; gradually stir into liquid in pan. Cook, stirring, until thickened. Pour over chicken.

Mrs. H. G. Moore, Arts and Crafts Section, Woman's Club, Avenal, Calif.

CHICKEN TARRAGON

Serves 4

¼ cup presifted flour
2 teaspoons salt
½ teaspoon pepper
2 pounds chicken parts
¼ cup butter
1 cup chopped onions
1 tablespoon chopped fresh or 1
  teaspoon dried tarragon
½ cup dry white wine
½ cup chicken broth

1. Combine flour, salt and pepper in paper bag. Add chicken; shake to coat well.
2. Melt butter in heavy skillet; sauté chicken and onion until chicken is browned on all sides.
3. Add remaining ingredients. Bring to boil; cover; simmer for 1½ hours.

*Mrs. R. H. Parker, Thursday Morning Club,
Madison, N.J.*

CHICKEN WITH CURRIED TOMATO SAUCE

Serves 5

½ cup shortening
4-pound frying chicken, cut into
  serving pieces
½ cup presifted flour
1 quart water
2½ cups peeled and seeded tomatoes
½ cup sliced mushrooms
½ cup finely chopped onions
¼ teaspoon thyme
1½ teaspoons salt
1 clove garlic, crushed
1 cup green peas
½ cup chopped celery
1 teaspoon curry powder
  Cooked rice
  Slivered toasted almonds

1. Melt shortening in large skillet; brown chicken on all sides over medium heat. Remove chicken; set aside.
2. Add flour to fat remaining in skillet. Gradually stir in water. Cook over medium heat, stirring constantly, until thickened and smooth. Stir in tomatoes, mushrooms, onions, thyme, salt, garlic, peas, celery, curry powder and chicken. Bring to boil; cover; simmer for 40 minutes.
3. Serve with rice topped with almonds.

*Mrs. Cled Gregory, President, Jaycettes,
Grenada, Miss.*

CHICKEN VÉRONIQUE
(Chicken with Green Grapes)

Serves 8

2 2½-pound broiler-fryers,
  quartered
¼ cup cooking oil
¼ cup presifted flour
1 teaspoon salt
1¾ teaspoons rosemary leaves
½ teaspoon poultry seasoning
¼ teaspoon pepper
¼ teaspoon thyme leaves
1 clove garlic, crushed
1 bay leaf, crushed
1¼ cups chicken broth

½ cup Chablis
3 cups seedless green grapes, halved
  Water cress sprigs (optional)

1. Wipe chicken with damp towel.
2. Heat oil in large heavy skillet; brown a few pieces of chicken at a time on all sides. Remove chicken; set aside.
3. Remove skillet from heat; stir in flour, seasonings, broth, Chablis and 1 cup of the grapes. Bring just to boil, stirring constantly. Add chicken; cover; simmer for about 40 minutes, turning occasionally. With slotted spoon, remove grapes; discard.
4. Add remaining grapes; simmer for 5 minutes longer.
5. Arrange chicken on serving dish. Pour sauce over it. Garnish with water cress, if desired.

Junior Woman's Club, North Arlington, N.J.

VINTAGE CHICKEN

Serves 4

2 tablespoons flour
1 teaspoon garlic salt
¼ teaspoon pepper
½ teaspoon rosemary
3-pound frying chicken, cut into
  serving pieces
⅓ cup butter
¾ cup dry white wine
¼ cup chopped scallions
1 cup sliced mushrooms

1. One piece of waxed paper combine flour, garlic salt, pepper and rosemary. Use to dredge chicken.
2. Melt butter in large skillet; brown chicken well on all sides. Add wine; cover; simmer for 15 minutes.
3. Stir in scallions and mushrooms. Simmer for 15 minutes longer.

*Mrs. Ray W. Maring, Women's Club,
South Pasadena, Calif.*

Stewed Chicken

CHICKEN FRICASSEE

Serves 6

5-pound stewing chicken, cut up
1 onion, quartered
1 carrot
2 stalks celery
4 peppercorns
2 quarts boiling water
2 teaspoons salt
½ cup presifted flour
12 Basic Baking Powder Biscuits
  (p. 119)

1. Put chicken, skin side down, in large 5- to 6-quart kettle. Add onion, carrot, celery and peppercorns. Add water and 1 teaspoon of the salt. Cover tightly; bring to boil; then simmer for 2 to 3 hours. Let cool in stock.
2. Remove chicken from stock; take meat off bones of breast, second joints and drumsticks. (Reserve smaller pieces for creamed chicken.) Skim chicken fat from stock; reserve. Strain stock; reserve.

3. Melt chicken fat in 2-quart saucepan over low heat. Stir in flour and remaining salt. Cook until bubbling. Gradually stir in 1 quart of reserved stock. Cook over low heat, stirring constantly, until thickened and smooth. Add chicken meat; heat thoroughly.

4. Arrange Basic Baking Powder Biscuits on serving platter; pour fricassee over them. Or serve biscuits separately.

Emily Cassell, Junior Woman's Club,
Cathedral City, Calif.

OLD-FASHIONED CHICKEN STEW
Serves 6

1 large chicken, cut into serving
  pieces
1½ teaspoons salt
2 potatoes, diced
5 carrots, sliced
4 ounces noodles or macaroni,
  cooked and drained
Old-Fashioned Dumplings (p. 460)

1. Put chicken in large kettle with water just to cover. Add salt; bring to boil; then simmer for 1 hour.

2. Remove chicken. Add potatoes and carrots to liquid in kettle. Simmer for 15 minutes, or until tender.

3. Return chicken to stew. Add noodles or macaroni. Heat to serving temperature.

4. Serve in large soup plates. Place a few Old-Fashioned Dumplings in each serving.

Mrs. Del De Forest, Junior Woman's Club,
Diamond Bar, Calif.

POLLO IN UMIDO CON POLENTA
(Chicken Stew with Polenta)
Serves 6

4- to 4¼-pound roasting chicken,
  cut into serving pieces
2 tablespoons butter
2 tablespoons olive oil
1 cup sliced onions
2 cloves garlic, minced
2 teaspoons salt
¼ cup chopped parsley
1 teaspoon rosemary or basil
2-pound 3-ounce can Italian plum
  tomatoes, undrained
1 cup chicken broth
Polenta (p. 464)

1. Wash and dry chicken.

2. Heat butter and oil in 6-quart Dutch oven; sauté a few pieces of chicken at a time until golden brown on all sides. Remove chicken; set aside.

3. Add onions and garlic to fat remaining in Dutch oven; sauté for 5 minutes, or until golden. Return chicken to Dutch oven. Add all remaining ingredients except Polenta.

5. Cover; simmer for 1¾ hours, stirring occasionally.

6. Invert Polenta onto center of large platter. Spoon chicken and sauce around and over Polenta.

Mrs. Albert E. Ward, Vice-President,
Woman's Club, Etheridge, N.C.

EXCELLENT CHICKEN À LA KING
Serves 6

3½-pound stewing chicken
  Butter
1 large green pepper, finely chopped
½ cup presifted flour
2 6-ounce cans sliced mushrooms
2 egg yolks
½ cup heavy cream
4-ounce can pimientos, drained and
  chopped
4 eggs, hard-cooked and sliced
6 baked patty shells

1. Stew chicken in water just to cover until tender. Cool. Reserve 2 cups chicken stock and ½ cup chicken fat, adding butter if necessary to total ½ cup. Discard skin and bones; cut meat into bite-size pieces; set aside.

2. Melt chicken fat in large skillet; sauté green pepper for 10 minutes. Stir in flour. Gradually stir in reserved stock. Cook over low heat, stirring constantly, until sauce is thickened and smooth.

3. Drain mushrooms. Stir liquid into sauce.

4. Blend egg yolks and cream. Gradually stir into sauce, but do not boil.

5. Add chicken, mushrooms, pimientos and eggs. Cook over very low heat until thoroughly hot.

6. Serve in patty shells.

Mrs. Frank Boone, Woman's Club, Hinton, W.Va.

CHICKEN PIE
Serves 8

4- to 5-pound chicken, poached
½ cup butter or margarine
½ cup presifted flour
1 cup milk
2 cups chicken broth
1½ teaspoons salt
½ teaspoon pepper
1 tablespoon Worcestershire
Pastry for a 1-Crust Pie (p. 548)

1. Preheat oven to 450° F. Lightly grease 1½-quart casserole or deep pie plate.

2. Remove chicken from bones; dice. Turn into casserole or pie plate.

3. Melt butter or margarine in large saucepan. Stir in flour. Gradually stir in milk and broth. Cook over low heat, stirring constantly, until sauce is thickened and smooth. Stir in salt, pepper and Worcestershire; correct seasoning. Pour sauce over chicken.

4. Top with Pastry for a 1-Crust Pie; make 2 slits in top to allow steam to escape.

5. Bake in preheated oven for 40 minutes.

Mrs. C. Mann, 20th Century Study Club,
Alexander City, Ala.

GRANDMOTHER'S CHICKEN PIE
Serves 6 to 8

3½- to 4-pound chicken, cut up
1 onion sliced
2 stalks celery, chopped

1 clove garlic, minced
2 sprigs parsley
  Salt and pepper to taste
  Flour
  Basic Baking Powder Biscuits
  dough (p. 119)

1. Put chicken, onion, celery, garlic and parsley in saucepan. Add water just to cover; bring to boil; cover; simmer for about 1½ hours, or until very tender. Season with salt and pepper.

2. Remove chicken; discard bones and excess fat; cut meat into large pieces.

3. Strain broth; measure. Mix 1 tablespoon flour for each cup of broth and a little water to a paste. Return broth to heat; thicken with paste.

4. Arrange chicken in baking pan; top with broth.

5. Preheat oven to 350° F.

6. Roll out Basic Baking Powder Biscuits dough ¼ inch thick; cut with floured biscuit cutter. Arrange on chicken. Bake in preheated oven for 15 to 20 minutes.

Mrs. Cora C. Moore, Mother's Study Club,
Weatherford, Okla.

BRUNSWICK STEW

Serves 6

4- to 5-pound chicken, cut up
  Salt and pepper to taste
3 tablespoons bacon drippings
2 cups water
1-pound 13-ounce can tomatoes
½ cup white wine
3 medium onions, sliced
½ teaspoon sugar
10-ounce package frozen Lima beans
12-ounce can whole-kernel corn
1 cup toasted bread crumbs
½ teaspoon salt
  Dash of pepper
  Dash of cayenne

1. Sprinkle chicken with salt and pepper.

2. Heat bacon drippings in heavy Dutch oven or cast-iron skillet; brown chicken on all sides.

3. Add water, tomatoes, wine, onions and sugar. Stir well. Bring to boil; cover; cook over low heat for 1½ to 2 hours.

4. Remove chicken; discard bones. Return chicken to sauce.

5. Add Lima beans and corn. Cook for 30 minutes longer, or until beans are tender. Add remaining ingredients.

6. Serve in individual casseroles or soup plates.

Mrs. Harry J. Keener, Woman's Civic Club,
Visalia, Calif.

ALABAMA BRUNSWICK STEW

Makes 5 to 6 Quarts

1 small stewing chicken, quartered
1 pound boneless chuck
1 pound onions
3 pounds potatoes
2 1-pound 13-ounce cans tomatoes

2 1-pound cans cream-style corn
1-pound can peas, drained
1-pound can Lima beans, drained
3 cups catsup
½ cup Worcestershire
½ cup vinegar
¾ cup lemon juice
1 tablespoon Tabasco
2 tablespoons salt
½ teaspoon black pepper

1. Put chicken and chuck in Dutch oven or large heavy saucepan. Cover with water. Bring to boil; cover; simmer for about 2 hours. Strain; reserve liquid. Remove chicken from bones.

2. Put chicken and meat through medium blade of meat grinder. Set aside.

3. Put onions and potatoes through medium blade of meat grinder; place in Dutch oven or saucepan. Stir in reserved liquid. Bring to boil; cover; simmer for about 15 minutes, or until vegetables are tender.

4. Stir in ground mixture and remaining ingredients. Cover; simmer for about 2 hours.

5. Serve immediately, or, if desired, cool, pour into containers and freeze.

Doris S. Dial, President, B.P.W., Fair Hope, Ala.

KENTUCKY BURGOO

Serves 12

Kentucky burgoo is a famous dish that is served to large crowds of people on Derby Day, at horse sales and at other large outdoor gatherings. The full recipe makes 1,200 gallons, but for convenience we have reduced this huge recipe to serve 12.

2-pound frying chicken
1 pound pork shank
1 pound beef shank
1 pound breast of lamb
1 pound veal shank
4 quarts water
1 cup chopped cabbage
1 medium green pepper, chopped
1-pound 13-ounce can tomatoes, drained
2 medium carrots, diced
2 potatoes, peeled and diced
2 medium onions, chopped
8-ounce can whole-kernel corn, drained
½ cup Lima beans
1 pod red pepper
  Salt and pepper to taste
¼ teaspoon cayenne
3 tablespoons Worcestershire

1. Put chicken and meats in large heavy saucepan. Add water. Bring to boil; cover; simmer for 2 hours.

2. Leave stock in pan; remove meats.

3. Discard bones, skin and gristle; dice meats; return to stock.

4. Add vegetables. Cover; simmer for 30 minutes, or until tender.

5. Season with salt and pepper. Stir in cayenne and Worcestershire. Simmer for 2 minutes.

Woman's Club, Newnan, Ga.

CHICKEN CHOP SUEY

Serves 10

5-pound stewing or 2 broiling chickens, cut up
2 quarts water
3 teaspoons salt
Celery tops
1 onion, sliced
1 pound boned pork shoulder, cut into ½-inch cubes
3 tablespoons butter
2 large onions
⅓ cup cornstarch
½ teaspoon paprika
2 cups bias-cut celery slices
1-pound 4-ounce can bean sprouts, drained
8-ounce can mixed Chinese vegetables, drained
5-ounce can water chestnuts, drained and sliced
6-ounce can mushrooms, drained
5-ounce can bamboo shoots, drained
¼ cups soy sauce
Cooked rice

1. Day before, poach chicken: Put chicken, with water, 2 teaspoons of the salt, celery tops and sliced onion in kettle. Bring to boil; cover; simmer for 1½ hours. Discard skin and bones; cut meat into medium pieces. Strain and cool broth. Refrigerate chicken in broth overnight.
2. Next day, melt butter in electric skillet or Dutch oven; brown pork well.
3. Meanwhile, to slice onions Chinese style, cut in half lengthwise; place cut surface on chopping board; cut lengthwise into thin slices. Add to pork; sauté until golden.
4. Remove chicken from broth. Mix cornstarch and ½ cup of the broth; add to pork. Stir in remaining broth, remaining salt and all remaining ingredients except soy sauce and rice; cook until celery is tender.
5. Add chicken and soy sauce. Heat.
6. Serve on rice.

Caroline Coffman, Three Arts Club, Marion, Ala.

CHICKEN ORIENTAL

Serves 6 to 8

5-pound stewing chicken, cut up
1 quart water
¾ cup butter
¾ cup presifted flour
Salt and pepper to taste
½ teaspoon monosodium glutamate
1 tablespoon soy sauce
¼ cup sweet white wine
1 cup sliced water chestnuts
½ cup chopped scallions
½ cup slivered blanched almonds
Chinese noodles

1. Put chicken and water in large saucepan. Bring to boil; cover; then simmer for 2½ hours.
2. Remove chicken; strain stock, adding water if necessary to total 4 cups; reserve.
3. Discard bones and skin; dice meat; set aside.
4. Prepare Oriental Sauce: Melt butter in saucepan; stir in flour. Gradually add reserved stock; cook over low heat, stirring constantly, until thickened and smooth. Season with salt and pepper. Stir in monosodium glutamate, soy sauce, wine, water chestnuts and scallions. Cook over low heat, stirring frequently, for 5 minutes.
5. Stir in chicken and almonds. Heat to serving temperature.
6. Serve with Chinese noodles.

*Lorrayn Krempel, Woman's Club,
Prospect Heights, Ill.*

EIGHT-BOY CURRY

Serves 8

4-pound stewing chicken
2 teaspoons salt
¼ teaspoon peppercorns
¼ cup butter or margarine
3 small onions, chopped
½ pound mushrooms, sliced
½ cup presifted flour
2 tablespoons curry powder
2 cups light cream
½ cup slivered blanched almonds
½ cup diced green pepper
Cooked rice
Condiments: chutney, salted toasted coconut, seedless raisins, chopped hard-cooked eggs, fried bananas and chopped onions

1. Day before, put chicken in Dutch oven or large saucepan. Add water just to cover. Add salt and peppercorns. Cover; simmer for 2½ hours. Cool chicken in stock.
2. Remove chicken; strain stock; reserve 3 cups.
3. Discard skin and bones; dice meat; set aside.
4. Melt butter or margarine in large skillet; sauté onions for 5 minutes. Stir in mushrooms; sauté for 5 minutes. Sprinkle in flour and curry powder; cook over low heat, stirring frequently, for 2 minutes. Gradually add reserved stock; cook over low heat, stirring constantly, until thickened and smooth. Stir in cream and chicken; simmer for 5 minutes.
5. Turn into large bowl; cover; refrigerate overnight. (This vastly improves flavor, although it is not essential.)
6. Next day, put curry in large saucepan; stir in almonds and green pepper. Simmer to serving temperature, stirring frequently.
7. Serve with rice and condiments.

Lois Davis, Women's Club, North Branford, Conn.

CHICKEN IN MILK

Serves 6

4 chicken breasts
5 chicken thighs
Salt and pepper to taste
Milk
Juice of 1½ lemons
Cooked rice

1. Sprinkle chicken with salt and pepper. Put in kettle. Add milk just to cover.
2. Bring slowly to boil. Add lemon juice; cover; simmer for 1 hour.
3. Serve with rice.

Margaret Zorraquinos, Woman's Club,
Temple City, Calif.

CREAM OF CHICKEN AND SWEETBREADS

Serves 10 to 12

4-pound chicken
2 pairs sweetbreads
1 tablespoon vinegar
8-ounce can whole mushrooms, drained
1 quart heavy cream
¼ cup butter
5 tablespoons flour
Freshly ground black pepper
Cayenne
Salt to taste
Buttered bread crumbs

1. Poach chicken in lightly salted water, to cover for 1½ hours, or until tender. Cool. Discard skin and bones; cut meat into small pieces.
2. Soak sweetbreads in salted water and vinegar for 1 hour. Drain. Cover with fresh water; simmer for 20 minutes, or until tender. Cool; cut into small pieces. Mix with chicken.
3. Cut each mushroom into 2 or 3 pieces. Mix with chicken and sweetbreads.
4. Preheat oven to 375° F. Grease 3-quart casserole.
5. Heat cream to simmering. Combine butter and flour to a smooth paste; gradually stir into cream. Cook, stirring constantly, until thickened and smooth. Pour over chicken mixture. Mix thoroughly; season very well with pepper and sufficient cayenne to bring out flavor. Add salt.
6. Pour chicken mixture into casserole; sprinkle with crumbs. Bake in preheated oven for 30 minutes.

Louise M. Graeber, Woman's Club, Eustis, Fla.

POT CHICKEN IN CASSEROLE

Serves 6

3-pound frying chicken, cut up
2 cups water
2 teaspoons salt
1 sprig celery top
1 slice lemon
1 bay leaf
1 tablespoon butter or margarine
1 small onion, chopped
1 cup chopped celery
10½-ounce can condensed cream of mushroom soup
1 tablespoon soy sauce

⅛ teaspoon Tabasco
½ cup chopped cashew nuts
2 3-ounce packages Chinese noodles

1. Put chicken, water, salt, celery top, lemon slice and bay leaf in large saucepan. Cover; bring to boil; then simmer for 1 hour. Cool chicken in broth.
2. Drain broth; reserve 1 cup. Discard chicken skin and bones; cut meat into large pieces; set aside.
3. Preheat oven to 350° F. Grease 2-quart casserole.
4. Melt butter or margarine in skillet; sauté onion and celery for 5 minutes. Stir in soup, reserved broth, soy sauce and Tabasco.
5. Remove from heat; stir in chicken and nuts. Turn into casserole. Bake in preheated oven for 30 minutes.
6. Serve on Chinese noodles.

Mrs. P. F. Haynes, Woman's Club,
Lakeworth, Fla.

SCALLOPED CHICKEN

Serves 12

5-pound chicken (reserve giblets)
1 carrot
1 onion, sliced
5 teaspoons salt
2 quarts boiling water
1½ loaves 2-day-old bread, trimmed
½ cup butter
6 sprigs parsley, chopped
6 scallions with tops, chopped
2 large stalks celery with tops, chopped
Dash of white pepper
1 teaspoon poultry seasoning
1 egg, lightly beaten
1 cup milk
1 cup flour
4 eggs, lightly beaten
1 cup bread crumbs
4 tablespoons melted butter

1. Poach chicken: Put chicken, carrot, onion, 2 teaspoons of the salt and water in large pot. Bring to boil; simmer for 2 to 2½ hours, or until meat begins to leave bones. Cool chicken in broth. When cool, remove chicken; take meat off bones. Remove skin; put through meat grinder, or cut finely with sharp knife. Strain broth; reserve.
2. Cook giblets in salted water until tender. Drain; chop.
3. Prepare stuffing: Crumble bread. Melt ½ cup butter in heavy skillet; cook parsley, scallions and celery over low heat for 5 minutes. Add to crumbled bread; mix lightly with fork. Add 1 teaspoon of the salt, pepper, poultry seasoning and giblets. Combine 1 egg and 6 tablespoons reserved broth. Add to stuffing; mix lightly.
4. Prepare sauce: Skim fat off remaining broth, adding butter, if necessary, to total 1 cup; heat in heavy saucepan. Heat 1 quart reserved broth and milk, but do not boil. Stir flour into fat. Gradually stir in broth mixture. Add remaining salt; cook, stirring constantly, until very thick. Com-

bine 4 eggs with a little hot sauce. (This is to keep eggs from curdling.) Add to rest of sauce; cook over low heat for 3 to 4 minutes longer, stirring constantly. Remove from heat. Stir in ground skin.

5. Preheat oven to 375° F. Grease 2 large casseroles.

6. Toss the crumbs in melted butter.

7. Put half the stuffing in each casserole. Pour half the sauce over each. Arrange chicken on top. Add remaining sauce. Top with crumbs.

8. Bake in preheated oven for 20 minutes, or until crumbs are golden brown and chicken is hot.

Fun and Fancy, Junior Round Table,
Placentia, Calif.

Chicken Breasts

KENTUCKY BAKED CHICKEN BREASTS

Serves 8

2 cups bread crumbs
¾ cup grated Parmesan or Romano cheese
¼ cup minced parsley
½ teaspoon white pepper
Salt to taste
½ teaspoon monosodium glutamate
4½ to 5 pounds chicken breasts, halved and boned
2 cups melted butter

1. Preheat oven to 325° F.

2. Combine crumbs, cheese, parsley and seasonings.

3. Dip chicken in butter; roll in crumb mixture until well coated. Arrange on baking sheet; spoon remaining butter over them.

4. Bake in preheated oven for 1½ hours, basting once or twice. Do not turn.

Mayme Mahon, President, Woman's Club,
Elmhurst, Ill.

CHICKEN BREASTS WITH POTATO STUFFING

Serves 8

¾ cup butter or margarine
1 large onion, finely chopped
1 cup finely chopped celery
4 cups mashed potatoes
2 eggs, lightly beaten
1 cup diced bread cubes
½ teaspoon poultry seasoning
½ cup chopped parsley
Salt
Pepper
4 chicken breasts, halved and boned
Paprika

1. Preheat oven to 375° F. Grease 13 x 9½ x 2-inch baking pan.

2. Prepare Potato Stuffing: Melt ½ cup of the butter or margarine in large skillet; sauté onion and celery for 5 minutes. Turn into mixing bowl. Add potatoes, eggs, bread, poultry seasoning, parsley, 1 teaspoon salt and ¼ teaspoon pepper; mix well. Spread in pan.

3. Arrange chicken, skin side up, on stuffing; dot with remaining butter or margarine. Sprinkle with salt, pepper and paprika.

4. Bake in preheated oven for 40 minutes.

Mrs. Henry Rabe, Woman's Club,
West Palm Beach, Fla.

CHICKEN BREASTS BAKED IN FOIL

Serves 1

1 chicken breast, halved
Salt and pepper to taste
½ cup diced potatoes
1 tablespoon chopped onion
2 tablespoons heavy cream
2 tablespoons dry sherry

1. Preheat oven to 350° F. Arrange square of aluminum foil on baking sheet.

2. Sprinkle chicken with salt and pepper; place on center of foil. Add potatoes; sprinkle with onion, cream and sherry. Fold foil to form sealed package.

3. Bake in preheated oven for 1 hour.

Dorothy Bassett, North Side Junior Woman's Club,
Atlanta, Ga.

CHICKEN BREASTS SUPREME GRILLED IN FOIL

Serves 4

Instead of being grilled over charcoal, these may be baked in preheated 350° F. oven for 1 hour.

½ cup presifted flour
1 teaspoon salt
⅛ teaspoon pepper
⅛ teaspoon nutmeg
4 chicken breasts, skinned and boned
1 egg, beaten with 1 tablespoon water
1 cup finely ground cashew nuts or walnuts
½ cup chopped chives
2 tablespoons chopped parsley
¼ cup melted butter or margarine

1. Prepare charcoal fire. Prepare 4 squares of heavy aluminum foil.

2. On piece of waxed paper combine flour, salt, pepper and nutmeg; use to coat chicken well. Dip in egg mixture; coat with nuts.

3. Arrange each breast on square of heavy aluminum foil. Sprinkle with remaining ingredients. Wrap foil around breasts to seal tightly.

4. Place foil packages on grill above charcoal. Cook for 1 hour, turning frequently.

Joan Dickson, Junior Woman's Club,
Glastonbury, Conn.

CHICKEN DELIGHT

Serves 6

2 cups boiling water
1 cup rice
1 teaspoon curry powder
4-ounce can mushrooms, undrained

2 tablespoons chopped parsley
2 chicken bouillon cubes
2 tablespoons butter or margarine
6 chicken breasts
½ cup orange marmalade
1 tablespoon lemon juice
1 teaspoon ground ginger
1 tablespoon grated lemon rind
6 peach halves

1. Preheat oven to 350° F. Grease 13 x 9½ x 2-inch baking pan.
2. Prepare rice mixture: Pour water into baking pan. Stir in rice, curry powder, mushrooms, parsley and bouillon cubes; mix well. Set aside.
3. Prepare chicken: Melt butter or margarine in skillet; brown chicken well on both sides; arrange on rice.
4. Cover with aluminum foil; bake in preheated oven for 50 minutes.
5. Meanwhile, in small bowl blend marmalade, lemon juice, ginger and lemon rind; use to fill peach halves; arrange on chicken.
6. Remove cover; bake for 15 minutes longer.

Mrs. Charles Richards, Woman's Club, Martinez, Calif.

CHICKEN KIEV

Serves 6

6 chicken breasts, boned
Salt and pepper to taste
½ cup ice-cold butter divided into 6 parts
1 tablespoon chopped parsley
Garlic salt
2 cups wheat germ or cracker crumbs
3 eggs, lightly beaten
Fat for deep frying

1. Place chicken breasts between 2 pieces of waxed paper; pound well to flatten. Remove paper; sprinkle with salt and pepper. Place portion of butter in center of each breast; sprinkle with parsley and garlic salt.
2. Fold short ends of breasts into center; then fold in sides. Make as tight a package as possible; secure with wooden pick.
3. Coat with wheat germ or crumbs. Dip in eggs; coat again with wheat germ or crumbs. Refrigerate for 1 hour.
4. Gently lower breasts into deep fat heated to 365° F. Fry for about 8 minutes, or until golden on all sides. Drain on absorbent paper.

Barbara McKee, Suburban Women's Club, Newark, Del.

CHICKEN MACADAMIA

Serves 6

3½-ounce jar macadamia nuts
2 tablespoons butter
2 eggs
2 tablespoons cooking oil
2 tablespoons soy sauce
1 teaspoon powdered ginger

¼ teaspoon pepper
2 tablespoons brandy
1 medium onion, minced
¼ cup water
½ cup presifted flour
¼ cup cornstarch
3 chicken breasts
Peanut oil

1. Preheat oven to 350° F.
2. Put nuts and butter in shallow baking pan. Bake in preheated oven for about 15 minutes, or until browned, stirring frequently. Be careful not to burn nuts.
3. In mixing bowl beat eggs. Beat in all remaining ingredients except chicken and peanut oil.
4. Cut chicken breasts in half lengthwise, then in half crosswise. Soak in batter for 20 minutes.
5. Fry chicken in skillet containing about ¼ inch peanut oil heated to 350° F. until browned on all sides.
6. Arrange on serving platter; sprinkle with nuts.

Mrs. William F. Nichols, Junior Civic Woman's Club, Parkersburg, W. Va.

CHICKEN BREASTS BAKED IN CREAM

Serves 6

3 tablespoons shortening
3 chicken breasts, halved
⅓ cup finely chopped onions
1 clove garlic, crushed
1½ teaspoons salt
½ teaspoon pepper
2 teaspoons Worcestershire
¾ cup chicken broth
1 cup heavy cream
3 tablespoons flour
1 cup water

1. Preheat oven to 300° F. Grease 2-quart casserole.
2. Melt shortening in skillet; brown chicken well on both sides. Place in casserole.
3. Sauté onions and garlic in fat remaining in skillet for 5 minutes. Stir in salt, pepper, Worcestershire, broth and cream. Bring to boil, stirring occasionally. Pour over chicken.
4. Cover; bake in preheated oven for 2 hours. Remove cover; bake for 15 minutes longer.
5. Place chicken on serving dish; keep in warm place.
6. In small bowl blend flour and water; stir into pan drippings. Cook over medium heat, stirring constantly, until thickened. Pour over chicken.

Mrs. Hollis Ellis, Island Woman's Club, Anna Maria, Fla.

CREAMED CHICKEN HOT DISH

Serves 6

3 chicken breasts, halved
Salt and pepper to taste
Butter
1-pound 4-ounce can tiny new
  potatoes, drained
½-pound diced cooked ham
4-ounce can sliced mushrooms,
  drained
¼ cup flour
2 cups light cream
1 cup dry white wine
2 ounces seedless green grapes

1. Preheat oven to 350° F. Grease 2-quart casserole.
2. Season chicken with salt and pepper. Melt ¼ cup butter in skillet; brown chicken on both sides. Place in casserole.
3. Sauté potatoes in fat remaining in skillet until brown on all sides; place on chicken. Sprinkle with ham and mushrooms.
4. Melt 3 tablespoons butter in skillet. Stir in flour. Gradually blend in cream, stirring constantly, over low heat, until thickened and smooth.
5. Stir in wine; season with salt and pepper. Pour over chicken. Cover; bake in preheated oven for 1¼ hours.
6. Stir in grapes; bake for 10 minutes longer.

Mrs. Donald H. Doig, President,
North Shore Junior Woman's Club,
Shorewood, Wis.

CHICKEN BREASTS WITH ARTICHOKE HEARTS

Serves 4

3 tablespoons flour
1½ teaspoons salt
¼ teaspoon pepper
½ teaspoon paprika
2 teaspoons orégano
2 chicken breasts, skinned and
  halved
10-ounce package frozen artichoke
  hearts, cooked and drained
4 slices bacon
½ cup sweet white wine
2 tablespoons water

1. Preheat oven to 350° F. Grease 10 x 6 x 1½-inch baking pan.
2. On piece of waxed paper combine flour, salt, pepper, paprika, and orégano; use to coat chicken.
3. Line pan with artichoke hearts. Top with chicken; arrange bacon slice on each half. Mix wine and water; pour over chicken.
4. Bake in preheated oven for 45 minutes.

Mrs. Bill Andrews, Junior Woman's Club,
Greenville, Miss.

CHICKEN BREASTS DIVAN

Serves 3

3 chicken breasts
1 bay leaf
1 slice lemon
1 teaspoon salt
1 stalk celery
10-ounce package frozen broccoli
1 cup medium Cream Sauce (p. 441)
¼ cup mayonnaise
2 tablespoons sherry
¼ cup heavy cream
½ teaspoon Worcestershire
¼ cup grated Parmesan cheese

1. Simmer chicken in water to cover with bay leaf, lemon, salt and celery until tender. Cool in broth. Discard skin and bones; cut meat into large slices.
2. Cook broccoli according to package directions until almost tender.
3. Combine all remaining ingredients except cheese.
4. Preheat oven to 350° F. Grease casserole.
5. Put broccoli in casserole; top with chicken. Pour sauce over chicken; sprinkle with cheese.
6. Bake in preheated oven for 20 to 30 minutes.

Mrs. P. F. Haynes, Woman's Club,
Lakeworth, Fla.

CHICKEN BREASTS WITH WINE AND MUSHROOM SAUCE

Serves 8

½ cup presifted flour
Salt
Pepper
4 large chicken breasts, halved
¾ cup heavy cream
½ cup butter
8-ounce can mushrooms
1 cup chicken broth
1 egg yolk
½ cup dry sherry

1. Preheat oven to 425° F. Grease 10 x 6 x 1½-inch baking pan.
2. On piece of waxed paper combine ¼ cup of the flour, 1 teaspoon salt and ¼ teaspoon pepper. Dip chicken in ¼ cup of the cream; dredge in seasoned flour.
3. Melt ¼ cup of the butter in large skillet; brown chicken on both sides. Arrange in pan. Pour butter from skillet over each portion.
4. Bake in preheated oven for 20 minutes, basting occasionally with pan juices.
5. Meanwhile, prepare Wine and Mushroom Sauce: Drain mushrooms; reserve liquid. Melt remaining butter in medium saucepan; stir in remaining flour. Gradually stir in reserved mushroom liquid, broth and remaining cream. Cook over low heat, stirring constantly, until thickened and smooth.
6. In small bowl beat egg yolk; stir in a little hot sauce. Add to rest of sauce; stir over low heat for 1 minute. Season with salt and pepper; stir in sherry and mushrooms; simmer, stirring constantly, for 2 minutes.
7. Arrange chicken on serving dish; spoon sauce over top.

Mrs. J. E. Neill, Sr., Book Club, Tallulah, La.

CHICKEN BREASTS WITH TARRAGON

Serves 6

3 chicken breasts, halved, skinned
  and boned
Salt and pepper to taste
¼ cup presifted flour
¼ cup butter or margarine
1 tablespoon finely chopped shallots
  or onion
¼ cup dry white wine
1 teaspoon freshly chopped or ½
  teaspoon dried tarragon
¼ cup chicken broth
¼ cup heavy cream

1. Season chicken with salt and pepper. Dredge in flour; reserve remaining flour.
2. Melt 3 tablespoons of the butter or margarine in large skillet; brown chicken on both sides. Transfer to heated platter.
3. Sauté shallots or onion in fat remaining in skillet for 2 minutes. Add wine; cook over high heat until wine is nearly evaporated, scraping loose all brown particles. Add reserved flour; stir to make a thick paste. Sprinkle with tarragon; stir in broth.
4. Return chicken to skillet. Cover; cook over low heat for 20 minutes.
5. Place breasts on serving dish; keep in warm place.
6. Add remaining butter and cream to skillet; heat to serving temperature, stirring constantly.
7. Pour sauce over chicken.

Flo Stahl, Junior Woman's Club, Simsbury, Conn.

CHINESE CHICKEN WITH THIN SPAGHETTI

Serves 4

2 tablespoons cooking oil
½ cup sliced water chestnuts
½ cup bamboo shoots
½ cup finely chopped celery
¼ cup finely chopped spinach
1 teaspoon sugar
1 teaspoon monosodium glutamate
1 tablespoon soy sauce
1 cup chicken broth
1½ tablespoons cornstarch
3 tablespoons water
1 chicken breast, cooked and thinly
  sliced
½ cup pineapple tidbits
8 ounces thin spaghetti

1. Heat oil in large skillet; sauté water chestnuts, bamboo shoots, celery and spinach for 5 minutes. Stir in sugar, monosodium glutamate, soy sauce and broth.
2. Bring to boil; then simmer.
3. In small bowl blend cornstarch and water to a smooth paste; stir into broth. Cook over low heat, stirring constantly, until thickened and clear.
4. Add chicken and pineapple tidbits; heat to serving temperature.

5. Meanwhile, cook thin spaghetti according to package directions. Drain.
6. Serve chicken mixture on spaghetti.

Mrs. Ernest Middleton, Junior Woman's Club,
Fort Myers, Fla.

CHICKEN WITH LOBSTER SAUCE

Serves 8

4 large chicken breasts, skinned
  and halved
Salt and pepper to taste
¼ cup butter or margarine
2 tablespoons dry sherry
½ pound mushrooms, sliced
2 tablespoons flour
1½ cups chicken broth
1 tablespoon tomato paste
1 bay leaf, crushed
1 tablespoon chopped chives
2 10-ounce packages frozen lobster
  tails, cooked according to package
  directions
3 ripe tomatoes, quartered

1. Preheat oven to 300° F. Grease 11 x 7 x 1½-inch baking pan.
2. Season chicken with salt and pepper.
3. Melt butter or margarine in large skillet; sauté chicken over medium heat until golden on both sides. Arrange in pan; sprinkle with sherry.
4. Cover with aluminum foil; bake in preheated oven for 25 to 30 minutes.
5. Meanwhile, prepare Lobster Sauce: Add mushrooms to fat remaining in skillet; sauté over medium heat, stirring frequently, until tender. Sprinkle with flour; gradually stir in broth. Cook over medium heat, stirring constantly, until thickened. Stir in tomato paste, bay leaf and chives; simmer, uncovered, for 15 minutes. Remove meat from lobster tails; cut into bite-size pieces. Add along with tomatoes to sauce. Simmer for 8 minutes.
6. Arrange chicken on serving dish; spoon sauce over top.

Joan Sobeck, Junior Women's Club, Tenafly, N.J.

CHICKEN BREASTS ROMANO

Serves 4

2 chicken breasts, halved
½ cup presifted flour
1 teaspoon salt
½ teaspoon garlic salt
¼ teaspoon pepper
4 tablespoons butter or margarine
½ cup chopped onions
1 cup sliced mushrooms
½ cup grated Parmesan cheese
2 tablespoons chopped parsley
1 cup sherry
¼ pound seedless green grapes,
  stemmed
Grape leaves and grapes (optional)

1. Remove skin and bones from chicken; cut each breast in half crosswise, making 8 pieces. Wash; drain; pat dry.
2. Combine flour, salt, garlic salt and pepper; use to coat chicken well.
3. Melt butter or margarine in heavy skillet; brown chicken lightly for 15 min-

utes on each side. Transfer chicken to warm plate; cover with aluminum foil.

4. Cook onions in fat remaining in skillet until tender but not browned. Add mushrooms, cheese, parsley and sherry. Cook over medium heat for 10 minutes. Add grapes; simmer for 10 minutes longer.

5. Pour sauce over chicken. Garnish with grape leaves and grapes, if desired.

Virginia Harrell, Allied Gardens Woman's Club,
San Diego, Calif.

CHICKEN BREASTS BAKED IN SOUR CREAM

Serves 8

¼ cup melted butter
1 tablespoon paprika
1 tablespoon lemon juice
8 small chicken breasts
  Garlic salt
3-ounce can mushroom pieces and
  stems, drained
1 teaspoon Worcestershire
¼ cup sweet sherry
¼ cup slivered almonds
2 tablespoons flour
½ cup sour cream

1. Preheat oven to 350° F. Grease 13 x 9½ x 2-inch baking pan.
2. In small bowl blend butter, paprika and lemon juice. Sprinkle chicken with garlic salt; dip in butter mixture. Arrange chicken, skin side up, in pan.
3. Bake in preheated oven for 30 minutes.
4. Blend mushrooms, Worcestershire and sherry; spread on chicken. Sprinkle with almonds. Bake for 30 minutes longer. Arrange chicken on serving dish; keep in warm place.
5. In small bowl blend flour and sour cream. Stir into pan juices. Cook over low heat, stirring constantly, until thickened and smooth. Pour over chicken.

Mrs. Lee Sawyer and Mrs. Doc Ponton,
Junior Woman's Club, Sylvester, Ga.

BREASTS OF CHICKEN SUPREME

Serves 6

6 chicken breasts
  Salt, pepper and paprika to taste
  Flour
3 tablespoons butter
2 large onions, minced
⅔ cup chopped green pepper
¼ cup water
1 cup sauterne
2 cups sour cream

1. Preheat oven to 350° F.
2. Sprinkle chicken with salt, pepper and paprika. Flour lightly.
3. Melt butter in skillet; sauté chicken until golden on both sides; transfer to casserole.
4. Sauté onions and green pepper in butter remaining in skillet for 5 minutes, or until onions are transparent. Add to casserole. Add water and sauterne. Cover; bake in preheated oven for 1 hour.

5. Stir in sour cream; bake until sauce is hot.

Mrs. Catherine Butera, Juniors, Saratoga, Fla.

POULET CINTRA

Serves 6

6 large chicken breasts
¼ cup presifted flour
1½ teaspoons salt
¼ teaspoon pepper
¼ cup butter or margarine
1 shallot or small onion, chopped
1 clove garlic, crushed
3 tablespoons brandy
½ cup Cintra or other quality port
½ cup dry white wine
2 egg yolks
1 cup heavy cream
1 truffle, sliced

1. Skin and bone chicken breasts. Cut each in half; pound to flatten slightly.
2. On piece of waxed paper combine flour, salt and pepper; use to coat chicken.
3. Melt butter in large skillet; sauté shallot or onion and garlic over low heat for 2 minutes. Add chicken; brown well on both sides.
4. Sprinkle with brandy; flame.
5. Add Cintra and white wine to skillet; bring to boil. Cover; simmer for 20 minutes. Arrange chicken on serving dish; keep in warm place.
6. In small bowl beat egg yolks and cream; gradually stir into pan drippings. Cook over low heat, stirring constantly, until sauce is thickened and smooth.
7. Strain sauce over chicken. Garnish with truffle.

Mrs. C. Hutchinson, Junior Woman's Club,
Scotch Plains, N.J.

Cooked Chicken Dishes

NOTE: Cooked turkey may be substituted for the chicken in any of the following recipes.

CHICKEN ALMOND

Serves 6

2½ cups chopped cooked white
  meat of chicken
10½-ounce can condensed cream of
  chicken soup
1 cup chopped celery
2 tablespoons grated onion
1 tablespoon lemon juice
5-ounce can water chestnuts,
  undrained
1 cup blanched almonds, halved
2 tablespoons mayonnaise
½ cup crushed potato chips

1. Preheat oven to 450° F. Grease 2-quart casserole.
2. Combine all ingredients except potato chips. Turn into casserole. Sprinkle with potato chips.
3. Bake in preheated oven for 20 to 30 minutes.

Irene Dehn, Anna Day Club, Troy, Mo.

CHICKEN À LA AVOCADO

Serves 6

10½-ounce can condensed cream of
chicken soup
2 tablespoons dry sherry
1 cup diced cooked chicken
1 cup cooked green peas
2 tablespoons chopped parsley
1 tablespoon lemon juice
2 tablespoons chopped pimientos
Salt and pepper to taste
2 tablespoons butter
1 cup fresh bread crumbs
3 large avocados, halved lengthwise
and pitted
½ cup water

1. Preheat oven to 375° F. Grease 11 x
7 x 1½-inch baking pan.
2. In saucepan blend soup and sherry.
Bring to boil, stirring frequently. Add
chicken, peas, parsley, lemon juice and
pimientos; blend carefully. Season with salt
and pepper. Simmer for 2 minutes, stirring
occasionally.
3. Meanwhile, melt butter in small skillet; sauté crumbs over medium heat, tossing frequently, until golden.
4. Arrange avocados, cut side up, in
pan. Add water. Fill avocados with chicken
mixture; sprinkle crumbs on top.
5. Bake in preheated oven for 15 minutes.

*Mrs. Billy Lanier, Athenian Study Club,
Daingerfield, Tex.*

CHICKEN AND BROCCOLI

Serves 6

2 10-ounce packages frozen broccoli
4 cups diced cooked chicken
2 10½-ounce cans condensed cream
of chicken soup
1 cup mayonnaise
1 teaspoon curry powder
2 tablespoons lemon juice
½ cup butter or margarine, melted
1 cup bread crumbs

1. Preheat oven to 350° F. Grease 11 x
7 x 1½-inch baking pan.
2. Cook broccoli according to package
directions until partially tender. Drain;
arrange in pan. Arrange chicken on broccoli.
3. Blend soup, mayonnaise, curry powder and lemon juice; spread on chicken.
4. Blend butter or margarine and
crumbs; sprinkle over sauce.
5. Bake in preheated oven for 50 minutes.

*Mrs. James T. Green, Golfview Hills
Woman's Club, Hinsdale, Ill.*

CLUB CHICKEN

Serves 8 to 10

¼ cup butter or margarine
¼ cup presifted flour
1 cup chicken broth
14½-ounce can evaporated milk
½ cup water

1½ teaspoons salt
2½ cups diced cooked chicken
3 cups cooked rice
3-ounce can sliced mushrooms,
drained
¼ cup chopped pimientos
⅓ cup finely chopped green pepper
½ cup slivered toasted almonds

1. Preheat oven to 350° F. Grease 13 x
9½ x 2-inch baking pan.
2. Melt butter or margarine in saucepan;
blend in flour. Gradually stir in broth, milk
and water; cook over medium heat, stirring constantly, until thickened and
smooth.
3. Remove from heat. Stir in salt,
chicken, rice, mushrooms, pimientos and
green pepper; mix well. Turn into baking
pan.
4. Bake in preheated oven for 30 minutes.
5. Sprinkle with almonds just before
serving.

*Sheilah Powers, Junior & Senior Woman's Clubs,
Grundy, Va.*

CHICKEN CROQUETTES

Makes 6

2 cups chopped cooked chicken
1 tablespoon minced or grated onion
½ teaspoon salt
Dash of cayenne
1 teaspoon lemon juice
1 tablespoon minced parsley
1 cup Thick White Sauce (p. 441)
1 egg
2 tablespoons water
1 cup fine bread or cracker crumbs
Fat for deep frying
Mushroom Sauce (p. 447), Egg
Cream Sauce (p. 441) or Cream
Sauce (p. 441)

1. Combine chicken, onion, salt, cayenne, lemon juice, parsley and Thick White
Sauce. Chill thoroughly.
2. Shape into 6 croquettes.
3. Beat egg with water.
4. Roll croquettes in crumbs; dip in egg
mixture to coat on all sides; roll again in
crumbs.
5. Fry in deep fat heated to 365° F. for
about 6 minutes, or until well browned.
Drain on absorbent paper. Serve with
Mushroom, Egg Cream or Cream Sauce.

VARIATIONS:

1. Add ½ cup chopped blanched almonds to croquette mixture in Step 1.
2. Make Thick White Sauce with ¾ cup
chicken broth and ¼ cup heavy cream
instead of 1 cup milk. Flavor sauce with 1
tablespoon sherry or 1 teaspoon curry
powder.

A. S.

CHICKEN ÉLÉGANTE

Serves 12

2 packages frozen or 12 baked
    patty shells
¼ cup butter
¼ cup presifted flour
10½-ounce can condensed cream of
    chicken soup
¼ cup crumbled blue cheese
½ teaspoon marjoram
1 cup grated Parmesan cheese
1 cup diced cooked chicken
10-ounce package frozen broccoli,
    cooked and drained
1 cup sour cream
Paprika

1. If using frozen patty shells, bake according to package directions.
2. Melt butter in saucepan. Stir in flour; cook, stirring, until smooth. Stir in soup, blue cheese, marjoram, ½ cup of the Parmesan cheese, chicken and broccoli; bring to boil, stirring constantly. Fold in sour cream; heat to serving temperature.
3. Preheat broiler.
4. Spoon mixture into patty shells. Sprinkle with remaining Parmesan cheese and paprika. Put under broiler heat until lightly browned and bubbling.

Louise Roth, Woman's Club, Chappaqua, N.Y.

CHICKEN CAN-CAN

Serves 8 to 10

4 cups diced cooked chicken
10½-ounce can condensed cream of
    chicken soup
10½-ounce can condensed cream of
    mushroom soup
10½-ounce can condensed cream of
    celery soup
10½-ounce can condensed chicken
    rice soup
14-ounce can evaporated milk
6-ounce can Chinese noodles
    Slivered blanched almonds

1. Preheat oven to 350° F. Grease shallow baking pan.
2. Combine all ingredients except almonds. Pour into pan; sprinkle with almonds.
3. Bake in preheated oven for 1 hour.

Mrs. William H. Hasebroock, Honorary President,
General Federation of Women's Clubs,
West Point, Neb.

CHICKEN CASSEROLE

Serves 4 to 6

2 10½-ounce cans condensed cream
    of mushroom soup
¼ cup water
8-ounce can water chestnuts,
    drained and sliced
1 cup chopped celery
¼ cup chopped scallions
2 cups diced cooked chicken
2 3-ounce cans Chinese noodles
¼ cup broken cashew nuts

1. Preheat oven to 325° F. Grease 2-quart casserole.

2. Combine soup and water; blend with water chestnuts, celery, scallions and chicken. Pour half into casserole; top with Chinese noodles. Add remaining chicken mixture; sprinkle with nuts.
3. Bake in preheated oven for 30 minutes.

Mrs. Floyd Barthel, Woman's Literary Club,
Pingree, N.D.

CHICKERONI BAKE

Serves 6 to 8

10½-ounce can condensed cream of
    mushroom soup
3 eggs, lightly beaten
½ cup chicken broth
¼ teaspoon salt
1 medium green pepper, finely
    chopped
1 cup diced Cheddar cheese
4 cups diced cooked chicken
2 cups cooked elbow macaroni
1 cup fresh bread crumbs

1. Preheat oven to 350° F. Grease 13 x 9½ x 2-inch baking pan.
2. In mixing bowl blend soup, eggs and broth. Stir in salt, green pepper, cheese, chicken and macaroni. Turn into pan; sprinkle with crumbs.
3. Bake in preheated oven for 30 minutes.

Mrs. Gerald Bemis, Junior Woman's Club,
De Kalb, Ill.

CHICKEN CURRY

Serves 4 to 6

5 tablespoons butter
½ cup minced onions
6 tablespoons flour
2½ teaspoons curry powder
1¼ teaspoons salt
1½ teaspoons sugar
¼ teaspoon ginger
1 chicken bouillon cube
1 cup boiling water
2 cups milk
4 cups diced cooked chicken
1 teaspoon lemon juice
    Cooked rice
    Condiments: raisins, crisp bacon
    bits, salted almonds, salted peanuts,
    sweet or sour pickles, shredded
    coconut and currant jelly

1. Melt butter in saucepan; sauté onions until tender. Stir in flour, curry powder, salt, sugar and ginger.
2. Dissolve bouillon cube in water; stir in. Gradually stir in milk; cook, stirring constantly, until thickened and smooth.
3. Stir in chicken and lemon juice; heat to serving temperature.
4. Serve on rice with an accompanying selection of condiments.

Mrs. J. K. Owens, Sr., Fourth District Director
Alabama Federation of Women's Clubs,
Gordo, Ala.

CHICKEN ENCHILADAS

Serves 6

1 tablespoon margarine
2 tablespoons minced onion
2 tomatoes, chopped
2 cups chopped cooked chicken
　Salt and pepper to taste
　Cooking oil
12 Tortillas (p. 136) or canned tortillas
5-ounce can green chili peppers,
　drained and chopped
1 pound Monterey Jack cheese,
　shredded
4 chicken bouillon cubes
1 pint half-and-half

1. Melt margarine in saucepan; brown onion. Add tomatoes; simmer for 5 minutes. Add chicken, salt and pepper; simmer for 20 minutes. Set aside.
2. Preheat oven to 350° F.
3. Heat oil; dip Tortillas in oil to soften, but do not brown. Drain on absorbent paper. Put spoonful of chicken mixture on each tortilla; sprinkle each with 1 teaspoon chilis. Roll up and fasten with wooden picks.
4. Arrange in baking pan; top with cheese; sprinkle remaining chilis on top.
5. Dissolve bouillon cubes in half-and-half; pour over enchiladas.
6. Bake in preheated oven for 25 minutes.

Mrs. Vernon Beloat, Woman's Club,
Buckeye, Ariz.

CHICKEN À LA KING, NEW ORLEANS STYLE

Serves 4

2 tablespoons butter
1½ tablespoons flour
1 cup heavy cream
½ cup dry sherry
3 eggs, lightly beaten
1 teaspoon salt
¼ teaspoon pepper
¼ cup finely chopped green pepper
¼ cup chopped pimientos
½ cup chopped mushrooms
¼ cup grated carrot
½ cup finely chopped scallions
½ teaspoon paprika
2 cups diced cooked chicken
2 eggs, hard-cooked and sliced
　Chopped parsley

1. Melt butter in top of double saucepan. Stir in flour. Gradually stir in cream and sherry. Cook over hot water, stirring constantly, until thickened and smooth.
2. Stir in beaten eggs, salt, pepper, green pepper, pimientos, mushrooms, carrot, scallions, paprika and chicken. Cook over hot water, stirring frequently, for 15 minutes.
3. Arrange in serving dish. Garnish with egg slices and parsley.

Dr. Diane Sartor Goggans, Cultural Club,
Alto, La.

CHICKEN HASH

Serves 4

2 tablespoons butter or margarine
½ cup thinly sliced celery
¼ cup chopped onion
10½-ounce can chicken broth
1 cup diced cooked chicken
　Dash of pepper
　Hot biscuits, cooked rice or baked
　patty shells

1. Melt butter or margarine in skillet; sauté celery and onion over medium heat for 10 minutes. Stir in broth and chicken; simmer for 5 minutes. Add pepper; simmer for 2 minutes.
2. Serve on biscuits, on rice or in patty shells.

Ann McMillin, Progressive Woman's Club,
Fresno, Calif.

SOUTH SEA CHICKEN

Serves 4 to 6

¼ cup butter or margarine
½ cup sliced scallions
1 clove garlic, crushed
2 tablespoons flour
1 teaspoon monosodium glutamate
1 teaspoon salt
1 cup dry white wine
5-ounce can water chestnuts, drained
　and sliced
4-ounce can mushrooms, drained
5-ounce can bamboo shoots, drained
1-pound 4-ounce can pineapple
　tidbits, drained
3 cups diced cooked chicken
1 pimiento, cut into strips
1 cup chopped macadamia nuts

1. Melt butter or margarine in large skillet; sauté scallions and garlic for 5 minutes. Stir in flour, monosodium glutamate and salt. Gradually stir in wine. Cook over low heat, stirring constantly, until thickened and smooth.
2. Stir in water chestnuts, mushrooms and bamboo shoots; simmer, stirring frequently, for 5 minutes. Stir in pineapple and chicken; heat to serving temperature.
3. Arrange on serving dish. Garnish with pimiento. Sprinkle nuts around edge.

Mrs. Roger K. Stewart, Woman's Club,
Sepulveda, Calif.

CHICKEN LOAF

Serves 4

4-pound stewing chicken, cooked
½ cup bread crumbs
1 egg
½ teaspoon salt
　Dash of pepper
¼ teaspoon paprika
　Chicken broth
　Mushroom Sauce (p. 447)

1. Preheat oven to 350° F. Grease 8-inch loaf pan.
2. Discard skin and bones of chicken; put meat through medium blade of meat grinder.

3. In mixing bowl combine chicken, crumbs, egg, salt, pepper and paprika; mix well. Stir in sufficient broth to moisten. Turn into pan.

4. Bake in preheated oven for 40 minutes. Cool for 5 minutes before removing from pan.

5. Serve with Mushroom Sauce.

Mrs. Margie Doss, President, Woman's Club, Madison, W.Va.

CHICKEN RICE LOAF SOUFFLÉ

Serves 6 to 8

2 cups fresh bread crumbs
4 cups diced cooked chicken
1 cup cooked rice
1½ teaspoons salt
1 tablespoon finely chopped pimiento
2 cups milk
1 cup chicken broth
4 eggs, lightly beaten
Easy Mushroom Sauce (p. 447)

1. Preheat oven to 325° F. Grease 10 x 6 x 1½-inch baking pan well.

2. Put crumbs, chicken and rice in mixing bowl. Add salt, pimiento, milk and broth; mix well. Add eggs; mix well. Turn into pan.

3. Bake in preheated oven for 1 hour.

4. Cut into squares; serve with Easy Mushroom Sauce.

Mabel H. Snyder, Civic Club, Shippenville, Pa.

CHICKEN RING WITH MUSHROOM VELOUTÉ SAUCE

Serves 6

4 cups diced cooked chicken
1 cup cooked rice
1½ teaspoons salt
2 cups fresh bread crumbs
3 cups milk or chicken broth
¼ cup finely chopped pimientos
4 eggs, lightly beaten
Mushroom Velouté Sauce (p. 447)

1. Preheat oven to 350° F. Grease 9-inch ring mold.

2. Combine chicken and rice in mixing bowl. Add salt, crumbs, milk or broth and pimientos; mix well. Add eggs; blend well. Turn into mold.

3. Set mold in pan containing 1 inch of hot water. Bake in preheated oven for 1 hour, or until set.

4. Let stand for 5 minutes; unmold onto serving dish. Serve with Mushroom Velouté Sauce.

Julia J. Behrens, Woman's Club, Greenview, Ill.

COMPANY CHICKEN AND RICE CASSEROLE

Serves 8

3 tablespoons butter or margarine
5 slices day-old bread, cut into 1-inch cubes
½ cup chopped celery
1 small onion, chopped
1½ cups cooked rice
4 cups diced cooked chicken
8-ounce can mushroom stems and pieces, undrained
½ cup chopped pimientos
1 cup slivered toasted almonds
2 cups Medium White Sauce (p. 441)
Salt, pepper and paprika to taste

1. Preheat oven to 350° F. Grease 3-quart casserole.

2. Melt butter or margarine in skillet; brown bread on all sides. Stir in celery and onion; sauté for 3 minutes. Arrange in casserole.

3. Combine rice, chicken, mushrooms, pimientos and almonds. Spoon into casserole. Season Medium White Sauce with salt and pepper; pour over chicken mixture. Sprinkle with paprika.

4. Bake in preheated oven for 45 minutes.

Mrs. John S. Perry, Woman's Club, Sepulveda, Calif.

SUNDAY CHICKEN PIE

Serves 4

Pastry for a 1-Crust Pie (p. 548)
⅓ cup butter or margarine
⅓ cup presifted flour
½ teaspoon salt
¼ teaspoon pepper
1½ cups chicken broth
½ cup heavy cream
2 cups diced cooked chicken
¼ cup diced pimientos

1. Preheat oven to 475° F. Grease baking sheet and 1½-quart casserole.

2. Roll out Pastry for a 1-Crust Pie on lightly floured board to fit top of casserole. Cut into quarters. Place on baking sheet. Prick with fork. Bake in preheated oven for 10 minutes.

3. Meanwhile, melt butter or margarine in saucepan. Stir in flour, salt and pepper. Gradually stir in broth. Cook over medium heat, stirring constantly, until thickened and smooth. Stir in cream; simmer for 1 minute.

4. Remove from heat. Stir in chicken and pimientos. Turn into casserole.

5. Top with pastry quarters. Bake in preheated oven for 10 minutes, or until hot and bubbling.

Ella McConnel, Pine River Pow Wow Club, Bayfield, Colo.

CHICKEN AND OYSTER PIE

Serves 6

¼ cup butter
¼ cup presifted flour
¼ teaspoon paprika
2 cups chicken broth
Salt and pepper to taste
2 eggs, hard-cooked and sliced
½ cup finely chopped celery
1 pint oysters, freshly shucked and drained
3 cups diced cooked chicken
Basic Baking Powder Biscuits dough (p. 119)

1. Preheat oven to 400° F. Grease 2-quart casserole.

2. Melt butter in saucepan; stir in flour and paprika. Gradually stir in broth. Cook over low heat, stirring constantly, until thickened and smooth.

3. Season with salt and pepper. Stir in eggs, celery, oysters and chicken. Pour into casserole. Set aside.

4. Turn Basic Baking Powder Biscuits dough onto lightly floured board. Knead gently 10 times; roll out to fit top of casserole. Fit dough on mixture in casserole.

5. Bake in preheated oven for 20 minutes, or until golden.

Colette Wirshing, Junior Woman's Club, Pompano Beach, Fla.

CHICKEN PIE WITH SWEET POTATO CRUST

Serves 4 to 6

3 cups diced cooked chicken
1 cup diced cooked carrots
6 small white onions, cooked
1 tablespoon chopped parsley
    Presifted flour
1½ teaspoons salt
⅛ teaspoon black pepper
1 cup evaporated milk
1 cup chicken broth
1 teaspoon baking powder
1 cup cooled mashed sweet potatoes
⅛ cup melted butter
1 egg, well beaten

1. Put chicken in shallow 1½-quart baking dish. Sprinkle with carrots, onions and parsley.

2. In saucepan combine 2 tablespoons flour, 1 teaspoon of the salt and pepper. Gradually stir in milk and broth. Bring to boil. Cook, stirring constantly, for 1 to 2 minutes.

3. Pour sauce over chicken.

4. Combine 1 cup flour, baking powder and remaining salt.

5. In mixing bowl combine sweet potatoes, butter and egg.

6. Stir in dry ingredients. Chill thoroughly.

7. Preheat oven to 350° F.

8. Roll out dough ¼ inch thick on lightly floured board; cut a little larger than dimensions of baking dish. Place over baking dish; flute edge.

9. Bake in preheated oven for about 40 minutes, or until lightly browned.

Mrs. M. F. Permenter, Women's Club, Arvin, Calif.

CHICKEN BREAD PUDDING

Serves 6

1 loaf white bread, cut into ½-inch cubes
3½- to 4-pound chicken, poached and cut into small pieces (including skin)
4 eggs, beaten
3 cups milk

1 cup chicken broth
1 tablespoon melted butter
    Salt and pepper to taste

1. Preheat oven to 350° F. Grease 13 x 9½ x 2-inch baking pan.

2. In pan alternate layers of bread and chicken, beginning and ending with bread.

3. Combine remaining ingredients. Pour over bread in pan.

4. Bake in preheated oven for 1 hour.

NOTE: Liquid should almost cover ingredients. If more is needed, it can be made in same proportions: 1 egg to ¾ cup milk and ¼ cup broth.

Mrs. Richard Joynson, Junior Woman's Club, Wauwatosa, Wis.

HENNY PENNY

Serves 4

2 cups diced cooked chicken
2 cups chopped celery
½ cup slivered toasted almonds
½ teaspoon salt
2 tablespoons grated onion
2 tablespoons lemon juice
1 cup mayonnaise
½ teaspoon monosodium glutamate
½ cup grated Cheddar cheese
1 cup crushed potato chips

1. Preheat oven to 450° F. Grease 1½-quart casserole.

2. Combine all ingredients except cheese and potato chips; toss lightly.

3. Turn into casserole. Sprinkle with cheese and potato chips.

4. Bake in preheated oven for 10 minutes, or until bubbling.

Velma Gill, Women's Club, Porterville, Calif.

BAKED CHICKEN SALAD

Serves 6

2 cups diced cooked chicken
10½-ounce can condensed cream of chicken soup
1 cup chopped celery
2 teaspoons grated onion
½ cup chopped walnuts
½ teaspoon salt
¼ teaspoon pepper
1 tablespoon lemon juice
3 eggs, hard-cooked and sliced
¾ cup mayonnaise
2 cups crushed potato chips

1. Preheat oven to 450° F. Lightly grease 2-quart casserole.

2. In mixing bowl combine all ingredients except potato chips. Pour into casserole. Top with potato chips.

3. Bake in preheated oven for 15 minutes.

Mrs. R. J. Swim, Town and Country League, Cheyenne, Wyo.

CHICKEN SQUARES
Serves 6 to 9

3 cups diced cooked chicken
1 cup cooked rice
2 cups soft bread crumbs
⅓ cup sliced celery
¼ cup chopped pimientos
4 eggs, lightly beaten
2 teaspoons salt
¼ teaspoon poultry seasoning
2 cups chicken broth
  Quick Mushroom Soup Sauce
  (p. 447)

1. Preheat oven to 350° F. Grease 9-inch square baking pan.
2. Combine chicken, rice, crumbs, celery and pimientos.
3. Combine eggs, salt, poultry seasoning and broth; stir into chicken mixture.
4. Pour into pan. Bake in preheated oven for 55 minutes.
5. Cut into squares. Serve with Quick Mushroom Soup Sauce.

Mrs. Garth Beal, Young Adult's Study Club,
Slater, Mo.

CHICKEN 'N' STUFFING SCALLOP
Serves 8 to 10

8-ounce package herb-seasoned
  bread stuffing
3 cups diced cooked chicken
½ cup butter or margarine
½ cup presifted flour
¼ teaspoon salt
  Dash of pepper
1 quart chicken broth
6 eggs, lightly beaten
  Quick Mushroom Pimiento
  Sauce (p. 447)

1. Preheat oven to 325° F. Grease 13 x 9½ x 2-inch baking pan.
2. Sprinkle stuffing in pan; top with chicken.
3. Melt butter in saucepan; blend in flour. Add salt and pepper. Gradually stir in broth. Cook over medium heat, stirring constantly, until sauce is thickened and smooth.
4. Combine eggs with a little sauce. Return to rest of sauce; blend well. Pour over chicken in pan.
5. Bake in preheated oven for 45 minutes, or until knife inserted in center comes out clean.
6. Let stand for 5 minutes. Cut into squares; serve with Quick Mushroom Pimiento Sauce.

Mrs. W. A. Brecht, Woman's Club,
Forest Hills, Pa.

SOPA DE FRITOS
Serves 4

1 medium onion, finely chopped
½ teaspoon orégano
¾ cup tomato juice
4 cups corn chips
2 cups diced cooked chicken
5 green chili peppers, diced
1 cup grated Cheddar cheese
2 cups chicken broth

1. Preheat oven to 350° F. Grease 1½-quart casserole.
2. In small saucepan combine onion, orégano and tomato juice. Bring to boil; cover; simmer for 10 minutes.
3. In casserole arrange alternate layers of corn chips, chicken, chilis and cheese. Pour in broth and tomato juice mixture.
4. Bake in preheated oven for 40 minutes.

Mrs. R. H. Daniel, Woman's Club, Roswell, N.M.

SUB GUM CHOW MEIN
Serves 6

⅓ cup peanut oil
1 clove garlic, crushed
1 cup diced canned water chestnuts
1 cup diced canned bamboo shoots
2 cups diced celery
1½ cups sliced Chinese cabbage
½ cup diced mushrooms
1 medium green pepper, diced
½ cup thinly sliced green beans
6 scallions, chopped
1 tablespoon salt
½ teaspoon pepper
1½ teaspoon sugar
2 cups chicken broth
2 tablespoons soy sauce
¼ cup water
2 tablespoons cornstarch
2 cups finely shredded cooked
  chicken
  Chinese noodles
½ cup blanched toasted almonds

1. Heat oil in large skillet.
2. Stir in garlic, water chestnuts, bamboo shoots, celery, cabbage, mushrooms, green pepper, beans, scallions, salt, pepper and sugar. Add broth; mix well. Bring to boil; cover; simmer for 10 minutes.
3. In small bowl blend soy sauce, water and cornstarch to a smooth paste. Stir into vegetables; stir until boiling and clear. Add chicken; simmer for 5 minutes.
4. Serve with Chinese noodles; sprinkle each serving with almonds.

Woman's Club, Palisade, N.J.

Chicken Livers

CHICKEN LIVER SAUTÉ
Serves 6

⅓ cup butter or margarine
1 pound fresh or defrosted chicken
  livers, halved
1 medium onion, sliced
3 tablespoons flour
1 teaspoon salt
  Dash of pepper
½ teaspoon ginger
10½-ounce can condensed beef
  consommé
4-ounce can mushrooms, drained
⅓ cup dry sherry
  Cooked rice (optional)

1. Melt butter or margarine in large skillet; sauté chicken livers over low heat for 8 minutes. Remove from pan; keep in warm place.

2. Sauté onion in fat remaining in skillet for 5 minutes. Stir in flour, salt, pepper and ginger. Gradually stir in consommé. Cook over low heat, stirring constantly, until thickened and smooth.

3. Stir in mushrooms, sherry and livers; simmer for 2 minutes.

4. Serve on rice, if desired.

Elizabeth Maxcy, Woman's Club, Sebring, Fla.

SAUTÉED CHICKEN LIVERS AND MUSHROOMS

Serves 6

¼ cup butter
¾ pound chicken livers, halved
¼ pound mushrooms, sliced
1 tablespoon finely chopped onion
1 tablespoon finely chopped green pepper
1 tablespoon finely chopped parsley
1 tablespoon flour
1 cup chicken broth
1 small bay leaf
Dash of thyme
Salt and pepper to taste
Dash of nutmeg
Cooked rice

1. Melt butter in large skillet. Add livers, mushrooms, onion, green pepper and parsley. Sauté over medium heat, stirring occasionally, for 4 minutes.

2. Sprinkle with flour; brown flour lightly. Gradually stir in broth; cook over medium heat, stirring constantly, until thickened. Add bay leaf and thyme. Cover; simmer for 15 minutes.

3. Season lightly with salt and pepper; stir in nutmeg. Serve on rice.

Milli Milillo, Junior Woman's Club,
Tullahoma, Tenn.

CHICKEN LIVERS IN SHERRY

Serves 4

1½ pounds chicken livers
Flour
½ teaspoon salt
⅛ teaspoon pepper
¼ teaspoon garlic powder
2 tablespoons butter or margarine
1 cup sherry
Cooked rice or buttered toast

1. Cut chicken livers into bite-size pieces. Sprinkle with 3 tablespoons flour, salt, pepper and garlic powder.

2. Melt butter or margarine in skillet; brown livers on all sides. Remove from pan.

3. Stir 1 teaspoon flour into fat remaining in pan. Gradually stir in wine; cook, stirring in brown bits from bottom and sides. Add livers; heat to serving temperature.

4. Serve on rice or toast, as desired.

Mrs. C. D. Hamilton, Woman's Club,
Morganton, N.C.

CHICKEN LIVERS IN SOUR CREAM

Serves 3 or 4

2 tablespoons butter or margarine
½ pound chicken livers, halved
1 medium onion, finely chopped
1 medium green pepper, finely chopped
½ teaspoon salt
⅛ teaspoon pepper
½ bay leaf
¼ cup water
1 cup sour cream
Toast or creamed potatoes

1. Melt butter in large skillet. Add chicken livers, onion and green pepper; sauté over medium heat, stirring occasionally, until lightly browned.

2. Add salt, pepper, bay leaf and water. Bring to boil; cover; simmer for 20 minutes.

3. Stir in sour cream; cook until bubbling.

4. Serve on toast or with potatoes, as desired.

Mrs. Ruth Hetrick, Woman's Club,
Slippery Rock, Pa.

Rock Cornish Game Hen

ROCK CORNISH GAME HENS WITH BACON STUFFING

Serves 2

2 frozen 1-pound Rock Cornish game hens, defrosted
Bacon Stuffing (p. 452)
¼ cup melted butter
Salt and pepper to taste
Gourmet Sauce (p. 444)

1. Preheat oven to 425° F.

2. Fill hen cavities loosely with Bacon Stuffing.

3. Arrange hens, breast up, on rack in shallow roasting pan. Brush well with butter; season with salt and pepper. Roast in preheated oven for 45 minutes.

4. Turn hens breast down; again brush with butter.

5. Serve with Gourmet Sauce.

Mrs. William F. Peifer, Greenfields Woman's Club,
Reading, Pa.

ROCK CORNISH GAME HENS WITH CELERY AND MUSHROOM DRESSING

Serves 8

8 frozen 1-pound Rock Cornish game hens, defrosted
½ cup melted butter
Salt and pepper to taste
Celery and Mushroom Dressing (p. 453)

1. Preheat broiler. Line broiler pan with aluminum foil.

2. Arrange hens, breast down, on pan; brush with butter. Season with salt and

pepper. Broil 6 to 7 inches from heat for 12 to 15 minutes.

3. Remove from pan; fill each hen with Celery and Mushroom Dressing. Replace hens, breast up, on pan; brush with remaining butter. Broil 6 to 7 inches from heat for 10 to 12 minutes, or until golden.

4. Turn temperature to 325° F. Place broiler pan in oven. Bake, basting occasionally with pan juices, for 20 minutes, or until tender.

Donna Tessendorf, Woman's Club, Dundee, Ill.

ROCK CORNISH GAME HENS STUFFED WITH WILD RICE

Serves 4

> 4 14-ounce Rock Cornish game hens (reserve giblets)
> Salt
> 2 cups cooked wild rice
> ½ pound mushrooms, sliced
> ½ cup chopped onions
> 1 egg
> 1 cup red wine
> ½ teaspoon poultry seasoning
> ¼ teaspoon pepper
> ¼ cup lemon juice
> ¼ cup melted butter
> 2 tablespoons soy sauce

1. Wash hens; drain; rub cavities with salt. Set aside.

2. Cook giblets in a little boiling salted water until tender. Drain and chop giblets.

3. Preheat oven to 400° F.

4. Prepare Wild Rice Stuffing: Combine wild rice, mushrooms, onions and giblets. Add egg, ½ cup of the wine, poultry seasoning, pepper and ½ teaspoon salt; mix well.

5. Rub outside of birds with lemon juice; stuff birds with rice mixture. Arrange in roasting pan.

6. Prepare basting sauce: Blend remaining wine, butter and soy sauce.

7. Brush birds with basting sauce; place pan in oven.

8. Reduce temperature to 350° F. Roast birds for about 1 hour. Brush frequently during roasting with basting sauce.

Mrs. E. L. Hay, Woman's Club, Lakeworth, Fla.

POTTED ROCK CORNISH GAME HENS

Serves 4

> 2 1-pound Rock Cornish game hens
> Salt and pepper to taste
> ¼ cup presifted flour
> ½ cup butter
> ¾ cup finely chopped onions
> ¼ cup dry sherry
> ¼ pound mushrooms, sliced
> Parsley

1. Split hens in half; season with salt and pepper. Dredge in flour.

2. Melt ¼ cup of the butter; in Dutch oven or heavy saucepan sauté onions for 5 minutes. Remove onions; set aside.

3. Brown hens well on both sides in butter remaining in pan. Add onions; stir

in sherry. Cover; simmer for 45 minutes, or until tender.

4. Meanwhile, melt remaining butter in skillet; sauté mushrooms. Set aside.

5. Arrange hens on serving dish; keep warm.

6. Stir mushrooms into pan drippings; simmer for 2 minutes. Pour over hens; garnish with parsley.

Marge Wroble, Woman's Club, Prospect Heights, Ill.

Guinea Fowl

GUINEAS GALA

Serves 4

> 2 3-pound guinea fowl, halved
> 3 tablespoons olive oil
> Salt and pepper to taste
> 1 cup water
> 1 tablespoon butter
> 1 medium onion, thinly sliced
> 1 cup canned tomatoes
> 2 medium green peppers, finely chopped
> ¼ cup finely chopped celery
> 4-ounce can sliced mushrooms, undrained
> 1½ cups heavy cream
> Dash of Tabasco
> Cooked wild rice

1. Preheat oven to 400° F. Grease 13 x 9½ x 2-inch baking pan.

2. Rub guinea fowl with oil; season with salt and pepper. Place in pan; add water.

3. Bake in preheated oven for 45 minutes, or until tender.

4. Remove birds from oven. Pour off broth; reserve.

5. Melt butter in skillet; sauté onion for 5 minutes. Stir in reserved broth, tomatoes, green peppers, celery, mushrooms, cream and Tabasco. Bring sauce to boil; remove from heat; season with salt and pepper.

6. Pour sauce over birds. Bake in preheated oven for 30 minutes, or until very tender, basting occasionally with sauce.

7. Serve with wild rice.

Elizabeth Jones, Woman's Club, Annandale, Va.

Squab

ROAST SQUABS

Serves 2

> 2 ¾-pound squabs
> Salt
> Pepper
> 1 cup water
> 2 cups fresh bread crumbs
> 1 egg, lightly beaten
> ½ teaspoon sage
> 2 slices bacon, halved

1. Place squabs in pan just large enough to hold them. Season with salt and pepper;

add water. Cover; simmer over very low heat for 30 minutes.

2. Preheat oven to 400° F.

3. Remove squabs from pan; cool. Reserve ¼ cup pan juices.

4. Combine crumbs, egg, sage, and reserved juices. Season with ½ teaspoon salt and a dash of pepper; mix lightly. Use to fill squab cavities. Sew or skewer openings.

5. Arrange squabs, breast up, on rack in shallow roasting pan. Arrange bacon on top.

6. Roast in preheated oven for 15 minutes, or until golden.

Mrs. W. B. Leslie, Jeffersonville Woman's Club, Tazewell, Va.

Turkey

ROAST TURKEY
Serves 14 to 16
10- to 12-pound turkey
Salt and pepper
12 cups Bon Secour Oyster Dressing (p. 454) or other favorite dressing
½ cup melted butter or margarine

1. Preheat oven to 325° F.

2. Rub inside of turkey with salt and pepper. Spoon dressing into neck and body cavities, securing with skewers. Brush turkey well with butter or margarine. Place, breast down, on rack in roasting pan.

3. Roast in preheated oven for 2½ hours.

4. Saturate large piece of cheesecloth with remaining butter. Turn bird breast up; cover with cheesecloth. Roast for 2 hours longer.

Edna Pearce Lockett, Woman's Club, Sebring, Fla.

TURKEY IN FOIL
Serves 12 to 16
10- to 12-pound turkey (reserve giblets)
⅓ cup butter
1 tablespoon salt
1 stalk celery with leaves, quartered
1 large onion, quartered

1. Preheat oven to 450° F.

2. Rub turkey well with butter; sprinkle with salt. Put celery and onion in cavity.

3. Place turkey in center of 2 long strips of heavy aluminum foil; wrap loosely.

4. Put turkey in large roasting pan. Roast in preheated oven for 3½ hours.

5. Meanwhile, put neck, gizzard and liver in saucepan; cover with salted water. Cover; simmer for 2 hours.

6. When turkey is cooked, open one corner of foil; pour liquid over giblets. Keep turkey sealed until ready to serve.

7. Strain liquid from giblets; correct seasoning; thicken as desired for gravy.

Mrs. Mary Alice Porter, Woman's Club, Newsoms, Va.

BAKED TURKEY
Serves 12
14-pound turkey
Salt and pepper
10 to 12 cups favorite dressing
1 cup butter or margarine
½ cup presifted flour

1. Wipe turkey with damp cloth; sprinkle cavity with salt and pepper. Fill neck and body cavities loosely with dressing. Secure with skewers or poultry pins.

2. Preheat oven to 350° F.

3. In medium bowl blend butter or margarine and flour to a smooth paste. Cover turkey completely with paste; arrange, breast down, on rack in shallow roasting pan.

4. Roast, uncovered, in preheated oven for 2 hours.

5. Reduce temperature to 300° F. Turn bird breast up; cover pan with aluminum foil. Roast, basting occasionally with pan juices, for 2 hours longer, or until tender. Allow about 25 minutes per pound.

Mrs. Rube Beard, Woman's Club, Cairo, Ga.

TURKEY AMANDINE
Serves 6
1 cup presifted flour
1 teaspoon baking powder
½ teaspoon salt
1 egg, lightly beaten
¾ cup milk
6 large slices cold cooked turkey
Fat for deep frying
¼ cup butter
½ cup chopped almonds

1. In mixing bowl combine flour, baking powder and salt.

2. Combine egg and milk; stir into dry ingredients to make batter.

3. Dip turkey in batter; fry in deep fat heated to 365° F. until golden brown. Drain on absorbent paper.

4. Melt butter in small pan; cook almonds until golden brown. Pour over turkey slices.

Mrs. Joseph Holton Jones, New Century Club, Wilmington, Del.

SLICED BREAST OF TURKEY MORNAY ON TOAST
Serves 4
2 cups Medium White Sauce (p. 441)
1 egg yolk
1 cup grated Cheddar cheese
Salt and pepper to taste
4 slices toast
4 large slices cooked turkey

1. Preheat oven to 375° F. Grease baking sheet.

2. Prepare Mornay Sauce: In saucepan bring Medium White Sauce to simmer. Remove from heat. Beat in egg yolk and ½ cup cheese. Season with salt and pepper.

3. Arrange toast on baking sheet; top each slice with turkey slice. Cover with Mornay Sauce; sprinkle with remaining cheese.

4. Bake in preheated oven for 12 minutes, or until browned.

Vivian Bates, Grant County Junior Woman's Club,
Williamstown, Ky.

TURKEY CASHEW CASSEROLE
Serves 6

3-ounce can Chinese noodles
2 cups diced cooked turkey
1 cup chopped celery
1 cup cashew nuts
½ cup chopped scallions
10½-ounce can condensed cream of
    mushroom soup
½ cup chicken broth
2 teaspoons soy sauce

1. Preheat oven to 325° F. Grease 1½-quart casserole.
2. Reserve ½ cup noodles. Place remaining noodles in mixing bowl. Add turkey, celery, nuts and scallions; toss lightly.
3. In small bowl blend soup, broth and soy sauce. Pour over turkey mixture; mix well. Turn into casserole; sprinkle with reserved noodles.
4. Bake in preheated oven for 30 minutes.

P. Webb, Junior Woman's Club,
Pacific Beach, Calif.

TURKEY CROQUETTES
Serves 4

2 cups finely diced cooked turkey
¼ cup fresh bread crumbs
2 tablespoons grated onion
2 tablespons chopped parsley
½ teaspon salt
⅛ teaspon pepper
10½-ounce can condensed cream
    of mushroom soup
1 egg, beaten with 2 tablespoons
    milk
1 cup dry bread crumbs
¼ cup milk
¼ cup chopped canned pimientos
Fat for deep frying

1. In mixing bowl combine turkey, fresh crumbs, onion, parsley, salt and pepper. Stir in half the soup; mix well. If mixture is too soft, add a few fresh crumbs. Shape into 8 patties or rolls.
2. Dip in egg mixture; coat completely with dry crumbs. Reshape, if necessary.
3. Meanwhile, to prepare sauce; in small saucepan blend remaining soup, milk and pimientos. Stir over low heat to serving temperature.
4. Fry croquettes in deep fat heated to 365° F. for 5 minutes, or until golden. Drain on absorbent paper. Serve with sauce.

Mrs. Charles Strother, Chairman, Elections
Committee, General Federation of Women's
Clubs, Madill, Okla.

CURRIED TURKEY
Serves 8

½ cup butter
1½ cups chopped onions
1 cup diced green pepper
2 tablespoons curry powder
1 cup presifted flour
1½ quarts turkey or chicken broth
2 teaspoons salt
½ cup orange marmalade
2 tablespoons lemon juice
4 cups diced cooked turkey
Almond Currant Rice (p. 474)

1. Melt butter in Dutch oven or large heavy saucepan; sauté onions and green pepper for 5 minutes. Stir in curry powder; sauté for 2 minutes. Stir in flour. Gradually add broth, stirring constantly, until thickened and smooth.
2. Add salt, marmalade and lemon juice. Cover; simmer for 15 minutes.
3. Add turkey. Heat to serving temperature, stirring occasionally.
4. Serve with Almond Currant Rice.

Ginnie Finkenaur, Junior Woman's Club,
Simsbury, Conn.

Goose

ROAST GOOSE
Serves 8

10- to 12-pound goose
Salt
Prune Stuffing (p. 454)

1. Preheat oven to 325° F.
2. Wipe goose with damp cloth. Sprinkle cavity with salt. Lightly fill body and neck cavities with Prune Stuffing. Sew or skewer opening; truss goose. Place, breast down, on rack in shallow roasting pan.
3. Roast in preheated oven for 3 hours. Remove fat from pan several times.
4. Turn goose breast up. Roast for 2 hours longer. Allow 25 minutes per pound.

Woman's Club, Palisade, N.J.

ROAST WATERTOWN GOOSE
Serves 8

10-pound goose
2 teaspoons salt
½ recipe for Apricot Stuffing (p. 452)
½ recipe for Wild Rice and Chestnut
    Stuffing (p. 455)
Juice and grated rind of 1 orange
3 tablespoons lemon juice

1. Preheat oven to 375° F.
2. Clean goose; wipe dry, but do not stuff. Place in roasting pan. Prick skin in fat layer around legs and wings. Roast, uncovered, in preheated oven for 15 minutes. Remove. Cool to room temperature. Repeat procedure twice more. Reduce temperature to 325° F.
3. Rub goose well with salt. Put Apricot Stuffing in neck cavity and Wild Rice and Chestnut Stuffing in body cavity. Truss. Weigh to estimate cooking time. Place, breast up, on rack in roasting pan. Roast, uncovered, allowing 35 minutes per pound.
4. When goose is half cooked, pour orange juice and rind and lemon juice over

breast. Baste occasionally with pan juices during rest of roasting.

Sethryn Hodges, Woman's Club, Elroy, Ariz.

Duck

BRAISED DUCK

Serves 4

> 4- to 5-pound duckling
> Salt and pepper
> 2 stalks celery with leaves, quartered
> 1 small apple, cored and quartered
> 2 small onions
> 1 clove garlic, finely slivered
> 2 tablespoons cooking oil
> 1 clove garlic
> ½ cup finely chopped green pepper
> 1 bay leaf
> ¼ teaspoon thyme
> Dash of Tabasco
> 1 teaspoon Worcestershire
> 1 cup water

1. Sprinkle cavity of duckling with salt and pepper. Place 1 of the celery stalks, apple and 1 of the onions in cavity. Pierce breast in several places; insert slivered garlic. Brush duck with oil.

2. Finely chop remaining celery stalk and remaining onion; sprinkle in Dutch oven or heavy saucepan. Add remaining ingredients.

3. Place rack in pan; arrange duck, breast up. Cover tightly; cook over very low heat, so that duck will steam, for 1½ hours, or until tender. Add water to bottom, if necessary, to prevent pan from burning.

4. Remove rack; place duck on serving platter.

5. Strain gravy, pressing through as much of vegetables as possible. Spoon a little gravy over duck; serve rest on side.

Junior Woman's Club, College Park, Md.

CREOLE DUCK

Serves 4

> 4- to 5-pound duckling
> 2 teaspoons salt
> ¼ teaspoon pepper
> ¼ cup presifted flour
> ¼ cup bacon drippings or shortening
> 1 large onion, sliced
> 2 cloves garlic, crushed
> 2 cups red wine
> 1 cup diced cooked ham
> Bouquet garni (see Glossary)
> 8-ounce can mushrooms
> 2 tablespoons cornstarch

1. Preheat oven to 375° F. Grease 13 x 9½ x 2-inch baking pan.

2. Cut duck into serving pieces; sprinkle with salt and pepper. Dredge well with flour.

3. Heat bacon drippings or shortening in large skillet; brown duck well on all sides. Arrange in pan.

4. Sauté onion and garlic in fat remaining in skillet for 5 minutes, scraping sides and bottom. Stir in wine, ham and bouquet garni; bring to boil. Pour over duck. Cover; bake in preheated oven for 1 hour.

5. Meanwhile, drain mushrooms. In small bowl blend cornstarch and mushroom liquid.

6. Transfer duck to serving dish; keep in warm place. Discard bouquet garni.

7. Stir cornstarch paste into pan drippings; cook over low heat, stirring constantly, until thickened and smooth. Stir in mushrooms; simmer for 2 minutes. Pour over duck.

Mrs. George Gerger, Sr., Book Club, Tallulah, La.

DUCK À L'ORANGE OR BIGARADE

Serves 2

> 5-pound duckling
> Salt and pepper to taste
> 2 oranges
> 3 teaspoons sugar
> ½ cup brown gravy
> 2 tablespoons cognac
> 1 teaspoon lemon juice

1. Preheat oven to 350° F.

2. Sprinkle duck inside and out with salt and pepper; truss for roasting. Place on rack in roasting pan. Roast in preheated oven for 2 hours, pouring off all fat from pan as it accumulates.

3. Meanwhile, remove thin rind from 1 of the oranges; cut into thin slivers; simmer in water to cover for 15 minutes. Drain; set aside.

4. Remove sections from both oranges; sprinkle with 2 teaspoons of the sugar; set aside.

5. Arrange duck on warm serving platter; keep warm.

6. Sprinkle pan with remaining sugar; stir over direct heat until caramel-colored.

7. Drain all juice from orange sections; stir into pan. Stir in gravy and cognac. Cook, stirring, for 3 minutes. Correct seasoning; stir in lemon juice and reserved orange rind and sections.

8. Pour sauce over duckling.

A. S.

DUCK OF THE FOUR SEASONS

Serves 2

> 4½- to 5-pound duckling
> Salt and pepper to taste
> 3 cloves garlic, sliced
> 1 medium onion, sliced
> 4-inch piece fresh ginger root or
> 4 pieces preserved ginger, chopped
> 1 cup water
> 1 cup sugar
> Cinnamon stick
> 1 lemon, sliced
> 2 ripe large peaches or any other fresh fruit in season, peeled, pitted and halved
> Water cress

1. Preheat oven to 350° F.
2. Prick skin of duck deeply with fork to allow fat to escape. Sprinkle inside and out with salt and pepper. Put garlic, onion and ginger in cavity. Truss duck; place on rack in roasting pan.
3. Roast in preheated oven for 1 hour. Pour off all fat from roasting pan. Roast for 1 hour longer. Before serving, turn temperature to 500° F. for a few minutes to brown and crisp duck skin, but watch carefully so it does not burn.
4. Meanwhile, combine water, sugar, cinnamon and lemon in saucepan. Bring to boil. Poach peach halves for 2 minutes on each side. Turn off heat. Let peaches steep in syrup until ready to serve.
5. Serve duck surrounded by water cress and peaches.

A. S.

Game Birds

Dove

BAKED DOVES WITH APPLE STUFFING

Serves 12

12 doves
3 cups fresh bread crumbs
2 cups tart apples, cubed
½ cup chopped celery
¼ cup melted butter or margarine
½ teaspoon salt
½ teaspoon poultry seasoning
1 small onion, finely chopped
½ cup milk or chicken broth

1. Put doves in large saucepan; add a little boiling salted water. Cover; simmer until tender. Drain; set aside.
2. Preheat oven to 425° F. Grease roasting pan.
3. Prepare Apple Stuffing: In mixing bowl combine remaining ingredients. Mix well; turn into pan. Arrange doves, breast down, in stuffing.
4. Bake in preheated oven for 25 minutes, or until browned.

Mrs. Milton T. Tathbun, NG,
Rebekah Magnolia Lodge No. 21,
Fitzgerald, Ga.

BAKED DOVES WITH RICE

Serves 6

¼ cup butter
½ cup chopped onions
½ cup chopped celery
1 cup rice
10½-ounce can condensed chicken broth
8-ounce can mushrooms, undrained
6 doves
12 slices bacon

1. Preheat oven to 325° F. Grease 13 x 9½ x 2-inch baking pan.
2. Melt butter in skillet. Add onions, celery and rice; sauté for 5 minutes, stirring

frequently. Stir in broth and mushrooms. Pour into pan. Top with doves. Arrange 2 slices of the bacon on each dove.
3. Cover with foil. Bake in preheated oven for 45 minutes, or until tender.

Mrs. Lemuel Parr, Junior Woman's Club,
Sylvester, Ga.

Grouse

ROAST GROUSE

Serves 4

4 1-pound grouse
Salt
½ teaspoon baking soda
1 large onion, finely chopped
3 tart apples, finely chopped
Pepper
1 cup water

1. Day before, place grouse in large bowl. Add water to cover; sprinkle with 1 teaspoon salt and baking soda. Cover; let stand overnight.
2. Next day, preheat oven to 375° F.
3. Drain grouse; pat dry.
4. Prepare Apple Stuffing: Combine onion, apples, dash of pepper and ½ teaspoon salt; mix well.
5. Sprinkle grouse inside and out with salt and pepper. Fill cavities with stuffing. Sew or skewer openings. Place on rack in roasting pan. Add water.
6. Cover; roast in preheated oven for 1 hour. Remove cover; roast for 20 minutes longer, or until tender.
7. Serve with pan juices.

Mrs. C. M. Adkins, Jeffersonville Woman's Club,
Tazewell, Va.

LARDED GROUSE

Serves 4

4 small grouse
Thinly sliced bacon
Melted butter
Flour
Salt and pepper to taste

1. Preheat oven to 400° F.
2. On each grouse arrange bacon until bird is completely covered. Tie with string to keep bacon in place.
3. Put birds in roasting pan. Pour sufficient water over them to provide for basting.
4. Roast in preheated oven for 25 minutes. Discard bacon. Brush birds with butter. Sprinkle with flour, salt and pepper. Roast for 15 minutes longer, or until birds are rich brown.

Wilton Manors Women's Club,
Fort Lauderdale, Fla.

Partridge

ROAST PARTRIDGE

Serves 4

4 ¾-pound partridges
Salt and pepper
4 slices bacon
1 cup sour cream

1. Preheat oven to 400° F.
2. Rub partridges inside and out with salt and pepper. Fasten bacon to breasts. Place birds, breast up, on rack in shallow roasting pan.
3. Bake in preheated oven for 30 minutes. Reduce temperature to 350° F. Roast for 50 minutes longer, or until tender.
4. Pour sour cream over birds. Return to oven until juices bubble.
5. Arrange birds on serving dish. Serve with pan juices.

Mrs. Bert Warner, Plum Lake Woman's Club,
Star Lake, Wis.

BRAISED PARTRIDGE

Serves 2

    2 ¾-pound partridges
    ½ teaspoon salt
    4 slices bacon, diced
    ¼ cup chopped celery
    ¼ cup chopped onion
    1 cup sliced mushrooms
    1 tablespoon flour
    1 cup water
    1 cup sour cream

1. Wash and dry partridges. Cut each in half; sprinkle with salt.
2. Cook bacon in large skillet over medium heat for 3 minutes. Add partridges; sauté well on all sides.
3. Remove partridges; set aside.
4. Sauté celery and onion in fat remaining in skillet for 5 minutes. Stir in mushrooms; cook over medium heat for 3 minutes. Stir in flour; gradually stir in water; cook over medium heat, stirring constantly, until sauce is thickened and smooth.
5. Return partridges to skillet. Cover; simmer, basting occasionally with sauce, for 1 hour, or until tender.
6. Arrange partridges on serving dish; keep in warm place.
7. Stir sour cream into skillet; bring to boil, stirring frequently. Pour over partridges.

Donna Hedman, Woman's Club, Nevis, Minn.

Pheasant

ROAST PHEASANT WITH APPLE STUFFING

Serves 2 to 4

    ¼ cup butter or margarine
    2 tablespoons finely chopped onion
    2 large apples, chopped
    4 slices toast, cubed
    1 teaspoon salt
    ¼ teaspoon pepper
    1 teaspoon sage
    1 egg
    2- to 4-pound pheasant
    2 thin strips salt pork

1. Preheat oven to 350° F.
2. Prepare Apple Stuffing: Melt butter or margarine in medium skillet; sauté onion and apple for 5 minutes. Remove from heat. Stir in toast, salt, pepper, sage and egg; mix well.

3. Spoon stuffing lightly into neck and body cavities of pheasant; truss bird.
4. Place pheasant in roasting pan; top with pork.
5. Roast in preheated oven for about 1 hour, basting occasionally with pan juices. Untruss.

Mrs. Harvey J. Brooks, Woman's Club,
Essex, Conn.

PHEASANT WITH RICE STUFFING

Serves 4

    2 2½-pound pheasants
    2 teaspoons salt
    1½ cups long-grain rice
    3 cups water
    ½ cup butter
    ½ cup finely chopped celery
    3 tablespoons minced onion
    ½ cup sliced mushrooms
    ⅛ teaspoon thyme
    ⅛ teaspoon crushed savory
      Melted butter
    6 slices bacon

1. Rub cavities of pheasants with 1 teaspoon of the salt.
2. Brown rice well in dry skillet. Transfer to saucepan; add water and remaining salt. Bring to boil; cover tightly; cook over low heat for 20 to 30 minutes, or until tender.
3. Preheat oven to 350° F.
4. Melt ½ cup butter in skillet; sauté celery, onion and mushrooms for 10 minutes, or until tender. Add to rice; mix lightly. Stir in herbs.
5. Stuff birds lightly; truss. Any extra stuffing may be baked in covered casserole during last 30 minutes of roasting time. Brush birds with melted butter; place on rack in roasting pan. Cover breasts of each bird with 3 slices of the bacon.
6. Roast in preheated oven, basting frequently with pan juices, for about 2 hours, or until tender.

Mrs. Isaac G. Cleaver, Women's Club,
Odessa, Del.

Quail

SHERRIED QUAIL

Serves 2 to 4

    4 quail
      Salt and pepper to taste
    ½ cup butter or margarine
    1 cup dry sherry

1. Thoroughly clean each bird; season with salt and pepper.
2. Melt butter or margarine in large skillet; brown quail well on all sides over medium heat.
3. Pour sherry over birds. Cover; simmer for 45 to 60 minutes, or until tender.

Mrs. Pete H. Rhymes, President, Home Arts Club,
Philadelphia, Miss.

COUNTRY FRIED QUAIL
Serves 8

12 quail
Salt
Pepper to taste
2 eggs
¼ cup milk
⅓ cup presifted flour
Fat for deep frying

1. Cut quail in half; season with salt and pepper.
2. In bowl combine eggs, milk, flour and ¼ teaspoon salt. Beat until batter is smooth.
3. Dip quail in batter. Fry in deep fat heated to 365° F. for about 8 minutes, or until golden brown. Drain on absorbent paper.

Mrs. Jimmy Holloway, President,
Possumneck H.D.C., West, Miss.

Wild Duck

ROAST WILD DUCK
Serves 2

To reduce the gamy flavor of a wild duck, insert a small piece of carrot into the cavity, and parboil before roasting. If duck is to be stuffed, use a peeled onion instead of carrot.

Wild duck
Salt and pepper
1 onion or favorite stuffing
Wine Sauce for Game (p. 451)

1. Preheat oven to 450° F.
2. Dry duck; rub inside and out with salt and pepper. Insert onion in cavity, or fill with stuffing.
3. Roast in preheated oven for about 20 minutes, turning occasionally to brown evenly.
4. Serve with Wine Sauce for Game.

Ethel Lee, Gentilly Woods Woman's Club,
New Orleans, La.

ROAST WILD DUCK WITH APPLES
Serves 2

Wild duck
Poultry seasoning
Onion slices
Apple wedges
1 carrot, diced
1 stalk celery, diced
Sliced bacon
Lemon juice
Worcestershire

1. Preheat oven to 500° F.
2. Rub duck inside with poultry seasoning; stuff with onion, apple, carrot and celery.
3. Place, breast up, on rack in roasting pan. Arrange bacon on breast and legs. Baste with lemon juice and Worcestershire.

4. Roast in preheated oven for 30 minutes.

Mrs. David Parsons, Junior Woman's Club,
Concord, Calif.

ROAST WILD DUCK WITH RICE
Serves 2 or 3

2½- to 3-pound wild duck
Salt and pepper to taste
2 cups cooked rice
2 thin strips salt pork

1. Preheat oven to 375° F.
2. Rinse duck well; pat dry. Season cavity with salt and pepper. Fill cavity with rice. Place in roasting pan. Cover breast with pork.
3. Roast in preheated oven for 45 minutes, or until tender.

Mrs. Howey Brooks, Woman's Club, Essex, Conn.

WILD DUCK CREOLE STYLE
Serves 3

1 medium wild duck
Salt and pepper
Gravy coloring
Bacon drippings
1 medium onion, chopped
2 stalks celery, chopped
1 clove garlic, crushed
1 cup water
1 chicken bouillon cube

1. Preheat oven to 325° F.
2. Rub duck inside and out with salt and pepper. Rub outside with gravy coloring and bacon drippings.
3. Cook duck in Dutch oven over medium heat until well browned on all sides. Remove duck.
4. Put onion, celery and garlic into pan; sauté for 5 minutes.
5. Return duck to pan; add water, bouillon cube, liver and gizzard. Bring to boil; cover; cook in preheated oven for 3 hours.
6. Place duck on serving dish in warm place.
7. Remove liver and gizzard; chop finely. Return to pan juices; season with salt and pepper. (If necessary, thicken slightly with flour.) Serve gravy with duck.

Mrs. Lawrence Rowe, President,
Beta Sigma Phi, Beta Psi Chapter,
Starkville, Miss.

POT-ROASTED WILD DUCK
Serves 4 or 5

1 wild duck
Salt and pepper
1 medium onion, chopped
1 green pepper, chopped
1 stalk celery, chopped
2 cloves garlic, crushed
1 medium turnip, peeled and chopped
1 medium tart apple, peeled and chopped
½ cup butter or margarine
Flour
Cooked rice

1. Season duck inside and out with salt and pepper.

2. In mixing bowl combine onion, green pepper, celery, garlic, turnip and apple; mix well; use to stuff cavity of duck. Truss, or sew opening.

3. Melt butter or margarine in Dutch oven or large heavy saucepan; brown duck well on all sides. Cover; simmer over very low heat for 3 to 4 hours, or until tender, turning occasionally. Add a little water at a time if duck begins to stick.

4. Arrange duck on serving dish; keep warm.

5. Thicken gravy with flour; simmer for a few minutes.

6. Serve duck and gravy with rice.

Mrs. W. T. Ewell, President, Wayside H.D.C., Vicksburg, Miss.

Wild Goose

BAKED WILD GOOSE WITH PRUNE STUFFING
Serves 6 to 8

36 prunes
2 cups chicken broth
¼ cup butter or margarine
1 large onion, finely chopped
1 cup fresh bread crumbs
½ pound sausage meat
1 egg, lightly beaten
Salt
Pepper
½ teaspoon sage
1 tablespoon chopped parsley
6- to 8-pound wild goose
2 tablespoons olive oil
Wine Sauce for Wild Goose or
Other Game (p. 451)

1. Place prunes in saucepan; add broth. Cover; simmer for 20 minutes, or until prunes are plump. Remove prunes; discard stones; chop prunes.

2. Preheat oven to 350° F.

3. Prepare Prune Stuffing: Melt butter or margarine in skillet; sauté onion over medium heat until golden.

4. Turn onion and butter into mixing bowl; add prunes, crumbs, sausage meat, egg, 1 teaspoon salt, ⅛ teaspoon pepper, sage and parsley. Mix well.

5. Sprinkle cavity of goose with salt and pepper; fill loosely with stuffing. Sew or skewer opening; place goose, breast up, on rack in shallow roasting pan. Brush goose with oil.

6. Roast in preheated oven, basting occasionally with pan juices, for 3 to 4 hours, or until tender.

7. Place goose on serving dish; remove thread or skewers; serve with Wine Sauce for Wild Goose or Other Game.

Mrs. Andy Griffith, Woman's Club, Manteo, N.C.

10. Meat

Meat supplies much-needed protein to the daily diet. Unfortunately, it is the most expensive item on the menu and can play havoc with the food budget unless care is taken in selecting, storing and cooking it to avoid wastage. Although the American people were once considered a strictly steak- and chop-eating nation, American homemakers have learned to take advantage of less expensive cuts of meat, drawing upon the cuisines of all countries of the world to make savory pot roasts, tender braised meats, delicious stews and an almost limitless variety of other meat dishes.

All About Meat

AMOUNT OF MEAT PER SERVING

Boneless meat, whole or ground: ⅓ pound per person
Meat with bone, such as rib roasts, steaks and chops: ½ pound per person
Bones surrounded by meat such as short ribs, spareribs and pigs' knuckles: 1 pound per serving

CARE OF MEAT IN REFRIGERATOR OR FREEZER

Store fresh meat in the coldest part of the refrigerator. Roasts, steaks and chops should be loosely covered or wrapped. Plastic wrappings on fresh prepackaged meats should be slit to allow air to circulate around the meat. Empty ground meat into a bowl, and cover it loosely with aluminum foil or transparent film.

Most fresh meat can be stored for several days in the refrigerator, but ground meat or variety meats should be used as soon as possible. Store cooked meat, tightly covered, in refrigerator, where it will keep safely for 4 to 5 days.

To freeze meat: Package the meat in moisture- and vaporproof paper, molding the paper closely to meat to eliminate air pockets, or package it in airtight freezer containers. Store at a constant 0° F. Keep meat wrapped while it is defrosting.

HINTS AND RULES FOR THE PREPARATION OF MEAT

Always have meat at room temperature before cooking. Always preheat the oven or broiler; this will seal in juices and flavor. Do not overcook choice cuts of meat, such as prime ribs or sirloin tip roast. All roasts from shoulder cuts should be cooked until well done, but be careful not to overcook.

In rotisserie barbecuing, most cuts of meat may be used. Balance the roast, and secure it tightly. A meat thermometer is helpful, particularly in outdoor cooking, where the temperature will vary with wind and weather.

Patronize a reliable butcher, and depend on his advice about the best cuts available at the time. The U.S. Department of Agriculture (USDA) inspects all meat for wholesomeness but does not grade all meat. Beware of fancy names, and depend on government grades and the word of a dependable butcher.

BASIC METHODS OF COOKING MEAT

ROASTING

Cooking meat in the dry heat of the oven in an open pan is known as roasting. The seasoned meat is placed, fat side up, on a rack in a shallow baking pan and is cooked either by a high-low heat method or by a constant heat method. The constant heat method results in less shrinkage. A small amount of liquid may be added to the pan, and the roast may be basted with pan juices throughout the cooking.

BROILING OR GRILLING

Cooking by direct heat, either in an oven or over charcoal, is known as broiling or grilling. For oven broiling, the broiler is usually preheated, the broiler rack is greased and the meat is cooked 2 to 5 inches from heat, depending on the type and thickness of the meat. The fat on steaks and chops should be slashed at intervals to prevent the meat from curling. Charcoal fires should be started well in advance of grilling meat and allowed to burn down until the coals are gray all over. Hardwood charcoal briquettes give the best results.

PAN BROILING AND PAN SAUTÉING

A heavy skillet is used for both these methods of cooking. For pan broiling, the meat is placed in a dry skillet without fat or liquid and is cooked over high heat until browned on both sides. The heat is then reduced to medium, and the meat is cooked until done to taste. The meat is turned occasionally, and the fat is poured out of the pan as it accumulates.

For pan sautéing, a small amount of butter, margarine, shortening, cooking oil or bacon drippings is heated in the pan, and the meat is cooked over moderate heat. Often meat is coated with flour or egg and crumbs before it is pan-sautéed.

BRAISING

This type of cooking can be done equally well on top of the stove or in a slow oven. The meat is usually browned well on all sides in a small amount of fat in a heavy kettle or Dutch oven. Seasonings and a small amount of liquid are then added, the kettle is covered with a tight-fitting lid to hold in the steam and the meat is cooked slowly until tender. The cooking time depends on the kind and quality of the meat.

STEWING

In this method of cooking a large quantity of liquid is used, but as in braising, meats may be stewed over direct heat or in a slow oven. The meat is cubed and browned well in a little fat. Sufficient liquid is then added to cover the meat, and seasonings are added. Finely chopped vegetables, designed to give more flavor to the sauce, may also be added at this time, but whole or sliced vegetables to serve with the meat should not be added until near the end of the cooking. Stews should never be allowed to boil; they should be cooked just at the simmering point, or barely bubbling.

MEAT AND CORRECT SAUCES

Roast beef: grated horseradish, tomato or cranberry sauce
Roast pork: applesauce
Boiled ham: mustard or currant jelly
Roast lamb: mint sauce
Mutton: caper sauce or tart jelly
Boiled tongue: sliced lemons or horseradish
Venison: currant jelly

Mrs. Cort A. Carter, Women's Club, Kirkland, Ariz.

Beef

Good beef is firm and fine-grained, well marbled with fat. The fat should be firm and creamy white.

GRADES OF BEEF

All beef is inspected and approved by the U.S. Department of Agriculture. The purple stamp on the fat will tell you what grade of meat you are buying.

Prime: This is the top grade of beef from choice steers.

Choice: This is an excellent grade of meat, not as heavily marbled as the prime.
Good: This grade of meat is best for braising or stewing. A steak graded good should be marinated before cooking to tenderize it.
Commercial and Utility: This meat is suitable only for braising or stewing.

CUTS OF BEEF AND HOW TO COOK THEM
Roast
  Standing rib roast
  Rolled rib roast
  Whole tenderloin
  Choice sirloin tip roast
Broil, Grill or Pan-Broil
  Porterhouse steak
  Sirloin steak
  T-bone steak
  Club steak or rib steak
  Tenderloin fillets
  Prime rump steak
  Prime chuck steak
  Choice round steak
  Choice chuck steak (marinate before cooking)
Braise
  Chuck steak
  Rolled roast from chuck
  Arm pot roast
  Short ribs
  Brisket
  Rolled rump
  Eye of round or bottom round
  Oxtails
  Tongue
Boil or Stew
  Brisket
  Shank
  Flank
  Short ribs
  Rump
  Tongue

How to Carve Beef Roasts

A *standing rib roast* is brought to the table on a platter. The cut side should be up, and the ribs should be to the carver's left. Insert a carving fork deep into the flesh between two ribs. Cut horizontally to the rib bone. With tip of knife, cut along length of rib bone, freeing slice of meat from bone.

A *rolled roast* is also placed cut side up on the platter. Since there is no need to cut along a bone, simply slice crosswise through the roast.

How to Carve a Steak

Steak is preferably served on a wooden platter with carved grooves and a gravy well.

Remove the T-shaped bone of a porterhouse steak by cutting around its edge with the point of a knife. Transfer it to small plate. Carve across the entire width of

Meat Cuts and Their Preparation

BEEF CHART

WHOLESALE CUTS OF BEEF AND THEIR BONE STRUCTURE

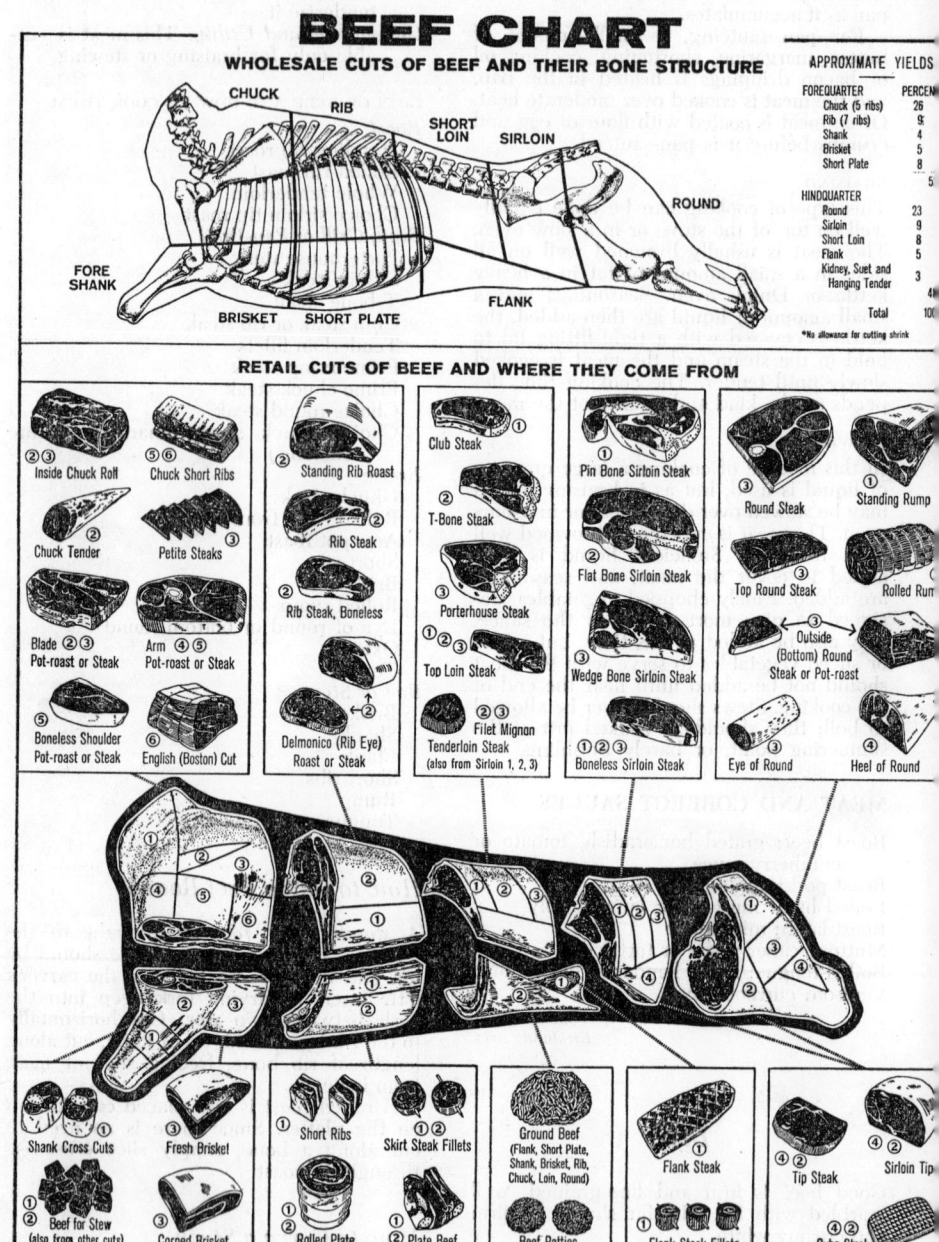

CHUCK

RIB

SHORT LOIN

SIRLOIN

ROUND

FORE SHANK

BRISKET   SHORT PLATE

FLANK

APPROXIMATE YIELDS

FOREQUARTER	PERCENT
Chuck (5 ribs)	26
Rib (7 ribs)	9
Shank	4
Brisket	5
Short Plate	8
	5
HINDQUARTER	
Round	23
Sirloin	9
Short Loin	8
Flank	5
Kidney, Suet and Hanging Tender	3
	4
Total	100

*No allowance for cutting shrink

RETAIL CUTS OF BEEF AND WHERE THEY COME FROM

② ③ Inside Chuck Roll

⑤ ⑥ Chuck Short Ribs

Chuck Tender

③ Petite Steaks

Blade **② ③** Pot-roast or Steak

Arm **④ ⑤** Pot-roast or Steak

⑤ Boneless Shoulder Pot-roast or Steak

⑥ English (Boston) Cut

② Standing Rib Roast

② Rib Steak

② Rib Steak, Boneless

Delmonico (Rib Eye) Roast or Steak ←②

Club Steak **①**

② T-Bone Steak

③ Porterhouse Steak

①②③ Top Loin Steak

②③ Filet Mignon Tenderloin Steak (also from Sirloin 1, 2, 3)

① Pin Bone Sirloin Steak

② Flat Bone Sirloin Steak

③ Wedge Bone Sirloin Steak

①②③ Boneless Sirloin Steak

③ Round Steak

① Standing Rump

③ Top Round Steak

① Rolled Rump

Outside (Bottom) Round Steak or Pot-roast

③ Eye of Round

④ Heel of Round

Shank Cross Cuts **①**

Fresh Brisket **③**

①② Beef for Stew (also from other cuts)

Corned Brisket **③**

① Short Ribs

①② Skirt Steak Fillets

①② Rolled Plate

② Plate Beef

Ground Beef (Flank, Short Plate, Shank, Brisket, Rib, Chuck, Loin, Round)

Beef Patties

Flank Steak

① Flank Steak Fillets

④② Tip Steak

④② Cube Steak

④② Sirloin Tip

NATIONAL LIVE STOCK AND MEAT BOARD

PORK CHART

WHOLESALE CUTS OF PORK AND THEIR BONE STRUCTURE

APPROXIMATE YIELDS*

NAME OF CUT	PERCENT
Fresh Hams, Skinned	18.5
Loins, Blade on	15.0
Boston Butts	6.5
Picnics, Regular	8.5
Bacon, Square Cut	17.5
Spareribs	3.0
Jowl, Trimmed	3.0
Feet, Tail, Neckbones	5.0
Fat Back, Clear Plate and all Fat Trimmings	18.0
Sausages Trimmings	5.0
Total	100

*Packer Dressed Hog, Head off, Leaf out
No allowance for cutting shrink

RETAIL CUTS OF PORK AND WHERE THEY COME FROM

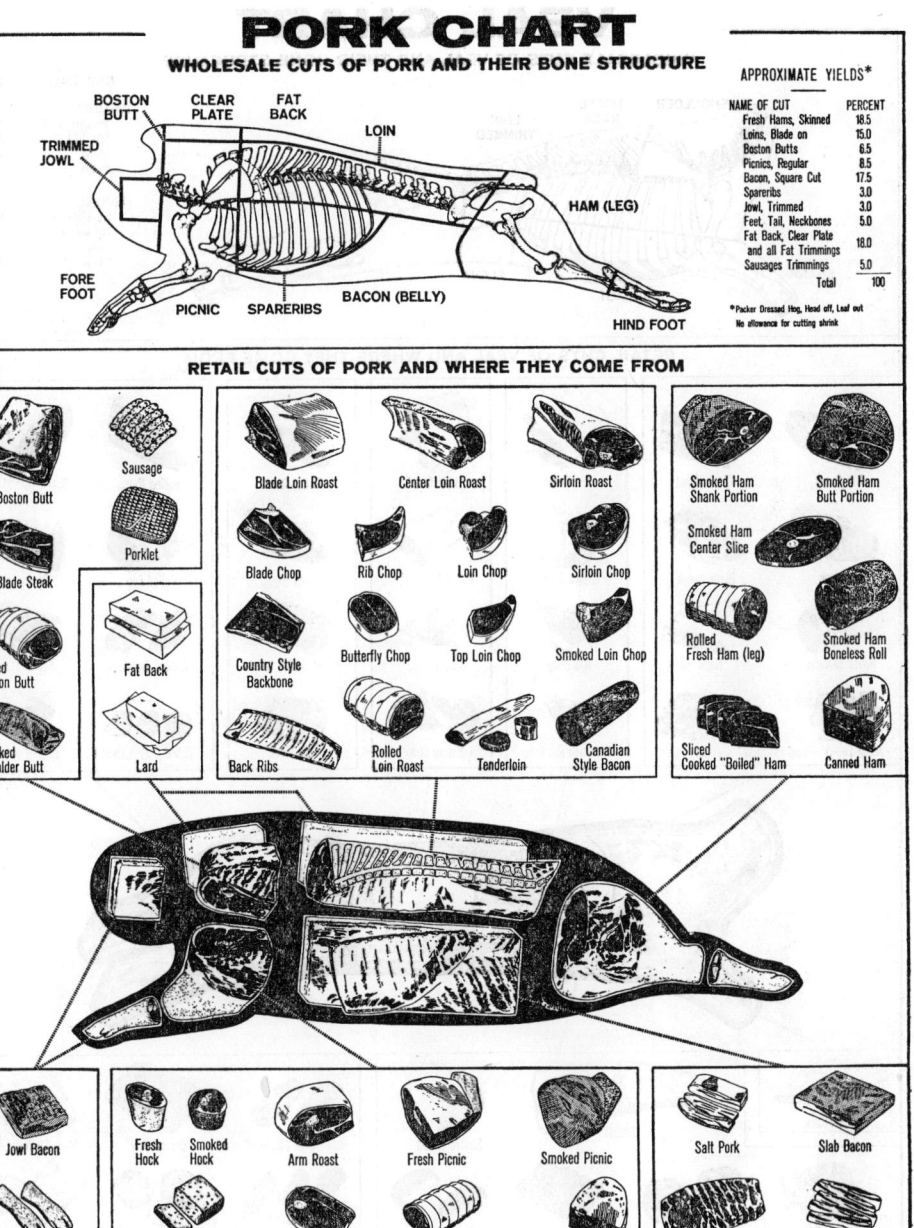

NATIONAL LIVE STOCK AND MEAT BOARD

VEAL CHART
WHOLESALE CUTS OF VEAL AND THEIR BONE STRUCTURE

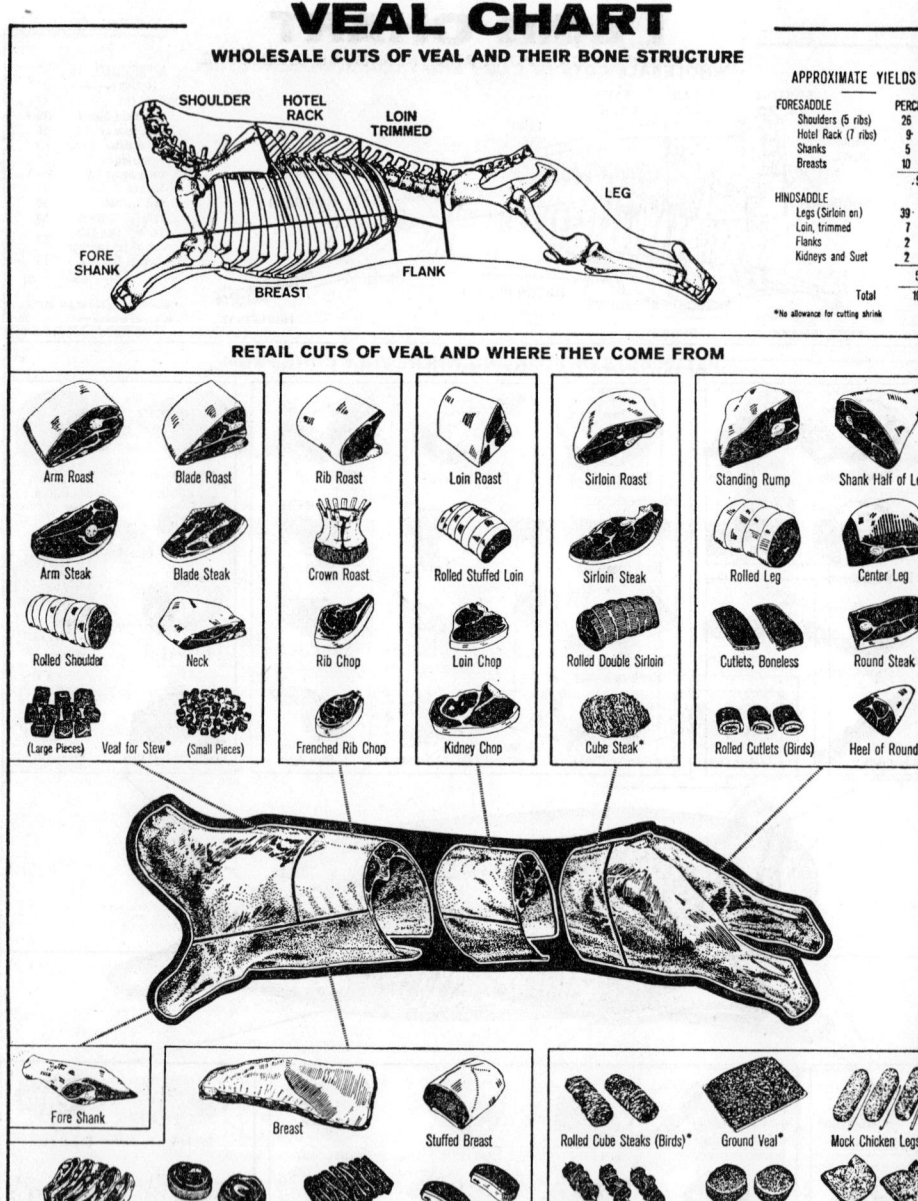

APPROXIMATE YIELDS*	
FORESADDLE	PERCENT
Shoulders (5 ribs)	25
Hotel Rack (7 ribs)	9
Shanks	5
Breasts	10
	.50
HINDSADDLE	
Legs (Sirloin on)	39
Loin, trimmed	7
Flanks	2
Kidneys and Suet	2
	50
Total	100

*No allowance for cutting shrink

Labels on diagram: SHOULDER, HOTEL RACK, LOIN TRIMMED, LEG, FORE SHANK, BREAST, FLANK

RETAIL CUTS OF VEAL AND WHERE THEY COME FROM

Arm Roast — Blade Roast — Rib Roast — Loin Roast — Sirloin Roast — Standing Rump — Shank Half of Leg

Arm Steak — Blade Steak — Crown Roast — Rolled Stuffed Loin — Sirloin Steak — Rolled Leg — Center Leg

Rolled Shoulder — Neck — Rib Chop — Loin Chop — Rolled Double Sirloin — Cutlets, Boneless — Round Steak

(Large Pieces) Veal for Stew* (Small Pieces) — Frenched Rib Chop — Kidney Chop — Cube Steak* — Rolled Cutlets (Birds) — Heel of Round

Fore Shank — Breast — Stuffed Breast — Rolled Cube Steaks (Birds)* — Ground Veal* — Mock Chicken Legs*

Riblets — Brisket Rolls — Brisket Pieces — Stuffed Chops — City Chicken* — Patties* — Choplets*

*VEAL FOR STEW, GRINDING OR CUBING MAY COME FROM ANY WHOLESALE CUT

NATIONAL LIVE STOCK AND MEAT BOARD

LAMB CHART

WHOLESALE CUTS OF LAMB AND THEIR BONE STRUCTURE

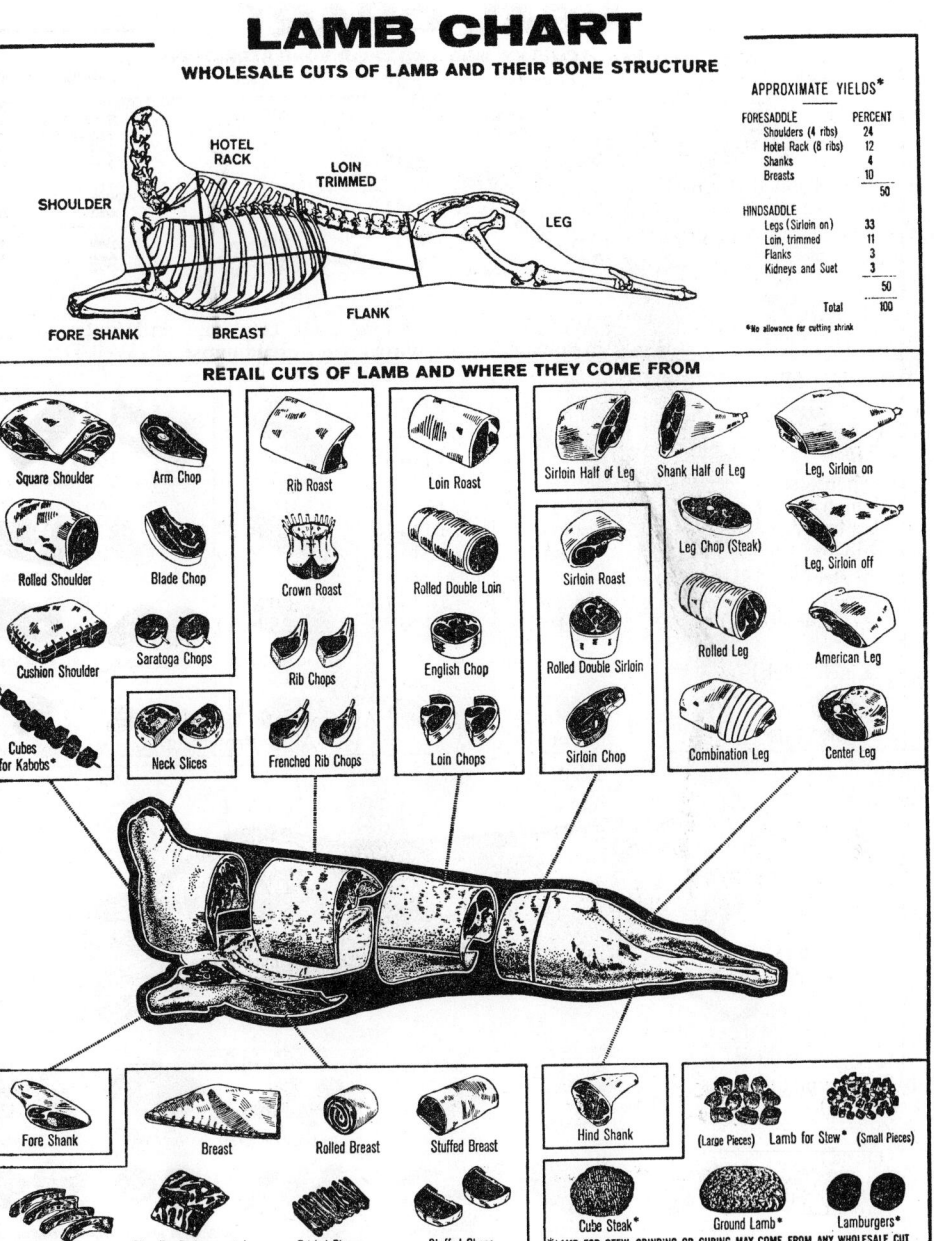

APPROXIMATE YIELDS*	
FORESADDLE	PERCENT
Shoulders (4 ribs)	24
Hotel Rack (8 ribs)	12
Shanks	4
Breasts	10
	50
HINDSADDLE	
Legs (Sirloin on)	33
Loin, trimmed	11
Flanks	3
Kidneys and Suet	3
	50
Total	100

*No allowance for cutting shrink

SHOULDER   HOTEL RACK   LOIN TRIMMED   LEG

FORE SHANK   BREAST   FLANK

RETAIL CUTS OF LAMB AND WHERE THEY COME FROM

Square Shoulder   Arm Chop   Rib Roast   Loin Roast   Sirloin Half of Leg   Shank Half of Leg   Leg, Sirloin on

Rolled Shoulder   Blade Chop   Crown Roast   Rolled Double Loin   Sirloin Roast   Leg Chop (Steak)   Leg, Sirloin off

Cushion Shoulder   Saratoga Chops   Rib Chops   English Chop   Rolled Double Sirloin   Rolled Leg   American Leg

Cubes for Kabobs*   Neck Slices   Frenched Rib Chops   Loin Chops   Sirloin Chop   Combination Leg   Center Leg

Fore Shank   Breast   Rolled Breast   Stuffed Breast   Hind Shank   (Large Pieces) Lamb for Stew* (Small Pieces)

Riblets   Ribs (for Barbecue, etc.)   Brisket Pieces   Stuffed Chops   Cube Steak*   Ground Lamb*   Lamburgers*

*LAMB FOR STEW, GRINDING OR CUBING MAY COME FROM ANY WHOLESALE CUT

NATIONAL LIVE STOCK AND MEAT BOARD

Timetable for Cooking Beef

ROASTING (325° F.)	Weight in Pounds	Approximate Time in Hours		
		Rare (140°)	Medium (160°)	Well Done (170°)
Rib roast	4	1¾	2½	3
	6	3¼	3¾	4¼
	8	3½	4½	5
Boned and rolled rib roast	4	2¾	3¼	3½
	6	3½	4¼	4¾
Prime or choice sirloin tip	3	1¾	2¼	2½
	5	2½	3	3½

BROILING OR GRILLING	Weight in Pounds	Approximate Total Time in Minutes		
		Rare	Medium	Well Done
Tenderloin fillet (1 inch thick)		6 to 8	10	12 to 14
Club steak (1 inch thick)	1½	10 to 12	14	16 to 18
Porterhouse steak (1 inch thick)	2½	12	16	22 to 24
(1½ inch thick)	2½ to 3	16 to 18	18 to 20	25 to 30
(2 inches thick)	3 to 3½	20 to 25	30 to 35	40 to 45
Sirloin steak (1 inch thick)	2⅓ to 3½	16 to 18	20	20 to 25
(1½ inches thick)	3½ to 4½	24 to 28	28 to 30	34 to 36
Patties (¾ inch thick)	¼	8	12	15

BRAISING	Weight in Pounds	Approximate Time in Hours After Browning
Flank steak	1½ to 2	1½
Pot roast	3 to 5	3½ to 4
Short ribs	2 to 2½	2 to 2½
Swiss steak (1 inch thick)	2	1½ to 2
Oxtails	1 to 1½	3 to 4

SIMMERING OR STEWING	Weight in Pounds	Approximate Total Time in Hours
Neck, chuck, plate, heel or round (1½-inch cubes)	2	2½ to 3
Brisket or plate (Fresh)	8	4 to 5
Brisket (cured)	8	6
Shanks (cross cut)	4	3 to 4
Tongue (fresh or smoked)	3 to 4	3 to 4

steak in 1-inch slices, keeping the knife at an angle. Each slice will have a portion of both the tenderloin and the sirloin.

A sirloin is cut in the same manner as a porterhouse. With a steak or boning knife, remove the small bone; then slice across the steak, holding the knife at a slant.

Large Cuts of Beef

STANDING RIBS OF BEEF
Serves 6

2- to 3-rib standing roast with
   chine removed
Salt and pepper to taste

1. Preheat oven to 300° F.
2. Arrange roast, fat side up, on rack in shallow roasting pan. If using meat thermometer, insert in thickest part of roast; make sure bulb is not in fat or resting on bone.
3. Season well with salt and pepper.
4. Roast in preheated oven for 2½ hours, or until done to taste. Allow 18 to 20 minutes per pound for rare; 22 to 25 minutes per pound for medium; 27 to 30 minutes per pound for well-done roast beef.

Mrs. C. H. Hatch, Cultural Club, Alto, La.

ROLLED ROAST BEEF
Serves 12

6-pound rib roast, boned and rolled
   Salt to taste
2 10½-ounce cans condensed beef
   consommé
1 tablespoon cornstarch
2 tablespoons water

1. Trim all fat from beef; place in roasting pan. Add 1 inch water; season beef with salt.
2. Put in cold oven; set temperature at 325° F. Bake for about 4 hours.
3. When beef is done to taste, place on serving dish; keep in warm place.
4. Stir consommé into pan juices; bring to boil.
5. Combine cornstarch and water; stir into consommé. Cook over low heat, stirring constantly, until smooth. Serve with beef.

Mrs. Lemuel Sharp, North Jacksonville Woman's Club, Jacksonville, Fla.

FILLET OF BEEF, "THE KING OF MEATS"
**Serves 6 to 10,
Depending on Size of Fillet**

1 fillet of beef
   Sliced bacon
   Broiled mushrooms
   Kumquats
   Parsley sprig

1. Remove all fat from fillet of beef; wrap bacon slices around it. Use no seasoning (salt and pepper tend to toughen meat and bacon is sufficient seasoning). Place beef in roasting pan.

2. Preheat oven to 400° F.
3. Roast in preheated oven for 30 minutes.
4. If guests are not ready and meat is done, remove from oven; cover beef with towel. Just before serving, place beef under broiler until just browned on both sides; bacon will become crisp.
5. Cut into 1-inch-thick slices; arrange on platter as if whole. There will be a variety of doneness from rare to well done. If further seasoning is desired, use some seasoned salt immediately before serving or after broiling.
6. Garnish with a mound of steaming mushrooms on one side of meat and a mound of cold kumquats on other side. Top meat with parsley sprig.

Mrs. Lyndon B. Johnson's recipe, submitted to Mrs. William Hasebroock, Honorary President, General Federation of Women's Clubs, West Point, Neb.

BAKED BEEF TENDERLOIN
Serves 10

1 cup French dressing
2 tablespoons seasoned salt
1 teaspoon monosodium glutamate
¼ cup grated onion
2 tablespoons lemon juice
4-pound beef tenderloin
½ cup butter
½ pound mushrooms, sliced

1. Prepare marinade: Blend French dressing, seasoned salt, monosodium glutamate, onion and lemon juice in bowl.
2. Arrange beef in shallow roasting pan; pour marinade over it. Marinate for 1 hour.
3. Preheat oven to 350° F.
4. Dot beef with ¼ cup of the butter. Bake in preheated oven for 45 minutes, or until done to taste.
5. Meanwhile, melt remaining butter in large skillet; sauté mushrooms.
6. Cut beef into 1-inch slices; arrange on serving dish. Cover with mushrooms.

Submitted to Woman's Club, Kankakee, Ill., by Mrs. Samuel H. Shapiro, Office of the Lieutenant Governor, Springfield, Ill.

BROILED WHOLE BEEF TENDERLOIN
Serves 8 to 10

If tenderloin has not been larded, the flavor is improved by marinating it for a few hours in olive oil and lemon juice, but if you tell your butcher you want it larded, he will wrap it in a thin layer of fat and tie it at intervals.

⅓ cup butter
2 medium onions, sliced
1 clove garlic, crushed
½ cup sliced mushrooms
½ pound ground beef
   Salt and pepper to taste
5- to 7-pound beef tenderloin, larded

1. Preheat broiler.
2. Melt butter in skillet; sauté onions, garlic and mushrooms until limp. Add

ground beef; cook until meat loses red color. Season with salt and pepper.

3. Place beef tenderloin on broiler pan; broil 2 inches from heat for 8 minutes. Turn tenderloin; broil for 7 minutes longer.

4. Turn temperature to 400° F.

5. Arrange tenderloin on rack in shallow roasting pan; season with salt and pepper. Spread ground beef mixture on tenderloin.

6. Roast in preheated oven for 10 minutes.

Mrs. Harold A. Reise, Woman's Club, Wilmette, Ill.

CHATEAUBRIAND

Serves 8 to 10

5- to 6-pound beef tenderloin
1 cup sweet white wine
½ cup butter
½ cup brandy
¼ teaspoon thyme
1 bay leaf
1 teaspoon salt
⅛ teaspoon pepper
1 small onion, thinly sliced
1 pound mushrooms, thinly sliced

1. Day before, place beef in large container; sprinkle with wine. Cover; marinate for 24 hours, turning occasionally.

2. Next day, preheat oven to 450° F.

3. Melt butter in large skillet. Stir in brandy, thyme, bay leaf, salt and pepper. Add onion; simmer until liquid is reduced by half. Add mushrooms; simmer for 4 minutes, stirring frequently.

4. Remove beef; reserve marinade. Cut pocket in beef; fill with mushroom mixture. Skewer opening.

5. Roast in preheated oven for 1 hour, basting frequently with pan juices and marinade. Beef will be rare. This may be spit-roasted, if desired.

Lee Merritt, Junior Women's Club, Tenafly, N.J.

BOLICHI (Stuffed Beef)

Serves 8 to 10

¼ pound peperoni
1 medium onion
½ medium green pepper
1 cup diced cooked ham
1 clove garlic
1 stalk celery
Salt and pepper to taste
⅛ teaspoon orégano
⅛ teaspoon basil
1 tablespoon Worcestershire
3- to 4-pound eye of round roast,
   with large pocket cut lengthwise
   through center
2 teaspoons paprika
2 teaspoons bacon drippings or
   shortening
2 tablespoons flour
2 cups water

1. Prepare filling: Put peperoni, onion, green pepper, ham, garlic and celery through medium blade of meat grinder. Turn into mixing bowl; season with salt and pepper. Add orégano, basil and Worcestershire; mix well.

2. Stuff pocket in roast with filling; skewer open end. Rub roast well with salt, pepper and paprika.

3. Preheat oven to 325° F. Put large square of heavy aluminum foil in center of roasting pan.

4. Melt bacon drippings or shortening in skillet; brown meat well on all sides.

5. Place meat in center of foil; wrap loosely to form package.

6. Roast in preheated oven for 2½ hours. Arrange roast on serving dish; keep warm.

7. Brown flour lightly in skillet, stirring frequently. Gradually stir in drippings from foil and water. Cook over medium heat, stirring constantly, until thickened and smooth. Correct seasonings. Serve with roast.

Mrs. A. L. Stathis, Woman's Club, Sebring, Fla.

ROAST PEPPERED RIB EYE

Serves 8 to 10

5- to 6-pound boneless eye of
   rib roast
½ cup coarsely cracked peppercorns
½ teaspoon ground cardamom
1 tablespoon tomato paste
½ teaspoon garlic powder
1 teaspoon paprika
1 cup soy sauce
¾ cup vinegar
1½ tablespoons cornstarch

1. Day before, trim fat from beef; press peppercorns and cardamom into beef with palm of hand. Arrange in shallow pan.

2. Prepare marinade: Blend tomato paste, garlic powder and paprika. Stir in soy sauce and vinegar. Pour over beef; cover; marinate in refrigerator for 24 hours, spooning marinade over beef several times.

3. Next day, remove meat from marinade; reserve marinade; let meat stand at room temperature for 1 hour. Preheat oven to 300° F.

4. Wrap beef in aluminum foil; place in shallow roasting pan.

5. Roast in preheated oven for 2 hours, for medium rare. Turn temperature to 350° F.

6. Open foil; spoon out juices from foil. Brown roast in oven for 15 minutes.

7. Meanwhile, prepare gravy: In saucepan blend ¼ cup water and cornstarch. Stir in beef juices and 1 cup water. Cook over medium heat, stirring constantly, until sauce is thickened and clear. If desired, some marinade may be added to gravy. Correct seasoning; skim off fat; simmer for 2 minutes.

8. Arrange beef on serving dish; serve with gravy.

Woman's Club, Erwin, Tenn.

BARBECUED BRISKET OF BEEF

Serves 6 to 8

4-pound brisket of beef
1 cup vinegar
2 tablespoons Worcestershire
1 tablespoon sugar

1 teaspoon salt
1 clove garlic, crushed
½ teaspoon Tabasco
½ cup catsup
1 teaspoon dry mustard
Beef consommé

1. Preheat oven to 350° F.
2. Wash beef; trim off excess fat.
3. Blend remaining ingredients in shallow roasting pan. Add beef.
4. Roast in preheated oven for 2 hours, allowing 30 minutes per pound. Baste meat frequently during cooking with pan juices. If sauce gets too thick, thin with a little consommé.

*Betty Grosslight, Junior Woman's Club,
Sunland, Calif.*

BRISKET OF BEEF AND SAUERKRAUT

Serves 6

2-pound brisket of beef
2 large onions, sliced
1 bay leaf
2 teaspoons salt
1-pound 11-ounce can sauerkraut, undrained
1 medium potato, grated
1 medium apple, sliced
1½ teaspoons caraway seeds

1. Place beef in Dutch oven or heavy kettle. Add water just to cover. Bring to boil; skim.
2. Add onions, bay leaf and salt. Cover; simmer for 2 hours.
3. Meanwhile, put sauerkraut, potato and apple in saucepan. Cover; simmer for 30 minutes.
4. Remove meat and onions from pan; set aside; reserve one-fourth of liquid.
5. Rinse pan; return meat, onions and reserved liquid. Stir in sauerkraut mixture; sprinkle with caraway seeds. Cover; simmer for 15 minutes longer, or until tender.

Mrs. Michael Kahn, Woman's Club, Sebring, Fla.

PEKING ROAST

Serves 6 to 8

3- to 5-pound brisket of beef
2 cloves garlic, slivered
1 cup vinegar
2 tablespoons shortening
2 cups strong black coffee
2 cups water
2 teaspoons salt
½ teaspoon pepper
1 tablespoon flour

1. 24 or 48 hours before, wipe beef with damp cloth. Cut slits in meat with sharp knife. Insert garlic slivers into slits; place beef in mixing bowl. Pour vinegar over beef; cover; refrigerate for 24 to 48 hours, turning occasionally.
2. When ready to use, remove meat from vinegar; wipe dry.
3. Melt shortening in Dutch oven or large kettle; brown beef on all sides over high heat.
4. Add coffee and water. Bring to boil. Season with salt and pepper. Cover; simmer for 4 to 6 hours, or until tender. Add water, if necessary, during cooking.
5. Arrange meat on serving dish; keep in warm place.
6. Sprinkle pan juices with flour; beat with whisk until smooth. Correct seasoning and consistency of gravy. Serve with meat.

*Vivian Bates, Grant County Junior Woman's Club,
Williamstown, Ky.*

BOILED BEEF OR POT-AU-FEU

Serves 6

3 pounds rump roast
2 pounds beef shank
4 quarts water
6 carrots, scraped
6 parsnips, scraped
3 onions, each stuck with clove
6 leeks (white parts only)
3 small hearts celery, halved
4 sprigs parsley
2 tablespoons salt
1 small head cabbage
Prepared mustard or horseradish
Boiled potatoes

1. Put meats in large kettle with water; bring to boil, skimming as scum rises to surface. Simmer for 2 hours, adding a little water occasionally to keep meat well submerged and skimming frequently.
2. Add carrots, parsnips, onions, leeks, celery, parsley and salt; cook over low heat for 1 to 1½ hours longer.
3. Skim all fat from surface of stock; reserve fat; continue to simmer meat.
4. Core cabbage; cut into wedges. Put in saucepan; cover with boiling water; then drain well. Add ½ cup of reserved fat and 1 cup stock. Cover; cook for 30 minutes.
5. Strain stock into soup tureen. Place meat in center of large platter; surround with vegetables, arranging cabbage wedges at each end. Serve with mustard or horseradish and potatoes.

A. S.

Steaks

BROILED STEAK

Serves 3 or 4

1½-pound 1½-inch-thick sirloin steak
Salt and pepper to taste
2 tablespoons melted butter
3 tablespoons water

1. Preheat broiler.
2. Wipe steak with damp cloth; remove excess fat and gristle. Slash edges to prevent curling.
3. Place steak on broiler pan. Broil 4 to 5 inches from heat for about 4 minutes on each side, or until done to taste.
4. Put steak on serving dish; sprinkle with salt, pepper and butter.
5. Swirl water into pan juices; bring to boil. Pour over steak.

Mrs. Bob Chambers, Woman's Club, Cornelia, Ga.

PLANKED STEAK
Serves 4
2½-pound 3-inch-thick sirloin steak
2 cups hot mashed potatoes
4 tablespoons melted butter or
   margarine
Salt
Pepper
1 egg
4 firm medium tomatoes, halved
4 large mushroom caps

1. Preheat oven to 425° F.
2. Trim fat from steak; remove bone.
3. Put fat on plank; place in preheated oven for 10 minutes, or until wood is saturated with grease.
4. Remove plank from oven; discard pieces of fat.
5. Put steak on plank. Roast in preheated oven for 20 minutes, or until done to taste.
6. Meanwhile, put potatoes in mixing bowl; add 2 tablespoons of the butter or margarine, ½ teaspoon salt, dash of pepper and egg. Beat well until smooth; then put potatoes in pastry bag with large fluted tube.
7. Remove plank from oven; press potatoes through pastry tube to form roses around steak. Return to oven; roast for 10 minutes longer.
8. Meanwhile, arrange tomato halves and mushroom caps on broiler pan. Sprinkle with salt and pepper; brush with remaining butter or margarine. Broil for 5 minutes, or until tender.
9. Remove plank from oven. Arrange tomatoes and mushrooms around steak.

Mrs. Robert S. Wagner, Woman's Club,
Bangor, Pa.

FILET MIGNON SEMIRAMIS
Serves 4
4 ¼-pound slices fillet of beef
4-ounce can pâté de foie gras
1 small truffle, quartered
4 slices bacon
2 tablespoons butter

1. Cut slit in side of each fillet to make pocket. Fill with pâté de foie gras and piece of truffle. Wrap each fillet in bacon slice; secure with wooden pick.
2. Melt butter in skillet; brown fillets on both sides over medium heat, about 5 minutes in all.

Mrs. O. N. Naylor, People's Church
Women's Club, Chicago, Ill.

LONDON BROIL WITH CLARET SAUCE
Serves 4
2-pound flank steak
Salt and pepper to taste
Claret Sauce (p. 443)

1. Preheat broiler.
2. Arrange steak on broiler pan. Broil 4 to 5 inches from heat for about 5 minutes on each side, or until done to taste.
3. Season with salt and pepper. Cut steak into 1-inch slices across grain.

4. Arrange slices on serving dish. Coat with Claret Sauce.

Madelaine Goldberg, Junior Woman's Club,
Tullahoma, Tenn.

PEPPER STEAK
Serves 4
2 tablespoons cracked peppercorns
2-pound 1½-inch-thick lean sirloin
   steak
⅓ cup olive oil
½ cup beef consommé
2 tablespoons Worcestershire
½ cup chopped parsley

1. Press pepper into both sides of steak.
2. Heat oil in large skillet; brown steak quickly on both sides. Reduce heat. Cook until done to taste. Arrange on serving platter.
3. Pour off oil from skillet; then combine consommé, Worcestershire and parsley in skillet. Bring to boil, stirring. Pour over steak.

Zella Berklan, Brainerd Junior Woman's Club,
Chicago, Ill.

EILEEN'S BAR-B-Q FLAT CHUCK ROAST
Serves 6
4 tablespoons olive oil
4 cloves garlic, crushed
½ teaspoon dry mustard
2 teaspoons soy sauce
1 teaspoon rosemary
½ cup vinegar
½ cup sauterne
4-pound 2½- to 3-inch-thick chuck
   roast
4 tablespoons catsup
3 teaspoons bottled steak sauce
1 teaspoon Worcestershire

1. Day before, heat oil in saucepan. Add garlic, mustard, soy sauce and rosemary. Cook for 1 minute, stirring constantly. Remove from heat. Stir in vinegar and sauterne.
2. Put beef in bowl or crock; pour vinegar mixture over it; refrigerate for 24 hours, turning 4 or 5 times.
3. Next day, prepare charcoal fire.
4. Remove meat from marinade. Add remaining ingredients to marinade; blend well; bring to simmer.
5. Brush meat well with marinade; grill over hot coals, basting frequently during cooking. Keep sauce simmering; if it gets too thick, add a little olive oil.
6. For rare in middle and charred on outside, grill for about 20 minutes on each side.

Mrs. Thomas Nickerson, Junior Women's Club,
Rye, N.H.

ORIENTAL FLANK STEAK
Serves 4 to 6
2 cloves garlic, crushed
½ cup olive oil
½ cup soy sauce
¾ cup red wine vinegar
3-pound flank steak

1. Prepare marinade: In shallow flat dish combine garlic, oil, soy sauce and vinegar; mix well.

2. Cut steak into 1-inch-wide pieces; add to marinade. Cover; marinate for at least 6 hours, turning occasionally.

3. Preheat broiler. Arrange steak slices on broiler pan.

4. Broil 3 to 4 inches from heat for 4 minutes on each side, or until done to taste.

Clarice McKinstry, East Glen Junior Women's Club, Portland, Ore.

EASY SUKIYAKI (Japanese Steak Dish)
Serves 4

1 teaspoon butter
2 medium onions, thinly sliced
1-pound sirloin steak or fillet of beef, cut into thin strips about 1 x 2 inches
1 tablespoon sugar
½ cup soy sauce
1 cup bamboo shoots, sliced
1 cup scallions, cut into 1½-inch lengths
½ cup sliced mushrooms
2 cups water cress
Cooked rice

1. Melt butter in large skillet; sauté onions for 3 minutes, stirring frequently. Stir in beef; cook over medium heat for 5 minutes, or until tender.

2. Add sugar and soy sauce; bring to boil. Add bamboo shoots, scallions and mushrooms; simmer for 5 minutes. Add water cress; simmer for 2 minutes.

3. Serve on rice.

Mrs. Gladys Robinson, Woman's Club, DeBary, Fla.

CHUCK STEAK WITH VEGETABLES IN GINGER SAUCE
Serves 8

¼ cup soy sauce
2 tablespoons dry white wine
2 teaspoons sugar
½ teaspoon powdered ginger
1½-pound chuck steak, cut into thin strips about ¼ x 1½ x 3 inches
¾ cup water
3-ounce can sliced mushrooms, undrained
2 10-ounce packages frozen French-cut string beans
1 tablespoon cooking oil
1 clove garlic, minced
1 tablespoon cornstarch

1. In shallow dish combine soy sauce, wine, sugar and ginger. Add beef; marinate for 30 minutes.

2. In saucepan combine water and mushrooms. Bring to boil. Add beans; cook for 5 minutes, or until almost tender. Set aside.

3. Heat oil in heavy skillet; brown garlic. Drain beef; reserve marinade. Add beef to skillet; brown quickly for 2 minutes, turning to cook on both sides.

4. Mix cornstarch and marinade; stir into meat.

5. Add mushroom-bean mixture with liquid. Cook, stirring constantly, until sauce is thickened and clear.

Audry Herbison, El Camino Women's Club, Ventura, Calif.

BEEF STROGANOFF
Serves 6

1½-pound lean top sirloin roast
3 tablespoons cooking oil
3 tablespoons vinegar
¼ cup butter or margarine
1 large onion, sliced
½ pound mushrooms, sliced
½ cup dry sherry
¼ cup water
2 teaspoons salt
¼ teaspoon pepper
1 cup sour cream
Cooked rice or noodles

1. Cut beef into ½-inch strips. Put in bowl; pour oil and vinegar over beef; marinate for several hours, stirring frequently. Drain beef; pat dry.

2. Melt butter or margarine; sauté in large skillet beef, onion and mushrooms over high heat, stirring frequently, until beef is browned.

3. Stir in sherry, water, salt and pepper. Bring to boil; then simmer for 5 minutes.

4. Remove from heat. Quickly stir in sour cream.

5. Serve at once with rice or noodles.

Mary Audsley, Woman's Club, Redwood City, Calif.

TENDERLOIN TIPS IN BURGUNDY
Serves 6

1½-pound beef tenderloin, cut into very thin 2- to 3-inch strips
Salt
6 tablespoons butter
1 medium onion, chopped
1 medium green pepper, chopped
1¼ cups canned or leftover beef gravy
Pepper to taste
2 tablespoons cornstarch
1 cup burgundy

1. Sprinkle beef with ½ teaspoon salt.

2. Melt 2 tablespoons of the butter in large skillet. Add about one-third of beef; brown on all sides over high heat; remove from pan. Cook rest of beef in same way, adding butter, if necessary.

3. Add remaining butter to pan; melt; sauté onion and green pepper for 5 minutes. Stir in beef gravy. Season with salt and pepper.

4. In small bowl blend cornstarch and burgundy; stir into sauce. Cook over medium heat, stirring constantly, until thickened and smooth. Simmer for 2 minutes; then stir in beef; heat thoroughly.

Fran Runyon, Junior Woman's Club, Jacksonville, Fla.

Pot Roasts

BEEF AT ITS BEST

Serves 12

2 teaspoons salt
1 teaspoon seasoned salt
½ teaspoon pepper
5- to 6-pound chuck or rump roast
2 tablespoons shortening
3 cups water
¼ cup presifted flour

1. Preheat oven to 275° F.
2. Rub salt, seasoned salt and pepper into surface of roast.
3. Melt shortening; in roasting pan brown beef well on all sides. Add 2 cups of the water. Cover pan, using heavy aluminum foil under lid to seal tightly.
4. Roast in preheated oven for 3½ hours. Remove cover; if necessary, add remaining water. (A total of 2 cups liquid is necessary for gravy.) Cover; roast for 1 hour longer.
5. Arrange meat on serving dish; keep in warm place.
6. Brown flour in skillet over medium heat, stirring frequently. Gradually stir in pan juices; cook over medium heat, stirring constantly, until thickened and smooth. Correct seasoning; serve with roast.

Mrs. Ike C. Hart, Woman's Club, Sebring, Fla.

BEEF ROAST SUPERB

Serves 8

3- to 4-pound chuck or arm roast
Bottled steak sauce
10½-ounce can condensed cream
of mushroom soup
½ envelope onion soup mix
Flour or cornstarch

1. Preheat oven to 300° F.
2. Brush roast generously with steak sauce; place in center of large piece of aluminum foil. Pour mushroom soup over meat; sprinkle with onion soup mix. Wrap tightly in foil; place in shallow baking pan.
3. Bake in preheated oven for about 3 hours.
4. Arrange meat on warm serving platter. Drain juices in foil into saucepan; thicken with flour or cornstarch to desired consistency; serve separately.

*Mrs. James P. Larsen, Junior Women's Club,
Bismarck, N.D.*

BEEF À LA VENISON

Serves 6 to 8

½ pound bacon, finely diced
1 large carrot, sliced
1 celery root, diced
1 parsley root, diced
1 large onion, chopped
2 bay leaves
Dash of thyme
5 peppercorns
5 whole allspice
1 teaspoon salt
2-pound rump roast
2½ cups boiling water
2 tablespoons flour

2 cups sour cream
Egg Dumplings (p. 460)

1. Cook bacon in Dutch oven or heavy kettle for 5 minutes. Add carrot, celery and parsley roots, onion, bay leaves, thyme, peppercorns and allspice; sauté until browned.
2. Rub salt into roast; add beef to pan; brown well on all sides.
3. Add ½ cup of the water. Cover; simmer for 2½ hours, or until tender, adding water, if necessary, so beef does not dry out.
4. Remove beef; keep in warm place.
5. Add remaining water to pan. Boil for 10 minutes. Strain juices; return to pan. Blend flour and sour cream; gradually stir into pan.
6. Return meat to pan; cook for a few minutes, or until sauce is thickened, stirring occasionally.
7. Serve with Egg Dumplings.

*Mrs. Charles Sindelar, Woman's Club,
Flagler Beach, Fla.*

DUDIE'S BOEUF FLAMBÉ

Serves 8

¼ cup presifted flour
2 teaspoons salt
½ teaspoon pepper
4-pound chuck roast
4 tablespoons butter
¼ cup brandy
½ cup beef broth

1. Preheat oven to 250° F.
2. On piece of waxed paper blend flour, salt, and pepper; use to dredge beef, rubbing in well.
3. Melt 2 tablespoons of the butter in skillet; brown meat on all sides.
4. Meanwhile, put remaining butter in 3-quart earthenware casserole; place in preheated oven.
5. Remove meat from heat; pour brandy over it. Ignite brandy; let flames die out. Put beef in casserole.
6. Add broth to skillet. Bring to boil; pour over beef. Cover; cook in preheated oven for 4 to 5 hours, or until tender.

Woman's Club, Wilmette, Ill.

BRAISED SIRLOIN TIP ROAST

Serves 6 to 8

3- to 4-pound sirloin tip roast
¼ cup presifted flour
2 tablespoons shortening
3½ teaspoons salt
¼ teaspoon pepper
1 medium onion, sliced
2 bay leaves
1 clove garlic, crushed
½ cup hot water
8 small white onions
8 small carrots
8 small potatoes

1. Preheat oven to 350° F.
2. Sprinkle roast with flour; rub in well.
3. Melt shortening in Dutch oven or heavy ovenproof pan; brown meat well on

all sides. Sprinkle with 2 teaspoons of the salt and pepper. Add sliced onion, bay leaves, garlic and water.

4. Cover; cook in preheated oven for 1½ hours.

5. Add whole onions, carrots and potatoes; sprinkle with remaining salt. Cover; cook for 1 hour longer, or until tender.

Mrs. Clyde Vick, Woman's Club, Newsoms, Va.

BAR-B-CUE POT ROAST

Serves 8

2 teaspoons salt
¼ teaspoon pepper
4- to 5-pound rump or sirloin roast
2 tablespoons butter or margarine
½ cup water
8-ounce can tomato sauce
3 medium onions, sliced
2 cloves garlic, crushed
2 tablespoons brown sugar
½ teaspoon dry mustard
¼ cup lemon juice
¼ cup vinegar
¼ cup catsup

1. In small bowl blend salt with pepper; rub over beef.

2. Melt butter or margarine in Dutch oven or heavy kettle; brown beef well on all sides over medium heat.

3. Add water, tomato sauce, onions and garlic. Cover; cook over low heat for 1½ hours.

4. Blend remaining ingredients; pour over beef. Cover; cook for 1½ to 2 hours longer, or until very tender.

5. Skim all fat from gravy; serve with sliced meat.

Carol Harm, Finneytown Junior Women's Club, Cincinnati, Ohio

POT ROAST WITH CHOCOLATE SAUCE

Serves 6

The chocolate gives a winy flavor to the sauce. This is a trick the conquistadors learned from the Aztecs.

3 tablespoons olive oil
3-pound bottom round roast
1 large onion, sliced
2 cloves garlic, crushed
1 tablespoon flour
Salt
2 cloves
2 bay leaves
½ cup white wine
1 cup water
½ tablespoon wine vinegar
1 tablespoon grated bitter chocolate

1. Heat oil in heatproof casserole or Dutch oven; brown roast well on all sides. Add onion and garlic; cook until vegetables are tender.

2. Add flour and 1½ teaspoons salt to fat; stir until blended. Add cloves, bay leaves, wine, water and vinegar. Cover; simmer for 2½ to 3 hours.

3. Place meat on serving dish; keep warm.

4. Add chocolate to sauce; cook until thickened and smooth. If necessary, add water to make 2 cups sauce. Correct seasoning with salt.

Mrs. Evelyn Cohen, Juniors of Eastchester Woman's Club, Eastchester, N.Y.

SAUERBRATEN (Spiced German Pot Roast)

Serves 10 to 12

This famous dish of the German cuisine is not sour, as the name implies. It is most often served with Rotkraut, or Red Cabbage (p. 397) and Kartoffel Puffer, or Potato Pancakes (p. 442) or Spaetzle, or German Parsley Dumplings (p. 462).

6-pound eye of round or rump roast
1 clove garlic, crushed
Salt and pepper to taste
4 bay leaves
12 cloves
1 large onion, thinly sliced
2 cups white vinegar
½ cup butter or margarine
2 tablespoons flour
½ cup red wine
2 cups sour cream

1. Day or two before, rub beef with garlic, salt and pepper; put in deep bowl (not metal). Sprinkle with bay leaves, cloves and onion.

2. In small saucepan bring vinegar to just below boiling point. Pour over beef. Cover; refrigerate for at least 24 hours. (This can be marinated for as long as 3 to 4 days.)

3. When ready to use, wipe roast dry. Strain marinade; reserve.

4. Preheat oven to 350° F.

5. Melt butter or margarine in Dutch oven or heavy kettle; brown beef well on all sides. Cover; roast in preheated oven for 3 hours, or until fork-tender, basting occasionally with marinade.

6. Slice beef thinly; keep in warm place.

7. Blend flour and wine. Stir into pan juices; cook over low heat, stirring constantly, until thickened and smooth. Gradually stir in sour cream; heat to serving temperature. Add beef; heat for 1 minute.

Mrs. Jess Tolerton, Junior Women's Club, Cheyenne, Wyo.

BEEF POT ROAST WITH LEMON FLAVOR

Serves 6

6-ounce can frozen lemonade concentrate
¾ cup white wine
2 slices onion
2 bay leaves
1 teaspoon peppercorns
1½ teaspoons salt
1 teaspoon cinnamon
1 teaspoon cloves
4-pound chuck roast
1 cup sour cream

1. Day before, combine lemonade concentrate and wine. Add onion slices, bay

leaves, peppercorns, salt, cinnamon and cloves. Pour marinade over beef; refrigerate for 12 hours or more.

2. Next day, drain off and reserve marinade.

3. Preheat oven to 300° F.

4. Brown meat in heavy kettle.

5. Put marinade in saucepan; bring to boil; pour over meat. Cover; cook in preheated oven for 3 hours, or until tender.

6. Just before serving, stir sour cream into liquid in kettle; serve with roast.

Mrs. Laurence B. Hickam, Woman's Club, Lantana, Fla.

PENNSYLVANIA POT ROAST
Serves 8

    3- to 5-pound chuck roast
    2 teaspoons salt
    ¼ teaspoon pepper
    1 teaspoon paprika
    3 tablespoons flour
    ½ pound bacon, diced
    1 cup sliced sweet gherkins
    1 large onion, chopped
    1 clove garlic, crushed
    1 cup water
    8-ounce can tomato sauce
    ½ cup sour cream

1. Rub roast with salt, pepper, paprika and flour.

2. Cook bacon in Dutch oven or heavy kettle until crisp; drain on absorbent paper; crumble.

3. Pour off fat from pan, leaving about 3 tablespoons; add roast; brown well on all sides.

4. Add gherkins, onion, garlic, water and tomato sauce. Bring to boil; cover; simmer for 2½ to 3 hours, or until tender.

5. Arrange meat on serving dish; keep in warm place.

6. Put sour cream in small bowl; gradually stir in about 1 cup of tomato gravy. Carefully stir into rest of gravy; heat to serving temperature, stirring frequently. Stir in bacon bits; serve with roast.

Delores Wallis, Junior Woman's Club, Pompano Beach, Fla.

LELAH'S SLOW-COOKED BEEF AND VEGETABLE DINNER
Serves 6 to 8

    1 cup red wine
    ½ cup olive oil
    1 medium onion, chopped
    ⅓ cup chopped celery
    2 cloves garlic, crushed
    ¼ teaspoon peppercorns
    1 bay leaf
    ½ teaspoon thyme
    ½ teaspoon marjoram
    1 tablespoon salt
    3-pound round or chuck roast
    6 slices carrot
    ½ pound sliced bacon
    3 large tomatoes, quartered
    1 cup pitted ripe olives

1. Day before, in saucepan combine wine, oil, onion, celery, garlic, pepper-

corns, bay leaf, thyme, marjoram and salt. Bring to boil; simmer for 15 minutes.

2. Put beef in bowl; add marinade. Refrigerate for at least 24 hours, turning occasionally.

3. Next day, remove beef. Strain and reserve marinade.

4. Preheat oven to 275° F.

5. Put beef in Dutch oven or heavy kettle; pour marinade over beef.

6. Top beef with carrots; cover with bacon. Cover; bake in preheated oven for 2½ hours.

7. Add tomatoes and olives; bake for 30 minutes longer, or until tender.

Mrs. Lauren Kelsey, Parliamentary Law Club, Glendale, Calif.

SHORT RIBS OF BEEF
Serves 4

    2 to 2½ pounds short ribs, cut into
        serving pieces
    ¼ cup presifted flour
    ½ teaspoon salt
    Dash of pepper
    2 tablespoons fat or bacon drippings
    10½-ounce can condensed cream
        of mushroom soup
    ½ cup water
    1 teaspoon horseradish

1. Trim all excess fat from short ribs.

2. Combine flour, salt and pepper; use to coat meat.

3. Heat fat or bacon drippings in heavy kettle; brown meat well on all sides.

4. Pour off any excess fat from kettle. Combine soup, water and horseradish; pour over meat. Cover; cook over low heat for 1½ hours.

Mrs. Robert L. Sheuermann, Thursday Morning Club, Madison, N.J.

BARBECUED SHORT RIBS
Serves 4

    1 cup tomato purée
    1 cup water
    ¼ cup vinegar
    1 tablespoon sugar
    1 tablespoon horseradish
    1 tablespoon prepared mustard
    1 teaspoon salt
    ¼ teaspoon pepper
    2 medium onions, finely chopped
    2 tablespoons chopped parsley
    3 pounds short ribs

1. Prepare marinade: Combine all ingredients except short ribs; mix well.

2. Arrange ribs in Dutch oven or roasting pan. Pour marinade over ribs; refrigerate for 4 hours.

3. Preheat oven to 350° F.

4. Cover pan; bake in preheated oven for 3 hours, or until tender. Skim excess fat from sauce; serve with ribs.

Marian Lieper, Woman's Club, Worland, Wyo.

OVEN CHUCK ROAST OR PRIME SHORT RIBS

Serves 6 or 7

2 tablespoons bacon drippings or cooking oil
4- to 5-pound chuck roast or 3½ to 4 pounds short ribs
1½ tablespoons butter
1 medium onion, chopped
1½ tablespoons Worcestershire
1½ tablespoons vinegar
2 tablespoons brown sugar
1½ teaspoons dry mustard
¾ teaspoon salt
¾ cup water
1 cup chili sauce
Dash of Tabasco
Several drops liquid hickory smoke flavoring (optional)

1. Heat drippings or oil in heavy skillet; brown meat on all sides.
2. Meanwhile, prepare sauce: Melt butter in saucepan; brown onion. Add remaining ingredients; simmer for 10 minutes.
3. Preheat oven to 325° F.
4. Place meat in baking dish; pour sauce over meat. Cover; cook in preheated oven for 2½ hours, or until tender, basting several times.

Mona Riffel, Allied Gardens Woman's Club, San Diego, Calif.

Corned Beef

CORNED BEEF BRISKET

Serves 8

4-pound corned brisket of beef
1 large onion
12 cloves
1 carrot, quartered
1 stalk celery, quartered
1 bay leaf
1 tablespoon salt

1. Put beef in Dutch oven or heavy kettle. Add water just to cover. Stick onion with cloves; add to pan. Add remaining ingredients.
2. Bring to boil; cover; simmer for 3 hours, or until fork-tender.
3. Remove from heat; cool.
4. When cold, slice beef. Serve cold, or reheat and serve hot.

Mamie B. Levy, Pathfinder Club, Compton, Calif.

BAKED CORNED BEEF

Serves 6

5-pound lean corned brisket of beef
4 carrots, quartered
1 large onion, quartered
4 stalks celery leaves, broken
10 peppercorns
¼ cup brown sugar
6 cassia buds
⅓ cup sweet sherry

1. Put beef in heavy saucepan or Dutch oven; cover with water. Bring to boil; drain off water.

2. Add carrots, onion, celery and peppercorns. Cover with hot water. Bring to boil; cover; simmer for 5 hours, allowing 1 hour per pound. Remove from heat. Cool in liquid; refrigerate until ready to use.
3. Preheat oven to 300° F. Grease 3-quart casserole.
4. Remove meat from liquid; place, fat side up, in casserole. Sprinkle with sugar, cassia buds and sherry.
5. Bake in preheated oven for 2 hours, or until top is glazed golden brown.

Mrs. Joseph Smith, Woman's Club, Wilmette, Ill.

CORNED BEEF AND CABBAGE
(New England Boiled Dinner)

Serves 8 to 10

4- to 5-pound corned brisket of beef
1 medium onion, sliced
1 tablespoon cloves
6 peppercorns
1 bay leaf
1 clove garlic
½ green pepper, sliced
½ teaspoon rosemary
1 stalk celery, coarsely cut
1 carrot, coarsely cut
Small potatoes
Small onions
Carrots
Cabbage wedges

1. Wipe beef with damp cloth; put in large kettle. Add water to cover. Add sliced onion, cloves, peppercorns, bay leaf, garlic, green pepper, rosemary, celery and cut carrot.
2. Bring to boil, removing any scum that rises to surface; cover; simmer for 3½ to 4½ hours, or until tender.
3. About 20 minutes before serving, add potatoes, onions, carrots and cabbage wedges; simmer until tender.
4. Slice meat; arrange on warm serving platter; surround with vegetables.

Mrs. Mike Sumara, Woman's Club, Wynnburg, Tenn.

CORNED BEEF CASSEROLE

Serves 4

12-ounce can corned beef, sliced
4 medium potatoes, quartered and cooked
10-ounce package frozen brussels sprouts, defrosted
½ teaspoon salt
⅛ teaspoon pepper
⅛ teaspoon marjoram
⅛ teaspoon thyme
1 cup beef or chicken consommé

1. Preheat oven to 350° F. Grease 1-quart casserole.
2. Arrange beef, potatoes and brussels sprouts in casserole. Sprinkle with salt, pepper, marjoram, and thyme. Pour consommé on top.
3. Cover; bake in preheated oven for 30 minutes.

Jay Stewart, Woman's Club, East Hartford, Conn.

RED FLANNEL HASH

Serves 4

¼ pound salt pork, diced
2 cups diced cooked potatoes
1 cup diced cooked beets
1 cup chopped cooked corned beef
1 medium onion, finely chopped
1½ teaspoons salt
¼ teaspoon pepper

1. Fry out pork in large skillet. Discard pieces.
2. Meanwhile, blend remaining ingredients in mixing bowl. Turn into fat in skillet; cook over low heat until well browned on under side. Turn; brown other side.

H. Lindfors, Woman's Club, La Crescenta, Calif.

CORNED BEEF AND LIMA BEANS

Serves 4

2 cups cooked Lima beans
4-ounce can mushrooms, drained
1 medium onion, chopped
8-ounce can tomato sauce
½ teaspoon dry mustard
¼ teaspoon thyme
⅛ teaspoon pepper
12-ounce can corned beef
⅓ cup grated Cheddar cheese

1. Preheat oven to 350° F. Grease 1½-quart casserole.
2. In mixing bowl combine all ingredients except beef and cheese. Turn into casserole.
3. Flake beef; arrange on vegetables.
4. Bake in preheated oven for 20 minutes.
5. Sprinkle cheese on top; bake for 10 minutes longer.

Mrs. Mark W. Emmel, President, Florida's Federation of Women's Clubs

HASH WITH PINEAPPLE TOPPING

Serves 4

1-pound can corned beef hash
⅓ cup butter or margarine
4 canned pineapple slices
⅔ cup brown sugar

1. Preheat broiler. Line broiler pan with aluminum foil.
2. Remove both ends from can of hash; push out contents so that shape of can is retained. Cut hash evenly into 4 rounds; place on foil. Spread each slice of hash with about 1 teaspoon of the butter or margarine.
3. Broil hash slices 3 to 4 inches from heat for 5 minutes, or until browned. Turn slices; top each with pineapple slice.
4. Blend remaining butter or margarine with sugar; spread on pineapple slices. Broil for 4 minutes longer, or until glazed.

Bywood Junior Women's Club, Upper Darby, Pa.

CORNED BEEF PATTIES

Makes 8

2 tablespoons butter or margarine
¼ cup chopped onion
Presifted flour

1-pound can tomatoes, drained
1¼ cups diced cooked corned beef
Dash of pepper
½ teaspoon salt
1 teaspoon baking powder
6 tablespoons shortening
1 egg yolk
⅓ cup milk

1. Preheat oven to 425° F. Lightly grease muffin cups.
2. Prepare filling: Melt butter or margarine in skillet; sauté onion for 5 minutes. Stir in 2 tablespoons flour; blend well. Stir in tomatoes, corned beef and pepper; mix well; set aside.
3. Prepare pastry: In mixing bowl sift together the 2 cups flour, salt and baking powder. Cut in shortening until mixture resembles fine crumbs. Add egg yolk and milk; mix with fork until dough is formed into ball.
4. Put dough on lightly floured board; knead 12 times, or until smooth. Divide into 8 parts; roll each piece into 9-inch circle.
5. Fit circles into cups; fill each with corned beef filling. Pinch dough on top to seal.
6. Bake in preheated oven for 20 minutes.

Edith Prickett, Home Club, Cromwell, Conn.

Dried Beef

CARACUS (Beef Rabbit)

Serves 2

½ cup chopped dried beef
1 cup canned tomatoes
2 cups shredded American cheese
2 eggs, lightly beaten
1 tablespoon onion juice
1 tablespoon butter
Dash of nutmeg
Hot salted crackers

1. In saucepan combine all ingredients except crackers. Stir over low heat until cheese is melted and mixture is hot.
2. Serve on crackers.

Mrs. Harry F. Schieman, Thursday Morning Club, Madison, N.J.

DRIED BEEF CREOLE

Serves 2 or 3

4 ounces dried beef, shredded
2 tablespoons butter or margarine
1 tablespoon grated onion
8-ounce can tomatoes
¼ cup grated Cheddar cheese
2 eggs
Cooked noodles

1. Put beef in mixing bowl; cover with boiling water. Let stand for 1 minute; then drain.
2. Melt butter or margarine in saucepan; sauté onion for 5 minutes. Stir in beef, tomatoes and cheese; cook over low heat, stirring frequently, until cheese is melted.

3. Beat eggs in small bowl; stir in some beef mixture; return to rest of beef mixture. Cook over low heat, stirring constantly, until thickened.

4. Serve on noodles.

Margaret Miller, Woman's Club,
Shell Beach, Calif.

LILA'S CHIPPED BEEF IN WINE SAUCE

Serves 4

4 ounces dried beef, shredded
2 tablespoons butter or margarine
2 tablespoons flour
10½-ounce can condensed cream of mushroom soup
½ cup dry white wine
3-ounce can mushroom stems and pieces, drained
½ cup grated Cheddar cheese
2 tablespoons chopped parsley
Salt and pepper to taste
1 tablespoon dry sherry
Toast

1. Put beef in mixing bowl; cover with boiling water. Let stand for 3 minutes; then drain well.

2. Melt butter or margarine in saucepan; sauté beef for 3 minutes. Sprinkle with flour; gradually stir in soup and white wine. Cook over medium heat, stirring constantly, until thickened and creamy.

3. Add mushrooms, cheese and parsley; cook, stirring frequently, until cheese is melted. Season with salt and pepper; stir in sherry.

4. Serve on toast.

Woman's Club, Wilmette, Ill.

Braised Steaks

BEEF DILL BIRDS

Serves 6

1 teaspoon salt
¼ teaspoon pepper
⅓ cup presifted flour
6 thin 4-ounce slices round steak
3 slices bacon, halved
3 medium dill pickles, halved lengthwise
2 tablespoons shortening
1 cup finely chopped onions
½ cup finely chopped celery
¼ cup water
¼ cup liquid from pickle jar
1 cup heavy cream

1. On piece of waxed paper combine salt, pepper and flour. Dredge beef in flour; pound in flour. Reserve remaining flour.

2. Arrange ½ slice bacon in center of each slice of beef; top with ½ pickle. Roll up like a jelly roll; secure with wooden picks.

3. Melt shortening in medium skillet; brown rolls well on all sides.

4. Add onions and celery; sauté for 5 minutes. Add water and pickle liquid.

Bring to boil; cover; simmer for 1½ hours, or until tender. Arrange beef rolls on serving dish; keep in warm place.

5. Blend reserved flour and cream; gradually stir into pan juices. Cook over low heat, stirring constantly, until thickened. Pour over beef rolls.

Janice Johnson, Woman's Club, Bartlett, Ia.

BEEF OLIVES

Serves 4

4 slices bread, crumbed
2 tablespoons chopped suet
1 tablespoon chopped parsley
Grated rind of ½ lemon
Salt and pepper to taste
Egg or milk to bind
1-pound thin slice top round steak
¼ cup presifted flour
2 tablespoons butter
1 cup beef consommé or broth
Mashed potatoes
Chopped parsley

1. Make Bread Stuffing: Combine crumbs; suet, parsley, lemon rind, salt and pepper. Moisten with egg or milk.

2. Cut beef into strips about 3 x 1 inches. Put a little stuffing on each strip; roll up; tie with coarse thread.

3. Roll meat in flour. Melt butter in heavy skillet; brown meat on all sides. Drain off excess fat. Add consommé or broth; season. Cover; simmer for 1½ hours, or until tender.

4. Remove thread. Arrange meat in center of serving dish; surround with potatoes. Pour gravy over meat; sprinkle with parsley.

Audrey D. Espinoso, Junior Woman's Club,
Concord, Calif.

BEEF ROULADES

Serves 6

½ cup butter
2 tablespoons chopped onion
1 clove garlic, crushed
1 cup fresh bread crumbs
1½ pounds ground beef
½ teaspoon celery salt
½ teaspoon pepper
3 teaspoons salt
2 tablespoons chopped parsley
1 teaspoon orégano
2 cups red wine
12 thin slices round steak
3 tablespoons flour
1-pound 4-ounce can tomatoes
8-ounce can sliced mushrooms, drained

1. Prepare Beef Filling: Melt ¼ cup of the butter in skillet; sauté onion and garlic for 5 minutes. Put in mixing bowl; add crumbs, ground beef, celery salt, pepper, 1 teaspoon of the salt, parsley and orégano; mix well. Add 1 cup of the wine; blend well.

2. Spread filling on beef slices; roll each like a jelly roll. Secure with wooden picks.

3. Preheat oven to 375° F. Grease 2½-quart casserole.

4. Dredge roulades in flour. Melt remaining butter in large skillet; brown roulades on all sides over medium heat; place in casserole.

5. In skillet combine tomatoes, mushrooms and remaining wine. Bring to boil. Pour over roulades. Add hot water, if necessary, to cover roulades completely.

6. Cover; bake in preheated oven for 1½ hours.

7. Put roulades on serving dish; remove picks; keep in warm place.

8. Pour sauce into saucepan; boil rapidly until reduced to about 3 cups. Pour over roulades.

Dagny Munday, Island Woman's Club, Anna Maria, Fla.

BEEF STROGANOFF WITH TOMATO

Serves 6

2-pound ¼-inch-thick round steak
3 tablespoons flour
2 teaspoons salt
¼ teaspoon pepper
¼ cup butter
¼ cup finely chopped onion
½ pound mushrooms, sliced
½ cup dry sherry or beef bouillon
2 cups sour cream
2 tablespoons tomato paste
½ teaspoon paprika
Buttered noodles

1. Cut beef into strips about 1 x 1½ inches.

2. On piece of waxed paper combine flour, salt and pepper; dip meat into mixture.

3. Melt butter in large skillet; brown meat well; push to side of pan. Stir in onion and mushrooms; cook over medium heat until mushrooms are soft. Return meat to center of pan; mix well with mushrooms.

4. Stir in sherry or bouillon; stir constantly until bubbling. Cover; simmer for about 15 minutes, or until meat is tender.

5. Add sour cream, tomato paste and paprika; blend well. Heat to serving temperature.

6. Serve on noodles or as desired.

Mrs. Robert W. Hunter, Suburban Woman's Club, West Hartford, Conn.

CHINESE PEPPER STEAK

Serves 4

2 tablespoons cooking oil
1-pound round steak, cut into thin strips
2 tablespoons minced onion
1 clove garlic, minced
2 green peppers, cut into strips
½ cup sliced celery
½ cup beef consommé
Salt and pepper to taste
2 teaspoons water
2 teaspoons cornstarch
1 teaspoon soy sauce
3 cups cooked rice

1. Heat oil in skillet; brown beef over low heat.

2. Add onion, garlic, peppers, celery and consommé; season with salt and pepper. Cover; simmer for 20 minutes.

3. Combine water, cornstarch and soy sauce. Stir into meat mixture; simmer for 5 minutes.

4. Serve with rice.

Mrs. Elsie Scott, Woman's Club, Azusa, Calif.

FLANK STEAK ROLL

Serves 6

2-pound 1½-inch-thick flank steak
2 cups bread crumbs
1 cup seedless raisins, scalded and drained
1 egg, lightly beaten
¼ teaspoon salt
¼ teaspoon pepper
⅛ teaspoon garlic powder or garlic salt
1 tablespoon grated Cheddar cheese
2 tablespoons shortening
16-ounce jar spaghetti sauce

1. Trim steak for even rolling.

2. Prepare Raisin Stuffing: Combine crumbs, raisins, egg, salt, pepper, garlic powder or salt and cheese. Stir in enough water to moisten.

3. Preheat oven to 350° F.

4. Spread steak evenly with stuffing. Roll up; tie or skewer to secure.

5. Melt shortening in skillet; brown meat well on all sides.

6. Place steak roll in baking dish; spread with spaghetti sauce. Cover; bake in preheated oven for 1 hour, or until tender. Slice beef; serve with sauce.

Mrs. George Thompson, President, Sorosis Club, Maple Rapids, Mich.

STUFFED ROUND STEAK

Serves 6

⅓ cup butter
1 onion, chopped
1 clove garlic, minced
3 cups coarse bread crumbs
½ cup minced celery
1½ tablespoons minced parsley
1 teaspoon salt
¼ teaspoon thyme
½ teaspoon sage
¼ teaspoon pepper
3-pound slice round steak
2 tablespoons hot fat
½ cup hot water

1. Prepare stuffing: Melt butter in skillet; sauté onion and garlic until golden. Combine with crumbs, celery, parsley, salt, thyme, sage and pepper.

2. Preheat oven to 350° F.

3. Spread stuffing on steak; roll up; tie securely.

4. Brown meat on all sides in fat in heavy casserole. Add water; cover; cook in preheated oven for 1½ hours. Remove cover; cook for 30 minutes longer.

5. Serve with pan juices, thickened, if desired.

Mrs. Ben Bakanec, Junior Woman's Club,
Diamond Bar, Calif.

VEGETABLE-STUFFED STEAK
Serves 6

2-pound ¾-inch-thick round or
  chuck steak
3 teaspoons salt
Flour
½ cup finely chopped green pepper
½ cup shredded carrots
1 cup finely chopped celery
1 small onion, finely chopped
2 tablespoons shortening
1 cup water

1. Remove bone from steak; place on lightly floured board. Sprinkle generously with 2 teaspoons of the salt and flour; pound with mallet or rolling pin.
2. In bowl blend remaining salt, green pepper, carrots, celery and onion; spread on half the steak; fold other half over filling; secure with wooden picks.
3. Melt shortening in heavy skillet; brown meat well on all sides. Add water; cover; simmer for 2 hours, or until tender. Remove picks before serving.

Mrs. Grace Palacio, Women's Club,
Lamoille, Nev.

SWISS STEAK
Serves 4

2-pound ¾-inch-thick round steak
1 clove garlic
3 tablespoons flour
1½ teaspoons salt
¼ teaspoon pepper
¼ cup bacon drippings or shortening
½ cup finely chopped onions
½ cup finely chopped carrots
½ cup finely chopped celery
½ cup finely chopped green pepper
1-pound can tomatoes, drained
1 cup beef broth

1. Preheat oven to 300° F.
2. Trim steak; slash edges to prevent curling; rub in flour, salt and pepper.
3. Heat bacon drippings or shortening in Dutch oven or heavy kettle; brown steak quickly on one side. Turn steak; add onions, carrots, celery and green pepper. Cook over high heat for 2 minutes.
4. Top with tomatoes and broth. Cover; bake in preheated oven for 2 hours, or until tender.

Mrs. Ben Crumbley, Junior Woman's Club,
Sylvester, Ga.

BEEF STEAK PARMIGIANA
Serves 3 or 4

1½-pound ⅜-inch-thick round steak
⅓ cup grated Parmesan cheese
⅓ cup fine bread crumbs
1 egg, lightly beaten
⅓ cup cooking oil
1 medium onion, finely chopped
6-ounce can tomato paste
2 cups hot water
1 teaspoon salt
½ teaspoon sugar
¼ teaspoon pepper
½ teaspoon powdered marjoram
½ pound sliced Mozzarella cheese

1. Pound steak until no more than ¼ inch thick. Trim off gristle and excess fat; cut into 6 or 8 serving pieces.
2. Combine Parmesan cheese and crumbs. Dip meat in egg; roll in crumbs.
3. Heat oil in skillet; brown steak on both sides over medium heat; transfer to shallow baking pan.
4. Preheat oven to 350° F.
5. Add onion to oil remaining in skillet; cook over low heat until tender. Stir in tomato paste, water, salt, sugar, pepper and marjoram. Bring to boil; cook for 5 minutes, scraping bottom and sides to blend in all browned bits. Pour over meat; reserve small amount for topping.
6. Cover meat with Mozzarella cheese; sprinkle with sauce.
7. Bake in preheated oven for 1 hour.

Rosemary Surgi, Gentilly Woods Woman's Club,
New Orleans, La.

LENORE'S BOEUF EN DAUBE
Serves 6

⅓ cup presifted flour
2 teaspoons salt
½ teaspoon pepper
3-pound round steak, cut into
  1½-inch cubes
3 tablespoons bacon drippings
2 cloves garlic, crushed
2 tablespoons brandy
12 medium mushroom caps
1 cup beef broth
1½ cups red wine
Herb bag (6 peppercorns, 4 cloves,
  1 bay leaf, 1 bunch parsley, dash
  of thyme and dash of marjoram
  tied in cheesecloth

1. Preheat oven to 300° F. Grease 3-quart casserole.
2. On piece of waxed paper combine flour, salt and pepper. Coat beef with flour.
3. Heat bacon drippings in large heavy skillet; brown meat on all sides. Add garlic and brandy; cook for 2 minutes; transfer meat to casserole.
4. Add mushrooms to skillet; cook until browned; transfer to casserole.
5. Add broth and wine to skillet; bring to boil, stirring and scraping bottom and sides to blend in all bits of meat glaze. Pour over meat; add herb bag. Cover; bake in preheated oven for 3 hours. If liquids have not thickened in 2 hours, bake, uncovered, for last hour. Discard herb bag before serving.

Woman's Club, Wilmette, Ill.

Beef Goulashes, Stews and Pies

BEEF BOURGUIGNONNE

Serves 6

¼ cup butter
2 pounds lean beef, cut into
    2-inch cubes
2 tablespoons dry sherry
    Salt and pepper to taste
24 small white onions
1 pound medium mushrooms
¼ cup presifted flour
1 tablespoon tomato paste
1 bay leaf
¼ teaspoon thyme
½ teaspoon marjoram
2 cups burgundy
2 tablespoons chopped parsley

1. Preheat oven to 325° F. Grease 3-quart casserole.
2. Melt butter in large skillet; brown beef quickly on all sides over high heat.
3. Put beef in casserole. Sprinkle with sherry, salt and pepper.
4. Add onions to butter remaining in skillet; brown well on all sides, turning frequently. Remove onions; set aside.
5. Add mushrooms to butter remaining in skillet; sauté over medium heat for 5 minutes. Remove mushrooms; set aside with onions.
6. Stir flour, tomato paste, bay leaf, thyme, marjoram and burgundy into butter still in skillet; cook over medium heat, stirring constantly, until bubbling. Pour over beef.
7. Cover; bake in preheated oven for 2 hours.
8. Stir in reserved onions and mushrooms. Bake, covered, for 1 hour longer, or until beef is fork-tender.
9. Sprinkle with parsley before serving.

Sandy Drennan, Lincoln Village Women's Club,
Columbus, Ohio

HERBED BEEF CASSEROLE DE LUXE

Serves 4

Serve with cooked noodles, brown rice or mashed potatoes, as desired.

1½ pounds lean beef shoulder, cut
    into 1½-inch cubes
1 tablespoon bacon drippings
4½ tablespoons flour
3 teaspoons salt
¼ teaspoon ground black pepper
1-pound can tomatoes
6-ounce can mushrooms
1½ cups sliced celery
1 pound carrots, diced
2 green peppers, cut into squares
3 tablespoons instant minced onion
1 teaspoon crumbled basil
1 teaspoon crumbled tarragon

1. In morning or day before, trim excess fat from beef; finely chop about 2 tablespoons fat; put with bacon drippings in heavy skillet; heat slowly for 5 minutes. Add beef; sprinkle with 1½ tablespoons of the flour, 1 teaspoon of the salt and pepper. Brown meat well on all sides.
2. Put meat in 2-quart casserole. Preheat oven to 325° F.
3. Stir remaining flour into fat remaining in skillet. Drain tomatoes and mushrooms; gradually stir their liquids into flour. Cook over medium heat, stirring constantly, until thickened and smooth. Pour over meat. Add tomatoes. Cover; bake in preheated oven for 1 hour.
4. Add celery, carrots, green peppers, remaining salt, onion and herbs. Cover; bake for 1 hour longer.
5. Cool. Add mushrooms. Refrigerate.
6. An hour before serving, preheat oven to 350° F.
7. Bake casserole for 40 to 50 minutes, or until hot and bubbling.

Shirley G. Hosman, Crafts and Hobbies Club,
St. Louis, Mo.

BEEF WITH MUSHROOMS

Serves 4

2 tablespoons shortening
1½ pounds chuck, cut into 2-inch
    cubes
1 medium onion, finely chopped
1 teaspoon salt
1 teaspoon monosodium glutamate
1 teaspoon sugar
1 tablespoon Worcestershire
¼ cup beef or water
8-ounce can tomato sauce
1 medium carrot, diced
1 stalk celery, diced
8-ounce can mushroom slices, drained

1. Melt shortening in Dutch oven or heavy kettle; brown beef on all sides over medium heat. Add onion; sauté until yellow.
2. Stir in all remaining ingredients except mushrooms. Bring to boil; cover; simmer for 2 hours, or until tender.
3. Add mushrooms 15 minutes before serving.

Mrs. Ben Levitt, President, Women's Club,
Dalton, Ga.

SMOTHERED BEEF

Serves 6

1 tablespoon shortening
2 pounds lean beef cut into 1-inch
    cubes
1 clove garlic or 1 teaspoon garlic
    salt
8-ounce can tomato sauce
1 cup water
1 teaspoon salt
1 teaspoon sugar
¼ teaspoon dry mustard
⅛ teaspoon black pepper
1 pound small white onions or
    1 large onion, chopped
    Cooked rice

1. Melt shortening in heavy kettle; brown beef on all sides over high heat. Add garlic or garlic salt, tomato sauce, water, salt, sugar, mustard and pepper. Bring to boil; cover; simmer for 1 hour.

2. Add onions; cook for 20 minutes longer, or until tender.

3. Serve on rice.

Mrs. Richard Beatty, Junior Woman's Club, Lombard, Ill.

CARNE CON CHILI VERDE

Serves 6

1½ pounds lean beef
1 tablespoon lard
Salt and pepper to taste
1 clove garlic, minced
2 scallions, chopped
2 tablespoons flour
2½ cups water
½ cup canned tomatoes
4-ounce can roasted green chili peppers, chopped

1. Cut beef into small pieces.

2. Melt lard in saucepan. Add meat; cover; cook for 15 minutes, stirring occasionally. Add salt, pepper, garlic and scallions. Cook for 5 minutes. Stir in flour; cook, stirring, for 2 minutes.

3. Add water, tomatoes and chilis. Bring to boil; cover; cook over low heat for 30 minutes, or until meat is tender.

Mrs. Gilbert Tosales, Woman's Club, Elroy, Ariz.

BENGAL CURRY

Serves 8

¼ cup shortening
4 pounds chuck, cut into 1-inch cubes
1 cup sliced onions
2 tablespoons curry powder
2 teaspoons salt
¼ teaspoon pepper
¼ teaspoon cloves
¼ cup slivered crystallized ginger
2 tablespoons chopped fresh or
1 teaspoon dried mint leaves
3 tablespoons flour
3 10½-ounce cans condensed beef bouillon
1 cup flaked coconut
¼ cup lime juice
1 cup light cream

1. Day before, melt shortening in heavy kettle or Dutch oven; sauté beef over high heat for about 20 minutes, or until browned on all sides. Remove cubes as they brown.

2. Add onions, curry powder, salt, pepper, cloves, ginger and mint to fat remaining in pan; sauté for about 5 minutes, or until onions are tender, stirring frequently.

3. Remove from heat; stir in flour. Gradually stir in bouillon. Return to heat; bring to boil. Cover; then simmer for 1½ hours, or until tender. Cool; refrigerate overnight.

4. Next day, about 40 minutes before serving, let curry stand at room temperature for 15 minutes. Reheat over medium heat for about 20 minutes, stirring occasionally. Stir in coconut, lime juice and cream; heat for 5 minutes longer.

5. Serve with rice.

Gladys Couch, Woman's Club, Buckeye, Ariz.

HUNGARIAN GOULASH

Serves 6 to 8

3 tablespoons shortening
¼ cup dehydrated onion flakes
3 pounds beef shoulder or chuck, cut into 1½-inch cubes
1 tablespoon paprika
½ teaspoon coarsely ground black pepper
2 teaspoons seasoned salt
Dash of cayenne
2 medium tomatoes peeled and cut into wedges
¼ cup tomato purée
1 cup water
3 slices bacon
Cooked noodles

1. Melt shortening in heavy kettle or Dutch oven; brown onion flakes. Remove onion flakes; set aside.

2. Add meat to shortening remaining in pan; brown well on all sides. Sprinkle with paprika, pepper, seasoned salt and cayenne.

3. Return onions to pan; add tomatoes, tomato purée and water. Place bacon on top. Cover; simmer for 2 hours, or until tender. Add water during cooking, if necessary.

4. Serve on noodles.

Mrs. William S. Shary, President, 2nd District Formers, New York State Federation of Women's Clubs and Former Federation President

RAGOUT OF BEEF WITH ONIONS

Serves 6 to 8

2 pounds top or bottom round
2 tablespoons butter or margarine
1 tablespoon sherry
24 small white onions
12 mushroom caps, quartered
3 tablespoons flour
1 cup beef broth
1 tablespoon tomato paste
1 teaspoon gravy coloring
1 cup red wine
Bouquet garni (see Glossary)
Salt and pepper to taste
2 tablespoons chopped parsley

1. Cut beef into strips.

2. Melt butter or margarine in Dutch oven or heavy kettle; brown beef on all sides over high heat. Stir in sherry. Remove beef; set aside.

3. Add onions to fat remaining in pan; cook over high heat until browned on all sides. Remove onions; set aside.

4. Add mushrooms to fat remaining in pan; sauté over low heat for 5 minutes.

5. Stir in flour; gradually stir in broth; cook over low heat, stirring constantly, until thickened. Stir in tomato paste, gravy coloring, ½ cup of the wine, bouquet garni, salt and pepper.

6. Return beef and onions to pan. Cover; simmer for 1¾ hours, or until tender. Stir in remaining wine, a little at a time, during cooking.

7. Discard bouquet garni; sprinkle with parsley.

Helen Harris, Leota Club, Englewood, Calif.

SAVORY BAKED STEW

Serves 4

2 pounds lean stewing beef, diced
   Salt and pepper to taste
2 tablespoons onion soup mix
6 medium potatoes, quartered
3 carrots, sliced
1 large onion, sliced
10½-ounce can condensed cream
   of celery soup
½ cup water
½ cup sherry

1. Preheat oven to 250° to 300° F.
2. Put meat in heavy casserole or Dutch oven; sprinkle with salt, pepper and onion soup mix. Add potatoes, carrots and onion.
3. Combine celery soup, water and sherry; pour over meat.
4. Cover; bake in preheated oven for 5 hours.

Mrs. Robert Bittourna, Junior Woman's Club,
Diamond Bar, Calif.

BLACK WALNUT STEW

Serves 8 to 12

6 pounds chuck, cut into large cubes
10½-ounce can condensed beef broth
1 large onion, halved
1 pound round steak, ground twice
3 8-ounce jars pickled black walnuts
   Browned flour
   Salt and pepper to taste
   Cooked rice or noodles

1. Put beef cubes in heavy kettle; add broth and enough water to cover. Add onion. Bring to boil; cover; cook over low heat for 3 hours.
2. Roll ground beef into small balls; add to stew.
3. Empty 1 of the walnut jars into bowl; mash; add to stew. Simmer for 1 hour longer, or until meat is tender.
4. Skim off excess fat from surface of liquid in kettle. Mix flour and water to a thin paste, using about 2 tablespoon flour per cup of liquid. Add to liquid to thicken.
5. Season with salt and pepper. Drain and chop remaining walnuts; add to stew.
6. Serve with rice or noodles.

Mrs. Barry Goldwater, Junior Woman's Club,
Scottsdale, Ariz.

ENGLISH BEEF STEW

Serves 6 to 8

3 tablespoons shortening
2 pounds chuck, cut into 1½-inch
   cubes
1 teaspoon sugar
¼ cup presifted flour
1 quart beef broth
¼ teaspoon thyme
1 tablespoon salt
¼ teaspoon pepper
1 medium green pepper, cut into
   strips
   Bouquet garni (see Glossary)
4 medium potatoes, quartered
4 carrots, quartered
1 pound small white onions

1. Melt shortening in Dutch oven or heavy kettle; brown beef over medium heat. Sprinkle with sugar; cook until well browned. Sprinkle with flour; brown flour lightly.
2. Add broth; bring to boil, stirring constantly. Add thyme, salt, pepper, green pepper and bouquet garni. Cover; simmer for 1½ hours.
3. Add potatoes, carrots and onions. Cover; simmer for 30 minutes longer, or until meat and vegetables are tender.
4. Discard bouquet garni before serving.

Ila Keenan, Monongahela, Pa.

FLEMISH CARBONADES

Serves 6

This is one of the best known of all Flemish dishes. The word "carbonades" originally meant meat grilled over hot coals, but it is now used to describe a method of slow stewing.

2½ pounds top beef shoulder or thin
   flank steak, cut into 1-inch cubes
   Salt and pepper to taste
⅓ cup lard
½ pound lean ham, coarsely chopped
2 tablespoons flour
2 cups beer
1 small clove garlic, crushed
½ teaspoon sugar
   Bouquet garni (see Glossary)
2 tablespoons butter or margarine
3 cups chopped onions
1 teaspoon vinegar

1. Preheat oven to 325° F. Grease 3-quart casserole.
2. Season beef with salt and pepper. Melt lard in large skillet; brown beef well on all sides. Stir in ham; sauté, stirring frequently, until browned. Remove meat; set aside.
3. Pour off excess fat from skillet, leaving about 2 tablespoons. Stir flour into fat remaining in skillet; cook over medium heat, stirring frequently, until browned.
4. Remove from heat; stir in beer, garlic, sugar and bouquet garni. Return to heat. Cook over medium heat, stirring constantly, until sauce is thickened and smooth. Pour into casserole.
5. Wipe skillet; melt butter or margarine in it; sauté onions over medium heat, stirring occasionally, until lightly browned.
6. Arrange alternate layers of meat and onions in sauce in casserole. Cover; bake in preheated oven for 2½ hours.
7. Just before serving, stir in vinegar; discard bouquet garni.

Doris McKinley, Woman's Club,
Breton Woods, N.J.

GONE-ALL-AFTERNOON STEW

Serves 6

2 pounds stewing beef, cubed
3 medium carrots, sliced
2 onions, chopped
3 potatoes, peeled and quartered
   Cooked or frozen peas or any
   leftover vegetables

10½-ounce can condensed tomato soup
½ soup can water
1 teaspoon salt
Sprinkle of pepper
1 bay leaf
¼ cup sweet or sour pickle juice
or cooking wine

1. Preheat oven to 275° F.
2. Put all ingredients in large casserole with lid to fit. There is no need to brown meat first. Mix ingredients.
3. Cover; bake in preheated oven for 5 hours.

Ione Minister, Women's Club, Yerington, Nev.
Tampa, Fla.

REAL IRISH STEW
Serves 6

This original recipe was brought to Mrs. Edwards from Ireland by Kathy O'Ryan, a colleen.

3 tablespoons bacon drippings or cooking oil
1½ pounds lean stewing beef, cut into 12 pieces
2 quarts water
3 teaspoons salt
¼ teaspoon pepper
1½ pounds green beans, trimmed
6 carrots, cut into 2-inch lengths
6 stalks celery broken into 2-inch lengths
6 small white onions
6 small potatoes
½ cup barley

1. Heat bacon drippings or oil in Dutch oven or heavy kettle; brown beef on all sides.
2. Drain off excess fat. Add water, salt, pepper, beans, carrots, celery and onions. Bring to boil; cover; simmer for 1½ hours, adding water, if necessary, to keep meat well covered at all times.
3. Add potatoes and barley; simmer for 30 minutes longer.

Mrs. Judson Edwards, Woman's Club,
Tampa, Fla.

RUSSIAN STEW
Serves 8

1½ pounds chuck, diced
1 marrow bone
2 cups sliced onions
1 cup sliced carrots
2 cups diced celery
2½ cups diced beets
1 pound cabbage, shredded
1 cup diced potatoes
1 tablespoon salt
⅛ teaspoon pepper
1-pound can tomatoes
Sour cream

1. In Dutch oven or heavy kettle combine beef, marrow bone, onions, carrots, celery, beets, cabbage and potatoes. Add water just to cover. Bring to boil; cover; simmer for 2 hours, or until tender.

2. Remove bone; add salt, pepper and tomatoes. Simmer for 5 minutes.
3. Top each serving with sour cream.

Mrs. W. L. Cannon, Tallulah Falls Circle and
Sylvester Woman's Club, Sylvester, Ga.

CORNISH PASTIES
Serves 6

Pastry for a 1-Crust Pie (p. 548)
1½-pound flank steak, cut into ½-inch cubes
8 medium potatoes, finely diced
2 medium onions, finely chopped
1½ teaspoons salt
¼ teaspoon pepper
1 cup finely diced turnip
2 tablespoons water

1. Prepare Pastry for a 1-Crust Pie.
2. Preheat oven to 425° F. Grease baking sheet.
3. Prepare filling: In mixing bowl combine all remaining ingredients; mix well.
4. Divide pastry into 6 parts; roll out each part to 10-inch circle. Place filling on half of each circle. Moisten edges of circles with water; fold dough over filling. Seal edges, flute.
5. Arrange pasties upright on folded side, so fluted edge stands up. Make slit in top of each pasty; place on baking sheet.
6. Bake in preheated oven for 15 minutes. Turn temperature to 350° F. Bake in preheated oven for 45 minutes longer.

Ruth Martrott, Progressive Woman's Club,
Adrian, Mich.

STEAK AND KIDNEY PIE
Serves 8

Flaky Puff Pastry (p. 580)
¼ cup shortening
3-pound round steak, cut into 1-inch cubes
1 cup sliced onions
¼ cup presifted flour
2 teaspoons salt
½ teaspoon pepper
1½ cups beef broth
1 beef kidney, cut into small pieces
Sliced mushrooms (optional)
Cooked sliced potatoes (optional)
1 egg yolk, beaten with 2 tablespoons milk

1. Prepare Flaky Puff Pastry. Chill.
2. Prepare filling: Melt shortening in Dutch oven or heavy saucepan; brown beef well on all sides. Add onions; sauté over medium heat for 5 minutes. Sprinkle with flour, salt and pepper. Add broth; cook, stirring constantly, until thickened. Cover; simmer for 1 hour. Sitr in kidney; cover; simmer for 30 minutes longer.
3. Turn filling into deep-dish pie pan; cool. Filling should come to within ¼ inch of top of pan. (Mushrooms and potatoes may be added to filling at this stage to help fill dish, if necessary.)
4. Preheat oven to 450° F.
5. Roll out pastry 1 inch larger than surface of pie pan. Cut 1-inch edge from around pastry; arrange on edge of pan.

Moisten with egg yolk mixture. Place pastry on top of pie pan. Press edges to seal; flute.

6. Roll out pastry scraps thinly; cut into leaves. Make hole in center of pastry; place leaves around it. Brush top of pastry with egg yolk mixture. Place pan on baking sheet.

7. Bake in preheated oven for 15 minutes. Turn temperature to 375° F. Bake for 30 minutes longer, or until golden and flaky.

A. C. R., Neighborly Club, Norfolk, Mass.

COUSIN JACK STEAK AND POTATO PIE

Serves 3 or 4

2 large potatoes, thinly sliced
2 medium onions, sliced
  Salt and pepper to taste
1-pound sirloin steak, cubed
2 tablespoons butter or margarine
  Pastry for a 1-Crust Pie (p. 548)

1. Preheat oven to 350° F. Grease 8-inch square baking dish.

2. Put layer of potatoes in baking dish; top with layer of onions. Sprinkle with salt and pepper. Arrange beef on onions; sprinkle again with salt and pepper. Dot with butter or margarine.

3. Roll out Pastry for a 1-Crust Pie thinly; cover contents in baking dish. Crimp edge; slit top to allow steam to escape.

4. Bake in preheated oven for 1 hour, or until potatoes are fork-tender and crust is browned.

Audrey Bishop, Woman's Club, Oceanside, Calif.

BEEF PIE

Serves 4 to 6

¼ cup presifted flour
1 teaspoon salt
⅛ teaspoon pepper
½ teaspoon tarragon or basil
¼ cup cooking oil
1 pound beef, cut into ½-inch cubes
½ cup chopped onions
½ cup chopped celery
2 cups water
1 bay leaf
2 cups cubed potatoes
1½ cups sliced carrots
  Pastry for a 1-Crust Pie (p. 548)

1. Combine flour, salt, pepper and tarragon or basil; use to coat beef.

2. Heat oil in saucepan; brown beef well. Add onions and celery; cook for 5 minutes, stirring occasionally.

3. Stir in remaining flour mixture. Gradually stir in water; cook, stirring constantly, until thickened. Add bay leaf; cover; cook over low heat for 20 minutes.

4. Add potatoes and carrots; cook for 20 minutes longer.

5. Preheat oven to 425° F.

6. Turn meat mixture into 1½-quart casserole. Top with Pastry for a 1-Crust

Pie; flute edge; slit top to allow steam to escape.

7. Bake in preheated oven for 30 minutes.

A. S.

BRAISED OXTAILS

Serves 4

1½ pounds oxtails, cut at joints
  Flour
2 tablespoons lard or bacon drippings
3¼ cups water
2½ cups tomato juice
1½ teaspoons dry mustard
  Salt to taste
4 potatoes, quartered
4 onions, halved
4 carrots, sliced

1. Dust oxtail pieces with flour. Melt lard or bacon drippings in heavy kettle; brown oxtails well on all sides.

2. Add 3 cups of the water; cover; simmer for 2 hours.

3. Add tomato juice, mustard and salt; simmer for 1 hour longer.

4. Add vegetables; simmer for 20 minutes longer, or until tender.

5. Combine 2 tablespoons flour and remaining water; stir into gravy. Cook, stirring constantly, until thickened.

Farina Jones, North Phoenix Woman's Club,
Phoenix, Ariz.

Hamburgers, Meat Balls and Meat Loaves

JUST PLAIN HAMBURGERS

It is hard to beat freshly ground lean beef shaped into patties and broiled or pan-broiled until browned on the outside and done to taste (but not overdone) on the inside. Count on from ⅓ to ½ pound meat per serving.

Freshly ground lean round or chuck
Butter
Salt and pepper to taste
Chopped parsley

1. Pat meat lightly into patties. Cook at high heat for about 5 minutes on each side, or until done to taste.

2. Arrange hamburgers on hot serving platter or individual plates. Put thin pat of butter on each; sprinkle with salt, pepper and parsley.

A. S.

GROUND BEEF PARMESAN

Serves 6

1½ pounds ground beef
1 egg, lightly beaten
1 medium onion, finely chopped
1 teaspoon salt
¼ teaspoon monosodium glutamate
⅛ teaspoon pepper
6-ounce can tomato paste
1 tablespoon Parmesan cheese
6 slices Mozzarella cheese

1. Preheat broiler.
2. Combine beef, egg, onion, salt, monosodium glutamate and pepper; mix well. Shape into large square, ¾ inch thick. Cut into 6 equal portions.
3. Arrange patties on broiler pan; broil 3 inches from heat for 10 minutes.
4. Meanwhile, mix tomato paste and Parmesan cheese. Turn patties; spread with tomato mixture. Top each with slice of Mozzarella cheese.
5. Broil for 4 minutes longer, or until cheese is melted and browned.

Junior Woman's Club, Pacific Beach, Calif.

NUT STEAK PATTIES

Serves 4

1 pound ground beef
¼ cup chopped walnuts
¾ teaspoon salt
¼ teaspoon pepper
¼ cup butter or margarine

1. Preheat broiler.
2. In mixing bowl combine beef, walnuts, salt and pepper. Mix well; shape into 4 flat patties.
3. Place on broiler pan; broil 3 to 4 inches from heat for 2 to 3 minutes on each side, or until done to taste.
4. Arrange on serving dish; spread patties with butter or margarine.

Mrs. J. Lucien Jones, Woman's Club,
Blacksburg, Va.

FRICADELLER (Danish Meat Cakes)

Serves 4

Serve with gravy and mashed potatoes, if desired.

1 pound ground beef
1 small onion, grated
½ cup cracker crumbs
1 teaspoon salt
¼ teaspoon pepper
1 egg
2 tablespoons flour
½ cup milk
⅓ cup shortening

1. In mixing bowl combine all ingredients except milk and shortening. Add milk; beat with wooden spoon. Shape into 8 oblong patties.
2. Melt shortening in large skillet; brown patties slowly over low heat on both sides.

Louise King, Woman's Club, South Amboy, N.J.

POTATO BURGERS

Serves 4

½ pound ground beef
1 cup grated potatoes
2 tablespoons grated onion
1 teaspoon salt
⅛ teaspoon pepper
3 tablespoons shortening

½ teaspoon dry mustard
1 tablespoon chopped parsley

1. In mixing bowl combine beef, potatoes, onion, salt and pepper. Shape into 4 flat patties.
2. Melt shortening in large skillet; brown patties well on both sides. Arrange patties on serving dish; keep in warm place.
3. Add mustard and parsley to fat remaining in skillet; heat. Pour over patties.

Mrs. Joe Determan, Pleasant Study Club,
Beresford, S.D.

SALISBURY STEAK

Serves 2

1 pound freshly ground beef
Salt and pepper to taste
Water cress
Mushroom Sauce (p. 447)

1. Divide beef in half. Pat each half into oval cake about 1 inch thick. Pan-broil or broil for 5 minutes on one side. Turn; cook for 5 minutes longer, or until done to taste.
2. Arrange on serving plate; sprinkle with salt and pepper; garnish with water cress. Serve with Mushroom Sauce.

A. S.

WILD WEST HAMBURGERS

Serves 2 or 3

1 pound ground beef
1 teaspoon crumbled dried sage
½ teaspoon minced herb seasoning
½ teaspoon monosodium glutamate
½ teaspoon sugar
Salt and pepper to taste
2 scallions, finely chopped
2 cloves garlic, minced
2 teaspoons India relish
2 tablespoons capers
1 tablespoon minced parsley
1 egg, lightly beaten
⅓ cup dry white wine
2 tablespoons cooking oil

1. Break up ground beef with fork; mix thoroughly with sage, herb seasoning, monosodium glutamate, sugar, salt, pepper, scallions, and garlic. Add relish, capers, parsley, egg and wine; mix well. Let stand at room temperature for 30 minutes to 1 hour.
2. Form into patties.
3. Heat oil in skillet until very hot but not smoking. Place patties in skillet; remove from heat for 1 minute. Turn heat to medium; sauté for 4 minutes. Turn heat to high; flip patties; let sizzle for 1 minute. Lower heat to medium; sauté for 3 minutes. Patties should be crisp and brown on both sides and pink in middle.

Mrs. E. J. Craigo, Maids and Matrons Club,
Jackson, Miss.

BARBECUED BAKED HAMBURGERS
Serves 6

½ cup milk
1½ cups bread crumbs
3 tablespoons margarine or
cooking oil
3 tablespoons minced onion
2 pounds ground beef
1½ teaspoons salt
¼ teaspoon pepper
Worcestershire
1 onion, chopped
½ cup chopped celery
1 green pepper, chopped (optional)
2 tablespoons vinegar
4 tablespoons lemon juice
1 cup catsup
½ teaspoon chili powder
½ teaspoon dry mustard
½ cup water
¼ teaspoon cayenne

1. Pour milk over crumbs; let soak until milk is absorbed.
2. Melt margarine or oil in skillet; brown minced onion; add to crumbs. Add beef, salt, pepper and ½ teaspoon Worcestershire. Mix; form into 6 patties.
3. Brown patties on both sides in fat remaining in skillet. Arrange in baking dish.
4. Sauté chopped onion, celery and green pepper in fat remaining in skillet for 5 minutes, or until onion is transparent. Add vinegar, lemon juice, catsup, 2 tablespoons Worcestershire, chili powder, mustard, water and cayenne. Simmer for 30 minutes, stirring occasionally.
5. Preheat oven to 350° F.
6. Pour sauce over patties; bake in preheated oven for 20 minutes, or until done to taste.

Mrs. Earl C. Tucker, Women's Reading Club,
Eolia, Mo.

SOUR CREAM PORCUPINES
Serves 6

1½ pounds ground beef
⅓ cup instant rice
1 teaspoon salt
¼ cup grated onion
2 tablespoons shortening
½ cup water
1 beef bouillon cube
1 tablespoon Worcestershire
10½-ounce can condensed cream
of mushroom soup
½ cup sour cream
Chinese noodles

1. Preheat oven to 350° F. Grease 1½-quart casserole.
2. Combine beef, rice, salt and onion; mix well. Shape into 1½-inch balls.
3. Melt shortening in large skillet; brown meat balls on all sides over medium heat. Arrange meat balls in casserole.
4. Drain fat from skillet; stir in water, bouillon cube, Worcestershire and soup. Cook over medium heat, stirring frequently, until thickened and smooth. Remove from heat; blend in sour cream. Pour over meat balls.

5. Bake in preheated oven for 45 minutes.
6. Serve with Chinese noodles.

Mary B. Moore, Woman's Club, Sepulveda, Calif.

BURGUNDY BEEF BALLS
Serves 8 to 10

2 tablespoons instant minced onion
or 1 onion, finely chopped
¾ cup milk
2 eggs
2 teaspoons salt
¼ teaspoon pepper
1 teaspoon prepared mustard
Dash of nutmeg
Dash of allspice
2 cups soft bread crumbs
2 pounds ground beef
3 tablespoons shortening
3 tablespoons flour
10½-ounce can condensed beef
consommé
¾ cup burgundy
½ cup sour cream
Chopped parsley

1. Combine onion and milk; set aside.
2. In mixing bowl beat eggs lightly. Add seasonings, crumbs, beef and milk mixture. Mix thoroughly. Shape into small balls.
3. Melt shortening in skillet; brown a few meat balls at a time. Remove when they are cooked.
4. Stir flour into fat remaining in skillet. Gradually stir in consommé and burgundy; cook, stirring constantly until thickened and smooth. Return meat balls to skillet; simmer for 15 minutes.
5. Just before serving, stir sour cream into gravy. Sprinkle with parsley.

Mrs. Barbara Sheppard, Women's Progressive
Club of Inglewood Acres, Inglewood, Calif.

MEAT BALLS IN RED WINE SAUCE
Serves 6

1 pound ground beef
½ pound ground pork
¾ cup bread crumbs
½ cup grated onions
1 tablespoon finely chopped parsley
1½ teaspoons salt
¼ teaspoon pepper
1 tablespoon Worcestershire
1 egg
½ cup milk
¼ cup shortening
2½ cups Red Wine Sauce (p. 451)

1. Preheat oven to 300° F. Grease 11 x 7 x 1½-inch baking pan.
2. In mixing bowl combine all ingredients except shortening and Red Wine Sauce. Mix well; shape into 1-inch balls.
3. Melt shortening in large skillet; brown meat balls well on all sides.
4. Arrange meat balls in pan; pour Red Wine Sauce over them. Cover with aluminum foil; bake in preheated oven for 1 hour.

Mrs. Franklin Ussery, Jr., Booklovers Club,
Alice, Tex.

ITALIAN MEAT BALLS

Serves 4

If desired, an Italian sausage may be added with the meat balls for additional flavor.

1 pound ground beef
2 eggs
1 clove garlic, minced
Chopped parsley
¾ cup grated Parmesan cheese
¾ cup bread crumbs
½ cup boiling water
Salt and pepper to taste
2 tablespoons cooking oil
1-pound 13-ounce can tomatoes, drained
8-ounce can tomato sauce
6-ounce can tomato paste
1½ 1-pound 13-ounce cans water

1. Combine beef, eggs, garlic, parsley, cheese, crumbs, boiling water, salt and pepper. Shape into oval balls. Heat oil in skillet; brown meat balls on all sides. Remove meat balls; set aside.
2. Strain fat from skillet into large saucepan. Add tomatoes, tomato sauce, tomato paste and 1½ cans water. Bring to boil; simmer for 45 minutes.
3. Add meat balls; simmer for 45 minutes longer.

Mrs. Marie Santaseiri, Juniors of Eastchester Woman's Club, Eastchester, N.Y.

MEAT BALL PANCAKES

Serves 4

½ pound ground beef
3 eggs, separated
¼ teaspoon baking powder
½ teaspoon salt
Dash of pepper
1 teaspoon lemon juice
1 tablespoon chopped parsley
1 tablespoon grated onion
Mushroom Sauce (p. 447)

1. Combine beef, egg yolks, baking powder, salt, pepper, lemon juice, parsley and onion; mix well.
2. In mixing bowl beat egg whites until stiff but not dry. Fold into beef mixture.
3. Grease and preheat griddle.
4. Drop beef mixture by tablespoons onto griddle. When cakes are puffed and brown, turn and brown other side.
5. Serve with Mushroom Sauce.

Mrs. Ruth J. Spitler, Trirosis Club, Canton, Ohio

MEAT BALLS ORIENTAL

Serves 4

1 pound ground beef
⅔ cup packaged bread stuffing
2 teaspoons instant minced onion
1 teaspoon salt
Dash of pepper
1 tablespoon minced parsley
1 egg
¾ cup water
Shortening
1 onion, diced
1 green pepper, diced
1 cup catsup
¼ cup vinegar
13½-ounce can pineapple chunks or tidbits
1½ tablespoons cornstarch
Cooked rice

1. Combine beef, stuffing, onion, ¾ teaspoon of the salt, pepper, parsley, egg and water. Blend well with fork. Shape into balls the size of walnuts.
2. Melt ¼ cup shortening in skillet; brown meat balls. Set aside on warm plate.
3. Wipe skillet; melt 1 tablespoon shortening; sauté onion and green pepper until onion is tender but not browned. Add catsup and vinegar.
4. Drain pineapple; combine ½ cup pineapple syrup and cornstarch, stirring to blend. Add to sauce; cook 3 to 5 minutes, stirring constantly, until thickened and clear.
5. Add meat balls and pineapple; cover; simmer for 15 minutes.
6. Serve on rice.

Mrs. Vernon L. Purchase, Woman's Club, Torrance, Calif.

SWEET AND SOUR MEAT BALLS

Serves 6 to 8

1 cup cubed bread
1 cup milk
⅓ cup minced onions
1½ pounds ground beef
½ pound ground pork
1 egg, lightly beaten
1 teaspoon salt
¼ teaspoon pepper
2 12-ounce bottles chili sauce
½ cup water
10-ounce jar grape jelly
1 cup sour cream

1. Soak bread in milk. Combine with onions, beef, pork, egg, salt and pepper. Shape into balls about the size of walnuts.
2. In large saucepan combine chili sauce, water and grape jelly. Heat to simmer.
3. Drop meat balls into sauce; simmer for about 1 hour. Skim excess fat from top of sauce.
4. Just before serving, stir in sour cream.

Ann and Linda, Junior Woman's Club, Bristol, Tenn.-Va.

SPANISH MEAT BALLS

Serves 6

1 pound ground beef
½ pound ground pork
½ cup rice
1 teaspoon salt
½ teaspoon pepper
1 egg
1-pound can tomatoes, undrained
2 cups water
1 tablespoon chili powder
1 clove garlic, crushed

1. Combine beef, pork, rice, salt, pepper and egg; mix well. Shape into 1-inch balls.
2. In large heavy skillet combine remaining ingredients. Bring to boil.

3. Add meat balls. Cover; simmer for 1 hour, stirring occasionally.

Mrs. Max Garbe, Centenarian Club, Valley Falls, Kan.

BEEF BALLS STROGANOFF

Serves 12

2 eggs
1½ cups milk
¾ cup fine bread crumbs
1 tablespoon salt
1 teaspoon pepper
3 tablespoons chopped parsley
3 pounds ground chuck
½ cup butter or margarine
1½ cups chopped onions
1½ cups sliced mushrooms
2 teaspoons paprika
6 tablespoons flour
2 quarts beef broth or consommé
1 tablespoon Worcestershire
Salt and pepper to taste
¾ cup sour cream

1. Beat eggs. Add milk, crumbs, salt and pepper; let stand for few minutes.
2. Add parsley and beef; mix thoroughly. Shape into 1-inch balls.
3. Melt ¼ cup of the butter or margarine in skillet; sauté meat balls for 10 minutes, or until browned. Remove from pan; set aside.
4. Add remaining butter or margarine, onions, mushrooms and paprika to skillet. Cook, stirring, until onions are lightly browned.
5. Stir in flour; cook for 2 to 3 minutes to brown flour lightly. Gradually stir in broth or consommé; cook, stirring, until sauce is thickened and smooth. Add Worcestershire, salt and pepper. Return meat balls to sauce; cover; cook over low heat for 20 minutes.
6. Stir in sour cream; heat gently, but do not boil.

Mrs. James McComber, Juniors, Saratoga, Fla.

SWEDISH MEAT BALLS

Serves 4 to 6

The cold mashed potatoes give these meat balls a light consistency. Since they are served as a meat course, the meat balls are rather large. Serve with mashed potatoes or cooked macaroni, Molded Cucumber Salad (p. 532) or lingenberries, as desired.

1 tablespoon shortening
½ cup grated or finely chopped onions
1 pound ground round or chuck
½ pound ground pork
1 cup loosely packed cold mashed or grated cooked potatoes
¼ cup fine bread crumbs
2½ teaspoons salt
¼ teaspoon pepper
1½ cups cream
¼ cup water
1 egg, lightly beaten
½ cup cooking oil
1 tablespoon flour

1. Melt shortening; sauté onions for 5 minutes. Turn into mixing bowl.
2. Add beef, pork, potatoes, crumbs, salt, pepper, ½ cup of the cream, water and egg. Mix well until smooth. Shape into balls with hands moistened with cold water, using tablespoon for measure.
3. Heat oil in skillet; brown meat balls well on all sides, shaking pan often to keep balls round.
4. As each batch is browned, transfer to hot serving dish; keep warm. Pour off excess fat from skillet after each batch.
5. When all meat balls are cooked, combine remaining cream and flour; add to skillet juices; cook, stirring constantly, until thickened and smooth. Correct seasoning. Strain over meat balls.

Women's Club, Mamaroneck, N.Y.

MEAT LOAF

Serves 8

2 cups fresh bread crumbs
¾ cup grated onions
¼ cup finely chopped green pepper
2 pounds ground beef
2 eggs
2 tablespoons horseradish
2½ teaspoons salt
1 teaspoon dry mustard
¼ cup milk
½ cup catsup

1. Preheat oven to 350° F. Grease 10 x 6 x 1½-inch baking pan.
2. In mixing bowl combine crumbs, onions, green pepper and beef; mix well.
3. In small bowl beat eggs; stir in horseradish, salt, mustard, milk and ¼ cup of the catsup. Add to meat mixture; mix well. Shape into loaf; put in pan. Top with remaining catsup.
4. Bake in preheated oven for 50 minutes.

Mrs. E. I. Schulz, Woman's Club, Washburn, N.D.

APPLE-POTATO MEAT LOAF

Serves 4 to 6

1 pound ground beef
1 medium potato, grated
1 medium apple, grated
¼ cup finely chopped onion
¼ cup finely chopped green pepper
½ teaspoon salt
½ teaspoon black pepper
1 egg

1. Preheat oven to 350° F. Line 8-inch loaf pan with aluminum foil.
2. In mixing bowl combine all ingredients; mix well.
3. Turn into pan; bake in preheated oven for 1 hour.

Mrs. M. Eccles, President, Ponderosa H.D.C., Picayune, Miss.

MEAT LOAF BARBECUE STYLE
Serves 4 to 6

1½ pounds ground beef
1 cup fresh bread crumbs
1 onion, finely chopped
1 egg, lightly beaten
1½ teaspoons salt
¼ teaspoon pepper
2 8-ounce cans tomato sauce
½ cup water
3 tablespoons vinegar
3 tablespoons brown sugar
3 tablespoons prepared mustard
2 teaspoons Worcestershire

1. Preheat oven to 350° F.
2. Combine beef, crumbs, onion, egg, salt, pepper and ½ can of the tomato sauce; mix well. Form into loaf; put in 10 x 6 x 1½-inch baking pan.
3. Combine remaining tomato sauce and remaining ingredients. Pour over loaf.
4. Bake in preheated oven for 1 hour and 15 minutes.

Joann Taylor, Home and Country Study Club,
Fayette, Mo.

ECONOMY MEAT LOAF
Serves 8

1 pound ground beef
¼ pound ground salt pork
1 cup rolled oats
¼ cup chopped onion
2 teaspoons salt
¼ teaspoon pepper
1 teaspoon dry mustard
1 egg
1 cup milk

1. Preheat oven to 350° F. Grease loaf pan.
2. Combine all ingredients. Pack firmly into pan.
3. Bake in preheated oven for 1 hour.

Mrs. James A. Holter, Woman's Club,
Casselton, N.D.

GOURMET MEAT LOAF
Serves 10 to 12

2 pounds ground beef
1 pound ground pork
1 pound ground veal
1 cup cottage cheese
1 cup bread crumbs
½ cup chili sauce
1 cup chopped onions
3 eggs, lightly beaten
2 tablespoons chopped green
  pepper
1 tablespoon salt
¼ teaspoon pepper
2 cloves garlic, chopped (optional)
1 tablespoon Worcestershire
¼ cup red wine
8-ounce can tomato sauce
2 slices bacon
  Beef broth
1 cup sour cream
⅓ cup crumbled crisply cooked bacon

1. Preheat oven to 400° F.
2. Combine beef, pork, veal, cheese, crumbs, chili sauce, onions, eggs, green

pepper, salt, pepper, garlic and Worcestershire; mix thoroughly. Form into loaf; place in shallow baking pan.
3. Bake in preheated oven for 30 minutes; turn heat to 325° F. Add wine to pan juices; bake for 30 minutes longer.
4. Pour tomato sauce evenly over loaf; top with bacon slices; bake for 30 minutes longer, or until well glazed.
5. Prepare gravy: Drain juices from pan into measuring cup; add enough broth to total 2 cups. Blend into sour cream; heat gently until smooth. Just before serving, stir in crumbled bacon.

Ruth Adams, Woman's Club, Oceanside, Calif.

ITALIAN MEAT LOAF
Serves 4 to 6

2 slices rye bread
2 slices white bread
1 cup water
1 pound ground beef
1 onion, minced
1 tablespoon chopped parsley
3 tablespoons grated Parmesan
  cheese
1 egg
1 teaspoon salt
½ teaspoon pepper
8-ounce can tomato sauce
1 teaspoon orégano

1. Preheat oven to 375° F. Grease shallow baking pan.
2. Put rye and white bread in large mixing bowl. Pour water over bread; let soak until bread has absorbed liquid.
3. Mash bread with fork; add beef, onion, parsley, cheese, egg, salt and pepper. Mix with hands. Shape into loaf; put in baking pan.
4. Bake in preheated oven for 30 minutes.
5. Pour tomato sauce over meat; sprinkle with orégano. Bake for 20 minutes longer.

Charlene Mosca, Junior Woman's Club,
Cathedral City, Calif.

STUFFED MEAT LOAF
Serves 8

2 pounds ground beef
2 eggs, lightly beaten
⅓ cup chili sauce
2 teaspoons salt
½ teaspoon dry mustard
4-ounce can mushroom stems and
  pieces, drained
½ cup finely chopped onions
½ cup grated sharp Cheddar cheese
⅛ teaspoon pepper
¼ teaspoon thyme

1. Preheat oven to 350° F. Grease 9-inch loaf pan.
2. Combine beef, eggs, chili sauce, salt and mustard; mix well.
3. Prepare Onion Filling: Combine mushrooms, onions, cheese, pepper and thyme; mix well.
4. Press half the meat mixture into pan.

5. Spread filling on meat in pan. Then spread remaining meat mixture evenly on filling.

6. Bake in preheated oven for 1½ hours.

Shirley Salls, Junior Woman's Club,
Glastonbury, Conn.

SWISS LOAF

Serves 8

2 pounds ground beef
1½ cups diced Swiss cheese
2 eggs, lightly beaten
½ cup finely chopped onions
½ cup finely chopped green pepper
1½ teaspoons salt
½ teaspoon pepper
1 teaspoon celery salt
½ teaspoon paprika
3 cups milk
1 cup bread crumbs

1. Preheat oven to 350° F. Grease 9-inch loaf pan.

2. In mixing bowl combine all ingredients; mix well. Press into pan.

3. Bake in preheated oven for 1½ hours.

Jean Phillips, Women's Club, Carol Stream, Ill.

Ground Beef Dishes

BEEF BOHEMIAN

Serves 4

2 tablespoons butter or margarine
1 pound ground beef
8-ounce can sliced mushrooms
1 teaspoon salt
¼ teaspoon pepper
1 cup sour cream
4 slices crisp toast

1. Melt butter or margarine in skillet; brown beef over medium heat, stirring occasionally.

2. Drain mushrooms; add liquid, salt and pepper to meat in skillet. Cover. Simmer for 20 minutes, or remove cover for last few minutes to allow liquid to evaporate.

3. Stir in sour cream and mushrooms; heat to serving temperature.

4. Serve on toast.

V. Speth, Woman's Club, Monterey Park, Calif.

BULGUR BARBECUE

Serves 8 to 10

1 cup bulgur (cracked wheat)
2 cups water
2 pounds ground beef
2 large onions, chopped
2 8-ounce cans tomato sauce
2 cups chopped celery
½ cup catsup
¾ cup brown sugar
2 teaspoons prepared mustard
2 tablespoons vinegar

1. Cook bulgur in water according to package directions.

2. Cook beef in skillet until it loses red color. Add onions; cook until golden.

3. Add remaining ingredients; cook over low heat for 30 minutes. Add bulgur; mix; simmer for 5 minutes longer.

Mrs. Lawrence Kaseberg, Women's Study Club,
Wasco, Ore.

COUNTRY CASSEROLE

Serves 6 to 8

1 pound ground beef
¼ pound sausage meat
½ teaspoon salt
¼ cup rice
1 medium cabbage, shredded
1-pound 11-ounce can sauerkraut, drained
1-pound 13-ounce can tomatoes, undrained
2 tablespoons sugar

1. Preheat oven to 350° F. Grease 4-quart casserole.

2. Combine beef, sausage meat, salt and rice; mix well. Put half the cabbage in casserole. Top with half the sauerkraut. Spread meat mixture on sauerkraut; top with remaining cabbage. Cover with remaining sauerkraut.

3. Pour tomatoes on top; sprinkle with sugar.

4. Bake in preheated oven for 1 hour. Turn temperature to 300° F. Cover; bake for 2 hours longer.

5. Cool; then skim off grease. Reheat.

Mrs. Ray Taylor, Woman's Club, Martinez, Calif.

STUFFED CABBAGE LEAVES

Serves 4

12 large cabbage leaves
1 pound ground beef
1 large onion, minced
2 tablespoons chopped parsley
¼ cup rice
Juice of ½ lemon
⅓ cup tomato purée
Salt and pepper to taste
2 tablespoons butter
1 cup sour cream
Five-Minute Tomato Sauce (p. 450)

1. Cover cabbage leaves with boiling water; soak until pliable. Drain.

2. Combine beef, onion, parsley, rice, lemon juice, tomato purée, salt and pepper.

3. Put about 3 tablespoons of meat mixture on each cabbage leaf; roll up, tucking in sides to make packages about 3 inches long and 1 inch thick. Secure with string or wooden picks.

4. Preheat oven to 350° F.

5. Melt butter in skillet; brown cabbage rolls on all sides. Arrange in rows in baking dish. Add a little hot water to skillet in which rolls were browned; pour over rolls.

6. Cover; bake in preheated oven for 1 hour.

7. Just before serving, pour sour cream over rolls; return casserole to oven just long enough to heat cream through. Serve with Five-Minute Tomato Sauce.

Gladys Reiner, Woman's Civic Club,
Roselle Park, N.J.

CABBAGE PIGEONS
Serves 6

1 medium cabbage
1 pound ground beef
½ pound ground pork
½ cup cooked rice
1 egg, lightly beaten
1½ teaspoons salt
¼ teaspoon pepper
¼ cup grated onion
1-pound 4-ounce can tomato juice

1. Put cabbage in mixing bowl; cover with boiling salted water. Let stand for 10 minutes; drain; cut out core of cabbage. Separate leaves. If they do not come off easily, return cabbage to boiling water for a few minutes. Trim down thick edge on back of leaves to make them easier to roll.
2. Prepare filling: Combine beef, pork, rice, egg, salt, pepper and onion; mix well.
3. Place a tablespoon of filling in center of each cabbage leaf. Roll up leaves like a jelly roll, folding in sides of leaves, to seal filling completely.
4. Place rolls in large skillet; add tomato juice.
5. Cover; simmer for 1½ hours.

Woman's Club, Mahanoy City, Pa.

OY-YOK-SUNG
(Chinese Beef and Beans)
Serves 4

1 tablespoon shortening
1 large onion, finely chopped
1 clove garlic, crushed
¾ pound ground beef
3 cups water
3 tablespoons soy sauce
1 pound green beans, diced
2½ tablespoons cornstarch
Cooked rice

1. Melt shortening in skillet; sauté onion and garlic over medium heat until golden. Add beef; cook, stirring occasionally, until browned.
2. Add 2¾ cups of the water and soy sauce; bring to boil. Add beans; cover; simmer for 10 minutes, or until tender.
3. In small bowl blend remaining water and cornstarch; stir into bean mixture. Cook, stirring constantly, until thickened and clear.
4. Serve on rice.

Mrs. William Rogers, Woman's Club,
Honesdale, Pa.

BEEF CHOW MEIN CASSEROLE
Serves 4 to 6

1 tablespoon butter
1 pound ground beef
1 green pepper, finely chopped
1 cup chopped celery
1 small onion, chopped
1 teaspoon salt
1 cup water
10½-ounce can condensed cream of mushroom soup
½ cup tomato juice
6-ounce can Chinese noodles

1. Preheat oven to 350° F. Grease 2-quart casserole.
2. Melt butter in large frying pan; brown beef over medium heat. Add green pepper, celery, onion and salt; cook over low heat until tender.
3. Add water, soup, tomato juice, and half the Chinese noodles. Stir to blend; pour into casserole.
4. Sprinkle with remaining noodles; bake in preheated oven for 30 minutes.

Mrs. Francis Hulett, Phi Lambda Club, Slater, Mo.

FARMER'S PIE
Serves 4 to 6

Leftover vegetables, such as cooked green beans, peas, carrots, etc., may be added to this casserole.

2 tablespoons butter
½ cup chopped onions
1½ pounds ground beef
Salt and pepper to taste
1-pound can cream-style corn
1 envelope instant mashed potatoes
1 egg, lightly beaten
Paprika

1. Preheat oven to 325° F.
2. Melt butter in skillet, sauté onions for 5 minutes, or until transparent. Add beef; cook until meat loses red color. Season with salt and pepper.
3. Turn into 1½-quart casserole; top with corn.
4. Prepare potatoes according to package directions. Stir in egg. Spoon potatoes on corn; sprinkle with paprika.
5. Bake in preheated oven for 30 to 35 minutes, or until hot and bubbling.

Mrs. Edna Fiala, Gold Coast Woman's Club,
North Palm Beach, Fla.

DUPYZA (Indian Curried Beef)
Serves 4 to 6

1 tablespoon shortening
1 large onion, finely chopped
1 tablespoon cumin
1 tablespoon ginger
1 tablespoon coriander
1 tablespoon turmeric
1 tablespoon sugar
1 pound ground beef
1-pound 4-ounce can tomato purée
1 tablespoon yogurt
2 tablespoons lemon juice
Salt to taste
½ cup slivered almonds
1 cup peas
Cooked rice

1. Melt shortening in Dutch oven or large skillet; sauté onion for 2 minutes. Stir in cumin, ginger, coriander and turmeric; sauté for 2 minutes, stirring frequently.
2. Add sugar and beef; cook over low heat until beef is browned. Stir in tomato purée, yogurt, lemon juice, salt and almonds. Cover; simmer for 30 minutes.

3. Stir in peas; simmer for 15 minutes longer, or until tender.

4. Serve on rice.

May Rutty, Woman's Club, Essex, Conn.

MEAT-A PIE

Serves 4

1 pound ground beef
½ teaspoon garlic salt
½ cup fine bread crumbs
⅔ cup evaporated milk
⅓ cup catsup or tomato paste
2-ounce can sliced mushrooms, drained
2 or 3 slices American or pizza cheese, cut into strips
¼ teaspoon orégano
2 tablespoons grated Parmesan cheese

1. Preheat oven to 400° F.

2. Combine beef, garlic salt, crumbs and milk in 9-inch pie plate. Mix with fork; spread evenly on bottom, raising rim about ½ inch around edge.

3. Spread catsup or tomato paste on meat mixture to rim. Cover with mushrooms; top with cheese strips in crisscross pattern. Sprinkle with orégano and grated cheese.

4. Bake in preheated oven for 20 minutes.

Pearl Wuthrich, Junior Women's Club, Vernon, Conn.

MOUSSAKA
(Greek Dish)

Serves 6 to 8

3 medium eggplants
½ cup olive oil
1½ pounds ground beef
3 large onions, sliced
Salt and pepper to taste
2 8-ounce cans tomato sauce
2 cups grated Cheddar cheese
1 cup Medium White Sauce (p. 441)
2 egg yolks

1. Leave skins on eggplants; cut into ½-inch-thick slices. Heat oil in large skillet; brown eggplant on both sides; drain; set aside.

2. Add beef and onions to oil remaining in skillet; cook over medium heat until meat is well browned. Season with salt and pepper; stir in tomato sauce.

3. Prepare Cheese Sauce: In saucepan blend cheese and Medium White Sauce. Cook over low heat, stirring constantly, until cheese is melted. Remove from heat; beat in egg yolks.

4. Preheat oven to 350° F. Grease 2½-quart casserole.

5. In casserole arrange alternate layers of eggplant with meat mixture. Pour Cheese Sauce on top.

6. Bake in preheated oven for 35 minutes.

Del Harvey, Finneytown Junior Women's Club, Cincinnati, Ohio

PIZZA HAMBURGER

Serves 4 to 6

1 pound ground beef
1½ teaspoons salt
¼ teaspoon pepper
1 teaspoon horseradish
1 teaspoon Worcestershire
1 teaspoon prepared mustard
1-pound 4-ounce can tomatoes, drained
2 tablespoons grated onion
1 cup grated Parmesan cheese
2 tablespoons chopped parsley
½ teaspoon basil
½ teaspoon orégano

1. Preheat oven to 375° F. Grease 9-inch pie plate.

2. In mixing bowl combine beef, salt, pepper, horseradish, Worcestershire and mustard; mix well. Press against bottom and sides of pie plate.

3. Spread tomatoes on meat mixture; sprinkle remaining ingredients on top.

4. Bake in preheated oven for 20 minutes.

5. Cool for 5 minutes; then cut into wedges.

Virginia Kirkpatrick, Woman's Club, Casey, Ia.

SHEPHERD'S PIE WITH BEEF

Serves 4 or 5

1 tablespoon cooking oil
1 pound ground beef
1 medium onion, chopped
1 teaspoon salt
½ teaspoon monosodium glutamate
¼ teaspoon black pepper
3 cups mashed potatoes
1 cup shredded Cheddar cheese

1. Preheat oven to 375° F.

2. Heat oil in skillet; sauté beef and onion until onion is transparent and meat has lost red color. Stir in salt, monosodium glutamate, and pepper.

3. Put meat mixture in 1½-quart baking dish; spread potatoes on top.

4. Sprinkle with cheese; bake in preheated oven for 30 minutes, or until cheese is melted and bubbling.

Mrs. L. T. Weatherly, Junior Woman's Club, Forest Park, Ga.

HAMBURGER STROGANOFF

Serves 4

¼ cup butter or margarine
½ cup minced onions
1 pound ground beef
1 clove garlic, minced
2 tablespoons flour
2 teaspoons salt
¼ teaspoon monosodium glutamate
¼ teaspoon pepper
¼ teaspoon paprika
1 pound mushrooms, sliced
10½-ounce can condensed cream of chicken soup
1 cup sour cream
Chopped parsley, chives or dill

1. Melt butter or margarine in saucepan or electric skillet; sauté onions until golden. Stir in beef, garlic, flour, salt, monosodium glutamate, pepper, paprika and mushrooms; sauté for 5 minutes, stirring frequently.

2. Add soup; bring to boil. Cover; simmer for 10 minutes.

3. Stir in sour cream; sprinkle with parsley, chives or dill.

Mrs. Paul O. Kempf, Crafts and Hobbies Club,
St. Louis, Mo.

TEXAS HASH

Serves 4

3 tablespoons butter or shortening
2 large onions, chopped
2 green peppers, chopped
1 pound ground beef
2 cups canned tomatoes
1 cup water
½ cup rice
1 tablespoon chili powder
1 teaspoon salt
¼ teaspoon pepper

1. Melt butter or shortening in saucepan; sauté onions and peppers until onions are golden. Add beef; cook, stirring, until meat loses red color.

2. Add remaining ingredients. Bring to boil; cover; simmer for 1½ hours.

Wanda Olsen, Allied Gardens Woman's Club,
San Diego, Calif.

TURKISH BEEF WITH OKRA

Serves 6

1 tablespoon shortening
3 medium onions, chopped
1 pound ground beef
2 pounds okra, sliced
1-pound can tomatoes
2 green peppers, chopped
½ cup lemon juice
3 cups water or beef broth
Salt to taste
Cooked rice

1. Melt shortening in saucepan; brown onions and beef.

2. Add all remaining ingredients except rice. Bring to boil; cover; simmer for 25 to 30 minutes.

3. Serve with rice.

Zeynep Kirdar, Junior Woman's Club,
Scottsdale, Ariz.

ZUCCHINI AND BEEF CASSEROLE

Serves 6

1 tablespoon shortening
1 medium onion, finely chopped
1 medium green pepper, finely chopped
1 pound ground beef
1 clove garlic, crushed
6 medium zucchini, cut into ½-inch slices
1-pound 13-ounce can tomatoes
8-ounce can tomato sauce
6-ounce can tomato paste
½ cup chopped pitted ripe olives
⅛ teaspoon orégano

Salt and pepper to taste
1 cup grated Cheddar cheese

1. Preheat oven to 350° F. Grease 2½-quart casserole.

2. Melt shortening in large skillet; sauté onion and green pepper for 5 minutes. Add beef and garlic; cook over low heat, stirring occasionally, until meat is browned. Add zucchini; simmer for 2 minutes. Add tomatoes, tomato sauce and tomato paste; cook for 10 minutes.

3. Remove from heat. Stir in olives and orégano. Season with salt and pepper.

4. Turn into casserole; sprinkle with cheese.

5. Bake in preheated oven for 45 minutes.

Phyllis Happ, Woman's Club,
Redwood City, Calif.

BARBECUED BEEF AND BEANS

Serves 6

1 pound ground beef
½ cup sliced onions
½ teaspoon salt
¼ teaspoon black pepper
1-pound 12-ounce can pork and beans
1 stalk celery, chopped, or ½ teaspoon celery salt
½ cup catsup
1 tablespoon Worcestershire
2 tablespoons vinegar
¼ teaspoon Tabasco
¼ teaspoon paprika
Grated cheese (optional)

1. Preheat oven to 350° F.

2. Brown beef and onions in large skillet or saucepan.

3. Pour off excess fat; add remaining ingredients; mix well.

4. Pour mixture into 1½-quart casserole; bake for 25 to 30 minutes. (Sprinkle cheese on mixture before baking, if desired.)

Mrs. Leon Norman, Woman's Federated Guild,
Moultrie, Ga.

KIDNEY BEANS BARBECUE

Serves 6

2 tablespoons bacon drippings or shortening
1 pound ground beef
1 medium green pepper, chopped
1 large onion, chopped
1 cup chopped celery
2 tablespoons flour
½ cup catsup
½ cup red wine
½ cup water
1 tablespoon red wine vinegar
1 tablespoon brown sugar
2 tablespoons Worcestershire
2 teaspoons chili powder
2 teaspoons salt
1-pound can kidney beans, drained

1. Melt bacon drippings or shortening in large skillet or Dutch oven; sauté beef, green pepper, onion and celery over medium heat, stirring frequently, until beef is browned.

2. Blend in flour; stir in all remaining ingredients except beans. Bring to boil; cover; simmer for 1 hour, stirring occasionally.

3. Add beans; cover; simmer for 10 minutes longer.

Mrs. Edna C. Matthews, Woman's Club, Van Nuys, Calif.

CHILI CON CARNE

Serves 6

2 tablespoons olive oil
3 medium onions, chopped
2 pounds ground beef
½ teaspoon salt
½ teaspoon cumin seeds
½ teaspoon orégano
2 tablespoons flour
¼ cup chili powder
2 cups beef broth
2 cups cooked pinto or kidney
    beans

1. Heat oil in Dutch oven or large heavy saucepan; brown onions over medium heat. Stir in beef; cook over medium heat, stirring occasionally, until browned.

2. Sprinkle with salt, cumin seeds, orégano, flour and chili powder. Gradually stir in broth; bring to boil, stirring constantly. Cover; simmer for 1 hour, stirring occasionally.

3. Add beans; cover; simmer for 30 minutes longer, stirring occasionally.

Esther McNally, Woman's Club, Roswell, N.M.

PEDERNALES RIVER CHILI

Makes 2½ Quarts

This is L. B. J.'s favorite.

4 pounds coarsely ground chuck
1 large onion, chopped
2 cloves garlic, crushed
2 tablespoons chili powder
1 teaspoon orégano
2 1-pound cans tomatoes
2 teaspoons salt
1 teaspoon ground cumin
2 cups hot water

1. In large skillet cook meat, onion and garlic until meat has lost red color, stirring frequently.

2. Add remaining ingredients; mix well. Cover; simmer for 1 hour.

Mrs. Lyndon B. Johnson, Junior Study Club, San Augustine, Tex.

ALL-DAY CHILI AND BEANS

Serves 6

8 ounces dried kidney beans
1 tablespoon bacon drippings
1 pound ground beef
1 large onion, chopped
2 cloves garlic, crushed
8-ounce can tomato sauce
2 tablespoons chili powder
    Salt to taste

1. Put beans in Dutch oven or large heavy saucepan. Add water so that level rises 1 inch above beans. Cover; simmer for 4 hours, adding water, if necessary.

2. Melt bacon drippings in large skillet; sauté beef, onion and garlic, stirring frequently, until meat has lost red color. Stir in tomato sauce and chili powder; simmer for 10 minutes.

3. Add meat mixture to beans; season with salt. Cover; simmer for 30 minutes, stirring frequently.

Pegge Barbarino, Junior Woman's Club, Sunland, Calif.

JAILHOUSE CHILI

Serves 6

½ pound ground beef suet
2 pounds diced round steak or
    ground beef
3 cloves garlic, chopped
3 tablespoons chili powder
1 tablespoon cumin seeds
1 tablespoon white pepper
3 cups water
1 tablespoon paprika
3 diced chili peppers
1 tablespoon salt
1 tablespoon diced sweet pepper

1. Fry out suet in heavy kettle. Discard scraps.

2. Add remaining ingredients. Bring to boil; cover; simmer for 3 to 4 hours, adding water as needed.

Sally Baker, Woman's Club, Temple City, Calif.

BEEF-FILLED BABKA

Serves 6

1½ cups presifted flour
¾ teaspoon salt
1 teaspoon baking powder
½ cup shortening
1 egg
3 tablespoons milk
1 tablespoon butter or margarine
⅓ cup chopped onion
½ pound ground beef
1 cup chopped celery
10½-ounce can condensed cream of
    mushroom soup
    Paprika

1. Into mixing bowl sift together flour, ¼ teaspoon of the salt and baking powder. Cut in shortening until mixture resembles fine crumbs.

2. Add egg and milk; mix to form into ball. Wrap in waxed paper. Refrigerate for several hours.

3. Preheat oven to 375° F. Grease baking sheet.

4. Prepare filling: Melt butter or margarine in skillet; sauté onion over medium heat for 5 minutes. Add beef and celery; sauté over medium heat, stirring occasionally, until meat is browned. Stir in remaining salt and ¾ cup of the soup; simmer for 10 minutes. Cool.

5. Turn dough onto lightly floured board; roll out ¼ inch thick. Spread filling on dough; roll up like a jelly roll. Seal ends of dough; place roll on baking sheet. Form into circle.

6. Bake in preheated oven for 40 minutes, or until golden.

7. Meanwhile, in small saucepan heat remaining soup to serving temperature.

8. Arrange babka on serving dish; pour hot soup over it; sprinkle with paprika.

Mrs. Alfred J. Thoman, Woman's Club,
Hudson, Mass.

BEEF PINWHEELS

Serves 6 to 8

3 cups biscuit mix
1½ teaspoons Tabasco
Milk
1½ pounds ground chuck
1 cup cornflakes
1 medium onion, chopped
2 teaspoons salt
1 tablespoon minced parsley
1 egg, lightly beaten
Quick Mushroom Soup Sauce
(p. 447)

1. Make rolled biscuit dough according to package directions, adding ½ teaspoon of the Tabasco to milk. Roll out on lightly floured board to rectangle about 10 x 15 inches.

2. Preheat oven to 375° F. Grease shallow baking pan.

3. Combine beef with remaining Tabasco, cornflakes, onion, salt, parsley and egg; spread on dough; roll up like a jelly roll. Cut roll into 12 slices about ¾ inch thick; arrange, cut side down, in pan.

4. Bake in preheated oven for about 30 minutes; allow 10 to 15 minutes' longer cooking time for frozen pinwheels.

5. Serve with Quick Mushroom Soup Sauce.

Mrs. Ray Remster, Woman's Club,
Devils Lake, N.D.

CORNISH PASTIES WITH GROUND BEEF

Makes 6

4 cups presifted flour
1½ teaspoons salt
¾ cup lard
¼ cup finely chopped suet
8 or 9 tablespoons water
1½ pounds ground round or flank steak
½ pound ground lean pork
8 medium potatoes, cubed
2 medium onions, chopped
1 cup finely cut turnips
Salt and pepper to taste
Butter

1. Preheat oven to 400° F.

2. Put flour and salt in mixing bowl. Add lard and suet; work by hand or with pastry blender until lard is broken into fine pieces. Stir in water to make a pastry-like dough.

3. Divide dough into 6 portions; roll out each to size of 10-inch plate.

4. Pasty filling: Mix together all remaining ingredients except butter; or ingredients, except butter, may be placed separately on dough in order given.

5. Put some filling, either mixed or one ingredient at a time, on half of each portion of dough. Fold other half of dough over filling; press edges together; crimp to seal.

6. Put pasties on baking sheet; cut a small slit in center top of each. Insert a piece of butter in each slit.

7. Bake in preheated oven for 1 hour.

Mrs. John J. Burke, President, Woman's Club,
Calumet Mich.

HAMBURGER-ONION PIE

Serves 6 to 8

1 cup biscuit mix
⅓ cup light cream
1 pound ground beef
2 medium onions, finely chopped
1 teaspoon salt
¼ teaspoon pepper
2 tablespoons flour
½ teaspoon gravy coloring
1 cup cream-style cottage cheese
2 eggs, lightly beaten
Paprika

1. Preheat oven to 375° F. Grease 9-inch pie plate.

2. Put biscuit mix in bowl; add cream. Mix with fork until dough holds together.

3. Turn onto lightly floured board; knead gently 10 times; roll out to 10-inch circle. Line pie plate with dough; crimp edges.

4. Cook beef and onions in skillet until meat has turned brown, stirring frequently. Stir in salt, pepper, flour and gravy coloring. Spread on dough.

5. Blend cheese with eggs; spread on meat. Sprinkle with paprika.

6. Bake in preheated oven for 30 minutes.

Peggy Czerwonka, Junior Woman's Club,
Glastonbury, Conn.

MEAT UPSIDE-DOWN PIE

Serves 6 to 8

1½ pounds ground beef
1 medium onion, chopped
1 cup whole-kernel corn
1-pound 4-ounce can tomatoes
1½ teaspoons salt
¼ teaspoon pepper
½ teaspoon garlic salt
¼ teaspoon chili powder
3 tablespoons flour
Basic Baking Powder Biscuits
dough (p. 119)

1. Preheat oven to 425° F. Lightly grease 9-inch pie plate.

2. Cook beef and onion in large skillet until meat is well browned.

3. Stir in corn, tomatoes, salt, pepper, garlic salt, chili powder and flour. Simmer for 15 minutes. Turn into pie plate.

4. Roll out Basic Baking Powder Biscuits dough to 10-inch circle. Place on meat.

5. Bake in preheated oven for 15 minutes, or until golden.

6. Invert onto large serving dish; cut into wedges.

C. Smith, Junior Womans' Club,
Pacific Beach, Calif.

RUBY MOUNTAIN SPECIAL CASSEROLE

Serves 6 to 8

1½ pounds ground beef
1 cup chopped celery
½ cup chopped onions
½ cup chopped green pepper
1 clove garlic, crushed
6-ounce can tomato paste
¾ cup water
1½ teaspoons salt
1 teaspoon paprika
½ teaspoon monosodium glutamate
1-pound can pork and beans
1-pound can chick-peas
1½ cups presifted flour
2 teaspoons baking powder
¼ cup butter or margarine
½ cup milk
½ cup sliced stuffed olives
½ cup slivered blanched almonds

1. Preheat oven to 425° F. Grease 11 x 7 x 1½-inch baking pan.
2. In large skillet cook beef, celery, onions, green pepper and garlic until vegetables are tender.
3. Stir in tomato paste, water, 1 teaspoon of the salt, paprika and monosodium glutamate. Set aside 1 cup of meat mixture.
4. Stir pork and beans and chick-peas into meat mixture in skillet; simmer for 10 minutes. Turn into pan.
5. Into mixing bowl sift together flour, baking powder and remaining salt. Cut in butter or margarine until mixture resembles fine crumbs. Add milk; blend until dry ingredients are moistened.
6. Turn onto lightly floured board; knead 12 times. Roll out dough to 12 x 9-inch rectangle.
7. Combine reserved meat mixture, olives and almonds. Spread on dough; roll up like a jelly roll, starting with 12-inch side. Cut into 1-inch pieces; place on meat mixture in pan.
8. Bake in preheated oven for 25 to 30 minutes, or until golden.

Claire Morrow, Women's Club, Lamoille, Nev.

FRIJOLE PIE

Serves 6

¼ cup cooking oil
1 onion, finely chopped
1 clove garlic, minced
1 pound ground beef
1 teaspoon monosodium glutamate
1 green pepper, finely chopped
1¼ cups cooked or canned pinto beans
1½ cups tomatoes
½ teaspoon chili powder
¼ teaspoon thyme
¼ teaspoon dry mustard
½ teaspoon celery seed
1 teaspoon salt
1 tablespoon cornstarch
3 tablespoons cold water
Pastry for a 2-Crust Pie (p. 548)

1. Heat oil in skillet; brown onion and garlic. Add beef; cook for 5 minutes, stirring frequently.
2. Add monosodium glutamate, green pepper, beans, tomatoes and seasonings. Mix well; cook for 5 minutes longer.
3. Mix cornstarch and water; stir into meat mixture.
4. Preheat oven to 350° F.
5. Line pie plate with pastry. Fill with meat mixture; cover with pastry; flute edge; slash top.
6. Bake in preheated oven for 35 minutes or until lightly browned.

Mrs. Eula F. Haley, Woman's Club,
Seligman, Ariz.

TAMALE CASSEROLE

Serves 6 to 8

10-ounce package frozen corn kernels, defrosted
7½-ounce can tomato sauce
10-ounce can hot chili sauce
1 cup milk
1 egg, lightly beaten
¾ cup corn meal
4-ounce can chopped ripe olives, drained
Salt and pepper to taste
1½ pounds ground beef
1 medium onion, chopped
1 green pepper, chopped

1. Preheat oven to 350° F. Grease 2-quart casserole.
2. In saucepan combine corn, tomato sauce, chili sauce, milk, egg, corn meal and olives. Bring to simmer; cook, stirring constantly, until thick. Stir in salt and pepper.
3. Sauté beef, onion and green pepper in skillet until meat loses red color and onions are transparent. Stir into cornmeal mixture; cook for 5 minutes longer, stirring occasionally.
4. Turn into casserole; cover; bake in preheated oven for 1 hour.

Helen Thrasher, El Camino Women's Club,
Ventura, Calif.

TAMALE PIE

Serves 12

¼ cup olive oil
3 cups diced celery
1 large onion, chopped
2 cloves garlic, crushed
1-pound 13-ounce can whole tomatoes, undrained
1-pound can whole-kernel corn, drained
1 tablespoon shortening
2 pounds ground beef
2 tablespoons chili powder
2 teaspoons salt
¼ teaspoon pepper
⅛ teaspoon cayenne
5 cups water
1½ cups yellow corn meal

1. Preheat oven to 425° F.
2. Heat oil in large skillet; sauté celery and onion for 10 minutes. Stir in garlic, tomatoes and corn; simmer for 20 minutes.
3. Meanwhile, melt shortening in saucepan; brown beef over medium heat, stirring frequently. Add chili powder, salt, pepper and cayenne; simmer for 5 minutes.
4. Meanwhile, blend 1 cup of the water with corn meal.
5. Bring remaining water to boil in saucepan. Stir in corn meal; cook over medium heat, stirring constantly, until very thick. Cool slightly.
6. Spread about two-thirds of corn meal mush on bottom and sides of 3-quart casserole. Arrange meat mixture in casserole; top with tomato mixture. Spread remaining corn meal mush on top to form crust.
7. Bake in preheated oven for 25 minutes.

Mrs. Jack Wright, Junior Forum, Seymour, Tex.

CORN CHIP PIE

Serves 6

2 tablespoons shortening
1 small onion, finely chopped
1 small green pepper, finely chopped
1 pound ground beef
1 teaspoon chili powder
1 teaspoon salt
⅛ teaspoon pepper
6-ounce can tomato paste
1 teaspoon sugar
1 cup grated Cheddar cheese
1½ cups corn chips

1. Preheat oven to 350° F. Grease 2-quart casserole.
2. Melt shortening in large skillet; sauté onion and green pepper over medium heat for 5 minutes. Add beef, chili powder, salt and pepper; cook over medium heat, stirring frequently, until meat loses red color. Stir in tomato paste and sugar; simmer for 5 minutes.
3. Turn into casserole; sprinkle with cheese and corn chips.
4. Bake in preheated oven for 25 minutes.

Myra Gail Walton, Junior Study Club,
San Augustine, Tex.

GREEN CHILI ENCHILADAS

Serves 4 to 6

1 pound ground beef
1 large onion, chopped
4-ounce can green chili peppers, chopped
1 pound mild Cheddar cheese, shredded
Cooking oil
12 Tortillas (p. 136) or canned tortillas
10-ounce can enchilada sauce
½ cup shredded American cheese
½ cup chopped olives

1. Brown beef and onion in skillet until meat loses red color. Add chilis and Cheddar cheese; heat until cheese is melted, stirring occasionally.

2. Heat about ¼ inch oil in another skillet: soften tortillas one at a time. (Oil should not be hot, for tortillas must be pliable.)
3. Preheat oven to 400° F.
4. Put 2 tablespoons meat mixture on each tortilla; roll up. Arrange rolls in deep baking dish.
5. Pour sauce over tortillas; sprinkle with American cheese. Bake in preheated oven for 10 minutes, or until cheese is melted.
6. Remove from oven; sprinkle with olives.

Evelyn Wilkerson, Junior Woman's Club,
Phoenix, Ariz.

ENCHILADAS WITH BEANS

Serves 6

1 pound ground beef
1-pound can kidney beans, drained
½ teaspoon salt
1 teaspoon chili powder
½ cup shortening
18 Tortillas (p. 136) or canned tortillas
1-pound can enchilada sauce
1 cup chopped onions
1 cup grated Cheddar cheese

1. Preheat oven to 375° F. Grease 10 x 6 x 1½-inch baking pan.
2. Brown beef well in saucepan over medium heat, stirring frequently. Stir in beans, salt and chili powder; simmer for 5 minutes.
3. Meanwhile, heat some of shortening in skillet; fry tortillas lightly on both sides.
4. Place a little beef mixture in center of each tortilla; roll up like a jelly roll. Arrange tortillas in pan; top with enchilada sauce. Sprinkle with onions and cheese.
5. Bake in preheated oven for 25 minutes.

Mrs. Don Greer, Junior Women's Club,
Cheyenne, Wyo.

TACOS

Makes 12

1 cup presifted flour
½ cup corn meal
Salt
1 egg
1½ cups water
1 large onion, finely chopped
2 tomatoes, peeled and diced
2 chili peppers, chopped
¼ teaspoon garlic powder
1 head lettuce, finely chopped
4 cups grated sharp Cheddar cheese
2 pounds ground beef
8-ounce can tomato sauce

1. This dish has four separate parts. First, prepare Tortillas: In mixing bowl combine flour, corn meal, ¼ teaspoon salt, egg and water; beat until smooth. Drop 3 tablespoons batter onto moderately hot ungreased griddle to make very thin 6-inch pancake. Turn when edges begin to look dry but not browned. Bake other side until

dry but not browned. Keep warm in covered pan.

2. Prepare onion mixture: In small bowl combine onion, tomatoes, chilis, garlic powder and 1 teaspoon salt; mix well. Chill.

3. Prepare lettuce mixture: In bowl mix lettuce and cheese lightly with hands. Chill.

4. Prepare meat filling: Cook beef in large skillet until browned. Stir in tomato sauce, salt and pepper to taste. Simmer for 15 minutes, stirring occasionally.

6. Spoon 3 tablespoons meat mixture in center of each tortilla; fold; secure with wooden pick. Keep warm in oven.

7. At the table, open each tortilla; sprinkle with onion mixture and lettuce mixture; roll again.

Mrs. John Myers, Women's Club, Canby, Minn.

Cooked Beef Dishes

INDIAN CURRY BOMBAY STYLE

Serves 4 to 6

1 tablespoon butter or margarine
1 large apple, peeled, cored and diced
1 large onion, chopped
1 cup chopped celery
1 tablespoon curry powder
1 cup beef broth
¼ cup seedless raisins
2 cups diced cooked beef
1 egg, lightly beaten
Cooked rice
Condiments: chutney, toasted coconut, roasted peanuts, bombay duck (dried flesh of Asian lizard fish) and lemon slices

1. Melt butter or margarine in heavy saucepan; sauté apple, onion and celery over medium heat for 5 minutes, stirring occasionally. Sprinkle with curry powder; sauté for 3 minutes, stirring frequently.

2. Stir in broth, raisins and beef. Cover; simmer for 15 minutes.

3. Remove from heat; stir in egg.

4. Serve with rice and condiments.

Natalie McLean, Woman's Club, Falls Church, Va.

BAKED BEEF HASH

Serves 6

¼ cup butter
½ cup chopped onions
4 cups diced cooked roast beef
½ cup red wine
6 large potatoes, cooked and diced
½ cup heavy cream
2 tablespoons soy sauce
2 tablespoons chopped parsley
¼ teaspoon marjoram
¼ teaspoon savory
Paprika

1. Preheat oven to 350° F. Grease 2-quart casserole.

2. Melt butter in large skillet; sauté onions for 10 minutes.

3. Remove from heat; stir in all remaining ingredients except paprika. Turn into casserole; sprinkle with paprika.

4. Bake in preheated oven for 30 minutes.

VARIATION: For Corned Beef Hash, substitute cooked corned beef for roast beef in above recipe.

Mrs. Paul K. Robertson, Woman's Club,
Wilmette, Ill.

SAUERBRATEN SLICES

Serves 6

Excellent served with Potato Drop Dumplings (p. 462).

2 cups water
½ cup vinegar
10 cloves
3 bay leaves
8 gingersnaps, crumbled
1 tablespoon sugar
½ teaspoon salt
¼ teaspoon gravy coloring
6 large slices cooked beef

1. In large skillet combine all ingredients except beef. Bring to boil; stir over low heat until smooth.

2. Add beef; heat to serving temperature.

P. Stookey, Junior Woman's Club,
Pacific Beach, Calif.

SHEPHERD PIE

Serves 4

Cooked roast beef
1 medium onion
1 medium green pepper
2 tablespoons shortening
½ cup thickened gravy
Salt and pepper to taste
3 cups mashed potatoes
1 cup grated Cheddar cheese
Paprika

1. Put enough beef through medium blade of meat grinder to make 3 cups ground beef; set aside.

2. Put onion and green pepper through medium blade of meat grinder.

3. Melt shortening in skillet; sauté onion and green pepper for 5 minutes. Stir in beef; simmer for 5 minutes.

4. Preheat oven to 375° F. Grease 2-quart casserole.

5. Stir gravy, salt and pepper into beef mixture; turn into casserole.

6. In mixing bowl beat potatoes with ½ cup of the cheese; spread on meat mixture. Sprinkle with remaining cheese and paprika.

7. Bake in preheated oven for 35 minutes.

Billie Simmons, Junior Woman's Club,
St. Cloud, Fla.

Frankfurters

BARBECUED FRANKFURTERS
Serves 4

1 tablespoon butter
1 small onion, finely chopped
½ cup catsup
¼ cup cider vinegar
¼ cup water
1 tablespoon sugar
1 teaspoon paprika
1 tablespoon Worcestershire
1 teaspoon prepared mustard
½ teaspoon pepper
8 frankfurters

1. Preheat oven to 400° F. Grease 10 x 6 x 1½-inch baking pan.
2. Melt butter in saucepan; sauté onion until tender. Stir in all remaining ingredients except frankfurters. Bring to boil; simmer for 2 minutes.
3. Slit frankfurters diagonally in 3 places; arrange in pan. Pour sauce over frankfurters.
4. Bake in preheated oven for 20 minutes, basting occasionally.

Gae Mallory, Thomas Jefferson Junior Woman's Club, Richmond, Va.

FRANKFURTER BEAN FARE
Serves 6

2 1-pound cans pork and beans
½ cup finely chopped onions
¼ cup molasses
¼ cup catsup
2 teaspoons horseradish
1 teaspoon dry mustard
6 frankfurters
1 tablespoon melted butter or margarine

1. Preheat oven to 350° F. Grease 1½-quart casserole.
2. Turn pork and beans into casserole. Add onions; mix well.
3. In small bowl blend molasses, catsup, horseradish and mustard. Spread on beans. Top with frankfurters; brush with butter or margarine.
4. Bake in preheated oven for 25 minutes, or until bubbling.

Bywood Junior Women's Club, Upper Darby, Pa.

CORN DOGS
Serves 8

1 cup presifted flour
2 tablespoons sugar
1½ teaspoons baking powder
1 teaspoon salt
⅔ cup corn meal
2 tablespoons cooking oil
1 egg
¾ cup milk
1 pound frankfurters
Fat for deep frying
Mustard or catsup

1. Into mixing bowl sift together flour, sugar, baking powder and salt. Blend in corn meal. Add oil, egg and milk; stir just until dry ingredients are moistened.

2. Meanwhile, cook frankfurters in boiling water for 5 minutes. Drain well; coat in batter.
3. Drop frankfurters into deep fat heated to 365° F. Cook for 5 minutes, or until golden.
4. Drain on absorbent paper; serve at once with mustard or catsup, as desired.

Mrs. William Kilpatrick, Civic Club, Fulton, Miss.

FRANKFURTER CROWN CASSEROLE
Serves 4

2 slices bacon
½ cup chopped onions
10½-ounce can condensed cream of mushroom soup
½ cup water
½ teaspoon salt
Dash of pepper
3 cups sliced cooked potatoes
1 cup cooked cut green beans
½ pound frankfurters, split and cut in half crosswise

1. Preheat oven to 350° F. Grease 1½-quart casserole.
2. Cook bacon in skillet until crisp. Drain on absorbent paper; crumble; set aside.
3. Sauté onions in fat remaining in skillet over medium heat until transparent. Stir in soup, water, salt, pepper, potatoes and beans. Mix well; turn into casserole.
4. Arrange frankfurters upright around edge of casserole.
5. Bake in preheated oven for 30 minutes. Just before serving, sprinkle with bacon.

Norma Taylor, Jahnke Road Woman's Club, Richmond, Va.

FRANKFURTERS DE LUXE
Serves 4 to 6

½ cup shortening
½ cup finely chopped onions
⅓ cup chopped green pepper
⅓ cup presifted flour
1-pound 12-ounce can tomatoes, drained
3 cups diced cooked carrots
3 tablespoons catsup
Salt and pepper to taste
8 frankfurters
⅓ cup fresh bread crumbs
2 tablespoons melted butter

1. Preheat oven to 350° F. Grease 2-quart casserole.
2. Melt shortening in skillet; sauté onions and green pepper for 5 minutes. Stir in flour; gradually stir in tomatoes. Cook over low heat, stirring occasionally, until thickened. Stir in carrots and catsup; season with salt and pepper.
3. Split frankfurters; place, cut side down, in casserole. Top with sauce. Combine crumbs and butter; sprinkle on top.
4. Bake in preheated oven for 30 minutes.

Carolyn Guthrie, Woman's Club, Selma, Ind.

ITALIAN CARTWHEEL

Serves 4

15½-ounce can marinara sauce
1⅓ cups water
1⅓ cups instant rice
¾ cup sweet pickle relish
3 tablespoons prepared mustard
8 frankfurters

1. Preheat oven to 350° F. Grease 1-quart casserole.
2. Pour marinara sauce, water and rice into casserole; stir to mix.
3. In small bowl blend pickle relish and mustard. Split frankfurters without cutting all the way through; fill with pickle mixture.
4. Arrange frankfurters on rice; bake in preheated oven for 20 minutes.
5. Place casserole under broiler; broil for 3 to 4 minutes, or until frankfurters are browned.

Alice J. Smith, Junior Woman's Club,
Pompano Beach, Fla.

GRACE'S SAUERKRAUT AND FRANKFURTER BAKE

Serves 6

1-pound 11-ounce can sauerkraut
1 cup applesauce
½ teaspoon caraway seeds
6 frankfurters

1. Preheat oven to 350° F. Grease 1-quart casserole.
2. Drain sauerkraut; rinse under cold water; drain again. In mixing bowl combine sauerkraut, applesauce and caraway seeds. Turn into casserole.
3. Score frankfurters; arrange on sauerkraut.
4. Cover; bake in preheated oven for 1 hour.

Mrs. G. I. Bennett, Parliamentary Law Club,
Glendale, Calif.

STUFFED HOT DOGS

Serves 8

4 cups mashed potatoes
Salt and pepper to taste
8 frankfurters
8 slices American cheese
Paprika
½ cup finely chopped scallions

1. Preheat broiler. Line broiler pan with aluminum foil.
2. Season potatoes with salt and pepper.
3. Simmer frankfurters in water for 5 minutes.
4. Drain frankfurters; cut lengthwise but not quite through.
5. Fill slits with potatoes; top each with cheese slice. Sprinkle with paprika; place on pan.

6. Broil about 5 inches from heat for 3 minutes, or until cheese is melted. Sprinkle with scallions.

Marjorie Seaman, Pathfinder Club,
Compton, Calif.

Pork

Pork is firmer in texture and less fatty from medium hogs than from extremely large hogs. The flesh of quality pork is light red and firm; the fat is firm and white. It should be cooked as soon as possible after it is purchased and not allowed to remain unfrozen in the refrigerator for more than a couple of days.

Pork and pork products must always be thoroughly cooked and must never be eaten if they show the slightest tinge of pink, for parasites, known as trichinae, exist in most pork and may be transmitted to the eater, causing a serious illness known as trichinosis. There is absolutely no danger of this, however, when pork is cooked to an internal temperature of 185° F. on a meat thermometer or until well done and white or gray in color.

If a meat thermometer is not used, follow either the timetable for cooking pork or the individual recipes which follow. Count on from 30 to 45 minutes per pound, depending on thickness of the pork, at a roasting temperature of 350° F. Broiling chops is not recommended, because they dry out before they are cooked in the center. The loin is the most succulent cut of pork for roasting; but a fresh ham can be equally good, and a shoulder is good either roasted or braised. Because of the high content of fat in these cuts of pork, no additional fat or oil is needed, and they are practically self-basting.

CUTS OF PORK AND HOW TO COOK THEM

Roast or Barbecue
   Whole baby pig
   Loin
   Leg (fresh ham)
   Shoulder (picnic roast) or Boston butt (boned rolled butt)
   Spareribs
Braise
   Loin chops
   Rib chops
   Shoulder chops or steak
   Ham steak
   Spareribs
Pan-Broil or Pan-Fry
   Rib chops
   Loin chops
   Salt pork
   Bacon
Stew
   Hock
   Foot
Broil
   Bacon

Timetable for Cooking Pork

ROASTING FRESH PORK	Weight in Pounds	Approximate Time in Hours (185°)
Fresh ham butt	4 to 6	3½ to 4
Whole fresh ham	10 to 14	6 to 7
Loin end	2½ to 3	2¼ to 2½
Loin	4 to 5	3¼ to 3½
Shoulder butt	4 to 6	3½ to 4
BRAISING	Weight in Ounces	Approximate Time After Browning
Rib or loin chops (¾ to 1 inch thick)	4 to 5 each	35 to 40 minutes
Shoulder steaks	5 to 6 each	35 to 40 minutes
STEWING	Weight in Pounds	Approximate Time in Hours
Hocks	¾	3

Pork Roasts

ROAST PIG

Serves 8 to 12

10- to 15-pound pig, dressed
1 tablespoon salt
1 teaspoon pepper
¾ teaspoon thyme
Bread Stuffing (p. 452)
1 potato
¼ cup prepared mustard
1 red apple

1. Preheat oven to 350° F.
2. Wash pig thoroughly inside and out; and wipe dry with paper towels.
3. In small bowl blend salt, pepper and thyme; rub inside pig cavity.
4. Fill cavity loosely with Bread Stuffing; skewer opening; lace with string. Place potato in mouth of pig; wrap aluminum foil around ears. Skewer forelegs forward and hind legs back. Place pig on rack in large shallow roasting pan.
5. Roast in preheated oven for 4 hours, or 18 minutes per pound.
6. About 30 minutes before pig is cooked, brush with mustard; roast for 30 minutes longer, or until tender.
7. Remove pig; arrange on large serving dish. Remove skewers, string and potato. Place apple in mouth; remove foil from ears.

Mrs. L. M. Hockenbery, Woman's Club,
Bangor, Pa.

ROAST SUCKLING PIG

Serves 16

1 cup butter or margarine
2 large onions, finely chopped
½ pound ground beef
1 small cabbage, shredded
1 quart milk, scalded
1-pound loaf white bread, crumbled
3 eggs, lightly beaten
2 teaspoons salt
¼ teaspoon pepper
1 teaspoon allspice

18-pound pig, dressed
1 red apple

1. Preheat oven to 375° F.
2. Prepare Beef and Cabbage Stuffing: Melt ½ cup of the butter or margarine in skillet; sauté onions over medium heat until golden. Add beef; cook, stirring frequently, until browned. Cover, simmer for 15 minutes. Meanwhile, cook cabbage in boiling salted water for 5 minutes; drain well. Pour milk over bread in mixing bowl; stir in eggs, salt, pepper, allspice, cabbage and meat mixture.
3. Fill pig cavity with stuffing; sew or skewer opening.
4. Put pig on rack in shallow roasting pan. Spread with remaining butter or margarine; cover with damp cloth.
5. Roast in preheated oven for 6 hours, basting pig frequently with pan juices.
6. Remove thread or skewers; arrange pig on serving dish. Place apple in mouth.

Helen Ambrose, Woman's Club,
Mahanoy City, Pa.

APRICOT PORK ROAST

Serves 8

6-pound pork loin roast
Salt and pepper to taste
1-pound can whole apricots
2 tablespoons cornstarch

1. Preheat oven to 350° F.
2. Place pork on rack in shallow roasting pan. Season with salt and pepper.
3. Roast in preheated oven for 2 hours. Spoon off excess fat.
4. Drain apricots; pour liquid over pork; bake for 1 hour longer, or until tender. Transfer pork to serving dish; keep warm.
5. Discard excess fat; strain pan juices into measuring cup; add water, if necessary, to total 2 cups; put in small saucepan. Blend cornstarch and 2 tablespoons water; stir into juices; cook over medium heat, stirring constantly, until sauce is thickened and clear.

6. Garnish roast with apricots; serve with sauce.

Carol Fehling, Whitfield Woman's Club, Reading, Pa.

ROAST RIBS OF PORK LOIN WITH BARBECUE SAUCE

Serves 8

8-ounce can tomato juice
½ cup catsup
½ cup vinegar
½ cup brown sugar
1 teaspoon chili powder
¼ cup dark corn syrup
½ cup water
1 tablespoon cornstarch
6-pound pork loin roast
Salt and pepper to taste

1. Preheat oven to 350° F.
2. Prepare Barbecue for Roast Pork Sauce: In saucepan combine tomato juice, catsup, vinegar, sugar, chili powder, corn syrup and water. Mix cornstarch with about 2 tablespoons of sauce; stir into rest of sauce. Cook over low heat for about 15 minutes or until slightly thickened, stirring occasionally.
3. Rub pork with salt and pepper. Place, fat side up, in shallow roasting pan.
4. Roast in preheated oven for 30 to 35 minutes per pound, basting frequently with a little sauce.
5. Serve roast with remaining sauce.

Meet Our Cooks, Arts Club, Aliceville, Ala.

ROAST FRESH HAM

A fresh ham may be cooked by any of the methods suitable for a roast suckling pig or a pork loin roast. Roast at 350° F. for 30 to 45 minutes per pound for a 10- to 14-pound whole ham; 40 to 45 minutes per pound for a 4- to 6-pound fresh ham butt.

A. S.

CROWN ROAST OF PORK

Serves 8

4½-pound (about 10 chops) crown roast of pork
Salt and pepper to taste
Corn Stuffing (p. 454)
About 10 spiced crab apples

1. Preheat oven to 325° F.
2. Season pork with salt and pepper; place in shallow roasting pan. Wrap pieces of aluminum foil around tips of bone.
3. Roast in preheated oven for 1 hour and 15 minutes.
4. Remove roast; fill center with Corn Stuffing. Bake for 1½ hours longer, or until well cooked.
5. Arrange roast on serving dish; remove foil; top each rib with crab apple.

Woman's Club, Moorestown, N.J.

GLAZED PORK LOIN

Serves 6 to 8

4- to 5-pound pork loin roast with backbone removed
¼ cup brown sugar
2 tablespoons flour
2 tablespoons vinegar
3 pineapple slices, halved
Parsley clusters

1. Preheat oven to 350° F.
2. Between each 2 ribs in roast, cut halfway into fat surface. Place, fat side up, in open roasting pan. (Do not add water or cover.)
3. Roast in preheated oven for 35 to 45 minutes per pound.
4. Combine sugar, flour and vinegar.
5. Remove roast from oven 10 minutes before it is done; insert pineapple half slices into cuts. Cover with sugar mixture. Roast for 10 minutes longer, or until nicely glazed. Garnish with parsley.

Ethel LaRue, Century Club, Coraopolis, Pa.

PORK ROAST WITH RUM

Serves 6

1 teaspoon ground cumin
1 teaspoon orégano
1½ teaspoons salt
¼ teaspoon pepper
½ teaspoon garlic powder
2 tablespoons water
4- to 5-pound pork loin roast
½ cup orange juice
2 tablespoons brown sugar
1 tablespoon grated orange rind
½ cup rum

1. Preheat oven to 400° F.
2. In small bowl combine cumin, orégano, salt, pepper, garlic powder and water to a paste.
3. Arrange pork on rack in roasting pan; spread paste on pork.
4. Roast, uncovered, in preheated oven for 30 minutes, or until browned.
5. Blend orange juice, sugar and orange rind; pour over pork. Turn temperature to 350° F. Cover; roast for 2 hours longer.
6. Pour rum over pork; roast for 30 minutes longer, or until cooked (185° F. on meat thermometer). Baste frequently during cooking. Add water, if necessary, to prevent juices from burning.

Mrs. Keith Kappmeyer, Federated Civic Club, Mount Vernon, Ill.

BAKED PORK TENDERLOIN

Serves 4

2-pound pork tenderloin
½ teaspoon salt
⅛ teaspoon pepper
4 slices bacon
1 cup apple juice
¼ teaspoon cinnamon
¼ teaspoon ground cloves

1. Preheat oven to 325° F.
2. Arrange pork on rack in shallow roasting pan; sprinkle with salt and pepper. Arrange bacon on pork.

3. In small saucepan combine apple juice, cinnamon and cloves; bring to boil. Remove from heat; brush pork with spiced apple juice.

4. Bake in preheated oven for 2 hours, or until tender, basting frequently with spiced apple juice.

Mrs. J. S. O'Sheal, Tallulah Falls Circle and Sylvester Woman's Club, Sylvester, Ga.

APPLE-STUFFED TENDERLOINS
Serves 6 to 8

1⅓ cups apple juice
1 tablespoon butter
1 teaspoon sage
¾ cup finely chopped apples
½ cup finely chopped onions
¾ cup packaged herb-seasoned
  bread stuffing
2 2-pound pork tenderloins
  Salt and pepper to taste
4 slices bacon, halved

1. Preheat oven to 350° F.
2. Prepare stuffing: Combine ⅓ cup of the apple juice, butter and sage. Bring to boil; remove from heat; stir in apples, onions and packaged stuffing.
3. Cut each tenderloin lengthwise, but not quite through. Flatten; season with salt and pepper. Arrange stuffing on one tenderloin; cover with other tenderloin. Secure with skewers; arrange on rack in shallow roasting pan. Pour remaining apple juice over top; cover with bacon.
4. Roast in preheated oven for 1½ hours, or until tender.
5. Serve with gravy made from pan juices, if desired.

Woman's Club, Bartlett, Ia.

Pork Chops

BAKED PORK CHOPS
Serves 6

6 1-inch-thick loin pork chops
¼ cup seasoned flour
1½ cups milk
¼ cup shortening
½ cup seedless raisins
½ teaspoon cinnamon
6 apples, cored
6 sweet potatoes, peeled and sliced

1. Preheat oven to 375° F.
2. Coat chops with flour. Dip in milk; coat again with flour.
3. Melt shortening in 11 x 7 x 1½-inch baking pan; brown meat on both sides. Remove from heat.
4. Combine raisins and cinnamon. Place apples around pork chops in pan; fill centers with raisin mixture. Place potatoes on chops. Pour in remaining milk.
5. Bake in preheated oven for 1½ hours, adding milk, if necessary, during cooking.

Beulah Cockrell, Woman's Club, Batchtown, Ill.

BARBECUED PORK AND BEAN BAKE
Serves 4

1-pound can pork and beans
  Salt and pepper to taste
4 pork chops
  Prepared mustard
  Brown sugar
  Catsup
4 onion slices
4 lemon slices

1. Preheat oven to 325° F.
2. Pour pork and beans into 13 x 9½ x 2-inch baking pan.
3. Sprinkle chops lightly with salt and pepper; arrange on beans. Brush each chop with mustard; sprinkle with sugar; spread with catsup. Place onion slice and lemon slice on each chop; secure with wooden pick.
4. Bake, uncovered, in preheated oven, for 1½ hours, or until fork-tender.

Mrs. L. E. Billings, Book Lovers Club, Kosciusko, Miss.

PORK CHOPS À LA BAUDOIN
Serves 6

2 tablespoons shortening
6 pork chops
1½ teaspoons salt
¼ teaspoon pepper
1 cup rice
3½ cups chicken broth
¼ teaspoon thyme
½ cup diced green pepper
½ cup diced onions

1. Preheat oven to 350° F.
2. Melt shortening in large skillet; brown chops on both sides. Remove from skillet; season with salt and pepper. If chops are very fat, drain off part of drippings.
3. Brown rice in fat remaining in skillet, stirring constantly. Add remaining ingredients.
4. Turn into 3-quart casserole; top with chops. Cover.
5. Bake in preheated oven for 1 hour.

Mrs. James Baudoin, La Clique d'Etude, Inc., Abbeville, La.

CHINESE PORK CHOPS
Serves 6

6 ¾-inch-thick pork chops
  Flour
1 tablespoon bacon drippings or fat
⅔ cup soy sauce
⅔ cup vinegar
⅓ cup sugar
½ teaspoon ginger
⅔ cup water

1. Dredge chops in flour. Heat drippings or fat in heavy skillet; brown chops well on both sides. Pour off excess fat.
2. Add remaining ingredients; bring to boil. Cover; simmer for 1 hour.

Mrs. S. E. Herbert, Woman's Club, Hilo, Hawaii

POOR MAN'S GOOSE

Serves 6

Serve with fresh applesauce, if desired.

6 medium potatoes, sliced
2 large onions, sliced
1-pound can cream-style corn
Salt and pepper to taste
Milk
6 loin pork chops
½ teaspoon monosodium glutamate

1. Preheat oven to 350° F. Grease 13 x 9½ x 2-inch baking pan.
2. In pan arrange layer of potatoes and layer of onions and layer of corn, sprinkling each layer with salt and pepper. Add milk just to cover top layer.
3. Arrange chops on top; season with salt, pepper and monosodium glutamate.
4. Bake in preheated oven for 1½ hours.

Doris Bossolt, Woman's Club, Paramus, N.J.

CRANBERRY PORK CHOPS

Serves 6

6 pork chops
¼ cup presifted flour
¾ teaspoon salt
1 tablespoon fat
1 small seedless orange, quartered
3 cups cranberries
¾ cup honey
½ teaspoon ground cloves
½ teaspoon nutmeg
Dash of cinnamon

1. Roll chops in flour; sprinkle with salt. Heat fat in large skillet, brown chops on both sides.
2. Meanwhile, put orange and cranberries through meat grinder; combine with remaining ingredients. Pour over chops.
3. Cover; cook over low heat for about 1 hour, or until well done.

Mrs. Marie Schaab, Women's Progressive Club of Inglewood Acres, Inglewood, Calif.

ORANGE-GLAZED PORK CHOPS

Serves 6

2 tablespoons shortening
6 pork chops
5 tablespoons sugar
1½ teaspoons cornstarch
¼ teaspoon salt
¼ teaspoon cinnamon
10 cloves
2 teaspoons grated orange rind
¼ cup orange juice
6 orange slices

1. Melt shortening in large skillet; brown pork chops on both sides. Cover; simmer for about 45 minutes, or until tender. Add a little water, if necessary, to prevent burning.
2. Meanwhile, prepare glaze: In small saucepan combine sugar, cornstarch, salt, cinnamon, cloves and orange rind. Blend in orange juice. Cook over low heat, stirring constantly, until thickened and smooth. Add orange slices; simmer for 2 minutes.

3. Drain chops; arrange on serving dish. Top each chop with orange slice; spoon glaze over it.

Mrs. Gertrude Myers, Salmagundi Federated Women's Club, Bloomington, Wis.

GERMAN CASSEROLE

Serves 4

A green vegetable and Sweet Potato Biscuits (p. 124) complete this meal.

1 large baking potato
1-pound can sauerkraut, drained
4 pork chops
Salt and pepper to taste

1. Preheat oven to 275° F. Grease casserole or baking pan.
2. Slice potato ½ inch thick; arrange in casserole or pan. Add sauerkraut; top with chops. Sprinkle with salt and pepper.
3. Bake in preheated oven for about 3 hours.

Mrs. L. J. Taylor, Woman's Club, Comer, Ga.

PEACH AND PORK CHOPS
BARBECUE SKILLET

Serves 6

1 tablespoon shortening
6 1-inch-thick loin pork chops
Salt and pepper to taste
1-pound 13-ounce can peach halves
¼ cup brown sugar
1 teaspoon cinnamon
½ teaspoon ground cloves
8-ounce can tomato sauce
¼ cup cider vinegar

1. Melt shortening in skillet; brown chops well on both sides. Drain off excess fat. Remove from heat; season with salt and pepper.
2. Drain peach halves; reserve ¼ cup syrup. Arrange peach halves on chops.
3. Prepare sauce: Combine syrup and remaining ingredients; mix well. Pour over pork and peaches.
4. Cover; simmer for 30 to 45 minutes, or until tender. Baste occasionally with sauce.

Mrs. E. Austin Hess, Woman's Club, Akron, Pa.

PORK CHOPS INDONESIAN

Serves 6

6 1-inch-thick loin pork chops
Salt and pepper to taste
3 tablespoons shortening
1-pound can peach slices
2 tablespoons brown sugar
1 tablespoon grated onion
2 tablespoons soy sauce
1 teaspoon ginger
⅛ teaspoon dry mustard
⅛ teaspoon garlic powder
1 large green pepper
Cooked rice

1. Season chops with salt and pepper. Melt shortening in large skillet; brown chops on both sides. Remove from heat; drain all but 2 tablespoons fat from skillet.
2. Drain peach slices; reserve syrup; set peach slices aside.

3. Blend peach syrup, sugar, onion, soy sauce, ginger, mustard and garlic powder. Pour over chops. Cover; simmer for 30 minutes.

4. Meanwhile, remove seeds and white membrane from green pepper; cut into slivers; add with peach slices to chops; simmer for 5 minutes longer.

5. Serve on rice.

Mrs. George J. Graf, Woman's Club,
Green River, Wyo.

PORK CHOPS WITH PRUNES

Serves 6

6 pork chops
Salt and pepper to taste
1 medium onion, sliced
12 dried prunes
½ cup water
2 tablespoons brown sugar
2 tablespoons cider vinegar
Dash of Tabasco

1. In skillet brown chops slowly on both sides in their own fat.

2. Sprinkle chops with salt and pepper; add remaining ingredients.

3. Cover; cook over low heat for 1 hour.

Jane Faust, Progressive Club, Hubbard, Ia.

SMOTHERED PORK CHOPS

Serves 6

1 tablespoon cooking oil
6 1-inch-thick loin pork chops
2 lemons, thinly sliced
2 medium onions, sliced
1 green pepper, cut into rings
Salt and pepper to taste
14-ounce bottle catsup
¾ cup water
1 tablespoon butter or margarine

1. Heat oil in large skillet; brown chops on both sides.

2. Top chops with lemon slices, onion slices and green pepper rings. Sprinkle with salt and pepper.

3. Blend catsup and water; pour over ingredients in skillet. Dot with butter or margarine.

4. Cover; simmer for 1 hour, or until tender.

Mrs. Bessie Childers, President, Homemakers
H.D.C., Vicksburg, Miss.

STUFFED PORK CHOPS

Serves 6

1 cup fresh bread crumbs
1 teaspoon salt
¼ teaspoon pepper
¼ teaspoon poultry seasoning
1 tablespoon grated onion
¼ cup melted shortening
1 egg
6 thick loin pork chops with pockets

1. Preheat oven to 350° F.

2. Prepare Bread Stuffing: Combine crumbs, salt, pepper, poultry seasoning and onion. Add 2 tablespoons of the shortening and egg; mix well.

3. Fill pockets of chops with stuffing; secure with wooden picks.

4. Heat remaining shortening in large skillet; brown chops well on both sides. Arrange pork in 10 x 6 x 1½-inch baking pan.

5. Bake in preheated oven for 1 hour, or until tender.

Mrs. Henry DeGooyer, Lower Naches
Woman's Club, Yakima, Wash.

PORK CHOPS WITH ORANGE STUFFING

Serves 4

1 small onion, finely chopped
½ stalk celery with leaves, finely chopped
¾ cup fresh bread crumbs
Grated rind of 1 orange
¼ cup orange juice
¼ teaspoon dry mustard
¼ teaspoon pepper
4 double rib pork chops with pockets
2 tablespoons flour
Salt and pepper to taste
2 tablespoons butter or margarine
½ cup hot water
1 bay leaf

1. Prepare Orange Stuffing: Combine onion, celery, crumbs, orange rind and juice, mustard and pepper; mix well.

2. Fill pockets of chops with stuffing.

3. Season flour with salt and pepper; coat chops. Melt butter or margarine in skillet; brown chops quickly on both sides.

4. Add water and bay leaf. Cover; simmer for 1 hour, or until tender.

Mrs. Arnold Rose, President, Garden Club,
Statesboro, Ga.

PORK 'N' SWEETS

Serves 8

4-pound loin of pork, cut into chops
Salt
Pepper
1-pound 4-ounce can crushed pineapple
¾ cup water
¼ cup vinegar
⅛ teaspoon pepper
¼ cup brown sugar
2 tablespoons lemon juice
2 tablespoons prepared mustard
2 tablespoons Worcestershire
2 tablespoons cornstarch
1-pound 13-ounce can potatoes
2 medium onions, thinly sliced

1. Remove excess fat from chops; sear well on both sides in skillet over moderate heat.

2. Transfer chops to 3-quart casserole; sprinkle with ½ teaspoon salt and ¼ teaspoon pepper.

3. Preheat oven to 350° F.

4. Drain and reserve crushed pineapple. Put syrup in saucepan. Add ½ cup of the water, vinegar, 1 teaspoon salt, ⅛ teaspoon pepper, sugar, lemon juice, mustard and Worcestershire.

5. Combine cornstarch and remaining water; stir into pineapple syrup. Bring to boil; cook, stirring constantly, until sauce is slightly thickened.

6. Drain sweet potatoes; arrange between chops. Separate onion slices into rings; arrange on potatoes and chops. Pour sauce over all.

7. Cover; bake in preheated oven for about 2 hours, or until tender.

8. Top with reserved pineapple; bake for 15 minutes longer.

Phyllis Bradford, El Camino Women's Club,
Ventura, Calif.

A Variety of Pork Dishes

ALL-AMERICA PORK AND BEAN CASSEROLE

Serves 6 to 8

1½ teaspoons salt
½ teaspoon pepper
¼ teaspoon poultry seasoning
2 pounds lean pork steak, cut into 1½-inch cubes
¼ cup cooking oil
1 medium onion, sliced
10½-ounce can condensed cream of mushroom soup
1¼ cups milk
10-ounce package frozen Italian-style green beans, defrosted
4-ounce package frozen French-fried onion rings

1. Preheat oven to 350° F. Grease 2½-quart casserole.

2. Mix salt, pepper and poultry seasoning; sprinkle over pork. Heat oil in large skillet; brown pork on all sides; transfer to casserole.

3. Sauté onion in oil remaining in skillet until tender. Add soup and milk; stir well, scraping bottom and sides to blend in all browned bits.

4. Spread beans on pork; cover with sauce.

5. Cover; bake in preheated oven for 1 hour.

6. Remove cover; sprinkle with onion rings. Bake for 15 minutes longer, or until rings are crisp.

Mrs. J. W. Chaplin, President, Woman's Club,
Wiley, Colo.

CHINESE BARBECUED PORK

Serves 4

½ teaspoon salt
¼ teaspoon pepper
1 teaspoon sugar
1 teaspoon Chinese Five-Spice
5 tablespoons chasu sauce
2 tablespoons soy sauce
1 clove garlic, crushed
2 tablespoons dry sherry
1 pound lean pork
Cooking oil

1. Day before, prepare marinade: Put salt, pepper, sugar, Five-Spice, chasu sauce, soy sauce, garlic and sherry in container of electric blender. Blend on high speed for few seconds. (If electric blender is unavailable, combine ingredients in mixing bowl; blend well with rotary beater.)

2. Cut pork into 4 lengthwise pieces, cutting with grain of meat. Arrange pork in shallow dish; cover with marinade. Refrigerate for at least 24 hours, turning occasionally.

3. Next day, preheat oven to 400° F. Remove pork from marinade; place on rack in roasting pan.

4. Brush with oil and some of marinade. Roast in preheated oven for 20 minutes.

5. Turn temperature to 250° F. Turn pork; roast for 40 minutes longer, brushing occasionally with oil and marinade.

6. Place pork under broiler for a few minutes to add crispness and to aid browning.

7. To serve pork, cut across grain into ¼-inch slices.

Junior Woman's Club, Coronado, Calif.

AMERICAN CHOP SUEY OR CHOW MEIN

Serves 4

¼ cup butter or margarine
1 medium onion, chopped
2 cups diced celery
1 teaspoon salt
Dash of pepper
1½ cups water
1-pound can bean sprouts, drained
2 cups cooked pork, cut into thin strips
2 tablespoons cornstarch
1 tablespoon soy sauce
1 teaspoon sugar
1 tablespoon gravy coloring
Cooked rice or Chinese noodles

1. Melt butter or margarine in large skillet; sauté onion for 3 minutes.

2. Stir in celery, salt, pepper and water. Bring to boil; cover; simmer for 5 minutes.

3. Add bean sprouts and pork; cover; cook for 5 minutes.

4. Meanwhile, in small bowl blend cornstarch, soy sauce, sugar and gravy coloring. Stir into meat mixture. Cook over low heat, stirring constantly, until thickened and clear. Simmer for 2 minutes.

5. Serve with rice or Chinese noodles.

NOTE: This dish is equally satisfying when made with thin strips of cooked beef, veal, chicken or turkey in place of pork.

Marion Greenberg, Junior Woman's Club,
Simsbury, Conn.

HAWAIIAN PORK

Serves 4

1 egg
2 tablespoons flour
½ teaspoon salt
⅛ teaspoon pepper
1 pound boneless pork, cut into 1-inch cubes
3 tablespoons shortening
3 medium green peppers

9-ounce can pineapple chunks
2½ tablespoons cornstarch
2½ tablespoons soy sauce
¼ cup sugar
¼ cup vinegar
Chinese noodles or cooked rice

1. In small bowl combine egg, flour, salt and pepper; use to coat pork thoroughly.
2. Melt shortening in skillet; brown pork well on all sides. Cover; simmer for 30 minutes.
3. Meanwhile, discard stems and seeds from green peppers; cut into 1-inch squares; cook in boiling salted water for 10 minutes; drain.
4. Drain pineapple; reserve syrup. Add green peppers and pineapple chunks to pork; cover; simmer for 10 minutes.
5. Meanwhile, in small saucepan blend cornstarch and reserved syrup. Stir in soy sauce, sugar and vinegar. Cook over low heat, stirring constantly, until sauce is thickened and clear. Pour over meat mixture; simmer for 5 minutes.
6. Serve pork and sauce on Chinese noodles or rice.

Donna Berg, Junior Woman's Club,
Brighton, Colo.

CHINESE SUB GUM

Serves 6

4 tablespoons butter
2 pounds lean pork, thinly sliced
1 medium onion, finely chopped
6 stalks celery, sliced
Salt and pepper to taste
2 cups hot water
8-ounce can Chinese vegetables with water chestnuts
6 scallions, sliced
2-ounce can sliced mushrooms
2 tablespoons cornstarch
2 tablespoons cold water
2 tablespoons soy sauce
Cooked rice
Chinese noodles

1 Melt butter in heavy kettle; brown pork and onion.
2. Add celery, salt and pepper; cook for 5 minutes. Add hot water, Chinese vegetables, scallions and mushrooms. Bring to boil; simmer for 10 minutes.
3. Combine cornstarch, water and soy sauce; Stir a little at a time into meat mixture; cook, stirring constantly, for about 5 minutes, or until thickened.
4. Serve on rice topped with Chinese noodles.

NOTE: Also excellent if 2 pounds shrimp, shelled and deveined, are substituted for the pork.

Leonore Kirchem, Gentilly Woods Woman's Club,
New Orleans, La.

GIZO

Serves 6 to 8

Danish adaptation of Spanish *guisado* (stew).

2 tablespoons shortening
2½ pounds lean pork, cut into ½-inch cubes
1 large onion, chopped
1-pound 13-ounce can tomatoes
2 teaspoons salt
¼ teaspoon pepper
1 teaspoon paprika
1 medium cabbage, shredded
2 small potatoes, peeled and diced
2 tablespoons flour
¼ cup water
1 teaspoon gravy coloring

1. Heat shortening in Dutch oven or heavy saucepan; sauté pork and onion over medium heat until pork is well browned. Stir in tomatoes, salt, pepper and paprika. Cover; simmer for 1 hour.
2. Stir in cabbage and potatoes; cover; simmer for 1 hour longer.
3. In small bowl blend flour with water; stir into stew. Cook over low heat, stirring constantly, until bubbling. Stir in gravy coloring; simmer for 2 minutes longer.

Helen Thomsen, Mendocino Study Club,
Little River, Calif.

PICKLED PIGS' FEET
(*Nalozene Veprove Nozicky*)

Serves 4 to 6

6 pigs' feet
Salt to taste
3 cups vinegar
1 medium onion, sliced
1 teaspoon mixed pickling spices

1. At least 2 days before, wash pigs' feet; place in Dutch oven or large heavy saucepan.
2. Cover with water; bring to boil. Cover; simmer for 2 hours, or until tender.
3. Drain; place pigs' feet in stone jar.
4. In saucepan combine vinegar, onion and spices; bring to boil. Pour over pigs' feet. Cover; let stand for at least 2 days before using.

Woman's Club, Clarkson, Neb.

SWEET AND SOUR PORK

Serves 4

½ cup presifted flour
2 eggs, lightly beaten
½ teaspoon salt
1 pound pork, cut into 1-inch cubes
Fat for deep frying
1 cup pineapple chunks
6 small sweet pickles
1 medium green pepper, cut into 1-inch pieces
3 small carrots, sliced
1 clove garlic, crushed
1 cup water
1 tablespoon cornstarch
2 tablespoons vinegar
1½ tablespoons sugar
1 tablespoon molasses

1. In mixing bowl blend flour, eggs and salt; beat until smooth; use to coat pork.

2. Fry pork in deep fat heated to 365° F. for 10 minutes. Drain on absorbent paper; put in large skillet.

3. Add pineapple, pickles, green pepper, carrots, garlic and ½ cup of the water. Bring to boil; cover; simmer for 10 minutes.

4. In small bowl blend remaining water and cornstarch to a paste. Stir in vinegar, sugar and molasses. Add to pork mixture; simmer for 5 minutes longer, stirring constantly, until thickened and clear.

Nancie Crabb, Junior Woman's Club, Jacksonville, Fla.

SARMI

Serves 6

1 large cabbage
1 pound ground pork
1 pound ground beef
1 cup cooked rice
1 teaspoon salt
1 teaspoon pepper
1-pound can sauerkraut, drained
1 large onion, sliced
1 large green pepper, sliced
1-pound 13-ounce can tomato juice

1. Separate leaves from cabbage; parboil in water to cover for 5 minutes. Drain; cool.

2. Combine pork, beef, rice, salt and pepper. Put large tablespoon of mixture in center of cabbage leaf; turn in sides; roll to close filling. Secure with wooden picks.

3. Line bottom of large roasting pan with sauerkraut. Arrange cabbage rolls on top. Add onion and green pepper. Add tomato juice and 1 quart water. Bring to boil; cover; simmer for 2 hours.

4. Arrange cabbage rolls on platter; drain juices from sauerkraut. Surround cabbage rolls with sauerkraut; serve pink gravy separately. (Gravy may be thickened, if desired, by adding a little flour or cornstarch mixed with a little water.)

Margaret Whitmer, Anna Day Club, Troy, Mo.

SWEDISH PORK BALLS IN BROWN SAUCE

Serves 6 to 8

1½ pounds ground pork
1 pound ground beef
2 cups fresh bread crumbs
2 eggs, lightly beaten
1 cup milk
1 cup brown sugar
1 teaspoon dry mustard
½ cup vinegar
½ cup water

1. Preheat oven to 325° F. Grease 10 x 6 x 1½-inch baking pan.

2. In mixing bowl combine pork, beef, crumbs, eggs and milk; mix well. Shape into 1½-inch balls; arrange in pan.

3. Combine remaining ingredients in saucepan. Cook over medium heat, stirring constantly, until sugar is dissolved and sauce is smooth. Pour over meat balls.

4. Bake in preheated oven for 1 hour, basting frequently with sauce.

Mrs. Louise Miller, Woman's Club, Durand, Wis.

TAMALE PORK PIE

Serves 10 to 12

½ cup olive oil
2 pounds ground pork
2 large onions, chopped
½ cup yellow corn meal
¼ cup milk
1-pound can whole-kernel corn, drained
1-pound can tomatoes, undrained
2 tablespoons chili powder
8-ounce can pitted ripe olives, drained and sliced

1. Preheat oven to 350° F. Grease 3-quart casserole.

2. Heat oil in large skillet; sauté pork and onions for 15 minutes. Stir in corn meal and milk; mix well.

3. Stir in corn, tomatoes and chili powder; simmer for 10 minutes. Stir in olives; turn into casserole.

4. Bake in preheated oven for 1 hour.

Mrs. Herbert Clark, Junior Women's Club, Cheyenne, Wyo.

Spareribs

BAKED SPARERIBS

Serves 4

3 to 4 pounds spareribs
4 cloves garlic, crushed
½ cup soy sauce
2 tablespoons brown sugar
2 teaspoons sugar
2 tablespoons vinegar
1½ cups beef broth
½ cup catsup
½ onion, grated
½ teaspoon salt
¼ teaspoon pepper

1. Day before, arrange spareribs in roasting pan. Combine remaining ingredients; pour over ribs; refrigerate for 24 hours.

2. Next day, preheat oven to 450° F.

3. Bake ribs in preheated oven for 10 minutes. Turn temperature to 325° F. Bake for 1 hour and 20 minutes longer, basting frequently. Just before serving, place under broiler heat for a minute to crisp.

Mrs. Marie Santaseiri, Juniors of Eastchester Woman's Club, Eastchester, N.Y.

BAKED BARBECUE SPARERIBS

Serves 4

Mrs. Arends' spareribs, served with cole-slaw and rye bread, is a favorite dish of many of her friends. The recipe has heretofore been her family secret.

3 pounds small spareribs
¾ cup vinegar
½ cup Barbecue Sauce for Spareribs, Pork Chops and Chicken (p. 442) or bottled barbecue sauce

3 tablespoons brown sugar
Dash of black pepper
Dash of cayenne
¼ teaspoon chili powder

1. Preheat oven to 250° F.
2. Wipe spareribs with damp cloth; arrange in large shallow roasting pan.
3. Bake in preheated oven for 2 hours, turning every half hour.
4. Meanwhile, in mixing bowl combine remaining ingredients.
5. Baste ribs with sauce. Bake for 30 minutes longer, turning and basting frequently.

Submitted to Woman's Club, Kankakee, Ill., on behalf of Mrs. Leslie Arends, Washington, D.C.

WESTERN BARBECUED SPARERIBS
Serves 4 or 5

⅓ cup vinegar
½ cup sweet sherry
⅓ cup chili sauce
2 tablespoons soy sauce
1 teaspoon horseradish
1 tablespoon Worcestershire
1 teaspoon Tabasco
½ cup pineapple juice
2 teaspoons dry mustard
¼ teaspoon paprika
¼ cup honey
2 teaspoons salt
5 pounds spareribs

1. Preheat broiler.
2. Prepare sauce: In saucepan combine all ingredients except spareribs. Bring to boil over high heat; set aside.
3. Arrange ribs on broiler pan; brown well on both sides. Drain off fat; reduce broiler heat.
4. Pour sauce over ribs. Broil for 30 minutes, basting frequently with sauce and turning occasionally.

Mrs. George Leckner, Woman's Club, South Pasadena, Calif.

CANTONESE SPARERIBS
Serves 6

5 pounds spareribs, cut into serving portions
1½ cups brown sugar
¾ cup soy sauce
¾ cup water
¼ cup bourbon

1. Put spareribs in large saucepan; cover with boiling water. Cover; simmer for 20 minutes. Drain; pat dry. Arrange in shallow pan.
2. Blend remaining ingredients; use to cover ribs; marinate for at least 4 hours. Turn occasionally; baste with marinade.
3. Preheat oven to 325° F. Grease large baking or roasting pan.
4. Arrange ribs in pan. Roast in preheated oven for 1 hour, basting occasionally with marinade.

Toby Van Petten, Woman's Club, Prospect Heights, Ill.

SPARERIBS BAKED IN CHERRY SAUCE
Serves 4

1 tablespoon shortening
4 pounds spareribs, cut into serving portions
1-pound 4-ounce can pie cherries
¼ teaspoon ground cloves
1 clove garlic, crushed
¼ cup brown sugar
¼ teaspoon dry mustard
½ teaspoon salt
2 tablespoons flour
3 tablespoons vinegar
1 cup water

1. Melt shortening in large skillet; brown spareribs well on all sides. Remove ribs; keep in warm place.
2. Drain cherries.
3. Add cherry liquid, cloves, garlic, sugar, mustard and salt to fat remaining in skillet.
4. In small bowl blend flour and vinegar to a smooth paste; stir with water into skillet. Cook over medium heat, stirring constantly, until sauce is thickened and smooth.
5. Return ribs to skillet; top with cherries. Cover; simmer for 1½ hours, basting occasionally with sauce.

Soani King, El Camino Real Junior Woman's Club, Capistrano Beach, Calif.

SPARERIBS DICK VAN DYKE
Serves 6

1 cup soy sauce
1 cup Cointreau
1 cup honey
13½-ounce can crushed pineapple, undrained
4 lemons, thinly sliced
4 teaspoons ginger
8 cloves garlic, crushed
6 pounds spareribs

1. Prepare marinade: In mixing bowl blend soy sauce, Cointreau, honey, pineapple, lemons, ginger and garlic.
2. Arrange spareribs in roasting pan; cover with marinade. Let stand for 2 hours, or preferably overnight.
3. Baste ribs with marinade while baking, broiling or barbecueing.

Marge Van Dyke, Junior Woman's Club, Fort Myers, Fla.

OVEN SPARERIBS
Serves 4

4 pounds spareribs
Salt and pepper to taste
½ cup finely chopped onions
¼ cup diced green pepper
2 8-ounce cans tomato sauce
1 tablespoon Worcestershire
⅓ cup cider or wine vinegar
1-pound 4-ounce can pineapple tidbits, undrained
¼ cup brown sugar
½ teaspoon dry mustard

1. Preheat oven to 350° F.
2. Cut partially through strips of spareribs after every third rib. Sprinkle with salt and pepper; place in shallow roasting pan.
3. Bake in preheated oven for 1¼ hours.
4. Meanwhile, combine remaining ingredients; let sauce stand to blend flavors.
5. Drain excess fat from roasting pan. Pour sauce over ribs. Bake for 50 minutes longer, basting frequently with sauce.

Carol Hunt, Junior Woman's Club,
Cathedral City, Calif.

ROAST SPARERIBS WITH APPLE STUFFING

Serves 8

6 cups fresh bread crumbs
2 cups chopped apples
1 cup finely chopped celery
1 cup finely chopped onions
2 teaspoons salt
¾ teaspoon sage
½ cup melted butter or margarine
2 sides spareribs
½ cup catsup
1 cup beef broth or consommé
2 tablespoons Worcestershire
1 teaspoon dry mustard
1 clove garlic, crushed
1 tablespoon finely chopped parsley
8 pineapple slices

1. Preheat oven to 450° F.
2. Prepare Apple Stuffing: In mixing bowl combine crumbs, apples, celery, onions, salt and sage; mix well. Add butter or margarine; mix well.
3. Arrange 1 of the sparerib sides in roasting pan. Spread with stuffing. Top with other side. Skewer sides together.
4. Brown in preheated oven for 10 minutes. Turn temperature to 375° F.
5. Meanwhile, prepare glaze: In saucepan combine catsup, broth or consommé, Worcestershire, mustard, garlic and parsley. Bring to boil. Pour over ribs. Bake for 1 hour and 10 minutes.
6. Arrange pineapple on ribs; bake for 10 minutes longer.

Junior Woman's Club, Pacific Beach, Calif.

Ham

Today much of the work has been taken out of the cooking of smoked hams, and a variety of processed hams are found in every market. These require no boiling to make them tender. Usually a processed ham needs from 1 to 2 hours of baking; but it is best to follow cooking directions on the wrapper, for the ideal baking time may vary with the brand.

Processed hams have become so popular with the homemaker that it is hard to find a good country-cured ham in many parts of the country. Country-cured, Virginia or Smithfield hams should be soaked for at least 6 hours or overnight to remove some of the high salt content and refresh the meat. During the soaking period the water may be changed one or more times if it tastes too salty. Country hams should be simmered, not boiled, in water to cover for about 30 minutes per pound, or until the meat shrinks away from the shank bone. If a ham is to be baked after it has been simmered, cook it until a meat thermometer registers 150° F. If it is not to be baked, the internal temperature of the ham should register 165° F.

How to Carve a Ham

Place the ham with the shank end at the carver's right. Cut a slice from the thin side, and turn the ham so that it rests steadily on the cut surface. Insert a carving fork at the thick butt end. With a sharp knife, cut and set aside a wedge in the fleshy part as close to the shank as possible. Slice down to the bone, cutting as many slices as may be needed for the first serving. Turn the knife, and insert it at base of wedge. Cut along the bone, freeing the slices.

HOW TO COOK A COUNTRY-CURED HAM

Serves 20 to 24

10- to 12-pound country-cured ham
½ cup vinegar
2 to 3 tablespoons brown sugar
1 tablespoon mixed pickling spices
Sweet pickle juice or cooking sherry
Ham Glaze (below)

1. Day before, put ham in cold water; soak overnight.
2. Next day, scrub ham well; trim. Put in large kettle; cover with lukewarm water. Add vinegar, sugar and spices. Bring to boil; cover; simmer for 3 to 3½ hours, or until meat is tender and bones are ready to drop out of hock.
3. Cool ham in liquid. When cool, remove ham from liquid; discard skin; trim off excess fat.
4. Preheat oven to 450° F.
5. Spread Ham Glaze over ham. Bake in preheated oven for 15 minutes, basting frequently with pickle juice or sherry.
6. Cool. Slice very thinly.

Mrs. Harry Lee Tartar, Junior Woman's Club,
Bristol, Tenn.-Va.

HAM GLAZE

Sufficient for a Whole Ham

2 cups light brown sugar
1 teaspoon dry mustard
½ teaspoon cloves

Combine ingredients; mix with a little fat from roasting pan or with water to make a stiff paste. Pat paste over entire surface of ham. Decorate as desired; bake until browned.

A. S.

BAKED HAM
Serves 20 to 24
10- to 12-pound country-style
    Virginia ham
¼ cup mixed pickling spices
2 cups brown sugar
½ cup vinegar
2 cups fresh bread crumbs
    Cloves and almonds (optional)

1. Put ham in large container; cover with boiling water. Cool; then remove ham. Scrub well with brush; place in large heavy kettle.
2. Add cold water to cover three-fourths of ham; add spices. Bring to boil; cover; simmer for 4 hours, turning ham occasionally.
3. Preheat oven to 325° F.
4. Remove ham from kettle; peel off skin. Place ham on rack in shallow roasting pan.
5. Bake in preheated oven for 2 hours.
6. Blend sugar with vinegar; spread on ham. Cook for 1 hour, basting frequently with sugar mixture.
7. Press crumbs onto ham; bake for 30 minutes longer, or until golden.
8. Arrange ham on serving dish; garnish shank with paper frill. Garnish ham with cloves and almonds, if desired.

Mrs. R. C. McCredie, State Women's Club,
Wash.

BAKED READY-TO-SERVE HAM
Serves 16 to 20
8- to 10-pound processed ham
1½ cups brown sugar
¼ teaspoon pepper
½ teaspoon cinnamon
1 tablespoon grated orange rind
¼ cup port
    Cloves
1 teaspoon dry mustard

1. Preheat oven to 400° F. Arrange large piece of aluminum foil in bottom of roasting pan.
2. Discard excess fat from ham; arrange in center of foil.
3. In small bowl blend ½ cup of the sugar, pepper, cinnamon, orange rind and port; spread over ham. Fold up foil to seal ham.
4. Bake ham in preheated oven for 2 hours.
5. Remove ham from foil. Pour off fat; reserve 1 tablespoon. Return ham to pan; stud with cloves.
6. Blend remaining sugar, mustard and reserved fat; spread on ham. Bake in preheated oven for 20 minutes, or until browned.

Mrs. W. W. Brown, Wilton Manors
Women's Club, Fort Lauderdale, Fla.

APRICOT-GLAZED HAM
Serves About 20
10-pound processed ham
1 cup light brown sugar
½ cup maple syrup
½ cup apricot nectar

1. Preheat oven to 325° F.
2. Place ham, fat side up, on rack in shallow roasting pan. Insert meat thermometer in center; do not let it touch bone.
3. Bake, uncovered, for 2½ to 3 hours, or until meat thermometer registers 130° F.
4. Meanwhile, prepare glaze: In small saucepan combine sugar, maple syrup and apricot nectar. Bring to boil, stirring; then simmer for 5 minutes.
5. Use some glaze to brush on ham 2 or 3 times during last hour of baking. Remove ham from oven; brush with remaining glaze. Cool. Refrigerate, covered, for several hours.

Woman's Club, North Arlington, N.J.

STUFFED HAM
Serves 12
This should be made the day before it is to be used.
7- to 8-pound processed ham
½ cup vinegar
½ cup brown sugar
2 stalks celery
3 medium onions
1-pound loaf bread
1 cup cracker crumbs
1 tablespoon granulated sugar
1 teaspoon mustard seed
½ cup chopped parsley
¼ cup sweet pickle relish
4 eggs, lightly beaten
1 cup sweet sherry
¼ teaspoon Tabasco

1. Put ham in large saucepan; cover with water. Add ¼ cup of the vinegar and brown sugar. Bring to boil; cover; simmer for 1 hour.
2. Cool ham in liquid. Remove from liquid. Trim fat; reserve 1 cup.
3. Carefully cut out and discard bone.
4. Put reserved fat, celery, onions and bread through medium blade of meat grinder. Turn into mixing bowl; add remaining ingredients and remaining vinegar; mix well; fill cavity in ham with dressing.
5. Tie securely with string; arrange ham on large square of cheesecloth. Spread remaining dressing on ham. Fold up cheesecloth; secure with string or wooden picks.
6. Preheat oven to 300° F. Arrange ham on rack in shallow roasting pan.
7. Bake in preheated oven for 1 hour.
8. Refrigerate for 24 hours; then remove cheesecloth and string or picks; slice thinly.

Mrs. Dan James, Book Club, Tallulah, La.

SPICE-CRUSTED HAM
Serves 8 to 10
5-pound can ham
1⅓ cups light brown sugar
¾ cup soft bread crumbs
2 teaspoons dry mustard
½ teaspoon cinnamon
½ teaspoon black pepper
¼ teaspoon ground cloves
¼ cup pineapple juice

1. Preheat oven to 325° F. Grease baking sheet.
2. Place ham on baking sheet. Bake for 1 hour in preheated oven. Remove from oven; score.
3. Turn oven temperature to 350° F.
4. Combine sugar, crumbs and spices. Add pineapple juice mix to form a thick paste. Spread over ham.
5. Return to oven. Bake for 30 minutes longer, or until browned.

Mrs. William H. Hasebroock, Honorary President,
General Federation of Women's Clubs,
West Point, Neb.

ROAST CANADIAN BACON
Serves 16 to 18

4- to 5-pound roll cooked Canadian
    bacon
1 quart pineapple juice
1 cup sugar
    Orange and lime slices

1. Preheat oven to 350° F.
2. Remove outer wrap from bacon; place roll in shallow roasting pan. Pour pineapple juice over bacon.
3. Roast in preheated oven for 1 hour, basting frequently with juice.
4. Transfer bacon to serving dish. Chill.
5. Pour juice into saucepan; stir in sugar. Bring to boil, stirring until sugar is dissolved. Boil for 10 minutes.
6. Cool syrup. Spoon over bacon to glaze.
7. Garnish with orange and lime slices. Chill until serving time.

Woman's Club, Erwin, Tenn.

MAMA'S FAVORITE GULYAS
(Stew)
Serves 6

2-pound cottage ham or smoked
    pork butt
1 quart water
1 cup dried navy beans
1 bay leaf
1-pound 4-ounce can tomatoes
1 cup sliced celery
1 cup sliced carrots
1 cup sliced onions
½ teaspoon paprika
1½ teaspoons salt
¼ teaspoon pepper
4 slices bacon, diced
1 teaspoon caraway seeds
3 tablespoons flour
¼ cup chopped parsley

1. Put ham in Dutch oven or large heavy saucepan. Add water; bring to boil. Cover; simmer for 45 minutes.
2. Remove ham from stock; cool stock. Trim fat from ham; skim fat from stock.
3. Return ham to stock; add beans and bay leaf. Bring to boil; cover; simmer for 45 minutes.
4. Add tomatoes, celery, carrots, onions, paprika, salt and pepper. Cover; simmer for 30 minutes.
5. Remove ham; cut into small pieces.

6. Remove about 2 cups broth; reserve.
7. Cook bacon in skillet until crisp; drain on absorbent paper; crumble; set aside. Pour off fat, leaving 3 tablespoons in skillet.
8. Add caraway seeds to fat remaining in skillet; toast over medium heat for 2 to 3 minutes. Sprinkle with flour; brown lightly. Gradually stir in reserved broth; bring to boil over medium heat, stirring constantly.
9. Stir into bean mixture. Add ham and bacon. Bring to boil; cover; simmer for 15 minutes.
10. Remove bay leaf. Sprinkle with parsley before serving.

Mrs. Joseph Brady, Woman's Club,
Morristown, N.J.

HAM AND ASPARAGUS ROLLS
WITH CHEESE SAUCE
Serves 2 or 4

12 cooked fresh or frozen asparagus
    spears
4 ⅛-inch-thick slices boiled ham
3 tablespoons butter or margarine
2 cups Cheese Sauce (p. 442)

1. Roll 3 asparagus spears in each slice of ham; secure with wooden pick.
2. Melt butter or margarine in large skillet; brown ham lightly on all sides.
3. Meanwhile, heat Cheese Sauce to serving temperature.
4. Arrange ham rolls on serving dish; cover with sauce.

Brainerd Junior Woman's Club, Chicago, Ill.

BAKED HAM SLICE
Serves 3 or 4

1½-pound 2-inch-thick slice
    cooked ham
12 cloves
2 tablespoons vinegar
½ cup water
½ cup brown sugar
1 tablespoon prepared mustard

1. Preheat oven to 350° F. Grease 10 x 6 x 1½-inch baking pan.
2. Put ham in pan; stud top with cloves.
3. In small saucepan combine remaining ingredients. Cook over low heat, stirring frequently, until smooth. Spread on ham.
4. Bake in preheated oven for 1 hour.

Mrs. Ray L. Hunter, President, Woman's Club,
Superior, Neb.

HAM BAKED IN MILK
Serves 4

½ teaspoon dry mustard
1 tablespoon flour
2-inch-thick slice cooked ham
2 tablespoons grated onion
2 cups milk
1 tablespoon butter
4 medium potatoes, sliced

1. Preheat oven to 375° F. Grease 10 x 6 x 1½-inch baking pan.
2. Combine mustard and flour; rub into ham. Put ham in pan; sprinkle with onion.

Top with milk; dot with butter. Arrange potatoes on ham.

3. Cover; bake in preheated oven for 1 hour.

4. Turn potatoes. Bake, uncovered, for 20 minutes longer.

Ester Nelson, Woman's Club, Shell Beach, Calif.

BAKED HAM SLICE WITH SWEET POTATOES

Serves 6

6 sweet potatoes
2-inch-thick slice cooked ham
8 cloves
1 cup maple syrup

1. Preheat oven to 450° F. Grease 11 x 7 x 1½-inch baking pan.

2. Peel potatoes; cut into 1-inch-thick slices. Parboil in boiling salted water for 5 minutes. Drain; set aside.

3. Trim skin from ham; stud fat with cloves.

4. Put ham in pan; surround with potatoes. Pour maple syrup over ham and potatoes.

5. Bake in preheated oven for 1 hour.

Mrs. T. A. Telfer, Morgan Park Woman's Club, Chicago, Ill.

STUFFED HAM STEAK

Serves 5 or 6

2 cups soft bread crumbs
½ cup chopped seedless raisins
½ cup broken walnuts
¼ cup brown sugar
½ teaspoon dry mustard
½ cup melted butter
2 large ½-inch-thick slices smoked ham
Cloves

1. Preheat oven to 300° F. Grease shallow baking pan.

2. Combine crumbs, raisins, walnuts, sugar, mustard and butter.

3. Place 1 slice of ham in pan; spread with crumb mixture. Put other slice of ham on top. Stud fat on ham with cloves.

4. Bake in preheated oven for about 1 hour.

Mrs. Hugh J. Gorman, Woman's Club, Peotone, Ill.

APPLE-STUFFED HAM STEAK

Serves 6

Butter
1 cup finely chopped celery
1 large onion, finely chopped
1-pound 4-ounce can pie-sliced apples, drained
1½ cups herb-seasoned bread stuffing
¼ cup chopped parsley
2 ½-inch-thick center-cut ham steaks
2 tablespoons apricot jam
2 10-ounce packages frozen Italian-style green beans

1. Preheat oven to 350° F.

2. Melt 2 tablespoons butter in skillet; sauté celery and onion until golden.

3. In large mixing bowl combine celery mixture, apples, stuffing, and parsley. Slowly add ½ cup butter, while tossing mixture with fork.

4. Put 1 steak in roasting pan. Top with apple mixture; cover with other ham steak. Spread jam on top.

5. Bake in preheated oven for 1 hour.

6. Cook beans according to package directions. Season to taste.

7. With two wide spatulas, lift meat to warm serving platter. Arrange beans along one side.

Mrs. H. T. Burfield, Junior Civic Woman's Club, Parkersburg, W.Va.

PAN-BROWNED HAM HASH

Serves 4 to 6

1 tablespoon shortening
1 small onion, chopped
2 tablespoons finely chopped green pepper
⅓ cup grated carrot
2 cups diced cooked potatoes
2 cups chopped cooked ham
½ teaspoon salt
½ teaspoon pepper
½ cup milk

1. Melt shortening in large skillet; sauté onion, green pepper and carrot over medium heat for 10 minutes.

2. Stir in potatoes; mix until flecked with brown. Add remaining ingredients.

3. Cook over low heat, without stirring, for 15 minutes.

NOTE: This dish may also be prepared by substituting chopped cooked roast beef for the ham.

Mrs. James L. Likes, Woman's Club, Kampsville, Ill.

HAM, PORK AND BEEF LOAF

Serves 12

1 pound smoked ham
1 pound lean pork
1 pound beef
2 tablespoons minced onion
1 teaspoon dry mustard
1 cup evaporated milk
½ cup catsup
1 cup bread crumbs
Salt and pepper to taste
1 cup brown sugar
2 tablespoons vinegar
2 tablespoons water

1. Put ham, pork and beef through meat grinder; mix together.

2. Add onion, mustard, milk, catsup, crumbs, salt and pepper. Shape into loaf; place in baking pan.

3. Preheat oven to 350° F.

4. In saucepan combine sugar, vinegar and water. Bring to boil; simmer for 10 minutes.

5. Bake loaf in preheated oven for 1 hour, basting every 15 minutes with syrup.

Mary Cole, Sorosis Club, Maple Rapids, Mich.

FRUITED HAM LOAF

Serves 4

2 cups ground cooked ham
¾ cup bread crumbs
½ cup milk
½ cup ground green pepper
4-ounce can pimientos, drained
    and chopped
2 eggs, lightly beaten
½ teaspoon ground cloves
½ teaspoon horseradish
¼ cup minced onion
2 tablespoons brown sugar
2 tablespoons apricot jam
8-ounce can crushed pineapple

1. Preheat oven to 350° F. Grease 10-inch loaf pan.
2. Combine all ingredients except jam and pineapple.
3. Pack into pan. Spread top with jam; cover with pineapple.
4. Bake in preheated oven for 1 hour.

Florence Cook, Woman's Club,
Temple City, Calif.

APPLESAUCE HAM LOAF

Serves 6

1 or more pineapple slices
2 pounds ground smoked ham
½ pound ground fresh ham
1 cup soft bread crumbs
1 egg
¼ cup milk
1 cup unsweetened applesauce
1 tablespoon applesauce
1 tablespoon vinegar
Freshly ground black pepper
¼ cup brown sugar
2 tablespoons melted butter
Cloves

1. Preheat oven to 375° F. Line 10-inch loaf pan with aluminum foil. Place pineapple in bottom.
2. Combine all ingredients except sugar, butter and cloves. Pack into pan with back of spoon; unmold into shallow baking pan.
3. Combine sugar and butter; spread on ham mixture. Dot with cloves.
4. Bake in preheated oven for 1 hour.

Mrs. Eugene J. Wallace, Wimodausis Study Club,
Cameron, Mo.

HAM LOAF WITH VINEGAR SAUCE

Serves 8 to 10

This is one of Astronaut John Glenn's favorite meat dishes, sent to the Fresno *Bee* by his mother.

2 eggs, lightly beaten
1¼ cups milk
⅔ cup cracker crumbs or rolled oats
⅓ cup tapioca
1 pound smoked ham
1 pound pork
¼ pound beef
½ cup brown sugar
1 tablespoon dry mustard
⅓ cup vinegar
¼ cup water

1. Combine eggs, milk, crumbs or oats and tapioca. Let stand for about 30 minutes, or until it begins to thicken.
2. Put ham, pork and beef through meat grinder; combine with egg mixture. Form into loaf; place in baking pan.
3. Combine remaining ingredients. Pour over loaf; bake in preheated oven for 2 hours, basting frequently.

Secrets of Coalinga Kitchens, Woman's Club,
Coalinga, Calif.

HAM AND SWEET POTATO ROLL

Serves 6

1½ pounds ground cooked ham
1 egg
1 teaspoon finely chopped onion
2 cups mashed sweet potatoes
½ cup milk
1 tablespoon melted butter
1½ teaspoons salt
⅛ teaspoon pepper

1. Preheat oven to 350° F.
2. Combine ham, egg and onion. Pat out ½ inch thick on piece of waxed paper.
3. Combine remaining ingredients; spread in center of meat mixture. Wrap meat around sweet potato mixture, making long roll. Place roll in baking pan; press edges of roll firmly to seal.
4. Bake in preheated oven for 45 minutes.

Mrs. T. O. Bjornson, Jr., Overlook Hills
Women's Clubs, Abington, Pa.

HAM BALLS

Serves 10 to 12

1 pound cooked ham
2 pounds lean pork
2 cups fresh bread crumbs
2 eggs
1 cup milk
1½ teaspoons salt
1½ teaspoons dry mustard
¼ teaspoon pepper
2 tablespoons finely chopped
    parsley
1 cup brown sugar
¾ cup water
¼ cup vinegar

1. Preheat oven to 400° F. Grease 10 x 6 x 1½-inch baking pan.
2. Put ham and pork through medium blade of meat grinder.
3. Put meat in mixing bowl; add crumbs, eggs, milk, salt, ½ teaspoon of the mustard, pepper and parsley; mix well. Shape into 1-inch balls; place in pan.
4. In small saucepan blend remaining mustard, sugar, water and vinegar. Cook over low heat, stirring frequently, until sugar is dissolved and sauce is smooth. Pour over ham balls.
5. Bake in preheated oven for 15 minutes. Turn temperature to 350° F. Bake for 45 minutes longer, basting frequently with sauce.

Mrs. Hazel M. West, Study Club, Northville, S.D.

OVEN HAM CROQUETTES

Serves 6

2 cups ground cooked ham
½ cup grated Cheddar cheese
1 cup fresh bread crumbs
¼ cup grated onion
1 egg, lightly beaten
1 teaspoon salt
¼ teaspoon pepper
¼ cup melted butter or margarine
1 cup cracker crumbs
    Pineapple Mustard Sauce (p. 449)

1. Preheat oven to 375° F. Grease 10 x 6 x 1½-inch baking pan.
2. In mixing bowl combine ham, cheese, bread crumbs, onion, egg, salt and pepper; mix well.
3. Divide into 12 parts; roll each into cone. Roll in butter or margarine; coat with cracker crumbs. Arrange in pan.
4. Bake in preheated oven for 45 minutes, or until golden. Turn once.
5. Serve with Pineapple Mustard Sauce.

Beta Alpha Latreian, Indianapolis, Ind.

HAM SOUFFLÉS

Serves 8

1 pound cooked ham
1 small green pepper
1 small onion
8-ounce package sharp American
    cheese
½ cup cracker crumbs
1½ cups milk
2 eggs, separated
    Salt and pepper to taste
    Mushroom Sauce for Ham (p. 447)

1. Preheat oven to 350° F. Grease 8 custard cups.
2. Put ham, green pepper, onion and cheese through medium blade of meat grinder; turn into mixing bowl. Add crumbs, milk and egg yolks; mix well. Season with salt and pepper.
3. In another mixing bowl beat egg whites until stiff but not dry. Fold into ham mixture; turn into cups.
4. Place cups on baking sheet; bake in preheated oven for 40 to 50 minutes, or until set.
5. Unmold onto serving dish; coat with Mushroom Sauce for Ham.

Helen R. Hogan, Service League, Lombard, Ill.

HAM TIMBALES

Serves 4

1 cup milk
1 cup fresh bread crumbs
2 tablespoons butter
1 tablespoon grated onion
½ teaspoon dry mustard
½ teaspoon salt
2 eggs, lightly beaten
    Dash of pepper
1 cup ground cooked ham
    Mushroom Sauce (p. 447)

1. Preheat oven to 350° F. Grease 4 custard cups well.
2. In saucepan combine milk, crumbs, butter and onion. Bring to boil.

3. Remove from heat. Stir in mustard, salt, eggs, pepper and ham; mix well. Pour into cups; set in pan of hot water.
4. Bake in preheated oven for 40 minutes, or until knife inserted in center comes out clean.
5. Serve with Mushroom Sauce.

Mrs. E. M. Hoke, Woman's Club, Sanford, Fla.

HAM BARBECUE

Serves 10 to 12

2 tablespoons butter
2 tablespoons brown sugar
2 tablespoons prepared mustard
2 tablespoons Worcestershire
1 medium onion, finely chopped
1-pound 4-ounce bottle catsup
1 cup water
2 pounds shaved ham

1. Melt butter in Dutch oven or heavy kettle. Blend in sugar, mustard and Worcestershire. Add onion, catsup and water; bring to boil.
2. Add ham; cover; simmer over very low heat for 2 hours, stirring occasionally.

Ann Gillespie, Civic League, Greenville, Pa.

CANTONESE HAM CASSEROLE

Serves 6

10-ounce package frozen French-style
    green beans
1 tablespoon butter
1 tablespoon flour
¾ cup milk
2 tablespoons soy sauce
1 cup sour cream
2 cups diced cooked ham
5-ounce can water chestnuts,
    drained and thinly sliced
½ cup buttered soft bread crumbs
    Paprika

1. Preheat oven to 350° F. Grease 1½-quart casserole.
2. Pour boiling water over beans to defrost. Drain well.
3. Melt butter in saucepan. Stir in flour. Gradually stir in milk and soy sauce; cook, stirring constantly, until sauce is slightly thickened.
4. Stir in sour cream; stir in ham, beans and water chestnuts. Pour into casserole; sprinkle with crumbs and paprika.
5. Bake in preheated oven for 30 to 35 minutes.

*Peanuts McKensie, Modern Study Club,
Mobile, Ala.*

BAKED HAWAIIAN HASH

Serves 5 or 6

3 tablespoons melted butter
3 cups diced cooked ham
3 cups diced cooked sweet potatoes
¼ cup finely chopped onion
½ teaspoon salt
¼ teaspoon pepper
½ cup pineapple juice
3 pineapple slices, halved
⅓ cup brown sugar
2 tablespoons softened butter

1. Preheat oven to 350° F. Grease 8-inch square baking pan.
2. Combine melted butter, ham, potatoes, onion, salt, pepper and pineapple juice, mixing lightly. Turn into pan; bake in preheated oven for 30 minutes.
3. Remove from oven. Top with pineapple slices; sprinkle with sugar; dot with softened butter.
4. Broil for about 7 minutes, or until pineapple is lightly browned.

Bernadean Ambrose, Woman's Club, St. Mary's, W.Va.

HAM À LA KING
Serves 4

¼ cup butter or margarine
2 tablespoons grated onion
¼ cup finely chopped celery
¼ cup presifted flour
1½ cups milk
1 cup diced cooked ham
1 teaspoon salt
⅛ teaspoon pepper
½ teaspoon Worcestershire
2 teaspoons prepared mustard
1 cup cooked mixed vegetables
4 slices buttered toast

1. Melt butter or margarine in large skillet; sauté onion and celery over medium heat for 5 minutes. Sprinkle with flour; gradually stir in milk. Cook over medium heat, stirring constantly, until thickened and smooth.
2. Add all remaining ingredients except toast. Cook over low heat, stirring frequently, until thoroughly heated.
3. Serve on toast.

Mrs. Ruth Roming, Woman's Club, Topton, Pa.

HAM, POTATO AND ONION CASSEROLE
Serves 6

1½ cups Medium White Sauce (p.441)
1 teaspoon salt
⅛ teaspoon pepper
1 cup grated Cheddar cheese
1 pound cooked ham, diced
2 cups diced cooked potatoes
1 large onion, thinly sliced
1 cup fresh bread crumbs
¼ cup melted butter or margarine

1. Preheat oven to 350° F. Grease 2-quart casserole.
2. Put Medium White Sauce in saucepan; stir in salt, pepper and cheese. Cook over medium heat, stirring occasionally, until cheese is melted.
3. Remove from heat; stir in ham, potatoes and onion. Turn into casserole. Sprinkle with crumbs and butter or margarine.
4. Bake in preheated oven for 40 minutes.

Mrs. William Darlington, Hickory Township Women's Club, Sharon, Pa.

BAKED HAM SALAD
Serves 4

3 cups diced cooked ham
½ cup chopped stuffed olives
2 tablespoons minced onion
1 tablespoon lemon juice
Dash of pepper
1 cup diced celery
2 eggs, hard-cooked and chopped
⅔ cup mayonnaise
2 teaspoons prepared mustard
1 cup crushed potato chips

1. Combine all ingredients except potato chips. Turn into large skillet; sprinkle with potato chips.
2. Cook over moderate heat for 25 minutes. If using electric skillet, cook at 220° F.

Mrs. L. H. Holden, Women's Club, Richland, Wash.

HAM BANANA ROLLS
Serves 6

6 slices boiled ham
¼ cup prepared mustard
6 firm bananas, peeled
2 tablespoons melted butter or margarine
2 cups Cheese Sauce (p. 442)

1. Preheat oven to 350° F. Grease 10 x 6 x 1½-inch baking pan.
2. Spread ham with mustard; wrap ham slice around each banana.
3. Arrange bananas in pan; sprinkle with butter or margarine.
4. Bake in preheated oven for 30 minutes.
5. Serve with Cheese Sauce.

Julia Force, Woman's Club, Chandlerville, Ill.

Sausage

GRANDFATHER'S SAUSAGE
Makes 48 Patties

12 pounds lean pork
5 tablespoons salt
2½ tablespoons freshly ground pepper
1 tablespoon sage

1. Put pork through medium blade of meat grinder twice.
2. Add remaining ingredients; and blend well with hands. Shape into 48 patties.
3. Fry at once, or wrap each patty in freezer paper and freeze until ready to use.

Mrs. James Dunlap, Woman's Club, Jacksonville, Ill.

HOMEMADE SAUSAGE
Makes 36 Patties

6 pounds lean pork
3 pounds fat pork
¼ cup sage
2 tablespoons pepper
2 tablespoons salt
2 teaspoons ground cloves
2 teaspoons mace
1 nutmeg, grated

1. Put pork through fine blade of meat grinder twice.
2. Put meat in mixing bowl; add remaining ingredients. Knead well with hands to

blend spices thoroughly. Shape into 36 patties.

3. Fry at once, or freeze.

Mrs. Edgar W. Greene, Reg. D.A.R.,
William R. King Chapter, Minter, Ala.

CORN SAUSAGE CASSEROLE

Serves 4

6 sausages, cooked and diced
1 egg, lightly beaten
1 cup milk
8½-ounce can cream-style corn
½ cup fresh bread crumbs
Salt and pepper to taste

1. Preheat oven to 350° F. Grease 1-quart casserole.
2. In mixing bowl combine all ingredients; mix well.
3. Turn into casserole; bake in preheated oven for 1 hour.

Cecile Davis, Women's Club, Durham, N.H.

DONATO MIX-UP

Serves 6

¼ cup olive oil
2½ cups cubed potatoes
4 medium onions, sliced
1 clove garlic, crushed
1 large stalk celery, cut into
    1-inch lengths
6-ounce can tomato paste
¾ cup water
1 teaspoon sugar
¼ teaspoon pepper
1 teaspoon orégano
1 pound Italian sausage, cut into
    1-inch lengths

1. Heat oil in large skillet; sauté potatoes, onions, garlic and celery for 15 minutes, stirring occasionally. Stir in remaining ingredients.
2. Cover; simmer for 30 minutes, lifting mixture from bottom occasionally to prevent sticking. Add water, if necessary, during cooking.

Donato Pignato, Beverly Hills Junior
Woman's Club, Chicago, Ill.

SAUSAGE LOAF

Serves 4

1 pound sausage meat
2 eggs, lightly beaten
2 cups grated potatoes
2 cups bread crumbs
1 small onion, grated
2 tablespoons green pepper, or
    to taste
¾ teaspoon celery seed
½ teaspoon salt
¼ teaspoon pepper
8-ounce can tomato sauce

1. Preheat oven to 350° F.
2. Combine all ingredients except tomato sauce; mix thoroughly. Pack into 8-inch loaf pan; pour tomato sauce over top.
3. Bake in preheated oven for 1¼ hours.

Mrs. E. O. Orleman, Woman's Club,
Whitefish, Mont.

SAUSAGE RING

Serves 6

2 pounds sausage meat
1 cup fine bread crumbs
2 eggs lightly beaten
½ cup milk
Scrambled eggs

1. Preheat oven to 350° F. Line baking sheet with aluminum foil.
2. Combine sausage meat, crumbs, eggs and milk.
3. Form meat mixture into ring on baking sheet.
4. Bake in preheated oven for 45 minutes.
5. Transfer ring to warm serving platter; fill center with scrambled eggs.

Mrs. Ralph Larson, Woman's Club,
Stromburg, Neb.

TOAD IN THE HOLE

Serves 4

1 cup presifted flour
½ teaspoon salt
2 eggs, lightly beaten
2 cups milk
1 pound sausages

1. Preheat oven to 375° F. Grease 10 x 6 x 1½-inch baking pan.
2. Into mixing bowl sift together flour and salt. Make well in center of flour; add eggs and 1 cup of the milk. Beat until smooth and bubbles form on top. Stir in remaining milk; cover; let stand for 1 hour.
3. Meanwhile, cook sausages in large skillet until crisp. Drain; arrange in pan.
4. Pour batter over sausages.
5. Bake in preheated oven for 40 minutes, or until puffed and golden.

Mrs. Wayne Harper, Zeta Chi Junior Club,
Atwood, Kans.

PORK-STUFFED GREEN PEPPERS

Serves 6

1 pound sausage meat
1 medium onion, finely chopped
½ cup chopped mushrooms
1 cup fresh bread crumbs
½ teaspoon salt
⅛ teaspoon pepper
6 medium green peppers
8-ounce can tomato sauce

1. Break up sausage meat; put in skillet; cook over medium heat, stirring frequently, for 10 minutes. Add onion; sauté for 5 minutes. Stir in mushrooms; sauté for 5 minutes longer.
2. Drain off excess fat; stir in crumbs, salt and pepper. Set aside.
3. Preheat oven to 350° F. Grease 10 x 6 x 1½-inch baking pan.
4. Cut slice from top of each green pepper; discard seeds. Cook in boiling salted water for 10 minutes. Drain well; place, cut side up, in pan.
5. Fill peppers with sausage mixture. Pour tomato sauce over peppers.
6. Bake in preheated oven for 30 minutes.

Lucy Newman, Woman's Club, Yakima, Wash.

Veal

The meat from young cattle not only is tender but also can be as delicate as chicken in flavor. The leg is considered the choice cut; from the leg come veal cutlets and the thin boneless slices known as veal scallops or scaloppine. The whole leg is excellent roasted; scallops are best sautéed in butter for only a minute or two on each side. Cutlets and all other cuts are best braised or stewed. The shoulder and breast of veal are frequently stuffed and braised.

VEAL ROAST ZURICH

Serves 8

4- to 5-pound boneless leg of veal
2 teaspoons salt
½ teaspoon pepper
1 teaspoon garlic salt
1 teaspoon monosodium glutamate
½ pound sliced bacon
2 large onions, thinly sliced
1 cup chopped parsley
⅓ cup heavy cream

1. Preheat oven to 300° F.
2. Trim veal; rub salt, pepper, garlic salt and monosodium glutamate into meat.
3. Line shallow roasting pan with bacon. Cover with onions; sprinkle with parsley. Place veal in center; sprinkle with a few tablespoons of the cream.
4. Roast in preheated oven for 2½ hours, or until tender, basting occasionally with remaining cream. Allow 30 minutes per pound.
5. Arrange veal on serving dish. Strain pan drippings; serve as gravy.

NOTE: Chop strained pan drippings; blend with ground beef to make flavorful hamburgers for another meal.

*Mrs. Robert E. Foster, Woman's Club,
Wilmette, Ill.*

SWEDISH VEAL ROAST

Serves 6

4½- to 5-pound veal rump with bone
2 teaspoons salt
¼ teaspoon pepper
2 tablespoons butter or margarine
1 bouillon cube
½ cup boiling water
2 carrots, sliced
2 onions, sliced
½ teaspoon allspice
2 tablespoons flour
¼ cup cold water
¾ cup cream

1. Rub veal with salt and pepper.
2. Melt butter or margarine in Dutch oven or heavy kettle; brown veal well on all sides. Remove from heat.
3. If cooking roast in oven, preheat oven to 325° F.
4. Dissolve bouillon cube in boiling water. Pour into kettle. Add carrots, onions and allspice. Cover tightly; cook in preheated oven for 30 to 35 minutes per pound. Or cover tightly; simmer for 1½ to 2 hours, or until tender.
5. Remove meat to hot serving platter.
6. Strain pan drippings into measuring cup; add water, if necessary, to total 1¼ cups; return to pan.
7. Combine flour and cold water. Stir into drippings. Add cream; cook over low heat, stirring constantly, until gravy is thickened and smooth.
8. Slice meat; serve with gravy.

Women's Club, Mamaroneck, N.Y.

GERMAN STUFFED BREAST OF VEAL

Serves 6

3 pounds breast of veal with pockets
1 tablespoon lemon juice
Pepper
½ loaf Italian bread, cut into chunks
⅓ cup shortening
½ cup chopped onions
½ cup chopped cooked ham
½ cup chopped parsley
¼ pound sausage meat
2 eggs
Curry powder
1 teaspoon salt

Timetable for Cooking Veal

ROASTING (325° F.)	Weight in Pounds	Approximate Time in Hours (170°)
Leg (center cut)	7 to 8	3 to 3½
Loin	4½ to 5	2½ to 3
Shoulder (boned and rolled)	3	3
	5 to 6	3½ to 4
BRAISING	Weight	Approximate Time After Browning
Cutlets or round steak	2 pounds	45 to 50 minutes
Loin or rib chops	3 to 5 ounces each	45 to 50 minutes
Shoulder pot roast	4 to 5½ pounds	2 to 2½ hours
STEWING	Weight in Pounds	Approximate Total Time
1½-inch cubes	2	1½ to 3 hours

1. Preheat oven to 500° F.
2. Sprinkle veal with lemon juice and ¼ teaspoon pepper.
3. Put bread in mixing bowl; moisten with a little water; set aside.
4. Melt 1 tablespoon of the shortening in skillet; sauté onions, ham and parsley over low heat for 15 minutes.
5. Add onion mixture to bread. Add sausage meat, eggs, 1 teaspoon curry powder, salt and ¼ teaspoon pepper; mix well.
6. Fill veal pockets with stuffing; secure with string or skewers.
7. Place on rack in shallow roasting pan; dot with remaining shortening. Add 1 cup water.
8. Roast in preheated oven for 10 minutes. Turn temperature to 375° F. Roast for 1½ hours longer, basting frequently with pan juices.
9. Arrange veal on serving dish; remove string or skewers. Slice; serve with gravy seasoned with curry powder, if desired.

Mrs. Alfred Walz, Junior New Century Club,
West Chester, Pa.

VEAL BIRDS

Serves 6

1½-pound ½-inch thick veal steak
  6 sausages, browned
  2 tablespoons shortening
1¼ cups water
  1 envelope onion soup mix
  ¼ cup sauterne
  ¼ cup minced parsley
  2 tablespoons flour

1. Cut veal into 6 portions; pound until thin.
2. Roll each piece around sausage; fasten with wooden picks.
3. Melt shortening in skillet; brown rolls on all sides.
4. Add 1 cup of the water, onion soup mix, sauterne and parsley. Cover; simmer for 45 minutes, or until tender.
5. Blend flour with remaining water. Add to skillet; cook until thickened and smooth.

Mrs. Philip P. Le Blanc, President, Hillsborough
County Federation of Women's Clubs,
Tampa, Fla.

VEAL CUTLETS

Serves 6

6 veal cutlets
1 egg, lightly beaten with
  2 tablespoons water
1 cup bread crumbs
½ teaspoon salt
¼ teaspoon pepper
½ cup grated Parmesan cheese
½ cup butter or margarine
6 slices boiled ham
1 cup milk
8-ounce can tomato sauce

1. Pound veal; dip in egg mixture.
2. On piece of waxed paper combine crumbs, salt, pepper and ¼ cup of the

cheese; use to coat veal; press crumbs into veal with back of knife.
3. Melt butter or margarine in large skillet; sauté veal for 5 minutes on each side.
4. Top each cutlet with ham slice; sprinkle with remaining cheese.
5. In small bowl blend milk and tomato sauce; pour over cutlets.
6. Cover; simmer for 30 minutes.

Ellen Patterson, Suburban Women's Club,
Newark, Del.

VEAL CUTLETS CORDON BLEU

Serves 6

12 thin veal scallops
  Salt and pepper to taste
  6 slices Swiss cheese
  6 thin slices boiled ham
  Flour
  3 eggs, lightly beaten
  ¾ cup bread crumbs
  ¾ cup butter or margarine

1. Pound veal with cleaver until very thin. Sprinkle with salt and pepper.
2. Put cheese slice and ham slice on each of 6 slices of veal. Top with remaining veal.
3. Pound edges together; dip in flour. Dip in eggs. Coat with crumbs; press crumbs into meat with back of knife.
4. Melt butter or margarine in large skillet; sauté veal over medium heat for about 4 minutes on each side.

Mrs. Jack McGuire, Martinez, Calif.

VEAL AU CRÈME AIGRE
(Veal with Sour Cream)

Serves 6 to 8

2 pounds veal scallops
3 tablespoons butter
½ pound mushrooms, sliced
2 tablespoons flour
1 cup sour cream
1 tablespoon grated onion
1 teaspoon salt
½ cup dry sherry

1. Preheat oven to 350° F. Grease 2-quart casserole.
2. Trim veal; cut into small pieces. Melt butter in large skillet; brown veal well on all sides. Turn into casserole.
3. Sauté mushrooms in butter remaining in skillet over medium heat for 5 minutes, stirring frequently. Arrange mushrooms on veal.
4. Sprinkle flour into skillet; scrape all browned bits from bottom to blend in. Stir in sour cream, onion and salt. Pour sauce over mushrooms. Sprinkle sherry on top.
5. Cover; bake in preheated oven for 1 hour.

Mrs. James P. Trueluck, Junior Woman's Club,
Spartanburg, S.C.

VEAL PARMESAN

Serves 4 to 6

6 tablespoons olive oil
1 medium onion, grated
3 cloves garlic, crushed
1-pound 4-ounce can tomatoes
1¼ teaspoons salt
¼ teaspoon pepper
¼ teaspoon thyme
8-ounce can tomato sauce
½ cup grated Parmesan cheese
¼ cup bread crumbs
1 pound thinly sliced veal scallops
1 egg, lightly beaten
8 ounces sliced Mozzarella cheese

1. Preheat oven to 350° F. Grease 13 x 9½ x 2-inch baking pan.
2. Prepare sauce: Heat 3 tablespoons of the oil in large skillet; sauté onion and garlic for 5 minutes. Stir in tomatoes; break up with spoon; simmer, uncovered, for 5 minutes. Stir in salt, pepper, thyme and tomato sauce. Cover; simmer for 20 minutes.
3. Meanwhile, on piece of waxed paper combine ¼ cup of the Parmesan cheese and crumbs. Dip veal into egg; coat with crumb mixture.
4. Heat remaining oil in large skillet; sauté veal until golden on both sides.
5. Arrange veal in pan; top with two-thirds of sauce. Arrange Mozzarella cheese on top; spoon remaining sauce over cheese. Sprinkle with remaining Parmesan cheese.
6. Bake in preheated oven for 35 minutes.

Mrs. Edward Ratcliffe, Senior Woman's Club, Dallas, Pa.

VEAL SCALOPPINE

Serves 6

Tell the butcher you want the veal for scaloppine; he will cut it and pound it for you. Have it cut into serving pieces.

4 tablespoons flour
1½ teaspoons salt
¼ teaspoon pepper
1½ pounds thinly cut loin or round of veal
2 tablespoons butter
¼ cup beef broth
2 tablespoons sweet sherry

1. Combine flour, salt and pepper; use to coat veal lightly on both sides.
2. Melt butter in skillet; brown veal quickly on both sides. Arrange on hot serving platter.
3. Stir broth and sherry into juices in skillet. When hot, pour over veal.

Mrs. Augustus J. Battaglia, Woman's Club, Elroy, Ariz.

ESCALOPES DE VEAU

Serves 4

2 tablespoons butter
1 medium onion, finely chopped
1 cup finely chopped mushrooms
1 clove garlic, crushed
½ cup grated carrots

1 teaspoon salt
¼ teaspoon pepper
½ bay leaf, crushed
1 tablespoon chopped parsley
½ cup dry white wine
½ cup beef bouillon
1½ pounds thinly sliced veal scallops

1. Melt 1 tablespoon of the butter in skillet; sauté onion, mushrooms and garlic for 5 minutes.
2. Stir in carrots, salt, pepper, bay leaf, parsley, wine and bouillon. Bring to boil; then simmer for 5 minutes.
3. Meanwhile, melt remaining butter in another skillet; sauté veal quickly on both sides; add to onion mixture. Cover; simmer for 25 minutes.

Mrs. Leroy Spilatore, Woman's Club, Mount Dora, Fla.

VEAL SCALLOPS

Serves 4 to 6

1½ pounds thinly sliced veal scallops
½ cup flour
¾ teaspoon monosodium glutamate
1 teaspoon salt
¼ teaspoon pepper
⅓ cup olive oil
1 medium green pepper, finely chopped
1 clove garlic, crushed
½ pound mushrooms, sliced
1-pound 13-ounce can tomatoes, undrained
1 tablespoon chopped parsley
¼ teaspoon orégano

1. Cut veal into 1-inch pieces.
2. On piece of waxed paper mix flour, monosodium glutamate, ½ teaspoon of the salt and ⅛ teaspoon of the pepper; use to coat veal well; set aside.
3. Heat oil in large skillet; sauté green pepper, garlic and mushrooms for 10 minutes.
4. Meanwhile, press tomatoes through sieve. Stir in remaining salt, remaining pepper, parsley and orégano; set aside.
5. Add veal to vegetables in skillet; cook over medium heat until browned. Stir in tomato mixture.
6. Cover; cook over low heat for 25 minutes, stirring occasionally.

Junior Woman's Club, Pacific Beach, Calif.

VEAL VENETO

Serves 4

4 slices Provolone cheese
8 thin 4-inch-square veal scallops
1 egg
2 tablespoons milk
1 cup cracker crumbs
¼ cup butter or margarine

1. Place cheese slice between 2 veal slices to form sandwich.
2. In shallow dish beat egg and milk; use to dip in veal sandwiches. Coat with crumbs; press crumbs into veal.
3. Melt butter or margarine in large skillet. Sauté veal sandwiches over low

heat for about 5 minutes on each side, or until golden brown.

Pauline Francis, Junior Woman's Club, Cheshire, Conn.

WIENER SCHNITZEL

Serves 4

1 pound veal scallops, thinly and evenly sliced
2 tablespoons flour
1 egg
2 tablespoons milk
1 teaspoon salt
¼ teaspoon pepper
1 cup fresh bread crumbs
¼ cup grated Parmesan cheese
⅓ cup butter or margarine
1 teaspoon lemon juice
2 teaspoons capers
Parsley sprigs

1. Pound veal until very thin. Dredge lightly in flour.
2. In shallow dish beat egg, milk, salt and pepper.
3. On piece of waxed paper blend crumbs and cheese.
4. Dip veal in egg mixture; coat with crumb mixture; press crumbs into veal with back of knife.
5. Melt butter or margarine in large skillet; brown veal quickly for about 3 minutes on each side. Arrange on serving dish; keep warm.
6. Stir lemon juice and capers into butter remaining in skillet; simmer over medium heat for 1 minute. Pour over veal.

Mildred Touchstone, Cadmean Club, Fort Worth, Tex.

WIENER SCHNITZEL HOLSTEIN

Serves 2

2 4-ounce slices veal, pounded thin
Flour
1 egg, beaten
½ cup bread crumbs
¼ cup cooking oil
2 eggs, fried

1. Roll veal in flour. Coat with beaten egg; roll in crumbs. Refrigerate for 30 minutes.
2. Heat oil in skillet; sauté veal for about 15 minutes on each side, or until well browned and fork-tender.
3. Top each serving with fried egg.

Fonda Ditch, Woman's Club, Sandy Springs, Ga.

PAPRIKA WIENER SCHNITZEL

Serves 4

1 pound ½-inch-thick veal cutlets
3 tablespoons flour
1 teaspoon salt
¼ teaspoon pepper
3 tablespoons shortening
1 medium onion, thinly sliced
1 clove garlic, crushed
⅓ cup beef consommé
1 cup sour cream
1 tablespoon paprika
Dash of Tabasco

1. Pound veal with mallet or edge of plate until very thin.
2. On piece of waxed paper combine flour, salt and pepper; use to dredge veal.
3. Melt shortening in large skillet; sauté onion and garlic over medium heat for 5 minutes. Remove onion; set aside.
4. Brown veal well on both sides in fat remaining in skillet. Top with onion; cover; simmer for 15 minutes.
5. Meanwhile, in small bowl blend remaining ingredients. Pour over veal.
6. Cover; simmer for 15 minutes longer.

Joan Santangelo, Lincoln Village Women's Club, Columbus, Ohio

VEAL CHOPS ARABIAN

Serves 6

1 clove garlic, crushed
Flour
Salt and pepper to taste
6 1-inch-thick loin veal chops
3 tablespoons cooking oil
2½ cups cooked tomatoes
1 onion, thinly sliced
¼ cup sherry
3 tablespoons butter
1 pound mushrooms, sliced
8 ripe olives, sliced

1. Rub inside of large skillet with garlic. Discard garlic.
2. Season flour with salt and pepper; roll chops in mixture.
3. Heat oil in skillet; brown chops on both sides. Add tomatoes, onion and sherry. Cover; simmer for 1½ hours.
4. Melt butter in another skillet; sauté mushrooms for 5 minutes. Add to veal. Add olives; simmer for 15 minutes longer.

Charlotte Wright, Woman's Club, Azusa, Calif.

FLAVORFUL VEAL CHOPS

Serves 4

4 1-inch-thick veal chops
⅓ cup olive oil
2 tablespoons vinegar
¼ teaspoon pepper
2 cloves garlic, crushed
3 tablespoons soy sauce

1. Trim chops; arrange in shallow dish.
2. Prepare marinade: Blend oil, vinegar, pepper, garlic and soy sauce. Pour over veal; let stand for at least 4 hours, turning occasionally.
3. Preheat broiler. Remove veal from marinade; reserve marinade.
4. Arrange veal on broiler pan; broil 4 to 5 inches from heat for about 10 minutes on each side, brushing veal frequently with reserved marinade.

Mrs. Sonny Goldstein, Junior Woman's Club, Milledgeville, Ga.

JELLIED VEAL

Serves 4

1 shoulder of veal with knuckle
  cracked
2 green peppers, chopped
1 cup chopped celery
3 bay leaves
1 teaspoon celery salt
1 teaspoon celery seed
2 teaspoons salt
1 teaspoon pepper
2 tablespoons dry mustard
  Lettuce leaves

1. Put veal in large saucepan; add water
just to cover. Bring to boil; cover; simmer
for 2 hours, or until meat falls from bone.
2. Add all remaining ingredients except
lettuce; cover; simmer for 1 hour longer.
Cool.
3. Remove meat; discard bones; chop
meat finely.
4. Put meat in 2-quart bowl; pour cooking liquid and vegetables over it; discard
bay leaves. Chill until set.
5. Unmold; cut into slices; serve on
lettuce.

Mrs. Blanche Seiter, Woman's Club, DeBary, Fla.

BLANQUETTE DE VEAU

Serves 4

1 tablespoon butter
1 pound stewing veal, cut into
  1½-inch cubes
1 tablespoon flour
6 small white onions
2 cloves garlic, crushed
8-ounce can mushrooms, drained
2 bay leaves
½ teaspoon thyme
½ teaspoon salt
  Dash of pepper
2 egg yolks, lightly beaten
  Cooked noodles or rice

1. Melt butter in large skillet; cook veal
over low heat, turning occasionally; do not
brown.
2. Sprinkle with flour; add water to
come halfway up veal. Add all remaining
ingredients except egg yolks and noodles or
rice. Bring to boil; cover; simmer for 1¼
hours.
3. Just before serving, remove from
heat; stir in egg yolks.
4. Serve on noodles or rice.

Markeeta Fayle, Federated Women's Club,
Levittown, Pa.

VEAL CALABRESE STYLE

Serves 4

5 tablespoons olive oil
1 pound veal rump, cut into
  1½-inch cubes
1 cup chopped mushrooms
2½ cups drained tomatoes
2 large green peppers, cut into
  strips
1 sweet red pepper, coarsely
  chopped

1. Heat 3 tablespoons of the oil in skillet; brown veal on all sides over medium
heat.
2. Add mushrooms and tomatoes; cover;
simmer for 10 minutes.
3. Meanwhile, heat remaining oil in
another skillet; sauté peppers for about 15
minutes, stirring occasionally. Add to meat;
cover; cook for 15 minutes longer.

Lola M. Beratta, Woman's Club,
Anchorage, Alaska

VEAL FRICASSEE

Serves 6

3 tablespoons butter or margarine
1½-pound boneless shoulder of veal,
  diced
1½ cups hot water
1 small onion, finely chopped
1 cup sliced mushrooms
1 teaspoon salt
  Dash of pepper
3 tablespoons flour
1 tablespoon lemon juice
1 cup light cream
4 eggs, hard-cooked and sliced
  Dash of cayenne

1. Melt butter or margarine in large
skillet or Dutch oven; brown veal well on
all sides over medium heat.
2. Stir in 1 cup of the water and onion.
Cover; simmer for 30 minutes, or until
veal is tender. Stir in mushrooms, salt and
pepper; simmer for 5 minutes.
3. Meanwhile, in small skillet brown
flour over medium heat, stirring frequently.
Stir in remaining water; cook over medium heat, stirring constantly, until sauce
is thickened and smooth.
4. Stir sauce into veal; add lemon juice
and cream. Simmer for 2 minutes, stirring
constantly.
5. Stir in eggs and cayenne; simmer for
2 minutes longer.

Mrs. Guignard Maxcy, Woman's Club,
Sebring, Fla.

MRS. CUTLER'S VEAL DELIGHT

Serves 6

1 tablespoon butter or margarine
3 medium onions, finely chopped
3 large tomatoes, sliced
2-pound shoulder of veal, cut
  into 1½-inch cubes
2 carrots, diced
2 tablespoons chopped parsley
1 tablespoon sugar
1 teaspoon salt
¼ teaspoon pepper
8-ounce can stewed tomatoes

1. Melt butter or margarine in large
skillet; sauté onions until golden.
2. Arrange tomatoes on onions; place
veal on tomatoes.
3. Add remaining ingredients. Bring to
boil; cover; simmer for 2 hours.

Senior Woman's Club, Highland Springs, Va.

KALBS GULYAS (Veal Goulash)
Serves 6 to 8

¼ cup butter or margarine
3 large onions, chopped
2-pound leg of veal, cut into
1-inch cubes
Salt and pepper to taste
1 tablespoon paprika
1 small green pepper, diced
1 large tomato, diced
2 tablespoons water
¼ cup capers with juice
1 cup sour cream
Cooked noodles or Potato
Drop Dumplings (p. 462)

1. Melt butter or margarine in Dutch oven or heavy saucepan; sauté onions over medium heat until golden.
2. Add veal; season with salt and pepper. Stir in paprika; cook over medium heat, stirring frequently, until browned.
3. Add green pepper, tomato and water. Cover; simmer for 45 minutes, adding water as required.
4. Stir in capers and sour cream; simmer for 5 minutes longer.
5. Serve with noodles or Potato Drop Dumplings.

Woman's Club, Newnan, Ga.

VEAL MADELEINE
Serves 6

2 tablespoons butter or margarine
2 pounds boneless veal, cut into
1-inch cubes
1 clove garlic, crushed
2 tablespoons flour
1 teaspoon salt
¼ teaspoon pepper
2 1-inch strips lemon peel
1 cup boiling water
1 cup heavy cream
Noodles Gratinée (p. 491)

1. Melt butter or margarine in large skillet; sauté veal and garlic until meat is browned.
2. Sprinkle with flour, salt and pepper; sauté over medium heat until flour browns lightly. Add lemon peel and water; stir for 1 minute. Cover; cook over low heat for 1 hour, stirring occasionally.
3. Remove lemon peel; stir in cream; heat to serving temperature.
4. Serve with Noodles Gratinée.

*Dorothy Kay, Blair Woman's Club,
Blairstown, N.J.*

RAGOUT OF VEAL
Serves 6

3 tablespoons bacon drippings
3 pounds lean stewing veal, cut
into ½-inch cubes
3 large onions, chopped
3 cloves garlic, crushed
½ pound bacon, chopped
10½-ounce can condensed tomato soup
1 tablespoon salt
½ pound mushrooms, sliced
1. Heat bacon drippings in heavy kettle. Add veal, onions, garlic and bacon; cook

over moderate heat, turning constantly, until rich brown.
2. Add soup, salt and water barely to cover. Cover; cook over low heat for 1 hour, stirring occasionally.
3. Add mushrooms; cook for 5 minutes longer.

*Mrs. Arthur Totton, Thursday Morning Club,
Madison, N.J.*

SPANISH VEAL CASSEROLE
Serves 6

2 pounds veal, cut into small pieces
Flour
Salt and pepper to taste
¼ cup olive oil
2 cups chicken or beef consommé
2 ripe tomatoes, sliced
1 bay leaf
Thyme and rosemary to taste
8 small onions
1 tablespoon butter
½ cup sliced mushrooms
1 cup sliced ripe olives
1 teaspoon chili powder
2 chorizos (sausages), sliced

1. Toss veal in flour; sprinkle with salt and pepper; brown in oil.
2. Preheat oven to 350° F.
3. Put meat in 2-quart casserole; add consommé, tomatoes, bay leaf, thyme and rosemary. Cover; bake in preheated oven for 1 hour.
4. Meanwhile, melt butter in skillet; sauté onions until lightly browned.
5. Add onions and remaining ingredients to casserole; stir to combine. Cover; bake for 1 hour longer.

*Dickie Gable, Junior Woman's Club,
Scottsdale, Ariz.*

WISCONSIN CASSEROLE
Serves 8

⅓ cup presifted flour
1 teaspoon paprika
2-pound veal round steak, cut into
2-inch cubes
¼ cup shortening
½ teaspoon salt
⅛ teaspoon pepper
2¾ cups water
10½-ounce can condensed cream
of chicken soup
1-pound can small white onions,
drained
Butter Crumb Dumplings (p. 461),
uncooked
Quick Chicken Cream Sauce
(p. 443)

1. On piece of waxed paper combine flour and paprika; use to dredge veal well.
2. Melt shortening in Dutch oven or heavy kettle; brown veal well on all sides.
3. Stir in salt, pepper and 1 cup of the water. Bring to boil; cover; simmer for 30 minutes.
4. Preheat oven to 425° F. Grease 3-quart casserole.
5. Pour veal mixture into casserole.

6. Stir soup and remaining water into kettle. Bring to boil. Remove from heat. Stir in onions.

7. Pour over veal; top with Butter Crumb Dumplings.

8. Bake in preheated oven for 20 to 25 minutes, or until golden brown.

9. Serve with Quick Chicken Cream Sauce.

Mrs. Richard Reid, Junior Woman's Club, Menomonee Falls, Wis.

VEAL LOAF

Serves 8

2½ pounds ground veal
½ pound salt pork, ground
4 eggs, lightly beaten
2 tablespoons lemon juice
⅓ cup catsup
1 cup cracker crumbs
2 teaspoons salt
¼ teaspoon pepper
½ teaspoon seasoned salt
⅛ teaspoon cayenne
1 tablespoon butter
Buttered cooked peas (optional)

1. Preheat oven to 350° F. Grease 9-inch loaf pan.

2. In mixing bowl combine all ingredients except butter. Mix well; pack into pan. Dot with butter; cover pan with aluminum foil.

3. Bake in preheated oven for 2 hours.

4. Let stand for 5 minutes; unmold onto serving dish. Garnish with peas, if desired.

Mrs. James P. Cronin, Woman's Club, Van Nuys, Calif.

VEAL LOAF WITH MASHED POTATOES

Serves 8

1 pound ground veal
½ pound ground pork
¾ pound ground beef
½ cup fresh bread crumbs
1 cup cooked thinly sliced carrots
1 cup cooked peas
¼ cup finely chopped onion
⅓ cup tomato juice
½ teaspoon pepper
1½ teaspoons salt
2 eggs, lightly beaten
2½ cups mashed potatoes
2 tablespoons flour
¾ cup catsup

1. Preheat oven to 350° F. Grease 9-inch loaf pan and baking sheet.

2. In mixing bowl combine veal, pork, beef, crumbs, carrots, peas, onion, tomato juice, pepper and salt; mix well. Reserve about 2 teaspoons of the eggs; stir remaining eggs into loaf mixture.

3. Turn loaf mixture into pan; bake in preheated oven for 1½ hours.

4. Unmold loaf onto baking sheet; reserve pan juices.

5. Turn temperature to 450° F.

6. Frost loaf with potatoes; brush top with reserved egg.

7. Bake for 10 minutes, or until golden.

8. Meanwhile, in small pan mix flour and pan juices to a paste; add water, if necessary, to total 1 cup. Stir in catsup. Cook over low heat, stirring constantly, until sauce is thickened and smooth. Serve with loaf.

Vera K. Cobb, Woman's Club, Sebring, Fla.

MUSHROOMS AND VEAL NEAPOLITAN

Serves 3 or 4

3 ripe tomatoes
5 tablespoons butter
1 pound mushrooms, sliced
Salt and pepper to taste
½ teaspoon Italian seasoning
1 pound ground veal
1 tablespoon chopped parsley
1 tablespoon dry vermouth
½ cup grated Parmesan cheese

1. Dip tomatoes into boiling water. Dip in cold water; peel; seed; chop.

2. Melt 2 tablespoons of the butter in saucepan; cook tomatoes over low heat until puréed.

3. Melt remaining butter in large skillet; sauté mushrooms over medium heat until lightly browned. Season with salt, pepper and Italian seasoning.

4. Add veal; cook, uncovered, for 12 minutes, stirring occasionally. Stir in tomato purée, parsley and vermouth; heat to serving temperature.

5. Serve with cheese on side.

Mrs. H. T. Burfield, Junior Civic Woman's Club, Parkersburg, W.Va.

Lamb

Lamb is graded like beef: Prime, Choice and Good. Prime is best, of course; but Choice is also excellent, and in the spring months when baby lamb is available, it is a real treat.

A saddle of baby lamb (a double loin), a baron of lamb (the saddle plus the two legs) or a crown roast (two racks, or ribs), of lamb shaped into a crown, is frequently served at very elegant dinner parties. But the most popular roasting cuts in the market all year round are the leg, shoulder and rack.

CUTS OF LAMB AND HOW TO COOK THEM

Roast
    Whole leg
    Shank half of leg
    Butt half of leg
    Boned and rolled shoulder
    Whole breast of lamb (excellent barbecued)
Broil, Grill or Pan-Fry
    Loin chops
    Rib chops (single or double rib)
    Shoulder chops
    Leg steaks

Timetable for Cooking Lamb

ROASTING (325° F.)	Weight in Pounds	Approximate Time in Hours Medium Rare
Leg (half)	3 to 4	1½ to 2
Leg (whole)	6 to 7	2 to 2½
Shoulder (bone in or stuffed)	4 to 5	2½ to 3½
Shoulder (boned and rolled)	4 to 6	2½ to 3½

BROILING OR GRILLING	Weight in Ounces	Approximate Time in Minutes
Chops, rib or loin (¾ inch thick)	3	14 to 15
Double rib (1½ inches thick)	4 to 5	22 to 25
Shoulder chops (¾ inch thick)	3 to 4	14 to 15
Patties (¾ inch thick)	3 to 4	14 to 15

BRAISING	Weight	Approximate Time After Browning
Shanks	1 pound each	1½ hours
Shoulder chops	4 to 5 ounces each	35 to 40 minutes
Shoulder pot roast (rolled)	3 to 5 pounds	2 to 2½ hours

STEWING	Weight in Pounds	Approximate Total Time in Hours
Shoulder or breast (1½-inch cubes)	2	1½ to 2

Braise or Stew
Breast
Shoulder
Shank
Neck (stew)

How to Carve Lamb Roasts

A *leg of lamb* should be placed on the table so that the thick, meaty section is near the carver. If a left leg, the shank should be to the carver's left, and vice versa. A thin slice from the thin side of the roast is removed so that the roast will rest firmly on this cut surface.

American style: Insert a carving fork into the meaty section. Cut a wedge out of the meaty section nearest the shank end, and remove. Slice as thinly as desired, down to the bone. Cut as many slices as needed to serve everyone. Insert the knife at the base of the wedge, and cut along the bone, freeing the slices.

French style: The leg of lamb is carved with the grain of the meat. At about 4 inches from the bone end, where thick, meaty portion begins, remove thin slice about size of a loin lamb chop, cutting toward the leg bone and leaving about 1 inch of meat and skin on the bone. The slice will be slightly curved on the cut side. Continue to slice, following the curve of the first cut, working away from the leg bone into the heavy meaty part. The slices will become larger as the carver works up the leg evenly and neatly. Two or three thin slices are considered better than one thick slice.

A *crown roast* is easy to carve. Insert the carving fork between the two ribs on the left. Beginning on the right side, slice between each two ribs.

Roast Lamb

ROAST LEG OF LAMB

Serves 10

3 tablespoons olive oil
1 tablespoon salt
2 teaspoons dry mustard
1 clove garlic, crushed
¼ teaspoon pepper
1 tablespoon flour
6-pound leg of lamb

1. Preheat oven to 500° F.
2. Prepare seasonings: In small bowl blend all ingredients except lamb.
3. Wipe lamb; arrange on rack in roasting pan. Spread seasonings on lamb.
4. Roast in preheated oven for 30 minutes. Turn temperature to 350° F. Roast for 1½ to 2 hours for well done, or until done to taste.

Chris Klein, Woman's Club,
Monterey Park, Calif.

SAVORY ROAST LEG OF LAMB
Serves 12 to 14

6- to 7-pound leg of lamb
4 cloves garlic, slivered
5 or 6 sprigs fresh mint or dried
   mint leaves
⅓ cup lemon juice
   Salt and pepper to taste
1 lemon, thinly sliced
   Parsley
   Mint Sauce for Roast Lamb (p. 446)

1. With pointed end of sharp knife, make deep slits in meaty part of lamb. Insert garlic and mint into slits.
2. Brown lamb on both sides in well-greased large skillet.
3. Preheat oven to 275° F. Grease roasting pan.
4. Put lamb in pan; pour lemon juice over it. Sprinkle with salt and pepper.
5. Roast in preheated oven for about 4 hours for well done, or until done to taste.
6. Arrange lamb on serving dish; garnish with lemon slices and parsley.
7. Serve with Mint Sauce for Roast Lamb.

Mrs. Earl E. Hurt, President, Garden Lovers Club, Brookhaven, Miss.

BAKED LEG OF LAMB
Serves 10

6-pound leg of lamb
   Garlic powder
   Salt
1 large onion, sliced
1 cup water

1. Preheat oven to 350° F.
2. Pierce lamb in about 6 places with skewers; fill holes with garlic powder.
3. Rub salt over lamb; place in roasting pan. Put onion and water around lamb.
4. Cover; roast in preheated oven for about 2¾ hours for well done, until done to taste. Remove cover; roast for 15 minutes longer, or until browned.

Mrs. H. P. Keith, Woman's Club, Clearwater, Fla.

LEG OF LAMB TEXAS STYLE
Serves 8

5- to 6-pound leg of lamb
1 clove garlic, slivered
1 tablespoon salt
1 teaspoon dry mustard
1 cup strong black coffee
2 teaspoons sugar
1 cup heavy cream
½ cup brandy
2 tablespoons water
5 tablespoons flour
2 tablespoons currant jelly

1. Preheat oven to 350° F.
2. Wipe lamb with damp cloth; make slits with sharp knife. Insert garlic into slits. Blend salt and mustard; rub over lamb. Place on rack in shallow roasting pan.
3. Roast in preheated oven for 1½ hours.
4. Meanwhile, in small bowl blend coffee, sugar, 2 tablespoons of the cream, brandy and water; use to baste lamb.

Roast for 1½ hours longer for well done, or until done to taste, basting frequently with coffee mixture.
5. Place lamb on serving dish in warm place. Remove rack; set pan on top of stove.
6. In small bowl mix remaining cream and flour to a smooth paste; stir into pan juices. Cook over low heat, stirring constantly, until thickened and smooth. Add currant jelly; simmer for 2 minutes. Serve with lamb.

Mrs. P. H. Bailey, Woman's Aladdin Club, Canutillo, Tex.

LEG OF LAMB IN FOIL
Serves 10

6- to 7-pound leg of lamb
1 clove garlic
1 clove
   Melted butter or olive oil
   Salt and freshly ground pepper
   to taste
1 small onion, quartered
   Few sprigs rosemary
½ cup dry red wine or ½ cup lemon
   juice combined with ¼ cup any
   other fruit juice
   Cooked potato balls or small
   new potatoes
   Cooked small carrots

1. Preheat broiler.
2. Put lamb on large sheet of heavy-duty aluminum foil; place shallow pan underneath. Fold foil loosely around lamb, so that it may be handled easily. Rub lamb with garlic; then stick garlic with clove; leave in foil. Brush lamb with butter or oil; sprinkle with salt and pepper. Put onion and rosemary in foil.
3. Put lamb under broiler heat until lightly browned on top and sides. Remove lamb.
4. Set temperature at 375° F.
5. Pour wine or fruit juice combination over lamb. Raise ends of foil on long sides of lamb; bring up over meat, overlapping about 3 inches. Close foil at each end; turn up, so juices cannot run out.
6. Roast in preheated oven for 2½ hours.
7. Open foil; fold back. Using bulb-type baster, siphon off fat from drippings; discard garlic and onion. Baste lamb with juices remaining in foil. Add potatoes and carrots; baste with juices. Cook for a few minutes longer to glaze vegetables. Serve in foil.

Mrs. Ann Caricone, Juniors of Eastchester Woman's Club, Eastchester, N.Y.

BARBECUED LEG OF LAMB
Serves 10

5-pound leg of lamb
1 teaspoon salt
½ teaspoon pepper
2 large onions, grated
¼ teaspoon garlic salt
1 tablespoon vinegar
3 tablespoons chili sauce
2 tablespoons Worcestershire

¼ teaspoon thyme
1 cup beef bouillon

1. Preheat oven to 425° F.
2. Rub lamb with salt and pepper. Arrange on rack in shallow roasting pan.
3. Roast in preheated oven for 30 minutes. Pour off fat.
4. Meanwhile, in saucepan combine remaining ingredients. Bring sauce to boil; remove from heat.
5. Turn temperature to 350° F. Pour sauce over lamb. Roast for 1½ hours longer for well done, or until done to taste, basting frequently with sauce.
6. Slice; serve with sauce.

Mary Audsley, Woman's Club,
Redwood City, Calif.

BONED BARBECUED LAMB

Serves 8

4-pound leg of lamb, boned
2 tablespoons olive oil
3 tablespoons soy sauce
⅓ cup dry vermouth
½ teaspoon garlic salt
1 tablespoon seasoned salt
½ teaspoon pepper
1 teaspoon dehydrated onion flakes
¼ teaspoon basil
¼ teaspoon rosemary
¼ teaspoon mint flakes

1. Preheat oven to 350° F.
2. Arrange lamb on rack in roasting pan.
3. In small bowl blend remaining ingredients; spread on lamb.
4. Roast in preheated oven for 1½ to 2 hours, or until done to taste, basting frequently with pan juices.

Sara Cotten, Junior Alpha Club, Lompoc, Calif.

CROWN ROAST OF LAMB

Serves 8

Have butcher prepare crown roast with 16 ribs by tying together rib sections of two loins of lamb in crown shape.

1 crown roast of lamb
8 slices bacon
6 cups favorite savory bread
    stuffing
Salt and pepper to taste
16 mushroom caps, broiled
2 tablespoons flour
1½ cups water

1. Preheat oven to 325° F.
2. Wrap bacon around bottom of roast; place on rack in shallow roasting pan. Fill center of roast with bread stuffing; wrap aluminum foil around tip of each bone to prevent burning. Season with salt and pepper.
3. Roast in preheated oven for about 1½ hours, or until done to taste, basting frequently with pan juices.
4. Place roast on serving dish. Remove foil; replace with mushroom caps. Keep in warm place.
5. Prepare gravy: Remove all but 2 tablespoons fat from pan. Stir in flour; cook over medium heat for 3 minutes, or

until browned. Gradually add water, stirring and scraping bottom and sides of pan to blend in browned bits. Simmer, stirring constantly, for 3 minutes. Season with salt and pepper. Strain gravy, if desired, before serving.

Eunice Myers, Woman's Club,
West Palm Beach, Fla.

Lamb Steaks and Chops

LAMB STEAK LUSCIOUS

Serves 4

2 tablespoons cooking oil
1 tablespoon vinegar
2 teaspoons Worcestershire
1 clove garlic, crushed
1 teaspoon salt
¼ teaspoon pepper
½ teaspoon celery seed
2 1¼- to 1½-inch-thick legs
    of lamb steak

1. In shallow dish combine all ingredients except lamb. Add lamb; refrigerate for 2 to 3 hours, turning occasionally.
2. Preheat broiler.
3. Remove lamb from marinade; broil 3 to 5 inches from heat for 10 to 12 minutes on each side, or until done to taste.

Mrs. Lilly M. Rank, Masonic Service Association,
Washington, D.C.

SHISH KEBAB

Serves 4

Mushroom caps and squares of eggplant may also be used when making kebabs.

½ cup lemon juice
½ cup olive oil
¼ cup grated onion
1 teaspoon salt
¼ teaspoon pepper
½ teaspoon rosemary
2 pounds leg of lamb, boned and
    cut into 1½-inch cubes
2 medium green peppers, cut into
    2-inch squares
8 small white onions, parboiled
2 medium tomatoes, quartered
Fluffy cooked rice

1. Prepare marinade: In small bowl blend lemon juice, oil, grated onion, salt, pepper and rosemary.
2. Prepare kebabs: On 4 large skewers alternate lamb, green peppers and white onions.
3. Arrange skewers flat in shallow roasting pan; pour marinade over them. Marinate for 2 to 3 hours, turning occasionally.
4. Preheat broiler. Arrange kebabs on broiler pan; reserve marinade.
5. Broil 4 to 5 inches from heat for about 12 minutes, brushing occasionally with marinade. Turn kebabs; broil for 7 minutes. Arrange tomatoes on ends of skewers; broil for 5 minutes longer, or until lamb is done to taste.
6. Serve on bed of rice.

Mrs. Martin J. Soovajian, Woman's Club,
East Hartford, Conn.

DEVILED LAMB CHOPS

Serves 6

6 1½-inch-thick loin lamb chops
1 tablespoon prepared mustard
¼ cup flour
2 teaspoons salt
Dash of pepper
½ teaspoon garlic salt
1 tablespoon shortening
1 medium green pepper, cut
into rings
2 medium onions, sliced
¼ cup water
Grated rind of 1 lemon

1. Spread one side of chops with mustard.
2. On piece of waxed paper combine flour, salt, pepper and garlic salt. Coat chops with mixture.
3. Melt shortening in large skillet; brown chops well on both sides.
4. Arrange green pepper and onions on chops. Sprinkle with water and lemon rind. Cover; simmer for 45 minutes, or until tender.

Mrs. Wallace Gray, Island Woman's Club,
Anna Maria, Fla.

DINNER LAMB CHOPS

Serves 6

2 tablespoons shortening
6 1-inch-thick lamb chops
Salt and pepper to taste
1 medium green pepper, cored and
cut into 6 rings
1 large onion, cut into 6 slices
1 lemon, cut into 6 slices
2 cups tomato juice

1. Preheat oven to 350° F. Grease 10 x 6 x 1½-inch baking pan.
2. Melt shortening in large skillet; brown chops well on both sides. Season with salt and pepper.
3. Arrange chops in pan; top each with a slice of green pepper, onion and lemon. Pour tomato juice over chops; cover pan with aluminum foil.
4. Bake in preheated oven for 1½ hours.

Carol Fehling, Whitfield Woman's Club,
Reading, Pa.

GRILLED TROPICAL LAMB CHOPS

Serves 6

6 1-inch-thick shoulder lamb chops
with pocket
1½ teaspoons salt
¼ teaspoon pepper
1 cup biscuit mix
2 tart apples, peeled and chopped
1 small onion, chopped
1 stalk celery, chopped
9-ounce can crushed pineapple,
drained
1 cup cooked rice
1 teaspoon chives
1 teaspoon curry powder
½ teaspoon sugar

1. Prepare charcoal fire. Cut 6 squares of heavy aluminum foil.

2. Rub chops with salt and pepper; dredge in biscuit mix.
3. Combine remaining ingredients. Fill pockets of chops with stuffing; secure with skewers.
4. Put each chop in center of foil square; fold foil to make package. Seal well.
5. Place on rack; cook over hot coals for 20 minutes. Turn foil packages; cook for 20 minutes longer.

Florence Martin, Woman's Club,
Redwood City, Calif.

POLLY'S BAKED LAMB CHOPS

Serves 4

4 ¾-inch-thick shoulder lamb chops
Salt and pepper to taste
½ cup water
3 medium tomatoes, sliced
1 large onion, thinly sliced
3 tablespoons chopped parsley
½ teaspoon orégano
Cooked rice

1. Preheat oven to 400° F. Grease 9-inch square baking pan.
2. Arrange chops in pan; sprinkle with salt and pepper.
3. Add water; top chops with tomatoes and onion. Season with salt and pepper; sprinkle with parsley and orégano.
4. Cover; bake in preheated oven for 1 hour. Remove cover; turn chops; bake, uncovered, for 20 minutes longer.
5. Serve chops and pan juices on rice.

Mrs. W. J. Hickman, Parliamentary Law Club,
Glendale, Calif.

Lamb Shanks

LAMB SHANKS

Serves 4

4 lamb shanks, cracked
6-ounce can tomato sauce
1 cup dry white wine
1 large onion, thinly sliced
¼ cup brown sugar
1 large clove garlic, crushed
1 teaspoon dillweed
½ teaspoon orégano
1 teaspoon rosemary
Cooked rice (optional)

1. Preheat oven to 300° F.
2. Arrange lamb in roasting pan.
3. In mixing bowl blend remaining ingredients. Pour over lamb.
4. Cover; bake in preheated oven for 3 hours. Remove cover; bake for 30 minutes longer.
5. Arrange lamb on serving dish; cover; keep in warm place.
6. Place pan over high heat; boil rapidly until sauce is reduced by half. Pour over lamb. Serve with rice, if desired.

Mrs. Albert Martin, Town and Country League,
Cheyenne, Wyo.

LAMB SHANKS AND CURRIED RICE

Serves 4

2 tablespoons shortening or
  cooking oil
4 lamb shanks
1 teaspoon salt
  Pepper to taste
3 cups hot water
½ teaspoon curry powder
1 cup diced onions
1 clove garlic, minced
1 cup rice

1. Preheat oven to 350° F.
2. Melt shortening or oil in baking pan; brown lamb. Sprinkle with salt and pepper. Add 1 cup of the water. Cover; bake in preheated oven for 1 hour.
3. Remove lamb. Add remaining water and curry powder to pan liquid; mix well. Add onions, garlic and rice. Place lamb on rice; cover; bake for 1 hour longer, or until shanks are tender and rice has absorbed liquid.

Bea Pippin, Woman's Club, Coalinga, Calif.

ARMENIAN LAMB SHANK STEW

Serves 4

2 tablespoons shortening
3 large lamb shanks
½ cup water
1 small onion, chopped
½ cup diced green pepper
1-pound can tomatoes
1 teaspoon salt
¼ teaspoon pepper
¾ cup bulgur (cracked wheat)

1. Melt shortening in Dutch oven or heavy kettle; brown lamb well on all sides. Add water. Bring to boil; cover; simmer for 1 hour.
2. Cool slightly; remove meat from bones; cut into large chunks. Return meat to pan; add remaining ingredients. Cover; simmer for 15 minutes, stirring occasionally and adding water, if necessary.

Florence J. Wilkins, Progressive Home Club,
Fresno, Calif.

Lamb Casseroles and Stews

ARMENIAN DINNER IN FOIL

Serves 4

4 ½-pound slices shoulder of lamb
1 green pepper, quartered
2 large tomatoes, halved
1 large onion, quartered
2 carrots, halved
2 potatoes, peeled and halved
  Salt and pepper to taste
½ teaspoon garlic powder

1. Preheat oven to 350° F. Cut 4 squares of heavy aluminum foil.
2. Arrange a slice of lamb in middle of each square of foil. Top each with green pepper quarter, tomato half, onion quarter, carrot half and potato half. Season with salt and pepper; sprinkle with garlic

powder. Fold each piece of foil to make a package; arrange in shallow roasting pan.
3. Pour cold water into pan to come ¼ inch up side of pan.
4. Bake in preheated oven for 2 hours, adding water, if necessary, during cooking.
5. Serve in foil packages.

Eleanor M. Holmes, Woman's Club,
South Pasadena, Calif.

LAMB CASSEROLE

Serves 6

⅓ cup presifted flour
2 teaspoons salt
½ teaspoon pepper
2½ pounds shoulder of lamb, boned
  and cut into 1-inch cubes
½ cup butter
1 large onion, finely chopped
1 cup finely chopped celery
1-pound can tomatoes, drained
2 cups chicken broth
1 bunch small carrots
4 pounds turnips, peeled and halved
12 small white onions
12 small potatoes
1 cup cooked peas
2 tablespoons chopped parsley

1. Preheat oven to 350° F. Grease 3-quart casserole.
2. On piece of waxed paper blend flour, salt and pepper; use to dredge lamb; reserve excess flour. Melt ¼ cup of the butter in large skillet; brown lamb well on all sides. Stir in onion and celery; sauté for 5 minutes, stirring frequently. Stir in reserved flour; gradually stir in tomatoes and broth.
3. Cook over medium heat, stirring constantly, until liquid thickens. Turn into casserole.
4. Cover; bake in preheated oven for 1 hour.
5. Melt remaining butter in skillet; sauté carrots, turnips, onions and potatoes until lightly browned.
6. Add vegetables to casserole; cover; bake for 1 hour.
7. Add peas; sprinkle with parsley. Cover; bake for 10 minutes longer.

Mrs. Charles A. Haskins, Woman's Club,
La Crescenta, Calif.

LAMB STEW

Serves 6

¼ cup presifted flour
2 teaspoons salt
¼ teaspoon pepper
2 pounds lean shoulder of lamb,
  boned and cut into 2-inch cubes
3 tablespoons shortening
¼ cup grated onion
2 cloves garlic, crushed
3 cups boiling water
2 teaspoons celery seed
8 medium carrots, quartered
3 medium potatoes, halved
12 small white onions
2 teaspoons Worcestershire
2 tablespoons chopped parsley

1. On piece of waxed paper combine flour, salt and pepper; use to dredge lamb; reserve excess flour.

2. Melt shortening in Dutch oven or heavy kettle; sauté grated onion and garlic over low heat for 5 minutes. Add lamb; cook over medium heat, stirring frequently, until well browned on all sides.

3. Stir in reserved flour; gradually stir in water. Cover; simmer for 1½ hours, or until fork-tender.

4. Add celery seed, carrots, potatoes and whole onions. Cover; simmer for 30 minutes, or until tender.

5. Just before serving, stir in Worcestershire and parsley.

Ozella F. Ruppersberger, Rodgers Forge Woman's Club, Baltimore, Md.

COUS-COUS
(Lamb Stew with Semolina)

Serves 8

Although this is the traditional dish of North Africa, the word "cous-cous" is Arabic for semolina which is steamed in a *couscousière*, or colander fitted over a heavy kettle containing the bubbling stew.

> 4 tablespoons olive oil
> 2 pounds shoulder of lamb, boned and cut into 1½-inch cubes
> 2 medium onions, chopped
> 1 clove garlic, minced
> 8 tomatoes, peeled, seeded and quartered
> 1½ pounds zucchini, split and cut into 1½-inch lengths
> ½ teaspoon thyme
> ½ teaspoon orégano
> 1 bay leaf
> Pinch of saffron
> 1 pound chick-peas, cooked or 1-pound 4-ounce can chick-peas, drained
> Salt and pepper to taste
> 2 pounds cous-cous (semolina)
> ¼ cup melted butter
> 8 small carrots, scraped
> 1 large rutabaga turnip, peeled and cut into eighths
> 3 green peppers, seeded and cut into strips
> 2 chili peppers
> Hot Sauce (opposite)

1. Heat oil in heavy kettle; brown lamb on all sides.

2. Add onions; brown lightly.

3. Add garlic, tomatoes, half the zucchini, herbs, and chick-peas.

4. Add water just to cover, salt and pepper. Bring to boil; simmer, without stirring, for 1 hour.

5. Meanwhile, moisten cous-cous with boiling water to make grains swell; stir with fork; let stand for 20 minutes. Repeat three times. Sprinkle with butter, salt and pepper. Place in large strainer or colander lined with cloth.

6. Add remaining zucchini, carrots, turnip, green peppers and chilis to stew. Add

water, if necessary, to cover meat and vegetables. Place strainer or colander containing cous-cous over kettle; cover; simmer for 1 hour longer.

7. Arrange cous-cous in cone-shaped pile on hot serving platter. Remove 1 cup liquid from kettle to make Hot Sauce (below). Drain rest of liquid from kettle; serve in gravy boat. Serve meat and vegetables in large tureen.

HOT SAUCE
Mix 1 cup liquid from stew, 2 tablespoons tomato paste, ½ teaspoon paprika, ¼ teaspoon ground coriander and ¼ to 1 teaspoon cayenne to taste. The sauce should be very hot.

A. S.

LANCASHIRE HOT POT

Serves 6

> 2 tablespoons butter or margarine
> 2½ pounds shoulder of lamb, cut into 1½-inch cubes
> 1 pound mushrooms, sliced
> 1 bunch carrots, sliced
> 2 large onions, sliced
> 2 pounds potatoes, thinly sliced
> 3 tablespoons flour
> 2 teaspoons salt
> ¼ teaspoon pepper
> 2 cups water
> 2 beef bouillon cubes
> ¼ cup chopped parsley
> ¼ teaspoon thyme

1. Preheat oven to 350° F. Grease 2½-quart casserole.

2. Melt butter or margarine in large skillet; brown lamb on all sides over medium heat.

3. Put lamb in casserole; reserve drippings. Arrange mushrooms on lamb; top with carrots and onions. Arrange potatoes on onions, overlapping the slices.

4. Add flour to reserved drippings in skillet. Stir in salt, pepper and water; cook over low heat, stirring constantly, until thickened and smooth. Add bouillon cubes, parsley and thyme; cook over low heat until cubes have dissolved. Pour over meat and vegetables.

5. Cover; bake in preheated oven for 2 hours.

6. Remove cover; bake for 20 minutes longer, or until potatoes are browned.

Gwenne Simpson, Junior Woman's Club, Simsbury, Conn.

BOMBAY CURRY

Serves 4

> 3 tablespoons shortening
> 1 medium onion, finely chopped
> 1 clove garlic, crushed
> 1 tart apple, peeled and chopped
> 1 tablespoon curry powder
> 1 teaspoon paprika
> ½ teaspoon ginger
> ¼ teaspoon sugar
> ¼ teaspoon chili powder
> 1 pound shoulder of lamb, boned and cubed

6-ounce can tomato paste
1 cup instant rice
¼ teaspoon turmeric

1. Melt shortening in large skillet or Dutch oven; sauté onion, garlic and apple over medium heat until golden brown.
2. Stir in curry powder, paprika, ginger, sugar and chili powder; sauté until well browned.
3. Add lamb; cook until browned, stirring frequently. Add tomato paste and boiling water to cover. Cover; simmer for 30 minutes, or until tender.
4. Meanwhile, cook rice according to package directions, adding tumeric to water.
5. Serve lamb curry on rice.

Emily Bowling, Civic Club, New Cumberland, Pa.

Ground Lamb Dishes

DOLMA ARMENIAN
(Stuffed Peppers)
						Serves 4
1 pound ground lamb
½ cup rice
1 large onion, finely chopped
1 large tomato, chopped
1 tablespoon chopped parsley
1½ teaspoons salt
¼ teaspoon pepper
4 large green peppers

1. Preheat oven to 350° F. Grease 8-inch square baking pan.
2. Combine all ingredients except green peppers; mix well.
3. Cut ½-inch slice from top of each pepper. Discard seeds. Fill peppers with lamb mixture; arrange in pan. Add water to come within ½ inch from top of pan.
4. Cover pan with aluminum foil; bake in preheated oven for 1 hour.

Mrs. Martin J. Soovajian, Woman's Club, East Hartford, Conn.

BAKED KIBBY
(Syrian Lamb and Wheat Patties)
						Serves 8
3 cups fine bulgur (cracked wheat)
2 pounds ground lean lamb
1 medium onion, finely ground
2½ teaspoons salt
½ teaspoon pepper
Butter
1 pound coarsely ground lamb
2 medium onions, finely chopped
½ teaspoon cinnamon
¼ cup pignolia (pine) nuts

1. Wash bulgur; drain well. Set aside for 1 hour.
2. In mixing bowl combine bulgur, ground lean lamb, ground onion, 1½ teaspoons of the salt and ¼ teaspoon of the pepper. Put through fine blade of meat grinder; return to mixing bowl.
3. Add sufficient ice water to soften; knead to form a dough. Set aside.
4. Preheat oven to 400° F. Grease 13 x 9½ x 2-inch baking pan.

5. Prepare filling: Melt 1 tablespoon butter in large skillet; add coarsely ground lamb; simmer, stirring occasionally, until excess liquid has evaporated. Add chopped onions; simmer for 10 minutes, stirring occasionally. Stir in remaining salt, remaining pepper and cinnamon; remove from heat. Melt 1 tablespoon butter in small skillet; brown nuts. Stir into filling; cool slightly.
7. To shape kibby, form bulgur dough into thin patties. Put 1 teaspoon filling in center of each patty; top with another patty. Flatten; press edges together. Repeat until all dough is used. Put in pan; dot with butter.
8. Bake in preheated oven for 30 minutes, or until bottoms are golden brown.
9. Place under broiler; broil for 2 minutes, or until tops are brown. Brush tops with melted butter.

Woman's Club, Monessen, Pa.

LAMBURGERS WITH PINE NUTS
						Serves 4
1 tablespoon butter or margarine
¼ cup pignolia (pine) nuts
1 pound ground lamb
¼ cup chopped parsley
1 medium onion, grated
1 teaspoon dried mint
1 teaspoon salt
¼ teaspoon pepper
12-ounce can tomato purée

1. Preheat oven to 350° F. Grease 8-inch square baking pan.
2. Melt butter in small skillet; brown nuts. Set aside.
3. Combine lamb, parsley, onion, mint, salt and pepper; mix well. Shape into round flat patties; press nuts into center of each patty.
4. Put in pan; top with tomato purée. Bake in preheated oven for 35 minutes.

Eleanore G. Crawford, Junior Woman's Club, Littleton, Colo.

LAMB LOAF
						Serves 8
3 pounds shoulder of lamb, skinned, boned and ground
1 cup bread crumbs
⅔ cup scalded milk
3 eggs, lightly beaten
⅓ cup chopped parsley
2½ teaspoons salt
¼ teaspoon pepper

1. Preheat oven to 350° F. Grease 2-quart casserole.
2. Put lamb and crumbs in mixing bowl; pour in milk. Add remaining ingredients; mix thoroughly. Turn into casserole.
3. Cover; bake in preheated oven for 2 hours.

Emily Barthold, Woman's Club, Moorestown, N.J.

LAMB MOUSSAKA
(Greek Casserole)

Serves 8

1 medium eggplant
½ cup shortening
4 tablespoons butter
4 medium onions, sliced
3 cloves garlic, crushed
1 pound ground lamb
¾ teaspoon salt
½ teaspoon thyme
½ teaspoon orégano
½ cup canned tomatoes
½ cup dry white wine
2 eggs, separated
1 cup fresh bread crumbs
2 tablespoons flour
1½ cups milk
⅛ teaspoon nutmeg

1. Preheat oven to 350° F. Grease 3-quart casserole.
2. Wash eggplant. Do not peel; cut into lengthwise slices.
3. Melt shortening in large skillet; brown eggplant on both sides. Set aside.
4. Heat 2 tablespoons of the butter in skillet; sauté onions and garlic for 5 minutes. Add lamb; cook over medium heat, stirring constantly, until lamb changes color. Stir in salt, thyme, orégano, tomatoes and wine. Cover; simmer for 30 minutes.
5. Cool; stir in egg whites and ½ cup of the crumbs.
6. Melt remaining butter in saucepan. Blend in flour; gradually stir in milk. Cook over medium heat, stirring constantly, until sauce is thickened and smooth.
7. Blend egg yolks with nutmeg; stir in a little sauce. Return to rest of sauce; simmer for 2 minutes, stirring constantly.
8. Sprinkle ¼ cup of the crumbs in casserole. Top with a layer of eggplant, then a layer of meat. Cover with half the sauce. Repeat layers of eggplant, meat, sauce, finishing with sauce. Sprinkle with remaining crumbs.
9. Bake in preheated oven for 1 hour.

Bernice Van Patten, Progressive Home Club, Fresno, Calif.

Cooked Lamb Dishes

LAMB CROQUETTES

Serves 4

2 cups chopped cooked lamb
¾ cup Thick White Sauce (p. 441)
½ teaspoon salt
Dash of paprika
1 egg yolk
¼ teaspoon celery salt
1 teaspoon lemon juice
Bread crumbs
1 egg, lightly beaten
Fat for deep frying
Barbecue Sauce for Lamb
Croquettes (p. 442)

1. Combine lamb, Thick White Sauce, salt, paprika, egg yolk, celery salt and lemon juice. Shape into croquettes.

2. Roll croquettes in crumbs; dip in egg; roll again in crumbs.
3. Fry in deep fat heated to 365° F. until well browned.
4. Serve with Barbecue Sauce for Lamb Croquettes.

Wilma Hougaard, Literary Club, Moab, Utah

CHEF'S LAMB AND MUSHROOMS

Serves 2

1 tablespoon butter or margarine
1 tablespoon grated onion
3-ounce can whole mushrooms, undrained
½ cup lamb gravy
1 cup diced roast lamb
1 teaspoon grated Parmesan cheese
1 teaspoon dry sherry
Hot mashed potatoes

1. Melt butter or margarine in skillet; sauté onion until golden. Stir in mushrooms, lamb gravy and lamb. Cook over low heat, stirring occasionally, for 5 minutes.
2. Remove from heat; stir in cheese and sherry.
3. Serve with potatoes.

Mrs. Robert Van Horn, Senior Woman's Club, Dallas, Pa.

LAMB SHEPHERD'S PIE

Serves 4

3 cups diced roast lamb
2 medium onions
4 tablespoons butter or margarine
½ cup lamb gravy
Salt and pepper to taste
2 cups mashed potatoes
1 egg
¼ cup grated Cheddar cheese
Paprika

1. Preheat oven at 375° F. Grease 1½-quart casserole.
2. Put lamb and onions through medium blade of meat grinder.
3. Melt 2 tablespoons of the butter in skillet; sauté lamb and onions over medium heat for 5 minutes, stirring frequently. Stir in gravy; season with salt and pepper. Turn into casserole.
4. In mixing bowl season potatoes with salt and pepper. Add egg and cheese; beat until smooth.
5. Spread potatoes on meat mixture. Dot with remaining butter; sprinkle with paprika.
6. Bake in preheated oven for 25 minutes, or until browned.

Selena Howard, Blair Woman's Club, Blairstown, N.J.

LAMB SHORTCAKES

Serves 6

Basic Baking Powder Biscuits dough (p. 119)
2 tablespoons shortening
⅓ cup bread crumbs
1 cup milk
3 tablespoons chopped green pepper

3 tablespoons chopped celery
2 tablespoons chopped onion
¾ teaspoon salt
¼ teaspoon pepper
2 cups ground cooked lamb
10½-ounce can condensed tomato soup
2 tablespoons butter
1 teaspoon Worcestershire
2 tablespoons pickle relish

1. Roll Basic Baking Powder Biscuits dough into rectangle about ¼ inch thick; cut into 12 squares.
2. Melt shortening in large skillet; brown crumbs. Add milk, green pepper, celery, onion, salt and pepper; cook over low heat for 10 minutes.
3. Preheat oven to 425° F. Grease large baking pan.
4. Add lamb to skillet; mix well.
5. Heap meat mixture on half the biscuit squares; arrange in baking pan. Top with remaining biscuit squares.
6. Bake in preheated oven for 15 minutes, or until golden brown.
7. Meanwhile, prepare tomato sauce: In saucepan combine soup, butter, Worcestershire and relish. Heat. Serve with lamb shortcakes.

Mrs. Julia Rohde, Women's Progressive Club of Inglewood Acres, Inglewood, Calif.

Specialty Meats

Brains

The brains of beef, calf, sheep and pig are considered delicacies, but calf's brains are the most desirable. They should be kept extremely cold and cooked and eaten as soon as possible. Before being braised or sautéed in butter, they must be parboiled in salted water, then plunged into cold water to firm the tissue. A little lemon juice or vinegar, some peppercorns, a bay leaf and other seasonings are frequently added to the water in which brains are parboiled.

BREADED CALF'S BRAINS

Serves 4

1 pound calf's brains
1 quart boiling water
Salt
1 tablespoon vinegar
1 cup bread crumbs
2 eggs, lightly beaten
¼ teaspoon pepper
¼ cup butter or margarine
2 tablespoons shortening

1. Wash brains; remove membrane.
2. Put water in saucepan; add 1 tablespoon salt and vinegar. Add brains; simmer for 10 minutes. Drain brains; plunge into cold water.
3. Cut brains into ¾-inch slices; coat with crumbs.

4. In shallow bowl mix eggs, 1 teaspoon salt and pepper: use to dip brains in; coat again with crumbs.
5. Melt butter or margarine and shortening in large skillet; sauté brains over medium heat for 10 minutes, or until golden on all sides.

Mrs. T. P. Stearns, State Women's Club, Wash.

SAUTÉED CALF'S BRAINS

Serves 2

1 pair calf's brains
¼ cup vinegar or lemon juice
Salt to taste
3 tablespoons butter or cooking oil
5 to 6 sprigs parsley
Paprika
Cooked peas

1. Simmer brains in boiling salted water for 15 minutes. Drain; remove outer membrane, being careful not to break brains.
2. Soak in cold water for 1 hour. Drain.
3. Sprinkle brains with a little of the vinegar or lemon juice; let stand for 30 minutes longer. Drain again.
4. Sprinkle brains with salt. Heat butter or oil in skillet; sauté brains until golden brown on all sides; place on warm serving plate.
5. Fry parsley in fat remaining in skillet until crisp. Add remaining vinegar or lemon juice. Heat. Pour over brains. Sprinkle with paprika; serve with peas.

Julia Hoff, Women's Club, Portsmouth, N.H.

BRAINS WITH SCRAMBLED EGGS
(*Michana Vejce s Mozkem*)

Serves 6

1 pound brains
3 tablespoons butter
½ teaspoon salt
5 eggs, lightly beaten
¼ teaspoon pepper

1. Wash brains; cover with warm water; soak for 30 minutes.
2. Drain; remove membrane. Pat dry with absorbent paper.
3. Melt butter in skillet. Add brains; sprinkle with salt; sauté over low heat, stirring occasionally, for 20 minutes.
4. Stir in eggs; cook, stirring frequently, until eggs are done to taste. Remove from heat; season with pepper.

Woman's Club, Clarkson, Neb.

Kidneys

The kidneys of all domestic farm animals, rich in protein and low in carbohydrates, are delicious if prepared well. Care must be taken when purchasing them, since they must be absolutely fresh. A good red color is a reliable guide; mottled kidneys should be avoided. If possible, buy them with the fat (suet) around them—the whiteness of the fat is a clue to their freshness. Since some people object to the strong odor of kidneys, soak them in cold water for 30 minutes. Pat dry; then skin them. Cut them in half, or into slices, and remove tubes.

The small *lamb kidneys* and the larger tender *veal kidneys* are usually broiled or braised. They should be cooked quickly, or they will be tough. After cooking, they should still be slightly pink in the center. When kidneys are cooked in a stew, they may be simmered for a longer period over very low heat.

The fatty white centers and tubes in *beef kidneys* must be removed. These kidneys are usually stewed. The flavor will be more delicate if they are soaked in cold water for 2 hours, then parboiled before being used in a recipe.

LAMB KIDNEYS IN WINE SAUCE

Serves 4

¼ cup butter
½ cup sliced onions
¼ cup finely chopped celery
8 lamb kidneys, cleaned
   and diced
3 tablespoons flour
1 teaspoon salt
¼ teaspoon pepper
1 cup red wine
½ cup beef broth
½ pound mushrooms, sliced
2 tablespoons chopped parsley
Cooked rice or noodles

1. Melt butter in skillet; sauté onions and celery for 10 minutes. Add kidneys; sauté, stirring frequently, until they change color.

2. Sprinkle with flour, salt and pepper; cook, stirring, until flour is lightly browned. Stir in wine and broth, cook, stirring constantly, until thickened. Add mushrooms; cover; simmer for 10 minutes.

3. Sprinkle with parsley. Serve on rice or noodles.

A. S.

VEAL KIDNEYS FLAMBÉ

Serves 4

3 tablespoons butter or margarine
¼ cup finely chopped scallions
4 veal kidneys, cleaned and
   thinly sliced
¼ pound mushrooms, sliced
2 tablespoons brandy
2 tablespoons dry sherry
1 teaspoon salt
Dash of pepper
2 tablespoons chopped parsley

1. Melt butter or margarine in skillet; sauté scallions for 5 minutes. Add kidneys and mushrooms; sauté over medium heat, stirring frequently, until kidneys are lightly browned on all sides.

2. Sprinkle with brandy; ignite. Allow flame to die out; stir in sherry, salt and pepper; simmer for 2 minutes.

3. Sprinkle with parsley.

A. S.

Liver

Calf's liver is considered most desirable liver, but the livers from beef, pork, and sheep may be prepared in many delicious ways and are highly nutritious. The thin membrane covering the outside of the liver and the tubes running through it should be removed before the liver is cooked.

BAKED LIVER AND ONIONS

Serves 3

2 large onions, sliced
½ cup butter or margarine
½ cup dry red wine
¼ cup chopped parsley
1 bay leaf, crumbled
1 teaspoon thyme
1 teaspoon salt
⅛ teaspoon pepper
½ cup water
6 slices calf's liver
½ cup presifted flour

1. Preheat oven to 350° F. Grease 10 x 6 x 1½-inch baking pan.

2. Arrange onions in pan; dot with butter or margarine. Add wine, parsley, bay leaf, thyme, salt, pepper and water. Cover pan with aluminum foil; bake in preheated oven for 30 minutes.

3. Coat liver with flour. Arrange on onion mixture. Cover; Bake for 30 minutes.

4. Remove foil; bake for 10 minutes longer.

Pat Heffron, Woman's Club, Dundee, Ill.

BROILED BEEF LIVER

Serves 4

½ cup butter
2 tablespoons finely chopped onion
2 tablespoons lemon juice
¼ teaspoon thyme
¼ teaspoon marjoram
1 pound beef liver, sliced

1. Preheat broiler.

2. Melt butter in small saucepan; sauté onion over medium heat until golden. Stir in lemon juice, thyme and marjoram; remove from heat.

3. Arrange liver on broiler pan; brush with sauce.

4. Broil 3 to 5 inches from heat for 4 minutes. Turn; brush with sauce. Broil for 5 minutes longer, or until done to taste.

5. Serve with remaining sauce.

Mrs. Milton D. Pattullo, Woman's Club, Wilmette, Ill.

CALF'S LIVER EN BROCHETTE

Serves 3 or 4

1 pound calf's liver, thickly sliced
4 slices bacon
2 egg whites, lightly beaten
½ cup bread crumbs
4 tablespoons olive oil
2 tablespoons vinegar
½ teaspoon dry mustard
1 tablespoon minced parsley
Salt and pepper to taste

1. Preheat broiler. Grease broiler pan.
2. Cut liver into squares. Cut bacon into squares. Alternate liver and bacon on 3 or 4 skewers.
3. Dip skewers in egg whites; roll in crumbs. Arrange on pan.
4. Broil slowly for 15 to 20 minutes; turning skewers occasionally until bacon is crisp.
5. Meanwhile, combine oil, vinegar, mustard, parsley, salt and pepper.
6. Arrange skewers on warm serving platter; pour sauce over meat.

Martha Sackett, Woman's Club, Durham, N.H.

LIVER AND ONIONS WITH FRENCH DRESSING

Serves 5 or 6

3 large onions, sliced and separated
    into rings
2⅓ cups water
1 tablespoon butter
1½ pounds lamb or beef liver,
    thinly sliced
2 tablespoons French dressing
½ teaspoon salt
¼ teaspoon pepper

1. Put onions and 2 cups of the water in large skillet; cook over medium heat for 15 minutes, stirring frequently, until water has evaporated and onions are lightly browned. Remove onions; set aside.
2. Melt butter in same skillet; brown liver quickly on both sides. Cover with onions.
3. In small bowl blend French dressing, remaining water, salt and pepper. Pour over liver and onions.
4. Cover; bring quickly to boil; then simmer for 3 minutes, or just until liver loses pink color.

Junior Service League, Statesville, N.C.

BRAISED LIVER

Serves 4 to 6

1 pound beef liver, cut into
    ½-inch-thick slices
¼ cup presifted flour
¼ cup bacon drippings or shortening
½ cup chopped onions
½ cup chopped celery
1 beef bouillon cube
¼ cup water
1 teaspoon salt
¼ teaspoon pepper
¼ teaspoon marjoram
¼ teaspoon rosemary

1. Dredge liver in flour.
2. Melt bacon drippings or shortening in large skillet; brown liver on both sides. Remove liver; set aside.
3. Add onions and celery to fat remaining in skillet; sauté for 5 minutes. Stir in remaining ingredients; cook over medium heat, stirring frequently, until bouillon cube is dissolved.

4. Return liver to skillet. Cover; simmer for 20 minutes, or until tender.

Mary Drummond, Pathfinder Club,
Compton, Calif.

BEEF LIVER STROGANOFF

Serves 4

3 tablespoons bacon drippings
¼ cup chopped onion
1 pound beef liver, cut into
    ½-inch strips
2 tablespoons flour
8-ounce can sliced mushrooms,
    undrained
⅓ cup water
1 beef bouillon cube
½ cup sour cream
    Salt and pepper to taste

1. Melt bacon drippings in large skillet; sauté onion over medium heat until golden. Remove onion; set aside.
2. Add liver to fat remaining in skillet; brown on all sides over medium heat. Sprinkle with flour; simmer.
3. Meanwhile, in bowl blend onion, mushrooms, water, bouillon cube and sour cream. Stir into skillet; cook over low heat, stirring constantly, until thickened and smooth. Season with salt and pepper.

Colette Gorychka, Service League, Lombard, Ill.

SCALLOPED LIVER

Serves 6

1½ cups fresh bread crumbs
½ pound beef liver, thinly sliced
¼ cup grated onion
¼ cup butter
    Salt and pepper to taste
2 cups canned tomatoes

1. Preheat oven to 350° F. Grease 1½-quart casserole.
2. Sprinkle about ½ cup of the crumbs in casserole. Top with a few slices of liver; sprinkle with a little of the onion; dot with butter. Season with salt and pepper. Add layer of tomatoes. Repeat layers until all ingredients have been used, finishing with crumbs.
3. Bake in preheated oven for 40 minutes.

Mrs. Roy Gruenhagen, Women's Club,
Stone Lake, Wis.

LIVER LOAF

Serves 6 to 8

1 pound beef liver
1 medium onion, quartered
½ pound sausage meat
1 cup bread crumbs
1 teaspoon Worcestershire
1 tablespoon lemon juice
1 teaspoon salt
⅛ teaspoon pepper
1 teaspoon celery salt
2 eggs, lightly beaten
4 slices bacon

1. Preheat oven to 350° F. Grease 10-inch loaf pan.

2. Put liver in saucepan; add water to cover. Bring to boil; cover; simmer for 5 minutes. Drain; reserve ½ cup liquid.

3. Put liver and onion through medium blade of meat grinder; turn into mixing bowl. Add all remaining ingredients except bacon; mix well. Pack into pan; cover with bacon.

4. Bake in preheated oven for 45 minutes.

5. Let stand for 10 minutes before removing from pan.

Berks County Federation of Women's Clubs, Pa.

Sweetbreads

Like brains, sweetbreads should be kept cold and cooked and eaten as soon as possible. Veal and lamb sweetbreads are the most desirable sweetbreads and, when correctly cooked, are splendid delicacies. Before cooking them, soak them in several changes of cold water for at least 1 hour to draw out any blood. Then parboil them in seasoned water for about 15 minutes, and plunge them into cold water (preferably ice water) to firm the tissue so they may be handled easily. The covering membrane and connecting tubes must be removed before the sweetbreads are baked, broiled, sautéed, braised or creamed.

BAKED SWEETBREADS

Serves 4

1 quart boiling water
1 teaspoon salt
1 tablespoon vinegar
1 pound sweetbreads
Sliced bacon
¼ cup melted butter
3 tablespoons dry sherry

1. Put water, salt and vinegar in large saucepan. Bring to boil; add sweetbreads. Cover; simmer for 20 minutes.

2. Drain; plunge sweetbreads into cold water. Remove membrane and tubes.

3. Preheat oven to 325° F. Grease 1-quart casserole.

4. Cut sweetbreads into uniform pieces; wrap each in bacon slice.

5. Put butter in casserole; arrange sweetbreads on top. Sprinkle with sherry.

6. Bake in preheated oven for 40 minutes.

Dale Carstens, Junior Woman's Club,
Glastonbury, Conn.

BROILED SWEETBREADS

Serves 4

1 pound sweetbreads
Salt
1 teaspoon vinegar
Pepper
¼ cup butter or margarine

1. Soak sweetbreads in cold water to cover with 1 teaspoon salt for 1 hour. Drain.

2. In saucepan bring 1 quart water, 1 teaspoon salt and vinegar to boil. Add sweetbreads; simmer for 20 minutes. Drain; cool; remove membrane and tubes.

3. Preheat broiler. Line broiler pan with aluminum foil.

4. Cut sweetbreads into slices; arrange on foil. Sprinkle with salt and pepper; dot with butter.

5. Broil 4 to 5 inches from heat for 3 minutes. Turn; broil for 2 minutes longer. Arrange on serving dish.

Laura Phillips, Woman's Club, Bangor, Pa.

CREAMED SWEETBREADS

Serves 4

1 quart water
1 tablespoon vinegar
1 slice lemon
Salt
1 bay leaf
¼ teaspoon peppercorns
1 pound sweetbreads
2 tablespoons butter
¼ cup presifted flour
Pepper to taste
1 egg, lightly beaten
1 teaspoon lemon juice
4 slices buttered toast

1. In saucepan combine water, vinegar, lemon slice, 1 teaspoon salt, bay leaf and peppercorns. Bring to boil; add sweetbreads. Cover; simmer for 20 minutes. Drain; reserve 2 cups liquid.

2. Plunge sweetbreads into cold water; remove membrane and tubes. Dice sweetbreads; set aside.

3. Melt butter in saucepan. Stir in flour. Gradually stir in reserved liquid; cook over low heat, stirring constantly, until sauce is thickened and smooth.

4. Season with salt and pepper; stir in egg. Cook over low heat, stirring constantly, for 2 minutes longer. Stir in lemon juice and sweetbreads; heat to serving temperature.

5. Serve on toast.

Laura Van Ness, Woman's Club, Sebring, Fla.

SWEETBREAD CROQUETTES

Serves 6

1 pound sweetbreads, cooked
Salt and pepper to taste
1 tablespoon finely chopped
cooked ham
4 eggs
¼ cup Thick White Sauce (p. 441)
¼ cup finely chopped mushrooms
1 cup cracker crumbs
Fat for deep frying
Mushroom Sauce (p. 447)
Five-Minute Tomato Sauce
(p. 450)

1. Remove membrane and tubes from sweetbreads. Chop finely; season well with salt and pepper.

2. Turn into saucepan; add ham, 2 of the eggs, Thick White Sauce and mushrooms. Mix well; cook over medium heat, stirring constantly, for 2 minutes. Spread on flat plate; cool.

3. With floured fingers, shape mixture into 1½-inch balls. Roll in crumbs; reshape, if necessary.

4. Fry in deep fat heated to 365° F. for 5 minutes, or until golden. Drain on absorbent paper.

5. Serve with Mushroom Sauce or Five-Minute Tomato Sauce.

Meals on Wheels, Woman's Club,
Greenwich, Conn.

SWEETBREADS VERSAILLES

Serves 4 or 5

1 pound sweetbreads
2 tablespoons lemon juice
2 stalks celery with leaves
¼ cup chopped onion
½ teaspoon salt
¼ teaspoon peppercorns
1 tablespoon butter or margarine
10½-ounce can condensed cream of
    mushroom soup
4-ounce can sliced mushrooms,
    drained
¼ cup milk
1 tablespoon dry white wine
¼ teaspoon seasoned salt
Toast points

1. Cover sweetbreads with cold water; soak for 20 minutes. Drain.

2. In large saucepan combine 1 quart water, lemon juice, celery, onion, salt and peppercorns. Bring to boil; add sweetbreads. Cover; simmer for 20 minutes. Drain; remove membrane and tubes. Cut sweetbreads into large chunks.

3. Melt butter in saucepan; sauté sweetbreads for 5 minutes. Stir in soup, mushrooms, milk, wine and seasoned salt. Cook over medium heat, stirring constantly, until smooth and bubbling.

4. Serve on toast points.

Mrs. William J. Lochhead, Woman's Club,
Wilmette, Ill.

Tongue

Beef, lamb, pork and veal tongue are delicious when properly prepared. Tongue must be braised or simmered over low heat to make it tender. When fork-tender, the tongue is removed from the water, the thick covering skin removed and the gristly part at the root end discarded.

BEEF TONGUE

Serves 6

1 fresh beef tongue
2 quarts boiling salted water or
    to cover
2 tablespoons salt
4 black peppercorns
12 white peppercorns
2 cloves
2 bay leaves
2 carrots, sliced
2 small onions, sliced
Tomatoes and parsley

1. Put tongue in kettle with water. Add salt, peppercorns, cloves, bay leaves, carrots and onions. Cover; simmer for 2½ hours, or until tender.

2. Remove tongue from broth. Remove skin and gristle at end.

3. Slice; arrange on serving platter. Garnish with tomatoes and parsley.

Mrs. Myron G. Johnson, Woman's Club,
Stromburg, Neb.

JELLIED NEAT'S TONGUE
(Boiled Smoked Tongue)

Serves 8 to 10

3½-pound smoked beef tongue
1 envelope gelatin
10½-ounce can jellied consommé

1. Day before, put tongue in large saucepan; add water to cover. Cover; simmer for about 3½ hours (allowing 1 hour per pound). Cool in liquid.

2. Remove skin and gristle; place tongue in bowl just large enough to hold it in circular shape.

3. In small saucepan soften gelatin in ½ cup water; cook over low heat, stirring, until dissolved. Stir into consommé.

4. Pour consommé over tongue; cover with plate; weight down. Refrigerate overnight.

5. Next day, unmold tongue; cut into thin slices to serve.

Elizabeth Ellis, Woman's Club, Durham, N.H.

BAKED TONGUE

Serves 6 to 8

3- or 4-pound smoked beef tongue
½ cup butter
1 cup chopped celery
1 cup chopped onions
1 cup diced carrots
⅓ cup presifted flour
¼ cup chopped parsley
1-pound 4-ounce can tomatoes,
    undrained
1 tablespoon Worcestershire
Salt and pepper to taste

1. Put tongue in Dutch oven or heavy saucepan; cover with boiling water. Cover; simmer for 2 hours. Drain; reserve 2 cups liquid.

2. Preheat oven to 325° F.

3. Skin tongue; arrange in shallow roasting pan.

4. Melt butter in skillet; sauté celery, onions and carrots for 5 minutes. Sprinkle with flour; gradually stir in reserved liquid. Cook over medium heat, stirring constantly, until sauce is thickened.

5. Remove from heat; stir in parsley, tomatoes and Worcestershire. Season with salt and pepper; pour over tongue.

6. Bake in preheated oven for 2 hours, basting occasionally with sauce.

Mrs. George D. Stevens, Woman's Club,
Wilmette, Ill.

BRAISED BEEF TONGUE

Serves 6

1 fresh beef tongue
2 carrots, diced
½ cup chopped onions
½ cup diced celery
¼ cup butter or margarine
¼ cup presifted flour
1-pound 4-ounce can stewed
    tomatoes
1 teaspoon Worcestershire
Salt and pepper to taste

1. Put tongue in Dutch oven or heavy saucepan; cover with boiling water. Cover; simmer for 3½ hours. Drain; reserve 2 cups liquid.
2. Cool tongue; remove skin and gristle.
3. Preheat oven to 300° F. Grease 11 x 7 x 1½-inch baking pan.
4. Put tongue in pan; surround with carrots, onions and celery.
5. Melt butter or margarine in saucepan; brown flour over medium heat, stirring frequently. Gradually stir in reserved liquid. Cook over medium heat, stirring constantly, until thickened and smooth.
6. Stir in tomatoes and Worcestershire; season with salt and pepper. Bring to boil; pour over tongue and vegetables.
7. Cover pan with aluminum foil; bake in preheated oven for 3 hours.

Mrs. Harold L. Stover, Woman's Club,
Ogunquit, Me.

Game

Deer (venison), moose, antelope and other game are still abundant in many states, and the meat from young animals may be cooked by any method suitable for beef. The choice cuts are frequently roasted or barbecued, and the less tender cuts are made into delicious stews and casseroles. Usually the meat from wild animals is marinated before cooking to remove any strong flavors and to ensure that the meat will be tender.

Dressed rabbits and squirrels may be cooked by any method suitable for chicken.

ANTELOPE STEAK SUPREME

Serves 6

3 medium ¾-inch-thick antelope
    round steaks
2 teaspoons salt
¼ cup vinegar
1 bay leaf (optional)
1 clove garlic, minced
Dash of black pepper
Dash of garlic salt
Flour
2 to 3 tablespoons cooking oil
10½-ounce can condensed cream
    of chicken or mushroom soup
1 soup can water

1. Put steaks in shallow pan with water to cover. Add salt, vinegar, bay leaf and garlic. Soak for 2 to 3 hours if meat has been processed and frozen. Soak longer is freshly slaughtered.
2. Remove steaks; drain. Sprinkle with pepper and garlic salt; dredge in flour.
3. Heat oil in skillet; brown steaks on both sides. Cover; simmer for 45 minutes, or until fairly tender, turning occasionally.
4. Add soup and water. Cover; simmer for 15 to 20 minutes.

Mrs. Oscar Dobbs, Anne Hutchinson
Study Club of Dora, Cordova, Ala.

MOOSE STEAK

Serves 2

2 tablespoons butter
½ cup finely chopped onions
1½-pound moose steak
2 tablespoons flour
½ cup sour cream
1 cup chopped mushrooms

1. Melt butter in large skillet; sauté onions for 5 minutes.
2. Turn heat to high; add steak to skillet; sear quickly on both sides. Cover; cook over low heat for 30 minutes.
3. Blend flour and sour cream in small bowl; add along with mushrooms to skillet; cover; simmer for 20 minutes longer, stirring occasionally.

Wilton Manors Women's Club,
Fort Lauderdale, Fla.

BRAISED MOOSE

Serves 8 to 12

4- to 6-pound moose roast
Salt pork, cut into strips
Claret or any other red wine
Salt
Pepper
Dash of cinnamon
Dash of ground cloves
1 bay leaf
1 small onion, sliced
Tart jelly

1. Day before, wipe roast with damp cloth.
2. Dip pork in wine; arrange on roast; tie in place. Sprinkle with salt, pepper, cinnamon and cloves; place in china bowl or crock. Partially cover with wine; refrigerate for at least 24 hours, turning occasionally.
3. Next day, preheat oven to 300° F.
4. Remove meat; reserve marinade. Brown meat well on all sides in heavy skillet or casserole over high heat, keeping track of cooking time.
5. Remove from heat; add ½ cup of the reserved marinade; bake in preheated oven for a total browning and baking time of 45 minutes per pound.
6. When half cooked, add 1 teaspoon salt, ½ teaspoon pepper, bay leaf, onion and a little more marinade.
7. Slice; serve with pan gravy and jelly.

Betty K. Batty, Woman's Club, Anchorage, Alaska

VENISON

VENISON STEAKS should be cut ¾ inch thick and may be broiled or fried. They may be served with brown gravy, but most people prefer a currant jelly sauce.

ROAST VENISON: The saddle or leg is best for roasting. Roast 10 minutes to the pound in the same way as you would roast lamb. Make a rich brown gravy, using pan drippings and stock made from the trimmings of the roast. Serve with currant or wild plum jelly.

Mrs. John Meyers, Woman's Literary Club,
Pingree, N.D.

VENISON ROAST

Serves 8 to 10

4-pound venison roast
1 teaspoon salt
1 teaspoon black pepper
1 envelope onion soup mix
10½-ounce can condensed cream of
    mushroom soup
½ cup water

1. Preheat oven to 350° F. Place large square of heavy aluminum foil in roasting pan.
2. Rub roast with salt and pepper. Arrange in center of foil. Sprinkle soup mix over meat; top with soup and water. Seal meat in foil, folding up sides to form package.
3. Roast in preheated oven for 3 hours, or until tender.

Mrs. H. S. Poole, President, W.S.C.S.,
Hartford, Ala.

VENISON POT ROAST

Serves 12

4- to 5-pound venison roast
2 teaspoons salt
½ teaspoon pepper
¼ cup presifted flour
¼ cup shortening
1½ cups chopped onions
12 potatoes, peeled
12 carrots

1. Day before, immediately after deer is dressed, place roast in salted water; soak overnight to remove strong taste or odor. (Meat may then be frozen, if desired.)
2. Rub salt, pepper and flour into meat.
3. Melt shortening in Dutch oven or heavy kettle; brown roast well on all sides. Add onions; sauté for 5 minutes. Stir in 1 cup water. Cover; simmer for about 3 hours, adding water, if necessary.
4. Meanwhile, put potatoes and carrots in saucepan. Add 2 cups boiling salted water; cook for 10 minutes. Drain well.
5. After roast has been cooking for 3 hours, add potatoes and carrots; cook for 1 hour longer, or until meat is fork-tender.

Mrs. Paul Weitman, Effingham County
Extension Clerk, Springfield, Ga.

BRAISED VENISON

Serves 4

1½ pounds shoulder or rump of
    venison, cubed
4 tablepoons flour
2 tablespoons cooking oil
2 medium onions, finely chopped
½ teaspoon thyme
½ teaspoon salt
½ teaspoon pepper
½ 6-ounce can tomato paste
2 cups beef broth
1 teaspoon chili powder
1 bay leaf
4-ounce can button or sliced
    mushrooms, drained

1. Preheat oven to 325° F.
2. Roll venison in flour. Heat oil in heavy kettle or Dutch oven; brown meat well. Add onions, thyme, salt and pepper; cook until onions are limp. Add tomato paste, broth, chili powder and bay leaf; mix well. Cover; cook in preheated oven for 1 hour, or until almost tender.
3. Add mushrooms; cover; cook for 30 minutes longer.

Mrs. William F. Allen, Women's Civic Club,
Visalia, Calif.

VENISON STEAK

Serves 4 or 5

2-pound venison steak
½ cup vinegar
1 cup water
¼ cup presifted flour
1 teaspoon salt
¼ teaspoon black pepper
½ teaspoon garlic salt
¼ cup shortening

1. Pound steak until tender. Put in bowl; cover with vinegar and water. Soak for 1 hour to draw out blood. Drain; dry.
2. On piece of waxed paper mix flour, salt, pepper and garlic salt; use to coat steak.
3. Heat shortening in large skillet; cook steak over medium heat until browned on both sides and tender.

Mrs. Mack Park, President, Green Thumb
Garden Club, Sylvester, Ga.

CASSEROLE OF VENISON STEAKS

Serves 4

4 venison steaks
    Salt and pepper to taste
    Thyme
    Marjoram
    Garlic powder
1 egg, lightly beaten
    Cornflake crumbs
2 tablespoons fat or shortening
1 medium onion, sliced
½ cup catsup
½ cup boiling water
1 teaspoon Worcestershire

1. Preheat oven to 325° F.
2. Rub steaks with salt, pepper, thyme, marjoram and garlic powder. Dip in egg; roll in crumbs.

3. Heat fat or shortening in skillet; brown steaks on both sides over high heat.

4. Put steaks in casserole. Add remaining ingredients; cover; bake in preheated oven for 1½ hours, or until tender.

Mrs. Perry W. Birdwell, Woman's Club,
Coalinga, Calif.

VENISON STEW

Serves 8

2 pounds venison stewing meat, cut into 2-inch cubes
1 cup water
1 red pepper
1 large onion, chopped
1 teaspoon salt
3 tablespoons bacon drippings or shortening
2 tablespoons flour
2 cups tomato juice
1 tablespoon Worcestershire

1. Put meat, water and red pepper in Dutch oven or heavy kettle. Cover; simmer for about 2 hours, or until tender. Add onion and salt; continue cooking.

2. Melt bacon drippings or shortening in skillet; add flour; stir over low heat until browned. Gradually stir in tomato juice and Worcestershire; cook over low heat, stirring constantly, until thickened and smooth.

3. Pour over meat. Cover; simmer for 1 hour.

Mrs. Thomas L. Smith, President, Cairo W.S.C.S.,
Athens, Ala.

VENISON TERIYAKI

Serves 2 or 3

Venison
¼ cup soy sauce
1 tablespoon brown sugar
1 tablespoon minced onion
1 tablespoon wine vinegar
½ teaspoon powdered ginger or grated ginger root
Dash of garlic powder (optional)
2 tablespoons bacon drippings
2 or 3 medium onions, sliced
1 teaspoon cornstarch
Chinese noodles or cooked rice

1. Trim enough venison meat to serve 2 or 3. Cut into thin strips. (Even tough cuts may be used when cooked this way.)

2. Combine soy sauce, sugar, minced onion, vinegar, ginger and garlic powder, if desired. Pour over meat; let stand for 2 hours. Drain; reserve marinade.

3. Melt bacon drippings in heavy skillet. Brown meat on all sides. Add sliced onions; cover; cook over low heat for 15 minutes, or until onions are tender.

4. Mix cornstarch with reserved marinade; pour over meat and onions; and cook until slightly thickened.

5. Serve with Chinese noodles or rice.

Mrs. Glenn K. Rogers, President, Wyoming
Federation of Women's Clubs, Cheyenne, Wyo.

VENISON CHILI WITH BEANS

Serves 12

3 tablespoons shortening
4 pounds ground venison
2 large onions, chopped
3 cloves garlic, crushed
3 tablespoons chili powder
1 teaspoon salt
½ teaspoon seasoned salt
1 tablespoon Worcestershire
1-pound 13-ounce can whole tomatoes, undrained
1-pound 4-ounce can stewed tomatoes, undrained
1-pound 13-ounce can kidney beans, undrained

1. Melt shortening in Dutch oven or heavy kettle; sauté venison, onions and garlic until meat is well browned, stirring frequently.

2. Stir in chili powder, salt, seasoned salt and Worcestershire. Add whole and stewed tomatoes and beans. Bring to boil; cover; simmer, stirring occasionally, for 2 hours.

Mrs. Ted Kohl, Junior Woman's Club,
Coronado, Calif.

VENISON MEAT BALLS IN SAUCE

Serves 8

1½ pounds ground venison
2 cups grated potatoes
⅔ cup chopped onions
1½ teaspoons salt
¼ teaspoon pepper
¼ cup milk
1 egg
¼ cup butter or margarine
3 cups water
3 tablespoons flour
2 cups sour cream
1 teaspoon dillweed
10-ounce package frozen peas, cooked

1. In mixing bowl combine venison, potatoes, onions, salt, pepper, milk and egg. Mix well; shape into 1½-inch balls.

2. Melt butter or margarine in large skillet; brown meat balls slowly on all sides.

3. Add ½ cup of the water. Cover; simmer for 20 minutes. Remove meat balls; keep in warm place.

4. Blend flour with ½ cup of the water in small bowl; stir into liquid in skillet along with remaining water. Cook over low heat, stirring constantly, until thickened and smooth.

5. Boil over high heat until sauce is reduced by about one-third. Reduce heat; slowly stir in sour cream and dillweed.

6. Add meat balls and peas; bring to serving temperature, but do not boil.

Mrs. Tristem Tyler, President, Magnolia
Study Club, Monroe, La.

VENISON LOAF

Serves 8 to 10

1½ cups fresh bread crumbs
½ cup beef or venison broth
2½ pounds ground venison
1 pound sausage meat
2 eggs
2 teaspoons salt
1 teaspoon pepper
¼ cup Worcestershire
1½ cups finely chopped onions

1. Preheat oven to 400° F. Grease 9-inch loaf pan.
2. In mixing bowl soak crumbs in broth for 10 minutes.
3. Add remaining ingredients; mix well. Turn into pan; bake in preheated oven for 1 hour.

Mrs. John H. Woolsey, President,
Riverdale H.D.C., Grenada, Miss.

RABBIT BAKED IN SOUR CREAM

Serves 4

1½-pound rabbit, quartered
Salt and pepper to taste
8 slices bacon
¼ cup melted butter or margarine
1½ tablespoons flour
1 cup sour cream
1 cup water
2 tablespoons lemon juice

1. Preheat oven to 475° F. Grease 2-quart casserole.
2. Season rabbit with salt and pepper; arrange in casserole. Top with bacon; bake in preheated oven for 25 minutes.
3. Turn temperature to 350° F.; sprinkle butter or margarine over rabbit; bake for 25 minutes longer.
4. Meanwhile, in bowl blend flour into sour cream. Stir in water and lemon juice.
5. Pour over rabbit; bake for 20 minutes longer, stirring sauce occasionally.

Peggy Bussard, Leota Club, Englewood, Colo.

RABBIT CREOLE STYLE

Serves 4

1 rabbit, cut into serving pieces
½ cup white wine
1 large onion, sliced
¼ teaspoon thyme
2 bay leaves
½ teaspoon nutmeg
Salt
1 tablespoon butter
12 small onions
2 tablespoons minced ham
2 tablespoons flour
3 tomatoes, peeled and chopped
2 cups beef consommé
½ cup red wine
Pepper to taste

1. Put rabbit in stone crock; add white wine, sliced onion, thyme, bay leaves, nutmeg and 1 tablespoon salt. Marinate for 6 hours or overnight.
2. Melt butter in saucepan; brown meat with small onions and ham. Stir in flour; cook until browned. Add tomatoes; cook for 10 minutes.

3. Add consommé and red wine; bring to boil, stirring. Correct seasoning; cook for 45 minutes longer.

Mrs. W. A. Parry, Jr., Woman's Club,
Anchorage, Alaska

RABBIT DE LUXE

Serves 6

5 tablespoons butter
1 rabbit, cut into serving pieces
2 to 4 ounces rye whiskey
1 tablespoon flour
1½ cups white wine
Salt and pepper to taste
1 tablespoon Worcestershire
Pinch of thyme
Bouquet of parsley (about size of carnation)
1 bay leaf
10 pitted green olives
10 small white onions
2 cloves garlic, crushed
Chicken broth
2 slices bacon, cooked and diced
¼ pound small mushrooms

1. Melt 4 tablespoons of the butter in saucepan. Brown rabbit on all sides.
2. Add whiskey, ignite. When flame burns out, set aside.
3. In another saucepan blend remaining butter and flour. Stir in wine; cook, stirring, until sauce is slightly thickened. Add salt, pepper, Worcestershire, thyme, parsley, bay leaf, olives, onions and garlic.
4. Pour sauce over rabbit. If it is not enough to cover, add broth. Cover; cook over medium heat for 30 minutes.
5. Add bacon; cook over low heat for 30 minutes longer. Add mushrooms; heat to serving temperature.

Betty Lombert, Women's Club,
Arroyo Grande, Calif.

HASENPFEFFER (Rabbit)

Serves 4

1 rabbit, cut into serving pieces
Vinegar and water
1 onion, sliced
1 teaspoon salt
6 peppercorns
1 bay leaf
Flour
Bacon drippings

1. Day before, put rabbit in stone crock or bowl; cover with equal parts vinegar and water. Add onion, salt, peppercorns and bay leaf. Refrigerate for at least 24 hours. (In Germany meat is marinated for 2 to 3 days.)
2. Next day, preheat oven to 325° F.
3. Remove meat; dry well. Roll in flour. Heat a little bacon drippings in heavy kettle or Dutch oven; brown meat.
4. Cover; cook in preheated oven for about 1 hour, or until very tender, adding a little water or broth if meat becomes too dry.

Mrs. Charles Bloodworth, Monday Study Club,
Poplar Bluffs, Mo.

HUNTER'S RABBIT

Serves 6

2 1-pound rabbits, cut into serving
  pieces
¼ cup presifted flour
2 tablespoons olive oil
1½ teaspoons salt
¼ teaspoon pepper
1½ cups dry white wine
1½ cups water
1 clove garlic
1 large onion, sliced
½ pound mushrooms, sliced
2 large tomatoes, peeled and sliced

1. Coat rabbits with flour.

2. Heat oil in large skillet; brown meat well on all sides. Sprinkle with salt and pepper; add wine and water. Bring to boil; add garlic and onion. Cover; simmer for 30 minutes.

3. Stir in mushrooms and tomatoes; cover; simmer for 30 minutes longer, or until meat is tender. Discard garlic before serving.

Mrs. Lois Shapiro, Junior Women's Club,
Fairview, Ill.

BAKED SQUIRREL

Serves 4

4 squirrels
  Flour
2 tablespoons butter or margarine
10½-ounce can condensed beef
  consommé
2 tablespoons Worcestershire
2 tablespoons chopped parsley
1 small onion, minced
1 clove garlic, minced
1 bay leaf
  Salt and pepper to taste

1. Preheat oven to 350° F.

2. Dredge squirrels in flour. Melt butter or margarine in roasting pan; brown meat well on all sides. Add remaining ingredients.

3. Bake in preheated oven for 45 minutes.

4. Turn temperature to 275° F. Bake for 45 minutes longer, or until tender.

A. S.

11. Vegetables

✿✿✿✿✿✿✿✿✿✿✿✿✿✿✿✿✿✿✿✿✿✿✿

It is just as easy to cook vegetables correctly as it is to overcook them to a lifeless mush. Whether you boil, steam or braise vegetables, they should be cooked as short a time as possible to be just fork-tender. If canned, heat gently.

To keep green vegetables green, do not cover; otherwise the best way to cook most vegetables is in a heavy saucepan with a tight-fitting lid. Only a small quantity of liquid—water, chicken broth, milk or tomato juice—is needed; the addition of a chunk of butter will keep vegetables from sticking. Cook tightly covered, so that the vegetables steam in their own juices until just crisply tender. Add salt or seasoned salt, pepper and a little monosodium glutamate, if desired. Sprinkle with chopped parsley, chives or sliced green onion tops.

Almost any partially cooked vegetable may be dipped in batter and deep-fried. When a variety of fried vegetables is served, the dish is known as *fritto misto*, mixed fry. The vegetables are often combined with deep-fried fish strips, shrimp or chicken livers.

Frying Batter for Vegetables

BASIC BATTER FOR FRYING VEGETABLES (FRITTER BATTER)
Makes About 2 Cups

Use to coat onion rings, eggplant, zucchini, etc. Then fry in hot deep fat.

  1¼ cups presifted flour
  1 teaspoon salt
  2 tablespoons shortening
  2 eggs, lightly beaten
  1 cup milk

1. Into mixing bowl sift together flour and salt. Cut in shortening until mixture resembles fine crumbs.
2. Add eggs and milk; beat until smooth.

Junior Women's Club, Riverside, N.J.

BEER BATTER FOR VEGETABLES
Makes About 2 Cups

  1¼ cups presifted flour
  1 teaspoon salt
  2 tablespoons shortening
  1 egg, lightly beaten
  1 cup stale beer

1. Into mixing bowl sift together flour and salt. Cut in shortening until mixture resembles fine crumbs.
2. Add egg and beer; beat until smooth.

Mrs. Jack Thomas, Golfview Hills Woman's Club,
Hinsdale, Ill.

Artichokes

The French artichoke is one of the most delicious of all vegetables. Artichokes range from 1 to 4 or 5 inches in diameter; the medium ones are best for serving whole, one to a person, either hot or cold. To eat an artichoke, pull the leaves from the head, one by one, and dip the tender nutty base of the leaf in hot melted butter, mayonnaise or Sauce Vinaigrette (p. 542). Finally, the heart, the most delicate and succulent part of the artichoke, is reached. The fuzzy hairs covering the surface of the artichoke base, known as the choke, should be discarded. Cut the bottom into bite-size pieces; dip them, with a fork, into the sauce or butter.

TO PREPARE AN ARTICHOKE

Wash the artichoke. With scissors or a heavy knife, cut off and discard the upper third of the leaves. Pull off and discard the outer tough leaves around the base. Trim the stalk to about ½ inch in length.

TO REMOVE THE CHOKE FROM A RAW ARTICHOKE

With the fingers, open the leaves of the artichoke from the center out. Pull out the yellowish leaves from the center. Then, with a teaspoon or melon ball cutter, scrape and pull out the fuzzy portion from the heart. Sprinkle the smooth bottom with lemon juice to keep it from darkening.

BOILED ARTICHOKES
Serves 4

  4 medium artichokes, ready to cook
  2 teaspoons salt
  Juice of 1 lemon
  Favorite sauce

1. Drop artichokes into a little boiling water; add salt and lemon juice.

383

2. Bring back to boil; cover; simmer for 40 minutes, or until an inner leaf pulls out easily from heart.

3. Serve hot or cold with sauce.

A. S.

BOILED ARTICHOKES ITALIAN STYLE

Serves 4

4 artichokes
4 small cloves garlic
4 tablespoons olive oil
Salt and pepper to taste

1. Cut off artichoke stems and about 1 inch off tops so that both bottom and top are flat. Place 1 garlic clove deep in center of each heart.

2. Arrange artichokes, upright compactly in a pot. Pour 1 tablespoon of the oil into center of each; sprinkle with salt and pepper.

3. Add 1 inch water; bring to boil. Cover; steam for about 45 minutes, or until tender.

4. Serve with or without dressing.

*S. M. Ferreira, Women's Club,
Arroyo Grande, Cailf.*

DEEP-FRIED ARTICHOKES

Serves 4 to 6

2 10-ounce packages frozen
artichoke hearts, defrosted
3 eggs
¼ cup presifted flour
1 teaspoon salt
⅛ teaspoon pepper
Fat for deep frying

1. Separate artichoke hearts.

2. Prepare batter: In mixing bowl beat eggs, flour, salt and pepper until smooth.

3. Dip artichokes in batter; coat completely.

4. Fry in deep fat heated to 365° F. for 5 to 6 minutes, or until golden brown.

5. Drain on absorbent paper.

*Marianne Tortora, Junior Woman's Club,
Glastonbury, Conn.*

ARTICHOKES SICILIAN STYLE

Serves 4

4 artichokes
½ small onion, chopped
1 tablespoon chopped parsley
2 tablespoons grated Romano
cheese
1 clove garlic, crushed
1 cup fresh bread crumbs
½ teaspoon salt
½ teaspoon pepper
Olive oil

1. Preheat oven to 325° F.

2. Cut off artichoke stalks and tips. Discard tough outer leaves. Spread open remaining leaves. Remove chokes.

3. Prepare filling: In mixing bowl combine onion, parsley, cheese, garlic, crumbs, salt, pepper, ¼ cup oil and 2 tablespoons water; mix well.

4. Place a little filling in center of each leaf and in center of each artichoke.

5. Arrange artichokes in shallow baking dish; sprinkle with a little oil. Pour a little water in bottom.

6. Bake in preheated oven for 45 minutes, or until bottoms of artichokes are fork-tender.

*Mrs. Joseph Di Benedetto, Women's Auxiliary to
the Chiropractic Association of New York,
New York, N.Y.*

ARTICHOKES AL FORNO
(with Peas)

Serves 4 to 6

2 10-ounce packages frozen artichoke
hearts, defrosted
1 cup frozen peas
1½ teaspoons salt
¼ teaspoon pepper
1 cup bread crumbs
½ cup grated Mozzarella cheese
½ cup water
⅓ cup butter or cooking oil

1. Preheat oven to 350° F. Grease 1-quart casserole.

2. Arrange artichokes and peas in casserole; sprinkle with salt, pepper and crumbs. Top with cheese; sprinkle water over surface. Dot with butter, or sprinkle with oil.

3. Cover; bake in preheated oven for 30 minutes.

4. Remove cover; bake for 15 minutes longer, or until crusty.

*Marianne Tortora, Junior Woman's Club,
Glastonbury, Conn.*

Jerusalem Artichokes

This tuberous vegetable, whose name derives from the Italian word for sunflower, *girasole* (its leaves and flowers are akin to those of the sunflower), is grown in most parts of the United States. When cooked, it provides an agreeable change from the ubiquitous potato, and it may be served in any way suitable for the white potato.

BOILED JERUSALEM ARTICHOKES

Serves 4 to 6

1½ pounds Jerusalem artichokes
2 tablespoons butter
Salt and pepper to taste
Chopped parsley (optional)

1. Wash artichokes; scrub with soft brush.

2. Put in saucepan; cover with boiling salted water. Bring to boil. Cover; cook for 25 to 30 minutes, or until fork-tender. Do not overcook, or artichokes will toughen.

3. Drain; peel off skin. Mash, slice or rice; season with butter, salt and pepper. Sprinkle with chopped parsley, if desired.

VARIATIONS:

1. Slice; add to creamed sauce.
2. Mash; mold in ring mold.

3. Mash with shredded cheese, form into patties; sauté.

4. Mash; form into balls; deep-fry.

5. Cool; slice or dice; serve as salad with mayonnaise or French Dressing (p. 541).

6. Slice; sauté in butter; season with a little lemon juice or vinegar.

A. S.

BAKED JERUSALEM ARTICHOKES
Serves 4

2 pounds Jerusalem artichokes
2 tablespoons butter or margarine
1 tablespoon brown sugar
1 tablespoon orange juice
2 teaspoons grated orange rind
½ teaspoon nutmeg

1. Preheat oven to 350° F. Grease 1½ quart casserole.

2. Scrub and trim artichokes; cook in boiling salted water until just tender. Drain.

3. Cut artichokes in half lengthwise; arrange in casserole. Dot with butter or margarine; sprinkle with remaining ingredients.

4. Bake in preheated oven for 20 minutes.

Marguerite Green, Pine River Pow Wow Club, Bayfield, Colo.

Asparagus

Fortunately the season for fresh asparagus gets longer every year, and when it is in season, it should be enjoyed as often as possible. Buy only crisp-looking green stalks. Limp stems and spreading tips indicate that the asparagus is old and flavorless. Canned or frozen asparagus stalks may be substituted in recipes for fresh; cook according to package directions.

STEAMED ASPARAGUS
Serves 4 to 6

2 pounds asparagus
⅓ cup melted butter
Salt, pepper and lemon juice to taste

1. Cut or snap off lower tough white part of stems. Some people like to peel stalks with vegetable parer; others prefer to leave skin on, feeling it contributes flavor. Either way, stand asparagus tips up in bottom of double saucepan. Tie into serving bundles, if desired. Add boiling water to come halfway up stems. Bring to rapid boil; cover with inverted upper part of double saucepan. Cook over high heat for about 12 minutes, or until fork-tender.

2. Drain. Serve immediately with butter, salt, pepper and lemon juice.

VARIATIONS:

1. Serve with Egg Cream Sauce (p. 441) or Hollandaise Sauce (p. 444).

2. Sauté 1 cup fresh bread crumbs in the butter; pour over cooked asparagus.

3. Cool; serve with French Dressing (p. 541) or Sauce Vinaigrette (p. 542).

4. Dice or slice leftover asparagus; add to Cream Sauce (p. 441) or Cheese Sauce (p. 442).

5. Arrange a thin slice of cooked ham on buttered toast or toasted English muffin; top with a serving of cooked asparagus; serve with Hollandaise Sauce (p. 444). Or sprinkle with shredded cheese; broil until cheese melts and bubbles.

6. Dip cooked stalks in Fritter Batter (p. 383); deep-fry.

A. S.

CHINESE ASPARAGUS
Serves 4

1 bunch asparagus
1 tablespoon olive oil
½ teaspoon salt
½ teaspoon monosodium glutamate
Dash of pepper

1. Clean asparagus.

2. Line up several stalks on cutting board; slice ¼ inch thick, cutting on extreme bias.

3. Heat oil in large skillet. Add asparagus; sprinkle with salt, monosodium glutamate and pepper.

4. Cover; cook over high heat for about 5 minutes, or until just tender, shaking skillet frequently as for popping corn.

Mrs. George Peterson, Golfview Hills Woman's Club, Hinsdale, Ill.

ASPARAGUS DAFFODIL
Serves 4 to 6

8-ounce package cream cheese
2 egg yolks
2 tablespoons lemon juice
⅛ teaspoon salt
2 pounds asparagus, cooked and hot

1. In small saucepan beat cheese until softened and smooth.

2. Add egg yolks, one at a time; beat well after each addition. Stir in lemon juice and salt.

3. Cover; cook over very low heat for 20 minutes. Raise heat slightly; cook for 1 minute, stirring constantly.

4. Arrange asparagus in serving dish; coat with sauce.

Woman's Club, Fort Wayne, Ind.

ASPARAGUS PARMESAN
Serves 6

3 pounds asparagus
1 egg
2 tablespoons dry white wine
½ cup presifted flour
1 cup bread crumbs
1 tablespoon grated Parmesan cheese
¼ teaspoon garlic powder
1 teaspoon salt
Freshly ground black pepper
½ cup olive oil

1. Break off tough ends of asparagus.
2. Beat egg with wine; combine crumbs, cheese, garlic powder, salt and pepper. Blend in egg mixture.
3. Dip stalks in flour, then in egg mixture, then in crumb mixture.
4. Heat oil in skillet; sauté asparagus for 10 minutes, or until tender and golden on all sides.

Century Club Cook Book, Coraopolis, Pa.

ASPARAGUS AMANDINE

Serves 6

1-pound 4-ounce can asparagus
   spears
10½-ounce can condensed cream of
   mushroom soup
½ teaspoon salt
¼ teaspoon pepper
1 cup grated American cheese
1 cup fresh bread crumbs
½ cup blanched almonds
¼ cup butter or margarine

1. Preheat over to 375° F. Grease 10 x 6 x 1½-inch baking pan.
2. Drain asparagus; reserve ½ cup liquid. Arrange asparagus in pan.
3. In bowl blend soup, reserved liquid, salt and pepper. Pour over asparagus; sprinkle with cheese. Sprinkle crumbs and almonds on top; dot with butter or margarine.
4. Bake in preheated oven for 35 minutes.

*Mrs. Bert Wilkes, Jr., Civic Woman's Club,
Picayune, Miss.*

ASPARAGUS CASSEROLE

Serves 6 to 8

10½-ounce can condensed cream of
   mushroom soup
¼ cup milk
¼ cup chopped pimientos
¼ cup slivered almonds
2 1-pound cans asparagus, drained
3 eggs, hard-cooked and sliced
1 cup crushed potato chips

1. Preheat oven to 350° F. Grease 11 x 7 x 1½-inch baking pan.
2. In saucepan blend soup and milk. Stir in pimientos and almonds; bring to boil over medium heat, stirring constantly.
3. Arrange asparagus in casserole; cover with eggs. Pour sauce over eggs and asparagus; sprinkle with potato chips.
4. Bake in preheated oven for 30 minutes.

*Mrs. Heister L. Reese, President,
Missouri Federation of Woman's Clubs*

ESCALLOPED ASPARAGUS

Serves 4

2 1-pound cans cut asparagus or
   4 cups cooked asparagus
6 tablespoons butter
6 tablespoons flour
2 tablespoons chopped onion
2 tablespoons chopped green
   pepper
1 cup milk

4 eggs, hard-cooked and chopped
Bread crumbs

1. Preheat over to 350° F. Grease 1½-quart casserole.
2. Drain asparagus; reserve 1 cup liquid.
3. Melt butter in saucepan over low heat. Add flour; stir until smooth. Add onion and green pepper; stir in milk and reserved asparagus liquid. Cook, stirring constantly, until thickened.
4. Put half the asparagus in casserole; sprinkle with eggs. Add remaining asparagus. Pour sauce over top; stir with fork.
5. Sprinkle with crumbs; bake in preheated oven for 20 to 25 minutes.

*Mrs. W. C. McClellan, Wimodausis Study Club,
Cameron, Mo.*

Avocado

Actually a fruit, not a vegetable, the avocado (sometimes referred to as the alligator pear) deserves mention in this chapter, if only briefly, because it is sometimes served, in place of potatoes or other starchy foods, to accompany chicken or veal. An avocado should never be cooked, but only gently heated to serving temperature, for cooking brings out an undesirable bitter flavor. It is, however, occasionally heated and served in soup and is sometimes halved, filled with creamed chicken or seafood and heated in a moderate oven. It is perhaps best appreciated for its lush buttery flavor in the Mexican dip called Guacamole (p. 72) and is also excellent in salads and molded mousses (see Index).

PURÉE OF AVOCADO

Serves 4

2 just ripe avocados
1 tablespoon lemon juice
1 tablespoon chopped chives or
   minced scallion
Salt and pepper to taste

1. Peel avocado; remove seed. Mash pulp with remaining ingredients.
2. Place in top of double sauce pan; heat over simmering water to serving temperature.

A. S.

ELEANOR'S BAKED AVOCADO
WITH SHRIMP

Serves 4

5 tablespoons butter
3 tablespoons flour
1 cup milk
¼ teaspoon gravy coloring
Salt and pepper to taste
1 cup diced cooked shrimp
2 large avocados
2 tablespoons lemon juice
1 cup fresh bread crumbs
½ cup hot water

1. Preheat over to 375° F.
2. Melt butter in saucepan. Stir in flour. Gradually stir in milk; cook over low heat, stirring constantly, until thickened and smooth.
3. Add gravy coloring; season with salt and pepper. Stir in shrimp; heat to serving temperature.
4. Cut avocados in half lengthwise. Remove seed, but do not peel.
5. Place avocado, cut side up, in shallow baking pan. Sprinkle with lemon juice; fill with shrimp mixture. Sprinkle with crumbs; pour water into bottom.
6. Bake in preheated oven for 20 minutes.

Mrs. J. Russell, Parliamentary Law Club, Glendale, Calif.

Bananas

Delicious eaten uncooked when fully ripe, the banana is a tropical fruit of many uses. It is included in this chapter because it is also excellent when prepared and cooked as a vegetable and served as an accompaniment to meat. Indeed, in Caribbean and South American countries the green banana is commonly regarded as a vegetable to be cooked in a variety of ways. Bananas make admirable dishes—baked, broiled, candied or deep-fried.

The *plantain* is a larger variety of banana that is widely used as a staple food in many tropical areas.

BAKED BANANAS

1 slightly green banana per person
Butter
Salt

1. Preheat oven to 375° F. Grease shallow baking dish.
2. Peel bananas, arrange in dish. Dot with butter; sprinkle lightly with salt.
3. Bake in preheated oven for 15 to 20 minutes, or until tender.

A. S.

BANANAS BAKED IN WINE HAWAIIAN STYLE
Serves 5

5 firm bananas
½ cup brown sugar
¾ teaspoon cinnamon
½ cup sweet white wine

1. Preheat oven to 350° F. Grease 10 x 6 x 1½-inch baking pan.
2. Peel bananas; cut in half lengthwise. Arrange in pan.
3. In small bowl mix sugar and cinnamon; sprinkle over bananas. Pour wine over bananas.
4. Bake in preheated oven for 15 minutes.

Mrs. J. E. Collins, Woman's Club, Ardmore, Pa.

EAST INDIAN CURRIED BANANAS
Serves 6

For something different to serve with baked ham, roast pork or poultry.

½ cup brown sugar
½ cup dry white wine
½ cup orange juice
2 tablespoons lime juice
3 tablespoons melted butter or margarine
¾ teaspoon curry powder
6 firm bananas, peeled

1. Preheat oven to 300° F. Grease 9-inch square baking pan.
2. In mixing bowl combine sugar, wine, orange and lime juice, butter or margarine and curry powder.
3. Arrange bananas side by side in pan. Pour wine mixture over bananas.
4. Bake in preheated oven for 30 to 35 minutes, basting frequently with sauce.

Linda Andes, North Side Junior Woman's Club, Atlanta, Ga.

FRIED BANANAS

Large firm bananas
Orange or lemon juice
Seasoned flour
Butter
Brown or confectioners' sugar

1. Peel bananas; cut in half crosswise and then lengthwise. Sprinkle with orange or lemon juice; roll in flour.
2. Melt butter in skillet; sauté bananas until delicately brown. Sprinkle with sugar.
3. Serve warm or cold.

Belair Women's International Cook Book, Belair, Md.

PLATANUTRI (Fried Plantains)
Serves 6

3 green plantains or bananas
Cooking oil
Salt

1. Peel plantains or bananas; cut on slant into very thin slices.
2. Soak in salted water for 30 minutes. Drain on absorbent paper.
3. Heat a little oil in large skillet; fry plantains, a few slices at a time, until golden on both sides.
4. Drain on absorbent paper; cool. Sprinkle with salt before serving.

Lillian T. de Canais, President, Puerto Rico Federation of Women's Clubs

Beans: For dried beans, see Index.

Snap or String Beans

The name "snap bean" refers to the green string bean or yellow wax bean. Most varieties grown for the market today are practically stringless and need be only trimmed and washed. They may be left whole, halved lengthwise, cut crosswise or slivered on the slant (French-style).

BOILED SNAP BEANS
Serves 4

1 pound snap beans (string or
   wax beans)
Butter
Salt and pepper to taste

1. Trim ends of beans; cut as desired. Cover with boiling water; boil rapidly, uncovered, for 15 to 20 minutes, or until barely tender. Remove any white foam or scum that rises to surface, since this will cause beans to discolor.
2. Drain. Toss with butter, salt and pepper.

VARIATIONS:

1. Add to Cream Sauce (p. 441) or Cheese Sauce (p. 442).
2. Sprinkle with chopped cashew nuts or toasted almonds.
3. Combine with sliced water chestnuts.
4. Add crisp bacon bits and sour cream.
5. Add sautéed mushrooms.
6. Season with orégano, savory, dill or nutmeg.

A. S.

GREEN BEANS
Serves 4 to 6

1 cup water
1 tablespoon vinegar
1 medium onion, finely chopped
2 pounds green beans
½ teaspoon salt
2 tablespoons bacon drippings

1. In saucepan combine water, vinegar and onion. Bring to boil; add beans.
2. Cover; simmer for 10 minutes, or until beans are tender. Add salt and bacon drippings. Cook, uncovered, over high heat for 5 minutes.

Pauline Hern, Woman's Club, Cumberland, Ky.

AUSTRIAN GREEN BEANS
Serves 6 to 8

3 tablespoons butter
¼ cup sugar
¼ teaspoon paprika
½ teaspoon salt
1 tablespoon water
6 cloves
½ lemon, thinly sliced and seeded
½ orange, thinly sliced and seeded
1 unpeeled apple, cored and cubed
1 medium onion, finely diced
2 1-pound cans green beans
1 tablespoon cornstarch

1. In saucepan combine butter, sugar, paprika, salt, water and cloves. Bring to boil; simmer for 3 minutes.
2. Add lemon and orange; simmer for 15 minutes, or until transparent.
3. Stir in apple and onion; simmer for 10 minutes longer, or until onion is tender.
4. Drain beans; reserve 1 tablespoon liquid. Add beans to saucepan.

5. Combine cornstarch and reserved liquid; stir into saucepan. Heat, stirring, until beans are hot.

Mrs. H. R. Beatty, Coterie Woman's Club,
Fort Collins, Colo.

GREEN BEANS AND GERMAN CABBAGE
Serves 4 to 6

3 slices bacon, cut into 1-inch
   pieces
½ cup vinegar
¼ cup sugar
3 tablespoons chopped onion
3 cups shredded cabbage
¾ teaspoon salt
¼ teaspoon pepper
1-pound can green beans, drained

1. Cook bacon in skillet until crisp. Remove bacon; drain on absorbent paper.
2. Add vinegar, sugar, onion, cabbage, salt and pepper to remaining fat in skillet. Cover; simmer for 5 minutes.
3. Stir in beans; cook for 5 minutes.
4. Spoon into serving dishes; top with bacon.

Mrs. L. E. Lapeyrouse, Woman's Club,
Houma, La.

GARLIC GREEN BEANS
Serves 6

⅔ cup cooking oil
½ cup sugar
5 cloves garlic
1 tablespoon salt
3 1-pound cans green beans,
   drained

1. Day before, combine oil, sugar, garlic and salt. Pour over beans; let stand overnight.
2. Next day, heat for 10 minutes before serving.

Mrs. J. W. Thurmon, Cosmos Club, Ruston, La.

HUNGARIAN STRING BEANS
Serves 6

1½ pounds green beans
1½ cups boiling water
½ teaspoon salt
6 slices bacon, chopped
1 onion, finely chopped
2 tablespoons flour
1 tablespoon vinegar
⅔ cup sour cream

1. Trim ends of beans; break into 1-inch lengths. Put in saucepan with water and salt. Bring to boil; cover; simmer for about 25 minutes, or until tender.
2. Meanwhile, cook bacon in skillet until crisp. Add onion; sauté until transparent.
3. Stir in flour. Stir in vinegar. Gradually stir in hot liquid from beans; cook, stirring, until creamy and smooth.
4. Add beans. Stir in sour cream. Cover; let stand for 2 minutes before serving.

Mrs. H. T. Burfield, Junior Civic Woman's Club,
Parkersburg, W. Va.

ITALIAN GREEN BEANS

Serves 3

10-ounce package frozen green
 beans
3 cloves garlic
½ teaspoon salt
⅛ teaspoon pepper
¼ cup red wine vinegar
2 tablespoons olive oil
¼ teaspoon monosodium glutamate
2 eggs, hard-cooked and sliced

1. Cook beans according to package directions. Drain.
2. Meanwhile, prepare Italian sauce: Mash garlic thoroughly with salt, pepper, vinegar, oil and monosodium glutamate. Or put these ingredients in container of electric blender; cover; blend on high speed until smooth.
3. Pour sauce over beans; cover; let stand for 1 hour.
4. Just before serving, heat over low heat. Turn into serving dish; garnish with eggs.

Frankie Polleschultz, Ruth Kelso Renfrow
Art Club, Glendale, Mo.

GREEN BEANS WITH POTATOES IN TOMATO SAUCE

Serves 6

1 tablespoon olive oil
1 clove garlic, crushed
1-pound 13-ounce can tomatoes,
 undrained
1 teaspoon salt
⅛ teaspoon pepper
1 teaspoon parsley flakes
½ teaspoon basil
¼ teaspoon sugar
10-ounce package frozen French-style
 green beans, cooked
1½ cups diced cooked potatoes

1. Heat oil in saucepan; sauté garlic for 5 minutes.
2. Stir in tomatoes, salt, pepper, parsley, basil and sugar. Bring to boil; simmer, uncovered, for 30 minutes.
3. Add beans and potatoes; cover; simmer for 15 minutes.

Bette Jane Camagna, Junior Woman's Club,
Springfield, Pa.

GREEN BEANS AMANDINE

Serves 6 to 8

2 10-ounce packages frozen
 French-style green beans
½ cup butter or margarine
¾ cup slivered almonds
2 tablespoons chopped parsley
1 cup finely chopped onions
1 cup finely chopped celery
1 grated carrot
½ cup condensed cream of
 mushroom soup
Buttered bread crumbs

1. Preheat oven to 350° F. Grease 1½-quart casserole.
2. Cook beans according to package directions until almost tender. Drain; set aside.

3. Melt butter or margarine in skillet; sauté almonds for 5 minutes over low heat. Stir in parsley, onions, celery and carrot; sauté for 5 minutes.
4. Stir in soup and beans. Pour into casserole.
5. Top with crumbs; bake in preheated oven for 30 minutes.

Mrs. H. Talley Brown, President, Woman's Club,
Hinton, W. Va.

GREEN BEANS AND SPROUTS NAPOLI

Serves 8

1 quart brussels sprouts, cleaned
2 1-pound cans French-style green
 beans, undrained
½ cup butter or margarine
½ cup coarsely crumbed day-old
 bread
1 teaspoon paprika
1 cup grated Parmesan cheese
1 tablespoon olive oil
½ teaspoon garlic salt

1. Cook sprouts in 1 inch of boiling salted water for 20 minutes, or until tender.
2. Heat beans.
3. Preheat oven to 450° F. Grease 2½-quart casserole.
4. Melt butter or margarine in small skillet. Add crumbs; stir over moderate heat until golden. Remove from heat; add paprika and cheese; toss lightly until blended.
5. Drain vegetables; toss with oil and garlic salt. Turn into casserole; top with crumb mixture.
6. Bake in preheated oven for 10 minutes.

V. Allison, Woman's Club, Ambridge, Pa.

GREEN BEAN CASSEROLE

Serves 6

10½ ounce can condensed cream of
 mushroom soup
1 teaspoon soy sauce
3½-ounce can French-fried onion
 rings
3 cups cooked French-style green
 beans
Dash of pepper

1. Preheat oven to 350° F.
2. Put soup and soy sauce in 1-quart casserole; stir until smooth.
3. Stir in 1½ cups of the onion rings, green beans and pepper.
4. Bake in preheated oven for 20 minutes. Top with remaining onion rings; bake for 5 minutes longer.

Mrs. Sheldon Fitts, Woman's Club, Marion, Ala.

CHINESE STRING BEANS
Serves 10 to 12
2 4-ounce cans mushrooms, drained
2 5-ounce cans water chestnuts, drained and sliced
4 cups drained bean sprouts
2 10-ounce packages frozen French-style green beans, cooked and drained
2 10½-ounce cans condensed cream of celery soup
½ cup heavy cream
4-ounce package frozen French-fried onion rings

1. Preheat oven to 375° F. Grease 3-quart casserole.
2. In mixing bowl combine mushrooms, water chestnuts, bean sprouts and green beans; toss lightly; turn into casserole.
3. In mixing bowl combine soup and cream; stir to blend. Pour over vegetables; top with onion rings.
4. Bake in preheated oven for 30 minutes.

Mrs. A. W. Engstrom, Coco Plum Woman's Club, Coral Gables, Fla.

DILL GREEN BEANS
Serves 6
2 1-pound cans French-style green beans
1 slice bacon, diced
1 teaspoon dill seed
½ cup butter or margarine
⅓ cup presifted flour
1¼ cups milk
¼ teaspoon Tabasco
1 teaspoon salt
¼ teaspoon pepper

1. Preheat oven to 350° F. Grease 1½-quart casserole.
2. Drain beans; reserve 1 cup liquid.
3. Cook bacon in skillet over medium heat for 5 minutes. Stir in beans and dill seed; cover; simmer for 10 minutes.
4. Meanwhile, melt butter or margarine in saucepan; blend in flour; gradually stir in milk and reserved liquid. Cook, stirring constantly, until thickened and smooth.
5. Add Tabasco, salt, pepper and bean mixture; mix well.
6. Turn into casserole; bake in preheated oven for 30 minutes.

Mrs. William Stewart, Woman's Club, Avondale, Ga.

FAVORITE GREEN BEAN CASSEROLE
Serves 6 to 8
2 tablespoons butter or margarine
2 tablespoons flour
1 teaspoon salt
¼ teaspoon pepper
1 teaspoon sugar
1 teaspoon dehydrated onion flakes
1 cup sour cream
2 1-pound cans French-style green beans, drained

1 cup grated Cheddar cheese
½ cup crushed cornflakes

1. Preheat oven to 350° F. Grease 1½-quart casserole.
2. Melt butter or margarine in medium saucepan; stir in flour, salt, pepper, sugar and onion flakes. Remove from heat.
3. Stir in sour cream and beans. Turn into casserole. Sprinkle with cheese and cornflakes.
4. Bake in preheated oven for 30 minutes.

Mrs. Ralph Pinkerton, President, Y. W. I. Club, Marion, Ind.

GREEN BEAN AND MUSHROOM CASSEROLE
Serves 10 to 12
¼ cup butter or margarine
1 pound mushrooms, sliced
1 medium onion, sliced
¼ cup presifted flour
2 cups milk
1 cup light cream
3 cups grated sharp Cheddar cheese
¼ teaspoon Tabasco
2 teaspoons soy sauce
1 teaspoon salt
½ teaspoon pepper
1 teaspoon monosodium glutamate
3 10-ounce packages frozen French-style green beans
5-ounce can water chestnuts, drained and sliced
¾ cup slivered toasted almonds

1. Preheat oven to 375° F. Grease 3-quart casserole.
2. Melt butter or margarine in saucepan; sauté mushrooms and onion for 5 minutes. Stir in flour; gradually stir in milk and cream; cook, stirring constantly, until thickened and smooth.
3. Stir in cheese, Tabasco, soy sauce, salt, pepper and monosodium glutamate; cook over low heat, stirring frequently, until cheese is melted.
4. Meanwhile, cook beans according to package directions; drain well.
5. Stir beans and water chestnuts into mushroom sauce; pour into casserole. Sprinkle with almonds.
6. Bake in preheated oven for 25 minutes, or until bubbling.

Lillian Wright, Woman's Club, Blandinsville, Ill.

CREAMED GREEN BEANS AND WATER CHESTNUTS
Serves 12
2 4-ounce cans sliced mushrooms
2 4-ounce cans water chestnuts
Milk
½ cup butter or margarine
1 medium onion, chopped
¼ cup presifted flour
⅛ teaspoon Tabasco
2 teaspoons soy sauce
1 teaspoon salt
½ teaspoon pepper
1 teaspoon monosodium glutamate

3 cups grated Cheddar cheese
3 10-ounce packages frozen
French-style green beans

1. Drain mushrooms and water chestnuts; reserve liquids.
2. Add sufficient milk to reserved liquids to total 3 cups.
3. Slice water chestnuts.
4. Melt butter in saucepan; sauté onion and water chestnuts over medium heat for 5 minutes.
5. Sprinkle with flour; gradually stir in reserved liquids. Cook over medium heat, stirring constantly, until sauce is thickened and smooth. Add Tabasco, soy sauce, salt, pepper, monosodium glutamate and cheese. Cook over low heat, stirring frequently, until cheese is melted.
6. Meanwhile, cook beans according to package directions. Drain; add to sauce.
7. Add mushrooms; simmer for 3 minutes.

Jean Henderson, Ruth Kelso Renfrow Art Club,
Glendale, Mo.

SAVORY WAX BEANS

Serves 6

1½ pounds wax beans
¼ cup cooking oil
1 clove garlic, minced
1 tablespoon chopped onion
¾ cup diced green pepper
¼ cup boiling water
1 teaspoon salt
1 teaspoon basil
½ cup grated Parmesan cheese

1. Trim ends of beans; cut into 1-inch pieces, or leave whole.
2. Heat oil and garlic in saucepan. Add onion and green pepper; cook for 3 minutes.
3. Add beans, water, salt and basil. Cover; simmer for about 15 minutes, or until beans are tender.
4. Stir in ¼ cup of the cheese. Turn into serving dish; sprinkle with remaining cheese.

Century Club, Coraopolis, Pa.

PICCADILLY WAX BEANS

Serves 4

1-pound can wax beans
¼ cup cider vinegar
2 tablespoons sugar
½ teaspoon salt
Dash of pepper
1 tablespoon diced pimiento

1. Drain beans; reserve ½ cup liquid.
2. In saucepan combine reserved liquid, vinegar, sugar, salt and pepper; mix well. Add beans and pimiento; let stand for 2 to 3 hours, stirring occasionally.
3. Simmer for a few minutes, or until thoroughly heated.

Ellen Bohannon, Woman's Club,
Temple Terrace, Fla.

Lima or Butter Beans

Lima beans are sold fresh in the pods, canned or dried. For cooking dried Limas, see Index. The frozen shelled Limas are so good and so plentiful that there is little reason for the homemaker to spend time shelling the fresh pods. If you do, cut a thin strip off the inner edge of the pod to make it easier to open; then remove the beans.

BOILED FRESH LIMAS

Serves 4

3 cups freshly shelled Lima beans
1 tablespoon butter
Salt and pepper to taste

1. Put beans in saucepan; cover generously with boiling salted water. Cover; boil over moderate heat for about 30 minutes, or until fork-tender.
2. Drain; return beans to heat. Add butter, salt and pepper; shake over heat until butter is melted.

VARIATIONS:

1. Add ½ cup heavy cream or warm sour cream to drained beans along with butter.
2. Add 1 tablespoon lemon juice and 1 tablespoon chopped chives, parsley or dill along with butter.
3. Combine with Cheese Sauce (p. 442).
4. Add ½ tablespoon flour to melted butter. Gradually stir in ½ cup chicken broth.
5. Cool; sprinkle with minced onion and parsley; marinate for several hours in French Dressing (p. 541) before serving.
6. Add celery, garlic or onion salt.
7. Add slivered tomatoes.
8. Add sautéed mushrooms.

A. S.

SUCCOTASH

Serves 6

2 cups cooked corn kernels
2 cups cooked Lima beans
2 tablespoons butter
Salt and pepper to taste

Combine all ingredients in saucepan. Heat to serving temperature.

VARIATION: Add ¼ cup cream to succotash. Cover; cook over very low heat for 10 minutes.

A. S.

LIMA BEANS IN SOUR CREAM

Serves 3 to 4

10-ounce package frozen Lima beans
2 tablespoons finely chopped onion
2 tablespoons chopped pimiento
2 tablespoon butter
½ cup sour cream
Salt and pepper to taste

1. Cook beans according to package directions; drain.

2. Stir in remaining ingredients.

Jo Ann Arnaud, Junior Solitic Club, Crowley, La.

LIMA BEAN CASSEROLE

Serves 4

10-ounce package frozen Lima beans, cooked and drained
½ cup finely chopped onions
½ teaspoon salt
⅛ teaspoon pepper
2 tablespoons melted butter or margarine
½ cup water
½ cup grated sharp Cheddar cheese
1 large tomato, sliced
2 tablespoons bread crumbs

1. Preheat oven to 375° F. Grease 1-quart casserole.

2. In mixing bowl combine beans, onions, salt, pepper, butter or margarine, water and cheese. Turn into casserole; top with tomato. Sprinkle with crumbs.

3. Bake in preheated oven for 40 minutes.

Bernice Hagedorn, Woman's Club, East Hartford, Conn.

LIMA BEAN AND MUSHROOM CASSEROLE

Serves 4

2 1-pound 4-ounce cans Lima beans
1 cup diced cooked ham
⅓ cup chopped green pepper
⅓ cup chopped onions
1 teaspoon Worcestershire
10½-ounce can condensed cream of mushroom soup
½ cup buttered bread crumbs

1. Preheat oven to 350° F. Grease 1½-quart casserole.

2. Drain beans; reserve ¼ cup liquid.

3. In mixing bowl combine beans, ham, green pepper and onions.

4. In measuring cup blend reserved liquid, Worcestershire and soup. Pour over beans; mix well. Turn into casserole.

5. Sprinkle with crumbs; bake in preheated oven for 35 minutes.

Clara Null, Woman's Club, Blandinsville, Ill.

Beets

Both the roots and the green leaves of garden beets are delicious cooked separately and served separately or combined. Select medium beets that are smooth and firm. Beets lose their color if they are peeled before cooking. They should be cooked in their skins with a couple of inches of stem left on.

BOILED BEETROOTS

Serves 4

8 medium beets
1 tablespoon butter
Salt and pepper to taste

1. Wash beets well; cut off tops, leaving 2 inches of stems. Cover with boiling water. Cover; boil for 30 to 45 minutes, or until fork-tender.

2. Drain; peel. Slice, quarter or chop; return beets to heat.

3. Add butter, salt and pepper; shake over heat until butter is melted.

VARIATIONS:

1. Add a little lemon or orange juice and grated rind. Add to Cream Sauce (p. 441).

2. Add ½ cup warm sour cream and a little lemon juice, vinegar or horseradish.

3. Cool; serve with French Dressing (p. 541).

A. S.

BEET GREENS

Beet greens
Butter
Salt and pepper to taste
Wine vinegar (optional)

1. Wash beet greens. Put in saucepan, using only water that clings to leaves. Cook, stirring occasionally, until wilted and tender.

2. Season with butter, salt and pepper. Add a little wine vinegar, if desired.

A. S.

DEVILED BEETS

Serves 6

3 tablespoons butter or margarine
2 tablespoons prepared mustard
½ teaspoon paprika
1 tablespoon honey
1 teaspoon Worcestershire
3 cups sliced cooked beets

1. Melt butter or margarine in medium saucepan. Stir in mustard, paprika, honey and Worcestershire.

2. Add beets; heat to serving temperature.

Mrs. Lena Aaron, Nautilus Club, DuBois, Pa.

GINGER BEETS

Serves 8

2 cups sugar
6 tablespoons cornstarch
3 teaspoons ginger
3 1-pound cans whole beets
1 cup vinegar
1 tablespoon butter
Dash of salt

1. In saucepan combine sugar, cornstarch and ginger. Drain liquid from beets into saucepan, stirring to mix liquid with sugar mixture. Add vinegar. Bring to boil; cook, stirring constantly, until thickened and clear.

2. Add butter, salt and beets. Heat to serving temperature.

Mrs. M. M. Fortenberry, Maids and Matrons Club, Jackson, Miss.

HARVARD BEETS

Serves 4

1-pound 4-ounce can beets
1 tablespoon cornstarch
½ cup sugar
½ cup cider vinegar
¾ teaspoon salt

1. Drain beets; reserve ½ cup liquid.
2. In saucepan combine cornstarch and sugar. Gradually stir in vinegar, reserved liquid and salt. Cook over medium heat, stirring constantly, until thickened and clear.
3. Add beets; heat to serving temperature.

Evelyn Emmett, Woman's Club, Glen Ellyn, Ill.

YALE BEETS

12 medium beets
2 tablespoons flour
¼ cup sugar
½ teaspoon salt
½ cup orange juice
2 tablespoons butter

1. Preheat oven to 400° F. Grease 1½-quart casserole.
2. Peel beets; slice thinly. Arrange in casserole.
3. Combine flour, sugar and salt. Stir in orange juice; pour over beets. Dot with butter.
4. Cover; bake in preheated oven for 45 minutes.

Mrs. R. F. Watts, Jr., Study Club, Collinsville, Ala.

BEETS IN HONEY SAUCE

Serves 4

1-pound 4-ounce can beets
1 tablespoon cornstarch
½ teaspoon salt
2 tablespoons vinegar
¼ cup honey
1 tablespoon butter

1. Drain beets; reserve 2 tablespoons liquid.
2. In saucepan combine reserved liquid and cornstarch to a smooth paste. Stir in salt, vinegar, honey and butter. Cook over low heat, stirring constantly, until thickened and clear.
3. Remove from heat; stir in beets. Cover; let stand for 10 minutes to allow flavors to blend.
4. Return to heat; heat to serving temperature, stirring occasionally.

Norma Adams, Woman's Club, Lincroft, N.J.

JELLY-GLAZED BEETS

Serves 4

3 cups sliced cooked or canned beets
2 tablespoons vinegar
2 tablespoons water or liquid drained from canned beets
1 tablespoon cooking oil
Dash of cloves
⅛ teaspoon salt
½ cup currant or grape jelly

1. In saucepan combine beets, vinegar, water or beet liquid, oil, cloves and salt. Bring to boil; simmer for 5 minutes.
2. Add jelly; simmer for 10 minutes longer, stirring and basting frequently until nicely glazed.

Mrs. Cornelius Smith, Woman's Club, Azusa, Calif.

BEETS AND RAISINS

Serves 4 to 6

¼ cup vinegar
1 cup sugar
3 tablespoons cornstarch
⅓ cup orange juice
1 tablespoon grated orange rind
1 cup seedless raisins
1-pound 4-ounce can beets, undrained

1. In top of double saucepan blend vinegar, sugar and cornstarch to a smooth paste. Stir in orange juice and rind and raisins. Cook over hot water, stirring constantly, until thickened and smooth.
2. Add beets. Cover; simmer over hot water for 1 hour, stirring occasionally.

Mrs. Glenn Dare, Federated Civic Club,
Mount Vernon, Ill.

SCALLOPED BEETS

Serves 4 to 6

3 cups sliced cooked beets
2 cups Medium White Sauce (p. 441)
½ cup grated Cheddar cheese
½ cup bread crumbs

1. Preheat oven to 375° F. Grease 1½-quart casserole.
2. Arrange beets in casserole; cover with Medium White Sauce. Sprinkle with cheese and crumbs.
3. Bake in preheated oven for 25 minutes.

Ruth B. Hurley, Women's Club, Beloit, Wis.

BEETS IN TURNIP CUPS

Serves 6

6 small white turnips
1 teaspoon lemon juice
1 cup diced cooked beets
¼ cup melted butter
½ teaspoon salt
Dash of pepper
2 tablespoons chopped parsley
2 tablespoons bread crumbs
1 tablespoon grated Parmesan cheese

1. Pare turnips; cook in boiling salted water with lemon juice for 25 minutes, or until just tender.
2. Preheat oven to 400° F. Grease 8-inch square baking pan.
3. Drain turnips; scoop out and chop centers; mix with beets, butter, salt and pepper. Arrange turnips in pan; fill with beet mixture.
4. In small bowl mix parsley, crumbs and cheese; sprinkle on turnips.
5. Bake in preheated oven for 15 minutes.

Mrs. Alice Weiler,
Roosevelt Neighborhood Woman's Club,
Phoenix, Ariz.

Broccoli

Select fresh broccoli with tightly closed flowers and crisp stalks. Stalks with yellowing or fading flowers are old and not worth eating. When fresh broccoli is out of season, frozen broccoli makes a fine substitute.

BOILED BROCCOLI

Serves 4 to 6

1 bunch broccoli
Salt and pepper to taste
⅓ cup melted butter
Lemon wedges

1. Discard tough bottoms of broccoli stems. Slit thicker stalks partially toward flower heads.
2. Soak in salted cold water for 10 minutes. Drain; put in saucepan with 1 inch boiling water. Cover; cook over moderate heat for 10 to 12 minutes, or until tender.
3. Drain; sprinkle with salt and pepper. Serve with butter and lemon wedges.

VARIATIONS:

1. Serve hot with Hollandaise Sauce (p. 444) or Cheese Sauce (p. 442).
2. Serve cold with French Dressing (p. 541), Sauce Vinaigrette (p. 542) or sour cream dressing.
3. Sprinkle with toasted almonds before serving.
4. Serve with fresh bread crumbs browned in the melted butter.
5. Flavor with minced onion, garlic, curry powder or marjoram.

A. S.

CREOLE BROCCOLI

Serves 4 to 6

2 tablespoons butter or margarine
½ cup diced celery
½ cup diced green pepper
¼ cup grated onion
1 teaspoon salt
1 teaspoon sugar
1 cup diced peeled tomatoes
2 10-ounce packages frozen broccoli, defrosted
1 teaspoon cornstarch
2 tablespoons water

1. Melt butter or margarine in large skillet; sauté celery, green pepper and onion for 5 minutes. Stir in salt, sugar and tomatoes; add broccoli. Cover; simmer for 7 minutes, or until broccoli is tender.
2. Arrange broccoli on serving dish; keep in warm place.
3. In small bowl blend cornstarch and water; stir into skillet. Cook over low heat, stirring constantly, until thickened.
4. Spoon sauce over broccoli.

Mrs. Tom Lett, Wednesday Club, Benton, Mo.

BROCCOLI À LA POLONAISE

Serves 2

1 bunch broccoli
½ cup butter

1 cup bread crumbs
1 egg, hard-cooked

1. Prepare broccoli; cook in boiling salted water for 25 minutes. Drain.
2. Melt butter in skillet; sauté crumbs and egg until butter and crumbs are browned.
3. Pour butter, crumbs and egg over broccoli.

Mrs. Paul Wilmot, Woman's Club, Roswell, N.M.

BROCCOLI WITH ZESTY SAUCE

Serves 4

1 bunch broccoli
2 tablespoons butter
2 tablespoons minced onion
1½ cups sour cream
2 teaspoons sugar
1 teaspoon white vinegar
½ teaspoon poppy seeds
¼ teaspoon salt
Dash of cayenne
½ teaspoon paprika
⅓ cup chopped cashew nuts

1. Cook broccoli in boiling salted water until just tender. Drain well; arrange on heated platter.
2. Melt butter in saucepan; sauté onion until tender. Remove from heat; stir in all remaining ingredients except nuts.
3. Pour sauce over broccoli; sprinkle with nuts.

Mrs. J. D. Hand, Novella Club, Columbiana, Ala.

GLAZED BROCCOLI WITH ALMONDS

Serves 6

2 pounds broccoli or 2 10-ounce packages frozen broccoli
Salt
1 chicken bouillon cube
¼ cup butter or margarine
¼ cup presifted flour
1 cup light cream
2 tablespoons dry sherry
2 tablespoons lemon juice
½ teaspoon monosodium glutamate
Pepper to taste
¼ cup grated Parmesan cheese
¼ cup slivered blanched almonds

1. Preheat oven to 375° F. Grease 10 x 6 x 1½-inch baking pan.
2. Separate broccoli; wash thoroughly. Put in saucepan with a little boiling water. Season with ½ teaspoon salt. Cover; boil over medium heat for 12 minutes, or until barely tender. Drain; arrange in pan.
3. Meanwhile, prepare Sherry Sauce: In small bowl dissolve bouillon cube in ¾ cup hot water. Melt butter or margarine in saucepan; blend in flour. Gradually stir in cream and dissolved bouillon cube; cook over medium heat, stirring constantly, until thickened and smooth. Remove from heat; stir in sherry, lemon juice and monosodium glutamate. Season with salt and pepper.
4. Pour sauce over broccoli. Sprinkle with cheese and almonds.

5. Bake in preheated oven for 20 minutes, or until golden brown.

Grace S. Forbes, Woman's Club, La Mesa, Calif.

BROCCOLI AND CHEESE CUSTARD

Serves 4

1 bunch broccoli
2 eggs
⅔ cup milk
1¼ cups shredded sharp Cheddar cheese
Salt and pepper to taste

1. Trim broccoli; slit stalks. Cook in boiling salted water until tender; drain.
2. Preheat oven to 325° F. Grease 1½-quart casserole.
3. Put broccoli in casserole.
4. Beat eggs; combine with milk, cheese, salt and pepper. Beat thoroughly. Pour over broccoli.
5. Set casserole in shallow pan containing about 1 inch hot water; bake in preheated oven for 25 to 30 minutes, or until knife inserted in center comes out clean.

Mrs. Sam White, Woman's Club, St. Mary's, W. Va.

BROCCOLI AND EGG CASSEROLE

Serves 4 to 6

10-ounce package frozen broccoli
2 cups packaged bread stuffing
6 eggs, hard-cooked and halved
3 cups Medium White Sauce (p. 441)
3 tablespoons grated onion
¼ cup hot water
¼ cup melted butter
½ teaspoon salt
1 cup grated Cheddar cheese
¼ cup grated Parmesan cheese

1. Cook broccoli according to package directions. Drain.
2. Preheat oven to 400° F. Grease 3-quart casserole.
3. Arrange 1 cup of the stuffing in casserole; top with broccoli. Arrange eggs on broccoli.
4. In mixing bowl blend Medium White Sauce with onion; pour over eggs.
5. Put remaining stuffing in mixing bowl; add water, butter, salt and Cheddar cheese. Mix well. Arrange on sauce in casserole. Sprinkle with Parmesan cheese.
6. Bake in preheated oven for 25 minutes.

NOTE: Cauliflower or asparagus may be substituted for the broccoli in this recipe.

Ruth Gaines, Junior Woman's Club, Jacksonville, Fla.

BROCCOLI MUSHROOM CASSEROLE

Serves 4

2 10-ounce packages frozen chopped broccoli
1 cup mayonnaise
1 cup shredded sharp cheese
2 eggs, lightly beaten

10½-ounce can condensed cream of mushroom soup
Cracker crumbs

1. Cook broccoli according to package directions, but for only 5 minutes. Drain.
2. Preheat oven to 350° F. Grease 2-quart casserole.
3. Combine mayonnaise, cheese, eggs and soup. Fold in broccoli. Turn into casserole; top with crumbs.
4. Bake in preheated oven for 45 minutes.

Mrs. Gerald F. Mabry, President, Woman's Club, Fort Meade, Fla.

Brussels Sprouts

These tiny cabbages have a delicious delicate flavor if they are not overcooked. Select sprouts that are hard and firm and that have a good green color. Loose large heads are apt to be stronger in flavor than small tight heads.

BOILED BRUSSELS SPROUTS

Serves 4

About 1 pint brussels sprouts
Salt and pepper to taste
2 tablespoons melted butter

1. Remove any wilted or yellow outer leaves from brussels sprouts. Cut crosswise gash in stem ends; soak in salted cold water for 10 minutes.
2. Drain; drop into rapidly boiling water. Cover; simmer for about 10 minutes, or until barely tender.
3. Drain. Sprinkle with salt and pepper; serve with butter.

VARIATIONS:

1. Add lemon juice, chopped chives or parsley to the melted butter.
2. Add grated Parmesan cheese to the melted butter.
3. Serve with Cream Sauce (p. 441) or Cheese Sauce (p. 442).
4. Add sautéed slivered almonds, sautéed mushrooms or seedless grapes.
5. Flavor with nutmeg or sage.

A. S.

DEVILED BRUSSELS SPROUTS

Serves 3 or 4

10-ounce package frozen brussels sprouts
¼ cup butter or margarine
2 teaspoons prepared mustard
1 teaspoon Worcestershire
¼ teaspoon salt
Dash of pepper

1. Cook brussels sprouts according to package directions.
2. Meanwhile, melt butter or margarine in small saucepan. Stir in remaining ingredients; simmer for 2 minutes.

3. Drain sprouts; arrange in serving dish. Pour sauce over sprouts.

Mrs. George Williams, Woman's Club, Emmaus, Pa.

BRUSSELS SPROUTS WITH GRAPES

Serves 6

2 cups fresh or frozen brussels sprouts
¾ cup seedless green grapes
2 tablespoons butter
½ teaspoon salt
⅛ teaspoon pepper

1. Cook brussels sprouts in boiling salted water until tender.
2. Add grapes; cook over low heat for 5 minutes longer. Drain; toss with butter, salt and pepper.

Mrs. R. H. Butler, Woman's Club, Albemarle, N.C.

TANGY BRUSSELS SPROUTS

Serves 10

1 quart fresh or 3 10-ounce packages frozen brussels sprouts
1 chicken or beef bouillon cube
½ cup sour cream
1 teaspoon lemon juice
¼ teaspoon Worcestershire
½ teaspoon salt
½ teaspoon paprika
Dash of pepper
¼ teaspoon dry mustard
¼ cup mayonnaise
6 slices bacon, cooked and crumbled

1. Cover brussels sprouts with boiling salted water; add bouillon cube. Cover; simmer for 10 to 15 minutes, or until tender. Drain; arrange in serving dish.
2. Meanwhile, prepare Sour Cream Sauce: In saucepan combine all remaining ingredients except bacon. Stir over low heat until sauce reaches serving temperature. Do not boil.
3. Spoon sauce over sprouts; sprinkle with bacon.

Mrs. William L. Mims, Sorosis Woman's Club, Orlando, Fla.

Cabbage

There are several types of cabbage—the early Dutch cabbage, the Savoy, the Jersey Wakefield and the Round Head—and all are excellent cooked or served raw in slaws or salads.

Select a cabbage head that is solid and hard with no worm-eaten or discolored outer leaves. The head should feel surprisingly heavy for its size. Use 1 pound cabbage for about 3 cups shredded raw or 2 cups cooked cabbage. Count on a good-size wedge or 1 cup shredded cabbage, cooked, per serving.

BOILED SHREDDED CABBAGE

Serves 4

2 pounds cabbage
Salt and white pepper to taste
4 tablespoons melted butter

1. Remove tough or discolored leaves from cabbage. Cut into quarters; discard core. Shred as thinly as possible.
2. Drop cabbage into rapidly boiling water; cover; simmer for 7 to 8 minutes.
3. Drain; sprinkle with salt and pepper. Turn into serving dish; sprinkle with butter.

A. S.

BOILED CABBAGE WEDGES

Serves 6

1 medium cabbage
Salt and white pepper to taste
4 tablespoons melted butter

1. Remove tough or discolored leaves from cabbage. Cut into 6 wedges. Cut away most of core; leave enough to hold leaves intact.
2. Heat ½ inch water in large skillet to boiling. Arrange wedges in water; cover; cook for about 10 minutes, or until translucent.
3. Arrange wedges on serving dish; sprinkle with salt, pepper and butter.

VARIATIONS:

1. Add a few drops lemon juice or vinegar to the melted butter.
2. Add 1 teaspoon caraway or poppy seeds to butter before melting.
3. Add 1 tablespoon chopped parsley or chives to the melted butter.
4. Add shredded cabbage to Cheese Sauce (p. 442) or Cream Sauce (p. 441).

A. S.

CABBAGE WITH ONIONS

Serves 6

2 pounds finely shredded cabbage
4 medium onions, sliced
Salt and pepper to taste
2 tablespoons butter

1. Grease Dutch oven or heavy saucepan. Arrange alternate layers of cabbage and onions; season each layer with salt and pepper. Dot final layer with butter.
2. Cover; steam over very low heat for 20 minutes, or until tender.

Woman's Club, Newnan, Ga.

FRIED CABBAGE

Serves 6

1 medium cabbage
¼ cup butter
1½ teaspoons salt
1 teaspoon paprika
½ cup heavy cream
1 tablespoon vinegar

1. Shred cabbage.
2. Melt buttter in large skillet. Add cabbage; toss in butter. Reduce heat to low; season with salt and paprika. Cook, un-

covered, for 15 minutes, stirring frequently.

3. Just before serving, stir in cream and vinegar; bring to boil.

Mrs. John J. Huff, Roosevelt Neighborhood Woman's Club, Phoenix, Ariz.

BAKED CABBAGE
Serves 6

1 medium cabbage
2 eggs, lightly beaten
6 tablespoons melted butter
3 tablespoons heavy cream
1 teaspoon salt
¼ teaspoon pepper
½ cup bread crumbs

1. Preheat oven to 375° F. Grease 2-quart casserole.
2. Cook cabbage in boiling salted water for 10 minutes, or until tender. Drain; cool; chop cabbage finely.
3. In mixing bowl blend eggs, 3 tablespoons of the butter, cream, salt and pepper. Stir in cabbage; turn into casserole. Blend remaining butter with crumbs; sprinkle over cabbage.
4. Bake in preheated oven for 30 minutes.

Mrs. J. C. Baird, Morgan Park Woman's Club, Chicago, Ill.

DRESSED-UP CABBAGE
Serves 4 to 6

1 large cabbage
2 eggs
1 cup light cream
1 teaspoon salt
Dash of pepper
1 tablespoon butter or margarine
¼ cup grated cheese

1. Preheat oven to 350° F. Grease 2-quart casserole.
2. Remove outer leaves from cabbage; shred cabbage.
3. Put in medium saucepan; cover with boiling water. Cover; boil over medium heat for 5 minutes. Drain well.
4. In mixing bowl beat eggs until foamy. Add cream, salt and pepper; beat until smooth.
5. Stir in cabbage; pour into casserole. Dot with butter or margarine; sprinkle with cheese.
6. Set in pan of hot water; bake in preheated oven for 30 minutes.

Dorothy Thresher, Women's Club, Yuba City, Calif.

SCALLOPED CABBAGE AND CHEESE
Serves 6

1 medium cabbage, shredded
2 cups grated Cheddar cheese
¼ cup presifted flour
1 teaspoon salt
¼ teaspoon pepper
½ cup butter
2 cups milk
½ cup bread crumbs

1. Preheat oven to 350° F. Grease 1½-quart casserole.
2. Put cabbage in saucepan; sprinkle with few tablespoons boiling salted water. Cover; simmer over medium heat for 8 minutes. Drain well.
3. In mixing bowl blend cheese, flour, salt and pepper.
4. Arrange alternate layers of cabbage, cheese mixture and small dots of butter, finishing with butter. Pour milk over all; sprinkle with crumbs.
5. Bake in preheated oven for 30 minutes.

Hazel J. Austin, Fortnightly Club, Hudson, N.H.

DILLED CABBAGE WITH SOUR CREAM
Serves 6

1 medium cabbage, cored and
  cut into 6 wedges
1 tablespoon butter
1 tablespoon dillweed
1 cup sour cream
1 tablespoon vinegar
Salt and pepper to taste

1. Cook cabbage in rapidly boiling salted water for 5 to 6 minutes. Drain well; keep hot.
2. Melt butter in saucepan; sauté dillweed for 1 minute. Stir in remaining ingredients; cook, stirring constantly, until hot.
3. Pour sauce over cabbage.

Mary McConnell, Woman's Club, Buckeye, Ariz.

Red Cabbage

Red cabbage may be prepared and cooked in the same manner as green cabbage, shredded or cut into wedges, but it must be cooked for a longer period of time than green cabbage to make it tender. It is usually best when cooked according to a specific recipe with chopped onion, brown sugar and vinegar or with sour apples.

ROTKRAUT (Red Cabbage)
Serves 8 to 10

1 tablespoon butter
3 slices bacon, diced
1 medium onion, chopped
1 medium red cabbage, shredded
6 cloves
¼ cup sugar
½ cup vinegar
1 apple, peeled and chopped
1 tablespoon flour

1. Melt butter in large saucepan; sauté bacon and onion for 5 minutes. Stir in cabbage; sauté for 5 minutes.
2. Add 3 cups water, cloves, sugar, vinegar and apple. Cover; cook over medium heat for about 10 minutes, or until tender.
3. Meanwhile, in small bowl blend ¼ cup water with flour; stir into cabbage

mixture. Cook over medium heat, stirring constantly, until thickened.

Mrs. Jess Tolerton, Junior Women's Club, Cheyenne, Wyo.

DANISH RED CABBAGE

Serves 6

1 medium red cabbage
2 tablespoons butter or margarine
1 small onion, finely chopped
1 beef bouillon cube
1 cup hot water
1 large apple, finely diced
1 teaspoon salt
¼ teaspoon pepper
1 tablespoon vinegar
1 tablespoon brown sugar

1. Chop cabbage finely.
2. Melt butter or margarine in saucepan; sauté cabbage and onion for 5 minutes.
3. Meanwhile, in small bowl dissolve bouillon cube in water. Add to cabbage with apple, salt and pepper. Cover; cook over low heat for 10 minutes.
4. Stir in vinegar and sugar; simmer for 5 minutes, or until tender.

Mrs. Arthur Pratt, Woman's Club, Mount Dora, Fla.

GRANDMA'S RED CABBAGE

Serves 4 or 5

3 cups shredded red cabbage
2 cups cubed unpeeled apples
¼ cup cider vinegar
¼ cup brown sugar
¼ cup water
1 teaspoon salt
⅛ teaspoon pepper
2 tablespoons olive oil
⅛ teaspoon caraway seeds

1. Combine all ingredients in saucepan.
2. Cover; steam over low heat for 30 minutes, or until cabbage is tender, stirring occasionally.

Mrs. E. C. Maynor, Westmoreland Woman's Club, Huntington, W. Va.

SWEET AND SOUR SPICED RED CABBAGE

Serves 4 to 6

2 tablespoons shortening
1 medium red cabbage, shredded
3 tart apples, peeled and sliced
Salt to taste
½ teaspoon pepper
4 cloves
½ teaspoon allspice
½ cup sugar
½ cup vinegar

1. Melt shortening in Dutch oven or heavy saucepan; sauté cabbage and apples over low heat for 3 minutes.
2. Sprinkle with salt, pepper, cloves, allspice and sugar. Cover; simmer for 1 hour.
3. Add vinegar; simmer for 1 hour longer.

Mrs. L. Behm, Junior Woman's Club, Newington, Conn.

Cabbage Palm

Cabbage palm grows profusely in the swamplands of Florida. When the mature trees are cut down, the tender part of the stem—the heart—is a great delicacy. It may be boiled and served with melted butter, but it is at its best when shredded raw and served as a salad with Mustard Mayonnaise Sauce (p. 448). The canned varieties of heart of palm are excellent substitutes for the fresh.

Chinese Cabbage

Chinese cabbage, also known as celery cabbage or by the Chinese name of wong bok, is a long tapered head with almost white leaves. It more closely resembles celery than it does cabbage, but it has a very delicate cabbage flavor. It may be cooked in the same manner as shredded green cabbage. It also makes an interesting addition to a tossed salad, or it may be shredded and used for coleslaw.

Carrots

Among the sweetest and most colorful members of the vegetable kingdom, carrots should be cooked only until barely fork-tender. They are available all year but are best in the spring, summer and early fall.

BOILED CARROTS

Serves 4

8 medium carrots
1 tablespoon butter
Salt and pepper to taste

1. Wash and scrape carrots, or peel very thinly with vegetable parer. If young, leave whole; otherwise, cut as desired.
2. Barely cover with water; bring to boil. Cover tightly; cook for 6 to 20 minutes, depending on size and age.
3. Drain; add butter, salt and pepper.

VARIATIONS:

1. Season with chopped mint, chervil, parsley, dill or chives, ginger, thyme or nutmeg.
2. Combine with cooked celery or peas.
3. Add to Cream Sauce (p. 441).
4. Sprinkle with crisp bacon bits.

A. S.

BAKED CARROTS

Serves 6 to 8

6 to 10 medium carrots, cooked
2 tablespoons grated onion
1 teaspoon sugar
½ teaspoon salt
⅛ teaspoon pepper

1 cup heavy cream
1 cup fresh bread crumbs
⅓ cup melted butter or margarine

1. Preheat oven to 350° F. Grease 1½-quart casserole.
2. In mixing bowl mash carrots until smooth. Stir in onion, sugar, salt, pepper and cream; turn into casserole.
3. In small bowl blend crumbs with butter or margarine; sprinkle over carrots.
4. Bake in preheated oven for 30 minutes.

Geri Condrey, Hull-Daisetta Study Club,
Hull and Daisetta, Tex.

CANDIED CARROTS WITH APPLES

Serves 4

8 large carrots, sliced
¼ cup granulated sugar
¼ cup brown sugar
1 teaspoon cinnamon
1 large cooking apple, peeled and sliced
2 tablespoons butter or margarine

1. Preheat oven to 325° F. Grease 1-quart casserole.
2. Put carrots in saucepan; cover with boiling salted water. Cover; cook until just tender. Drain.
3. Combine granulated sugar, brown sugar and cinnamon.
4. Arrange alternate layers of carrots and apple in casserole, sprinkling sugar mixture over layers. Dot with butter or margarine.
5. Bake in preheated oven for 45 minutes, or until apples are tender.

Teddy Jean Greenwald, Junior Solitic Club,
Crowley, La.

CREAMED CARROTS

Serves 4

6 medium carrots, sliced
1 cup sour cream
3-ounce package cream cheese
1 tablespoon chopped scallions
1 tablespoon finely chopped green pepper
½ teaspoon salt
½ teaspoon grated lemon rind

1. Preheat oven to 350° F. Grease 1-quart casserole.
2. Cook carrots, covered, in boiling salted water until tender. Drain.
3. In mixing bowl blend remaining ingredients. Add carrots; mix lightly. Turn into casserole.
4. Bake in preheated oven for 15 minutes.

Junior Women's Club, Porterville, Calif.

DEVILED CARROTS

Serves 6

6 large carrots, quartered
½ cup butter
2 tablespoons brown sugar
1 teaspoon salt
Dash of pepper
Dash of Tabasco

1. Cook carrots in boiling salted water until just tender. Drain.
2. Melt butter in saucepan; sauté carrots over low heat for 5 minutes.
3. Sprinkle with sugar, salt, pepper and Tabasco. Cook over low heat, stirring occasionally, for 10 minutes.

Jan Sayles, Junior Woman's Club, Vista, Calif.

BROWN SUGAR-GLAZED CARROTS

Serves 6

1 pound carrots
2 tablespoons cooking oil
¼ cup water
3 tablespoons brown sugar
¼ teaspoon salt

1. Cut carrots into thin strips. Heat oil in saucepan; brown carrots lightly over medium heat.
2. Combine remaining ingredients; pour over carrots. Cover; cook over low heat for about 10 minutes, or until just tender.

Mrs. Paul Pumphrey, President, Woman's Club,
Ovid, Colo.

SHOESTRING CARROTS

Serves 6

2 small bunches carrots
6 slices bacon, diced
2 onions, chopped
1 tablespoon flour
1¼ cups water
2 teaspoons sugar
Salt and pepper to taste
2 small bay leaves

1. Cut carrots into thin strips.
2. Cook bacon in skillet until crisp and golden. Drain on absorbent paper.
3. Add onions to fat remaining in skillet; sauté until golden. Stir in flour. Gradually stir in water. Add carrots, bacon and remaining ingredients. Cover; cook over low heat for about 15 minutes, or until carrots are tender, stirring frequently.

Flossie Young, Woman's Club, Ambridge, Pa.

STUFFED CARROTS

Serves 6

12 large carrots
3 tablespoons butter
1 cup finely chopped onions
1 cup finely chopped green pepper
¼ cup finely chopped parsley
Salt and pepper to taste
½ cup grated Cheddar cheese
1 cup fresh bread crumbs

1. Preheat oven to 325° F. Grease 11 x 7 x 1½-inch baking pan.
2. Cook carrots in boiling salted water until tender. Drain.
3. Meanwhile, melt butter in skillet; sauté onions and green pepper over medium heat for 10 minutes. Remove from heat; stir in parsley; season with salt and pepper. Add cheese; mix well.
4. Cut a thin slice from top of each carrot; scoop out center, lengthwise. Fill carrots with cheese mixture; place in pan. Sprinkle with crumbs.

5. Bake in preheated oven for 20 minutes.

Mrs. George Cragin, Woman's Aladdin Club, Canutillo, Tex.

VITAMIN CARROTS

Grated peeled carrots
Salt to taste
Butter

1. Preheat oven to 350° F. Grease baking dish.
2. Fill dish with carrots. Season with salt; dot with a tablespoon or so of butter.
3. Cover; bake in preheated oven for 30 minutes.

Mrs. C. E. Boone, Arts and Crafts Section, Woman's Club, Avenal, Calif.

SCALLOPED CARROTS AND CELERY

Serves 6

3 cups diced cooked carrots
1½ cups diced cooked celery
½ cup shredded sharp Cheddar cheese
½ cup bread crumbs
2 cups Medium White Sauce (p. 441)

1. Preheat oven to 350° F. Grease 2-quart baking dish.
2. Combine carrots and celery.
3. Combine cheese, crumbs and Medium White Sauce.
4. Fill dish with alternate layers of vegetables and cheese mixture, ending with cheese mixture.
5. Bake in preheated oven for 30 minutes.

Rita Whalen, Anna Day Club, Troy, Mo.

CARROT SOUFFLÉ

Serves 6

1 cup bread crumbs
1 cup milk
3 eggs, separated
1 cup mashed cooked carrots
1 tablespoon grated onion
1 cup shredded cheese
Salt and pepper to taste

1. Soak crumbs in milk for 10 minutes.
2. Preheat oven to 350° F. Grease 1-quart casserole.
3. Combine crumb mixture, egg yolks, carrots, onion, cheese, salt and pepper.
4. Beat egg whites until stiff but not dry; fold into carrot mixture.
5. Turn into casserole; bake in preheated oven for 40 minutes, or until set.

Ida Gardner, Arts Club, Aliceville, Ala.

ZESTY CARROTS

Serves 6

1 cup crushed potato chips
8 medium carrots, cooked and sliced
2 tablespoons grated onion
2 tablespoons horseradish
1½ cups mayonnaise
½ teaspoon salt
¼ teaspoon pepper

1. Preheat oven to 375° F. Grease 1-quart casserole.

2. Sprinkle ½ cup of the potato chips in casserole. Arrange carrots on top.
3. Blend onion, horseradish, mayonnaise, salt and pepper. Spread on carrots; sprinkle with remaining potato chips.
4. Bake in preheated oven for 20 minutes.

Mrs. Richard Eike, Junior Woman's Club, De Kalb, Ill.

Cauliflower

This member of the cabbage family has a mild flavor if properly cooked. Select a creamy-white solid head surrounded by fresh green leaves. Any yellowing or browning of the head indicates that it is not fresh. Cauliflower may be cooked whole or separated into flowerets, but either way it should be cooked until just barely tender, for overcooking gives it a strong flavor and an unattractive mushy texture. The cooked cauliflowerets (or defrosted frozen cauliflower) are excellent dipped into batter and deep-fried.

BOILED CAULIFLOWER

Serves 4

1 medium cauliflower
Salt and pepper to taste
3 to 5 tablespoons melted butter
Juice of ½ lemon (optional)

1. Remove outer green leaves from cauliflower; cut away tough end of stem. Soak, head down, in salted cold water for 15 to 20 minutes. Drain. Break into flowerets, or cut deep gashes in stalk if left whole.
2. Put cauliflower, head up, in pot; almost cover with boiling water. Cook, uncovered, for 12 to 15 minutes, or until stalk is barely fork-tender.
3. Drain; empty into serving dish. Sprinkle with salt and pepper; pour butter over it. Sprinkle with lemon juice, if desired.

VARIATIONS:

1. Sauté 3 tablespoons bread crumbs in the butter before pouring over cauliflower.
2. Sauté slivered blanched almonds in butter before pouring over cauliflower.
3. Season with nutmeg.
4. Serve with Cream Sauce (p. 441), Cheese Sauce (p. 442) or Egg Cream Sauce (p. 441).

A. S.

BLUSHING CAULIFLOWER

Serves 6

1 large cauliflower
2½ cups tomato juice
1 tablespoon salt
¼ teaspoon pepper
¾ cup grated Cheddar cheese
Chopped parsley

1. Trim outer leaves from cauliflower; place cauliflower, stem end up, in saucepan.

2. Pour tomato juice over cauliflower; sprinkle with salt and pepper. Bring to boil; cover; simmer for 20 minutes, or until tender.

3. Drain; arrange in serving dish. Sprinkle with cheese and parsley.

Mrs. Leonard Wells, Lower Naches Woman's Club, Yakima, Wash.

CAULIFLOWER AU GRATIN
Serves 6

1 large cauliflower, cooked
3 tablespoons flour
2 cups cream-style cottage cheese
½ teaspoon salt
¼ teaspoon pepper
1 teaspoon Worcestershire
1 tablespoon chopped scallions
¼ cup grated Cheddar cheese

1. Preheat oven to 350° F. Grease 1-quart casserole.

2. Break cauliflower into small pieces; turn into mixing bowl.

3. In another bowl blend flour, cottage cheese, salt, pepper, Worcestershire and scallions.

4. Combine cottage cheese mixture and cauliflower; turn into casserole. Sprinkle with grated cheese.

5. Bake in preheated oven for 30 minutes, or until golden.

Junior Women's Club, Porterville, Calif.

BAKED STUFFED CAULIFLOWER
Serves 5

1 large cauliflower
2 tablespoons butter
2 tablespoons flour
1 cup milk
½ teaspoon salt
¼ teaspoon pepper
2 eggs, hard-cooked and chopped
2 tablespoons chopped pimiento
¾ cup chopped scallions
¼ cup buttered bread crumbs
2 tablespoons grated cheese

1. Leave cauliflower whole. Cook, covered, in boiling salted water for 20 minutes, or until just tender. Drain; cool.

2. Preheat oven to 375° F. Grease baking dish.

3. Melt butter in saucepan. Stir in flour. Gradually stir in milk; cook, stirring constantly, until sauce is thickened and smooth. Stir in salt, pepper, eggs, pimiento and scallions.

4. Put cauliflower in baking dish. Cut deep round wedge from top. Fill center with sauce; replace top; pour remaining sauce over top. Sprinkle with crumbs and cheese.

5. Bake in preheated oven for about 20 minutes.

Marianne Scherle, Woman's Club, Palmdale, Calif.

COMPANY CAULIFLOWER
Serves 6 to 8

1 medium cauliflower
⅓ cup butter or margarine
¼ cup diced green pepper
½ pound mushrooms, sliced
¼ cup presifted flour
2 cups milk
1 teaspoon salt
2 cups grated Cheddar cheese
6 slices pimiento
Paprika to taste

1. Preheat oven to 400° F. Grease 1½-quart casserole.

2. Cook cauliflower in boiling salted water for 15 minutes, or until tender. Drain; break into flowerets.

3. Melt butter or margarine in saucepan; sauté green pepper and mushrooms for 5 minutes. Blend in flour; gradually stir in milk. Cook over low heat, stirring constantly, until sauce is thickened and smooth. Add salt.

4. Arrange half the cauliflower in casserole; sprinkle with 1 cup of the cheese and 3 of the pimiento slices. Cover with half the sauce. Repeat layers, finishing with sauce. Sprinkle with paprika.

5. Bake in preheated oven for 15 minutes, or until browned and bubbling.

Mrs. Lee Hogue, Woman's Club, Sheffield Lake, Ohio

CAULIFLOWER TIMBALES
Serves 6

1 medium cauliflower
2 eggs
½ teaspoon salt
Dash of pepper
2 tablespoons melted butter
1 cup milk
6 tablespoons shredded cheese
Paprika

1. Separate cauliflower into flowerets. Cover with salted water, bring to boil; boil for 10 minutes. Drain.

2. Preheat oven to 325° F. Grease 6 custard cups.

3. Divide cauliflower into custard cups, floweret heads down.

4. Beat eggs. Stir in salt, pepper, butter, milk and 3 tablespoons of the cheese.

5. Pour egg mixture into cups, covering cauliflower but not quite filling cups.

6. Set cups in shallow pan containing about 1 inch hot water. Bake in preheated oven for 30 to 40 minutes, or until knife inserted in center comes out clean.

7. Loosen edges with sharp knife; invert into serving dish. Sprinkle with remaining cheese; top each timbale with a dash of paprika.

Mrs. E. L. Williamson, New Century Club, Pine Apple, Ala.

Celery

Celery is often considered a vegetable to be served only raw or stuffed with Roquefort or blue cheese. Actually it is a delicate vegetable when braised. Select heads with crisp stalks that are easy to snap and with fresh-looking leaves. The outer tough stalks should be removed but not discarded, for they add flavor to soups, stews and casseroles. The yellow leaves are delicious chopped and used as a garnish for hot dishes or added to salads.

BRAISED CELERY

Serves 4

2 medium bunches celery
Hot chicken broth
1 tablespoon butter
Salt and pepper to taste

1. Wash celery thoroughly; set aside outer heavy stalks. Cut hearts in half lengthwise; put in shallow pan or skillet.
2. Add broth barely to cover; cover; cook over low heat for about 20 minutes, or until fork-tender. Remove cover; add butter. Continue to cook over very low heat until most of liquid has been absorbed, basting frequently.
3. Season with salt and pepper.

VARIATIONS:

1. Serve with a generous sprinkling of grated Parmesan cheese.
2. Serve with Cream Sauce (p. 441) or Cheese Sauce (p. 442).
3. Braise in cream instead of broth, and, if desired, season with a little curry powder.

A. S.

CELERY AMANDINE

Serves 8

¼ cup boiling water
4 cups sliced celery
Salt and pepper to taste
¼ cup butter
1 tablespoon chopped chives
1 tablespoon grated onion
1½ tablespoons flour
1 cup light cream
½ cup chicken broth
½ cup slivered almonds

1. In saucepan combine water and celery. Cover; simmer for 10 minutes.
2. Season lightly with salt and pepper; add butter. Cover; simmer for 10 minutes, shaking frequently to prevent scorching.
3. Sprinkle with chives and onion; continue to cook until celery is tender.
4. Add flour; gradually stir in cream and broth, stirring constantly, until thickened and smooth.
5. Stir in almonds; simmer for 1 minute longer.

Mrs. William Roderick, Woman's Club,
West Palm Beach, Fla.

BAKED CELERY

Serves 6

1 bunch celery, thinly sliced
½ cup chopped toasted almonds
½ cup grated sharp Cheddar cheese
2 10½-ounce cans condensed cream of celery soup
½ teaspoon salt
½ teaspoon paprika
⅛ teaspoon pepper
½ cup buttered bread crumbs

1. Preheat oven to 375° F. Grease 9-inch square baking pan.
2. Arrange celery in pan; sprinkle with almonds and cheese.
3. Blend soup, salt, paprika and pepper. Pour over celery; and sprinkle with crumbs.
4. Bake in preheated oven for 45 minutes.

Woman's Club, Newark, Ill.

GOLDEN BAKED CELERY LOAF

Serves 6

For a delicious dish to serve with roast turkey or chicken, omit Five-Minute Tomato Sauce and serve with gravy.

1½ cups sliced celery
¼ bunch parsley
1 large white onion
½ green pepper
¾ cup walnuts
2 eggs, lightly beaten
1 cup fine whole wheat bread crumbs
3 tablespoons melted butter
1 teaspoon salt
1½ cups milk
Five-Minute Tomato Sauce (p. 450)

1. Grease 1½-quart baking dish.
2. Put celery, parsley, onion, green pepper and walnuts through coarse blade of meat grinder.
3. Combine ground mixture with remaining ingredients; turn into baking dish. Let stand in dish for 20 minutes.
4. Preheat oven to 350° F.
5. Bake in preheated oven for about 1 hour, or until set. Serve with Five-Minute Tomato Sauce.

Mae Ketchum, Women's Club,
Arroyo Grande, Calif.

SCALLOPED CELERY

Serves 6

1 bunch celery
2 cups Medium White Sauce (p. 441)
2 eggs, lightly beaten
1 cup fresh bread crumbs
2 tablespoons butter or margarine

1. Preheat oven to 375° F. Grease 2-quart casserole.
2. Wash celery; cut stalks into 2-inch lengths. Put in saucepan with boiling salted water to half cover. Cover pan; simmer for 15 minutes, or until tender.
3. Drain; arrange celery in casserole.

4. Combine Medium White Sauce and eggs; pour over celery; sprinkle with crumbs. Dot with butter or margarine.

5. Bake in preheated oven for 30 minutes.

Harriet Gold Armstrong, Morgan Park Woman's Club, Chicago, Ill.

Celery Root (Celeriac)

This tuberous vegetable is not common throughout America but should be more widely cultivated, for its delicate celery-like flavor is agreeable to almost everyone. It is good either raw or cooked. It may be mashed, creamed, baked au gratin, or served cold with Sauce Vinaigrette (p. 542). It is especially good cooked and mashed with an equal quantity of potatoes, and like celery, it is excellent braised in chicken broth. Select small or medium roots that feel heavy. Large or light knobs are likely to be woody or hollow.

BOILED CELERY ROOT
Serves 4
  4 small to medium celery roots
  Melted butter
  Salt and pepper to taste
  Minced parsley

1. Scrub roots with stiff brush; put in deep pot.

2. Cover with boiling water. Bring to boil; simmer for about 25 minutes, or until fork-tender.

3. Drain; peel while hot. Slice into serving bowl; sprinkle with butter, salt, pepper and parsley.

VARIATIONS:

1. Slice cooked celery roots into a serving dish; sprinkle with minced parsley and onion. Moisten with French Dressing (p. 541); marinate in refrigerator for several hours before serving.

2. Peel, dice and cook celery roots until tender. Add to Cream Sauce (p. 441).

3. Peel raw celery roots; cut into thin strips. Moisten with Sauce Rémoulade (p. 446) or Mustard Mayonnaise Sauce (p. 448).

A. S.

Chard (Swiss Chard)

Swiss chard belongs to the beet family, but only the stalks and leaves are eaten, not the roots. The leaves may be prepared like spinach greens, and the heavy white stems may be prepared in any way suitable for asparagus or cooked celery.

Chayote (Mexican Squash)

This Mexican member of the squash family, now being cultivated in Florida, is becoming increasingly popular in the United States. It may be halved and baked in the oven like acorn squash; or it may be peeled, cut into strips, dipped in batter and deep-fried like eggplant or summer squash. It may be peeled, diced, boiled and added to Cream Sauce (p. 441) or mashed with butter and seasonings. The seeds should not be removed, since they become very tender when cooked.

BRAISED CHAYOTE
Serves 4
  2 medium or about 1 pound chayotes
  1 cup water
  2 tablespoons melted butter
  Salt and pepper to taste

1. Peel chayotes; slice or cube.

2. Put in saucepan with water; bring to boil. Cover tightly; cook over low heat for about 20 minutes, or until tender.

3. Drain; empty into serving dish. Sprinkle with butter, salt and pepper.

A. S.

Chestnuts

Chestnuts are not normally eaten raw but are holiday favorites roasted, parboiled and cooked in poultry stuffing, braised in chicken broth or boiled and mashed. The mashed purée is a favorite gourmet accompaniment to wild game. Chestnuts are time-consuming to prepare, but fortunately for those who appreciate their flavor, they are available in specialty stores in several forms—glacéed, preserved in heavy vanilla or rum syrup or puréed plain or flavored with vanilla. To serve as a vegetable, do not buy *purée de marrons au vanille*, since this purée contains considerable sugar, as well as vanilla, and is used only for desserts.

CHESTNUT PURÉE
Serves 6
  2 pounds chestnuts
  3 stalks celery with leaves
  1 small onion
  2 tablespoons softened butter
  Salt and pepper to taste
  2 or more tablespoons hot cream,
    milk or chicken broth

1. Make two crosscut gashes on flat side of each chestnut. Put in saucepan; cover with boiling water. Bring to boil; boil for 15 to 20 minutes.

2. Remove from heat; do not drain. Peel chestnuts as soon as they are cool enough to handle; remove inner skins. Keep unpeeled chestnuts covered with hot water.

3. Return peeled chestnuts to saucepan; again cover with boiling water. Add celery

and onion; bring to boil; simmer for 15 to 20 minutes longer, or until tender.

4. Drain; discard celery and onion. Purée chestnuts through food mill, or press through strainer.

5. Beat butter into purée; season with salt and pepper. Stir in cream, milk or broth; keep hot over simmering water until ready to serve.

A. S.

DROOL DISH

Serves 6 to 8

1½ pounds chestnuts
½ pound mushrooms, sliced
2½ cups Medium White Sauce (p. 441)
 Salt and pepper to taste
½ cup heavy cream
1 cup grated Cheddar cheese

1. Preheat oven to 350° F. Grease 2-quart casserole.

2. Boil and blanch chestnuts; peel; turn into casserole. Top with mushrooms; mix lightly.

3. Prepare Medium White Sauce in saucepan. Season with salt and pepper; stir in cream. Cook over low heat, stirring constantly, until bubbling.

4. Pour sauce over chestnuts and mushrooms; sprinkle with cheese.

5. Bake in preheated oven for 20 to 25 minutes.

Virginia Moore, Woman's Club,
West Palm Beach, Fla.

Corn

Sweet corn—also known as maize and Indian corn—is a native of the New World and, like the potato, squash and tomato, was unknown in Europe until the discovery of America.

Whole-kernel sweet corn is available in canned and frozen forms, but nothing surpasses the flavor of an ear of garden-fresh corn. Fortunately, the season for fresh sweet corn has been lengthened, and it arrives in excellent condition in most major markets for 6 to 8 months of the year. Fresh corn on the cob should never be allowed to boil. Each kernel is filled with corn milk which will curdle, just as cow's milk will, if cooked at too high a temperature. Buy only ears with plump shiny kernels. To keep for any length of time before cooking, wrap in moist absorbent paper, and store in the crisper of the refrigerator.

CORN ON THE COB

1 or 2 ears corn per person, depending on size
 Butter
 Salt and freshly ground pepper to taste

1. Remove husks and silk from ears of corn. Keep ears covered at all times with moist absorbent paper.

2. Bring large pot of water to rapid boil. Drop in ears; bring back to simmer. The moment bubbles begin to rise from bottom of pot, cover tightly, turn off heat and let corn coddle in for 10 minutes.

3. Drain; serve with butter, salt and pepper.

A. S.

REALLY ROASTED CORN ON THE COB PICNIC STYLE

Corn on the cob
Butter

1. Remove silk from ears of corn; leave husks on. Soak corn in cold water for few minutes; then tie husks securely around ears, using long grass, if possible (string will do).

2. Place in hot ashes of wood fire that has died down to coals; roast until husks are nearly blackened.

3. Remove from ashes; discard husks, which will fall away easily. Spread ears with butter.

Mrs. Joseph Holton Jones, New Century Club,
Wilmington, Del.

OVEN CORN ON THE COB

Serves 4

Softened butter
1 tablespoon prepared mustard
1 teaspoon horseradish
1 teaspoon salt
 Dash of pepper
4 ears corn
 Chopped parsley

1. Preheat oven to 450° F. Arrange 4 squares of aluminum foil on baking sheet.

2. Prepare seasoned butter: In medium bowl blend ½ cup butter, mustard, horseradish, salt and pepper until smooth.

3. Husk corn; spread seasoned butter on all sides.

4. Place each ear in center of each foil square. Wrap loosely to form packages.

5. Bake in preheated oven for 25 minutes.

6. Open foil; sprinkle with parsley. Serve in foil with additional butter.

Jane Pedrick, Junior Woman's Club,
Jacksonville, Fla.

FRIED CORN

Serves 8

10 ears corn
3 tablespoons bacon drippings
6 cups water
2 teaspoons salt
¼ teaspoon pepper

1. Cut corn kernels from cob into bowl, scraping cob well to extract all corn milk.

2. Heat bacon drippings in skillet. Add corn, 2 cups of the water, salt and pepper.

3. Simmer for at least 1 hour, stirring frequently and adding remaining water, a cup at a time, as mixture becomes dry.

Phyllis Alford, Woman's Club, Lavalette, W. Va.

NUGEN'S CORN OYSTERS

Serves 8

12 large ears corn (matured beyond
  milky roasting-ear stage)
12 soda crackers, crushed
 3 eggs, separated
   Salt to taste
   Butter

1. Grate corn ears lightly; then scrape, so that nothing but creamy part is collected in mixing bowl.
2. Stir in crackers, egg yolks and salt.
3. In another mixing bowl beat egg whites until stiff but not dry. Fold into corn mixture.
4. Drop batter by tablespoons into butter; fry for about 3 to 4 minutes, or until golden on all sides.

Mrs. Albert Zimmer, Woman's Club,
Newcomerstown, Ohio

CORN FRITTERS

Makes 25

Serve as a vegetable or with syrup, as desired.

 1 egg
 ¼ cup milk
 1 cup pancake mix
 12-ounce can whole-kernel corn,
   drained
   Fat for deep frying

1. Beat egg and milk. Add to pancake mix; stir just until smooth. Fold corn into batter.
2. Drop by spoons into deep fat heated to 365° F. Fry until golden brown.

Mrs. Paul Pumphrey, President, Woman's Club,
Ovid, Colo.

FLUFFY CORN FRITTERS

Makes 12

8-ounce can cream-style corn
1 egg, separated
5 tablespoons presifted flour
1½ teaspoon baking powder
 ¼ teaspoon salt
   Fat for deep frying

1. In mixing bowl blend corn and egg yolk.
2. Into same bowl, sift together flour, baking powder and salt; mix well.
3. In another bowl beat egg white until stiff but not dry; fold into corn mixture.
4. Drop batter by teaspoons into deep fat heated to 365° F. Fry for 2 to 3 minutes, or until golden brown on all sides.

Olga Forrest, 20th Century Club, Nephi, Utah

SOUTHERN CORN CASSEROLE

Serves 4 to 6

6 tablespoons butter or margarine
2 tablespoons sugar
2 tablespoons flour
1 teaspoon salt
4 eggs, well beaten
1¾ cups milk
 2 cups fresh or canned whole-kernel
   corn

1. Preheat oven to 325° F. Grease 1½-quart casserole.
2. Combine butter or margarine, sugar, flour and salt. Stir in eggs, milk and corn.
3. Pour into casserole; bake in preheated oven for 45 minutes, or until lightly browned. Stir once during baking.

Mrs. Marvin Price, 20th Century Club,
Gordo, Ala.

CORN BALLS

Makes About 12

 ¼ cup margarine
 ½ cup chopped onions
 ½ cup chopped celery
 13-ounce can cream-style corn
 1 cup water
 1 teaspoon salt
 ¼ teaspoon pepper
 1½ teaspoons poultry seasoning
  2 cups packaged bread stuffing
  3 egg yolks, lightly beaten
 ½ cup melted butter

1. Preheat oven to 375° F.
2. Melt margarine in saucepan; sauté onions and celery until tender but not browned. Add corn, water and seasonings; bring to boil.
3. Pour mixture over stuffing; mix lightly. Stir in egg yolks.
4. Shape into 12 balls. Put balls in baking dish; pour butter over them.
5. Bake in preheated oven for 15 minutes.

Genevieve Phelps, Woman's Club,
Oceanside, Calif.

BAKED CORN CUSTARD

Serves 6

6 tablespoons butter or margarine
1 medium onion, finely chopped
1 cup diced celery
3 tablespoons flour
2 cups milk
1 cup grated Cheddar cheese
1-pound 4-ounce can whole-kernel
  corn, drained
2 eggs, lightly beaten
1 teaspoon sugar
  Salt and pepper to taste
1 cup fresh bread crumbs

1. Preheat oven to 350° F. Grease 2-quart casserole.
2. Melt 3 tablespoons of the butter or margarine in saucepan; sauté onion and celery over medium heat for 5 minutes.
3. Sprinkle with flour; gradually stir in milk. Cook over medium heat, stirring constantly, until thickened and smooth.
4. Remove from heat; stir in cheese, corn, eggs and sugar. Season with salt and pepper; turn into casserole. Sprinkle with crumbs; dot with remaining butter or margarine.
5. Bake in preheated oven for 35 minutes.

Lullaby Club, Canton, Ohio

CORN AND MUSHROOM CASSEROLE

Serves 6

4-ounce can sliced mushrooms, drained
Light cream
1 tablespoon butter or margarine
1-pound 4-ounce can cream-style corn
1 egg, lightly beaten
Salt and pepper to taste
½ cup cracker crumbs

1. Preheat oven to 350° F. Grease 1½-quart casserole.
2. Drain mushrooms; reserve liquid. Add sufficient cream to total ⅔ cup liquid.
3. Melt butter or margarine in skillet; sauté mushrooms for 5 minutes.
4. Remove from heat; stir in corn, egg and reserved liquid. Season with salt and pepper; stir in crumbs. Turn into casserole.
5. Cover; bake in preheated oven for 45 minutes. Remove cover; bake for 15 minutes longer.

Evelyn McKirgan, Woman's Club, Hinckley, Ill.

CORN PUDDING

Serves 6

3 eggs
2 cups milk
1 tablespoon melted butter or margarine
1 tablespoon flour
2 tablespoons sugar
1 teaspoon salt
2 cups whole-kernel corn

1. Preheat oven to 400° F. Grease 1½-quart casserole.
2. In mixing bowl beat eggs and milk until smooth.
3. Add butter or margarine, flour, sugar and salt; beat until blended. Stir in corn; pour into casserole.
4. Bake in preheated oven for 45 minutes, or until set.

Mrs. Henry W. Bromblett, Woman's Club,
Mount Sterling, Ky.

FLORIDA CORN PUDDING

Serves 4

2 cups whole-kernel corn
1 egg, lightly beaten
1 tablespoon sugar
½ teaspoon salt
1 tablespoon cornstarch
1 cup milk
1 tablespoon butter

1. Preheat oven to 350° F. Grease 1-quart casserole.
2. In mixing bowl combine corn, egg, sugar and salt.
3. In small bowl blend cornstarch and a little of the milk to a paste. Stir in remaining milk. Stir into corn; pour into casserole. Dot with butter.
4. Bake in preheated oven for 1 hour, or until set.

Barbara Hale, Junior Woman's Club,
St. Cloud, Fla.

SCALLOPED CORN WITH CHEESE

Serves 4

1-pound can cream-style corn
1 egg, separated
½ cup cracker crumbs
⅔ cup milk
½ cup grated Cheddar cheese
Salt and pepper to taste
3 tablespoons butter or margarine

1. Preheat oven to 425° F. Grease 1-quart casserole.
2. In mixing bowl combine corn, egg yolk, crumbs, milk and cheese. Season with salt and pepper; mix well.
3. In another bowl beat egg white until stiff but not dry; fold into corn mixture; turn into casserole. Dot with butter or margarine.
4. Bake in preheated oven for 20 minutes.

Clara Norrid, Wednesday Club, Benton, Mo.

CORN LOAF

Serves 8

1-pound can cream-style corn
1 cup yellow corn meal
1 cup diced canned tomatoes
1 medium green pepper, finely chopped
1 medium onion, minced
1 cup grated Cheddar cheese
Salt and pepper to taste
2 cups Olive Sauce (p. 448)

1. In mixing bowl combine corn, corn meal and tomatoes; let stand for 20 minutes.
2. Add green pepper, onion and cheese; season with salt and pepper; mix well. Cover; let stand for 6 hours or overnight.
3. Preheat oven to 350° F. Grease 8-inch square baking pan.
4. Stir corn mixture; pour into pan.
5. Bake in preheated oven for 1 hour.
6. Cut into squares; serve with Olive Sauce.

Mrs. Chud Wendle, Civic Club, Sandpoint, Ida.

CORN PIE

Serves 4

3 tablespoons butter
4-ounce can green chili peppers, drained and chopped
1-pound can cream-style corn
1 tablespoon sugar
½ cup corn meal
1 cup shredded cheese
½ cup milk
½ teaspoon salt

1. Preheat oven to 375° F. Grease shallow 1½-quart baking dish.
2. Melt butter in skillet; sauté chilis for 5 minutes.
3. Combine remaining ingredients. Stir in chilis.
4. Pour into baking dish; bake in preheated oven for 30 minutes.

Mrs. Mabel Swan, Woman's Club,
McFarland, Calif.

Cucumbers

Select firm well-shaped cucumbers. If a cucumber is puffy-looking, withered or yellowed, the seeds will be extremely large and inedible, and the flesh will be rubbery. In addition to the valuable place cucumbers have in salads, they may be cooked in many interesting ways. Boiled and served with parsley or dill butter, they are an excellent accompaniment to fish; they may be creamed, sautéed, deep-fried or stuffed and baked and may also be cooked in any manner suitable for zucchini.

BOILED CUCUMBERS

Serves 4

2 to 3 medium cucumbers
2 tablespoons melted butter
Salt and pepper to taste
Minced parsley, dill or chives

1. Peel cucumbers; cut into half lengthwise; discard seeds. Cut flesh into thin strips, or form into little olive shapes with paring knife.
2. Put cucumber in saucepan; barely cover with boiling water. Bring to boil; then simmer for 5 minutes.
3. Drain; empty into serving dish. Sprinkle with butter, salt, pepper and parsley, dill or chives.

VARIATIONS:

1. Follow recipe above. Add ½ cup warm sour cream to butter and seasonings; heat over simmering water.
2. Add 2 cups cooked cucumber strips or "olives" to ¾ cup Cream Sauce (p. 441). Season with nutmeg, lemon juice or chopped herbs.

A. S.

BAKED CUCUMBERS

Serves 6

6 cucumbers
4 slices bacon, cubed
1 thin slice garlic
1 green pepper, diced
1-pound can whole-kernel corn, drained
6 medium tomatoes, peeled and diced
Salt and pepper to taste
Bread crumbs
Shredded cheese

1. Preheat oven to 325° F. Grease shallow baking dish.
2. Cut cucumbers in half lengthwise; scoop out and discard seeds. Set cucumber aside.
3. Cook bacon in skillet until crisp. Add garlic, green pepper, corn and tomatoes; cook until fairly thick. Stir in salt and pepper.
4. Pour off excess juice from vegetable mixture; stuff cucumber halves. Arrange in baking dish; sprinkle with crumbs and cheese.
5. Bake in preheated oven for 1½ hours.

Mrs. C. B. Griffith, Woman's Club, Azusa, Calif.

FRIED CUCUMBERS

Firm cucumbers
Salt and pepper to taste
Flour
Fat for deep frying

1. Pare cucumbers; cut into slices about ½ inch thick. Let stand in ice water for 10 to 15 minutes; drain; dry.
2. Sprinkle cucumbers with salt and pepper; roll in flour.
3. Fry in skillet containing ½ inch fat heated to 365° F. until golden brown. Drain on absorbent paper.

Mrs. Walter Rush, Woman's Club, Eustis, Fla.

CUCUMBERS POULETTE

Serves 6

6 large cucumbers
2 tablespoons butter
2 tablespoons flour
4 egg yolks, lightly beaten and then mixed with 2 tablespoons water
Salt and pepper to taste
Juice of 1 lemon
Chopped mint

1. Peel cucumbers; cut in half lengthwise; scoop out and discard seeds. Simmer in boiling salted water for 5 minutes, or until barely tender. Carefully remove cucumbers; reserve 2 cups liquid.
2. Melt butter in saucepan. Stir in flour. Gradually stir in reserved liquid; cook, stirring, until sauce is thickened and smooth.
3. Stir in egg yolk mixture; cook over low heat, stirring, for 3 minutes. Do not boil. Season with salt and pepper, stir in lemon juice.
4. Arrange cucumbers in shallow serving dish; strain sauce over them. Sprinkle with mint.

*Evangeline Atwood, Woman's Club,
Anchorage, Alaska*

Dasheen

This tuberous vegetable is a relative of taro, from which the Hawaiians make their poi. The dasheen is cooked in any way suitable for a potato: boiled without paring, or peeled, boiled and mashed or riced. It is excellent fried like potato chips, and it may be baked, but only after it has been parboiled for about 15 minutes.

Eggplant

The eggplant was first grown in southern Asia but is popular today in all parts of the world. Select medium specimens with a uniform dark color and shiny skin. Eggplants should be firm and heavy, not soft and flabby. The flesh discolors quickly when cut. Use a stainless steel knife, and cook as soon as possible after cutting. Eggplant is delicious dipped in egg and crumbs or in batter, then sautéed in oil or deep-fried. It is also good baked and mashed or stuffed. Mashed cooked eggplant makes an excellent soufflé.

FRIED EGGPLANT

Serves 4

1 medium eggplant
1 cup cracker crumbs
1 egg, beaten with 2 tablespoons milk
½ cup butter or margarine

1. Peel eggplant; cut into ½-inch-thick slices. Put in mixing bowl; cover with salted cold water. Let stand for 30 minutes. Drain; pat dry with absorbent paper.
2. Dip eggplant in crumbs, then in egg mixture. Coat again with crumbs, patting in crumbs with back of knife.
3. Melt butter or margarine in large skillet; sauté eggplant for about 5 minutes on each side until golden.

Women's Club, Monroe, Ia.

OVEN-CRISP EGGPLANT

Serves 6

½ cup cracker crumbs
¼ teaspoon orégano
½ teaspoon paprika
½ teaspoon salt
1 egg
1 tablespoon water
2 1-pound eggplants
¼ cup melted butter or margarine

1. Preheat oven to 400° F. Grease 10 x 6 x 1½-inch baking pan.
2. On piece of waxed paper blend crumbs, orégano, paprika and salt; set aside.
3. In small bowl blend egg and water; set aside.
4. Peel eggplants; cut each lengthwise into 6 segments. Dip in egg; coat with crumbs.
5. Arrange in pan; let stand for 30 minutes. Sprinkle butter or margarine over eggplant.
6. Bake in preheated oven for 20 minutes, or until crisp.

Mrs. Charles Yeargin, President, Little League Auxiliary, Ellierton, Ga.

EGGPLANT CAKES

Serves 4

1 medium eggplant
1 egg
½ teaspoon baking powder
1 tablespoon melted butter
Flour
Fat for deep frying

1. Peel and dice eggplant. Put in saucepan; add boiling salted water to half cover. Cover; simmer over medium heat for 15 minutes, or until tender.
2. Drain; turn into mixing bowl. Mash eggplant; add egg, baking powder, butter and sufficient flour to make a thick batter.
3. Drop by tablespoons into deep fat

heated to 365° F. Fry for 4 minutes, or until golden. Drain on absorbent paper.

Mrs. Carlisle Atkinson, Senior Woman's Club, Highland Springs, Va.

EGGPLANT À LA MEXICAN WAY

Serves 4

1 medium eggplant
⅓ cup butter or margarine
½ cup water
1½ teaspoons chili powder
   Salt to taste
½ cup sour cream

1. Peel eggplant; cut into 2-inch cubes.
2. Melt butter or margarine in large skillet; sauté eggplant until well coated in butter.
3. Add water and chili powder. Cover; simmer for 15 minutes, or until tender.
4. Sprinkle with salt; remove from heat. Stir in sour cream.

Mrs. Harold Cramer, Woman's Club, Fort Wayne, Ind.

SCALLOPED EGGPLANT

Serves 6

1 medium eggplant
1 egg, lightly beaten
2 tablespoons melted butter or
   margarine
1 small onion, finely chopped
   Salt and pepper to taste
1 cup dry bread crumbs
½ cup buttered bread crumbs

1. Peel eggplant; cut into 1-inch cubes. Put in saucepan with boiling salted water; cover; cook until tender. Drain.
2. Preheat oven to 375° F. Grease 1-quart casserole.
3. In large bowl blend egg, butter or margarine, onion, salt and pepper. Stir in eggplant and dry crumbs. Turn into casserole; sprinkle with buttered crumbs.
4. Bake in preheated oven for 30 minutes.

Evaline Kahlke, Beverly Hills Junior Woman's Club, Chicago, Ill.

EGGPLANT AMANDINE

Serves 4 to 6

1 medium eggplant
½ cup salted water
½ cup butter
¾ cup slivered almonds
1 medium onion, finely chopped
¼ cup chopped parsley
¾ cup cracker crumbs
2 eggs
2 tablespoons milk
1 cup grated Cheddar cheese

1. Preheat oven to 400° F. Grease 1-quart casserole.
2. Peel eggplant; cut into 2-inch cubes. Put in saucepan with water. Bring to boil; cover; simmer for 15 minutes, or until tender.
3. Drain; turn into mixing bowl; mash and beat until fluffy.

4. Melt butter in skillet; sauté almonds until a light gold. Remove almonds; set aside.

5. Add onion to butter remaining in skillet; cook over low heat for 5 minutes. Stir in parsley and crumbs. Remove from heat; stir into eggplant.

6. In mixing bowl beat eggs and milk; stir into eggplant mixture. Add almonds; mix well. Turn into casserole; sprinkle with cheese.

7. Bake in preheated oven for 30 minutes.

*Mildred Moss, Gulf Beach Woman's Club,
St. Petersburg, Fla.*

EGGPLANT AND MUSHROOM CASSEROLE

Serves 4

2 tablespoons butter
1 pound mushrooms
1 small eggplant
½ of 10½-ounce can condensed
   cream of celery soup
Dash of sherry

1. Melt butter in skillet; sauté mushrooms, stirring frequently, for 5 minutes, or until tender.

2. Peel eggplant; boil in salted water to cover for 5 minutes. Drain; cut into chunks.

3. Preheat oven to 375° F.

4. Combine mushrooms and eggplant in casserole. Add soup and sherry; stir to mix.

5. Bake in preheated oven for 15 minutes.

*Mrs. John M. Ericson, Thursday Morning Club,
Madison, N.J.*

EGGPLANT OLIVE CASSEROLE

Serves 6

1 large eggplant
Salt
1 tablespoon olive oil
1 medium green pepper, chopped
1 clove garlic, crushed
½ cup chopped ripe olives
½ cup bread crumbs
⅔ cup grated Cheddar cheese

1. Preheat oven to 325° F. Grease 1½-quart casserole.

2. Peel and dice eggplant; put in mixing bowl. Sprinkle with salt; let stand for 30 minutes.

3. Drain eggplant well; cover with boiling water. Cover; cook over medium heat for 15 minutes, or until tender. Drain well; turn into mixing bowl.

4. Heat oil in skillet; sauté green pepper and garlic for 5 minutes. Add to eggplant; mix well.

5. Add 1½ teaspoons salt, olives, half the crumbs and half the cheese; mix well; turn into casserole.

6. Mix remaining crumbs and remaining cheese; sprinkle over eggplant mixture.

7. Bake in preheated oven for 30 minutes.

*Mrs. J. S. Brengle, Sr., Woman's Club,
Tampa, Fla.*

AUBERGINE PROVENÇALE
(Eggplant and Tomatoes)

Serves 6

1 large eggplant
Salt to taste
⅓ cup olive oil
4 large tomatoes, peeled and sliced
3 cloves garlic, thinly sliced

1. Peel eggplant; cut into ¼-inch-thick slices. Sprinkle with salt; let stand for 1 hour. Drain well; pat dry with absorbent paper.

2. Preheat oven to 375° F. Grease 2-quart casserole.

3. Heat a little oil in large skillet; fry a few eggplant slices at a time until browned on all sides. Add oil as needed.

4. Arrange alternate layers of eggplant, tomatoes and garlic in casserole, finishing with eggplant.

5. Cover; bake in preheated oven for 1 hour.

*Mrs. C. P. Heffenger, Woman's Aladdin Club,
Canutillo, Tex.*

EGGPLANT PARMESAN

Serves 6 to 8

½ cup presifted flour
1½ teaspoons salt
¼ teaspoon pepper
2 medium eggplants, peeled and cut
   into ½-inch slices
¾ cup olive oil
½ cup finely chopped onions
½ cup finely chopped green pepper
1 clove garlic, crushed
2 tablespoons chopped parsley
2 8-ounce cans tomato sauce
8 ounces sliced Mozzarella cheese
¼ cup grated Parmesan cheese

1. Preheat oven to 350° F. Grease 10 x 6 x 1½-inch baking pan.

2. On piece of waxed paper mix flour, 1 teaspoon of the salt and ⅛ teaspoon of the pepper; use to dip eggplants.

3. Heat about 2 tablespoons of the oil in large skillet; fry a few eggplant slices at a time until browned on both sides. Add oil to skillet as needed, reserving 2 tablespoons oil. Drain on absorbent paper.

4. Add reserved oil to skillet; sauté onions, green pepper and garlic for 5 minutes. Stir in parsley, tomato sauce, remaining salt and remaining pepper. Simmer for 5 minutes.

5. Spoon half the sauce into pan. Top with eggplant slices. Cover with Mozzarella cheese; spoon remaining sauce on top. Sprinkle with Parmesan cheese.

6. Bake in preheated oven for 30 minutes, or until golden.

*Mrs. Warren Daubert, Senior Woman's Club,
Dallas, Pa.*

EGGPLANT AND BEEF PARMESAN

Serves 6 to 8

1 tablespoon shortening
1 pound ground beef
8 ounces Italian sweet sausage, diced
2 large onions, chopped
2 cloves garlic, crushed
2 1-pound 4-ounce cans tomatoes, undrained
6-ounce can tomato paste
1 teaspoon orégano
Salt and pepper to taste
2 eggs
2 tablespoons water
1 large eggplant, peeled and thinly sliced
Flour
Cooking oil
1 cup grated Parmesan cheese
8 ounces sliced Mozzarella cheese

1. Melt shortening in Dutch oven or large heavy saucepan. Add beef, sausage, onions and garlic; cook over medium heat until meat is browned.
2. Stir in tomatoes, tomato paste, orégano, salt and pepper. Simmer, uncovered, for 1 hour.
3. Meanwhile, in small bowl beat eggs and water. Dip eggplant in egg; coat with flour.
4. Heat oil in large skillet; fry eggplant slices until browned on both sides. Sprinkle each slice with salt.
5. Preheat oven to 375° F. Grease 13 x 9½ x 2-inch baking pan.
6. Spread some sauce in pan; top with layer of eggplant. Sprinkle with Parmesan cheese. Repeat layers, finishing with sauce. Top with Mozzarella cheese.
7. Bake in preheated oven for 25 minutes.

Mrs. Ed Patrie, Palm Springs Woman's Club, Hialeah, Fla.

EGGPLANT PIE

Serves 4

1 medium eggplant, peeled
2 medium potatoes, peeled
4 small green peppers
¼ cup olive oil
1 large onion, sliced
2 cloves garlic, crushed
1¼ teaspoons salt
½ teaspoon pepper
4 eggs
¼ cup grated Romano cheese
2 tablespoons chopped parsley

1. Cut eggplant and potatoes into 1-inch cubes. Cut green peppers into 1-inch squares.
2. Heat oil in large skillet; add prepared vegetables, onion, garlic, 1 teaspoon of the salt and ¼ teaspoon of the pepper. Cover; sauté over low heat for about 20 minutes.
3. Meanwhile, preheat oven to 400° F. Grease 8-inch pie plate.
4. In mixing bowl beat eggs; stir in cheese, parsley, remaining salt and remaining pepper.

5. Arrange vegetables in pie plate; top with egg mixture.
6. Bake in preheated oven for 15 minutes, or until eggs are browned.

Mary Licata, Palm Springs Woman's Club, Hialeah, Fla.

SOUTHERN-STYLE EGGPLANT

Serves 2

1 medium eggplant, unpeeled
3 tablespoons shortening
¼ cup finely chopped onion
1-pound can whole-kernel corn, drained
½ cup fresh bread crumbs
Salt and pepper to taste
4 slices bacon, halved

1. Preheat oven to 400° F. Grease baking sheet.
2. Cut eggplant in half lengthwise. Arrange, cut side down, on baking sheet. Bake in preheated oven for 25 minutes, or until tender.
3. Carefully scoop out eggplant pulp; place shells, right side up, on baking sheet.
4. Prepare filling: Melt shortening in skillet; sauté onion for 5 minutes. Remove from heat; stir in corn, crumbs, salt and pepper. Chop eggplant pulp finely; stir into onion mixture.
5. Fill shells with filling; top with bacon.
6. Bake in preheated oven for 20 minutes.

Mrs. Fredrick Sleight, Woman's Club, Mount Dora, Fla.

STUFFED EGGPLANT

Serves 8

2 medium eggplants, unpeeled
2½ teaspoons salt
¼ teaspoon black pepper
5 tablespoons flour
4 tablespoons olive oil
3 tablespoons butter or margarine
1 cup sliced onions
Dash of cayenne
¾ cup milk
2 tablespoons grated Parmesan cheese
2 tablespoons grated Gruyère cheese
¼ cup heavy cream
1 teaspoon dry mustard
1 cup sliced mushrooms

1. Cut eggplants in half lengthwise. Cut gashes in pulp; sprinkle each half with ½ teaspoon of the salt. Let stand for 30 minutes. Squeeze out excess water from eggplant; wipe dry.
2. On piece of waxed paper combine pepper and flour. Dredge eggplant halves; reserve remaining flour mixture.
3. Heat 2 tablespoons of the oil in large skillet. Add 2 eggplant halves, cut side down; sauté over low heat for 10 minutes. Turn; cook for 10 minutes longer. Remove; repeat with remaining oil and eggplant.
4. Add 2 tablespoons of the butter or margarine to skillet; sauté onions until limp. Blend in reserved flour mixture, remaining salt and cayenne. Stir in milk;

cook over low heat, stirring constantly, until sauce is thickened.

5. In small bowl combine cheeses; stir half into sauce. Stir in 3 tablespoons of the cream and mustard; remove from heat.

6. Melt remaining butter or margarine in another skillet; sauté mushrooms for 5 minutes. Stir into sauce.

7. Scoop out eggplant pulp, leaving ½-inch adhering to shell. Chop eggplant pulp; add to sauce; mix well. Spoon into shells; sprinkle with remaining cheese mixture.

8. Preheat broiler. Arrange eggplant halves on broiler pan.

9. Broil 5 to 6 inches from heat for 6 to 7 minutes, or until golden brown.

10. Just before serving, sprinkle with remaining cream.

Peggy Shores, Senior Woman's Club,
Wytheville, Va.

Endive: See Lettuce, opposite.

Fennel

This plant belongs to the parsley family but resembles celery in appearance. It has the taste and aroma of anise, and it may be cooked or used in any manner suitable for celery. It is excellent served raw and in salads.

Greens

Turnip greens, mustard greens, beet greens, kale and so on may be cooked and served in any manner suitable for spinach.

GREENS

Serves 4

6 cups leaves of white mustard, spinach, water cress, cowslips, dandelions and beet greens
1 teaspoon salt
¼ cup butter

1. If leaves are not fresh, soak in salted cold water for 30 minutes. Drain well.

2. Put greens in saucepan; add 1 cup boiling water and salt. Cover; simmer for 15 minutes, or until greens sink to bottom.

3. Drain; add butter. Toss lightly.

Women's Club, Monroe, Ia.

Kale

Cook like spinach, but a little longer—until fork-tender.

Kohlrabi (Turnip Cabbage)

Another member of the prolific cabbage family, kohlrabi resembles a white turnip in appearance and flavor. The leaves may be cooked like spinach, but the bulbs are the choice part of the vegetable. Select young small bulbs from 1½ to 2½ inches in diameter; bulbs more than 3 inches in diameter may be tough. Boil kohlrabi in the skin, and peel later; or insert a knife under the skin at the base of the raw bulb, strip off the skin, then slice, dice or quarter, and cook. The cooked root may be marinated in French Dressing, like celery root.

BOILED KOHLRABI

Serves 4

8 medium kohlrabi
2 tablespoons melted butter
Salt and pepper to taste

1. Wash kohlrabi, cut off tops; peel. Slice into rapidly boiling water. Bring back to boil; cover; simmer for 15 to 20 minutes, or until tender. Drain.

2. If desired, chop stalks; cook separately in boiling water for 10 minutes, or until tender. Drain; combine with roots.

3. Turn into serving dish; sprinkle with butter, salt and pepper.

VARIATIONS: Serve in Cream Sauce (p. 441) or Chicken Sauce (p. 441).

A. S.

Leeks

Leeks belong to the onion family but are milder in flavor than onions. They may be steamed like asparagus or braised like celery. The coarse green stalks are discarded, and only the thick white part is cooked. Usually it is full of sand, and it must be washed carefully. If it is very sandy, it is best to split it lengthwise and rinse out the sand between the layers. Leeks are excellent creamed, cooked in chicken broth, cooked and added to Cream Sauce (p. 441) or served cold with French Dressing (p. 541).

Lentils: See Index.

Lettuce

Leafy lettuce is seldom cooked unless it is shredded and stewed with green peas or tomatoes, but head lettuce, such as iceberg and Belgian endive, is delicious and delicate braised. For cooking lettuce, select firm heads that look fresh, not wilted.

Belgian endive stalks should also be crisp and moist-looking, not wilted or dry. Leeks and celery may be braised by the same method as that used for lettuce.

BRAISED LETTUCE OR ENDIVES

Serves 4

1 medium lettuce or 8 stalks
    Belgian endive
Boiling chicken broth
1 tablespoon butter
Salt and pepper to taste
Dash of lemon juice (optional)

1. Cut lettuce into quarters; leave endives whole. Arrange in shallow saucepan; add a little broth. Cover; braise for about 8 minutes, or until just tender.

2. Add butter; cook for a few minutes longer, or until most of liquid has been absorbed. Sprinkle with salt, pepper and lemon juice, if desired.

A. S.

ENDIVES PRINTEMPS

Serves 6

2 cups ground cooked chicken
½ cup finely chopped mushrooms
1 cup fresh bread crumbs
2 egg yolks
    Salt
    Pepper
¼ teaspoon thyme
½ teaspoon orégano
2½ cups Thick White Sauce (p. 441)
12 stalks Belgian endive, washed,
    drained and trimmed
½ cup butter or margarine
½ cup boiling water
1 teaspoon lemon juice
1 cup grated Romano cheese
    Paprika

1. Prepare stuffing: In mixing bowl combine chicken, mushrooms, crumbs, egg yolks, ½ teaspoon salt, ¼ teaspoon pepper, thyme, orégano and 1 cup of the Thick White Sauce. Mix well.

2. Gently open endives; spread insides with stuffing. Fold leaves around stuffing.

3. Preheat oven to 350° F. Grease large ovenproof skillet.

4. Arrange endives in skillet; dot with butter or margarine. Pour water over endives. Cover; simmer for 10 minutes. Remove cover; sprinkle with salt and pepper.

5. Put skillet in preheated oven; cover; bake for 45 minutes.

6. Meanwhile, prepare sauce: Blend remaining Thick White Sauce, mayonnaise and lemon juice.

7. Remove skillet; turn temperature to broil.

8. Spread endives with sauce. Sprinkle with cheese; dust with paprika.

9. Broil 5 inches from heat for 5 minutes, or until top is puffed and golden.

Meals on Wheels, Woman's Club,
Greenwich, Conn.

Mushrooms

Fresh mushrooms require little preparation except a gentle rinsing in cold water. Dry thoroughly. They do not need to be peeled unless they are old and yellow. The bottom tough portion of the stems should be cut off, but should not be discarded, for they add flavor to stocks and soups. Because overcooking toughens mushrooms, they should be cooked briefly and rapidly; 4 to 5 minutes is plenty. To keep mushrooms pale, add lemon juice to the poaching water, or sprinkle on both sides with lemon juice when sautéeing them. Mushrooms may be sautéed in butter and used as a garnish for other vegetables, fish, meat, poultry, eggs or pasta.

Imported dried mushrooms are used frequently in soups, stews and Oriental dishes. Canned mushrooms make a fine substitute when the fresh vegetable is not in season.

MUSHROOMS AU GRATIN

Serves 4 to 6

1 pound large mushrooms
1 teaspoon salt
1 teaspoon onion juice
½ cup cracker crumbs
3 tablespoons butter or margarine

1. Preheat oven to 375° F. Grease 10 x 6 x 1½-inch baking pan.

2. Remove stems from mushrooms; cut stems into uniform slices.

3. Arrange caps and stems in pan. Sprinkle with salt and onion juice; cover with crumbs. Dot with butter or margarine.

4. Cover; bake in preheated oven for 20 minutes.

Lorraine K. Myers, Woman's Club, Dundee, Ill.

CREAMED MUSHROOMS

Serves 6

1 pound mushrooms
¼ cup butter
2 tablespoons flour
2 cups milk
½ teaspoon salt
1½ teaspoons Worcestershire

1. Cut mushrooms into 4 or 6 pieces, depending on size. Rinse once in salted water, then twice in clear water.

2. Cover with boiling water; simmer for 5 minutes. Drain in colander.

3. Melt butter in saucepan. Stir in flour. Gradually stir in milk; cook, stirring constantly, until slightly thickened and smooth. Stir in salt, Worcestershire and mushrooms.

4. Keep warm for at least 30 minutes, stirring occasionally, before serving.

Claire Harrison, Culture Club, Columbiana, Ala.

MUSHROOMS PIQUANTE

Serves 8

6 tablespoons butter
3 onions, finely diced
2 pounds mushrooms, thinly sliced
Salt and paprika to taste
¼ cup minced parsley
2 tablespoons flour
3 cups sour cream
Hot buttered toast or waffles

1. Melt butter in skillet; sauté onions until lightly browned. Add mushrooms; cook for 5 to 10 minutes, or until liquid has evaporated.
3. Sprinkle with salt, paprika, parsley and flour. Stir in sour cream. Bring to boil.
4. Serve on toast or waffles, as desired.

Mrs. Joseph Holton Jones, New Century Club,
Wilmington, Del.

MUSHROOMS WITH SOUR CREAM

Serves 4

½ cup butter or margarine
2 scallions, finely chopped
2 pounds mushrooms, sliced
2 tablespoons flour
¼ cup dry sherry
1½ cups sour cream
Salt and pepper to taste
Toast triangles

1. Melt butter or margarine in large skillet; sauté scallions over medium heat for 5 minutes. Stir in mushrooms; sauté for 5 minutes, stirring frequently.
2. Sprinkle with flour; stir in sherry; cook, stirring constantly, for 2 minutes. Add sour cream, salt and pepper; heat to serving temperature.
3. Serve on toast triangles.

Cleo Gardner, Service League, Lombard, Ill.

BAKED STUFFED MUSHROOMS

Makes 24

24 large mushrooms
Lemon juice
½ cup butter
1 clove garlic, crushed
¼ cup grated onion
1 cup fresh bread crumbs
¼ cup chopped parsley
¼ cup grated Swiss cheese
½ teaspoon salt
⅛ teaspoon pepper
¼ cup dry sherry

1. Preheat oven to 350° F. Grease baking sheet.
2. Wash mushrooms; remove and reserve stems. Put caps, stem side up, on baking sheet; sprinkle with lemon juice; set aside. Chop stems finely.
3. Melt ¼ cup of the butter in skillet; sauté reserved stems, garlic and onion for 5 minutes.
5. Remove from heat; stir in ½ cup of the crumbs and remaining ingredients; mix well. Fill mushroom caps with mixture.
6. Melt remaining butter in small saucepan; remove from heat; stir in remaining crumbs. Sprinkle over mushroom caps.

7. Bake in preheated oven for 15 minutes.

Ruth Sears, Women's Club, North Branford, Conn.

STUFFED MUSHROOMS

Serves 4

12 medium mushrooms
Butter or margarine
Salt and pepper to taste
5 slices bacon
1 tablespoon finely chopped onion
1 egg
1 tablespoon lemon juice
1 tablespoon chopped parsley
1 cup fresh bread crumbs
10½-ounce can condensed cream
of mushroom soup
½ cup water

1. Preheat oven to 400° F. Grease baking sheet.
2. Wash mushrooms; remove stems; chop stems finely; set aside.
3. Put caps, stem side up, on baking sheet; dot each with ½ teaspoon butter or margarine. Sprinkle with salt and pepper. Bake in preheated oven for 10 minutes.
4. Cook bacon in skillet until crisp. Drain on absorbent paper; crumble; set aside.
5. Sauté stems and onion in fat remaining in skillet for 5 minutes.
6. In mixing bowl beat egg; stir in lemon juice, parsley, crumbs, sautéed stems and onion and bacon; mix well. Season with salt and pepper; mix; use to fill mushroom caps. Top each with ½ teaspoon butter or margarine.
7. Put baking sheet under broiler. Broil about 5 inches from heat for 5 minutes.
8. Meanwhile, prepare sauce: In saucepan blend soup and water; heat to serving temperature, stirring occasionally. Arrange mushrooms on deep serving dish; top with sauce.

Carol Pitman, Junior Woman's Club,
Jacksonville, Fla.

Okra

Okra is the seed pod of an ornamental plant, originally native to Africa but now cultivated in the Southern United States. Fresh pods are 2 to 4 inches long, are moist-looking and snap easily when broken. Pods too old to cook are dry and woody. Okra, which is extensively used in stews, soups and gumbos, is excellent simply boiled and served with lemon butter, creamed or scalloped; it may also be pan-fried or dipped in batter and deep-fried. It is a natural accompaniment to tomatoes, onions and corn.

BOILED OKRA

Serves 4

1 pound okra
½ teaspoon salt
½ cup water
Melted butter

1. Wash okra thoroughly. Trim stem ends, but do not cut pods.
2. Put okra in heavy saucepan with salt and water. Bring to boil; cover; cook over low heat for 12 to 15 minutes.
3. Serve with butter.

Mrs. E. S. Griffith, Woman's Club, Azusa, Calif.

CREOLE OKRA

Serves 8 to 10

2 slices bacon, diced
2 tablespoons butter or margarine
2 large onions, chopped
2 large green peppers, chopped
2 6-ounce cans tomato paste
1-pound 13-ounce can tomatoes
8-ounce can tomato sauce
⅛ teaspoon garlic salt
1 teaspoon paprika
Dash of Tabasco
Salt and pepper to taste
2 tablespoons shortening
6 cups sliced fresh, canned or defrosted okra

1. Cook bacon in large skillet for 2 minutes. Add butter or margarine, onions and green peppers; sauté for 5 minutes, stirring frequently. Stir in tomato paste, tomatoes, tomato sauce, garlic salt, paprika and Tabasco. Bring to boil; then simmer for 5 minutes.
2. Season with salt and pepper; cover; simmer for 20 minutes longer.
3. Meanwhile, melt shortening; in another large skillet; sauté okra for 5 minutes. Stir into cooked tomato mixture; cover; simmer for 15 minutes longer.

Mrs. Ruth Richard Levy, Tuesday Literary Club, Bolivar, Tenn.

FRIED OKRA

Serves 4

1 pound okra
½ cup presifted flour
¼ cup corn meal
1 teaspoon salt
Bacon drippings

1. Simmer okra in lightly salted water for 5 minutes. Drain.
2. Combine flour, corn meal and salt; use to roll each pod.
3. Melt bacon drippings in skillet; pan-fry okra until browned.

Mignonne Griggs, Woman's Club, Bent Mountain, Va.

SOUTHERN BROWNED OKRA

Serves 6

¼ cup shortening
3 pounds okra, sliced crosswise
1 large onion, chopped
1 teaspoon lemon juice
1 large tomato, diced
Salt to taste
⅛ teaspoon cayenne

1. Melt shortening in large skillet; cook okra over low heat, stirring, until it starts to brown.

2. Stir in onion and lemon juice; cook, stirring frequently, until okra is browned and mixture has been reduced.
3. Add tomato; season with salt; add cayenne. Cover; simmer for 10 minutes, stirring frequently.

Jaynette Taylor, Aggressive Study Club, De Quincy, La.

Onions

The importance of onions in cooking can scarcely be overestimated, as every cook knows. Chives, scallions, shallots and leeks —all belong to the onion family, but it is the white- or yellow-skinned bulb that is used most widely in cooking. The smallest onion, known as the pearl onion, may be white- or yellow-skinned and is often referred to as the pickling onion. The medium onion, 1 to 1½ inches in diameter, is the best size for boiling, braising or serving creamed or in stews and ragouts. The largest white- and yellow-skinned onion is used primarily for grating, mincing or chopping to add flavor to other dishes. The mild-flavored Spanish or Bermuda onion and the purple Italian onion are delicious served raw, in salads or in vegetables vinaigrette.

To avoid tears, peel onions under running cold water; or cook them in their skins, and peel them when partially cooked. If the small pickling onions are covered with boiling water and allowed to stand for 5 minutes, the skins will come off easily and without tears.

FRIED ONIONS AND GREEN TOMATOES

Serves 4

¼ cup shortening
2 cups sliced onions
2 cups sliced green tomatoes
½ teaspoon curry powder
Salt and pepper to taste

1. Melt shortening in skillet; sauté onions over medium heat for 5 minutes.
2. Stir in tomatoes; sauté for 5 minutes. Sprinkle with curry powder; season well with salt and pepper.
3. Cover; cook over low heat for 5 minutes, or until onions are tender.

Helen Remick, Woman's Club, Ogunquit, Me.

FRENCH-FRIED ONION RINGS

Serves 6 to 8

6 large Bermuda onions
½ cup milk
1 egg, well beaten
1 cup presifted flour
½ teaspoon salt
1 teaspoon sugar
1 tablespoon melted shortening
Fat for deep frying

1. Peel onions; cut into ¼-inch-thick slices. Cover with water; let stand for 30

minutes. Drain; wipe dry. Separate slices into rings.

2. Combine milk and egg. Stir in dry ingredients to make a batter. Stir in shortening.

3. Dip onion rings in batter; fry in deep fat heated to 365° F. until lightly browned. Drain on absorbent paper.

Mrs. Otis Durham, Woman's Federated Guild, Moultrie, Ga.

STEWED ONIONS

Serves 4

3 cups thinly sliced onions
1 cup water
2 tablespoons butter
½ teaspoon salt
Dash of pepper
1 cup heavy cream

1. In skillet combine onions, water, butter, salt and pepper. Bring to boil; cover; simmer for 20 minutes, or until tender.

2. Remove cover; cook over high heat until liquid has evaporated.

3. Reduce heat; stir in cream. Heat to serving temperature; do not boil.

Mrs. Brewster, Friday Reading Club, Thayer, Kans.

BAKED ONIONS

Serves 6

24 small white onions
3 cups fresh bread crumbs
1 teaspoon salt
¼ teaspoon pepper
½ cup butter
2 cups milk

1. Preheat oven to 350° F. Grease 2-quart casserole.

2. Cook onions in boiling salted water for 10 minutes; drain.

3. Mix crumbs with salt and pepper.

4. Arrange about one-third of the onions in casserole; sprinkle with 1 cup of the crumbs. Dot with one-third of the butter. Repeat layers until all ingredients have been used, finishing with crumbs dotted with butter. Pour milk over all.

5. Bake in preheated oven for 45 minutes.

Mrs. Alex Hoover, Woman's Club, Ligonier, Pa.

SCALLOPED ONIONS WITH CHEESE SAUCE

Serves 6

5 or 6 medium onions
¼ cup butter
¼ cup presifted flour
2 cups milk
½ teaspoon salt
2 cups grated American cheese

1. Preheat oven to 350° F.

2. Slice onions thinly into 1½-quart casserole.

3. Melt butter in saucepan. Stir in flour. Gradually stir in milk; cook over moderate heat, stirring constantly, until thickened

and smooth. Add salt and cheese; cook, stirring, until melted. Pour over onions.

4. Bake in preheated oven for 1 hour.

Phyllis Edwards, Woman's Club, Sandy Springs, Ga.

SPANISH ONIONS

Serves 4 to 6

6 medium onions
½ cup finely chopped celery
1 teaspoon salt
¼ teaspoon pepper
1-pound 4-ounce can tomatoes
1 tablespoon butter

1. Preheat oven to 350° F. Grease 1-quart casserole.

2. Peel onions; arrange in casserole.

3. In mixing bowl combine celery, salt, pepper and tomatoes; mix well. Pour over onions; dot with butter.

4. Cover; bake in preheated oven for 2 hours.

Mrs. Paul Kammerer, Woman's Club, Emmaus, Pa.

BAKED STUFFED ONIONS

Serves 6

6 large onions
½ cup Medium White Sauce (p. 441)
1 cup grated Cheddar cheese
4-ounce can mushrooms, drained and finely chopped
½ cup fresh bread crumbs
½ teaspoon salt
¼ teaspoon pepper
1 teaspoon dry mustard
½ cup buttered bread crumbs

1. Preheat oven to 375° F. Grease 9-inch square baking pan.

2. Peel onions; put in saucepan. Cover with boiling salted water; cover; cook over medium heat for about 15 minutes, or until tender; drain.

3. Scoop out onion centers, leaving several layers as shell. Arrange shells in pan; set aside.

4. Chop onion centers finely; put in bowl. Stir in all remaining ingredients except buttered crumbs.

5. Fill onion shells with cheese mixture; sprinkle with buttered crumbs. Add enough water to total about ½ inch.

6. Bake in preheated oven for 35 minutes, or until golden.

Mary Ballentine, Finneytown Junior Women's Club, Cincinnati, Ohio

ONION PIE

Serves 6

Pastry for a 1-Crust Pie (p. 548)
3 tablespoons butter or margarine
2½ cups sliced onions
1 cup pitted ripe olives
2 eggs
1 cup sour cream
1 teaspoon salt
⅛ teaspoon pepper
Paprika

1. Preheat oven to 350° F. Roll out Pastry for a 1-Crust Pie; fit into 9-inch pie plate.

2. Melt butter or margarine in skillet; add onions; cover; sauté over low heat for 10 minutes, or until transparent, stirring occasionally. Arrange in pie shell; top with olives.

3. In mixing bowl beat eggs lightly. Add sour cream, salt and pepper; beat until smooth. Pour over onions; sprinkle with paprika.

4. Bake in preheated oven for 25 to 30 minutes.

Mrs. H. R. Bresnahan, Woman's Club, Sebring, Fla.

Oyster Plant (Salsify)

This root vegetable, similar in shape to a parsnip, has a sweet mild flavor somewhat reminiscent of an oyster: hence, its name. It may be boiled, mashed, sautéed, creamed, deep-fried or prepared in any manner suitable for carrots. Oyster plant discolors rapidly. Scrape the roots, and drop immediately into cold water to which a little vinegar or lemon juice has been added.

Parsnips

Parsnips are a late fall and winter vegetable too little used in American kitchens. They do not appear in the market until after a severe frost, for they need to be frostbitten to develop their full flavor. Resembling carrots in shape, parsnips have a brownish yellow skin and, when cooked, have a marvelous sweet nutty flavor. Select smooth firm roots. Small or medium parsnips are best, for oversize ones may be woody in the center. Like oyster plants, they may be cooked in any manner suitable for carrots.

BOILED PARSNIPS

Serves 4

8 medium parsnips
2 tablespoons melted butter
Salt and pepper to taste
Minced parsley

1. Wash parsnips; scrub with stiff brush. Put in saucepan; cover with water. Bring to boil; cook for 20 to 25 minutes, or until fork-tender.

2. Drain; peel; slit lengthwise. If core is mushy, scoop it out, since it will have little flavor.

3. Sprinkle with butter, salt, pepper and parsley.

VARIATIONS:

1. Rice the peeled cooked parsnips, and serve in place of potatoes.

2. Sauté cooked parsnips in butter until golden brown on all sides.

3. Dip in batter, and French-fry.

4. Add to Cream Sauce (p. 441) or Cheese Sauce (p. 442).

A. S.

BAKED PARSNIPS

Serves 6

2 pounds parsnips
½ pound salt pork, diced
1 tablespoon sugar
½ cup beef broth

1. Preheat oven to 350° F. Grease 1½-quart casserole.

2. Peel and slice parsnips. Put in saucepan; add 2 inches salted water; bring to boil. Cover; parboil for 10 minutes. Drain.

3. Arrange alternate layers of parsnips and pork in casserole. Blend sugar and broth; pour over parsnips.

4. Bake in preheated oven for 35 minutes.

Mrs. R. L. Coin, Woman's Club, Waynesville, N.C.

CANDIED PARSNIPS

Serves 4 to 6

4 medium parsnips, scraped and quartered
¾ cup brown sugar
½ teaspoon salt
Dash of pepper

1. Preheat oven to 325° F. Grease 1-quart casserole.

2. Cook parsnips in boiling salted water for 20 minutes, or until tender.

3. Drain parsnips; arrange in casserole. Combine sugar, salt and pepper; sprinkle over parsnips.

4. Bake in preheated oven for 40 minutes, or until browned and slightly candied.

Mrs. Alice Weiler, Roosevelt Neighborhood Woman's Club, Phoenix, Ariz.

Peas

There is no more delectable vegetable than garden-fresh peas. They are at their peak of perfection when braised in very little water or broth with butter, salt and pepper and cooked only until just tender. They should not be drained but should be served with the pan liquid. A pound of peas, shelled, makes about 1 cup or 2 servings.

Cooked peas are delicious added to Cream Sauce (p. 441) or sour cream or combined with sliced water chestnuts or cooked tiny onions. They may also be flavored with mint or sprinkled with curry powder or chopped chives. Canned or frozen green peas may be substituted for fresh, and the tiny petits pois are especially delicious.

For dried peas, see Index.

NEW PEAS

Serves 4

1 pound peas
½ cup boiling water
½ teaspoon salt
⅔ cup heavy cream
1 tablespoon butter or margarine
1 teaspoon sugar

1. Shell peas; put in saucepan; add water and salt. Cover; simmer for 20 minutes.
2. Add cream, butter or margarine and sugar; simmer for 2 minutes longer.

Mrs. G. M. Cowles, Women's Club, Monroe, Ia.

PEAS DELICIOUS

Serves 6 to 8

2 tablespoons butter or margarine
2 tablespoons water
1 clove garlic, impaled on
wooden pick
6 small white onions
3 large lettuce leaves, quartered
1 teaspoon sugar
¾ teaspoon salt
⅛ teaspoon pepper
2 10-ounce packages frozen peas

1. Melt butter or margarine in large skillet. Stir in water, garlic, onions, lettuce, sugar, salt and pepper. Cover; simmer for 30 minutes.
2. Add peas; cover; simmer for 30 minutes longer.
3. Discard garlic; stir well.

Junior Woman's Club, Pacific Beach, Calif.

TASTY PEAS AND CELERY

Serves 6

¼ cup butter or margarine
½ cup bias-cut sliced celery
¼ cup finely chopped onion
1 cup sliced mushrooms
2 tablespoons chopped pimiento
½ teaspoon salt
Dash of pepper
1-pound 4-ounce can peas, drained

1. Melt butter or margarine in saucepan; sauté celery and onion over medium heat for 5 minutes. Add mushrooms; sauté for 5 minutes longer.
2. Add pimiento, salt and pepper; simmer, uncovered, for 5 minutes. Add peas; heat to serving temperature.

Mrs. E. Wilson, Pierian Study Club, Vivian, La.

FRENCH PEAS

Serves 6

4 slices bacon, chopped
1 tablespoon chopped onion
1 tablespoon flour
2½ cups cooked peas
½ cup light cream
2 tablespoons butter
1 cup chopped mushrooms
Salt and pepper to taste

1. Sauté bacon in saucepan until partially cooked. Add onion; cook until onion is tender and bacon is crisp.

2. Stir in flour. Add peas and cream; cook until thickened, stirring occasionally.
3. Melt butter in skillet; sauté mushrooms for 5 minutes. Add to peas; season with salt and pepper.

Modern Study Club Cook Book, Mobile, Ala.

ENGLISH PEA CASSEROLE

Serves 8

3 1-pound cans peas
¾ cup butter
¾ cup chopped scallions
1½ cups chopped celery
2 tablespoons flour
5-ounce can water chestnuts,
drained and sliced
Salt and pepper to taste
1 cup fresh bread crumbs

1. Preheat oven to 375° F. Grease 2-quart casserole.
2. Drain peas; reserve liquid. Arrange peas in casserole.
3. Melt ½ cup of the butter in saucepan; sauté scallions and celery for 5 minutes. Sprinkle with flour; gradually stir in reserved liquid. Cook, stirring constantly, until sauce is thickened. Add water chestnuts; season with salt and pepper.
4. Pour sauce over peas; sprinkle with crumbs. Dot with remaining butter.
5. Bake in preheated oven for 20 minutes, or until golden.

*Mrs. Guy Black, Sorosis Woman's Club,
Orlando, Fla.*

CREOLE PEAS

Serves 6

¼ cup butter or margarine
½ cup chopped green pepper
½ cup chopped celery
1 small onion, chopped
1-pound can peas, drained
4-ounce can sliced mushrooms,
drained
4-ounce jar pimientos, drained
and diced
2 eggs, hard-cooked and chopped
10½-ounce can condensed tomato soup
¼ teaspoon Worcestershire
Salt and pepper to taste
½ cup cracker crumbs

1. Preheat oven to 350° F. Grease 1½-quart casserole.
2. Melt butter or margarine in skillet; sauté green pepper, celery and onion for 10 minutes.
3. Turn into mixing bowl; add peas, mushrooms, pimientos and eggs; toss lightly. Add soup, Worcestershire, salt and pepper. Mix well; turn into casserole. Sprinkle with crumbs.
4. Bake in preheated oven for 40 minutes.

*Mrs. Johnny Arrington, Veritas Club,
Greensboro, Ala.*

Peppers, Green and Red

Green peppers, also known as sweet bell peppers, are available almost all year. They should be firm, crisp and a shiny bright green. They are widely used in stews, soups, casseroles and salads, and they add flavor and color to stewed tomatoes and corn. They make an excellent luncheon dish, stuffed with rice, meat, chicken or fish and baked.

Just before the first frost green peppers are allowed to remain on the vine to ripen and turn red. These red peppers may be eaten or cooked in any way suitable for green peppers.

Curried peppers are superb. To make them, wash and seed peppers; cut them into large dice or long strips. Braise in butter with a heaping teaspoon curry powder for about 10 minutes, or until wilted. Serve as an accompaniment to roast lamb or chops.

ITALIAN FRIED PEPPERS

Serves 2

2 large green peppers
3 tablespoons olive oil
1 clove garlic, crushed
½ teaspoon orégano
Salt to taste

1. Wash and seed peppers. Cut into strips.
2. Heat oil in skillet; sauté garlic for 2 minutes. Add peppers; coat well with oil. Stir in orégano and salt.
3. Cover; simmer for 20 minutes, stirring frequently.

Joan M. Williams, Woman's Club, Essex, Conn.

BEST-EVER STUFFED PEPPERS

Serves 6

6 large green peppers
1 tablespoon olive oil
1½ pounds ground beef
1 medium onion, chopped
8-ounce can whole-kernel corn, drained
Salt and pepper to taste
¼ teaspoon basil
1 cup grated Cheddar cheese
10½-ounce can condensed tomato soup
⅓ cup water
8-ounce package noodles, cooked and drained

1. Wash peppers thoroughly; remove tops, seeds and membranes. Chop tops.
2. Heat oil in large skillet; sauté beef, onion and pepper tops over medium heat until meat is browned.
3. Stir in corn, salt, pepper and basil. Turn into large bowl; clean skillet.
4. Arrange peppers in skillet; fill with meat mixture. Sprinkle with cheese; pour soup and water over all.
5. Cover; simmer for 40 minutes, or until tender. Serve with noodles.

Mrs. Dale Martin, Palm Springs Woman's Club, Hialeah, Fla.

GREEN PEPPERS STUFFED WITH HAM

Serves 8

8 large green peppers
1 cup diced cooked ham
1 small onion, grated
1 cup cooked rice
½ cup condensed cream of mushroom soup
1 teaspoon Worcestershire
½ teaspoon salt
1 cup fresh bread crumbs
⅓ cup melted butter or margarine

1. Preheat oven to 350° F. Grease 13 x 9½ x 2-inch baking pan.
2. Cut slice from top of each pepper; remove membranes and seeds.
3. Put peppers in large bowl; cover with boiling water. Let stand for 8 minutes; drain well.
4. Combine ham, onion, rice, soup, Worcestershire and salt.
5. Arrange peppers, cut side up, in pan. Fill with ham mixture. In small bowl blend crumbs with butter or margarine; sprinkle over peppers. Add water to cover bottom of pan.
6. Bake in preheated oven for 40 minutes.

Ruth Anderson, Leroy Fidelis Club, Crown Point, Ind.

MACARONI-STUFFED PEPPERS

Serves 6

6 large green peppers
2 cups cooked elbow macaroni
1 cup condensed tomato soup
¾ cup grated Cheddar cheese
1 egg, lightly beaten
¾ cup bread crumbs

1. Preheat oven to 400° F. Grease 10 x 6 x 1½-inch baking pan.
2. Cut slice from top of each pepper; remove seeds and membranes.
3. Cook peppers in boiling salted water in large saucepan for 5 minutes. Drain well; arrange, cut side up, in pan.
4. Chop macaroni; turn into mixing bowl. Add soup, cheese and egg; mix well.
5. Fill peppers with macaroni mixture; sprinkle with crumbs.
6. Bake in preheated oven for 12 minutes.

Shirley Vilsmeier, Junior Woman's Club, Lansdale, Pa.

Potatoes

The potato is one of the most important foods that America has given the world. The early Spanish explorers found it growing in Peru and took it back to Spain. From there it was introduced into Central Europe and rapidly spread into Germany. Auguste Parmentier introduced it into France and England, and English colonists brought it back with them to America.

Like bread and rice, potatoes are a major staple food and are harvested yearly by the billions of bushels.

There are two main types of potato: the long mealy potato, such as the Idaho, which is best for baking and mashing, and the harder, waxier potato, such as the Irish Cobbler, which is suitable for all other uses. New potatoes, or potatoes dug before they are fully mature, have a delicate flavor and thin tender skin. They do not keep long and should be cooked as soon as possible after they are purchased. They are delicious cooked whole, either peeled or in their jackets. Lately dehydrated potatoes have become popular for a quick mashed potato dish, and small potato balls are available in cans. These are convenient to keep on hand for a last-minute addition to a soup or stew. Several prepared potato products, such as French fries and potato puffs, are found in frozen food counters and need only be heated according to package directions.

Basic Ways to Cook Potatoes

BOILED POTATOES

Select potatoes of uniform size. Use medium potatoes, or cut large ones into uniform pieces so they will cook evenly. Small new potatoes do not need to be peeled unless desired, but in peeling any potato, peel very thinly, for much of the valuable nutrient lies just under the skin. Drop the peeled potato immediately into cold water to cover so that its surface will not turn black.

When ready to cook, cover with salted water; bring to boil; boil for about 20 minutes for medium potatoes, or until potatoes are tender when tested with a fork. Drain thoroughly; shake pan with potatoes over the heat for 2 to 3 minutes, to dry them. Turn into serving dish; sprinkle with salt, pepper and melted butter. Sprinkle with chopped parsley or fresh dill, if desired; finely chopped scallion tops or chives are also an excellent addition. If potatoes were cooked in their jackets, strip off skins while they are hot; finish as for peeled potatoes.

MASHED POTATOES

Peel and boil potatoes until very tender. Drain; dry thoroughly over heat. Press potatoes through potato ricer into warm mixing bowl. Beat in a chunk of softened butter or some melted butter; season to taste with salt and pepper. Beat until light and fluffy, adding a little hot milk or cream if desired. Serve immediately, or set mixing bowl in a pan of simmering water to keep potatoes hot until ready to serve.

BAKED POTATOES

Scrub uniformly sized potatoes; prick each in several places with a fork to allow steam to escape. Idahos are best for baking. Bake in preheated 425° F. oven for 40 to 60 minutes, or until potatoes feel tender when pressed on each side by hand protected by potholder. For soft skins, rub potatoes with a little cooking oil or butter before baking. Remove potatoes from oven; cut a cross in center top of each. Push ends of potatoes toward center to open cross. Put a chunk of butter in each cross; sprinkle with salt, pepper or parika and chopped chives or parsley, as desired. Some people like baked potatoes topped with a big dollop of sour cream.

COTTAGE FRIED POTATOES

Dice cold boiled potatoes. Sauté in hot butter or bacon drippings in heavy skillet until browned on all sides. Season with salt and pepper. If desired, sauté a little minced onion or garlic in the hot fat before adding potatoes.

FRANCONIA POTATOES

Peel small or medium potatoes, or cut large potatoes into uniform pieces. Cook in boiling salted water for 10 minutes; drain. About 1 hour before a beef or lamb roast is ready to serve, arrange potatoes in pan drippings. Baste occasionally with drippings; turn once to brown evenly on all sides.

FRENCH-FRIED POTATOES

Peel firm potatoes of good size. Cut lengthwize into uniform strips no thicker than ½ inch and preferably thinner. Very thin strips are known as julienne fried potatoes. Drop strips immediately into cold water to cover; refrigerate for 30 minutes. Heat cooking oil or fat in deep-fat fryer to 365° F. Drain potatoes; dry well between paper towels. Drop a few potatoes at a time into oil or fat; fry for about 20 minutes, or until crisp and golden brown. Skim potatoes out of oil or fat with slotted spoon; drain on absorbent paper. Keep hot; sprinkle with salt before serving.

Twice-fried potatoes are fried as above until soft and just beginning to color. Drain on absorbent paper; set aside. When ready to serve, reheat oil or fat to 365° F. Fry for 2 minutes, or until hot, crisp and golden.

POTATOES LYONNAISE

Serves 6

3 tablespoons butter or bacon drippings
2 tablespoons minced onion
3 cups diced cooked potatoes
Salt and pepper to taste
1 tablespoon minced parsley

1. Melt butter or bacon drippings in skillet; sauté onion for 10 minutes, or until transparent and beginning to turn golden.

2. Add potatoes, salt and pepper. Toss to coat potatoes in fat. Cover; cook for 5 minutes. Remove cover; cook until browned. Sprinkle with parsley.

A. S.

Baked Potatoes

BAKED POTATOES WITH RUSSIAN CAVIAR

Serves 4

4 medium baking potatoes
Butter
4 ounces Russian caviar
1½ cups sour cream

1. Preheat oven to 400° F.
2. Bake potatoes in preheated oven for about 1 hour, or until soft.
3. Cut a deep cross in each potato; squeeze from sides to open top.
4. Insert a dab of butter in each potato; top with 2 tablespoons of the caviar. Serve sour cream separately.

Mrs. Achille Capecelatro, Thursday Morning Club, Madison, N.J.

SPUD 'N' ONION BAKE

Serves 4

4 medium baking potatoes
¼ cup butter or margarine
2 medium onions, sliced
Salt and pepper to taste
2 tablespoons chopped parsley

1. Preheat oven to 375° F. Cut 4 double-thickness squares of aluminum foil; place on baking sheet.
2. Peel potatoes; cut each into 4 crosswise slices. Spread each with butter or margarine.
3. Reassemble potatoes, arranging onion slices between potato slices. Secure with wooden picks.
4. Sprinkle generously with salt and pepper; wrap each potato in foil square.
5. Arrange on baking sheet; bake in preheated oven for 1 hour.
6. Open foil; sprinkle with parsley.

Mrs. James S. O'Daniel, Jr., Junior Woman's Club, Conover, N.C.

BAKED STUFFED POTATOES

Serves 8

4 large baking potatoes, baked
¼ cup butter or margarine
¾ cup milk
1 teaspoon salt
½ cup grated Cheddar cheese
Paprika to taste

1. Preheat oven to 375° F.
2. Cut potatoes in half lengthwise; scoop out pulp, leaving thin shell.
3. Whip pulp with butter and milk until light and fluffy. Add salt; pile into shells. Put on baking sheet; sprinkle with cheese.
4. Bake in preheated oven for 15 minutes. Sprinkle with paprika just before serving.

Mrs. Jennie Selid, Book & Thimble Club, Portland, N.D.

BAKED STUFFED POTATOES WITH CHIVES

Serves 4

4 medium baking potatoes
3 tablespoons butter
½ teaspoon salt
¼ teaspoon white pepper
¼ cup hot milk
2 teaspoons minced chives or scallion tops
1 egg white, stiffly beaten
Grated cheese

1. Preheat oven to 400° F.
2. Bake potatoes in preheated oven for 50 minutes, or until tender. Cut slice off top of each potato; scoop out pulp.
3. Mash pulp well; add butter, salt, pepper, milk and chives or scallion tops; beat until fluffy. Fold in egg white. Pile lightly into shells; sprinkle with cheese.
4. Bake for 5 to 8 minutes longer, or until browned.

Jewel Roberts, North Long Beach Women's Club, Long Beach, Calif.

STUFFED POTATOES WITH SHRIMP

Serves 4

4 medium baking potatoes
4 tablespoons butter
½ cup milk
½ teaspoon salt or to taste
2 cups diced cooked shrimp
2-ounce can sliced mushrooms, drained
1 cup shredded Cheddar cheese
Cooked whole shrimp

1. Preheat oven to 450° F.
2. Bake potatoes in preheated oven for about 1 hour, or until tender. Remove potatoes; turn temperature to 400° F.
3. Cut potatoes in half lengthwise; scoop out pulp, being careful not to break shells.
4. Mash pulp; beat in butter, milk and salt. Fold in diced shrimp and mushrooms. Pile lightly into shells, mounding up slightly. Sprinkle with cheese.
5. Bake in preheated oven for 15 minutes, or until cheese is melted and potatoes are very hot. Garnish with whole shrimp.

Mrs. Vance V. Omohundro, President, Crafts and Hobbies Club, St. Louis, Mo.

BAKED SHOESTRING POTATOES

Serves 4 to 6

4 medium potatoes
3 tablespoons butter or margarine
½ cup grated Cheddar cheese
2 tablespoons chopped parsley
1½ teaspoons salt
Dash of pepper
½ cup heavy cream

1. Preheat oven to 450° F. Cut 48 inches of aluminum foil; fold in half. Place on baking sheet.
2. Peel potatoes; cut lengthwise into thin strips as for French fries.

3. Place potatoes in center of foil; dot with butter. Sprinkle with cheese, parsley, salt and pepper. Pull up edges of foil; pour cream over potatoes. Fold foil to make package.

4. Bake in preheated oven for 1 hour.

Louise West, Junior Sorosis, Canton, Ohio

TOASTED POTATOES

Serves 8

8 medium potatoes
½ cup softened butter
1½ cups cracker crumbs
1 egg, lightly beaten
1 teaspoon salt
¼ teaspoon pepper

1. Preheat oven to 400° F. Grease casserole.

2. Peel potatoes; wash and dry well.

3. Brush potatoes with ¼ cup of the butter; roll in crumbs; dip in egg; roll again in crumbs.

4. Place potatoes in casserole; sprinkle with salt and pepper. Dot with remaining butter.

5. Bake in preheated oven for 1 hour, or until tender.

Florence Morrison, Century Club, Coraopolis, Pa.

Fried Potatoes

HERB FRIED POTATOES

Serves 4

3 tablespoons butter
3 large potatoes, peeled and
    cut into ⅛-inch-thick slices
½ teaspoon orégano
2 teaspoons finely chopped celery
2 teaspoons finely chopped onion
2 teaspoons chopped parsley
Salt and pepper to taste

1. Melt butter in large skillet. Add potatoes; cover; cook over medium heat for 10 minutes.

2. Carefully turn potatoes; cook, uncovered, for 10 minutes.

3. Sprinkle with remaining ingredients; cook for 5 minutes longer.

Lucy Schoff, Junior Woman's Club, St. Cloud, Fla.

BEER POTATOES

Serves 6

2 1-pound cans whole potatoes
Beer Batter for Vegetables (p. 383)
Fat for deep frying

1. Drain potatoes; wipe dry with absorbent paper. Dip into Beer Batter for Vegetables, coating completely.

2. Fry potatoes in deep fat heated to 365° F. for about 5 minutes, or until golden. Drain on absorbent paper.

*Mrs. Jack Thomas, Golfview Hills Woman's Club,
Hinsdale, Ill.*

OVEN-BAKED FRENCH FRIES

Serves 6

6 potatoes, peeled and cut into
    ⅜-inch-thick strips

⅓ cup melted shortening
Salt and pepper to taste

1. Preheat oven to 450° F.

2. Dip potatoes in shortening. Arrange in large shallow baking pan; do not overlap.

3. Bake in preheated oven for 45 minutes, or until crisp. Sprinkle with salt and pepper. (If cooked but not browned enough, place under broiler for a few minutes.)

Kathryn Hartl, Study Club, La Crosse, Wis.

OVEN HASHED BROWN POTATOES

Serves 10 to 12

3 pounds potatoes, unpeeled
½ cup butter or margarine
2 large onions, chopped
2 tablespoons Worcestershire
2 teaspoons salt
1 tablespoon paprika
½ teaspoon pepper
2 tablespoons chopped parsley

1. Preheat oven to 425 °F. Grease 10 x 6 x 1½-inch baking pan.

2. Put potatoes in saucepan; add boiling salted water to half cover them. Cover; boil for 20 minutes, or until tender.

3. Drain; cool; then peel and cube. Place in baking pan.

4. Melt butter or margarine in skillet; sauté onions for 2 minutes. Remove from heat; stir in remaining ingredients. Pour over potatoes; stir with fork to mix.

5. Bake in preheated oven for 1 hour. Just before serving, put under broiler for a few minutes to brown.

*Jane Hoffman, Woman's Club,
Monterey Park, Calif.*

SESAME POTATO SPEARS

Serves 6 to 8

Halved broiling chickens may be baked along with potatoes for dinner.

6 to 8 medium potatoes
¼ cup melted butter
2 teaspoons salt
2 teaspoons paprika
¼ cup sesame seeds

1. Preheat oven to 400° F. Grease baking sheet.

2. Peel potatoes; cut lengthwise into thick strips. Dip in butter to coat completely.

3. On piece of waxed paper mix together salt, paprika and sesame seeds; use to coat potatoes. Arrange on baking sheet.

4. Bake in preheated oven for 1 hour, or until tender.

*Joz Hostage, Junior Woman's Club,
Cheshire, Conn.*

Potato Pancakes

POTATO LATKES
Serves 4

A traditional dish at Hanukkah, the Jewish Festival of Lights.

6 medium potatoes, peeled
1 small onion
2 eggs
2 tablespoons flour
1 teaspoon salt
¼ teaspoon baking powder
Dash of pepper
Fat for deep frying
Sour cream or applesauce

1. Grate potatoes and onion; turn into mixing bowl.
2. Stir in eggs, flour, salt, baking powder and pepper; mix well.
3. Drop by tablespoons into deep fat heated to 365° F. Fry for 3 to 4 minutes, or until golden, turning once.
4. Drain on absorbent paper. Serve with sour cream or applesauce, as desired.

Lee M. Grower, Home Club, Cromwell, Conn.

KARTOFFEL PUFFER
(German Potato Pancakes)
Serves 6

4 large potatoes, peeled
1 small onion
2 eggs
2 tablespoons flour
Salt and pepper to taste
Dash of nutmeg

1. Put potatoes and onion through medium blade of meat grinder.
2. Put in mixing bowl; add eggs, one at a time, beating well after each addition. Stir in remaining ingredients.
3. Grease and preheat griddle. Drop batter by tablespoons onto griddle. Cook for about 3 minutes on each side, or until browned.

Mrs. Jess Tolerton, Junior Women's Club, Cheyenne, Wyo.

SHALLOW-FRIED POTATO PANCAKES
Makes 12

3 large potatoes, peeled
1 small onion
2 eggs
½ cup presifted flour
¾ teaspoon salt
Dash of pepper
Fat for shallow frying

1. Grate potatoes and onion, using medium grater. Mix.
2. Add eggs; stir until well blended. Stir in flour, salt and pepper.
3. Heat enough fat in skillet to measure about ½ inch when melted. When very hot, spoon in potato mixture, using about ¼ cup for each pancake. Pat lightly with spoon to spread to desired thickness. Fry until golden brown on both sides.

Gloria Hooper, Woman's Club, Temple City, Calif.

Raw Potato Dishes

PEEKET POTATOES
Serves 8

6 large potatoes, peeled and grated
1 teaspoon salt
3 eggs, lightly beaten
½ cup milk
½ teaspoon baking powder
2 tablespoons flour
8 ounces sliced bacon
Applesauce on tart salad

1. Preheat oven to 350° F. Grease 10 x 6 x 1½-inch baking pan.
2. In mixing bowl combine potatoes, salt, eggs and milk; stir well.
3. In small bowl blend baking powder and flour; stir into potato mixture.
4. Arrange half the bacon in pan. Pour in potato mixture; top with remaining bacon.
5. Bake in preheated oven for 50 minutes.
6. Serve with applesauce or salad, as desired.

Mrs. Ruth Anne Ceder, Woman's Club, Blandinsville, Ill.

LITHUANIAN POTATO PUDDING
Serves 6 to 8

1 tablespoon butter or margarine
½ pound smoked ham, cubed
1 medium onion, chopped
10 medium potatoes, peeled and grated
2 eggs
2 teaspoons salt
¼ teaspoon pepper

1. Preheat oven to 350° F. Grease 1½-quart casserole.
2. Melt butter or margarine in skillet; sauté ham until golden. Add onion; sauté for 5 minutes.
3. In mixing bowl combine potatoes, eggs, salt and pepper. Stir in ham mixture.
4. Turn into casserole; bake in preheated oven for 1 hour. (If top is not golden brown, place under broiler for about 5 minutes.)

Mrs. Milton J. Stipek, American Home Chairman, Woman's Club, 6th District of Illinois, Cicero, Ill.

O'BRIEN POTATOES
Serves 4

2 cups diced potatoes
¼ cup finely chopped onion
1 teaspoon parsley flakes
¼ cup chopped pimientos
¼ cup finely chopped green pepper
Salt and pepper to taste
¼ cup melted butter

1. Preheat oven to 350° F. Grease 1-quart casserole.
2. Cook potatoes in a little boiling salted water for 10 minutes, or until just tender. Drain; turn into casserole.
3. Add onion, parsley, pimientos and green pepper. Season with salt and pepper; toss lightly. Sprinkle with butter.

4. Bake in preheated oven for 20 minutes.

Woman's Club, Newark, Ill.

POTATOES PIMIENTO

Serves 6

6 large potatoes
3 tablespoons butter or margarine
2 medium onions, finely chopped
    Salt and pepper to taste
4-ounce can pimientos, drained
    and diced
1 cup grated sharp Cheddar cheese
    Paprika

1. Preheat oven to 375° F. Grease 1½-quart casserole.
2. Peel and cube potatoes. Cook in boiling salted water for about 15 minutes, or until tender. Drain; set aside.
3. Meanwhile, melt butter or margarine in skillet; sauté onions for 10 minutes.
4. Combine potatoes and onions; season with salt and pepper. Stir in pimientos; turn into casserole. Sprinkle with cheese and paprika.
5. Bake in preheated oven for 30 minutes.

*Peg Bowman, Woman's Club,
Temple Terrace, Fla.*

GRATIN DAUPHINOISE

Serves 6

2 pounds potatoes
½ clove garlic
5 tablespoons butter
1 teaspoon salt
⅛ teaspoon pepper
1 cup shredded Swiss cheese
1 cup hot cream
    Milk

1. Preheat oven to 350° F.
2. Peel potatoes; cut into slices about ⅛ inch thick. Put in bowl of cold water.
3. Rub shallow (no more than 2-inch-deep) baking dish with garlic; grease with 1 tablespoon of the butter. Mince garlic; set aside.
4. Drain potatoes; dry on absorbent paper. Spread half in baking dish. Sprinkle with garlic; dot with 2 tablespoons of the butter; sprinkle with ½ teaspoon of the salt, ¼ teaspoon of the pepper and ½ cup of the cheese. Arrange remaining potatoes on first layer. Dot with remaining butter; sprinkle with remaining salt, pepper and cheese.
5. Pour cream over potatoes. Add milk just to cover; cook over low heat until simmering.
6. Put potatoes in preheated oven; bake for 50 to 60 minutes, or until most of milk and cream have been absorbed and top of potatoes is browned.

*Belair Women's International Cook Book,
Belair, Md.*

POTATOES AU GRATIN

Serves 4 to 6

3 tablespoons butter
3 tablespoons whole wheat flour
1½ cups milk
1 teaspoon salt
1 cup shredded Cheddar cheese
1 tablespoon grated onion
4 cups thinly sliced potatoes

1. Melt butter in saucepan. Stir in flour; cook, stirring, until well blended. Gradually stir in milk; cook, stirring constantly, until sauce is thickened and smooth.
2. Stir in salt and cheese; cook until melted. Remove from heat; stir in onion.
3. Preheat oven to 350° F. Grease 1½-quart baking dish.
4. Arrange alternate layers of potatoes and sauce in baking dish, finishing with sauce.
5. Bake in preheated oven for 1 hour. Turn top potatoes under; bake for 1 hour longer.

*Kathryn Saywell, North Long Beach Women's
Club, Long Beach, Calif.*

POTATOES, MUSHROOMS, ONIONS— AU GRATIN

Serves 10 to 12

5 pounds potatoes
½ teaspoon salt
⅓ cup butter or margarine
1 pound mushrooms, sliced
4 tablespoons flour
2 cups milk
½ cup light cream
10½-ounce can condensed beef
    consommé
2 cups grated Cheddar cheese
½ teaspoon seasoned salt
¼ teaspoon pepper
1 teaspoon Worcestershire
2 1-pound cans small white onions,
    drained

1. Peel potatoes; cut into ½-inch cubes. Put in large saucepan; add water to half cover potatoes. Add salt. Cover; cook over medium heat for 15 minutes, or until tender; drain.
2. Meanwhile, preheat oven to 350° F. Grease 4-quart casserole.
3. Melt butter or margarine in saucepan; sauté mushrooms for 5 minutes. Blend in flour. Gradually stir in milk, cream and consommé. Cook over medium heat, stirring constantly, until sauce is thickened and smooth.
4. Add cheese, seasoned salt, pepper and Worcestershire; cook over low heat, stirring, until cheese is melted.
5. Arrange potatoes and onions in casserole; top with sauce.
6. Bake in preheated oven for 45 minutes, or until golden brown.

*Coleen Govig, Finneytown Junior Women's Club,
Cincinnati, Ohio*

MASHED POTATOES À LA PHYFE
Serves 6

9 medium potatoes
1 teaspoon olive oil
2 tablespoons butter
½ clove garlic, grated
Few dashes of paprika
¼ teaspoon salt
Pinch of pepper
⅛ teaspoon celery seed
½ cup light cream

1. Peel potatoes; cook in boiling salted water until tender. Drain; mash.
2. Heat oil and butter in deep saucepan; sauté garlic for 1 minute.
3. Add paprika, salt, pepper, celery seed and potatoes. Beat with spoon, occasionally adding a dash of cream until all cream is used and potatoes are light and fluffy.

Helen Urbany, Carmichaels and Cumberland Township Civic Club, Carmichaels, Pa.

GUISADO DE PAPAS
(Stewed Potatoes)
Serves 4

2 tablespoons shortening
1 large onion, chopped
1 clove garlic, crushed
3 large tomatoes, diced
½ cup chopped parsley
12 small new potatoes, unpeeled
Salt and pepper to taste

1. Melt shortening in large skillet; sauté onion and garlic over medium heat for 5 minutes.
2. Stir in tomatoes and parsley; cover; simmer for 15 minutes.
3. Add potatoes; cover; cook over low heat for 20 minutes, or until tender. Season with salt and pepper.

Mrs. Vernon Knapp, Woman's Club, Roswell, N.M.

SCALLOPED POTATOES
Serves 4 to 6

10½-ounce can condensed cream of
celery or mushroom soup
¾ cup milk
Dash of pepper
4 cups thinly sliced potatoes
1 medium onion, thinly sliced
1 cup grated Cheddar cheese
1 tablespoon butter or margarine

1. Preheat oven to 375° F. Grease 2-quart casserole.
2. Blend soup, milk and pepper.
3. Arrange alternate layers of potatoes, onion and cheese in casserole. Pour soup mixture over all; dot with butter or margarine.
4. Cover; bake in preheated oven for 1 hour. Remove cover; bake for 15 minutes longer, or until tender.

Mrs. Carrol Bauske, Fortnightly Club, Dawson, N.D.

ESCALLOPED POTATOES AND HAM
Serves 6

4 cups thinly sliced potatoes
2 cups diced cooked ham

1 cup shredded Cheddar cheese
Salt and pepper to taste
¼ cup butter
About 2 cups scalding-hot milk

1. Preheat oven to 350° F. Grease 2½-quart casserole.
2. In casserole arrange alternate layers of potatoes, ham, and cheese: sprinkle with salt and pepper. Repeat until all ingredients have been used, finishing with potatoes.
3. Dot with butter; pour in sufficient milk to come just below top layer of potatoes.
4. Bake in preheated oven for 1¼ hours.

Viola M. Smith, Women's Club, Durham, N.H.

Cooked Potato Dishes

COTTAGE POTATOES
Serves 6

5 large potatoes, cooked and diced
1 cup grated Cheddar cheese
1 medium onion, chopped
½ cup chopped parsley
½ cup chopped pimientos
½ green pepper, chopped
½ cup fresh bread crumbs
1 teaspoon salt
¼ teaspoon pepper
½ cup melted butter or margarine
½ cup milk
½ cup cornflakes

1. Preheat oven to 400° F. Grease 2-quart casserole.
2. In mixing bowl combine potatoes, cheese, onion, parsley, pimientos, green pepper and crumbs; mix well; turn into casserole.
3. In measuring cup blend salt, pepper, butter or margarine and milk; pour over potato mixture. Sprinkle with cornflakes.
4. Bake in preheated oven for 30 minutes.

Lucille Peckman, Junior Woman's Club, Turtle Creek, Pa.

OLIVE CREAMED POTATOES
Serves 6

2 cups sour cream
6 medium potatoes, cooked and diced
3 tablespoons grated onion
2 tablespoons chopped stuffed olives
1 teaspoon salt
½ teaspoon pepper
½ teaspoon paprika
1 tablespoon chopped parsley

1. Pour sour cream into large skillet; stir in potatoes, onion and olives. Cook over low heat, stirring frequently, until potatoes are thoroughly heated.
2. Season with salt and pepper; turn into serving dish. Garnish with paprika and parsley.

Junior Woman's Club, Teaneck, N.J.

DELMONICO POTATOES

Serves 6

2 cups Thin White Sauce (p. 441)
⅛ teaspoon celery salt
  Salt and pepper to taste
¼ cup grated Parmesan cheese
¼ cup finely chopped pimientos
6 cups cubed cooked potatoes

1. Season Thin White Sauce with celery salt, salt and pepper; bring to simmer.
2. Stir in cheese and pimientos, cook over medium heat, stirring constantly, until sauce is bubbling and cheese is melted.
3. Add potatoes; heat to serving temperature, stirring occasionally.

Mrs. John Hudson, President, Woman's Club, Malta, Ill.

POTATOES ROMANOFF

Serves 8

6 large baking potatoes, baked
1 bunch scallions, chopped
1½ cups grated sharp Cheddar cheese
4 cups sour cream
1½ teaspoons salt
¼ teaspoon pepper
  Paprika

1. Day before or 3 hours before cooking, grease 10 x 6 x 1½-inch baking pan.
2. Peel potatoes; cut into cubes. Put in mixing bowl. Add all remaining ingredients except paprika; mix well. Turn into pan; refrigerate overnight or for at least 3 hours.
3. When ready to use, preheat oven to 350° F.
4. Sprinkle potato mixture with paprika. Bake in preheated oven for 30 minutes.

Brigitte Sanborn, Modern Arts Club, Libby, Mont.

POTATO CASSEROLE

Serves 6

10½-ounce can condensed cream of
  chicken soup
¼ cup shredded cheese
¼ cup minced onion
1 teaspoon onion juice
2 tablespoons finely chopped
  pimiento
  Salt and pepper to taste
4 cups diced cooked potatoes
½ cup buttered bread crumbs
  Pimiento strips (optional)

1. Preheat oven to 325° F. Grease casserole or loaf pan.
2. Combine soup, cheese, onion, onion juice, chopped pimiento, salt and pepper.
3. In casserole or loaf pan arrange alternate layers of potatoes and soup mixture until all ingredients are used. Sprinkle with crumbs; garnish with pimiento strips, if desired.
4. Bake in preheated oven for 45 minutes, or until sauce is bubbling and top is lightly browned.

Mrs. Sam Davis, Sr., 20th Century Club, Gordo, Ala.

POTATO, EGG AND SALAMI CASSEROLE

Serves 8 to 10

4 cups Medium White Sauce (p. 441)
  Salt and pepper to taste
4 cups grated sharp Cheddar cheese
10 medium potatoes, cooked and
  sliced
8 eggs, hard-cooked and sliced
1 pound sliced salami

1. Preheat oven to 375° F. Grease 3-quart casserole.
2. Prepare Medium White Sauce; leave in pan; season with salt and pepper. Add cheese; cook over medium heat, stirring frequently, until melted.
3. Arrange half the potatoes in casserole. Add half the eggs, then half the salami. Top with half the cheese sauce. Repeat layers, finishing with sauce.
4. Bake in preheated oven for 25 minutes, or until browned and bubbling.

Mrs. Richard Cunningham, Valamont Woman's Club, Chattanooga, Tenn.

SPANISH POTATOES

Serves 6

2 cups Medium White Sauce (p. 441)
1 tablespoon chopped onion
2 tablespoons chopped green pepper
2 tablespoons chopped pimiento
  Salt and pepper to taste
3 cups diced cooked potatoes

1. Put Medium White Sauce in saucepan; and bring to boil, stirring frequently. Stir in onion, green pepper and pimiento; season with salt and pepper. Remove from heat; cover; let stand.
2. Just before serving, add potatoes; simmer, stirring occasionally, until thoroughly heated.

Mrs. Layward S. Watts, Woman's Club, Nitro, W. Va.

Mashed Potato Dishes

CHANTILLY POTATOES

Serves 6 to 8

4 cups mashed potatoes
  Salt and pepper to taste
½ cup heavy cream, whipped
½ cup grated Parmesan cheese

1. Preheat oven to 450° F. Grease 10 x 6 x 1½-inch baking pan.
2. Season potatoes with salt and pepper; spread in pan.
3. Spread cream on potatoes; sprinkle with cheese.
4. Bake in preheated oven for 10 minutes, or until browned.

Mrs. Ralph Andrew, Woman's Club, Albemarle, N.C.

DUTCH POTATOES

Serves 6 to 8

4 cups mashed potatoes
    Salt and pepper to taste
3 chicken bouillon cubes
½ cup water
2 tablespoons grated onion
⅓ cup chopped parsley
2 eggs, lightly beaten

1. Preheat oven to 350° F. Grease 1½-quart casserole.
2. Turn potatoes into mixing bowl; season well with salt and pepper.
3. Put bouillon cubes and water in small saucepan; heat until dissolved. Add to potatoes. Add onion, parsley and eggs; mix well. Turn into casserole.
4. Bake in preheated oven for 1 hour.

Junior Woman's Club, Muhlenberg, Pa.

PEANUTATOES

Serves 4

3 cups mashed potatoes
4 tablespoons peanut butter
1 tablespoon grated onion
    Salt and pepper to taste
1 egg, lightly beaten
1 tablespoon butter or margarine

1. Preheat oven to 350° F. Grease 1-quart casserole.
2. Put potatoes, 3 tablespoons of the peanut butter and onion in mixing bowl. Beat well until smooth; season with salt and pepper.
3. Add egg; beat well. Turn into casserole.
4. In small bowl blend remaining peanut butter with butter or margarine; use to dot potato mixture.
5. Bake in preheated oven for 30 minutes, or until browned.

Mrs. S. A. Allen, Simi Valley Woman's Club,
Simi, Calif.

POTATO NESTS WITH PEAS

Serves 4

3 cups mashed potatoes
    Salt and pepper to taste
2 tablespoons butter
2 tablespoons heavy cream
1 egg, lightly beaten
1½ cups New Peas (p. 417)

1. Preheat oven to 450° F. Line 4 custard cups with aluminum foil.
2. Put potatoes in mixing bowl; season with salt and pepper. Add butter and cream; beat until smooth.
3. Fill cups with potato mixture; make a nest in center of each. Brush with egg; bake in preheated oven for 15 minutes, or until golden.
4. Remove nests from cups; arrange on serving dish. Fill with New Peas.

Alice Blodgett, Judith Lyford Woman's Club,
Cabot, Vt.

POTATO SOUFFLÉ

Serves 4

2 eggs, separated
2 cups mashed potatoes
¼ cup milk
½ cup grated Cheddar cheese
¼ cup grated onion
2 tablespoons melted butter or margarine
1 teaspoon salt
¼ teaspoon pepper

1. Preheat oven to 375° F. Grease 1½-quart casserole.
2. In mixing bowl blend all ingredients except egg whites.
3. In another mixing bowl beat egg whites until stiff but not dry. Fold into potato mixture; turn into casserole.
4. Bake in preheated oven for 35 minutes, or until browned.

Annette Boulanger, Woman's Club,
East Hartford, Conn.

Sweet Potatoes

The sweet potato is the root of a creeping vine, indigenous to tropical America. There are two types. One is pale-fleshed and is dry and mealy when cooked; the other, incorrectly called a yam, has a deep-orange flesh and is moist and very sweet when cooked. A true yam is the root of a climbing plant used extensively for food in the West Indies. Although it resembles our moist sweet type of sweet potato and may be cooked in the same manner, it is much larger, often growing to 30 pounds or more. The potato grown in the southern United States and marketed as a true yam is really a large sweet potato.

When possible, cook sweet potatoes in their scrubbed jackets either in the oven or in boiling salted water. If peeled before cooking, they must be dropped immediately into salted cold water and cooked as soon as possible to prevent their darkening. Sweet potatoes may be baked or boiled in the same manner as white potatoes.

To boil: Scrub well; boil in salted water to cover for 45 to 60 minutes, depending on size, or until fork-tender; drain; peel while hot.

To mash: Put through ricer to remove any fibrous tissue; beat in a little hot milk or cream and butter; season to taste with salt and pepper.

To bake: Scrub; prick deeply with fork to allow steam to escape; bake in preheated 425° F. oven for 45 to 60 minutes, depending on size, or until fork-tender.

SWEET POTATOES ON HALF SHELL

Serves 6

6 medium sweet potatoes
¼ cup evaporated milk
¼ cup water
3 tablespoons softened butter
½ teaspoon salt
¼ cup chopped blanched almonds
12 marshmallows

1. Bake potatoes in a 400° F. oven for 40 minutes, or until soft. Remove potatoes; leave oven on.

2. Cut potatoes in half lengthwise; scoop out and mash pulp; beat in milk, water, butter, salt and almonds. Return pulp to shells; top each half with 2 marshmallows.

3. Arrange on baking sheet; bake for 5 minutes, or until marshmallows are melted and browned.

Mrs. Walter Rush, Woman's Club, Eustis, Fla.

BACONIZED SWEET POTATOES
Serves 12

6 sweet potatoes, cooked
12 slices bacon
12 pineapple slices
¾ cup brown sugar
Salt and pepper to taste

1. Preheat oven to 375° F. Grease 13 x 9½ x 2-inch baking pan.

2. Peel potatoes; cut each in half lengthwise.

3. Wrap each half in bacon slice; secure with wooden pick.

4. Arrange pineapple in pan; sprinkle with sugar. Place potato half on each pineapple slice; season with salt and pepper.

5. Bake in preheated oven for 45 minutes.

Mrs. Bjorn Garnaas, Town & County Study Club, Sheyenne, N.D.

SWEET POTATOES IN ORANGE CUPS
Serves 6

Mrs. Pearce writes: "This recipe is my favorite because it combines sweet potatoes, so often associated with my native Southland, and oranges, a major agricultural product of my home state of Florida."

3 oranges
6 medium sweet potatoes, cooked
4 tablespoons butter
½ teaspoon salt
½ cup orange juice
½ cup seedless raisins
6 marshmallows

1. Cut oranges in half crosswise. Cut around inside of shells; scoop out pulp; press through sieve or ricer to extract juice. Set aside shells and juice.

2. Mash potatoes; beat in butter, salt, ½ cup reserved orange juice and raisins.

3. Preheat oven to 350° F.

4. Fill orange cups with potato mixture, piling up high in center.

5. Top each with marshamallow; bake in preheated oven for 15 minutes, or until lightly browned.

Mrs. E. D. Pearce, President, General Federation of Women's Clubs, Washington, D.C.

SHREDDED YAMS
Serves 6

4 medium sweet potatoes, peeled
½ cup salt
2 cups sugar

½ cup light corn syrup
Orange juice and grated orange rind, or pineapple juice and pineapple chunks or lacing of vanilla

1. Cut potatoes lengthwise into thin strips. Soak in 2 quarts water with salt for 1½ hours. Drain; rinse.

2. Preheat oven to 350° F.

3. In saucepan combine 1 cup water, sugar and corn syrup. Bring to boil; boil for 5 minutes; turn into baking pan.

4. Add potatoes. Add a little orange juice and rind, or pineapple juice and chunks or vanilla, as desired.

5. Bake in preheated oven for 35 minutes. Do not stir. When potato edges are transparent, remove from oven.

Mildred Mills, Women's Club, Warner Robins, Ga.

SUPER CANDIED SWEET POTATOES
Serves 8 to 10

2 teaspoons cornstarch
1 cup sugar
⅛ teaspoon salt
2 cups water
¼ cup butter or margarine
10 medium sweet potatoes, boiled, peeled and quartered

1. Preheat oven to 350° F. Grease 2-quart casserole.

2. In saucepan blend cornstarch, sugar and salt. Gradually stir in water; cook over low heat, stirring constantly, until sauce is thickened and clear. Simmer for 15 minutes, stirring frequently. Remove from heat; stir in butter or margarine.

3. Arrange potatoes in casserole; top with sauce.

4. Bake in preheated oven for 30 minutes.

Alice Ruppert, Gardens Century Club, Wilmington, Del.

SCALLOPED SWEET POTATOES AND APRICOTS
Serves 8

4 cups sliced peeled boiled sweet potatoes
1-pound can apricot halves, drained
1½ cups sour cream
½ teaspoon salt
Dash of cinnamon

1. Preheat oven to 350° F. Grease 2-quart casserole.

2. Arrange potatoes in casserole; top with apricots.

3. In bowl blend sour cream, salt and cinnamon. Spread on apricots and potatoes.

4. Cover; bake in preheated oven for 30 to 35 minutes.

Mrs. Robert McClinton, Federated Civic Club, Mount Vernon, Ill.

SWEET POTATO AND ORANGE CASSEROLE

Serves 10 to 12

10 large sweet potatoes, boiled,
    peeled and sliced
1 cup brown sugar
½ cup butter
3 oranges, unpeeled and thinly sliced
1 cup orange juice
½ cup honey
½ cup fresh bread crumbs

1. Preheat oven to 350° F. Grease 3-quart casserole.
2. Arrange half the potatoes in casserole. Sprinkle with ⅓ cup of the sugar. Dot with 2 tablespoons of the butter. Arrange half the orange slices on top; cover with remaining potatoes. Sprinkle with ⅓ cup of the sugar; dot with 2 tablespoons of the honey. Top with remaining orange slices.
3. Blend orange juice and remaining honey in small bowl; pour into casserole.
4. Combine remaining sugar and crumbs; sprinkle on top. Dot with remaining butter.
5. Cover; bake in preheated oven for 45 minutes. Remove cover; bake for 15 minutes longer.

Mrs. Olga Wilson, Woman's Club, Essex, Conn.

TROPICAL SWEET POTATOES

Serves 6

6 medium sweet potatoes, boiled,
    peeled and sliced
9-ounce can crushed pineapple,
    undrained
½ cup light corn syrup
2 tablespoons melted butter or
    margarine

1. Preheat oven to 375° F. Grease 1½-quart casserole.
2. Arrange potatoes in casserole.
3. In small bowl mix pineapple, corn syrup and butter or margarine. Pour over potatoes.
4. Bake in preheated oven for 30 minutes.

Mrs. George H. Chilcote, Woman's Club of Mount Washington, Baltimore, Md.

TIPSY SWEET POTATOES

Serves 6

¾ cup sugar
3 tablespoons cornstarch
1½ cups water
⅓ cup butter
3 tablespoons bourbon
½ teaspoon cinnamon
¼ teaspoon nutmeg
6 medium sweet potatoes, boiled,
    peeled and sliced

1. Preheat oven to 325° F. Grease 10 x 6 x 1½-inch baking pan.
2. In saucepan combine sugar and cornstarch. Gradually stir in water to make a smooth paste.
3. Add butter, bourbon, cinnamon and nutmeg; cook over medium heat, stirring constantly, until sauce is thickened and smooth.
4. Arrange potatoes in pan; cover with sauce.
5. Bake in preheated oven for 20 minutes.

Charlotte Faulconer, Cutler Ridge Woman's Club, Miami, Fla.

LOUISIANA YAM GOODIES

Serves 6

3 cups mashed yams or sweet
    potatoes
½ cup sugar
¾ cup flaked coconut
2 eggs, lightly beaten
1 teaspoon cinnamon
½ teaspoon nutmeg
½ teaspoon ground cloves
½ teaspoon allspice
Marshmallows
2 cups crushed cornflakes
¼ cup shortening

1. In mixing bowl combine potatoes, sugar, coconut, eggs, cinnamon, nutmeg, cloves and allspice; mix well.
2. Shape into 2-inch balls; place marshmallow in center of each. Coat completely with cornflakes.
3. Melt shortening in large skillet; fry balls until golden on all sides.

Mrs. Phil James, President, Woman's Club, Ferriday, La.

BANANA SWEET POTATO CASSEROLE

Serves 6

4 medium sweet potatoes, boiled
    and mashed
½ cup melted butter
½ cup chopped walnuts or pecans
½ cup flaked coconut
1 cup brown sugar
4 bananas, mashed
½ cup crushed cornflakes

1. Preheat oven to 350° F. Grease 1-quart casserole.
2. In mixing bowl blend potatoes, ⅓ cup of the butter, nuts, coconut and ¾ cup of the sugar.
3. Spread half the potato mixture in casserole. Top with bananas; spread remaining potato mixture on bananas.
4. Sprinkle with cornflakes, then with remaining butter and remaining sugar.
5. Bake in preheated oven for 20 minutes.

Mrs. Erma L. Wade, President, Mount Carmel H.D.C., Cordele, Ga.

GINGER-SHERRIED SWEET POTATOES

Serves 6

4 cups mashed sweet potatoes
¼ cup sugar
¼ cup melted butter or margarine
½ teaspoon salt
½ teaspoon ginger
½ teaspoon nutmeg
¼ cup sherry
½ cup milk

1. Preheat oven to 375° F. Grease 1-quart casserole.
2. Combine all ingredients; beat until fluffy.
3. Turn into casserole; bake in preheated oven for 45 minutes, or until lightly browned.

Mrs. Murray Snoddy, Magazine Club, Roanoke, Ala.

SWEET POTATO PONE

2½ cups grated peeled sweet potatoes
1 cup dark corn syrup or molasses
2 eggs, lightly beaten
2 cups milk or evaporated milk
1 tablespoon melted butter
1 teaspoon ginger or grated orange rind
1 tablespoon brown sugar
½ teaspoon cinnamon

1. Preheat oven to 350° F. Grease 1½-quart casserole.
2. Combine potatoes, syrup or molasses, eggs, milk, butter and ginger or orange rind.
3. Turn into casserole; bake in preheated oven for 20 minutes.
4. Sprinkle top with sugar and cinnamon; bake for 25 minutes longer.

Mrs. Bess Burns, Woman's Club, Starke, Fla.

SWEET POTATO PUDDING

Serves 4

3 medium sweet potatoes, boiled, peeled and washed
½ cup sugar
½ cup orange juice
½ teaspoon cinnamon
½ teaspoon allspice
½ teaspoon nutmeg
½ cup melted butter or margarine
3 eggs, lightly beaten

1. Preheat oven to 350° F. Grease 1-quart casserole.
2. Put potatoes in mixing bowl; stir in all remaining ingredients except eggs.
3. Add eggs; beat until smooth. Turn into casserole.
4. Bake in preheated oven for 30 minutes, or until firm.

Marge Watts, Annakusa Club, Kingston, Tenn.

SWEET POTATO RING

Serves 6 to 8

3 pounds sweet potatoes, boiled, peeled and mashed
3 eggs, separated
2 tablespoons melted butter
1 teaspoon salt
1 cup milk
½ cup walnut halves
⅓ cup brown sugar
Buttered cooked peas or Lima beans

1. Preheat oven to 350° F. Grease 8-inch ring mold.
2. In mixing bowl blend potatoes, egg yolks, butter, salt and milk.

3. In another mixing bowl beat egg whites until stiff but not dry. Fold into potato mixture.
4. Arrange walnuts in mold; sprinkle with sugar. Spoon in potato mixture.
5. Bake in preheated oven for 45 minutes.
6. Invert onto serving dish; let stand for 5 minutes. Remove mold; fill center of ring with peas or beans.

Mrs. Donald Cleary, Woman's Club, East Hartford, Conn.

SWEET POTATO SOUFFLÉ

Serves 4

3 medium sweet potatoes, boiled and peeled
½ cup cream
⅓ cup sugar
½ teaspoon salt
2 tablespoons melted butter
2 eggs, lightly beaten
1 teaspoon nutmeg
Chopped pecans (optional)
Marshmallows

1. Preheat oven to 350° F. Grease 1-quart casserole.
2. Beat potatoes until light and smooth.
3. Beat in cream, sugar, salt, butter, eggs and nutmeg. Stir in pecans, if desired. Turn into casserole; top with marshmallows.
4. Bake in preheated oven for 30 minutes.

Elfie Muncy, Culture Club, Columbiana, Ala.

Radish

This crisp root vegetable is generally eaten as an appetizer or is sliced raw in a mixed salad. It is, however, delicious simmered in salted water, drained and added to a cream sauce or sliced and simmered in soups and stews. Either the red-skinned round root or the white spindle-rooted radish may be cooked. The flavor is reminiscent of a mild white turnip. Radishes should be scrubbed and trimmed, but not peeled, before cooking.

Sauerkraut

Fresh sauerkraut is available in the fall and winter at many butcher stores and delicatessens. During the rest of the year it is available in cans. Sauerkraut may be eaten raw in salads (see Chapter 17), but it is generally cooked and served hot.

Before cooking, always taste sauerkraut to make sure it is not too salty. If it is, rinse it well in water, separating the shreds with the fingers. Drain well; then braise or bake according to recipe instructions.

TO MAKE SAUERKRAUT

Cabbage
Salt

1. Shred cabbage; pack firmly in sterilized quart jars.
2. Fill to top with cooled boiled water.
3. Add 1 teaspoon salt to each quart.
4. Seal; store in cool dark place. Place jars on paper, for they will leak until fermentation is finished. Sauerkraut will be ready to use in about 5 weeks.

Mrs. O. J. Murray, Woman's Club,
Thompson Falls, Mont.

CREAMED SAUERKRAUT

Serves 6

1-pound 11-ounce can sauerkraut
2 tablespoons bacon drippings
1 teaspoon salt
¼ teaspoon pepper
½ teaspoon caraway seeds
1 large potato, peeled and grated

1. Drain and rinse sauerkraut. Turn into saucepan; add water just to cover.
2. Add bacon drippings, salt, pepper and caraway seeds. Cover; simmer for 15 minutes.
3. Stir in potato; cover; simmer for 15 minutes longer.

Mrs. Herbert Beyer, Woman's Club,
Royersford, Pa.

SAUERKRAUT AND SPLIT PEAS

Serves 8

8-ounce package split peas
1-pound 11-ounce can sauerkraut,
undrained
Salt and pepper to taste

1. Put peas in saucepan; cover with water. Bring to boil; cover; simmer for 1 hour, or until tender and mushy. Add water if necessary.
2. Put sauerkraut in Dutch oven or large heavy saucepan. Season lightly with salt and pepper; simmer for 5 minutes.
3. Stir peas into sauerkraut. Cover; simmer for 30 minutes longer.

Thelma McCready, Junior Woman's Club,
Runnemede, N.J.

Spinach

Frozen whole-leaf or chopped spinach is an excellent product but, like most other vegetables, can never quite match the flavor of fresh spinach, briefly cooked in the water clinging to its leaves. Fresh spinach should be moist and green, not wilted or yellowing. Two pounds spinach make about 1½ cups cooked, or enough to serve 3.

BRAISED SPINACH

Serves 3

2 pounds spinach
2 tablespoons butter

Salt and freshly ground pepper to taste

1. Cut tough stems and roots from spinach; Wash thoroughly in several rinses of cool water until free of sand.
2. Lift from water with hands; put in heavy pot. Do not add water; cook over moderate heat, turning spinach with long fork from bottom to top of pot. When wilted, cover; then simmer for 3 to 4 minutes.
3. Drain off excess water, but leave moist. Stir in butter, salt and pepper.

VARIATIONS:

1. Add mushrooms or chopped onion sautéed in butter.
2. Flavor with a dash of nutmeg.
3. Add to Cream Sauce (p. 441).
4. Sprinkle with crisp bacon bits.

A. S.

SPINACH PALO ALTO

½ cup water
1 teaspoon salt
10-ounce package frozen spinach
3-ounce package cream cheese
Salt and pepper to taste

1. In saucepan bring water and salt to boil. Add spinach; cover; cook for 10 minutes.
2. Meanwhile, mash cheese until soft and fluffy.
3. Drain spinach; return to pan; add cheese; cook, stirring, until cheese is melted and blended with spinach. Season with salt and pepper.

Audrey Ovington, Woman's Club,
Palmdale, Calif.

SPINACH AND SOUR CREAM

Serves 6

2 10-ounce packages frozen
    chopped spinach
2 tablespoons butter
2 tablespoons flour
1 cup sour cream
1 teaspoon dehydrated onion flakes
1 teaspoon monosodium glutamate
1 teaspoon salt
¼ teaspoon pepper

1. Cook spinach according to package directions; drain thoroughly.
2. Meanwhile, melt butter in saucepan. Stir in flour; gradually stir in sour cream. Cook over low heat, stirring constantly, until thickened and smooth.
3. Stir in remaining ingredients. Stir in spinach. Heat to serving temperature, stirring occasionally.

Mrs. Lunn Easten, Woman's Club,
Clearwater, Fla.

BAKED SPINACH

Serves 6 to 8

3 pounds spinach
6 slices bacon, cut into 1-inch
    squares
½ cup chopped onions

½ teaspoon cinnamon
2 tablespoons red wine vinegar
1 teaspoon salt
Freshly ground black pepper

1. Wash spinach; cut off tough stems and roots; slice leaves into ½-inch strips.
2. Preheat oven to 350° F. Grease large casserole.
3. Sauté bacon and onion until bacon is crisp and onion is lightly browned. Remove from heat; stir in remaining ingredients.
4. Combine bacon mixture with spinach. Put in casserole; cover; bake in preheated oven for 30 minutes, or until tender.

Dorothy Keller, Century Club, Coraopolis, Pa.

OKLAHOMA SPINACH CASSEROLE
Serves 8

10-ounce package frozen chopped
  spinach
4 eggs
1 cup milk
1 tablespoon dehydrated onion
  flakes
1 tablespoon Worcestershire
2 teaspoons salt
¼ cup melted butter
3 cups cooked rice
3 cups grated Cheddar cheese

1. Preheat oven to 350° F. Grease 2-quart casserole.
2. Cook spinach according to package directions. Drain.
3. In mixing bowl beat eggs; stir in milk, onion flakes, Worcestershire and salt.
4. Add butter, rice, cheese and spinach; mix well. Turn into casserole.
5. Bake in preheated oven for 35 minutes.

Lola Kudrna, Woman's Club, Northridge, Calif.

SPINACH DISH
Serves 4 to 6

1 pound spinach, cooked and
  chopped
1 cup cracker crumbs
1 cup milk
1 egg, lightly beaten
1 teaspoon salt
¼ teaspoon pepper
1 teaspoon Worcestershire
½ cup grated Cheddar cheese

1. Preheat oven to 350° F. Grease 1½-quart casserole.
2. In mixing bowl combine all ingredients, except cheese.
3. Turn into casserole; sprinkle with cheese.
4. Set casserole in shallow pan containing 1 inch hot water. Bake in preheated oven for 45 minutes, or until set.

Mrs. William C. Kampe, Woman's Club, Royal Oak, Mich.

SPINACH PARMESAN
Serves 6

3 pounds spinach, cooked,
  drained and chopped

½ cup grated Parmesan cheese
⅓ cup minced onions
⅓ cup heavy cream
½ cup melted butter or margarine
1 teaspoon salt
¼ teaspoon pepper
½ cup cracker crumbs

1. Preheat oven to 400° F. Grease 2-quart casserole.
2. In mixing bowl combine spinach, cheese, onions, cream, ¼ cup of the butter or margarine, salt and pepper; mix well. Turn into casserole.
3. In small bowl blend remaining butter or margarine and crumbs; sprinkle over spinach.
4. Bake in preheated oven for 15 minutes, or until golden.

Submitted by Mrs. Lyndon B. Johnson to Twentieth Century Woman's Club, Beaver Dam, Ky.

SPINACH AU GRATIN
Serves 2 or 3

½ pound spinach, finely chopped, or
  10-ounce package frozen chopped
  spinach
½ cup shredded Cheddar cheese
¾ cup hot Medium White Sauce
  (p. 441)
4 slices bacon, crisply cooked
Buttered fresh bread crumbs

1. Cook spinach; drain.
2. Preheat oven to 350° F.
3. Add cheese to Medium White Sauce; heat, stirring, until melted. Combine spinach and sauce; turn into baking dish.
4. Crumble bacon; sprinkle on top. Sprinkle with crumbs.
5. Bake in preheated oven for 20 minutes.

Mrs. John Karl, Thursday Morning Club, Madison, N.J.

SPINACH LOAF
Serves 6

10-ounce package frozen spinach,
  defrosted
1 medium onion, grated
1 clove garlic, crushed
4 slices toast, crumbled
¼ cup melted butter or margarine
2 eggs, lightly beaten
1 teaspoon salt
Dash of nutmeg

1. Preheat oven to 350° F. Grease 1½-quart casserole.
2. In mixing bowl combine all ingredients; mix well. Turn into casserole.
3. Place in shallow pan containing about 1 inch water; bake in preheated oven for 1 hour, or until set.

Elta Dorris, Tuesday Literary Club, Bolivar, Tenn.

Squash

There are three varieties of the tender-skinned summer squash: the white disk-shaped cymling squash known as pattypan; the yellow crookneck squash, which in recent years has been cultivated in a more regular shape; and the green or green-and-white-striped squash known as Italian squash or zucchini. (For zucchini recipes, see p. 437 and Index.)

The seeds of tender-skinned squash soften in cooking and may be eaten along with the flesh. Yellow squash and zucchini need not be peeled, for the skin is edible and adds flavor. Receipes for summer squash and zucchini are interchangeable.

There are four varieties of the hard-skinned winter squash: the small dark-green fluted acorn squash; the medium pale-green streaked-with-white squash known as the sweet potato squash; the large dark-green or dark-yellow rough-skinned Hubbard squash; and the golden dumbbell-shaped butternut squash.

The seeds of the hard-skinned varieties are hard and must be removed, along with the fibrous tissue found in the center of the squash when cut. If separated from the fibrous tissue, squash seeds, like pumpkin seeds, may be dried or toasted in the oven.

SAVORY SUMMER SQUASH

Serves 6 to 8

2 pounds summer squash, sliced
2 large onions, thinly sliced
1 teaspoon salt
1 teaspoon sugar
⅛ teaspoon pepper
4 large tomatoes, peeled and thinly sliced
2 tablespoons prepared mustard

1. Preheat oven to 350° F. Grease 2-quart casserole.
2. Arrange squash in casserole; top with onions. Sprinkle with salt, sugar and pepper.
3. Arrange tomatoes on top; spread with mustard.
4. Cover; bake in preheated oven for 45 minutes. Remove cover; bake for 5 minutes longer, or until tender.

Mrs. Olga B. Gerner, Woman's Club, DeBary, Fla.

COLOCHI (Vegetable Stew)

Serves 6

2 tablespoons bacon drippings
⅓ cup minced onion
3 cups diced summer squash
1 cup whole-kernel corn
½ small tomato, cubed
Pinch of orégano
Salt and pepper to taste
1 cup shredded Tillamook or Cheddar cheese

1. Heat bacon drippings in heavy skillet; sauté onion until transparent. Add squash; cook, stirring frequently, until wilted.

2. Add corn, tomato, orégano, salt and pepper. Cover; simmer for 30 minutes.
3. Add cheese; cover; simmer for 15 minutes longer.

Eliza Terrill, Women's Club, Arroyo Grande, Calif.

SCALLOPED SQUASH

Serves 8

8 medium summer squash
1 large onion, sliced
1 egg, lightly beaten
½ teaspoon pepper
½ cup milk
2 tablespoons melted butter
1 teaspoon salt
1 cup fresh bread crumbs
2 cups grated sharp Cheddar cheese

1. Preheat oven to 350° F. Grease 2½ quart casserole.
2. Wash squash; cut into 2-inch cubes. Put with onion in large saucepan; cook in a little boiling salted water for about 10 minutes, or until tender; drain. Arrange in casserole.
3. In mixing bowl combine egg, pepper, milk, butter, salt, crumbs and 1 cup of the cheese; mix well; pour over squash. Sprinkle with remaining cheese.
4. Bake in preheated oven for 30 minutes.

Hazel H. Thompson, Woman's Club, Temple Terrace, Fla.

SERENDIPITY CASSEROLE

Serves 4

¼ cup bacon drippings
1 cup sliced onions
3 small summer squash, sliced
1 cup whole-kernel corn
1 cup sliced Vienna sausages

1. Melt bacon drippings in skillet; brown onions over medium heat. Add squash; sauté for 5 minutes. Cover; simmer for 15 minutes, or until tender.
2. Add corn; cover; simmer for 5 minutes longer. Stir in sausages; heat to serving temperature.

Beverly Dunklee, Thomas Jefferson Junior Woman's Club, Richmond, Va.

BAKED SQUASH

Serves 4

4 tablespoons butter
1 medium onion, grated
½ cup finely chopped celery
1 pound winter squash, cooked and mashed
1 egg, lightly beaten
½ cup milk
¼ teaspoon garlic powder
1 teaspoon salt
⅛ teaspoon pepper
1 cup cracker crumbs

1. Preheat oven to 350° F. Grease 1½-quart casserole. Melt 2 tablespoons of the butter in skillet; sauté onion and celery over medium heat for 5 minutes.

2. Turn into mixing bowl; add squash, egg, milk, garlic powder, salt, pepper, and ½ cup of the crumbs; mix well. Turn into casserole; sprinkle with remaining crumbs.

3. Dot with remaining butter. Bake in preheated oven for 25 minutes.

Sammye Baker, Study Club, Wink, Tex.

BAKED WINTER SQUASH WITH WALNUTS
Serves 6

2 pounds winter squash, peeled and thinly sliced
1 medium onion, chopped
1 cup water
2 teaspoons salt
¼ cup butter
2 tablespoons flour
1 cup light cream
1 egg, lightly beaten
1 tablespoon grated orange rind
2 tablespoons orange juice
½ cup chopped walnuts
¼ cup cracker crumbs

1. Preheat oven to 325° F. Grease 1½-quart casserole.

2. Put squash, onion, water and salt in saucepan. Bring to boil; cover; simmer for 12 minutes, or until tender. Drain; mash with fork.

3. Melt butter in saucepan; stir in flour. Gradually stir in cream; cook over low heat, stirring constantly, until sauce is thickened and smooth.

4. Put egg in small bowl; stir in a little sauce; add to rest of sauce; simmer for 2 minutes. Remove from heat; stir in squash, orange rind and juice and walnuts. Turn into casserole; sprinkle with crumbs.

5. Bake in preheated oven for 35 minutes, or until browned.

Mary Harris, Director, Pilot Club, Tuscumbia, Ala.

SQUASH CASSEROLE
Serves 6

1 cup scalded milk
2 eggs, lightly beaten
1½ cups mashed cooked winter squash
1 cup diced American cheese
3 tablespoons chopped pimiento
1 tablespoon grated onion
3 tablespoons melted butter or margarine
¼ teaspoon salt
2 tablespoons chopped parsley
1 cup fresh bread crumbs

1. Preheat oven to 350° F. Grease 1½-quart casserole.

2. Pour milk into mixing bowl; stir in eggs, squash and cheese. Add pimiento, onion, butter or margarine, salt and parsley; mix. Blend in crumbs; turn into casserole.

3. Bake in preheated oven for 45 minutes.

Mrs. Lena A. Armour, Literary and Civic Club, Houlka, Miss.

SQUASH-PEANUT PIE
Serves 6

¼ cup bread crumbs
2 pounds winter squash, peeled and thinly sliced
½ teaspoon salt
Dash of pepper
2 tablespoons melted butter or margarine
1 small onion, grated
1 cup heavy cream
1 cup Spanish or salted peanuts, toasted
8 slices bacon, crisply cooked and crumbled

1. Preheat oven to 350° F. Grease 9-inch pie plate; sprinkle bottom and sides with crumbs.

2. Cook squash in a little boiling salted water in saucepan until tender. Drain; mash with fork. Stir in salt, pepper, butter or margarine, onion and cream.

3. Turn into pie plate; bake in preheated oven for 50 minutes.

4. Just before serving, sprinkle with peanuts and bacon.

Mrs. Wilma Crapps, President, Woman's Club, Fort Gaines, Ga.

BUTTERNUT SQUASH SOUFFLÉ
Serves 6

4 cups diced peeled butternut squash
1 cup water
½ teaspoon salt
½ cup melted butter
1 cup brown sugar
½ teaspoon cinnamon
½ cup evaporated milk
1 cup marshmallows

1. Preheat oven to 350° F. Grease 1½-quart casserole.

2. Put squash, water and salt in saucepan. Cover; bring to boil; boil for 15 minutes, or until tender. Drain; put in mixing bowl. Mash.

3. Add remaining ingredients; mix well. Turn into casserole.

4. Bake in preheated oven for 30 minutes.

Mrs. Clyde Rumsey, North Jacksonville Woman's Club, Jacksonville, Fla.

APPLESAUCE SQUASH SCALLOP
Serves 6

1-pound can applesauce
1½ cups cooked winter squash
¼ cup brown sugar
Dash of nutmeg
½ teaspoon salt
¼ teaspoon melted butter or margarine
½ cup evaporated milk
2 eggs, lightly beaten
½ cup slivered toasted almonds
1½ cups buttered soft bread crumbs

1. Preheat oven to 375° F. Grease 1½-quart shallow baking dish.

2. Combine all ingredients except almonds and crumbs. Pour into baking

dish. Sprinkle almonds around edge; top with crumbs.

3. Bake in preheated oven for 45 minutes.

Mrs. John Gloor, Junior Women's Club, Rye, N.H.

SQUASH TIMBALES

Serves 4

1 cup mashed winter squash
2 eggs
3 tablespoons milk
2 tablespoons melted butter or margarine
½ teaspoon salt
Dash of pepper
Medium White Sauce (p. 441) or Cheese Sauce (p. 442)

1. Preheat oven to 350° F. Grease 4 custard cups.

2. In mixing bowl combine all ingredients; beat until smooth. Turn into cups; place cups in pan containing about 1 inch hot water.

3. Bake in preheated oven for 30 minutes, or until centers are firm.

4. Unmold onto serving dish; serve with Medium White Sauce or Cheese Sauce, as desired.

Mrs. A. S. Thompson, Women's Club, Beloit, Wis.

STUFFED ACORN SQUASH

Serves 6

3 medium acorn squash
1 pound sausage meat
¼ cup sweet pickle relish
1 tablespoon dry mustard
½ cup bread crumbs
½ cup heavy cream
¼ teaspoon salt

1. Preheat oven to 425° F. Grease 13 x 9½ x 2-inch baking pan.

2. Cut squash in half lengthwise; discard seeds. Place, cut side down, in pan. Add water to come ½ inch up side of pan.

3. Bake in preheated oven for 20 minutes.

4. Meanwhile, fry sausage in skillet, stirring into small pieces, for 15 minutes.

5. Remove from heat; drain off fat. Put sausage in mixing bowl. Add remaining ingredients; mix well.

6. Remove squash; turn cut side up; fill with sausage mixture.

7. Bake for 25 minutes longer.

Mrs. Douglas Stenstrom, Woman's Club, Sanford, Fla.

Tomatoes

When tomatoes are lush and allowed to ripen on the vine, there is no more attractive fruit to serve as a vegetable simply sliced raw or cooked in any number of ways. Unfortunately, most of the year, except for a short time in the spring when some excellent-flavored beefsteak tomatoes arrive in the markets, the usual kind sold is the hothouse tomato, which is sadly lacking in flavor and color. When only hothouse tomatoes are available, canned whole tomatoes are better for cooking, for they are canned in season.

The tiny cherry tomatoes, which have rapidly gained in favor, are fortunately available most of the year. If they are pale, let them sit in a bright window until ripe. They make a delicious dish stewed very briefly in garlic butter, or they may be sautéed in butter and sprinkled with chives or dill. They should be peeled first, and this is simple: Put them in a saucepan; cover with boiling water. Let stand for 30 seconds; drain; skins will strip off quickly.

SPANISH TOMATOES

Serves 4 to 6

2 tablespoons butter
1 cup chopped celery
6 firm large tomatoes, quartered
1 teaspoon salt
¼ teaspoon pepper
1 tablespoon sugar
1 small green pepper, finely chopped
¼ teaspoon aromatic bitters

1. Melt butter in skillet; sauté celery over medium heat for 5 minutes. Stir in tomatoes; simmer, uncovered, for 20 minutes, stirring occasionally.

2. Add salt, pepper, sugar and green pepper; simmer for 5 minutes longer. Remove from heat; stir in bitters.

Mrs. Harry Cottman, Woman's Club, Jessup, Md.

STEWED TOMATOES

Serves 6

2 tablespoons bacon drippings
1 cup chopped onions
½ cup chopped celery
12 large tomatoes, peeled and sliced
1 teaspoon sugar
2 teaspoons salt
¼ teaspoon pepper
½ teaspoon basil

1. Melt bacon drippings in saucepan. Sauté onions and celery over medium heat for 5 minutes.

2. Add remaining ingredients; cover; simmer for 15 minutes.

Mrs. George Bozie, Woman's Club, Chula Vista, Calif.

FRIED TOMATOES

Serves 4

4 firm large tomatoes
Salt and pepper to taste
3 tablespoons sugar
1 cup cracker crumbs
½ cup butter or margarine

1. Cut tomatoes into ¾-inch-thick slices. Sprinkle with salt, pepper and sugar. Dip in crumbs.

2. Melt butter or margarine in large skillet; fry tomatoes over medium heat for 2 to 3 minutes on each side, or until golden.

Mrs. Hineline, Women's Club, Beloit, Wis.

TOMATOES BROILED WITH FRENCH DRESSING

Serves 6

6 firm medium tomatoes
½ cup cooking oil
4 teaspoons sugar
1½ teaspoons salt
2 tablespoons minced onion
2 teaspoons dry mustard
2 teaspoons vinegar
2 tablespoons cracker crumbs
2 tablespoons melted butter

1. Preheat broiler.
2. Wash tomatoes. Cut thin slice from top of each tomato; discard. Hollow out tomatoes slightly.
3. Combine oil, sugar, salt, onion, mustard and vinegar; put 1 tablespoon in hollow of each tomato.
4. Combine crumbs and butter; sprinkle on tomatoes.
5. Broil for 10 minutes, basting occasionally. (Or bake in preheated 350° F. oven for 20 minutes.)

Arline Sparks and Mrs. Morgan Washburn, Arts and Crafts Section, Woman's Club, Avenal, Calif.

BAKED TOMATOES

Serves 4

2 ripe medium tomatoes
½ teaspoon prepared mustard
1 small onion, grated
1 teaspoon Worcestershire
Salt to taste
2 tablespoons buttered bread crumbs

1. Preheat oven to 375° F. Lightly grease 8-inch square baking pan.
2. Cut stems from tomatoes; cut in half crosswise.
3. Arrange tomatoes, cut side up in pan; spread with mustard. Sprinkle with onion, Worcestershire and salt. Sprinkle with crumbs.
4. Bake in preheated oven for 20 minutes.

Pat Laughlin, Ingram Civic Club, Junior Section, Pittsburgh, Pa.

ANCHOVY-STUFFED BAKED TOMATOES

Serves 6

6 large tomatoes
1 cup fresh bread crumbs
7-ounce can tuna, drained and flaked
2-ounce can anchovies, drained and chopped
1 clove garlic, crushed
½ teaspoon basil
¼ teaspoon salt
3 tablespoons grated Parmesan cheese
3 tablespoons melted butter or margarine

1. Preheat oven to 375° F. Grease 10 x 6 x 1½-inch baking pan.
2. Cut slice from top of each tomato; discard. Scoop out insides; chop pulp

finely. Turn tomatoes upside down to drain.
3. Turn pulp into mixing bowl; add crumbs, tuna, anchovies, garlic and basil; mix well.
4. Arrange tomatoes; hollow side up in pan, sprinkle insides lightly with salt. Fill with anchovy mixture. Sprinkle with cheese and butter or margarine.
5. Bake in preheated oven for 20 minutes.

Rose Fernandez, Woman's Club, Paramus, N.J.

BAKED TOMATOES WITH CRAB MEAT FILLING

Serves 6

6 ripe medium tomatoes
Salt
1 tablespoon butter
1 tablespoon flour
Dash of pepper
¼ teaspoon paprika
½ cup light cream
1 cup flaked crab meat
1 tablespoon finely chopped green pepper
1 tablespoon diced pimiento
¼ cup chopped toasted almonds
1 cup buttered bread crumbs

1. Wash tomatoes. Cut slice from top of each tomato; discard. Scoop out pulps, leaving thick shells; sprinkle insides with salt to taste; invert tomatoes to drain.
2. Preheat oven to 375° F. Grease shallow baking dish.
3. Melt butter in skillet. Stir in flour, ½ teaspoon salt, pepper and paprika. Gradually stir in cream; cook, stirring constantly until thickened and smooth.
4. Stir in crab meat, green pepper, pimiento and almonds. Fill shells with crab meat mixture; sprinkle with crumbs.
5. Arrange in baking dish. Bake in preheated oven for 20 to 25 minutes.

Mrs. M. C. Daetzel, South Side Woman's Club, Denver, Colo.

BAKED TOMATOES STUFFED WITH RICE

Serves 6

6 firm large tomatoes
Salt and pepper to taste
2 tablespoons butter or margarine
2 tablespoons grated onion
2 tablespoons finely chopped green pepper
2 tablespoons chopped parsley
1½ cups cooked rice
½ cup chopped green olives
1 egg
¼ cup light cream
⅓ cup bread crumbs

1. Preheat oven to 375° F. Grease 10 x 6 x 1½-inch baking pan.
2. Wash tomatoes. Cut ½-inch slice from top of each tomato; discard. Scoop out pulps, leaving ½-inch shells. Sprinkle insides with salt and pepper; arrange, cut side up, in pan.

3. Melt butter or margarine in skillet; sauté onion and green pepper for 5 minutes.

4. Remove from heat; stir in parsley, rice and olives; mix well.

5. In small bowl mix egg and cream; pour over rice mixture; mix; use to fill shells. Sprinkle crumbs over tops.

6. Bake in preheated oven for 20 minutes, or until tops are browned and tomatoes tender.

Mrs. Doris Steed Smith, Woman's Club, Sparta, Ga.

GREEN TOMATO PIE

Serves 6

2½ cups thinly sliced green
    tomatoes
2 tablespoons light corn syrup
1 teaspoon cinnamon
½ teaspoon nutmeg
½ teaspoon ground cloves
¼ cup brown sugar
2 tablespoons lemon juice
2 tablespoons water
    Pastry for a 1-Crust Pie (p. 548)
3 tablespoons flour

1. Preheat oven to 425° F.

2. Put tomatoes in mixing bowl; add syrup, cinnamon, nutmeg, cloves, sugar, lemon juice and water; mix well.

3. Roll out pastry for a 1-Crust Pie to fit 9-inch pie plate.

4. Turn tomatoes into pie shell; sprinkle with flour.

5. Bake in preheated oven for 25 minutes, or until tender.

Mrs. Charles Hill, Lancaster County Federation of Women's Clubs, Pa.

SCALLOPED CHEESE TOMATOES

Serves 8

½ cup packaged herb bread stuffing
½ teaspoon garlic salt
¼ teaspoon orégano
2 teaspoons sugar
1-pound 13-ounce can tomatoes
1 cup grated Cheddar cheese
1 large onion, thinly sliced
2 tablespoons butter or margarine

1. Preheat oven to 350° F. Grease 10 x 6 x 1½-inch baking pan.

2. In mixing bowl combine bread stuffing, garlic salt, orégano and sugar; mix well.

3. Arrange half the tomatoes in pan; top with layer of bread stuffing. Sprinkle with ½ cup of the cheese and onion. Spread with remaining tomatoes; sprinkle with remaining cheese. Dot with butter or margarine.

4. Bake in preheated oven for 30 minutes.

Judy Montgomery, Junior Woman's Club, Pompano Beach, Fla.

TOMATO PUDDING

Serves 4

10-ounce can tomato purée
¼ cup boiling water

1 cup light brown sugar
¼ teaspoon salt
1 cup 1-inch white bread cubes
¼ cup melted butter

1. Preheat oven to 375° F.

2. In saucepan combine tomato purée, water, sugar and salt. Bring to boil; simmer for 5 minutes.

3. Put bread in small casserole. Pour butter over bread. Add tomato mixture.

4. Cover; bake in preheated oven for 30 minutes.

Mrs. Dwight D. Eisenhower, Gettysburg, Pa.

TOMATO SOUFFLÉ

Serves 4

8-ounce can tomatoes
1 small onion, quartered
1 teaspoon salt
3 tablespoons butter
3 tablespoons flour
3 eggs, separated
¼ cup grated Cheddar cheese
    Paprika to taste

1. Preheat oven to 350° F. Grease 1-quart casserole.

2. In saucepan combine tomatoes, onion and salt. Bring to boil; cover; simmer for 20 minutes.

3. Force vegetables through sieve; set aside to cool.

4. Melt butter in saucepan; blend in flour. Gradually stir in tomato mixture; cook over medium heat, stirring constantly, until thickened. Cool.

5. Beat egg yolks until thick and lemon-colored.

6. Beat egg whites until stiff but not dry.

7. Stir egg yolks into tomato mixture; fold in egg whites. Turn into casserole; sprinkle with cheese and paprika.

8. Bake in preheated oven for 25 minutes, or until puffed and golden.

Mrs. P. L. Murkland, Women's Club, Beloit, Wis.

Turnips

There are two types of turnips; the small white bulbs frequently streaked with purple and the large yellow knobs known as rutabagas. The white turnips are mild in flavor and are generally peeled and boiled. They may be diced or sliced and served with melted butter or added to a cream sauce.

The stronger-flavored rutabaga turnip may be baked like a regular baking potato. When tender, gash tops; sprinkle with salt and pepper; add a big chunk of butter. Boiled rutabagas are delicious mashed with butter and cream. People who do not like the flavor of turnips usually find them palatable when combined half and half with boiled potatoes.

TURNIP BALLS

Large white turnips
Butter
Salt and pepper to taste

1. Peel turnips; cut balls from turnips with melon ball cutter.
2. Cook balls in boiling salted water for 15 to 20 minutes, or until fork-tender. Drain.
3. Melt a little butter in skillet; sauté turnip until golden brown on all surfaces. Sprinkle with salt and pepper.

*Hilda Skidmore, Women's Club,
Arroyo Grande, Calif.*

TURNIP FLUFF

Serves 4

2 pounds yellow turnips, peeled and cubed
¼ cup light cream
1 egg, lightly beaten
2 tablespoons melted butter
¼ cup light brown sugar
2 tablespoons cream of wheat
Salt and pepper to taste

1. Cook turnips in 1 inch boiling salted water until tender. Drain thoroughly; mash.
2. Preheat oven to 350° F. Grease 1-quart casserole.
3. Add remaining ingredients to turnips. Turn into casserole; bake in preheated oven for 40 minutes.

Vera Sweterlitsch, Century Club, Coraopolis, Pa.

TURNIP AND APPLE CASSEROLE

Serves 6

6 cups grated yellow turnips
1 apple, peeled and chopped
2 tablespoons brown sugar
1 teaspoon salt
¼ teaspoon pepper
¼ cup butter

1. Preheat oven to 350° F. Grease 1½-quart casserole.
2. Combine turnips, apple, sugar, salt and pepper; mix well. Turn into casserole; dot with butter.
3. Cover; bake in preheated oven for 1½ hours.

*Margaret Knoll Gardner, Woman's Club,
Emmaus, Pa.*

TURNIP PUFFS IN GREEN PEPPERS

Serves 8

2 cups diced yellow turnips
3 cups diced potatoes
4 large green peppers
2 eggs, lightly beaten
1 tablespoon sugar
Salt and pepper to taste

1. Cook turnips in boiling salted water for 20 minutes, or until tender; drain.
2. Cook potatoes in boiling salted water for 10 minutes, or until tender; drain.
3. Preheat oven to 375° F. Grease 10 x 6 x 1½-inch baking pan.
4. Cut green peppers in half lengthwise; discard seeds; parboil in boiling salted water for 5 minutes; turn cut side down to drain for a few minutes.
5. Arrange peppers, cut side up, in pan.
6. Combine turnips and potatoes in mixing bowl. Add eggs and sugar; toss lightly. Season with salt and pepper. Fill peppers with turnip mixture.
7. Bake in preheated oven for 25 to 30 minutes.

*Mrs. Ruth Gurresh, Junior Woman's Club,
Glastonbury, Conn.*

Water Chestnuts

Until recently the water chestnut, the bulb of a marshy plant, was used almost exclusively in Oriental cuisine. Now the canned form is readily available in markets throughout the country and is used by American homemakers as a crisp complement to other cooked vegetables, such as string beans, peas, carrots or cauliflower, and in many cooked dishes with a Polynesian or Oriental flavor. Here is one unusual and very good recipe using water chestnuts, but many other recipes in this book call for water chestnuts as an ingredient.

WATER CHESTNUT FRITTERS

Serves 6

1½ cups presifted flour
1½ teaspoons baking powder
¼ teaspoon salt
⅛ teaspoon pepper
1 egg, lightly beaten
1 tablespoon melted butter
¾ cup milk
1 cup finely chopped water chestnuts
Fat for deep frying

1. Into mixing bowl sift together flour, baking powder, salt and pepper. Add egg, butter and milk; beat until smooth. Stir in water chestnuts.
2. Drop by teaspoons into deep fat heated to 365° F. Fry for 2 to 3 minutes, or until golden. Drain on absorbent paper.

Mrs. A. Kulik, Woman's Club, Palisade, N.J.

Zucchini

For general information about zucchini and other squash, see page 432.

ZUCCHINI IN SKILLET

Serves 4 to 6

2 tablespoons cooking oil
1 small onion, sliced
2 tomatoes, peeled and quartered
1 teaspoon salt
¼ teaspoon pepper
1 pound zucchini, sliced
1 tablespoon chopped pimiento
1 bay leaf
½ teaspoon basil

1. Heat oil in large skillet; sauté onion for 5 minutes. Stir in tomatoes, salt and pepper. Cover; simmer for 5 minutes.

2. Stir in remaining ingredients; cover; simmer for 20 minutes longer. Remove bay leaf before serving.

Phil Karam, Junior Woman's Club,
Glastonbury, Conn.

ZUCCHINI AND PEPPERS

Serves 4 to 6

1 tablespoon cooking oil
1 clove garlic, minced
4 medium zucchini, sliced
1 green pepper, seeded and sliced
1-pound 12-ounce can tomatoes, sieved
¼ teaspoon salt
¼ teaspoon pepper

1. Heat oil in saucepan; brown garlic lightly. Add zucchini and green pepper; cook until zucchini are lightly browned.

2. Add remaining ingredients; cover; simmer for about 30 minutes, or until tender.

Angela Amantia, Junior Woman's Club,
Scottsdale, Ariz.

ZUCCHINI ROMA

Serves 8

4 medium zucchini, parboiled
1 egg
1 cup cream-style cottage cheese
1 small onion, grated
½ teaspoon salt
1 tablespoon chopped parsley
½ cup cooked rice
Dash of Tabasco
2 cups Cheese Sauce (p. 442)

1. Preheat oven to 325° F. Grease baking sheet.

2. Trim ends of zucchini; cut in half lengthwise. Scoop out centers; chop finely. Arrange shells, right side up, on baking sheet.

3. Put chopped zucchini in mixing bowl. Stir in egg, cheese, onion, salt, parsley, rice and Tabasco; mix well; spoon into shells.

4. Bake in preheated oven for 30 minutes.

5. Meanwhile, heat Cheese Sauce to serving temperature. Arrange zucchini on serving dish; top with sauce.

Mrs. H. W. Staffelbach, Woman's Club,
Martinez, Calif.

BAKED ZUCCHINI CASSEROLE

Serves 4 to 6

4 tablespoons butter
1 small onion, chopped
3 large zucchini, sliced and steamed
   until tender but still crisp
1 cup grated Cheddar cheese
2 eggs, lightly beaten
¼ cup fresh bread crumbs

1. Preheat oven to 325° F. Grease 1½-quart casserole.

2. Melt 2 tablespoons of the butter in skillet. Sauté onion until golden. Add zucchini, cheese and eggs; mix well.

3. Turn mixture into casserole. Sprinkle with crumbs; dot with remaining butter.

4. Bake in preheated oven for 45 minutes.

Barbara Seeburger, Gerlach-Empire Women's
Club, Empire, Nev.

ZUCCHINI SOUFFLÉ

Serves 6

6 medium zucchini, finely chopped
6 scallions, finely chopped
1 medium green pepper, finely
   chopped
¼ cup chopped pimientos
1 teaspoon salt
⅛ teaspoon pepper
1 cup fresh bread crumbs
1 cup grated Cheddar cheese
5 eggs, separated

1. Preheat oven to 350° F. Grease 2-quart casserole.

2. In mixing bowl combine zucchini, scallions, green pepper and pimientos; mix well. Add salt, pepper, crumbs, ½ cup of the cheese and egg yolks; mix well.

3. In another mixing bowl beat egg whites until stiff but not dry; fold into vegetable mixture. Pour into casserole. Sprinkle with remaining cheese.

4. Set in pan of hot water; bake in preheated oven for 1½ hours.

Gertrude Clements, Woman's Club,
Cupertino, Calif.

Mixed Vegetable Dishes

ALASKAN MIXED VEGETABLES

Serves 4 to 6

Especially good with wild game, moose or caribou, as well as with salmon.

2 cups sliced carrots
1 cup chopped celery
1 cup chopped onions
4 cups coarsely chopped cabbage
1 tablespoon sugar
1½ teaspoons salt
¼ cup cooking oil
½ cup hot water

1. Put all vegetables in order given in large saucepan. Add sugar, salt and oil. Pour water over top.

2. Cover; cook over medium heat for about 25 minutes, or until tender.

Mrs. Robert E. Lee, Woman's Club,
Anchorage, Alaska

OLIVE CHOW YUK
(Sautéed Vegetables with Olives)

Serves 4

2 tablespoons olive oil
1 medium green pepper, cut into
   strips
2 medium onions, sliced
1 stalk celery, cut into 1-inch slices
1 cup beef consommé

1 tablespoon cornstarch
1 tablespoon soy sauce
2 cups sliced pitted ripe olives
Cooked rice

1. Heat oil, in large skillet; sauté green pepper, onions and celery over medium heat for 10 minutes. Add consommé; bring to boil.

2. In small bowl combine cornstarch and soy sauce to a smooth paste. Stir into vegetables; cook over low heat, stirring constantly, until thickened and clear.

3. Stir in olives. Serve on rice.

Mrs. R. A. Pellage, People's Church Women's Club, Chicago, Ill.

CREOLE VEGETABLES

Serves 8

⅔ cup olive oil
4 large summer squash, cut into
    ¾-inch slices
6 large tomatoes, cut into ¾-inch
    slices
3 Bermuda onions, cut into ¼-inch
    slices
3 medium green peppers, cut into
    ½-inch rings
2 teaspoons salt
¼ teaspoon pepper

1. Heat oil in large skillet; add vegetables. Sprinkle with salt and pepper.

2. Cover; simmer for 30 minutes, or until tender.

Mrs. John K. J. Kirk, Vermont Federation of Women's Clubs

MACÉDOINE OF VEGETABLES

Serves 6

3 medium carrots
1 turnip
3 tablespoons butter
3 tablespoons flour
¾ cup chicken broth
½ cup milk
    Salt and pepper to taste
2 egg yolks
2 teaspoons lemon juice
1¼ cups cooked peas

1. Clean carrots and turnip; cut into thin strips or fancy shapes. There should be enough to total 1¼ cups carrots and ½ cup turnip.

2. Cook carrots and turnip separately in boiling salted water until tender. Drain; set aside.

3. Melt butter in saucepan; blend in flour. Gradually stir in broth and milk; cook over medium heat, stirring constantly, until sauce is thickened and smooth. Season with salt and pepper; simmer for 2 minutes.

4. In small bowl blend egg yolks and lemon juice; stir in a little sauce; stir into rest of sauce. Add carrots, turnip and peas. Cook over low heat, stirring constantly, for 3 minutes.

Mrs. L. D. Wervely, Sr., Woman's Club, Emmaus, Pa.

RATATOUILLE (Vegetables Stewed in Olive Oil)

Serves 6

1 medium eggplant, peeled and
    sliced
    Salt and pepper to taste
½ cup olive oil
2 small summer squash, sliced
3 cloves garlic, crushed
3 medium onions, sliced
2 medium green peppers, cut into
    strips
3 large tomatoes, peeled, seeded
    and diced
½ cup chopped parsley

1. Sprinkle eggplant with salt; let stand for 30 minutes. Drain; wipe dry with absorbent paper.

2. Heat a little oil at a time in large skillet; sauté eggplant and squash until golden on both sides; remove eggplant and squash, set aside.

3. Heat remaining oil in skillet; sauté garlic, onions and green peppers over medium heat for 10 minutes, stirring frequently.

4. Sprinkle with salt and pepper. Top with tomatoes; simmer for 5 minutes. Cover; simmer for 10 minutes longer.

5. Arrange alternate layers of eggplant and squash, tomato mixture and parsley in 2-quart saucepan. Cover; simmer for 15 minutes. If there is too much liquid, remove cover, and simmer until excess has been absorbed. (This may also be layered in a casserole and baked, covered, in preheated 350° F. oven for 30 minutes.)

6. Serve hot or cold.

Woman's Club, Clearfield, Pa.

UPSIDE-DOWN VEGETABLE CAKE

Serves 8

2 cups presifted flour
2 teaspoons baking powder
½ teaspoon salt
¼ cup shortening
1 egg, lightly beaten
1 cup milk
4 cups cooked mixed vegetables
    (peas, carrots, celery, Lima beans)
½ cup stock from vegetables
2 tablespoons butter or margarine
    Quick Tomato Sauce (p. 451) or
    Mushroom Sauce (p. 447)

1. Preheat oven to 425° F. Grease 10 x 6 x 1½-inch baking pan well.

2. Prepare biscuit topping: Into mixing bowl sift together flour, baking powder and salt. Cut in shortening until mixture resembles fine crumbs. Add egg and milk; beat until smooth. Set aside.

3. Arrange vegetables in pan. Add stock; dot with butter or margarine. Pour biscuit topping over vegetables.

4. Bake in preheated oven for 20 to 25 minutes.

5. Cool for 5 minutes; invert onto serving dish.

6. Cut into squares; serve with Quick Tomato Sauce or Mushroom Sauce.

Mrs. Martin Kelly, Junior Woman's Club, Elyria, Ohio

VEGETABLE MEDLEY

Serves 6

¼ cup butter or margarine
¾ cup chopped green pepper
1 clove garlic, crushed
¼ cup presifted flour
1 cup milk
¾ teaspoon salt
⅛ teaspoon pepper
⅛ teaspoon basil
⅛ teaspoon orégano
¼ teaspoon sugar
1 cup grated Cheddar cheese
1-pound can tomatoes, well drained
10-ounce package frozen whole-kernel corn, defrosted
1-pound can whole small onions, drained

1. Preheat oven to 350° F. Grease 2-quart casserole.
2. Melt butter or margarine in saucepan; sauté green pepper and garlic for 5 minutes. Stir in flour, gradually stir in milk; cook, stirring constantly, until thickened and smooth.
3. Stir in salt, pepper, basil, orégano, sugar and ½ cup of the cheese. Cook over medium heat, stirring constantly, until cheese is melted.
4. Remove from heat; stir in tomatoes, corn and onions. Turn into casserole; sprinkle with remaining cheese.
5. Bake in preheated oven for 45 minutes.

Helen Mullineaux, Crest Century Club, Wilmington, Del.

12. Sauces for Fish, Poultry, Meat and Vegetables

❦❦❦❦❦❦❦❦❦❦❦❦❦❦❦❦❦❦❦❦❦❦❦

Hundreds of sauces are included as integral parts of the recipes in this book. In this chapter, for quick reference, you will find basic sauces, which stand on their own. For other sauces, see Index.

Thick or thin, mildly seasoned, piquant or robust, a sauce can make all the difference between a poor dish and an inspired one. Often an extra pinch of salt, a dash of pepper or nutmeg or a drop of lemon juice is all it takes to make a sauce perfect. So always season a sauce to taste, for no recipe can specify the exact amount of seasoning to suit every palate.

Sauces are easy to make; by carefully following directions, you need not fear that your sauce will be lumpy or that an addition of egg yolks will curdle.

Sauces should not be too thick. Use Medium White Sauce for general use or when adding capers, horseradish, mustard or herbs. Use Thick White Sauce only when you plan to thin it with cream, sherry, wine or any other liquid.

THICK WHITE SAUCE (SAUCE BÉCHAMEL)

Makes About 1 Cup

2 tablespoons butter
3 tablespoons flour
1 cup hot milk
½ teaspoon salt
⅛ teaspoon pepper
Special herbs and spices (optional)

1. Melt butter in heavy saucepan. Add flour; cook, stirring constantly, for 2 minutes, or until mixture, known as a roux, is smooth and begins to bubble.

2. Remove saucepan from heat. Add milk all at once. Return saucepan to heat; stir vigorously with wooden spoon or wire whisk. Sauce will be thickened and smooth in about 1 minute.

3. Add salt and pepper; cook over low heat for 10 minutes, stirring occasionally.

4. Correct seasoning, adding special herbs or spices, if desired.

VARIATIONS:

Medium White Sauce: Follow directions for Thick White Sauce, using only 2 tablespoons flour.

Thin White Sauce: Follow directions for Thick White Sauce, using only 1 tablespoon each of butter and flour.

Meat Sauce or Gravy: Substitute Beef Stock (p. 170) or broth or juices from meat for part or all of milk.

Chicken Sauce (Chicken Velouté): Substitute Chicken Stock (p. 170) or broth for part or all of milk.

Fish Sauce (Fish Velouté): Substitute Fish Stock (p. 171) for part or all of milk.

Curry Sauce: Follow directions for Medium or Thick White Sauce, adding 1 teaspoon curry powder along with flour. If using Thick White Sauce, stir ½ cup cream into cooked sauce; heat to serving temperature.

Cheese Sauce (Cheddar): Add ½ cup grated sharp Cheddar cheese to 1 cup Medium White Sauce. Cook, stirring constantly, until melted.

Cheese Sauce (Mornay): Add 2 tablespoons each grated Swiss and Parmesan cheese and ¼ cup heavy cream to 1 cup Thick White Sauce. Cook, stirring constantly, until melted.

A. S.

CREAM SAUCE

Makes About 1½ Cups

1 cup Thick White Sauce (opposite)
½ cup heavy cream

Combine ingredients; cook over low heat until hot, stirring occasionally.

VARIATIONS:

Caper Cream Sauce: Stir 2 tablespoons chopped capers and a little caper juice into hot Cream Sauce.

Egg and Caper Sauce: Add 2 eggs, hard-cooked and chopped, to hot Caper Cream Sauce.

Egg Cream Sauce: Add 2 eggs, hard-cooked and sliced, to hot Cream Sauce.

Herb Cream Sauce: Add 1 tablespoon any chopped fresh or 1 teaspoon any dried herb to hot Cream Sauce. Cook over low heat for 3 minutes, stirring occasionally.

Horseradish Cream Sauce: Stir drained horseradish to taste into hot Cream Sauce.

Mustard Cream Sauce: Add 1 tablespoon prepared or 1 teaspoon dry mustard to hot Cream Sauce; cook, stirring constantly for 1 minute.

Sherry Cream Sauce: Stir 2 tablespoons sherry into hot Cream Sauce.

Often a cream sauce is enriched by the addition of egg yolks. To add egg yolks, without fear of their curdling, beat lightly; stir in a few tablespoons of the hot sauce. Turn heat under sauce to very low, or place saucepan over simmering (but not boiling) water. Stir egg mixture into sauce with wooden spoon; cook, stirring constantly, for 2 to 3 minutes, or until egg is cooked and sauce is thoroughly hot. Do not boil.

A. S.

BABCOCK SAUCE

Makes About 1 Cup

Serve with steamed clams.

3 tablespoons butter or margarine
1 tablespoon flour
½ teaspoon dry mustard
1 cup clam liquor, strained
¼ teaspoon salt
½ teaspoon coarsely ground black pepper

1. Melt butter or margarine in saucepan; blend in flour and mustard.
2. Gradually stir in clam liquor; cook over medium heat, stirring constantly, until thickened and smooth.
3. Season with salt and pepper.

Betty Cook, Woman's Club, Breton Woods, N.J.

BARBECUE SAUCE FOR SPARERIBS, PORK CHOPS AND CHICKEN

Makes About 3 Cups

1 cup catsup
½ cup chili sauce
¼ cup vinegar
⅓ cup brown sugar
½ large onion, chopped
1 teaspoon dry mustard
2 teaspoons Worcestershire
½ cup chopped celery
½ teaspoon salt
Pepper to taste
Garlic (optional)

Combine all ingredients in saucepan. Bring to boil; then simmer for 15 minutes.

Mrs. James O'Dell, Woman's Club, Wildwood, Fla.

ORONO BARBECUE SAUCE

Makes About 3 Quarts

Ideal for spareribs, chicken or pork chops.

2 14-ounce bottles catsup
12-ounce bottle chili sauce
⅓ cup prepared mustard
1½ cups brown sugar
2 teaspoons black pepper

1 cup lemon juice
½ cup bottled thick steak sauce
¼ teaspoon Tabasco
1 tablespoon soy sauce
2 tablespoons olive oil
1 cup sweet sherry
2 cloves garlic, crushed

1. Combine all ingredients in large bowl; mix well.
2. Turn into covered containers; store in refrigerator, where it will keep for several weeks; if stored in freezer, it will keep longer.

Mrs. Robert C. Lovell, Woman's Club, Orono, Me.

BARBECUE SAUCE FOR LAMB CROQUETTES

Makes About 2 Cups

3 tablespoons butter
⅓ cup minced onion
1 cup catsup
⅓ cup lemon juice or vinegar
2 tablespoons brown sugar
½ teaspoon salt
½ cup water
2 teaspoons prepared mustard
2 tablespoons Worcestershire

1. Melt butter in saucepan; sauté onion until tender.
2. Add remaining ingredients. Bring to boil; then simmer for 10 minutes.

Wilma Hougaard, Literary Club, Moab, Utah

BUTTER SAUCE FOR FISH, SEAFOOD AND VEGETABLES

Makes About 1 Cup

1 cup butter
1½ tablespoons lemon juice
Dash of Tabasco
½ tablespoon Worcestershire

1. Melt butter over low heat.
2. Stir in remaining ingredients.

VARIATIONS:

Beurre Noir (Brown Butter Sauce): Follow directons for Butter Sauce, but let butter turn dark gold before adding remaining ingredients.

Almond Butter Sauce for Fish or Chicken: Follow directions for Butter Sauce, adding ¼ cup slivered blanched almonds to butter; brown lightly before adding remaining ingredients.

Wine Butter Sauce: Add 2 tablespoons dry white wine to Butter Sauce above.

A. S.

CHEESE SAUCE

Makes About 2 Cups

1 cup milk
2 cups grated Cheddar cheese
1 tablespoon butter or margarine
½ teaspoon salt
⅛ teaspoon pepper
¼ teaspoon dry mustard
Dash of cayenne

1. Put all ingredients in top of double saucepan. Cook over hot water, stirring frequently, until cheese is melted.

2. Remove from heat; beat for 1 minute.

Mrs. Dalton Wheeler, Woman's Club, Basin, Wyo.

CHEESE PIMIENTO SAUCE
Makes About 2 Cups

2 tablespoons butter or margarine
2 tablespoons flour
  Dash of pepper
  Dash of Tabasco
1¼ cups milk
½ cup grated Cheddar cheese
4-ounce can pimientos, drained
  and chopped
½ teaspoon salt

1. Melt butter or margarine in saucepan. Stir in flour, pepper and Tabasco. Gradually stir in milk; and cook, stirring constantly, until thickened and smooth.

2. Add cheese, pimientos and salt; cook, stirring constantly, until cheese is melted.

Mrs. John F. Olszewski, Woman's Club,
North Arlington, N.J.

QUICK CHICKEN CREAM SAUCE
Makes About 2 Cups

10½-ounce can condensed cream of
  chicken soup
1 cup sour cream
2 tablespoons chopped parsley
2 tablespoons chopped chives

Blend all ingredients in saucepan. Cook over low heat, stirring frequently, until smooth and hot. Do not boil.

Mrs. Richard Reid, Junior Woman's Club,
Menomonee Falls, Wis.

RED CHILI SAUCE
Makes About 3½ Cups

7-ounce can red chili peppers, drained
½ cup tomato sauce
1 clove garlic, crushed
¼ cup olive oil
1½ teaspoons salt
1 teaspoon orégano
¼ teaspoon cumin

1. Preheat oven to 400° F. Grease baking sheet.

2. Arrange chilis on baking sheet; bake in preheated oven for 4 minutes. Cool.

3. Rinse chilis in cold water; remove seeds. Cover with hot water; let stand for 1 hour.

4. In container of electric blender, blend chilis and water to cover to make a smooth paste; or rub chilis through strainer.

5. Add water to chilis to total of 3 cups. Put in saucepan. Stir in remaining ingredients; bring to boil; then simmer for 10 minutes, stirring occasionally.

Mrs. Joseph Glider, Women's Improvement Club,
Blythe, Calif.

CLARET SAUCE
Makes About 2 Cups

Serve on London Broil (p. 310) with Claret Sauce or any other desired meat.

1 tablespoon butter
1 cup sliced mushrooms
1 tablespoon flour
½ cup claret or dry red wine
¼ cup water
  Salt and pepper to taste

1. Melt butter in saucepan; sauté mushrooms over medium heat for 5 minutes. Sprinkle with flour; brown slightly, stirring frequently.

2. Stir in wine and water; cook over medium heat, stirring constantly, until thickened.

3. Season lightly with salt and pepper; simmer for 2 minutes.

Madelaine Goldberg, Junior Woman's Club,
Tullahoma, Tenn.

HOT CRANBERRY SAUCE FOR HAM
Makes About 3 Cups

2 cups whole cranberry sauce
½ cup brown sugar
1 cup crushed pineapple
½ cup chopped nuts
½ teaspoon ground cloves
  Orange juice (optional)

1. In saucepan combine all ingredients except orange juice. Heat, stirring occasionally, until well blended.

2. If thinner sauce is desired, stir in a little orange juice.

Jackie Cates, Culture Club, Columbiana, Ala.

CREOLE SAUCE
Makes About 1 Quart

This may be used with all kinds of seafood and with spaghetti and noodles. It may be frozen for future use.

4 slices bacon, diced
2 large onions, chopped
1 cup chopped celery
2 8-ounce cans tomato sauce
2 cups water
4 cloves garlic, crushed
2 teaspoons sugar
  Dash of allspice
  Salt and pepper to taste
¼ cup chopped parsley

1. Cook bacon in large skillet or Dutch oven for 3 minutes. Add onions and celery; sauté for 5 minutes.

2. Stir in tomato sauce, water, garlic, sugar, allspice, salt and pepper. Bring to boil; cover; simmer for 2 to 3 hours.

3. Stir in parsley just before serving.

Kay Kraft, Palm Springs Woman's Club,
Hialeah, Fla.

QUICK CREOLE SAUCE
Makes About 1¼ Cups

8-ounce can tomato sauce
½ teaspoon salt
4-ounce can sliced mushrooms, drained

Combine all ingredients in saucepan. Bring to boil; simmer for 10 minutes.

Mrs. Claude Williamson, Junior Women's Club, Rye, N.H.

CUCUMBER BUTTER FOR FISH
Makes About 1 Cup

This hard sauce melts when put on hot fish.

1 medium cucumber
½ cup butter
2 teaspoons lemon juice
Salt and pepper to taste

1. Peel cucumber; discard seeds. Grate cucumber; squeeze juice out of pulp.
2. Beat remaining ingredients until fluffy.
3. Add cucumber pulp; blend thoroughly. Refrigerate until ready to use.

Mrs. C. W. Coulter, Woman's Club, Durham, N.H.

CUCUMBER SAUCE FOR SALMON
Makes 1½ Cups

1 large cucumber
½ cup heavy cream
2 tablespoons vinegar
Few grains cayenne

1. Peel cucumber; cut into fine strips; drain for 20 minutes.
2. Whip cream until stiff; stir in salt, vinegar, cayenne and cucumber.

Mrs. LaFell Dickinson, Honorary President, General Federation of Women's Clubs, West Hartford, Conn.

DEEP-SEA SAUCE
Makes About 1 Cup

For fish, oysters and scallops.

1 tablespoon butter
1 tablespoon flour
3 tablespoons water
1 teaspoon vinegar
2 tablespoons chili sauce
1 tablespoon chopped pimiento
⅛ teaspoon celery seed
½ teaspoon minced onion
3 tablespoons mayonnaise

1. Melt butter in saucepan. Stir in flour; cook over low heat until lightly browned.
2. Stir in all remaining ingredients except mayonnaise. Cook until thick, stirring constantly.
3. Remove from heat; blend in mayonnaise.

Marian B. Diehl, Woman's Club, Las Vegas, N.M.

GOURMET SAUCE
Makes About 2 Cups

Serve with roast Rock Cornish game hens or roast chicken.

3 tablespoons butter
¼ cup finely chopped onion
3 tablespoons flour
1 teaspoon salt
1 teaspoon parsley flakes
¼ teaspoon pepper

½ cup nonfat dry milk solids
1½ cups water
3-ounce can sliced mushrooms, undrained
2 tablespoons dry sherry

1. Melt butter in saucepan; sauté onion until transparent. Sprinkle with flour, salt, parsley flakes, pepper and milk solids. Gradually stir in water; cook over low heat, stirring constantly, until thickened.
2. Stir in mushrooms and sherry; simmer for 3 minutes.

Mrs. William H. Peifer, Greenfields Woman's Club, Reading, Pa.

HOLLANDAISE SAUCE
Makes About ¾ Cup

½ cup butter
1 tablespoon lemon juice
4 egg yolks
¼ teaspoon paprika (optional)
Pinch of cayenne (optional)

1. Cream butter thoroughly in top of double saucepan. Add lemon juice; beat in egg yolks, one at a time; mix well.
2. Cook over simmering water, stirring constantly, just long enough to heat thoroughly. If sauce should be a bit overcooked, beat in 2 teaspoons water.
3. Season with paprika and cayenne, if desired.

Letitia Morris, Bedford Hills Woman's Club, Chappaqua, N.Y.

BÉARNAISE SAUCE
Makes 1 Cup

1 teaspoon chopped shallot or scallion
¼ teaspoon dried tarragon
4 peppercorns
¼ cup tarragon vinegar
Hollandaise Sauce (above)
1 teaspoon minced parsley

1. Simmer shallot or scallion, tarragon and peppercorns in vinegar until vinegar is reduced by half.
2. Strain into Hollandaise Sauce.
3. Stir in parsley.

A. S.

HORSERADISH SAUCE FOR FISH
Makes About 2 Cups

1 cup heavy cream
2 tablespoons horseradish
2 tablespoons lemon juice
⅛ teaspoon salt
¼ cup chopped parsley

1. In mixing bowl whip cream until stiff. Fold in remaining ingredients.
2. Chill well before serving.

Marie Dobler, Junior Woman's Club, Floral Park, N.Y.

LEMON BUTTER
Makes ½ Cup

Serve on fish.

½ cup butter
2 tablespoons lemon juice

1 teaspoon grated lemon rind
¼ teaspoon salt

1. In small bowl blend all ingredients. Shape into square; chill.
2. When ready to serve, cut into slices.

VARIATIONS:

Lemon Parsley Butter: Add ¼ cup chopped parsley to Lemon Butter.

Lemon Caper Butter: Stir 2 tablespoons chopped drained capers into Lemon Butter.

> *Mrs. Harvey Brooks, Woman's Club, Essex, Conn.*

SAUCE MAISON FOR STEAKS OR CHOPS

Makes About ½ Cup

    1 tablespoon mayonnaise
    1 teaspoon sweet pickle relish
    3 tablespoons bottled barbecue
      sauce
    1 tablespoon catsup
    ½ teaspoon Worcestershire
    1 teaspoon soy sauce
    2 drops Tabasco

Combine all ingredients.

> *Meals on Wheels, Woman's Club, Greenwich, Conn.*

1916 SAUCE FOR HAM

Makes About ¼ Cup

Serve with baked ham. Good hot or cold.

    2 tablespoons catsup
    2 tablespoons dry sherry
    ½ teaspoon dry mustard
    1 tablespoon Worcestershire

Combine all ingredients in small saucepan. Bring to boil over low heat, stirring occasionally.

> *Rosann Crandal, En Avant Society, Potosi, Mo.*

ORIENTAL MARINADE FOR BEEF OR CHICKEN

Makes About ½ Cup

Use to marinate beef or chicken for 30 minutes before cooking.

    2 cloves garlic, crushed
    ½ cup soy sauce
    1 tablespoon cooking oil
    ½ teaspoon salt
    ½ teaspoon pepper
    ¼ teaspoon ginger
    ½ teaspoon monosodium glutamate

Combine all ingredients.

> *Joan Dice, Junior Woman's Club, Cheshire, Conn.*

WINE MARINADE

Makes About 2½ Cups

Use to marinate spareribs, beef, chicken, pork, turkey, etc., for at least 2 hours before cooking.

    1 cup dry white wine
    3 tablespoons vinegar
    ⅓ cup olive oil

⅓ cup soy sauce
1 tablespoon sugar
¼ teaspoon pepper
¼ teaspoon marjoram
¼ teaspoon basil
1 clove garlic, crushed
⅓ cup bottled barbecue sauce
1 teaspoon salt
½ teaspoon orégano

Combine all ingredients.

> *Junior Women's Club, Portersville, Calif.*

WHOLE EGG MAYONNAISE

Makes 2 Cups

For thinner mayonnaise, use 2 eggs.

    1 teaspoon salt
    1 teaspoon sugar
    ½ teaspoon paprika
    ½ teaspoon dry mustard
      Dash of black pepper
    1 egg
    2 cups cooking oil
    2 tablespoons lemon juice

1. In mixing bowl or electric mixer blend salt, sugar, paprika, mustard and pepper. Add egg; beat (on medium speed if using electric mixer) until fluffy.
2. Gradually beat in oil until mixture is stiff. Beat in lemon juice.

CUCUMBER MAYONNAISE: Add 1 medium cucumber, peeled, seeded and chopped, to Whole Egg Mayonnaise above.

> *Bebe Dent, Junior Woman's Club, Jacksonville, Fla.*

BLENDER MAYONNAISE

Makes 1¼ Cups

    1 egg
    ½ teaspoon dry mustard
    ½ teaspoon salt
    2 tablespoons vinegar
    1 cup cooking oil

1. Break egg into container of electric blender.
2. Add mustard, salt, vinegar and ¼ cup of the oil. Cover.
3. Turn motor on low speed. Immediately remove cover; pour in remaining oil in steady stream. Blending should not take more than a total of 18 seconds. If a few drops of oil remain on surface of mayonnaise, stir in with rubber spatula.

VARIATIONS:

Lemon Mayonnaise: Substitute lemon juice for vinegar.

Garlic Mayonnaise: Add 1 small clove garlic along with mustard.

Herb Mayonnaise: Add ½ teaspoon any dried herb along with mustard.

Curry Mayonnaise: Add 1 teaspoon curry powder, ¼ teaspoon ginger, ½ small clove garlic and 1 tablespoon honey along with mustard. Use lemon or lime juice in place of vinegar.

Sauce Verte (Green Mayonnaise): Add 1½ tablespoons cut chives, 1 teaspoon dillweed, ¼ teaspoon dried tarragon and 2 tablespoons chopped parsley along with mustard.

A. S.

SAUCE GRIBICHE

Makes About 3 Cups

Blender Mayonnaise (p. 445)
2 tablespoons parsley clusters
1 teaspoon dillweed
1 small sour pickle, coarsely cut
1 tablespoon coarsely cut onion
1 tablespoon lemon juice
3 drops Tabasco
3 eggs, hard-cooked and chopped

1. Prepare Blender Mayonnaise; leave in container of blender.
2. Add all remaining ingredients except eggs; stir to combine.
3. Cover; blend on high speed for 6 seconds.
4. Fold in eggs.

A. S.

SAUCE RAVIGOTE

Makes 1½ Cups

Blender Mayonnaise (p. 445)
2 tablespoons capers
2 tablespoons parsley clusters
1 clove garlic
2 tablespoons coarsely cut onion
⅓ cup white wine
1 tablespoon lemon juice
1 egg, hard-cooked and chopped

1. Prepare Blender Mayonnaise; leave in container of blender.
2. In saucepan combine all remaining ingredients except egg. Bring to boil; simmer for 15 minutes; add to Blender Mayonnaise; stir to combine.
3. Cover; blend on high speed for 3 seconds.
4. Fold in egg.

A. S.

SAUCE RÉMOULADE

Makes 1½ Cups

Blender Mayonnaise (p. 445)
1 tablespoon capers
¼ cup coarsely cut sour pickles
½ teaspoon dry mustard
1 tablespoon parsley clusters
½ teaspoon dried tarragon

1. Prepare Blender Mayonnaise; leave in container of blender.
2. Add remaining ingredients; stir to combine.
3. Cover; blend on high speed for 6 seconds.

A. S.

SAUCE À LA RITZ

Makes About 1¾ Cups

Blender Mayonnaise (p. 445)
¼ teaspoon Worcestershire
1 ripe tomato, peeled and quartered
1 tablespoon chili sauce
1 clove garlic
2 tablespoons parsley clusters

1. Prepare Blender Mayonnaise; leave in container of blender.
2. Add remaining ingredients; stir to combine.
3. Cover; blend on high speed for 6 seconds.

A. S.

SAUCE TARTARE

Makes 1½ Cups

Blender Mayonnaise (p. 445)
1 tablespoon parsley clusters
2 cloves garlic
5 sweet gherkins
3 pitted olives
½ teaspoon dried tarragon
¼ teaspoon coarsely ground pepper

1. Prepare Blender Mayonnaise; leave in container of blender.
2. Add remaining ingredients; stir to combine.
3. Cover; blend on high speed for 6 seconds.

A. S.

MINT SAUCE FOR ROAST LAMB

Makes 1 Cup

½ cup water
2 tablespoons sugar
½ cup vinegar
½ teaspoon salt
3 tablespoons chopped mint

1. In saucepan bring water, sugar, vinegar and salt to boil.
2. Remove from heat; add mint; let stand for 3 to 4 hours before serving.

Edna Larimer, Century Club, Coraopolis, Pa.

PAT'S MORNAY SAUCE

Makes About 2 Cups

2 cups Medium White Sauce (p. 441)
½ cup grated Gruyère cheese
½ cup grated Parmesan cheese
1 teaspoon prepared mustard
1 teaspoon Worcestershire
Salt and pepper to taste
2 tablespoons butter or margarine

1. Prepare Medium White Sauce; leave in saucepan.
2. Stir in cheeses, mustard and Worcestershire; season with salt and pepper. Cook over low heat, stirring constantly, until cheeses are melted.
3. Remove from heat; add butter or margarine, a small piece at a time, beating well after each addition.

Pat Pollard, Suburban Women's Club, Newark, Del.

SAUCE MOUSSELINE FOR COOKED VEGETABLES

Makes About ¾ Cup

2 egg yolks
⅓ cup cream
⅛ teaspoon nutmeg
Juice of 1 lemon
2 tablespoons butter

1. In top of double saucepan combine all ingredients except butter. Cook over simmering water, stirring constantly for 5 minutes, or until mixture coats spoon.

2. Stir in butter.

Mrs. D. C. Norton, Thursday Morning Club, Madison, N.J.

MUSHROOM SAUCE

Makes About 2 Cups

¼ cup butter or margarine
1 teaspoon grated onion
1 cup sliced mushrooms
¼ cup presifted flour
½ teaspoon salt
¼ teaspoon pepper
2 cups milk

1. Melt butter or margarine in saucepan; sauté onion and mushrooms for 5 minutes. Stir in flour, salt and pepper; cook for 1 minute.

2. Gradually stir in milk; cook over low heat, stirring constantly, until thickened and smooth.

Mrs. John W. Crabb, President, Iowa Federation of Women's Clubs, Jamaica, Ia.

MUSHROOM CREAM SAUCE

Makes About 3 Cups

Serve with Macaroni Loaf (p. 499) or as desired.

4 tablespoons butter or margarine
1 pound mushrooms, sliced
3 tablespoons flour
2 cups heavy cream
Salt to taste

1. Melt 2 tablespoons of the butter or margarine in large skillet; sauté mushrooms over low heat, stirring frequently, until tender.

2. Meanwhile, melt remaining butter or margarine in saucepan; blend in flour. Gradually stir in cream; cook over low heat, stirring constantly, until thickened and smooth.

3. Season with salt; add mushrooms. Simmer for 1 minute.

Mrs. J. C. Davis, Junior and Senior Woman's Clubs, Grundy, Va.

MUSHROOM VELOUTÉ SAUCE

Makes About 3 Cups

Serve with Chicken Ring with Mushroom Velouté Sauce (p. 288) or as desired.

¼ cup butter or margarine
½ pound mushrooms, sliced
¼ cup presifted flour
2 cups chicken broth
½ cup light cream
⅛ teaspoon paprika
1 teaspoon salt
1 tablespoon chopped parsley
1 tablespoon lemon juice

1. Melt butter or margarine in saucepan; sauté mushrooms over medium heat until wilted.

2. Sprinkle with flour; gradually stir in broth. Cook, stirring constantly, until thickened.

3. Stir in cream, paprika, salt and parsley; simmer for 5 minutes. Remove from heat; stir in lemon juice.

Julia J. Behrens, Woman's Club, Greenview, Ill.

MUSHROOM SAUCE FOR HAM

Makes About 2 Cups

Serve with Ham Soufflés (p. 355) or broiled ham steaks.

1½ cups Medium White Sauce (p. 441)
1 tablespoon grated onion
2 tablespoons chopped parsley
3-ounce can mushroom pieces, undrained
Salt and pepper to taste

1. Put Medium White Sauce in saucepan; stir in onion, parsley and mushrooms.

2. Simmer, stirring frequently, for 5 minutes. Season with salt and pepper.

Helen R. Hogan, Service League, Lombard, Ill.

EASY MUSHROOM SAUCE

Makes About 3 Cups

Serve with Chicken Rice Loaf Soufflé (p. 288) or fried chicken or as desired.

10½-ounce can condensed cream of mushroom soup
2 cups chicken broth
¼ cup heavy cream
⅛ teaspoon paprika
1 tablespoon finely chopped parsley
2 teaspoons lemon juice
Salt to taste

1. Put soup, broth and cream in saucepan; stir; cook over low heat until smooth and bubbling.

2. Stir in paprika, parsley and lemon juice; simmer for 1 minute. Remove from heat; season with salt.

Mabel H. Snyder, Civic Club, Shippenville, Pa.

QUICK MUSHROOM PIMIENTO SAUCE

Makes About 3 Cups

Serve with Chicken 'n' Stuffing Scallop (p. 290) or as desired.

10½-ounce can condensed cream of mushroom soup
¼ cup milk
1 cup sour cream
¼ cup chopped pimientos

1. In saucepan blend soup, milk and sour cream.

2. Stir in pimientos; heat to serving temperature, stirring occasionally.

Mrs. W. A. Brecht, Woman's Club, Forest Hills, Pa.

QUICK MUSHROOM SOUP SAUCE

Makes About 2 Cups

10½-ounce can condensed cream of mushroom soup
½ cup milk
¼ teaspoon Tabasco

Combine all ingredients in saucepan. Stir over medium heat until smooth and hot.

Mrs. Ray Remster, Woman's Club,
Devils Lake, N.D.

HOT SWEDISH MUSTARD
Makes About 1½ Cups

Make this 2 weeks ahead.

½ cup dry mustard
¼ cup presifted flour
½ cup sugar
¼ cup milk
¼ cup vinegar

1. Combine mustard, flour and sugar in small saucepan. Gradually stir in milk and vinegar. Cook over medium heat, stirring constantly, until thickened and smooth.
2. Remove from heat; cool, stirring occasionally.
3. Refrigerate in airtight container for 2 weeks to ripen.

Ethel Jansson, Woman's Club, Natick, Mass.

MUSTARD SAUCE
Makes About 2½ Cups

Serve with ham loaf, broiled fish or as desired.

⅓ cup sugar
½ cup dry mustard
½ cup vinegar
1 egg, lightly beaten
Dash of salt
1 cup mayonnaise

1. Blend sugar and mustard in top of double saucepan. Gradually stir in vinegar, egg and salt. Cook over hot water, stirring constantly, until thickened and smooth.
2. Stir in mayonnaise; simmer for 1 minute.

Elaine Haown, Junior Woman's Club,
Chester, Va.

MUSTARD MAYONNAISE SAUCE
Makes About ½ Cup

⅓ cup mayonnaise
4 teaspoons horseradish
1 tablespoon prepared mustard

Blend all ingredients in small bowl.

Anna H. McCollum, Island Woman's Club,
Anna Maria, Fla.

MUSTARD TOMATO SAUCE
Makes About 2 Cups

Serve on meat loaf or as desired.

3 egg yolks
½ cup prepared mustard
½ cup vinegar
½ cup condensed tomato soup
½ cup sugar
½ cup butter or margarine

1. In top of double saucepan beat egg yolks lightly.
2. Stir in remaining ingredients; cook over hot water, stirring constantly, until thickened and smooth.

Mrs. Bill Williams, Secretary and Treasurer,
Woman's Club, Okeechobee, Fla.

OLIVE SAUCE
Makes About 2½ Cups

Serve with Corn Loaf (p. 406) or as desired.

2 cups Medium White Sauce (p. 441)
Dash of cayenne
1 teaspoon Worcestershire
½ cup sliced stuffed olives
Salt and pepper to taste

1. In saucepan combine Medium White Sauce, cayenne, Worcestershire and olives. Heat to serving temperature, stirring occasionally.
2. Season with salt and pepper.

Mrs. Chud Wendle, Civic Club, Sandpoint, Ida.

ONION SAUCE FOR ROAST BEEF
Makes About 1 Cup

1 large mild Spanish onion,
    grated or thinly sliced
⅓ cup sugar
1 or 2 tablespoons vinegar
Salt and freshly ground pepper
    to taste

Combine all ingredients. Let stand for a few hours before serving.

Mrs. W. Humes, Century Club, Coraopolis, Pa.

ONION BUTTER SAUCE FOR STEAK
Makes About ½ Cup

2 tablespoons butter
2 tablespoons grated onion
½ teaspoon chopped parsley
½ teaspoon Worcestershire
1 beef bouillon cube
¼ cup boiling water

1. Melt butter in small saucepan; sauté onion until golden.
2. Stir in remaining ingredients; cook over medium heat, stirring constantly, until sauce bubbles and bouillon cube is dissolved.

Kay Sharrow, Fine Arts Club, Monongahela, Pa.

ORANGE RAISIN SAUCE
Makes About 2 Cups

Serve with baked him or as desired.

1 tablespoon flour
¼ cup brown sugar
1 cup water
¼ cup frozen orange juice
    concentrate, defrosted
1 tablespoon butter
1 tablespoon vinegar
⅓ cup seedless raisins

1. In saucepan combine flour and sugar. Gradually stir in water. Add remaining ingredients.
2. Cook over medium heat, stirring constantly, until thickened and smooth.

Gertrude Fisher, Fernwood Woman's Club,
Chicago, Ill.

PECAN SAUCE

Makes About 1½ Cups

Serve with Fish Soufflé with Pecan Sauce (p. 224) or as desired.

2 tablespoons butter
¼ cup chopped pecans
2 tablespoons flour
1 cup light cream
Salt to taste

1. Melt butter in saucepan; brown pecans lightly, stirring frequently.
2. Blend in flour; gradually stir in cream. Cook over low heat, stirring constantly, until thickened. Remove from heat; season lightly with salt.

Mrs. William Sager, Junior Women's Club, Orange, N.J.

PINEAPPLE SAUCE

Makes About 3 Cups

Serve with Chinese Meat Balls (p. 69) or as desired.

½ cup sugar
3 tablespoons cornstarch
1 cup chicken broth
½ cup vinegar
2 tablespoons soy sauce
½ cup pineapple juice
1 green pepper, cut into strips
1 cup pineapple chunks

1. In saucepan combine sugar and cornstarch. Stir in broth, vinegar and soy sauce to make a smooth paste.
2. Stir in pineapple juice; cook over medium heat, stirring constantly, until thickened and clear.
3. Add green pepper and pineapple chunks; simmer for 2 minutes.

Mrs. Frederick Ziesenheim, Women's Club, Forest Hills, Pa.

PINEAPPLE MUSTARD SAUCE

Makes About 2 Cups

Serve with Oven Ham Croquettes (p. 355) or favorite ham loaf.

1 cup brown sugar
1½ tablespoons cornstarch
2 tablespoons dry mustard
½ cup water
½ cup pineapple juice
½ cup vinegar

1. In saucepan combine sugar, cornstarch and mustard. Blend in water to make a smooth paste.
2. Stir in pineapple juice and vinegar; cook over low heat, stirring constantly, until thickened and clear.

Beta Alpha Latreian, Indianapolis, Ind.

PIQUANT SAUCE

Makes About 2½ Cups

10½-ounce can condensed cream of mushroom soup
1 cup sour cream
2 tablespoons chili sauce
⅛ teaspoon cayenne

Combine all ingredients in saucepan. Heat to serving temperature, stirring occasionally.

Mrs. Paul Willingham, Woman's Club, Wynnburg, Tenn.

RÉMOULADE SAUCE

Makes About 5 Cups

Serve on cold cooked shrimp on bed of lettuce.

¾ cup Dijon mustard
1½ cups cooking oil
½ cup vinegar
Red pepper to taste
Few drops Tabasco
Salt to taste
2 tablespoons minced parsley
3 tablespoons grated onion
2 eggs, hard-cooked and sieved
1¼ cups minced celery
½ teaspoon paprika
1 tablespoon lemon juice
1 tablespoon prepared hot mustard

Combine all ingredients; mix well. Chill.

Mrs. E. C. Riall, Kuwot Study Club, Mooringsport, La.

QUICK SHRIMP SAUCE

Makes About 2 Cups

Serve with Salmon Loaf with Shrimp Sauce (p. 232) or as desired.

10-ounce can frozen condensed cream of shrimp soup
½ cup milk
1 tablespoon dry sherry

Heat soup according to package directions. Stir in milk and sherry; simmer for 1 minute.

Mrs. H. Powell, New Century Club, Parkside, Pa.

SOUR CREAM NO-COOK SAUCE

Makes About ½ Cup

With the addition of chopped sweet pickle, this sauce is good on well-drained vegetables—spinach, cauliflower or broccoli—along with fish and other seafood.

¼ cup sour cream
¼ cup French dressing
Rind of ½ lemon, grated
Juice of ½ lemon
¾ teaspoon grated onion
⅛ teaspoon monosodium glutamate
Pinch of garlic

Combine all ingredients.

Shirley Duncan, Anna Day Club, Troy, Mo.

TART CREAM DRESSING FOR VEGETABLES

Makes About 1 Cup

2 eggs
1 teaspoon sugar
1 teaspoon salt
Pepper to taste
2 tablespoons vinegar
Pinch of dry mustard
2 tablespoons butter
½ cup heavy cream

Combine all ingredients in top of double saucepan. Cook over simmering water until thickened and smooth, stirring frequently.

Edna Larimer, Century Club, Coraopolis, Pa.

SOUR CREAM CAPER SAUCE FOR SHRIMP

Makes About 1¼ Cups

½ cup sour cream
½ cup mayonnaise
2 tablespoons finely chopped capers
2 teaspoons caper juice
1½ teaspoons onion juice
½ teaspoon salt
2 tablespoons catsup

Combine all ingredients. Let stand for at least 30 minutes to blend flavors.

Mrs. Norman Herren, Woman's Club, Naples, Fla.

SWEET SOUR SAUCE FOR FRIED CHICKEN

Makes About 5 Cups

3 tablespoons cornstarch
1 cup vinegar
1 cup sugar
¼ teaspoon Tabasco
1 tablespoon Worcestershire
1 tablespoon prepared mustard
2 medium green peppers, cubed
4-ounce can pimientos, drained
   and cubed
1-pound 13-ounce can pineapple
   chunks, undrained

1. In small saucepan blend cornstarch and a little of the vinegar. Stir in remaining vinegar and sugar. Cook over medium heat, stirring constantly, until thickened and clear.
2. Stir in Tabasco, Worcestershire, mustard and green peppers. Cook over low heat, stirring occasionally, for 10 minutes.
3. Add pimientos and pineapple; heat to serving temperature.

Mrs. John A. Gronouski, Woman's Club, Washington, D.C.

SWEET SOUR PINEAPPLE SAUCE

Makes About 1 Quart

Serve with Sweet Sour Pineapple Fish Balls (p. 223) or as desired.

1-pound 13-ounce can pineapple
   chunks
3 tablespoons cornstarch
¼ cup sugar
1 tablespoon soy sauce
½ cup vinegar
½ cup dry white wine
½ cup thinly sliced celery
½ cup thinly sliced scallions
1 large tomato, cut into small
   wedges

1. Drain pineapple; reserve syrup. Add water to syrup to total 1 cup.
2. In saucepan blend cornstarch and sugar; stir in reserved syrup to make a smooth paste. Stir in soy sauce, vinegar and wine; cook over medium heat, stirring constantly, until thickened and clear.

3. Add celery and scallions; simmer for 5 minutes. Add pineapple chunks and tomato; simmer for 2 minutes.

Valene Klamt, Woman's Club, St. Anthony, Ida.

TARTAR SAUCE FOR FISH

Makes About 1 Cup

1 cup mayonnaise
1 teaspoon finely chopped green
   pepper
1 teaspoon finely chopped olives
1 teaspoon finely chopped pickle

Mix all ingredients; chill until ready to serve.

Bicentennial Cook Book, Berks County Federation of Women's Clubs, Pa.

HOT TARTAR SAUCE

Makes About 1 Cup

Serve with fried fish.

½ cup Medium White Sauce (p. 441)
½ cup mayonnaise
2 tablespoons vinegar
2 tablespoons chopped green olives
2 tablespoons chopped dill or
   sweet pickle
1 teaspoon grated onion

Combine all ingredients in saucepan. Heat to serving temperature over low heat, stirring occasionally.

Mrs. Harold Nordwall, Study Club, Turtle Lake, N.D.

TERIYAKI SAUCE

Makes 1¼ Cups

Very good overnight marinade for chicken, round steak, pork steaks or spareribs. Best when barbecued.

½ cup soy sauce
½ cup water
½ cup sugar
1 tablespoon vinegar
½ teaspoon garlic powder or 2 cloves
   garlic, minced
1 tablespoon grated or thinly sliced
   ginger root
½ teaspoon monosodium glutamate

Combine all ingredients in saucepan; bring to boil.

VARIATION: Marinade may be thickened with a little cornstarch softened in water. Serve thickened sauce on cooked rice.

Pauline Romero, El Camino Women's Club, Ventura, Calif.

FIVE-MINUTE TOMATO SAUCE

Makes About 1½ Cups

2 tablespoons butter
2 tablespoons flour
½ cup hot water
1 cup strained tomatoes
¼ teaspoon onion juice
Salt and pepper to taste

1. Melt butter in saucepan; stir in flour: cook, stirring, until smooth. Add water; cook over medium heat, stirring vigorously, until thickened and smooth.

2. Add remaining ingredients. Bring to boil; then simmer for 5 minutes.

Gladys Reiner, Woman's Civic Club,
Roselle Park, N.J.

QUICK TOMATO SAUCE

Makes About 1¼ Cups

10½-ounce can condensed tomato soup
2 tablespoons shortening
¼ teaspoon salt
Dash of pepper
Dash of cayenne
2 tablespoons chopped chives
  or scallion tops
1 tablespoon grated cheese
1 tablespoon lemon juice

1. In saucepan combine all ingredients except lemon juice. Bring to boil; cook, stirring, until cheese is melted and mixture is smooth.
2. Remove from heat; stir in lemon juice.

Marion Weeks, Women's Club, Portsmouth, N.H.

SAUCE VERONICA

Makes About 2 Cups

Serve with Roast Whole Boneless Chicken with Wild Rice and Foie Gras Stuffing and Sauce Veronica (p. 262) or with broiled chicken.

2 tablespoons butter
2 tablespoons flour
1½ teaspoons lemon juice
1½ cups chicken broth
2 egg yolks, lightly beaten
  Salt and pepper to taste
1 cup seedless white grapes

1. Melt butter in saucepan; blend in flour. Gradually stir in lemon juice and broth; cook over medium heat, stirring constantly, until thickened and smooth.
2. Put egg yolks in small bowl; beat with a little sauce. Add to rest of sauce; cook over low heat, stirring constantly, until mixture starts to bubble.
3. Season with salt and pepper; stir in grapes. Cook, stirring, for 1 minute.

Mrs. Alan Grubbs, Junior Woman's Club,
Spartansburg, Pa.

WINE SAUCE FOR GAME

Makes 1½ Cups

Especially good with venison.

½ cup currant jelly
½ cup water
1 tablespoon butter
1 teaspoon salt
  Juice of ½ lemon

Pinch of cayenne
3 cloves
½ cup port

1. In saucepan combine all ingredients except port. Bring to boil; simmer for a few minutes.
2. Strain; stir in port.

Ethel Lee, Gentilly Woods Woman's Club,
New Orleans, La.

WINE SAUCE FOR WILD GOOSE OR OTHER GAME

Makes About 2 Cups

3 cups chicken broth
¼ cup goose drippings
3 tablespoons flour
1 tablespoon brandy
1 tablespoon dry white wine
1 tablespoon gin
  Salt and pepper to taste

1. Boil broth over high heat until reduced to about 2 cups.
2. Heat goose drippings in heavy saucepan; blend in flour. Gradually stir in broth; cook over medium heat, stirring constantly, until thickened and smooth.
3. Stir in brandy, wine and gin; simmer for 2 minutes. Remove from heat; stir in salt and pepper.

Mrs. Andy Griffith, Woman's Club, Manteo, N.C.

RED WINE SAUCE

Makes About 2½ Cups

Serve on Meat Balls in Red Wine Sauce (p. 326), or use for basting broiled chicken, as desired.

⅓ cup butter or margarine
¼ cup grated onion
⅓ cup presifted flour
1½ cups dry red wine
½ cup catsup
½ cup beef broth
½ teaspoon salt
⅛ teaspoon pepper
  Dash of garlic salt
1 tablespoon brown sugar
1 tablespoon prepared mustard
  Dash of ground cloves

1. Melt butter in saucepan; sauté onion until golden. Sprinkle with flour; gradually stir in wine; cook over medium heat, stirring constantly, until thickened and smooth.
2. Stir in remaining ingredients; simmer for 5 minutes.

Mrs. Franklin Ussery, Jr., Booklovers Club,
Alice, Tex.

13. Stuffings and Garnishes for Fish, Poultry, Meat and Vegetables

Stuffings

Many people like a little stuffing with their turkey! Indeed, stuffings in meat, fish and poultry add a delicious savory accompaniment to the main course and extend the number of servings carved from a roast. Purists prefer to bake their stuffing in a separate casserole, in the belief that the stuffing robs the roast of juices, but others believe that it contributes flavor to meat.

Basically, there are two types of stuffings —moist and dry—and the choice is one of personal preference. Bread is the usual base, but other starchy substitutes—cooked rice, mashed potatoes or chestnuts, bulgur (cracked wheat) or corn meal or noodles —are often used. To the base are added butter or some other fat, herbs, spices, vegetables, sometimes an egg and often sausage meat, oysters, chestnuts or fruit.

All stuffings expand during cooking. Room must be left for expansion, or the roast will burst.

HOW TO STUFF A BIRD

Prepare the stuffing according to recipe directions. Unless the bird is to be cooked immediately, the stuffing should be cooled before it is used.

First fill the crop of a ready-to-cook bird with stuffing. Pull back the skin of the neck over the opening; fasten with a skewer. Fill the body cavity lightly with the remaining stuffing; sew or skewer opening. Finally, truss the bird (p. 261), and it is ready for the oven.

Recipes for some excellent stuffings, erroneously but commonly called dressings, follow, and there are many other throughout the book. For these, consult the Index. Most stuffings may be used for stuffing vegetables, such as tomatoes and green peppers, as well as for roasts.

APRICOT STUFFING

Sufficient to Stuff 5-Pound Duck
or 10-Pound Goose

½ pound dried apricots
2 cups bread crumbs
½ cup cracker crumbs
1½ teaspoons salt
¼ teaspoon paprika
4 tablespoons chopped celery
1 tablespoon minced parsley
4 tablespoons butter or other fat, melted

1. Wash apricots. Cover with water; bring to boil; cook until tender. Drain; reserve liquid.
2. Cut up apricots; combine with remaining ingredients, moistening with apricot liquid if too dry.

Sethryn Hodges, Woman's Club, Elroy, Ariz.

BACON STUFFING

Sufficient to Stuff 2 Rock Cornish
Game Hen or 1 Small Chicken

5 slices bacon, diced
1 small onion, finely chopped
2 cups fresh bread crumbs
¼ cup nonfat dry milk solids
2 tablespoons chopped parsley
1 teaspoon poultry seasoning
½ teaspoon salt
⅛ teaspoon pepper

1. Cook bacon in skillet over low heat for 3 minutes. Add onion; sauté for 5 minutes longer, or until bacon is crisp.
2. Remove from heat; stir in remaining ingredients. Mix well; cool.

Mrs. William H. Peifer, Greenfields Woman's Club, Reading, Pa.

BREAD STUFFING

Sufficient to Stuff
10-Pound Pig or Turkey

½ cup butter or margarine
1 cup chopped onions
1 cup chopped celery
1 cup chopped mushrooms
2 teaspoons salt
½ teaspoon pepper
½ teaspoon thyme
¼ teaspoon mace
2 tablespoon chopped parsley
8 cups fresh bread crumbs

1. Melt butter or margarine in large skillet; sauté onions and celery over

medium heat for 10 minutes. Add mushrooms; sauté for 5 minutes longer.

2. Turn into mixing bowl; add remaining ingredients; mix well.

Mrs. L. M. Hockenbery, Woman's Club,
Bangor, Pa.

INDIAN BREAD STUFFING

Sufficient to Stuff 10- to 12-Pound Turkey

¾ cup butter or margarine
1 cup finely chopped onions
¾ cup finely chopped chili peppers
½ cup finely chopped celery
5½ cups fresh white bread crumbs
5 cups fresh dark bread crumbs
1 cup chicken broth
¾ pound sausages, sliced
1½ teaspoons salt
¼ teaspoon pepper
2 eggs, lightly beaten
1 cup chopped walnuts

1. Melt butter or margarine in skillet; add onions, chilis and celery; sauté over medium heat for 10 minutes, stirring occasionally.

2. Turn into mixing bowl; add crumbs and broth; toss lightly.

3. Brown sausages well in fat remaining in skillet; add to crumb mixture. Add remaining ingredients; toss lightly.

Mrs. Roy Purchase, Golfview Hills Woman's Club,
Hinsdale, Ill.

RYE BREAD AND CHESTNUT FILLING FOR TURKEY

Sufficient to Stuff 12- to 15-Pound Turkey

1 pound chestnuts
1 loaf rye bread, diced
½ cup water
1 large onion, finely chopped
½ cup melted butter or margarine
2 teaspoons salt
¼ teaspoon pepper
3 eggs, lightly beaten
½ cup milk

1. Roast chestnuts; peel; cut into thin slices.

2. Put bread in mixing bowl; sprinkle with water. Add remaining ingredients; mix well.

Marge Lawlor, Woman's Club, Mahanoy City, Pa.

BULGUR STUFFING

Makes About 4 Cups

For meat, fish, poultry, game birds and vegetables.

⅓ cup butter
⅓ cup chopped onions
⅓ cup chopped celery
⅓ cup diced peeled tart green apple
    Chopped cooked turkey giblets
13-ounce can bulgur (cracked wheat) or 1 cup dry bulgur, cooked according to package directions
⅓ cup slivered blanched almonds
½ teaspoon salt

⅛ teaspoon pepper
½ teaspoon poultry seasoning
¾ cup chicken broth or water

1. Melt butter in saucepan; sauté onions, celery, apple and giblets until onions are golden.

2. Stir in remaining ingredients; cover; cook over moderate heat until liquid is absorbed.

Mrs. Walter Bruckert, Women's Club, Wasco, Ore.

CELERY DRESSING

Sufficient to Stuff 5-Pound Fish or Roasting Chicken

¼ cup melted butter or margarine
¼ cup boiling water
1½ cups cracker crumbs
¼ teaspoon salt
1 tablespoon grated onion
2 tablespoons finely chopped parsley
¼ cup finely chopped celery leaves
¼ teaspoon poultry seasoning

Combine all ingredients in mixing bowl; mix well.

Mrs. Henry Bourne, Junior Wednesday Club,
Danville, Va.

CELERY AND MUSHROOM DRESSING

Makes about 4 Cups, Sufficient to Stuff 8 Rock Cornish Game Hens or 2 Roasting Chickens

2 tablespoons butter or margarine
4 cups finely chopped celery
4 cups finely chopped mushrooms
2 teaspoons salt
½ teaspoon rosemary
½ teaspoon thyme
⅛ teaspoon pepper
⅔ cup sliced water chestnuts

1. Melt butter or margarine in large skillet; add celery, mushrooms, salt, rosemary, thyme and pepper; sauté over low heat for 10 minutes, stirring occasionally.

2. Stir in water chestnuts.

Dona Tessendorf, Woman's Club, Dundee, Ill.

CHESTNUT DRESSING

Makes about 14 Cups, Sufficient to Stuff 12- to 14-Pound Turkey

4 cups corn bread crumbs
1 cup fresh bread crumbs
2½ cups hot chicken broth or bouillon
1 cup butter or margarine
1½ cups chopped celery
½ cup chopped onions
¼ cup chopped parsley
1 cup chopped chestnuts
1 teaspoon thyme
2 teaspoons pepper
2 teaspoons salt
4 eggs, lightly beaten

1. Combine crumbs in large mixing bowl. Pour broth or bouillon over crumbs; set aside.

2. Melt butter or margarine in skillet; sauté celery, onions and parsley for 10 minutes.

3. Stir in remaining ingredients; mix well. Add to crumbs; stir well.

NOTE: This dressing is also excellent when 1 cup sausage meat or 1 cup drained oysters is substituted for chestnuts.

Mrs. J. P. King, Sr., Woman's Club,
Dahlonega, Ga.

CORN STUFFING

Sufficient to Stuff Crown Roast of Pork or Lamb

1-pound can cream-style corn
1½ cups whole-kernel corn
1 egg, lightly beaten
1 cup fresh bread crumbs
½ cup finely chopped onions
Dash of pepper
½ cup finely chopped green pepper
2 tablespoons chopped pimiento
1½ teasoons salt

Combine all ingredients in mixing bowl; mix well.

Woman's Club, Moorestown, N.J.

CORN BREAD DRESSING

Sufficient to Stuff 4-Pound Chicken

1 egg, lightly beaten
2 cups crumbled corn bread
⅓ cup finely chopped onions
1 teaspoon salt
⅛ teaspoon pepper
⅓ cup melted butter or margarine

Combine all ingredients in mixing bowl; mix well.

Mrs. Perry O'Neal, Sr., President, American
Legion Auxiliary, Moultrie, Ga.

STUFFING FOR FISH

Sufficient to Stuff 3-Pound Fish

2 tablespoons fat
1 medium onion, minced
4 slices bacon, diced
1 large tomato, peeled, seeded and chopped
1 cup bread crumbs
½ teaspoon pepper
½ teaspoon salt
About ½ cup hot water

1. Melt fat in skillet; sauté onion, bacon and tomato for 10 minutes, or until vegetables are tender and bacon is cooked.
2. Add to crumbs; add pepper and salt. Stir in enough water to moisten.

Hoke County Cook Book, Woman's Club,
Raeford, N.C.

BON SECOUR OYSTER DRESSING

Sufficient to Stuff 4-Pound Chicken

For a 10- to 15-pound turkey, triple quantity of each ingredient.

½ cup butter
4 tablespoons chopped parsley
½ cup chopped onions
4 cups crustless white or corn bread crumbs
⅛ teaspoon poultry seasoning
¾ teaspoon salt
¼ teaspoon pepper
½ teaspoon paprika
2 cups chicken broth or oyster liquor
3 eggs, lightly beaten
1 pint oysters, freshly shucked and chopped

1. Melt butter in saucepan; sauté parsley and onions for 5 minutes, or until onions are transparent. Add crumbs and seasonings; mix thoroughly.
2. Add broth or oyster liquor and eggs. Cook for 3 minutes, stirring occasionally.
3. Add oysters; cook for 2 to 3 minutes longer, stirring constantly.

A. S.

PRUNE STUFFING

Sufficient to Stuff 10- to 12-Pound Goose

1 cup large dried prunes
2 cups water
1 tablespoon shortening
½ cup chopped onions
2 cups ground cooked pork
1 teaspoon salt
¼ teaspoon pepper
1 egg yolk, lightly beaten
¼ cup chopped pitted green olives

1. Put prunes in saucepan; cover with water. Soak for 1 hour. Cover; cook over medium heat for 45 minutes, or until plump and tender. Drain; carefully slit prunes; discard pits; set aside.
2. Melt shortening in skillet; sauté onions over medium heat for 5 minutes. Stir in pork; sauté for 2 minutes longer.
3. Remove from heat; add salt, pepper and egg yolk; mix well.
4. Put ¼ cup of pork mixture in small bowl; blend in olives; use to stuff prunes.
5. Gently mix prunes with remaining pork mixture.

Woman's Club, Palisade, N.J.

RICE ALMOND STUFFING

Sufficient to Stuff 4-Pound Chicken

¼ cup butter or margarine
¼ cup minced onion
½ cup rice
1 cup chicken broth
1 teaspoon salt
½ cup chopped almonds

1. Melt butter or margarine in large skillet; add onion and rice, sauté over low heat, stirring frequently, until rice is golden.
2. Stir in broth and salt; cover; simmer for 15 minutes, stirring occasionally, or until rice is tender.
3. Remove from heat; stir in almonds.

Mrs. Alex Wood, Athenaeum Club,
Kansas City, Mo.

RICE AND MUSHROOM STUFFING

Sufficient to Stuff 4- to 5-Pound Chicken

3 tablespoons butter or margarine
3 tablespoons chopped onion
½ cup sliced mushrooms
1⅓ cups instant rice
1 chicken bouillon cube
½ teaspoon marjoram
¼ teaspoon paprika
Dash of pepper
1½ cups water

1. Melt butter or margarine in saucepan; sauté onion and mushrooms for about 5 minutes, or until onion is tender.
2. Add remaining ingredients; bring to boil, fluffing rice gently with fork. Cover; remove from heat; let stand for about 10 minutes. Cool.

Mrs. Stanley Thomson, Woman's Club, Anchorage, Alaska

RHODE ISLAND BROWN RICE TURKEY DRESSING

Sufficient to Stuff 10- to 12-Pound Turkey

3 cups cooked brown rice
3 cups whole wheat bread crumbs
½ cup melted butter
2 medium onions, finely chopped
2 stalks celery, finely chopped
2 teaspoons salt
¼ teaspoon pepper
4 eggs, lightly beaten
1 cup gravy or milk

Combine all ingredients in mixing bowl in order given; toss lightly.

D. Frances Webb, Woman's Club, Bellows Falls, Vt.

SAUSAGE APPLE STUFFING

Sufficient to Stuff 12- to 15-Pound Turkey

1 pound sausage meat
1 cup minced onions
1 cup chopped celery
8 cups soft bread crumbs
2 cups diced peeled apples
1 teaspoon salt
¼ teaspoon sage

1. In skillet sauté sausage meat, onions and celery for about 10 minutes, or until onions and celery are golden.
2. Stir in remaining ingredients; cook, stirring, until crumbs begin to brown.

Margaret Ovington, Woman's Club, Palmdale, Calif.

WATER CHESTNUT STUFFING

Sufficient to Stuff 10-Pound Turkey

1 cup butter or margarine
1 cup chopped onions
½ cup chopped green pepper
½ cup chopped celery
1 tablespoon soy sauce
1 tablespoon chopped candied ginger
2 cups sliced water chestnuts
8 cups toasted bread cubes

1. Melt butter or margarine in skillet; sauté onions, green pepper and celery for 10 minutes, stirring occasionally.
2. Remove from heat; turn into mixing bowl. Add remaining ingredients; toss lightly.

Marion Block, Pathfinder Club, Compton, Calif.

WILD RICE STUFFING

Sufficient to Stuff 6-Pound Fish or Baby Turkey

¼ cup butter or margarine
½ cup chopped green pepper
¼ cup chopped onion
4 cups cooked wild rice
10½-ounce can condensed cream of mushroom soup

1. Melt butter or margarine in skillet; sauté green pepper and onion over medium heat for 10 minutes.
2. Turn into mixing bowl; add rice and soup; mix well.

Mrs. Laurence R. Ellerman, Plum Lake Woman's Club, Star Lake, Wis.

WILD RICE STUFFING FOR CHICKEN

Sufficient to Stuff 4-Pound Chicken

⅓ cup melted butter
½ cup wild rice
1 small onion, finely chopped
1 bay leaf
¼ cup finely chopped celery
½ teaspoon salt
¼ teaspoon pepper
1½ cups chicken broth
1 chicken liver, chopped
2 tablespoons chopped chives
2 tablespoons dry sherry

1. Preheat oven to 350° F. Grease 1-quart casserole.
2. In mixing bowl combine butter, rice, onion, bay leaf, celery, salt, pepper and broth. Mix well; turn into casserole.
3. Bake in preheated oven for 30 minutes, or until liquid has been absorbed.
4. Remove from oven; stir in remaining ingredients.

Woman's Club, Pikeville, Ky.

WILD RICE AND CHESTNUT STUFFING

Sufficient to Stuff 4-Pound Fowl

1 cup wild rice
3 cups water
1 teaspoon salt
½ pound chestnuts, cooked and peeled
½ cup butter or other fat, melted
¼ teaspoon salt
⅛ teaspoon pepper
2 tablespoons minced onion

1. Wash rice; put in saucepan with water and salt. Bring to boil; simmer for 40 minutes, or until tender. Drain.
2. Combine rice and remaining ingredients. Mix well.

Sethryn Hodges, Woman's Club, Elroy, Ariz.

WILD RICE AND FOIE GRAS STUFFING

Sufficient to Stuff 6-Pound Chicken or 2 Small Boned Broiling Chickens

8-ounce package wild rice
¼ cup pâté de foie gras
½ cup brandy
½ teaspoon salt
Dash of pepper

1. Cook rice according to package directions.
2. Drain; combine with remaining ingredients.

Mrs. Alan Grubbs, Junior Woman's Club, Spartansburg, Pa.

WILD RICE AND OYSTER DRESSING

Sufficient to Stuff 6-Pound Chicken

3 tablespoons bacon drippings
1 medium onion, minced
2 cups cooked wild rice
  Salt and freshly ground pepper to taste
1 teaspoon crushed thyme
1 teaspoon chopped parsley
½ bay leaf, crumbled
1 tablespoon minced ham
24 oysters, freshly shucked
1 egg, well beaten

1. Melt bacon drippings in large skillet; sauté onion for 5 minutes, or until transparent. Add rice and seasonings; sauté for 5 minutes longer.
2. Cut oysters in half; add with ham to rice mixture. Cook for 3 minutes, stirring constantly.
3. Remove from heat; add egg. Mix gently but thoroughly.

A. S.

TOMATO STUFFING

Sufficient to Stuff 4-Pound Chicken

2 tablespoons butter or margarine
1 small onion, finely chopped
½ cup rice
1-pound can tomatoes
1 teaspoon salt
¼ teaspoon pepper
½ teaspoon chili powder

1. Melt butter or margarine in skillet; sauté onion and rice, stirring frequently, until rice is golden.
2. Stir in remaining ingredients. Bring to boil; cover; simmer for 15 minutes, or until liquid has been absorbed and rice is tender.
3. Cool slightly before stuffing chicken.

Mrs. J. R. Burnett, En Avant Society, Potosi, Mo.

Garnishes

In Pennsylvania Dutch country, seven sweets and seven sours are traditionally served at every meal. This may be going a little too far for the average homemaker, but certainly a serving of one or more sweet preserves, garnishes, sour pickles, or relishes piques the appetite and heightens the flavor contrast of the meal.

Chapter 25 contains some special recipes for preserves, any one of which will make a memorable contribution to most main courses. In addition, the shelves of grocery stores burgeon with a vast assortment of jellies, jams, pickled and preserved fruits, chow-chows, piccalillis, etc., and among these are many that will surely please the most fastidious palate.

The following section presents a tempting selection of recipes for favorite garnishes of American cooks.

MEAT GARNISHES

WITH BAKED HAM: hot spiced peaches; cinnamon orange slices; fried pineapple slices; hot spiced applesauce.

WITH FRESH PORK ROAST OR CHOPS: cinnamon apples; fried apple slices; whole apples simmered in grape juice; spiced hot applesauce; hot baked peaches; broiled pineapple slices.

WITH ROAST LAMB OR BROILED CHOPS: pears filled with mint jelly and broiled; minted green-tinted pineapple slices.

WITH VEAL: spiced rhubarb sauce; any of the sweet pickled fruits.

WITH BEEF: sautéed mushroom caps; mustard pickles; corn relish; broiled apricots.

Century Club Cook Book, Coraopolis, Pa.

APPLE RELISH

Makes About 2 Cups

Serve well chilled with pork or turkey.

1 pound large red apples
2 dill pickles
1 medium onion
½ cup sugar
¼ cup vinegar

1. Core but do not peel apples. Put apples, pickles and onion through meat grinder.
2. Stir in sugar and vinegar. Chill.

Mrs. Otis Durham, Woman's Federated Guild, Moultrie, Ga.

APPLE CINNAMON RELISH

Makes About 3 Cups

2 cups canned applesauce
½ cup chopped celery
½ cup seedless raisins
½ cup red cinnamon candies

1. Combine all ingredients in mixing bowl.
2. Chill for several hours, stirring occasionally, until candies are dissolved.

Marietta Schif, Woman's Club, Paxton, Ill.

RED APPLE SLICES

Serve with pork, ham, fowl or curries.

2 cups sugar
2 cups water

Juice of 1½ lemons
Rind of 1 lemon, grated
1 cinnamon stick
⅛ teaspoon ground cardamom or
  seeds from 2 hulls cardamom
½ teaspoon red food coloring
8 large or 12 small cooking apples

1. In skillet combine all ingredients except apples. Bring to boil; then simmer for 5 minutes.
2. Meanwhile, peel and core apples. Cut crosswise into slices about 1 inch thick.
3. Put several apple slices in syrup. Do not crowd. Cook over low heat for 10 to 12 minutes, or until edges seem transparent, spooning syrup over apples as they cook.
4. Lift out cooked slices gently; arrange in serving dish. Cook apple slices as long as there is syrup to cook them in; syrup eventually thickens and cooks away.
5. Spoon any syrup remaining in skillet over apples; cover; store in refrigerator, where they will keep well.

Mrs. Violet Bailey, President, Sorosis Club,
Harvey, N.D.

APPLE FRITTERS

Serves 6

Serve as an accompaniment to meat.
1½ cups presifted flour
¼ teaspoon salt
2 teaspoons baking powder
2 tablespoons sugar
1 egg, lightly beaten
¾ cup milk
4 medium tart apples
  Fat for deep frying

1. Sift together dry ingredients.
2. In mixing bowl combine egg and milk. Gradually stir in dry ingredients.
3. Peel and core apples; cut into eighths.
4. Dip apples in batter; drop into deep fat heated to 365° F. Fry until golden brown, turning once.
5. Drain on absorbent paper.

North Phoenix Woman's Club, Phoenix, Ariz.

APPLESAUCE

Makes 2 Cups

2 pounds apples
¼ cup water or fruit juice
  Dash of salt
  Sugar to taste

1. Wash and quarter apples, but do not peel or core. Put in saucepan with water or juice; cook over low heat until soft.
2. Put apples and liquid through a coarse strainer or food mill.
3. Stir in salt and sugar.

A. S.

GOLDEN JELLIED APRICOTS

Makes About 4 Cups

Delicious with turkey, ham or game.
3½ cups canned peeled apricot halves
  with syrup

¼ cup vinegar
1 teaspoon cloves
4-inch cinnamon sticks
3-ounce package orange gelatin

1. Drain syrup from apricots into saucepan. Add vinegar, cloves and cinnamon; bring to boil. Add apricots; simmer for 10 minutes. Remove apricots with slotted spoon; place each in small mold.
2. Strain syrup into large measuring cup; add boiling water to total 2 cups. Add gelatin; stir until dissolved. Pour over apricots; chill until firm.

NOTE: For a salad, serve on pineapple slice on bed of lettuce; top with Sour Cream Dressing (p. 544).

Mrs. Maiben Williams, Three Arts Club,
Monroeville, Ala.

MUSTARD WAX BEANS

Serves 4

Serve as relish, in a salad or as an accompaniment to meat.
1 cup sugar
½ cup cider vinegar
3 tablespoons prepared mustard
½ teaspoon dehydrated onion flakes
¼ teaspoon salt
1-pound can wax beans, drained,
  or 10-ounce package frozen wax
  beans, cooked and drained

1. Day before, in saucepan combine all ingredients except beans. Bring to boil, stirring until sugar is dissolved.
2. Add beans; simmer, uncovered, for 5 minutes.
3. Cool. Cover; refrigerate overnight.

Marge Leiner, Junior Woman's Club,
Lombard, Ill.

PICKLED BEET RELISH

Makes About 2 Cups

2 cups chopped cooked beets
1 tablespoon horseradish
½ cup chopped sweet pickles
½ teaspoon salt
  Dash of pepper
2 tablespoons liquid from pickle jar
1 tablespoon sugar

1. Put beets in bowl or jar. Add remaining ingredients; mix gently but well with fork.
2. Cover; refrigerate for several hours.

Jean Baurers, Woman's Club, Oceanside, Calif.

CRANBERRY RELISH

Makes 5 Cups

1 pound cranberries
3 winesap apples
1 large orange
2 cups sugar

1. Several days or a week before, wash and sort cranberries. Quarter and seed unpeeled apples and orange. Put fruits through medium blade of meat grinder. Stir in sugar.

2. Put in container; cover refrigerate for at least a few days to 1 week. Flavor improves with age.

Mrs. Del De Forest, Junior Woman's Club, Diamond Bar, Calif.

CRANBERRY SAUCE

Makes About 4 Cups

4 cups fresh or frozen cranberries
1⅓ cups water
2 cups sugar

1. Day before, put cranberries and water in saucepan. Bring to boil; cover; simmer until soft.
2. Press through coarse strainer; return purée to saucepan. Add sugar; boil for 5 minutes.
3. Turn into serving dish; refrigerate for 24 hours.

Ruth Feidler, Woman's Club, Batchtown, Ill.

SPICED CRANBERRIES

Makes About 5 Cups

1 cup water
1¼ cups brown sugar
¾ cup granulated sugar
½ cup vinegar
2 teaspoons cloves
2 cinnamon sticks
4 cups cranberries

1. In saucepan combine all ingredients except cranberries. Bring to boil; boil rapidly over high heat for 5 minutes.
2. Strain; return syrup to saucepan. Add cranberries; cook over medium heat, stirring occasionally, for about 5 minutes, or until cranberries pop. Cool well before serving.

Mrs. George Oram, Junior Woman's Club, Scotch Plains, N.J.

MELANZANE SATT ACETO
(Pickled Eggplant)

Makes About 1 Quart

This will keep a week or longer in refrigerator. Excellent with lamb.

1 large eggplant
2 cloves garlic
1 teaspoon salt
½ cup wine vinegar
½ teaspoon black pepper
½ teaspoon basil
½ teaspoon orégano
¼ cup olive or cooking oil

1. Day before cut unpeeled eggplant into large cubes. Cook in boiling salted water for 10 minues. Drain thoroughly.
2. In large mixing bowl mash garlic with salt. Add vinegar and seasonings. Add eggplant. Refrigerate overnight or longer.
3. Just before serving, stir in oil.

Jane Von Wicklin, Probieren Club, Weatherford, Okla.

CURRIED FRUITS

Serves 18 to 20

1-pound 4-ounce can peach halves, drained

1-pound 4-ounce can pear halves, drained
1-pound 4-ounce can apricots, drained
1-pound 4-ounce can pineapple chunks, drained
⅓ cup butter or margarine
¾ cup brown sugar
2 teaspoons curry powder

1. Grease 3-quart casserole or baking dish.
2. Arrange fruits in casserole dish.
3. Melt butter or margarine in small saucepan. Remove from heat; stir in sugar and curry powder. Pour over fruits. Let stand for 1 hour.
4. Preheat oven to 350° F.
5. Bake in preheated oven for 20 minutes.

Mrs. Ann Umbehr, Ladies Reading Circle, Alma, Kans.

BAKED ORANGES

Serves 4

Serve wth poultry or meat.

4 large oranges
¼ cup sugar
4 teaspoons butter or margarine

1. Wash oranges; grate rinds slightly.
2. Put in saucepan; cover with boiling water. Cover; simmer over medium heat for 30 minutes.
3. Cool. Cut off a small slice at blossom end of each orange; remove core.
4. Preheat oven to 350° F. Grease 8-inch square baking pan.
5. In small mixing bowl cream sugar with butter or margarine; put some in center of each orange. Place in pan; add water to half fill pan.
6. Cover; bake in preheated oven for 2 hours.

Woman's Club, Newnan, Ga.

BAKED PEACH HALVES

Serves 6

Serve with baked ham.

1-pound can peach halves, drained
1 cup mincemeat

1. Preheat oven to 350° F. Grease 10 x 6 x 1½-inch baking pan.
2. Arrange peaches, cut side up, in pan. Fill centers with mincemeat.
3. Bake in preheated oven for 15 minutes.

Eula Jorgensen, Cutler Ridge Woman's Club, Miami, Fla.

BAKED CRUSHED PINEAPPLE

Serves 6

Delicious with ham or lamb.

¾ cup sugar
1 teaspoon cinnamon
Dash of nutmeg
Dash of ground cloves
¼ cup cornstarch
1-pound 4-ounce can crushed pineapple, undrained

2 eggs, lightly beaten
2 tablespoons melted butter
Marshmallows

1. Preheat oven to 350° F. Grease 8-inch square baking pan.
2. In mixing bowl combine sugar, cinnamon, nutmeg, cloves and cornstarch. Stir in pineapple, eggs and butter. Pour into pan; top with marshmallows.
3. Bake in preheated oven for 25 to 35 minutes, or until set and lightly browned.

Mrs. James Martin, Woman's Club,
Ebensburg, Pa.

ESCALLOPED PINEAPPLE

Serves 6

Use as an additional vegetable dish.

1 pineapple, peeled, cored and
thinly sliced
Butter
Brown sugar
2 tablespoons water
Cracker crumbs

1. Preheat oven to 350° F. Grease 1½-quart casserole.
2. In casserole arrange a layer of pineapple; dot with butter; sprinkle with sugar, water and crumbs. Repeat for 3 or 4 layers, ending with crumbs.
3. Bake in preheated oven for 30 minutes, or until browned.

Olive M. Chamberlain, South Side Woman's
Club, Denver, Colo.

PINEAPPLE FRITTERS

Serves 4

If teaspoon is dipped in the hot fat before being dipped in the batter, the fritter will slip off more easily and will maintain a more uniform shape. Serve with meat, chicken or duck.

1 cup presifted flour
½ teaspoon salt
1 teaspoon baking powder
1 egg
¼ cup milk
1 tablespoon melted shortening
1 cup drained crushed pineapple
Fat for deep frying
Confectioners' sugar

1. In mixing bowl combine flour, salt and baking powder.
2. In another mixing bowl beat egg; stir in milk, shortening and pineapple. Add to dry ingredients; mix lightly.
3. Drop by teaspoons into deep fat heated to 365° F. Fry for 3 to 5 minutes, or until cooked through and golden.
4. Drain on absorbent paper; sprinkle with confectioners' sugar.

Mrs. George Gaull, Woman's Club,
Newtown Square, Pa.

HORSERADISH (*Kren*)

Makes About 2 Cups

1 cup grated horseradish
¼ cup sugar
½ cup vinegar
¼ teaspoon salt

Combine all ingredients. Turn into container; cover; store in refrigerator, where it will keep indefinitely.

VARIATION: 1 part grated apple may be added to 2 parts horseradish mixture.

Woman's Club, Clarkson, Neb.

CHINESE SWEET AND SOUR RADISHES

Serves 4

Serve as a relish.

1 bunch radishes with leaves
1 teaspoon salt
2 teaspoons soy sauce
2 tablespoons vinegar
2 tablespoons sugar
1 teaspoon sesame oil

1. Wash and trim radishes; set leaves aside. With flat side of cleaver or heavy knife gently crush radishes, but do not break into pieces.
2. Wash leaves; cut into ½-inch pieces.
3. Put radishes and leaves in bowl; sprinkle with salt. Let stand for 10 minutes. Drain; return to bowl.
4. Blend remaining ingredients; pour over radishes. Refrigerate until serving time.

Junior Woman's Club, West Essex, N.J.

FIRE AND ICE TOMATOES

Serves 8

6 ripe tomatoes
1 large green pepper
1 large red onion
¾ cup vinegar
1½ teaspoons celery salt
1½ teaspoons mustard seed
½ teaspoon salt
4½ teaspoons sugar
⅛ teaspoon red pepper
⅛ teaspoon black pepper
¼ cup ice water

1. Peel and quarter tomatoes. Seed green pepper; cut into strips. Slice onion; separate into rings.
2. Put vegetables in bowl. Add remaining ingredients; refrigerate until serving time.

Mrs. Donald Wolfe, Juniors, Saratoga, Fla.

14. Dumplings and Other Starch Substitutes

Dumplings

There are many substitutes for the ubiquitous potato in daily menus. Among these are dumplings, spoon breads, hominy grits, barley, bulgur (cracked wheat), beans, rice and pasta. The last two—rice and pasta—and the many dishes and casseroles based on these staples will be found in Chapters 15 and 16 and as ingredients in many recipes throughout this book. Here we deal with the other starch substitutes, beginning with dumplings. In this category, however, the potato creeps back, for it makes one of the most delicious of all dumplings.

Dumplings are usually leavened to make them light and fluffy, and they usually contain egg to bind the dry ingredients and hold the dumplings together as they steam in simmering water, broth, soup or gravy. They are excellent in soups and are wonderful when added to stews and ragouts or served with creamed chicken or pot roasts.

BUTTER BALLS

Makes About 1 Cup

    2 cups presifted flour
    ½ teaspoon baking powder
    Pinch of salt
    ¼ cup butter
    About ⅔ cup milk or water

1. In mixing bowl combine flour, baking powder and salt. Cut in butter. Stir in enough milk or water to make a firm dough.
2. Roll dough into small balls; add to boiling soup 5 minutes before serving.

Woman's Club, Eustis, Fla.

EGG DUMPLINGS

Makes About 18

    1 cup milk
    1 tablespoon butter
    ½ teaspoon salt
    Dash of nutmeg
    1 cup presifted flour
    2 eggs

1. In saucepan combine milk, butter, salt and nutmeg. Bring to boil; remove from heat.

2. Add flour all at once; beat until dough leaves side of pan. Add eggs, one at a time, beating well after each addition.
3. Drop by teaspoons into simmering soup. Cover; simmer for 30 minutes.

Mrs. Michael Gray, Golfview Hills Woman's Club, Hinsdale, Ill.

FLUFFY DUMPLINGS

Serves 4 to 6

    ¾ cup milk
    1 egg
    2 cups presifted flour
    3 teaspoons baking powder
    ½ teaspoon salt
    1 tablespoon melted butter

1. In mixing bowl beat milk and egg.
2. Sift together flour, baking powder and salt. Gradually stir into egg mixture. Stir in butter.
3. Drop by spoons into simmering water. Cover; steam for 10 minutes.

CORN MEAL DUMPLINGS: Use 1 cup corn meal in place of 1 cup presifted flour in above recipe.

Mrs. Joan Lorge, Junior Woman's Club, Port Washington, Wis.

OLD-FASHIONED DUMPLINGS

Makes 30 to Serve 6

Float dumplings in each serving of soup or stew. Especially good in Old-Fashioned Chicken Stew (p. 276).

    1 cup water
    ½ cup margarine
    1 cup presifted flour
    4 eggs
    ½ teaspoon salt
    ⅛ teaspoon nutmeg
    1 teaspoon sugar

1. In saucepan bring water and margarine to rapid boil. Add flour all at once; stir rapidly until paste forms ball in center of pan.
2. Remove from heat; beat in eggs, one at a time, beating well after each addition. Beat in salt, nutmeg and sugar.
3. Bring water to boil in a skillet; reduce heat. Shape paste into oblong dumplings with teaspoon. Place spoon in simmering water; gently slide off batter. Dip

spoon in water for each dumpling; keep water simmering gently.

4. Cook dumplings for about 5 minutes, or until they float.

Mrs. Del De Forest, Junior Woman's Club, Diamond Bar, Calif.

THREE-MINUTE WATER DUMPLINGS

Serves 4 to 6

2 cups presifted flour
2 teaspoons baking powder
½ teaspoon salt
1 egg, lightly beaten
2 tablespoons melted shortening
⅔ cup water

1. Into mixing bowl sift together flour, baking powder and salt. Add remaining ingredients; mix until blended.
2. Drop by spoons into boiling salted water; cover; boil for 3 minutes; drain.

Alice Pierson, Garden Century Club, Wilmington, Del.

BUTTER CRUMB DUMPLINGS

Makes About 15

2 cups presifted flour
4 teaspoons baking powder
½ teaspoon salt
1 teaspoon poultry seasoning
1 teaspoon celery seed
1 teaspoon dehydrated onion flakes
1 tablespoon poppy seeds
¼ cup olive oil
1 cup milk
¼ cup melted butter or margarine
1 cup bread crumbs

1. Preheat oven to 425° F. Grease baking sheet.
2. In mixing bowl combine flour, baking powder, salt and poultry seasoning. Stir in celery seed, onion flakes, poppy seeds, oil and milk; mix just until moistened.
3. Drop by tablespoons into butter or margarine to coat. Dredge in crumbs.
4. Arrange on baking sheet; bake in preheated oven for 20 to 25 minutes, or until golden.

Mrs. Richard Reid, Junior Woman's Club, Menomonee Falls, Wis.

ONION DUMPLINGS

Serves 6

1½ cups presifted flour
2 teaspoons baking powder
1 egg
⅔ cup milk
2 teaspoons dehydrated onion flakes
2 tablespoons chopped parsley

1. Into mixing bowl sift together flour and baking powder.
2. In measuring cup beat egg and milk.
3. Stir milk mixture, onion flakes and parsley into flour just until dry ingredients are moistened.
4. Drop by tablespoons into simmering stew; cook, uncovered, for 10 minutes.
5. Cover; cook for 10 minutes longer.

Madeline Hoss, Women's Club, Morton Grove, Ill.

RAISED BOHEMIAN DUMPLINGS

Serves 6 to 8

½ envelope active dry yeast
1½ cups lukewarm milk
1 teaspoon sugar
About 5 cups presifted flour
½ teaspoon baking powder
1 teaspoon melted butter
1 teaspoon salt
2 eggs, lightly beaten
3 slices white bread, cubed

1. In small bowl soften yeast in ½ cup of the milk. Let stand for 5 minutes; add sugar; stir until yeast is dissolved.
2. Into mixing bowl sift together 2 cups of the flour and baking powder. Add yeast and remaining milk. Stir in butter, salt and eggs; beat well.
3. Cover; set aside in warm place for 1 hour.
4. Add bread cubes and remaining flour to make a soft dough. Turn onto lightly floured board; knead until smooth.
5. Shape into 4 oblong pieces. Cover; let rise for 1 hour.
6. Gently lower oblongs into large saucepan of boiling water; cover; boil for 10 minutes. Turn rolls; cover; boil for 10 minutes longer.
7. Remove rolls; slice with thread.

Submitted to Kankakee Woman's Club by Mrs. Otto Kerner, Executive Mansion, Springfield, Ill.

CHICKEN CURRY DUMPLINGS

Serves 6 to 8

2 cups presifted flour
1 tablespoon baking powder
1 teaspoon salt
½ teaspoon curry powder
2 tablespoons shortening
1½ cups diced cooked chicken
1 cup milk
2 cups chicken broth

1. Into mixing bowl sift together flour, baking powder, salt and curry powder. Cut in shortening until mixture resembles fine crumbs.
2. Add chicken; stir in milk just until dry ingredients are moistened.
3. Bring broth to boil in large skillet.
4. Drop by tablespoons into broth. Cover; steam over very low heat for 12 minutes.

Mrs. W. D. Provine, Modern Study Club, Wolfe City, Tex.

PIROHI

Serves 4 to 6

Serve with pot cheese and seasoned with salt and pepper to taste.

3 medium potatoes, boiled and mashed
1½ pounds pot cheese
Salt to taste
3 cups presifted flour
2 eggs
¼ pound sliced bacon, diced
1 medium onion, grated
½ cup butter

1. Prepare filling: In mixing bowl combine potatoes and cheese; mix well; season with salt. Set aside.

2. Mound flour on board; make a well in center.

3. In small bowl blend eggs and water; pour into well in flour. Knead into a soft dough. Roll out ⅛-inch thick on lightly floured board.

4. Cut dough in 3½-inch circles; moisten edges with water. Place a spoonful of filling in center of each circle; fold over. Pinch edges together to seal and form half circle. Dry for about 20 minutes on board.

5. Meanwhile, fill 6-quart saucepan two-thirds full of water; bring to boil. Drop half circles, or pirohi, into water gradually so that water keeps boiling. Cook until pirohi float; lift out with slotted spoon; drain.

6. Meanwhile, prepare bacon mixture: Cook bacon in large skillet over medium heat, stirring frequently, for 5 minutes. Add onion; sauté over medium heat for 5 minutes. Add butter; allow to melt.

7. Drop pirohi into bacon mixture; spoon mixture over them. Keep hot over low heat for about 10 minutes.

Mrs. Norma G. Boykis, Woman's Club,
Clearfield, Pa.

PIROSHKI

Serves 6

3 eggs
2½ cups presifted flour
1¾ cups finely chopped cooked chicken
1 tablespoon grated onion
½ teaspoon salt
¼ teaspoon pepper
Grated Parmesan cheese
Melted butter

1. In mixing bowl beat 2 of the eggs until light. Stir in ½ cup water; gradually stir in flour.

2. Turn dough onto lightly floured board; knead until smooth.

3. Divide dough in half; roll out each half ¹⁄₁₆ inch thick.

4. Prepare filling: In mixing bowl combine remaining egg, chicken, onion, salt and pepper.

5. Place filling in mounds 2 inches apart on dough half; cover with second half; cut into 2-inch squares. Seal edges.

6. Drop piroshki into large saucepan of boiling salted water; boil for 12 to 15 minutes.

7. Drain well; serve with cheese and butter.

Mrs. Robert Austin, Lower Naches Woman's
Club, Yakima, Wash.

SPAETZLE (German Parsley Dumplings)

Serves 4 to 6

4 egg yolks
2 cups milk
¼ teaspoon salt
2½ cups presifted flour
⅓ cup butter
3 tablespoons chopped parsley

1. In mixing bowl beat egg yolks and milk.

2. Add salt; gradually stir in flour to make a paste thinner than biscuit dough.

3. Place colander with large holes over large saucepan with boiling salted water. Force dough through holes into water. Boil for 10 minutes, shaking pan occasionally. Drain; rinse.

4. Melt butter in clean saucepan; sauté parsley and spaetzle for about 3 minutes.

Mrs. Jess Tolerton, Junior Women's Club,
Cheyenne, Wyo.

POTATO DROP DUMPLINGS

Serves 4

4 medium potatoes, cooked and mashed
2 eggs
1 clove garlic, minced
½ cup presifted flour
Salt and pepper to taste

1. Put potatoes in mixing bowl. Add eggs and garlic; beat until smooth.

2. Stir in flour, salt and pepper; mix well.

3. Bring salted water to hard boil in large saucepan.

4. Drop potato mixture by teaspoons into water; cook for 2 minutes. Drain.

POTATO PUFFS: Use above recipe, but instead of boiling drop dumplings in deep fat heated to 365° F., fry until browned on all sides.

Palm Springs Woman's Club, Hialeah, Fla.

GNOCCHI (Italian Dumplings)

Serves 8 to 12

4 pounds potatoes
Salt to taste
5 cups presifted flour
Quick Tomato Sauce (p. 451)
Grated Romano cheese

1. Boil, drain and dice potatoes. Turn into mixing bowl. Season with salt. Gradually add flour, kneading after each addition to make a smooth dough.

2. Roll dough into ropelike strips about ¾ inch thick. Cut into ¾-inch pieces. Use fork prong to make design in each piece.

3. Drop into rapidly boiling salted water; cook for about 10 minutes.

4. Drain; serve with Quick Tomato Sauce and cheese.

Mrs. Gasper Zaffuto, Woman's Club,
Ebensburg, Pa.

SWEDISH POTATO DUMPLINGS

Serves 8

¾ pound ground beef
¼ pound ground salt pork
1 small onion, finely chopped
3 teaspoons salt
¼ teaspoon pepper
6 cups mashed potatoes
1 egg
1 egg yolk
About 1½ cups presifted flour
Favorite sauce or melted butter

1. Prepare meat stuffing: In skillet sauté beef, pork and onion until beef has lost pink color. Season with 1 teaspoon of the salt and pepper; set aside.

2. Prepare potato mixture: Into mixing bowl combine potatoes, remaining salt, egg and egg yolk; mix well. Add sufficient flour to make mixture easy to handle.

3. Shape mixture into ½-inch-thick cakes; put 1 teaspoon of meat stuffing in center of each.

4. Press potato mixture over to cover and seal stuffing completely.

5. Drop into boiling salted water in large saucepan; cover; simmer for 30 minutes. Lift out with slotted spoon; arrange on serving dish.

6. Serve with favorite sauce or butter, as desired.

Mrs. Ernest Fredlund, Twentieth Century Club,
Iron River, Mich.

SPANISH VANISH
(Cheese Dumplings in Tomato Sauce)

Serves 6

The sauce in which dumplings are cooked explains the first part of the name of this dish; the steadily emptied bowl explains the last part.

   3 tablespoons cooking oil
   1½ tablespoons chopped green pepper
   3 tablespoon chopped onion
     Presifted flour
   1-pound 12-ounce can tomatoes
   1 tablespoon chopped celery tops
   1 teaspoon sugar
     Salt
   3 teaspoons baking powder
   6 tablespoons shortening
   ¾ cup shredded Cheddar cheese
   1½ tablespoons chopped parsley
   ¾ cup milk

1. Heat oil in large skillet; sauté green pepper and onion for 10 minutes, or until tender. Stir in 3 tablespoons flour; cook, stirring, until flour and oil are combined.

2. Add tomatoes, celery tops, sugar and ½ teaspoon salt. Bring to boil, stirring constantly; then simmer for 5 minutes, stirring occasionally.

3. Make dumplings: In mixing bowl combine 1½ cups flour, baking powder and ¾ teaspoon salt. Cut in shortening until mixture resembles fine crumbs.

4. Stir in cheese and parsley. Add milk; stir with fork just until dry ingredients are moistened.

5. Dip tablespoon in cold water; drop batter from spoon into tomato sauce. Cover tightly; cook over low heat, without removing cover, for 20 minutes.

Dorothy Neidhart, Junior Woman's Club,
Cathedral City, Calif.

KNEDLICH (Matzo Balls)

Serves 6

   4 eggs, lightly beaten
   ½ cup water
   2 tablespoons melted chicken fat
     or shortening

   1 tablespoon salt
     Dash of pepper
   2 cups matzo meal
     Clear chicken soup

1. In mixing bowl beat eggs, water, fat or shortening, salt and pepper. Stir in matzo meal; beat until smooth. Let stand for 10 minutes.

2. Bring soup to boil in large saucepan. Drop batter by tablespoons into boiling liquid. Cover; simmer for 15 minutes.

Lillian Downs, Lincoln Village Women's Club,
Columbus, Ohio

Cereals

Corn meal, farina (cream of wheat) and hominy are cereals made of corn.

Corn meal, either yellow or white, is used extensively in corn breads, muffins, corn sticks and pancakes, and these recipes will be found in Chapters 3 and 4. Here we deal with those light creamy corn puddings known as spoon bread, because they are served hot from the oven with a spoon, and with other corn meal dishes.

Corn meal mush, known in Italy as polenta and in Rumania as mamaliga, is a simple combination of corn meal cooked in salted water or in milk and served hot with milk or cream and with sugar as a breakfast cereal or with butter and grated cheese in place of a starchy vegetable. Sometimes the mush is poured into a loaf pan and allowed to cool. It is then sliced, sautéed in butter and served hot with tomato sauce and grated cheese, with gravy, with syrup or with any other preferred sauce.

Farina (cream of wheat) is finely ground white corn used primarily as a breakfast food and in milky desserts.

Hominy: There are various types of hominy on the market, differing mainly in the fineness of grind. Coarse-ground hominy is called grits. It is cooked like corn meal and served in place of rice or potatoes.

Whole hominy (hulled corn) is made by soaking kernels of corn in water with lye until the hulls are loosened. The hulls are then removed, and the kernels are washed and boiled until tender. Cooked whole hominy is available in cans.

Barley, a cereal often added to soups, is also delicious when cooked like rice and served as a substitute for a starchy vegetable.

Bulgur consists of cooked and dried particles of wheat. It is generally soaked in cold water. It may then be eaten raw as a salad, mixed with a little olive oil, chopped onion and chopped parsley, or it may be mixed with ground meat and baked.

Semolina is known throughout the Near East as cous-cous. Like bulgur, it is the hard central part of wheat grains remaining after the finer portions are removed in the bolting process. When finely ground, it is used in the manufacture of some types of pasta. The coarser particles are generally steamed over a bubbling stew and served with the stew in place of rice or potatoes. See Index for cous-cous.

Kasha (buckwheat groats), a grain native to India, is also known as Saracen wheat. It may be cooked like rice and served as a starchy vegetable substitute.

Corn Meal

CORN MEAL MUSH

Serves 8

7 cups water
2 cups corn meal
2 teaspoons salt
Brown sugar, milk and sugar
or syrup

1. In mixing bowl blend 2 cups of the water and corn meal.
2. Pour remaining water into saucepan; add salt; bring to boil.
3. Stir in corn meal; cook over medium heat, stirring constantly, until thickened and smooth. Reduce heat; cook, stirring occasionally, for about 1 hour.
4. Serve with sugar, milk and butter. Or pour into loaf pan; cool; cut into slices; then fry in hot greased skillet until browned; serve with syrup.

Margaret Knoll Gardner, Woman's Club,
Emmaus, Pa.

POLENTA

Serves 6

4 cups water
1 tablespoon salt
2 cups yellow corn meal

1. In heavy 3-quart saucepan bring water and salt to full rolling boil. Slowly stir in corn meal, using wooden spoon. Reduce heat; cook, stirring constantly, until thin crust forms around edge of pan and mixture is firm.
2. Cover; cook, without stirring, for 15 to 20 minutes longer.

Mrs. Albert E. Ward, Vice-President,
Woman's Club, Etheridge, N.C.

MUSHROOM POLENTA

Serves 6

1 cup corn meal
1 quart water
1 teaspoon salt
4 egg yolks
¼ cup heavy cream
1 cup grated American cheese
Mushroom Sauce (p. 447)

1. In top of double saucepan blend corn meal and 1 cup of the water. Gradually stir in remaining water and salt. Bring to boil over hot water, stirring constantly. Cook over hot water for 30 minutes longer, stirring occasionally.
2. Meanwhile, preheat oven to 350° F. Grease 2-quart casserole.
3. Remove corn meal mixture from heat; stir in egg yolks, cream and cheese.

4. Pour into casserole; bake in preheated oven for 25 minutes.
5. Serve with Mushroom Sauce.

Mrs. Harry C. Parker, Simi Valley Woman's Club,
Simi, Calif.

SPOON BREAD

Serves 6 to 8

2 cups milk
½ cup corn meal
1 teaspoon salt
½ teaspoon baking powder
½ teaspoon sugar
2 tablespoons melted butter or
margarine
3 eggs, separated

1. Preheat oven to 375° F. Grease 1½-quart casserole.
2. Scald milk in saucepan. Stir in corn meal; cook, stirring constantly, until thickened.
3. Remove from heat; stir in salt, baking powder, sugar and butter or margarine.
4. Beat egg yolks; stir into corn meal mixture.
5. Beat egg whites until stiff but not dry; fold into corn meal mixture.
6. Turn into casserole; bake in preheated oven for 25 to 30 minutes.

Mrs. T. J. Arant, Woman's Colonial Club,
South Charleston, W. Va.

CHEESE SPOON BREAD

Serves 6 to 8

2 cups milk
2 tablespoons butter or margarine
1⅓ cups yellow corn meal
2 eggs, separated
1½ cups grated Cheddar cheese
½ teaspoon salt

1. Preheat oven to 375° F. Grease 1½-quart casserole.
2. Bring milk in saucepan to just below boiling point. Add butter or margarine; gradually stir in corn meal. Cook over medium heat, stirring constantly, for 2 minutes, or until thickened.
3. Remove from heat; beat in egg yolks, cheese and salt.
4. Beat egg whites until stiff but not dry; fold into corn meal mixture.
5. Turn into casserole; bake in preheated oven for 35 minutes.

Mrs. C. J. Aders, Woman's Club, Pikeville, Ky.

OLD VIRGINIA BUTTERMILK SPOON BREAD

Serves 8

2 cups milk
2 cups buttermilk
1 cup yellow corn meal
1 teaspoon baking soda
1 teaspoon salt
3 tablespoons melted butter or
margarine
2 eggs, separated

1. In saucepan combine milk and buttermilk. Bring to just below boiling point; gradually stir in corn meal. Cook

over medium heat, stirring constantly, for 15 minutes. Cool slightly.

2. Preheat oven to 350° F. Grease 2-quart casserole.

3. Add baking soda, salt, butter or margarine and egg yolks to corn meal; beat well.

4. Beat egg whites until stiff but not dry; fold into corn meal mixture.

5. Turn into casserole; bake in preheated oven for 30 minutes.

Mrs. J. Harden Howell, Woman's Club, Waynesville, N.C.

MEXICAN SPOON BREAD WITH CHEESE TOPPING

Serves 6

1-pound can cream-style corn
⅓ cup shortening
1 cup corn meal
¾ cup milk
2 eggs, lightly beaten
½ teaspoon baking soda
4-ounce can green chili peppers, drained
1½ cups grated Cheddar cheese

1. Preheat oven to 400° F. Grease 8-inch square baking pan.

2. In mixing bowl combine corn and shortening. Stir in corn meal, milk, eggs and baking soda.

3. Turn half the batter into pan. Arrange strips of chilis on top; cover with half the cheese. Add remaining batter; sprinkle with remaining cheese.

4. Bake in preheated oven for 20 to 25 minutes.

Mrs. Frank Ryan, Junior Woman's Club, Benson, Ariz.

CORN MEAL SOUFFLÉ

Serves 6

2 cups milk
⅓ cup white corn meal
1 cup finely diced American cheese
Dash of pepper
1 tablespoon butter
1 teaspoon salt
¼ teaspoon paprika
4 eggs, separated

1. Preheat oven to 350° F. Grease 8-inch pie plate.

2. Bring milk to boil in saucepan. Stir in corn meal, cheese, pepper, butter, salt and paprika. Cook over medium heat, stirring constantly, for 5 minutes.

3. Remove from heat; stir in egg yolks; cool slightly.

4. In mixing bowl beat egg whites until stiff but not dry; fold into corn meal mixture.

5. Turn into pie plate; bake in preheated oven for 25 minutes.

Mrs. George Ross, Woman's Club, Covington, Ky.

MAMALIGUTA CU BRANZA
(Mush with Meat)

Serves 4

This is an old Rumanian dish—quick, nutritious, and good for using up leftover meat.

1 tablespoon salt
3 cups boiling water
1 cup yellow corn meal
1 tablespoon butter or margarine
2 cups diced cooked ham, beef, lamb or chicken
2 cups grated Cheddar cheese
Sour cream or Quick Tomato Sauce (p. 451)

1. Preheat oven to 350° F. Grease 2-quart casserole.

2. Add salt to boiling water in saucepan. Gradually stir in corn meal; cook over medium heat, stirring constantly, until thickened and smooth. Remove from heat; stir in butter or margarine.

3. In casserole arrange alternate layers of corn meal, meat and cheese, finishing with cheese.

4. Bake in preheated oven for 30 minutes.

5. Serve with sour cream or Quick Tomato Sauce, as desired.

Mrs. Alvaro Ferlini, Suburban Woman's Club, West Hartford, Conn.

AMERICAN SCRAPPLE

Serves 8

4 cups hot water
1 tablespoon salt
1 tablespoon garlic powder
1 tablespoon sage
2 cups yellow corn meal
1 pound sausage meat

1. Grease 9½-inch loaf pan.

2. In top of double saucepan combine water, salt, garlic powder and sage. Cook over hot water for 10 minutes.

3. Gradually stir in corn meal; cook, stirring constantly, until smooth.

4. Add sausage, breaking it up with back of wooden spoon to distribute it evenly through corn meal. Cover; steam over hot water for 3 hours, adding water to bottom of double saucepan, as necessary.

5. Pour into pan; chill. Remove scrapple from pan; wrap in aluminum foil; chill until ready to use.

6. Cut into slices; fry as desired.

Mrs. Ralph H. Fish, Sr., Woman's Club, Flagstaff, Ariz.

Farina (Cream of Wheat)

FRETTURA DOLCE
(Lemon Almond Fritters)

Serves 6

Delicious as an accompaniment to meat, chicken or veal, this dish may also be served as an appetizer.

2 cups milk
½ cup farina (cream of wheat)
½ cup sugar
Rind of 1 lemon, grated
1 teaspoon almond extract
2 eggs, lightly beaten
1 cup bread crumbs
Fat for deep frying

1. Scald milk in saucepan; gradually stir in farina and sugar. Add lemon rind; cook over low heat, stirring constantly, until thickened and smooth.

2. Remove from heat; stir in almond extract. Pour onto dinner plate; cool.

3. Cut into squares or oblong pieces; dip in eggs; coat with crumbs.

4. Fry in deep fat heated to 365° F. until golden on all sides. Drain on absorbent paper.

Mrs. S. James Bessole, President, Michigan State Federation of Women's Clubs, Negaunee, Mich.

Hominy

BAKED HOMINY

Serves 6

¼ teaspoon salt
1 quart boiling water
1 cup hominy
1 egg
1 cup milk
1 tablespoon sugar

1. Add salt to water in saucepan. Stir in hominy; boil over medium heat, stirring occasionally, for 1 hour. Cool.

2. Preheat oven to 400° F. Grease 1½-quart casserole.

3. Stir egg, milk and sugar into hominy. Turn into casserole.

4. Bake in preheated oven for 30 minutes.

Mrs. J. L. Warner, Clio Club, Roselle, N.J.

HOMINY CASSEROLE

Serves 4

1 cup chili sauce
1 clove garlic, crushed
½ teaspoon orégano
1-pound can hominy, drained
1 cup grated onions
1 cup grated Cheddar cheese

1. Preheat oven to 300° F. Grease 1-quart casserole.

2. In bowl blend chili sauce, garlic and orégano.

3. Arrange layers of chili sauce, hominy, onions and cheese in casserole.

4. Bake in preheated oven for 30 minutes.

Mrs. L. A. Burns, Woman's Aladdin Club, Canutillo, Tex.

HOMINY BEEF CASSEROLE

Serves 2

2 teaspoons cooking oil
½ pound ground beef
1 small onion, chopped
¼ green pepper, chopped
½ 6-ounce can tomato paste
1-pound 13-ounce can hominy, undrained

1. Preheat oven to 350° F. Grease 1½-quart casserole.

2. Heat oil in skillet; sauté beef, onion and green pepper over low heat until browned.

3. Add tomato paste and hominy. Bring to boil, stirring.

4. Pour into casserole; bake in preheated oven for 30 minutes.

Selma S. Brown, Woman's Club, Azusa, Calif.

HOMINY CHEESE BAKE

Serves 4 to 6

2 eggs
1 cup milk
1 cup soft bread crumbs
1 teaspoon salt
3 cups drained canned hominy
1 cup shredded American cheese
1 tablespoon chopped parsley

1. Heat oven to 325° F. Grease 2-quart casserole.

2. In mixing bowl beat eggs lightly. Stir in remaining ingredients.

3. Turn into casserole; bake in preheated oven for 55 to 65 minutes, or until firm when tested with tip of knife.

Mrs. Victor Jost, Senior Study Club, Potwin, Kans.

NEW ENGLAND BACON AND HOMINY

Serves 8

2 tablespoons butter or margarine
1 small onion, chopped
1 medium green pepper, chopped
1-pound can tomatoes, drained
1 teaspoon salt
Dash of pepper
2 teaspoons sugar
3 cups cooked hominy
½ pound sliced bacon

1. Preheat oven to 325° F. Grease 11 x 7 x 1½-inch baking pan.

2. Melt butter or margarine in skillet; sauté onion and green pepper for 10 minutes. Stir in tomatoes, salt, pepper and sugar; simmer for 10 minutes.

3. Arrange hominy in pan; cover with tomato mixture. Arrange bacon on top.

4. Bake in preheated oven for 30 minutes, or until bacon is crisp and browned.

Nancy Replogle, Woman's Club, New Johnsonville, Tenn.

HOMINY DISH

Serves 6

¾ pound sliced bacon, diced
1 medium onion, finely chopped
1-pound can hominy, drained
1-pound 4-ounce can tomatoes, drained
3 tablespoons sugar
½ teaspoon celery seed
Salt to taste

1. Sauté bacon in skillet over medium heat until crisp. Drain off all but 3 tablespoons fat.

2. Stir in onion, hominy, tomatoes, sugar and celery seed. Season with salt. Cover; simmer for 15 minutes, or until liquid has been absorbed.

Mrs. Frank Jutten, Woman's Club, St. Joseph, Mo.

HOMINY PIE

Serves 6

3 tablespoons shortening
1½ pounds ground beef
1 tablespoon flour
1-pound 4-ounce can tomatoes, drained
1 teaspoon chili powder
1½ teaspoons salt
¼ teaspoon pepper
1-pound 4-ounce can hominy, drained
1 medium onion, chopped
1 cup grated Cheddar cheese

1. Preheat oven to 350° F. Grease 2-quart casserole.
2. Melt 1 tablespoon of the shortening in large skillet; brown beef over medium heat, stirring frequently.
3. Stir in flour, tomatoes, chili powder, salt and pepper; simmer for 5 minutes. Turn into mixing bowl; wipe skillet.
4. Melt remaining shortening in skillet; sauté hominy and onion over medium heat, stirring frequently, until browned.
5. Remove from heat; stir into meat mixture. Turn into casserole; sprinkle with cheese.
6. Bake in preheated oven for 30 minutes.

Mrs. Frank Williams, Woman's Club,
Bakersfield, Calif.

GRITS DE LUXE

Serves 8 to 10

1½ quarts boiling water
1½ cups grits
2 teaspoons salt
2 teaspoons seasoned salt
Dash of Tabasco
½ cup butter or margarine
1 pound grated American cheese
3 eggs, lightly beaten

1. Preheat oven to 300° F. Grease 13 x 9½ x 2-inch baking pan.
2. In large saucepan combine water and grits. Cook over medium heat, stirring frequently, for 20 minutes.
3. Remove from heat; stir in all remaining ingredients except eggs; stir until blended. Stir in eggs; mix well.
4. Pour into pan; bake in preheated oven for 1 hour.

Mrs. R. L. Richard, Contact Study Club,
De Quincy, La.

GARLIC CHEESE GRITS

Serves 10 to 12

1 cup instant grits
1 quart boiling water
1 teaspoon salt
½ cup butter or margarine
3 cloves garlic, crushed
3 cups grated sharp Cheddar cheese
2 eggs, lightly beaten
⅔ cup milk

1. Preheat oven to 325° F. Grease 3-quart casserole.
2. In large saucepan combine grits, water and salt. Cook over medium heat, stirring frequently, until thickened and smooth.
3. Meanwhile, melt butter or margarine in small skillet; sauté garlic for 3 minutes. Add garlic, fat in skillet, 2 cups of the cheese, eggs and milk to grits; blend well.
4. Turn into casserole; cover; bake in preheated oven for 40 minutes.
5. Remove cover; sprinkle with remaining cheese. Bake, uncovered, for 20 minutes longer.
6. Let stand for 15 minutes before serving.

Mrs. William Campbell, President, Fine Arts Club,
Harlingen, Tex.

Barley

BARLEY CASSEROLE

Serves 12

½ cup butter
1¾ cups pearl barley
2 medium onions, chopped
8-ounce can sliced mushrooms
4 cups chicken broth
½ cup slivered toasted almonds

1. Preheat oven to 325° F. Grease 3-quart casserole.
2. Melt butter in skillet; sauté barley, stirring frequently, until golden.
3. Turn into casserole; add onions, mushrooms and 3 cups of the broth; stir to mix.
4. Bake in preheated oven for 1 hour.
5. Stir in remaining broth and almonds. Cover; bake for 1½ hours longer.

Connie Holland, Culture Club, Essex, Ia.

BARLEY PILAF

Serves 6

4 tablespoons butter
½ pound mushrooms, thinly sliced
2 medium onions, chopped
1¾ cups pearl barley
5 to 6 cups chicken broth

1. Melt 2 tablespoons of the butter in heavy skillet or Dutch oven; sauté mushrooms over low heat for about 5 minutes; remove mushrooms; set aside.
2. Add remaining butter to pan; sauté onions for 10 minutes, or until transparent. Add barley; brown very slowly, stirring frequently.
3. Preheat oven to 350° F.
4. Add mushrooms and 4 cups of the broth to barley mixture. Cover tightly; bake in preheated oven for 30 minutes.
5. Add 1¾ cups of the broth; bake for 30 minutes longer.
6. If barley looks dry, add a little broth; cook until tender but not mushy.

Mrs. Herb Hilscher, Woman's Club,
Anchorage, Alaska

Bulgur (Cracked Wheat)

Bulgur has been known to peoples of other lands—particularly those of the Near East and North Africa—for centuries and is highly prized by them as the staff of life. It is America's turn to discover this form of wheat.

Bulgur is either soft or hard wheat that is soaked in water and then cooked in steam or water under pressure or at normal air pressure. After this water treatment it is dried, and the bran is partially removed. The kernels either are left whole or are cracked to suitable size (fine, medium or coarse). Bulgur is not a flour. The processed wheat particles are very hard and therefore keep well in a loosely covered container stored in a cool place. Bulgur appears on food market shelves under various trade names. In some states canned bulgur may be bought at local markets.

In addition to the recipes that follow, see bulgur in the Index for other recipes using cracked wheat.

Mrs. Lawrence Kaseberg, Women's Study Club, Wasco, Ore.

BULGUR PILAF

Serves 6

½ cup butter
1 medium onion, chopped
2 cups bulgur (cracked wheat)
1 quart hot chicken broth
1 teaspoon salt
¼ teaspoon pepper

1. Preheat oven to 350° F.
2. Melt butter in Dutch oven or heavy saucepan until soft and yellow but not browned.
3. Stir in bulgur; cover; cook over low heat for 10 minutes.
4. Add broth, salt and pepper; cover, bake in preheated oven for 30 minutes. Stir gently with fork; bake for 15 minutes longer, or until liquid is absorbed and bulgur is moist and fluffy.

A. S.

TAB ULEE (Salad with Wheat)

Serves 6 to 8

1 cup bulgur (cracked wheat)
1 cucumber, diced
2 medium tomatoes, diced
⅓ cup chopped scallions
¼ cup chopped parsley
1 medium green pepper, diced
10 large radishes, sliced
½ cup lemon juice
¼ cup olive oil
1 tablespoon salt
½ teaspoon pepper
1 tablespoon crushed mint leaves

1. Wash bulgur three times. Soak in water to cover for 1 hour.
2. Meanwhile, put cucumber, tomatoes, scallions, parsley, green pepper and radishes in salad bowl. Toss lightly. Chill until serving time.
3. Just before serving, drain bulgur; squeeze out all moisture. Sprinkle over vegetables.

4. In small bowl blend lemon juice, oil, salt and pepper. Pour over salad; toss lightly. Garnish with mint.

Mrs. Sol Bayouth, Home Representative Club, Collinsville, Okla.

Kasha (Buckwheat Groats)

BAKED KASHA

Serves 6

2 tablespoons butter
1½ cups coarse kasha (buckwheat groats)
1 teaspoon salt

1. Preheat oven to 400° F.
2. Melt butter in heavy skillet; cook kasha over moderate heat for 10 minutes, stirring constantly.
3. Transfer kasha to casserole; add salt and boiling water to cover kasha by 1 inch. Cover; bake in preheated oven for 30 minutes.
4. Remove cover; add a little boiling water if kasha seems dry. Turn temperature to 300° F. Bake for 30 minutes longer.

A. S.

Dried Beans, Peas and Lentils

Dried beans and peas are frequently served in place of a fresh starchy vegetable at tables throughout the world. Valued by cooks for their versatility in a great variety of dishes, they are highly nutritious and are an excellent source of protein.

The familiar white bean, used for baked beans, varies somewhat in size and shape but is generally known as *navy* or *pea* bean. The large flat greenish or yellow beans are shelled and *dried Lima beans.* Tiny dried Lima beans are called *flageolets;* imported from France, they are usually available only in specialty food shops. *Kidney beans* are large red kidney-shaped beans used for baking and stewing; they are also excellent served cold with French Dressing (p. 541) for salad. *Pinto beans,* the frijoles of Mexico, are small pink beans with a brownish-black dot. *Cowpeas,* or *black-eyed peas,* are small white beans with a black spot on the side, used extensively in Southern states in a variety of Creole dishes and in the Southern specialty known as Hopping John.

Dried peas, usually split, come in yellow and green varieties. Most are the quick-cooking type and should be cooked according to package directions. If they are not specified as quick-cooking, they should be soaked overnight in water to cover.

Lentils are now grown in America; but originally the dark red variety was imported from Egypt, and the larger green lentil came from central Europe. The American lentils usually are quick-cooking and do not need overnight soaking. To cook, follow the instructions on package.

TO COOK WHOLE BEANS AND PEAS

Pick over the beans and peas, discarding any foreign particles or shriveled ones. Wash in several changes of water. The usual preparation requires beans and peas to soak overnight in water to cover generously, but the U.S. Department of Agriculture recently suggested a quicker method: Put beans, or peas in kettle with water to cover; bring to boil; boil rapidly for 2 minutes. Remove from heat; cover; let soak for 1 hour. Then proceed to cook as directed in recipe.

OLD-FASHIONED BAKED BEANS
Serves 6

1 pound dried navy or pea beans
2 quarts water
¼ cup molasses
2 tablespoons brown sugar
1 tablespoon salt
½ teaspoon dry mustard
¼ pound salt pork, scored

1. Day before, wash beans, place in water to cover in large saucepan. Cover; soak overnight.
2. Next day, bring to boil; cover; simmer for 30 minutes. Drain; reserve 2 cups liquid.
3. Preheat oven to 275° F. Grease 2-quart casserole.
4. Arrange beans in casserole; stir in reserved liquid, molasses, sugar, salt and mustard. Press pork into center of beans.
5. Cover; bake in preheated oven for 4 hours, adding water, if necessary. Remove cover; bake for 15 minutes longer.

Victoria Orpik, Woman's Club, East Hartford, Conn.

VERMONT BAKED BEANS
Serves 8

2 pounds dried yellow-eye beans
4 teaspoons salt
1 teaspoon baking soda
1 pound lean salt pork or slab
  bacon with rind
1¼ to 1½ cups maple syrup (if pure
  maple syrup, use only 1 cup)
½ teaspoon dry mustard

1. Day before, wash beans; soak overnight in water to cover.
2. Next day, drain beans; cover with fresh water; add salt. Bring to boil; simmer for about 20 minutes. About 3 minutes before removing from heat, stir in baking soda. Drain beans.
3. Preheat oven to 325° F.
4. Score pork or bacon; place half in bean pot or heavy earthenware baking dish. Cover with beans.
5. Mix syrup and mustard with a little boiling water. Pour over beans; top with remaining pork or bacon. Add boiling water to cover.
6. Cover; bake in preheated oven for 6

hours. Remove cover; bake for 30 minutes longer.

Junior Century Club, Manchester, Conn.

BAKED PORK AND BEANS
Serves 4 to 6

1-pound 4-ounce can pork and beans
4 slices bacon, diced
½ cup chopped onions
¼ cup chopped green pepper
1 tablespoon molasses
3 tablespoons brown sugar
½ teaspoon salt
¼ teaspoon pepper
2 teaspoons Worcestershire

1. Preheat oven to 400° F. Grease 1-quart casserole.
2. In mixing bowl combine all ingredients; mix well.
3. Turn into casserole; bake in preheated oven for 1 hour.

Mrs. Art Zaiser, Fortnightly Club, Dawson, N.D.

BOURBON STREET BAKED BEANS
Serves 8

4 1-pound cans Boston baked beans
¾ teaspoon dry mustard
½ cup chili sauce
1 tablespoon molasses
⅓ cup bourbon
⅓ cup strong black coffee
12 pineapple slices (optional)
Brown sugar

1. In baking dish combine all ingredients except pineapple and sugar. Let stand for 3 hours.
2. Preheat oven to 375° F.
3. Arrange pineapple on beans, if desired; sprinkle with sugar.
4. Bake, uncovered, in preheated oven for 40 minutes.

Mrs. Robert E. Baumgarten, Thursday Morning Club, Madison, N.J.

GOLDEN-TOPPED BAKED BEANS
Serves 4

2 1-pound cans baked beans
1 teaspoon minced onion
1 teaspoon prepared mustard
1 teaspoon horseradish
8 ¼-inch-thick slices Canadian
  bacon
4 ¼-inch-thick slices orange,
  halved
¼ cup brown sugar
1 tablespoon butter
Cloves

1. Preheat oven to 400° F.
2. In deep 9-inch pie plate or shallow casserole combine beans, onion, mustard and horseradish. Arrange bacon and orange slices on beans. Sprinkle with sugar; dot with butter; stud with cloves.
3. Bake in preheated oven for 25 minutes.

Darlene Lutz, Junior Women's Club, Papillion, Neb.

SPICY BAKED BEANS

Serves 6

1 tablespoon shortening
2 small onions, thinly sliced
1 cup diced cooked ham
2 1-pound cans baked beans
¼ cup brown sugar
2 tablespoons sweet pickle relish
1 teaspoon dry mustard
  Dash of cinnamon
  Dash of pepper

1. Preheat oven to 350° F. Grease 1½-quart casserole.
2. Melt shortening in large skillet; sauté onions and ham over medium heat for 5 minutes.
3. Remove from heat; stir in remaining ingredients; mix well. Turn into casserole.
4. Bake in preheated oven for 25 minutes, or until bubbling.

Donna J. Fields, Junior Woman's Club,
Vista, Calif.

BEAN RAREBIT

Serves 2

8-ounce can baked beans
2 tablespoons butter
½ teaspoon salt
¼ teaspoon paprika
½ cup milk
1 cup grated Cheddar cheese
½ teaspoon Worcestershire
2 slices rye toast

1. Force beans through sieve or blend in electric blender until puréed.
2. Melt butter in saucepan; stir in salt, paprika and puréed beans. Heat over low heat, stirring frequently.
3. Gradually stir in milk, cheese and Worcestershire; cook, stirring, until cheese is melted and smooth.
4. Serve on toast.

Rosann Crandal, En Avant Society, Potosi, Mo.

RIPE OLIVE BEAN BAKE

Serves 10 to 12

2 cups pitted ripe olives
2 1-pound cans kidney beans
2 1-pound cans pork and beans
2 1-pound cans Lima beans, drained
¼ cup catsup
1 tablespoon vinegar
2 tablespoons dehydrated onion flakes
1 teaspoon dry mustard
½ teaspoon salt
⅛ teaspoon pepper
2 cups grated Cheddar cheese
1 medium green pepper, cut into rings

1. Preheat oven to 350° F. Grease 3-quart casserole.
2. Reserve 6 olives for garnish. Chop remaining olives; put in mixing bowl.
3. Drain kidney beans; reserve ½ cup liquid. Add kidney beans, reserved liquid and all remaining ingredients except cheese and green pepper to olives. Mix well; turn into casserole.
4. Cover; bake in preheated oven for 45 minutes.
5. Remove cover; sprinkle with cheese. Garnish with reserved olives and green pepper.
6. Bake, uncovered, for 15 minutes longer, or until cheese is melted.

Mrs. W. T. Hoskins, Junior Study Club,
San Augustine, Tex.

BURGUNDY BEANS

Serves 6

2 cups or 1 pound dried kidney beans
1 large onion, mined
1 cup chopped bacon
1 cup burgundy
8-ounce can tomato sauce
1 teaspoon salt
1 teaspoon pepper
1 bay leaf, crumbled
2 teaspoons chopped parsley
  Pinch of thyme
1 large clove garlic, minced

1. Day before, wash beans. Put in Dutch oven or heavy kettle with tight-fitting lid; cover generously with water. Soak overnight.
2. Next day, preheat oven to 325° F.
3. Drain beans; add remaining ingredients. Add water to cover ingredients by 2 inches.
4. Cover; bake in preheated oven for 6 to 7 hours, adding water, if necessary, to keep beans moist.

Adelaide Foster, Woman's Club,
Temple City, Calif.

FANCY KIDNEY BEANS

Serves 6

8 slices bacon, diced
1 medium onion, chopped
1 cup brown sugar
⅓ cup catsup
3 tablespoons sweet pickle relish
2 1-pound cans kidney beans

1. Preheat oven to 350° F. Grease 1½-quart casserole.
2. Sauté bacon and onion in skillet until onion is tender. Remove from heat; stir in sugar, catsup and pickle relish.
3. Drain beans; reserve 1 cup liquid. Add beans and reserved liquid to bacon mixture; mix well. Turn into casserole.
4. Bake in preheated oven for 1 hour.

Mrs. J. Steven Rutledge, Golfview Hills
Woman's Club, Hinsdale, Ill.

SAVORY LIMA BEAN SCALLOP

Serves 4

1 pound dried Lima beans
1 small onion, diced
½ teaspoon salt

1 cup chopped celery
2 tablespoons green pepper
10½-ounce can condensed tomato soup
8-ounce can tomato sauce
2 tablespoons melted butter
  Sliced bacon

1. Soak beans in water to cover generously for 6 to 8 hours.
2. Add onion; bring to boil; then simmer for 1 to 1½ hours, or until tender. Drain.
3. Preheat oven to 375° F.
4. Add salt, celery, green pepper, soup, tomato sauce and butter to beans. Pour into casserole.
5. Top with bacon; bake in preheated oven for about 40 minutes.

Mrs. Fred G. Weimer, Thursday Morning Club,
Madison, N.J.

LIMA BEANS IN SOUR CREAM

Serves 6

1 cup dried Lima beans
2 tablespoons butter
6 slices Canadian bacon
1 medium onion, sliced
3 tablespoons brown sugar
1 teaspoon dry mustard
  Dash of pepper
2 tablespoons chopped parsley
1 cup sour cream

1. Day before, put beans in saucepan; cover with water; soak overnight.
2. Next day, bring to boil; then simmer for 1 hour, adding water, if necessary. Drain; set aside.
3. Preheat oven to 375° F. Grease 10 x 6 x 1½-inch baking pan.
4. Melt butter in skillet; sauté bacon for 3 to 4 minutes on each side.
5. Arrange bacon in pan. Top with beans.
6. Sauté onion in fat remaining in skillet over medium heat for 5 minutes. Stir in sugar, mustard, pepper and parsley; simmer for 2 minutes. Remove from heat; stir in sour cream. Pour sauce over beans.
7. Bake in preheated oven for 30 minutes.

Mrs. Carlton Jones, Contact Study Club,
De Quincy, La.

ARIZONA RANCH-STYLE FRIJOLES

Serves 10

These frijoles are easily converted into a delicious chili con carne by the addition of 2 pounds chopped beef and 1 large onion, chopped, which are browned in any kind of fat. Add to beans after the first hour of cooking.

2 pounds dried pinto beans
2 teaspoons salt
½ teaspoon black pepper
2 large onions, diced

4 cloves garlic, chopped
4-ounce can roasted green chili
  peppers, chopped
8-ounce can tacos sauce
1-pound 12-ounce can tomatoes
½ teaspoon cumin seeds

1. Day before, wash beans; soak overnight in water to cover generously.
2. Next day, drain beans; cover with fresh water by 2 inches. Add salt; bring to boil; simmer over moderate heat for about 1 hour, adding water, if needed.
3. Add remaining ingredients; cook over low heat for 1 to 1½ hours, or until beans are tender and sauce is reduced.

Mrs. Barry Goldwater, Junior Woman's Club,
Scottsdale, Ariz.

HOPPING JOHN

Serves 8

⅓ pound bacon, diced
2 quarts water
2 cups or 1 pound dried cowpeas
  (black-eyed peas) soaked
  overnight
1¼ cups rice
1-pound can tomatoes
½ green pepper, chopped
6 scallions, chopped

1. Sauté bacon in heavy saucepan until crisp and golden. Add water; bring to boil. Add peas; cook until almost tender.
2. Add rice; cook for about 20 minutes longer, or until tender. Drain; put in warm oven for a few minutes to dry.
3. Meanwhile, in another saucepan combine remaining ingredients; bring to boil; then simmer for 10 minutes, or until vegetables are tender.
4. Turn peas and rice into hot serving dish; serve with tomato mixture.

Mrs. Albert S. Johnston, Thursday Morning
Club, Madison, N.J.

BLACK-EYED PEAS AND TOMATOES

Serves 8

2 tablespoons olive oil
1 medium onion, finely chopped
2 1-pound cans black-eyed peas,
  drained
2 1-pound cans tomatoes, drained
10½-ounce can condensed cream of
  chicken soup
½ teaspoon salt
  Dash of pepper
1 teaspoon sugar
1 teaspoon Worcestershire

1. Heat oil in saucepan; sauté onion until tender.
2. Stir in remaining ingredients; bring to boil. Cover; simmer over low heat for 15 minutes.

Joan Gregory, Thomas Jefferson Junior Woman's
Club, Richmond, Va.

LENTILS

Serves 8 to 12

Serve as a side dish with Mexican food or as a main dish.

1 pound dried lentils
4 slices bacon, diced
1 medium onion, chopped
½ cup chopped celery
4-ounce can green chili peppers, drained and diced
2 8-ounce cans tomato sauce

1. Put lentils in large saucepan; add water to cover. Cover; cook over low heat for 2 to 3 hours, or until tender. Drain.

2. Meanwhile, sauté bacon, onion and celery in large skillet. Stir in chilis and tomato sauce; mix well.

3. Combine lentils and chili mixture; heat to serving temperature.

Junior Woman's Club, Pacific Beach, Calif.

15. Rice and Rice Dishes

Since American homemakers embraced the foods of other countries, rice has become increasingly important in everyday meals and menus. For example, ten years ago it would have been difficult to find even one recipe for pilaf in a general cook book, but today almost every cook book contains one or more recipes for this simple and delicious rice dish from the Near East.

In addition to the dishes in this chapter, there are throughout this book many recipes, including desserts, which contain rice. For these, consult the Index.

Several types of rice are grown in America. Among the varieties of *white rice* are the long-grained rice, the round-grained or Japanese rice and the short-grained rice. All require moisture and from 15 to 25 minutes of cooking.

Brown rice contains practically all the bran removed in the usual hulling and milling operations; it therefore contains more nutritive elements than white rice.

Converted rice is in between white and brown, for less of the bran is removed than in white rice, and the milled grains are slightly yellow. Brown rice and converted rice are cooked in the same way as white rice.

In recent years *instant rice* has become popular. This is white rice that has been completely cooked, then dehydrated. It needs little cooking, and for the best results one should follow the directions on the package.

The old-fashioned American method of cooking rice in a large quantity of rapidly boiling water has been completely outmoded in favor of the classic method of letting it steep in a measured amount of liquid (from 2 to 2½ cups liquid to 1 cup of rice). One cup of rice makes from 3½ to 4 cups cooked.

Rice may be cooked in advance and kept hot and moist for a considerable time by putting it in a sieve or colander over a saucepan of steaming water. The sieve or colander should be covered with a clean kitchen towel to keep the rice on top from drying out.

HOW TO COOK RICE

Serves 4 to 6

Don't peek when boiling rice; this lets out steam and cools the rice. Don't stir after rice comes to boil; this makes a mush of rice. Don't leave rice in the cooking pan more than 10 minutes after it is done; this causes packy rice.

1 cup rice
1 teaspoon salt
2 cups water

1. Combine all ingredients in 3-quart saucepan with tight-fitting lid.
2. Bring to boil, stirring only once as water comes to boil.
3. Lower heat to simmer; cover; cook for 15 to 20 minutes, without stirring or removing lid.

FOR DRIER RICE: After cooking, fluff rice lightly with fork; let stand in covered pan for 5 to 10 minutes to steam-dry.

Marie Treme, Aggressive Study Club, De Quincy, La.

Rice—A Variety of Dishes

BAKED RICE

Serves 4 to 6

3 tablespoons butter
1 cup rice
3 chicken bouillon cubes
3 cups boiling water
3 tablespoons dried parsley flakes

1. Preheat oven to 350° F.
2. Melt butter in skillet; cook rice until lightly browned, stirring constantly. Turn into 1-quart casserole.
3. Dissolve bouillon cubes in water; pour over rice. Sprinkle with parsley.
4. Cover tightly; bake in preheated oven for 50 minutes.

Sarah Hardin, Arts Club, Aliceville, Ala.

ALMOND RICE

Serves 4

½ cup butter or margarine
1 cup rice
2 10½-ounce cans condensed beef consommé
½ teaspoon salt
½ cup slivered almonds

1. Preheat oven to 350° F. Grease 1½-quart casserole.
2. Melt butter in skillet; cook rice over medium heat, stirring occasionally, until browned.

3. Stir in remaining ingredients; pour into casserole.

4. Cover; bake in preheated oven for 1 hour. Remove cover; bake for 30 minutes longer.

Mrs. Howard O'Neal, President, Women's Club,
LaGrange, Ga.

ALMOND CURRANT RICE

Serves 8

2⅔ cups instant rice
1 teaspoon salt
⅓ cup currants
4 tablespoons butter
½ cup slivered blanched almonds

1. Boil 2⅔ cups water in saucepan; stir in rice, salt, currants and 2 tablespoons of the butter. Cover; remove from heat; let stand for 5 minutes.

2. Meanwhile, melt remaining butter in small skillet; sauté almonds over low heat, stirring frequently, until golden.

3. Stir almonds into rice.

Ginnie Finkenaur, Junior Woman's Club,
Simsbury, Conn.

ARMENIAN RICE

Serves 6

1 cup rice
¼ cup shortening
½ teaspoon salt
Dash of Tabasco
1 quart water, milk or beef broth

1. Put rice in sieve; set in bowl of water. Rub rice between hands, lifting sieve from bowl and changing water until water is clear. Drain.

2. Preheat oven to 350° F. Grease 1½-quart baking dish.

3. Melt shortening in heavy skillet; sauté rice until golden brown, stirring constantly. Turn into baking dish. Add remaining ingredients.

4. Cover; bake in preheated oven for 30 minutes.

Joyce Abreu, Woman's Club, Oceanside, Calif.

BROWN RICE

Serves 4

½ cup butter or margarine
1 small onion, chopped
½ cup chopped celery
⅔ cup rice
1 teaspoon salt
¼ teaspoon pepper
10½-ounce can condensed beef
        consommé

1. Preheat oven to 350° F. Grease 1-quart casserole.

2. Melt butter or margarine in skillet; sauté onion, celery and rice over medium heat until rice is browned.

3. Stir in salt, pepper and consommé. Pour into casserole.

4. Cover; bake in preheated oven for 1 hour.

Mrs. E. J. Hill, President, Better Homemakers
HDC, Pinehurst, Ga.

CURRIED RICE

Serves 4

2 cups water
1 cup rice
1 teaspoon salt
1 teaspoon shortening
2 tablespoons butter
½ cup minced onions
4-ounce can sliced mushrooms,
        drained
½ cup minced celery
½ teaspoon curry powder

1. Bring water to rapid boil in heavy saucepan with tight-fitting lid. Add rice, salt and shortening. Cover; cook over very low heat for 22 minutes, without raising lid.

2. Meanwhile, melt butter in skillet; sauté onions and mushrooms until lightly browned.

3. Remove rice from heat; stir in celery, onions and mushrooms with butter from skillet and curry powder.

4. Turn into greased casserole; keep hot, or reheat in 325° F. oven.

Mrs. Steve Marshall, Woman's Club,
Roswell, N.M.

INDIAN CURRIED RICE

Serves 6 to 8

¼ cup olive oil
2 medium onions, chopped
3 tart apples, peeled, and chopped
½ cup chopped celery
½ cup chopped green pepper
1½ cups rice
3½ cups chicken broth
2 teaspoons curry powder
1 clove garlic, crushed
1 teaspoon mustard seed
8 peppercorns
½ teaspoon paprika
¼ teaspoon ginger
½ teaspoon chili powder
¼ teaspoon turmeric
3 tablespoons tomato paste
½ cup flaked coconut

1. Heat oil in large skillet or Dutch oven; add onions, apples, celery and green pepper; sauté over medium heat, stirring occasionally, until golden.

2. Stir in all remaining ingredients except coconut. Bring to boil; cover; simmer for 20 minutes, or until rice is tender and liquid is absorbed.

3. Just before serving, stir in coconut.

Mae Dister, Woman's Club. Slippery Rock, Pa.

GREEN RICE

Serves 6 to 8

This dish needs no gravy.

2 cups rice
⅔ cup finely chopped green pepper
1 cup chopped scallions
⅓ cup chopped parsley
¼ cup olive oil
1½ tablespoons Worcestershire
1 teaspoon salt
¼ teaspoon cayenne
1 quart beef or chicken broth

1. Preheat oven to 350° F. Grease 2-quart casserole.
2. In mixing bowl combine all ingredients; mix well. Turn into casserole.
3. Cover; bake in preheated oven for 45 minutes.
4. Remove cover; toss.

Mrs. S. L. Wright II, Attakapas Study Club,
Crowley, La.

MEXICAN RICE

Serves 4

2 tablespoons butter
1/3 cup chopped onions
1/4 cup green pepper
1 cup rice
2 10½-ounce cans condensed
    beef consommé
3/4 teaspoon cumin seeds
3/4 teaspoon salt
1 teaspoon Worcestershire

1. Melt butter in saucepan; sauté onions, green pepper and rice until lightly browned.
2. Add remaining ingredients; bring to boil. Cover tightly; cook over low heat for 20 minutes.

Charlene Lewis, Altruistic Club,
Carlisle, Ark.

POLKA DOT RICE

Serves 6

3 cups hot cooked rice
2 cups hot cooked peas
1/3 cup melted butter
Salt and pepper to taste

Toss all ingredients together; keep hot until ready to serve.

Mrs. Philip LeBlanc, President, Hillsborough
County Federation of Women's Clubs,
Tampa, Fla.

POLYNESIAN MINGLE

Serves 8

1½ cups instant rice
1½ cups sliced celery
1/4 cup grated onion
2 10-ounce packages frozen peas,
    defrosted
4 chicken bouillon cubes
1 tablespoon soy sauce
1 teaspoon sugar
1 teaspoon salt
2 cups water

1. Preheat oven to 375° F. Grease 2-quart casserole.
2. Combine rice, celery, onion and peas in casserole.
3. Put remaining ingredients in saucepan; bring to boil. Remove from heat; pour over ingredients in casserole; stir well.
4. Cover; bake in preheated oven for 30 minutes. Remove cover; stir; bake, uncovered, for 15 minutes longer.

Mrs. Roy Hayes, Wednesday Club,
Benton, Mo.

RAISIN RICE

Serves 6

1⅓ cups rice
2 tablespoons butter
1/4 cup finely chopped onion
1/4 cup slivered almonds
1 teaspoon salt
1/4 cup seedless raisins

1. Cook rice (p. 473).
2. Meanwhile, melt butter, in saucepan; sauté onion and almonds until almonds are golden. Stir in salt and raisins; cook over low heat for 2 minutes.
3. Stir into rice.

Fran Runyon, Junior Woman's Club,
Jacksonville, Fla.

WAIKIKI RICE

Serves 6

1⅓ cups water
9-ounce can pineapple tidbits,
    undrained
1/4 cup brown sugar
1/8 teaspoon cinnamon
1/2 teaspoon salt
2 tablespoons butter or margarine
1⅓ cups instant rice

1. In saucepan combine water, pineapple, sugar, cinnamon, salt and butter or margarine. Bring to boil; stir in rice.
2. Cover; simmer for 10 minutes.

Ella Taylor, Island Woman's Club,
Anna Maria, Fla.

RICE PILAF

Serves 8

3/4 cup butter or margarine
1 medium onion, chopped
2 teaspoons orégano
2 cups rice
2 10½-ounce cans condensed
    beef consommé
4-ounce can mushroom stems and
    pieces, undrained

1. Preheat oven to 400° F. Grease 3-quart casserole.
2. Melt butter or margarine in large skillet; sauté onion, orégano and rice over low heat for 20 minutes, stirring occasionally.
3. Combine consommé and mushrooms in casserole. Stir in rice mixture.
4. Cover; bake in preheated oven for 1½ hours, stirring occasionally.

Mrs. John W. Cherry, Woman's Club,
Avondale, Ga.

ARMENIAN RICE PILAF

Serves 6

1/2 cup butter or margarine
1/4 cup fine noodles, broken into
    small pieces
1 cup rice
2¾ cups hot water
1 teaspoon salt

1. Melt butter or margarine in saucepan; fry noodles until golden, stirring frequently.

2. Stir in rice, water and salt. Cover; cook over low heat for 15 minutes, or until all liquid is absorbed. Do not stir.

3. Remove from heat; let stand, covered, for 15 minutes.

Mrs. George Melickian, Junior Woman's Club, Cahokia, Ill.

TURKISH PILAF

Serves 4 to 6

2 tablespoons shortening
1 cup rice
1½ cups boiling water
2 cups stewed tomatoes
Salt and pepper to taste

1. Melt shortening in skillet; brown rice over medium heat, stirring occasionally.

2. Stir water. Cover; cook over very low heat for about 10 minutes, or until liquid is absorbed.

3. Stir in tomatoes; cook, uncovered, over low heat until rice is soft. Season with salt and pepper.

Mrs. Noel C. Carr, Woman's Club, DeBary, Fla.

RISOTTO

Serves 6 to 8

½ cup butter
1 small onion, grated
1½ cups rice
¼ teaspoon saffron
2 teaspoons salt
4½ cups chicken broth
Grated Parmesan cheese

1. Melt ¼ cup of the butter in large skillet; sauté onion over medium heat until golden. Stir in rice; sauté, stirring occasionally, until butter is absorbed. Add saffron and salt.

2. Gradually stir in broth. Bring to boil; cover; simmer for 30 minutes, or until broth is absorbed. Remove from heat; stir in remaining butter.

3. Serve with cheese.

Mrs. Richard Benenti, Junior Woman's Club, New Britain, Conn.

RISOTTO ALL'ERBE

Serves 4

2 tablespoons butter
2 tablespoons olive oil
1 cup rice
1 medium onion, finely chopped
1 clove garlic, crushed
½ cup dry white wine
2 cups beef bouillon
½ teaspoon pepper
1 teaspoon salt
1 teaspoon paprika
¼ teaspoon thyme
¼ teaspoon basil
¼ teaspoon marjoram
¼ teaspoon dried parsley flakes
¼ teaspoon rosemary

1. Heat butter and oil in large skillet or Dutch oven; stir in rice, onion and garlic; sauté over medium heat, stirring frequently, until rice is browned.

2. Stir in remaining ingredients; bring to boil. Cover; simmer for 20 minutes, or until rice is cooked and liquid is absorbed.

Faye Higgins, Woman's Club, Essex, Conn.

RICE RING

Serves 4

Fill with creamed mushrooms and crab meat or desired filling.

2¼ cups water
1 teaspoon salt
1 cup rice
¼ cup butter or margarine

1. Lightly grease 8-ring mold.

2. Bring water and salt in 2-quart saucepan to boil. Add rice; cover; cook over low heat for 20 minutes, or until water is absorbed.

3. Stir in butter or margarine; toss until melted. Spoon into ring mold; press down lightly. Let stand in warm place for 5 minutes.

4. Invert onto serving dish.

Mrs. Hugh Lee Nathurst, Junior Woman's Club, Fort Myers, Fla.

Fried Rice

YANKEE FRIED RICE

Serves 4

3 chicken bouillon cubes
3 cups boiling water
½ cup butter
1 medium onion, chopped
1¼ cups rice

1. Dissolve bouillon cubes in water. Set aside.

2. Melt butter in heavy skillet; sauté onion until golden but not browned. Add rice; sauté until golden but not browned.

3. Add bouillon; bring to rapid boil. Cover; cook over medium to low heat for 20 minutes.

Mrs. Fred Muller, Jr., Thursday Morning Club, Madison, N.J.

FRIED RICE

Serves 6

2 cups rice
10 slices bacon
½ cup thinly sliced water chestnuts
½ cup finely diced bamboo shoots
½ cup grated or minced onions
½ cup finely diced green pepper
1 tablespoon soy sauce
1½ teaspoons Worcestershire
Peanut oil

1. Cook rice (p. 473). Cool thoroughly in freezer for a couple of hours.

2. Cook bacon in skillet until golden and crisp. Drain on absorbent paper.

3. Crumble bacon; mix with all remaining ingredients except oil.

4. Pour enough oil into skillet to cover bottom. Heat; add rice mixture. Cook over

moderate heat, turning with spatula until very hot.

Mrs. Wally Hartman, Monday Study Club, Poplar Bluffs, Mo.

ALMOND FRIED RICE
Serves 8

¼ cup cooking oil
1 cup chopped scallions or 2 large onions, chopped
1 cup chopped green pepper
1 clove garlic, finely grated
1 teaspoon salt
½ teaspoon black pepper
4 cups cooked rice
¼ cup soy sauce
1 cup blanched almonds, shredded

1. Heat oil in large skillet; sauté scallions or onions, green pepper, garlic, salt and pepper until lightly browned.
2. Add remaining ingredients; sauté for about 10 minutes longer.

Belair Women's Club International Cook Book, Belair, Md.

FRIED RICE WITH MUSHROOMS AND ALMONDS
Serves 6 to 9

2 tablespoons cooking oil
4 large onions, sliced
4 ounces seedless raisins
4 tablespoons butter
2 pounds mushrooms, sliced
2 chicken bouillon cubes, dissolved in 2 tablespoons boiling water
4 cups cooked rice
5 ounces toasted almonds
Salt and pepper to taste

1. Heat 1 tablespoon of the oil in skillet; sauté onions until golden brown; drain on absorbent paper.
2. Heat remaining oil; sauté raisins until slightly crisp and shiny; drain; set aside.
3. Melt 2 tablespoons of the butter in skillet; sauté mushrooms for 3 to 4 minutes. Add bouillon; cover; simmer for 5 minutes.
4. Melt remaining butter in saucepan; heat rice thoroughly. Stir in onions, raisins, mushrooms and almonds. Season with salt and pepper.

Gretchen Bickerstaff, Century Club, Coraopolis, Pa.

FRIED RICE WITH SHRIMP
(*Ha Chow Foo*)
Serves 4

3 tablespoons olive oil
1 pound shrimp, shelled, deveined and cut into ½-inch pieces
⅓ cup chopped scallions
3-ounce can sliced mushrooms, drained
1 tablespoon salt
Dash of pepper
2 eggs, lightly beaten
½ cup drained bean sprouts
4 cups cooked rice
2 tablespoons soy sauce
1 tablespoon gravy coloring

1. Heat oil in large heavy skillet; add shrimp, scallions, mushrooms, salt and pepper; cook over medium heat for 10 minutes, stirring constantly.
2. Push to one side of skillet; add eggs; stir well until cooked. Mix eggs and shrimp mixture.
3. Add remaining ingredients; cook over medium heat, stirring frequently, until rice is thoroughly heated.

Mrs. George Flewelling, Junior Women's Club, Nashua, N.H.

JAVANESE FRIED RICE
Serves 4

2 tablespoons butter
1 cup rice
2 teaspoons curry powder
2 cups chicken broth
½ pound ground beef
2 tablespoons bread crumbs
1 egg, lightly beaten
1¼ cups chopped onions
Salt and pepper to taste
3 tablespoons cooking oil
1 cup diced celery
½ pound shrimp, shelled and deveined

1. Melt butter in saucepan; cook rice and curry powder until browned. Add broth; bring to boil; cover tightly; cook over low heat for 25 minutes.
2. Meanwhile, combine beef, crumbs, eggs, ¼ cup of the onions, salt and pepper. Roll into small balls; set aside.
3. Heat oil in large skillet; sauté celery and remaining onions for 5 minutes, or until onions are transparent. Add shrimp; sauté for 3 to 5 minutes, stirring constantly, until shrimp turns pink. Remove shrimp and vegetables.
4. Brown meat balls well on all sides in fat remaining in skillet. Stir in shrimp mixture and rice. Cover; heat until piping hot.

Wynetta Miller, Woman's Club, Atascadero, Calif.

PORK FRIED RICE
Serves 4 or 5

2 slices bacon
4 scallions, white and green parts chopped separately
¾ cup rice
2 10½-ounce cans condensed chicken broth
Dash of sage
1 cup diced cooked pork
1 teaspoon salt
¼ teaspoon pepper

1. Cook bacon in large skillet until crisp. Drain on absorbent paper; crumble. Mix with scallion greens; set aside.
2. Add white parts of scallions and rice to fat remaining in skillet; sauté over medium heat, stirring frequently, until rice is golden.
3. Stir in broth, sage, pork, salt and pepper. Bring to boil; cover; simmer for 20 minutes, or until liquid is absorbed, stirring occasionally.

4. Turn into serving dish; sprinkle with bacon and scallion greens.

Mrs. Ivan Bartley, Junior Woman's Club, Kennewick, Wash.

RICE CROQUETTES
Serves 4

1 cup cooked rice
3 tablespoons grated Parmesan cheese
2 tablespoons butter or margarine
¼ teaspoon salt
Dash of pepper
1 egg, lightly beaten
⅔ cup bread crumbs
Fat for deep frying

1. Put rice, cheese, butter or margarine, salt and pepper in mixing bowl. Mix well; shape into 1-inch balls.
2. Dip in egg; coat with crumbs.
3. Fry in deep fat heated to 365° F. for 3 minutes, or until golden. Drain on absorbent paper.

Edmee L. Enders, Woman's Club, Basin, Wyo.

Baked Rice Dishes

TOASTED RICE CASSEROLE
Serves 8

2 cups rice
2 cups chopped onions
2 cups chopped celery
2 cups chopped green peppers
2 teaspoons salt
1 tablespoon poultry seasoning
5 cups chicken broth
2 eggs, well beaten
½ cup minced parsley or celery tops
1 cup sliced mushrooms or broken pecans

1. Preheat oven to 350° F. Grease 3-quart casserole.
2. Spread rice in shallow baking pan; toast in preheated oven for about 25 minutes, stirring occasionally.
3. In saucepan combine onions, celery, green peppers, salt, poultry seasoning and broth. Bring to boil. Stir in rice. Cover; cook over low heat for about 25 minutes, or until liquid is absorbed and rice is tender.
4. Remove from heat. Fold in eggs, parsley or celery tops and mushrooms or pecans.
5. Turn into casserole; bake in preheated oven for 15 minutes, or until eggs are done to taste.

Mrs. C. H. Hutcheson, Jonesboro, Ga.

RICE AND PINEAPPLE
Serves 6

3 cups cooked rice
1-pound 4-ounce can pineapple chunks, drained
1½ cups sugar
½ cup melted butter or margarine

1. Preheat oven to 450° F. Grease 1½-quart casserole.
2. In mixing bowl combine all ingredients; mix well.
3. Turn into casserole; bake for 20 minutes, or until browned.

Mrs. W. D. Peavy, 20th Century Club, Atmore, Ala.

RICE AND CORN CASSEROLE
Serves 8 to 10

½ cup butter or margarine
1 medium onion, chopped
1 medium green pepper, chopped
2 tablespoons flour
1-pound can tomatoes, undrained
½ teaspoon Tabasco
2 teaspoons salt
2 cups cooked rice
2 eggs, hard-cooked and chopped
2 cups whole-kernel corn
1 tablespoon Worcestershire
1 cup grated Cheddar cheese

1. Preheat oven to 350° F. Grease 3-quart casserole.
2. Melt butter or margarine in skillet; sauté onion and green pepper until tender.
3. Stir in flour; add tomatoes. Cook, stirring, until mixture comes to boil and thickens. Remove from heat; turn into mixing bowl.
4. Add all remaining ingredients except cheese; turn into casserole; sprinkle with cheese.
5. Bake in preheated oven for 40 minutes.

Mrs. Joel Glass, 20th Century Club, Gordo, Ala.

RICE AND EGGPLANT ON PARADE
Serves 6

1 large or 3 small eggplants
¼ cup bacon drippings or shortening
1 small green pepper, chopped
1 cup chopped celery
1 medium onion, chopped
1 cup rice
4-ounce can shrimp, drained
3 beef bouillon cubes

1. Preheat oven to 375° F. Grease 2-quart casserole.
2. Peel eggplant; cube. Cook in boiling salted water for 7 minutes, or until tender. Drain.
3. Melt bacon drippings or shortening in large skillet; sauté green pepper, celery and onion for 5 minutes. Remove from heat; turn into mixing bowl.
4. Add eggplant, rice and shrimp; mix well.
5. Blend 2 cups boiling water with bouillon cubes; stir until dissolved. Pour over eggplant mixture; mix well. Turn into casserole.
6. Cover; bake in preheated oven for 1 hour and 15 minutes.

Mrs. S. L. Wright II, Attakapas Study Club, Crowley, La.

RICE AND VEGETABLE CASSEROLE

Serves 5 or 6

4-H Blue Ribbon winner originated by Peggy Sue Foreman.

4 tablespoons margarine
½ cup grated onions
½ cup chopped green pepper
½ cup chopped celery
2 cloves garlic, minced
½ cup chopped scallions
¼ cup dried parsley flakes
2 cups canned mixed vegetables
2 cups cooked rice
2 6½-ounce cans crab meat, drained and flaked
⅓ cup milk
¼ teaspoon Worcestershire
2 10½-ounce cans condensed cream of celery soup
½ cup grated sharp Cheddar cheese
Crushed crisp rice cereal crumbs or bread crumbs

1. Preheat oven to 325° F.
2. Melt margarine in skillet; sauté grated onions, green pepper, celery and garlic until wilted. Add scallions and parsley flakes; simmer for 3 minutes.
3. Add mixed vegetables and rice; mix well. Turn into 2½-quart casserole.
4. Spread crab meat evenly on top.
5. Combine milk, Worcestershire, and soup. Pour over crab meat. Sprinkle evenly with cheese; top with crumbs.
6. Bake in preheated oven for 25 minutes.

Mrs. Carrol Spell, La Clique d'Etude, Inc., Abbeville, La.

SAVORY RICE AND CHEESE

Serves 4

¾ cup rice
2 tablespoons shortening or cooking oil
½ cup diced celery
¼ cup minced green pepper
2 tablespoons minced onion
1¼ teaspoons salt
¼ teaspoon pepper
2 cups grated sharp American cheese
⅔ cup milk

1. Cook rice (p. 473).
2. Preheat oven to 425° F. Grease 1½-quart casserole.
3. Heat shortening or oil in skillet; sauté celery, green pepper and onion for 5 minutes, or until partially tender. Stir in salt and pepper.
4. In casserole arrange alternate layers of rice, vegetables and cheese, finishing with cheese. Pour in milk.
5. Bake, uncovered, in preheated oven for 35 minutes, or until golden brown.

Our Best to You Cook Book, Woman's Club, Willingboro, N.J.

SPANISH RICE

Serves 4

½ cup butter or margarine
1 cup chopped onions
⅓ cup rice
1-pound can tomatoes
1 cup water
1 teaspoon salt
⅛ teaspoon cayenne
¼ cup chopped stuffed olives
½ cup grated Cheddar cheese

1. Preheat oven to 350° F. Grease 1½-quart casserole.
2. Melt butter or margarine in large skillet; sauté onions for 5 minutes. Add rice; sauté, stirring occasionally, for 5 minutes.
3. Stir in tomatoes, water, salt, cayenne and olives; bring to boil.
4. Remove from heat; stir in cheese. Turn into casserole.
5. Cover; bake in preheated oven for 1 hour, or until tender.

Mrs. E. L. Fenton, Woman's Club, Marlinton, W.Va.

SOUR CREAM RICE

Serves 6

2 cups sour cream
2 teaspoons salt
½ teaspoon pepper
1 tablespoon sugar
3 cups cooked rice
4 cups grated Cheddar cheese

1. Preheat oven to 425° F. Grease 2-quart casserole.
2. In mixing bowl blend sour cream, salt, pepper and sugar.
3. In casserole arrange alternate layers of rice, 3½ cups of the cheese and sour cream. Sprinkle remaining cheese on top.
4. Bake in preheated oven for 30 minutes.

Mrs. Jorgen Storm, Woman's Club, Clearwater, Fla.

CALEXICO RICE

Serves 8 to 10

3 cups sour cream
Tabasco, salt and pepper to taste
¼ teaspoon monosodium glutamate
7-ounce can green chili peppers, drained and diced
4 cups cooked rice
1 pound Monterey Jack cheese, cubed
⅓ pound sharp Cheddar cheese, shredded

1. Preheat oven to 350° F. Grease large flat baking pan.
2. Combine sour cream, Tabasco, salt, pepper and monosodium glutamate. Stir in chilis.
3. Arrange 2 cups of the rice in pan; cover with half the sour cream mixture and half the Monterey Jack cheese. Repeat layers; sprinkle Cheddar cheese on top.
4. Cover pan with aluminum foil; bake in preheated oven for 45 minutes.

Bee McFarland, Woman's Club, McFarland, Calif.

PARSLEY RICE RING

Serves 6

Fill center with creamed chicken, fish or any desired filling.

2 eggs, lightly beaten
¼ cup melted butter or margarine
1 cup grated Cheddar cheese
½ cup chopped parsley
2 tablespoons grated onion
1 teaspoon Worcestershire
1 teaspoon salt
1 cup milk
3½ cups cooked rice

1. Preheat oven to 350° F. Grease 8-inch ring mold well.
2. In mixing bowl combine all ingredients except rice. Mix well. Stir in rice. Pour into mold.
3. Set mold in pan of hot water; bake in preheated oven for 45 minutes, or until knife inserted in center comes out clean.
4. Let stand for 5 minutes; unmold onto serving dish.

*Mrs. F. D. Gassmere, Chicago Lawn
Woman's Club, Chicago, Ill.*

BRAZILIAN RICE

Serves 8

¼ cup butter
4 eggs, lightly beaten
1 pound sharp Cheddar cheese, shredded
1 cup milk
10-ounce package frozen chopped spinach, cooked and drained
1 tablespoon chopped onion
2 teaspoons salt
1 tablespoon Worcestershire
1 teaspoon marjoram
1 teaspoon thyme
1 teaspoon rosemary
3 cups cooked rice

1. Preheat oven to 350° F. Grease 2-quart casserole.
2. Melt butter in saucepan. Stir in eggs, cheese, milk, spinach and onion. Cook, stirring, until cheese is melted.
3. Remove from heat; combine with remaining ingredients.
4. Turn into casserole; bake in preheated oven for 35 minutes.

*Marian Ruebel, Woman's Club,
Temple City, Calif.*

GREEN RICE WITH BROCCOLI

Serves 8

14½-ounce can evaporated milk
2 eggs, lightly beaten
¼ cup melted butter or margarine
4 cups cooked rice
1 cup grated Cheddar cheese
⅓ cup grated onions
1½ teaspoons salt
⅛ teaspoon monosodium glutamate
¼ teaspoon pepper
2 cups cooked chopped broccoli

1. Preheat oven to 325° F. Grease 2½-quart casserole.

2. In mixing bowl beat milk and eggs. Stir in remaining ingredients; mix well. Turn into casserole.
3. Set in pan of hot water; bake in preheated oven for 1 hour, or until set.

*Mrs. M. Oliver, Study Club,
Montgomery City, Mo.*

GREEN RICE WITH CHEESE

Serves 4

⅓ cup cooking oil
1 cup chopped parsley
1 clove garlic, minced
2 small onions, diced
2 eggs, lightly beaten
2 cups milk
1 teaspoon salt
1 teaspoon Worcestershire
2 cups shredded sharp cheese
2 cups cooked rice

1. Heat oil in skillet; sauté parsley, garlic and onions over low heat for 10 minutes, or until onions are tender but not browned.
2. Preheat oven to 350° F.
3. In mixing bowl combine eggs and milk. Stir in salt, Worcestershire, vegetable mixture, cheese and rice.
4. Turn into 1½-quart casserole; bake in preheated oven for 30 minutes, or until set.

*Mrs. Jordan Lindsey, Woman's Club,
Harrisonville, Mo.*

GREEN RICE MOLD

Serves 8

1 cup rice, cooked and fluffed (p. 473)
1½ cups evaporated milk
3 eggs, separated
1 cup chopped parsley
½ cup chopped green pepper
½ cup chopped celery
2 teaspoons grated onion
Salt and cayenne to taste

1. Preheat oven to 350° F. Grease 1½-quart mold.
2. Combine rice and milk.
3. Beat egg yolks; stir with parsley, green pepper, celery, onion, salt and cayenne into rice.
4. Beat egg whites until stiff but not dry; fold into rice mixture. Turn into mold. Chill, if desired.
5. Set mold in shallow pan containing about 1 inch hot water; bake in preheated oven for 30 to 40 minutes, or until set. Turn onto warm serving plate.

*Helen Lamphere, Woman's Club,
Falls Church, Va.*

Rice Dishes with Fish or Seafood

RISOTTO WITH CLAMS

Serves 4

¼ cup olive oil
1 onion, finely chopped
1 clove garlic

2 cups tomatoes
8-ounce bottle clam juice
2 tablespoons chopped parsley
Pinch of sweet basil
Pinch of saffron
8-ounce can minced clams, undrained
1 cup rice
¾ teaspoon salt
Fresh cherrystone or little neck
  clams, washed

1. Heat oil in saucepan; sauté onion and garlic for 5 minutes, or until onion is transparent.
2. Add tomatoes, clam juice, parsley, basil and saffron. Bring to boil; simmer for 30 minutes.
3. Add minced clams; bring to boil.
4. Stir in rice and salt. Bring back to boil. Arrange fresh clams on rice; cover; cook over low heat for 20 minutes, or until rice is cooked and clams have opened.

Marguerite Doyle, Junior Woman's Club,
Concord, Calif.

FISH WITH RICE

Serves 4 to 6

4 tablespoons olive oil
1½ cups rice
3 cups boiling water
2 teaspoons salt
¼ cup butter
1 cup chopped onions
1 clove garlic, crushed
4 fillets of sole, cut into 4-inch
  squares
½ teaspoon pepper
¼ teaspoon orégano
¼ teaspoon allspice
3 tablespoons chopped parsley
1 cup chopped peeled tomatoes

1. Heat 2 tablespoons of the oil in saucepan; sauté rice over low heat, stirring constantly, until golden.
2. Add water and salt; cover; cook over low heat for 15 minutes. Drain well, if any water remains.
3. Meanwhile, heat remaining oil and butter in large skillet; sauté onions and garlic over medium heat until onions are transparent.
4. Add fish, pepper, orégano and allspice; sauté for 5 minutes longer. Add rice, parsley and tomatoes; mix lightly. Cook over low heat for 15 minutes, stirring frequently.

Mrs. Felix A. Buskey, Greenfields Woman's Club,
Reading, Pa.

SHRIMP RICE BILOXI

Serves 6

1 cup rice
¼ cup butter
2 cups Cheese Sauce (p. 442)
1½ cups diced cooked shrimp

1. Grease 6 6-ounce custard cups.
2. Cook rice (p. 473).
3. Add butter to rice; toss to mix. Press rice into cups; keep in warm place for 5 minutes.

4. Put Cheese Sauce in saucepan; stir in shrimp. Simmer, stirring frequently, for 5 minutes.
5. Turn rice molds onto serving dish; top with shrimp sauce.

Barbara Montgomery, Service League,
Lombard, Ill.

GUM SOOZLE

Serves 2 or 4

1 cup cooked rice
1 large onion, chopped and
  sautéed in butter
1 cup heavy cream
½ cup catsup
1 cup shrimp, shelled, deveined,
  cooked and diced
Baked patty shells

1. In top of double saucepan combine rice, onion and cream. Cook over simmering water for 10 minutes, stirring occasionally.
2. Add catsup and shrimp; cook for 30 minutes longer.
3. Serve in patty shells.

Mrs. Frederick W. Marriner, President,
Woman's Club, Watertown, Mass.

JAMBALAYA

Serves 8

3 slices bacon, chopped
2 small onions, chopped
3 tablespoons chopped green
  pepper
2 tablespoons chopped parsley
2 tablespoons chopped celery
1 tablespoon flour
3 cups cooked or canned tomatoes
1 cup chicken broth
1 teaspoon salt
Dash of cayenne
1 teaspoon chili powder
3 cups cooked rice
3 cups coarsely chopped cooked
  shrimp
12 oysters, parboiled

1. Cook bacon in large saucepan until golden. Add onions, green pepper, parsley and celery; cook until onions are golden.
2. Stir in flour. Add tomatoes, broth, salt, cayenne and chili powder. Bring to boil; cook over low heat, stirring occasionally, until thickened.
3. Add rice, shrimp and oysters; mix well. Heat to serving temperature.

Gulf Coast Gourmet, Woman's Club, Foley, Ala.

JAMBALAYA À LA CREOLE

Serves 6

2 tablespoons shortening
1 medium onion, finely chopped
2 cups brown rice
1 pound shrimp, shelled and
  deveined
1 quart chicken broth or water
1 tablespoon chopped parsley
1 tablespoon finely chopped
  scallions
¼ teaspoon cayenne
Salt and pepper to taste

1. Melt shortening in large heavy skillet; sauté onion over low heat for 5 minutes. Stir in rice; sauté, stirring constantly, until rice begins to pop and whiten.

2. Stir in remaining ingredients. Bring to boil; cover. Cook over low heat for about 20 minutes, or until liquid is absorbed.

NOTE: Minced beef, ham, chicken, any other leftover meat or oysters may be substituted for the shrimp.

Junior Woman's Club, Pacific Beach, Calif.

SHRIMP PILAU

Serves 4

1-pound 4-ounce can tomatoes
½ cup chopped onions
½ cup chopped celery
2 teaspoons lemon juice
2 teaspoons salt
2 tablespoons catsup
2 tablespoons Worcestershire
2 tablespoons butter or margarine
1 cup rice
1 pound shrimp, shelled and deveined

1. In large saucepan combine tomatoes, onions and celery. Bring to boil; cover; simmer for 15 minutes.

2. Add lemon juice, salt, catsup, Worcestershire and butter or margarine. Bring to boil; stir in rice. Cover; simmer for 15 minutes.

3. Stir in shrimp; cook, uncovered, for 15 minutes, or until liquid is absorbed.

Ruth Gaines, Junior Woman's Club, Jacksonville, Fla.

SHRIMP PURLO

Serves 6

2 pounds shrimp, shelled and deveined
1 cup rice
1 cup water
2 slices bacon, diced
1 medium onion, chopped
1 green pepper, seeded and chopped
2 tablespoons melted butter
1 teaspoon salt
Dash of pepper

1. Cut shrimp into two or three pieces, according to size; put with rice and water in heavy saucepan.

2. Cook bacon in skillet until crisp. Add onion and green pepper; sauté until onion is lightly browned; add to rice. Add butter, salt and pepper. Mix well.

3. Cover tightly; cook over low heat for about 40 minutes, or until tender.

Mrs. H. L. Gatlin, Jr., Woman's Club, Raeford, N.C.

OYSTERS AND RICE

Serves 6

1 pint oysters, freshly shucked
¼ cup cooking oil
1 medium onion, chopped
2 stalks celery, chopped
1 small green pepper, chopped

4 chicken bouillon cubes
1 bay leaf, crushed
½ teaspoon thyme
¼ teaspoon Tabasco
1 teaspoon Worcestershire
1½ cups rice
¼ cup chopped parsley
¼ cup chopped scallions

1. Preheat oven to 350° F. Grease 2½-quart casserole.

2. Drain oysters; reserve liquor. Remove any pieces of shell; cut oysters in half, if large; set aside.

3. Heat oil in large skillet; sauté onion, celery and green pepper for 5 minutes.

4. Strain and measure reserved liquor; add hot water to total 2½ cups. Stir in bouillon cubes; stir until dissolved. Stir into vegetables in skillet. Bring to boil; remove from heat.

5. Stir in remaining ingredients and oysters; mix well. Turn into casserole.

6. Cover; bake in preheated oven for 45 minutes. Remove cover; stir once; cover again; bake for 15 minutes longer.

Mrs. S. L. Wright II, Attakapas Study Club, Crowley, La.

Rice Dishes with Poultry

CHICKEN RICE BAKE

Serves 6 to 8

2 tablespoons butter
¼ cup sliced mushrooms or 4-ounce can mushrooms, drained
½ cup blanched almonds
3 cups cooked rice
2-ounce jar pimientos, drained and chopped
1½ cups diced cooked chicken
½ cup sliced celery
1½ cups chicken broth
1½ tablespoons flour
Salt and pepper to taste

1. Preheat oven to 350° F. Grease 1½-quart casserole.

2. Melt butter in skillet; sauté mushrooms and almonds until almonds are lightly browned. Set aside.

3. Combine rice and pimientos; spoon one-third into casserole. Add alternate layers of chicken, celery, almond mixture and remaining rice mixture.

4. Combine broth, flour, salt and pepper. Pour into casserole.

5. Cover; bake in preheated oven for 1 hour.

Mrs. Ralph Brubaker, Junior Woman's Club, Torrance, Calif.

CHICKEN PILAF

Serves 4

¼ cup butter
1 medium onion, chopped
⅓ cup diced celery
¼ cup sliced mushrooms
1 cup rice

2 cups chicken broth
2 cups cubed cooked chicken
1 teaspoon salt
¼ teaspoon pepper

1. Preheat oven to 350° F.
2. Melt butter in skillet; sauté onion, celery, mushrooms and rice for about 10 minutes, or until onion and rice are golden.
3. Turn into 1½-quart casserole. Add remaining ingredients; mix.
4. Cover; bake in preheated oven for 45 minutes.

Mrs. Farel Wykoff, Woman's Club, Palmdale, Calif.

CHICKEN RODGER
Serves 4

3 tablespoons butter
3½-pound frying chicken, cut into serving pieces
Salt and pepper to taste
1 cup rice
1 onion, chopped
8-ounce can mushroom pieces, undrained
2½ cups chicken broth

1. Melt 2 tablespoons of the butter in large skillet; sauté chicken until golden on all sides. Sprinkle lightly with salt and pepper; set aside.
2. Preheat oven to 350° F. Grease baking dish.
3. Put rice in dish; sprinkle with onion. Add mushrooms; top with chicken. Add broth; dot with remaining butter.
4. Bake in preheated oven for 1 hour.

Lydia Weber, Woman's Club, Ashley, N.D.

CHICKEN AND RICE IN FOIL
Serves 8

3 cups water
2 beef bouillon cubes
1½ tablespoons soy sauce
1 cup rice
8 chicken breasts, skinned
½ cup heavy cream
½ cup butter or margarine
1 envelope onion soup mix

1. Preheat oven to 300° F. Grease 2-quart casserole.
2. Put water, bouillon cubes, soy sauce and rice in casserole; stir.
3. Bake in preheated oven for 1 hour.
4. Cut 8 12-inch squares of aluminum foil. Place one-eighth of rice mixture in center of each piece of foil. Top each with 1 of chicken breasts; sprinkle each with 1 tablespoon of the cream. Put pat of butter or margarine on top; sprinkle with soup mix. Fold foil to form package; place on baking sheet.
5. Turn oven up to 350° F. Bake in preheated oven for 1 hour.

Ethel Prestage, President, Women's Club, Porterville, Calif.

CHICKEN PEUFFLE
Serves 4

2 cups cooked rice
1 cup finely chopped cooked chicken
½ cup heavy cream
½ cup chicken broth
½ teaspoon salt
Dash of pepper
Dash of mace

1. Preheat oven to 350° F. Grease 1-quart casserole.
2. Turn all ingredients into mixing bowl; mix well. Turn into casserole.
3. Bake in preheated oven for 30 minutes.

Mrs. J. W. Venemon, Mothers' Club, Tieton, Wash.

RICE AND CHICKEN SUPREME
Serves 12

¼ cup melted butter
¾ cup presifted flour
1 quart hot chicken broth
3 cups hot milk
6 cups cooked chicken, cut into 1-inch pieces
6 cups cooked rice
1 cup sliced blanched almonds
4-ounce can pimientos, drained and finely chopped
2 4-ounce cans sliced mushrooms, drained
Salt and pepper to taste
1 cup buttered bread crumbs

1. In large saucepan combine butter and flour. Add broth and milk; cook over moderate heat, stirring rapidly, until sauce is thickened and smooth.
2. Preheat oven to 350° F. Grease large casserole.
3. Combine sauce and all remaining ingredients except crumbs. Pour into casserole; sprinkle with crumbs.
4. Bake in preheated oven for 45 minutes.

Ava Thompson, Federated Woman's Club, Bailey, Colo.

ARROZ CON POLLO
(Chicken with Yellow Rice)
Serves 4

½ cup olive oil
2½-pound frying chicken, cut into serving pieces
1 large onion, finely chopped
1 medium green pepper, chopped
2 cloves, garlic, crushed
1 cup rice
2½ cups water
1 bay leaf
1 tablespoon salt
⅛ teaspoon saffron
1-pound can tomatoes, drained
2 pimientos, sliced
8-ounce can peas, drained

1. Preheat oven to 375° F. Grease 3-quart casserole.

2. Heat oil in large skillet; brown chicken well on all sides. Put in casserole.

3. Sauté onion, green pepper and garlic in oil remaining in skillet for 5 minutes. Add rice; sauté for 5 minutes.

4. Stir in water, bay leaf, salt, saffron and tomatoes; bring to boil. Pour over chicken.

5. Bake in preheated oven for 40 minutes, or until rice is cooked and liquid is absorbed.

6. Garnish with pimientos and peas.

Mrs. Benjamin Wait, Junior Women's Club,
Fort Myers, Fla.

CHICKEN JAMBALAYA

Serves 6

  ⅓ cup olive oil
  3-pound frying chicken, cut into
    serving pieces
  1 cup finely chopped onions
  6 shallots, chopped
  2 cloves garlic, crushed
  1 green pepper, chopped
  ¼ teaspoon pepper
  1 bay leaf, crushed
  1 tablespoon salt
  Dash of Tabasco
  8-ounce can mushrooms, undrained
  1-pound can tomatoes, undrained
  5 cups water
  2½ cups rice
  ½ cup dry sherry
  8-ounce can small peas, drained

1. Preheat oven to 400° F.

2. Heat oil in dutch oven or heavy saucepan; brown chicken well on all sides. Remove chicken; set aside.

3. Sauté onions, shallots, garlic and green pepper in oil remaining in pan for 5 minutes. Stir in pepper, bay leaf, salt, Tabasco, mushrooms and tomatoes. Bring to boil; then simmer for 5 minutes.

4. Stir in water, rice, sherry and peas. Return chicken to pan.

5. Cover; bake in preheated oven for 45 minutes.

Gene Knobloch, Junior Woman's Club,
Thibodaux, La.

PAELLA CON VINO

Serves 6

  ½ cup olive oil
  2½-pound frying chicken, cut into
    serving pieces
  1 large onion, finely chopped
  ½ teaspoon saffron
  ½ teaspoon paprika
  1 bay leaf
  ½ cup dry white wine
  1½ cups chicken broth
  2 tablespoons lemon juice
  1½ cups rice
  1½ teaspoons salt
  ⅛ teaspoon pepper
  1½-pound lobster, cut into pieces
  6 clams in shells
  6 mussels in shells
  ¾ pound shrimp, shelled and
    deveined

1. Heat oil in Dutch oven or large heavy saucepan; brown chicken well on all sides. Remove chicken; set aside.

2. Sauté onion in oil remaining in pan for 5 minutes. Stir in saffron, paprika, bay leaf, wine, broth, lemon juice, rice, salt and pepper. Bring to boil; return chicken to pan. Stir well to mix.

3. Top with lobster, clams, mussels and shrimp. Cover with aluminum foil; cover with lid of pan. Simmer for 15 minutes.

4. Remove lid and foil; cook for 5 minutes longer, or until liquid is absorbed and chicken is tender.

Mrs. D. Landau, Woman's Club, Hannibal, Mo.

RICE MILANESE

Serves 4 to 6

  6 tablespoons butter or margarine
  1 tablespoon olive oil
  1 medium onion, grated
  1 cup rice
  1¼ cups boiling beef consommé
  ½ cup dry white wine
  ½ cup water
  Salt and pepper to taste
  ½ pound chicken livers
  ½ pound mushrooms, sliced

1. Preheat oven to 350° F. Grease 2½-quart casserole.

2. Heat 2 tablespoons of the butter and oil in large skillet; sauté onion over medium heat for 5 minutes. Stir in rice; sauté over medium heat, stirring frequently, until golden.

3. Stir in consommé, wine and water. Season with salt and pepper; turn into casserole.

4. Cover; bake in preheated oven for 30 minutes.

5. Melt 2 tablespoons of the butter in same skillet; sauté livers, stirring frequently, for about 5 minutes.

6. Melt remaining butter in another large skillet; sauté mushrooms over medium heat for 5 minutes.

7. Season livers and mushrooms with salt and pepper; stir into rice.

Winnie Smith, Woman's Club, Falls Church, Va.

CREOLE RICE

Serves 4

  2 tablespoons shortening
  ½ pound chicken livers, diced
  1 large onion, chopped
  1 green pepper, chopped
  ½ pound chicken gizzards, chopped
  ½ cup chopped celery
  1 clove garlic, crushed
  1 teaspoon Worcestershire
  ½ teaspoon orégano
  1 teaspoon salt
  ⅛ teaspoon black pepper
  Dash of cayenne
  ½ cup water
  1 tablespoon chopped parsley
  ½ cup chopped scallions
  2 cups cooked rice

1. Melt shortening in large skillet. Add livers, onion, green pepper, gizzards, celery and garlic; sauté until all is browned.

2. Add Worcestershire, orégano, salt, pepper, cayenne and water; stir. Cover; simmer for 40 minutes, stirring occasionally. Add water during cooking, if necessary.

3. Stir in parsley and scallions; simmer for 10 minutes longer.

4. Add rice; toss lightly. Heat to serving temperature.

Junior Woman's Club, Pacific Beach, Calif.

BAYOU LEFTOVER TURKEY RICE DINNER

Serves 6

3 cups cooked rice
2 medium green peppers, finely chopped
2 cups diced cooked turkey
1-pound 4-ounce can tomatoes
2 cups turkey gravy
1 teaspoon salt
¼ teaspoon pepper
Dash of Tabasco
2 tablespoons melted butter or margarine

1. Preheat oven to 350° F. Grease 2½-quart casserole.

2. Arrange alternate layers of rice, green peppers, turkey and tomatoes in casserole.

3. In bowl blend remaining ingredients; pour over layers in casserole.

4. Bake in preheated oven for 30 minutes, or until bubbling.

Mary Russell Cunningham, Treasurer, D.A.R., Conecuh Chapter, Evergreen, Ala.

TURKEY RICE POM-POMS

Serves 4

2 cups cooked rice
½ cup diced celery
½ cup chopped walnuts
2 tablespoons minced onion
¾ teaspoon salt
¾ teaspoon poultry seasoning
Dash of pepper
2 cups diced cooked turkey
¼ cup melted butter
2 eggs, lightly beaten
¾ cup fine bread crumbs

1. Preheat oven to 425° F. Grease baking pan.

2. Combine rice, celery, walnuts, onion, seasonings and turkey.

3. Stir in butter and eggs. Shape into 2-inch balls; roll in crumbs.

4. Arrange in baking pan; bake in preheated oven for 30 minutes, or until crisp.

Mrs. Harland Patton, Coterie Woman's Club, Fort Collins, Colo.

Rice Dishes with Meat

CHOW CASSEROLE

Serves 6

1 pound ground beef
½ cup rice
4 teaspoons soy sauce
1 cup chopped celery
1 cup chopped onions
10½-ounce can condensed cream of chicken soup
10½-ounce can condensed cream of mushroom soup
1½ cups water
1 teaspoon salt
3-ounce can Chinese noodles

1. Preheat oven to 350° F. Grease 2-quart shallow baking dish.

2. In mixing bowl combine all ingredients except Chinese noodles. Mix well. Turn into dish; sprinkle with Chinese noodles.

3. Bake in preheated oven for 1½ hours.

Mrs. Myron S. Hinkle, Woman's Study Club, Lubbock, Tex.

FLUFF

Serves 6

1½ pounds ground beef
¾ cup rice
1-pound 12-ounce can tomatoes
2½ cups water
1 medium onion, chopped
Salt and pepper to taste

1. Preheat oven to 350° F. Grease 2-quart casserole.

2. Combine all ingredients; mix well. Turn into casserole.

3. Bake in preheated oven for 1½ hours.

Mrs. G. O. Barr, Woman's Club, American Home and Garden Dept., Silvis, Ill.

FU CHU

Serves 6

1 tablespoon olive oil
1 pound ground beef
2 cups chopped celery
1 cup chopped onions
10½-ounce can condensed cream of mushroom soup
1¼ cups water
1 cup rice
1-pound can bean sprouts, drained
4-ounce can mushrooms, drained
¼ cup soy sauce

1. Preheat oven to 350° F. Grease 2-quart casserole.

2. Heat oil in skillet; sauté beef, celery and onions over medium heat, stirring frequently, until meat is browned.

3. Remove from heat. Stir in remaining ingredients. Turn into casserole.

4. Bake in preheated oven for 1 hour.

Mrs. John Scofield, Woman's Club, Shell Beach, Calif.

CHEROKEE CASSEROLE
Serves 4

1 pound ground beef
1 tablespoon olive oil
¾ cup chopped onions
¼ teaspoon orégano
½ bay leaf, crumbled
¼ teaspoon garlic powder
1½ teaspoons salt
¼ teaspoon thyme
2 cups canned tomatoes
10½-ounce can condensed cream of
  mushroom soup
1 cup instant rice
6 stuffed olives, sliced
Sliced Monterey Jack cheese

1. Preheat broiler.
2. Heat oil in large skillet; brown beef.
Add onions; cook until tender.
3. Add all remaining ingredients except
olives and cheese; mix well. Add half the
olives; simmer, stirring frequently, for 5
minutes.
4. Spoon into 2-quart casserole or baking dish; top with cheese and remaining
olives.
5. Cook under broiler until cheese is
melted.

Mrs. J. A. Chandler, Book Lovers Club,
Kosciusko, Miss.

SPANISH RICE WITH BEEF
Serves 6

2 tablespoons butter
1 medium onion, finely chopped
1 pound ground beef
1-pound 13-ounce can tomatoes,
  undrained
1 teaspoon salt
1 teaspoon celery salt
¼ teaspoon pepper
1 tablespoon sugar
3 cups cooked rice
2 cups grated American cheese

1. Preheat oven to 325° F. Grease 2½-
quart casserole.
2. Melt butter in large skillet; sauté
onion and beef, stirring occasionally, until
meat is browned and crumbly.
3. Add tomatoes, salt, celery salt, pepper
and sugar; simmer for 20 minutes.
4. Remove from heat. Stir in rice and
cheese. Turn into casserole.
5. Bake in preheated oven for 1 hour.
6. Keep in warm place for 20 minutes
before serving.

Mrs. George H. Cannon, Friendly Hour Home
Demonstration Club, Bremen, Ind.

BEEF AND RICE CASSEROLE
Serves 6 to 8

1 tablespoon shortening
1 medium onion, chopped
1 medium green pepper, chopped
1½ pounds ground beef
1-pound can tomatoes, undrained
1-pound can kidney beans, drained
1 cup rice
Salt and pepper to taste
3 slices American cheese, halved

1. Preheat oven to 350° F. Grease 3-
quart casserole.
2. Melt shortening in large skillet; sauté
onion and green pepper over medium heat
for 5 minutes. Add beef; sauté, stirring
frequently, until browned.
3. Stir in tomatoes, beans and rice.
Season with salt and pepper. Turn into
casserole.
4. Bake in preheated oven for 1 hour.
5. Remove from oven; top with cheese.
Bake for 10 minutes longer.

Natalie Leonchik, Argo Summit Woman's Club,
Summit, Ill.

RISOTTO WITH MEAT
Serves 6 to 8

⅓ cup olive oil
¼ cup chopped onion
2 cloves garlic, crushed
2 cups rice
½ pound ground beef
½ pound Italian sweet or hot sausage,
  sliced
2 teaspoons salt
¼ teaspoon pepper
⅛ teaspoon saffron
½ teaspoon orégano
2 tablespoons chopped parsley
5 cups chicken or beef broth
Grated Parmesan cheese

1. Heat oil in large skillet; sauté onion
and garlic for 5 minutes. Stir in rice, beef
and sausage; sauté over medium heat, stirring frequently, until meat is browned.
2. Stir in salt, pepper, saffron, orégano,
parsley and broth; bring to boil; cover;
simmer, stirring occasionally, for 20 minutes, or until liquid is absorbed.
3. Serve with cheese.

Carol Meskell, Junior Woman's Club,
Glastonbury, Conn.

OLYMPIAN RICE
Serves 6

6 tablespoons butter
2 cups rice
4 cups chicken broth
3 ripe tomatoes, peeled and diced
1 cup chopped onions
1 cup julienne strips salami
6 to 8 mushrooms, sliced
⅛ teaspoon pepper
2 teaspoons salt
10-ounce package frozen peas,
  cooked and drained

1. Melt butter in heavy kettle; sauté rice
until golden.
2. Add all remaining ingredients except
peas. Cover tightly; cook over moderate
heat for 30 to 40 minutes, or until rice is
tender and has absorbed broth.
3. Add peas; toss.

Mrs. R. C. Ennis, Women's Club,
Richland, Wash.

RUSSIAN FLUFF

Serves 25

1 clove garlic
¼ cup olive oil
2 pounds ground beef
1 pound ground pork
2 large onions, chopped
2 medium green peppers, diced
4 cups chopped celery
2 1-pound cans peas, drained
4 10½-ounce cans condensed tomato
   soup
4-ounce jar pimientos, drained and
   chopped
6 cups cooked rice
1 tablespoon salt
½ teaspoon pepper
1 teaspoon basil
1 teaspoon orégano
1 teaspoon sugar
¼ cup chopped parsley

1. Rub inside of very large saucepan with garlic. Heat oil in pan; sauté beef and pork until meat loses red color.

2. Add onions, green peppers and celery; sauté over medium heat for 10 minutes, stirring occasionally.

3. Stir in remaining ingredients; mix well. Bring to boil; cover; simmer for 30 minutes, stirring occasionally.

Sally Ortolani, Community Woman's Club, Annandale, Va.

Wild Rice

Wild rice or Indian rice grows in the northern states of America, particularly in Minnesota and Wisconsin. The crop is limited, depending entirely on the whims of nature, and wild rice is therefore expensive. A little goes a long way, however —1 cup making a good 3 cups cooked rice. When cooked, it can be extended by adding about 1 cup cooked white rice to each 2 or 3 cups wild rice. Wild rice has a natural affinity for richly flavored foods, such as wild game and game birds, chicken livers and mushrooms. It is apt to be dusty and should be washed carefully in several changes of clear water. The usual way to cook wild rice is to boil it in a large quantity of salted water for 40 to 45 minutes; then it is drained and tossed with butter. However, it is much better cooked according to the Indian method.

TO COOK WILD RICE INDIAN STYLE

Serves 4

1 cup wild rice
Salt
Butter
Freshly ground black pepper

1. Wash rice thoroughly; soak in cold water for 5 to 6 hours, changing water occasionally.

2. Put rice in heavy saucepan; pour boiling salted water over it, using about 4 cups water to each cup rice; cover; let stand for 20 minutes; drain. Repeat this step three times.

3. A few minutes before serving, cover again with boiling salted water; simmer for 3 minutes. Drain; place in hot oven for a few minutes to dry out.

4. Toss with big nugget of butter; season to taste with salt and pepper.

A. S.

WILD RICE

Serves 8 to 10

2 quarts water
1 pound wild rice
½ cup butter or margarine
Salt and pepper to taste

1. Combine water and rice in saucepan. Bring to boil; simmer for 1 hour. Drain; rinse under running cold water.

2. Melt butter or margarine in large skillet. Stir in rice; sauté over medium heat for 10 minutes, stirring frequently. Season with salt and pepper.

Mrs. Olive Gooch, Woman's Club, Hugoton, Kans.

SPECIAL WILD RICE

Serves 6

1½ cups wild rice
1 quart water
1 teaspoon salt
1 small onion
4 slices bacon, diced
4 scallions, chopped
6 mushrooms, thinly sliced
Salt and freshly ground black
   pepper to taste

1. Rinse rice thoroughly. Put in saucepan with water, salt and onion. Bring to boil; simmer, uncovered, for 40 to 45 minutes, or until tender. Discard onion; drain in colander.

2. Cook bacon in skillet until crisp. Drain on absorbent paper. Sauté scallions and mushrooms in fat remaining in skillet for about 8 minutes, or until tender.

3. Add rice, bacon, salt and pepper. Heat through, tossing occasionally.

VARIATIONS: Cook ½ cup white rice separately; add to wild rice. This provides a sufficient quantity to serve 8 or 9 people generously.

Mona Boner, Three Arts Club, Marion, Ala.

WILD RICE CONSOMMÉ

Serves 4

1 cup wild rice
2 tablespoons butter or margarine
½ cup finely chopped onions
½ cup finely chopped celery
4-ounce can sliced mushrooms,
   drained
10½-ounce can condensed beef
   consommé

1. Wash rice well; cover with water. Soak for 1 hour; drain.

2. Melt butter or margarine in skillet; sauté onions and celery over medium heat for 5 minutes.

3. Remove from heat. Stir in mushrooms, consommé and rice. Let stand for 3 hours.

4. Preheat oven to 350° F. Grease 1½-quart casserole.

5. Turn rice mixture into casserole.

6. Bake in preheated oven for 1½ hours.

Mrs. Roger Ostroot, Women's Club,
Canby, Minn.

WILD RICE CASSEROLE

Serves 8

1½ cups wild rice
1 quart chicken broth
2 tablespoons butter
½ cup chopped green pepper
½ cup chopped onions
½ cup chopped celery
¼ cup slivered almonds
2 tablespoons soy sauce
1 teaspoon salt
Pepper to taste
10½-ounce can condensed cream of
  mushroom soup

1. Combine rice and broth in saucepan. Bring to boil; cover; simmer for about 25 minutes, or until liquid is absorbed. Set aside.

2. Preheat oven to 350° F. Grease 2-quart casserole.

3. Melt butter in skillet; sauté green pepper, onions and celery for about 10 minutes, or until soft. Stir into rice.

4. Combine rice mixture with remaining ingredients. Turn into casserole.

5. Bake in preheated oven for 30 minutes.

Jane Culbertson, El Camino Women's Club,
Ventura, Calif.

WILD RICE RING MOLD

Serves 8

This is good served with creamed mushrooms and shrimp or crab meat.

1½ cups wild rice
6 slices bacon
1 medium onion, chopped
¼ teaspoon pepper
¼ teaspoon salt
¼ teaspoon celery salt
1 tablespoon chopped parsley
1 egg yolk, lightly beaten
½ cup sugar
1 cup grated carrots
2 tablespoons melted butter

1. Wash rice; soak for several hours in salted water, changing water several times. When ready to cook, drain; cover with fresh water; bring to boil; then simmer for 20 minutes. Drain.

2. Preheat oven to 350° F. Grease 2-quart ring mold.

3. Cook bacon in skillet until crisp. Drain on absorbent paper. Crumble; set aside.

4. Sauté onion in fat remaining in skillet for about 10 minutes, or until tender. Combine rice, bacon, onion and remaining ingredients.

5. Turn into mold; cover with aluminum foil.

6. Bake in preheated oven for 40 to 45 minutes. Turn out of mold to serve.

Mrs. John Whalen, Woman's Club,
Whitefish, Mont.

WILD RICE HOT DISH

Serves 8

10½-ounce can condensed cream of
  mushroom soup
10½-ounce can condensed cream of
  celery soup
8-ounce can mushroom caps,
  drained
1 teaspoon curry powder
2 tablespoons minced green pepper
2 tablespoons diced pimiento
3 cups cooked wild rice
4½-ounce can shrimp, drained
7¾-ounce can lobster, drained and
  flaked
2 eggs, hard-cooked
3 tablespoons melted butter or
  margarine
½ cup chopped almonds

1. Preheat oven to 350° F. Grease 2½-quart casserole.

2. In mixing bowl blend soups, mushrooms, curry powder, green pepper and pimiento. Stir in rice, shrimp and lobster.

3. Separate egg yolks from whites. Chop whites; add to rice mixture.

4. Turn into casserole; force egg yolks through sieve over rice mixture.

5. Bake in preheated oven for 45 minutes. Just before serving, sprinkle with butter or margarine and almonds.

Mrs. Edgar Massee, L'Etudier Club,
East Grand Forks, Minn.

CHICKEN AND WILD RICE CASSEROLE

Serves 10

½ cup butter or margarine
½ pound mushrooms, sliced
¼ cup presifted flour
½ teaspoon rosemary
Salt and pepper to taste
1½ cups chicken broth
⅓ cup dry sherry
6-ounce package mixed long grain
  and wild rice
5 chicken breasts, boned and halved
Paprika

1. Preheat oven to 350° F. Grease 3-quart casserole.

2. Melt butter or margarine in large skillet; sauté mushrooms until tender. Sprinkle flour, rosemary, salt and pepper over mushrooms.

3. Gradually stir in broth; cook over low heat, stirring constantly, until sauce is thickened. Remove from heat. Stir in sherry.

4. Put rice in casserole. Top with chicken. Sprinkle with salt, pepper and paprika. Pour sauce over chicken and rice.

5. Cover; bake in preheated oven for 30 minutes. Remove cover; bake for 30 minutes longer.

Mrs. Joseph Glider, Women's Improvement Club, Blythe, Calif.

WILD RICE AND TURKEY RING

Serves 6

½ pound wild rice
1¼ teaspoons salt
2 tablespoons finely chopped green pepper
2 tablespoons finely diced celery
1 tablespoon diced onion
2 tablespoons butter
Salt to taste
4-ounce can mushrooms, undrained
1 tablespoon minced parsley
10½-ounce can condensed cream of mushroom soup
1 soup can milk
1 egg yolk, lightly beaten
2 cups diced cooked turkey
1 clove garlic, impaled on wooden pick
2 tablespoons diced pimiento
¼ cup slivered toasted almonds

1. Wash rice thoroughly. Put in heavy saucepan with water to cover generously. Add 1 teaspoon of the salt. Bring to boil; cover; cook for 45 minutes, or until rice is tender and water is absorbed.

2. Preheat oven to 325° F. Grease 6-cup ring mold generously.

3. Press rice firmly into mold; set mold in shallow pan of hot water; bake in preheated oven for 30 minutes.

4. Meanwhile, simmer green pepper, celery and onion in butter for 10 minutes, or until tender. Add salt, mushrooms and parsley.

5. Combine soup, milk and egg yolk; stir into vegetable mixture.

6. Add turkey, garlic and pimiento; heat, but do not boil.

7. Unmold onto warm serving platter. Discard garlic; fill center of mold with turkey mixture. Sprinkle with almonds.

Mrs. Glenn K. Roger, President, Wyoming Federation of Women's Clubs, Cheyenne, Wyo.

WILD RICE CASSEROLE WITH SAUSAGE

Serves 8

1 pound sausage
2 medium onions, chopped
2 4-ounce cans button mushrooms, drained and left whole or sliced
2 cups washed wild rice
¼ cup presifted flour
½ cup heavy cream
2½ cups chicken broth
1 teaspoon monosodium glutamate
1 tablespoon salt
⅛ teaspoon pepper
Pinch each of orégano, thyme and marjoram
½ cup slivered toasted blanched almonds

1. Brown sausage in skillet. Drain on absorbent paper; crumble.

2. Sauté onions in fat remaining in skillet, until transparent. Add mushrooms and sausage; set aside.

3. Cook rice, covered, in briskly boiling salted water for 20 to 25 minutes. Remove cover; cook over low heat for 10 to 15 minutes. Drain off excess water.

4. Preheat oven to 350° F. Grease casserole.

5. Combine flour and cream in saucepan. Add broth. Bring to boil, stirring constantly, until thickened. Add seasonings and herbs. Combine with sausage mixture, turn into casserole.

6. Bake in preheated oven for 25 to 30 minutes. Before serving, sprinkle with almonds.

Mrs. Orville L. Freeman, Chevy Chase, Md.

16. Pasta Dishes and Sauces for Pasta

No other category of food is more versatile than the various forms of pasta products available today. With a pound of any one of them, almost any leftover in the refrigerator and a touch of imagination, a homemaker can produce a nutritious and appetizing dish for her family.

Noodles, macaroni and spaghetti are so closely related that they may usually be interchanged in a pasta recipe. Noodles differ only in that they contain eggs and are most frequently made in flat strips of varying widths; whereas spaghetti, which comes in several thicknesses, is tubular, and macaroni, usually a hollow tube in assorted sizes, also comes in many other shapes and forms, such as shells, bow ties, ruffles, etc. However, the same method of preparing the more common shapes of pasta can be applied to these as well. They all are good when cooked according to package directions, drained and served hot with a savory sauce and grated Parmesan cheese.

Cooking time varies with the type and thickness of the pasta, but the important thing to remember is to use a large quantity of rapidly boiling salted water and to cook until the pasta is barely tender or, as the Italians would say, *al dente*.

Some forms of pasta, such as the large shells, rigatoni, large tubes, and cannelloni, wide strips, are usually stuffed with meat, cheese, spinach or chicken fillings after they are cooked, then sauced, reheated and served with grated cheese.

HOW TO COOK PASTA

Use plenty of water, about 8 times the amount of pasta.

WEIGHT OF PASTA	AMOUNT OF WATER
4 ounces	1 quart
8 ounces	2 quarts
1 pound	4 quarts

1. Bring water to rapid boil.
2. Add 1 tablespoon each of salt and cooking oil.
3. Add pasta very slowly, so that water never stops boiling.
4. Cook according to package directions, stirring occasionally and lifting pasta

from bottom of pan, until tender but still chewy.
5. Pour carefully into colander to drain.
6. Rinse with cold water when serving cold in salads; with hot water when cooked ahead of time or when combining with other hot ingredients.

APPROXIMATE COOKING TIME

PRODUCT	MINUTES, OR ACCORDING TO PACKAGE DIRECTIONS
Spaghetti	15
Thin spaghetti	10 to 12
Macaroni, long, elbow or shells	12 to 15
Noodles, wide	9 to 12
Noodles, fine, medium and alphabet	7 to 8

Noodles

HOMEMADE NOODLES

Serves 4

The secret of making delicious noodles is to have the dough kneadable. It should be soft and very workable.

2 eggs
1 teaspoon salt
About 1¼ cups presifted flour
Boiling salted water or broth

1. Beat eggs until very frothy. Add salt; work in flour.
2. Knead well. Roll out thinly on lightly floured board; dust with flour. Cut into strips about ¼ inch wide.
3. Scatter strips on board; let dry for about 1 hour before cooking.
4. Cook in water or broth for about 12 minutes.

GREEN NOODLES: These are available in many stores throughout the country. If you wish to make your own, mix ½ cup finely chopped cooked spinach with the eggs and

490

salt in above recipe before working in the flour.

Mary Rost, Literary Club, Moab, Utah

NOODLES GRATINÉE
Serves 6

12-ounce package medium noodles
⅓ cup butter
¾ cup grated Parmesan cheese

1. Preheat broiler. Grease 10 x 6 x 1½-inch baking pan.
2. Cook noodles according to package directions; drain.
3. Mix noodles, butter and cheese. Stir until butter is melted.
4. Turn into pan; broil 3 to 4 inches from heat for 5 minutes, or until crusty and browned.

Dorothy Kay, Blair Woman's Club,
Blairstown, N.J.

NOODLE PUDDING
Serves 5

8-ounce package wide noodles
3 eggs, lightly beaten
½ cup melted butter
Salt and pepper to taste

1. Preheat oven to 350° F. Grease 2-quart casserole.
2. Cook noodles according to package directions. Drain well; rinse; turn into mixing bowl.
3. Add eggs and butter; season with salt and pepper. Mix well; turn into casserole.
4. Bake in preheated oven for 30 minutes.

Eileen Pearlstine, Junior Woman's Club,
Lansdale, Pa.

NOODLE PUDDING WITH SOUR CREAM
Serves 6

8-ounce package medium noodles
2 cups cream-style cottage cheese
1 cup sour cream
1 tablespoon sugar
4 eggs, separated
½ cup melted butter or margarine
Salt and pepper to taste

1. Preheat oven to 325° F. Grease 2½-quart casserole.
2. Cook noodles according to package directions; drain; rinse.
3. In mixing bowl blend cheese, sour cream, sugar and egg yolks. Fold in noodles and butter or margarine; season with salt and pepper.
4. In another mixing bowl beat egg whites until stiff but not dry; fold into noodle mixture.
5. Turn into casserole; bake in preheated oven for 30 minutes. Turn temperature to 300° F. Bake for 30 minutes longer.

Mrs. Henry W. Grossberg, Woman's Club,
Bradenton, Fla.

NOODLE RING
Serves 6

Fill center with creamed chicken, fish or shrimp, as desired.

3 eggs, separated
1½ teaspoons Worcestershire
1 tablespoon catsup
1 cup milk
1 teaspoon salt
¼ teaspoon pepper
2 cups cooked noodles

1. Preheat oven to 350° F. Grease well and flour 8-inch ring mold.
2. Put egg yolks in mixing bowl; beat with Worcestershire, catsup, milk, salt and pepper. Stir in noodles.
3. In another mixing bowl beat egg whites until stiff but not dry. Fold into noodle mixture; turn into mold.
4. Set mold in pan of hot water; bake in preheated oven for 45 minutes, or until set.
5. Let stand on top of stove for 20 minutes. Carefully loosen sides from mold. Unmold onto serving dish.

Mrs. Edward E. Meyers, Woman's Club,
Bakersfield, Calif.

NOODLES ROMANOFF
Serves 6

1 cup cream-style cottage cheese
1 cup sour cream
½ small onion, minced
1 clove garlic, crushed
Dash of Worcestershire
Dash of Tabasco
½ teaspoon salt
3 cups cooked medium noodles
½ cup grated Cheddar cheese
Paprika

1. Preheat oven to 350° F. Grease 2-quart casserole.
2. In mixing bowl blend cottage cheese, sour cream, onion, garlic, Worcestershire, Tabasco and salt. Add noodles; toss lightly. Turn into casserole. Sprinkle with Cheddar cheese; dust with paprika.
3. Bake in preheated oven for 40 minutes.

Lila Blanchette, L'Etudier Club,
East Grand Forks, Minn.

HUNGARIAN NOODLES
Serves 6

8-ounce package fine noodles
1 cup cream-style cottage cheese
1 cup sour cream
2 eggs, lightly beaten
¼ cup finely chopped onion
1 clove garlic, crushed
2 teaspoons Worcestershire
Dash of Tabasco
½ teaspoon salt
Dash of pepper
¾ cup grated Cheddar cheese

1. Preheat oven to 350° F. Grease 1½-quart casserole.
2. Cook noodles according to package directions; drain; rinse.

3. In mixing bowl blend cottage cheese, sour cream and eggs. Stir in onion, garlic, Worcestershire, Tabasco, salt and pepper. Add noodles and ¼ cup of the Cheddar cheese; mix well. Turn into casserole.

4. Set casserole in pan of hot water; bake in preheated oven for 30 minutes. Sprinkle remaining cheese on top; bake for 10 minutes longer.

Donna Sutton, Lincoln Village Women's Club, Columbus, Ohio

NOODLES WITH WATER CHESTNUTS

Serves 6

8-ounce package medium noodles
10½-ounce can condensed cream
    of celery soup
¼ cup milk
¾ teaspoon salt
¼ teaspoon pepper
5-ounce can water chestnuts,
    drained and sliced
¼ cup slivered blanched almonds

1. Preheat oven to 375° F. Grease 1½-quart casserole.

2. Cook noodles according to package directions; drain; rinse. Turn into mixing bowl.

3. In another bowl blend soup, milk, salt and pepper; pour over noodles.

4. Add water chestnuts; mix well. Turn into casserole; sprinkle with almonds.

5. Bake in preheated oven for 30 minutes.

Mrs. J. E. Casey, Woman's Club, Ardmore, Pa.

BAKED NOODLES AND CRAB MEAT

Serves 6

2 tablespoons butter
1 onion, chopped
4-ounce can mushrooms
1 green pepper, chopped
8-ounce package medium noodles,
    cooked
1½ cups flaked crab meat
2½ cups drained tomatoes
1 cup sour cream

1. Preheat oven to 350° F. Grease 2½-quart casserole.

2. Melt butter in saucepan; brown onion, mushrooms and green pepper lightly.

3. Combine vegetables, noodles, crab meat and tomatoes. Turn into casserole; spread sour cream on top.

4. Bake in preheated oven for 45 minutes.

Mrs. Paul Kaatz, Woman's Club, Anchorage, Alaska

OYSTERS TETRAZZINI

Serves 8

1 quart oysters, freshly shucked
4 cups fine noodles
7 tablespoons butter or margarine
1 cup soft bread crumbs
⅓ cup grated Parmesan cheese
¼ cup presifted flour
2½ teaspoons salt
¼ teaspoon pepper
2 teaspoons Worcestershire
3 cups milk
¼ cup sherry
½ teaspoon paprika

1. Drain oysters; reserve ½ cup liquor. Chill.

2. Cook noodles according to package directions. Drain; rinse with cold water; put in 2-quart baking dish. Refrigerate.

3. In top of double saucepan melt butter or margarine. Remove 3 tablespoons; mix with crumbs and cheese. Refrigerate.

4. Stir flour, 2 teaspoons of the salt and ⅛ teaspoon of the pepper into remaining butter or margarine. Gradually stir in reserved liquor, Worcestershire and milk; cook, stirring constantly, until sauce is thickened and smooth. Stir in sherry. Refrigerate.

5. About 1 hour before serving, preheat oven to 400° F.

6. Arrange oysters on noodles in dish; sprinkle with remaining salt, remaining pepper and paprika. Pour sauce over oysters; top with crumb mixture.

7. Bake in preheated oven for about 50 minutes, or until bubbling.

Martha Pippin Cannon, Woman's Federated Guild, Moultrie, Ga.

BAKED NOODLES YUKON

Serves 6

8-ounce package medium noodles
1 cup Medium White Sauce (p. 441)
1-pound can salmon, drained
    and flaked
    Dash of Tabasco
    Salt and pepper to taste
1 cup fresh bread crumbs
¼ cup melted butter or margarine

1. Cook noodles according to package directions. Drain well; rinse.

2. Preheat oven to 350° F. Grease 2-quart casserole.

3. Combine Medium White Sauce, salmon, Tabasco, salt and pepper.

4. Arrange alternate layers of salmon sauce and noodles in casserole, finishing with sauce.

5. In small bowl mix crumbs with butter or margarine; sprinkle over mixture in casserole.

6. Bake in preheated oven for 30 minutes.

Mrs. E. C. Jones, Jr., Woman's Club, Paxton, Mass.

TUNA NOODLE CASSEROLE

Serves 4

4 tablespoons fat
4 tablespoons flour
½ teaspoon salt
2 cups hot milk
7-ounce can tuna, drained
    and flaked
8-ounce package medium noodles,
    cooked
1 cup shredded sharp cheese

1. Preheat oven to 375° F. Grease 2-quart baking dish.
2. Melt fat in saucepan. Stir in flour and salt. Add milk; cook, stirring constantly, over moderate heat until sauce is thickened and smooth.
3. Combine sauce and tuna; toss with noodles. Turn into dish; sprinkle with cheese.
4. Bake in preheated oven for 20 minutes, or until cheese is melted and sauce is bubbling.

Mrs. Dorothy Piner, Senior Study Club,
Potwin, Kans.

CHICKEN NOODLE CASSEROLE
Serves 10 to 12

2 6-ounce packages green noodles
4 cups diced cooked chicken
½ cup butter or margarine
1 cup finely chopped celery
1 cup finely chopped onions
1 cup finely chopped green pepper
¼ cup presifted flour
2 cups chicken broth
  Salt and pepper to taste
8-ounce package American cheese, diced
½ cup sliced stuffed olives
8-ounce can sliced mushrooms, drained
½ cup slivered blanched almonds

1. Preheat oven to 350° F. Grease 13 x 9½ x 2-inch baking pan.
2. Cook noodles according to package directions. Drain well; rinse; turn into pan. Add chicken; mix well.
3. Melt butter or margarine in skillet; sauté celery, onions and green pepper over medium heat for 10 minutes.
4. Sprinkle with flour; gradually stir in broth; cook, stirring constantly, until thickened. Season with salt and pepper. Stir in cheese; cook over low heat, stirring constantly, until melted. Remove from heat. Stir in olives and mushrooms.
5. Pour over noodles and chicken. Sprinkle with almonds.
6. Bake in preheated oven for 45 minutes.

Mrs. W. H. Cromwell, Woman's Club,
Batesville, Miss.

NOODLE SOUFFLÉ WITH CREAMED CHICKEN SAUCE
Serves 6

1 cup cooked medium noodles
3 eggs, lightly beaten
1 cup scalded milk
1 cup grated Cheddar cheese
¼ cup melted butter
1 cup fresh bread crumbs
1 tablespoon grated onion
1 teaspoon salt
¼ cup chopped pimientos
½ cup finely chopped celery
10½-ounce can condensed cream of chicken soup
½ cup light cream

1. Preheat oven to 350° F. Grease 11 x 7 x 1½-inch baking pan.
2. Put noodles in mixing bowl; add all remaining ingredients except soup and cream. Mix well; turn into pan.
3. Set baking pan in pan of hot water; bake in preheated oven for 45 minutes, or until set and browned.
4. Meanwhile, in saucepan blend soup and cream; heat to serving temperature, stirring occasionally.
5. Cut noodle soufflé into squares; top with sauce.

Myrtle Haugom, Book & Thimble Club,
Portland, N.D.

FETTUCINI ALFREDO
Serves 4

8 ounces fettucini (medium noodles)
4 tablespoons butter
½ cup grated Parmesan cheese
½ cup grated Swiss or Gruyère cheese
½ cup heavy cream
  Freshly ground black pepper

1. Cook fettucini according to package directions. Drain; rinse; turn into hot serving dish or chafing dish.
2. Add butter; toss. Continue to toss while gradually adding cheeses and cream.
3. Sprinkle with plenty of pepper; toss again.

A. S.

NOODLES NAPOLI
Serves 6

2 tablespoons olive oil
1 medium onion, finely chopped
1 clove garlic, crushed
1 pound ground beef
4-ounce can sliced mushrooms, undrained
1½ 8-ounce cans tomato sauce
6-ounce can tomato paste
2 teaspoons salt
1 teaspoon orégano
2 eggs
8-ounce package wide noodles, cooked, drained and rinsed
10-ounce package frozen chopped spinach, defrosted and drained
1 cup large-curd cottage cheese
½ cup grated Parmesan cheese
8-ounce package American cheese, cut into strips

1. Preheat oven to 450° F. Grease 13 x 9½ x 2-inch baking pan.
2. Heat 1 tablespoon of the oil in skillet; sauté onion and garlic over medium heat until golden. Add beef; cook, stirring occasionally, until browned.
3. Stir in mushrooms, tomato sauce, tomato paste, 1 teaspoon of the salt and orégano. Cover; simmer for 15 minutes.
4. Meanwhile, beat 1 of the eggs; mix with noodles. Set aside.
5. In mixing bowl beat remaining egg; stir in spinach, remaining oil, cottage cheese, Parmesan cheese and remaining salt; mix well.

6. Spread half the meat mixture in pan. Spread with half the noodles; cover with spinach mixture; top with remaining noodles. Pour remaining meat mixture on top.

7. Cover pan with aluminum foil; bake in preheated oven for 45 minutes.

8. Discard foil; arrange strips of American cheese on top. Bake for 5 minutes longer.

Bette Nordstrom, Woman's Club,
Annandale, Pa.

HACIENDA HAMBURG

Serves 4

  ½ cup olive oil
  1 pound ground beef
  ¾ cup chopped onions
  1 cup chopped celery
  1½ teaspoons salt
  ¼ teaspoon pepper
    Dash of orégano
  1-pound 4-ounce can tomatoes, undrained
  ¾ cup sliced pitted ripe olives
  2 cups wide noodles
  1 cup diced American cheese

1. Heat oil in large skillet; brown beef over medium heat, stirring occasionally.

2. Add onions and celery; sauté for 5 minutes. Stir in remaining ingredients. Cover; bring to boil over medium heat.

3. Stir thoroughly. Simmer, covered, for 20 minutes, or until tender.

Mabel V. Lewis, Community Woman's Club,
Annandale, Va.

JACKPOT NOODLE

Serves 6

  2 tablespoons shortening
  1 pound ground beef
  ¼ cup chopped onion
  10½-ounce can condensed tomato soup
  1½ cups water
  2 cups medium noodles
    Salt and pepper to taste
  1-pound 4-ounce can cream-style corn
  ¼ cup chopped ripe olives
  1½ cups grated American cheese
  1 cup fresh bread crumbs
  ¼ cup melted butter or margarine

1. Preheat oven to 350° F. Grease 2-quart casserole.

2. Melt shortening in large skillet; sauté beef and onion over medium heat until meat is browned.

3. Stir in soup, water and noodles. Cook over low heat, stirring frequently, until noodles are tender.

4. Season with salt and pepper; stir in corn, olives and cheese. Turn into casserole; sprinkle with crumbs and butter or margarine.

5. Bake in preheated oven for 45 minutes.

Lucille Warren, Women's Club, Braintree, Mass.

ROUND STEAK ROYALE

Serves 4 to 6

  ¼ cup butter or margarine
  1-pound round steak, cut into 1-inch cubes
  1 clove garlic, crushed
  1 medium onion, chopped
  1½ teaspoons salt
  ¼ teaspoon pepper
  4-ounce can mushroom stems and pieces, undrained
  1 bay leaf
  1 teaspoon Worcestershire
  1½ cups water
  8-ounce package medium noodles, cooked, drained and rinsed
  ½ cup grated Parmesan cheese
  ½ cup fresh bread crumbs

1. Melt butter or margarine in large skillet or Dutch oven; sauté beef, garlic and onion over medium heat until meat is browned on all sides.

2. Stir in salt, pepper, mushrooms, bay leaf, Worcestershire and water. Bring to boil; cover; simmer for 40 minutes, or until meat is tender.

3. Meanwhile, preheat oven to 375° F. Grease 3-quart casserole.

4. Discard bay leaf; stir noodles into meat mixture. Turn into casserole; sprinkle with cheese and crumbs.

5. Bake in preheated oven for 20 minutes.

Mary H. Foster, Woman's Club,
Van Nuys, Calif.

SPANISH DELIGHT

Serves 4 to 6

  ¼ cup shortening
  ½ cup chopped onions
  2 green peppers, seeded and chopped
  1½ pounds ground beef
  6-ounce can tomato paste
  2 4-ounce cans mushrooms, drained
  8-ounce can whole-kernel corn
  2 tablespoons chili sauce
  8-ounce package wide noodles, cooked, drained and rinsed
  ½ pound shredded mild cheese
  ¼ cup sliced stuffed olives

1. Melt shortening in skillet; sauté onions and green peppers until onions are golden brown. Add beef; cook until lightly browned, stirring occasionally. Add tomato paste, mushrooms, corn and chili sauce; heat.

2. Preheat oven to 300° F.

3. Mix meat sauce with noodles; turn into 2-quart baking dish. Sprinkle with cheese and olives.

4. Bake in preheated oven for 20 minutes.

Mrs. Homer Garner, Monday Study Club,
Poplar Bluffs, Mo.

BAKED DRIED BEEF AND NOODLES

Serves 8

2 cups Thin White Sauce (p. 441)
1 cup grated sharp Cheddar cheese
Salt and pepper to taste
8-ounce package fine noodles,
  cooked, drained and rinsed
½ pound dried beef

1. Preheat oven to 350° F. Grease 2½-quart casserole.
2. Put Thin White Sauce in saucepan. Add cheese; cook over medium heat, stirring frequently, until melted.
3. Remove from heat. Season with salt and pepper. Stir in noodles and beef; turn into casserole.
4. Bake in preheated oven for 30 minutes.

Mrs. C. Edward Thorney, Woman's Club, Wilmette, Ill.

NOODLES WITH FRANKFURTERS

Serves 4 to 6

8-ounce package wide noodles
4 tablespoons butter
1 pound skinless frankfurters
1 large onion, sliced
4 tablespoons flour
2½ cups canned tomatoes
1 teaspoon sugar
1 teaspoon prepared mustard
Salt and pepper to taste

1. Cook noodles according to package directions. Drain; rinse; keep warm.
2. Melt butter in saucepan; brown frankfurters and onion. Remove frankfurters; keep hot.
3. Stir flour into saucepan. Stir in remaining ingredients. Simmer for 10 to 15 minutes.
4. Arrange frankfurters on noodles; cover with sauce.

Mary Rouse, Tuesday Club, Dunshore, Pa.

MAZETTI

Serves 12

¾ cup finely chopped celery
½ cup butter
1 cup minced onions
¾ cup minced green pepper
1 pound ground lean pork
1 pound ground beef
1½ teaspoons salt
½ teaspoon pepper
12-ounce package wide noodles
4-ounce can sliced mushrooms,
  undrained
2 10½-ounce cans condensed tomato
  soup
Grated Parmesan cheese

1. In saucepan cook celery in boiling salted water to cover for 15 minutes, or until tender. Drain.
2. Melt ¼ cup of the butter in large skillet; sauté onions and green pepper for 5 minutes. Stir in pork, beef, salt and pepper; cook until meat loses red color.

3. Cook noodles according to package directions. Drain; rinse; turn into 3-quart casserole. Toss with remaining butter.
4. Stir in meat mixture, celery, mushrooms and soup. Mix well; sprinkle with cheese. Cover; refrigerate.
5. When ready to serve, preheat oven to 350° F.
6. Bake, uncovered, in preheated oven for 45 minutes.

Mrs. Walter Vreeland, Pueblo Junior Woman's Club, Tucson, Ariz.

NOODLE CASSEROLE WITH PORK

Serves 4

1 tablespoon butter or margarine
1-pound pork tenderloin, cut
  into thin strips
3 tablespoons chopped green pepper
1½-ounce envelope cream of
  mushroom soup
2 cups milk
½ cup water
¼ cup crumbled blue cheese
2 cups cooked medium noodles
Chopped parsley

1. Preheat oven to 350° F. Grease 10 x 6 x 1½-inch baking pan.
2. Melt butter or margarine in large skillet; brown pork on all sides. Add green pepper; cover; cook over low heat for 20 minutes. Remove meat; set aside.
3. Stir soup mix into fat remaining in skillet. Slowly stir in milk and water. Cook over low heat, stirring constantly, until sauce is thickened and smooth. Stir in cheese.
4. Arrange noodles in pan; top with pork. Pour sauce over pork and noodles; sprinkle with parsley.
5. Bake in preheated oven for 30 minutes.

Florence Martin, Woman's Club, Redwood City, Calif.

BULGARIAN NOODLES

Serves 4

Serve with Mushroom Sauce (p. 447), if desired.

8-ounce package wide noodles
2 tablespoons butter or margarine
4 onions, chopped
1 pound lean pork, coarsely ground
½ pound sharp cheese, coarsely grated
1 cup tomato sauce
½ cup chili sauce
Salt and pepper to taste

1. Preheat oven to 325° F. Grease shallow casserole.
2. Melt butter or margarine in skillet; sauté onions until transparent.
3. Combine remaining ingredients; stir in onions; mix; turn into casserole.
4. Bake in preheated oven for 45 minutes.

Mrs. A. B. Nixon, New Century Club, Wilmington, Del.

NOODLE, COTTAGE CHEESE AND HAM CASSEROLE

Serves 6

1 cup medium noodles
2 tablespoons butter or margarine
¼ cup chopped green pepper
½ cup chopped celery
½ cup chopped onions
2 tablespoons flour
2 cups milk
½ teaspoon salt
1½ cups cream-style cottage cheese
1 cup chopped cooked ham

1. Preheat oven to 350° F. Grease 2-quart casserole.
2. Cook noodles according to package directions. Drain; rinse.
3. Melt butter or margarine in large skillet; sauté green pepper, celery and onions over medium heat for 5 minutes.
4. Blend in flour. Gradually stir in milk; cook over medium heat, stirring constantly, until thickened and smooth.
5. Stir in remaining ingredients. Add noodles; toss lightly. Turn into casserole.
6. Bake in preheated oven for 30 minutes, or until golden and bubbling.

Senior Woman's Club, Beaver Falls, Pa.

NOODLES AND ZUCCHINI ITALIANO

Serves 6 to 8

½ pound sausage meat
3 tablespoons olive oil
2 tablespoons butter
1 cup chopped onions
1 clove garlic, crushed
1 green pepper, cut into strips
1-pound can tomatoes
8-ounce can tomato sauce
1 teaspoon salt
⅛ teaspoon pepper
1 teaspoon orégano
½ teaspoon crushed red pepper
1¼ pounds zucchini, sliced
8-ounce package medium noodles
2 cups grated Cheddar cheese

1. Shape sausage meat into ½-inch balls. Brown on all sides in skillet over low heat; drain off excess fat as it accumulates.
2. Meanwhile, prepare tomato sauce: Heat oil and butter in large skillet; sauté onions, garlic and green pepper for 5 minutes. Stir in tomatoes, tomato sauce, salt, pepper, orégano and red pepper. Simmer for 5 minutes. Stir in zucchini; cover; simmer for 15 minutes, or until zucchini is tender.
3. Meanwhile, cook noodles according to package directions; drain; rinse.
4. Add noodles, sausage balls and cheese to tomato sauce. Simmer, uncovered, stirring occasionally, until cheese is melted.

Mrs. Hugh S. Ginger, Coco Plum Woman's Club, Coral Gables, Fla.

Filled Pasta Dishes

LASAGNE

Serves 8 to 10

3 tablespoons olive oil
1 cup finely chopped onions
1 clove garlic, crushed
1 pound ground beef
2 teaspoons salt
1-pound 14-ounce can tomatoes
8-ounce can tomato sauce
6-ounce can tomato paste
¾ cup water
½ teaspoon basil
½ teaspoon orégano
1 teaspoon sugar
1 tablespoon dried parsley flakes
1-pound package lasagne (wide noodles)
1 pound ricotta cheese
1 egg
1 pound Mozzarella cheese, thinly sliced
1 cup grated Parmesan cheese

1. Heat 2 tablespoons of the oil in Dutch oven or large heavy saucepan; sauté onions and garlic for 5 minutes. Stir in beef; cook over medium heat until browned.
2. Add salt, tomatoes, tomato sauce, tomato paste, water, basil, orégano, sugar and parsley flakes. Bring sauce to boil; then simmer for 45 minutes.
3. Meanwhile, cook lasagne according to package directions. Add remaining oil while cooking lasagne, to prevent it from sticking. Drain; rinse; cool.
4. In bowl blend ricotta cheese and egg.
5. Preheat oven to 375° F. Grease 13 x 9½ x 2-inch baking pan.
6. In pan arrange alternate layers of sauce, lasagne, ricotta cheese and Mozzarella cheese, finishing with sauce. Sprinkle with Parmesan cheese.
7. Bake in preheated oven for 35 minutes.
8. Let stand for 10 minutes before serving.

Susan Wilkinson, Junior Woman's Club, Jacksonville, Fla.

OLD-FASHIONED NEAPOLITAN LASAGNE

Serves 4 to 6

2 slices bacon, diced
¼ cup butter
1 clove garlic
1 medium onion, finely chopped
2 tablespoons finely chopped carrot
1 tablespoon finely chopped celery
½ pound ground beef
2 Italian sausages without casing
½ cup dry white wine
¼ teaspoon marjoram
2 cups fresh or canned peeled tomatoes, diced
6-ounce can tomato paste
Salt and pepper
1 tablespoon chopped parsley
8 ounces ricotta cheese

1 egg
½ cup grated Parmesan cheese
8 ounces lasagne (wide noodles),
cooked, drained and rinsed

1. Preheat oven to 375° F. Grease 10 x 6 x 1½-inch baking pan.
2. Sauté bacon, butter, garlic, onion, carrot and celery in skillet for 5 minutes.
3. Discard garlic; add beef and sausages; cook until meat is browned. Stir in wine; cook until evaporated.
4. Add marjoram, tomatoes, tomato paste, salt and pepper to taste; simmer, uncovered, for 30 minutes, stirring occasionally. Stir in parsley; correct seasoning.
5. In bowl blend ricotta cheese, egg, Parmesan cheese, ¼ teaspoon of the salt and dash of pepper.
6. In pan arrange alternate layers of lasagne, meat sauce and cheese mixture finishing with sauce.
7. Bake in preheated oven for 25 minutes.

Mrs. William C. Cuartero, North Jacksonville Woman's Club, Jacksonville, Fla.

MANICOTTI

Serves 4 to 6

4 eggs
1 cup presifted flour
¾ cup water
  Butter
1 pound ricotta cheese
1 pound Mozzarella cheese, grated
¼ cup chopped parsley
2 cups tomato sauce
½ cup grated Parmesan cheese

1. Preheat oven to 350° F. Grease 13 x 9½ x 2-inch baking pan.
2. Prepare pancake batter: In mixing bowl combine 2 of the eggs, flour and water; beat until smooth.
3. Melt about 1 teaspoon butter in 6-inch skillet. When it starts to brown, pour in about 1 tablespoon batter, swirling skillet to coat bottom. Cook over medium heat for about 2 minutes. Turn; brown other side. Cool on absorbent paper. Repeat with remaining batter.
4. Prepare filling: In mixing bowl combine remaining eggs, ricotta cheese, Mozzarella cheese and parsley; mix well.
5. Spread pancakes with filling; roll up.
6. Arrange in pan; cover with tomato sauce. Sprinkle with Parmesan cheese.
7. Bake in preheated oven for 30 minutes.

Audrey Testa, Pine Ridge Woman's Club, Fairfax, Va.

CANNELLONI WITH CHICKEN FILLING

Serves 4

2 tablespoons olive oil
2 tablespoons minced onion
2 tablespoons minced celery
2 tablespoons minced carrot
2 tablespoons minced parsley
2 cups ground cooked chicken
¾ teaspoon salt

¼ teaspoon orégano
¼ teaspoon basil
½ teaspoon white pepper
¾ cup dry white wine
2 cups Thick White Sauce (p. 441)
8 cannelloni
4 tablespoons tomato sauce
½ cup cream
½ cup grated Parmesan cheese

1. Prepare filling: Heat oil in skillet; stew onion, celery, carrot and parsley for about 10 minutes, or until tender. Add chicken, salt, orégano, basil, pepper and wine. Bring to boil; then simmer until wine is reduced by half. Stir in ½ cup of the thick White Sauce.
2. Preheat oven to 450° F. Grease baking dish.
3. Cook cannelloni in boiling salted water for 8 minutes. Drain; rinse with cold water. Put 2 tablespoons filling on each cannelloni. Roll up; arrange in a layer in dish.
4. Stir tomato sauce and cream into remaining Thick White Sauce. Pour over cannelloni; sprinkle with cheese.
5. Bake in preheated oven for 10 minutes.

A. S.

RAVIOLI WITH CHEESE FILLING

Serves 8

6 cups presifted flour
  Salt
6 eggs
1 cup lukewarm water
1 pound ricotta cheese
  Dash of pepper
  Grated Parmesan cheese
1 tablespoon finely chopped parsley
  Tomato sauce

1. Onto board sift together flour and ¾ teaspoon salt. Make a well in center of flour; put 4 of the eggs in it. Mix eggs lightly with fingers; then work in flour. Gradually knead in water. Cover with warm bowl for 15 minutes.
2. Knead again until dough is smooth; re-cover with warm bowl.
3. Repeat twice more.
4. Roll out half the dough ⅛ inch thick on lightly floured board; set aside. Roll out second half of dough ⅛ inch thick.
5. Meanwhile, prepare Ricotta Cheese Filling for Ravioli: In mixing bowl mash ricotta cheese with fork. Add remaining eggs, ½ teaspoon salt, pepper, ½ cup Parmesan cheese and parsley; mix until smooth.
6. Drop filling by teaspoons about 3 inches apart onto one of dough halves. Cover with other dough half; gently press around each mound of filling to form little filled squares. Cut apart with pastry wheel.
7. Cook in boiling water in very large saucepan for about 15 minutes, or until tender.

8. Drain; turn onto serving dish. Top with tomato sauce; sprinkle with grated Parmesan cheese, if desired.

Mrs. Walter Darby, Neptunian Club,
Manhattan Beach, Calif.

MEAT FILLING FOR RAVIOLI

¼ cup cooking oil
1 small onion, minced
2 tablespoons minced parsley
2 cups ground cooked beef
2 eggs, lightly beaten
Salt and pepper to taste

1. Heat oil in skillet; sauté onion and parsley until onion is transparent.
2. Add meat and eggs; cook for about 5 minutes, stirring constantly. Season with salt and pepper.

CHICKEN AND SPINACH FILLING FOR RAVIOLI

1 cup cooked spinach, well drained
1 cup cooked chicken
¼ cup grated Parmesan cheese
Salt and pepper to taste

Put spinach and chicken through medium blade of meat grinder. Stir in cheese, salt and pepper.

A. S.

RIGATONI

Serves 10 to 12

1-pound package rigatoni
2 tablespoons olive oil
1½ pounds ground beef
2 10-ounce packages frozen chopped spinach, defrosted
1 cup grated Romano cheese
2 eggs, lightly beaten
Salt and pepper to taste
2 quarts Tomato and Meat Sauce (p. 507)

1. In large saucepan cook rigatoni according to package directions. Drain; rinse; cool.
2. Meanwhile, prepare filling: Heat oil in skillet; brown beef over medium heat. Stir in spinach; simmer for 5 minutes. Remove from heat; stir in ¼ cup of the cheese. Cool. Stir in eggs; season with salt and pepper.
3. Stuff each rigatoni with filling.
4. Preheat oven to 375° F. Grease 13 x 9½ x 2-inch baking pan.
5. Arrange a layer of rigatoni in pan; spoon a generous layer of Tomato and Meat Sauce on top. Sprinkle with ¼ cup of the cheese. Repeat layers, finishing with sauce. Sprinkle with remaining cheese.
6. Bake in preheated oven for 40 minutes.

Nell Rees, Finneytown Junior Women's Club,
Cincinnati, Ohio

Macaroni

AUNT LYDIA'S MACARONI AND CHEESE

Serves 4

½ cup elbow macaroni
1 cup sharp Cheddar cheese, diced
1 egg, lightly beaten
4 salted crackers, crushed
¼ cup heavy cream
Salt and pepper to taste
2 tablespoons butter or margarine

1. Preheat oven to 350° F. Grease 1-quart casserole.
2. Cook macaroni according to package directions. Drain; rinse; turn into mixing bowl.
3. Add cheese, egg, half the crackers and cream. Season with salt and pepper; mix lightly. Turn into casserole. Sprinkle with remaining crackers; dot with butter or margarine.
4. Bake in preheated oven for 30 minutes.

Mrs. Clyde Beale, Woman's Club,
Jainesville, Fla.

MACARONI AND CHEESE SUPREME

Serves 6

3½ cups cooked elbow macaroni
4-ounce can sliced mushrooms, drained
¼ cup chopped pimientos
1¼ cups cubed American cheese
¾ cup evaporated milk
3 tablespoons grated onion
2 teaspoons dry mustard
1 teaspoon salt
¼ teaspoon Worcestershire
4 slices American cheese
1 large tomato, sliced

1. Preheat oven to 350° F. Grease 1½-quart casserole.
2. Put macaroni, mushrooms, pimientos and cubed cheese in casserole; mix well.
3. Combine milk, onion, mustard, salt and Worcestershire. Pour over macaroni mixture. Top with cheese slices and tomato.
4. Bake in preheated oven for 30 minutes.

Mrs. John Zodrow, Eastmont Junior
Women's Club, East Wenatchee, Wash.

DEVILED MACARONI

Serves 4 to 6

10½-ounce can condensed cream of mushroom soup
¼ cup grated sharp Cheddar cheese
¼ cup chopped pimientos
¼ teaspoon salt
2 teaspoons prepared mustard
8 ounces elbow macaroni, cooked, drained and rinsed
4 eggs, hard-cooked and sliced
2 tablespoons melted butter
¼ cup bread crumbs

1. Preheat oven to 350° F. Grease 2-quart casserole.

2. In mixing bowl blend soup, cheese, pimientos, salt and mustard. Add macaroni; mix well.

3. Pour half the macaroni mixture into casserole; cover with eggs; top with remaining macaroni mixture.

4. In small bowl mix butter and crumbs; sprinkle on macaroni mixture.

5. Bake in preheated oven for 40 minutes.

Florence Martin, Woman's Club,
Redwood City, Calif.

CHESTERFIELD PIE

Serves 4

Serve with Mushroom Cream Sauce (p. 447) if desired.

1 cup cooked elbow macaroni
1 cup soft bread crumbs
1 cup grated sharp cheese
3 tablespoons chopped green pepper
3 tablespoons chopped pimiento
1½ cups cream
3 eggs, separated
Salt and pepper to taste

1. Preheat oven to 350° F. Grease 1½-quart casserole.

2. Combine macaroni, crumbs, cheese, green pepper and pimiento.

3. Combine cream and egg yolks. Stir into macaroni mixture; season with salt and pepper.

4. Beat egg whites until stiff but not dry; fold into macaroni mixture.

5. Turn into casserole; bake in preheated oven for 50 minutes, or until set.

Mrs. Dan Traner, Woman's Club,
Ogonquit, Me.

MACARONI LOAF

Serves 6

½ cup butter
1 cup heavy cream
3 eggs
1 cup fresh bread crumbs
2 tablespoons chopped parsley
1 tablespoon grated onion
½ cup grated Cheddar cheese
4-ounce can pimientos, drained
and diced
1 teaspoon salt
2 cups cooked elbow macaroni,
chopped
Mushroom Cream Sauce (p. 447)

1. Preheat oven to 350° F. Grease 1½-quart mold.

2. In mixing bowl cream butter until soft. Add cream; beat until blended. Add eggs; beat until smooth.

3. Stir in all remaining ingredients except Mushroom Cream Sauce; mix well; turn into mold.

4. Set mold in pan of hot water; bake in preheated oven for 1 hour.

5. Let stand for 5 minutes; unmold onto serving dish; serve with Mushroom Cream Sauce.

Mrs. J. C. Davis, Junior and Senior
Woman's Clubs, Grundy, Va.

MACARONI OMELET WITH CREOLE SAUCE

Serves 4

1 cup elbow macaroni
½ cup finely diced sharp American
cheese
½ teaspoon salt
4 eggs, separated
2 tablespoons butter
Quick Creole Sauce (p. 443)

1. Cook macaroni according to package directions until just tender. Drain; rinse.

2. Combine cheese and macaroni; set aside.

3. Beat egg yolks with salt until thickened and pale. Stir into macaroni mixture.

4. Beat egg whites until stiff but not dry; fold into macaroni mixture.

5. Melt butter in heavy 10-inch skillet. Pour in macaroni mixture; cook over low heat for about 20 minutes, or until set and lightly browned on bottom.

6. Loosen omelet; cut partly in half through center; fold in half.

7. Turn onto hot serving platter; serve with Quick Creole Sauce.

Mrs. Claude Williamson, Junior Women's Club,
Rye, N.H.

MACARONI RING

Serves 6

1½ cups cooked elbow macaroni
1 cup grated Parmesan cheese
1 cup fresh bread crumbs
1 tablespoon finely chopped parsley
3 tablespoons finely chopped
pimiento
1 tablespoon grated onion
3 tablespoons melted butter or
margarine
1 egg, lightly beaten
1 teaspoon salt
1 cup scalded milk
⅛ teaspoon pepper

1. Preheat oven to 375° F. Grease 8-inch ring mold well.

2. Chop macaroni; turn into mixing bowl.

3. Add cheese, crumbs, parsley, pimiento and onion; mix well. Add remaining ingredients; mix well. Turn into mold.

4. Bake in preheated oven for 35 minutes.

5. Let stand for 5 minutes; unmold onto serving dish.

Mrs. P. W. Metz, Woman's Club,
Basin, Wyo.

MACARONI AND CHEESE WITH OLIVES

Serves 6

    8 ounces macaroni
    ½ pound sharp cheese, shredded
    ¼ cup chopped pimientos
    ½ cup chopped green olives
    ¼ cup juice from olive jar
    ¼ cup chopped parsley
      Celery salt and paprika to taste

1. Cook macaroni according to package directions until tender. Drain; rinse.
2. Preheat oven to 350° F. Grease 3-quart casserole.
3. Combine half the cheese, pimientos, olives, olive juice, parsley and macaroni. Pour into casserole; sprinkle with celery salt and paprika. Top with remaining cheese.
4. Bake in preheated oven for 30 minutes.

Mrs. J. Raynn Carrow, New Century Club, Wilmington, Del.

CHEESE-A-RONI CASSEROLE

Serves 4

    8 ounces elbow macaroni
    3 tablespoons butter or margarine
    1 medium onion, sliced
    ½ green pepper, diced
    1 stalk celery, diced
    1-pound 4-ounce can tomatoes
    1 bay leaf, crushed
    1 teaspoon salt
    ¼ teaspoon pepper
    6-ounce can tomato paste
    ¼ cup water
    1 cup grated Cheddar cheese
    2 slices American cheese, cut
      into strips

1. Preheat oven to 350° F. Grease 2-quart casserole.
2. Cook macaroni according to package directions. Drain; rinse; turn into casserole.
3. Meanwhile, melt butter or margarine in large skillet; sauté onion, green pepper and celery for 5 minutes. Stir in tomatoes, bay leaf, salt, pepper, tomato paste and water. Bring to boil; then simmer for 5 minutes.
4. Remove from heat; stir in grated cheese. Pour over macaroni; mix.
5. Bake in preheated oven for 45 minutes.
6. Arrange cheese strips on top; bake for 5 minutes longer.

Junior Women's Club, Porterville, Calif.

MACARONI DELIGHT

Serves 4

    1 cup macaroni
    1 cup soft bread crumbs
    1½ cups milk
    ¾ cup butter
    ½ cup shredded sharp cheese
    1 pimiento, chopped
    1 teaspoon grated onion
      Salt
    3 eggs, well beaten
    ½ cup chopped green pepper
    2 tablespoons minced onion
    2 tablespoons flour
    1 cup hot milk
      Pepper to taste

1. Cook macaroni according to package directions. Drain; rinse; toss with crumbs.
2. Preheat oven to 350° F. Grease 1½-quart baking dish.
3. Heat the 1½ cups milk. Add ½ cup of the butter, cheese, pimiento, grated onion and 1 teaspoon salt; cook, stirring constantly, until cheese is melted. Stir into macaroni. Stir in eggs.
4. Pour into dish; bake in preheated oven for 45 minutes.
5. Meanwhile, melt remaining butter in saucepan; sauté green pepper and minced onion until tender. Stir in flour. Gradually stir in hot milk; cook, stirring constantly, until sauce is thickened and smooth. Season with salt and pepper. Cook over low heat for 5 minutes.
6. Cut macaroni into squares; serve with sauce.

Mrs. Paul A. Wolk, Woman's Club, Whitefish, Mont.

MACARONI, CORN AND OYSTER CASSEROLE

Serves 6

    2 cups cooked macaroni
    1-pound can whole-kernel corn,
      drained
    2 8-ounce cans oysters, drained
    2 cups light cream
    1 teaspoon salt
    ¼ teaspoon pepper
    ¼ teaspoon dry mustard
      Dash of Tabasco
    ½ cup grated Cheddar cheese

1. Preheat oven to 350° F. Grease 2-quart casserole.
2. In mixing bowl combine macaroni, corn and oysters; mix well.
3. Combine cream, salt, pepper, mustard and Tabasco.
4. Turn macaroni mixture into casserole; top with cream mixture.
5. Bake in preheated oven for 20 minutes.
6. Sprinkle with cheese; bake for 10 minutes longer.

Kate Miller, Woman's Club, Culbertson, Neb.

ASPARAGUS MACARONI CASSEROLE

Serves 6

    8 ounces elbow macaroni
    1-pound can asparagus tips
      Milk
    ¼ cup butter or margarine
    ¼ cup presifted flour
      Salt and pepper to taste
    1 cup grated American cheese
    2 cups diced cooked chicken
      or turkey

1. Preheat oven to 375° F. Grease 2-quart casserole.
2. Cook macaroni according to package directions. Drain; rinse.

3. Drain asparagus; reserve liquid; add milk to total 2 cups.

4. Melt butter or margarine in saucepan; blend in flour. Gradually stir in reserved asparagus liquid; cook over medium heat, stirring constantly, until sauce is thickened and smooth.

5. Season with salt and pepper. Stir in cheese; cook, stirring, until melted.

6. Arrange alternate layers of macaroni, asparagus, chicken or turkey and sauce in casserole, finishing with sauce.

7. Cover; bake in preheated oven for 35 minutes.

Mrs. Jerome Stevens, Study Club, Washburn, N.D.

MACARONI HAMBURGER UPSIDE-DOWN CASSEROLE

2½ cups elbow macaroni
3 tablespoons butter
½ cup minced onions
1 pound ground beef
8-ounce can tomato sauce
2 teaspoons salt
½ teaspoon pepper
½ teaspoon orégano
8-ounce package grated cheese
3 eggs, lightly beaten
¾ cup milk

1. Cook macaroni according to package directions until just tender. Drain; rinse.

2. Melt butter in skillet; sauté onions until transparent. Add beef, cook, stirring, until browned. Stir in tomato sauce, salt, pepper and orégano; simmer for 10 minutes.

3. Preheat oven to 350° F. Grease 2-quart casserole.

4. Spread meat mixture in casserole. Toss macaroni with cheese; spread on meat, packing down well.

5. Combine eggs and milk; pour over macaroni.

6. Bake in preheated oven for 1½ hours. Let stand for 15 minutes; loosen edges; carefully unmold onto serving plate. Serve in pie-shaped wedges.

Mrs. Robert Bittourna, Junior Woman's Club, Diamond Bar, Calif.

OVERNIGHT ITALIAN CASSEROLE

Serves 8 to 10

8 ounces elbow macaroni
1 cup butter or margarine
3 medium onions, finely chopped
1 green pepper, chopped
2 pounds ground beef
1 clove garlic, crushed
3 8-ounce cans tomato sauce
12-ounce can whole-kernel corn, drained
4-ounce can sliced mushroom, undrained
1 tablespoon brown sugar
1 tablespoon chili powder
1 tablespoon Worcestershire
2 teaspoons salt
¼ teaspoon black pepper

1. Day before, cook macaroni according to package directions. Drain; rinse.

2. Grease 3-quart casserole.

3. Melt butter or margarine in large skillet; sauté onions and green pepper until soft. Add beef and garlic; cook until meat is browned. Stir in remaining ingredients.

4. Turn meat mixture into casserole. Add macaroni; toss lightly to mix.

5. Cover; refrigerate overnight, to allow flavors to mellow.

6. Next day, preheat oven to 325° F. Place casserole in preheated oven; bake for 1½ hours.

Mrs. George G. Townsend, La Petite Fortnightly Club, Forest, Miss.

MACARONI BURGER CASSEROLE

Serves 4

1 pound ground beef
1 large onion, chopped
1 green pepper, chopped
Salt and chili powder to taste
10½-ounce can condensed tomato soup
1-pound can cream-style corn
1-pound can green beans, drained
1½ cups cooked macaroni
½ cup diced Cheddar cheese
2 tablespoons butter

1. Preheat oven to 350° F.

2. Sauté beef, onion and green pepper in skillet until meat loses red color and onion is transparent. Add salt and chili powder.

3. Add soup, corn and beans; mix well. Add macaroni and cheese; mix lightly.

4. Turn into 2-quart casserole; dot with butter.

5. Bake in preheated oven for 20 minutes, or until cheese is melted.

Mrs. Ellis Schmidt, Tri L C Club, Fleming, Colo.

MACARONI AND MEAT BALLS

Serves 6

1 pound ground beef
1 egg
½ cup fresh bread crumbs
Salt
Pepper to taste
2 tablespoons butter or margarine
8 ounces elbow macaroni
10½-ounce can condensed tomato soup
1½ teaspoons chili powder

1. In mixing bowl combine beef, egg, crumbs, salt to taste and pepper; mix well. Shape into 1½-inch balls.

2. Melt butter or margarine in large skillet; brown meat balls on all sides over medium heat. Add water to cover. Bring to boil. Stir in macaroni; cover; cook over medium heat for 10 minutes.

3. Stir in soup, chili powder and ½ teaspoon salt. Cover; simmer for 5 minutes.

Mrs. Donald Larson, Woman's Club, Sterling, Colo.

PASTICCIO WITH KIMA
(Baked Macaroni with Greek Meat Sauce)

Serves 6 to 8

½ cup butter
1 large onion, chopped
1 pound ground beef
8-ounce can tomato sauce
1 teaspoon salt
¼ teaspoon pepper
½ teaspoon cinnamon
¾ cup red wine
1-pound package elbow macaroni
3 eggs, lightly beaten
2 cups grated Parmesan cheese
3 recipes for Thick White Sauce
   (p. 441)
1 teaspoon dry mustard

1. Melt 2 tablespoons of the butter in large skillet; sauté onion for 5 minutes. Stir in beef; cook over medium heat, stirring occasionally, until meat is browned and crumbly.
2. Add tomato sauce, salt, pepper, cinnamon and wine. Bring to boil; cover; simmer for 20 minutes.
3. In large saucepan cook macaroni according to package directions. Drain; rinse; turn into mixing bowl.
4. Add eggs, ½ cup of the cheese and remaining butter; mix well.
5. Preheat oven to 375° F. Grease 13 x 9½ x 2-inch baking pan.
6. Prepare Thick White Sauce in saucepan. Stir in 1 cup of the cheese and mustard.
7. Turn macaroni into baking pan. Top with meat sauce. Cover with sauce. Sprinkle with remaining cheese.
8. Bake in preheated oven for 40 minutes.
9. Cool for 5 minutes; cut into squares to serve.

*Leah Petropoulos, Woman's Club,
Prospect Heights, Ill.*

MACARONI CHIPPED BEEF CASSEROLE

Serves 6

10½-ounce can condensed cream
   of mushroom soup
1 cup milk
1 teaspoon dry mustard
1 small onion, finely chopped
½ pound Cheddar cheese, diced
¾ pound chipped beef, minced
4 eggs, hard-cooked and diced
4 cups cooked elbow macaroni

1. Preheat oven to 350° F. Grease 2-quart casserole.
2. In mixing bowl combine soup, milk, mustard and onion.
3. Add remaining ingredients; mix well. Turn into casserole.
4. Bake in preheated oven for 30 minutes.

Elsie H. Clark, Fortnightly Club, Dawson, N.D.

SCALLOPED HAM AND MACARONI

Serves 4 to 6

2 cups Thin White Sauce (p. 441)
1 cup finely chopped boiled ham
½ teaspoon dry mustard
   Salt and pepper to taste
   Dash of cayenne
1 egg, lightly beaten
4 cups cooked elbow macaroni
½ cup bread crumbs
3 tablespoons butter or margarine

1. Preheat oven to 400° F. Grease 2-quart casserole.
2. Heat Thin White Sauce; stir in ham and mustard. Season with salt and pepper; stir in cayenne and egg.
3. Arrange alternater layers of sauce and macaroni in casserole. Sprinkle with crumbs; dot with butter or margarine.
4. Bake in preheated oven for 25 minutes.

*Mrs. F. G. Wright, Roselle and Roselle Park
Clio Club, Roselle, N.J.*

RIGATONI WITH SAUSAGE

Serves 4 to 6

¼ cup olive oil
1 pound Italian sausage, sliced
1 large onion, sliced
1 clove garlic, crushed
1 pound mushrooms, sliced
1 bay leaf
1½ teaspoons salt
¼ teaspoon pepper
6-ounce can tomato paste
3 cups water
1 teaspoon orégano
1 teaspoon sugar
1-pound package rigatoni
½ cup grated Parmesan cheese
¼ pound Muenster cheese, sliced

1. Heat oil in large skillet; sauté sausage, onion and garlic until meat is browned. Add mushrooms, bay leaf, salt, pepper, tomato paste, water, orégano and sugar. Bring to boil. Cover; simmer for 1 hour, stirring occasionally.
2. Meanwhile, cook rigatoni according to package directions. Drain; rinse.
3. Preheat oven to 400° F. Grease 3-quart casserole.
4. Arrange rigatoni in casserole; top with sauce. Sprinkle with Parmesan cheese; cover with Muenster cheese.
5. Bake in preheated oven for 20 minutes, or until cheese is melted.

*Barbara Dion, Junior Woman's Club,
Simsbury, Conn.*

Spaghetti

RING OF PLENTY

Serves 6 to 8

Fill center with creamed vegetable or fish.

8 ounces spaghetti
2 cups diced mild cheese

2 cups soft bread crumbs
3 tablespoons minced pimiento
2 tablespoons chopped onion
2 eggs, lightly beaten
¼ teaspoon pepper
2 tablespoons minced parsley
6 tablespoons butter
2 cups hot milk
2 teaspoons salt

1. Break spaghetti into short pieces; cook according to package directions. Drain; rinse.
2. Preheat oven to 350° F. Grease 10-inch ring mold.
3. Combine spaghetti and remaining ingredients.
4. Turn into mold. Set mold in pan containing 1 inch hot water. Bake in preheated oven for 35 minutes, or until set.
5. Unmold.

Mrs. L. E. Knoedler, Woman's Club,
Roswell, N.M.

SPAGHETTI GIOVANNI

Serves 4

3 tablespoons butter
1 large onion, minced
1 green pepper, finely chopped
½ cup mushrooms, sliced
2 cups canned tomatoes, drained
1½ cups flaked crab meat
1 cup sour cream
1 cup grated sharp cheese
8 ounces spaghetti, cooked, and rinsed

1. Preheat oven to 350° F. Grease 1½-quart casserole.
2. Melt butter in skillet; sauté onion, green pepper and mushrooms for about 5 minutes, or until wilted.
3. Add tomatoes, crab meat, sour cream, ½ cup of the cheese and spaghetti. Turn into casserole; sprinkle with remaining cheese.
4. Bake in preheated oven for 45 minutes.

Mrs. Charles Thompson, Junior Woman's Club,
Concord, Calif.

SAN FRANCISCO CHICKEN AND SPAGHETTI

Serves 8

1 cup butter or chicken fat
¾ cup presifted flour
1 quart chicken broth
1 cup milk
1 cup finely chopped celery
1 cup sliced mushrooms
4-ounce can pimientos, drained and chopped
6-ounce can tomato paste
2 cloves garlic, halved
Salt, pepper and orégano to taste
⅔ pound spaghetti, cooked, drained and rinsed

3 cups chopped cooked chicken
1 cup shredded sharp or grated Parmesan cheese

1. Melt butter or fat in saucepan. Stir in flour. Gradually stir in broth and milk; cook, stirring constantly, until thickened.
2. Add celery, mushrooms, pimientos, tomato paste, and garlic, salt, pepper and orégano. Stir to blend; remove from heat; set aside for 1 hour.
3. Preheat oven to 350° F. Grease 13 x 9½ x 2-inch baking pan.
4. Spread spaghetti in pan; sprinkle with chicken. Cover with sauce; top with cheese.
5. Bake in preheated oven for 45 minutes.

Mrs. Thomas S. Sterrett, Woman's Club,
Charlotte, N.C.

CHICKEN TETRAZZINI

Serves 10

4- to 5-pound stewing chicken
Salt
3 stalks celery, quartered
1 large onion, quartered
½ cup butter or margarine
½ pound mushrooms, sliced
⅓ cup presifted flour
1 cup heavy cream
3 tablespoons sherry
1½ teaspoons monosodium glutamate
1 cup grated Parmesan cheese
1-pound package spaghetti, cooked, drained and rinsed

1. Put chicken in Dutch oven or large heavy saucepan; add water to cover. Add 2 teaspoons salt, celery and onion. Bring to boil; cover; simmer for 2 hours, or until tender.
2. Drain chicken; reserve 3½ cups stock. Discard bones and skin; cut meat into bite-size pieces.
3. Prepare Tetrazzini Sauce: Melt butter or margarine in saucepan, sauté mushrooms for 5 minutes. Stir in flour. Gradually stir in reserved stock; cook over low heat, stirring constantly, until thickened and smooth. Stir in cream, sherry, monosodium glutamate, ½ teaspoons salt and ½ cup of the cheese. Simmer, stirring constantly, for 5 minutes.
4. Preheat oven to 425° F. Grease 4-quart casserole.
5. Arrange one-third of spaghetti in casserole; sprinkle with half the chicken; top with one-third of sauce. Repeat. Cover with remaining spaghetti; spoon rest of sauce over top. Sprinkle with remaining cheese.
6. Bake in preheated oven for 35 minutes.

Mrs. A. B. Chernosky, Sigma Sorosis Club,
Woodward, Okla.

MRS. STUART SYMINGTON'S CHICKEN TETRAZZINI

Serves 4

Butter
¼ pound mushrooms, thinly sliced
2 cups diced cooked chicken
2 cups heavy cream
1 tablespoon sherry
2 tablespoons white wine
Salt and pepper to taste
2 tablespoons flour
4 ounces thin spaghetti
2 tablespoons grated Parmesan cheese

1. Melt ¼ pound butter in skillet; sauté mushrooms for 2 to 3 minutes. Add chicken, cream, sherry, white wine, salt and pepper; bring to simmer.
2. Mix flour and 2 tablespoons butter to a smooth paste. Stir, bit by bit, into chicken mixture; cook, stirring constantly, until slightly thickened. Cook over low heat for 5 minutes.
3. Meanwhile, cook spaghetti according to package directions until just tender. Drain; rinse with cold water.
4. Preheat oven to 375° F. Grease shallow casserole. Spread spaghetti in casserole; pour chicken mixture over it. Sprinkle with cheese.
5. Bake in preheated oven for 20 minutes, or until golden.

NOTE: Medium noodles may be substituted for spaghetti in this recipe.

Mrs. Harry Leopold, Study Club, Auxvasse, Mo.

CUBAN SPAGHETTI

Serves 8

8 ounces spaghetti
14 slices bacon
1 pound ground beef
4 large onions, chopped
4 green peppers
3 teaspoons chopped garlic
Salt and pepper to taste
½ pound cheese, shredded

1. Cook spaghetti according to package directions until tender. Drain; rinse.
2. Cook bacon until crisp and golden. Drain on absorbent paper.
3. Pour off excess bacon drippings. Cook beef and onions in drippings remaining in pan until onions are transparent, and meat has lost red color.
4. Meanwhile, put green peppers, bacon and garlic through meat grinder.
5. Preheat oven to 325° F.
6. Combine spaghetti, meat mixture and green pepper mixture; season with salt and pepper. Turn into 2-quart casserole; sprinkle with cheese.
7. Bake in preheated oven for 1½ hours, stirring occasionally.

Mrs. Fred Durden, Junior Woman's Club, Forest Park, Ga.

DEVILED SPAGHETTI

Serves 4 to 6

1½ pounds ground beef
⅛ teaspoon red pepper
Chili powder to taste
¼ cup dried celery flakes
Salt to taste
8 ounces thin spaghetti
2 1-pound cans kidney beans, undrained

1. Brown beef well in skillet. Add water just to cover. Add red pepper, chili powder and celery flakes. Simmer for 1 hour, stirring frequently. Season with salt.
2. Cook spaghetti according to package directions. Drain; rinse.
3. Heat beans until steaming hot.
4. Make a nest of spaghetti on warm serving plate. Fill with beans; top with a generous serving of meat sauce.

Mrs. Roy E. Tomlinson, Women's Club, Richland, Wash.

SPAGHETTI WITH MEAT BALLS

Serves 4 to 6

2 slices bread
Water or milk
1 pound ground beef
½ pound ground pork
2 tablespoons chopped parsley
Grated cheese
1 egg
Salt and pepper to taste
¼ cup olive oil
2 cloves garlic, minced
1 medium onion, finely chopped
¼ cup dry red wine
1-pound 13-ounce can tomatoes, undrained
2 6-ounce cans tomato paste
1 bay leaf
Pinch of sugar
1-pound package thin spaghetti or spaghettini

1. Soak bread in water or milk. Squeeze dry; combine with beef and pork. Mix well; mix in parsley, 2 tablespoons grated cheese, egg, salt and pepper. Shape into balls.
2. Heat oil in skillet or saucepan; brown meat balls on all sides. Remove.
3. Add garlic and onion to oil remaining in pan; cook until browned. Return meat balls to pan.
4. Add wine, tomatoes, tomato paste, bay leaf, sugar, salt and pepper. Cook over low heat for 1 hour or longer, or until thickened.
5. Cook spaghetti or spaghettini according to package directions. Drain; rinse; serve with sauce. Serve grated cheese on side.

Mrs. Joel Tessitore, New Century Club, Wilmington, Del.

SPAGHETTI WITH ITALIAN MEAT BALLS

Serves 8

1½ pounds ground beef
¼ cup chopped celery
¾ cup finely chopped onions
1 clove garlic, crushed
1-pound 13-ounce can tomatoes, undrained

1 teaspoon sugar
Salt
Pepper
3 bay leaves, crushed
½ teaspoon orégano
3 6-ounce cans tomato paste
2 cups water
2 4-ounce cans mushrooms,
   undrained
½ cup fresh bread crumbs
1 egg
Grated Parmesan cheese
1 teaspoon garlic salt
2 tablespoons olive oil
1 pound hot or sweet, diced
   Italian sausage
1-pound package spaghetti

1. Brown ½ pound of the beef in heavy saucepan. Add celery, ¼ cup of the onions, garlic, tomatoes, sugar, 1 teaspoon salt, pepper to taste, bay leaves, orégano, tomato paste, water and mushrooms. Stir well; bring to boil. Cover; simmer for 2 hours, stirring occasionally.
2. Meanwhile, combine remaining beef, remaining onions, crumbs, egg, 1 table-spoon cheese, garlic salt, ½ teaspoon salt and ⅛ teaspoon pepper. Mix well; shape into 1-inch balls.
3. Heat oil in large skillet; brown meat balls and sausage. Stir into meat sauce; cover; simmer for 1 hour longer.
4. Meanwhile, cook spaghetti according to package directions. Drain; rinse; turn into serving dish.
5. Serve spaghetti with meat balls, sauce and additional Parmesan cheese, if desired.

Shirley Mondus, Woman's Club,
Prospect Heights, Ill.

ALL-IN-ONE SPAGHETTI CASSEROLE

Serves 8

8 ounces spaghetti
2 tablespoons bacon drippings
½ cup chopped onions
½ cup diced green pepper
2 pounds ground beef
1 cup cream-style corn
1-pound 4-ounce can tomatoes,
   undrained
2 10½-ounce cans condensed
   tomato soup
½ cup grated sharp Cheddar cheese
1½ teaspoons salt
½ teaspoon Worcestershire
Bread crumbs
Grated Parmesan cheese

1. Cook spaghetti according to package directions. Drain; rinse with cold water.
2. Heat bacon drippings in skillet; brown onions and green pepper. Add beef; cook, stirring occasionally, until browned.
3. Preheat oven to 375° F. Grease 4-quart casserole.
4. Combine meat mixture and spaghetti. Add corn, tomatoes, soup, Cheddar cheese, salt and Worcestershire; mix well.

5. Pour into casserole; bake in preheated oven for 1 hour.

Mrs. Walter J. Russell, Thursday Morning Club,
Madison, N.J.

Sauces for Pasta

FRENCH SPAGHETTI SAUCE

Makes About 1½ Pints

2 tablespoons cooking oil
1 large onion, finely chopped
1 clove garlic, crushed
6-ounce can tomato paste
2 cups water
1 teaspoon salt
¼ teaspoon pepper
1 bay leaf
½ teaspoon basil
⅛ teaspoon thyme
2 tablespoons chopped parsley

1. Heat oil in saucepan. Sauté onion and garlic for 5 minutes. Stir in remaining ingredients; mix well.
2. Bring to boil; simmer, uncovered, for 45 minutes, stirring occasionally.

Jackie Wilkinson, Junior Woman's Club,
Jacksonville, Fla.

GARLIC SAUCE

Makes Enough to Serve 2

¼ cup butter
¼ cup cooking oil
½ cup minced parsley
Salt and pepper to taste
4 cloves garlic, thinly sliced

1. Heat butter and oil in skillet; sauté parsley for 5 minutes. Sprinkle with salt and pepper.
2. Add garlic; sauté until lightly browned.

Helen Boone, Woman's Club, Buckeye, Ariz.

MARINARA SAUCE

Makes Enough to Serve 4 to 6

1-pound 13-ounce can tomatoes
½ cup olive oil
2 cloves garlic, chopped
2 tablespoons chopped parsley
2 basil leaves, chopped
½ teaspoon orégano
Salt and pepper to taste

1. Drain tomatoes. Chop finely; set aside.
2. Heat oil in saucepan; simmer garlic over low heat until partially cooked. Add parsley and basil; cook until garlic is golden brown.
3. Add tomatoes; cook over low heat for 25 minutes.
4. Add orégano, salt and pepper. Stir to combine.

Mrs. Joel Tessitore, New Century Club,
Wilmington, Del.

QUICK SPAGHETTI SAUCE WITHOUT MEAT

Makes Enough to Serve 2

¼ cup olive oil
1 large onion, chopped
1 clove garlic, minced
¼ pound mushrooms, sliced
1-pound 4-ounce can Italian
   tomatoes, drained
6-ounce can tomato paste
Salt and pepper to taste

1. Heat oil in saucepan; sauté onion, garlic and mushrooms for 10 minutes, or until tender.
2. Add tomatoes and tomato paste; bring to boil; then simmer over low heat for 20 minutes.
3. Season with salt and pepper.

Madelaine Goldberg, Junior Woman's Club,
Tullahoma, Tenn.

WHITE CLAM SAUCE

Makes Enough to Serve 4

¼ cup olive oil
½ cup butter
6 cloves garlic, crushed
¼ cup finely chopped parsley
1 tablespoon basil
3 tablespoons grated Parmesan
   cheese
Dash of cayenne
Dash of pepper
10 to 12 freshly shucked large
   cherrystone clams with liquor,
   chopped

1. Heat oil in saucepan. Add butter; simmer for 2 minutes. Add garlic, parsley, basil, cheese, cayenne and pepper. Bring to boil; stir in clams.
2. Bring back to boil.

RED CLAM SAUCE: Add 1 cup tomato sauce along with clams in above recipe.

Mary Lake, Women's Club, Linwood, N.J.

OIL AND GARLIC SAUCE

Makes Enough to Serve 2

½ cup olive oil
2 cloves garlic, thinly sliced
Salt and freshly ground black
   pepper to taste

Heat oil in skillet; sauté garlic until golden brown. Season with salt and pepper.

A. S.

MEAT SAUCE FOR SPAGHETTI

Makes Enough to Serve 8 to 10

1 tablespoon shortening
1 pound ground beef
1½ cups chopped onions
¾ cup chopped green peppers
1 clove garlic, crushed
3 8-ounce cans tomato sauce
⅓ cup water
1½ teaspoons salt
1 teaspoon celery seed
½ teaspoon dry mustard
2 teaspoons Worcestershire
Dash of pepper

4-ounce can sliced mushrooms,
   undrained
1 teaspoon horseradish

1. Melt shortening in Dutch oven or heavy saucepan; brown beef well, stirring occasionally.
2. Add onions, green peppers and garlic; sauté over medium heat for 5 minutes.
3. Stir in tomato sauce, water, salt, celery seed, mustard, Worcestershire and pepper. Bring to boil; cover; simmer for 30 minutes, stirring occasionally.
4. Stir in mushrooms and horseradish; cover; simmer for 30 minutes longer.

Mrs. Wallace G. Porter, Woman's Club,
Riverdale, N.J.

ITALIAN SPAGHETTI SAUCE

Makes Enough to Serve 6

¼ cup olive oil
1 large onion, chopped
¼ cup chopped parsley
1 stalk celery with leaves, finely
   chopped
1 pound ground beef
1-pound 4-ounce can tomatoes
6-ounce can tomato paste
¾ cup water
1 bay leaf
1 clove garlic, crushed
1½ teaspoons salt
¼ teaspoon pepper
1 carrot, grated
Dash of Tabasco

1. Heat oil in large skillet; sauté onion, parsley and celery over medium heat for 5 minutes. Add beef; brown over medium heat, stirring occasionally.
2. Add remaining ingredients; mix well. Cover; simmer for 2 hours, stirring occasionally.

Evelyn Fowler, Monday Club, Spencer, Mass.

NEAPOLITAN SPAGHETTI SAUCE

Makes About 1½ Quarts

1 tablespoon shortening
1 pound ground beef
1 large onion, chopped
3 cloves garlic, crushed
2 8-ounce cans tomato sauce
2 6-ounce cans tomato paste
1½ cups water
1 cup grated Romano cheese
1 teaspoon orégano
2 teaspoons basil
3 tablespoons dried parsley flakes
1 tablespoon sugar
1½ teaspoons salt
¼ teaspoon pepper
½ teaspoon monosodium glutamate
1 bay leaf

1. Melt shortening in Dutch oven or large heavy saucepan; sauté beef, onion and garlic over medium heat, stirring occasionally, until meat is browned.
2. Stir in remaining ingredients; bring to boil; then simmer, uncovered, for 3 hours, stirring occasionally.

Nancy Standlee, Junior Woman's Club,
Lompoc, Calif.

ITALIAN SPAGHETTI SAUCE WITH BEEF AND PORK

Makes Enough to Serve 6

2 tablespoons olive oil
5 medium onions, finely chopped
2 green peppers, finely chopped
1½ pounds ground beef
½ pound ground pork
1-pound 13-ounce can tomatoes, undrained
2 6-ounce cans tomato paste
½ teaspoon sugar
Pinch of orégano
½ teaspoon prepared mustard
1 teaspoon minced fresh or ¼ teaspoon dried basil
Dash of red pepper
1 clove garlic, minced

1. Heat oil in skillet or heavy saucepan; sauté onions and green peppers for 10 minutes, or until soft and tender.
2. Add beef and pork; cook until lightly browned, stirring frequently.
3. Add remaining ingredients. Bring to boil; then simmer for about 3 hours, stirring occasionally.

Kitty McDaniel, North Phoenix Woman's Club, Phoenix, Ariz.

CARTER'S SPECIAL SPAGHETTI SAUCE

Makes About 1 Quart

2 tablespoons butter or margarine
1 small green pepper, chopped
½ cup chopped celery
1 large onion, sliced
1 clove garlic, crushed
1½ pounds ground beef
2 10½-ounce cans condensed tomato soup
6-ounce can tomato paste
1 cup water
4-ounce can sliced mushrooms, undrained
1 teaspoon cinnamon
1 teaspoon pepper
Dash of cayenne
1 cup sliced pitted ripe olives
½ cup grated Cheddar cheese
Salt to taste

1. Melt butter or margarine in Dutch over or large heavy saucepan. Add green pepper, celery, onion and garlic; sauté for 5 minutes. Add beef; cook over low heat, stirring frequently, until well browned.

2. Stir in soup, tomato paste, water, mushrooms, cinnamon, pepper, cayenne and olives. Bring to boil; simmer, uncovered, for 30 minutes.
3. Stir in cheese; season with salt. Simmer for 5 minutes longer.

Mrs. Harry H. Nash, Jr., Junior Woman's Club, Coronado, Calif.

TOMATO AND MEAT SAUCE

Makes About 4 Quarts

¼ cup olive oil
1 large onion, chopped
1 pound ground beef
1 pound link sausages, diced
3 1-pound 13-ounce cans tomatoes, undrained
3 6-ounce cans tomato paste
1 cup tomato purée
3 cloves garlic, crushed
2 teaspoons salt
¼ teaspoon pepper
1½ teaspoons sugar
¼ teaspoon thyme
¼ teaspoon mint
2 tablespoons chopped parsley

1. Heat oil in large heavy saucepan or Dutch oven; sauté onion for 5 minutes. Stir in beef and sausage; cook until browned.
2. Add remaining ingredients. Bring to boil; then simmer for about 5 hours, stirring occasionally. Add water during cooking, if necessary, to keep consistency of gravy.

Nell Rees, Finneytown Junior Women's Club, Cincinnati, Ohio

BEEF GRAVY SAUCE FOR SPAGHETTI

Makes Enough to Serve 4

3 tablespoons olive oil
2 tablespoons butter
2 tablespoons chopped onion
2 tablespoons chopped parsley
½ pound mushrooms, sliced, or 2 4-ounce cans mushrooms, drained
3 tablespoons white wine
1 cup beef gravy
1 cup tomato juice

1. Heat oil and butter in saucepan; sauté onion until tender. Sprinkle with parsley.
2. Add remaining ingredients. Bring to boil; then simmer for 20 minutes.

Louise Caprio, Woman's Club, Falls Church, Va.

17. Salads and Salad Dressings

Tossed Green Salads

There are many different types of salad, and each has its place in our daily menus. The universally popular tossed green salad is served either as a first course, with the main course or after the main course with crusty bread and often with cheese. Its success depends on several factors, the most important of which is selection of the greens. Lettuce is, of course, the main ingredient, but there are many other kinds of salad greens than iceberg or Boston lettuce. They include escarole (broad-leaf endive), chicory (curly endive), romaine, Bibb lettuce, Belgian endive, water cress, fresh spinach leaves, field salad and dandelion greens.

A TOSSED SALAD

1. Use a variety of crisp fresh salad greens. They should be well washed, thoroughly dried and well chilled.
2. To the greens you may add thinly sliced cucumbers, onions, scallions, radishes, green peppers, carrots and other raw vegetables and a favorite herb, fresh, if possible, or dried.
3. Rub the inside of a large salad bowl with a cut clove of garlic, or when you toss the salad, add a heel of French bread rubbed with garlic. The French call this a *chapon*.
4. Tear the salad greens into the bowl, add other vegetables as desired and keep cold.
5. When ready to serve, add a few tablespoons of your favorite salad dressing, and toss the greens lightly. Use just enough dressing to coat the greens without leaving any residue in the bottom of the bowl.
6. Serve tossed salads immediately after the greens and vegetables have been mixed with the dressing.

VARIATION FOR A TOSSED SALAD: The salad dressing may be mixed in the bowl first, then the greens added and tossed at serving time.

1. Into the salad bowl sprinkle ½ teaspoon salt, some freshly ground pepper and ½ teaspoon dry or 1 teaspoon prepared mustard. Add 1 tablespoon wine vinegar. Stir vigorously with the back of a wooden salad spoon until the ingredients are well mixed.
2. Gradually add 3 to 4 tablespoons salad oil, stirring vigorously. Set aside.
3. When ready to serve, tear in the salad greens; toss lightly. This salad dressing is enough to coat salad greens to serve from 4 to 6.

A. S.

CAESAR SALAD

Serves 6

¼ cup olive oil
1 clove garlic, crushed
1 teaspoon salt
⅛ teaspoon pepper
2 slices bread, cubed
8 cups torn salad greens (lettuce, romaine, endive, etc.)
8 anchovy fillets, diced
¼ cup grated Parmesan cheese
2 tablespoons lemon juice
1 egg

1. Preheat oven to 300° F.
2. Mix oil, garlic, salt and pepper in salad bowl.
3. Arrange bread on baking sheet; bake in preheated oven for 15 minutes, or until croutons are golden.
4. When ready to serve, put greens on oil in bowl. Sprinkle with anchovies, cheese and lemon juice.
5. Break egg in middle of salad. Toss lightly until greens are well coated. Add croutons; toss lightly.

Mrs. Leonard H. Havens, Suburban Woman's Club, West Hartford, Conn.

DALEEN'S CAESAR SALAD

Serves 8 to 12

1 clove garlic
¾ cup salad oil
2 cups bread cubes
2 heads romaine
1 head Boston lettuce
1 bunch water cress
¾ cup grated Parmesan cheese
¼ teaspoon dry mustard
¼ teaspoon black pepper
⅓ cup lemon juice
2 eggs, lightly beaten
Dash of Worcestershire
16 anchovy fillets

1. Crush garlic; add to oil; set aside for at least 1 hour. Discard garlic.

2. Heat ¼ cup of the garlic oil; sauté bread until golden. Drain on absorbent paper.

3. Tear romaine, lettuce and water cress into salad bowl. Sprinkle with cheese, mustard and pepper.

4. Combine remaining garlic oil and lemon juice. Pour over greens. Add eggs, Worcestershire, anchovies and bread. Toss gently.

Mrs. Daleen Sutton, Juniors, Saratoga, Fla.

GREEN SALAD WITH HERRING DRESSING

Serves 4 to 6

1½ quarts torn crisp lettuce
2 tablespoons chopped dill
7-ounce jar herring fillets in wine
   sauce or sour cream

1. Put lettuce and dill in salad bowl.

2. Strain sauce from herring over greens. Cut herring into bite-size pieces; add to salad; toss lightly.

Betty Connolly, Woman's Club,
Anchorage, Alaska

SALADE VERTE

Serves 8

½ cup olive oil
2 tablespoons wine or tarragon
   vinegar
½ teaspoon salt
¼ teaspoon black pepper
1 clove garlic, crushed
1 head romaine
1 head escarole
2 heads Belgian endive, sliced

1. In mixing bowl combine oil, vinegar, salt, pepper and garlic. Beat vigorously with rotary beater until well blended.

2. Tear romaine and escarole into salad bowl. Add endive. Chill until serving time.

3. Just before serving, pour dressing over greens; toss lightly.

Orptec Club, Aberdeen, S.D.

WILTED LETTUCE

Serves 6

6 slices bacon, cut into small pieces
¼ cup vinegar
2 teaspoons brown sugar
½ teaspoon salt
Dash of pepper
1 head iceberg lettuce, shredded

1. Cook bacon in skillet until crisp; drain on absorbent paper; crumble.

2. Drain off bacon drippings, leaving about 3 tablespoons in skillet. Stir vinegar, sugar, salt and pepper. Bring to boil; pour over lettuce; toss lightly.

3. Sprinkle with bacon.

Emily Schaffer, Women's Club, Durham, N.H.

ZUCCHINI TOSSED SALAD

Serves 8

½ head iceberg lettuce
½ head romaine
2 medium zucchini, thinly sliced
1 cup sliced radishes
3 scallions, sliced
⅓ cup French dressing
1 clove garlic, crushed
1 ounce blue cheese, crumbled

1. Tear iceberg lettuce and romaine into bite-size pieces into salad bowl. Add zucchini, radishes and scallions; toss lightly.

2. Prepare Blue Cheese Dressing: In small container combine French dressing, garlic and cheese. Cover container; shake well.

3. Pour dressing over salad in bowl; toss lightly.

C. Myers, Junior Woman's Club,
Pacific Beach, Calif.

GREENEST SALAD IN TOWN

Serves 4

1 quart spinach
1 cup shredded Cheddar cheese
4 slices bacon, crisply cooked
   and crumbled
¼ cup French dressing
½ cup croutons

1. Wash and dry spinach. Tear small pieces into salad bowl.

2. Add cheese, bacon and French dressing; toss lightly. Sprinkle with croutons.

Jayne Rodriques, Tuesday Club, Assonet, Mass.

Bean and Vegetable Salads Vinaigrette

BEAN SALAD

1½ cups vinegar
½ cup water
1¾ cups sugar
1-pound can whole green beans,
   drained
1-pound can wax beans, drained
1-pound can garbanzos (chick-peas)
   drained
1-pound can kidney beans, drained
1 green pepper, chopped
2 medium onions, shredded
2 stalks celery, chopped

1. Day before, combine vinegar, water and sugar in saucepan. Bring to boil; then simmer for 3 minutes. Cool slightly.

2. In china bowl or crock combine remaining ingredients. Pour vinegar mixture over them; refrigerate for at least 24 hours before serving.

Mrs. Leah M. Jolmes, American History
Forum and History and Literature Club,
Tulsa, Okla.

BEAN RELISH SALAD

Serves 10 to 12

1 small cauliflower, broken
  into flowerets
3 cups sugar
2 cups vinegar
1 teaspoon salt
2 cups sliced celery
1-pound can kidney beans,
  drained
1-pound can green beans, drained
1-pound can wax beans, drained
1-pound can Lima beans, drained
1-pound can garbanzos (chick-peas),
  drained
1 green pepper, cut into strips
1 cup pickled sweet onions, drained
1 or 2 large sweet onions, cut into
  rings

1. Day before, pour boiling water over cauliflower; set aside.
2. In saucepan combine sugar, vinegar, salt and ½ cup water. Bring to boil; boil for 3 minutes. Remove from heat; add celery.
3. In bowl or crock combine remaining ingredients. Drain cauliflower; add to mixture.
4. Pour vinegar mixture over salad mixture; toss lightly. Refrigerate overnight.

Mrs. Dellis Schrock, Woman's Club,
Casselton, N.D.

GREEN BEAN AND BACON SALAD

Serves 8

2 cups cut green beans
½ cup olive or salad oil
¼ cup vinegar
2 tablespoons minced onion
1 teaspoon seasoned salt
8 slices bacon
1 head lettuce, shredded

1. Cook beans in boiling salted water until just tender. Drain; cool.
2. Combine oil, vinegar, onion and salt. Pour over beans; chill.
3. Cook bacon in skillet until crisp; drain on absorbent paper; crumble.
4. Combine beans and lettuce. Add bacon; toss.

Mrs. George Erwin, Junior Woman's Club,
Wauwatosa, Wis.

BEANS AND BEETS

Serves 6 to 8

1-pound jar pickled beets
1-pound can French-style green
  beans, drained
1 tablespoon vinegar
3 tablespoons olive oil
1 tablespoon sugar
1 tablespoon lemon juice
  Salt and pepper to taste
  Lettuce leaves

1. Drain beets; reserve ½ cup liquid.
2. Mix beets and beans in salad bowl.
3. In small bowl blend reserved liquid, vinegar, oil, sugar, lemon juice, salt and

pepper. Pour over vegetables; refrigerate for 4 hours.
4. Serve on lettuce.

Ellen Griffee, Woman's Club, Colonia, N.J.

CRUNCHY KIDNEY BEAN SALAD

Serves 4

1-pound can kidney beans
½ cup diced celery
½ cup diced green pepper
¼ cup grated onion
¼ cup favorite salad dressing
½ teaspoon salt
¼ teaspoon pepper
  Lettuce leaves

1. Drain beans; rinse in cold water; drain again.
2. Turn into bowl; add all remaining ingredients except lettuce; mix well; chill for at least 1 hour.
3. Line salad bowl with lettuce; spoon bean mixture into center.

Carol Wider, Junior Woman's Club,
Newington, Conn.

CABBAGE SALAD WITH SWEET OIL DRESSING

Serves 4

3 cups chopped cabbage
¼ cup chopped green pepper
1 tablespoon chopped pimiento
1 tablespoon chopped onion
3 tablespoons salad oil
⅓ cup vinegar
1 teaspoon salt
¼ teaspoon black pepper
½ teaspoon dry mustard
1 teaspoon celery salt
2 tablespoons sugar
  Sliced stuffed olives

1. In salad bowl combine all ingredients except olives. Mix well; cover; chill thoroughly.
2. When ready to serve, garnish with olives.

Mrs. R. E. York, Woman's Club, Hugoton, Kans.

TWENTY-FOUR-HOUR CABBAGE SALAD

Serves 6 to 8

1 large cabbage, shredded
1 large onion, very thinly sliced
1 cup sugar
1 cup vinegar
⅔ cup olive oil
1 tablespoon celery seed
1 tablespoon dry mustard

1. Day before, in mixing bowl arrange alternate layers of cabbage and onion. Sprinkle with sugar.
2. In saucepan combine remaining ingredients; bring to boil. Pour over cabbage and onion.
3. Cover; refrigerate for 24 hours.

Mrs. Jerry Surber, Phil Avant Study Club,
Kanawa, Okla.

TEXAS COLESLAW

Serves 6

1 medium cabbage, shredded
1 medium green pepper, finely
  chopped
1 large onion, finely chopped
1 carrot, grated
½ cup salad oil
½ cup vinegar
1 cup sugar
1 teaspoon salt
½ teaspoon dry mustard
2 tablespoons chopped parsley
¼ teaspoon pepper

1. Day before, put cabbage, green pepper, onion and carrot in mixing bowl; toss lightly.
2. In another bowl combine remaining ingredients. Beat until smooth and blended.
3. Pour dressing over vegetables; toss lightly. Cover; refrigerate overnight.

*Mrs. C. J. Vanzandt, Wheeler Wednesday
Study Club, Mobeetie, Tex.*

MARINATED CARROTS

Serves 8

1 bunch carrots, sliced
2 cloves garlic, minced
½ teaspoon salt
¼ cup olive oil
2 tablespoons wine vinegar
1 teaspoon orégano
½ teaspoon pepper

1. Cook carrots in boiling salted water in saucepan until tender. Drain; put in mixing bowl.
2. Meanwhile, in small bowl blend remaining ingredients. Pour over carrots. Cover; marinate for 12 hours.
3. Serve at room temperature.

*Barbara P. Ray, Toastmistress Club,
Huntsville, Ala.*

SUSAN'S RAW MUSHROOM SALAD

Serves 6 to 8

1 pound mushrooms
6 stalks celery with leaves, cut into
  1-inch pieces
2 eggs, hard-cooked and cut into
  eighths
2 tablespoons chopped scallions
¼ cup diced pimientos
⅓ cup olive oil
2 tablespoons wine vinegar
1 teaspoon salt
¼ teaspoon freshly ground black
  pepper
Romaine leaves

1. Wash and dry mushrooms. Cut into halves or quarters, depending on size; put in mixing bowl.
2. Add celery, eggs, scallions and pimientos; toss lightly.
3. In small bowl blend oil, vinegar, salt and pepper. Pour over salad; toss lightly; chill.

4. When ready to serve, line salad bowl with romaine; pile mushroom mixture in center.

Junior Woman's Club, Pompano Beach, Fla.

NEW ENGLAND SALAD BOWL

Serves 4 to 6

½ clove garlic, crushed
½ teaspoon salt
½ cup finely diced bread, fried in
  cooking oil
¼ cup sliced onion
¼ cup cooked peas
1 cup cauliflowerets
1 sweet or dill pickle, sliced
1 tomato, peeled and sectioned
½ head lettuce, torn
1 egg, hard-cooked and sliced
3 tablespoons olive oil
  Dash of pepper
1 teaspoon brown sugar
1 teaspoon vinegar

1. In salad bowl combine garlic and salt to a paste.
2. Add all remaining ingredients except vinegar. Toss lightly; chill for 15 minutes.
3. Sprinkle with vinegar; toss again.

*Joy Hostage, Junior Woman's Club,
Cheshire, Conn.*

LOUIS PAPPAS' FAMOUS GREEK SALAD

Serves 6 to 8

You may convert this into a main course to serve 4 if you add many more shrimp.

6 medium potatoes, cooked and
  peeled
2 medium onions, sliced
¼ cup finely chopped parsley
2 medium green peppers
  Salt to taste
½ cup favorite salad dressing
1 large head lettuce, shredded
  Water cress
2 medium tomatoes, each cut into
  6 wedges
1 medium cucumber, peeled and
  cut lengthwise into 8 fingers
1 medium avocado, peeled and cut
  into wedges
8 ounces feta cheese, cut into fingers
4 canned beets, sliced
8 large shrimp, shelled, deveined
  and cooked
4 anchovy fillets
12 ripe olives
12 medium hot preserved peppers
4 radishes, cut into roses
4 scallions
½ cup white vinegar
¼ cup olive oil
¼ cup vegetable oil
  Orégano

1. Prepare potato salad: Slice potatoes into mixing bowl. Add onions and parsley. Cut 1 of the green peppers into thin slices; add to potatoes. Sprinkle lightly with salt. Add salad dressing; toss lightly. Chill while preparing rest of ingredients.

2. Cut remaining green pepper into rings.

3. Just before serving, arrange lettuce and water cress on large serving dish.

4. Start building a mound by placing potato salad in center of lettuce. Add alternate layers of tomatoes, cucumber, avocado and cheese.

5. Garnish with green pepper rings, beets, shrimp, anchovies, olives, hot preserved peppers, radishes and scallions.

6. Prepare dressing: In bowl blend vinegar, olive oil and vegetable oil. Sprinkle over salad; sprinkle orégano on top.

Nancie Crabb, Junior Woman's Club, Jacksonville, Fla.

SAUERKRAUT SALAD

Serves 6 to 8

1-pound 11-ounce can sauerkraut
½ cup chopped onions
½ cup chopped green pepper
½ cup chopped celery
4-ounce jar pimientos, drained and chopped
1 teaspoon celery seed
½ teaspoon mustard seed
1 cup sugar
1 tablespoon vinegar

1. Drain sauerkraut well. Chop finely; turn into mixing bowl. Add remaining ingredients; mix well.

2. Chill well before serving.

Mrs. L. Simmons, President, Woman's Club, Clinton, Ia.

ITALIAN TOMATO SALAD

Serves 4

5 medium tomatoes
1 teaspoon salt
Dash of pepper
½ teaspoon garlic salt
½ large onion, thinly sliced
1 teaspoon chopped parsley
1 teaspoon orégano
½ cup olive oil

1. Cut tomatoes into eighths; arrange on serving dish.

2. Combine remaining ingredients in bowl; mix well. Pour over tomatoes; chill.

G. Filippelli, Totowa Junior Women's Club, Wayne, N.J.

BULGARIAN SALAD

Serves 6 to 8

8 large green peppers
8 firm large tomatoes
2 large onions
1 cup vinegar
½ cup olive oil
1 teaspoon salt
¼ teaspoon pepper

1. Char green peppers over flame; cool.

2. Clean charred skin from peppers; core and slice peppers.

3. Cut tomatoes into quarters; mix with peppers in salad bowl. Chop onions finely; sprinkle over tomatoes and peppers.

4. In small bowl blend vinegar, oil, salt and pepper. Pour over vegetables; marinate in refrigerator for at least 2 hours.

Junior Woman's Club, West Essex, N.J.

CROCK SALAD

Serves 6

2 green peppers, seeded and cut into rings
2 tomatoes, thinly sliced
2 Spanish onions, sliced and separated into rings
1½ cups vinegar
1½ cups salad oil
½ cup sugar
2 tablespoons salt
1 teaspoon celery seed

1. Day before, put vegetables in crock or enamel bowl.

2. Combine remaining ingredients. Pour over vegetables; refrigerate overnight.

Lida Moses, Woman's Club, Lavalette, W.Va.

SALSA

This Mexican salad is good served with Spanish Rice (p. 479) and Chili con Queso on Tortillas (p. 215).

1½ cups chopped ripe tomatoes
4-ounce can hot chili peppers, chopped
1 clove garlic, minced
1 cup chopped onions
Dash of cider vinegar
Salt to taste

Day before, combine ingredients; refrigerate overnight.

Mrs. Stephen Skidmore, Woman's Club, Azusa, Calif.

Bean and Vegetable Salads with Cream or Mayonnaise

CRUNCHY BEAN SALAD WITH MAYONNAISE

Serves 4

1-pound can kidney beans
½ cup chopped celery
⅓ cup chopped sweet pickles
2 tablespoons chopped onion
⅓ cup sliced stuffed olives
¼ cup mayonnaise
3 tablespoons chili sauce
½ teaspoon salt

1. Drain beans; rinse in cold water. Put in bowl.

2. Add remaining ingredients; mix well. Chill until serving time.

Joanne Davis, Woman's Club, Glasgow, Mo.

HOT SLAW

Serves 6

1 tablespoon shortening
1 medium cabbage, shredded
¼ cup water
½ teaspoon salt

Dash of pepper
1 egg
½ cup vinegar
½ cup sour cream

1. Melt shortening in saucepan. Add cabbage, water, salt and pepper. Bring to boil; cover; simmer for 10 minutes.

2. Remove cover; cook over medium heat until water has evaporated. Remove from heat.

3. Blend egg, vinegar and sour cream. Pour over cabbage; cover; let stand for 5 minutes before serving.

Mrs. Phil R. Easterday, Woman's Club,
Lincoln, Neb.

SOUR CREAM COLESLAW

Serves 6 to 8

1 medium cabbage, finely shredded
2 cups sour cream
½ teaspoon salt
¼ cup sugar
3 tablespoons vinegar
½ teaspoon dry mustard

1. Put cabbage in mixing bowl; add remaining ingredients. Beat hard with wooden spoon (do not use mixer) until frothy and creamy.

2. Chill; serve within a few hours.

Katherine E. Carlin, Junior Woman's Club,
Coronado, Calif.

TRIPLE VEGETABLE SLAW

Serves 6 to 8

4 cups shredded cabbage
6 tablespoons No-Cook Boiled
    Dressing (p. 545)
2 cups shredded turnips
1 small red apple, chopped
½ cup shredded beets

1. In mixing bowl toss cabbage with 3 tablespoons of the No-Cook Boiled Dressing.

2. In another bowl toss remaining dressing, turnips and apple.

3. Spoon cabbage into salad bowl; mound turnip mixture on top. Garnish with cone of beets.

Woman's Club, Belle, W. Va.

TURKISH CAULIFLOWER SALAD

Serves 6

1 cauliflower, separated into
    flowerets
4 carrots, sliced
Salad greens
1 cup yogurt
1 tablespoon olive oil
Salt to taste

1. In separate saucepans cook cauliflower and carrots in boiling salted water until just tender. Drain; cool.

2. Arrange vegetables on bed of salad greens; top with a mixture of yogurt, oil and salt.

Zeynep Kirdar, Junior Woman's Club,
Scottsdale, Ariz.

PENNSYLVANIA DUTCH CUCUMBERS

Makes About 1 Pint

1 large cucumber, sliced
1 large onion, sliced
½ tablespoon salt
1 cup heavy cream
1 tablespoon vinegar
1 tablespoon sugar
Black pepper to taste

1. Put cucumber and onion in bowl. Sprinkle with salt; add water just to cover. Let stand for at least 1 hour; drain well.

2. Combine cream, vinegar and sugar; pour over cucumber and onion.

3. Sprinkle with pepper. Chill.

Pea Hocker, Gardens Century Club,
Wilmington, Del.

CUCUMBERS IN SOUR CREAM

Serves 6 to 8

6 medium cucumbers, peeled
1 small onion
1 tablespoon salt
1 tablespoon vinegar
1 tablespoon olive oil
1 cup sour cream
Pepper to taste

1. Grate cucumbers and onion into mixing bowl. Sprinkle with salt, vinegar and oil. Chill for several hours.

2. Drain vegetables; add sour cream; mix well. Sprinkle with pepper; correct seasoning. Chill until serving time.

Barbara Sampl, Junior Woman's Club,
Newington, Conn.

GURKENSALAT (Cucumbers in Sour Cream)

Serves 6 to 8

2 medium cucumbers
Salt
1 large onion, thinly sliced
1 cup sour cream
1 teaspoon sugar
½ teaspoon dillweed
¼ teaspoon caraway seeds
Salt and pepper to taste

1. Score and slice unpeeled cucumbers. Arrange in layers in bowl, sprinkling each layer with salt. Cover with plate; weight down. Let stand for 1 hour.

2. Drain thoroughly. Arrange alternate layers of cucumber and onion in salad bowl.

3. In small bowl blend remaining ingredients. Pour over cucumbers and onion.

Mrs. Fred Young, Junior Women's Club,
Cheyenne, Wyo.

GREEN GODDESS SALAD

Serves 4 to 6

10 anchovy fillets, minced
1 scallion, minced
¼ cup minced parsley
1 tablespoon minced fresh tarragon
or 1 tablespoon dried tarragon,
soaked in vinegar and strained
1 tablespoon chopped chives
½ clove garlic
1½ large heads romaine
Mrs. Hasebroock's Green Goddess
Salad Dressing (p. 543)
Lettuce or romaine leaves
Cooked lobster, shrimp, crab
meat or turkey

1. Combine anchovies, scallion, parsley, tarragon and chives.
2. Rub salad bowl with garlic; add anchovy mixture.
3. Tear romaine into bite-size pieces into salad bowl.
4. Pour enough Green Goddess Salad Dressing over salad to moisten; toss lightly.
5. Spoon onto chilled salad plates lined with lettuce or romaine; garnish with shellfish or turkey.

Mrs. William H. Hasebroock, Honorary President,
General Federation of Women's Clubs,
West Point, Neb.

STUFFED ICEBERG LETTUCE

Serves 6

1 large head iceberg lettuce
3-ounce package cream cheese
3 tablespoons mayonnaise
½ teaspoon salt
⅛ teaspoon pepper
½ teaspoon paprika
2 tablespoons grated carrot
2 tablespoons grated onion
2 tablespoons finely chopped
tomato
1 tablespoon finely chopped green
pepper
1 tablespoon finely chopped pimiento
Favorite salad dressing

1. Remove core from lettuce. Wash and drain lettuce well, keeping it whole.
2. Remove soft outer leaves; where core has been removed, scoop out a hole about 5 inches deep.
3. Blend cheese, mayonnaise, salt, pepper and paprika until smooth. Add remaining ingredients; mix well.
4. Fill hole in lettuce with cheese filling.
5. Wrap lettuce in aluminum foil; refrigerate for 6 hours.
6. Remove foil; cut lettuce into serving slices. Serve with dressing.

Shirley Earl, Mendocino Study Club,
Little River, Calif.

MUSHROOM AND LIMA BEAN SALAD

Serves 8

10-ounce package frozen baby
Lima beans
8 mushrooms, thinly sliced
1 large onion, chopped
1 tablespoon chopped parsley
½ teaspoon orégano
1 cup chopped celery
½ cup tiny cauliflowerets
½ cup sour cream
4 tablespoons mayonnaise
2 tablespoons lemon juice
2 teaspoons horseradish mustard
Salt and pepper to taste

1. Cook Lima beans according to package directions. Drain; cool.
2. Combine Lima beans, mushrooms, onion, parsley, orégano, celery and cauliflowerets.
3. Mix sour cream, mayonnaise, lemon juice and mustard. Stir into vegetables; season with salt and pepper.

Charlotte Turnbull, Anna Day Club,
Troy, Mo.

ONION SALAD

Serves 4

4 large onions, chopped
1 teaspoon vinegar
2 tablespoons mayonnaise
2 tablespoons sugar
½ teaspoon salt
½ teaspoon pepper

1. Put onions in colander; pour boiling water over them.
2. Plunge onions into bowl of ice water; drain.
3. In mixing bowl blend remaining ingredients. Add onions; mix well.

Dorothy Longman, Woman's Club,
La Crescenta, Calif.

PEA SALAD

Serves 4

1-pound can peas, drained
2 eggs, hard-cooked and chopped
¼ cup cubed sharp Cheddar cheese
¼ cup sweet pickle relish
¼ cup mayonnaise

1. In mixing bowl combine peas, eggs, cheese and pickle relish. Chill until serving time.
2. Just before serving, add mayonnaise; toss lightly.

Fran Runyon, Junior Woman's Club,
Jacksonville, Fla.

SWISS SALAD ROLLS

Serves 6

1 cup cottage cheese
½ cup chopped nuts
½ cup grated carrots
4 teaspoons mayonnaise
⅔ tablespoon chopped chives
½ teaspoon salt
Cabbage leaves

1. Combine all ingredients except cabbage; mix well.
2. Spread mixture from ¼ to ½ inch thick on cabbage leaves. Roll up; secure with cocktail picks.
3. When ready to serve, cut each roll into slices about 2 inches thick; discard picks.

NOTE: These are easier to slice if they are refrigerated all day.

Mrs. Frances Jacquat, Women's Progressive Club of Inglewood Acres, Inglewood, Calif.

STUFFED TOMATO CLOWNS
Serves 6

6 medium tomatoes
6 eggs, hard-cooked and finely chopped
⅓ cup finely chopped celery
⅓ cup sliced olives
¼ cup finely chopped scallions
½ teaspoon salt
Dash of pepper
⅓ cup mayonnaise
Lettuce leaves

1. Peel tomatoes; with sharp knife at slant, cut out a cone from end opposite stem of each tomato. Reserve cones.
2. Scoop out half the center from each tomato. Invert; chill.
3. In mixing bowl combine eggs, celery, olives, scallions, salt and pepper. Chill.
4. Just before serving, combine egg mixture with mayonnaise. Arrange tomatoes on lettuce-lined serving dish. Fill each tomato with egg mixture; perch cones on top.

Frieda Disch, Home Representative Club, Collinsville, Okla.

MIXED VEGETABLE SALAD
Serves 6

2 cups torn lettuce
2 cups torn chicory (curly endive)
2 cups torn spinach
6 tablespoons mayonnaise
1 medium red or white onion, thinly sliced
3 teaspoons sugar
¾ teaspoon salt
Freshly ground pepper to taste
1½ cups drained cooked peas
1 cup julienne strips Monterey Jack cheese
6 slices bacon, crisply cooked and crumbled

1. Put half the greens in salad bowl. Dot with 2 tablespoons of the mayonnaise. Top with one-third of onion slices; sprinkle with 1 teaspoon of the sugar, ¼ teaspoon of the salt and pepper. Add one-third of peas and cheese.
2. Repeat layers twice more, seasoning each layer. Do not toss. Chill for 2 hours.
3. Just before serving, top with bacon; toss.

Mrs. George McMillan, Junior Woman's Club, Diamond Bar, Calif.

Macaroni, Potato and Rice Salads

MACARONI SALAD
Serves 6

1½ tablespoons lemon juice
1 tablespoon salad oil
2 cups cooked elbow macaroni
2 tablespoons chopped chives

1 cup chopped celery with leaves
1 cup chopped parsley
½ cup chopped stuffed olives
¾ teaspoon salt
Freshly ground pepper to taste
2 tablespoons chopped pimiento
¼ cup sour cream
Lettuce leaves

1. In large mixing bowl beat lemon juice and oil. Add macaroni; toss lightly. Chill for 1 hour.
2. Add all remaining ingredients except lettuce; toss lightly. Chill.
3. Arrange lettuce on serving dish; top with macaroni mixture.

Ruby Fulton, Brook Run Junior Woman's Club, Richmond, Va.

MACARONI SEAFOOD SALAD
Serves 12

1-pound package elbow macaroni
6½-ounce can crab meat, drained and flaked
1½ cups diced cooked shrimp
4 eggs, hard-cooked and diced
1 large onion, chopped
4-ounce can pimientos, drained and diced
2 cups diced cucumbers
1 cup sliced pitted ripe olives
2 cups mayonnaise
1 cup sour cream
1 tablespoon salt
1 teaspoon pepper
Paprika

1. Cook macaroni according to package directions. Drain; rinse well in cold water.
2. Put macaroni in large salad bowl; add crab meat, shrimp, eggs, onion, pimientos, cucumbers and olives; toss lightly.
3. In another bowl blend mayonnaise, sour cream, salt and pepper. Pour over macaroni mixture; toss lightly but well.
4. Sprinkle with paprika; chill.

Mrs. J. A. Fosland, Woman's Club, Scobey, Mont.

TANGY MACARONI SALAD
Serves 12

8 ounces shell or elbow macaroni
1-pound garbanzos (chick-peas), drained
6-ounce can tuna fish, drained and flaked
1 medium dill pickle, chopped
4 scallions, chopped
⅓ cup chopped parsley
1 clove garlic, minced
2 tablespoons capers with liquid
2-ounce bottle stuffed olives, undrained and halved
⅓ cup lemon juice
Dash of black pepper
1 cup mayonnaise
Salt to taste

1. Cook macaroni according to package directions. Drain; rinse in cold water.

2. Combine macaroni with remaining ingredients. Toss lightly. Chill until ready to serve.

Emmy Warp, Woman's Club, West Chicago, Ill.

CHICKEN MACARONI SALAD

Serves 6

3 cups diced cooked chicken
1½ cups chopped celery
½ cup sliced ripe olives
¼ cup chopped almonds
3 medium apples, unpeeled and diced
3 cups cooked shell macaroni
1 cup mayonnaise
¼ cup heavy cream
1½ teaspoons salt
¼ teaspoon pepper
Dash of cayenne
1 tablespoon grated onion
Lettuce leaves
2 eggs, hard-cooked and sliced
Paprika

1. In mixing bowl combine chicken, celery, olives, almonds, apples and macaroni; toss lightly.
2. In small bowl blend mayonnaise, cream, salt, pepper, cayenne and onion.
3. Pour dressing over chicken mixture; toss lightly but well.
4. Line salad bowl with lettuce; pile chicken mixture in center. Garnish with egg; sprinkle with paprika. Chill for at least 1 hour before serving.

Mrs. Francis Toti, Twentieth Century Club, Iron River, Mich.

COTTAGE CHEESE POTATO SALAD

Serves 6

3 cups diced cooked potatoes
½ cup chopped celery
1 tablespoon chopped green pepper
1 tablespoon chopped pimiento
2 tablespoons grated onion
1¼ teaspoons salt
⅛ teaspoon dry mustard
1 tablespoon lemon juice
½ cup mayonnaise
1 cup cream-style cottage cheese
Lettuce leaves
Parsley

1. In mixing bowl combine potatoes, celery, green pepper, pimiento and onion. Chill for 30 minutes.
2. Meanwhile, in small bowl mix 1 teaspoon of the salt, mustard, lemon juice and mayonnaise. Add to potato mixture; toss lightly.
3. In small bowl blend cheese with remaining salt. Add to potato mixture; toss lightly. Chill.
4. Line salad bowl with lettuce; fill with potato mixture. Garnish with parsley.

Mrs. Norman Forehand, Palm Springs Woman's Club, Hialeah, Fla.

POTATO SALAD

Serves 6

Mrs. Freeman writes: "President Eisenhower served this salad hot. Perle Mesta let the salad blend overnight in refrigerator and served it cold. It's delicious either way."

6 medium potatoes, scrubbed
4 slices bacon, diced
¼ cup chopped onion
¼ cup chopped celery
1 dill pickle, chopped
¼ cup water
½ teaspoon dry mustard
½ teaspoon sugar
½ cup vinegar
⅛ teaspoon paprika

1. Cook potatoes in boiling salted water until tender. Drain; peel. While still hot, cut into slices. Put in bowl; keep warm.
2. Meanwhile, cook bacon in skillet for 5 minutes. Add onion, celery and pickle; sauté until golden. Stir in remaining ingredients; bring to boil.
3. Pour over potatoes; toss lightly.

Ruth Freeman, Woman's Club, Chicopee Falls, Mass.

RICH POTATO SALAD

Serves 8

¼ cup olive oil
2 tablespoons vinegar
1½ teaspoons salt
⅛ teaspoon pepper
4 cups hot sliced cooked potatoes
1 cup ripe olives, cut into large pieces
2 eggs, hard-cooked and diced
1 cup sliced celery
¼ cup chopped dill pickle
¼ cup diced pimientos
1 small onion, minced
½ cup mayonnaise

1. Combine oil, vinegar, salt and pepper. Pour over potatoes; set aside to cool.
2. When cool, add remaining ingredients; toss. Chill until serving time.

Mrs. Alan Cree, Thursday Morning Club, Madison, N.J.

SOUR CREAM POTATO SALAD

Serves 6

4 cups sliced cooked potatoes
1 cup diced celery
¼ cup chopped onion
¼ cup chopped radishes
1 cup sour cream
¼ cup vinegar
1 tablespoon blue cheese salad dressing
Sliced radishes
Parsley

1. Combine potatoes, celery, onion and chopped radishes.
2. Blend sour cream, vinegar and salad dressing. Pour over vegetables. Toss gently to blend.

3. Garnish with radishes and parsley. Chill for several hours.

Mrs. P. F. Haynes, Woman's Club, Lakeworth, Fla.

SOUR CREAM POTATO EGG SALAD

Serves 8 to 10

6 cups sliced cooked potatoes
⅓ cup Italian dressing
¾ cup diced celery
⅓ cup chopped scallions
4 eggs, hard-cooked and chopped
1 cup mayonnaise
½ cup sour cream
1½ teaspoons horseradish
1 tablespoon prepared mustard

1. Put potatoes in mixing bowl; sprinkle with Italian dressing; toss lightly; chill for 2 hours.
2. Add celery, scallions and eggs; toss lightly.
3. In mixing bowl blend remaining ingredients; pour over vegetables; toss lightly. Chill for 2 hours.

Mrs. W. P. Rochelle, Band Boosters Club, Lonoke, Ark.

SILLSALLAD (Swedish Herring Salad)

Serves 6

This salad makes a satisfying main dish served with dark bread and green vegetables.

2 cups pickled herring, cut into small pieces
2 cups cubed cooked potatoes
2 cups cubed cooked beets
1 cup cubed peeled apples
¼ cup chopped onion
1 tablespoon sugar
¼ teaspoon black pepper
2 cups mayonnaise
2 eggs, hard-cooked and sliced
1 medium cucumber, sliced

1. In mixing bowl combine herring, potatoes, beets, apples and onion; toss lightly.
2. Sprinkle with sugar and pepper; add mayonnaise. Blend well; arrange on serving dish.
3. Garnish with eggs and cucumber. Chill until serving time.

Helen Crozier, Pine Ridge Woman's Club, Fairfax, Va.

TURKISH POTATO SALAD

Serves 6 to 8

5 large potatoes, scrubbed
1 cup chopped boiled beef tongue
1-pound can green beans, drained
1-pound can peas, drained
½ cup chopped celery
2 eggs, hard-cooked and chopped
1 dill pickle, chopped
3 tablespoons mayonnaise
1 tablespoon lemon juice
1 tablespoon olive oil
Salad greens

1. Boil potatoes until tender. Drain. When cool enough to handle, peel; cut into small pieces.
2. Mix potatoes, tongue, vegetables, eggs and pickle.
3. Combine mayonnaise, lemon juice and oil; stir into potato mixture. Chill. Before serving, garnish with greens.

Zeynep Kirdar, Junior Woman's Club, Scottsdale, Ariz.

RICE SALAD

Serves 4 to 6

2 cups cold cooked rice
½ cup chopped celery
1 cup grated Cheddar cheese
10-ounce package frozen peas, cooked and drained
¼ cup diced pimientos
1 teaspoon grated onion
¼ cup sweet pickle relish
2 tablespoons French dressing

1. In mixing bowl combine rice, celery, cheese, peas and pimientos; toss lightly.
2. In small bowl combine remaining ingredients; mix well. Pour over vegetables; toss lightly. Turn into serving dish; chill until serving time.

Mrs. John Mooradian, Woman's Club, Wood-Ridge, N.J.

FAVORITE RICE SALAD

Serves 4

½ cup mayonnaise
¼ cup sour cream
1 tablespoon chopped chives
¼ cup chopped parsley
1 teaspoon salt
⅛ teaspoon pepper
1 tablespoon olive oil
1 tablespoon white wine vinegar
½ cup finely chopped celery
2 cups cooked brown or white rice
2 eggs, hard-cooked and chopped

1. In mixing bowl blend mayonnaise, sour cream, chives, parsley, salt, pepper, oil and vinegar.
2. Add remaining ingredients; toss lightly. Chill for 2 hours to blend flavors.

Mrs. Paul Lampley, Woman's Club, Campo, Tex.

RICE AND SHRIMP SALAD

Serves 4

¼ cup grated onion
2 tablespoons olive oil
1 tablespoon vinegar
½ teaspoon curry powder
1 tablespoon chopped parsley
1 teaspoon salt
¼ teaspoon pepper
1½ cups cooked rice
1 cup chopped celery
1 pound shrimp, shelled, deveined and cooked
¼ cup chopped green pepper
½ cup mayonnaise

1. In mixing bowl combine onion, oil, vinegar, curry powder, parsley, salt and pepper; mix well.

2. Add rice; toss lightly. Chill for 2 hours.

3. Add remaining ingredients; toss lightly. Chill until serving time.

Mrs. Dewey Ashford, Bogue Country Club,
Yuba City, Calif.

RICE, HAM AND CHEESE SALAD

Serves 4 to 6

10-ounce package frozen peas
1⅓ cups boiling salted water
1⅓ cups instant rice
Mayonnaise
½ cup chopped dill pickle
1 teaspoon grated onion
Lettuce leaves
1 cup slivered Swiss cheese
1 cup slivered cooked ham
Tomato slices

1. In saucepan combine peas and water. Cover; bring back to boil. Stir in rice. Cover; remove from heat; let stand for 10 minutes.

2. With a fork stir in ¾ cup mayonnaise, pickle and onion. Chill thoroughly.

3. When ready to serve, pile into lettuce-lined salad bowl; top with cheese and ham. Garnish with tomato; serve with additional mayonnaise on side.

Evelyn Boren, Woman's Club, West Chicago, Ill.

Fish and Shellfish Salads

CRAB SALAD

Serves 6

6½-ounce can crab meat, drained and flaked
1 cup finely chopped celery
1 tablespoon minced or grated onion
4 eggs, hard-cooked and chopped
1 cup mayonnaise
1 cup catsup
1 cup heavy cream, whipped
Shredded lettuce

1. Combine all ingredients except lettuce; chill for serveral hours.

2. Serve on lettuce.

Mabel Riese, Woman's Club, McFarland, Calif.

CRAB SALAD DIABLO

Serves 6

2 6½-ounce cans crab meat, drained
1 cup French dressing
1 cup mayonnaise
2 tablespoons finely chopped celery
3 tablespoons sliced stuffed olives
½ cup thinly sliced cucumber
2 tablespoons chili sauce
1 teaspoon horseradish
½ tablespoon Worcestershire
Salt and cayenne to taste
Lettuce leaves
2 eggs, hard-cooked and sliced
2 tomatoes, sliced
6 radishes

1. Remove membranes from crab meat, keeping chunks whole. Marinate in French dressing for 1 hour.

2. Prepare Sauce Diablo: Put mayonnaise in bowl. Add celery, olives, cucumber, chili sauce, horseradish, Worcestershire, salt and cayenne. Mix; put in serving bowl.

3. Drain crab meat; arrange on lettuce-lined salad plate. Garnish with eggs, tomatoes and radishes. Serve Sauce Diablo separately.

Mrs. William H. Hasebroock, Honorary President,
General Federation of Women's Clubs,
West Point, Neb.

CRAB LOUIE

Serves 6

1 pound fresh lump crab meat
1 head lettuce
½ teaspoon salt
4 tomatoes, quartered
3 eggs, hard-cooked and cut into eighths
1 cucumber, sliced
1 cup mayonnaise
3 tablespoons catsup
2 tablespoons chopped sweet pickle
2 tablespoons lemon juice

1. Remove any shell or cartilage from crab meat, being careful not to break meat into too small pieces.

2. Shred lettuce; arrange in large shallow salad bowl. Sprinkle with salt.

3. Arrange crab meat, tomatoes, eggs and cucumber on lettuce.

4. Prepare Louie Dressing: Combine mayonnaise, catsup, pickle and lemon juice.

5. Spread dressing on salad; chill thoroughly.

Gulf Coast Gourmet, Woman's Club, Foley, Ala.

CRAB RAVIGOTE

Serves 6

1 pound fresh or canned crab meat
¼ cup basil wine vinegar
1 teaspoon salt
½ teaspoon pepper
3 tablespoons chopped pimiento
2 tablespoons chopped chives or scallions
¾ cup Special Salad Dressing for Seafood (p. 545)
6 lettuce cups (optional)
2 tablespoons chopped capers

1. Day before, flake crab meat into bowl. Sprinkle with vinegar; refrigerate overnight.

2. Next day, drain crab meat well, pressing gently.

3. Add salt, pepper, pimiento, chives or scallions and ½ cup of Special Salad Dressing for Seafood. Mix lightly.

4. Pile into 6 scallop shells or lettuce cups, if desired. Cover with remaining dressing; sprinkle with capers.

Rose Harrington, Longvue Women's Club,
Pittsburgh, Pa.

LOBSTER SALAD

Serves 6

2½ cups shredded cooked lobster
½ cup diced celery
2 tablespoons grated onion
2 tablespoons French dressing
⅓ cup mayonnaise
1 tablespoon capers
2 tablespoons chopped parsley
Lettuce leaves

1. In mixing bowl combine lobster, celery, onion and French dressing. Chill for 30 minutes.
2. Add mayonnaise, capers and parsley; toss lightly.
3. Line salad bowl with lettuce; fill with lobster mixture.

Mrs. Mack Chastain, Woman's Club, Cairo, Ga.

SALMON EGG SALAD

Serves 4

7¾-ounce can salmon, drained and
    flaked
¼ cup chopped scallions
½ cup chopped celery
½ cup chopped cucumber
3 eggs, hard-cooked and chopped
⅓ cup mayonnaise
1 teaspoon salt
¼ teaspoon thyme
¼ teaspoon basil
¼ teaspoon tarragon
⅓ cup dry white wine
2 tablespoons chopped parsley

1. Put salmon in mixing bowl. Add scallions, celery, cucumber and eggs; mix lightly.
2. In small bowl combine remaining ingredients. Mix well.
3. Pour over salmon; toss lightly. Arrange on serving dish; chill until serving time.

Ann Neiburg, Woman's Club, Paxton, Ill.

SALMON AND EGGS À LA WRIGLEY

Serves 6

1-pound can salmon, drained,
    boned and flaked
2 6½-ounce cans tuna, drained
    and flaked
1½-ounce can sardines, drained
½ cup mayonnaise
3 tablespoons French dressing
3 tablespoons chili sauce
6 eggs, hard-cooked
    Lettuce leaves
    Parsley
    Thousand Island Dressing (p. 544)

1. Combine salmon, tuna and sardines in mixing bowl; mix well. Add mayonnaise, French dressing and chili sauce; mix to a smooth paste.
2. Cut eggs in half lengthwise; remove small slice of white from the bottom of each half to make a steady base.
3. Arrange lettuce on serving dish; top with egg halves. Spoon fish mixture on each egg half; garnish with parsley and Thousand Island Dressing.

Theba Cockreham, Pine River Pow Wow Club, Bayfield, Colo.

SALMON FRUIT SALAD

Serves 6

1-pound can salmon, drained
1 tablespoon lemon juice
2 oranges, peeled and sectioned
1 banana, sliced
1 red apple, unpeeled and diced
½ teaspoon salt
½ cup toasted blanched almonds
3 cups shredded lettuce
    Mayonnaise
    Additional orange sections
    Water cress

1. Break salmon into bite-size chunks. Sprinkle with lemon juice.
2. Combine fruits. Add salmon, salt, almonds, lettuce and 1 cup mayonnaise. Toss lightly; arrange on cold salad plates; top with orange sections and a dab of mayonnaise. Garnish with water cress.

Margaret G. Miekle, Woman's Club, Anchorage, Alaska

SEAFOOD PIERRE

Serves 6

½ pound crab meat, cooked
1 pound shrimp, shelled, deveined
    and cooked
2 tablespoons French dressing
1 cup diced celery
½ cup diced cucumber
2 tablespoons chopped radishes
1 tablespoon chopped capers
3 tablespoons lemon juice
½ cup mayonnaise
    Salt and freshly ground pepper
    to taste
    Lettuce leaves

1. Flake crab meat, removing any bits of shell or cartilage.
2. Combine shrimp and crab meat. Add French dressing. Chill for 15 minutes.
3. Add all remaining ingredients except lettuce; toss lightly. Serve on lettuce.

Gulf Coast Gourmet, Woman's Club, Foley, Ala.

SHRIMP ARNAUD

Serves 6 to 8

½ clove garlic
½ cup catsup
¼ cup vinegar
½ cup olive oil
1 teaspoon prepared mustard
1 teaspoon horseradish
1 teaspoon salt
¼ teaspoon pepper
2½ pounds shrimp, shelled, deveined
    and cooked
    Lettuce leaves

1. Rub salad bowl with garlic.
2. In bowl combine catsup, vinegar, oil, mustard, horseradish, salt and pepper; mix well.
3. Add shrimp; toss well. Chill for 6 hours, stirring occasionally.

4. Remove shrimp; wipe bowl. Line bowl with lettuce; fill with shrimp.

Pierian Study Club, Vivian, La.

SHRIMP RÉMOULADE

Serves 8 or 9

Shrimp will absorb flavor of sauce more quickly if freshly cooked and added to sauce while still warm.

    3 pounds shrimp, shelled, deveined
      and cooked
    6 tablespoons olive oil
    2 tablespoons vinegar
    1 tablespoon paprika
    4 tablespoons Creole mustard
    2 tablespoons grated fresh
      horseradish
    3 tablespoons pepper vinegar
    ½ teaspoon white pepper
    ½ teaspoon salt
    1 teaspoon sugar
    ¼ teaspoon cayenne
    ½ onion, grated
    1 clove garlic, grated
    2 tablespoons minced parsley
      Dash of lemon juice
      Lettuce leaves
      Stuffed olives and anchovy fillets
      (optional)

1. Put shrimp in serving bowl.
2. Combine remaining ingredients. Pour over shrimp. Chill thoroughly.
3. Serve on lettuce. Garnish with olives and anchovies, if desired.

Marjorie H. Jordan, Modern Study Club, Mobile, Ala.

TUNA FISH SALAD

Serves 2

    7-ounce can tuna, drained and
      flaked
    3 eggs, hard-cooked and chopped
    ¼ cup chopped pecans
    ½ cup chopped celery
    ¼ cup chopped sweet mixed pickles
      A little minced onion and garlic
      Mayonnaise
      Salt and pepper to taste
      Lettuce leaves

1. Combine tuna, chopped ingredients, onion and garlic; moisten with mayonnaise. Season with salt and pepper.
2. Serve on lettuce.

Nell Nollman, Woman's Club, Starke, Fla.

MANDARIN TUNA SALAD

Serves 6

    2 6½-ounce cans tuna, drained
    ½ cup finely chopped celery
    3 tablespoons French dressing
    1 tablespoon grated onion
    1 tablespoon chopped parsley
    ½ teaspoon curry powder
    ⅓ cup mayonnaise
    ¼ cup walnuts
    11-ounce can mandarin oranges,
      drained
      Salad greens

1. Put tuna in mixing bowl; break into large chunks. Add celery and French dressing; toss lightly. Chill.
2. Add onion, parsley, curry powder and mayonnaise; mix well. Add walnuts and mandarin oranges; toss lightly.
3. Arrange on greens.

Ruth Spencer, E. O. F. Club, Jesop, Ia.

RONDA JO'S SALAD

Serves 4

    7-ounce can solid-pack tuna,
      drained
    1 red apple, cored and diced
    1 cup chopped celery
    ½ cup seedless raisins
    ¼ cup mayonnaise
      Salad greens
    ¼ cup chopped walnuts or pecans

1. Put tuna in mixing bowl; break into large chunks. Add apple, celery, raisins and mayonnaise; toss lightly. Chill for 1 hour.
2. Arrange greens on serving dish; top with tuna mixture. Sprinkle with nuts.

Lois Smith, Woman's Club, Temple Terrace, Fla.

Chicken and Meat Salads

NOTE: Cooked turkey meat may be substituted for the chicken in all the following chicken salad recipes.

CHICKEN SALAD

Serves 6

    3 cups cubed cooked chicken
    1½ cups diced celery
    1 teaspoon salt
    3 eggs, hard-cooked and quartered
    3 sweet pickles, chopped
      Mayonnaise
      Lettuce leaves
      Sliced stuffed olives

1. Combine chicken, celery, salt, eggs and pickles. Moisten with mayonnaise.
2. Serve on lettuce; garnish with olives.

Emily E. Harrington, Woman's Club, West Chicago, Ill.

CHICKEN ALMOND SALAD

Serves 8

    4 cups diced cooked chicken
    4 cups diced celery
    ½ cup split blanched almonds
    ¼ cup chopped pimientos
    1 teaspoon salt
    ¼ teaspoon paprika
    1 cup mayonnaise
    1 cup whipped cream
      Lettuce leaves
      Hard-cooked eggs
      Stuffed olives

1. In mixing bowl combine chicken, celery, almonds, pimientos, salt and paprika.

2. Blend mayonnaise and cream. Add half to chicken mixture; blend lightly. Chill.

3. Serve on lettuce. Garnish with eggs and olives; top with remaining dressing.

Mrs. C. E. Hutchings, South Side Woman's Club, Denver, Colo.

CURRIED CHICKEN SALAD
Serves 4

2 cups cubed cooked chicken
½ cup chopped celery
1 pink grapefruit, sectioned
½ cup thinly shredded skinned
   green pepper
12 small cucumber balls
½ cup French dressing
   Mayonnaise
1 teaspoon curry powder
1 tablespoon grated onion
1 tablespoon chopped parsley
1 tablespoon chopped chives
   Water cress
   Paprika
2 tablespoons capers

1. In mixing bowl combine chicken, celery, grapefruit, green pepper, cucumber and French dressing. Toss well; chill.

2. Just before serving, press out excess dressing.

3. Toss salad with ½ cup mayonnaise, curry powder, onion, parsley and chives.

4. Line salad bowl with water cress; spoon in salad. Garnish with mayonnaise forced through pastry tube. Sprinkle with paprika and capers.

Mrs. John Postel, Palm Springs Woman's Club, Hialeah, Fla.

ELEGANT CHICKEN SALAD
Serves 6

3 cups cubed cooked chicken
1 cup diced celery
½ cup seedless grapes
¼ cup flaked coconut
½ cup pecans or toasted almonds
¼ cup heavy cream, whipped
½ cup mayonnaise
½ teaspoon salt
6 lettuce cups

1. In large bowl combine chicken, celery, grapes and coconut. Chill.

2. Just before serving, add nuts; toss lightly.

3. In small bowl blend cream, mayonnaise and salt. Add to chicken mixture; toss lightly. Serve in lettuce cups.

Mrs. Robert C. Magley, Woman's Club, Edensburg, Pa.

HAWAIIAN CHICKEN SALAD
Serves 6

8-ounce can pineapple tidbits
3 cups diced cooked chicken
1 cup diced celery
½ cup almonds
1 cup seedless grapes (optional)
1 tablespoon olive oil
1 teaspoon vinegar
½ cup mayonnaise

1 teaspoon salt
6 lettuce cups
   Olives
   Sweet pickles
   Parsley

1. Drain pineapple; reserve 1 tablespoon syrup.

2. In large mixing bowl lightly toss chicken, celery, pineapple, almonds and grapes.

3. In small bowl mix reserved syrup, oil, vinegar, mayonnaise and salt. Pour over chicken; toss lightly.

4. Arrange in lettuce cups. Garnish with olives, pickles and parsley or as desired.

Mrs. William Wenstrand and Mrs. Marvin Hillman, Tomorrow's Club, Essex, Ia.

PARSNIP CHICKEN SALAD
Serves 6

1 clove garlic, cut
   Lettuce leaves
2 cups grated parsnips
1 cup chopped cooked chicken
¼ cup chopped scallions
2 eggs, hard-cooked and chopped
¾ cup mayonnaise
2 tablespoons prepared mustard
1 tablespoon lemon juice
½ teaspoon salt
   Dash of pepper

1. Rub salad bowl with garlic.

2. Line bowl with lettuce.

3. In mixing bowl combine parsnips, chicken, scallions and eggs. Blend mayonnaise, mustard, lemon juice, salt and pepper. Add to chicken mixture; toss lightly.

4. Pile into salad bowl; chill until serving time.

Mrs. Loraine Cook, Woman's Club, Spencer, Wis.

SWEETHEART CHICKEN SALAD
Serves 6

1½ cups diced cooked chicken
1½ cups diced celery
1 small white onion, minced
4 eggs, hard-cooked and coarsely
   chopped
1½ cups diced peeled apples
½ cup mayonnaise
¾ teaspoon salt
2 tablespoons vinegar
   Lettuce leaves
   Jellied cranberry sauce

1. Combine chicken, celery, onion, eggs and apples.

2. Combine mayonnaise, salt and vinegar. Add to chicken mixture; toss lightly. Chill for 30 minutes.

3. Arrange on lettuce. Garnish with heart cut out of cranberry.

Mrs. L. G. Abraham, Thursday Morning Club, Madison, N.J.

GILDE SALAD (Roast Beef and Herring Salad)

Serves 8

1½-pound salted herring
1½ pounds roast beef
2 cups diced cooked beets
2½ cups diced cooked potatoes
2 apples, cored and diced
Dash of pepper
⅛ teaspoon sugar
1 dill pickle, diced
5 tablespoons vinegar
2 eggs, hard-cooked and sliced
1 cup heavy cream, whipped
3 tablespoons beet juice

1. Day before, put herring in mixing bowl; cover with water. Soak overnight.
2. Next day, drain herring; bone; dice.
3. Dice beef; turn with herring into mixing bowl. Add beets, potatoes and apples; sprinkle with pepper and sugar. Add pickle; sprinkle with vinegar; toss lightly.
4. Turn into serving dish; garnish with eggs.
5. Blend cream with beet juice; serve with salad.

Jean Peterson, People's Church Women's Club, Chicago, Ill.

CORNED BEEF AND CABBAGE SALAD

Serves 4

2½ cups shredded cabbage
¼ teaspoon salt
2 tablespoons chopped celery
1 tablespoon finely chopped onion
1 tablespoon finely chopped green pepper
3 tablespoons French dressing
¾ cup diced cooked corned beef
¼ cup mayonnaise
4 lettuce leaves

1. In mixing bowl combine cabbage, salt, celery, onion, green pepper and French dressing. Chill for 1 hour.
2. Add corned beef and mayonnaise; toss lightly.
3. Arrange lettuce on serving dish; fill each leaf with meat mixture.

Mrs. Ernest E. Johnson, Woman's Club, Flagstaff, Ariz.

HAM AND PEAS SALAD

Serves 6

1 cup chilled canned peas drained
1 tablespoon minced Bermuda onion
5 eggs, hard-cooked and chopped
½ cup chopped celery
1 to 1½ cups chopped cooked ham
Salt to taste
About 4 tablespoons mayonnaise
6 lettuce cups
Potato chips or cheese-flavored wafers

1. Combine peas, onion, eggs, celery and ham. Sprinkle with salt; moisten with mayonnaise.

2. Serve in lettuce cups accompanied by potato chips or wafers, as desired.

Joy Smith, Junior Study Club, San Augustine, Tex.

Fruit Salads

APPLE SALAD

Serves 6

5 medium apples, peeled, cored and diced
½ cup chopped walnuts
¼ cup finely chopped celery
2 tablespoons minced onion
⅓ cup mayonnaise
1 ounce blue cheese, crumbled
Dash of Tabasco
6 lettuce cups

1. In mixing bowl combine apples, walnuts, celery and onion.
2. In small bowl blend mayonnaise, cheese and Tabasco. Pour over apples; toss lightly.
3. Fill lettuce cups.

Mrs. Emma Tucker, Judith Lyford Woman's Club, Cabot, Vt.

APPLE BACON SALAD

Serves 4

10 slices lean bacon, cut into 1-inch pieces
1 cup diced red apples
1 cup diced celery
½ cup broken walnuts or pecans
½ cup cubed Cheddar cheese
½ cup mayonnaise
4 lettuce cups
Paprika

1. Cook bacon until golden and crisp. Drain on absorbent paper; crumble.
2. In mixing bowl combine bacon, apples, celery, nuts and cheese. Stir in mayonnaise.
3. Serve in lettuce cups. Sprinkle with paprika.

Mrs. Arthur Messenger, Thursday Morning Club, Madison, N.J.

STUFFED CINNAMON APPLE SALAD

Serves 6

2 cups sugar
2 cups water
1 cup cinnamon candies
6 medium apples, peeled and cored
2 3-ounce packages cream cheese
2 tablespoons mayonnaise
¼ cup finely chopped walnuts
Lettuce leaves

1. In skillet combine sugar, water and candies. Bring to boil; then simmer for 5 minutes.
2. Add apples; cover; simmer for 5 minutes, or until tender. Drain apples; chill.

3. In small bowl blend cheese and mayonnaise until smooth. Stir in walnuts; use to fill centers of apples.

4. Arrange on lettuce.

Mrs. Lloyd Haynes, Women's Club,
Cumberland, Ky.

WALDORF SALAD

Serves 4

2 cups diced peeled apples
1 cup finely diced celery
½ cup coarsely chopped walnuts
½ cup mayonnaise
1 teaspoon lemon juice
Salt and pepper to taste
Lettuce leaves

1. Combine apples, celery and walnuts.
2. Combine mayonnaise and lemon juice. Stir into apple mixture; season with salt and pepper.
3. Serve on lettuce.

A. S.

AVOCADO SALAD

Serves 6

3 avocados
1 cup pineapple cubes
1 cup seedless grapes, halved
2 oranges, peeled and sectioned
½ cup grapefruit sections (optional)
French dressing
Lettuce leaves
Mint

1. Cut avocados in half lengthwise. Discard pits; scoop out pulp with melon ball cutter. Reserve shells.
2. Combine avocado balls and other fruits; moisten with French dressing. Chill for about 20 minutes.
3. Fill avocado shells; arrange on individual salad plates garnished with lettuce. Garnish salad with mint.

Mrs. Charles Young, Woman's Club,
Chappaqua, N.Y.

STUFFED CANTALOUPE SALAD

Serves 4

1 medium cantaloupe
½ cup diced orange
½ cup diced banana
1 tart apple, cored and diced
½ cup crushed pineapple
⅓ cup French dressing
½ cup mayonnaise
Lettuce

1. Chill all fruits.
2. Just before serving, cut cantaloupe in quarters. Pare off rind; scrape out seeds. Arrange on salad plates.
3. Combine orange, banana, apple, pineapple and French dressing; mix lightly. Pile on cantaloupe; top with mayonnaise. Garnish with lettuce.

Mrs. Demi Mack, Woman's Club, Nitro, W.Va.

CRANBERRY APPLE ORANGE SALAD

Serves 8

1 pound fresh or frozen canberries
6 tart apples, cored

1 orange, pitted
1½ cups sugar
1 cup heavy cream

1. Day before, put cranberries, apples and orange through large blade of meat grinder. Turn into mixing bowl; stir in sugar. Refrigerate overnight.
2. Next day in mixing bowl whip cream until stiff; fold into cranberry mixture. Turn into serving dish. Chill until serving time.

Mrs. K. E. Underhill, Akitsa Club,
Centralia, Wash.

CRANBERRY GRAPE SALAD

Serves 8

1 pound cranberries
2 cups sugar
1 pound seedless grapes, finely cut
1 cup chopped nuts
Pinch of salt
2 cups heavy cream, whipped

1. Put cranberries through meat grinder. Stir in sugar and grapes; let stand for at least 2 hours or overnight.
2. Drain cranberries and grapes; combine with nuts.
3. Add salt to cream; fold in fruit mixture. Chill for 2 hours before serving.

Mrs. O. Hall, Woman's Club, Eolia, Mo.

CRANBERRY PINEAPPLE NUT SALAD

Serves 8

1 quart or 1 pound fresh or frozen cranberries
1½ cups sugar
1 cup chopped nuts
1½ cups crushed pineapple, drained
1 cup tiny marshmallows

1. Put cranberries through meat grinder (if frozen they are easier to grind).
2. Combine with remaining ingredients; chill until serving time.

Mrs. Howard Bossaller, Young Adults'
Study Club, Slater, Mo.

TOKAY CUCUMBER RELISH SALAD

Makes About 1 Pint

1½ cups Tokay grapes, halved and seeded
½ cup diced cucumber
½ cup sour cream
1½ tablespoons vinegar
2 teaspoons sugar
⅛ teaspoon salt

1. In bowl mix grapes and cucumber.
2. Blend sour cream, vinegar, sugar and salt.
3. Pour over grapes and cucumber; mix well. Chill until serving time.

Mrs. Harley L. Dangremond, Chairman,
General Federation of Women's Clubs,
Home Life Department, Teaneck, N.J.

INDIVIDUAL GRAPE-CLUSTER SALAD

Serves 4

2 cups red grapes
3-ounce package cream cheese
2 tablespoons mayonnaise
4 canned pear halves
4 lettuce leaves

1. Cut grapes in half; discard seeds.
2. In small bowl blend cheese and mayonnaise until smooth.
3. Arrange each pear half, cut side down, on lettuce leaf on serving dish. Spread cheese mixture generously over pear halves; stud with grape halves, being careful to follow outline of pear so it resembles a bunch of grapes. Chill until serving time.

Civic Culture Club, Madison, Kans.

PEACH BANANA FAN SALAD

Serves 4

4 lettuce leaves
4 peach halves
4 maraschino cherries
4 ripe bananas
Water cress
Favorite tart or sweet salad dressing

1. Arrange lettuce leaf on each salad plate.
2. Place peach half on lettuce; put cherry in center of peach.
3. Peel bananas; cut into 3 sections; cut each section in half lengthwise. Arrange banana slices around half the peach, fanning them out over lettuce.
4. Garnish with water cress. Serve with dressing.

Mrs. Steve Rose, Wolfe County Woman's Club, Campton, Ky.

PINEAPPLE BANANA SALAD

Serves 4

1-pound can pineapple chunks
¼ cup sugar
2 tablespoons flour
1 egg, well beaten
1 tablespoon butter
2 tablespoons cider vinegar
1½ cups tiny marshmallows
4 bananas, sliced

1. Drain pineapple syrup into saucepan or top of double saucepan. Stir in sugar, flour and egg. Cook over low heat or simmering water, stirring constantly, until dressing is thickened and smooth.
2. Remove from heat. Stir in butter and vinegar. Cool.
3. Combine dressing, pineapple, marshmallows and bananas. Chill until serving time.

Mrs. W. E. Arrington, Quest Club, Bowling Green, Mo.

PINEAPPLE CHERRY CHEESE SALAD

Serves 4

½ cup softened cream cheese
¼ cup French dressing

½ pound tiny marshmallows
1-pound can Royal Ann cherries
½ cup crushed pineapple, drained
½ teaspoon salt
1 cup heavy cream

1. Combine cheese and French dressing; beat thoroughly.
2. Add to marshmallows, cherries and pineapple; mix well.
3. Add salt to cream; beat until stiff. Fold into fruit mixture; chill for at least 2 hours.

Mrs. C. C. Grage, Woman's Club, Hugoton, Kans.

HIGH HAT SALAD

Pineapple slices
Cottage cheese
Cranberry sauce, sliced
Water cress
Mayonnaise

1. For each serving, arrange pineapple slice on serving dish. Top with large spoonful of cheese, then cranberry slice and small spoonful of cheese.
2. Garnish with water cress. Serve with mayonnaise.

Mrs. Russel Murton, Woman's Club, Lantana, Fla.

TWENTY-FOUR-HOUR FRUIT SALAD WITH SOUR CREAM

Serves 4 to 6

8-ounce can mandarin orange sections, drained
8-ounce can pineapple tidbits, drained
1½ cups shredded coconut
1 cup tiny marshmallows
1½ cups chopped pecans (optional)
¾ cup sour cream
4 maraschino cherries, chopped

1. Day before, in mixing bowl combine marshmallows and pecans, if desired. Fold in sour cream. Refrigerate overnight.
2. Next day, turn into serving bowl. Sprinkle with cherries.

Inez Valdois, La Cadena Club, Haven, Kans.

SUMMER FRESH FRUIT SALAD

½ watermelon
Cantaloupe balls
Seedless grapes
Peach slices
Pear slices
Strawberries
Red and black raspberries
Banana slices
Pineapple cubes
Black cherries
Apple cubes
Delicious Salad Dressing for Fruit Salads (p. 546)

1. Scoop red flesh from watermelon with melon ball cutter. Drain shell well.
2. Fill shell with watermelon balls combined with the other fruits and berries. Chill until serving time.
3. Serve with Delicious Salad Dressing for Fruit Salads.

NOTE: For a small party use a large cantaloupe or honeydew melon instead of a watermelon. Put the melon on a platter, and decorate it with large leaves.

Mrs. Fred Buettner, Woman's Club,
Crystal Lake, Ill.

TWENTY-FOUR-HOUR FRUIT SALAD WITH CUSTARD DRESSING

Serves 6

2 eggs
¼ cup vinegar
¼ cup sugar
2 tablespoons butter or margarine
2 cups white cherries, halved
2 cups pineapple chunks
2 oranges, peeled and sectioned
1 cup seedless grapes
2 cups tiny marshmallows
1 cup heavy cream, whipped

1. Day before, prepare custard dressing: In top of double saucepan combine eggs, vinegar and sugar. Cook over hot water, stirring constantly, until thickened and smooth. Remove from heat. Beat in butter or margarine. Cool.
2. Meanwhile, toss fruits lightly in serving dish. Add marshmallows; toss lightly.
3. Fold cream and custard dressing into fruits. Refrigerate for 24 hours.

Mrs. E. Lee Ozbirn, Honorary President,
General Federation of Women's Clubs,
Oklahoma City, Okla.

Frozen Salads

FROZEN FRUIT SALAD

Serves 6

3-ounce package cream cheese
2 tablespoons cream
⅓ cup mayonnaise
2 tablespoons lemon juice
Pinch of salt
1 cup canned pineapple, cut into small pieces
1 cup orange sections, sliced
½ cup Royal Ann cherries, pitted and quartered
½ cup chopped maraschino cherries
½ cup chopped pecans
1 cup heavy cream, whipped
2 tablespoons sugar

1. Mix cheese and 2 tablespoons cream thoroughly. Stir in mayonnaise, lemon juice and salt.
2. Combine fruits and pecans; stir into cheese mixture.
3. Mix whipped cream and sugar. Fold into mixture. Pour into refrigerator tray; freeze without stirring.

Mrs. D. C. Hungerford, Thursday Morning Club,
Madison, N.J.

FROZEN CRANBERRY APPLE SALAD

Serves 10 to 12

1 pound cranberries
3 red apples
1 cup sugar
1 cup chopped pecans
1 package tiny marshmallows
1 cup heavy cream, whipped

1. Wash cranberries; drain well.
2. Quarter apples; core, but do not peel.
3. Put cranberries and apples through meat grinder into bowl. Stir in sugar; let stand for 30 minutes.
4. Fold fruit mixture, pecans and marshmallows into cream. Spoon into 8-inch square baking pan; cover with aluminum foil; freeze.
5. To serve, remove foil; cut into squares.

Billie Atchison, Culture Club, Columbiana, Ala.

PINK ARCTIC SALAD

Serves 6 to 8

2 3-ounce packages cream cheese
2 tablespoons sugar
Dash of salt
2 tablespoons mayonnaise
1-pound can cranberries, undrained
9-ounce can crushed pineapple, drained
½ cup chopped pecans
2 cups heavy cream, whipped

1. In mixing bowl beat cheese, sugar, salt and mayonnaise until smooth.
2. Stir in cranberries, pineapple and pecans until well mixed. Fold in cream.
3. Pour into refrigerator trays; freeze, stirring occasionally.

Mrs. Fenley Mass, 20th Century Club,
Ackerman, Miss.

FROZEN GINGER ALE SALAD

Serves 6

1 envelope gelatin
¼ cup orange juice
2 tablespoons lemon juice
¼ cup sugar
1 cup ginger ale
¼ cup crushed strawberries or raspberries
¼ cup diced pears
¾ cup mayonnaise
1 cup heavy cream, whipped
Lettuce leaves

1. Soak gelatin in orange juice in top of double saucepan for 5 minutes; heat over simmering water until dissolved.
2. Add lemon juice, sugar and ginger ale; stir until sugar is dissolved. Add fruits; cool until slightly thickened.
3. Fold in mayonnaise and cream. Pour into refrigerator tray; freeze.
4. Cut into squares. Serve on lettuce.

Mrs. Olive Gooch, Woman's Club, Hugoton, Kans.

FROZEN GRAPE SALAD

Serves 6 to 8

1-pound 4-ounce can pineapple
   tidbits
2 3-ounce packages cream cheese
2 tablespoons favorite salad dressing
2 cups tiny marshmallows
2 cups green grapes, halved and
   seeded
1 cup heavy cream, whipped

1. Drain pineapple; reserve 2 tablespoons syrup.
2. In bowl blend reserved syrup, cheese
and salad dressing until smooth.
3. Stir in marshmallows and grapes; fold
in cream. Turn into refrigerator tray;
freeze for 2 to 3 hours, or until firm.
4. Cut into squares.

Margaret Edminson, Federated Civic Club,
Mount Vernon, Ill.

FROZEN PEACH SALAD

Serves 6 to 8

1 cup crushed macaroons
2 cups finely chopped peaches
1 tablespoon lemon juice
1¼ cups sugar
1 cup heavy cream, whipped

1. Arrange ½ cup of the macaroons in 1-
quart refrigerator tray.
2. In mixing bowl mix peaches, lemon
juice and sugar. Fold in cream. Turn into
tray. Sprinkle with remaining macaroons.
3. Freeze for 4 to 6 hours, or until firm.

Mrs. D. F. Davis, Woman's Club,
Newcomerstown, Ohio

FROZEN PEAR SALAD

Serves 6

1-pound can sliced pears
3-ounces package cream cheese
3 tablespoons French dressing
   Chopped nuts
   Chopped maraschino cherries
   Lettuce leaves

1. Drain syrup from pears; mix syrup
and cheese. Add French dressing; beat
until creamy. Add nuts and cherries.
2. Arrange pears in refrigerator tray;
pour cheese mixture on top. Freeze for 4 to
5 hours, or until firm.
3. Cut into squares; serve on lettuce.

Mrs. David Broadfoot, Junior Woman's Club,
Wauwatosa, Wis.

RECEPTION SALAD

Serves 12 to 14

2 3-ounce packages lemon gelatin
1-pound 4-ounce can crushed
   pineapple
8-ounce package cream cheese
4-ounce can pimientos, drained
1 cup chopped nuts
1 cup finely chopped celery
1 cup heavy cream, whipped
   Lettuce leaves

1. Put gelatin in mixing bowl.
2. Drain pineapple syrup into large
measuring cup; add water to total 1½
cups. Pour into saucepan; bring to boil.

Pour over gelatin; stir until dissolved. Chill
until gelatin begins to set.
3. Meanwhile, cream the cheese and
pimientos.
4. Fold cheese mixture into gelatin mixture. Stir in pineapple, nuts and celery.
Fold in cream. Pour into individual molds
or baking pan; freeze.
5. Cut into squares; serve on lettuce.

Mrs. J. A. Chandler, Book Lovers Club,
Kosciusko, Miss.

YELLOW CHEESE AND
PINEAPPLE SALAD

Serves 8 to 12

1 envelope gelatin
½ cup water
1-pound 4-ounce can crushed
   pineapple, undrained
½ cup sugar
1 cup chopped nuts
1 cup shredded American cheese
1 cup mayonnaise
1 cup heavy cream, whipped
   Lettuce leaves or water cress

1. Soak gelatin in water.
2. In saucepan combine pineapple and
sugar. Bring to boil; boil for 3 minutes.
Remove from heat. Stir in gelatin. Cool
until syrupy.
3. Fold in remaining ingredients. Pour
into 2-quart baking dish; freeze.
4. Remove from freezer about 30 minutes before serving time. Slice; serve on
lettuce or water cress, as desired.

Mrs. Lena A. Armour, Literary and Civic Club,
Houlka, Miss.

Molded Salads

MOLDED AMBROSIA SALAD

Serves 10

3-ounce package orange gelatin
1 cup boiling water
1 cup undrained crushed pineapple
1 cup chopped pecans
1 cup mandarin orange sections
½ cup grated coconut
1 cup sour cream
⅓ cup sugar

1. Dissolve gelatin in water. Add pineapple. Cool.
2. Stir in remaining ingredients.
3. Pour into 6-cup mold; chill until firm.

Mrs. L. Rogers, Inter Se Circle, Marion, Ala.

CINNAMON CANDY APPLE SALAD

Serves 12

½ cup red cinnamon candies
3 cups water
2 3-ounce packages cherry gelatin
2 cups chopped peeled apples
2 cups chopped celery
1 cup chopped pecans or walnuts

1. Combine candies and water in saucepan; bring to boil. Remove from heat; stir

until dissolved. Pour over gelatin in bowl; stir until dissolved. Chill until partially set.

2. Fold in remaining ingredients. Turn into 8-cup mold or 12 individual molds. Chill.

Mrs. W. E. Arrington, Quest Club, Bowling Green, Mo.

JELLIED WALDORF LUNCHEON SALAD

Serves 6

3-ounce package apple gelatin
1 cup boiling water
¾ cup apple cider
Lemon juice
1 large apple
⅓ cup slivered toasted almonds
¼ cup minced celery
Salad greens
Cottage cheese
Blanched almonds
Cider Dressing (p. 543)

1. Dissolve gelatin in water. Add cider and 3 tablespoons lemon juice. Chill until syrupy.
2. Core apple; cut into thin slices. Cut slices into small wedges to total 1 cup. Sprinkle remaining slices with lemon juice; reserve.
3. Fold apple wedges, toasted almonds and celery into gelatin. Pour into 8-inch ring mild; chill until set.
4. Unmold on greens. Fill center with cheese; garnish with reserved apple slices and blanched almonds. Serve with Cider Dressing.

Mrs. George Habbenggar, Junior Woman's Club, Wauwatosa, Wis.

APPLESAUCE PINEAPPLE SALAD

Serves 6

1-pound can applesauce
3-ounce package lime gelatin
8-ounce can crushed pineapple, undrained
½ cup ginger ale
2 tablespoons lemon juice
1 cup chopped pecans

1. Combine applesauce and gelatin. Stir in pineapple and ginger ale. Stir over low heat until gelatin is completely dissolved.
2. Remove from heat. Stir in lemon juice and pecans.
3. Pour into 6-cup mold or 6 individual molds; chill until set. Unmold when ready to serve.

Ellen D. Rodgers, Tuesday Study Club, Aliceville, Ala.

APRICOT SALAD

Serves 8

2 3-ounce packages orange gelatin
2 cups boiling water
10 marshmallows, chopped
½ cup undrained crushed pineapple
1 cup apricot nectar or juice
½ cup sugar
3 tablespoons flour
1 egg, lightly beaten
2 tablespoons butter

½ cup heavy cream, whipped
Grated Cheddar cheese

1. Put gelatin in bowl; add water and marshmallows; stir until marshmallows are dissolved. Cool.
2. Drain pineapple into measuring cup; add water to total ½ cup; reserve.
3. Stir ½ cup of the apricot nectar or juice, apricots and pineapple into marshmallow mixture. Pour into 2-quart mold; chill until firm.
4. Meanwhile, in saucepan or top of double saucepan combine sugar, flour, egg, reserved pineapple liquid, and remaining apricot nectar or juice. Cook over low heat or simmering water, stirring constantly, until thickened. Remove from heat. Stir in butter. Cool.
5. Fold in cream. Spread on molded salad; sprinkle with cheese. Chill until serving time.

Mrs. Pat Cronan, Cosmos Club, Vandalia, Mo.

APRICOT NECTAR SALAD

Serves 6

12-ounce can apricot nectar
3-ounce package pineapple or orange gelatin
8-ounce can crushed pineapple, undrained
½ cup chopped nuts
2 bananas, sliced

1. Heat 1 cup of the apricot nectar. Add gelatin; stir until dissolved. Add remaining nectar and pineapple; cool until slightly thickened.
2. Add nuts and bananas. Pour into 1-quart mold or dish; chill.

Mrs. Clyde Adams, Woman's Club, Clinton, Mo.

ASPARAGUS CUP SALAD

Serves 8

2 envelopes gelatin
¼ cup water
1 cup asparagus juice
1 cup chopped canned asparagus
1 cup slivered almonds
1 cup finely chopped celery
1¼ cups mayonnaise
½ cup heavy cream, whipped
8 pineapple slices
8 ripe olives

1. In small saucepan soften gelatin in water. Stir in asparagus juice; bring to boil; simmer until dissolved. Chill to consistency of egg whites.
2. Stir asparagus, almonds and celery into gelatin. Fold in 1 cup of the mayonnaise and cream. Turn into 8 individual molds. Chill until firm.
3. Arrange pineapple on serving dish; top each slice with unmolded salad. Top each with 1 teaspoon of the mayonnaise and olive.

Mrs. Louis Kilpatrick, Civic Club, Fulton, Miss.

AVOCADO MOLD

Serves 6 to 8

1½ envelopes gelatin
½ cup cold water
¾ cup boiling water
2 tablespoons lemon juice
1¼ teaspoons salt
1 teaspoon grated onion
2 dashes Tabasco
2½ cups sieved ripe avocados
1 cup sour cream
1 cup mayonnaise

1. Lightly oil 6-cup mold.
2. In bowl soften gelatin in cold water. Add boiling water; stir until dissolved.
3. Stir in lemon juice, salt, onion and Tabasco; cool.
4. Stir in avocados, sour cream and mayonnaise. Turn into mold; chill until firm.
5. Unmold onto serving dish; garnish as desired.

Mrs. Thomas S. Arms, Jr., Woman's Club,
McLean, Va.

AVOCADO RING MOLD

Serves 6 to 8

Fill center with diced fruits or as desired.

3-ounce package lemon gelatin
3-ounce package lime gelatin
3 cups boiling water
¼ cup lemon juice
¼ teaspoon salt
1 cup mashed avocado
9-ounce can crushed pineapple, drained
1 cup mayonnaise
½ cup heavy cream, whipped

1. Lightly oil 8-inch ring mold.
2. In bowl stir gelatins in water until dissolved.
3. Cool; stir in lemon juice, salt, avocado and pineapple. Chill until mixture starts to thicken.
4. Fold in mayonnaise and cream; turn into mold. Chill until firm.
5. Unmold onto serving dish.

Mrs. J. T. Coatsworth, Senior Woman's Club,
Dallas, Pa.

BANANA MARSHMALLOW SALAD

Serves 4 to 6

3-ounce package lemon gelatin
2 cups boiling water
8-ounce can crushed pineapple
2 large bananas, sliced
1½ cups tiny marshmallows
1 egg, lightly beaten
3 tablespoons flour
2 tablespoons butter
1 or 2 tablespoons sugar
1 cup heavy cream, whipped
Grated Cheddar cheese

1. Dissolve gelatin in water; cool until syrupy.
2. Drain pineapple into measuring cup; add water to total 1 cup; reserve.

3. Stir pineapple, bananas and marshmallow into gelatin. Pour into 2-quart mold; chill.
4. Meanwhile, in saucepan or top of double saucepan combine egg, flour and butter. Gradually stir in reserved pineapple liquid. Cook over low heat or over simmering water, stirring constantly, until thickened. Cool.
5. Combine sugar and cream; fold into egg mixture. Pour over molded salad; sprinkle with cheese. Chill until serving time.

Mrs. W. W. Backus, Atheneum Club,
Springfield, Colo.

COLESLAW SOUFFLÉ SALAD

Serves 7 or 8

1 cup boiling water
3-ounce package lemon gelatin
½ cup cold water
2 tablespoons vinegar
½ cup mayonnaise
¼ teaspoon salt
Dash of pepper
2 cups finely chopped cabbage
2 tablespoons minced green pepper
1 tablespoon minced onion
¼ teaspoon celery seed
Salad greens

1. Pour boiling water over gelatin. Stir until dissolved.
2. Add cold water, vinegar, mayonnaise, salt and pepper. With egg beater, beat until well blended. Pour into refrigerator tray; quick-chill in freezing unit for 15 to 20 minutes, or until firm about 1 inch from edges but soft in center.
3. Turn into bowl. With egg beater, beat until fluffy. Fold in cabbage, green pepper, onion and celery seed.
4. Pour into 1-quart mold or 7 or 8 individual molds. Refrigerate until firm.
5. Unmold onto greens.

Mrs. Matt Hjort, Richfield Study and
Social Club, Rolla, Kans.

VEGETABLE DELIGHT SALAD

Serves 8

8-ounce can crushed pineapple
3-ounce package vegetable-flavored gelatin
1 cup boiling water
1 tablespoon lemon juice
4 ice cubes
¼ cup mayonnaise
2 tablespoons minced green pepper
1 stalk celery, finely chopped
1 cup finely shredded cabbage
2 medium carrots, grated

1. Drain pineapple; reserve syrup.
2. Dissolve gelatin in water. Stir in lemon juice, ice cubes and reserved syrup. Cool until mixture begins to set.
3. Whip gelatin until frothy. Add mayonnaise; beat until thickened. Fold in remaining ingredients and pineapple.
4. Turn into 6-cup mold; chill until set.

Mrs. T. W. Creager, Woman's Club, Ovid, Colo.

CONGEALED CORNED BEEF SALAD

Serves About 15

3-ounce package lemon gelatin
1 cup boiling water
1 envelope plain gelatin
1 cup cold water
2 beef bouillon cubes
1 teaspoon salt
3 eggs, hard-cooked and chopped
2 cups chopped celery
1 medium onion, chopped
1 large red or green pepper, chopped
1 cup diced corned beef
Lettuce leaves
½ cup mayonnaise
Sliced olives

1. Dissolve lemon gelatin in boiling water. Soften plain gelatin in ¼ cup of the cold water; add with bouillon cubes to lemon gelatin. Stir until gelatin and bouillon are dissolved.
2. Stir in remaining cold water and salt. Stir in eggs, celery, onion, red or green pepper and corned beef.
3. Turn into 13 x 9½ x 2-inch baking pan; chill until set.
4. Cut into squares; serve on lettuce. Put dab of mayonnaise on top of each square; garnish with olives.

Woman's Club, Evergreen, Ala.

CHERRY JELLY SALAD

Serves 6

1-pound can sweet black cherries
13½-ounce can crushed pineapple
3-ounce package black cherry gelatin
1 cup boiling water
¼ cup cold water
½ cup chopped celery
½ cup chopped pecans
Whipped cream

1. Drain cherries and pineapple into bowl; reserve ½ cup combined syrup.
2. Dissolve gelatin in boiling water. Stir in cold water, reserved syrup, cherries, pineapple, celery and pecans. Pour into 6-cup mold; chill until firm.
3. Unmold onto serving dish; decorate with cream.

Mrs. C. W. Peterson, Jr., Woman's Club, Maynard, Mass.

BING CHERRY COLA SALAD

Serves 8 to 12

1-pound can Bing cherries
13½-ounce can crushed pineapple
3-ounce package black cherry gelatin
3-ounce package raspberry, cherry or strawberry gelatin
2 6-ounce bottles cola
1 cup finely diced celery
1 cup coarsely chopped nuts
½ cup flaked coconut
2 3-ounce packages cream cheese
Salad greens

1. Drain cherries and pineapple into measuring cup; add water to total 2 cups. Turn into saucepan. Bring to boil.
2. Add gelatins; stir until dissolved. Add cola; chill until slightly thickened.
3. Meanwhile, pit cherries; combine with pineapple, celery, nuts and coconut.
4. Beat cheese until soft; combine with fruits and nuts.
5. When gelatin starts to set, fold in cheese mixture. Turn into 8-cup mold or individual molds; chill until set.
6. Unmold onto greens.

Mrs. S. D. Davis, Sr., 20th Century Club, Gordo, Ala.

MOLDED CHICKEN LOAF

Serves 6

2 envelopes gelatin
2½ cups chicken broth
4 cups diced cooked chicken
Salt and pepper to taste
2 teaspoons lemon juice
2 tablespoons chopped parsley
¾ cup finely chopped celery
2 tablespoons sweet pickle relish
¼ cup chopped pimientos
1 cup mayonnaise
Green pepper rings
Tomato slices

1. Lightly oil 6-cup mold.
2. In small bowl soften gelatin in ½ cup of the broth.
3. Put remaining broth in saucepan; bring to boil. Stir in gelatin; stir until dissolved.
4. Add chicken; season with salt and pepper. Chill until mixture starts to thicken.
5. Fold in lemon juice, parsley, celery, pickle relish, pimiento and mayonnaise. Turn into mold; chill until firm.
6. Unmold onto serving dish; garnish with green pepper and tomato.

Mrs. Wayne Growell, President, East Side Library Club, Grand Rapids, Mich.

CHICKEN EGG SALAD

Serves 8

4- to 5-pound chicken
1 large onion
3 stalks celery with leaves
10 eggs, hard-cooked
2 canned pimientos
10 to 12 pieces mixed sweet pickles
1 teaspoon celery seed
2 envelopes gelatin
½ cup water
Lettuce leaves
Tomato slices
Mayonnaise

1. Put chicken, onion and celery in large kettle. Add water almost to cover; bring to boil; then simmer until chicken is very tender and broth is reduced to about 1 cup.
2. Put chicken meat, eggs, pimientos and pickles through meat grinder. Sprinkle with celery seed.

3. Soften gelatin in water; add broth; stir until dissolved. Add to chicken mixture; mix well. Turn into 8-inch square baking pan; chill until set.

4. Cut into squares; arrange on lettuce; garnish with tomato; pass mayonnaise.

Mrs. J. F. Rainer, 20th Century Club,
Gordo, Ala.

CHICKEN AND SOUR CREAM SALAD

Serves 6

1 envelope gelatin
2½ cups chicken broth
2 tablespoons grated onion
1 teaspoon salt
Dash of pepper
2 cups diced cooked chicken
½ cup slivered toasted almonds
½ cup sliced ripe olives
2 cups sour cream
Shredded lettuce

1. Sprinkle gelatin over 1 cup of the broth to soften. Place over low heat; stir until dissolved.

2. Remove from heat. Stir in remaining broth, onion, salt and pepper.

3. Chill to consistency of egg whites; fold in all remaining ingredients except lettuce. Pour into 6-cup mold; chill until firm.

4. Unmold; garnish with lettuce.

Mrs. Wayne Fairman, American Home and
Garden Department, Woman's Club,
Silvis, Ill.

OUT OF THIS WORLD SALAD

Serves 6

3-ounce package lemon gelatin
½ cup boiling water
1 cucumber, finely chopped
1 small onion, finely chopped
½ cup chopped pecans
½ cup mayonnaise
1 teaspoon vinegar
¼ teaspoon salt
2 cups cream-style cottage cheese

1. Lightly oil 1½-quart mold.

2. In mixing bowl dissolve gelatin in water.

3. Stir in remaining ingredients; turn into mold. Chill until firm.

4. Unmold onto serving dish; garnish as desired.

Nina Sackett, Woman's Club, Ithaca, Mich.

COTTAGE CHEESE PINEAPPLE SALAD

Serves 8

1-pound 4-ounce can crushed
pineapple
24 marshmallows
3-ounce package cherry gelatin
2 cups cottage cheese
1 cup broken nuts
1 cup heavy cream, whipped

1. Drain pineapple syrup into saucepan. Add marshmallows; heat until melted, stirring occasionally. Add gelatin; stir until dissolved. Cool.

2. When partially set, fold in cheese, nuts and cream.

3. Turn into 2-quart mold; chill until set.

Eleanor Burdick, Present Day Study Club,
Northport, Ala.

MRS. EATO'S SPECK SALAD

Serves 8

3-ounce package lemon or
lime gelatin
1 cup boiling water
1 cup tiny marshmallows or 12 large
marshmallows, quartered
1 apple, finely chopped
8-ounce can crushed pineapple,
drained
1 cup cottage cheese
½ cup minced celery
1 cup grated carrot
½ cup mayonnaise

1. In small bowl combine gelatin, water and marshmallows. Stir until gelatin is dissolved; chill until just beginning to set.

2. Combine remaining ingredients. Stir into gelatin; turn into 2-quart mold. Chill until set.

Mrs. Fred Eato, Woman's Club, Lantana, Fla.

COTTAGE CHEESE TUNA SALAD

Serves 6

3-ounce package lime gelatin
1½ cups boiling water
3 tablespoons vinegar
½ teaspoon salt
1 cup cottage cheese
½ cup chopped celery
7-ounce can tuna fish, drained
and flaked
3 tablespoons chopped onion
½ cup thinly sliced radishes
¼ cup mayonnaise
Salad greens
Additional cottage cheese and
radish roses (optional)

1. Dissolve gelatin in water. Stir in vinegar and salt. Chill until slightly thickened.

2. Fold in remaining ingredients. Pour into 8-inch ring mold. Chill until firm.

3. Unmold on greens. Garnish with cottage cheese and radish roses if desired.

Mrs. L. W. Carter, Women's Study Club,
Daphne, Ala.

CRANBERRY APPLE NUT SALAD

Serves 8

4 cups cranberries
1½ cups sugar
2 tablespoons gelatin
½ cup orange juice
1 cup finely chopped celery
1 cup diced unpeeled red apples
1 cup broken nuts

1. Wash and pick over cranberries. Put through meat grinder. Stir in sugar; let stand for 15 minutes, stirring occasionally.

2. In top of double saucepan soften gelatin in orange juice for 5 minutes; stir over hot water until dissolved.

3. Combine gelatin; cranberries, celery, apples and nuts. Pour into 2-quart pan or mold; chill until set.

Minnie Blanchard, Woman's Club, Crawford, Ga.

PRIZE CHRISTMAS CRANBERRY SALAD

Serves 8

3-ounce package raspberry gelatin
1 cup boiling water
½ cup cold water
2 oranges, diced
9-ounce can crushed pineapple, drained
1-pound can whole cranberry sauce
¼ cup chopped pecans

1. Dissolve gelatin in boiling water. Stir in cold water; chill until slightly thickened.

2. Stir in remaining ingredients; mix well. Pour into 1½-quart mold; chill until set.

3. Unmold; garnish as desired.

*Muriel Woodfin, Woman's Club,
West Concord, N.H.*

MOLDED CRANBERRY BANANA SPECIAL

Serves 14 to 20

1½ envelopes gelatin
¼ cup water
4 cups cranberies, ground
2 ripe bananas, mashed
2 cups sugar
1 cup drained crushed pineapple
½ cup chopped nuts
12 marshmallows, melted
2 cups heavy cream, whipped
Lettuce leaves

1. Soften gelatin in water in top of double saucepan; stir over simmering water until thoroughly dissolved.

2. Combine cranberries, bananas, sugar, pineapple and nuts. Stir in marshmallows and gelatin. Fold in cream.

3. Fill individual molds; chill for 2 or 3 hours.

4. Unmold on lettuce.

*Katie T. Boswell, Worthwhile Club,
Thomasville, Ala.*

MOLDED CRANBERRY PARTY SALAD

Serves 4 to 6

2 cups cold water
1 cup sugar
2 cups cranberries
3-ounce package strawberry gelatin
1 cup boiling water
2 tablespoons lemon juice
3-ounce package cream cheese, cubed
½ cup chopped nuts
1 cup chopped celery

1. In saucepan combine 1 cup of the cold water, sugar and cranberries. Bring to boil. Remove from heat; cover; let stand for 5 minutes.

2. Meanwhile, dissolve gelatin in boiling water. Add remaining cold water, cranberry mixture and lemon juice. Chill until syrupy.

3. Fold in remaining ingredients. Pour into 1-quart mold; chill until firm.

Belle White, Woman's Club, Vandalia, Mo.

CRANBERRY JUICE PEACH SALAD

Serves 8

2 envelopes gelatin
2 cups cranberry juice
1-pound can sliced peaches
½ cup chopped walnuts
¼ cup water
3-ounce package cream cheese
1 tablespoon lemon juice
⅛ teaspoon salt
Mayonnaise
1 cup chopped celery
Walnut halves for garnish

1. Soften three-fourths of the gelatin in ½ cup of the cranberry juice.

2. Bring remaining cranberry juice to boil; stir into gelatin until dissolved. Chill until slightly thickened.

3. Meanwhile, drain peaches; reserve syrup. Chop peaches.

4. Add peaches and chopped walnuts to cranberry mixture. Turn into 8 individual molds; chill until firm.

5. Soften remaining gelatin in water.

6. Bring reserved syrup to boil; stir into gelatin until dissolved. Chill until slightly thickened.

7. In small bowl blend cheese, lemon juice and salt. Stir in ⅓ cup mayonnaise, celery and peach syrup mixture. Spoon over cranberry mixture in molds. Chill until firm.

8. Unmold; garnish with mayonnaise and walnut halves.

*Mrs. John W. Crabb, President, Iowa
Federation of Women's Clubs*

CRANBERRY, PINEAPPLE AND SOUR CREAM SALAD

Serves 8

8-ounce can crushed pineapple
½ envelope plain gelatin
3-ounce package raspberry gelatin
1½ cups boiling water
2 cups sour cream
1-pound can cranberry sauce

1. Drain pineapple; add plain gelatin to syrup; let soak for 5 minutes.

2. Combine raspberry gelatin and water. Add gelatin; stir until dissolved. Cool.

3. Combine sour cream, pineapple and cranberry sauce; beat until well blended. Combine with gelatin mixture. Pour into 8-cup mold; chill until firm.

*Mrs. J. K. Owens, Sr., Fourth District Director,
Alabama Federation of Women's Clubs,
Gordo, Ala.*

FRESH CUCUMBER SQUARES
Serves 8

1½ envelopes gelatin
¼ cup cold water
1 cup boiling water
Few drops green food coloring
4 teaspoons lemon juice
2 cups shredded unpeeled cucumber
2 teaspoons grated onion
1 teaspoon salt
Lettuce leaves
French Dressing (p. 541) or
Sour Cream Dressing (p. 544)

1. Lightly oil 9-inch loaf pan.
2. In mixing bowl soften gelatin in cold water; add boiling water; stir until dissolved. Stir in food coloring to make mixture emerald green. Chill to consistency of egg whites.
3. Stir in lemon juice, cucumber, onion and salt; mix well. Pour into pan; chill until set.
4. Unmold; cut in half lengthwise. Cut each half into squares. Serve on lettuce with French Dressing or Sour Cream Dressing, as desired.

Study and Civic Club, Reedley, Calif.

MOLDED CUCUMBER SALAD
Serves 6

3-ounce package lime gelatin
1 cup boiling water
¼ cup cold water
1 tablespoon vinegar
½ teaspoon salt
½ teaspoon grated onion
1 cup diced peeled cucumber
3-ounce package cream cheese
1 cup diced celery
¼ cup diced green pepper
Lettuce leaves

1. Dissolve gelatin in boiling water; add cold water, vinegar, salt, onion and cucumber. Chill until slightly thickened.
2. Turn half the gelatin mixture into 4-cup mold; chill until firm.
3. Soften cheese with fork. Stir in remaining gelatin mixture. Fold in celery and green pepper. Spread on gelatin in mold; chill until firm.
4. Unmold on lettuce.

Mrs. Robert Hanson, Woman's Club,
Turtle Lake, N.D.

DEVILED EGG MOLD
Serves 4

1 envelope gelatin
½ cup water
1 teaspoon salt
2 tablespoons lemon juice
¼ teaspoon Worcestershire
⅛ teaspoon cayenne
¾ cup mayonnaise
1½ teaspoons grated onion
½ cup finely diced celery
¼ cup chopped pimientos
4 eggs, hard-cooked and chopped

1. Sprinkle gelatin into water to soften; dissolve over low heat.

2. Remove from heat. Stir in salt, lemon juice, Worcestershire and cayenne. Cool.
3. Stir in remaining ingredients. Pour into 3-cup mold or individual molds; chill until set.

Molded Salads and Dressings, Woman's Club,
Silver Spring, Md.

PARTY PINK CONGEALED SALAD
Serves 4

3-ounce package raspberry gelatin
2 cups boiling water
5-ounce package tiny marshmallows
3-ounce package cream cheese
8-ounce can fruit cocktail, drained
1 cup heavy cream, whipped

1. Dissolve gelatin in water. Cool.
2. Add marshmallows, cheese and fruit cocktail. Chill until mixture begins to congeal.
3. Stir until smooth; fold in cream. Pour into 1-quart mold; chill for several hours or overnight.

Mrs. E. A. Stokes, Jr., Three Arts Club,
Reform, Ala.

SPRINGTIME SALAD
Serves 8

2 large grapefruits
3-ounce package lime gelatin
1 cup boiling water
½ cup grapefruit juice
1½ tablespoons lemon juice
½ cup mayonnaise
½ teaspoon paprika
1½ cups diced avocados
¾ cup slivered toasted almonds
Salad greens

1. Cut grapefruits in half. Cut out sections; set aside. Take out membranes; drain any juice in grapefruit shells onto sections.
2. Dissolve gelatin in water. Drain off ½ cup juice from grapefruit sections; add to gelatin. Add lemon juice, mayonnaise and paprika. Beat until smooth.
3. Pour into refrigerator tray; freeze until firm around edges. Whip until fluffy. Fold in grapefruit sections, avocados and almonds. Spoon into shells; chill until firm.
4. Cut each shell in half; serve on greens.

Mrs. William H. Hasebroock, Honorary President,
General Federation of Women's Clubs,
West Point, Neb.

LOBSTER OR CRAB RING
Serves 8

2 envelopes gelatin
¼ cup water
10½-ounce can condensed tomato soup
3 8-ounce packages cream cheese
1 cucumber, peeled and minced
1 teaspoon grated onion
4 cups flaked cooked lobster or crab meat
Salt and pepper to taste
Salad greens

1. Soften gelatin in water.

2. Heat soup; add gelatin; stir until completely dissolved.

3. Put cheese through ricer; stir into soup mixture. Stir in cucumber and onion. Fold in lobster or crab meat; season with salt and pepper.

4. Spoon into 2½-quart mold; chill until set.

5. Unmold onto serving plate; garnish with greens.

Mrs. Harold I. Schlenker, Thusrday Morning Club, Madison, N.J.

OLIVE WREATH MOLD

Serves 8 to 10

2½ cups crushed pineapple
3-ounce package lime gelatin
½ cup shredded American cheese
½ cup chopped pimientos
½ cup finely chopped celery
⅔ cup chopped walnuts
¼ teaspoon salt
1 cup heavy cream, whipped
Small stuffed olives, sliced
Chicory (curly endive)

1. Drain pineapple into saucepan; bring to boil. Add gelatin; stir until dissolved. Cool.

2. When gelatin begins to thicken, stir in pineapple, cheese, pimientos, celery, walnuts and salt. Fold in cream.

3. Arrange a row of olives in 9-inch ring mold. Pour in gelatin mixture; chill until firm.

4. Unmold onto platter lined with chicory.

Molded Salads and Dressings, Woman's Club, Silver Spring, Md.

ORANGE GELATIN SALAD

Serves 4 to 6

2 3-ounce packages orange gelatin
1 cup boiling water
6-ounce can frozen orange juice concentrate
12-ounce bottle lemon-lime soda
Dash of salt
11-ounce can mandarin oranges, drained
Salad greens

1. Dissolve gelatin in water. Stir in orange juice concentrate, soda and salt. Cool to consistency of egg whites.

2. Stir in oranges; pour into 1-quart mold. Chill until set.

3. Unmold; serve on greens.

Mrs. Elmo Collins, Woman's Study Club, Lubbock, Tex.

ORANGE WATER CHESTNUT SALAD

Serves 6

3-ounce package peach flavored gelatin
8-ounce can mandarin oranges, drained
4-ounce can water chestnuts, drained and sliced paper-thin
Endive

1. Prepare gelatin according to package directions. Cool until it begins to thicken.

2. Fold in oranges and water chestnuts. Pour into 4-cup mold; chill until firm.

3. Unmold on bed of endive.

Alice Ann Younger, Anna Day Club, Troy, Mo.

MY FAVORITE SUMMER SALAD

Serves 8

2 3-ounce packages orange gelatin
2 cups boiling water
1 pint orange sherbet
13½ ounce can crushed pineapple, undrained
11-ounce can mandarin oranges, drained

1. Dissolve gelatin in water. Add sherbet; blend well. Chill until slightly thickened.

2. Fold in pineapple and oranges. Turn into 2-quart mold; chill until firm.

3. Unmold; garnish as desired.

Mrs. W. F. Frank, Woman's Club, New Millport, Pa.

PEACHES AND CREAM SALAD

Serves 8

1 cup syrup from canned peaches
3-ounce package lemon gelatin
⅔ cup cream-style cottage cheese
2 cups sliced peaches
½ cup chopped pecans
2 cups heavy cream, whipped

1. In saucepan bring peach syrup to boil. Add gelatin; stir until completely dissolved. Cool until slightly thickened.

2. Fold in cheese, peaches and pecans.

3. Fold into cream. Pour into 2-quart mold; chill for 3 hours.

Mrs. P. F. Haynes, Woman's Club, Lakeworth, Fla.

PEACHY GELATIN SALAD

Serves 12

2 3-ounce packages peach gelatin
3½ cups boiling water
4 cups chopped canned peaches
1 cup syrup from canned peaches
½ cup sugar
2 tablespoons flour
1 egg, lightly beaten
3-ounce package cream cheese, softened
1 cup heavy cream, whipped, or
1 package dessert topping mix
1 cup chopped nuts
½ cup tiny marshmallows
Shredded Cheddar cheese

1. Dissolve gelatin in water; chill until mixture begins to set.

2. Fold in peaches; turn into 3-quart mold; chill until firm.

3. In top of double saucepan combine peach syrup, sugar, flour and egg. Cook over simmering water, stirring constantly, until thickened. Cool.

4. Fold in cream cheese and cream or dessert topping mix. Fold in nuts and marshmallows. Spread on gelatin; sprinkle with cheese. Chill for several hours before serving.

Mrs. Jackie Lynch, Bas Bleu Federated Club,
Hugoton, Kans.

PINEAPPLE CABBAGE NUT SALAD

Serves 8

3-ounce package lime gelatin
1 cup boiling water
1 cup tiny marshmallows
½ cup mayonnaise
1 cup pineapple juice
1 cup drained crushed pineapple
1 cup finely shredded cabbage
1 cup chopped walnuts
1 cup heavy cream, whipped

1. Dissolve gelatin in water. Add marshmallows; stir until melted. Cool.
2. Combine mayonnaise, pineapple juice, pineapple, cabbage and walnuts; stir into gelatin mixture. Fold in cream.
3. Pour into 2-quart mold; chill until set.

Mrs. J. C. Wiseman, Priscilla Club, Butler, Mo.

LIME PINEAPPLE SALAD

Serves 4 to 6

3-ounce package lime gelatin
1 cup boiling water
½ cup chopped nuts
8-ounce can crushed pineapple, undrained
1 cup tiny marshmallows
½ cup grated cheese
1 cup heavy cream, whipped

1. Dissolve gelatin in water.
2. Add nuts, pineapple, marshmallows and cheese. Cool to room temperature; fold in cream. Pour into 6-cup mold; chill.
3. Cut into squares to serve.

Mrs. W. C. Newell, Brookridge Woman's Club,
Atlanta, Ga.

GINGER ALE PINEAPPLE NUT SALAD

Serves 12

2 3-ounce packages lemon gelatin
2 cups boiling water
2 6-ounce bottles ginger ale
1 tablespoon sugar
4-ounce can pimientos, drained and chopped
1-pound 4-ounce can crushed pineapple, drained
1 cup chopped celery
2 cups chopped pecans
Lettuce leaves
Mayonnaise

1. Dissolve gelatin in water. Cool until mixture begins to thicken.
2. Stir in ginger ale, sugar, pimientos, pineapple, celery and pecans. Pour into individual molds; chill until set.

3. Unmold onto lettuce; garnish with mayonnaise.

Mrs. Marvin Price, 20th Century Club,
Gordo, Ala.

FROSTED PINEAPPLE, LIME AND WALNUT SALAD

Serves 9

3-ounce package lime gelatin
1 cup boiling water
1-pound 4-ounce can crushed pineapple, undrained
1 cup cream-style cottage cheese
½ cup finely chopped celery
1 tablespoon chopped pimiento
½ cup chopped walnuts
3-ounce package cream cheese
1 tablespoon mayonnaise
1 teaspoon lemon juice
Lettuce leaves
Walnut halves

1. In mixing bowl dissolve gelatin in water. Cool to consistency of egg whites.
2. Stir in pineapple, cottage cheese, celery, pimiento and chopped walnuts; mix well. Turn into 9-inch baking pan; chill until set.
3. Meanwhile, prepare Cheese Salad Frosting: In mixing bowl blend cream cheese, mayonnaise and lemon juice.
4. Spread on gelatin.
5. Cut into squares; serve on lettuce. Garnish with walnut halves.

Ginny Wrigley, Woman's Club, Springfield, Pa.

RED VELVET SALAD

Serves 8

3-ounce package lemon gelatin
2 cups boiling water
16 marshmallows, chopped
8-ounce can crushed pineapple, undrained
1 cup mayonnaise
3-ounce package cream cheese
3-ounce package black raspberry gelatin

1. Dissolve lemon gelatin in water. Add marshmallows; stir until melted. Cool until syrupy.
2. Stir in pineapple.
3. Combine mayonnaise and cheese; stir into pineapple mixture. Pour into 8-cup serving dish; chill until set.
4. Make raspberry gelatin according to package directions. Cool. Pour over congealed salad; chill until topping is set.

Mrs. C. W. Gibson, Woman's Club,
St. Joseph, Mo.

PINEAPPLE SOUR CREAM SALAD

Serves 8

2 3-ounce packages lime gelatin
1 cup boiling water
1-pound 4-ounce can crushed pineapple, drained
1 pint sour cream
⅔ cup chopped pecans

1. Lightly oil 1½-quart mold.
2. In mixing bowl dissolve gelatin in water. Chill until syrupy; fold in remaining ingredients. Turn into mold; chill until set.
3. Unmold; garnish as desired.

Lois Brach, Woman's Club, Colonia, N.J.

SOUR CREAM FRUIT MOLD
Serves 6

3-ounce package lemon gelatin
1 cup boiling water
8-ounce can crushed pineapple, drained
1 cup finely chopped peaches, drained
⅓ cup shredded coconut (optional)
Sour cream
2 3-ounce packages cream cheese
Shredded coconut or chopped pecans

1. Dissolve gelatin in water. Chill until partially set.
2. Fold in pineapple, peaches, coconut and 1 cup sour cream. Turn into 5-cup fancy mold; chill until firm.
3. Mash cheese with enough sour cream to make a workable mixture. Shape into balls the size of walnuts; roll in coconut or pecans.
4. Unmold; garnish with cream cheese balls.

Mrs. Eric Rogers, Present Day Study Club,
4th District, Northport, Ala.

CONSTANT COMMENT PINEAPPLE-ORANGE SALAD
Serves 8

2 3-ounce packages orange-pineapple gelatin
2 cups boiling water
13-ounce can crushed pineapple, undrained
11-ounce can mandarin oranges, drained
1 medium banana, finely chopped
1 cup tiny marshmallows
1 cup heavy cream, whipped

1. Lightly oil 2-quart mold.
2. In mixing bowl dissolve gelatin in water. Stir in pineapple and oranges. Chill until slightly thickened.
3. Fold in remaining ingredients; pour into mold. Chill until firm.
4. Unmold; garnish as desired.

Mary Beth Jensen, Woman's Club,
Cheyenne, Wyo.

ROQUEFORT RING SALAD
Serves 6

¼ pound Roquefort cheese
1 pint cream-style cottage cheese
¼ teaspoon salt
1 teaspoon Worcestershire
Dash of Tabasco
½ cup spicy salad dressing
2 envelopes gelatin
¼ cup water
1 cup heavy cream, whipped
Water cress

1. Mash Roquefort cheese; beat into cottage cheese until very smooth. Stir in salt, Worcestershire, Tabasco and salad dressing.
2. In top of double saucepan, soften gelatin in water; stir over hot water until dissolved. Slowly beat into cheese mixture.
3. Fold in cream. Pour into 6-inch ring mold; chill until set.
4. Unmold; garnish with water cress.

Mrs. H. H. Hurst, Thursday Morning Club,
Madison, N.J.

MOLDED SALMON
Serves 4

7¾-ounce can salmon, drained
½ teaspoon salt
1 tablespoon sugar
½ teaspoon flour
1 teaspoon dry mustard
Few grains cayenne
2 egg yolks
1½ tablespoons butter
¾ cup milk
¼ cup vinegar
1 envelope gelatin
2 tablespoons water
Lettuce leaves
Cucumber Sauce for Salmon (p. 444)

1. Flake salmon; set aside.
2. In top of double saucepan combine salt, sugar, flour, mustard, cayenne, egg yolks, butter, milk and vinegar. Cook over simmering water until slightly thickened, stirring occasionally.
3. Soften gelatin in water; add to thickened mixture; stir until thoroughly dissolved. Remove from heat. Stir in salmon. Turn into 3-cup ring mold; chill until set.
4. Unmold on lettuce. Serve with Cucumber Sauce for Salmon.

Mrs. LaFell Dickinson, Honorary President,
General Federation of Women's Clubs,
West Hartford, Conn.

LIME COTTAGE CHEESE MOLD WITH SHRIMP
Serves 8

2 3-ounce packages lime gelatin
2 cups boiling water
1 cup cold water
½ cup mayonnaise
1 pint small-curd cream-style cottage cheese
1 tablespoon horseradish
1 teaspoon grated onion
2 to 4 drops Tabasco
Salad greens
2 pounds shrimp, shelled, deveined and cooked, or 1 pound cooked shrimp
Sour Cream Chili Dressing (p. 544)

1. Dissolve gelatin in boiling water. Add cold water. Chill until slightly thickened.
2. Combine mayonnaise, cheese, horseradish, onion and Tabasco; beat until

smooth. Stir into gelatin mixture. Pour into 1½-quart ring mold; chill until firm.

3. Unmold on greens. Fill center with shrimp. Serve with Sour Cream Chili Dressing.

Study Club, Bay Minette, Ala.

SHRIMP EGG SALAD

Serves 4

3-ounce package lemon gelatin
½ cup boiling water
1 cup light cream
½ cup mayonnaise
3-ounce jar pimiento cheese spread
Dash of salt
1 teaspoon grated onion
2 tablespoons finely chopped green pepper
5½-ounce can shrimp, drained and chopped
3 eggs, hard-cooked and chopped
Salad greens

1. Lightly oil 1½-quart mold.
2. Stir gelatin into water; stir until dissolved. Cool until slightly thickened.
3. Meanwhile, blend cream, mayonnaise and cheese spread until smooth.
4. Add gelatin, salt, onion and green pepper; stir until blended. Fold in shrimp and eggs; turn into mold. Chill until set.
5. Unmold; garnish with greens.

Ruth Garrett, Woman's Club, Bartlett, Ia.

PEPPY SHRIMP RING

Serves 6

2 envelopes gelatin
½ cup water
1½ teaspoons salt
¼ cup catsup
2 cups sour cream
¼ cup lemon juice
2 tablespoons horseradish
3 cups diced cooked shrimp
1 cup chopped green peppers
1 cup chopped celery
Salad greens

1. Lightly oil 8-inch ring mold.
2. In top of double saucepan soften gelatin in water. Cook over hot water, stirring occasionally, until dissolved.
3. Cool. Stir in salt, catsup, sour cream, lemon juice and horseradish. Add shrimp, green peppers and celery; mix well. Turn into mold; chill until firm.
4. Unmold onto serving dish; fill center with greens.

Evelyn Smith, Woman's Club, Van Nuys, Calif.

STRAWBERRY RHUBARB SALAD

Serves 6 to 8

10-ounce package frozen rhubarb
3-ounce package strawberry gelatin
1 cup boiling water
1 envelope plain gelatin
¼ cup cold water
1 package frozen sliced strawberries, defrosted
Salad greens

Sour Cream Pecan Dressing for Fruit Salads (p. 544)

1. Cook rhubarb without water until tender. Mash; set aside.
2. Dissolve strawberry gelatin in boiling water. Soften plain gelatin in cold water; add to strawberry gelatin; stir until thoroughly dissolved. Cool until partially set.
3. Stir in rhubarb and strawberries. Pour into 1-quart mold; chill until set.
4. Unmold onto bed of greens; serve with Sour Cream Pecan Dressing for Fruit Salads.

Mrs. Jack S. Lee, Thursday Morning Club, Madison, N.J.

STRAWBERRIES AND CREAM SALAD

Serves 8

3-ounce package strawberry gelatin
1 cup boiling water
2 10-ounce packages frozen strawberries
13½-ounce can crushed pineapple, drained
2 large bananas, mashed
1½ cups sour cream
Additional sour cream and whole strawberries (optional)

1. Dissolve gelatin in water. Add frozen strawberries; stir; mash until well separated.
2. Stir in pineapple and bananas; pour half into 2-quart mold; chill until set.
3. Spread sour cream on gelatin in mold; top with remaining gelatin. Chill until set.
4. Unmold; garnish with sour cream and strawberries, if desired.

Mrs. William McClain, Studere Club, Wellville, Mo.

ARLETTE'S ORIGINAL "WATER-MELON-FEED" SALAD

Serves 6 to 8

6-ounce package raspberry gelatin
2 cups boiling water
1 cup tiny marshmallows
1 cup drained crushed pineapple
1 cup diced mixed fruits
1½ cups cubed watermelon

1. Dissolve gelatin in water. Add marshmallows; stir until dissolved. Chill until slightly thickened.
2. Fold in pineapple, mixed fruits and watermelon. Turn into serving dish; chill until set.

Mrs. Vernon Palm, The Tomorrow's Club, Essex, Ia.

WHITE FRUIT SALAD

Serves 8 to 12

1-pound 4-ounce can grapefruit sections
1-pound 4-ounce can pineapple cubes
1-pound 4-ounce can white cherries
2 envelopes gelatin
1 cup mayonnaise
1 cup heavy cream, whipped

1. Day before, drain grapefruit, pineapple and cherries; reserve 1½ cups combined liquid.
2. In small bowl soften gelatin in ½ cup of the reserved liquid.
3. In small saucepan bring remaining liquid to boil. Stir into gelatin until dissolved. Chill until slightly thickened.
4. Blend mayonnaise into gelatin; fold in cream and fruits. Turn into 10 x 6 x 1½-inch baking pan; refrigerate overnight.
5. Next day, cut into squares.

Mrs. Joe L. Seitz, President, Woman's Culture Club, West Point, Miss.

Aspics

A true aspic is a rich flavorful broth or stock that is made from fish, seafood, meat, poultry or vegetables and that contains sufficient gelatin to congeal the liquid as it cools. The hot liquid is clarified by adding egg whites and straining it through a sieve lined with a damp cloth.

The word "aspic" applies not only to foods arranged in a mold filled with aspic but also to fillets of fish, seafood, slices of meat or poultry coated with sparkling clear aspic. Generally the food is arranged in a formal pattern on a cold platter and is chilled before it is coated with the cool but still liquid aspic. As each of usually two, but sometimes three, layers is ladled over the fish or meat, the dish is refrigerated until the thin layer sets. The food is often decorated exquisitely and painstakingly with tiny cutouts of sliced truffle, radish, pimiento or green pepper. Each bit of decoration is first dipped in liquid aspic before it is put in place; then a final coat of aspic is applied over the decoration.

The stocks used in preparing an aspic depend to a certain extent on the foods to be coated. Beef Stock (p. 170) is used to make an aspic to coat a beef fillet. Fish Stock (p. 171) is used to make an aspic destined only for poached fish or seafood. Chicken Stock (p. 170), on the other hand, produces a versatile aspic that may be used for beef, fish or chicken.

Sparkling, tender and delicately flavored aspics may be quickly made by using canned broths and bottled tomato juice.

BASIC ALL-PURPOSE ASPIC

Makes About 1 Quart

2 cups canned chicken broth
2 cups canned tomato juice
4 envelopes gelatin
1 teaspoon salt
¼ teaspoon coarsely ground pepper
¼ teaspoon sugar
3 sprigs parsley
1 bay leaf
Pinch of thyme
2 egg whites, lightly beaten
2 egg shells, crushed
Dash of sherry, Madeira or brandy (optional)

1. Combine all ingredients except wine or brandy in 2-quart saucepan. (Gelatin does not need to be softened, for it softens and dissolves as mixture is heated.)
2. Stir over medium heat until mixture boils up. Immediately remove from heat; let stand for 10 minutes.
3. Strain through sieve lined with flannel wrung out of hot water. (Flannel produces clearest aspic, but several layers of cheesecloth or a clean kitchen towel may also be used.) Strained liquid is pale gold, for clarification process removes not only all sediment but color from tomato juice as well.
4. Correct seasoning; if desired, stir in sherry, Madeira or brandy.

VARIATIONS:

White Wine Aspic: Substitute 1 cup dry white wine for 1 cup of the broth or the tomato juice.

Red Wine Aspic: Substitute 1 cup dry red wine for 1 cup of the tomato juice. Clarification of liquid will remove color from wine as it does from juice. If pale rose color is desired, add 1 or 2 drops red food coloring.

Beef Aspic: Substitute strong beef broth or consommé for chicken broth. Since beef aspics are generally used to coat robust dishes, add a few onion slices to basic ingredients.

Fish Aspic: Substitute Fish Stock (p. 171) for broth in basic recipe.

Clam Stock (substitute for Fish Stock): Bottled clam juice makes an excellent substitute for Fish Stock (p. 171). However, it is very strong in flavor and should be diluted with water and dry white wine for delicately flavored aspic. Substitute ¼ cup clam juice, 1¼ cups water and ½ cup dry white wine for broth in basic recipe.

Tarragon Aspic: Omit bay leaf and thyme from basic recipe; add 1 teaspoon dry or 4 or 5 sprigs fresh tarragon.

A. S.

RED BEET ASPIC

Serves 6

2 envelopes gelatin
½ cup water
⅔ cup sugar
½ cup vinegar
1 teaspoon salt
2 cups boiling beet juice or combined beet juice and water
2 cups shredded cooked beets
2 cups finely chopped celery
1 tablespoon horseradish

1. Soften gelatin in water.
2. Combine sugar, vinegar, salt and beet juice or combined beet juice and water. Stir in gelatin until dissolved. Chill until partially set.
3. Stir in remaining ingredients. Pour into 6-cup ring mold; chill until set.

Ethel Woodward, Woman's Club, East Chicago, Ill.

BROCCOLI SALAD IN ASPIC

Serves 6 to 8

1 pound broccoli
1 envelope gelatin
¼ cup water
10½-ounce can condensed chicken
   consommé
4 eggs, hard-cooked and chopped
2 tablespoons lemon juice
3 tablespoons Worcestershire
   Dash of Tabasco
¾ cup mayonnaise
   Radish Roses (below)
   Iceberg lettuce leaves or
   romaine

1. Wash broccoli; trim only small bit off stem end. If stalks are large, split each stalk lengthwise almost through to flowerets to permit quicker cooking. Cook, covered, in a little boiling salted water until just tender. Drain. Reserve a few flowerets for garnish. Chop remaining broccoli to total 2 cups.

2. Soften gelatin in water; bring consommé to boil; add gelatin; stir to dissolve. Add chopped broccoli, eggs, lemon juice, Worcestershire and Tabasco. Fold in mayonnaise (do not worry if it curdles). Mix well. Pour into 1½-quart ring mold; chill until set.

3. Unmold on plate; garnish with broccoli flowerets, Radish Roses and lettuce or romaine.

RADISH ROSES: To make radish roses, cut thin strips of red peel, beginning at root end, and work through almost to stem. Place radishes in ice water; "rose petals" will fold back. For extra color, leave some of small leaves and stem intact.

Mrs. Philip LeBlanc, President, Hillsborough County Federation of Women's Clubs, Tampa, Fla.

PRESSED CHICKEN

Serves 10 to 12

2 5-pound stewing chickens
1 stalk celery with leaves, quartered
1 large onion, quartered
¼ teaspoon peppercorns
   Salt
4 envelopes gelatin
¾ cup water
2 tablespoons lemon juice
1½ cups finely chopped celery
½ cup finely chopped stuffed olives
½ cup slivered almonds
2 eggs, hard-cooked and chopped
¼ cup finely chopped green pepper
   Pepper to taste
   Favorite mayonnaise dressing
   (optional)

1. Put chickens in large heavy saucepan. Add quartered celery, onion, peppercorns and 2 teaspoons salt. Add water to cover. Bring to boil; cover; simmer for 2 hours, or until meat falls from bones.

2. Remove chickens; cool. Boil stock over high heat until reduced to 1 quart; strain; set aside.

3. Soften gelatin in water; add to stock; stir until dissolved. Add lemon juice; cool.

4. Remove bones, skin and gristle from chicken; cut meat into bite-size pieces.

5. Add chicken, chopped celery, olives, almonds, eggs and green pepper to stock; mix well. Season with salt and pepper. Turn into 13 x 9½ x 2-inch baking pan. Chill until firm.

6. Unmold; slice; serve with mayonnaise dressing, if desired.

Mrs. A. Hugo Kimball, Junior Service League, Statesville, N.C.

HAM IN ASPIC

Serves 6 to 8

1½ envelopes gelatin
½ cup water
3 cups tomato juice
   Dash of salt
1 teaspoon sugar
½ bay leaf
1 tablespoon chopped onion
3 cups minced cooked ham

1. Soften gelatin in water.

2. In saucepan combine tomato juice, salt, sugar, bay leaf and onion. Bring to boil; then simmer for 10 minutes. Strain into mixing bowl.

3. Add gelatin; stir until dissolved. Cool.

4. Stir in ham. Pour into 2-quart mold; chill until set.

Molded Salads and Dressings, Woman's Club, Silver Spring, Md.

SWEDISH SALMON IN ASPIC

Serves 12

6-pound whole salmon
2-pound salmon steak
¾ cup mixed onion, carrot and celery
   slices
2 sprigs dill
8 peppercorns
2 teaspoons salt
½ cup dry white wine
3 cups water
¾ pound butter, creamed
   Salt and pepper to taste
2 egg whites, stiffly beaten but
   not dry
2 teaspoons tomato paste
3 envelopes gelatin
1 pound rice, cooked and chilled
   Cooked shrimp
   Stuffed eggs
   Sliced truffle
   Water cress

1. Clean and wash salmon. Put with salmon steak in long fish kettle. Scatter vegetables on top; add dill, peppercorns, salt, wine and water. Cover; bring slowly to boil; then simmer for 45 to 50 minutes. Cool in stock.

2. Carefully remove whole salmon; wrap in freezer paper; chill.

3. Strain stock; reserve.

4. Skin, bone and chop salmon steak; put through meat grinder; blend with butter; season with salt and pepper.

5. Put stock, with egg whites, tomato paste and gelatin in saucepan. Bring to boil, stirring constantly. Remove from heat; let stand for 10 minutes without moving. Strain liquid through a sieve lined with damp cloth (flannel is best) to make a clear aspic. Refrigerate until syrupy.

6. Arrange bed of rice on long platter. Place whole salmon upright on rice, balancing it with cocktail picks, if necessary.

7. Carefully remove skin of salmon; spoon enough cool, but still liquid, aspic over fish until coated. Chill until set. (If aspic became too stiff in refrigerator, melt it; then stir over ice until cold and just beginning to set.)

8. Fill pastry bag with salmon and butter mixture; pipe large scallops of this mousse down back of fish. Pipe a nest of mousse all around base of fish.

9. Garnish with shrimp, eggs, truffle and water cress.

10. Coat fish, mousse and garnish with more cool, but still liquid, aspic; chill until serving time.

Women's Club International Cook Book, Belair, Md.

MOLDED SALMON ASPIC

Serves 4 to 6

3-ounce package lemon gelatin
1 cup boiling water
3 tablespoons vinegar
½ teaspoon salt
½ cup cold water
1 cup flaked salmon
2 tablespoons horseradish
1 cup cooked peas
1 cup diced cooked carrots

1. Dissolve gelatin in boiling water. Add vinegar, salt and cold water.

2. Pour 1 cup of gelatin into 6-cup mold; chill until set.

3. Mix salmon and horseradish; use to cover gelatin in mold with thick layer. Pour a little of remaining gelatin mixture over salmon; chill until it begins to set.

4. Add layer of peas; chill until firm.

5. Add layer of carrots and remaining gelatin. Chill until firm.

Molded Salads and Dressings, Woman's Club, Silver Spring, Md.

SHRIMP AND POTATO SALAD IN TOMATO ASPIC

Serves 6

2 envelopes gelatin
½ cup water
2½ cups hot tomato juice
1 tablespoon salt
Dash of pepper
1 cup diced cooked shrimp
1½ cups diced cooked potatoes
⅓ cup finely chopped celery
2 tablespoons minced green pepper
Mayonnaise
1 tablespoon vinegar
1 teaspoon grated onion
Chopped chives or water cress

1. Soften gelatin in water. Dissolve in tomato juice; stir in salt and pepper. Chill until syrupy.

2. Meanwhile, combine shrimp, potatoes, celery, green pepper, ½ cup mayonnaise, vinegar and onion. Mix well. Fold into tomato mixture. Pour into 6-cup mold rinsed in cold water. Chill until firm.

3. Serve with additional mayonnaise and chives or water cress or as desired.

Mrs. Gardner C. Hudson, Woman's Club, Ridgewood, N.J.

BEST TOMATO ASPIC

Serves 8

6-ounce package lemon gelatin
3 cups tomato juice
Dash of Tabasco
1 tablespoon lemon juice
1 teaspoon Worcestershire
Dash of white pepper
¼ teaspoon salt
1 cup finely chopped celery
¼ cup sliced stuffed olives
½ cup finely diced cucumber
2 tablespoons chopped scallions
Texas Coleslaw (p. 511)

1. Lightly oil 8-inch ring mold.

2. In saucepan stir gelatin into 1 cup of the tomato juice. Cook over medium heat, stirring frequently, until dissolved.

3. Remove from heat. Stir in remaining tomato juice, Tabasco, lemon juice, Worcestershire, pepper and salt. Chill to consistency of egg whites.

4. Stir in celery, olives, cucumber and scallions; mix well. Pour into mold; chill until set.

5. Unmold onto serving dish; fill center with Texas Coleslaw.

Study Civic Club, Reedley, Calif.

TOMATO ASPIC WITH CHEESE BALLS

Serves 6

2 cups tomato juice
2 tablespoons vinegar
¼ teaspoon salt
½ teaspoon sugar
3-ounce package lemon gelatin
3-ounce package cream cheese
2 tablespoons chopped nuts
1 teaspoon grated onion with juice
Salad greens
Mayonnaise or favorite salad dressing

1. In saucepan combine tomato juice, vinegar, salt and sugar. Bring to boil. Pour over gelatin; stir until dissolved. Chill until partially set.

2. Fill 6 individual molds half full of gelatin mixture; chill until firm.

3. Combine cheese, nuts and onion; put spoonful in each mold. Add remaining gelatin mixture to fill mold; chill until firm.

4. Unmold onto a bed of greens. Serve with mayonnaise or salad dressing, as desired.

Susan Lepper, Woman's Club, West Chicago, Ill.

Savory Mousses

Mousses may be hot or cold, sweet or savory. This chapter includes only the savory cold mousses which are served in place of a molded salad or may be combined with several other types of salad on a buffet table.

A mousse means a dish which is light and frothy, and savory cold mousses are given this light texture by means of whipped cream or sour cream (sometimes combined with mayonnaise) and occasionally by beaten egg whites.

Sweet mousses, both hot and cold, will be found in the Chapter 22. Hot savory mousses—vegetable, fish, chicken or meat —will be found by consulting the Index.

AVOCADO MOUSSE

Serves 8

1 envelope plain gelatin
2 tablespoons cold water
2 cups boiling water
3-ounce package lime gelatin
1 cup mashed ripe avocado
½ cup mayonnaise
½ cup heavy cream, whipped

1. Lightly oil 1½-quart mold.
2. In mixing bowl soften plain gelatin in cold water. Add boiling water and lime gelatin; stir until dissolved. Chill until partially set.
3. Stir in remaining ingredients; pour into mold. Chill until set. Unmold; garnish as desired.

Woman's Culture Club, West Point, Miss.

CHICKEN MOUSSE

Serves 6 to 8

4 eggs, separated
2 cups milk
2 envelopes gelatin
½ cup water
1 cup hot chicken broth
2 cups ground cooked chicken
1 teaspoon salt
¼ teaspoon white pepper
Dash of Tabasco
1 cup heavy cream, whipped
Salad greens

1. Lightly oil 9-inch ring mold.
2. In top of double saucepan beat egg yolks; stir in milk. Cook over hot water, stirring constantly, until thickened and smooth. Cool.
3. In small saucepan soften gelatin in water. Add broth; cook over low heat, stirring constantly, until dissolved.
4. Stir in chicken, salt, pepper and Tabasco; combine with egg yolk mixture. Cool thoroughly.
5. Meanwhile, in mixing bowl beat egg whites until stiff but not dry. Fold with cream into chicken mixture. Turn into mold; chill until firm.

6. Unmold; fill center with greens.

LOBSTER MOUSSE: Use 2 cups ground cooked lobster instead of chicken in above recipe.

Mrs. Gregory Comstock, Woman's Club, Essex, Conn.

CRAB MOUSSE

Serves 6

1 envelope gelatin
2 tablespoons tarragon vinegar
½ cup mayonnaise
1 teaspoon Worcestershire
Salt and pepper to taste
½ cup heavy cream, whipped
¾ cup seedless grapes
½ cup grated peeled cucumber
1½ cups flaked crab meat
Water cress
Cherry tomatoes

1. Lightly oil 1½-quart mold.
2. In small saucepan soften gelatin in vinegar and 2 tablespoons water.
3. Add ½ cup water; cook over low heat, stirring frequently, until gelatin is dissolved. Cool until slightly thickened.
4. Stir in mayonnaise and Worcestershire; season with salt and pepper. Fold in cream; stir in grapes, cucumber and crab meat. Turn into mold; cover with aluminum foil. Freeze until firm.
5. Remove from freezer 1 hour before serving; unmold. Garnish with water cress and cherry tomatoes. Chill until serving time.

Jo Henne, Lincoln Village Women's Club, Columbus, Ohio

HAM MOUSSE

Serves 4

1 envelope gelatin
½ cup water
2 cups ground boiled ham
1 teaspoon prepared mustard
Dash of cayenne
½ cup heavy cream, whipped
Tomato slices
Parsley sprigs

1. Lightly oil 1-quart mold.
2. In small bowl soften gelatin in water; cook over hot water, stirring constantly, until dissolved.
3. Remove from heat. Turn into mixing bowl. Stir in ham, mustard and cayenne. Cool.
4. Fold cream into ham mixture; turn into mold. Chill until set.
5. Unmold; garnish with tomato and parsley.

Mrs. Preston H. Hadley, Woman's Club, Bellows Falls, Vt.

SALMON MOUSSE

Serves 8

2 envelopes gelatin
½ cup water
⅛ teaspoon paprika
½ cup lemon juice
¾ teaspoon salt

1-pound can salmon, drained,
   boned and flaked
1 cup heavy cream, whipped
Tomato slices
Cucumber slices
Mayonnaise

1. Lightly oil 9-inch loaf pan; line bottom with waxed paper.
2. In top of double saucepan soften gelatin in water; stir over hot water until dissolved.
3. Stir in paprika, lemon juice and salt. Add salmon; mix. Fold in cream; turn into pan. Chill until set.
4. Unmold; garnish with tomato and cucumber. Serve with mayonnaise.

Mrs. Clyde Rumsey, North Jacksonville Woman's Club, Jacksonville, Fla.

SEAFOOD MOUSSE LOAF

Serves 8

2 envelopes gelatin
2 tablespoons cold water
2 chicken bouillon cubes
½ cup boiling water
1½ cups cooked seafood
½ small onion, grated
1 cup chopped celery
1 cup seedless grapes or ½ cup
   chopped ripe olives
Salt, pepper and monosodium
   glutamate to taste
1 cup mayonnaise
1 cup heavy cream, whipped
Spiced peaches or pears

1. Lightly oil 8-cup mold.
2. Soften gelatin in cold water.
3. Dissolve bouillon cubes in boiling water. Add gelatin; stir until completely dissolved.
4. Add seafood, onion, celery, grapes or olives, salt, pepper and monosodium glutamate. Add mayonnaise and cream; fold until well mixed. Pour into mold; chill until set.
5. Unmold; serve with peaches or pears.

Mrs. Jack Stengall, Woman's Club, St. Petersburg, Fla.

Salad Dressings

For other mayonnaise dressings, see Chapter 12.

FRENCH DRESSING

Makes 1 Cup

1 teaspoon salt
½ teaspoon sugar
¼ teaspoon pepper
½ teaspoon paprika
½ teaspoon dry mustard
¾ cup salad oil
¼ cup vinegar

1. Measure ingredients into jar in order given. Cover; shake well.
2. Chill. Shake well before using.

VARIATIONS:

Anchovy French Dressing: Add 2 tablespoons anchovy paste and 1 tablespoon each finely chopped parsley and onion.

Catsup French Dressing: Add ½ cup catsup.

Chiffonade French Dressing: After chilling, add 1 egg, hard-cooked and chopped; 1 cooked small beet, finely chopped; and 1 small onion, finely chopped.

Curried French Dressing: Add ½ teaspoon curry powder along with mustard.

Garlic French Dressing: Add 1 clove garlic at least 1 hour before serving. Discard garlic.

Herb French Dressing: Add 1 tablespoon mixed dried herbs at least 1 hour before serving.

Mint French Dressing: Use lemon juice instead of vinegar. Add ¼ cup finely chopped mint leaves.

Peanut Butter French Dressing: Use lemon juice instead of vinegar. Add ¼ cup peanut butter.

Roquefort French Dressing: Add ¼ cup crumbled Roquefort or blue cheese.

What's Cookin' in Hapeville?, Woman's Club, Hapeville, Ga.

CATSUP SALAD DRESSING

Makes About 3 Cups

1 cup chili sauce or catsup
1 cup salad oil
⅔ cup vinegar
⅔ cup sugar
1 teaspoon paprika
1 teaspoon dry mustard
1 teaspoon pepper
1 teaspoon salt
Juice of 1 lemon
2 cloves garlic

1. Combine all ingredients in quart jar. Refrigerate.
2. Discard garlic after a day or so. Shake well before using.

Mrs. Fran Glover, Home and Country Study Club, Fayette, Mo.

CHIFFONADE DRESSING

Makes About 1 Cup

Serve on wedge of lettuce, or as desired.

½ cup French Dressing (opposite)
2 eggs, hard-cooked and chopped
2 tablespoons chopped green pepper
2 tablespoons chopped parsley
2 teaspoons chopped chives
1 teaspoon grated onion

Combine all ingredients; mix well.

Mary Donella, Okolona Woman's Club, Louisville, Ky.

GARLIC SALAD DRESSING
Makes 1 Cup
¾ cup salad oil
¼ cup vinegar
1 teaspoon salt
½ teaspoon sugar
1 teaspoon garlic powder
½ teaspoon dry mustard
½ teaspoon paprika
¼ teaspoon red pepper

Put all ingredients in pint jar; shake well. Chill; store in refrigerator. Shake again before using.

Mrs. Darald Holleman, Athenia Study Club, Tuscaloosa, Ala.

ORÉGANO CHEESE DRESSING FOR GREEN SALAD
Makes About 1½ Cups
Serve on green salad; toss lightly.

¼ cup water
2 teaspoons aromatic bitters
1½ teaspoons garlic salt
1½ teaspoons sugar
½ teaspoon cumin
1 teaspoon Worcestershire
½ teaspoon orégano
½ teaspoon garlic powder
½ teaspoon monosodium glutamate
¼ teaspoon pepper
6 tablespoons olive oil
3 tablespoons wine vinegar
⅔ cup grated Parmesan cheese

Combine all ingredients in large container. Cover; shake well until blended.

Janet Pettinotti, Woman's Club, La Habra, Calif.

POPPY SEED DRESSING FOR FRUIT SALAD
Makes About 1½ Cups
¾ cup sugar
1 teaspoon dry mustard
1 teaspoon salt
⅓ cup vinegar
⅓ small onion, grated
1 cup salad oil
1 tablespoon poppy seeds

1. In mixing bowl combine sugar, mustard, salt, vinegar and onion. Beat well with rotary beater.
2. Gradually add oil, beating constantly.
3. Stir in poppy seeds. Refrigerate. Shake well before using.

NOTE: If made in electric blender, add poppy seeds after removing dressing from blender container.

Mrs. J. R. Cudworth, Quest Club, Tuscaloosa, Ala.

CREAMY ROQUEFORT CHEESE DRESSING
Makes About 1 Cup
3 ounces Roquefort cheese
½ teaspoon salt
Dash of pepper
Dash of paprika
⅔ cup olive oil
1 teaspoon lemon juice
1 teaspoon vinegar
½ teaspoon Worcestershire

1. Mash cheese with fork. Add salt, pepper and paprika.
2. Beat in oil, drop by drop, to form a thin paste.
3. Beat in lemon juice, vinegar and Worcestershire by drops. Correct seasoning to taste.

Betsy Rees, Woman's Club, Escondido, Calif.

TANGY FRUIT SALAD DRESSING
Makes About 1 Cup
⅓ cup lime juice
⅓ cup honey
⅓ cup olive oil
1 teaspoon celery seed

Combine all ingredients in small bowl; beat until blended and smooth. Store in jar with tight-fitting cover in refrigerator. Shake well before using.

Audrey Berglund, Woman's Club, Mar Vista, Calif.

SAUCE VINAIGRETTE
Makes ¾ Cup
Serve on tossed green salad. Or heat in top of double saucepan, and serve on broccoli, asparagus, etc.

1 teaspoon salt
⅛ teaspoon pepper
Dash of cayenne
¼ teaspoon paprika
3 tablespoons vinegar
½ cup olive oil
1 tablespoon finely chopped pickle
½ tablespoon finely chopped parsley
½ tablespoon finely chopped chives

1. Put salt, pepper, cayenne and paprika in bowl. Blend in vinegar.
2. Gradually add oil; beat until well blended.
3. Stir in remaining ingredients; mix well.

Carolyn Beauchamp, Okolona Woman's Club, Louisville, Ky.

VINAIGRETTE DRESSING WITH OLIVES
Makes 1 Cup
1 cup French Dressing (p. 541)
1 teaspoon finely chopped green olives
1 teaspoon finely chopped pimiento
1 teaspoon finely chopped chives

Combine all ingredients. Shake well before using.

Mrs. Peyton I. Lingle, Woman's Club, Avondale Estates, Ga.

LOW-CALORIE BUTTERMILK SALAD DRESSING
Makes 1 Cup
1 cup buttermilk
½ teaspoon onion juice
¾ teaspoon salt
Dash of pepper
1½ tablespoons lemon juice

Put all ingredients in jar or bottle. Shake thoroughly; store in refrigerator. Shake well before using.

Mary Vlack, Woman's Club, Lemon Grove, Calif.

PEPPY LOW-CALORIE TOMATO DRESSING

Makes About 1 Cup

8-ounce can tomato sauce
1 tablespoon tarragon vinegar
1 tablespoon lemon juice
½ teaspoon grated onion
½ teaspoon Worcestershire
½ teaspoon salt
½ teaspoon basil
⅛ teaspoon celery seed

1. Combine all ingredients in jar with tight-fitting lid. Shake until thoroughly blended.
2. Chill; shake well before using.

Progressive Woman's Club, Adrian, Mich.

GREEK SALAD DRESSING FOR RAW VEGETABLES

Makes About 1 Cup

Serve on cucumber slices, green pepper rings, onion rings or tomato wedges.

1 cup sugar
1 teaspoon salt
¼ teaspoon pepper
½ teaspoon celery seed
½ cup vinegar
¼ cup water

1. Combine all ingredients in saucepan. Bring to boil; then simmer for 5 minutes.
2. Cool; chill. Shake well before using.

Nancy Beltz, La Cadena Club, Haven, Kans.

MAYONNAISE DRESSING

Makes About 2 Cups

1 teaspoon dry mustard
1 teaspoon salt
1 teaspoon confectioners' sugar
½ teaspoon paprika
Dash of cayenne
2 egg yolks
2 tablespoons vinegar
1½ cups olive oil
2 tablespoons lemon juice

1. In mixing bowl blend mustard, salt, sugar, paprika, cayenne and egg yolks. When smooth, stir in about 1 teaspoon of the vinegar.
2. Beat constantly; add oil in thin stream. As mixture thickens, gradually add remaining vinegar and lemon juice.

NOTE: If oil is added too rapidly, mixture will curdle. Beat in another egg yolk; add oil in a thin stream, until all oil is added. It is a good idea to place bowl in another bowl containing cracked ice.

Mrs. Leasure, Woman's Club, Rocky Ford, Colo.

BELGIAN MAYONNAISE

Makes About 1 Quart

2 hard-cooked egg yolks
2 raw egg yolks

3 cups corn or peanut oil
½ cup vinegar
1 teaspoon prepared mustard
Salt and pepper to taste
A little garlic powder (optional)

1. In mixing bowl mash hard-cooked and raw egg yolks to a smooth paste.
2. By hand or on low speed of electric beater, add oil very slowly by drops. Beat constantly, or oil will separate from eggs.
3. As mayonnaise thickens, add a few drops of the vinegar from time to time until all vinegar is used.
4. Beat in seasonings last.
5. Store tightly covered in refrigerator, where it will keep for months.

NOTE: For fruit salad blend in ½ to 1 cups heavy cream.

Mrs. L. J. Goossens, Woman's Club,
Crystal Lake, Ill.

CIDER DRESSING

Makes About ½ Cup

⅓ cup mayonnaise
2 tablespoons apple cider
1½ teaspoons lemon juice

Combine all ingredients; chill.

Mrs. George Habbenggar, Junior Woman's Club,
Wauwatosa, Wis.

GREEN GODDESS SALAD DRESSING

Makes About 2 Cups

1 cup mayonnaise
½ cup sour cream
3 tablespoons tarragon vinegar
1 tablespoon lemon juice
⅓ cup finely chopped parsley
3 tablespoons grated onion
3 tablespoons mashed anchovy fillets
1 tablespoon chopped capers
1 tablespoon chopped chives
1 clove garlic, crushed
⅛ teaspoon salt
⅛ teaspoon black pepper

Blend all ingredients thoroughly in mixing bowl. Turn into covered container; chill for 3 to 4 hours.

Meals on Wheels, Woman's Club,
Greenwich, Conn.

MRS. HASEBROOCK'S GREEN GODDESS SALAD DRESSING

Makes About 1 Quart

½ cup finely cut chives
3 cups sour cream
1 tablespoon mayonnaise (optional)
¼ cup tarragon wine vinegar
1 drop green food coloring

Mix all ingredients well. Chill.

Mrs. William H. Hasebroock, Honorary President,
General Federation of Women's Clubs,
West Point, Neb.

LAMAIZE SAUCE
Makes About 1 Quart

Excellent for shrimp, lobster and crab meat salads.

      2 cups mayonnaise
      2 cups chili sauce
      ½ cup sweet pickle relish
      2 eggs, hard-cooked and chopped
      1 teaspoon chives
      1 tablespoon prepared mustard
      Salt and pepper to taste

Blend all ingredients. Put in covered container. Store in refrigerator.

Joan Biel, Junior Woman's Club, Cheshire, Conn.

OLD-COUNTRY KITCHEN DRESSING
Makes About 2 Cups

      1 cup mayonnaise
      ¾ cup catsup
      2 teaspoons grated Parmesan cheese
      1 egg yolk
      Dash of paprika
      1 clove garlic, crushed
      2 teaspoons vinegar

Beat all ingredients thoroughly with rotary beater; store in refrigerator.

Mrs. Harriet E. Lopaus, Wednesday Morning Club, Cranford, N.J.

THOUSAND ISLAND DRESSING
Makes About 2½ Cups

      2 cups mayonnaise
      ½ cup chili sauce
      1 teaspoon finely chopped green pepper
      1 teaspoon chopped pimiento
      1 tablespoon chopped parsley
      1 tablespoon chopped chives

Blend all ingredients. Chill until serving time.

Theba Cockreham, Pine River Pow Wow Club, Bayfield, Colo.

COCONUT GROVE THOUSAND ISLAND DRESSING
Makes 2 Quarts

      2 medium onions
      2 medium green peppers
      4 eggs, hard-cooked
      4-ounce jar pimientos, drained
      1 quart mayonnaise
      2 cups catsup
      1½ cups chili sauce
      2 tablespoons Worcestershire
      ¼ teaspoon Tabasco
      2 tablespoons chopped parsley
      1 tablespoon salt
      ½ teaspoon pepper

1. Couple of days before, put onions, green peppers, eggs and pimientos through medium blade of meat grinder.
2. Turn into mixing bowl; add remaining ingredients. Mix well. Turn into covered container; refrigerate.

Bonnie Taylor, Woman's Club, La Habra, Calif.

SOUR CREAM DRESSING
Makes About 1 Cup

      1 cup sour cream
      1 tablespoon white vinegar
      1 to 2 tablespoons sugar or sugar to taste
      ½ teaspoon salt
      Grated orange peel (optional)

Combine sour cream and vinegar. Add sugar and salt. If desired, sprinkle with orange peel.

Mrs. Maiben Williams, Three Arts Club, Monroeville, Ala.

SOUR CREAM CHILI DRESSING
Makes 1½ Cups

      1 cup sour cream
      ½ cup chili sauce or catsup
      2 teaspoons horseradish

Combine all ingredients; chill.

Study Club, Bay Minette, Ala.

SOUR CREAM PECAN DRESSING FOR FRUIT SALADS
Makes 1¼ Cups

      1 cup sour cream
      ¼ cup confectioners' sugar
      2 teaspoons vanilla
      ¼ cup chopped pecans

Combine all ingredients; chill.

Mrs. Jack S. Lee, Thursday Morning Club, Madison, N.J.

BLUE CHEESE SOUR CREAM DRESSING
Makes About 3 Cups

      ¼ pound blue cheese, crumbled
      1 cup sour cream
      1 cup mayonnaise
      ¼ teaspoon monosodium glutamate
      ⅓ cup pickle vinegar
      ½ teaspoon garlic powder or 1 clove garlic, minced
      ½ teaspoon Worcestershire
      Salt and pepper to taste

Blend all ingredients in mixing bowl. Store in covered container in refrigerator.

Mrs. Tom Garcia, Junior Woman's Club, Fort Myers, Fla.

RANCHO SALAD DRESSING
Makes About 2 Cups

      2 cups sour cream
      ⅓ cup finely chopped scallions
      ¼ cup crumbled Roquefort cheese
      ¼ cup lemon juice
      1 teaspoon salt
      ¼ teaspoon pepper

Day before, blend all ingredients; cover. Refrigerate for 24 hours.

Janette H. Fletcher, Woman's Club, La Crescenta, Calif.

ROQUEFORT DRESSING
Makes About 2 Cups

      1 cup sour cream
      1 cup mayonnaise

1 teaspoon garlic powder
½ teaspoon onion powder
1½ ounces Roquefort cheese, crumbled
    Dash of wine vinegar
1 tablespoon dried parsley flakes

Combine all ingredients. Refrigerate for a few hours before serving to allow flavors to blend.

Mrs. Ben Bakanec, Junior Woman's Club,
Diamond Bar, Calif.

RUSSIAN DRESSING

Makes 1 Cup

½ cup mayonnaise
¼ cup chili sauce
¼ cup India relish

Combine all ingredients. Refrigerate.

A. S.

NO-COOK BOILED DRESSING

Makes About 2½ Cups

1 egg
1 tablespoon dry mustard
1 teaspoon salt
½ teaspoon paprika
    Dash of cayenne
1 cup vinegar
¼ cup melted butter
14-ounce can sweetened condensed
    milk

1. In mixing bowl beat egg until thickened. Add mustard, salt, paprika and cayenne; beat until smooth.
2. Slowly beat in vinegar. Stir in milk and butter. Store in refrigerator in airtight container.

Woman's Club, Belle, W. Va.

SPECIAL SALAD DRESSING FOR SEAFOOD

Makes 1½ Cups

2 tablespoons flour
2 tablespoons sugar
1¼ teaspoons salt
    Pinch of red pepper
1 teaspoon prepared mustard
1 tablespoon corn oil
1 cup water
2 eggs
4 tablespoons basil or white wine
    vinegar

1. In top of double saucepan combine all ingredients except eggs and vinegar. Cook over hot water, stirring constantly, until thickened.
2. Beat eggs lightly in small bowl. Gradually beat in vinegar. Slowly beat in half the sauce. Stir into rest of sauce.
3. Cook over hot water, stirring constantly, until mixture coats spoon. (Overcooking after eggs have been added will curdle dressing.
4. Pour into jar. When cool, cover; refrigerate.

Rose Harrington, Longvue Women's Club,
Pittsburgh, Pa.

FRUITY CREAM CHEESE TOPPING

Makes About 1 Cup

Serve on molded fruit salads or as desired.

3-ounce package cream cheese
½ cup orange juice
4 teaspoons lemon juice
¼ teaspoon salt
1 teaspoon sugar
¼ teaspoon paprika

Beat cheese until soft and fluffy. Add remaining ingredients; beat until blended and smooth.

Mrs. Glenn Morrow, Phil Avant Study Club,
Kanawa, Okla.

NORMANDY DRESSING

Makes About 2½ Cups

Serve on grapefruit or other fruit salad.

2 3-ounce packages cream cheese
3 tablespoons lemon juice
2 tablespoons currant jelly
½ cup heavy cream, whipped

1. Beat cheese and lemon juice until smooth. Add jelly; beat until smooth.
2. Fold in cream.

M. Sutton, Woman's Club, Ogunquit, Me.

CINNAMON CREAM SALAD DRESSING

Makes About 2 Cups

¼ cup confectioners' sugar
1 teaspoon cinnamon
2 tablespoons maraschino cherry
    juice
1 tablespoon lemon juice
1 cup heavy cream, whipped

Combine sugar, cinnamon, cherry juice and lemon juice; chill for 1 hour; fold into cream.

Mayme Mahon, President, Woman's Club,
Elmhurst, Ill.

LEMON DRESSING FOR FRUIT SALADS

Makes About 1½ Cups

1 cup sugar
1 tablespoon flour
1 tablespoon grated lemon rind
    Juice of lemon
2 eggs, well beaten
1 cup water

1. Combine all ingredients in saucepan. Cook, stirring constantly, until thickened. Cool.
2. Store in covered container in refrigerator.

Mrs. Edward C. Holt, Woman's Club,
Casselton, N.D.

COOKED PINEAPPLE SALAD DRESSING FOR FRUIT SALAD

Makes About 1 Cup

¼ cup sugar
¾ teaspoon salt
1½ tablespoons flour
1 egg, lightly beaten
¾ cup pineapple juice
2 tablespoons lemon juice

1. In saucepan combine sugar, salt and flour. Stir in egg. Gradually stir in pineapple and lemon juices.
2. Cook over medium heat, stirring constantly, until very thick. Chill.

Geneva Masterson, El Camino Women's Club, Ventura, Calif.

FRUIT SALAD DRESSING

Makes About 3 Cups

Use as dressing on fruit salad or on gingerbread.

2 eggs
½ cup sugar
Dash of dry mustard
1½ tablespoons flour
1 cup pineapple juice
1 cup heavy cream, whipped

1. In top of double saucepan blend eggs, sugar, mustard and flour. Stir in pineapple juice. Cook over hot water, stirring constantly, until thickened and smooth.
2. Remove from heat. Cool, stirring occasionally.
3. Fold in cream.

Doris Gerkins, Women's Club, Linwood, N.J.

DELICIOUS SALAD DRESSING FOR FRUIT SALADS

Makes About 2 Cups

3 egg yolks
6 tablespoons sugar
3 tablespoons pineapple juice
2 tablespoons white vinegar
1 cup heavy cream, whipped

1. In saucepan or top of double saucepan combine egg yolks and sugar. Gradually stir in pineapple juice and vinegar. Cook over low heat or simmering water, stirring constantly, until fairly thickened and smooth. Cool.
2. Fold in cream.

Mrs. Fred Buettner, Woman's Club, Crystal Lake, Ill.

18. Pies and Pastries

Many countries have favorite rich pastry desserts, but no country in the world has the appetite for so wide a variety of pies that the United States has.

Although baked crumb and meringue crusts are popular for chiffon and creamy pie fillings, every homemaker prides herself on the flaky quality of her favorite piecrust. Piecrust recipes in this chapter are generally interchangeable. Therefore, no cross references are made when a pie recipe specifies pastry for a 1- or 2-crust pie.

Equipment for Pie Baking

Every kitchen should be equipped with:
Pastry board
Rolling pin
Several 8- or 9-inch (or 8½- and 9½-inch) pie plates
Rectangular baking pan (10 x 6 x 1½ inches) for deep-dish pies
Variety of fluted tart or individual pie pans
Pastry wheel
Pastry blender

But the most important pieces of pie-making equipment are a heavy canvas cloth for rolling out the dough and a stocking for the rolling pin. These are packaged in a set, available at all housewares stores, and they greatly simplify pastry rolling and cutting.

Baking Temperatures for Pies

Many homemakers prefer two baking temperatures for pies: they begin with a preheated 450° F. oven for 10 to 20 minutes to set the crust and then reduce the temperature to 350° or 325° F. (depending on the type of filling) to bake the pie until it is done. Modern techniques advocate a constant temperature of 400° or 425° F. throughout the baking.

Common Causes of Failure in Making Pies

1. Pastry crumbles if flour and shortening are overmixed.

2. Pastry is tough if too much water is used or dough is overmixed.
3. Pies fail to brown because they are not baked long enough at a high enough temperature.

Anniversary Cookbook, Women's Club,
Ashland, Mass.

How to Make a 2-Crust Pie

1. Make Pastry for a 2-Crust Pie (p. 548).
2. On lightly floured board roll out half the pastry to circle ⅛ inch thick and about 1½ inches larger than pie plate.
3. Gently fit circle in pie plate; trim off overhanging edge.
4. Put filling in pastry-lined plate.
5. Roll out remaining pastry to circle ⅛ inch thick. Fold in half; cut several slits for steam to escape.
6. Unfold pastry; place over filling in pie plate.
7. Trim off extra edge, leaving ½ inch overhanging.
8. Fold overhanging edge of top pastry under edge of lower pastry; press together to seal.
9. Flute edge: Take rim of pastry between thumb and forefinger of both hands held ½ inch apart; pull rim held in right hand down and toward you, holding rim in place with other hand; place thumb and finger of left hand in ripple made by right hand. Repeat all around edge of pie.
10. Bake according to recipe directions.

How to Make a 1-Crust Pie

1. Make Pastry for a 1-Crust Pie (p. 548).
2. On lightly floured board roll out pastry to a circle ⅛ inch thick.
3. Fit pastry loosely into pie plate; trim off edge, leaving ½ inch overhanging. Fold overhanging edge back and under.
4. Make standing fluted edge: Place left forefinger against inside of pastry rim; pinch outside with right thumb and forefinger. Repeat all around rim.
5. Put filling in pastry-lined plate. Bake according to recipe directions.

How to Make a Pie Shell

1. Make Pastry for a 1-Crust Pie (p. 548). Fit into pie plate; flute edge as above,

2. Prick bottom and sides of pastry generously with fork.

3. Bake in preheated 425° F. oven for 12 to 15 minutes, or until golden brown.

4. Cool before filling.

How to Make a Lattice-Topped Pie

1. Make Pastry for a 2-Crust Pie (below). (There will be some left over for tarts or turnovers.)

2. Begin in same way as for 1-crust pie, leaving half of pastry overhanging pie plate by ½ inch.

3. Put filling in pastry-lined pie plate.

4. Roll out remaining pastry; cut into strips from ⅜ to ½ inch wide. For fluted strips, cut with pastry wheel.

5. Weave top crust: Place a strip lightly across center of pie, dividing pie in half. Place another strip at right angles to first. Pie is now divided into quarters, with second strip overlapping first strip in center. Place another strip on each side of first strip. Lift strips when necessary to allow strip being woven to run under. Weave 10 strips in all, 5 running in each direction.

6. Turn overhanging pastry over ends of strips; flute deeply.

7. Bake according to recipe directions.

Piecrusts

PASTRY FOR A 2-CRUST PIE

2¼ cups presifted flour
1 teaspoon salt
¾ cup shortening
6 tablespoons water

1. In mixing bowl combine flour and salt. With pastry blender or two knives, cut in shortening until mixture resembles coarse meal.

2. Sprinkle water over mixture, a tablespoon at a time; mix lightly with fork until all flour is moistened.

3. With hands, gather dough into a ball; cut in half.

FOR RICHER PASTRY: Increase shortening to 1 cup.

PASTRY FOR A 1-CRUST PIE OR BAKED PIE SHELL

1¼ cups presifted flour
½ teaspoon salt
½ cup shortening
3 tablespoons water

Follow directions in preceding recipe.

A. S.

HOT WATER PIE PASTRY

Makes Pastry for 2-Crust Pie

½ cup boiling water
1 cup shortening
3 cups presifted flour

1 teaspoon salt
1 teaspoon baking powder

1. In mixing bowl pour water over shortening; stir until creamy.

2. Combine flour, salt and baking powder.

3. Add dry ingredients to shortening; mix to a smooth dough. Chill before rolling out and cutting.

Mrs. Frank G. Tallman, New Century Club, Wilmington, Del.

HEIRLOOM PIE PASTRY

Makes Pastry for 4 or 5
2-Crust Pies

Use dough as required; unused pieces may be returned to original piece of dough. There is no waste, since dough can be handled without damage; if stored in refrigerator, it will keep for months.

5 cups presifted flour
1½ tablespoons salt
2 cups lard
½ cup milk
¼ cup cider vinegar

1. In large mixing bowl combine flour and salt. Cut in lard until mixture resembles fine crumbs.

2. Add milk and vinegar; mix with fork until dough cleans sides of bowl.

3. Form dough into oblong shape; wrap in double layer of waxed paper. Close ends; secure with rubber bands. Store in refrigerator.

Mrs. R. Sheldon Weist, Women's Auxiliary to the Chiropractic Association of New York, New York, N.Y.

NEVER-FAIL PIE PASTRY

Makes Pastry for 2
2-Crust Pies

If well wrapped to prevent drying, this dough may be kept in refrigerator for several days. It also freezes well. Defrost it gradually if frozen.

3 cups presifted flour
1 teaspoon salt
1 cup lard
1 egg, lightly beaten
5 tablespoons cold water
1 tablespoon vinegar

1. Put flour, salt and lard in large bowl of electric mixer. Blend well on low speed.

2. Combine egg, water and vinegar; stir into flour mixture.

3. Gather up dough with hands; wrap in waxed paper; chill for easier handling.

Mrs. G. S. Garland, Friday Club, Barlow, N.D.

PERFECT PIE PASTRY

Makes Pastry for 2-Crust
and 1-Crust Pie

3 cups presifted flour
1⅓ cups shortening
1 egg
1 tablespoon vinegar
⅓ cup water

1. Put flour in mixing bowl. Cut in shortening until mixture resembles coarse meal.

2. Beat egg, vinegar and water. Add to flour mixture; mix lightly with fork until dough cleans sides of bowl.

Mrs. John P. Burke, Federated Woman's Club, Bailey, Colo.

RICH PIE PASTRY

Makes Pastry for 2-Crust Pie

2 cups presifted flour
¼ cup cold milk
⅔ cup shortening
⅓ cup butter

1. Combine ⅓ cup of the flour with milk to make a paste. Set aside.

2. Cut shortening and butter into remaining flour until mixture resembles coarse meal.

3. Add paste; blend well.

Mayme Mahon, President, Woman's Club, Elmhurst, Ill.

CHEESE PASTRY

Makes Pastry for 1-Crust Pie

1 cup presifted flour
½ teaspoon salt
⅓ cup (plus 1 tablespoon, if hydrogenated) shortening
¼ cup shredded American cheese
2 tablespoons water

1. In mixing bowl combine flour and salt. Cut in shortening until mixture resembles coarse crumbs.

2. Lightly stir in cheese.

3. Sprinkle with water; stir with fork until all ingredients are moistened and can be gathered into a ball.

Nana Miller, Junior Woman's Club, Corning, N.Y.

CREAM CHEESE PASTRY

Makes Pastry for 2-Crust Pie or 36 3-Inch Squares

8-ounce package cream cheese
1 cup butter or margarine
2 cups presifted flour

1. In mixing bowl beat cheese and butter or margarine until fluffy.

2. Stir in flour; mix until blended. Chill for 3 hours.

Mrs. Dale Ackerman, Atheneum Club, Marysville, Kans.

FLAKY PUFF PASTRY

Makes Pastry for 2-Crust Pie or 12 Tart Shells

To freeze puff pastry, wrap in aluminum foil.

3 cups presifted flour
¼ teaspoon salt
1 cup shortening
½ cup butter
1 teaspoon lemon juice
Ice water

1. Into mixing bowl sift together flour and salt. Cut ¼ cup of the shortening and

2 tablespoons of the butter until mixture resembles fine crumbs.

2. Make a well in center; add lemon juice and about ⅓ cup ice water. Blend with back of knife; work together until dough leaves sides of bowl (if necessary, add a little more water).

3. Turn onto lighter floured board; roll out to rectangle 12 x 4 inches.

4. Lightly mark dough into 3 even squares. Spread ¼ cup of the shortening evenly over top two-thirds of dough. Dot evenly with 2 tablespoons of the butter.

5. Fold unbuttered third of dough over middle third; fold remaining third on top to form a square. Press edges lightly with rolling pin; give dough quarter turn to left.

6. Roll out to 12 x 6-inch rectangle; repeat steps 4 and 5.

7. Repeat Step 6; wrap dough in waxed paper; chill for 30 minutes.

8. Roll and fold 3 more times.

9. Chill dough for 30 minutes. Roll out and use as desired.

Women's Club, Cheney, Kans.

BUTTER CRUST PASTRY

Makes 9-Inch Pie Shell

1 cup presifted flour
Dash of salt
2 tablespoons sugar
½ cup butter

1. Preheat oven to 375° F.

2. In mixing bowl combine flour, salt and sugar; mix well. Cut in butter; work until dough forms a ball.

3. With fingers press dough onto bottom and sides of 9-inch pie plate. Chill for 15 minutes.

4. Bake in preheated oven for 15 minutes.

Mrs. Burton Winkler, Junior Women's Club, Nashua, N.H.

CANADIAN PIE PASTRY

Makes Pastry for 4 or 5 1-Crust Pies

5 cups presifted flour
3 tablespoons brown sugar
1 teaspoon salt
1 teaspoon baking powder
1 pound lard
1 egg
2 tablespoons vinegar

1. In mixing bowl combine flour, sugar, salt and baking powder. Cut in lard until mixture resembles coarse crumbs.

2. In measuring cup combine egg and vinegar; add sufficient water to total ⅔ cup. Add to flour mixture; work together until dough forms a ball.

Mrs. H. M. Walker, Tillicum Club, Boardman, Ore.

RICH COOKY CRUST

Makes Pastry for 1-Crust Pie

1 cup presifted flour
½ cup butter
2 egg yolks
3 tablespoons sugar
1 teaspoon vanilla
½ teaspoon salt

1. Put flour in mixing bowl; make a well in center.
2. Slice butter into well; add remaining ingredients. With hands, mix ingredients in center well to a smooth paste; gradually work in surrounding flour to make a firm dough.
3. This dough is difficult to handle. Chill for 30 minutes before rolling out; use well-floured stocking on rolling pin and pastry board fitted with well-floured canvas cloth. Or, if desired, use fingers to press dough onto bottom and sides of pie plate or baking pan.

Mrs. Clifford Williams, President, Woman's Club, Lidgerwood, N.D.

PANTRY SHELF PIE PASTRY

Makes Pastry for 6 1-Crust Pies or 6 Pie Shells

4½ cups presifted flour
1½ teaspoons salt
1½ cups shortening

1. Combine all ingredients in mixing bowl; work together until crumbly.
2. Put in covered container; place on shelf. Use as desired.

TO MAKE 1 PIE SHELL:

1. Preheat oven to 450° F.
2. Put 1½ cups of above mixture in mixing bowl.
3. Put 3 tablespoons of mixture in small bowl with 3 tablespoons ice water.
4. Work together; return to rest of mixture. Work with hands to form a smooth dough.
5. Put dough between two sheets of waxed paper; roll out ⅛ inch thick.
6. Remove top sheet; invert pastry into 9-inch pie plate. Peel off remaining paper; fit pastry lightly into pie plate. Flute edge.
7. Bake in preheated oven for 10 minutes.

Mrs. Paul E. Long, Woman's Club, Albany, N.Y.

TART PASTRY

Makes 12 3-Inch Tart Shells

Fill with favorite cream filling or fruits, as desired.

1½ cups presifted flour
¼ teaspoon salt
1 tablespoon sugar
½ cup shortening
2 tablespoons butter or margarine
Ice water

1. Into mixing bowl sift together flour, salt and sugar. Cut in shortening and butter or margarine until mixture resembles fine crumbs.

2. Sprinkle with about 4 tablespoons ice water; mix until dough is formed.
3. Turn onto lightly floured board; roll out ⅛ inch thick. Cut out with floured 5-inch cooky cutter; fit into 12 3-inch tart pans.
4. Prick pastry with fork tines. Chill for 15 minutes.

BAKED TART SHELLS: Preheat oven to 425° F. Place tart pans on baking sheet; bake in preheated oven for 2 minutes, or until golden.

Ruth Whitney, Woman's Club, Athol, Mass.

ALMOND PASTRY

Makes Pastry for 1-Crust Pie

¼ cup butter
¼ teaspoon salt
2 tablespoons sugar
1 egg yolk
¾ cup presifted flour
¼ cup ground almonds

1. In mixing bowl cream butter, salt and sugar until light and fluffy.
2. Add egg yolk; beat thoroughly.
3. Stir in flour and almonds to make a firm dough.
4. With fingers, press dough onto bottom and sides of 9-inch pie plate. Chill for 30 minutes.

Mrs. Donald Ohleyer, Bogue Country Club, Yuba, Calif.

BUTTER CRUNCH FOR PIE SHELL AND TOPPING

Makes 2½ Cups

½ cup butter
¼ cup brown sugar
1 cup presifted flour
½ cup chopped pecans, chopped walnuts or flaked coconut

1. Preheat oven to 400° F.
2. Combine all ingredients by hand; spread in 13 x 9½ x 2-inch baking pan.
3. Bake in preheated oven for 15 minutes.
4. Remove from oven; stir with spoon.
5. Use hot to line pie plate. Or cool and then store in covered container in refrigerator for later use.

Mrs. Vernon L. Purchase, Junior Woman's Club, Torrance, Calif.

CEREAL CRUNCH PIECRUST

Makes Crust for 9-Inch Pie or 10 x 6 x 1½-Inch Baking Pan

1 egg white
1 cup crushed wheat flakes or cornflakes
½ cup finely chopped walnuts or pecans
¼ cup brown sugar

1. Preheat oven to 300° F.
2. Beat egg white until stiff peaks form.
3. Fold in remaining ingredients.
4. Spread onto bottom and sides of 9-inch pie plate or 10 x 6 x 1½-inch baking pan.

5. Bake in preheated oven for 10 minutes. Cool before filling.

Alice Jeffries, Junior Woman's Club, Phoenix, Ariz.

WHEAT CRUST

Makes 8- or 9-Inch Pie Shell

1 cup finely crushed wheat cereal
¼ cup sugar
¼ teaspoon cinnamon
¼ cup melted butter or margarine

1. Combine all ingredients thoroughly.
2. Pat out in 8- or 9-inch pie plate; chill until ready to fill.

Elma Gray Holtam, Worthwhile Club,
Thomasville, Ala.

CHOCOLATE SHELL

Makes 9-Inch Pie Shell

¾ cup semi-sweet chocolate pieces
¼ cup shortening
¼ cup finely chopped walnuts

1. Preheat oven to 300° F.
2. Line 9-inch pie plate with aluminum foil, smoothing sides and rim with fingers. Trim foil.
3. Put chocolate and shortening in pie plate; heat in oven for 4 minutes, or until chocolate softens.
4. Remove from oven; stir in walnuts; blend well. Cool for 12 to 15 minutes, or until thick enough to spread.
5. Spread evenly over bottom and sides of plate to make a pie shell. Chill for about 1 hour, or until firm.
6. Carefully peel foil from shell; slip shell back into plate. Chill until ready to fill.

Mrs. Harvey Porter, Round Table Club of
Camden and Wyoming, Delaware
Federation of Women's Clubs

BAKED CHOCOLATE CRUMB CRUST

Makes 9-Inch Pie Shell

25 chocolate wafers, crushed
1 tablespoon sugar
⅓ cup melted butter

1. Preheat oven to 350° F. Grease 9-inch pie plate.
2. Combine all ingredients. Press onto bottom and sides of pie plate.
3. Bake in preheated oven for 7 minutes. Cool.

Mrs. B. F. Burns, Jr., Thursday Study Club,
Iuka, Miss.

CHOCOLATE OR VANILLA WAFER CRUST

Makes 9-Inch Pie Shell

1½ cups chocolate or vanilla wafer crumbs
¼ teaspoon cinnamon
2 tablespoons sugar
⅓ cup melted butter or margarine

1. Lightly grease 9-inch pie plate.
2. In mixing bowl combine crumbs, cinnamon and sugar. Stir in butter or margarine; mix well.

3. Press mixture onto bottom and sides of pie plate. Chill for 1 hour before filling.

Mrs. Warren Ringer, Junior New Century Club,
Needham Heights, Mass.

COCONUT MACAROON PIE SHELL

Makes 10-Inch Pie Shell

Fill with Coconut Sherry Chiffon filling (p. 568) or other filling, as desired.

26 large coconut macaroons
¼ cup sweet sherry

1. Arrange macaroons in bottom and on sides of 10-inch pie plate, flattening with fingers so they take shape of plate.
2. Sprinkle with sherry; chill for 30 minutes.

Mrs. S. S. Stoaks, President, Parnassus Club,
Jackson, Miss.

MACAROON CRUMB CRUST

Makes 9-Inch Pie Shell

24 macaroons
½ cup softened margarine

1. Few days before, buy macaroons; dry thoroughly. Roll into fine crumbs.
2. Mix crumbs with margarine; press evenly onto bottom and sides of 9-inch pie plate. Chill before filling.

Marjorie Meredith, Modern Culture Club,
Tuscaloosa, Ala.

GINGERSNAP CRUST

Makes 9-Inch Pie Shell

Fill with Peach Rice filling (p. 572) or other filling, as desired.

¼ cup melted butter or margarine
2 tablespoons sugar
¼ teaspoon ginger
1¼ cups crushed gingersnaps

1. Preheat oven to 325° F. Grease 9-inch pie plate.
2. Pour butter or margarine into mixing bowl; stir in sugar, ginger and crumbs.
3. Mix well; press onto bottom and sides of pie plate.
4. Bake in preheated oven for 10 minutes.
5. Cool before filling.

Edna Storms, Book and Needle Club, Oradell, N.J.

GRAHAM CRACKER CRUMB CRUST

Makes 9-Inch Pie Shell

20 graham cracker squares
¼ cup softened butter
¼ cup sugar

1. Roll crackers (or blend in electric blender) to even fine crumbs.
2. Pour crumbs into mixing bowl; add butter and sugar. Blend well with fingers or fork.
3. Pour into 9-inch pie plate; press firmly to make even layer on bottom and sides. Chill for 45 minutes before filling.

Ima Carl Clements, Modern Culture Club,
Tuscaloosa, Ala.

ICE CREAM PASTRY FOR FRUIT TARTS OR TURNOVERS

Makes Pastry for 4 1-Crust Pies

4 cups presifted flour
2 tablespoons sugar
1 pound butter
1 pint vanilla ice cream, partially
   melted

1. Day before, in mixing bowl combine flour and sugar. Cut in butter until mixture resembles fine meal.
2. Stir in ice cream to make a stiff dough.
3. Wrap in aluminum foil; refrigerate overnight.

Mrs. Claire Crawford, Junior Woman's Club,
Lombard, Ill.

MERINGUE NEST

Makes 9-Inch Pie Shell

4 egg whites
¼ teaspoon salt
1 teaspoon lemon juice
1 cup sugar

1. Preheat oven to 275° F. Grease well and flour 9-inch pie plate.
2. In mixing bowl beat egg whites and salt until foamy.
3. Add lemon juice; gradually beat in sugar, about 2 tablespoons at a time; beat until stiff and glossy.
4. Spread in pie plate, hollowing out center.
5. Bake in preheated oven for 1 hour and 15 minutes.
6. Carefully remove shell from pie plate. Cool before filling.

Mrs. Earl Hampton, Home Life Chairman,
Oregon Federation of Women's Clubs,
Zenith Women's Club, Salem, Ore.

MERINGUE PIE SHELL

Makes 8- or 9-Inch Pie Shell

3 egg whites
¼ teaspoon cream of tartar
1 cup sugar
½ cup soda crackers, broken up
½ cup chopped nuts, flaked coconut
   or chocolate chips

1. Preheat oven to 350° F.
2. Beat egg whites and cream of tartar until soft peaks form.
3. Gradually beat in sugar; beat until thickened and glossy. Fold in remaining ingredients.
4. Spread onto bottom and sides of 8- or 9-inch pie plate.
5. Bake in preheated oven for 15 minutes, or until lightly browned. Cool before filling.

Myrtle Haugom, Book and Thimble Club,
Portland, N.D.

MERINGUE TOPPINGS

For extravagant toppings: Use 4 or 5 egg whites.
For everyday toppings: Use 2 or 3 egg whites.
For garnish: Use 1 egg white.

Egg whites
¼ teaspoon cream of tartar
Sugar

1. Preheat oven to desired temperature (see Step 6).
2. In mixing bowl beat egg whites until frothy.
3. Add cream of tartar; beat until stiff peaks form.
4. Gradually beat in 2 tablespoons of the sugar for each egg white. Beat until stiff and glossy.
5. Pile meringue lightly on cooled pie, making sure it touches edge of pastry to prevent it from shrinking. Swirl into large curls.
6. Bake at 425° F. for 5 to 6 minutes or at 325° F. for about 12 minutes.

Mrs. Maxwell Kelley, Nineteenth Century Club,
Bangor, Me.

2-EGG-WHITE COOKED MERINGUE

Makes About 2 Cups

2 egg whites
½ cup sugar
2 tablespoons water
Dash of salt

1. In top of double saucepan combine all ingredients. Beat with rotary beater until thoroughly mixed.
2. Place over rapidly boiling water; beat for 1 minute.
3. Remove from heat. Beat for 2 minutes longer, or until stiff peaks form.

Mrs. A. L. Shuck, President, 4th District,
Oklahoma Federation of Women's Clubs,
Weatherford, Okla.

5-EGG-WHITE FRUIT MERINGUE

Makes About 5 Cups

5 egg whites
½ teaspoon baking powder
4 tablespoons sugar
¾ cup well-drained fruit preserves

1. Preheat oven to 350° F.
2. Beat egg whites until frothy. Add baking powder; beat until stiff but not dry.
3. Gradually beat in sugar, a tablespoon at a time; beat until smooth and glossy. Fold in preserves.
4. Spread lavishly over pie filling. Bake in preheated oven until browned.

Mrs. R. L. Perry, Woman's Cooperative Club,
New Augusta, Miss.

CREAM PUFF PASTRY

Makes 8 to 10 Cream Puffs

½ cup butter or margarine
1 cup boiling water
1 cup presifted flour
¼ teaspoon salt
4 eggs

1. Put butter or margarine and water in small saucepan; stir over high heat until butter or margarine is melted and liquid is boiling rapidly.
2. Add flour and salt all at once; raise saucepan a few inches above heat; stir

briskly. (Paste will come away from sides of pan and form a smooth ball in center.) Cook, stirring, for 30 seconds longer.

3. Remove from heat. Break 1 of the eggs into paste; beat vigorously until smooth and fluffy. Break in remaining eggs, one at a time; beat vigorously after each addition until smooth and glossy.

Mrs. Nellie Partridge, Women's Club,
Osage, Wyo.

2-Crust Pies

MOM'S APPLE PIE

Makes 9-Inch Pie

Pastry for 2-crust pie
6 medium tart apples, peeled, cored and sliced
2 tablespoons flour
2 tablespoons butter
2 teaspoons vanilla
1 cup sugar
1 egg
1 cup heavy cream
Dash of salt
½ cup chopped black walnuts

1. Preheat oven to 400° F.
2. Line 9-inch pie plate with half the pastry.
3. Arrange apples in pastry-lined plate.
4. In bowl combine flour, butter and vanilla. Add sugar, egg, cream and salt; beat until smooth. Pour over apples. Sprinkle with walnuts.
5. Roll out remaining pastry; make 3 slashes in center; place on apples. Seal edges; flute.
6. Bake in preheated oven for 30 minutes, or until apples are tender.

Mrs. E. M. Platt, Women's Club, Nemaha, Ia.

RICH APPLE PIE

Makes 9-Inch Pie

Pastry for 2-crust pie
½ cup butter
1 cup sugar
2 tablespoons flour
Winesap apples

1. Preheat oven to 450° F.
2. Line 9-inch pie plate with half of pastry.
3. Slice ¼ cup of the butter into pastry-lined plate.
4. Combine sugar and flour; sprinkle half over butter.
5. Peel, core and chop enough apples to fill pie plate to heaping; sprinkle with remaining sugar mixture; slice remaining butter onto top.
5. Cover with lattice topping.
6. Bake in preheated oven for 10 minutes. Turn temperature to 350° F..; bake for 25 to 30 minutes longer, or until well browned.

Mrs. Duncan Hines, Woman's Club,
Williamsburg, Ky.

MOCK APPLE PIE

Makes 9-Inch Pie

Pastry for 2-crust pie
30 salted crackers
1¾ cups water
1½ cups sugar
1¾ teaspoons cinnamon
2¼ teaspoons cream of tartar
1 tablespoon lemon juice
¼ teaspoon grated lemon rind
Butter

1. Preheat oven to 425° F.
2. Line 9-inch pie plate with half of pastry.
3. Break crackers into pastry-lined plate.
4. Combine remaining ingredients; pour over crackers. Dot with butter. Cover with remaining pastry; cut several 1-inch slits. Flute edge.
5. Bake in preheated oven for 30 minutes. Serve hot.

Mrs. I. Rubin, Civic League, Greenville, Pa.

APRICOT PIE

Makes 9-Inch Pie

1-pound 13-ounce can apricots, drained
¾ cup sugar
1 teaspoon cinnamon
2 tablespoons tapioca
Pastry for 2-crust pie

1. Preheat oven to 425° F.
2. Mix apricots, sugar, cinnamon and tapioca.
3. Line 9-inch pie plate with half of pastry. Put filling in pastry-lined plate. Cover with remaining pastry; cut slits for steam to escape; flute edge.
4. Bake in preheated oven for about 45 minutes.

Barbara Kirby, Marri-eds Junior Women's Club,
Santa Cruz, Calif.

BLUEBERRY OR CHERRY PIE

Makes 9-Inch Pie

Pastry for 2-crust pie
¾ to 1 cup sugar
¼ cup presifted flour
2½ cups blueberries or pitted cherries with juice
1⅓ teaspoons butter

1. Preheat oven to 425° F.
2. Line 9-inch pie plate with half of pastry.
3. In saucepan combine sugar, flour and blueberries or cherries. Bring to boil over moderate heat, stirring constantly, until thickened.
4. Pour filling into pastry-lined plate; dot with butter. Cover with remaining pastry; cut slits for steam to escape; flute edge.
5. Bake in preheated oven for 30 to 40 minutes. Cool until slightly warm, not hot, before serving.

Bette H. Simmons, New Century Club,
Wilmington, Del.

TAPIOCA CHERRY PIE

Makes 9-Inch Pie

1-pound 4-ounce can water-packed
    sour red cherries
1 cup sugar
2½ tablespoons quick-cooking tapioca
⅛ teaspoon salt
6 drops red food coloring
¼ teaspoon almond extract
1 tablespoon margarine
Pastry for 2-crust pie

1. Drain juice from cherries into mixing
bowl. Stir in sugar, tapioca, salt, food
coloring and almond extract.
2. Let stand for 15 minutes; stir in cherries.
3. Preheat oven to 425° F.
4. Line 9-inch pie plate with half of
pastry.
5. Pour in filling; dot with margarine.
6. Cover with remaining pastry, either
closed and slashed or lattice topped. (For
glazed crust, sprinkle lightly with sugar.)
7. Bake in preheated oven for 50
minutes.

Mrs. W. B. Wallace, Entre Nous Study Club,
Shreveport, La.

RAISIN CRANBERRY PIE

Makes 9-Inch Pie

1¼ cups sugar
3 tablespoons cornstarch
½ teaspoon salt
1½ cups water
2 cups cranberries
1½ cups seedless raisins
1 tablespoon grated orange rind
¼ cup chopped almonds
1 tablespoon butter
Pastry for 2-crust pie

1. In saucepan blend sugar, cornstarch
and salt. Gradually stir in water; cook over
medium heat, stirring constantly, until
thickened and smooth.
2. Remove from heat. Add cranberries,
raisins, orange rind, almonds and butter.
Mix well. Cool.
3. Preheat oven to 425° F.
4. Line 9-inch pie plate with half of
pastry; fill with cranberry mixture.
5. Roll out remaining pastry; cover filling. Seal; flute edges. Make 2 slashes in
top to allow steam to escape.
6. Bake in preheated oven for 30 minutes, or until browned.

Mrs. Charles Strother, Chairman, Elections
Committee, General Federation of
Women's Clubs, Madill, Okla.

OLD-FASHIONED CONCORD GRAPE PIE

Makes 9-Inch Pie

Concord grapes
1¼ cups sugar
2½ teaspoons quick-cooking tapioca
Pastry for 2-crust pie
2 tablespoons flour

1. Wash grapes; pull enough off stems
to make rounded mound in 9-inch pie
plate.

2. Squeeze pulp from grapes into saucepan; reserve skins. Bring pulp to boil;
strain out seeds; mix puréed pulp with
skins. Stir in 1 cup of the sugar and
tapioca.
3. Preheat oven to 500° F.
4. Line 9-inch pie plate with half of
pastry.
5. Combine remaining sugar and flour;
sprinkle into pastry-lined plate. Add grape
filling. Cover with lattice topping.
6. Bake in preheated oven for 10 minutes. Reduce temperature 25° every 10
minutes, for a total baking time of 50 to 60
minutes.

Mayme Mahon, President, Woman's Club,
Elmhurst, Ill.

EARLY SETTLER'S ORANGE PIE

Makes 8-Inch Pie

10 to 12 oranges
½ cup sugar
2 tablespoons flour
½ teaspoon cinnamon
Pastry for 2-crust pie

1. Peel and section oranges to total 5
cups.
2. Put oranges in mixing bowl; sprinkle
with sugar, flour and cinnamon.
3. Preheat oven to 400° F.
4. Line 8-inch pie plate with half of
pastry.
5. Arrange oranges in pastry-lined plate.
Cover with remaining pastry; cut slits in
top; flute edge.
6. Bake in preheated oven for 30 minutes, or until golden.

Mrs. H. H. Mallory, Woman's Club,
Mount Dora, Fla.

BUTTERSCOTCH PEACH PIE

Makes 8-Inch Pie

Pastry for 2-crust pie
5 or 6 ripe peaches
¼ cup brown sugar
2 tablespoons flour
2 teaspoons lemon juice
6 tablespoons butter, melted

1. Line 8-inch pie plate with half of
pastry.
2. Peel peaches; cut in half. Discard
pits. Slice peaches thickly into pastry-lined
plate.
3. Preheat oven to 450° F.
4. Combine remaining ingredients; pour
over peaches. Cover with lattice topping.
5. Bake in preheated oven for 15 minutes. Turn temperature to 350° F. Bake for
30 minutes longer.

Betty Larson, Woman's Club, Ambridge, Pa.

GOLDEN PEACH PIE

Makes 9-Inch Pie

4 cups canned sliced peaches
    with juice
½ cup sugar
2 tablespoons flour
¼ teaspoon nutmeg

Dash of salt
2 tablespoons butter
1 tablespoon lemon juice
½ teaspoon grated orange peel
⅛ teaspoon almond extract
Pastry for 2-crust pie

1. Drain peaches; reserve ⅓ cup syrup.
2. In saucepan combine sugar, flour, nutmeg and salt. Stir in reserved syrup; bring to boil. Cook, stirring constantly, until thickened.
3. Remove from heat; stir in butter, lemon juice, orange peel and almond extract.
4. Preheat oven to 400° F.
5. Line 9-inch pie plate with half of pastry. Add peach filling. Cover with lattice topping.
6. Bake in preheated oven for 40 to 45 minutes.

Virginia Costa, Marri-eds Junior Women's Club, Santa Cruz, Calif.

RHUBARB CUSTARD PIE

Makes 9-Inch Pie

Pastry for 2-crust pie
1½ cups sugar
3 tablespoons flour
½ teaspoon nutmeg
1 tablespoon softened butter
2 eggs
3 cups rhubarb, cut into 1-inch pieces
Confectioners' sugar

1. Preheat oven to 450° F.
2. Line 9-inch pie plate with half of pastry.
3. Combine sugar, flour, nutmeg, butter and eggs. Beat until smooth.
4. Put rhubarb in pastry-lined plate; pour egg mixture on top. Cover with lattice topping; flute edge.
5. Bake in preheated oven for 10 minutes. Turn temperature to 350° F. Bake for 30 minutes longer.
6. Before serving, dust with confectioners' sugar.

Theresa Gamperoli, Cabot Club, Middleboro, Mass.

RHUBARB AND LEMON PIE

Makes 9-Inch Pie

Pastry for 2-crust pie
3 cups diced rhubarb
1 cup sugar
1 tablespoon flour
1 egg, lightly beaten
1 teaspoon grated lemon rind
½ cup water
1 tablespoon lemon juice

1. Preheat oven to 425° F.
2. Line 9-inch pie plate with half of pastry.
3. Spread rhubarb on pastry-lined plate.
4. In top of double saucepan blend sugar and flour. Gradually stir in remaining ingredients. Cook over hot water, stirring constantly, until thickened and smooth.

5. Remove from heat; pour over rhubarb. Cover with lattice topping.
6. Bake in preheated oven for 40 minutes.
7. Cool slightly before serving.

Mrs. William P. Apgar, Woman's Club, Orono, Me.

1-Crust Pies

APPLE CRUMB PIE

Makes 8-Inch Pie

Pastry for 2-crust pie
4 large tart apples, peeled and cored
1 cup sugar
1 teaspoon cinnamon
¾ cup presifted flour
⅓ cup butter

1. Preheat oven to 450° F.
2. Line 8-inch pie plate with pastry.
3. Slice apples into pastry-lined plate; sprinkle with ½ cup of the sugar and cinnamon. Into small bowl sift together remaining sugar and flour. Cut in butter until mixture resembles fine crumbs; sprinkle over apples.
5. Bake in preheated oven for 10 minutes; turn temperature to 350° F. Bake for 40 minutes longer.

Mrs. Dave Robinson, Women's Club, Riverdale, N.D.

DUTCH APPLE PIE

Makes 8-Inch Pie

½ cup butter
2 tablespoons flour
½ cup granulated sugar
½ cup brown sugar
1 teaspoon cinnamon
4 apples, peeled, cored and sliced
1 egg white
Pastry for 1-crust pie

1. Preheat oven to 350° F.
2. Combine butter, flour and sugars to make crumbs; put half in 8-inch pie plate.
3. Arrange apples over crumbs.
4. Beat egg white until stiff but not dry; fold in remaining crumb mixture; spoon over apples.
5. Roll out pastry; make lattice topping.
6. Bake in preheated oven for about 50 minutes.

Mrs. Erwin Burt, Veritas Club, Greensboro, Ala.

FRENCH APPLE PIE

Makes 9-Inch Pie

Pastry for 1-crust pie
6 cups sliced cored peeled cooking apples
Presifted flour
1¼ cups granulated sugar
½ teaspoon cinnamon
1 tablespoon lemon juice
¼ teaspoon salt
¼ cup brown sugar
½ cup butter or margarine
Whipped cream or ice cream

1. Preheat oven to 450° F.
2. Line 9-inch pie plate with pastry.
3. Combine apples, 2 tablespoons flour, 1 cup of the granulated sugar, cinnamon and lemon juice; spread in pastry-lined plate.
4. In mixing bowl combine 1 cup flour, remaining granulated sugar, salt and brown sugar. Cut in butter or margarine until mixture resembles coarse crumbs; sprinkle over apples.
5. Bake in preheated oven for 10 minutes. Turn temperature to 400° F. Bake for 40 minutes longer.
6. Serve warm with whipped cream or ice cream.

Mrs. Irene Schofield, Woman's Club, Northborough, Mass.

PAPER BAG APPLE PIE

Makes 9-Inch Pie

Pastry for 1-crust pie
5 cups sliced cored peeled cooking apples
1 cup sugar
Presifted flour
½ teaspoon nutmeg
2 tablespoons lemon juice
½ cup butter or margarine

1. Preheat oven to 425° F.
2. Line 9-inch pie plate with pastry.
3. Arrange apples in pastry-lined plate.
4. In small bowl combine ½ cup of the sugar, 2 tablespoons flour, nutmeg and lemon juice; mix well. Sprinkle over apples.
5. Combine remaining sugar, ½ cup flour and butter or margarine to make crumbs; sprinkle over apples.
6. Slide pie into large brown paper bag. Fold end over twice; secure with paper clips.
7. Put on baking sheet. Bake in preheated oven for 1 hour.

Mrs. Iris Meseke, Ladies Reading Circle, Alma, Kans.

BUTTERMILK PIE

Makes 9-Inch Pie

Pastry for 1-crust pie
3 eggs
⅔ cup buttermilk
2 cups sugar
1 tablespoon flour
½ cup melted butter
1 teaspoon vanilla

1. Preheat oven to 375° F.
2. Line 9-inch pie plate with pastry.
3. In mixing bowl beat eggs until smooth. Add buttermilk; mix well.
4. Add sugar, flour, butter and vanilla; mix to blend. Pour into pastry-lined plate.
5. Bake in preheated oven for 1 hour, or until knife inserted in center comes out clean.

Ruth Longabaugh, Woman's Club, Ruidoso, N.M.

BUTTERMILK LEMON PIE

Makes 9-Inch Pie

Pastry for 1-crust pie
2 cups sugar
3 tablespoons flour
¼ teaspoon nutmeg
½ cup melted butter
3 eggs, lightly beaten
1 cup buttermilk
Juice of 1 lemon
1 teaspoon vanilla

1. Preheat oven to 400° F.
2. Line 9-inch pie plate with pastry.
3. In mixing bowl combine sugar, flour and nutmeg. Add butter; beat until creamy. Stir in eggs, buttermilk, lemon juice and vanilla.
4. Pour filling into pastry-lined plate. Bake in preheated oven for 10 minutes. Turn temperature to 325° F. Bake for 30 minutes longer.

Mrs. Lola L. Carter, Literary and Civic Club, Houlka, Miss.

BAKED BUTTERSCOTCH PIE

Makes 8- or 9-Inch Pie

Pastry for 1-crust pie
¼ cup butter
⅓ cup flour
½ teaspoon salt
2 cups sugar
4 eggs, lightly beaten
3 cups milk
1 teaspoon vanilla

1. Preheat oven to 450° F.
2. Line 8- or 9-inch pie plate with pastry. Flute edge.
3. In saucepan combine butter, flour, salt, sugar, eggs and milk. Cook over low heat, stirring constantly, until thickened and smooth.
4. Remove from heat; stir in vanilla. Pour into pastry-lined plate.
5. Bake in preheated oven for 15 minutes. Turn temperature to 325° F. Bake for 30 to 35 minutes longer.

Mrs. Arthur E. J. Johnson, Chairman, Division of Americas, State Federation of Women's Clubs; President, Rebecca Pollard Study Club, Fort Madison, Ia.

CARROT PIE

Makes 9-Inch Pie

Pastry for 1-crust pie
1¼ cups cooked carrots
3 tablespoons butter or margarine
¾ cup sugar
2 eggs
1 tablespoon flour
¼ teaspoon ginger
¼ teaspoon cinnamon
¼ teaspoon nutmeg
½ teaspoon salt
1 teaspoon vanilla
1½ cups milk

1. Preheat oven to 425° F.
2. Line 9-inch pie plate with pastry.
3. Force carrots through ricer or sieve; set aside.

4. In mixing bowl cream butter or margarine and sugar until light and fluffy. Add eggs; beat until smooth.

5. Add flour, seasonings and vanilla; beat until smooth.

6. Add milk and carrot purée; blend. Pour into pastry-lined plate.

7. Bake in preheated oven for 10 minutes. Turn temperature to 350° F. Bake for 30 minutes longer, or until set.

Mrs. H. M. Walters, Civic Club, Galva, Ia.

DUTCH CHERRY PIE

Makes 9-Inch Pie

1 cup presifted flour
1½ teaspoons baking powder
2 tablespoons sugar
¼ cup shortening
1 egg
Milk
1-pound can cherry pie filling

1. Preheat oven to 400° F.

2. In mixing bowl combine flour, baking powder and sugar. Cut in shortening until mixture resembles crumbs.

3. Break egg into measuring cup. Add milk to total ½ cup; add to flour mixture. Stir quickly with fork until dry ingredients are moistened.

4. Pat dough into bottom and sides of 9-inch pie plate.

5. Pour pie filling into pastry-lined plate. Bake in preheated oven for 20 minutes.

Mrs. James Reed, Flamingo Woman's Club, North Dade, Fla.

CHESS PIE

Makes 8-Inch Pie

Pastry for 1-crust pie
½ cup butter or margarine
1½ cups sugar
1 tablespoon vinegar
3 eggs
1 teaspoon vanilla
Dash of salt

1. Preheat oven to 375° F.

2. Line 8-inch pie plate with pastry.

3. Melt butter or margarine in small saucepan. Stir in sugar and vinegar; bring to boil.

4. In mixing bowl beat eggs; stir in vinegar mixture. Stir in vanilla and salt; pour into pastry-lined plate.

5. Bake in preheated oven for 35 minutes, or until set.

Mrs. Ossie B. Armour, Tuesday Literary Club, Bolivar, Tenn.

LEMON CHESS PIE

Makes 9-Inch Pie

Pastry for 1-crust pie
2 cups sugar
1 tablespoon flour
1 tablespoon corn meal
4 eggs
¼ cup melted butter or margarine
¼ cup milk
¼ cup grated lemon rind
¼ cup lemon juice

1. Preheat oven to 375° F.

2. Line 9-inch pie plate with pastry.

3. In mixing bowl combine sugar, flour and corn meal. Add eggs, butter or margarine, milk, lemon rind and juice; beat until blended and smooth. Pour into pastry-lined plate.

4. Bake in preheated oven for 35 to 45 minutes, or until golden brown.

Mrs. Orville E. Carnes, Tri-Arts Federated Club, Cameron, Mo.

NEW ENGLAND CRANBERRY PIE

Makes 8- or 9-Inch Pie

Pastry for 1-crust pie
1 cup cranberries
1 cup seedless raisins
½ cup water
1 cup sugar
Pinch of salt
3 tablespoons flour
1 teaspoon vanilla

1. Preheat oven to 350° F.

2. Line 8- or 9-inch pie plate with pastry.

3. In saucepan combine cranberries, raisins and ¼ cup of the water. Bring to boil; then simmer for 10 minutes, or until cranberries burst. Stir in sugar and salt.

4. Combine remaining water and flour; stir into cranberry mixture; cook for 3 minutes, stirring constantly.

5. Remove from heat; stir in vanilla. Pour into pastry-lined plate.

6. Bake in preheated oven for 25 to 30 minutes.

A.S.

MINNESOTA BAKED CREAM CHEESE PIE

Makes 9-Inch Pie

Graham Cracker Crumb Crust
(p. 551)
2 eggs
½ cup sugar
8-ounce package softened cream cheese
3-ounce package softened cream cheese
1 teaspoon vanilla
Fresh fruit
Ice cream

1. Preheat oven to 350° F.

2. Line 9-inch pie plate with Graham Cracker Crumb Crust.

3. Beat eggs and sugar until thickened and pale. Add cheese and vanilla; beat until smooth.

4. Turn into crumb-lined plate. Bake in preheated oven for 20 to 30 minutes, or until set. Cool.

5. Serve with fresh fruit and ice cream.

Mrs. Cecil Jones, Young Matrons Study Club, Slater, Mo.

VELVETY CUSTARD PIE

Makes 9-Inch Pie

Pastry for 1-crust pie
4 eggs, lightly beaten
½ cup sugar
¼ teaspoon salt
1¼ teaspoons vanilla
2½ cups scalding-hot milk
Nutmeg

1. Preheat oven to 475° F.
2. Line 9-inch pie plate with pastry.
3. Thoroughly mix eggs, sugar, salt and vanilla. Gradually stir in milk. Pour at once into pastry-lined plate (to avoid spilling, fill at oven). Sprinkle with nutmeg.
4. Bake in preheated oven for 5 minutes. Turn temperature to 425° F. Bake for about 30 minutes longer, or until knife inserted halfway between edge and center comes out clean.

Mrs. Cury Palmer, Present Day Study Club, Northport, Ala.

EGG CUSTARD PIE

Makes 9-Inch Pie

Pastry for 1-crust pie
2¾ cups milk
¼ cup margarine
5 eggs
1 cup sugar
1 teaspoon vanilla
Nutmeg

1. Preheat oven to 450° F.
2. Line 9-inch pie plate with pastry.
3. In saucepan combine milk and margarine; bring to simmer.
4. In mixing bowl beat eggs and sugar until thickened and pale. Gradually stir in milk mixture and vanilla. Pour into pastry-lined plate. Sprinkle with nutmeg.
5. Bake in preheated oven for 10 minutes. Turn temperature to 350° F. Bake for 20 minutes longer, or until set.

VARIATIONS:

Almond Custard Pie: Brown 1 cup chopped almonds in 2 tablespoons butter. Sprinkle on pastry before adding filling.
Coconut Custard Pie: Sprinkle 1 cup flaked coconut on pastry before adding filling.

Mrs. A. H. Wright, Mother's Study Club, Weatherford, Okla.

OLD ENGLISH DATE PIE

Makes 9-Inch Pie

Serve with cinnamon-flavored whipped cream or ice cream, as desired.

Pastry for 1-crust pie
1½ cups diced dates
1½ cups heavy cream
3 eggs
1 cup sugar
1½ teaspoons cinnamon
½ teaspoon nutmeg
¼ teaspoon ground cloves
½ teaspoon salt
2 tablespoons bread crumbs
2 teaspoons vanilla
¾ cup flaked coconut

1. Preheat oven to 400° F.
2. Line 9-inch pie plate with pastry. Arrange dates in pastry-lined plate.
3. In mixing bowl combine all remaining ingredients except coconut; beat just until blended.
4. Pour into pastry-lined plate. Bake in preheated oven for 15 minutes. Turn temperature to 325° F. Sprinkle coconut on pie. Bake for 30 to 35 minutes longer, or until silver knife inserted 1 inch from edge comes out clean.

Dorothy Liphart, Woman's Club, Ebensburg, Pa.

LEMON PIE

Makes 8-Inch Pie

Butter
Flour
Pastry for 1-crust pie
½ cup milk
Grated rind of 2 lemons
Juice of 2 lemons
¼ cup melted butter
1 tablespoon corn meal
2 cups sugar
4 eggs
Dash of salt

1. Preheat oven to 375° F.
2. Grease 8-inch pie plate; dust with flour; line with pastry.
3. In mixing bowl combine milk, lemon rind and juice and butter.
4. In bowl of electric mixer combine 1 tablespoon flour, corn meal, sugar, eggs and salt; beat until well blended. Gradually beat in lemon mixture.
5. Pour into pastry-lined plate. Bake in preheated oven for 40 to 45 minutes.

Alma Ruth Durham, Woman's Club, Rockville, Va.

COLONIAL LEMON PIE

Makes 9-Inch Pie

This is very rich, so cut small slices.

3 lemons
3 cups sugar
Pastry for 1-crust pie
6 eggs
Dash of salt
½ cup melted butter or margarine
Whipped cream

1. Cut 1 of the lemons into paper-thin slices; cut each slice into quarters.
2. Squeeze juice from remaining lemons; put with lemon slices and sugar in mixing bowl. Marinate for 3 hours, stirring occasionally.
3. Preheat oven to 450° F.
4. Line 9-inch pie plate with pastry.
5. Beat eggs and salt until frothy; stir with butter or margarine into marinade. Pour into pastry-lined plate.
6. Bake in preheated oven for 15 minutes. Turn temperature to 350° F. Bake for 30 minutes longer.
7. Cool. Serve topped with whipped cream.

Woman's Club, Kewaunee, Wis.

MACADAMIA NUT PIE

Makes 9-Inch Pie

Pastry for 1-crust pie
3 eggs
1 cup light corn syrup
⅔ cup sugar
1½ cups chopped salted macadamia
nuts
2 tablespoons melted butter
1 teaspoon vanilla
Whipped cream

1. Preheat oven to 350° F.
2. Line 9-inch pie plate with pastry.
3. Beat eggs, corn syrup and sugar well. Stir in nuts, butter and vanilla; mix well.
4. Pour into pastry-lined plate. Bake in preheated oven for 50 minutes, or until crust is golden and filling is set.
5. Cool; then chill. Serve topped with whipped cream.

Jane Von Wicklin, Probieren Club,
Weatherford, Okla.

OATMEAL PIE

Makes 9-Inch Pie

Pastry for 1-crust pie
2 eggs, lightly beaten
1 cup sugar
½ cup light corn syrup
¾ cup quick-cooking oats
¾ cup flaked or shredded coconut
½ cup evaporated milk
¼ cup melted margarine

1. Preheat oven to 400° F.
2. Line 9-inch pie plate with pastry.
3. Combine all ingredients.
4. Pour into pastry-lined plate. Bake in preheated oven for 15 minutes. Turn temperature to 200° F. Bake for 40 to 45 minutes, or until set.

Mrs. C. W. Gibson, Federated Women's Clubs,
St. Joseph, Mo.

PEACH PIE

Make 8-Inch Pie

Pastry for 1-crust pie
2 cups canned sliced peaches
3 egg yolks, lightly beaten
1 cup sugar
½ cup melted margarine
2 tablespoons flour
2-Egg-White Cooked Meringue
(p. 552)

1. Preheat oven to 350° F.
2. Line 8-inch pie plate with pastry.
3. Combine peaches, egg yolks, sugar, margarine and flour.
4. Pour into pastry-lined plate. Bake in preheated oven for 35 minutes, or until set.
5. Cool. Top with 2-Egg-White Cooked Meringue. Brown in oven.

Mrs. Blake Smith, Veritas Club, Greensboro, Ala.

DEEP-DISH FRESH FRUIT PIE

Serves 6

6 cups sliced peaches or 4 cups
blueberries or pitted cherries
1 cup sugar
¼ teaspoon salt
1½ tablespoons quick-cooking tapioca
2 tablespoons butter or margarine
Pastry for 1-crust pie

1. Preheat oven to 425° F.
2. In mixing bowl combine fruit, sugar, salt and tapioca. Turn into 1-quart casserole; dot with butter or margarine.
3. Roll pastry ⅛ inch thick; cover filling; trim; turn under; flute edge. Cut gash in center for steam to escape.
4. Bake in preheated oven for 30 to 40 minutes, or until browned. Serve warm or cold.

Billie Scott, Junior Woman's Club, Norfolk, Va.

STREUSEL CREAM PEACH PIE

Makes 9-Inch Pie

Pastry for 1-crust pie
10 peaches
½ cup granulated sugar
½ teaspoon nutmeg
2 eggs
¼ cup heavy cream
¼ cup brown sugar
½ cup presifted flour
¼ cup butter or margarine

1. Preheat oven to 425° F.
2. Line 9-inch pie plate with pastry.
3. Peel, pit and quarter peaches. Arrange in pastry-lined plate. Combine granulated sugar and nutmeg; sprinkle over peaches.
4. In small bowl beat eggs and cream; pour over peaches.
5. Blend brown sugar and flour; cut in butter or margarine until mixture resembles coarse crumbs; sprinkle on peaches.
6. Bake in preheated oven for 35 to 40 minutes.

Mrs. Judd Theirolf, Delphian Junior
Woman's Club, Beloit, Kans.

PEANUT BUTTER CUSTARD PIE

Makes 9-Inch Pie

Pastry for 1-crust pie
1 cup dark corn syrup
1 cup sugar
3 eggs, lightly beaten
½ teaspoon vanilla
⅓ cup creamy or chunk-style
peanut butter

1. Preheat oven to 400° F.
2. Line 9-inch pie plate with pastry.
3. In mixing bowl combine remaining ingredients; blend until smooth. Pour into pastry-lined plate.
4. Bake in preheated oven for 15 minutes. Turn temperature to 350° F. Bake for 30 minutes longer. (Filling in center will appear a little less set than filling around edge.)

Mrs. Hobart Haywood, Woman's Social and
Benevolent Club, Lyons, Ind.

AMBER PECAN PIE
Makes 8-Inch Pie

⅓ recipe for Perfect Pie Pastry
    (p. 548)
½ cup butter
1 cup brown sugar
3 eggs, well beaten
¼ teaspoon salt
1 cup light corn syrup
1 cup pecan halves
1 teaspoon vanilla

1. Preheat oven to 325° F.
2. Line 8-inch plate with pastry.
3. Cream butter and sugar. Stir in remaining ingredients.
4. Pour into pastry-lined plate. Bake in preheated oven for 45 minutes, or until set.

Mrs. John P. Burke, Federated Woman's Club,
Bailey, Colo.

GEORGIA PECAN PIE
Makes 9-Inch Pie

Pastry for 1-crust pie
2½ tablespoons flour
⅔ cup sugar
4 eggs, lightly beaten
¼ cup softened butter
Pinch of salt
1⅓ cups corn syrup
⅔ cup broken pecans
Whipped cream

1. Preheat oven to 375° F.
2. Line 9-inch pie plate with pastry.
3. Combine flour and sugar.
4. Combine eggs and butter. Stir in flour mixture. Stir in salt, corn syrup and pecans. Pour into pastry-lined plate.
5. Bake in preheated oven for 10 minutes. Turn temperature to 350° F. Bake for 50 minutes longer.
6. Serve warm or cool with whipped cream.

Mrs. J. W. Gholston, Woman's Club, Comer, Ga.

PINEAPPLE PIE
Makes 8-Inch Pie

Pastry for 1-crust pie
2 eggs, separated
⅓ cup butter or margarine
⅔ cup sugar
2 teaspoons flour
13½-ounce can crushed pineapple
⅔ cup heavy cream

1. Preheat oven to 450° F.
2. Line 8-inch pie plate with pastry.
3. In mixing bowl combine egg yolks, butter or margarine and sugar; beat until creamy and smooth. Stir in flour, pineapple and cream.
4. In another mixing bowl beat egg whites until stiff but not dry; fold into pineapple mixture. Turn into pastry-lined plate.
5. Bake in preheated oven for 10 minutes. Turn temperature to 350° F. Bake for 30 minutes longer, or until firm.
6. Serve warm or cold.

Mrs. O. L. Beale, Woman's Club, Holland, Va.

PINEAPPLE CHESS PIE
Makes 9-Inch Pie

Pastry for 1-crust pie
½ cup butter or margarine
1½ cups sugar
2 tablespoons flour
2 eggs, lightly beaten
1 teaspoon vanilla
1 cup milk
1-pound can crushed pineapple,
    well drained

1. Preheat oven to 400° F.
2. Line 9-inch pie plate with pastry.
3. In mixing bowl cream butter or margarine, sugar and flour until light and fluffy.
4. Add eggs and vanilla; beat until smooth. Slowly stir in milk; blend until smooth. Stir in pineapple. Pour into pastry-lined plate.
5. Bake in preheated oven for 10 minutes. Turn temperature to 350° F. Bake for 30 minutes longer.

Mrs. Jess Thacker, Futuristic Study Club,
Sunray, Tex.

PUMPKIN PIE
Makes 9-Inch Pie

Pastry for 1-crust pie
1½ cups mashed cooked pumpkin
⅔ cup brown sugar
2 tablespoons molasses
½ teaspoon ginger
1 teaspoon cinnamon
1 teaspoon salt
3 eggs, separated
14½-ounce can evaporated milk or
    1¾ cups cream

1. Preheat oven to 450° F.
2. Line 9-inch pie plate with pastry.
3. In mixing bowl blend pumpkin, sugar, molasses, ginger, cinnamon and salt.
4. Blend egg yolks and milk or cream; stir into pumpkin mixture.
5. In another mixing bowl beat egg whites until stiff but not dry; fold into pumpkin mixture. Turn into pastry-lined plate.
6. Bake in preheated oven for 10 minutes. Turn temperature to 325° F. Bake 30 minutes longer, or until firm.

Mrs. Bernard L. Deering, Woman's Club,
Orono, Me.

CARAMEL PECAN PUMPKIN PIE
Makes 9-Inch Pie

Pastry for 1-crust pie
2½ cups mashed cooked pumpkin
¼ cup heavy cream
2 eggs, lightly beaten
1 cup granulated sugar
1 tablespoon flour
¼ teaspoon salt
¼ teaspoon cinnamon
¼ teaspoon nutmeg
¼ teaspoon allspice
½ teaspoon lemon flavoring
½ teaspoon vanilla

⅓ cup butter
1 cup pecan halves
1 cup brown sugar

1. Preheat oven to 450° F.
2. Line 9-inch pie plate with pastry.
3. In mixing bowl combine pumpkin, cream and eggs. Stir in granulated sugar, flour, salt, spices, lemon flavoring and vanilla; mix well.
4. Melt 1 tablespoon of the butter in small saucepan; stir into pumpkin mixture.
5. Pour into pastry-lined plate. Bake in preheated oven for 10 minutes. Turn temperature to 350° F. Bake for 40 minutes longer, or until set.
6. Prepare topping: In small bowl combine remaining butter, pecans and brown sugar; blend. Spread on baked pie.
7. Place in broiler about 4 inches from heat; broil until topping is caramelized.

Evelyn Rudolchick, Ingram Civic Club, Junior Section, Pittsburgh, Pa.

SOUR CREAM RAISIN PIE

Makes 8-Inch Pie

Pastry for 1-crust pie
2 eggs
¾ cup sugar
¼ teaspoon salt
1 teaspoon cinnamon
½ teaspoon nutmeg
¼ teaspoon ground cloves
1 cup sour cream
1 cup seedless raisins
Pecan halves

1. Preheat oven to 450° F.
2. Line 8-inch pie plate with pastry.
3. In mixing bowl beat eggs. Stir in sugar, salt and spices.
4. Blend in sour cream and raisins; pour into pastry-lined plate. Sprinkle with pecans.
5. Bake in preheated oven for 10 minutes. Turn temperature to 350° F. Bake for 30 minutes longer, or until knife inserted in center comes out clean.
6. Serve warm or cold.

Nelle Crissey, Civic Club, New Cumberland, Pa.

RHUBARB CREAM PIE

Makes 9-Inch Pie

Pastry for 1-crust pie
3 eggs
2-Egg-White Cooked Meringue (p. 552)
1 cup sugar
3 tablespoons flour
1 teaspoon grated lemon rind
¼ teaspoon salt
1 tablespoon melted butter or margarine
3 cups diced rhubarb

1. Preheat oven to 450° F.
2. Line 9-inch pie plate with pastry.
3. Separate 2 of the eggs; use egg whites to prepare 2-Egg-White Cooked Meringue.

4. In mixing bowl combine sugar, flour, lemon rind and salt. Add egg yolks and remaining egg; beat until smooth.
5. Stir in butter or margarine and rhubarb; mix well. Pour into pastry-lined plate.
6. Bake in preheated oven for 10 minutes. Turn temperature to 350° F. Bake for 30 minutes longer.
7. Spread meringue on baked pie. Turn temperature to 325° F. Bake for 12 minutes, or until golden.

Mrs. Maxwell Kelley, Nineteenth Century Club, Bangor, Me.

OAT CRUMBLE RHUBARB PIE

Makes 9-Inch Pie

Pastry for 1-crust pie
6 cups diced rhubarb
1⅓ cups sugar
⅔ cup presifted flour
1 cup quick-cooking oats
½ teaspoon cinnamon
¼ teaspoon salt
⅓ cup melted butter or margarine
Whipped cream or vanilla ice cream

1. Preheat oven to 375° F.
2. Line 9-inch pie plate with pastry.
3. Combine rhubarb, 1 cup of the sugar and 3 tablespoons of the flour; mix well. Spoon into pastry-lined plate, piling high in center.
4. Combine all remaining ingredients except whipped or ice cream; mix well with pastry blender. Sprinkle over rhubarb.
5. Bake in preheated oven for 45 to 50 minutes, or until rhubarb is tender and syrup is hot and bubbling.
6. Cool. Serve with whipped cream or ice cream.

Mrs. Cassius M. Goens, Woman's Club, Marion, Ind.

GÂTEAU ST.-HONORÉ

Serves 8

Called a cake in French, this is really a very rich pie.

Pastry for 1-crust pie
Cream Puff Pastry (p. 552)
1 egg yolk, beaten with
1 tablespoon milk
Crème Patissière (p. 630)
Crème St.-Honoré (p. 679)
1 cup sugar
⅓ cup water
¼ teaspoon cream of tartar
1 cup heavy cream, whipped
Candied cherries, halved

1. Preheat oven to 425° F.
2. Roll out pie pastry ¼ inch thick to 10-inch circle. Place on baking sheet; moisten edge with water.
3. Put Cream Puff Pastry in pastry bag; force ¾-inch-thick ring of paste around edge of pie pastry. Brush puff pastry with egg yolk mixture.
4. Bake in preheated oven for 10 minutes. Turn temperature to 300° F. Bake for 20 to 30 minutes longer, or until edge is light and browned. Cool.

5. Make small cream puffs with remaining puff pastry; cook. Cool; then fill with Crème Patissière.

6. Arrange pastry ring on serving dish; fill center with Crème St.-Honoré.

7. In small saucepan mix sugar, water and cream of tartar. Boil over medium heat until light golden; dip in cream puffs; arrange around pastry edge.

8. Decorate pastry with cream. Top each puff with cherry.

Submitted to Woman's Club, Kankakee, Ill., on behalf of Mrs. John F. Kennedy

SHOOFLY PIE

Makes 2 8-Inch Pies

Pastry for 2 1-crust pies
1 cup molasses
1½ cups hot water
1 teaspoon baking soda
3 cups presifted flour
1 cup brown sugar
1 teaspoon baking powder
½ cup shortening

1. Preheat oven to 350° F.
2. Line 2 8-inch pie plates with pastry.
3. Blend molasses, water and baking soda.
4. In mixing bowl combine flour, sugar and baking powder. Cut in shortening until mixture resembles coarse crumbs.
5. Arrange alternate layers of crumb mixture and molasses mixture in pastry-lined plates.
6. Bake in preheated oven for 30 to 40 minutes, or until browned.

Leah Clark, Junior Woman's Club, Hamburg, Pa.

SYRUP PIE

Makes 9-Inch Pie

Pastry for 1-crust pie
1½ cups molasses
2 tablespoons butter
3 eggs, lightly beaten
½ cup sugar
¼ teaspoon allspice
½ teaspoon cinnamon
½ cup chopped pecans
Whipped cream or ice cream

1. Preheat oven to 400° F.
2. Line 9-inch pie plate with pastry.
3. Cook molasses in saucepan over moderate heat until it starts to thicken.
4. Remove from heat; beat in all remaining ingredients except whipped or ice cream. Pour into pastry-lined plate.
5. Bake in preheated oven for 10 minutes. Turn temperature to 325° F. Bake for 50 minutes longer, or until set.
6. Cool slightly. Serve with whipped cream or ice cream.

Mrs. Gladys Hamrick, Modern Study Club, Wolfe City, Tex.

PRIZE SWEET POTATO PECAN PIE

Makes 9-Inch Pie

Pastry for 1-crust pie
1½ cups mashed sweet potatoes
1 cup brown sugar
1 teaspoon cinnamon
¼ teaspoon salt
Dash of mace
3 eggs, well beaten
1½ cups scalded milk
¼ cup butter
¾ cup chopped pecans
Whipped cream

1. Preheat oven to 350° F.
2. Line 9-inch pie plate with pastry.
3. In mixing bowl combine potatoes, ½ cup of the sugar, cinnamon, salt and mace. Add eggs; mix well. Stir in milk.
4. Pour into pastry-lined plate. Bake in preheated oven for 20 minutes.
5. Combine remaining sugar, butter and pecans; mix well, sprinkle over partially cooked pie. Bake for about 25 minutes longer, or until set.
6. Serve topped with whipped cream.

Mrs. T. J. Bridges, President, Woman's Club, McColl, S.C.

SOUR CREAM WALNUT PIE

Makes 8-Inch Pie

Pastry for 1-crust pie
⅓ cup butter or margarine
½ cup brown sugar
¾ cup granulated sugar
4 eggs, lightly beaten
½ cup sour cream
¼ cup light corn syrup
1 teaspoon vanilla
⅔ cup chopped walnuts

1. Preheat oven to 350° F.
2. Line 8-inch pie plate with pastry.
3. Melt butter or margarine in saucepan. Stir in all remaining ingredients except vanilla and walnuts. Cook over low heat, stirring constantly, for 5 minutes.
4. Remove from heat; stir in vanilla and walnuts. Pour into pastry-lined plate.
5. Bake in preheated oven for 55 minutes.

Mrs. Dinny Larson, L'Etudier Club, East Grand Forks, Minn.

WASHINGTON NUT PIE

Makes 9-Inch Pie

Pastry for 1-crust pie
3 eggs
½ cup sugar
1 cup light corn syrup
¼ cup melted butter
1 teaspoon vanilla
½ teaspoon salt
1 cup ground nuts

1. Preheat oven to 350° F.
2. Line 9-inch pie plate with pastry.
3. In mixing bowl, beat eggs until smooth. Add all remaining ingredients except nuts; beat until smooth. Stir in nuts; pour into pastry-lined plate.
4. Bake in preheated oven for 50 minutes, or until set.

Carol Romer, Women's Club, Idaho Falls, Ida.

Pie Fillings for Baked Pie Shells and Crumb Crusts

BASIC CREAM PIE AND VARIATIONS

Makes 8- or 9-Inch Pie

8- or 9-inch baked pie shell
⅓ cup presifted flour or ¼ cup
   cornstarch
⅔ cup sugar
½ teaspoon salt
½ cup cold milk
3 egg yolks (use whites for
   meringue topping)
1½ cups hot milk
½ teaspoon vanilla
2 tablespoons butter

1. Prepare pie shell.
2. In top of double saucepan combine flour or cornstarch, sugar, salt and cold milk.
3. Beat egg yolks; stir into sugar mixture. Gradually stir in hot milk. Cook over simmering water, stirring frequently, until thickened and smooth.
4. Remove from heat; stir in vanilla and butter. Cool slightly. Pour into pie shell.

BANANA CREAM PIE: Stir 3 bananas, mashed, into cooked filling.

BUTTERSCOTCH CREAM PIE: Use brown sugar in place of granulated sugar in above recipe. Increase butter to 3 tablespoons.

CARAMEL CREAM PIE: Heat ¼ cup of the sugar in above recipe until it turns dark brown; stir into cooked filling.

CHOCOLATE CREAM PIE: Increase sugar to 1 cup in above recipe. Add 2 1-ounce squares unsweetened chocolate, melted, along with hot milk.

COCONUT CREAM PIE: Stir 1 cup shredded coconut into cooked filling. If pie is topped with meringue, sprinkle meringue with ½ cup shredded coconut before browning in oven.

DATE CREAM PIE: Stir 1 cup cut dates into cooked and cooled filling.

PINEAPPLE CREAM PIE: Stir ½ cup drained crushed pineapple into cooked and cooled filling.

Ruth Caskey, Woman's Club, Yale, Ia.

ANGEL FOOD PIE

Makes 2 9-Inch Pies

2 9-inch baked pie shells
1¼ cups sugar
¼ cup cornstarch
   Pinch of salt
2 cups boiling water
3 egg whites
   Shredded coconut
   Whipped cream

1. Prepare pie shells.
2. In saucepan combine sugar, cornstarch, salt and water. Cook over moderate heat, stirring constantly, until thickened and clear.
3. Beat egg whites until stiff, but not dry; gradually pour in cornstarch mixture, beating constantly.
4. Divide filling into pie shells. Sprinkle generously with coconut; cover with whipped cream.

Mrs. Hugh Cowan, Bas Bleu Federated Club,
Hugoton, Kans.

REFRIGERATOR APPLE PIE

Makes 13 x 9½-Inch Pie

2 tablespoons melted butter
½ pound vanilla wafers, crumbed
½ cup butter
1 cup confectioners' sugar
2 eggs, well beaten
1 envelope gelatin
1 tablespoon cold apple juice
¼ cup hot apple juice
1 cup heavy cream, whipped
2 cups applesauce

1. Day before, combine melted butter and wafers; spread two-thirds in 13 x 9½ x 2-inch baking pan.
2. Cream ½ cup butter and sugar; beat in eggs; spread on crumbs.
3. Soften gelatin in cold apple juice. Add hot apple juice; stir until thoroughly dissolved.
4. Combine cream and applesauce. Stir in gelatin. Spread on egg mixture; sprinkle with remaining crumbs.
5. Refrigerate for at least 24 hours before serving.

Mrs. Stewart Harrison, Thursday Study Club,
Napoleon, N.D.

APRICOT CREAM PIE

Makes 9-Inch Pie

9-inch baked pie shell
1½ cups cooked dried apricots
   Sugar
5 tablespoons flour
   Pinch of salt
   Butter
2 egg yolks
1 cup milk
½ teaspoon vanilla
   Whipped cream

1. Prepare pie shells.
2. In saucepan mash apricots; beat in 3 tablespoons sugar, 2 tablespoons of the flour and salt. Cook over moderate heat, stirring constantly, until very thick. Remove from heat; stir in 1 tablespoon butter. Cool.
3. In saucepan beat egg yolks and milk. Combine ¼ cup sugar and remaining flour; stir into egg mixture. Cook over moderate heat until custard coats spoon. Remove from heat; stir in vanilla and ½ teaspoon butter.
4. Spread apricot mixture in pie shell. Pour custard over it. Serve topped with whipped cream.

Mrs. J. H. Gooding, New Century Club,
Wilmington, Del.

NEIMAN-MARCUS CREAM PIE

Makes 9-Inch Pie

9-inch baked pie shell
½ cup sugar
¼ teaspoon salt
3 tablespoons flour
1½ cups milk
2 eggs
1 teaspoon butter
½ teaspoon vanilla
1½ cups heavy cream, whipped
3 medium bananas, sliced

1. Prepare pie shell.
2. In small bowl combine sugar, salt and flour. Stir in ½ cup of the milk to make a smooth paste.
3. Put remaining milk in top of double saucepan; scald. Stir in paste; cook over hot water, stirring constantly, until thickened and smooth.
4. In small bowl beat eggs; stir in a little of hot mixture. Return to rest of hot mixture; cook over hot water, stirring constantly, for 5 minutes.
5. Remove from heat; stir in butter and vanilla. Cool custard, stirring occasionally.
6. Fold in half the cream. Arrange half the bananas in pie shell; cover with half the custard. Top with remaining bananas; cover with remaining custard.
7. Spread remaining cream on top; refrigerate for at least 1 hour.

Mrs. W. A. Spurlock, Futuristic Study Club,
Sunray, Tex.

BANANA SPLIT PIE

Makes 8-Inch Pie

8-inch baked pie shell
½ cup butter or margarine
1½ cups confectioners' sugar, sifted
2 eggs
1 teaspoon vanilla
2 large bananas
1 tablespoon lemon juice
1-ounce square sweetened chocolate, grated
½ cup chopped walnuts
Banana slices (optional)

1. Prepare pie shell.
2. In mixing bowl cream butter or margarine and sugar until light and fluffy.
3. Add eggs, one at a time, beating well after each addition. Add vanilla; beat well.
4. Slice bananas into bowl; sprinkle with lemon juice.
5. Stir bananas and chocolate into creamed mixture; pour into pie shell. Sprinkle with walnuts. Refrigerate for 2 to 3 hours.
6. Decorate with banana slices, if desired.

Amy Mack, Saturday Review Club, Utica, Ohio

BAVARIAN CREAM PIE

Makes 9-Inch Pie

9-inch Chocolate Wafer Crust
  (p. 551)
1 envelope gelatin
¼ cup water
3 eggs, separated
¼ teaspoon salt
¾ cup sugar
1 cup scalded milk
1 teaspoon vanilla
1 cup heavy cream, whipped
Shaved chocolate

1. Prepare Chocolate Wafer Crust.
2. Soften gelatin in water.
3. In top of double saucepan blend egg yolks, salt and sugar. Gradually stir in milk; cook over hot water, stirring constantly, until thickened and smooth. Add gelatin; cook, stirring constantly, until dissolved.
4. Remove from heat; stir in vanilla. Cool.
5. In mixing bowl beat egg whites until stiff but not dry; fold in gelatin mixture and then cream. Pour into crust; sprinkle with chocolate. Refrigerate until set.

Mrs. Warren Ringer, Junior New Century Club,
Needham Heights, Mass.

BLACK BOTTOM PIE

Makes 11 x 7-Inch Pie

Gingersnap Crust (p. 551)
1½ cups milk
1½ cups sugar
1 tablespoon cornstarch
3 eggs, separated
1 envelope gelatin
3 tablespoons water
1 teaspoon vanilla
1½ 1-ounce squares unsweetened chocolate, melted
3 tablespoons whiskey
1 cup heavy cream, whipped
Grated unsweetened chocolate

1. Preheat oven to 300° F.
2. Prepare Gingersnap Crust; spread firmly in 11 x 7 x 1½-inch glass baking pan.
3. Bake in preheated oven for 10 minutes, or until set. Remove; cool.
4. Heat milk in top of double saucepan.
5. Combine sugar, cornstarch and egg yolks; stir into milk. Cook over simmering water, stirring constantly, until thickened.
6. Soak gelatin in water; add to custard; stir until dissolved. Remove from heat; stir in vanilla.
7. Add melted chocolate to one-third of custard; spread on crust.
8. Cool remaining custard; stir in whiskey.
9. Beat egg whites until stiff but not dry; fold into remaining custard. Spread on chocolate custard in pie shell; refrigerate until firm.
10. Spread with whipped cream; sprinkle with grated chocolate. Refrigerate until ready to serve.

Mrs. J. R. Cudworth, Quest Club,
Tuscaloosa, Ala.

FRESHY'S BLUEBERRY OR HUCKLEBERRY PIE

Makes 9-Inch Pie

9-inch baked pie shell
¾ cup granulated sugar
2½ tablespoons cornstarch
¼ teaspoon salt
⅔ cup water
3 cups fresh or frozen blueberries or huckleberries
2 tablespoons butter
1½ tablespoons lemon juice (when using blueberries)
1 cup heavy cream, whipped
2 tablespoons confectioners' sugar
½ teaspoon vanilla

1. Prepare pie shell.
2. In saucepan combine granulated sugar, cornstarch and salt. Stir in water and 1 cup of the berries. Bring to boil; cook, stirring constantly, until very thick. Remove from heat; stir in butter and lemon juice, if using blueberries. Cool.
3. Stir in remaining berries; chill thoroughly.
4. Combine cream, confectioners' sugar and vanilla; spread half in pie shell. Top with berry mixture. Refrigerate for 1 to 2 hours.
5. Before serving, garnish with remaining whipped cream.

Mrs. Dale Skatrud, Modern Arts Club, Libby, Mont.

KENTUCKY BOURBON PIE

Makes 9-Inch Pie

9-inch Graham Cracker Crumb Crust (p. 551)
1 envelope gelatin
¼ cup water
¼ cup bourbon
1 teaspoon vanilla
2 eggs, separated
1 cup sugar
1 cup heavy cream, whipped
½ cup chopped pecans

1. Prepare Graham Cracker Crumb Crust.
2. In small saucepan soften gelatin in water. Cook over low heat, stirring constantly, until dissolved.
3. Remove from heat; stir in bourbon and vanilla. Cool until slightly thickened.
4. In mixing bowl beat egg yolks and sugar until thickened and lemon-colored.
5. In another mixing bowl beat egg whites until stiff but not dry; fold along with cream, gelatin mixture and pecans into egg yolk mixture. Turn into crust. Refrigerate until set.

Mrs. Clyde Stigall, President, Southland Woman's Club, Louisville, Ky.

COCONUT BUTTERSCOTCH PIE

Makes 8-Inch Pie

8-inch baked pie shell
¼ cup butter
¾ cup sugar
2 cups milk
½ cup presifted flour
½ teaspoon salt
2 eggs
¼ teaspoon vanilla
1 cup flaked coconut

1. Prepare pie shell.
2. Melt butter in saucepan. Stir in ½ cup of the sugar; and cook over medium heat, stirring constantly, for 2 minutes, or until browned. Stir in 1½ cups of the milk to dissolve syrup. Set aside.
3. In small bowl blend remaining sugar, flour and salt. Stir in remaining milk. Stir into milk in saucepan; cook over medium heat, stirring constantly, until thickened and smooth.
4. Beat eggs lightly; stir in a little of hot mixture. Return to rest of hot mixture; cook over low heat, stirring constantly, for 2 minutes.
5. Remove from heat; stir in vanilla and coconut. Cool for 5 minutes.
6. Pour into pie shell. Cool.

Mrs. William K. Bodell, President, Women's Club, Frankfort, Ky.

CARAMEL CREAM MERINGUE PIE

Makes 8-Inch Pie

8-inch baked pie shell
3 tablespoons butter or margarine
¼ cup presifted flour
1 cup brown sugar
1 cup evaporated milk
¾ cup water
2 eggs, separated (use whites for meringue)
1 teaspoon salt
1 tablespoon vanilla
2-Egg-White Meringue Topping (p. 552)

1. Prepare pie shell.
2. Melt butter or margarine in top of double saucepan. Blend in flour, sugar, milk and water. Cook over hot water, stirring constantly, until thickened and smooth.
3. Beat egg yolks and salt in small bowl; stir in a little of hot mixture. Return to rest of hot mixture; cook, stirring constantly, for 2 minutes.
4. Remove from heat; stir in vanilla. Cool, stirring occasionally. Pour into pie shell.
5. Preheat oven to 300° F.
6. Cover pie with 2-Egg-White Meringue Topping; brown in preheated oven for 15 minutes, or until golden.

Mrs. Thomas A. Massey, Sesame Club, Birmingham, Ala.

EASY CHERRY CHEESE PIE

Makes 8-Inch Pie

8-inch baked pie shell
3-ounce package cream cheese
½ cup confectioners' sugar, sifted
Dash of salt
1 cup heavy cream, whipped
1-pound 6-ounce can cherry pie filling

1. Prepare pie shell.
2. In mixing bowl blend cheese, sugar and salt until smooth. Fold in cream; turn into pie shell.
3. Top with cherry filling; refrigerate until serving time.

Submitted to Woman's Club, Kankakee, Ill., by H. Barnes, President, Illinois Federation of Women's Clubs

MERINGUE-TOPPED CHERRY PIE
Makes 9-Inch Pie

9-inch baked pie shell
1-pound 4-ounce can sour cherries
3 tablespoons cornstarch
¾ cup sugar
¾ cup water
1 tablespoon butter or margarine
½ teaspoon almond extract
　Few drops red food coloring
3-Egg-White Meringue Topping
　(p. 552)

1. Prepare pie shell.
2. Drain cherries; put liquid in saucepan. Set cherries aside.
3. Blend cornstarch into cherry liquid; stir in sugar and water. Cook over medium heat, stirring constantly, until thickened and clear. Stir in butter or margarine, almond extract, food coloring and cherries.
4. Cool slightly. Pour into pie shell.
5. Preheat oven to 350° F.
6. Spread filling with 3-Egg-White Meringue Topping; bake in preheated oven for 12 minutes, or until golden.

Mrs. Harry Kraner, Woman's Club, Brandenton, Fla.

CHERRY NUT PARFAIT PIE
Makes 9-Inch Pie

9-inch baked pie shell
1¼ cups water
2 tablespoons lemon juice
3-ounce package cherry gelatin
1 pint butter pecan ice cream
½ cup chopped walnuts
¼ cup chopped maraschino cherries
1 cup heavy cream, whipped
　Whole maraschino cherries

1. Prepare pie shell.
2. Bring water and lemon juice to boil in saucepan. Remove from heat; stir in gelatin until dissolved.
3. Add ice cream by spoonfuls, stirring after each addition.
4. Stir in walnuts and chopped cherries; refrigerate until thickened.
5. Turn into pie shell; refrigerate until set. Decorate with whipped cream and whole cherries; refrigerate until serving time.

Mrs. Ralph Stoops, Woman's Club, Riverdale, N.J.

CHOCOLATE CREAM CHEESE PIE
Makes 9-Inch Pie

9-inch baked pie shell
8-ounce package cream cheese
½ cup brown sugar

2 eggs, separated
6-ounce package semi-sweet
　chocolate chips, melted
⅛ teaspoon salt
1 teaspoon vanilla
¼ cup granulated sugar
1 cup heavy cream, whipped

1. Prepare pie shell.
2. In mixing bowl beat cheese and brown sugar until smooth. Beat in egg yolks, chocolate, salt and vanilla.
3. In another mixing bowl beat egg whites until foamy. Gradually add granulated sugar; beat until stiff and glossy; fold into chocolate mixture.
4. Turn into pie shell; top with whipped cream. Refrigerate well before serving.

Ingram Civic Club, Junior Section, Pittsburgh, Pa.

CHOCOLATE BAR PIE
Makes 9-Inch Pie

9-inch Baked Chocolate Crumb
　Crust (p. 551)
½ cup milk
5 1¼-ounce chocolate almond bars
15 marshmallows
¼ teaspoon vanilla
1 cup heavy cream, whipped

1. Prepare Baked Chocolate Crumb Crust.
2. Combine milk, chocolate, and marshmallows. Cook over low heat, stirring occasionally, until melted. Cool.
3. Fold in vanilla and cream. Turn into crust. Refrigerate for at least 3 hours or overnight.

Mrs. B. F. Burns, Jr., Thursday Study Club, Iuka, Miss.

CHOCOLATE PECAN CREAM PIE WITH MERINGUE TOPPING
Makes 9-Inch Pie

9-inch baked pie shell
¼ cup presifted flour
1 cup sugar
½ teaspoon salt
2 cups milk
2 1-ounce squares unsweetened
　chocolate
3 eggs, separated (use whites for
　meringue)
2 tablespoons butter or margarine
1 teaspoon vanilla
½ cup chopped pecans
3-Egg-White Meringue Topping
　(p. 552)

1. Prepare pie shell.
2. In saucepan blend flour, sugar and salt. Gradually stir in milk to make a smooth paste. Cook over medium heat, stirring constantly, until thickened and smooth. Add chocolate; cook over low heat, stirring frequently, until melted.
3. Beat egg yolks in small bowl; and stir in a little of chocolate mixture. Return to rest of chocolate mixture; cook over low heat, stirring constantly, for 2 minutes.

4. Remove from heat; stir in butter or margarine, vanilla and pecans. Cool for 5 minutes. Pour into pie shell.

5. Preheat oven to 375° F.

6. Spread with 3-Egg-White Meringue Topping; brown in preheated oven for 12 minutes.

Mrs. Lois Mathis, Junior Women's Club, Carlsbad, N.M.

BUTTER CRUST PARFAIT PIE

Serves 6

1 cup presifted flour
½ cup butter
⅝ cup sugar
1 cup semi-sweet chocolate pieces
¼ cup light corn syrup
½ cup water
1 egg white
1 teaspoon vanilla
1 teaspoon lemon juice
1 cup heavy cream

1. Preheat oven to 375° F.

2. In mixing bowl combine flour, butter and 2 tablespoons of the sugar. Cut in butter with pastry blender, or use electric mixer at lowest speed, until mixture resembles fine crumbs; sprinkle ⅓ cup in small pan. With well-floured fingers, press remaining crumbs onto sides and bottom of 9-inch pie plate. Bake both crumbs and crust in preheated oven for 10 to 12 minutes. Remove; cool.

3. In saucepan combine chocolate, corn syrup and ¼ cup of the water. Cook over low heat, stirring constantly, until chocolate is melted and mixture is smooth.

4. In mixing bowl combine remaining sugar, remaining water, egg white, vanilla and lemon juice. Beat until mixture stands in soft peaks. (Use electric beater if available.)

5. Whip cream until thick; fold with half the chocolate mixture into egg white mixture. Pour half into crust; drizzle with half the remaining chocolate mixture. Add remaining filling; drizzle with remaining chocolate. Cut through filling with knife to eliminate air holes; sprinkle top with crumbs.

6. Freeze for 4 to 6 hours, or until firm.

Mrs. William H. Hasebroock, Honorary President, General Federation of Women's Clubs, West Point, Neb.

FRENCH SILK PIE

Makes 9-Inch Pie

9-inch baked pie shell
½ cup softened butter
¾ cup sugar
1-ounce square unsweetened chocolate, melted
Pinch of salt
1 teaspoon vanilla
2 eggs
1 cup heavy cream, whipped
Chopped toasted almonds

1. Prepare pie shell.

2. Beat butter in mixing bowl until fluffy. Gradually beat in sugar until well blended. Add chocolate, salt and vanilla; blend well.

3. Add eggs, one at a time, beating for 3 minutes after each addition.

4. Pour into pie shell; spread with whipped cream. Refrigerate well.

5. Just before serving, sprinkle with almonds.

Mrs. W. Willard Wirtz, Washington, D.C.

COCOA CREAM PIE

Makes 8-Inch Pie

8-inch baked pie shell
⅜ cup presifted flour
3 tablespoons cocoa
1½ cups sugar
2 egg yolks, lightly beaten (use whites for meringue)
1½ cups evaporated milk
3 tablespoons butter
1 teaspoon vanilla
2-Egg-White Meringue Topping (p. 552)

1. Prepare pie shell.

2. In top of double saucepan combine flour, cocoa and sugar. Stir in egg yolks and milk. Add butter and vanilla; cook over simmering water, stirring constantly, until thickened. Cool slightly.

3. Pour into baked pie shell.

4. Preheat oven to 375° F.

5. Spread filling with 2-Egg-White Meringue Topping; brown in preheated oven for 12 minutes.

Mrs. Mabel S. Lancaster, Literary and Civic Club, Houlka, Miss.

HOLLYWOOD PIE

Makes 9-Inch Pie

12 graham crackers, crumbed
¼ cup butter
1 cup confectioners' sugar
3 eggs, separated
½ cup chocolate syrup
12 marshmallows, cut up
1 cup chopped nuts
1 teaspoon vanilla

1. Grease 9-inch pie plate; sprinkle bottom and sides with half the crumbs.

2. Cream butter and sugar.

3. Beat egg yolks; stir into butter mixture. Stir in chocolate syrup, marshmallows, nuts and vanilla.

4. Beat egg whites until stiff but not dry; fold into chocolate mixture. Turn into crumb-sprinkled pie plate; sprinkle with remaining crumbs. Refrigerate for several hours before serving.

Mrs. Al Fortman, Junior Women's Club, Bismarck, N.D.

COCONUT SHERRY CHIFFON PIE
Makes 10-Inch Pie

10-inch Coconut Macaroon Pie
  Shell (p. 551)
1 envelope gelatin
¼ cup water
4 eggs, separated
1 cup sugar
1¾ cups milk
⅛ teaspoon almond extract
½ teaspoon vanilla
¼ cup sweet sherry
1 cup heavy cream, whipped

1. Prepare Coconut Macaroon Pie Shell.
2. Soften gelatin in water.
3. In top of double saucepan beat egg yolks and ¾ cup of the sugar; stir in milk. Cook over hot water, stirring constantly, until thickened and smooth. Add gelatin; stir until dissolved.
4. Remove from heat; stir in almond extract, vanilla and sherry. Refrigerate, stirring occasionally, until mixture starts to mound when dropped from spoon.
5. Meanwhile, in mixing bowl beat egg whites until foamy. Gradually add remaining sugar; beat until stiff and glossy; fold in sherry mixture and cream. Spoon into pie shell.
6. Refrigerate until set. Freeze for 5 minutes before serving.

Mrs. S. S. Stoaks, President, Parnassus Club, Jackson, Miss.

CREAM CHEESE PIE
Makes 8-Inch Pie

20 graham crackers, crushed
⅜ cup butter, melted
2 8-ounce packages cream cheese
2 eggs
3 teaspoons vanilla
  Sugar
1 cup sour cream

1. Day before, combine crackers and butter. Press into 8-inch pie plate.
2. Preheat oven to 350° F.
3. In mixing bowl combine cheese, eggs, 2 teaspoons of the vanilla and ¾ cup sugar. Beat until smooth. Pour into crumb-lined pie plate.
4. Bake in preheated oven for 17 minutes. Remove from oven; cool for 5 minutes.
5. Combine sour cream, 3½ tablespoons sugar and remaining vanilla. Spread on pie; return to oven; bake for 10 minutes longer. Cool. Refrigerate overnight.

Mrs. James Himes, Junior Woman's Club, Diamond Bar, Calif.

DANISH PIE
Makes 9-Inch Pie

9-inch baked pie shell
3-ounce package Danish junket
  dessert
2 cups boiling water or any fruit
  juice
8-ounce package cream cheese
3 tablespoons sugar

Dash of salt
½ teaspoon vanilla
¼ cup heavy cream, whipped
1 cup sliced sweetened strawberries

1. Prepare pie shell.
2. Add junket to water or fruit juice; beat for 1 minute. Cool to room temperature.
3. Meanwhile, cream cheese, sugar, salt and vanilla until fluffy. Fold in cream. Reserve a little for garnish; spread rest in pie shell.
4. Fold strawberries into junket; spoon into pie shell. Refrigerate for 3 to 4 hours.
5. Before serving, garnish with reserved cheese mixture.

Dorothy Baum, Woman's Club, Niles, Ill.

HOLIDAY MACAROON PIE
Makes 9-Inch Pie

9-inch Macaroon Crumb Crust
  (p. 551)
½ cup milk
2 eggs, lightly beaten
½ cup sugar
  Pinch of salt
½ envelope gelatin
¼ cup water
1 cup heavy cream, whipped
¼ cup finely chopped pecans
4 marshmallows, cut into small
  pieces
1 slice canned pineapple, cut into
  small pieces
¼ cup chopped candied cherries
  Whipped cream and candied
  cherries for garnish

1. Day before, prepare Macaroon Crumb Crust.
2. In top of double saucepan combine milk, eggs, sugar and salt. Cook over simmering water, stirring constantly, until custard coats spoon. Remove from heat.
3. Soften gelatin in water. Add to custard; stir until thoroughly dissolved. Chill until syrupy.
4. Fold in cream, pecans, marshmallows, pineapple and chopped cherries. Pour into crust; refrigerate overnight.
5. Before serving, garnish with mounds of whipped cream and cherries.

Marjorie Meredith, Modern Culture Club, Tuscaloosa, Ala.

CRÈME DE MENTHE PIE
Makes 9-Inch Pie

9-inch Graham Cracker Crumb
  Crust (p. 551)
3 egg yolks
¼ cup sugar
⅛ teaspoon salt
1 envelope gelatin
⅓ cup water
2 cups heavy cream, whipped
⅓ cup crème de menthe
  Shaved chocolate

1. Prepare Graham Cracker Crumb Crust.

2. In mixing bowl beat egg yolks, sugar and salt until thickened and lemon-colored.

3. In small saucepan soften gelatin in water. Cook over low heat until dissolved. Cool; fold into egg mixture.

4. Fold in 1 cup of the cream and crème de menthe. Turn into crust; refrigerate until set.

5. Top with remaining cream; decorate with chocolate.

June Ehr, Gulf Beach Woman's Club,
St. Petersburg, Fla.

ANGEL LEMON CREAM
Makes 9-Inch Pie

9-inch Meringue Nest (p. 552)
4 egg yolks
⅔ cup sugar
Grated rind of 2 lemons
⅓ cup lemon juice
Dash of salt
1 cup heavy cream

1. Prepare Meringue Nest.

2. In top of double saucepan beat egg yolks and sugar until light. Add lemon rind and juice and salt. Cook over hot water, stirring constantly, until thickened and smooth. Cool.

3. Whip cream until stiff; spread half in nest. Top with lemon mixture. Cover with remaining cream. Refrigerate for 2 hours.

Mrs. Earl Hampton, Home Life Chairman,
Oregon Federation of Woman's Clubs;
Zenith Woman's Club, Salem, Ore.

HEAVENLY LEMON PIE
Makes 9-Inch Pie

1½ cups sugar
¼ teaspoon cream of tartar
4 eggs, separated
2 tablespoons flaked coconut
3 tablespoons lemon juice
1 tablespoon lemon rind
Pinch of salt
2 cups heavy cream
Strawberries

1. Day before, preheat oven to 225° F. Grease 9-inch pie plate.

2. Sift together 1 cup of the sugar and cream of tartar. Beat egg whites until stiff peaks form. Gradually beat in sugar mixture; beat until stiff and glossy.

3. Spread meringue in pie plate, making sides 1 inch thick and bottom ¼ inch thick. Sprinkle top edge with coconut.

4. Bake in preheated oven for 1 hour. Cool.

5. Meanwhile, in top of double saucepan beat egg yolks. Stir in remaining sugar, lemon juice, lemon rind and salt. Cook over simmering water, stirring constantly, for 10 minutes, or until thickened. Cool.

6. Whip 1 cup of the cream until thickened; fold into custard. Pour into meringue shell; refrigerate for at least 12 (preferably 24) hours before serving.

7. Next day, whip remaining cream; use to top pie. Garnish with strawberries.

Mrs. Jack Lasseter, Junior Woman's Club
Macon, Ga.

LEMON CHIFFON PIE OR FAIRY TART
Makes 9-Inch Pie

9-inch baked pie shell
1 envelope gelatin
¼ cup water
1 cup sugar
½ cup lemon juice
¼ teaspoon salt
4 eggs, separated
1 cup heavy cream, whipped

1. Prepare pie shell.

2. In top of double saucepan soften gelatin in water. Stir in ½ cup of the sugar, lemon juice, salt and egg yolks. Cook over hot water, stirring constantly, until thickened and smooth. Cool, stirring occasionally.

3. Meanwhile, beat egg whites until foamy. Gradually add remaining sugar; beat until stiff and glossy.

4. Beat cooled egg yolk mixture until fluffy; fold with cream into egg whites. Pour into pie shell. Refrigerate until set.

Woman's Club, Kewaukee, Wis.

CARMELITA'S FAVORITE LEMON PIE
Makes 8- or 9-Inch Pie

8- or 9-inch baked pie shell
1½ cups sugar
½ cup cornstarch
½ teaspoon salt
2½ cups hot water
5 eggs, separated (use whites for meringue)
¼ cup butter
½ cup lemon juice
Grated rind of 1 lemon
Few drops yellow food coloring (optional)
5-Egg-White Meringue Topping (p. 552)
½ teaspoon grated lemon rind

1. Prepare pie shell.

2. In saucepan combine sugar, cornstarch and salt. Stir in water. Cook over medium heat for about 5 minutes, stirring constantly, until thickened and smooth. Cover; cook over low heat for a few minutes longer.

3. Combine egg yolks and ½ cup of sugar mixture; stir into rest of mixture. Cook over low heat, stirring, for 1 minute longer. Remove from heat; stir in butter, lemon juice, rind of 1 lemon and food coloring, if desired. Cool.

4. Preheat oven to 350° F. Prepare 5-Egg White Meringue Topping.

5. Pour filling into pie shell. Cover with meringue, piling it high in pretty swirls; sprinkle with ½ teaspoon lemon rind.

6. Bake in preheated oven for 20 to 25 minutes.

Carmelita Kelley, El Camino Women's Club, Ventura, Calif.

MILE-HIGH LEMONADE PIE
Makes 9-Inch Pie

3 tablespoons butter or margarine
1½ cups flaked coconut
14½-ounce can evaporated milk
1 envelope gelatin
¼ cup water
¾ cup sugar
6-ounce can frozen lemonade concentrate

1. Melt butter or margarine in skillet. Stir in coconut; cook over medium heat, stirring constantly, until golden; press onto bottom and sides of 9-inch pie plate. Cool.
2. Pour milk into refrigerator tray. Freeze for about 15 minutes, or until ice crystals form at edges.
3. Meanwhile, in small saucepan soften gelatin in water. Stir in sugar; cook over low heat, stirring frequently, until dissolved.
4. Remove from heat; stir in lemonade concentrate. Chill until slightly thickened.
5. Scrape milk into large mixing bowl; beat vigorously for 5 minutes, or until stiff. Fold in gelatin mixture. Turn into pie shell. Refrigerate for 3 hours, or until set.

Joyce Wolfe, Woman's Club, Scobey, Mont.

LIME PIE
Makes 8-Inch Pie

8-inch baked pie shell
4 eggs, separated
15-ounce can sweetened condensed milk
2 tablespoons butter
½ cup lime juice
½ cup sugar
¼ teaspoon vanilla

1. Prepare pie shell. Preheat oven to 325° F.
2. Put egg yolks in mixing bowl; add milk, butter and lime juice; beat until smooth.
3. In another mixing bowl beat egg whites until foamy. Gradually add sugar; beat until meringue is stiff and glossy.
4. Fold a few tablespoons of meringue into lime filling; turn into pie shell.
5. Stir vanilla into rest of meringue; spread on filling.
6. Bake in preheated oven for 20 minutes, or until golden.

Submitted to Woman's Club, Kankakee, Ill., by Mrs. Dexter Otis Arnold, Honorary President, General Federation of Women's Clubs

FROSTED DAIQUIRI PIE
Makes 9-Inch Pie

9-inch baked pie shell
1 envelope gelatin
1 cup sugar
½ teaspoon salt
3 eggs, separated
¼ cup water
½ cup lime juice
1 teaspoon grated lime rind
Few drops green food coloring
⅓ cup light rum
Whipped cream
Shaved chocolate

1. Prepare pie shell.
2. In top of double saucepan combine gelatin, ⅔ cup of the sugar and salt. Stir in egg yolks, water and lime juice. Cook over hot water, stirring constantly, until thickened and smooth.
3. Remove from heat; stir in lime rind, food coloring and rum. Chill until slightly thickened, stirring occasionally.
4. In mixing bowl beat egg whites until foamy. Gradually add remaining sugar; beat until stiff and glossy. Fold into rum mixture; turn into pie shell. Refrigerate for 2 to 3 hours.
5. Decorate with whipped cream and chocolate.

Mrs. Everett Ray Williams, President, Glenbrook Woman's Club, Louisville, Ky.

MINT CHIFFON PIE
Makes 9-Inch Pie

9-inch baked pie shell
1 envelope gelatin
¼ cup water
1 cup milk
1¼ cups after-dinner mints
3 eggs, separated
½ teaspoon salt
½ teaspoon vanilla
¼ teaspoon cream of tartar
½ cup sugar
1 cup heavy cream, whipped
Few drops green food coloring

1. Prepare pie shell.
2. In saucepan soften gelatin in water. Add milk and mints; cook over low heat, stirring occasionally, until dissolved.
3. Beat egg yolks; stir into mint mixture; cook over low heat, stirring constantly, until thickened and smooth. Stir in salt and vanilla. Cool.
4. In mixing bowl beat egg whites and cream of tartar until foamy. Gradually add sugar; beat until stiff and glossy; fold with cream into mint custard. Stir in food coloring.
5. Turn into pie shell. Refrigerate until set.

Mrs. Jessie Frazier, Tuesday Evening Women's Club, Emington, Ill.

GLAMOROUS NESSELRODE PIE
Makes 9-Inch Pie

9-inch baked pie shell
1 envelope gelatin
⅔ cup sugar
⅛ teaspoon salt
3 eggs, separated
1¼ cups milk
1 cup heavy cream
3 tablespoons rum

1 tablespoon chopped maraschino
  cherries
Shaved chocolate

1. Prepare pie shell.
2. In top of double saucepan blend gelatin, ⅓ cup of the sugar and salt.
3. In large measuring cup blend egg yolks, milk and cream; gradually stir into gelatin. Cook over hot water, stirring constantly, until custard is thickened and smooth and gelatin is dissolved.
4. Remove from heat; stir in rum and cherries. Chill, stirring occasionally, until mixture mounds when dropped from spoon.
5. In mixing bowl beat egg whites until foamy. Gradually add remaining sugar; beat until stiff and glossy; fold into gelatin mixture.
6. Turn into pie shell; sprinkle with chocolate. Refrigerate until set.

Mrs. Adolf Linse, Woman's Club,
Billings, Mont.

ORANGE MERINGUE PIE

Makes 8-Inch Pie

8-inch baked pie shell
1⅜ cups sugar
⅓ cup presifted flour
¼ teaspoon salt
  Grated rind of 1 orange
1 cup orange juice
3 eggs, separated
2 tablespoons butter
¼ teaspoon baking powder

1. Prepare pie shell.
2. In top of double saucepan combine 1 cup of the sugar, flour and salt. Stir in orange rind and juice; cook over simmering water for 10 minutes, stirring constantly.
3. Beat egg yolks lightly. Pour in orange mixture; return to saucepan; add butter. Cook over simmering water for 2 minutes longer, stirring constantly. Cool. Pour into pie shell.
4. Preheat oven to 425° F.
5. Beat egg whites until soft peaks form. Gradually beat in remaining sugar and baking powder; beat until thickened and glossy.
6. Spread meringue on filling in pie shell; bake in preheated oven for 5 to 6 minutes.

Edna Smith, Women's City Club,
Portsmouth, N.H.

ORANGE CREAM PIE

Makes 9-Inch Pie

9-inch Graham Cracker Crumb
  Crust (p. 551)
1 cup orange juice
3-ounce package orange gelatin
¼ cup sugar
⅔ cup evaporated milk
2 tablespoons lemon juice

1. Prepare Graham Cracker Crumb Crust.
2. In small saucepan bring orange juice to boil. Remove from heat; stir in gelatin until dissolved. Stir in sugar. Refrigerate.

3. Meanwhile, put milk in refrigerator tray. Freeze for about 15 minutes, or until ice crystals form at edges.
4. Scrape milk into mixing bowl; beat until thickened. Stir in lemon juice; beat for 2 minutes. Fold into gelatin mixture. Turn into crust. Refrigerate until set.

Mrs. Sue Holbrook, President, Woman's Club,
Groveland, Fla.

AMBROSIA PIE

Makes 9-Inch Pie

9-inch baked pie shell
½ cup presifted flour
¼ teaspoon salt
¾ cup sugar
1¼ cups water
2 eggs, separated (use whites for
  meringue)
½ cup orange juice
2 tablespoons grated orange rind
1 tablespoon grated lemon rind
2-Egg-White Cooked Meringue
  (p. 552)
5 orange sections, free of membranes
40 seedless grapes
¾ cup flaked coconut

1. Prepare pie shell.
2. In top of double saucepan combine flour, salt and sugar. Stir in water and egg yolks; mix well. Cook over hot water, stirring constantly, until thickened and smooth.
3. Remove from heat; stir in orange juice and rinds. Cool.
4. Pour into pie shell. Pile 2-Egg-White Cooked Meringue lightly on pie.
5. Arrange orange sections on pie, one in center of each slice. Place 1 of the grapes at end of each orange section near center of pie. Arrange remaining grapes around pie. Sprinkle with coconut.

Mrs. A. L. Shuck, President, 4th District,
Oklahoma Federation of Women's Clubs,
Weatherford, Okla.

PEACH MERINGUE PIE

Makes 9-Inch Pie

9-inch baked pie shell
5 eggs, separated (use whites for
  meringue)
1 cup sugar
¼ cup cornstarch
2 cups scalding-hot milk
3 tablespoons butter
1 teaspoon vanilla
5-Egg-White Fruit Meringue (p.
  552), made with peach preserves

1. Prepare pie shell. Beat egg yolks lightly.
2. In saucepan combine sugar and cornstarch. Gradually stir in milk. Add butter and egg yolks. Cook over moderate heat, stirring constantly, until thickened. Do not boil.
3. Remove from heat; stir in vanilla. Cool.
4. Preheat oven to 375° F.

5. Pour filling into pie shell; spread with 5-Egg-White Fruit Meringue.

6. Bake in preheated oven until browned.

Mrs. R. L. Perry, Woman's Cooperative Club, New Augusta, Miss.

PEACH PARFAIT PIE

Makes 9-Inch Pie

9-inch baked pie shell
1 cup diced peaches
½ cup sugar
1 tablespoon lemon juice
3-ounce package orange gelatin
1¼ cups boiling water
1 pint vanilla ice cream
1 cup flaked coconut
1 cup heavy cream, whipped
Diced peaches and flaked coconut
for garnish

1. Prepare pie shell.
2. Put 1 cup peaches in bowl; sprinkle with sugar and lemon juice. Let stand for 15 minutes, stirring occasionally.
3. Meanwhile, dissolve gelatin in water; gradually add ice cream, stirring until smooth.
4. Drain peaches; stir liquid into gelatin mixture. Chill until slightly thickened.
5. Stir in peaches and 1 cup coconut; turn into pie shell. Refrigerate until set.
6. Spread with whipped cream. Decorate with peaches and coconut.

Adelaide J. Haman, Woman's Club, Red Lodge, Mont.

PEACH RICE PIE

Makes 9-Inch Pie

9-inch Gingersnap Crust (p. 551)
1¼ cups peach nectar
3-ounce package lemon gelatin
1 pint vanilla ice cream
2 cups cooked rice
1-pound 13-ounce can sliced peaches,
drained
1 cup heavy cream
2 tablespoons confectioners' sugar,
sifted
½ teaspoon almond extract

1. Prepare Gingersnap Crust.
2. In saucepan bring peach nectar to boil; turn into mixing bowl. Add gelatin; stir until dissolved.
3. Add ice cream by spoonfuls, stirring after each addition until smooth. Add rice. Chill until slightly thickened.
4. Chop half the peach slices; stir into rice mixture. Spoon into crust; refrigerate until firm.
5. Beat cream until stiff but not dry; fold in sugar and almond extract; use to decorate pie. Arrange remaining peach slices on top. Refrigerate until serving time.

Edna Storms, Book and Needle Club, Oradell, N.J.

PEANUT BUTTER PIE

Makes 8-Inch Pie

8-inch baked pie shell or Graham
Cracker Crumb Crust (p. 551)
½ cup brown sugar
½ cup granulated sugar
½ cup peanut butter
2 eggs
2 tablespoons flour
1½ cups milk
½ teaspoon vanilla

1. Prepare pie shell or Graham Cracker Crumb Crust.
2. In saucepan combine sugars, peanut butter, eggs and flour. Gradually stir in milk. Cook over moderate heat, stirring constantly, until thickened; do not boil.
3. Remove from heat; stir in vanilla. Pour into pie shell or crust.

Mrs. J. E. Crockett, Civic League, Sugar City, Colo.

MOCHA PECAN CHIFFON PIE

Makes 9-Inch Pie

9-inch baked pie shell
1 envelope gelatin
1 cup water
3 tablespoons cocoa
1 cup sugar
2 teaspoons instant coffee
3 eggs, separated
½ teaspoon vanilla
½ teaspoon rum extract
¼ teaspoon salt
¾ cup finely chopped pecans
Whipped cream
Pecan halves

1. Prepare pie shell.
2. Soften gelatin in ¼ cup of the water.
3. In heavy saucepan combine cocoa, ¾ cup of the sugar, coffee and remaining water. Bring to boil; then simmer for 4 to 5 minutes, stirring constantly.
4. Beat egg yolks lightly; gradually pour in cocoa mixture, stirring constantly. Return to saucepan; stir over low heat until thickened; do not boil.
5. Remove from heat; add gelatin, vanilla and rum extract; stir until completely dissolved. Chill until mixture mounds slightly.
6. Beat egg whites and salt until soft peaks form. Gradually beat in remaining sugar; beat until stiff and glossy. Fold meringue and chopped pecans into gelatin mixture. Turn into pie shell; refrigerate until set.
7. Before serving, garnish with whipped cream and pecan halves.

Dottie Chapman, El Camino Women's Club, Ventura, Calif.

PEPPERMINT BONBON PIE

Makes 9-Inch Pie

9-inch Chocolate Shell (p. 551)
2 cups coarsely crushed peppermint
stick candy
1 cup evaporated milk
1 envelope gelatin

2 tablespoons water
2 cups heavy cream

1. Prepare Chocolate Shell.
2. Reserve 2 tablespoons of the candy for topping. In top of double saucepan combine remaining candy and milk; cook over hot water until candy melts and mixture is smooth.
3. Soften gelatin in water; add to candy mixture; stir until thoroughly dissolved. Cool until syrupy.
4. Whip 1½ cups of the cream until stiff. Fold in gelatin mixture. Turn into shell; refrigerate for about 2 hours, or until firm.
5. Just before serving, whip remaining cream until stiff; spoon petal-fashion on pie. Sprinkle with reserved candy.

Mrs. Harvey Porter,
Round Table Club of Camden and Wyoming,
Delaware Federation of Women's Clubs

PINEAPPLE PIE

Makes 9-Inch Pie

9-inch baked pie shell
2 eggs, well beaten
1½ cups sugar
8-ounce can crushed pineapple
3-ounce package lemon gelatin
14-ounce can evaporated milk
1 teaspoon vanilla

1. Prepare pie shell.
2. In saucepan combine eggs, sugar and pineapple. Mix well; bring to simmer, stirring constantly.
3. Remove from heat; stir in gelatin. Cool until syrupy.
4. Whip milk until very stiff; fold into pineapple mixture. Fold in vanilla. Pour into pie shell; refrigerate until set.

Mrs. H. C. Taylor, Progressive Study Club,
Bay Minette, Ala.

PINEAPPLE CREAM PIE

Makes 9-Inch Pie

9-inch baked pie shell
3 tablespoons flour
1 cup sugar
2 eggs, separated (use whites for meringue)
2 cups milk
1 tablespoon butter
1 cup cubed pineapple
2-Egg-White Meringue Topping (p. 552)

1. Prepare pie shell.
2. In top of double saucepan combine flour and sugar. Stir in egg yolks and milk. Cook over boiling water, stirring constantly, until thickened.
3. Remove from heat; stir in butter and pineapple. Cool. Pour into pie shell.
4. Preheat oven to 375° F.
5. Spread filling with 2-Egg-White Meringue Topping; brown in preheated oven.

Mrs. O. P. Armour, Jr., Literary and Civic Club,
Houlka, Miss.

PINEAPPLE SOUR CREAM PIE

Makes 9-Inch Pie

9-inch baked pie shell
¾ cup sugar
¼ cup presifted flour
½ teaspoon salt
1-pound 4-ounce can crushed pineapple, undrained
1 cup sour cream
1 tablespoon lemon juice
2 eggs, separated (use whites for meringue)
½ teaspoon vanilla
2-Egg-White Meringue Topping (p. 552)

1. Prepare pie shell.
2. In saucepan blend sugar, flour and salt. Stir in pineapple, sour cream and lemon juice. Cook over medium heat, stirring constantly, until thickened.
3. Beat egg yolks. Stir in a little of pineapple mixture; return to rest of pineapple mixture; cook over low heat for 2 minutes, stirring constantly. Cool. Pour into pie shell.
4. Preheat oven to 400° F.
5. Spread filling with 2-Egg-White Meringue Topping; bake in preheated oven for 12 minutes, or until golden.

Mrs. Malcolm Hesse, Study Club,
Farber, Mo.

PINEAPPLE CHEESE ICEBOX PIE

Makes 9-Inch Pie

4 cups cornflakes
1 cup sugar
¼ cup melted butter or margarine
1 envelope gelatin
¼ cup water
3 eggs, separated
9-ounce can crushed pineapple, undrained
1 teaspoon grated lemon rind
2 tablespoons lemon juice
1 cup cream-style cottage cheese
¼ teaspoon salt

1. Crush cornflakes; turn into mixing bowl. Add ¼ cup of the sugar and butter or margarine; mix well.
2. Reserve 3 tablespoons crumb mixture for topping; press remaining crumbs on bottom and sides of 9-inch pie plate. Refrigerate for 1 hour.
3. Meanwhile, soften gelatin in water; set aside.
4. In top of double saucepan beat egg yolks lightly; stir in pineapple, ½ cup of the sugar and lemon rind and juice. Cook over boiling water, stirring constantly, until thickened.
5. Add gelatin; stir until dissolved. Cool.
6. Force cheese through sieve; stir into egg yolk mixture.
7. In mixing bowl beat egg whites until foamy; gradually add salt and remaining sugar; beat until stiff and glossy. Fold into pineapple mixture; turn into crust.

8. Sprinkle with reserved crumbs. Refrigerate for 3 hours.

Ernestine Fahnestock, Gulf Beach Woman's Club,
St. Petersburg, Fla.

COCONUT PUMPKIN CHIFFON PIE

Makes 9-Inch Pie

9-inch baked pie shell
1¼ cups canned mashed pumpkin
¾ cup evaporated milk
¾ cup water
2 eggs, separated
¾ cup brown sugar
½ teaspoon salt
¼ teaspoon ginger
½ teaspoon cinnamon
½ teaspoon nutmeg
1 envelope gelatin
½ teaspoon vanilla
1 cup toasted flaked coconut
Whipped cream

1. Prepare pie shell.
2. In saucepan combine pumpkin, milk, ½ cup of the water, egg yolks, ½ cup of the sugar, salt, ginger, cinnamon and nutmeg. Cook over moderate heat, stirring constantly, for about 10 minutes, or until slightly thickened.
3. Soften gelatin in remaining water.
4. Remove pumpkin mixture from heat; add gelatin; stir until dissolved. Chill until mixture begins to set.
5. Beat egg whites until soft peaks form. Add remaining sugar; beat until stiff and glossy. Fold into pumpkin mixture. Fold in vanilla and ¾ cup of the coconut. Chill until set.
6. Before serving, garnish with whipped cream; sprinkle with remaining coconut.

Mrs. D. E. Golden, Woman's Club,
Tampa, Fla.

RASPBERRY PIE

Makes 9-Inch Pie

9-inch Graham Cracker Crumb
  Crust (p. 551)
½ cup milk
35 marshmallows
10-ounce package frozen raspberries,
  defrosted
1 cup heavy cream, whipped
Whipped cream (optional)

1. Day before, prepare Graham Cracker Crumb Crust.
2. In top of double saucepan combine milk and marshmallows; cook over hot water, stirring occasionally, until dissolved. Remove from heat; cool.
3. Stir in raspberries; fold in cream. Pour into crust; refrigerate overnight.
4. Before serving, decorate with whipped cream, if desired.

Myrtle Muir, Athenaeum Club,
Kansas City, Mo.

RASPBERRY POUF PIE

Makes 9-Inch Pie

Ladyfingers
¾ cup orange juice
¾ pound marshmallows
1½ cups heavy cream, whipped
10-ounce package frozen raspberries,
  defrosted
Whipped cream (optional)

1. Line 9-inch pie plate with ladyfingers.
2. Heat orange juice in top of double saucepan. Add marshmallows; cook over boiling water, stirring occasionally, until marshmallows are melted and mixture is smooth. Remove from heat; cool; refrigerate until partly set.
3. Fold in cream and raspberries. Pour into pie plate; refrigerate until set.
4. Garnish with whipped cream, if desired.

Maude Stewart, Woman's Club,
Harwich Port, Mass.

RHUBARB CUSTARD PIE

Makes 9-Inch Pie

9-inch baked pie shell
1 cup sugar
1 tablespoon flour
1 teaspoon cornstarch
¼ teaspoon salt
2 eggs, separated (use whites for
  meringue)
Juice of ½ lemon
3 cups sliced rhubarb
2-Egg-White Meringue Topping
  (p. 552)

1. Prepare pie shell.
2. In saucepan combine sugar, flour, cornstarch, salt, egg yolks and lemon juice. Add rhubarb; cook over low heat, stirring constantly, until rhubarb is soft and custard is thickened. Pour into pie shell; cool.
3. Preheat oven to 375° F.
4. Spread filling with 2-Egg-White Meringue Topping; brown in preheated oven.

Mrs. L. L. Morgan, Woman's Club,
Hugoton, Kans.

RUM CHIFFON PIE

Makes 9-Inch Pie

9-inch Chocolate or Vanilla Wafer
  Crust (p. 551)
⅓ cup rum
1 cup sugar
1 tablespoon cornstarch
2 envelopes gelatin
4 eggs, separated
½ cup water
2 cups milk
1 teaspoon vanilla
1 cup heavy cream, whipped

1. Prepare Chocolate or Vanilla Wafer Crust; sprinkle with 1 tablespoon of the rum. Chill.
2. In top of double saucepan combine ½ cup of the sugar, cornstarch and gelatin. Add egg yolks and water to make a smooth paste. Stir in milk; cook over hot water, stirring constantly, until thickened and smooth. Cool.
3. Beat egg whites until foamy; gradually beat in remaining sugar; beat until stiff

and glossy; fold with vanilla and remaining rum into custard.

4. Turn into crust; top with whipped cream, flavored to taste. Refrigerate for 2 hours.

Mrs. T. L. Aldrich, Glendale Estates Woman's Club, Decatur, Ga.

SHERRY CREAM PIE

Makes 8-Inch Pie

8-inch Graham Cracker Crumb
   Crust (p. 551)
1 pound marshmallows
1 cup sweet sherry
2 cups heavy cream, whipped

1. Prepare Graham Cracker Crumb Crust.
2. In top of double saucepan cook marshmallows and sherry over boiling water, stirring occasionally, until melted. Cool.
3. Fold in cream; turn into crust. Refrigerate for at least 1 hour.

Marjorie Yokley, North Carolina Federation of Women's Clubs, Mount Airy, N.C.

FRESH STRAWBERRY PIE

Makes 8-Inch Pie

8-inch baked pie shell
3 tablespoons cornstarch
¾ cup sugar
¼ cup water
4 cups strawberries
½ teaspoon lemon juice
   Few drops red food coloring
   Whipped cream

1. Prepare pie shell.
2. In saucepan combine cornstarch, ½ cup of the sugar, water and 2 cups of the strawberries. Bring to boil; cook, stirring constantly, until thickened and clear.
3. Add remaining sugar; stir until dissolved. Stir in lemon juice, food coloring and remaining strawberries. Turn into pie shell; refrigerate.
4. Before serving, garnish with whipped cream.

Mrs. Marshall Smith, Woman's Club, Geff, Ill.

STRAWBERRY BAVARIAN PIE

Makes 9-Inch Pie

9-inch Wheat Crust (p. 551)
1 envelope gelatin
¼ cup cold water
¾ cup boiling water
¾ cup sugar
1 cup crushed strawberries with juice
2 tablespoons lemon juice
1 cup heavy cream

1. Prepare Wheat Crust.
2. Soften gelatin in cold water; add boiling water and sugar; stir until dissolved. Cool.
3. Stir in strawberries; refrigerate until syrupy.
4. Combine lemon juice and cream; whip until stiff; fold in gelatin mixture.

Chill until slightly thickened; then pile lightly into crust. Refrigerate until firm.

Elma Gray Holtam, Worthwhile Club, Thomasville, Ala.

STRAWBERRY CHEESE PIE

Makes 9-Inch Pie

9-inch baked pie shell
3 tablespoons heavy cream
8-ounce package cream cheese
1 quart strawberries
¾ cup sugar
2 tablespoons cornstarch
   Pineapple juice
   Whipped cream

1. Prepare pie shell.
2. In small bowl blend cream and cheese. Spread in pie shell. Chill.
3. Slice half the strawberries, using largest berries. Set aside.
4. Put remaining strawberries in mixing bowl; mash with fork. Stir in sugar; let stand for 10 minutes.
5. Force mashed strawberries through sieve, or blend in electric blender until puréed. Stir in cornstarch; add sufficient pineapple juice to total 1½ cups.
6. Pour into saucepan; cook over medium heat, stirring constantly, until thickened and clear. Cool.
7. Pour half the strawberry mixture over cheese in pie shell; top with sliced strawberries. Pour remaining strawberry mixture over sliced strawberries. Refrigerate.
8. Just before serving, top with whipped cream.

Mrs. Carl Rice, Fidelis Club, Overbrook, Kans.

STRAWBERRY MINUTE PIE

Makes 8- or 9-Inch Pie

8-or 9-inch baked pie shell
3-ounce package strawberry
   gelatin
1 cup boiling water
10-ounce package frozen sliced
   strawberries
   Whipped cream

1. Prepare pie shell.
2. Dissolve gelatin in water. Add strawberries; stir, breaking up strawberries with fork. As strawberries defrost, gelatin thickens.
3. When partially set, pour into pie shell. Refrigerate until completely set.
4. Serve garnished with whipped cream.

RASPBERRY MINUTE PIE: Follow recipe above, using raspberry gelatin in place of strawberry gelatin and frozen raspberries in place of strawberries.

Mrs. Clabe Howard, Janus Junior Women's Club, Columbus, Ohio

Crustless Pies

CRUMB-TOPPED APPLE PIE
Makes 8-Inch Pie

3 cups sliced peeled tart apples
1½ cups sugar
3 tablespoons flour
1 cup graham cracker crumbs
½ cup melted butter or margarine

1. Preheat oven to 400° F. Lightly grease 8-inch pie plate.
2. In mixing bowl combine apples, sugar and flour; toss lightly.
3. Arrange apples in pie plate. Top with crumbs. Sprinkle with butter or margarine.
4. Bake in preheated oven for 25 minutes.

Mrs. Joe G. Chaney, President, Woman's Club, Wingate, N.C.

NORWEGIAN APPLE PIE (CRUSTLESS)
Makes 2 9-Inch Pies

1½ cups sugar
1 cup presifted flour
2 eggs
2 teaspoons baking powder
½ teaspoon salt
½ teaspoon vanilla
2 cups chopped apples
1 cup chopped walnuts
Whipped cream or ice cream

1. Preheat oven to 350° F. Grease 2 9-inch pie plates.
2. In mixing bowl combine sugar and flour. Add eggs, baking powder, salt and vanilla; beat until smooth.
3. Stir in apples and walnuts. Pour into pie plates.
4. Bake in preheated oven for 30 minutes.
5. Serve warm with whipped cream or ice cream.

Mary Lunden, Carmichaels and Cumberland Civic Women's Club, Carmichaels, Pa.

BROWNIE PIE
Makes 8-Inch Pie

3 egg whites
¾ cup sugar
½ cup chopped walnuts or pecans
½ cup chocolate cooky crumbs
1 cup heavy cream, whipped

1. Preheat oven to 325° F. Grease 8-inch pie plate.
2. In mixing bowl beat egg whites until foamy. Gradually add sugar; beat until stiff and glossy. Fold in nuts and crumbs; turn into pie plate.
3. Bake in preheated oven for 35 minutes.
4. Cool. Top with whipped cream. Refrigerate. Cut into wedges to serve.

Mrs. Elta Dorris, Tuesday Literary Club, Bolivar, Tenn.

NO-CRUST COCONUT PIE
Serves 6 to 8

1 cup cornflake crumbs
1 cup flaked coconut

4 egg whites
⅛ teaspoon salt
1 cup sugar
1 teaspoon vanilla
8½-ounce can crushed pineapple, well drained
Sweetened whipped cream

1. Preheat oven to 325° F. Grease 9-inch square baking pan.
2. Combine crumbs and coconut.
3. Beat egg whites and salt until soft peaks form. Gradually beat in sugar; beat until stiff peaks form. Add vanilla. Fold in crumb mixture. Stir in pineapple.
4. Pour into pan; bake in preheated oven for 45 to 50 minutes. Cool.
5. Serve with whipped cream.

Mrs. William H. Hasebroock, Honorary President, General Federation of Women's Clubs, West Point, Neb.

CRACKER PIE
Makes 8-Inch Pie

3 egg whites
1 cup sugar
1 cup unsalted cracker crumbs
1 teaspoon baking powder
1 teaspoon vanilla
1 cup chopped pecans or walnuts
1 cup heavy cream, whipped

1. Preheat oven to 350° F. Grease 8-inch pie plate.
2. In mixing bowl beat egg whites until foamy. Gradually add sugar; beat until stiff and glossy.
3. Fold in crumbs, baking powder, vanilla and nuts. Turn into pie plate.
4. Bake in preheated oven for 35 minutes.
5. Cool. Cover with whipped cream. Refrigerate for 2 hours.

Mrs. Lester Blackshaw, Studere Club, Wellsville, Mo.

MACAROON PIE
Makes 8- or 9-Inch Pie

3 eggs, separated
1 cup sugar
1 cup graham cracker crumbs
½ cup chopped nuts
1 tablespoon almond extract
Pistachio ice cream

1. Preheat oven to 300° F. Grease 8- or 9-inch pie plate.
2. Combine egg yolks, ½ cup of the sugar, crumbs, nuts and almond extract.
3. Beat egg whites until stiff but not dry. Gradually add remaining sugar; beat until stiff and glossy. Fold into egg yolk mixture; turn into pie plate.
4. Bake in preheated oven for 1 hour.
5. Serve topped with scoops of ice cream.

Mrs. C. H. Hunsdorfer, President, Woman's Auxiliary to the Chiropractic Association of New York, New York, N.Y.

NO-CRUST CUSTARD PIE
Makes 9-Inch Pie

4 eggs
1 teaspoon vanilla

2 cups milk
4½ tablespoons flour
⅓ cup sugar
¼ teaspoon salt
Nutmeg

1. Preheat oven to 325° F. Grease 9-inch glass pie plate.
2. In mixing bowl beat eggs. Stir in vanilla and 1½ cups of the milk.
3. In small bowl blend remaining milk, flour, sugar and salt. Stir into egg mixture. Pour into pie plate; sprinkle with nutmeg.
4. Bake in preheated oven for 35 to 40 minutes, or until knife inserted inch from edge comes out clean.

Mrs. Richard Robinson, Semper Fidelis
Study Club, Clarinda, Ia.

FUDGE PIE

Makes 9-Inch Pie

3 eggs
1 cup sugar
¼ cup presifted flour
½ cup butter
2 1-ounce squares unsweetened chocolate
½ cup chopped pecans
1 teaspoon vanilla
Whipped cream

1. Preheat oven to 350° F. Grease 9-inch pie plate well.
2. Beat eggs and sugar until thickened and pale. Stir in flour.
3. Melt butter and chocolate, stirring constantly until smooth. Stir into egg mixture. Fold in pecans and vanilla.
4. Pour into pie plate. Bake in preheated oven for 20 minutes.
5. Serve with whipped cream.

Mrs. L. J. Taylor, Woman's Club,
Comer, Ga.

AMISH LEMON SPONGE PIE

Makes 1-Quart Casserole Pie

2 tablespoons butter or margarine
1 cup sugar
3 eggs, separated
3 tablespoons flour
½ teaspoon salt
2 teaspoons grated lemon rind
2 tablespoons lemon juice
1½ cups hot milk

1. Preheat oven to 400° F. Grease 1-quart casserole.
2. Put butter or margarine and sugar in mixing bowl; cream until light and fluffy. Add egg yolks; beat until smooth. Stir in flour, salt, lemon rind and juice and milk.
3. In another mixing bowl beat egg whites until stiff but not dry. Fold into batter; pour into casserole.
4. Bake in preheated oven for 40 minutes, or until puffed and golden.

Mrs. Clarence Shonk, Lancaster County
Federation of Woman's Clubs, Lancaster, Pa.

Tarts, Turnovers and Small Pastries

APPLE SLICES

Serves 10

Presifted flour
½ teaspoon baking powder
¾ teaspoon salt
½ cup butter or margarine
¼ cup shortening
½ cup milk
2 egg yolks
4 large tart apples, peeled and sliced
1 tablespoon lemon juice
1 cup granulated sugar
½ teaspoon cinnamon
1 cup confectioners' sugar, sifted and mixed with 2 to 3 tablespoons water

1. Preheat oven to 350° F. Grease large baking sheet.
2. Into mixing bowl sift together 2 cups flour, baking powder and ½ teaspoon of the salt; cut in butter or margarine and shortening until mixture resembles fine crumbs.
3. In small bowl beat milk and egg yolks; add to flour mixture. Work together to make a smooth dough.
4. Divide dough in half; roll out each half to 15 x 10-inch rectangle. Place one sheet of dough on baking sheet.
5. In mixing bowl combine apples, 3 tablespoons flour, remaining salt, lemon juice, granulated sugar and cinnamon; mix lightly.
6. Spread apple mixture on dough on baking sheet. Top with other sheet of dough; press edges to seal.
7. Bake in preheated oven for 1 hour.
8. Cool. Spread top with confectioners' sugar. Cut into 5 x 3-inch slices.

Barbara Wharton, Progressive Art Club,
South Bend, Ind.

APPLE STRUDEL HOME STYLE

Serves 8

1½ cups presifted flour
½ teaspoon baking powder
⅓ teaspoon salt
1 large egg, lightly beaten
⅓ cup apple cider
Melted butter
8 cups ground peeled cored apples
1 cup seedless raisins
½ cup currants
1 cup finely chopped almonds
1 cup sugar
1½ teaspoons cinnamon

1. Into mixing bowl sift together flour, baking powder and salt.
2. Make a well in center; put in egg and cider. Mix with fork until dough holds together.
3. Turn onto lightly floured board; knead until dough leaves board clean.
4. Brush dough with a little of the butter; return to mixing bowl. Cover; let stand over hot water for 30 minutes.

5. Preheat oven to 400° F. Grease baking sheet.

6. Place dough in center of well-floured cloth on table. With hands, palms down, under dough, pull and stretch gently until dough becomes as large as possible and as thin as paper.

7. Spread apples evenly over dough. Sprinkle raisins, currants and almonds over apples.

8. In small bowl blend sugar and cinnamon; sprinkle over fruit mixture. Drip more butter over filling; trim edges of dough.

9. Roll up like a jelly roll; place on baking sheet.

10. Bake in preheated oven for 25 minutes. Brush with butter; bake for 10 minutes longer, or until browned and crisp.

11. Brush again with butter. Serve hot or warm.

*Doris McKinley, Woman's Club,
Breton Woods, N.J.*

LITTLE FRIED PIES

Makes 12

Pastry for 2-crust pie
2 cups drained cooked apricots or apples
½ cup granulated sugar
½ pound fat for deep frying
Confectioners' sugar

1. Roll out pastry ⅛ inch thick on lightly floured board; cut into circles about 5 inches in diameter.

2. Combine fruit and granulated sugar; place 1½ tablespoons on one side of each round. Moisten edges with water; fold into semi-circle, enclosing filling. Press edges with fork to seal.

3. Heat fat to 365° F. in deep skillet.

4. Fry pies for 3 to 4 minutes, or until browned.

5. Drain on absorbent paper; sprinkle with confectioners' sugar.

*Katie Slocum, Dixieland Women's
Improvement Club, Madera, Calif.*

APRICOT TURNOVERS

Makes 12

Pastry for 2-crust pie
8-ounce package dried apricots
1½ cups water
⅛ teaspoon salt
1 cup sugar
3 tablespoons melted butter

1. Prepare apricot filling: In saucepan combine apricots, water, salt and ¾ cup of the sugar. Bring to boil; boil over high heat for 5 minutes; cover; simmer for 10 minutes longer. Force through ricer or sieve. Chill.

2. Preheat oven to 375° F.

3. Roll out pastry ⅛ inch thick on lightly floured board. Cut 2½-inch circles with floured cooky cutter.

4. Place filling in center of each circle. Fold over to form half circle; seal edges well.

5. Flute edges; place on baking sheet. Brush tops with butter; sprinkle with remaining sugar.

6. Bake in preheated oven for 15 minutes, or until golden.

*Melba Jenkins, Beta Study Club,
Shreveport, La.*

SWEET BANANA PASTRY PUFFS FROM INDIA

Makes About 18

Pastry for 2-crust pie
3 ripe medium bananas, mashed
⅓ cup flaked coconut
Water
Fat for deep frying
Confectioners' sugar

1. Roll out pastry ⅛ inch thick on lightly floured board. Cut out with floured 3-inch cooky cutter.

2. Mix bananas and coconut.

3. Place spoonful of banana mixture in center of each pastry circle. Moisten edges slightly with water; fold over, pressing edges well to seal.

4. Drop into deep fat heated to 365° F. Fry for 4 minutes, or until golden.

5. Drain on absorbent paper. Sprinkle with confectioners' sugar. Serve hot or cold.

*Josie and Delila Baird, Pierian Study Club,
San Saba, Tex.*

BANBURY TARTS

Makes 8 to 12

Pastry for 2-crust pie
1 cup currant jelly
Juice and rind of 2 lemons
1 cup sugar
1 cup chopped seedless raisins
5 crackers, crumbed
2 teaspoons cinnamon
Pinch of salt

1. Preheat oven to 400° F.

2. Roll out pastry thinly; cut into 4-inch circles.

3. Combine remaining ingredients; place spoonful on each pastry circle. Fold into semi-circle; seal edges. Prick each tart with fork 3 or 4 times.

4. Arrange on baking sheet. Bake in preheated oven for 15 minutes, or until browned.

*Mrs. C. Richard Powers, New Century Club,
Wilmington, Del.*

BLUEBERRY TARTS

Makes 8

8 Baked Tart Shells (p. 550)
1-pound can blueberries
½ cup sugar
2 tablespoons flour
½ teaspoon salt
¼ teaspoon cinnamon
1½ tablespoons butter
1 cup heavy cream, whipped

1. Prepare Baked Tart Shells.

2. Drain blueberries; reserve liquid.

3. In saucepan combine sugar, flour, salt and cinnamon. Gradually blend in reserved liquid. Cook over medium heat, stirring constantly, until thickened and smooth.

4. Remove from heat; beat in butter. Stir in blueberries; cool.

5. Fill shells with blueberry mixture; top each with whipped cream. Refrigerate until ready to serve.

Mrs. Doug Perdue, Les Causeuses Women's Club,
Hillsboro, Tex.

BUTTER TARTS

Makes 12

Pastry for 2-crust pie
⅓ cup butter
⅓ cup light corn syrup
½ cup brown sugar
½ teaspoon vanilla
1 egg, lightly beaten
½ cup seedless raisins or chopped nuts

1. Preheat oven to 375° F.
2. Line 12 small tart pans with pastry.
3. Combine remaining ingredients; spoon into pans.
4. Bake in preheated oven for 15 to 20 minutes.

Mrs. J. J. Hickam, Junior Woman's Club,
Bristol, Tenn.

SEAFOAM CANTALOUPE TARTS

Makes 12

12 Baked Tart Shells (p. 550)
1 cup sugar
⅓ cup cornstarch
⅛ teaspoon salt
1½ cups water
3 egg yolks
¼ cup lime juice
1 tablespoon grated lime rind
Few drops green food coloring
2 tablespoons butter or margarine
1½ cups small cantaloupe balls

1. Prepare Baked Tart Shells.
2. In top of double saucepan combine sugar, cornstarch and salt. Gradually stir in water to make a smooth paste. Cook over moderate heat, stirring constantly, until sauce is thickened and smooth.
3. In small bowl beat egg yolks and some of sauce. Stir into rest of sauce; cook over hot water, stirring constantly, until just below boiling point.
4. Remove from heat; stir in lime juice and rind, food coloring and butter or margarine. Cool, stirring occasionally.
5. Fold in melon balls; spoon into tart shells.

Ruth Whitney, Woman's Club,
Athol, Mass.

CHERRY TARTS

Makes 18

18 Baked Tart Shells (p. 550)
1-pound 4-ounce can sour red cherries
3 tablespoons cornstarch
¾ cup sugar
Whipped cream

1. Prepare Baked Tart Shells.
2. Drain cherries; reserve liquid.
3. In saucepan combine cornstarch and sugar. Gradually stir in reserved liquid to make a smooth paste. Add cherries; cook over low heat, stirring constantly, until thickened and clear. Cool slightly, stirring occasionally.
4. Fill tart shells with cherry mixture; cool until serving time.
5. Just before serving, top with whipped cream.

Gayle Miles, Younger Woman's Club,
Barbourville, Ky.

TEATIME TASSIES

Makes 24

½ cup butter or margarine
3-ounce package cream cheese
1 cup presifted flour
1 tablespoon butter
1 egg
¾ cup brown sugar
1 teaspoon vanilla
⅔ cup chopped pecans

1. Preheat oven to 325° F. Grease 24 1¾-inch muffin cups well.
2. Combine butter or margarine and cheese; beat until smooth. Blend in flour. Refrigerate for 15 minutes.
3. Divide dough into 24 pieces; roll each into a ball. Press each ball onto bottom and sides of muffin cup. Refrigerate.
4. In mixing bowl cream 1 tablespoon butter, egg, sugar and vanilla until smooth. Sprinkle pecans in lined muffin cups; top with egg mixture.
5. Bake in preheated oven for 25 minutes, or until set. Cool. Remove from cups.

Mae Wheaton, Woman's Club,
Olympia, Wash.

CREAM PUFFS

Makes 8 to 10

Cream Puff Pastry (p. 552)
Whipped cream or favorite filling

1. Preheat oven to 450° F. Grease baking sheet.
2. Drop Cream Puff Pastry by tablespoons into large mounds 2 inches apart on baking sheet.
3. Bake in preheated oven for 15 minutes. Turn temperature to 325° F. Bake for 20 minutes longer, or until pastry is puffed, golden brown and dry.
4. Cook. Split puffs horizontally two-thirds of way through; fill with whipped cream or favorite filling, as desired.

PROFITEROLES

Makes 32

Cream Puff Pastry (p. 552)
Whipped cream, custard filling or ice cream

1. Preheat oven to 450° F. Grease baking sheet.
2. Drop Cream Puff Pastry by teaspoons onto baking sheet.

3. Bake in preheated oven for 10 minutes. Turn temperature to 325° F. Bake for 15 minutes longer.

4. Cool. Split. Fill with whipped cream, custard filling or ice cream, as desired.

Mrs. Nellie Partridge, Women's Club, Osage, Wyo.

LEMON-FILLED CREAM PUFFS

Serves 12

12 Baked Cream Puffs (p. 552)
3½-ounce package lemon pie filling mix
2 cups water
2 3-ounce packages cream cheese
Confectioners' sugar

1. Prepare Cream Puffs.
2. In saucepan blend lemon mix and 1½ cups of the water. Cook over medium heat, stirring constantly, until thickened and smooth. Remove from heat; cool.
3. In small saucepan bring remaining water to boil. Remove from heat; add cheese; beat until smooth. Cool.
4. Combine cheese mixture and lemon mix; beat until smooth.
5. Fill puffs with cooled lemon filling; sprinkle with sugar.

Mrs. A. R. Smeek, Woman's Club, Vienna, W. Va.

ECLAIRS

Makes 10 to 12

1 cup water
½ cup butter
¼ teaspoon salt
1 cup presifted flour
4 eggs
Rich Custard Filling (p. 631)
Chocolate Frosting (p. 623)

1. Preheat oven to 425° F. Grease baking sheet.
2. In saucepan combine water, butter and salt. Bring to full rolling boil; add flour. Beat vigorously over low heat until mixture forms a ball and leaves sides of saucepan.
3. Remove from heat; beat in eggs, one at a time, beating well after each addition.
4. Fill pastry tube with dough, using large nozzle; press dough onto baking sheet, forming strips 1 x 4 inches.
5. Bake in preheated oven for 20 minutes. Turn temperature to 350° F. Bake for 20 minutes longer.
6. Remove from baking sheet; slit side of each eclair. Scoop out moist dough in center. Cool.
7. Fill with Rich Custard Filling. Frost tops with Chocolate Frosting.

Norma Rankin, Champaign Urbana Junior Woman's Club, Champaign, Ill.

PETITS MILLEFEUILLES OR NAPOLEONS

Makes 6

Flaky Puff Pastry (p. 549)
Quick Custard Filling (p. 631) or 2
cups heavy cream, whipped and sweetened to taste
Sifted confectioners' sugar

1. Line baking sheet with several layers of heavy brown paper.
2. Roll out Flaky Puff Pastry to 8 x 12-inch rectangle ⅛ inch thick; cut into three strips 2½ inches wide, arrange on baking sheet. Prick surfaces with fork; chill thoroughly.
3. Preheat oven to 450° F.
4. Bake pastry in preheated oven for 10 minutes. Turn temperature to 350° F.; bake for 10 minutes more. Place cold baking sheet under baking sheet with pastry; turn temperature to 300° F.; bake for 20 minutes longer, or until dry and golden brown. Cool.
5. Put 3 strips together, one on top of the other, with Quick Custard Filling or whipped cream between. Sprinkle top strip generously with sugar; cut crosswise with serrated knife into slices 2 inches wide.

A. S.

RAGALACH (Hungarian Cream Cheese Pastry)

Makes About 60

1 cup butter
8-ounce package cream cheese
¼ teaspoon salt
2 cups presifted flour
1 cup chopped walnuts
½ cup sugar
1 tablespoon cinnamon

1. Day before, beat butter, cheese and salt in mixing bowl until creamy. Add flour; mix well. Shape into 14 balls; refrigerate overnight.
2. Next day, preheat oven to 350° F.
3. Prepare filling: In bowl mix walnuts, sugar and cinnamon.
4. Roll out each pastry ball on lightly floured board to 6-inch circle; cut each in fourths.
5. Drop teaspoonful of filling in center of each quarter. Pinch edges over filling; shape into crescents. Place on baking sheets.
6. Bake in preheated oven for about 12 minutes, or until lightly browned. Cool on wire racks.

Woman's Club, Palisade, N. J.

KOLACHY (Fruit Turnovers)

Makes 36

Cream Cheese Pastry (p. 549)
Favorite fruit filling

1. Prepare Cream Cheese Pastry; refrigerate.
2. Preheat oven to 425° F. Grease baking sheets.
3. Roll out dough ⅛ inch thick on lightly floured board; cut into 3-inch squares.
4. Place a spoonful of filling in center of each square. Fold in corners to center; seal. Place on baking sheets.
5. Bake in preheated oven for 20 minutes.

Mrs. Dale Ackerman, Atheneum Club, Marysville, Kans.

NUT-FILLED HORNS
Makes About 72

2 cups butter
Dash of salt
1 cup sour cream
12 egg yolks
7 to 8 cups sifted cake flour
6 egg whites
1 pound confectioners' sugar, sifted
2 cups ground walnuts

1. Day before, beat butter, salt, sour cream and egg yolks until blended. Gradually work in sufficient flour to make a stiff dough.
2. Roll dough into 1½-inch balls; refrigerate overnight.
3. Next day, preheat oven to 350° F. Lightly grease baking sheet.
4. Beat egg whites until foamy. Gradually beat in sugar; beat until stiff and glossy. Fold in walnuts.
5. Roll out balls to circles ⅛ inch thick on lightly floured surface. Place a little meringue in center of each circle; roll up to form horn. Place on baking sheet.
6. Bake in preheated oven for 15 to 20 minutes, or until lightly browned. Cool on wire racks.

Mrs. John Hawksworth, Woman's Club,
Ebensburg, Pa.

FRIED PEACH PIES
Makes About 12

Pastry for 1-crust pie
2 cups finely chopped peeled peaches
½ cup granulated sugar
2 tablespoons cornstarch
1 teaspoon lemon juice
1 tablespoon butter or margarine
Shortening
Confectioners' sugar
Whipped cream or boiled custard

1. Prepare pastry.
2. Put peaches in saucepan; sprinkle with granulated sugar and cornstach. Cook over low heat, stirring constantly, until thickened and clear. Remove from heat; stir in lemon juice and butter or margarine. Cool.
3. Roll out pastry ¹⁄₁₆ inch thick; cut with floured cooky cutter into 3-inch circles. Moisten edges with water and place a teaspoon of peach filling in the center of each. Fold over to form half circles; press edges to seal well.
4. Melt shortening in deep skillet to depth of 1 inch. Heat to 365° F.
5. Fry a few pies at a time over medium heat for about 4 to 5 minutes on each side or until crisp and golden.
6. Drain on absorbent paper; sprinkle with confectioners' sugar. Serve at once with whipped cream or custard, as desired.

Mrs. Lillie W. Wilderman, Women's Club,
Freeburg, Ill.

PLUM JELLY TARTS
Makes 18 Small Tarts

Pastry for 18 small tarts
4 egg yolks
2 cups sugar
1 cup heavy cream
½ cup butter
¼ cup plum jelly

1. Preheat oven to 425° F.
2. Line small tart pans with pastry.
3. In top of double saucepan blend egg yolks and sugar. Add cream and butter; cook over hot water, stirring constantly, until thickened and smooth.
4. Remove from heat; spoon about 1 tablespoon into each pan; top with ½ teaspoon of the jelly.
5. Place on baking sheet; bake in preheated oven for 10 minutes. Turn temperature to 325° F. Bake for 20 minutes longer, or until filling is set and pastry is golden.

Mrs. E. Gerrard, Younger Woman's Club,
Barbourville, Ky.

PUMPKIN FANCHONETTES (Tartlets)
Makes 18 Small Tarts

Pastry for 18 small tarts
2 cups mashed cooked pumpkin
1 teaspoon salt
2 cups milk
2 eggs, lightly beaten
¾ cup sugar
1¼ teaspoons cinnamon
½ teaspoon nutmeg
¼ teaspoon ginger
¼ teaspoon allspice
¼ cup currant jelly
1 cup heavy cream, whipped

1. Preheat oven to 450° F.
2. Line small tart pans with pastry.
3. In mixing bowl combine all remaining ingredients except jelly and cream; blend well; pour into pans.
4. Bake in preheated oven for 10 minutes. Turn temperature to 325° F. Bake for 25 minutes longer.
5. Cool. Spread surface with jelly; top with spoonful of whipped cream.

Helen Adams, Women's Club, Cheney, Kans.

STRAWBERRY TARTS
Makes 12

12 Baked Tart Shells (p. 550)
1⅓ cups sugar
1¼ cups water
¼ cup cornstarch
⅛ teaspoon salt
1 tablespoon lemon juice
Red food coloring (optional)
1 quart strawberries
Whipped cream

1. Prepare Baked Tart Shells.
2. Bring sugar and ½ cup of the water to boil.
3. Dissolve cornstarch in remaining water. Add to syrup. Cook for about 10 minutes, or until clear, stirring occasionally.

4. Blend in salt, lemon juice and, if desired, enough food coloring to produce a light red shade.

5. Pour syrup over strawberries; mix gently. Cool. Spoon into tart shells. Garnish with whipped cream.

Betty Warren, Woman's Club, Starke, Fla.

SWEDISH PASTRIES

Makes 12

1 cup butter or margarine
1¾ cups presifted flour
3 eggs
1 cup confectioners' sugar, sifted
2 tablespoons shortening
1 teaspoon vanilla
Cream

1. Preheat oven to 350° F. Grease baking sheet.

2. In mixing bowl cream ½ cup of the butter or margarine, 1 cup of the flour and 1 tablespoon water until smooth.

3. Divide dough in half; pat each half onto baking sheet in strip 3½ inches wide.

4. In saucepan combine remaining butter or margarine and 1 cup water. Bring to boil; remove from heat; add remaining flour. Beat until smooth. Add eggs, one at a time, beating well after each addition.

5. Spread on strips of dough.

6. Bake in preheated oven for 1 hour. Cool on wire rack.

7. Blend sugar, shortening, vanilla and sufficient cream to make a smooth frosting. Spread on pastries. Cut into 2-inch bars.

Ellen Collins, Culture Club, Essex, Ia.

WALNUT TARTS

Makes 8

Pastry for 8 tart shells
1 cup brown sugar
2 tablespoons butter
1 egg
1 cup chopped walnuts

1. Preheat oven to 375° F.

2. Prepare tart shells.

3. In mixing bowl beat sugar, butter and egg until bubbling. Stir in walnuts; mix well. Pour into shells, filling them half full.

4. Place on baking sheet; bake in preheated oven for 20 minutes, or until golden.

Helen Mason, Woman's Club, Patten, Mass.

19. Cakes

The way in which a cake is frosted, decorated and presented can be a work of art; but the actual making of the cake is a science, and there are a few rules that must be followed to ensure success.

Cakes can be divided into two basic categories:

1. *Butter-Type Cakes* in which sugar is blended into butter, margarine or shortening until light and fluffy before the other ingredients are added. This creaming may be done with a wooden spoon or with an electric mixer. When butter is used, the sugar will blend in more readily if the butter is at room temperature.

2. *Sponge-Type Cakes* in which either no shortening is used or shortening in liquid form is carefully folded into a spongy batter.

How to Make Good Cakes

1. Read and follow recipe exactly.

2. Preheat oven to correct temperature. Invest in oven thermometer if oven does not have a regulator.

3. Assemble all ingredients and utensils.

4. Use the correct size cake pan. If correct pan is not available, fill pans only half full of batter. Any remaining batter may be baked as cupcakes. For cake pan substitutes, see page 584. If a glass baking pan is used, increase oven temperature by 25° F.

5. Prepare pans: Grease sides and bottom of pan with shortening or cooking oil; sprinkle lightly with flour, and tap and swirl pan to coat it evenly with flour; shake out any excess flour. Or blend equal parts of shortening and flour to a smooth paste, and brush this onto bottom and sides of pan with a pastry brush. If recipe calls for it, line bottom of pan with waxed paper or heavy brown paper cut to fit, according to directions.

6. Measure accurately. Dry ingredients should be level in either cup or spoon. This is done by filling cup or spoon heaping and leveling off across top with knife or spatula.

7. Mix carefully: Cream, beat or fold exactly as recipe specifies.

8. Turn batter into prepared pans, and spread to edge. When layer pans are used, divide batter evenly. Tap pans gently on table top to remove large air pockets in batter.

9. Place pans in oven: Place oven rack in center of oven, and put cake pan in center of rack. When baking two layers, arrange them in opposite corners of the rack, allowing 2 to 3 inches of space around each pan. When baking three layers, place the third on another rack a few inches above or below the first rack, making sure that no cake pan is directly above another.

10. Test for doneness: Test cake at minimum baking time or a few minutes before end of specified baking time as follows:

(a) Touch center of cake lightly with finger. If surface springs back, cake is done. If impression remains, bake for a few minutes longer; test again.

(b) Insert a wooden pick in center of cake. If pick comes out clean, cake is done. If pick is moist, check again after 5 minutes.

(c) Cake is done when it begins to pull away from sides of pan.

11. Remove cake from oven. Set on wire rack to let air circulate around pan. Allow cake to stand in pan for 5 to 10 minutes unless recipe specifies immediate removal. Run a spatula carefully around edge of cake to loosen it from sides of pan. Invert cake onto wire rack. Immediately turn cake right side up. This is easily done by placing another wire rack on top. Tip cake and racks over, and remove the first rack.

Frosting the Cake

Be sure both the cake and the frosting are completely cooled. Place cake, top or rounded side down, in center of serving plate. Slide 4 strips of waxed paper under edge of cake to protect plate while cake is frosted.

Frost top of layer with icing or filling. If a 2-layer cake, put second layer on first layer bottom or flat side down. This places the bottoms or flat sides of both cakes together in center of cake. Frost first the sides of cake, then the top.

If layers tend to slide during frosting (this may happen if 2 or more layers are used), insert a skewer or wooden dowel through center of all layers. Remove the skewer or dowel when frosting sets.

Freezing Cakes

Most cakes freeze well. If unfrosted, they should be wrapped in aluminum foil, freezer paper or transparent film and placed in 0° F. storage, where they will stay fresh and flavorful for 2 to 3 months. Defrost before unwrapping.

Butter and fudge frostings freeze well, but frosted cakes must be completely frozen before being wrapped for storage. They will keep well for 1 to 2 months. Unwrap before defrosting.

Storing Cakes

Cakes may be stored in a cake keeper, in a large airtight container, or under a deep bowl inverted over cake on the plate.

Any cake with a whipped cream or custard filling should be refrigerated.

Fruit cakes should be sprinkled with brandy, rum or sherry and wrapped tightly in aluminum foil. Stored in an airtight container in a cool place, preferably in the refrigerator, they will keep for a long time.

Simplified Chart for High-Altitude Cake Baking

Adjustments	Altitude in Feet		
	3,500–5,000	5,000–6,500	6,500–8,000
Increase flour	1 tablespoon	2 tablespoons	3 tablespoons
Decrease leavening	1/3 to 1/2 teaspoon	1/2 to 2/3 teaspoon	2/3 to 3/4 teaspoon
Increase baking temperature	25° F.	25° F.	25° F.

Cake Pan Substitutes

The cake pan suggested for a recipe is the ideal pan for that cake. Most cakes, however, can be successfully baked in a different type or shape of pan. This is not true of poundcakes, which should always be baked in a loaf or tube pan. Pans should be filled only half full. Bake leftover batter in cupcake pans.

IF CAKE BAKES AS	IT WILL ALSO BAKE AS
Two 8-inch layers	Two thin 8 x 8 x 2-inch squares; 18 to 24 cupcakes 2½ inches in diameter
Three 8-inch layers	Two 9 x 9 x 2-inch squares
Two 9-inch layers	Two 8 x 8 x 2-inch squares; three thin 8-inch layers, one 15½ x 10½ x 1-inch rectangle; 30 cupcakes 2½ inches in diameter
One 8 x 8 x 2-inch square	One 9-inch layer
Two 8 x 8 x 2-inch squares	Two 9-inch layers; one 13 x 9½ x 2-inch rectangle
One 9 x 9 x 2-inch square	Two thin 8-inch layers
Two 9 x 9 x 2-inch squares	Three 8-inch layers
One 13 x 9½ x 2-inch rectangle	Two 9-inch layers; two 8 x 8 x 2-inch squares
One 9½ x 5¼ x 2¾-inch loaf pan, called 9-inch loaf pan	One 9 x 9 x 2-inch square; 24 to 30 cupcakes 2½ inches in diameter
One 8½ x 4½ x 2½-inch loaf pan, called 8-inch loaf pan	One 8 x 8 x 2-inch square
One 9 x 3½-inch tube pan	Two 9-inch layers; 24 to 30 cupcakes 2½ inches in diameter
One 10 x 4-inch tube pan	Two 9½ x 5¼ x 2¾-inch loaf pans; one 13 x 9½ x 2-inch rectangle; two 15½ x 10½ x 1-inch rectangles

COMMON CAUSES OF FAILURE IN CAKES

1. Cracks and uneven surfaces may be caused by too much flour, too hot an oven and sometimes too cold an oven at start of baking.

2. Dryness may be caused by too much flour, too little shortening, too much baking powder or baking at too low a temperature.

3. A heavy cake means that too much sugar has been used or that cake has been baked for too short a period.

4. A sticky surface on a cake is caused by too much sugar.

5. A coarse-grained cake may be caused by too little mixing, too much shortening, too much baking powder, using too soft shortening, or baking at too low a temperature.

6. Falling may be caused by insufficient flour, under-baking, too much sugar, too much shortening or not enough baking powder.

7. Uneven browning may be caused by baking at too high a temperature, crowding the oven rack (allow at least 2 inches around pans) or using dark pans (use bright-finish smooth-bottomed pans).

8. Uneven color is caused by not mixing well. Mix thoroughly, but do not overmix.

Anniversary Cook Book, Women's Club, Ashland, Mass.

White Cakes

AMBROSIA CAKE

Makes 3 9-Inch Layers

3½ cups presifted flour
4 teaspoons baking powder
  Dash of salt
1 cup butter
2 cups sugar
1 cup milk
1 teaspoon vanilla
6 egg whites
  Orange Pineapple Filling (p. 632)

1. Preheat oven to 350° F. Grease and flour 3 9-inch layer cake pans.
2. Onto piece of waxed paper sift together flour, baking powder and salt.
3. In mixing bowl cream butter and sugar until light and fluffy.
4. Add flour mixture and milk alternately to creamed mixture, beating well after each addition. Stir in vanilla.
5. In another mixing bowl beat egg whites until stiff but not dry. Fold into cake batter. Pour batter into pans; spread evenly.
6. Bake in preheated oven for 30 minutes.
7. Cool for 5 minutes; remove from pans; cool on wire racks. Spread Orange Pineapple Filling between layers.

Mrs. R. L. Perry, Women's Co-operative Club,
New Augusta, Miss.

WHITE CAKE FOR TWO

Makes 8-Inch Layer

⅔ cup cake flour
1 teaspoon baking powder
  Dash of salt
3 tablespoons butter
½ cup sugar
3 tablespoons milk
½ teaspoon vanilla
2 egg whites

1. Preheat oven to 350° F. Grease and flour 8-inch layer cake pan.
2. Onto piece of waxed paper sift together flour, baking powder and salt.
3. In mixing bowl cream butter and sugar until light and fluffy.
4. Add flour mixture alternately with milk, beating well after each addition. Stir in vanilla.
5. In another bowl beat egg whites until stiff but not dry; fold into batter. Pour batter into pan; spread evenly.
6. Bake in preheated oven for 25 to 30 minutes.
7. Cool for 5 minutes; remove from pan; cool on wire rack. Cut in half; fill and frost to make half a layer cake.

L. Cleaves, Woman's Literary Club,
Bar Harbor, Me.

WHITE BUTTERMILK CAKE

Makes 2 9-Inch Layers

½ cup shortening
2 cups sugar
2 egg whites
1¾ cups buttermilk
2¾ cups sifted cake flour
½ teaspoon baking powder
½ teaspoon salt
1 teaspoon baking soda
1 teaspoon vanilla

1. Preheat oven to 350° F. Grease and flour 2 9-inch layer cake pans.
2. In mixing bowl cream shortening and sugar until light and fluffy. Add egg whites; beat until light.
3. Add 1 cup of the buttermilk, 2 cups of the flour, baking powder and salt; beat until smooth.
4. Add remaining buttermilk, remaining flour, baking soda and vanilla; beat until blended. Turn into pans.
5. Bake in preheated oven for 25 to 30 minutes.
6. Cool for 5 minutes; remove from pans; cool on wire racks. Fill and frost with favorite frosting.

Gloria Lewis, E.O.F. Club, Jesop, Ia.

ICE WATER WHITE CAKE

Makes 3 8-Inch Layers

½ cup shortening
2 cups sugar
½ teaspoon salt
3 cups cake flour, sifted
1½ cups ice water
2 teaspoons vanilla
3 teaspoons baking powder
3 egg whites

1. Preheat oven to 350° F. Grease and flour 3 8-inch layer cake pans.
2. In mixing bowl cream shortening, 1½ cups of the sugar and salt until light and fluffy. Add 1 cup of the flour, ½ cup of the ice water and vanilla; beat until smooth.
3. Sift together remaining flour and baking powder into mixture. Add remaining ice water; beat until smooth.
4. In another mixing bowl beat egg whites until foamy. Gradually add remaining sugar; beat until stiff and glossy. Fold into batter; pour into pans.
5. Bake in preheated oven for 25 to 30 minutes.
6. Cool for 5 minutes; remove from pans; cool on wire racks. Fill and frost with favorite frosting.

Naomi Bauer, I.Q. Study Club, Hudson, Kans.

LEMON AND PINEAPPLE WHITE CAKE

Makes 3 8-Inch Layers

Butter
3 cups sugar
1 cup milk
3 cups presifted flour
3 teaspoons baking powder
1 teaspoon vanilla
8 egg whites, stiffly beaten
8 egg yolks
8-ounce can crushed pineapple
  Grated rind of 2 lemons
  Juice of 2 lemons

1. Preheat oven to 350° F. Grease and flour 3 8-inch layer cake pans.
2. In mixing bowl cream 1 cup butter and 2 cups of the sugar until light and fluffy; gradually stir in milk.
3. Sift together flour and baking powder three times; stir into butter mixture. Stir in vanilla. Fold in egg whites.
4. Pour batter into pans; bake in preheated oven for 25 to 30 minutes. Remove from pans to wire racks to cool.
5. Meanwhile, prepare Pineapple Custard: In top of double saucepan combine egg yolks and remaining sugar. Stir in pineapple and lemon rind and juice. Cook over simmering water, stirring constantly, until thickened. Remove from heat; add 2 tablespoons butter; cool.
6. Fill and frost cake layers with custard.

Joan W. Thompson, Ethan Club, Dadeville, Ala.

QUEEN OF MAY CAKE

Makes 2 9-Inch Layers

2¾ cups cake flour
3 teaspoons baking powder
¾ teaspoon salt
½ cup shortening
1½ cups sugar
1½ teaspoons vanilla
½ cup milk
½ cup water
4 egg whites
  Pineapple Cream Filling (p. 632)
  Never-Fail Three-Minute Frosting
  (p. 626)

1. Preheat oven to 350° F. Grease and flour 2 9-inch layer cake pans.
2. Onto piece of waxed paper sift together flour, baking powder and salt.
3. In mixing bowl cream shortening and sugar until light and fluffy.
4. In measuring cup combine vanilla, milk and water.
5. Add flour mixture and milk mixture alternately to creamed mixture, beating well after each addition.
6. In another mixing bowl beat egg whites until stiff but not dry. Fold into batter; pour into pans.
7. Bake in preheated oven for 25 to 30 minutes.
8. Cool for 5 minutes; remove from pans; cool on wire racks.
9. Split each layer in half. Fill layers with Pineapple Cream Filling. Frost sides and top of cake with Never-Fail Three-Minute Frosting.

Mrs. Carl Eder, Woman's Club, Globe, Ariz.

VIENNA CAKE

Makes 10-Inch Ring

6 eggs, separated
½ cup water
1½ cups sugar
½ teaspoon vanilla
½ teaspoon orange extract
1½ cups presifted flour
¼ teaspoon salt
¾ teaspoon cream of tartar

  Vienna Frosting (p. 625)
½ cup toasted coconut

1. Preheat oven to 350° F. Grease and flour 10-inch tube pan.
2. Beat egg yolks until very thick and pale. Gradually beat in water. Slowly add sugar, beating constantly; beat until thickened. Stir in vanilla and orange extract. Stir in flour and salt.
3. Beat egg whites until foamy. Add cream of tartar; beat until stiff peaks form. Fold into egg yolk mixture.
4. Spoon batter into pan; bake in preheated oven for 45 to 50 minutes. Remove from pan to wire rack to cool.
5. Cut in half crosswise. Fill and frost with Vienna Frosting. Sprinkle with coconut.

Jerry Wagner, Junior's Woman's Club, Phoenix, Ariz.

Yellow Cakes

BOSTON CREAM PIE

Makes 9-Inch Layer

1 tablespoon shortening
½ cup milk
1 cup sifted cake flour
1 teaspoon baking powder
½ teaspoon salt
2 eggs
1 cup sugar
1 teaspoon vanilla
  Custard Cream Filling for
  Boston Cream Pie (p. 631)
  Shiny Chocolate Frosting for
  Boston Cream Pie (p. 629)

1. Preheat oven to 350° F. Grease and flour 9-inch layer cake pan.
2. In top of double saucepan combine shortening and milk; heat over simmering water.
3. Sift together flour, baking powder and salt.
4. In mixing bowl beat eggs until light. Add sugar; beat until thickened and pale. Add vanilla; gradually beat in milk mixture. Fold in flour mixture, blending thoroughly.
5. Turn batter into pan; bake in preheated oven for 25 to 30 minutes. Turn onto wire rack to cool slightly.
6. While still warm, split and fill with Custard Cream Filling for Boston Cream Pie. Frost with Shiny Chocolate Frosting for Boston Cream Pie.

Jessie M. Witbeck, Cabot Club, Middleboro, Mass.

REGAL BUTTER CAKE

Makes 2 9-Inch Layers

2¼ cups sifted cake flour
2¼ teaspoons baking powder
½ teaspoon salt
¾ cup butter
1½ cups sugar

3 eggs
⅔ cup milk
1 teaspoon vanilla
Never-Fail Three-Minute
Frosting (p. 626)

1. Preheat oven to 375° F. Grease and flour 2 9-inch layer cake pans; line bottoms with circles of waxed paper.
2. Onto piece of waxed paper sift together flour, baking powder and salt.
3. In mixing bowl cream butter until fluffy. Add sugar; beat until light and fluffy. Add eggs, one at a time, beating well after each addition.
4. Add flour mixture and milk alternately, beating well after each addition. Add vanilla; blend well. Turn into pans.
5. Bake in preheated oven for 20 minutes.
6. Cool for 5 minutes; remove from pans; cool on wire racks. Fill and frost with Never-Fail Three-Minute Frosting.

Herriete Chambers, Current Literature Club, Burkburnett, Tex.

TOASTED BUTTER PECAN CAKE
Makes 2 8-Inch Layers

1⅓ cups chopped pecans
Butter
1⅓ cups granulated sugar
2¼ teaspoons vanilla
2 eggs
2 cups presifted flour
1½ teaspoons baking powder
¼ teaspoon salt
⅔ cup milk
3 cups sifted confectioners' sugar
2½ to 3 tablespoons light cream

1. Preheat oven to 350° F. Grease and flour 2 8-inch layer cake pans.
2. Spread pecans in shallow pan; dot with 3 tablespoons butter. Toast in preheated oven for 15 minutes, stirring occasionally.
3. In mixing bowl beat ⅔ cup butter until soft. Gradually beat in sugar until light and fluffy. Stir in 1½ teaspoons of the vanilla. Add eggs, one at a time, beating well after each addition.
4. Combine flour, baking powder and salt. Stir alternately with milk into butter mixture. Stir in 1 cup of pecans.
5. Pour batter into pans; bake in preheated oven for 30 to 35 minutes. Remove from oven; cool for 10 minutes; turn onto wire racks to cool completely.
6. Meanwhile, prepare Butter Pecan Frosting: Combine 3 tablespoons butter, confectioners' sugar, cream and remaining vanilla: mix until smooth. Stir in remaining pecans.
7. Fill and frost layers with Butter Pecan Frosting.

Rosemary Riemer, Anna Day Club, Troy, Mo.

BUTTERSCOTCH CAKE
Makes 2 8-Inch Layers

2¼ cups sifted cake flour
2½ teaspoons baking powder
1 teaspoon salt
1½ cups brown sugar
½ cup shortening
1 cup milk
1 teaspoon vanilla
2 eggs
Penuche Icing (p. 628)

1. Preheat oven to 350° F. Grease and flour 2 8-inch layer cake pans.
2. Into mixing bowl sift together flour, baking powder and salt. Add sugar, shortening and ⅔ cup of the milk. Beat at medium speed with electric mixer for 2 minutes, or 100 hand strokes.
3. Add remaining milk, vanilla and eggs; beat for 2 minutes longer, or 100 hand strokes. Turn into pans.
4. Bake in preheated oven for 30 to 35 minutes.
5. Cool for 5 minutes; remove from pans; cool on wire racks. Fill and frost layers with Penuche Icing.

Mrs. O. T. Collins, Ploma Collins Study Club, Waco, Tex.

COCONUT LAYER CAKE
Makes 2 9-Inch Layers

2½ cups sifted cake flour
1½ cups sugar
3 teaspoons baking powder
¼ teaspoon salt
½ cup butter or margarine
1 cup milk
2 eggs
1 teaspoon vanilla
Never-Fail Three-Minute
Frosting (p. 626)
8 ounces ground coconut

1. Preheat oven to 350° F. Grease and flour 2 9-inch layer cake pans. Line bottoms with circles of waxed paper.
2. Into mixing bowl sift together flour, sugar, baking powder and salt.
3. In another mixing bowl beat butter or margarine until creamy and soft. Add flour mixture and ¾ cup of the milk; beat for 2 minutes.
4. Add eggs, vanilla and remaining milk; beat for 1 minute longer. Pour into pans.
5. Bake in preheated oven for 25 to 30 minutes.
6. Remove from pans; cool on wire racks.
7. Cover one layer with Never-Fail Three-Minute Frosting; sprinkle with some of the coconut. Top with other layer. Frost sides and top with remaining frosting; sprinkle with remaining coconut.

Kay Beatty, Woman's Club, Springfield, Pa.

DANISH LAYER CAKE

Makes 4-Layer Cake

¾ cup milk
⅓ cup butter
3 eggs
1½ cups sugar
1½ cups sifted cake flour
1½ teaspoons baking powder
¼ teaspoon salt
1 teaspoon vanilla
Mary's Chocolate Filling (p. 630)
1½ cups chopped nuts

1. Preheat oven to 375° F. Grease and flour 2 8-inch layer cake pans.
2. In saucepan bring milk and butter to boil.
3. Beat eggs until thickened and lemon-colored (use electric beater if possible). Gradually add sugar; beat vigorously for 5 minutes (on high speed).
4. Gradually beat in flour, baking powder and salt (low speed). Gradually add milk mixture, beating constantly; add vanilla. When batter is bubbling and thin, turn into pans.
5. Bake in preheated oven for 25 to 30 minutes.
6. Turn onto wire racks to cool.
7. Split each layer. Fill cake and frost sides and top with Mary's Chocolate Filling. Sprinkle sides with nuts.

Mary Greiner, Woman's Club, Willsboro, N.J.

VANILLA WAFER CRUMB CAKE

Makes 9-Inch Layer

½ cup butter
1 cup sugar
½ teaspoon baking powder
1½ cups vanilla wafer crumbs
3 eggs
1⅓ cups shredded coconut
1 cup chopped nuts

1. Preheat oven to 325° F. Grease and flour 9-inch layer cake pan.
2. Cream butter and sugar well. Stir in baking powder and crumbs.
3. Add eggs, one at a time, beating well after each addition. Stir in coconut and nuts.
4. Turn batter into pan. Bake in preheated oven for 35 to 40 minutes.
5. Turn onto wire rack to cool.

Mrs. Calmer Buen, Study Club, Hatton, N.D.

HOT MILK CAKE

Makes 9-Inch Loaf

2 eggs
1 cup sugar
Pinch of salt
¼ cup butter
½ cup hot milk
1 cup presifted flour
1 teaspoon baking powder
1 teaspoon lemon extract

1. Preheat oven to 350° F. Line 9-inch loaf pan with waxed paper.
2. In mixing bowl beat eggs and sugar until thickened and pale. Stir in salt.

3. Melt butter in milk; stir into egg mixture. Combine flour and baking powder; stir into batter. Stir in lemon extract.
4. Turn batter into pan; bake in preheated oven for 45 to 50 minutes.
5. Turn onto wire rack to cool.

Juna McCreary, Grandview Woman's Club,
Phoenix, Ariz.

ICELANDIC VINARTARTA

Makes 4-Layer Cake

3 cups sugar
1 cup butter or margarine
2 eggs
3 cups presifted flour
1½ teaspoons baking powder
¼ teaspoon ground cardamom
¼ cup milk
1½ pounds prunes, cooked and drained
1 teaspoon vanilla

1. Preheat oven to 375° F. Grease 2 15½ x 10½ x 1-inch jelly roll pans.
2. Cream 1 cup of the sugar and butter or margarine until light and fluffy. Add eggs; beat until blended.
3. Onto piece of waxed paper sift together flour, baking powder and ⅛ teaspoon of the cardamom; add alternately with milk to creamed mixture, beating well after each addition. Spread in pans.
4. Bake in preheated oven for 10 to 15 minutes, or until lightly browned.
5. Turn onto wire racks at once; discard waxed paper. Cool.
6. Meanwhile, prepare Prune Filling: Chop prunes; discard pits. Put in saucepan with remaining sugar and remaining cardamom. Cook over medium heat, stirring occasionally, until sugar dissolves. Remove from heat; stir in vanilla. Cool.
7. Split each layer; reassemble with Prune Filling between.

Mrs. Raymond Josephson, Study Club,
Washburn, N.D.

LAZY DAISY CAKE

Makes 8-Inch Square

3 eggs, lightly beaten
1½ cups granulated sugar
1½ teaspoons vanilla
1½ cups presifted flour
1½ teaspoons baking powder
¾ teaspoon salt
¾ cup milk
5 tablespoons butter
3 tablespoons brown sugar
2 tablespoons cream
½ cup shredded coconut or chopped nuts

1. Preheat oven to 350° F. Grease and flour 8-inch square baking pan.
2. Beat eggs, granulated sugar and vanilla until thickened and pale.
3. Sift together flour, baking powder and salt three times; stir into egg mixture.
4. Heat milk and 2 tablespoons of the butter until very hot; stir into batter.
5. Pour batter into pan; bake in preheated oven for 30 to 40 minutes.

6. Meanwhile, prepare Nut Topping: Combine remaining butter, brown sugar, cream and coconut or nuts.

7. Remove cake from oven; spread with topping. Return to oven for 5 minutes, or until browned.

Bonnie Schnittger, Home and Country Study Club, Fayette, Mo.

MINCEMEAT TEA LOAF

Makes 9-Inch Loaf

2 cups presifted flour
½ teaspoon salt
½ teaspoon baking soda
1 teaspoon baking powder
¼ cup butter or margarine
⅔ cup brown sugar
2 eggs
3 tablespoons sour cream
1 cup mincemeat
½ cup chopped pecans

1. Preheat oven to 350° F. Grease and flour 9-inch loaf pan well.

2. Into mixing bowl sift together flour, salt, baking soda and baking powder.

3. In another mixing bowl cream butter or margarine and sugar until light and fluffy. Add eggs, one at a time, beating well after each addition. Add sour cream; blend until smooth.

4. Pour creamed mixture over dry ingredients; mix until well blended. Stir in mincemeat and pecans; turn into pan. Spread evenly in pan.

5. Bake in preheated oven for 50 to 60 minutes.

6. Cool for 5 minutes; remove from pan; cool on wire rack.

Mrs. Herman Babel, Bellevue Woman's Club, Ingomar, Pa.

EASY PUDDING AND CAKE

Makes 4 Thin 8-Inch Layers

1½ cups presifted flour
½ teaspoon baking powder
¼ teaspoon salt
½ cup butter
¾ cup sugar
1 egg
1 teaspoon vanilla
4-ounce package chocolate pudding
½ cup heavy cream, whipped

1. Preheat oven to 375° F. Grease and flour 4 8-inch layer cake pans. Line bottoms with circles of waxed paper.

2. Onto piece of waxed paper sift together flour, baking powder and salt.

3. In mixing bowl cream butter and sugar until light and fluffy. Add egg and vanilla; beat until smooth. Add flour mixture; beat until smooth.

4. Turn batter into pans; spread evenly.

5. Bake in preheated oven for 8 to 10 minutes, or until light golden. Remove from pans; cool on wire racks.

6. Make pudding according to package directions. Cool.

7. Arrange cake layer on serving dish; spread with one-third of pudding. Repeat,

finishing with cake layer. Frost top with whipped cream; refrigerate until serving time.

Mrs. Bill Mattison, Three Arts Club, Reform, Ala.

RUM CAKE

Makes 9-Inch Ring

1 cup butter or margarine
2½ cups sugar
5 eggs
2 cups presifted flour
3 teaspoons rum extract
½ cup water

1. Preheat oven to 300° F. Grease and flour 9-inch tube pan or fluted ring mold.

2. In mixing bowl cream butter or margarine and 1½ cups of the sugar until light and fluffy. Beat in eggs, one at a time.

3. Gradually beat in flour and 1 teaspoon of the rum extract. Turn into pan or mold.

4. Bake in preheated oven for about 1 hour and 15 minutes.

5. Meanwhile, prepare Rum Syrup: In saucepan combine remaining sugar and water. Bring to boil; boil for 3 minutes. Remove from heat; stir in remaining rum extract.

6. Cool cake for 10 minutes; turn onto serving dish.

7. Spoon Rum Syrup over hot cake.

Mrs. A. T. Cocanougher, Woman's Study Club, Lubbock, Tex.

CALIFORNIA SUNSHINE CAKE

Makes 10-Inch Ring

1 cup cake flour
1 teaspoon salt
6 large eggs, separated
1 cup sugar
2 teaspoons grated lemon rind
1 tablespoon lemon juice
½ teaspoon orange extract

1. Preheat oven to 325° F. Grease and flour 10-inch tube pan.

2. Onto piece of waxed paper sift together flour and salt; repeat three more times.

3. In mixing bowl beat egg whites until foamy. Gradually add ½ cup of the sugar; beat until stiff and glossy.

4. In another mixing bowl beat egg yolks and remaining sugar until thickened and lemon-colored. Stir in remaining ingredients.

5. Spoon egg yolk mixture on egg whites; beat very slowly to blend well. Sift in flour mixture, a little at a time; blend carefully. Turn into pan.

6. Bake in preheated oven for 45 to 50 minutes.

7. Cool for 10 minutes; remove from pan; cool on wire rack.

Elsie P. Martin, Woman's Club, La Crescenta, Calif.

TARTA BABA
Makes 9-Inch Ring

4 eggs, separated
2 cups granulated sugar
½ pound butter
2½ cups presifted flour
2 teaspoons baking powder
1 cup milk
1 teaspoon vanilla
Confectioners' sugar

1. Preheat oven to 350° F.
2. Beat egg whites until stiff but not dry. Set aside.
3. In mixing bowl cream granulated sugar and butter until light and fluffy. Stir in egg yolks.
4. Combine flour and baking powder; stir alternately with milk into creamed mixture. Stir in vanilla. Fold in egg whites.
5. Turn batter into 9-inch tube pan; bake in preheated oven for 1 hour.
6. Cool for 15 minutes; remove from pan; cool on wire rack. Sprinkle with confectioners' sugar.

Mrs. Edward Hitchler, Junior Woman's Club, Elgin, Ill.

WALNUT WONDER CAKE
Makes 13 x 9½-Inch Layer

1 cup butter
1½ cups granulated sugar
2 eggs
1 teaspoon vanilla
2 cups presifted flour
1 teaspoon baking powder
1 teaspoon baking soda
½ teaspoon salt
1 cup sour cream
⅓ cup brown sugar
1 teaspoon cinnamon
1 cup chopped nuts
Dash of powdered ginger

1. Preheat oven to 350° F. Grease and flour 13 x 9½ x 2-inch baking pan.
2. Cream butter and 1 cup of the granulated sugar until light and fluffy. Beat in eggs and vanilla.
3. Sift together flour, baking powder, baking soda and salt; stir alternately with sour cream into egg mixture. Turn half the batter into pan.
4. Combine brown sugar, remaining granulated sugar, cinnamon, nuts and ginger; sprinkle half over batter in pan. Top with remaining batter; sprinkle with remaining nut mixture.
5. Bake in preheated oven for 35 minutes.
6. Cool in pan.

Elaine Besgrove, Home and Country Study Club, Fayette, Mo.

Chocolate Cakes

CHOCOLATE FUDGE CAKE
Makes 13 x 9½-Inch Layer

4 1-ounce squares unsweetened chocolate

½ cup butter or margarine
4 eggs
2 cups sugar
1 teaspoon vanilla
1¾ cups cake flour, sifted
1 teaspoon baking powder
1 cup chopped walnuts
Chocolate frosting

1. Preheat oven to 375° F. Grease and flour 13 x 9½ x 2-inch baking pan. Line bottom with waxed paper.
2. Melt chocolate and butter or margarine in top of double saucepan over hot water. Cool.
3. In mixing bowl beat eggs and sugar until thickened and lemon-colored. Stir in chocolate and vanilla until blended.
4. Add flour and baking powder; mix well. Stir in walnuts. Pour into pan.
5. Bake in preheated oven for 25 to 30 minutes.
6. Cool for 5 minutes; remove from pan; cool on wire rack. Frost with chocolate frosting.

Mrs. Ralph Summey, Jr., Junior Woman's Club, Dallas, N.C.

KATHRYN'S FUDGE CAKE
Makes 3 8-Inch Layers

½ cup plus 1 tablespoon butter
2½ cups sugar
1½ teaspoons vanilla
3 eggs
3 1-ounce squares unsweetened chocolate, melted
3 cups cake flour
1¼ teaspoons baking soda
¾ teaspoon salt
1½ cups ice water
Kathryn's Chocolate Frosting (p. 628)

1. Preheat oven to 350° F. Grease and flour 3 8-inch layer cake pans; line with waxed paper.
2. Cream butter, sugar and vanilla until light and fluffy. Beat in eggs, one at a time. Stir in chocolate.
3. Sift together flour, baking soda and salt; stir alternately with water into egg mixture. Pour into pans.
4. Bake in preheated oven for 30 to 35 minutes.
5. Turn onto wire racks to cool. Fill and frost with Kathryn's Chocolate Frosting.

Mrs. R. D. Bruce, Junior Women, Coos Bay, Ore.

$100 CHOCOLATE CAKE
Makes 2 9-Inch Layers

2 cups cake flour
2 teaspoons baking powder
½ teaspoon salt
½ cup butter
2 cups sugar
2 eggs
4 1-ounce squares unsweetened chocolate, melted
1½ cups milk
1 teaspoon vanilla
1 cup chopped walnuts
Chocolate Nut Frosting (p. 623)

1. Preheat oven to 350° F. Grease and flour 2 9-inch layer cake pans.

2. Onto piece of waxed paper sift together flour, baking powder and salt.

3. In mixing bowl cream butter and sugar until light and fluffy. Beat in eggs, one at a time. Stir in chocolate.

4. Add flour mixture and milk alternately to creamed mixture, beating after each addition. Stir in vanilla and walnuts. Pour into pans.

5. Bake in preheated oven for 30 to 35 minutes.

6. Cool for 10 minutes; remove from pans; cool on wire racks. Fill and frost with Chocolate Nut Frosting.

Mildred Wells, Woman's Social & Benevolent Club, Lyons, Ind.

EGGLESS CHOCOLATE CAKE

Makes 8-Inch Square

½ cup butter
3 1-ounce squares unsweetened chocolate
1 cup granulated sugar
1½ cups sifted cake flour
Pinch of salt
1 teaspoon baking soda
1 cup buttermilk
1 cup sifted confectioners' sugar

1. Preheat oven to 350° F. Grease and flour 8-inch square baking pan.

2. Melt ¼ cup of the butter in top of double saucepan. Add 1½ squares of the chocolate; heat over simmering water, stirring occasionally, until chocolate is melted and mixture is smooth.

3. Remove from heat. Add granulated sugar; stir well.

4. Combine flour, salt and baking soda; stir alternately with buttermilk into chocolate mixture; stirring to blend after each addition.

5. Turn batter into pan; bake in preheated oven for 30 to 35 minutes.

6. Remove from pan; cool on wire rack.

7. Melt remaining butter and remaining chocolate. Remove from heat; stir in confectioners' sugar. Spread on top of cake.

Pat McFadden, Junior Woman's Club, Norfolk, Va.

DOMINICAN CAKE

Makes 2 8-Inch Layers

½ cup butter
4 1-ounce squares unsweetened chocolate
1 cup boiling water
1¼ cups sugar
1½ teaspoons baking soda
½ cup sour milk
2 cups presifted flour
2 eggs
Brown Sugar Frosting (p. 627)

1. Preheat oven to 350° F. Grease and flour 2 8-inch layer cake pans.

2. In mixing bowl combine butter and chocolate; add water; stir until blended. Stir in sugar.

3. Dissolve baking soda in milk; add alternately with flour to chocolate mixture, beating after each addition. Add eggs; beat until smooth.

4. Turn batter into pans; bake in preheated oven for 25 to 30 minutes.

5. Cool for 10 minutes; remove from pans; cool on wire racks. Frost with Brown Sugar Frosting.

Mrs. Carroll E. Miller, Chairman, Public Affairs Department and Crusade for Light Division, General Federation of Women's Clubs, Washington, D.C.

CHOCOLATE BEER CAKE

Makes 2 8-Inch Layers

¾ cup beer
1¾ cups sifted cake flour
1½ teaspoon baking powder
¼ teaspoon baking soda
½ teaspoon salt
½ cup butter
1 cup sugar
2 eggs
2 1-ounce squares unsweetened chocolate, melted
Favorite frosting

1. Pour out beer; let stand to come to room temperature. Preheat oven to 375° F. Grease well and flour 2 8-inch layer cake pans.

2. Onto piece of waxed paper sift together flour, baking powder, baking soda and salt.

3. In mixing bowl cream butter and sugar until light. Beat in eggs, one at a time. Stir in chocolate.

4. Add flour mixture and beer alternately to creamed mixture, beating well after each addition.

5. Pour batter into pans; bake in preheated oven for 25 to 30 minutes.

6. Cool for 5 minutes; remove from pans; cool on wire racks. Frost as desired.

Yvonne Zink, Beverly Hills Junior Woman's Club, Chicago, Ill.

VERY FLUFFY CHOCOLATE CAKE

Makes 2 9-Inch Layers

½ envelope active dry yeast
¼ cup lukewarm water
1 cup shortening
2 cups sugar
3 eggs, separated
3 1-ounce squares unsweetened chocolate, melted
1 cup milk
2¾ cups sifted cake flour
½ teaspoon salt
¾ cup chopped walnuts
½ teaspoon baking soda
3 tablespoons boiling water
1½ teaspoons vanilla
Favorite frosting

1. Day before, in small bowl soften yeast in lukewarm water; let stand for 5 minutes. Stir until dissolved.

2. In mixing bowl cream shortening and sugar until light and fluffy. Add egg yolks; beat well.

3. Stir in and blend yeast, chocolate and milk. Gradually beat in flour and salt until batter is smooth.

4. In another mixing bowl beat egg whites until stiff but not dry; fold with walnuts into flour mixture.

5. Cover. Refrigerate overnight.

6. Next day, let batter come to room temperature.

7. Preheat oven to 350° F. Grease and flour 2 9-inch layer cake pans.

8. Dissolve baking soda in boiling water; stir in vanilla. Stir into batter. Turn into pans.

9. Bake in preheated oven for 35 to 40 minutes.

10. Cool for 10 minutes; remove from pans; cool on wire racks. Fill and frost as desired.

Zoe Billings, Tillicum Club, Boardman, Ore.

STARLIGHT DOUBLE DELIGHT CAKE

Makes 2 9-Inch Layers

    2 3-ounce packages cream cheese
    ¾ cup shortening
    ½ teaspoon vanilla
    ½ teaspoon peppermint extract
    6 cups confectioners' sugar (sift
        if lumpy)
    ¼ cup hot water
    4 1-ounce squares unsweetened
        chocolate, melted
    3 eggs
    2¼ cups sifted cake flour
    1½ teaspoons baking soda
    1 teaspoon salt
    ¾ cup milk

1. Preheat oven to 350° F. Grease and flour 2 9-inch layer cake pans.

2. Blend cheese, ½ cup of the shortening, vanilla and peppermint extract until smooth and fluffy. Gradually beat in 3 cups of the sugar until smooth.

3. In another mixing bowl blend water and chocolate; beat in remaining sugar. Add cheese mixture; beat until smooth.

4. Remove half the chocolate mixture (2 cups); reserve for frosting.

5. Add remaining shortening to remaining chocolate mixture; beat until smooth. Add eggs, one at a time; beating well after each addition.

6. Onto piece of waxed paper sift together flour, baking soda and salt; add alternately with milk to chocolate mixture, beating well after each addition. Turn into pans.

7. Bake in preheated oven for 25 to 30 minutes.

8. Cool for 5 minutes; remove from pans; cool on wire racks. Fill and frost with reserved chocolate mixture.

Mrs. E. L. Hudson, Junior Woman's Club,
South Boston, Va.

EXQUISITE CHOCOLATE MINT SQUARES

Makes 9 3-Inch Squares

    2 1-ounce squares unsweetened
        chocolate

    ½ cup butter
    2 eggs
    1 cup sugar
    ¼ teaspoon peppermint extract
    ½ cup presifted flour
        Dash of salt
    ½ cup chopped nuts
        Chocolate Mint Topping (p. 630)
        Chocolate Glaze (p. 629)

1. Preheat oven to 350° F. Grease and flour 9-inch square baking pan.

2. Melt chocolate and butter in top of double saucepan.

3. In mixing bowl beat eggs until frothy. Stir in sugar, peppermint extract and chocolate.

4. Add flour, salt and nuts; mix well. Pour into pan.

5. Bake in preheated oven for 20 to 25 minutes.

6. Cool for 10 minutes; remove from pan; cool on wire rack. Spread top with Chocolate Mint Topping; refrigerate for 15 minutes. Dribble Chocolate Glaze over topping; tip cake back and forth to cover surface completely.

7. Mark into 3-inch squares; refrigerate for at least 5 minutes.

Mrs. Max Lyons, Jr., Woman's Club,
Higginsville, Mo.

CRAZY CHOCOLATE CAKE

Makes 13 x 9½-Inch Layer

    3 cups sifted cake flour
    2 cups sugar
    6 tablespoons cocoa
    2 teaspoons baking soda
    1 teaspoon salt
    ¾ cup cooking oil
    2 tablespoons vinegar
    2 teaspoons vanilla
    2 cups water
        Sammye's Chocolate Frosting
        (p. 628)

1. Preheat oven to 350° F. Grease and flour 13 x 9½ x 2-inch baking pan.

2. Into mixing bowl sift together flour, sugar, cocoa, baking soda and salt. Add oil, vinegar, vanilla and water; beat until smooth. Turn into pan.

3. Bake in preheated oven for 25 to 30 minutes.

4. Cool for 5 minutes; remove from pan; cool on wire rack. Frost sides and top with Sammye's Chocolate Frosting.

Sammye Baker, Study Club, Wink, Tex.

RED DEVIL'S FOOD

Makes 13 x 9½-Inch Layer

    2¼ cups presifted flour
    3 tablespoons cocoa
    1 teaspoon salt
    2 cups sugar
    ½ cup shortening
    3 eggs
    1 tablespoon baking soda
    ½ cup milk
    1 cup boiling water
        Special Fruit-Nut Frosting (p. 629)
        or Peppermint Frosting (p. 627)

1. Preheat oven to 350° F. Grease and lightly flour only bottom of 13 x 9½ x 2-inch baking pan.
2. Sift together flour, cocoa and salt. Set aside.
3. In mixing bowl gradually add sugar to shortening; cream well. Add eggs, one at a time, beating well after each addition.
4. Combine baking soda and milk; add alternately with flour mixture to creamed mixture, beating well after each addition. Stir in water.
5. Pour batter into pan; bake in preheated oven for 40 to 45 minutes.
6. Turn onto wire rack to cool. Frost with Special Fruit-Nut or Peppermint Frosting.

Martha Moore, North Morris Woman's Club,
Wharton, N.J.

WALNUT-FILLED COCOA CAKE
Makes 3 9-Inch Layers

    3 cups sifted cake flour
    ¼ teaspoon salt
    4 cups sugar
    ¾ cup butter or margarine
    3 eggs
    3 tablespoons cocoa
    ½ cup hot water
    1 teaspoon baking soda
    ½ cup buttermilk
    1 teaspoon vanilla
    1 cup heavy cream
    1 cup chopped black walnuts
    1 apple, peeled and finely chopped
      Mrs. Hood's Chocolate Frosting
      (p. 628)

1. Preheat oven to 375° F. Grease and flour 3 9-inch layer cake pans.
2. Onto piece of waxed paper sift together flour and salt.
3. In mixing bowl cream 2 cups of the sugar and ½ cup of the butter or margarine until light and fluffy. Beat in eggs, one at a time.
4. Dissolve cocoa in water; cool. Dissolve baking soda in buttermilk.
5. Stir cocoa and vanilla into creamed mixture.
6. Add flour mixture and buttermilk alternately, beating well after each addition. Pour into pans.
7. Bake in preheated oven for 25 to 30 minutes.
8. Cool for 10 minutes; remove from pans; cool on wire racks.
9. Meanwhile, prepare Walnut Apple Filling: In saucepan combine remaining sugar, remaining butter or margarine and cream. Cook over low heat, stirring constantly, until sugar is dissolved. Cook without stirring to soft-ball stage (236° F. on candy thermometer). Cool. Stir in walnuts and apple.
10. Spread filling between cake layers. Frost with Mrs. Hood's Chocolate Frosting.

Mrs. A. R. Hood, Delphian Literary Club,
Amory, Miss.

ALL CHOCOLATE CAKE
Makes 2 9-Inch Layers

    3 cups sifted cake flour
    1 teaspoon salt
    ½ cup cocoa
    ¾ cup hot water
    ½ cup shortening
    2 cups sugar
    1 teaspoon vanilla
    2 eggs
    1 teaspoon baking soda
    1 cup sour milk
      Chocolate frosting

1. Preheat oven to 350° F. Grease and flour 2 9-inch layer cake pans.
2. Onto piece of waxed paper sift together flour and salt.
3. In saucepan blend cocoa and water; cook over medium heat for 5 minutes, stirring occasionally. Cool.
4. In mixing bowl cream shortening and sugar until light and fluffy. Add vanilla; blend well. Add eggs, one at a time, beating well after each addition. Stir in cocoa; blend until smooth.
5. Stir baking soda into milk; add alternately with flour mixture to creamed mixture, beating well after each addition. Pour into pans.
6. Bake in preheated oven for 25 to 30 minutes.
7. Cool for 5 minutes; remove from pans; cool on wire racks. Fill and frost with chocolate frosting.

Mrs. H. M. Berry, Research Club, Topeka, Kans.

FRENCH CHOCOLATE CAKE
Makes 2 8-Inch Layers

    ½ cup cocoa
    ¾ cup boiling water
    ½ cup butter
    2 cups sugar
    ½ teaspoon baking soda
    ½ cup sour cream
    2½ cups sifted cake flour
    3 egg whites, stiffly beaten
    1 teaspoon vanilla
      French Cocoa Filling and
      Frosting (p. 629)

1. Preheat oven to 350° F. Grease and flour 2 8-inch layer cake pans.
2. Add cocoa to water; stir until smooth. Cool.
3. In mixing bowl cream butter and sugar. Stir in cocoa.
4. Combine baking soda and sour cream; stir alternately with flour into chocolate mixture. Fold in egg whites and vanilla.
5. Turn batter into pans; bake in preheated oven for 25 to 30 minutes.
6. Turn onto wire racks to cool. Fill and frost with French Cocoa Filling and Frosting.

Mrs. J. D. McCullough, Jr., Junior Woman's Club,
Smyrna, Ga.

CHOCOLATE MACAROON CAKE

Makes 10-Inch Ring

1 egg white
2 teaspoons vanilla
2¼ cups sugar
2 cups finely flaked coconut
2 cups plus 1 tablespoon cake
　flour, sifted
½ cup cocoa
¾ cup hot black coffee
3 eggs, separated
1 teaspoon baking soda
½ cup sour cream
½ cup shortening
1 teaspoon salt
Chocolate Fudge Icing (p. 628)

1. Preheat oven to 350° F. Grease 10-inch tube pan.
2. Beat 1 egg white and 1 teaspoon of the vanilla until foamy. Gradually beat in ½ cup of the sugar; beat until stiff and glossy. Stir in coconut and 1 tablespoon of the flour; set coconut meringue aside.
3. Dissolve cocoa in coffee; set aside.
4. Beat 3 egg whites until foamy. Gradually beat in ½ cup of the sugar; beat until stiff peaks form; set meringue aside.
5. Dissolve baking soda in sour cream; set aside.
6. In mixing bowl combine shortening, salt, remaining sugar, egg yolks, remaining vanilla and half the cocoa mixture. Beat for about 4 minutes.
7. Add remaining flour, sour cream mixture and remaining cocoa mixture; blend well. Fold in meringue.
8. Pour one-third of batter into pan. Spread with half the coconut meringue. Cover with half the remaining batter; spread with remaining coconut mixture. Top with remaining batter.
9. Bake in preheated oven for 55 to 65 minutes.
10. Cool in pan; remove from pan; frost sides and top with Chocolate Fudge Icing.

Mrs. A. M. Furr, Castalian Club, Tupelo, Miss.

BLIND DATE CAKE

Makes 9-Inch Square

1 cup finely cut dates
1¼ cups boiling water
1 teaspoon baking soda
½ cup shortening
1½ cups sugar
2 eggs, lightly beaten
1 teaspoon vanilla
1¼ cups presifted flour
1 tablespoon cocoa
1 teaspoon salt
1 cup semi-sweet chocolate pieces
½ cup chopped walnuts

1. Preheat oven to 325° F. Grease and flour 9-inch square baking pan.
2. Prepare date filling: In small saucepan mix dates and water. Bring to boil; then simmer for 5 minutes. Cool; stir in baking soda.
3. In mixing bowl cream shortening, 1 cup of the sugar, eggs and vanilla until blended and smooth.

4. Onto piece of waxed paper sift together flour, cocoa and salt; add with dates to creamed mixture; beat until blended. Turn into pan.
5. Prepare Chocolate Nut Topping: Mix remaining sugar, chocolate pieces and walnuts. Sprinkle on batter.
6. Bake in preheated oven for 30 to 35 minutes. Cool cake in pan.

*Pauline Moldrup, Athenaeum Club,
Sapulpa, Okla.*

MARBLE CAKE

Makes 13 x 9½-Inch Layer

2 cups plus 2 tablespoons presifted
　flour
1½ cups sugar
3½ teaspoons baking powder
1 teaspoon salt
½ cup shortening
1 cup milk
1 teaspoon vanilla
½ to ⅔ cup egg whites
1-ounce square unsweetened
　chocolate, melted
¼ teaspoon baking soda
2 tablespoons warm water
¼ teaspoon red food coloring
Favorite frosting

1. Preheat oven to 350° F. Grease and flour 13 x 9½ x 2-inch baking pan.
2. Into mixing bowl sift together flour, sugar, baking powder and salt. Add shortening, milk and vanilla; beat for 2 minutes.
3. Add egg whites; beat for 2 minutes longer.
4. Pour two-thirds of batter into pan. Add remaining ingredients to remaining batter; mix well. Pour chocolate batter here and there over white batter. Cut through batter several times with knife.
5. Bake in preheated oven for 25 to 30 minutes.
6. Turn onto wire rack to cool. Frost with favorite frosting.

Betty Kane, Women's Club, Milton Junction, Wis.

Butterscotch and Caramel Cakes

BUTTERSCOTCH CAKE

Makes 13 x 9½-Inch Layer

2¼ cups sifted cake flour
2½ teaspoons baking powder
1 teaspoon salt
1½ cups brown sugar
½ cup shortening
1 cup milk
1 teaspoon vanilla
2 eggs
Favorite frosting

1. Preheat oven to 350° F. Grease and flour 13 x 9½ x 2-inch baking pan.
2. Into mixing bowl sift together flour, baking powder and salt. Add sugar, shortening, ⅔ cup of the milk and vanilla; beat

vigorously by hand or on medium speed of electric mixer for 2 minutes. Add remaining milk and eggs; beat for 2 minutes longer. Turn into pan.

3. Bake in preheated oven for 25 to 30 minutes.

4. Cool for 5 minutes; remove from pan; cool on wire rack. Frost as desired.

Ramona Weenink, Junior Woman's Club,
Coolidge, Ariz.

SOUTHERN CARAMEL CAKE

Makes 13 x 9½-Inch Layer

½ cup brown sugar
¼ cup hot water
1½ cups granulated sugar
⅔ cup butter
3 eggs, separated
3 cups sifted cake flour
2 teaspoons baking powder
¼ teaspoon salt
1 cup cold water
1½ teaspoons vanilla
Caramel Sauce De Luxe (p. 700)

1. Preheat oven to 350° F. Grease and flour 13 x 9½ x 2-inch baking pan.

2. Cook brown sugar in small saucepan over low heat until sugar is melted and turns dark brown. Add hot water; simmer until syrupy. Cool.

3. In mixing bowl cream granulated sugar and butter until light and fluffy. Add egg yolks; beat well. Blend in caramel syrup.

4. Onto piece of waxed paper sift together flour, baking powder and salt; repeat four more times; add alternately with cold water to creamed mixture, beating well after each addition.

5. In another mixing bowl beat egg whites until stiff but not dry; fold with vanilla into batter.

6. Turn batter into pan; bake in preheated oven for 25 to 30 minutes. Cool; cut into squares; serve with Caramel Sauce De Luxe.

Mrs. Velton Williams, Study Club, Farber, Mo.

LEATHER CAKE

Makes 3 8-Inch Layers

The name refers to the color of the cake.

1 cup brown sugar
1¼ cups boiling water
½ cup butter
2½ cups granulated sugar
1 cup warm water
2½ cups presifted flour
2 egg yolks
1½ teaspoons vanilla
2 teaspoons baking powder
4 egg whites

1. In heavy saucepan heat brown sugar, stirring until melted. Cook until syrup smokes. Add 1 cup of the boiling water; cook, stirring occasionally, until syrup spins a thread. Set aside.

2. Preheat oven to 350° F. Grease and flour 3 8-inch layer cake pans.

3. In mixing bowl cream butter and 1½ cups of the granulated sugar until smooth. Add warm water, 2 cups of the flour and egg yolks. Beat vigorously by hand for 5 minutes or one medium speed of mixer for 2 minutes.

4. Stir in 3 tablespoons of brown sugar syrup, 1 teaspoon of the vanilla, baking powder and the remaining flour. Beat 3 of the egg whites stiffly. Fold into batter.

5. Turn batter into pans; bake in preheated oven for 25 to 30 minutes. Turn onto wire racks to cool.

6. Meanwhile, prepare **Brown Sugar Meringue Frosting:** In saucepan combine the remaining granulated sugar and remaining boiling water. Bring to boil; cook until syrup spins a thread. Beat remaining egg white stiffly; gradually pour into syrup, beating constantly until thickened and cool. Stir in 2 tablespoons of brown sugar syrup and remaining vanilla.

7. Fill layers; frost sides and top.

Sara Thompson, Pineville Junior Woman's Club,
Miracle, Ky.

MARDI GRAS PARTY CAKE

Makes 2 9-Inch Layers

2¼ cups presifted flour
1 teaspoon salt
1 teaspoon baking soda
½ teaspoon baking powder
⅔ cup butterscotch pieces
¼ cup water
½ cup shortening
1¼ cups sugar
3 eggs
1 cup buttermilk
Butterscotch Filling (p. 630)
Seafoam Frosting (p. 627)

1. Preheat oven to 350° F. Grease and flour 2 9-inch layer cake pans.

2. Onto piece of waxed paper sift together flour, salt, baking soda and baking powder.

3. In top of double saucepan melt butterscotch and water; cool.

4. In mixing bowl cream shortening and sugar until light and fluffy. Add eggs, one at a time, beating well after each addition. Add butterscotch; beat until smooth.

5. Add flour mixture and buttermilk alternately, beating well after each addition. Turn into pans.

6. Bake in preheated oven for 25 to 30 minutes.

7. Cool for 5 minutes; remove from pans; cool on wire racks.

8. Split layers; sandwich 4 layers together with Butterscotch Filling. Frost sides and top with Seafoam Frosting.

Mrs. Julian W. Walton, Kentuck Woman's Club,
Ringgold, Va.

Fruit-Flavored Cakes

APPLE CAKE
Makes 13 x 9½-Inch Layer

3 cups presifted flour
1 teaspoon ground cloves
1 teaspoon cinnamon
1 teaspoon allspice
1 teaspoon baking soda
1 teaspoon baking powder
2 cups sugar
½ cup shortening
2 eggs
½ cup water
2 large tart apples, peeled and
    finely chopped
½ cup chopped pecans
½ cup seedless raisins
Whipped cream

1. Preheat oven to 350° F. Grease and flour 13 x 9½ x 2-inch baking pan.
2. Onto piece of waxed paper sift together flour, spices, baking soda and baking powder.
3. In mixing bowl cream sugar and shortening until light and fluffy. Add eggs; beat until blended.
4. Add flour mixture and water alternately to creamed mixture, beating well after each addition. Stir in apples, pecans and raisins; mix well. Pour into pan.
5. Bake in preheated oven for 40 to 45 minutes. Serve warm and topped with whipped cream.

Lillian Kraut, Woman's Club, Batchtown, Ill.

QUICKIE APPLE CAKE
Makes 9-Inch Square

1-pound can apple pie filling
1-pound 2½-ounce package white
    cake mix
½ cup melted butter or margarine
Whipped cream or ice cream

1. Preheat oven to 350° F. Grease and flour 9-inch square baking pan.
2. Arrange pie filling in pan; sprinkle with cake mix. Pour butter or margarine over top, making sure to cover entire surface.
3. Bake in preheated oven for 30 minutes. Cool for 10 minutes; cut into squares; serve with whipped cream or ice cream.

Study Club, Bay Minette, Ala.

APPLESAUCE CAKE
Makes 13 x 9½-Inch Layer

2⅔ cups presifted flour
2 cups sugar
¼ teaspoon baking powder
1½ teaspoons baking soda
1½ teaspoons salt
¾ teaspoon cinnamon
½ teaspoon ground cloves
½ teaspoon allspice
½ cup soft shortening
½ cup water
1½ cups unsweetened applesauce
1 large egg

1. Preheat oven to 350° F. Grease and flour 13 x 9½ x 2-inch baking pan.
2. Into mixing bowl sift together dry ingredients. Add shortening and water; beat for 2 minutes. Add applesauce and egg; beat for 2 minutes longer.
3. Turn batter into pan; bake in preheated oven for 25 to 30 minutes. Turn onto wire rack to cool.

Mrs. John Wells, Young Adults' Study Club,
Slater, Mo.

BANANA CAKE
Makes 3 9-Inch Layers

3½ cups sifted cake flour
¾ teaspoon salt
¾ teaspoon baking powder
¾ cup shortening
2¼ cups sugar
3 eggs, lightly beaten
1½ cups mashed ripe bananas
1½ teaspoons vanilla
1½ teaspoons baking soda
½ cup buttermilk
1 cup chopped walnuts
Banana Cream Cheese Filling
    (p. 624)

1. Preheat oven to 350° F. Grease and flour 3 9-inch layer cake pans.
2. Onto piece of waxed paper sift together flour, salt and baking powder.
3. In mixing bowl cream shortening and sugar until light and fluffy. Stir in eggs, bananas and vanilla.
4. Dissolve baking soda in buttermilk; add alternately with flour mixture to creamed mixture, beating well after each addition. Stir in walnuts; turn into pans.
5. Bake in preheated oven for 25 to 30 minutes.
6. Cool for 5 minutes; remove from pans; cool on wire racks. Spread Banana Cheese Filling between layers and on top.

Woman's Club, Evergreen, Ala.

CHERRY MERINGUE CAKE
Makes 8-Inch Square

2 cups canned sour cherries, drained
1 cup sugar
2 tablespoons flour
Grated rind and juice of ½ orange
1 cup cake flour
1 teaspoon baking powder
¼ teaspoon salt
2 eggs, separated
1 tablespoon melted butter
½ cup milk

1. Preheat oven to 425° F. Grease 8-inch square baking pan well.
2. Arrange cherries in pan. Sprinkle ¼ cup of the sugar, 2 tablespoons flour and orange rind and juice over cherries.
3. Into mixing bowl sift together ½ cup of the sugar, cake flour, baking powder and salt. Add egg yolks, butter and milk; beat until smooth; pour over cherries.
4. Bake in preheated oven for 25 to 30 minutes.

5. Meanwhile, prepare meringue: Beat egg whites until soft peaks form; gradually add remaining sugar; beat until stiff and glossy.
6. Invert cake onto wire rack. Cover top with meringue. Turn temperature to 325° F.
7. Bake cake in oven for 12 minutes, or until meringue is golden.

Mrs. W. H. Chamberlain, Wednesday Study Club, Racine, Minn.

DATE NUT CAKE
Makes 9-Inch Square
1 cup presifted flour
1½ teaspoons baking powder
½ teaspoon salt
1 cup sugar
2 cups coarsely chopped pecans
3 8-ounce packages dates, chopped
4 eggs, separated
1 teaspoon vanilla

1. Preheat oven to 350° F. Grease 9-inch square baking pan; line bottom with waxed paper.
2. Into mixing bowl sift together flour, baking powder, salt and sugar. Stir in pecans and dates.
3. In small bowl beat egg yolks and vanilla until light.
4. In another mixing bowl beat egg whites until stiff but not dry; pour in egg yolk mixture; fold in. Add flour mixture; fold in. Turn into pan.
5. Bake in preheated oven for 40 to 45 minutes. Cool for 10 minutes; remove from pan; cool on wire rack.

Mrs. Edna Thomason, Cultural Club, Alto, La.

QUEEN ELIZABETH CAKE
Makes 9-Inch Square
1 cup chopped dates
1 teaspoon baking soda
1 cup boiling water
1 cup granulated sugar
⅓ cup butter or margarine
1 egg
1½ cups presifted flour
1 teaspoon baking powder
¼ teaspoon salt
1 cup chopped walnuts
⅓ cup brown sugar
⅓ cup milk

1. Preheat oven to 350° F. Grease and flour 9-inch square baking pan.
2. In small bowl combine dates and baking soda; cover with water.
3. In mixing bowl cream granulated sugar and half the butter or margarine. Add egg; beat well.
4. Beat in flour, baking powder, salt and ½ cup of the walnuts. Add date mixture; beat until well blended.
5. Turn batter into pan; bake in preheated oven for 30 to 40 minutes. Cool for 5 minutes; remove from pan; cool on wire rack.
6. Meanwhile, prepare Brown Sugar Topping: In small saucepan combine remaining butter or margarine, brown sugar

and milk. Bring to boil, stirring. Boil for 3 minutes. Spread on top of cake. Sprinkle with remaining walnuts.

Delphian Literary Club, Amory, Miss.

FIG CAKE WITH LEMON ORANGE GLAZE
Makes 13 x 9½-Inch Layer
3 eggs
2 cups sugar
1 cup cooking oil
½ cup milk
1 teaspoon baking soda
1 teaspoon cinnamon
1 teaspoon nutmeg
1 teaspoon vinegar
2 cups presifted flour
1 cup chopped pecans
1 cup seedless raisins
1 cup mashed canned figs or fig preserves
¼ cup lemon juice
1 teaspoon grated lemon rind
1 teaspoon grated orange rind

1. Preheat oven to 350° F. Grease and flour 13 x 9½ x 2-inch baking pan.
2. In large mixing bowl combine eggs, 1 cup of the sugar, oil, milk, baking soda, cinnamon, nutmeg and vinegar; mix well.
3. In another bowl mix flour, pecans and raisins; add to egg mixture; mix well. Stir in figs. Pour into pan.
4. Bake in preheated oven for about 1 hour.
5. Meanwhile, prepare Lemon Orange Glaze: In saucepan combine remaining sugar, lemon juice and rind and orange rind. Bring to boil; boil for 5 minutes.
6. Spread glaze on warm cake.

Sis Chaillot, Junior Solitic Club, Crowley, La.

FRUIT COCKTAIL CAKE
Makes 13 x 9½-Inch Layer
2 cups presifted flour
2 cups granulated sugar
2 teaspoons baking soda
½ teaspoon salt
Dash of cinnamon
1-pound 13-ounce can fruit cocktail, undrained
2 eggs, lightly beaten
1 cup brown sugar
1 cup chopped pecans

1. Preheat oven to 300° F. Grease and flour 13 x 9½ x 2-inch baking pan.
2. Into mixing bowl sift together flour, granulated sugar, baking soda, salt and cinnamon. Add fruit cocktail and eggs; mix to blend.
3. Pour batter into pan; sprinkle with brown sugar and nuts.
4. Bake in preheated oven for about 1 hour. Cool for 10 minutes; remove from pan; cool on wire rack.

Mrs. Gerald F. Mabry, President, Polk County Federation of Women's Clubs, Fla.

LEMON LOAF CAKE

Makes 10-Inch Loaf

1½ cups presifted flour
1 teaspoon baking powder
1 teaspoon salt
1¾ cups sugar
½ cup butter
2 eggs
½ cup milk
Grated rind of 1 lemon
½ cup chopped walnuts
3 tablespoons lemon juice

1. Preheat oven to 350° F. Grease 10-inch loaf pan; line with waxed paper.
2. Onto piece of waxed paper sift together flour, baking powder and salt.
3. In mixing bowl cream 1 cup of the sugar and butter until light and fluffy. Add eggs, one at a time, beating well after each addition.
4. Add milk and flour mixture alternately, beating after each addition. Stir in lemon rind and walnuts; turn into pan.
5. Bake in preheated oven for about 1 hour.
6. Meanwhile, prepare Lemon Glaze: In small saucepan blend remaining sugar and lemon juice; cook over low heat, stirring frequently, until melted.
7. Remove cake from pan as soon as it comes from oven. Place on wire rack; pour glaze over it.

Gladys Hogan, Beta Study Club, Shreveport, La.

QUICK LEMON CAKE

Makes 13 x 9½-Inch Layer

1-pound 2½-ounce package yellow
    cake mix
3-ounce package lemon gelatin
4 eggs, lightly beaten
¾ cup cooking oil
¾ cup water
½ cup lemon juice
2 cups confectioners' sugar
    Whipped cream

1. Preheat oven to 350° F. Grease and flour 13 x 9½ x 2-inch baking pan.
2. Combine cake mix and gelatin. Add eggs, oil and water; mix well.
3. Pour batter into pan; bake in preheated oven for about 40 minutes. Remove from oven; let stand for 20 minutes.
4. Beat lemon juice and sugar until well blended. Poke holes throughout cake with fork; pour the lemon mixture over cake.
5. Serve topped with whipped cream.

Mrs. Richard Beatty, Junior Woman's Club, Lombard, Ill.

LEMON TREASURE CAKE

Makes 10-Inch Ring

6 eggs
2⅔ cups sugar
2¼ teaspoons salt
¼ cup cornstarch
1 cup water
4 teaspoons grated lemon rind
3 tablespoons lemon juice
2 tablespoons butter

3 to 4 drops yellow food coloring
½ teaspoon baking soda
3 cups presifted flour
1 cup shortening
1 cup buttermilk
¾ cup graham cracker crumbs

1. Prepare Lemon Custard: Beat 1 of the eggs lightly. In saucepan combine ⅔ cup of the sugar, ¼ teaspoon of the salt and cornstarch. Stir in water, 1 teaspoon of the lemon rind, lemon juice and beaten egg. Cook over moderate heat, stirring constantly, until thickened. Stir in butter and food coloring. Cool. Reserve one-fourth for frosting.
2. Sift together 1 teaspoon of the salt, baking soda and flour. Set aside.
3. Preheat oven to 375° F. Grease and flour 10-inch tube pan.
4. In mixing bowl cream shortening and remaining sugar. Stir in remaining lemon rind. Add remaining eggs, one at a time, beating well after each addition.
5. Stir in flour mixture alternately with buttermilk, blending well after each addition (at low speed if using electric mixer).
6. Turn two-thirds of batter (about 4½ cups) into pan. Cover with three-fourths of the custard. Add remaining batter. Sprinkle with all but 2 tablespoons of crumbs.
7. Bake in preheated oven for 55 to 60 minutes.
8. Remove from pan; cool on wire rack. Frost top with reserved custard; sprinkle with remaining crumbs. Store in refrigerator.

Mrs. William E. La Prade, Jr.,
Junior Woman's Club, Bristol, Tenn.-Va.

FRESH ORANGE LAYER CAKE

Makes 2 9-Inch Layers

2¼ cups sifted cake flour
1½ cups sugar
2 teaspoons baking powder
¼ teaspoon baking soda
    Juice of 1 orange
    Milk
½ cup shortening
    Rind of 1 orange, grated
2 eggs
    Creamy Nut Filling and
    Frosting (p. 626)

1. Preheat oven to 350° F. Grease and flour 2 9-inch layer cake pans.
2. Into mixing bowl sift together flour, sugar, baking powder and baking soda.
3. Put orange juice in measuring cup; add milk to total 1 cup. Add with shortening and orange rind to flour mixture. Beat for 2 minutes (on medium speed with electric beater). Add eggs; beat for 2 minutes longer. Turn into pans.
4. Bake in preheated oven for 25 to 30 minutes.
5. Cool for 10 minutes; remove from pans; cool on wire racks. Fill and frost with Creamy Nut Filling and Frosting.

Mrs. W. C. Cornelius, Woman's Colonial Club,
South Charleston, W. Va.

GRAND MARNIER CAKE

Makes 9-Inch Ring

1 cup softened butter
1½ cups sugar
3 eggs, separated
2 cups presifted flour
1 teaspoon baking powder
1 teaspoon baking soda
1 cup sour cream
    Rind of 1 orange, grated
½ cup chopped nuts
¼ cup orange juice
⅓ cup Grand Marnier
2 tablespoons slivered blanched
    almonds

1. Preheat oven to 350° F. Grease 9-inch tube pan.
2. Cream butter and 1 cup of the sugar until light and fluffy. Beat in egg yolks, one at a time.
3. Combine flour, baking powder and baking soda; add alternately with sour cream to egg mixture, mixing well after each addition. Stir in orange rind and chopped nuts.
4. Beat egg whites until stiff but not dry; fold into batter.
5. Turn batter into pan; bake in preheated oven for 45 to 50 minutes.
6. Combine remaining sugar, orange juice and Grand Marnier; spoon over hot cake in pan; decorate with almonds. Cool before removing from pan.

Woman's Club, Mamaroneck, N.Y.

"I SMELL CHRISTMAS" CAKE

Serves 6 to 8

1 medium orange
1½ cups sugar
¾ cup walnuts
1 cup pitted dates
2 cups presifted flour
1 teaspoon baking soda
1 teaspoon salt
½ cup shortening
2 eggs
¾ cup buttermilk
    Candied cherries (optional)

1. Day before, preheat oven to 300° F. Grease 2-quart casserole.
2. Squeeze juice from orange; mix with ½ cup of the sugar; set aside.
3. Remove membrane and white pulp from orange rind; put with walnuts and dates through medium blade of meat grinder.
4. Onto piece of waxed paper sift together flour, baking soda and salt.
5. In mixing bowl cream remaining sugar and shortening until light and fluffy. Add eggs, one at a time, beating well after each addition.
6. Add buttermilk alternately with flour mixture, beating well after each addition. Stir in fruit mixture; blend well. Turn into casserole.
7. Bake in preheated oven for about 1½ hours.

8. As soon as cake comes from oven, pour reserved orange juice over it. Cool overnight in casserole before cutting.
9. Next day, decorate top with cherries, if desired.

Mrs. L. Schlosser, Woman's Club, Palisade, N.J.

QUICK ORANGE CAKE

Makes 10-Inch Ring

1-pound 2½-ounce package
    white cake mix
3-ounce package orange gelatin
⅔ cup cooking oil
⅔ cup water
4 eggs
    Confectioners' sugar or favorite
    frosting

1. Preheat oven to 325° F. Grease and flour 10-inch tube pan.
2. Combine cake mix and gelatin in mixing bowl. Add oil and water; beat for 2 minutes (medium speed with electric beater).
3. Add eggs, one at a time, beating well after each addition. Turn into pan.
4. Bake in preheated oven for about 1 hour.
5. Cool for 5 minutes; remove from pan; cool on wire rack. Sprinkle with confectioners' sugar, or frost with favorite frosting, as desired.

*Mrs. Lena Armour, Literary and Civic Club,
Houlka, Miss.*

PINEAPPLE PARFAIT CAKE

Makes 2 9-Inch Layers

½ cup shortening
¾ teaspoon salt
1 teaspoon grated lemon rind
1 egg yolk
1½ cups sugar
    3 cups sifted cake flour
    3 teaspoons baking powder
¾ cup pineapple juice
¼ cup water
4 egg whites
    Pineapple Parfait Frosting (p. 627)

1. Preheat oven to 350° F. Grease and flour 2 9-inch layer cake pans.
2. In mixing bowl beat shortening, salt, lemon rind and egg yolk until smooth. Add sugar; beat until light and fluffy.
3. Onto piece of waxed paper sift together flour and baking powder; add alternately with pineapple juice and water to shortening mixture, beating well after each addition.
4. In another mixing bowl beat egg whites until stiff but not dry; fold into batter; turn into pans.
5. Bake in preheated oven for 25 to 30 minutes.
6. Cool for 10 minutes; remove from pans; cool on wire racks. Fill and frost with Pineapple Parfait Frosting.

Pearl Henry, Women's Club, Pawpaw, Ill.

QUICK PINEAPPLE CAKE
Makes 13 x 9½-Inch Layer
1-pound 13-ounce can crushed
    pineapple
1-pound 2½-ounce package yellow
    cake mix
1 cup butter or margarine, melted
1 cup chopped pecans

1. Preheat oven to 400° F.
2. Empty can of crushed pineapple into
13 x 9½ x 2-inch baking pan. Sprinkle with
cake mix. Pour butter or margarine over
cake mix; sprinkle with pecans.
3. Bake in preheated oven for 25 to 30
minutes. Serve warm.

Lucille de Villiers, Athenia Study Club,
Tuscaloosa, Ala.

PRUNE CAKE
Makes 2 8-Inch Layers
1½ cups sugar
3 tablespoons melted butter or
    margarine
2 eggs
2 cups sifted cake flour
1 teaspoon baking soda
1 teaspoon ground cloves
2 teaspoons cinnamon
½ teaspoon salt
2 cups mashed prunes
    Whipped cream

1. Preheat oven to 350° F. Grease well
and flour 2 8-inch layer cake pans. Line
bottoms with circles of waxed paper.
2. In mixing bowl beat sugar and butter
or margarine until fluffy. Add eggs; beat
well.
3. Onto piece of waxed paper sift together flour, baking soda, cloves, cinnamon
and salt; add to creamed mixture; beat
until smooth. Stir in prunes. Turn into
pans.
4. Bake in preheated oven for 35 to 40
minutes. Cool on wire rack for 10 minutes;
remove from pans to finish cooling.
5. Fill and frost layer with whipped
cream.

Mrs. Marshall E. Jones, Woman's 20th
Century Club, St. Cloud, Minn.

SUGAR PLUM CAKE
Makes 13 x 9½-Inch Layer
3 eggs
2½ cups sugar
1 cup cooking oil
2 cups presifted flour
1½ cups buttermilk
1 cup cooked prunes or chopped
    dates
1 cup chopped pecans
1½ teaspoons baking soda
½ teaspoon salt
2 teaspoons vanilla
1 teaspoon cinnamon
1 teaspoon nutmeg
¼ cup margarine
1 tablespoon light corn syrup

1. Preheat oven to 325° F. Grease and
flour 13 x 9½ x 2-inch baking pan.

2. In large mixing bowl combine eggs,
1½ cups of the sugar and oil. Stir in flour,
1 cup of the buttermilk, prunes or dates,
pecans, 1 teaspoon of the baking soda, salt,
1 teaspoon of the vanilla, cinnamon and
nutmeg.
3. Turn batter into pan; bake in preheated oven for 1 hour.
4. Meanwhile, prepare Buttermilk
Glaze: In saucepan combine remaining
sugar, remaining buttermilk, margarine,
remaining baking soda, corn syrup and remaining vanilla. Bring to boil; and cook
to soft-ball stage (236° F. on candy thermometer).
5. Turn cake onto wire rack. While hot,
make holes in cake with knife point; pour
glaze over it.

Mrs. J. H. Robertson, Present Day Study Club,
4th District, Northport, Ala.

FRESH RHUBARB CAKE
Makes 11 x 7-Inch Layer
½ cup shortening
1½ cups brown sugar
1 egg
2 cups presifted flour
1 teaspoon baking soda
1 cup sour milk or buttermilk
1 teaspoon vanilla
2 cups chopped rhubarb

1. Preheat oven to 350° F. Grease and
flour 11 x 7 x 1½-inch baking pan.
2. In mixing bowl cream shortening and
sugar. Beat in egg.
3. Sift together flour and baking soda;
stir alternately with milk or buttermilk into
egg mixture. Stir in vanilla and rhubarb.
4. Turn batter into pan; bake in preheated oven for 45 to 50 minutes. Turn
onto wire rack to cool.

Mrs. C. P. Johnson, Study Club, Hatton, N.D.

STRAWBERRY CAKE DELICIOUS
Makes 3 9-Inch Layers
1-pound 2½-ounce package
    white cake mix
½ cup cooking oil
4 eggs
3-ounce package strawberry gelatin
3 tablespoons flour
10-ounce package frozen strawberries,
    defrosted
    Strawberry Frosting (p. 625)

1. Preheat oven to 350° F. Grease and
flour 3 9-inch layer cake pans.
2. Put cake mix, oil and eggs in mixing
bowl; beat for 2 minutes (on medium
speed with electric beater).
3. Combine gelatin and flour; set aside.
4. Drain strawberries well; reserve ½
cup syrup.
5. Add gelatin mixture, strawberries and
reserved syrup to batter in bowl; beat for 1
minute. Turn into pans.
6. Bake in preheated oven for 25 to 30
minutes.

7. Cool for 5 minutes; remove from pans; cool on wire racks. Fill and frost with Strawberry Frosting.

Mrs. Al Fortman, Junior Women's Club,
Bismarck, N.D.

Spice Cakes

CARROT CAKE

Makes 13 x 9½-Inch Layer

2 cups sugar
4 eggs
1⅓ cups cooking oil
2 cups presifted flour
2 teaspoons baking soda
2 teaspoons baking powder
2 teaspoons cinnamon
4 cups grated carrots
¾ cup broken nuts
Cream Cheese Frosting (p. 624)

1. Preheat oven to 350° F. Grease and flour 13 x 9½ x 2-inch baking pan.
2. Beat sugar and eggs until thickened and pale. Stir in oil.
3. Sift together flour, baking soda, baking powder and cinnamon; stir into egg mixture. Fold in carrots and nuts.
4. Spoon batter into pan; bake in preheated oven for 35 to 40 minutes.
5. Turn onto cake rack to cool. Frost with Cream Cheese Frosting.

Mrs. Davis Hoggard,
Home and Country Study Club, Fayette, Mo.

CROFTS CAKE

Makes 2 9-Inch Loaves

1 cup butter
1 cup sugar
1 cup molasses
3 eggs, lightly beaten
3½ cups presifted flour
1 teaspoon baking soda
1 teaspoon ground cloves
1 teaspoon cinnamon
1 cup sour milk
2 cups seedless raisins
¼ cup chopped citron

1. Preheat oven to 350° F. Grease and flour 2 9-inch loaf pans.
2. In mixing bowl beat butter and sugar until fluffy. Beat in molasses and eggs.
3. Sift together flour, baking soda, cloves and cinnamon; add alternately with milk to butter mixture, blending well after each addition. Fold in raisins and citron.
4. Turn batter into pans; bake in preheated oven for about 1 hour.

Mrs. La Fell Dickinson, Honorary President,
General Federation of Women's Clubs,
West Hartford, Conn.

EGGLESS, MILKLESS AND BUTTERLESS RAISIN SPICE CAKE

Makes 2 9-Inch Layers

2 cups brown sugar
¼ cup shortening
2 cups hot water
12 ounces seedless raisins, chopped
2 teaspoons cinnamon
2 teaspoons ground cloves
2 teaspoons baking soda
1 tablespoon lukewarm water
3 cups presifted flour
Mrs. Sharp's Caramel Icing (p. 628)

1. Preheat oven to 300° F. Grease and flour 2 9-inch layer cake pans.
2. In saucepan combine sugar, shortening, hot water, raisins, cinnamon and cloves. Bring to boil; boil for 5 minutes, stirring occasionally. Cool.
3. Dissolve baking soda in lukewarm water; stir into mixture in saucepan; turn into mixing bowl. Gradually add flour, beating well after each addition.
4. Turn batter into pans; bake in preheated oven for about 45 minutes.
5. Cool for 10 minutes; remove from pans; cool on wire racks. Fill and frost with Mrs. Sharp's Caramel Icing.

Mrs. J. Robert Sharp, Home Fire-Lites Club,
7th District, Indianapolis, Ind.

HILLBILLY CAKE

Makes 13 x 9½-Inch Layer

½ cup shortening
1 cup sugar
1 cup water
½ teaspoon cinnamon
½ teaspoon allspice
½ teaspoon ground cloves
½ cup chopped walnuts
½ cup seedless raisins
½ cup chopped pitted dates
½ teaspoon vanilla
2 cups sifted cake flour
1 teaspoon baking soda
½ teaspoon salt
Coconut Nut Topping (p. 630)

1. Preheat oven to 375° F. Grease and flour 13 x 9½ x 2-inch baking pan.
2. Melt shortening in saucepan. Stir in sugar, water, spices, walnuts, raisins and dates. Bring to boil over medium heat, stirring occasionally. Boil for 1 minute. Remove from heat; stir in vanilla; cool.
3. Onto piece of waxed paper sift together flour, baking soda and salt; add to fruit mixture; blend well. Turn into pan.
4. Bake in preheated oven for 25 to 30 minutes.
5. Spread Coconut Nut Topping over cake; place under broiler heat for 4 to 5 minutes, or until golden and bubbling.

Mrs. William Burchfield, Junior Woman's Club,
Torrance, Calif.

BLACK CURRANT JAM CAKE
Makes 3 8-Inch Layers

3 cups presifted flour
1 teaspoon baking soda
1 teaspoon cinnamon
1 teaspoon ground cloves
1 teaspoon ginger
1 teaspoon allspice
1 teaspoon cocoa
½ teaspoon salt
1 cup shortening
1 cup sugar
4 egg yolks
1 cup buttermilk
1 cup black currant jam
1 teaspoon vanilla
Favorite frosting

1. Preheat oven to 325° F. Grease and flour 3 8-inch layer cake pans.
2. Onto piece of waxed paper sift together flour, baking soda, spices, cocoa and salt.
3. In mixing bowl cream shortening and sugar until light and fluffy. Add egg yolks; beat until smooth.
4. Add flour mixture and buttermilk alternately to creamed mixture, beating well after each addition. Add jam and vanilla; beat until smooth. Turn into pans.
5. Bake in preheated oven for 25 to 30 minutes.
6. Cool for 5 minutes; remove from pans; cool on wire rack. Fill and frost with favorite frosting.

Mrs. Charles G. Paris, President,
Senior Woman's Club, Sturgis, Ky.

NEVER-FAIL SOUR CREAM SPICE CAKE
Makes 8-Inch Square

1 cup sour cream
1 cup sugar
2 eggs, lightly beaten
1½ cups presifted flour
1 teaspoon baking soda
1 teaspoon baking powder
½ teaspoon salt
1 teaspoon cinnamon
½ teaspoon ground cloves
½ teaspoon nutmeg
¼ cup chopped nuts or dates
    or ½ cup chopped seedless raisins

1. Preheat oven to 350° F. Grease and flour 8-inch square baking pan.
2. Put sour cream in mixing bowl; stir in sugar and eggs.
3. Sift together dry ingredients and spices; stir into sour cream mixture. Stir in nuts, dates or raisins.
4. Pour batter into pan; bake in preheated oven for 25 to 30 minutes. Turn onto wire rack to cool.

Mrs. Milford Andres, Woman's Literary Club,
Pingree, N.D.

OATMEAL SPICE CAKE
Makes 10 x 6-Inch Layer

1 cup quick-cooking rolled oats
1½ cups boiling water
1 cup granulated sugar
1 cup brown sugar
½ cup butter or margarine
2 eggs
1 teaspoon vanilla
1½ cups presifted flour
1 teaspoon baking soda
1 teaspoon nutmeg
1 teaspoon cinnamon
Nut Topping (p. 630)

1. Preheat oven to 350° F. Grease and flour 10 x 6 x 1½-inch baking pan.
2. In saucepan combine oats and water. Bring to boil, stirring constantly; cook until thickened and smooth. Remove from heat; cool.
3. In mixing bowl cream sugars and butter or margarine until light and fluffy. Add eggs and vanilla; beat until smooth.
4. Onto piece of waxed paper sift together flour, baking soda, nutmeg and cinnamon; add alternately with oatmeal to creamed mixture, beating well after each addition. Turn into pan.
5. Bake in preheated oven for 35 to 40 minutes.
6. Spread with Nut Topping. Broil 5 to 6 inches from heat for 3 to 4 minutes, or until browned.

Mrs. Clyde Corrello, Home Life Chairman,
Michigan State Federation of Women's Clubs;
Woman's Study Club, Ypsilanti, Mich.

ORLEANS MERINGUE CAKE
Makes 13 x 9½-Inch Layer

3 cups presifted flour
1 teaspoon baking soda
1 teaspoon salt
1½ teaspoons cinnamon
½ teaspoon nutmeg
½ teaspoon allspice
½ teaspoon ground cloves
¼ teaspoon mace
¾ cup butter or margarine
1¼ cups granulated sugar
1 cup brown sugar
4 eggs
1⅔ cups buttermilk or sour milk
Meringue Crunch Topping (p. 630)

1. Preheat oven to 350° F. Grease and flour 13 x 9½ x 2-inch baking pan.
2. Onto piece of waxed paper sift together flour, baking soda, salt and spices.
3. In large mixing bowl cream butter or margarine. Add sugars; beat until light and fluffy. Beat in 2 whole eggs and 2 egg yolks. (Reserve remaining egg whites for topping.)
4. Add flour mixture and milk alternately to creamed mixture, beating well after each addition.
5. Pour batter into pan; bake in preheated oven for 50 to 55 minutes.
6. Spread Meringue Crunch Topping over cake; bake for 20 minutes longer, or until golden.

Mrs. Ross Parsons, Victor Valley Women's Club,
Victorville, Calif.

SQUASH SPICE CAKE

Makes 2 8-Inch Squares

2 cups sifted cake flour
¼ teaspoon baking soda
½ teaspoon nutmeg
¼ teaspoon ground cloves
½ teaspoon cinnamon
2 teaspoons baking powder
½ teaspoon salt
½ cup butter or margarine
1½ cups brown sugar
2 eggs
¼ cup buttermilk
¾ cup thickly sieved cooked squash
½ cup currants
½ cup chopped walnuts

1. Preheat oven to 350° F. Grease and flour 2 8-inch square baking pans.
2. Into bowl sift together flour, baking soda, spices, baking powder and salt.
3. In mixing bowl cream butter or margarine and sugar until light and fluffy. Add eggs, one at a time, beating well after each addition.
4. Add flour mixture, buttermilk and squash alternately to creamed mixture, beating after each addition. Stir in currants and walnuts; pour into pans.
5. Bake in preheated oven for 25 to 30 minutes. Cool for 5 minutes; remove from pans; cool on wire racks.

Velma Tourczyk, Woman's Club, Chicopee Falls, Mass.

Poundcakes

POUNDCAKE

Makes 9-Inch Loaf

1 cup butter
1½ cups sugar
5 eggs
1½ cups presifted flour
1 teaspoon vanilla

1. Preheat oven to 350° F. Grease and flour 9-inch loaf pan.
2. Cream butter until soft and fluffy. Gradually add sugar; beat until light.
3. Add eggs, one at a time, alternately with flour, beating well after each addition. Stir in vanilla.
4. Turn batter into pan; bake in preheated oven for 1 hour.
5. Turn onto wire rack to cool.

Portia Palsa, Altruistic Club, Carlisle, Ark.

OLD-FASHIONED POUNDCAKE

Makes 9-Inch Ring

1 pound presifted flour
½ teaspoon salt
1 teaspoon baking powder
1 pound butter
8 large eggs, separated
1 pound sugar
1 tablespoon vanilla
1 teaspoon lemon extract

1. Preheat oven to 300° F. Grease and flour 9-inch tube pan.
2. Onto piece of waxed paper sift together flour, salt and baking powder.
3. In mixing bowl cream butter until light and fluffy. Gradually beat in flour mixture until smooth.
4. In another mixing bowl beat egg yolks until lemon-colored. Gradually add sugar; beat until thickened. Stir egg yolk mixture into creamed mixture. Add vanilla and lemon extract; beat until smooth.
5. Beat egg whites until stiff but not dry; fold into batter; turn into pan.
6. Bake in preheated oven for about 1 hour.
7. Cool for 10 minutes; remove from pan; cool on wire rack.

Mrs. L. E. Maloney, Woman's Club, Beckley, W. Va.

CHERRY POUNDCAKE

Makes 2 9-Inch Loaves

6 cups sifted cake flour
2 teaspoons baking powder
¼ teaspoon salt
2 cups butter
2 cups sugar
10 eggs
½ cup pineapple juice
1 pound chopped candied cherries
4 ounces chopped candied pineapple
½ cup chopped walnuts

1. Preheat oven to 275° F. Grease and flour 2 9-inch loaf pans.
2. Onto piece of waxed paper sift together flour, baking powder and salt.
3. In mixing bowl cream butter and sugar until light and fluffy. Add eggs, one at a time, beating well after each addition.
4. Add flour mixture and pineapple juice alternately, beating after each addition. Beat for 20 minutes (on medium speed with electric mixer).
5. Add cherries, pineapple and walnuts; mix to blend. Turn into pans.
6. Bake in preheated oven for about 1½ hours.
7. Cool for 10 minutes; remove from pans; cool on wire racks.

Frances Martin, Inter Se Circle, Marion, Ala.

CHOCOLATE POUNDCAKE

Makes 9-Inch Ring

1 cup margarine
½ cup shortening
3 cups sugar
5 eggs
3 cups presifted flour
½ cup cocoa
½ teaspoon baking powder
Dash of salt
1¼ cups milk
1 teaspoon vanilla

1. Preheat oven to 325° F. Grease and flour 9-inch tube pan.
2. Cream margarine, shortening and sugar until light and fluffy. Add eggs, one at a time, beating well after each addition.

3. Sift together flour, cocoa, baking powder and salt; add alternately with milk to egg mixture, stirring after each addition until well blended. Stir in vanilla.

4. Turn batter into pan; bake in preheated oven for 1½ hours. Turn onto wire rack to cool.

Mrs. H. E. Shurett, Athenia Study Club, Tuscaloosa, Ala.

PECAN POUNDCAKE

Makes 9-Inch Ring

2 cups presifted flour
½ teaspoon mace
1 teaspoon salt
1 cup shortening
1½ cups sugar
5 eggs
3 tablespoons milk
¾ cup chopped pecans, toasted
2 teaspoons lemon juice
1 teaspoon grated lemon rind

1. Preheat oven to 325° F. Grease and flour 9-inch tube pan.
2. Onto piece of waxed paper sift together flour, mace and salt.
3. In mixing bowl cream shortening and sugar until light and fluffy. Add eggs, one at a time, beating well after each addition.
4. Add milk and flour mixture; beat until smooth. Stir in pecans and lemon juice and rind; pour into pan.
5. Bake in preheated oven for about 1½ hours. Cool for 5 minutes; remove from pan; cool on wire rack.

Mrs. Herbert L. Anders, Springfield Improvement Association and Woman's Club, Jacksonville, Fla.

RAISIN HONEY POUNDCAKE

Makes 9-Inch Loaf

1 cup seedless raisins
1 cup shortening
1 cup honey
4 eggs, lightly beaten
3 cups presifted flour
3 teaspoons baking powder
½ teaspoon salt
1 teaspoon vanilla
1 teaspoon lemon extract
¾ cup chopped walnuts

1. Preheat oven to 300° F. Line 9-inch loaf pan with paper.
2. Rinse raisins; dry on towel; slice finely.
3. Cream shortening thoroughly; gradually add honey, continuing to cream. Add eggs; blend.
4. Sift together flour, baking powder and salt; add to creamed mixture; beat. Add vanilla, lemon extract, raisins and walnuts; stir to blend.
5. Pour batter into pan; bake in preheated oven for about 2 hours.

Mrs. Leland H. Goss, Woman's Club, Franklin, Me.

SOUR CREAM POUNDCAKE

Makes 9-Inch Loaf

3 cups presifted flour
¼ teaspoon baking soda
¼ teaspoon salt
1 cup butter
3 cups granulated sugar
6 large eggs
1 cup sour cream
½ teaspoon vanilla
½ teaspoon lemon extract

1. Preheat oven to 325° F. Grease and flour 9-inch loaf pan.
2. Onto piece of waxed paper sift together flour, baking soda and salt three times.
3. In mixing bowl cream butter until light. Gradually beat in sugar until light and fluffy. Add eggs, one at a time, beating well after each addition.
4. Add flour mixture and sour cream alternately, beating after each addition. Stir in vanilla and lemon extract. Turn into pan.
5. Bake in preheated oven for about 1½ hours.
6. Cool for 10 minutes; remove from pan; cool on wire rack.

Mrs. J. W. Chaplin, President, Woman's Club, Wiley, Colo.

Coffee Cakes

APPLE PAN COFFEE CAKE

Makes 11 x 7-Inch Layer

3 cups sliced peeled apples
½ cup presifted flour
½ teaspoon salt
Sugar
3 eggs
½ cup milk
½ teaspoon cinnamon
Juice of 1 lemon

1. Preheat oven to 450° F. Lightly grease 11 x 7 x 1½-inch baking pan.
2. Arrange apples in pan. Bake in preheated oven for 15 minutes.
3. Meanwhile, into mixing bowl sift together flour, salt and 1 teaspoon sugar.
4. In another bowl beat eggs and milk; stir into flour mixture.
5. Pour batter over apples; bake in oven for 15 minutes longer.
6. Meanwhile, in small bowl combine ½ cup sugar and cinnamon; sprinkle on cake. Bake for 5 minutes longer.
7. Just before serving, sprinkle with lemon juice.

Jeannie May, Brook Run Junior Woman's Club, Richmond, Va.

CHERRY COBBLER COFFEE CAKE

Makes 9-Inch Square

1 cup presifted flour
2 teaspoons baking powder

⅛ teaspoon salt
¼ cup butter or margarine
1 cup sugar
½ cup milk
1-pound can pitted sour red
  cherries
Cream or ice cream

1. Preheat oven to 375° F. Grease 9-inch square baking pan.
2. Onto piece of waxed paper sift together flour, baking powder and salt.
3. In mixing bowl cream butter or margarine and ½ cup of the sugar until light and fluffy. Add milk and flour mixture; beat until smooth. Spread in pan.
4. Drain cherries; reserve syrup. Arrange cherries evenly on batter. Pour syrup on top; sprinkle with remaining sugar.
5. Bake in preheated oven for 40 to 45 minutes. Serve warm or cold, cut into squares, with cream or ice cream, as desired.

Mrs. A. Hathaway, Woman's Club,
Hugoton, Kans.

RAISIN PRALINE COFFEE CAKE

Makes 9- or 10-Inch Ring

½ cup shortening
¾ cup granulated sugar
1 teaspoon vanilla
3 eggs
1½ cups seedless dark raisins, chopped
2 cups presifted flour
1 teaspoon baking powder
1 teaspoon baking soda
1 teaspoon salt
1 cup sour cream
⅓ cup butter
1 cup brown sugar
2 teaspoons cinnamon
¾ cup coarsely chopped pecans

1. Preheat oven to 350° F. Grease and flour 9- or 10-inch tube pan.
2. Beat shortening, granulated sugar and vanilla until light and fluffy. Add eggs, one at a time, beating well after each addition. Stir in raisins.
3. Sift together flour, baking powder, baking soda and salt; stir alternately with sour cream into egg mixture.
4. In small bowl combine butter, brown sugar and cinnamon. Rub together until crumbled. Stir in pecans.
5. Spread half the batter in pan; sprinkle with half the crumbs. Add remaining batter; sprinkle with remaining crumbs.
6. Bake in preheated oven for about 50 minutes.
7. Cool in pan for 10 minutes; remove from pan; cool on wire rack. Serve reheated or cold.

Mrs. Earl Rhyne, Veritas Club, Greensboro, Ala.

COWBOY CAKE

Makes 2 9-Inch Layers

Mrs. Chaplin writes: "This recipe is similar to those used by the cowboys of the old West. They always used baking soda as the leavening agent, but I also use baking powder. I keep several batches as a mix in glass jars. I mix all the ingredients except the baking soda, buttermilk and eggs. I place the ½ cup 'crumbs' for topping in a small plastic bag in the top of each jar, along with a notation to add ½ teaspoon baking soda, 1 cup buttermilk and 2 beaten eggs."

2½ cups presifted flour
2 cups brown sugar
½ teaspoon salt
2 teaspoon baking powder
  Cinnamon
½ teaspoon nutmeg
⅔ cup shortening
½ teaspoon baking soda
1 cup buttermilk
2 eggs, well beaten
  Finely chopped nuts (optional)

1. Preheat oven to 350° F. Grease 2 9-inch layer cake pans.
2. In mixing bowl combine flour, sugar, salt, baking powder, 1 teaspoon cinnamon and nutmeg. Cut in shortening until mixture resembles fine crumbs; reserve ½ cup for topping.
3. Dissolve baking soda in buttermilk; add along with eggs to batter. Stir well until blended.
4. Pour batter into pans; sprinkle with reserved crumbs. Some nuts and cinnamon may also be added on top, if desired.
5. Bake in preheated oven for 15 to 20 minutes. Serve warm or reheated.

Mrs. J. W. Chaplin, President, Woman's Club,
Wiley, Colo.

CRUMB CAKE

Makes 8-Inch Square

¾ cup brown sugar
¾ cup granulated sugar
2½ cups presifted flour
  Dash of salt
¾ cup shortening
1 egg
1 teaspoon baking powder
1 teaspoon baking soda
1 cup sour milk or buttermilk
1 teaspoon cinnamon
½ teaspoon mace or nutmeg
½ cup chopped nuts

1. Preheat oven to 350° F. Grease 8-inch square baking pan.
2. In mixing bowl combine sugars, flour and salt. Cut in shortening until mixture resembles very fine crumbs; reserve ½ cup for topping.
3. Add egg and baking powder to remaining crumbs. Combine baking soda and milk or buttermilk; add to crumbs. Add cinnamon and mace or nutmeg; mix thoroughly.
4. Spread batter in pan. Mix reserved crumbs and nuts; sprinkle over batter.
5. Bake in preheated oven for 25 to 30 minutes.

Mrs. Edward C. Schock, President's Aide,
General Federation of Women's Clubs,
Kansas City, Mo.

FAVORITE COFFEE CAKE
Makes 8-Inch Square

½ cup shortening
½ cup granulated sugar
½ teaspoon vanilla
1 egg
1½ cups sifted cake flour
½ teaspoon salt
1½ teaspoons baking powder
½ cup milk
½ cup brown sugar
1 tablespoon flour
1 tablespoon cinnamon
¼ cup melted butter or margarine
¼ cup chopped walnuts
½ cup chopped dates

1. Preheat oven to 350° F. Grease 8-inch square baking pan.
2. In mixing bowl beat shortening and granulated sugar until light and fluffy. Add vanilla and egg; beat well.
3. Onto piece of waxed paper sift together cake flour, salt and baking powder; add alternately with milk to sugar mixture, beating well after each addition. Spread half in pan.
4. In another bowl, combine remaining ingredients; reserve about 3 tablespoons; spread rest of filling over batter in pan. Top with remaining batter. Dot with reserved filling.
5. Bake in preheated oven for 40 to 45 minutes.

Mrs. Roy E. Metsker, Woman's Club,
Englewood, Colo.

SNICKERDOODLE COFFEE CAKE
Makes 13 x 9½-Inch Layer

1 cup sugar
½ cup shortening
1 egg
1 cup milk
2½ cups presifted flour
4 teaspoons baking powder
½ teaspoon salt
½ cup cut dates
½ cup broken nuts
   Mixed sugar and cinnamon

1. Preheat oven to 375° F. Grease 13 x 9½ x 2-inch baking pan.
2. Cream sugar and shortening until light and fluffy.
3. Combine egg and milk; stir into sugar mixture. Stir in dry ingredients. Fold in dates and nuts.
4. Pour batter into pan; sprinkle with mixed sugar and cinnamon.
5. Bake in preheated oven for 30 minutes.

Carolyn Brown, Women's Club,
Milton Junction, Wis.

JEWISH COFFEE CAKE
Makes 9-Inch Ring

½ cup butter
1 cup granulated sugar
3 eggs
1 teaspoon baking powder
1 teaspoon baking soda

2⅓ cups presifted flour
⅛ teaspoon salt
1 cup sour cream
1 teaspoon vanilla
1 cup brown sugar
¾ cup chopped nuts
3 teaspoons melted butter
1 teaspoon cinnamon

1. Preheat oven to 350° F. Grease 9-inch tube pan.
2. In mixing bowl cream ½ cup butter and granulated sugar. Add eggs, one at a time, beating well after each addition.
3. Combine baking powder, baking soda, 2 cups of the flour and salt. Add to egg mixture; mix well. Stir in sour cream and vanilla.
4. In a separate bowl mix brown sugar, remaining flour, nuts, melted butter and cinnamon until crumbed; put half in pan. Add half the batter; sprinkle with remaining crumbs; top with remaining batter.
5. Bake in preheated oven for 1 hour.

Mrs. Ginny Kartheiser, Junior Woman's Club,
Port Washington, Wis.

MINCEMEAT COFFEE CAKE
Makes 9-Inch Ring

2 cups presifted flour
¾ cup granulated sugar
2½ teaspoons baking powder
½ teaspoon salt
⅓ cup shortening
1 egg, lightly beaten
½ cup cold milk
¾ cup moist mincemeat
2 tablespoons butter
3 tablespoons hot milk
1 cup confectioners' sugar (sift if lumpy)

1. Preheat oven to 375° F. Grease 9-inch tube pan.
2. Into mixing bowl sift together flour, granulated sugar, baking powder and salt. Cut in shortening until mixture resembles fine crumbs.
3. Add egg, cold milk and mincemeat; stir until blended. Turn into pan.
4. Bake in preheated oven for 30 to 35 minutes. Cool for 5 minutes; turn onto wire rack.
5. Meanwhile, prepare Butter Frosting: In small bowl blend butter, hot milk and confectioners 'sugar until smooth.
6. Spread frosting on ring while still warm.

Mrs. Joseph Mitchell, Woman's Study Club,
Ypsilanti, Mich.

COFFEE RING
Makes 10-Inch Ring

½ cup shortening
1 cup granulated sugar
¾ cup brown sugar
2 eggs
2 cups presifted flour
1 teaspoon baking powder
1 teaspoon baking soda
1 teaspoon vanilla
1 cup sour cream

½ cup chopped walnuts
1 teaspoon cinnamon

1. Preheat oven to 350° F. Grease 10-inch tube pan.
2. In mixing bowl cream shortening, granulated sugar and ½ cup of the brown sugar until light and fluffy. Add eggs, one at a time, beating well after each addition.
3. Onto piece of waxed paper sift together flour, baking powder and baking soda.
4. Stir vanilla into sour cream.
5. Add flour mixture alternately with sour cream to egg mixture, beating well after each addition.
6. Pour half the batter into pan.
7. In small bowl mix remaining brown sugar, walnuts and cinnamon.
8. Sprinkle half the nut mixture over batter in pan.
9. Pour in remaining batter; and sprinkle with remaining nut mixture.
10. Bake in preheated oven for about 45 minutes.
11. Cool for 5 minutes; remove from pan; serve warm.

Mrs. Claire Hiltz, Woman's Club, Woodland, Me.

RADIO CAKE
Makes 10 x 6-Inch Layer

1¼ cups cake flour
1 teaspoon baking powder
Dash of salt
3 eggs
½ cup butter
1 cup granulated sugar
½ cup milk
1 cup chopped walnuts
2 cups brown sugar, sifted

1. Preheat oven to 300° F. Grease 10 x 6 x 1½-inch baking pan.
2. Onto piece of waxed paper sift together flour, baking powder and salt.
3. Separate 2 of the eggs.
4. In mixing bowl cream butter and granulated sugar until light and fluffy. Add 2 egg yolks and remaining egg; beat until smooth.
5. Add flour mixture and milk alternately, beating after each addition. Spread in pan; sprinkle with walnuts.
6. In mixing bowl beat egg whites until stiff but not dry; fold in brown sugar; spread on walnuts.
7. Bake in preheated oven for 40 to 45 minutes. Cool in pan; cut into squares to serve.

Mrs. Ruby King, Women's Club, Clinton, Mont.

SOUR CREAM COFFEE CAKE
Makes 10 x 6-Inch Layer

1½ cups presifted flour
1¼ cups sugar
2 teaspoons baking powder
¼ teaspoon salt
2 eggs

½ teaspoon baking soda
1 cup sour cream
¼ cup butter or margarine
½ teaspoon cinnamon
½ cup chopped walnuts

1. Preheat oven to 350° F. Grease 10 x 6 x 1½-inch baking pan.
2. Onto piece of waxed paper sift together flour, 1 cup of the sugar, baking powder and salt.
3. In mixing bowl beat eggs, baking soda and sour cream until smooth. Stir in flour mixture; beat until smooth. Pour into pan.
4. Bake in preheated oven for 25 to 30 minutes.
5. Meanwhile, prepare Nut Topping: In small bowl cream remaining sugar and butter or margarine until fluffy. Add cinnamon and walnuts; mix well.
6. When cake comes from oven, spread topping on cake. Cut into squares; serve warm.

Mrs. Jane Sweeder, Woman's Fortnightly Reading Club, Cincinnati, Ohio

SPICY MARBLE COFFEE CAKE
Makes 9-Inch Square

½ cup shortening
¾ cup granulated sugar
1 egg
Presifted flour
2 teaspoons baking powder
½ teaspoon salt
¾ cup milk
2 tablespoons molasses
2 teaspoons cinnamon
¼ teaspoon nutmeg
½ teaspoon ground cloves
½ cup brown sugar
½ cup chopped nuts
2 tablespoons melted butter

1. Preheat oven to 350° F. Grease and flour 9-inch square baking pan.
2. Cream shortening and granulated sugar well. Beat in egg.
3. Combine 2 cups flour, baking powder and salt; stir alternately with milk and molasses into egg mixture.
4. Divide batter in half. Stir 1 teaspoon of the cinnamon, nutmeg and cloves into one half.
5. Turn plain batter into pan. Add spiced batter; swirl spiced batter through plain batter.
6. Combine remaining cinnamon, brown sugar, nuts, 2 tablespoons flour and butter; sprinkle over batter.
7. Bake in preheated oven for 30 minutes. Serve warm.

Mrs. Warren E. Peterson, Thursday Morning Club, Madison, N.J.

STREUSEL-FILLED COFFEE CAKE
Makes 8-Inch Layer

½ cup brown sugar
Presifted flour
2 tablespoons cinnamon
½ cup chopped nuts
2 tablespoons melted butter
¾ cup granulated sugar
3 teaspoons baking powder
½ teaspoon salt
¼ cup shortening
1 egg
½ cup milk
1 teaspoon vanilla

1. Preheat oven to 375° F. Grease 8-inch square or layer cake pan.
2. Combine brown sugar, 2 tablespoons flour, cinnamon, nuts and butter; reserve for topping.
3. Into mixing bowl sift together granulated sugar, 1½ cups flour, baking powder and salt. Cut in shortening.
4. Beat egg; combine with milk and vanilla. Add to flour mixture; stir only until dry ingredients are moistened.
5. Spread half the batter in pan; sprinkle with half the reserved topping. Add remaining batter; sprinkle with remaining topping. (Or, if desired, reserve remaining topping until cake is baked; then spread on cake, and place under broiler until sugar bubbles.)
6. Bake in preheated oven for 25 to 30 minutes.

Mrs. John Kuhn, Junior Woman's Club,
Benson, Ariz.

Upside-Down Cakes

APPLE UPSIDE-DOWN CAKE
Makes 8-Inch Square

Brown sugar
Cinnamon
2 tablespoons butter
Sliced peeled apples
3 eggs, separated
1 cup granulated sugar
½ cup cooking oil
1 cup presifted flour
2 teaspoons baking powder
½ teaspoon salt
1 teaspoon vanilla or almond extract

1. Grease 8-inch square baking pan. Sprinkle lightly with brown sugar and cinnamon; dot with butter. Arrange apples on top.
2. Preheat oven to 350° F.
3. Beat egg yolks and granulated sugar until thickened and pale. Add oil; mix well.
4. Sift together flour, baking powder and salt.
5. Beat egg whites until stiff but not dry; fold alternately with flour mixture into egg yolk mixture. Stir in vanilla or almond extract.

6. Pour over apples; bake in preheated oven for 40 minutes.
7. Remove from oven. Place large plate upside down over cake; invert pan to drop cake onto plate.

Lottie Kula, Woman's Club, Chatham, N.J.

CHERRY UPSIDE-DOWN CAKE
Makes 8-Inch Square

1-pound 4-ounce can pitted sour red cherries
2½ tablespoons cornstarch
⅔ cup sugar
1¾ cups sifted cake flour
½ teaspoon salt
¼ teaspoon baking soda
2 teaspoons baking powder
⅓ cup shortening
1 egg
½ cup all-bran
1 teaspoon grated orange rind
½ cup orange juice
¼ cup milk
Whipped cream or hard sauce

1. Preheat oven to 375° F. Grease 8-inch square baking pan.
2. Drain cherries; reserve syrup.
3. In small saucepan combine cornstarch and sugar; blend in reserved syrup to make a smooth paste. Cook over medium heat, stirring constantly, until thickened and clear. Stir in cherries; pour into pan.
4. Onto piece of waxed paper sift together flour, salt, baking soda and baking powder.
5. In mixing bowl cream shortening. Add egg; beat until smooth. Stir in all-bran and orange rind.
6. Add flour mixture alternately with orange juice and milk, beating well after each addition. Pour over cherries.
7. Bake in preheated oven for 40 to 45 minutes. Cool for 5 minutes; invert onto serving dish. Serve warm, with whipped cream or hard sauce, as desired.

Mrs. Bernard Law, Woman's Club, Wallkill, N.Y.

PINEAPPLE UPSIDE-DOWN CAKE
Makes 10-Inch Layer

½ cup butter or margarine
1 cup brown sugar
1-pound 4-ounce can pineapple slices
Maraschino cherries
1 cup walnut halves
3 eggs, separated
1 cup granulated sugar
1 cup sifted cake flour
½ teaspoon salt
1 teaspoon baking powder
¼ teaspoon cream of tartar

1. Preheat oven to 350° F.
2. Melt butter or margarine in 10-inch layer cake or square pan over medium heat. Stir in brown sugar; cook until golden brown. Remove from heat.
3. Drain pineapple; reserve ⅓ cup syrup. Arrange pineapple in pan; place

cherry in center of each. Arrange walnuts between slices.

4. In mixing bowl beat egg yolks and granulated sugar until thickened and lemon-colored. Stir in flour, salt and baking soda; blend well. Stir in reserved syrup.

5. In another mixing bowl beat egg whites and cream of tartar until stiff but not dry. Fold into egg yolk mixture. Spread over fruit in pan.

6. Bake in preheated oven for about 1 hour. Cool for 5 minutes; invert onto serving dish.

Mrs. T. La Buz, Ken-Rose Evening
Woman's Club, Glenwood, Ill.

STRAWBERRY UPSIDE-DOWN CAKE

Makes 11 x 7-Inch Layer

1 cup presifted flour
¼ teaspoon salt
1 teaspoon baking powder
2 eggs
2½ cups sugar
½ cup milk
2 tablespoons butter or margarine
1 quart strawberries
6 tablespoons cornstarch
Whipped cream or ice cream

1. Preheat oven to 350° F. Grease and flour 11 x 7 x 1½-inch baking pan.

2. Onto piece of waxed paper sift together flour, salt and baking powder.

3. In mixing bowl beat eggs until frothy. Add 1 cup of the sugar; beat until thickened and lemon-colored.

4. Add flour mixture to egg mixture; beat until blended.

5. In small saucepan combine milk and 1 tablespoon of the butter or margarine. Cook over low heat until butter is melted. Add to batter; beat until blended and smooth. Pour into pan.

6. Bake in preheated oven for 25 to 30 minutes. Cool for 15 minutes; remove from pan; cool on wire rack.

7. Meanwhile, stem and wash strawberries; sprinkle with ½ cup of the sugar; let stand for 15 minutes.

8. Drain strawberries; add water to juice to total 1 cup; reserve.

9. In small saucepan blend remaining sugar and cornstarch. Gradually stir in reserved juice to make a smooth paste. Cook over medium heat, stirring constantly, until thickened and clear. Remove from heat; stir in strawberries and remaining butter or margarine.

10. Wash pan in which cake was baked; spread strawberry mixture in bottom. Top with cake; refrigerate until serving time.

11. Turn cake, strawberry side up, out of pan; cut into squares; serve with whipped cream or ice cream.

Mrs. B. Macy Bugg, Woman's Club,
Plant City, Fla.

Angel, Chiffon and Sponge Cakes

ANGEL FOOD CAKE

Makes 9-Inch Ring

1 cup sifted cake flour
1¼ cups sifted confectioners' sugar
1½ cups egg whites
1½ teaspoons cream of tartar
¼ teaspoon salt
1½ teaspoons vanilla
¼ teaspoon almond extract
1 cup granulated sugar

1. Preheat oven to 375° F.

2. Sift flour and confectioners' sugar together three times.

3. In large mixing bowl beat egg whites, cream of tartar, salt, vanilla and almond extract until soft peaks form. Beat in 2 tablespoons of the granulated sugar at a time; beat until stiff and glossy. Fold in flour mixture very gradually.

4. Spoon batter into 9-inch tube pan; bake in preheated oven for 30 to 35 minutes.

5. Invert pan; cool for 1 hour; remove from pan.

Ann Duerr, Woman's Club of Baldwin Borough,
Pittsburgh, Pa.

BITS OF GOLD ANGEL CAKE

Makes 9-Inch Ring

1 cup cake flour
1½ cups plus 2 tablespoons sugar
1½ cups egg whites
1½ teaspoons cream of tartar
¼ teaspoon salt
1 teaspoon orange extract
¼ cup grated orange rind

1. Preheat oven to 350° F.

2. Onto piece of waxed paper sift flour; add ¾ cup of the sugar. Sift three times.

3. In mixing bowl beat egg whites until foamy. Add cream of tartar and salt; beat until soft peaks form. Gradually beat in remaining sugar until stiff and glossy.

4. Gently fold in flour mixture, a little at a time. Add orange extract and rind; fold in just to distribute the rind. Spoon into 9-inch tube pan.

5. Bake in preheated oven for 35 to 40 minutes.

6. Invert pan; cool cake in pan.

Mrs. H. J. Dudley, Woman's Club,
Windsor, Colo.

DAFFODIL CAKE

Makes 9-Inch Ring

¾ cup sifted cake flour
¾ cup egg whites
¼ teaspoon salt
¾ teaspoon cream of tartar
1 cup plus 1½ tablespoons sugar
¼ teaspoon vanilla
¼ teaspoon grated orange rind
4 egg yolks

1. Preheat oven to 325° F.

2. Sift flour four times.

3. Beat egg whites and salt until foamy. Add cream of tartar; continue to beat until stiff but not dry.

4. Carefully fold 1 cup of the sugar into egg whites, 2 tablespoons at a time.

5. Sift flour over egg white mixture, a little at a time; fold in carefully.

6. Divide batter in half. Stir vanilla into one half. Fold orange rind into other half.

7. Beat egg yolks and remaining sugar until very thick and pale. Fold into orange batter.

8. Drop vanilla and orange batter alternately into 9-inch tube pan, filling pan about half full.

9. Bake in preheated oven for about 1 hour.

10. Invert pan; cool.

Elizabeth Carroll, Women's City Club,
Portsmouth, N.H.

LEMON CHIFFON CAKE

Makes 10-Inch Ring

2 cups sifted cake flour
1½ cups sugar
3 teaspoons baking powder
1 teaspoon salt
½ cup cooking oil
5 eggs, separated
¾ cup water
1 teaspoon vanilla
2 teaspoons grated lemon rind
½ teaspoon cream of tartar
Favorite frosting

1. Preheat oven to 325° F. Grease and flour 10-inch tube pan.

2. In large mixing bowl sift together flour, sugar, baking powder and salt.

3. Make a well in center; add oil, egg yolks, water, vanilla and lemon rind; beat until smooth.

4. In another mixing bowl beat egg whites and cream of tartar until stiff but not dry; fold into batter. Turn into pan.

5. Bake in preheated oven for about 1½ hours.

6. Cool for 10 minutes; remove from pan; cool on wire rack. Frost with favorite frosting.

Mrs. Carmella Di Santo, Ken-Rose Evening
Woman's Club, Glenwood, Ill.

MAHOGANY CHIFFON CAKE

Makes 10-Inch Ring

¾ cup boiling water
½ cup cocoa
1¾ cups sifted cake flour
1¾ cups sugar
1½ teaspoons baking soda
1 teaspoon salt
½ cup olive oil
7 eggs, separated
2 teaspoons vanilla
½ teaspoon cream of tartar

1. Preheat oven to 325° F.

2. Blend water and cocoa; cool.

3. Into mixing bowl sift together flour, sugar, baking soda and salt.

4. Make a well in center of flour mixture; add cocoa, oil, egg yolks and vanilla; beat until smooth.

5. In another mixing bowl beat egg whites and cream of tartar until stiff but not dry. Pour egg yolk mixture over egg whites; gently fold until blended. Pour into 10-inch tube pan.

6. Bake in preheated oven for 65 to 70 minutes.

7. Invert pan; cool cake in pan.

Mrs. George R. Krempels, Junior Women's
Civic Club, Indiana, Pa.

JIFFY SPONGE CAKE

Makes 10-Inch Ring

4 eggs, separated
1½ cups sugar
2 teaspoons cold water
½ cup hot water
1 teaspoon vanilla
1⅔ cups sifted cake flour
¼ teaspoon salt
¼ teaspoon baking powder
Favorite frosting

1. Preheat oven to 325° F.

2. Beat egg whites; set aside.

3. Beat egg yolks until light and fluffy. Gradually beat in sugar (on high speed with electric beater). Beat in cold water, hot water and vanilla.

4. Sift together flour, salt and baking powder; fold into egg yolk mixture; fold in egg whites.

5. Turn batter into 10-inch tube pan; bake in preheated oven for about 40 minutes.

6. Invert pan onto wire rack to cool; remove from pan; frost with favorite frosting.

A. S.

PINEAPPLE CREAM CAKE

Makes 10-Inch Ring

1 cup cake flour
½ teaspoon salt
1 teaspoon baking powder
4 eggs, separated
1 cup sugar
½ cup milk
1 tablespoon butter or margarine
1 teaspoon vanilla
1 cup heavy cream
8-ounce can crushed pineapple, drained

1. Preheat oven to 350° F.

2. Onto piece of waxed paper sift together flour, salt and baking powder.

3. In mixing bowl beat egg whites until foamy. Gradually add ⅓ cup of the sugar; beat until soft peaks form.

4. In another mixing bowl beat egg yolks and remaining sugar until thickened and lemon-colored. Add flour mixture; stir until well blended.

5. Bring milk and butter or margarine to just below boiling point. Add to batter with vanilla; stir until mixed.

6. Fold in egg whites; turn into 10-inch tube pan.

7. Bake in preheated oven for 30 to 40 minutes. Cool for 20 minutes; remove from pan; cool on wire rack.

8. Split cake; whip cream until stiff; fold in pineapple; use to fill and frost cake. Refrigerate until serving time.

Mildred Dearborn, President, Woman's Progress Club, Meredith, N.H.

MAGIC CAKE

Makes 2 8-Inch Layers

5 eggs, separated
5 tablespoons confectioners' sugar
3 tablespoons cocoa
Whipped cream

1. Preheat oven to 350° F. Grease 2 8-inch layer cake pans. Line with waxed paper.

2. Beat egg yolks until thickened and pale.

3. Sift together sugar and cocoa; stir into egg yolks.

4. Beat egg whites until stiff but not dry; fold into egg yolk mixture.

5. Pour batter into pans; bake in preheated oven for 35 to 40 minutes.

6. Remove from oven, turn onto wire rack to cool; remove waxed paper.

7. When thoroughly cool, fill and top with whipped cream. Refrigerate until serving time.

Mrs. J. E. Rupert, Woman's Club, St. Mary's, W. Va.

CHOCOLATE ROLL

Serves 8

5 eggs, separated
1 cup confectioners' sugar (sift if lumpy)
1 tablespoon presifted flour
¼ cup cocoa
1 teaspoon vanilla
Granulated sugar
1 cup heavy cream, whipped
Chocolate frosting

1. Preheat oven to 350° F. Grease 15½ x 10½ x 1-inch jelly roll pan. Line with waxed paper; grease again.

2. Combine egg yolks and sugar in mixing bowl; beat until thickened and lemon-colored. Carefully fold in flour, cocoa and vanilla.

3. In another mixing bowl beat egg whites until stiff but not dry; fold into egg yolk mixture. Spread evenly in pan.

4. Bake in preheated oven for 12 to 15 minutes.

5. Loosen paper carefully; invert onto piece of waxed paper sprinkled with granulated sugar. Cover with damp towel; cool.

6. Remove paper; spread with cream. Roll up sideways to form a long roll. Frost with chocolate frosting.

Mrs. Carl Westby, Senior Woman's Club, Culbertson, Mont.

MOTHER'S ORANGE ROLL

Serves 8

1 cup cake flour
2 teaspoons baking powder
4 eggs
1 cup granulated sugar
¼ cup orange juice
Confectioners' sugar
Orange Filling (p. 632)

1. Preheat oven to 425° F. Grease 15½ x 10½ x 1-inch jelly roll pan; line bottom with waxed paper; grease paper.

2. Onto piece of waxed paper sift together flour and baking powder.

3. In mixing bowl beat eggs until thickened and lemon-colored. Add sugar, flour mixture and orange juice; fold in carefully. Spread in pan.

4. Bake in preheated oven for 12 to 15 minutes. Turn out at once onto clean cloth sprinkled with confectioners' sugar.

5. Carefully remove paper; spread with Orange Filling. Roll up like a jelly roll, starting at 15-inch side. Cool on wire rack. Sprinkle with confectioners' sugar.

Mrs. D. D. Fluke, Seminar Club, Cuba, Mo.

OLD-FASHIONED JELLY ROLL

Serves 8

2 cups sifted cake flour
2 teaspoons baking powder
4 eggs
2 cups sugar
2 teaspoons lemon extract
1 cup boiling water
1 cup currant jelly
Confectioners' sugar

1. Preheat oven to 400° F. Grease 15½ x 10½ x 1-inch jelly roll pan. Line with waxed paper; grease again.

2. Onto piece of waxed paper sift together 1 cup of the flour and baking powder; set aside.

3. In mixing bowl beat eggs until foamy. Add sugar; beat until thickened. Stir in lemon extract. Add remaining flour; beat until smooth. Add flour mixture; stir in lightly. Gradually stir in water. Pour into pan.

4. Bake in preheated oven for 15 to 20 minutes.

5. Invert cake onto dry cloth dusted with confectioners' sugar. Carefully remove waxed paper. Roll up like a jelly roll in towel; cool on wire rack.

6. Unroll cake; spread jelly over center, coming to within inch of all edges. Reroll. Place, seam side down, on serving dish. Dust with sifted confectioners' sugar.

Mrs. Charles Adan, Junior Woman's Club, Berlin, Conn.

Fruitcakes

FRUITCAKE
Makes About 7 Pounds
3½ cups sifted cake flour
½ teaspoon baking soda
1 teaspoon cinnamon
½ teaspoon nutmeg
1 teaspoon baking powder
1 teaspoon salt
1 teaspoon mace
½ teaspoon ground cloves
¾ cup candied orange peel, sliced
1¾ cups currants
1¾ cup dates, sliced
¾ cup candied pineapple, sliced
1½ cups candied citron, sliced
1½ cups seedless raisins
1½ cups candied cherries
1½ cups chopped walnuts
1½ cups shortening
1 cup brown sugar
5 eggs
½ cup molasses
½ cup fruit juice
½ cup honey

1. At least 1 week before, preheat oven to 250° F. Grease 4 8-inch loaf pans. Line bottoms and sides with 3 layers of waxed paper. Grease paper.
2. Into mixing bowl sift together flour, baking soda, cinnamon, nutmeg, baking powder, salt, mace and cloves.
3. In another large bowl mix orange peel, currants, dates, pineapple, citron, raisins, cherries and walnuts; sprinkle with 1 cup of flour mixture.
4. In another mixing bowl cream shortening and sugar until light and fluffy. Add eggs, one at a time, beating well after each addition.
5. In measuring cup blend molasses, fruit juice and honey; add alternately with remaining flour mixture to egg mixture, beating well after each addition. Stir in fruit mixture; blend well. Turn into pans, filling each three-fourths full.
6. Bake in preheated oven for about 2½ hours. If cakes become browned before end of cooking period, top with greased waxed paper.
7. Cool for 15 minutes; remove from pans; cool on wire racks.
8. Store cakes in airtight containers for 1 week before using.

Mrs. Elizabeth Ash, Woman's Country Club, Orleans, Ill.

TROPICAL CAKE
Makes 9-Inch Loaf
3 cups Brazil nuts
1 pound pitted dates
1 cup maraschino cherries
¾ cup sifted cake flour
¾ cup sugar
½ teaspoon baking powder
½ teaspoon salt
3 eggs
1 teaspoon vanilla

1. Preheat oven to 300° F. Grease 9-inch loaf pan well. Line with waxed paper. Grease paper.
2. Put nuts, dates and cherries in mixing bowl; mix well. Sift together flour, sugar, baking powder and salt into bowl; mix well.
3. Beat eggs and vanilla until frothy; pour into bowl; mix well. Pour into pan.
4. Bake in preheated oven for about 1¾ hours. Cool for 10 minutes; remove from pan; cool on wire rack.

Fern Kaland, Woman's Club, Nevis, Minn.

CANDIED FRUITCAKE
Makes 2 9-Inch Loaves
1 pound candied pineapple
1½ pounds pitted dates
1 pound candied cherries
2 cups presifted flour
2 teaspoons baking powder
½ teaspoon salt
4 eggs
1 cup sugar
2 pounds pecan halves

1. Preheat oven to 275° F. Grease 2 9-inch loaf pans. Line bottoms and sides with waxed paper. Grease paper.
2. Cut pineapple and dates into large mixing bowl; add cherries.
3. Onto piece of waxed paper sift together flour, baking powder and salt. Add to fruits, stirring until well coated.
4. In another mixing bowl beat eggs until frothy. Gradually add sugar; beat for 2 to 3 minutes. Stir into fruits; mix well. Add pecans; mix well. Turn into pans; press down with fingers.
5. Bake in preheated oven for 1½ hours (tops will look dry).
6. Cool; remove from pans.

Mrs. E. J. Pacey, Woman's Club, Paxton, Ill.

COCONUT FRUITCAKE
Makes 10-Inch Ring
½ pound butter
1 pound sugar
1 pound presifted flour
1 teaspoon baking powder
12 egg whites
¼ cup brandy
½ pound freshly grated coconut
½ pound blanched almonds
½ pound candied pineapple wedges
½ pound candied cherries

1. Preheat oven to 325° F. Grease and flour 10-inch tube pan.
2. Cream butter and sugar until light and fluffy.
3. Sift together flour and baking powder.
4. Beat egg whites until stiff but not dry.
5. Fold half the flour mixture and half the egg whites into creamed mixture. Add brandy, coconut, half the almonds, half the pineapple and half the cherries. Fold in remaining flour mixture, remaining egg whites and remaining almonds and fruits.

6. Spoon batter into pan; bake in pre-heated oven for about 1½ hours.

Mrs. O. S. Anderson, Thursday Morning Club, Madison, N.J.

HOLIDAY FRUITCAKE

Makes 2 4-Pound Loaves

These cakes will keep in the refrigerator for a year or more.

1 pound candied pineapple, diced
1 pound candied cherries
1 pound pitted dates, cut
7 cups broken pecans
1 cup presifted flour
½ teaspoon salt
¼ teaspoon ground cloves
¼ teaspoon allspice
2 cups condensed milk
1 cup moist flaked coconut

1. Preheat oven to 300° F. Line 2 2-pound baking pans with heavy paper. Grease paper.
2. In mixing bowl combine pineapple, cherries, dates and pecans. Sift together flour, salt and spices over fruit mixture; mix.
3. Add milk and coconut; mix thoroughly. Spoon into pans.
4. Bake in preheated oven for 1¼ hours. Remove from pans; cool on wire racks; wrap in aluminum foil. Store in refrigerator.

Thelma Miles, Culture Club, Columbiana, Ala.

GOLDEN FRUITCAKE

Makes 8 Pounds

6 cups presifted flour
3 teaspoons baking powder
1 teaspoon salt
2 teaspoons cinnamon
1 pound seedless raisins
½ pound candied citron, diced
½ pound candied cherries, chopped
¼ pound candied lemon peel, diced
½ pound candied orange peel, diced
1 pound figs, diced
1 pound chopped walnuts or pecans
2 cups butter or margarine
2 cups brown sugar
1 cup grape jelly
8 eggs
1 cup milk
2 teaspoons vanilla

1. Preheat oven to 275° F. Grease 4 8-inch loaf pans. Line bottoms with brown paper; grease paper.
2. Into mixing bowl sift together flour, baking powder, salt and cinnamon; reserve half.
3. Add raisins, citron, cherries, lemon peel, orange peel, figs and nuts to remaining flour mixture in bowl; mix well.
4. In another mixing bowl cream butter or margarine and sugar until light and fluffy. Add jelly; beat well to blend. Add eggs, one at a time, beating well after each addition.
5. Combine milk and vanilla; add alternately with reserved flour mixture to creamed mixture, beating well after each addition. Stir in fruit mixture.
6. Fill pans two-thirds full; make well in center of batter. Cover with brown paper.
7. Bake in preheated oven for 2 to 3 hours, depending on size. Cool in pans.

Mrs. George Shepherd, Sr., Woman's Club, Mound, Minn.

WHITE FRUITCAKE

Makes 10-Inch Ring

3 cups cake flour, sifted
1 pound seedless raisins
1¼ pounds candied cherries
1¼ pounds candied pineapple, chopped
4 cups chopped pecans
1 cup butter
1½ cups sugar
6 eggs, separated
½ teaspoon vanilla
½ teaspoon almond extract
½ teaspoon lemon extract

1. Preheat oven to 275° F. Grease 10-inch tube pan. Line with waxed paper. Grease paper.
2. Put 1 cup of the flour in mixing bowl; add raisins, cherries, pineapple and pecans; mix well.
3. In another mixing bowl cream butter and sugar until light and fluffy. Add egg yolks, one at a time, beating well after each addition. Stir in remaining flour; blend well.
4. In another mixing bowl beat egg whites until stiff but not dry; fold with vanilla, almond extract and lemon extract into egg yolk mixture.
5. Stir in fruit mixture; blend well. Turn into pan.
6. Bake in preheated oven for about 3 hours. Cool in pan.

Mrs. Malcolm Stubblefield, Civic Club, Fulton, Miss.

BISHOP'S CAKE

Makes 9-Inch Loaf

1½ cups sifted cake flour
1½ teaspoons baking powder
¼ teaspoon salt
6-ounce package semi-sweet chocolate pieces
2 cups chopped walnuts
1 cup chopped dates
1 cup halved candied cherries
1 cup diced candied pineapple
2 eggs
1 cup sugar
2 tablespoons rum

1. Preheat oven to 325° F. Grease 9-inch loaf pan. Line bottom with waxed paper. Grease paper.
2. Into mixing bowl sift together flour, baking powder and salt. Stir in chocolate, walnuts, dates, cherries and pineapple.
3. In another mixing bowl beat eggs and sugar until thickened and lemon-colored. Stir in fruit mixture; blend well. Stir in rum. Turn into pan.

4. Bake in preheated oven for about 1½ hours. Cool for 10 minutes; remove from pan; cool on wire rack.

Myrna McQuillen, Buechel Woman's Club, Louisville, Ky.

CHRISTMAS CHERRY CAKE

Makes 9-Inch Loaf

1 cup presifted flour
1 teaspoon baking powder
½ teaspoon salt
1 pound pitted dates, chopped
½ pound candied cherries
1 pound pecan halves
2 slices candied pineapple, chopped
4 eggs
1 cup sugar
1 teaspoon vanilla

1. Preheat oven to 275° F. Grease 9-inch loaf pan. Line bottom and sides with waxed paper. Grease paper.
2. Into mixing bowl sift together flour, baking powder and salt. Add dates, cherries, pecans and pineapple; mix well.
3. In another mixing bowl beat eggs until foamy. Add sugar and vanilla; beat until thickened and lemon-colored. Add flour mixture; blend well. Turn into pan; cover with piece of waxed paper.
4. Bake in preheated oven for 2 hours. Cool for 15 minutes; remove from pan; cool on wire rack.

Dixie Garison, Woman's Club, Abbeville, La.

EGGNOG CAKE

Makes 10-Inch Ring

4 cups presifted flour
1 pound candied pineapple, diced
1 pound candied cherries, halved
2 teaspoons baking powder
1 cup butter
2½ cups sugar
6 eggs
1 cup whiskey

1. Preheat oven to 325° F. Grease 10-inch tube pan well. Line bottom with waxed paper. Grease paper.
2. Put 1 cup of the flour in mixing bowl; add pineapple and cherries; mix well.
3. Onto piece of waxed paper sift together remaining flour and baking powder.
4. In another mixing bowl cream butter and sugar until light and fluffy. Add eggs, one at a time, beating well after each addition.
5. Add flour mixture and whiskey alternately, beating well after each addition. Stir in fruit mixture; turn into pan.
6. Bake in preheated oven, with pan of hot water on lower shelf, for about 2½ hours. Cool for 15 minutes; remove from pan; cool on wire rack.

Mrs. Wilson Smith, Woman's Club, Huntington, N.Y.

KING'S CAKE

Makes 9-Inch Ring

1 cup butter
5 eggs, separated

1½ cups sugar
2 tablespoons lemon juice
2 teaspoons grated lemon rind
½ cup rum
1 teaspoon salt
¾ cup seedless raisins
2¾ cups cake flour
1 tablespoon cornstarch
½ cup chopped almonds
Dash of almond extract
1 teaspoon baking powder

1. Preheat oven to 350° F. Grease and flour 9-inch tube pan well.
2. In mixing bowl cream butter until light. Stir in egg yolks, sugar, lemon juice and rind, rum, salt and raisins.
3. Onto piece of waxed paper sift together flour and cornstarch; stir into batter. Beat for 5 minutes.
4. In another mixing bowl beat egg whites until stiff but not dry; fold in almonds, almond extract and baking powder into batter. Turn into pan.
5. Bake in preheated oven for about 1 hour. Cool for 15 minutes; remove from pan; cool on wire rack.

Mrs. Billy Ginn, Glendale Estates Woman's Club, Decatur, Ga.

SAUSAGE CAKE

Makes 9-Inch Ring

1 pound sausage meat
1½ cups brown sugar
1½ cups granulated sugar
2 eggs, lightly beaten
3 cups presifted flour
1 teaspoon powdered ginger
1 teaspoon baking powder
1 teaspoon pumpkin pie spice
1 teaspoon baking soda
1 cup strong black coffee
1 cup seedless raisins
1 cup chopped walnuts

1. Preheat oven to 350° F. Grease and flour 9-inch tube pan.
2. In mixing bowl combine sausage meat and sugars; stir until well blended. Add eggs; mix well.
3. Onto piece of waxed paper sift together flour, ginger, baking powder and pumpkin pie spice.
4. Stir baking soda into coffee.
5. Add flour mixture and coffee alternately to sausage meat mixture, beating well after each addition.
6. Pour boiling water over raisins; let stand for 5 minutes; drain well; dry in cloth. Fold with walnuts into batter. Turn into pan.
7. Bake in preheated oven for about 1 hour. Test cake for doneness; if necessary, turn temperature to 275° F.; bake for 20 minutes longer. Cool in pan.

Mrs. Robert Fenton, 2nd District, New York State Federation of Woman's Clubs

Cheesecakes

BILL'S CHEESECAKE

Makes 9-Inch Square

1½ cups graham cracker crumbs
1 cup sugar
½ cup chopped pecans
⅓ cup melted shortening
3 eggs, separated
3 8-ounce packages cream cheese
1 teaspoon vanilla
1½ tablespoons flour
⅔ cup heavy cream, whipped
¼ cup currants

1. Preheat oven to 300° F. Grease 9-inch square baking pan.
2. In mixing bowl combine crumbs, ⅓ cup of the sugar, pecans and shortening; mix well. Press into bottom of pan; reserve about ¼ cup for topping.
3. Beat egg yolks well; gradually beat in remaining sugar, cheese, vanilla and flour.
4. Beat egg whites until stiff but not dry; fold two-thirds with cream into cheese mixture. Stir in currants.
5. Pour filling into crust. Fold remaining egg whites into reserved crumb mixture; spread over filling.
6. Bake in preheated oven for 1 hour. Cool.

Helen Munson, Masonic Service Association, Washington, D.C.

BLUEBERRY CHEESECAKE

Makes 8-Inch Cake

1½ cups graham cracker crumbs
1 cup sugar
¼ cup melted butter or margarine
8-ounce package cream cheese
2 eggs
1-pound can blueberry pie mix
1 cup heavy cream, whipped

1. Preheat oven to 350° F. Grease 8-inch spring-form pan.
2. In mixing bowl blend crumbs, ½ cup of the sugar and butter or margarine.
3. Press into bottom and sides of pan. Bake in preheated oven for 10 minutes.
4. In mixing bowl beat cheese until soft and fluffy. Add eggs and remaining sugar; beat until blended.
5. Pour into crust; bake for 20 minutes longer.
6. Cool. Top with blueberry pie mix. Spread whipped cream on top. Refrigerate until serving time.

Joyce Roth, Cynosure Women's Club, Casselton, N. D.

CHERRY CHEESECAKE

Makes 9-Inch Cake

1 cup plus 3 tablespoons sugar
½ pound cottage cheese
8-ounce package cream cheese
2 eggs
1 teaspoon vanilla
1 to 1½ cups crushed graham crackers

¼ cup butter, melted
1-pound 3-ounce can pitted sour red cherries
1 tablespoon cornstarch
Few drops red food coloring (optional)

1. Grease 9-inch spring-form pan.
2. In mixing bowl combine ¾ cup of the sugar, cottage cheese, cream cheese, eggs and vanilla. Beat for 15 minutes. (Use electric beater if possible.)
3. Combine crackers, ¼ cup of the sugar and butter. Press into bottom and sides of pan.
4. Preheat oven to 350° F.
5. Pour cheese filling into crust; bake in preheated oven for 25 minutes.
6. Remove from oven; cool. Drain cherry syrup into saucepan; and arrange cherries on cake.
7. Stir cornstarch, remaining sugar, and food coloring, if desired, into cherry syrup. Bring to boil, stirring. Spoon on cherries. Refrigerate until serving time.

Mrs. Frances Westley, Juniors of Eastchester Woman's Club, Eastchester, N.Y.

COTTAGE CHEESECAKE

Makes 10-Inch Cake

½ pound graham crackers, crushed
½ cup confectioners' sugar
⅓ cup melted butter
4 eggs
2 pounds large-curd cottage cheese, finely ground
1 cup heavy cream
1 teaspoon vanilla
2 tablespoons flour
1½ cups granulated sugar
Pinch of salt

1. Preheat oven to 350° F. Grease 10-inch spring-form pan.
2. Combine crackers, confectioners' sugar and butter; use to line bottom and sides of pan. Reserve a few crumbs for topping.
3. Beat eggs until light. Stir in remaining ingredients in order given.
4. Pour into crust; sprinkle with reserved crumbs; bake in preheated oven for 1 hour. Refrigerate until serving time.

Mrs. Roger Paulson, Junior Woman's Club, Wauwatosa, Wis.

CRANBERRY CHEESECAKE

Makes 8-Inch Cake

1¼ cups finely crushed vanilla wafers
¾ cup sugar
¼ cup melted butter
2 8-ounce packages cream cheese
½ teaspoon cinnamon
1 teaspoon vanilla
3 eggs, lightly beaten
½ envelope gelatin
3 tablespoons water
1-pound can whole cranberry sauce
1 cup sour cream
2 tablespoons chopped pecans

1. Preheat oven to 350° F. Grease 8-inch spring-form pan.
2. In mixing bowl combine wafers, ¼ cup of the sugar and butter; press into bottom and sides of pan. Bake in preheated oven for 10 minutes. Cool.
3. Meanwhile, in mixing bowl beat cheese until fluffy. Add remaining sugar, cinnamon and vanilla; beat well. Blend in eggs; pour into crust.
4. Bake for 35 to 40 minutes longer. Cool.
5. Soak gelatin in water; stir over hot water until dissolved. Stir into cranberry sauce; cool.
6. Spread cranberry mixture on cheesecake. Spread sour cream over cranberry mixture; refrigerate until serving time. Just before serving, sprinkle with pecans.

Mrs. William Huey, Suburban Club,
Sandborn, Ind.

Tortes

Torte (plural: *Torten*) is a German word for a flat cake or tart. Usually a torte is a shallow cake, rich with beaten eggs and lavishly flavored with chopped nuts, but today the word is used to denote a cake that is very rich and delicious.

BLITZ TORTE
Makes 2 8-Inch Layers

1 cup presifted flour
1 teaspoon baking powder
4 eggs, separated
½ cup butter or margarine
1½ cups sugar
5 tablespoons water
1 teaspoon vanilla
½ teaspoon cream of tartar
½ cup thinly sliced blanched almonds
Lemon Filling (p. 631)

1. Preheat oven to 325° F. Grease 2 8-inch layer cake pans. Line bottoms with circles of waxed paper. Grease paper.
2. Onto piece of waxed paper sift together flour and baking powder.
3. In bowl beat egg yolks until thickened and lemon-colored.
4. In mixing bowl cream butter or margarine and ½ cup of the sugar until light and fluffy. Add egg yolks; beat until smooth. Add water and vanilla; stir until blended.
5. Fold in flour mixture; spread in pans.
6. Beat egg whites and cream of tartar until foamy. Gradually beat in remaining sugar until stiff and glossy. Spread evenly on batter. Sprinkle with almonds.
7. Bake in preheated oven for 50 minutes. Cool for 10 minutes; remove from pans; cool on wire rack.
8. Put layers together with Lemon Filling.

Indiana Harbor Junior Woman's Club,
East Chicago, Ind.

BLUEBERRY TORTE
Makes 10 x 6-Inch Layer

1 cup presifted flour
Sugar
½ cup butter or margarine
1-pound can blueberries
¼ cup cornstarch
½ cup water
4 egg whites
Whipped cream (optional)

1. Preheat oven to 350° F. Grease and flour 10 x 6 x 1½-inch baking pan.
2. In mixing bowl blend flour and 1½ tablespoons sugar. Cut in butter or margarine until mixture resembles fine crumbs; press into pan. Bake in preheated oven for 20 minutes.
3. Meanwhile, drain blueberries; reserve syrup.
4. In saucepan combine 1 cup sugar and cornstarch; blend in water to make a smooth paste. Stir in reserved syrup. Cook over medium heat, stirring constantly, until thickened and clear. Remove from heat; stir in blueberries. Cool.
5. In mixing bowl beat egg whites until stiff but not dry; fold into blueberry mixture; pour over crust.
6. Bake in preheated oven for 15 to 20 minutes. Cool. Serve with whipped cream, if desired.

Mrs. Mary Brogren, Woman's Club,
Crystal Lake, Ill.

BITS AND PIECES TORTE
Serves 10 to 12

2 tablespoons gelatin
¼ cup cold water
1 cup boiling water
1 cup orange juice
1 tablespoon lemon juice
Sugar
Pinch of salt
2 cups heavy cream
Baked Angel Food Cake (p. 609)
Slivered almonds

1. Day before, soften gelatin in cold water; add boiling water; stir until completely dissolved.
2. Stir in orange juice, lemon juice, 1 cup sugar and salt. Chill until thickened and just beginning to set.
3. Whip 1 cup of the cream; fold into gelatin mixture; refrigerate remaining cream.
4. Line large round bowl with waxed paper. Tear Angel Food Cake into chunks; put in bowl in layers, alternating layer of cake and layer of cream mixture. Refrigerate overnight.
5. Next day, whip remaining cream; sweeten to taste. Unmold cake; frost with sweetened cream; garnish with almonds.

Mrs. Ben Bakanec, Junior Woman's Club,
Diamond Bar, Calif.

PRISM TORTE
Makes 9-Inch Torte

3-ounce package lime gelatin
4½ cups boiling water

2 3-ounce packages cherry gelatin
3-ounce package lemon gelatin
1 cup hot pineapple juice
¼ cup sugar
½ cup cold water
1 cup heavy cream, whipped
1 cup graham cracker crumbs
¼ cup melted butter

1. Day before, dissolve lime gelatin in 1½ cups of the boiling water; turn into 8-inch square baking pan; chill until firm.
2. Dissolve cherry gelatin in remaining boiling water; turn into 2 8-inch square baking pans; chill until firm.
3. Next day, dissolve lemon gelatin in pineapple juice. Stir in sugar and cold water; chill until slightly thickened. Fold in cream.
4. Cut lime and cherry gelatins into ½-inch cubes; fold into lemon gelatin.
5. Mix crumbs and butter; press into bottom of 9-inch spring-form pan. Pour gelatin mixture over crust; chill until firm.
6. Remove sides of pan; cut into slices.

Mrs. Edith Vinyard and Mrs. Donna Casey,
Sorosis Club, Shattuck, Okla.

RED-LETTER DAY TORTE

Makes 11 x 7-Inch Layer

2 cups presifted flour
1 teaspoon salt
1 cup shortening
4 eggs
1-pound can pie cherries
1½ cups sugar
3 tablespoons tapioca
¼ teaspoon red food coloring
2 teaspoons lemon juice
1 teaspoon vanilla
¼ teaspoon cream of tartar
¾ cup chopped nuts

1. Preheat oven to 425° F. Grease and flour 11 x 7 x 1½-inch baking pan.
2. Into mixing bowl sift together flour and salt. Cut in shortening until mixture resembles fine crumbs.
3. Separate 3 of the eggs; reserve.
4. Stir in remaining egg into flour mixture; mix to form a soft dough. Spread in pan.
5. Bake in preheated oven for 20 minutes. Remove from oven; set aside. Turn temperature to 350° F.
6. Meanwhile, prepare cherry filling: Drain cherries; reserve syrup; add water to total 1 cup; put in saucepan. Stir in egg yolks, ¾ cup of the sugar, tapioca and food coloring. Cook over low heat, stirring constantly, until thickened and smooth. Remove from heat; stir in cherries and lemon juice.
7. Prepare meringue: Put egg whites in mixing bowl. Add vanilla and cream of tartar; beat until foamy. Gradually beat in remaining sugar until stiff and glossy. Fold in nuts.
8. Pour cherry filling into crust; spread with meringue.

9. Bake in preheated oven for 20 minutes, or until golden. Cool. Cut into squares.

Dorothy K. Sumnick, Woman's Club,
Waterloo, Neb.

BLACK FOREST TORTE

Serves 16

1½ cups egg whites
½ teaspoon salt
2½ cups sugar
4 1-ounce squares semi-sweet chocolate
3 cups heavy cream
2 cups finely chopped toasted almonds

1. Preheat oven to 250° F. Trace 3 9-inch circles on waxed paper; arrange on baking sheets.
2. Beat egg whites and salt until stiff peaks form. Gradually beat in 1½ cups of the sugar by tablespoons; beat until very stiff; spread evenly over 3 circles.
3. Bake in preheated oven for 2½ hours. Cool.
4. Melt 3 of the chocolate squares; spread on cake; let stand until firm.
5. Whip cream until stiff but not dry, gradually adding remaining sugar. Fold in almonds.
6. Fill meringue layers with whipped cream mixture. Shave remaining chocolate over top. Refrigerate until ready to serve, or freeze.

Mrs. E. T. Fulkerson, Morning Study Club,
Victoria, Tex.

CHOCOLATE TORTE LILI

Serves 10 to 12

1 cup strong black coffee
1½ tablespoons sugar
2 tablespoons Grand Marnier
1 cup butter
2 large eggs
12 ounces semi-sweet chocolate, melted
Vanilla wafers
1 cup heavy cream, whipped and lightly flavored with Grand Marnier
Candied cherries, angelica and sugar crystals (optional)

1. Combine coffee, sugar and Grand Marnier.
2. Cream butter until fluffy; beat in eggs and chocolate.
3. Line 9-inch loaf pan with aluminum foil. Arrange layer of wafers on bottom; sprinkle generously with coffee mixture. Spread chocolate mixture on top. Continue in layers, finishing with wafers.
4. Cover top with aluminum foil; set another loaf pan on torte; weigh it down with a heavy stone. Refrigerate for at least 12, but preferably 24, hours.
5. To serve, frost sides and top with whipped cream. If desired, garnish with cherries, angelica and sugar crystals. Slice thinly; it is very rich.

Mrs. David Tolan, Junior Woman's Club,
Wauwatosa, Wis.

HELLO DOLLY TORTE

Makes 8-Inch Square

½ cup butter
1½ cups graham cracker crumbs
14-ounce can sweetened condensed milk
4-ounce can flaked coconut
1 cup chopped pecans
6-ounce package semi-sweet chocolate pieces

1. Preheat oven to 350° F. Grease 8-inch square baking pan.
2. In mixing bowl mix butter and crumbs; press into pan. Spread milk over crumbs. Top with coconut, then with pecans. Sprinkle chocolate on top.
3. Bake in preheated oven for 20 to 30 minutes. Cool in pan; cut into squares.

Mrs. Harry B. Hill, Jr., Book Lovers' Club and the Aliceans, Alice, Tex.

VIENNA SACHER TORTE

Makes 8-Inch Layer

½ cup butter
4 eggs, separated
1 cup sugar
1 cup presifted flour
8 ounces semi-sweet chocolate, melted
¼ cup jam
2 tablespoons shortening
Whipped cream

1. Preheat oven to 350° F. Grease and flour 8-inch spring-form pan.
2. In mixing bowl cream butter until light and fluffy. Add egg yolks, one at a time, beating well after each addition. Add sugar; beat until light and fluffy. Add flour and half the chocolate; blend well.
3. In another mixing bowl beat egg whites until stiff but not dry; fold into batter; turn into pan.
4. Bake in preheated oven for 1 hour.
5. Cool in pan; invert onto serving dish. Spread top with jam.
6. Melt shortening; stir into remaining chocolate; use to frost sides and top of cake.
7. Serve each slice topped with whipped cream.

Mrs. Paul Gerth, Community Woman's Club, Lake Zurich, Ill.

FRUIT TORTE

Serves 12

1 cup sugar
3 eggs, well beaten
1 cup cut dates
1 cup broken walnuts
2 tablespoons water
⅔ cup presifted flour
½ teaspoon baking soda
1 teaspoon baking powder
3 bananas, sliced
1 orange, sectioned
Red grapes, halved and seeded
1-pound can crushed pineapple, undrained
1 cup heavy cream, whipped

1. Preheat oven to 300° F. Grease and flour 13 x 9½ x 2-inch baking pan.
2. Beat sugar and eggs until thickened and pale. Fold in dates, walnuts, water, flour, baking soda and baking powder.
3. Turn batter into pan; bake in preheated oven for 20 to 25 minutes.
4. Combine fruits; spread on cake. Top with whipped cream. Refrigerate for several hours before serving.

Janet Arnold, Women's Club, Milton Junction, Wis.

PINEAPPLE TORTE

Makes 13 x 9½-Inch Layer

12-ounce package vanilla wafers, crumbed
½ cup butter
1½ cups confectioners' sugar
2 eggs
1-pound 14-ounce can crushed pineapple, well drained
2 cups heavy cream
½ cup chopped walnuts

1. Day before, grease 13 x 9½ x 2-inch baking pan.
2. Sprinkle half the crumbs in pan.
3. Cream butter and sugar until light and fluffy. Add eggs; beat well; spread on crumbs in pan. Spread pineapple on egg mixture.
4. Whip 1 cup of the cream until stiff but not dry; fold in walnuts. Spread on pineapple. Top with remaining crumbs. Cover; refrigerate with remaining cream overnight.
5. Next day, just before serving, whip remaining cream; spread on top.

Mrs. Frederick Fullam, Junior Women's Club, Nashua, N.H.

VIENNA PLUM TORTE

Makes 8-Inch Square

½ cup butter
1 cup sugar
2 eggs
1 cup presifted flour
1 teaspoon baking powder
¼ teaspoon salt
10 red or blue plums
2 teaspoons cinnamon

1. Preheat oven to 375° F. Grease and flour 8-inch square baking pan.
2. In mixing bowl cream butter. Add ½ cup of the sugar; cream until pale. Add eggs, one at a time, beating well after each addition.
3. Combine flour, baking powder and salt; beat into egg mixture. Spread in pan.
4. Cut plums in half; discard pits. Press plums, cut side up, in rows into pan.
5. Combine remaining sugar and cinnamon; spoon a little into each plum half.
6. Bake in preheated oven for 30 minutes. Serve hot or cold.

Mrs. Edwin Bollinger, Women's Civic Club, Richardson Park, Wilmington, Del.

BRAZIL NUT TORTE
Makes 9-Inch Layer

1 cup butter
2 cups sugar
4 eggs, separated
2¼ cups presifted flour
1 teaspoon baking powder
1 teaspoon baking soda
Pinch of salt
1 cup milk
1 teaspoon vanilla
1 cup chopped Brazil nuts
12 to 14 maraschino cherries, cut up
Favorite butter frosting

1. Preheat oven to 350° F. Grease and flour 9-inch spring-form pan.
2. Cream butter and sugar thoroughly. Beat in egg yolks.
3. Sift together flour, baking powder, baking soda and salt; add alternately with milk to egg yolk mixture, stirring until smooth after each addition. Stir in vanilla, nuts and cherries.
4. Beat egg whites until stiff but not dry; fold into batter.
5. Turn batter into pan; bake in preheated oven for about 1 hour. Remove sides of pan; cool.
6. Frost with favorite butter frosting.

Mrs. John Walker Crossett, Thursday Morning Club, Madison, N.J.

WALNUT TORTE
Makes 2 9-Inch Layers

12 eggs, separated
¾ cup sugar
¾ cup ground walnuts
1½ 1-ounce squares unsweetened chocolate, ground
¼ cup fresh bread crumbs
1 teaspoon baking powder
1 teaspoon lemon extract
Chocolate Rum Frosting (p. 623)

1. Preheat oven to 350° F. Grease 2 9-inch layer cake pans. Line bottoms with circles of waxed paper. Grease and flour paper.
2. In mixing bowl beat egg whites until stiff but not dry.
3. In another mixing bowl beat egg yolks and sugar until thickened and lemon-colored; blend into egg whites. Add walnuts, chocolate, crumbs, baking powder and lemon extract; fold in to blend well. Spread evenly in pans.
4. Bake in preheated oven for 30 minutes. Remove from pans; carefully peel off paper; cool on wire racks.
5. Fill and frost with Chocolate Rum Frosting.

Betty Windish, Woman's Club, Linglestown, Pa.

HUNGARIAN WALNUT TORTE
Makes 2 9-Inch Layers

½ cup presifted flour
½ teaspoon cocoa
½ teaspoon instant coffee
3½ cups ground walnuts
6 eggs, separated
1 cup sugar
1 teaspoon grated lemon rind
½ teaspoon vanilla
1 teaspoon rum
Favorite butter frosting

1. Preheat oven to 350° F. Grease and flour bottoms of 2 9-inch layer cake pans or pans with removable bottoms.
2. Into mixing bowl sift together flour, cocoa and coffee. Add walnuts; mix well.
3. In another mixing bowl beat egg yolks and ½ cup of the sugar until thickened and lemon-colored. Stir in lemon rind, vanilla and rum; set aside.
4. In another mixing bowl beat egg whites until foamy. Gradually beat in remaining sugar until stiff and glossy.
5. Add egg yolk mixture. Spoon one-fourth of flour mixture over egg yolk mixture; gently fold in with a few strokes until only partially blended. Repeat with second and third portions of flour mixture. Spoon remaining one-fourth of flour mixture over batter; gently fold in until just blended. Do not overmix. Gently turn batter into pans; spread to edges.
6. Bake in preheated oven for 20 to 30 minutes. Cool; remove from pans.
7. Fill and frost with favorite butter frosting.

Woman's Club, Palisade, N.J.

Cupcakes

CUPCAKES
Makes 36

3 cups presifted flour
3 teaspoons baking powder
1 cup butter
2 cups sugar
5 eggs
1 teaspoon vanilla
¼ cup milk (optional)
Confectioners' Sugar Icing (p. 622)

1. Sift together flour and baking powder twice.
2. Preheat oven to 375° F. Arrange 36 cupcake liners on baking sheet.
3. Cream butter until light; gradually beat in sugar until fluffy. Add eggs, one at a time, beating after each addition until smooth.
4. Fold in flour mixture. Stir in vanilla. If mixture is too thick, stir in milk. (This depends on size of eggs.)
5. Spoon batter into cupcake liners, filling them two-thirds full.
6. Bake in preheated oven for 12 to 15 minutes.
7. Cool on wire rack. Frost tops with Confectioners' Sugar Icing.

Mrs. Amelia Cabot, Woman's Club, Key West, Fla.

CHERRY CHEESE CUPS

Makes About 43

8-ounce box vanilla wafers
1 pound softened cream cheese
3 eggs, lightly beaten
½ cup sugar
1 teaspoon vanilla
1-pound can cherry pie filling

1. With scissors, trim wafers to fit bottoms of small cupcake liners. Arrange on baking sheet.
2. Preheat oven to 350° F.
3. Combine cheese, eggs, sugar and vanilla.
4. Fill cupcake liners about three-fourths full, using about 1 tablespoon of cheese mixture in each.
5. Bake in preheated oven for 15 to 20 minutes. Remove from oven; cool.
6. Top each cupcake with a few cherries and a little juice.

Woman's Club, Westwood, Mass.

BLACK BOTTOM CUPS

Makes 24

8-ounce package cream cheese
1 egg
1⅓ cups sugar
6-ounce package semi-sweet
    chocolate pieces
1½ cups presifted flour
¼ cup cocoa
1 teaspoon baking soda
1 teaspoon salt
1 cup water
⅓ cup cooking oil
1 tablespoon vinegar
1 teaspoon vanilla
1 cup chopped peanuts

1. Preheat oven to 350° F. Arrange 24 cupcake liners in muffin cups.
2. In small bowl blend cheese, egg, and ⅓ cup of the sugar until smooth. Stir in chocolate.
3. Into mixing bowl sift together remaining sugar, flour, cocoa, baking soda and salt. Stir in water, oil, vinegar and vanilla; beat until smooth.
4. Fill cupcake liners one-third full with chocolate batter. Spoon cheese mixture on top; sprinkle with peanuts.
5. Bake in preheated oven for 30 to 35 minutes.
6. Turn onto wire racks to cool.

*Mrs. Frank Moskel, Junior Women's
Civic Club, Indiana, Pa.*

CHOCOLATE CUPCAKES

Makes 18

½ cup shortening
1 cup sugar
2 1-ounce squares unsweetened
    chocolate, melted
2 eggs, lightly beaten
1 teaspoon vanilla
1 cup presifted flour
1 teaspoon baking powder
Pinch of salt
½ cup milk
Chocolate frosting

1. Preheat oven to 375° F. Line muffin pans with cupcake liners.
2. In mixing bowl cream shortening and sugar. Add chocolate, eggs and vanilla; mix well.
3. Combine flour, baking powder and salt; add alternately with milk to egg mixture, stirring well after each addition.
4. Spoon batter into cupcake liners, filling each two-thirds full.
5. Bake in preheated oven for 18 minutes.
6. Cool for 5 minutes; remove from pans; cool on wire racks. Frost tops with chocolate frosting.

*Mrs. Thomas Jackson, Janus Junior Women's Club,
Columbus, Ohio*

CREAM CUPCAKES

Makes 30

1¾ cups cake flour
1 cup sugar
2 teaspoons baking powder
¼ teaspoon salt
1 cup heavy cream
1 teaspoon vanilla
3 eggs

1. Preheat oven to 350° F. Arrange 30 cupcake liners on baking sheet.
2. Into mixing bowl sift together flour, sugar, baking powder and salt. Add cream and vanilla; beat for 1 minute (medium speed with electric beater).
3. In another bowl beat eggs until frothy; stir into flour mixture; beat for 1 minute. Place teaspoon of batter in each cupcake liner.
4. Bake in preheated oven for 12 to 15 minutes.
5. Turn onto wire racks to cool.

*Mrs. Robert Bristol, Konnaheeta Woman's Club,
Andrews, N.C.*

RUM CAKES

Makes 24

2 cups presifted flour
2 tablespoons cocoa
1 teaspoon ground cloves
1 teaspoon allspice
1 teaspoon cinnamon
1½ cups mixed candied cherries and
    candied pineapple
1 cup pecans
½ cup margarine
1 cup sugar
1 egg
1 cup applesauce
½ cup orange juice
1 teaspoon baking soda
½ cup hot water
1 teaspoon rum extract
12 ounces semi-sweet chocolate
    pieces
½ block paraffin

1. Preheat oven to 325° F. Grease 24 small muffin cups.
2. Combine 1 cup of the flour, cocoa and spices.
3. Mix candied fruits, pecans and remaining flour; set aside.

4. In mixing bowl cream margarine and sugar until light and fluffy. Stir in egg and applesauce. Add flour mixture alternately with orange juice.

5. Dissolve baking soda in water; stir into batter. Add rum extract; fold in fruit mixture.

6. Spoon into muffin cups; bake in preheated oven for 10 minutes.

7. Melt chocolate over hot water with paraffin; use to frost cakes.

Mrs. Edwin Hodge, Cosmos Club, Ruston, La.

SNOWBALLS

Makes About 30

4 8-ounce boxes butter cookies
1 cup finely chopped pecans
12-ounce pacakage dates, finely
  chopped

8 ounces marshmallows, finely cut
1-pound 12-ounce can crushed
  pineapple, undrained
1 quart heavy cream, whipped
  Shredded coconut

1. 2 days before, crumble 4 of the cookies into large mixing bowl; add pecans, dates, marshmallows, and pineapple; mix well. Refrigerate filling overnight.

2. Next day, spread a little filling on cooky; top with another cooky. Repeat until each snowball has 4 cookies and 3 layers of filling.

3. Frost sides and top of each snowball with whipped cream; roll in coconut. Refrigerate overnight to set.

Mrs. Robert Macfarlane, Woman's Club, Charleston, W. Va.

20. Frostings and Fillings

Cakes may be simply or lavishly embellished. Some people like only a dusting of confectioners' sugar on top of a plain poundcake; others like gobs of a rich butter frosting on a 1-layer cake; still others prefer a towering layer cake, filled and frosted with mountains of fluffy frosting. A layer cake usually means 2 layers, either round or square, put together with a filling between. However, when specified in a recipe, they may be 3 or even 4 layers high.

Basically, there are five different cake frostings:

1. *Sugar frostings* are easy to make and are suitable as a thin icing on small or large cakes. Usually they are very sweet.

2. *Creamy butter frostings* are rich and luxurious. A little of these goes a long way. They are easy to spread and may be used both to fill and to frost a layer cake.

3. *Cooked fluffy frostings* are based on beaten egg whites and cooked sugar syrup. They are, perhaps, the prettiest frostings and, like butter frostings, may be used both to fill and to frost layers. Sometimes the layers are put together with a custard-like filling; then the sides and top are lavishly coated with fluffy frosting

4. *Fudge frostings* are popular, though they are a little tricky to make and to spread. When cooked to the right degree as registered on a candy thermometer, they are a delicious sweet complement to small cakes or the larger one- or two-layer cakes. They may be used as both filling and frosting.

5. *Sweet toppings*, baked or boiled directly on a cake, are quick, easy and satisfying. These are usually suitable for one layer.

The correct way to fill and frost cakes is explained in the preceding chapter.

Sugar Frostings

CONFECTIONERS' SUGAR ICING

Makes About ½ Cup, or Sufficient
to Frost 9-Inch Layer Cake

1 cup confectioners' sugar (sift if lumpy)
4 teaspoons warm water
½ teaspoon lemon juice

Combine all ingredients in medium bowl; blend until smooth.

Mildred M. Dicker, Order of the Eastern Star,
Waukomis, Okla.

ORANGE ICING

Sufficient to Frost 9-Inch Layer Cake

1 tablespoon grated orange rind
½ teaspoon orange juice
1 tablespoon lemon juice
1 cup confectioners' sugar (sift if lumpy)

Combine all ingredients; blend until smooth.

Dorothy Buckminster, Woman's Club,
West Concord, N.H.

BONBON FROSTING

Sufficient to Frost 48 Cookies

1 cup confectioners' sugar (sift if lumpy)
1 teaspoon butter
2 tablespoons lemon juice
Food coloring

1. Combine sugar, butter and lemon juice; blend until smooth.

2. Tint with drop of food coloring. Or, if desired, divide frosting into three parts; color each with different shade of food coloring.

Mrs. Albert Goss, Janus Junior Women's Club,
Columbus, Ohio

MIRACLE ICING

Sufficient to Frost 8-Inch Layer Cake

1 cup sugar
1 egg white
¼ teaspoon cream of tartar
½ cup boiling water
2 tablespoons strawberry gelatin
1 teaspoon vanilla

1. In mixing bowl combine all ingredients except vanilla. Beat vigorously until peaks form (on high speed with electric beater).

2. Stir in vanilla.

Mrs. John P. Burke, Federated Woman's Club,
Bailey, Colo.

Creamy Frostings

BUTTER CREAM FROSTING

Sufficient to Fill and Frost 8-Inch Layer Cake

Mrs. Rizzo writes: "Not like the bakery butter cream, but almost like whipped cream. It can be refrigerated for some time; just let it soften slightly before using."

½ cup margarine
½ cup shortening
1 cup sugar
¾ cup lukewarm milk
1 teaspoon vanilla

1. In mixing bowl cream margarine and shortening. Beat in sugar and milk alternately.
2. Beat vigorously until granules cannot be felt between fingers (on high speed with electric beater for 10 minutes). Blend in vanilla.

Mrs. Joseph Rizzo, Junior Woman's Club, Lombard, Ill.

BUTTER NUT FILLING

Sufficient to Fill 10-Inch 3-Layer Cake

½ cup butter or margarine
2 cups sifted confectioners' sugar
⅔ tablespoon evaporated milk
1 tablespoon vanilla
1 cup chopped toasted almonds

1. In mixing bowl cream butter or margarine until soft. Gradually beat in sugar until light and fluffy.
2. Add milk and vanilla; beat until blended. Stir in almonds; mix well.

Mrs. James Riddle, Woman's Guild, Moultrie, Ga.

CHERRY ICING

Sufficient to Frost 24 Cupcakes or 8- or 9-Inch Layer Cake

4 tablespoons softened butter
1 teaspoon vanilla
½ teaspoon almond extract
¼ teaspoon salt
4 cups confectioners' sugar, sifted
4 to 6 tablespoons scalded cream
Few drops red food coloring

1. Combine butter, vanilla, almond extract and salt.
2. Blend in ½ cup of the sugar. Add cream alternately with remaining sugar, beating well after each addition. Add only enough cream to give good spreading consistency.
3. Stir in food coloring to make icing delicate pink.

Mrs. D. Howard Moreau, Woman's Club, Flemington, N.J.

CHOCOLATE FROSTING

Sufficient to Frost 10 to 12 Eclairs or 8-Inch Layer Cake

1 egg
⅓ cup melted butter
1½ 1-ounce squares unsweetened chocolate, melted
1 teaspoon vanilla
1½ cups confectioners' sugar, sifted

1. In mixing bowl beat egg until foamy. Add butter, chocolate and vanilla; stir until blended.
2. Add sugar; beat until smooth. If mixture is too thin, add a little sugar.

Norma Rankin, Champaign Urbana Junior Woman's Club, Champaign, Ill.

CHOCOLATE NUT FROSTING

Sufficient to Fill and Frost 9-Inch Layer Cake Generously

½ cup butter or margarine
2 1-ounce squares unsweetened chocolate, melted
1 egg
1 pound confectioners' sugar, sifted
1 teaspoon vanilla
1 teaspoon lemon juice
1 cup chopped walnuts

1. In mixing bowl beat butter or margarine until fluffy. Blend in chocolate and egg.
2. Gradually beat in sugar; beat until smooth. Stir in remaining ingredients.

Mildred Wells, Woman's Social and Benevolent Club, Lyons, Ind.

CHOCOLATE CHIP FROSTING

Sufficient to Frost and Fill 9-Inch Layer Cake

6-ounce package semi-sweet chocolate pieces
½ cup shortening
2 eggs
½ cup chopped walnuts
10 chopped candied cherries

1. Melt chocolate in top of double saucepan over hot water.
2. Beat shortening in mixing bowl. Add eggs, one at a time, beating well after each addition. Add chocolate; beat until thickened and smooth.
3. Stir in walnuts and cherries.

Mrs. Paul Manzoline, Women's Club, Negaunee, Mich.

CHOCOLATE RUM FROSTING

Sufficient to Fill and Frost 9-Inch Layer Cake

6-ounce package semi-sweet chocolate pieces
½ cup butter
1 egg
1 pound confectioners' sugar, sifted
¼ cup rum

1. Melt chocolate in top of double saucepan.
2. In mixing bowl cream butter until soft. Add egg; beat until smooth. Gradually beat in sugar and chocolate. Add rum; beat until smooth.

Betty Windish, Woman's Club, Linglestown, Pa.

MOCHA FILLING AND FROSTING
Sufficient to Fill and Frost 9-Inch Layer Cake

½ cup butter or margarine
1½ cups confectioners' sugar, sifted
1-ounce square unsweetened
    chocolate, melted
1 tablespoon instant coffee
¼ teaspoon vanilla

1. In mixing bowl cream butter or margarine until soft. Gradually add sugar; beat until smooth.
2. Add chocolate, coffee and vanilla; beat until blended.

Mrs. G. H. Graham, Woman's Club,
Bakersfield, Calif.

MOCHA BUTTER FROSTING
Sufficient to Fill and Frost 8- or 9-Inch Layer Cake or 20 Brownies

1 pound confectioners' sugar (sift
    if lumpy)
2 teaspoons instant coffee
¼ cup boiling water
¼ cup melted butter
1 teaspoon vanilla
3 tablespoons cocoa

Mix all ingredients in order given. Blend until smooth.

Elizabeth Rife, Donald District Woman's Club,
Wapato, Wash.

PARTY FROSTING
Sufficient to Fill and Frost 9-Inch 4-Layer Cake

1 cup butter
1 pound confectioners' sugar, sifted
5 eggs, separated
¼ cup lemon juice

1. Cream butter in mixing bowl until soft. Gradually beat in sugar until light and fluffy.
2. Add egg yolks, one at a time, beating well after each addition. Add lemon juice; beat until smooth.
3. In another mixing bowl beat egg whites until stiff but not dry; fold into creamed mixture.
4. Fill and frost cake as desired. Refrigerate for 6 hours or overnight.

Camilla Marm, South Hills Civic Club,
Bridgeville, Pa.

PINEAPPLE FROSTING
Sufficient to Fill and Frost 9-Inch Layer Cake

½ cup butter, melted
1 pound confectioners' sugar (sift
    if lumpy)
1-pound can crushed pineapple,
    drained

1. Add butter to sugar; mix well.
2. Beat in pineapple.
NOTE: If desired, a little syrup from can of crushed pineapple may be dribbled over cake layers before they are frosted.

Fern Beaty, Altruistic Club, Carlisle, Ark.

VANILLA BUTTER FROSTING
Sufficient to Fill and Frost 8-Inch Layer Cake

1 pound confectioners' sugar (sift
    if lumpy)
2 egg whites
½ cup butter or margarine
1 teaspoon vanilla

In mixing bowl beat all ingredients for 5 minutes, or until very creamy. If too dry and too thick, add few drops milk. Frosting should still be thick.

CHOCOLATE BUTTER FROSTING: Beat 1-ounce square unsweetened chocolate, melted, into above recipe.

Mrs. Del De Forest, Junior Woman's Club,
Diamond Bar, Calif.

CREAM CHEESE FROSTING
Sufficient to Fill and Frost 9-Inch Layer Cake

8-ounce package cream cheese
½ cup margarine
1 teaspoon vanilla
1 pound confectioners' sugar (sift
    if lumpy)

Beat all ingredients until well blended and velvety.

Anita M. Ferraez, International City Women's Club
(Gentilly Branch), New Orleans, La.

BANANA CREAM CHEESE FILLING
Sufficient to Fill and Frost 9-Inch 3-Layer Cake

½ cup butter or margarine
8-ounce package cream cheese
1 cup mashed ripe bananas
1 teaspoon vanilla
1 pound confectioners' sugar, sifted

1. In mixing bowl cream butter until soft. Add cheese, bananas and vanilla; beat until smooth.
2. Gradually add sugar; beat until smooth.

Woman's Club, Evergreen, Ala.

CHOCOLATE CREAM CHEESE FROSTING
Sufficient to Fill and Frost 8-Inch Layer Cake

¼ cup milk
3-ounce package cream cheese
2½ cups confectioners' sugar, sifted
1-ounce square unsweetened
    chocolate, melted
1 teaspoon vanilla
Dash of salt

1. In mixing bowl beat milk and cheese until smooth.
2. Gradually add sugar; beat until smooth.
3. Stir in chocolate, vanilla and salt; beat until blended.

Mrs. D. K. Hardy, Junior Federation of Women,
Fremont, Ohio

PEANUT BUTTER FROSTING
Sufficient to Frost 27 3 x 1-Inch Pan Cookies

1 cup confectioners' sugar (sift if lumpy)
¼ cup peanut butter
About ¼ cup evaporated milk

Combine all ingredients. Blend until smooth.

Mrs. Billie Wooster, Junior Woman's Club, Smyrna, Ga.

PRUNE ICING
Sufficient to Fill and Frost 8- or 9-Inch Layer Cake

2 cups confectioners' sugar (sift if lumpy)
2 tablespoons softened butter
⅛ teaspoon cinnamon
Pinch of salt
1 tablespoon lemon juice
2 tablespoons prune juice

Combine all ingredients thoroughly.

NOTE: If desired, decorate with candied fruits.

Mrs. F. M. Holden, Thursday Morning Club, Madison, N.J.

RAISIN FROSTING
Sufficient to Frost 9-Inch Square Cake

Spread on gingerbread cake, or use as desired.

2 tablespoons softened butter
2 tablespoons strong black coffee
1 teaspoon vanilla
¼ teaspoon cinnamon
⅛ teaspoon salt
1½ cups sifted confectioners' sugar
½ cup seedless raisins

Put all ingredients in mixing bowl; beat for 3 minutes. Let stand for 10 minutes; beat again until creamy.

Mrs. Leo Pollak, Woman's Club, Lincoln, Neb.

STRAWBERRY FROSTING
Sufficient to Fill and Frost 9-Inch 3-Layer Cake

½ cup butter or margarine, melted
1 pound confectioners' sugar, sifted
10-ounce package frozen strawberries, defrosted and drained

1. Pour butter or margarine into mixing bowl. Gradually add sugar; beat until smooth.
2. Add strawberries; beat until blended and smooth.

Mrs. Al Fortman, Junior Women's Club, Bismarck, N.D.

CHOCOLATE WHIPPED CREAM FROSTING
Sufficient to Fill and Frost 9-Inch Layer Cake

1 cup heavy cream
2 tablespoons cocoa
2 tablespoons confectioners' sugar (sift if lumpy)
¼ teaspoon vanilla

In mixing bowl beat cream until stiff. Fold in cocoa, sugar and vanilla.

Mrs. C. E. Reeves, Woman's Club, Merchantville, N.J.

Cooked Frostings

NEVER-FAIL BUTTER ICING
Sufficient to Fill and Frost 9-Inch Layer Cake

2½ tablespoons flour
½ cup milk
½ cup sugar
½ cup shortening
½ teaspoon vanilla
Dash of salt
Chopped nuts, melted chocolate or crushed pineapple

1. In small saucepan blend flour and milk to make a smooth paste. Cook over low heat, stirring constantly, until thickened and smooth. Cool.
2. In mixing bowl cream sugar, shortening, vanilla and salt until fluffy. Add milk mixture, a tablespoon at a time; beat until fluffy and thickened.
3. Stir in nuts, chocolate or pineapple.

Hariette Adams, Beverly Hills Junior Woman's Club, Chicago, Ill.

VIENNA FROSTING
Sufficient to Fill and Frost 9-Inch Layer or 10-Inch Ring Cake

⅞ cup sugar
½ cup presifted flour
2¼ cups milk
½ teaspoon vanilla
½ cup butter

1. In saucepan combine sugar, flour and milk. Bring to boil, stirring constantly; cook over low heat until very thick. Cool. Stir in vanilla.
2. Beat butter until light and fluffy; beat in milk mixture.

Jerry Wagner, Junior Woman's Club, Phoenix, Ariz.

EASY CHOCOLATE FROSTING
Sufficient to Frost 16 Fudge Bars

½ cup brown sugar
¼ cup water
2 1-ounce squares unsweetened chocolate
1 tablespoon butter
1 teaspoon vanilla
1½ cups sifted confectioners' sugar
Evaporated milk

1. In saucepan combine brown sugar, water and chocolate. Bring to boil; then simmer for 3 minutes.
2. Remove from heat; stir in butter and vanilla. Stir in confectioners' sugar and a little milk to give good spreading consistency.

Wilda Matthews, Plum Creek Valley Woman's Club, Pittsburgh, Pa.

CHOCOLATE PECAN FROSTING

Sufficient to Fill and Frost 9-Inch
Layer Cake

½ cup butter or margarine
¼ cup cocoa
⅓ cup milk
1 pound confectioners' sugar, sifted
1 teaspoon vanilla
1 cup chopped pecans

1. In saucepan combine butter or margarine, cocoa and milk; bring to boil.
2. Turn confectioners' sugar into mixing bowl; gradually stir in milk mixture. Add vanilla; beat until smooth. Stir in pecans.

Mrs. W. H. Clem, W.I.A.,
Las Cruces, N.M.

CREAMY NUT FILLING AND FROSTING

Sufficient to Fill and Frost 9-Inch
Layer Cake

2½ tablespoons flour
½ cup milk
½ cup butter
½ cup granulated sugar
½ cup chopped nuts
½ teaspoon vanilla
1 cup confectioners' sugar (sift if lumpy)

1. Combine flour and milk in saucepan. Cook over medium heat, stirring constantly, until thickened and smooth. Cool.
2. Meanwhile, in mixing bowl beat butter and granulated sugar until light and fluffy. Add milk mixture; beat until fluffy and smooth. Stir in nuts and vanilla.
3. Use one-third of mixture to fill cake.
4. Blend confectioners' sugar into remaining mixture; use to frost sides and top of cake.

Mrs. W. C. Cornelius, Woman's Colonial Club,
South Charleston, W. Va.

GERMAN FROSTING

Sufficient to Frost 8-Inch Cake

¾ cup sugar
2 egg yolks, lightly beaten
⅓ cup evaporated milk
1 tablespoon butter
Dash of salt
½ teaspoon vanilla
¾ cup chopped nuts
½ cup flaked coconut

1. In saucepan combine sugar, egg yolks and milk. Cook over moderate heat, stirring constantly, until thickened. Do not boil.
2. Remove from heat; stir in remaining ingredients.

Mrs. Vern McNeese, Junior Women's Club,
West Covina, Calif.

NEVER-FAIL THREE-MINUTE FROSTING

Sufficient to Frost 9-Inch Layer Cake

1 cup sugar
¼ teaspoon salt
½ teaspoon cream of tartar
2 egg whites

3 tablespoons water
1 teaspoon vanilla

1. In top of double saucepan combine all ingredients except vanilla. Cook over hot water; beat for 3 minutes, or until stiff peaks form.
2. Remove from heat; beat in vanilla.

Junior Woman's Club, Corpus Christi, Tex.

DIVINITY NEVER-FAIL ICING

Sufficient to Fill and Frost 9-Inch
Layer Cake

Mrs. Wilson writes: "I like to use this icing on a white cake or angel food cake and sprinkle with flaked coconut."

1½ cups granulated sugar
½ cup water
16 marshmallows
2 egg whites
½ teaspoon cream of tartar
About 1½ cups confectioners' sugar (sift if lumpy)

1. In saucepan combine granulated sugar, water and marshmallows. Cover; bring to boil over low heat. Remove cover; cook rapidly for 3 minutes.
2. Beat egg whites until frothy. Add cream of tartar; beat until soft peaks form. Gradually beat in hot syrup; beat until thickened.
3. Fold in confectioners' sugar (enough to give good spreading consistency).

Shirley Wilson, Anna Day Club, Troy, Mo.

CARMELITA'S LEMON MERINGUE FROSTING

Sufficient to Fill and Frost 9-Inch
Layer Cake Generously

5 egg whites
½ teaspoon cream of tartar
Pinch of salt
½ cup sugar
1 teaspoon lemon juice
½ teaspoon grated lemon rind

1. With electric beater beat egg whites until foamy. Add cream of tartar and salt; beat until stiff peaks form.
2. Gradually beat in remaining ingredients; beat until stiff and glossy.

Carmelita Kelly, El Camino Women's Club,
Ventura, Calif.

FLUFFY APPLE JUICE FROSTING

Sufficient to Fill and Frost 9-Inch
Layer Cake

1 cup sugar
½ cup apple juice
Dash of salt
1 tablespoon lemon juice
2 egg whites

1. In saucepan blend all ingredients except egg whites. Bring to boil; cook over medium heat to soft-ball stage (236° F. on candy thermometer).
2. Meanwhile, in mixing bowl beat egg whites until stiff but not dry. Gradually beat in apple syrup; beat until soft peaks form.

Chelan County Club, Chelan, Wash.

MELODY FROSTING

Sufficient to Fill and Frost 9-Inch Layer Cake

2 egg whites
1½ cups sugar
3 tablespoons maraschino cherry
    syrup
2 tablespoons water
1 teaspoon light corn syrup
Dash of salt
1 teaspoon vanilla
½ teaspoon almond extract

1. In top of double saucepan combine egg whites, sugar, cherry syrup, water, corn syrup and salt. Beat over rapidly boiling water until mixture holds peak.
2. Remove from heat; stir in vanilla and almond extract; beat until stiff enough to spread.

Mary Olander, Woman's Club, Nevis, Minn.

PEPPERMINT FROSTING

Sufficient to Frost 8-Inch Layer Cake

1½ cups sugar
1 tablespoon light corn syrup
5 tablespoons water
2 egg whites
½ cup crushed peppermint stick
    candy

1. In top of double saucepan combine all ingredients except candy. Beat over boiling water for 3 minutes.
2. Remove from heat; but leave over hot water; beat for 7 minutes longer.
3. Blend in candy.

*Mrs. Frank Brede, Woman's Club,
Flagler Beach, Fla.*

PINEAPPLE PARFAIT FROSTING

Sufficient to Fill and Frost 9-Inch Layer Cake

2 egg whites
1½ cups sugar
5 tablespoons pineapple juice
1 teaspoon light corn syrup
1 teaspoon grated lemon rind

1. In top of double saucepan combine all ingredients except lemon rind. Beat over hot water for about 7 minutes, or until mixture holds peak.
2. Remove from heat; stir in lemon rind.

Pearl Henry, Women's Club, Pawpaw, Ill.

SEAFOAM FROSTING

Sufficient to Fill and Frost 9-Inch Layer Cake

⅓ cup granulated sugar
⅓ cup brown sugar
⅛ cup water
1 tablespoon light corn syrup
1 egg white
¼ teaspoon cream of tartar

1. In saucepan combine sugars, water and corn syrup. Cook over medium heat, stirring constantly, until dissolved. Cook to soft-ball stage (236° F. on candy thermometer).

2. Meanwhile, in mixing bowl beat egg white and cream of tartar until stiff but not dry. Gradually beat in syrup; beat until stiff peaks form.

*Mrs. Julian W. Walton, Kentuck
Woman's Club, Ringgold, Va.*

BROWN SUGAR FROSTING

Sufficient to Frost 8-Inch Cake

2 cups brown sugar
2 tablespoons flour
½ cup milk
1 tablespoon butter
1 teaspoon vanilla
1 cup chopped walnuts, optional

1. In saucepan blend sugar and flour. Stir in milk. Bring to boil over medium heat; boil for 2 minutes, or to soft-ball stage (236° F. on candy thermometer).
2. Remove from heat; stir in butter and vanilla. Beat to good spreading consistency. If desired, add walnuts before frosting cake.

*Mrs. Carroll E. Miller, Chairman, Public Affairs
Department, General Federation of Women's
Clubs, and Crusade for Light Division,
Washington, D.C.*

BROWN SUGAR ICING

Sufficient to Frost 8-Inch Cake

½ cup butter
½ cup brown sugar
Few drops maple flavoring
2 tablespoons cream
Confectioners' sugar

1. Melt butter in saucepan. Stir in brown sugar; bring to boil; boil for 3 minutes.
2. Remove from heat; stir in maple flavoring and cream.
3. Beat in enough confectioners' sugar to give good spreading consistency.

Lena Burkley, Woman's Club, Salem, Ia.

CARAMEL CAKE FILLING

Sufficient to Fill 8- or 9-Inch Layer Cake

1 cup buttermilk
2 cups granulated sugar
½ teaspoon baking soda
½ cup butter or margarine
½ cup brown sugar
1 tablespoon vanilla

1. In saucepan blend all ingredients except vanilla. Cook over medium heat, stirring occasionally, until sugars are dissolved. Cook without stirring to soft-ball stage (236° F. on candy thermometer).
2. Remove from heat; cool. Add vanilla; beat until creamy.

*Mrs. W. C. Chick, Twentieth Century
Woman's Club, Beaver Dam, Ky.*

MRS. KITTLER'S CARAMEL FROSTING

Sufficient to Frost 9-Inch Cake

1 cup granulated sugar
1 cup brown sugar
¼ cup margarine
1 teaspoon vanilla
1 tablespoon flour
½ cup milk

1. Combine all ingredients in large saucepan. Bring to boil, stirring constantly; boil rapidly to soft-ball stage (236° F. on candy thermometer).
2. Remove from heat; beat to good spreading consistency.

Mrs. Chester Kittler, Altruistic Club, Carlisle, Ark.

MRS. SHARP'S CARAMEL ICING

Sufficient to Fill and Frost 9-Inch Layer Cake

½ cup butter or margarine
1 cup brown sugar
¼ cup milk
2½ cups confectioners' sugar, sifted
½ teaspoon vanilla

1. In saucepan combine butter or margarine and brown sugar. Bring to boil, stirring occasionally. Boil over medium heat for 2 minutes. Add milk; bring back to boil.
2. Remove from heat; gradually beat in confectioners' sugar. Stir in vanilla.

Mrs. J. Robert Sharp, Home Fire-lites Club, 7th District, Indianapolis, Ind.

PENUCHE ICING

Sufficient to Fill and Frost 8-Inch Layer Cake

2 cups brown sugar
½ cup milk
½ cup shortening
½ teaspoon salt
½ teaspoon vanilla

1. In saucepan combine sugar, milk, shortening and salt. Bring to boil over medium heat, stirring constantly; boil rapidly for 1 minute.
2. Remove from heat; beat until lukewarm. Add vanilla; beat until icing begins to lose its gloss and is thick enough to spread.

Mrs. O. T. Collins, Ploma Collins Study Club, Waco, Tex.

KATHRYN'S CHOCOLATE FROSTING

Sufficient to Frost 8-Inch Cake

1 cup cream
2 cups sugar
1-ounce square unsweetened chocolate
1 tablespoon butter
1 teaspoon vanilla

1. Combine all ingredients except vanilla in large saucepan. Bring to boil; cook rapidly to soft-ball stage (236° F. on candy thermometer).
2. Remove from heat; stir in vanilla. Cool; beat until creamy.

Mrs. R. D. Bruce, Junior Women, Coos Bay, Ore.

SAMMYE'S CHOCOLATE FROSTING

Sufficient to Frost 13 x 9½-Inch Cake

2 cups sugar
½ cup milk
¼ cup light corn syrup
3 tablespoons cocoa
½ cup chopped walnuts
1 teaspoon vanilla

1. In saucepan combine sugar, milk, corn syrup and cocoa. Bring to boil, stirring frequently. Boil to soft-ball stage (236° F. on candy thermometer).
2. Remove from heat; add walnuts and vanilla; beat until frosting loses gloss.

Sammye Baker, Study Club, Wink, Tex.

MRS. HOOD'S CHOCOLATE FROSTING

Sufficient to Frost 9-Inch 3-Layer Cake

1 cup milk
3 cups sugar
3 tablespoons butter or margarine
⅛ teaspoon salt
4 eggs yolks
4 1-ounce squares unsweetened chocolate, melted
1 teaspoon vanilla

1. In saucepan combine milk, sugar, butter or margarine and salt. Stir over medium heat until sugar is dissolved. Cover; cook for about 3 minutes.
2. Remove cover; cook to soft-ball stage (236° F. on candy thermometer).
3. In mixing bowl beat egg yolks. Add syrup in steady stream, beating constantly. Add chocolate and vanilla; beat until thickened. If frosting becomes too thick to spread, beat in few drops hot water.

Mrs. A. R. Hood, Delphian Literary Club, Amory, Miss.

FUDGE FROSTING

Sufficient to Frost 8-Inch Square Cake

2 cups sugar
1-ounce square unsweetened chocolate
⅔ cup milk
1 tablespoon butter

1. Combine all ingredients in saucepan. Cook over low heat, stirring constantly, until sugar is dissolved. Bring to boil; cook to soft-ball stage (236° F. on candy thermometer). Cool.
2. Beat until frosting has spreading consistency.

Jessie Carson, Woman's Club, Paxton, Ill.

CHOCOLATE FUDGE ICING

Sufficient to Frost 10-Inch Ring Cake

2 cups sugar
1 cup water
¼ teaspoon salt
2 1-ounce squares unsweetened chocolate
2 tablespoons light corn syrup
2 tablespoons butter or margarine
1 teaspoon vanilla

1. In saucepan combine sugar, water, salt, chocolate and corn syrup. Cook over low heat, stirring constantly, until sugar dissolves. Cover; cook for 2 minutes.

2. Remove cover; cook over medium heat to soft-ball stage (236° F. on candy thermometer).

3. Remove from heat; beat in butter or margarine. Cool; stir in vanilla.

4. Beat to good spreading consistency. If frosting becomes too stiff, beat in few drops hot water.

Mrs. A. M. Furr, Castalian Club, Tupelo, Miss.

SHINY CHOCOLATE FROSTING FOR BOSTON CREAM PIE

Sufficient to Frost 8-Inch Cake

1-ounce square unsweetened
    chocolate
2 teaspoons butter
¼ cup milk
1 cup confectioners' sugar
½ teaspoon vanilla

1. In saucepan combine chocolate, butter and milk. Heat slowly, stirring constantly, until chocolate is melted and mixture is smooth. Cool to lukewarm.

2. Beat in confectioners' sugar to give a good spreading consistency. Stir in vanilla. Frosting should be soft and glossy.

Jessie M. Witbeck, Cabot Club, Middleboro, Mass.

FRENCH COCOA FILLING AND FROSTING

Sufficient to Fill and Frost 9-Inch Layer Cake

1½ cups sugar
½ cup butter
½ cup heavy cream
⅛ teaspoon flour
¼ cup cocoa

1. Put all ingredients in heavy skillet; bring to boil, stirring constantly. Cook, stirring occasionally, until thickened.

2. Remove from heat; beat to good spreading consistency.

Mrs. J. D. McCullough, Jr., Junior Woman's Club, Smyrna, Ga.

SPECIAL FRUIT-NUT FROSTING

Sufficient to Frost 13 x 9½-Inch Cake

3 egg yolks
⅔ cup sugar
½ cup softened butter or margarine
½ cup seedless raisins
½ cup chopped coconut
½ cup chopped nuts

1. Combine egg yolks and sugar; beat until thickened and pale. Pour into heavy saucepan.

2. Add butter or margarine and raisins. Bring to boil; cook over moderate heat, stirring constantly, for 5 to 7 minutes, or until thickened.

3. Stir in coconut and nuts; spread immediately.

Martha Moore, North Morris Woman's Club, Wharton, N.J.

LEMON FROSTING

Sufficient to Frost 9-Inch Layer Cake

1 cup sugar
2½ tablespoons cornstarch
    Dash of salt
⅔ cup water
⅓ cup lemon juice
1 egg yolk
1 teaspoon grated lemon rind
3 tablespoons butter or margarine

1. In top of double saucepan combine ¾ cup of the sugar, cornstarch and salt. Slowly stir in water and lemon juice. Cook over hot water, stirring constantly, until thickened and smooth.

2. In small bowl blend remaining sugar and egg yolk; stir in a little lemon mixture; return to rest of lemon mixture. Cook over hot water, stirring constantly, for 2 minutes longer.

3. Remove from heat; stir in lemon rind and butter or margarine. Cool.

Mrs. J. W. Johnson, Jr., Junior Woman's Club, Elizabeth City, N.C.

Glazes and Toppings

GLAZE

Sufficient to Glaze 4 9-Inch Fruitcakes

2 tablespoons brown sugar
1 tablespoon light corn syrup
2 tablespoons water

1. Combine all ingredients in small pan. Bring to boil; then simmer for 3 minutes.

2. Remove from heat; cool slightly.

Mrs. W. A. Hailey, Junior Woman's Club, South Boston, Va.

CHOCOLATE GLAZE

Sufficient to Glaze 9-Inch Square Cake

1-ounce square unsweetened
    chocolate
1 tablespoon butter

Cook ingredients in top of double saucepan over hot water until melted and smooth.

Mrs. Max Lyons, Jr., Woman's Club, Higginsville, Mo.

CONFECTIONERS' SUGAR ORANGE GLAZE

Sufficient to Glaze 9-Inch Square Cake

1½ cups sifted confectioners' sugar
2 tablespoons softened butter
1 to 2 teaspoons grated orange rind
2 to 3 tablespoons cream

Combine ingredients.

Lorna Maycock, Woman's Club, Orem, Utah

VANILLA GLAZE

Sufficient to Glaze 48 Drop Cookies

1½ cups sifted confectioners' sugar
1 tablespoon melted butter
½ teaspoon vanilla
⅛ teaspoon salt
2½ tablespoons light cream

Combine all ingredients to good spreading consistency.

Charlotte Acton, Home and Country
Study Club, Fayette, Mo.

COOKED TOPPING FOR WHITE CAKE

Sufficient to Top 2 8-Inch Square Cakes

1 cup sugar
½ cup presifted flour
½ teaspoon salt
1½ cups water
1 teaspoon butter
½ pound dates, cut up
½ cup chopped walnuts
1 teaspoon vanilla
½ teaspoon lemon extract
8-ounce can crushed pineapple, drained

1. In saucepan combine sugar, flour and salt. Gradually stir in water. Add butter; cook over moderate heat, stirring constantly, until very thick.
2. Remove from heat; while hot, stir in remaining ingredients. Cool.

Normandine Leo, Woman's Club, Yale, Ia.

CHOCOLATE MINT TOPPING

Sufficient to Top 8-Inch Square Cake

2 tablespoons softened butter or margarine
1 cup sifted confectioners' sugar
1 tablespoon heavy cream
¾ teaspoon peppermint extract

In mixing bowl beat all ingredients until smooth.

Mrs. Max Lyons, Jr., Woman's Club,
Higginsville, Mo.

MERINGUE CRUNCH TOPPING

Sufficient to Top 13 x 9½-Inch Cake

2 egg whites
¼ teaspoon salt
1 cup brown sugar
½ cup chopped walnuts

In mixing bowl beat egg whites and salt until soft peaks form. Gradually add sugar; beat until stiff and glossy. Fold in walnuts.

Mrs. Ross Parsons, Victor Valley Women's
Club, Victorville, Calif.

NUT TOPPING

Sufficient to Top 10 x 6-Inch Cake

3 tablespoons butter or margarine
3 tablespoons water
1 cup ground walnuts
¾ cup brown sugar
1 egg, lightly beaten

1. In saucepan combine butter or margarine and water. Bring to boil over medium heat.
2. Remove from heat; stir in remaining ingredients.
3. Spread on top of cake; place under broiler heat until bubbling.

Mrs. Clyde Corrello, Home Life Chairman,
Michigan State Federation of Women's Clubs;
Woman's Study Club, Ypsilanti, Mich.

COCONUT NUT TOPPING

Sufficient to Top 13 x 9½-Inch Cake

¼ cup butter or margarine
⅔ cup brown sugar
1 tablespoon cream
½ cup flaked coconut
½ cup chopped nuts

1. Melt butter or margarine in small saucepan. Add sugar; stir over low heat until dissolved.
2. Remove from heat; stir in cream, coconut and nuts.

Mrs. William Burchfield, Junior Woman's
Club, Torrance, Calif.

Soft Cooked Fillings

BUTTERSCOTCH FILLING

Sufficient to Fill 9-Inch Layer Cake

½ cup sugar
1 tablespoon cornstarch
½ cup evaporated milk
⅓ cup water
⅓ cup butterscotch pieces
1 egg yolk
2 tablespoons butter
1 cup flaked coconut
1 cup chopped walnuts

1. In saucepan combine sugar and cornstarch. Gradually stir in milk and water to make a smooth paste. Add butterscotch and egg yolk; cook over low heat, stirring constantly, until thickened and smooth.
2. Remove from heat; stir in butter, coconut and walnuts.

Mrs. Julian W. Walton, Kentuck Woman's Club,
Ringgold, Va.

MARY'S CHOCOLATE FILLING

Sufficient to Fill 8- or 9-Inch 4-Layer Cake

2⅓ cups milk
½ cup granulated sugar
½ cup presifted flour
¼ cup cocoa
1 cup butter
1 cup confectioners' sugar (sift if lumpy)
2 teaspoons vanilla

1. In top of double saucepan combine ⅓ cup of the milk, granulated sugar, flour and cocoa.
2. In saucepan bring remaining milk to boil; gradually stir into cocoa mixture; cook over boiling water, stirring constantly, until thickened. Remove from heat; cool to room temperature.
3. Cream butter and confectioners' sugar thoroughly; add along with vanilla to cocoa mixture; beat until smooth.

Mary Greiner, Woman's Club, Willingboro, N.J.

CREAM FILLING

Sufficient to Fill 48 Sandwich Cookies

⅓ cup presifted flour
1 cup milk

Dash of salt
1 cup butter
2½ cups sifted confectioners' sugar
1 teaspoon vanilla

1. In saucepan blend flour and a little of the milk to make a smooth paste. Stir in remaining milk; cook over medium heat, stirring constantly, until thickened and smooth. Cool.

2. In mixing bowl cream salt, butter, sugar and vanilla until light and fluffy. Add milk mixture, a tablespoon at a time; beat until smooth.

Mrs. Patrick J. McCann, Woman's Club, Ebensburg, Pa.

CRÈME PATISSIÈRE

Makes About 2 Cups

2 cups milk
1-inch stick vanilla bean
⅓ cup presifted flour
1 teaspoon cornstarch
½ cup sugar
4 egg yolks

1. In saucepan heat milk and vanilla bean to just below boiling point.

2. In another saucepan blend remaining ingredients. Gradually stir in milk; cook over low heat, stirring constantly, until thickened and smooth.

3. Cool, stirring occasionally; discard vanilla bean. Consistency should be that of thick mayonnaise.

Submitted to Woman's Club, Kankakee, Ill., on behalf of Mrs. John F. Kennedy

CUSTARD CREAM FILLING FOR BOSTON CREAM PIE

Sufficient to Fill 9-Inch Cake

¼ cup sugar
¼ cup presifted flour
¼ teaspoon salt
2 cups milk
2 tablespoons butter
2 eggs or 4 egg yolks, well beaten
1½ teaspoons vanilla

1. In top of double saucepan combine sugar, flour and salt. Gradually stir in milk; cook over simmering water, stirring constantly, until thickened and smooth. Cover; cook for 10 minutes.

2. Add butter and eggs or egg yolks. Stir vigorously; cook, stirring constantly, for 1 minute longer. Remove from heat; cool; stir in vanilla.

Jessie M. Witbeck, Cabot Club, Middleboro, Mass.

QUICK CUSTARD FILLING

Sufficient to Fill 6 Petits Mille-feuilles or Napoleons

3-ounce package vanilla pudding mix
1 cup milk
½ cup heavy cream, whipped

In saucepan combine pudding mix and milk. Bring to boil over medium heat, stirring constantly. Remove from heat; cover surface with waxed paper; chill for 1 hour. Fold in cream.

A. S.

RICH CUSTARD FILLING

Sufficient to Fill 10 to 12 Eclairs

½ cup sugar
½ teaspoon salt
6 tablespoons flour
1 cup milk
1 cup light cream
4 egg yolks
2 teaspoons vanilla

1. In saucepan combine sugar, salt and flour. Gradually stir in milk and cream; cook over low heat, stirring constantly, until sauce is thickened and smooth.

2. In small bowl beat egg yolks; stir in a little sauce. Return to rest of sauce. Bring to boil, stirring constantly.

3. Remove from heat; stir in vanilla. Cool, stirring occasionally.

Norma Rankin, Champaign Urbana Junior Woman's Club, Champaign, Ill.

LEMON FILLING

Sufficient to Fill 8-Inch Layer Cake

2 egg yolks
½ cup sugar
1 tablespoon cornstarch
½ cup water
¼ cup lemon juice
2 teaspoons grated lemon rind
1 tablespoon butter or margarine

1. Beat egg yolks in top of double saucepan. Stir in sugar and cornstarch to make a smooth paste. Add water; cook over hot water, stirring constantly, until thickened and smooth.

2. Remove from heat; stir in remaining ingredients. Cool, stirring occasionally.

Indiana Harbor Junior Woman's Club, East Chicago, Ind.

LEMON BUTTER FILLING

Makes 2 Cups

Serve on angel food cake or in bite-size pastry shells.

3 eggs
1 cup sugar
Grated rind and juice of 2 lemons
1 tablespoon butter or margarine

1. In top of double saucepan beat eggs and sugar until thickened and pale. Add remaining ingredients.

2. Cook over hot water, stirring constantly, until thickened and smooth.

Mrs. A. M. Furr, Castalian Woman's Club, Tupelo, Miss.

MARSHMALLOW FILLING

Sufficient to Fill 48 Sandwich Cookies or 2 Layer Cakes

½ cup shortening
1 cup marshmallow cream
1 teaspoon vanilla
1 pound confectioners' sugar, sifted
Milk

In mixing bowl cream shortening, marshmallow cream and vanilla until smooth. Gradually beat in sugar and sufficient milk to give good spreading consistency.

Ruth Crowley, Woman's Club,
West Jonesport, Me.

ORANGE FILLING

Sufficient to Fill Jelly Roll or 9-Inch Layer Cake

2 tablespoons cornstarch
¼ cup water
1 cup sugar
2 eggs
Dash of salt
1 tablespoon grated orange rind
¼ cup orange juice
1 tablespoon butter

1. In small saucepan blend cornstarch and water to make a smooth paste. Stir in sugar, eggs, salt and orange rind and juice. Cook over low heat, stirring constantly, until thickened and smooth.
2. Remove from heat; beat in butter.

Mrs. D. D. Fluke, Seminar Club, Cuba, Mo.

ORANGE CUSTARD FILLING

Sufficient to Fill 8- or 9-Inch 4-Layer Cake

1 cup sugar
6 tablespoons flour
¾ cup orange juice
2 tablespoons lemon juice
2 tablespoons butter or margarine
Dash of salt
2 tablespoons grated orange rind
2 eggs
1 cup heavy cream, whipped

1. In top of double saucepan combine sugar and flour. Stir in orange juice to make a smooth paste. Add all remaining ingredients except cream. Cook over hot water, stirring constantly, until thickened and smooth.
2. Remove from heat; cool, stirring occasionally. Fold in cream; refrigerate until ready to use.

Mrs. Ralph Brubaker, Junior Woman's Club,
Torrance, Calif.

ORANGE PINEAPPLE FILLING

Sufficient to Fill 9-Inch 3-Layer Cake

1-pound can crushed pineapple
5 tablespoons cornstarch
2 cups sugar
¼ cup butter or margarine
1 cup orange juice
3 tablespoons grated orange rind
4 eggs
Dash of salt
1 cup flaked coconut

1. Drain pineapple. Add water, if necessary, to syrup, to total 1 cup.
2. In saucepan combine cornstarch and sugar. Gradually stir in syrup to make a smooth paste. Add butter or margarine and orange juice and rind; cook over medium heat, stirring constantly, until thickened and smooth.

3. In mixing bowl beat eggs and salt with a little of cooked mixture. Return to rest of mixture; cook over low heat, stirring constantly, for 3 minutes.
4. Remove from heat; stir in pineapple and coconut. Cool, stirring occasionally.

Mrs. R. L. Perry, Women's Co-Operative Club,
New Augusta, Miss.

PINEAPPLE FILLING

Sufficient to Fill 9-Inch Layer Cake

½ cup sugar
3 tablespoons cornstarch
½ teaspoon salt
¾ cup pineapple juice
9-ounce can crushed pineapple, drained
1 tablespoon butter
½ teaspoon lemon juice

1. In saucepan combine sugar, cornstarch and salt. Gradually stir in pineapple juice to make a smooth paste. Stir in pineapple; cook over medium heat, stirring constantly, until thickened and clear.
2. Remove from heat; stir in butter and lemon juice. Cool.

Mrs. Sheldon Mentch, Woman's Club,
Ebensburg, Pa.

PINEAPPLE CREAM FILLING

Sufficient to Fill 9-Inch Layer Cake

2 tablespoons cornstarch
⅔ cup sugar
1 cup water
8-ounce can crushed pineapple, undrained
3 egg yolks
1 teaspoon butter
1 tablespoon lemon juice

1. In top of double saucepan blend cornstarch and sugar. Stir in water and pineapple. Cook over hot water, stirring constantly, until thickened and clear.
2. In small bowl beat egg yolks; stir in a little pineapple mixture. Return to rest of pineapple mixture; bring to boil over hot water, stirring constantly.
3. Remove from heat; stir in butter and lemon juice.

Lyoce McCann, Woman's Club, Globe, Ariz.

FLAVORFUL WINE FILLING

Sufficient to Fill 9-Inch Layer Cake

¼ cup butter or margarine
½ cup sugar
4 egg yolks
¼ cup sweet white wine or sauterne
½ cup chopped nuts
½ cup finely chopped dates
½ cup chopped seedless raisins

1. Melt butter or margarine in saucepan.
2. Remove from heat; stir in sugar and egg yolks. Add remaining ingredients. Cook over low heat, stirring constantly, until thickened.
3. Cool.

Mrs. Joe Jobson, Southern Culture Club,
Northport, Ala.

21. Cookies

Most American homes keep a supply of cookies on hand, either in the cooky jar, readily available to eager hands, or in the refrigerator or freezer, ready to bake and serve warm and sweet-smelling from the oven. The material sent in by members of Federated Women's Clubs from every state contained enough cooky recipes to fill many books. Here is a happy cross section of America's favorite cookies.

There are six types of cookies:

Rolled cookies are made from a dough soft but firm enough to roll out easily on a lightly floured board. For ease in rolling, use a floured canvas to cover the board and a floured stocking on the rolling pin. Cut into a variety of shapes, arrange fairly close together on a baking sheet and bake according to recipe directions.

Drop cookies are made from a dough, firm yet soft enough to be pushed from a spoon directly onto a baking sheet. The softer the dough, the more the cooky will spread in the baking; mounds of dough should therefore be kept at least 1 inch apart. Bake according to recipe directions.

Molded or pressed cookies are made from a stiff dough that can be shaped with the palms of the hands into balls, sticks or crescents. The same dough may be forced through a cooky press onto a baking sheet in a variety of fancy shapes. Cooky presses are available in the housewares department of department stores. There are several types, but adequate instructions are enclosed with the press. Most molded cooky doughs should be refrigerated for at least 1 hour before being shaped.

Refrigerator cookies are sliced from a roll or rectangle of dough that has been chilled until very firm. Most refrigerator doughs may be kept in the refrigerator for weeks and sliced and baked as needed. Molded cooky dough may also be used to make refrigerator cookies (see p. 650).

Pan cookies are halfway between a cooky and a rich cake. The soft dough is spread into a greased pan, baked and then cut into squares or bars, while still in the pan. Usually the dough is filled with chopped fruits or nuts.

No-bake cookies are becoming increasingly popular in America. This type of cooky originated with bourbon balls, those fragrant unbaked confections that are part cooky and part candy. The state of Kentucky may rightly take credit for the origination of this sweet, even though rum and brandy are frequently substituted for Kentucky bourbon.

TO STORE COOKIES

Soft cookies should be stored in a container with a tight-fitting lid, but crisp cookies should be stored in a container with a loose-fitting lid. If they lose their crispness, they may be crisped in a slow oven for about 5 minutes. Store pan cookies in the pan in which they were cooked, covered with transparent film or aluminum foil.

TO FREEZE COOKIES

All cookies freeze well, but unbaked cooky doughs make the best use of valuable freezer space, for most baked cookies keep well at room temperature. Freeze rolled and cut cookies on baking sheets. When frozen, pack in refrigerator cartons, separating each layer with two pieces of waxed paper. Drop cooky batters directly onto the baking sheet in the same manner as if you were going to bake them, but instead freeze them. When frozen, pack in plastic refrigerator bags and return to freezer. Wrap refrigerator doughs in aluminum foil or transparent film and freeze; slice them when they are still frozen. Bake all frozen cookies directly from freezer according to recipe directions.

TO MAKE COOKIES

1. Read the recipe.
2. Assemble ingredients and utensils.
3. Grease baking sheet lightly with shortening or cooking oil. Generally two sheets are needed. While one is in the oven, the other may be filled. If only one baking sheet is available, let it cool, remove crumbs with a spatula and regrease it before using it again.
4. Preheat the oven.
5. Cream shortening and butter until light and fluffy. All or part margarine may be used.
6. Beat in beaten eggs.
7. Stir in combined dry ingredients alternately with liquid and flavorings specified in recipe, mixing thoroughly after each addition.
8. Drop, roll and cut or chill dough according to directions.

9. Bake according to directions, but watch baking time carefully, for cookies burn easily. It's difficult to give the exact time since a great deal depends on the size and thickness of the cookies. Crisp cookies are done when they are delicately browned. Drop cookies are done when an impression made by touching the center lightly with a finger does not remain. If your oven does not bake evenly, turn the baking sheet halfway through baking period.

10. Remove the cookies from the sheet with a spatula as soon as they come from oven; place them on a wire rack to cool.

Rolled Cookies

SUGAR COOKIES
Makes About 48

3 cups presifted flour
1 teaspoon baking soda
1 cup sugar
½ teaspoon salt
2 eggs, lightly beaten
3 tablespoons milk
1 teaspoon cream of tartar
1 teaspoon vanilla
1½ cups shortening

1. Sift together flour, baking soda, sugar and salt.
2. Combine eggs, milk, cream of tartar and vanilla; gradually mix alternately with dry ingredients into shortening.
3. Chill dough until firm.
4. Preheat oven to 350° F.
5. Roll out dough thinly on lightly floured board; cut with floured cooky cutters. Place on baking sheets.
6. Bake in preheated oven for 5 to 8 minutes, or until light brown.

Jeannine Schrank, Women's Club, Milton Junction, Wis.

MRS. EISENHOWER'S SUGAR COOKIES
Makes About 36

2 cups presifted flour
1 teaspoon baking powder
½ teaspoon salt
½ cup butter
1 cup sugar
2 egg yolks
1 tablespoon heavy cream
1 tablespoon vanilla

1. Grease baking sheets.
2. Onto piece of waxed paper sift together flour, baking powder and salt.
3. Cream butter and sugar in mixing bowl until light and fluffy. Add egg yolks; beat well. Add cream and vanilla; beat until smooth.
4. Gradually work in flour mixture to a smooth dough. Chill for 1 hour.
5. Preheat oven to 375° F.
6. Roll out dough to ¼ inch thick on floured board. Cut with floured 3-inch cooky cutter; place on baking sheets.

7. Bake in preheated oven for 10 to 12 minutes, or until light golden.

Tri-County Woman's Club, Venango County, Pa.

OLD-TIME BROWN SUGAR COOKIES
Makes About 72

4 cups presifted flour
1 teaspoon baking soda
1 teaspoon baking powder
½ teaspoon salt
2 cups brown sugar
1 cup butter
3 eggs, well beaten

1. Preheat oven to 350° F. Grease baking sheets.
2. Combine flour, baking soda, baking powder and salt. Stir in sugar.
3. Cut in butter.
4. Stir in eggs. Dough should be rather stiff.
5. Roll out dough thinly on lightly floured board; cut into desired shapes.
6. Arrange on baking sheets; bake in preheated oven for 10 to 12 minutes, or until delicately browned.

Ida LeNord, Artemisia Club 1960, Fallon, Nev.

BIZCOCHOS
Makes 144

This thin, crisp and delicately spiced Spanish cooky is a great favorite at fiestas and other special occasions.

6 cups sifted cake flour
2 tablespoons baking powder
1 teaspoon salt
1 pound lard
1¾ cups sugar
3 tablespoons cinnamon
¾ cup water
1 teaspoon aniseeds

1. Preheat oven to 375° F.
2. Onto piece of waxed paper sift flour. Sift again with baking powder and salt.
3. In mixing bowl beat lard until fluffy. Add ¾ cup of the sugar and 1 tablespoon of the cinnamon; beat until smooth.
4. Add flour mixture and water alternately to creamed mixture, beating after each addition until smooth. Work in aniseeds.
5. Put dough on lightly floured board; cut into 18 pieces. Knead each piece lightly; roll out to circle ⅛ inch thick. Cut each circle into 8 pie-shaped wedges.
6. Place on baking sheets; bake in preheated oven for 15 minutes, or until golden.
7. Meanwhile, mix remaining sugar and remaining cinnamon; dip in cookies, while still hot.

Mrs. Merle Creech, W.I.A., Las Cruces, N.M.

MRS. RICHARD NIXON'S CHOCOLATE BUTTER COOKIES
Makes About 96

2 cups butter
1 cup sugar
2 eggs, well beaten

1 teaspoon vanilla
4 cups presifted flour
½ cup cocoa

1. Cream butter and sugar in mixing bowl until light and fluffy.
2. Beat in eggs and vanilla.
3. Stir in flour and cocoa. Chill thoroughly.
4. Preheat oven to 400° F. Grease baking sheets.
5. Roll out dough thinly on lightly floured board; cut into desired shapes.
6. Arrange on baking sheets; bake in preheated oven for 12 to 15 minutes.

VARIATION: Use 3 1-ounce squares semisweet chocolate, melted, in place of cocoa in above recipe; add to creamed mixture.

Junior Woman's Club, Edgewood, R.I.

CREAM CHEESE COOKIES

Makes About 36

¼ pound softened butter
4 ounces softened cream cheese
Sugar
¼ teaspoon salt
2 eggs
1 teaspoon vanilla
1½ cups presifted flour
1 teaspoon baking powder

1. Cream butter and cheese in mixing bowl until fluffy.
2. Stir in ½ cup sugar, salt, 1 of the eggs and vanilla.
3. Combine flour and baking powder; stir into cheese mixture.
4. Roll out dough thinly on lightly floured board; cut with floured cooky cutter. Arrange on baking sheets.
5. Preheat oven to 325° F.
6. Beat remaining egg; use to brush surface of cookies. Sprinkle with sugar.
7. Bake in preheated oven for 12 to 15 minutes, or until light brown.

Mrs. D. C. Norton, Thursday Morning Club,
Madison, N.J.

FINSKA KAHAR

(Scandinavian Almond Cooky)

Makes About 48

¾ cup butter
¼ cup sugar
1 teaspoon almond extract
2 cups presifted flour
1 egg white
⅓ cup finely chopped almonds,
    mixed with 1 tablespoon sugar

1. Cream butter, ¼ cup of the sugar and almond extract in mixing bowl until light and fluffy.
2. Gradually work in flour to form dough. Chill for 30 minutes.
3. Preheat oven to 350° F.
4. Turn dough onto lightly floured board; roll out ⅛ inch thick. Brush with egg white; sprinkle with almond mixture.
5. Cut into ½-inch squares; place on baking sheets.
6. Bake in preheated oven for 15 minutes, or until light golden.

7. Cool for 2 minutes; remove from baking sheets.

Jeannie Worthing, Woman's Club,
Thompson Falls, Mont.

GERMAN CHRISTMAS COOKIES

Makes About 60

2 cups presifted flour
1 cup sugar
½ teaspoon cinnamon
½ teaspoon ground cloves
½ teaspoon nutmeg
¼ teaspoon baking soda
3 eggs
2 teaspoons grated lemon rind
½ cup finely chopped almonds
½ cup finely chopped candied citron
½ cup black coffee

1. Day before, into mixing bowl sift together flour, sugar, cinnamon, cloves, nutmeg and baking soda.
2. Separate 1 of the eggs; in small bowl beat egg white and remaining eggs. Add with lemon rind, almonds and citron to flour mixture; work together to form dough.
3. Turn onto lightly floured board; roll out ¼ inch thick. Cut with floured cooky cutter. Leave on board; cover with clean towel. Let stand overnight. Refrigerate egg yolk.
4. Next day, preheat oven to 375° F. Grease baking sheets.
5. Beat egg yolk and coffee. Arrange cookies on baking sheets; brush with coffee mixture.
6. Bake in preheated oven for 12 minutes, or until golden.

Mrs. R. F. Robinson, Daughters of Indiana,
Chicago, Ill.

HERMITS

Makes About 60

1 cup very finely chopped seedless
    raisins
⅔ cup shortening
1 cup sugar
⅔ cup milk
1 egg
1½ teaspoons baking soda
½ teaspoon nutmeg
½ teaspoon ground cloves
2 to 3 cups presifted flour

1. Preheat oven to 400° F. Grease baking sheets.
2. Put raisins in mixing bowl.
3. Melt shortening in small saucepan until it starts to bubble; remove from heat; pour over raisins. Stir in sugar, milk, egg, baking soda, nutmeg and cloves; mix well.
4. Add sufficient flour to make a dough stiff enough to roll.
5. Knead a few times on lightly floured board until smooth.
6. Roll out ⅛ inch thick; cut with floured 2-inch cooky cutter. Place cookies on baking sheets.

7. Bake in preheated oven for 10 minutes.

Mrs. William Horr, New Century Grange,
East Holden, Me.

OATMEAL COOKIES

Makes About 36

2 cups presifted flour
½ teaspoon salt
3 cups quick-cooking oats
½ cup butter
½ cup shortening
1½ cups brown sugar
⅓ cup milk
1 teaspoon baking soda

1. Into mixing bowl sift together flour and salt. Blend in oats. Cut in butter and shortening until mixture resembles coarse crumbs. Mix in sugar.
2. Blend milk and baking soda; stir into dry ingredients. Mix well; chill for 30 minutes.
3. Preheat oven to 375° F.
4. Roll out dough ¼ inch thick on lightly floured board. Cut with floured cooky cutter; place on baking sheets.
5. Bake in preheated oven for 10 to 12 minutes, or until golden.

Elinore Sooy, Junior Woman's Club,
Millville, N.J.

PEPPARKAKOR

(Swedish Ginger Cookies)

Makes About 96

⅔ cup brown sugar
⅔ cup dark corn syrup
1 teaspoon ginger
1 teaspoon cinnamon
½ teaspoon ground cloves
2¼ teaspoons baking soda
⅔ cup butter
1 egg
4 cups presifted flour

1. In saucepan combine sugar, corn syrup, ginger, cinnamon and cloves. Bring to boil, stirring frequently. Remove from heat; stir in baking soda.
2. Put butter in mixing bowl; pour sugar mixture over it; stir until melted. Add egg; blend well.
3. Gradually stir in flour to make a smooth soft dough.
4. Knead gently a few times on lightly floured board. Chill for 30 minutes.
5. Preheat oven to 325° F. Grease baking sheets.
6. Roll out dough ⅛ inch thick on lightly floured board; cut with floured cooky cutters. Place on baking sheets.
7. Bake in preheated oven for 8 to 10 minutes.

Mrs. Emil Johnson, Community Woman's Club,
Lake Zurich, Ill.

SAND TARTS

Makes About 36

1¾ cups presifted flour
2 teaspoons baking powder
½ cup butter
1½ cups sugar

1 egg
1 egg white
2 teaspoons cinnamon
Pecan or walnut halves

1. Day before, onto piece of waxed paper sift together flour and baking powder.
2. Cream butter and 1 cup of the sugar in mixing bowl until light and fluffy. Add egg; beat until smooth.
3. Gradually work in flour mixture to make a smooth dough. Refrigerate overnight.
4. Next day, preheat oven to 350° F. Grease baking sheets.
5. Roll out dough ¼ inch thick on lightly floured board; cut with floured 2-inch cooky cutter. Place on baking sheets; brush with egg white.
6. In small bowl combine remaining sugar and cinnamon; sprinkle on cookies. Press nut half in center of each cooky.
7. Bake in preheated oven for 10 to 15 minutes, or until golden.

Mrs. Frank Walther, Woman's Club,
Columbia, Pa.

SHORT'NIN' BREAD

Makes About 30

4 cups presifted flour
Dash of salt
1 cup brown sugar
2 cups butter

1. Preheat oven to 350° F.
2. In mixing bowl combine flour, salt and sugar; mix well.
3. Cut in butter until mixture resembles fine crumbs. Work together with hands until dough forms a ball.
4. Pat or roll out ½ inch thick on lightly floured board. Cut circles with floured 2-inch cooky cutter; place on baking sheets.
5. Bake in preheated oven for 25 minutes, or until golden.

Woman's Club, Newnan, Ga.

SCOTTISH SHORTBREAD

Makes About 36

Sugar
Dash of salt
2¼ cups presifted flour
1 cup butter

1. Preheat oven to 350° F. Grease baking sheets.
2. Combine ⅔ cup sugar, salt, flour, and butter together in mixing bowl; rub with hands until mixture resembles fine crumbs. Work with hands until pliable and smooth. (A little more flour may be necessary if weather is warm.)
3. Turn dough onto lightly floured board; roll out ¼ inch thick. Prick surface with fork. Cut with floured cooky cutter; place on baking sheets.
4. Bake in preheated oven for 15 minutes, or until just golden.
5. Remove from oven; sprinkle with sugar. Cool for 2 minutes.

Lucille Chastain, President, State Federation
of Women's Organization, Spokane, Wash.

SWEDISH CREAM WAFERS

Makes 60

1¼ cups softened butter
⅓ cup cream
2 cups presifted flour
Granulated sugar
¾ cup sifted confectioners' sugar
1 egg yolk
1 teaspoon vanilla
Food coloring

1. Mix 1 cup of the butter, cream and flour to a soft dough. Chill.
2. Preheat oven to 375° F.
3. Cover piece of waxed paper heavily with granulated sugar.
4. Roll out one-third of dough ⅛ inch thick on lightly floured board; cut into 1½-inch rounds. Keep remaining dough refrigerated until ready to use, rolling out only one-third at a time.
5. Transfer cooky cutouts to sugar-coated waxed paper; cover well with sugar.
6. Arrange on baking sheets; bake in preheated oven for 7 to 9 minutes, or until light browned. Cool.
7. Combine remaining butter and confectioners' sugar, egg yolk, vanilla and food coloring as desired; use to sandwich two cookies in pairs.

Carol Zuck, Woman's Club, Yakima, Wash.

VIENNESE SPECIALS

Makes 48

2 cups sifted cake flour
¾ teaspoon cinnamon
½ teaspoon ground cloves
Dash of salt
1 cup shortening
1 cup sugar
2 egg yolks
1 teaspoon grated lemon rind
1 cup ground walnuts
1 cup jam or jelly

1. Onto piece of waxed paper sift together flour, cinnamon, cloves and salt.
2. Cream shortening and sugar in mixing bowl until light and fluffy. Add egg yolks; beat well.
3. Gradually add flour mixture; beat until smooth. Add lemon rind and walnuts; mix well. Refrigerate for 1 hour.
4. Preheat oven to 400° F.
5. Roll out dough ⅛ inch thick between 2 sheets of waxed paper. Cut 48 circles with floured 2-inch cooky cutter; place on baking sheets. Spread tops with thin layer of jam or jelly.
6. Cut remaining dough into thin strips, 2 x ½ inch, rerolling dough if necessary. Press 2 strips of dough on each cooky to form a cross.
7. Bake in preheated oven for 10 to 15 minutes, or until light golden.

Ruth Mitchell, Woman's Club, West Frankfort, Ill.

Drop Cookies

FRESH APPLE COOKIES

Makes About 48

½ cup soft shortening
1⅓ cups brown sugar
½ teaspoon salt
1 teaspoon cinnamon
1 teaspoon ground cloves
½ teaspoon nutmeg
1 egg
2 cups presifted flour
1 teaspoon baking soda
1 cup chopped nuts
1 cup finely chopped apples
1 cup seedless raisins
¼ cup apple juice or milk
Vanilla Glaze (p. 629)

1. Preheat oven to 400° F. Grease baking sheets.
2. In mixing bowl combine shortening, sugar, salt, spices and egg. Beat well.
3. Sift together flour and baking soda; stir into egg mixture. Stir in nuts, apples and raisins. Blend in apple juice or milk; stir in remaining flour mixture.
4. Drop dough by tablespoons onto baking sheets; bake in preheated oven for 11 to 14 minutes, or until light brown.
5. Remove from sheets; spread while hot, with Vanilla Glaze.

Charlotte Acton, Home and Country
Study Club, Fayette, Mo.

BUTTERSCOTCH COOKIES

Makes About 36

⅔ cup shortening
1½ cups brown sugar
2 eggs
1 teaspoon vanilla
1 tablespoon vinegar
1 cup evaporated milk
2½ cups presifted flour
1 teaspoon baking soda
½ teaspoon baking powder
½ teaspoon salt
1 cup chopped walnuts
Confectioners' Sugar Icing (p. 622)
Walnut halves

1. Preheat oven to 350° F. Grease baking sheets.
2. Cream shortening and sugar in mixing bowl until light and fluffy. Add eggs; beat until smooth.
3. In small bowl mix vanilla, vinegar and milk.
4. Onto piece of waxed paper sift together flour, baking soda, baking powder and salt.
5. Add milk mixture and flour mixture alternately to creamed mixture, beating well after each addition. Stir in chopped walnuts.
6. Drop dough by tablespoons about 2 inches apart, onto baking sheets.
7. Bake in preheated oven for 15 minutes, or until golden.

8. Frost tops with Confectioners' Sugar Icing. Top each with walnut half.

Iris L. Cushing, President, Hancock County Republican Woman's Club, Bucksport, Me.

COOKED CARROT COOKIES

Makes About 36

1 cup sugar
½ cup shortening
1 cup mashed cooked carrots
1 egg
2 cups presifted flour
¼ teaspoon salt
2 teaspoons baking powder
2 tablespoons grated orange rind

1. Preheat oven to 350° F. Grease baking sheets.
2. Cream sugar and shortening in mixing bowl until light and fluffy. Add carrots and egg; beat until blended.
3. Into mixing bowl sift together flour, salt and baking powder; blend until smooth. Stir in orange rind; drop dough by spoon 2 inches apart, onto baking sheets.
4. Bake in preheated oven for 20 minutes.

Mrs. M. Crocker, Marble Hill-Lutesville Junior Woman's Club, Lutesville, Mo.

CHERRY COOKIES

Makes About 96

2 cups sugar
1 cup shortening
3 eggs
4 cups presifted flour
Pinch of salt
2 teaspoons baking soda
1 quart can pie cherries, drained
  (reserve 3 tablespoons liquid)
1 cup chopped nuts
1 teaspoon maple flavoring

1. Cream sugar and shortening in mixing bowl. Add eggs, one at a time, beating well after each addition.
2. In another large mixing bowl combine flour, salt and soda. Stir in cherries, nuts, reserved cherry liquid and maple flavoring. Stir in egg mixture. Chill.
3. Preheat oven to 375° F. Grease baking sheets.
4. Drop dough by teaspoons onto baking sheets; bake in preheated oven for 15 minutes.

Melba Kofford, Woman's Club, Orem, Utah

CHOCOLATE ACORNS

Makes About 36

3 egg whites
1 teaspoon vinegar
¼ teaspoon salt
1 cup sugar
1 teaspoon vanilla
½ pound blanched almonds,
  coarsely ground
½ pound unsweetened chocolate,
  coarsely grated
¼ pound semi-sweet chocolate
½ cup finely chopped blanched
  pistachio nuts

1. Preheat oven to 250° F. Grease baking sheets.
2. In mixing bowl combine egg whites, vinegar and salt; beat until soft peaks form. Gradually add sugar; beat until stiff and glossy.
3. Fold in vanilla, almonds and unsweetened chocolate.
4. Drop mixture by teaspoons, 1 inch apart, onto baking sheets; shape into ovals about the size of a large pecan.
5. Bake in preheated oven for 30 minutes, or until firm.
6. In top of double saucepan melt semi-sweet chocolate. When cool, dip each cooky halfway in chocolate; sprinkle dipped ends with pistachio nuts.

Mrs. Cheron, Woman's Club, Palisades Park, N.J.

CHEWY CHOCOLATE COOKIES

Makes About 30

2 1-ounce squares unsweetened
  chocolate
15-ounce can condensed milk
1 teaspoon vanilla
½ cup chopped walnuts
Pecan halves

1. Preheat oven to 350° F. Grease and flour baking sheets.
2. Cook chocolate in top of double saucepan over hot water until melted.
3. Add milk; cook over hot water, stirring frequently, until very thick. Remove from heat; stir in vanilla and walnuts.
4. Drop mixture by teaspoons 2 inches apart, onto baking sheets. Put pecan half in center of each cooky.
5. Bake in preheated oven for 10 to 12 minutes.
6. Remove at once from baking sheets; place on serving dish.

Mrs. Ray H. Nourie, Office of Mayor, Woman's Club, Kankakee, Ill.

CHOCOLATE CHIPPERS

Makes 42

½ cup shortening
½ cup granulated sugar
¼ cup brown sugar
1 egg
1 teaspoon vanilla
1 cup presifted flour
¾ teaspoon salt
½ teaspoon baking soda
6-ounce package semi-sweet
  chocolate pieces
½ cup broken nuts
½ cup crushed peppermint stick
  candy (optional)

1. Preheat oven to 375° F. Grease baking sheets.
2. Cream shortening, sugars, egg and vanilla in mixing bowl.
3. Sift together flour, salt and baking soda; stir into creamed mixture, blending well. Add chocolate and nuts. If desired, add candy.
4. Drop dough by teaspoons, 2 inches apart, on baking sheets.

5. Bake in preheated oven for 10 to 12 minutes. Remove from heat at once.

Mrs. F. F. Stump, Woman's Club, Starke, Fla.

MRS. NIXON'S WALNUT CLUSTERS

Makes About 30

½ cup presifted flour
½ teaspoon salt
¼ teaspoon baking powder
¼ cup butter
½ cup sugar
1½ 1-ounce squares unsweetened chocolate, melted
1 egg
1½ teaspoons vanilla
2 cups chopped walnuts

1. Preheat oven to 375° F. Grease baking sheets.
2. Onto piece of waxed paper sift together flour, salt and baking powder.
3. Cream butter and sugar in mixing bowl until light and fluffy. Add chocolate; beat until smooth. Add egg and vanilla; beat until blended.
4. Add flour mixture; beat until smooth; fold in walnuts.
5. Drop dough by teaspoons, 1 inch apart, onto baking sheets.
6. Bake in preheated oven for 10 minutes.

Tri-County Woman's Club, Venango County, Pa.

GOBS (SANDWICH COOKY)

Makes About 48

2 cups sugar
½ cup shortening
2 eggs
1 cup buttermilk
1 cup boiling water
4 cups sifted cake flour
2 teaspoons baking soda
½ teaspoon salt
½ teaspoon baking powder
½ cup cocoa
Cream Filling (p. 630)

1. Preheat oven to 375° F.
2. Cream sugar and shortening in mixing bowl until fluffy. Add eggs; beat until fluffy. Stir in buttermilk and water.
3. Onto piece of waxed paper sift together flour, baking soda, salt, baking powder and cocoa; stir into creamed mixture only until smooth.
4. Drop dough by teaspoons, 3 inches apart, onto baking sheets.
5. Bake in preheated oven for 10 minutes, or until golden.
6. Cool; sandwich in pairs with Cream Filling.

Mrs. Patrick J. McCann, Woman's Club, Ebensburg, Pa.

WHOOPIE COOKY PIES

Makes About 48

3½ cups presifted flour
2 teaspoons baking soda
1 teaspoon baking powder
4 teaspoons cream of tartar

1 teaspoon salt
¾ cup cocoa
2 cups sugar
1 cup shortening
3 eggs
2 teaspoons vanilla
1½ cups milk
Marshmallow Filling (p. 631)

1. Preheat oven to 375° F. Grease baking sheets.
2. Onto piece of waxed paper sift together flour, baking soda, baking powder, cream of tartar, salt and cocoa.
3. Cream sugar and shortening in mixing bowl until light and fluffy. Add eggs, one at a time, beating well after each addition.
4. Blend vanilla and milk; add alternately with flour mixture to egg mixture, beating well after each addition.
5. Drop dough by teaspoons, 2 inches apart, onto baking sheets.
6. Bake in preheated oven for 10 to 12 minutes.
7. Cool; sandwich in pairs with Marshmallow Filling.

Ruth Crowley, Woman's Club, West Jonesport, Me.

COCONUT COOKIES

Makes About 48

1½ cups sweetened condensed milk
4 cups shredded coconut
½ teaspoon salt
2 teaspoons vanilla
¼ teaspoon almond extract

1. Combine all ingredients; let stand for several hours.
2. Preheat oven to 350° F. Grease baking sheets.
3. Drop dough by teaspoons onto baking sheets; bake in preheated oven for 10 minutes, or until light brown.

Dorothy Halleman, Woman's Club, Elmwood Park, Ill.

FIG HONEY COOKIES

Makes 36

1 cup dried figs
½ cup shortening
¾ cup sugar
½ cup honey
2 eggs, well beaten
2 tablespoons milk
2¾ cups presifted flour
3 teaspoons baking powder
½ teaspoon salt
½ cup flaked coconut
1 teaspoon lemon extract
3 tablespoons chopped orange rind

1. Wash figs; cover with water. Bring to boil; simmer for 10 minutes. Drain; cut into small pieces.
2. Preheat oven to 425° F. Grease baking sheets.
3. Cream shortening and sugar in mixing bowl until light and fluffy. Stir in honey, eggs and milk; mix thoroughly.

4. Combine flour, baking powder and salt; stir into creamed mixture. Stir in figs and remaining ingredients.

5. Drop dough by teaspoons onto baking sheets; bake in preheated oven for 12 to 15 minutes.

Suburban Cookie Book, Mutual Improvement Club, Ronceverte, W. Va.

HOT CRUNCHIES

Makes About 36

1½ cups presifted flour
½ teaspoon baking soda
½ teaspoon salt
½ cup shortening
¼ cup sugar
1 egg
½ cup chopped nuts
½ cup seedless raisins

1. Preheat oven to 375° F.
2. Sift together flour, baking soda and salt.
3. Cream shortening and sugar in mixing bowl until fluffy. Stir in flour mixture. Stir in egg, nuts, and raisins.
4. Drop dough by teaspoons onto baking sheets.
5. Bake in preheated oven for 15 minutes.

Decie Faupell, Artemisia Club, Fallon, Nev.

ENGLISH BREAKFAST COOKIES

Makes About 24

1 cup brown sugar
½ cup shortening
2 eggs
½ teaspoon baking soda
½ cup cold black coffee
1½ cups presifted flour
½ teaspoon baking powder
1 teaspoon cinnamon
½ teaspoon ground cloves
½ teaspoon nutmeg
½ teaspoon salt
1 cup chopped walnuts
½ cup seedless raisins

1. Preheat oven to 350° F. Grease baking sheets.
2. Cream sugar and shortening in mixing bowl until light and fluffy. Add eggs, one at a time, beating after each addition.
3. Dissolve baking soda in coffee; let stand for a few minutes.
4. Onto piece of waxed paper sift together flour, baking powder, cinnamon, cloves, nutmeg and salt.
5. Add flour mixture and coffee mixture alternately to creamed mixture, beating after each addition. Stir in walnuts and raisins.
6. Drop dough by tablespoons, 3 inches apart, onto baking sheets.
7. Bake in preheated oven for 15 minutes, or until golden.

Mrs. Arlene Smith, Tuesday Evening Woman's Club, Emington, Ill.

MOTHER'S CRUMPETS

Makes About 24

⅔ cup butter or margarine
1 cup brown sugar
2 eggs
1½ cups presifted flour
½ teaspoon salt
½ teaspoon cinnamon
1 teaspoon baking soda
¼ cup hot water
½ cup chopped dates
⅓ cup chopped walnuts
½ teaspoon vanilla

1. Preheat oven to 350° F. Grease baking sheets.
2. Cream butter or margarine and sugar in mixing bowl until fluffy. Add eggs; beat well.
3. Onto piece of waxed paper sift together flour, salt and cinnamon.
4. Dissolve baking soda in water.
5. Add flour mixture and water mixture alternately to creamed mixture, beating after each addition. Stir in dates, walnuts and vanilla.
6. Drop dough by tablespoons onto baking sheets.
7. Bake in preheated oven for 25 minutes.

Mrs. Leona Murphy, St. Andrews Episcopal Guild, Mount Desert, Me.

DATE HERMITS

Makes About 72

3 cups sifted cake flour
1 teaspoon baking soda
1 teaspoon ground cloves
½ teaspoon salt
1 teaspoon cinnamon
1 cup butter or margarine
1½ cups brown sugar
3 eggs, lightly beaten
1 tablespoon molasses
1 tablespoon grated orange rind
1 cup chopped walnuts
1 cup chopped seedless raisins
1 cup chopped dates

1. Preheat oven to 400° F. Grease baking sheets.
2. Onto piece of waxed paper sift together flour, baking soda, cloves, salt and cinnamon.
3. Cream butter or margarine and sugar in mixing bowl until light and fluffy. Add eggs and molasses; beat until smooth.
4. Add flour mixture; beat until blended. Stir in orange rind, walnuts, raisins and dates; mix well.
5. Drop from spoon tip onto baking sheets.
6. Bake in preheated oven for 7 to 8 minutes, or until golden.

Mrs. W. H. Dempewolf, Woman's Club, Henderson, Ky.

NOELS

Makes 36

⅓ cup softened butter
2 teaspoons vanilla
¾ cup light brown sugar

1 egg
1¼ cups presifted flour
½ teaspoon salt
¼ teaspoon baking powder
½ cup sour cream
36 pitted dates
36 walnut halves
2 tablespoons butter
1 cup confectioners' sugar
1 tablespoon cream

1. Cream softened butter, 1 teaspoon of the vanilla and sugar well. Add egg; beat thoroughly.
2. Combine flour, salt and baking powder; add alternately with sour cream to creamed mixture.
3. Preheat oven to 400° F. Grease baking sheets.
4. Stuff each date with walnut half; coat with dough. Drop from fork onto baking sheets.
5. Bake in preheated oven for about 10 minutes. Cool.
6. Meanwhile, combine 2 tablespoons butter, confectioners sugar, remaining vanilla and cream; use to spread top of each cooky.

Joyce Conway, Junior Woman's Club,
Phoenix, Ariz.

CHRISTMAS COOKIES

Makes About 48

¾ pound candied red cherries, chopped
4 slices candied green pineapple slices, chopped
1 cup chopped pecans
1 cup chopped black walnuts
1 cup chopped Brazil nuts
½ cup presifted flour
3 egg whites
½ cup sugar
1 teaspoon vanilla
½ teaspoon salt

1. Preheat oven to 350° F. Grease baking sheets.
2. In mixing bowl combine cherries, pineapple, pecans, walnuts and Brazil nuts; mix well. Add flour; mix well.
3. In another mixing bowl beat egg whites until foamy. Gradually add sugar; beat until stiff and glossy.
4. Fold in fruit mixture, vanilla and salt.
5. Drop by teaspoons onto baking sheets.
6. Bake in preheated oven for 15 minutes, or until golden. Cool for a few minutes; remove from baking sheets.

Mrs. Otto Braner, Woman's Club, New Berlin, Ill.

PRIZEWINNING KANSAS ROCKS

Makes 60

1½ cups presifted flour
¼ teaspoon baking soda
¼ teaspoon salt
1 egg
1 teaspoon cinnamon
¼ teaspoon ground cloves
¼ teaspoon nutmeg

¼ teaspoon allspice
½ cup part shortening and part butter
½ cup granulated sugar
½ cup brown sugar
¼ cup milk
½ pound candied cherries
3 cup pecans
1 cup chopped dates
½ cup candied pineapple, chopped
½ cup chopped mixed candied fruits

1. Preheat oven to 325° F. Grease baking sheets well.
2. In mixing bowl combine all ingredients except cherries, pecans, dates, pineapple and mixed fruits. Beat until well blended.
3. Combine remaining ingredients in large mixing bowl. Add dough; mix.
4. Drop by teaspoons onto baking sheets; bake in preheated oven for 20 to 25 minutes.

Mrs. Iva D. Deering, Research Club,
Topeka, Kans.

FROSTED GINGER CREAMS

Makes About 72

1 cup granulated sugar
½ cup shortening
2 eggs
½ cup molasses
1 teaspoon baking soda
1 cup hot black coffee
3 cups presifted flour
1 teaspoon ginger
1 teaspoon cinnamon
1 teaspoon ground cloves
1 cup seedless raisins
Juice and grated rind of 1 orange
Confectioners' sugar

1. Preheat oven to 350° F. Grease baking sheets.
2. Cream granulated sugar and shortening in mixing bowl. Add eggs, one at a time, beating well after each addition. Stir in molasses.
3. Dissolve baking soda in coffee; stir into egg mixture.
4. Combine flour and spices; stir into egg mixture. Stir in raisins.
5. Drop dough by teaspoons onto baking sheets; bake in preheated oven for 20 minutes.
6. Combine orange rind and juice; stir in enough confectioners' sugar to make a creamy orange frosting.
7. Remove cookies from oven; frost tops while still warm.

Mrs. Allen Brandt, Cultura Club,
Hankinson, N.D.

ALMOND LACE WAFERS

Makes About 24

¾ cup finely ground almonds
½ cup butter
½ cup sugar
1 tablespoon flour
2 tablespoons cream

1. Preheat oven to 350° F. Grease baking sheets well; dust with flour.

2. Combine all ingredients in saucepan. Cook over medium heat, stirring frequently, until butter is melted and mixture bubbles.

3. Drop by teaspoons, about 3 inches apart, onto baking sheets.

4. Bake in preheated oven for about 7 minutes, or until edges are light brown.

5. Cool on sheets for 2 minutes, or until firm enough to lift with spatula.

Mrs. John R. Merz, Woman's Club,
Worland, Wyo.

LEMONADE COOKIES

Makes 54

1 cup butter or margarine
  Sugar
2 eggs
3 cups presifted flour
1 teaspoon baking soda
6-ounce can frozen lemonade
  concentrated, defrosted

1. Preheat oven to 400° F.

2. Cream butter or margarine and 1 cup sugar in mixing bowl. Add eggs, one at a time, beating well after each addition.

3. Combine flour and baking soda; stir alternately with ½ cup of the lemonade concentrate into egg mixture.

4. Drop dough by teaspoons, 2 inches apart, onto ungreased baking sheets.

5. Bake in preheated oven for about 8 minutes, or until edges are light brown.

6. Remove from oven; brush hot cookies lightly with remaining concentrate; sprinkle with sugar.

Mrs. W. Raymond Jones, Past President,
Woman's Club, Lawrence, Mass.

COCONUT MACAROONS

Makes About 36

2 eggs whites
1 cup sugar
2 cups cornflakes
1 cup flaked coconut
1 teaspoon vanilla

1. Preheat oven to 350° F. Line baking sheets with waxed paper.

2. In mixing bowl beat egg whites until foamy. Gradually beat in sugar; beat until stiff and glossy.

3. Fold in cornflakes, coconut and vanilla.

4. Drop by tablespoons onto baking sheets.

5. Bake in preheated oven for 12 to 15 minutes, or until light brown. Remove from baking sheets with spatula.

Mrs. Marshall Millbourn, Kloves Reading Klub,
Greenfield, Ind.

POLKA DOT MACAROONS

Makes About 36

3 egg whites
½ teaspoon salt
¾ cup sugar
3 cups cornflakes
1 cup semi-sweet chocolate pieces
1 teaspoon vanilla

1. Preheat oven to 350° F. Grease baking sheets.

2. In mixing bowl beat egg whites and salt until foamy. Gradually beat in sugar; beat until stiff and glossy.

3. Fold in cornflakes, chocolate and vanilla.

4. Drop by teaspoons onto baking sheets.

5. Bake in preheated oven for 15 minutes. Cool on sheets.

Junior Woman's Club, Corpus Christi, Tex.

RICEAROONS

Makes About 36

3 egg whites
½ teaspoon salt
¼ teaspoon almond extract
1 cup sugar
2 cups crisp bite-size rice cereal
2½ cups flaked coconut

1. Preheat oven to 300° F. Line baking sheets with heavy paper.

2. Beat egg whites, salt and almond extract until soft peaks form. Gradually beat in sugar; beat until thickened and glossy.

3. Fold in rice cereal and coconut.

4. Drop from spoon tip onto baking sheets; bake in preheated oven for 18 to 20 minutes, or until delicately browned.

Mrs. C. W. Johnson, Land o' Lakes
Woman's Club, Lutz, Fla.

SURPRISE MERINGUES

Makes About 36

2 egg whites
⅛ teaspoon cream of tartar
⅛ teaspoon salt
¼ teaspoon vanilla
¾ cup sugar
6-ounce package semi-sweet
  chocolate pieces
¼ cup chopped nuts

1. Preheat oven to 300° F. Line baking sheets with brown paper; grease lightly.

2. In mixing bowl combine egg whites, cream of tartar, salt and vanilla; beat until soft peaks form. Gradually beat in sugar; beat until stiff and glossy.

3. Fold in chocolate and nuts.

4. Drop by teaspoons onto baking sheets.

5. Bake in preheated oven for 25 minutes, or until meringues can be easily lifted from paper.

Dorothy Kerr, Woman's Literary Club,
Winthrop, Ia.

MRS. JOHN KENNEDY'S HAZELNUT MERINGUES

Makes About 96

1 pound confectioners' sugar, sifted
1 pound ground hazelnuts
8 egg whites, stiffly beaten
  Grated rind and juice of 1 lemon
2 teaspoons cinnamon

1. Preheat oven to 325° F. Grease and flour baking sheets.

2. Gradually fold sugar and hazelnuts into egg whites. Fold in lemon rind and juice and cinnamon.

3. Drop by spoons onto baking sheets; bake in preheated oven for 10 minutes. Remove from baking sheets immediately to cool.

Junior Women's Club, Edgewood, R.I.

PECAN DAINTIES

Makes About 36

1 egg white
Dash of salt
1 cup brown sugar
1½ cup pecan halves

1. Preheat oven to 250° F. Grease baking sheets well.
2. In mixing bowl beat egg white and salt until soft peaks form. Gradually add sugar; beat until stiff and glossy. Stir in pecans.
3. Drop by teaspoons, 3 inches apart, onto baking sheets.
4. Bake in preheated oven for 30 minutes. Remove from baking sheets at once to cool.

Mrs. J. M. Mitchell, Book Lovers' Club and Aliceans, Alice, Tex.

NUT CRISPIES

Makes About 60

½ cup shortening
½ cup butter
2½ cups brown sugar
2 eggs, lightly beaten
2½ cups presifted flour
¼ teaspoon salt
½ teaspoon baking soda
1 cup chopped pecans or walnuts

1. Preheat oven to 350° F. Grease baking sheets.
2. Cream shortening, butter and sugar in mixing bowl. Add eggs; beat well.
3. Combine flour, salt and baking soda; stir into egg mixture. Add nuts.
4. Drop dough by teaspoons, about 2 inches apart, onto baking sheets.
5. Bake in preheated oven for 11 to 12 minutes.

Jean Cuillier, Woman's Club, Yakima, Wash.

OATMEAL DROP COOKIES

Makes About 24

1 cup seedless raisins
¾ cup water
¾ cup shortening
1 cup sugar
2 eggs
2 cups presifted flour
1 teaspoon baking soda
½ teaspoon salt

1. Preheat oven to 400° F.
2. In saucepan combine raisins and water. Bring to boil; boil for 5 minutes. Drain raisins; reserve ¼ cup liquid.

3. Cream shortening in mixing bowl until soft. Gradually add sugar; beat until light and fluffy. Add eggs; beat well. Stir in oats.
4. Combine flour, baking soda and salt; add alternately with reserved liquid to egg mixture, beating after each addition. Stir in raisins.
5. Drop dough by tablespoons, 2 inches apart, onto baking sheets.
6. Bake in preheated oven for 12 to 15 minutes.

Joanne Davis, Woman's Club, Glasgow, Mont.

CRISP OATMEAL WAFERS

Makes About 36

2 eggs
1 cup sugar
1 tablespoon melted butter
or margarine
1 teaspoon vanilla
2 teaspoons baking powder
2 cups quick-cooking oats
½ teaspoon salt

1. Preheat oven to 375° F. Grease and flour baking sheets.
2. In mixing bowl beat eggs until frothy. Add sugar; beat until thickened and lemon-colored. Stir in butter or margarine and vanilla.
4. On piece of waxed paper combine baking powder, oats and salt; add to egg mixture; blend well.
5. Drop dough by teaspoons, 3 inches apart, onto baking sheets.
6. Bake in preheated oven for 10 to 15 minutes, or until golden.

Mrs. Alfred R. Webb, Colony Club, Ambler, Pa.

BANANA NUGGETS

Makes About 48

1½ cups presifted flour
1 cup sugar
½ teaspoon baking soda
1 teaspoon salt
¼ teaspoon nutmeg
¾ teaspoon cinnamon
¾ cup shortening
1 egg, lightly beaten
1 cup mashed ripe bananas
1¾ cups quick-cooking oats
6-ounce package semi-sweet
chocolate pieces

1. Preheat oven to 400° F. Grease baking sheets.
2. Into mixing bowl sift together flour, sugar, baking soda, salt, nutmeg and cinnamon. Cut in shortening until mixture resembles fine crumbs.
3. Add remaining ingredients; mix well.
4. Drop dough by teaspoons onto baking sheets.
5. Bake in preheated oven for 12 minutes, or until browned.

Hester Peoples, Civic Club, Belleville, Pa.

BANANA RAISIN DROPS

Makes 42

¾ cup butter
1 tablespoon grated orange peel
1 cup sugar
1 egg
1 cup mashed ripe banana
1½ cups rolled oats
1 cup seedless raisins
½ cup chopped walnuts
1½ cups presifted flour
1 teaspoon salt
½ teaspoon baking soda

1. Preheat oven to 375° F.
2. Cream butter, orange peel and sugar in mixing bowl. Beat in egg. Stir in bananas, oats, raisins and walnuts.
3. Sift together remaining ingredients. Add to banana mixture; mix well.
4. Drop dough by tablespoons onto baking sheets; bake in preheated oven for 10 to 12 minutes, or until golden brown.

Mrs. William H. Hasebroock, Honorary President, General Federation of Women's Clubs, West Point, Neb.

ROLLED WHEAT COOKIES

Makes 108 to 120

1 cup butter
1 cup brown sugar
1 cup granulated sugar
2 eggs, lightly beaten
1¾ cups presifted flour
½ teaspoon salt
½ teaspoon baking soda
3 cups rolled wheat
1 teaspoon vanilla
1¼ cups seedless raisins

1. Preheat oven to 375° F. Grease baking sheets.
2. Cream butter and sugars in mixing bowl. Add eggs; beat.
3. Sift together flour, salt and baking soda. Add to egg mixture. Mix well.
4. Add remaining ingredients; mix.
5. Drop dough by teaspoons, 2 inches apart, onto baking sheets.
6. Bake in preheated oven for 10 to 12 minutes.

Mrs. Robert E. Musgrove, Richfield Study and Social Club, Rolla, Kans.

ORANGE COOKIES

Makes About 48

¾ cup shortening
1 cup granulated sugar
¾ cup frozen orange juice concentrate, defrosted
2 eggs, lightly beaten
1 cup flaked coconut
2¼ cups presifted flour
½ teaspoon baking powder
3-ounce package cream cheese
½ cup water
Confectioners' sugar

1. Preheat oven to 375° F. Grease baking sheets.
2. Cream shortening and granulated sugar in mixing bowl. Stir in ½ cup of the orange concentrate, eggs and coconut.

3. Combine flour and baking powder; stir into egg mixture.
4. Drop dough by teaspoons onto baking sheets; bake in preheated oven for 10 minutes, or until browned.
5. Meanwhile, prepare Orange Icing: Cream the cheese until fluffy. Combine remaining orange concentrate and water; gradually beat into cheese. Beat in enough confectioners' sugar to give good spreading consistency.
6. Frost cookies while warm with icing.

Mrs. Grover Price, Quest Club, Bowling Green, Mo.

PINEAPPLE COCONUT DROP COOKIES

Makes About 72

1½ cups sugar
1 cup shortening
3 eggs or ¼ cup cream and 2 eggs
1 teaspoon baking soda
2 teaspoons baking powder
1 cup drained crushed pineapple
1 cup shredded coconut
¼ teaspoon salt
3½ cups presifted flour

1. Preheat oven to 375° F. Grease baking sheets.
2. Cream sugar and shortening in mixing bowl. Beat in eggs.
3. Stir in remaining ingredients.
4. Drop dough by spoons onto baking sheets; bake in preheated oven for 10 to 12 minutes, or until toasty brown.

Anna M. Hicks, Sorosis Club, Maple Rapids, Mich.

PRUNE COOKIES

Makes 42

1½ cups dried prunes
5 eggs
1 cup brown sugar
1 cup granulated sugar
1 cup butter
⅓ cup milk
4¼ cups presifted flour
1 teaspoon baking soda
½ teaspoon salt
1 teaspoon cinnamon
½ teaspoon ground cloves
½ teaspoon ginger
1 teaspoon vanilla
2-Egg-White Cooked Meringue (p. 552)

1. Cover prunes with boiling water; cover; let stand for 15 minutes. Drain; dry well on towel; cut flesh into small pieces.
2. Break 3 of the eggs into small bowl. Add yolks of remaining eggs; use whites for frosting.
3. Preheat oven to 400° F. Grease baking sheets.
4. Cream sugars and butter in mixing bowl. Beat in combined eggs and yolks. Stir in milk.
5. Combine flour, baking soda, salt and spices. Add to egg mixture; beat well. Stir in prunes and vanilla.

6. Drop dough by tablespoons, 3 inches apart, onto baking sheets. Bake in preheated oven for 12 to 15 minutes.

7. When cool, frost tops with 2-Egg-White Cooked Meringue.

Helen Doornink, Donald District Woman's Club, Wapato, Wash.

PUMPKIN COOKIES
Makes About 36

2¼ cups sifted cake flour
¼ teaspoon nutmeg
½ teaspoon cinnamon
2¼ teaspoons baking powder
¼ teaspoon ground cloves
½ cup shortening
1½ cups sugar
1 egg
1⅓ cups mashed cooked pumpkin
1 cup chopped seedless raisins

1. Preheat oven to 375° F. Grease baking sheets.

2. Onto piece of waxed paper sift together flour, nutmeg, cinnamon, baking powder and cloves.

3. Cream shortening and sugar in mixing bowl until light and fluffy. Add egg; beat until smooth.

4. Add flour mixture and pumpkin alternately, beating well after each addition. Stir in raisins.

5. Drop dough by tablespoons, 2 inches apart, onto baking sheets.

6. Bake in preheated oven for 15 minutes.

Alice Baiardi, Woman's Club, Southwick, Mass.

STIR-AND-DROP SUGAR COOKIES
Makes 36

2 eggs
⅔ cup cooking oil
2 teaspoons vanilla
1 teaspoon grated lemon rind
¾ cup sugar
2 cups presifted flour
2 teaspoons baking powder
½ teaspoon salt

1. Preheat oven to 400° F. Grease baking sheets.

2. In mixing bowl beat eggs until well blended. Stir in oil, vanilla and lemon rind. Add sugar; blend until thickened.

3. Combine flour, baking powder and salt; stir into egg mixture.

4. Drop dough by teaspoons dipped in sugar onto baking sheets.

5. Bake in preheated oven for 8 to 10 minutes, or until delicately browned.

Rita Stifle, Woman's Club, Paxton, Ill.

SOUR CREAM SUGAR COOKIES
Makes About 60

5 cups sifted cake flour
1 teaspoon baking soda
2 teaspoons baking powder
½ teaspoon salt
1 cup butter or margarine
1 cup sugar
2 eggs
2 cups sour cream

1. Preheat oven to 375° F. Grease baking sheets.

2. Onto piece of waxed paper sift together flour, baking soda, baking powder and salt.

3. In mixing bowl combine butter or margarine and sugar; beat until fluffy. Beat in eggs.

4. Add flour mixture and sour cream alternately to egg mixture; beating well after each addition.

5. Drop dough by teaspoons onto baking sheets.

6. Bake in preheated oven for 12 to 15 minutes, or until golden.

Mrs. Mary Kozub, South Woman's Club, Canton, Ohio

Molded or Pressed Cookies

ALMOND DELIGHT COOKIES
Makes 60

2 cups presifted flour
¼ teaspoon baking powder
¼ teaspoon baking soda
Dash of salt
1 cup butter or margarine
1 cup confectioners' sugar
(sift if lumpy)
1 egg yolk
½ teaspoon vanilla
½ teaspoon almond extract
3 tablespoons heavy cream
60 blanched almonds

1. Onto piece of waxed paper sift together flour, baking powder, baking soda and salt.

2. Cream butter or margarine and sugar in mixing bowl until light and fluffy. Add egg yolk, vanilla and almond extract; beat until smooth.

3. Add flour mixture; work together to make a smooth dough. Chill for at least 1 hour.

4. Preheat oven to 375° F. Grease baking sheets.

5. Roll dough into ½-inch balls; place about 2 inches apart on baking sheets. Brush with cream; press almond into center of each ball.

6. Bake in preheated oven for 10 to 12 minutes, or until just brown.

Mrs. Edna I. Waller, Woman's Club, Scobey, Mont.

BERLINER KRANZER
Makes 100

1 pound butter
1 cup granulated sugar
8 egg yolks
1 tablespoon water
1 teaspoon almond extract
4 cups presifted flour
1 teaspoon baking powder
2 egg whites, lightly beaten
Crushed loaf sugar

1. Cream butter and granulated sugar thoroughly.

2. Beat egg yolks until thickened and pale. Beat in water and almond extract.

3. Combine flour and baking powder.

4. Add egg mixture alternately with flour mixture to creamed mixture, beating well after each addition to make a firm dough.

5. Preheat oven to 350° F. Grease baking sheets.

6. Take piece of dough about the size of small egg; roll into rope; shape rope into crown or figure 8. Brush with egg white; sprinkle with loaf sugar.

7. Arrange on baking sheets; bake in preheated oven for 8 to 10 minutes, or until light brown.

*Mrs. Oscar Sanbo, Woman's Club,
Milan, Minn.*

DANISH EGG RINGS

Makes About 48

½ cup butter
½ cup sugar
3 egg yolks
2 cups presifted flour
2 teaspoons baking powder
1 teaspoon vanilla
1 tablespoon cream
Melted butter
Mixed sugar and cinnamon

1. Preheat oven to 325° F. Grease baking sheets.

2. Cream ½ cup butter and sugar in mixing bowl. Beat in egg yolks.

3. Stir in flour, baking powder, vanilla and cream.

4. Form dough into pencil strips about 3 inches long; shape into rings. Arrange on baking sheets. Brush with melted butter; sprinkle with mixed sugar and cinnamon.

5. Bake in preheated oven for 8 to 10 minutes, or until golden.

*Grace Honnold, Junior Woman's Club,
North Canton, Ohio*

MELTING MOMENTS

Makes 36

1 cup butter
1 teaspoon vanilla
1⅓ cups cornstarch
1 cup presifted flour
Favorite frosting

1. In mixing bowl beat butter and vanilla until light.

2. Beat in cornstarch and flour; beat until smooth. Chill for 1 hour.

3. Preheat oven to 350° F.

4. Roll dough into long sausage shape; cut into 36 pieces. Roll each piece of dough into ball; place about 2 inches apart on baking sheets. Flatten each ball slightly with fork tines.

5. Bake in preheated oven for 12 to 15 minutes. When cool, frost with favorite frosting.

*Mary Moskel, Junior Women's Civic Club,
Indiana, Pa.*

CRISP BROWN SUGAR COOKIES

Makes About 48

½ cup butter or margarine
⅔ cup brown sugar
1 egg yolk
2 cups presifted flour
1 teaspoon vanilla
Walnut or pecan halves

1. Cream butter or margarine and sugar in mixing bowl until smooth.

2. Stir in egg yolk, flour and vanilla. Chill for 30 minutes.

3. Preheat oven to 350° F. Grease baking sheets.

4. Form dough into balls about ½ inch in diameter; place on baking sheets; flatten with fork. Press nut half into center.

5. Bake in preheated oven for 12 to 15 minutes.

Alice Whitefield, Reading Club, Demopolis, Ala.

CHOCOLATE PIXIES

Makes About 48

2 cups presifted flour
2 teaspoons baking powder
½ teaspoon salt
¼ cup butter or margarine
4 1-ounce squares unsweetened chocolate
2 cups granulated sugar
4 eggs
½ cup chopped walnuts
Confectioners' sugar
(sift if lumpy)

1. On piece of waxed paper sift together flour, baking powder and salt.

2. In small saucepan combine butter or margarine; cook over low heat, stirring occasionally, until chocolate is melted. Pour into mixing bowl; cool.

3. Add granulated sugar; beat to blend. Add eggs, one at a time, beating well after each addition.

4. Add walnuts and flour mixture; mix well. Chill for 30 minutes.

5. Preheat oven to 300° F. Grease baking sheets.

6. Shape dough into 1-inch balls; roll in confectioners' sugar. Place 2 inches apart on baking sheets.

7. Bake in preheated oven for 18 to 20 minutes.

*Mary Anderson, Mid Century Study Club,
Montpelier, Ohio*

YULETIDE COCONUT BALLS

Makes About 36

¾ cup seedless raisins
¾ cup nuts
2 cups shredded coconut
1 egg
½ cup brown sugar
2 tablespoons flour
Dash of salt

1. Preheat oven to 350° F. Grease baking sheets.

2. Rinse and drain raisins. Put raisins, nuts and ¾ cup of the coconut through medium blade of meat grinder.

3. Beat egg lightly; mix with sugar, flour and salt. Add raisins, nuts and coconut; mix well.

4. Shape dough into balls about ½ inch in diameter; roll in remaining coconut.

5. Place on baking sheets; bake in preheated oven for about 10 minutes. Cool for a few minutes; remove from sheets.

Ella Ashby, Crafts and Hobbies Club,
St. Louis, Mo.

WOODCHUCKS

Makes About 24

2 cups walnut halves
1 cup pitted dates
1 cup brown sugar
2 eggs, lightly beaten
2½ cups shredded coconut

1. Preheat oven to 375° F.
2. Put walnuts and dates through coarse blade of meat grinder; turn into mixing bowl. Add sugar, eggs and 1½ cups of the coconut; mix well.
3. Shape dough into 2 x ¾-inch oblong rolls. Roll each in remaining coconut; place on baking sheets.
4. Bake in preheated oven for 12 to 15 minutes, or until golden.

Mrs. Moore, Athenian Study Club,
Daingerfield, Tex.

CASSEROLE COOKIES

Makes 40 to 60

2 eggs
1 cup sugar
1 cup dates, cut into small pieces
1 cup shredded coconut
1 cup nuts, coarsely chopped
1 teaspoon vanilla
¼ teaspoon almond extract (optional)
⅛ teaspoon salt
Sugar or decorettes

1. Preheat oven to 350° F.
2. Beat eggs; add sugar; beat well. Blend in all remaining ingredients except sugar or decorettes.
3. Turn into 2-quart casserole; bake in preheated oven for 30 minutes. While still hot, beat well with wooden spoon.
4. Cool; form into small balls; roll in sugar or decorettes (chocolate is good), as desired.

Mrs. Ethel Nunn, Fortnightly Club, Dawson, N.D.

CRACKLY GINGERSNAPS

Makes 48

¾ cup shortening
1 cup brown sugar
½ cup dark molasses
1 egg
2¼ cups presifted flour
1½ teaspoons baking soda
1 teaspoon cinnamon
1 teaspoon ginger
¼ teaspoon ground cloves
¼ teaspoon salt
Granulated sugar

1. Cream shortening and brown sugar in mixing bowl until well blended. Add molasses and egg; beat thoroughly.

2. Sift together flour, baking soda, spices and salt. stir into molasses mixture. Cover; chill until firm.

3. Preheat oven to 375° F. Grease baking sheets.

4. Shape dough into balls the size of a small walnut, Swiftly dip balls in cold water; dip tops in granulated sugar. (Sugar forms crackly top when baked.)

5. Arrange on baking sheets; bake in preheated oven for 12 to 15 minutes.

Bertha Peterson, Woman's Club,
Brownstown, Ill.

NORWEGIAN JELLY COOKIES

Makes About 24

⅓ cup butter
⅓ cup brown sugar
1 egg, separated
1 cup presifted flour
1 cup finely chopped nuts
Mint or red currant jelly

1. Preheat oven to 350° F. Grease baking sheets.

2. Cream butter and sugar in mixing bowl until light and fluffy. Add egg yolk; beat until smooth. Add flour; mix to make a smooth dough.

3. Roll dough into 1-inch balls; dip in egg white. Roll in nuts; place on baking sheets; press down center of each to form small hollow.

4. Bake in preheated oven for 8 minutes.

5. Remove from oven; press down centers again. Bake in preheated oven for 10 minutes longer.

6. Before serving, fill centers with jelly.

Mrs. L. L. Hyde, Library Club,
Robbinsdale, Minn.

LEMON BONBON COOKIES

Makes 48

1 cup butter
⅓ cup confectioners' sugar
¾ cup cornstarch
1¼ cups presifted flour
½ cup chopped pecans
Bonbon Frosting (p. 622)

1. In mixing bowl beat butter and sugar until light and fluffy.

2. Add cornstarch and flour; mix well. Chill until easy to handle.

3. Preheat oven to 350° F.

4. Sprinkle pecans onto piece of waxed paper.

5. Shape dough into 1-inch balls. Place balls on pecans; flatten with bottom of glass dipped in flour.

6. With spatula, transfer cookies, nut side up, to baking sheets.

7. Bake in preheated oven for 15 minutes. Cool; frost with Bonbon Frosting.

Mrs. Albert Goss, Janus Junior Women's Club,
Columbus, Ohio

MOLASSES CRINKLES
Makes About 60
    1 cup soft shortening
    1 cup brown sugar
    1 egg
    ¼ cup molasses
    ¼ cup milk
    2½ cups presifted flour
    2 teaspoons baking soda
    ¼ teaspoon salt
    ½ teaspoon ground cloves
    1 teaspoon cinnamon
    1 teaspoon ginger
    6-ounce package semi-sweet
      chocolate pieces
      Granulated sugar

1. In mixing bowl combine shortening, brown sugar, egg, molasses and milk thoroughly.
2. Combine flour, baking soda, salt and spices; stir into sugar mixture.
3. Fold in chocolate. Chill for at least 1 hour.
4. Preheat oven to 375° F. Grease baking sheets.
5. Roll dough into balls the size of walnut. Dip top side of each ball in granulated sugar; arrange, sugar side up, about 3-inches apart on baking sheets.
6. Bake in preheated oven for about 10 minutes.

Mrs. Harold Hendrix, Junior Civic Woman's Club, Parkersburg. W.Va.

NUTMEG BUTTER BALLS
Makes 48 to 60
    1 cup butter
    ½ cup granulated sugar
    1 teaspoon vanilla
    1⅓ cups chopped pecans
    2 cups presifted flour
    ½ cup sifted confectioners' sugar
    2 teaspoons nutmeg

1. Cream butter and granulated sugar in mixing bowl until light and fluffy. Stir in vanilla and pecans.
2. Gradually add flour; blend well. Chill for 30 minutes.
3. Preheat oven to 325° F. Lightly grease baking sheets.
4. Shape dough into 1¼-inch balls; place about 2 inches apart on baking sheets.
5. Bake in preheated oven for 15 to 20 minutes, or until light golden.
6. Combine confectioners' sugar and nutmeg; roll warm cookies in mixture.

Mrs. Ruth Smith, Culture Club, Hueytown, Ala.

MEXICAN WEDDING COOKIES
Makes About 48
    1 cup butter
    2 cups presifted flour
    3 tablespoons confectioners' sugar
    1 cup finely chopped walnuts
    1 teaspoon vanilla

1. Preheat oven to 350° F. Lightly grease baking sheets.
2. Cream butter in mixing bowl until light. Mix in flour. Stir in sugar, walnuts and vanilla.

3. Shape dough into 1-inch balls; place about 2 inches apart on baking sheets.
4. Bake in preheated oven for 15 to 20 minutes, or until golden.

Mrs. Hanes W. Hall, Woman's Club, Worland, Wyo.

DICK MORROW'S PECAN PUFFS
Makes About 24
    ½ cup butter
    2 tablespoons granulated sugar
    1 teaspoon vanilla
    1 cup ground pecans
    1 cup sifted cake flour
      Confectioners' sugar

1. Preheat oven to 300° F. Grease baking sheets.
2. Cream butter and granulated sugar in mixing bowl until light and fluffy.
3. Add vanilla; mix well. Stir in pecans and flour; mix well.
4. Shape dough into 1-inch balls; place 1 inch apart on baking sheets.
5. Bake in preheated oven for 30 minutes, or until light golden.
6. Roll in confectioners' sugar as soon as puffs come from oven. Cool; roll again in confectioners' sugar.

Ailene Morrow, South Hills Civic Club, Bridgeville, Pa.

SNOWDROPS
Makes About 36
    1 cup butter
    ½ cup confectioners' sugar
      (sift if lumpy)
    ¼ teaspoon salt
    2¼ cups presifted flour
    ¾ cup finely chopped walnuts

1. Cream butter and sugar in mixing bowl until light and fluffy. Add remaining ingredients; mix until smooth.
2. Chill for 30 minutes; roll into 1-inch balls.
3. Preheat oven to 400° F.
4. Place dough balls about 2 inches apart on baking sheets.
5. Bake in preheated oven for 10 to 12 minutes, or until set but not browned.

Mrs. Goodwin Gilman, Woman's Club, Newport, Me.

OATMEAL COCONUT COOKIES
Makes About 72
    1 cup butter or margarine
    1 cup granulated sugar
    1 cup brown sugar
    2 eggs
    1 teaspoon vanilla
    1 cup presifted flour
    ½ teaspoon baking soda
    1 cup flaked coconut
    4 cups rolled oats

1. Preheat oven to 325° F. Grease baking sheets.
2. Cream butter or margarine and sugar in mixing bowl. Beat in eggs and vanilla.
3. Stir in flour, baking soda, coconut and oats.

4. Roll dough into balls about ½ inch in diameter; arrange on baking sheets.

5. Bake in preheated oven for 15 to 20 minutes, or until light brown.

Jennie Bennett, Woman's Club, Ovid, Colo.

ORANGE CRISPS

Makes About 60

2 cups presifted flour
½ teaspoon baking powder
⅛ teaspoon baking soda
½ teaspoon salt
⅔ cup shortening
2 tablespoons grated orange rind
½ cup brown sugar
⅓ cup granulated sugar
1 egg

1. Preheat oven to 400° F.

2. Onto piece of waxed paper sift together flour, baking powder, baking soda and salt.

3. Cream shortening, orange rind and sugars in mixing bowl until light and fluffy. Add egg; beat well.

4. Gradually add flour mixture; blend thoroughly.

5. Shape dough in ¾-inch balls; place about 3 inches apart on baking sheets. Flatten with fork tines, making crisscross pattern by pressing fork first one way, then opposite way.

6. Bake in preheated oven for 6 to 8 minutes, or until light brown.

Woman's Progress Club, Meredith, N.H.

PEANUT BLOSSOMS

Makes About 36

1¾ cups presifted flour
1 teaspoon baking soda
½ teaspoon salt
½ cup shortening
½ cup peanut butter
1 cup granulated sugar
½ cup brown sugar
1 egg
2 tablespoons milk
1 teaspoon vanilla
Chocolate kisses

1. Preheat oven to 375° F. Grease baking sheets.

2. Onto piece of waxed paper sift together flour, baking soda and salt.

3. Cream shortening, peanut butter, ½ cup of the granulated sugar and brown sugar in mixing bowl until light and fluffy. Stir in egg, milk and vanilla; beat until blended.

4. Stir in flour mixture; mix well.

5. Shape dough into 1½-inch balls; roll in remaining granulated sugar. Place about 2 inches apart on baking sheets.

6. Bake in preheated oven for 8 minutes. Top each cooky with chocolate kiss; bake for 2 minutes longer.

Mrs. Raymond Walker, President, Contemporary Club, Salem, N.H.

PFEFFERNÜSSE

Makes About 100

2 cups dark corn syrup
2 cups sugar
2 cups lard
2 cups cold black coffee
1 teaspoon baking soda
1 teaspoon baking powder
1 teaspoon salt
1½ teaspoons black pepper
1½ teaspoons nutmeg
1½ teaspoons ginger
1½ teaspoons ground cloves
12 to 13 cups presifted flour

1. In large mixing bowl combine all ingredients except flour. Blend well.

2. Gradually add flour, 2 cups at a time; work in until dough is smooth and slightly stiffer than pie pastry. Chill for 30 minutes.

3. Preheat oven to 375° F.

4. Roll out dough with hands into pencil-thick ropes. Cut into 1-inch pieces. Place on baking sheets.

5. Bake in preheated oven for 15 to 20 minutes, or until golden.

Erwina Newman, Sorosis Club, Shattuck, Okla.

RAISIN COOKIES

Makes About 72

1½ cups seedless raisins
1 cup water
1½ cups sugar
1 cup shortening
3 eggs, lightly beaten
1 teaspoon vanilla
3½ cups presifted flour
1 teaspoon baking powder
1 teaspoon baking soda
½ teaspoon salt

1. Simmer raisins in water for 20 minutes, or until water is absorbed.

2. Preheat oven to 350° F. Grease baking sheets.

3. Cream sugar and shortening in mixing bowl. Beat in eggs and vanilla.

4. Stir in flour, baking power, baking soda and salt. Fold in raisins.

5. Roll dough into 1-inch balls; place on baking sheets. Press down with bottom of glass dipped in sugar.

6. Bake in preheated oven for 10 to 12 minutes.

Mrs. John Lee, Fortnightly Club, Dawson, N.D.

ITALIAN SESAME SEED COOKIES

Makes About 72

1 cup butter
1 cup sugar
3 eggs
1 teaspoon vanilla
4 teaspoons baking powder
½ teaspoon salt
4 cups presifted flour
Milk
Sesame seeds

1. Preheat oven to 350° F. Grease and flour baking sheets.

2. Cream butter in mixing bowl until light. Add sugar; beat until light and fluffy. Beat in eggs and vanilla.

3. Combine baking powder, salt and flour; sift together once; gradually stir into egg mixture.

4. Turn dough onto lightly floured board; knead as for making bread.

5. Roll dough into long ropelike strips about ¾ inch thick; cut into 2-inch pieces. Dip in milk, then in sesame seeds; arrange on baking sheets.

6. Bake in preheated oven for 20 minutes, or until golden brown.

Mrs. Russell F. Rabone, Thursday
Morning Club, Madison, N.J.

SPRITZ COOKIES

Makes About 96

2½ cups presifted flour
¼ teaspoon salt
1 cup butter
½ cup granulated or brown sugar
1 egg
1 teaspoon vanilla

1. Preheat oven to 375° F.
2. Combine flour and salt.
3. Cream butter and sugar in mixing bowl. Beat in egg and vanilla. Gradually blend in flour mixture.
4. Press mixture through cooky press onto baking sheets.
5. Bake in preheated oven for 7 to 10 minutes.

Beth Stickland, Woman's Club, Starke, Fla.

SNICKERDOODLES

Makes About 48

1 cup butter
1½ cups sugar
2 eggs
2¾ cups presifted flour
1 teaspoon baking soda
2 teaspoons cream of tartar
½ teaspoon salt
Mixed sugar and cinnamon

1. Preheat oven to 400° F. Grease baking sheets.
2. Cream butter and 1½ cups sugar in mixing bowl. Beat in eggs.
3. Add flour, baking soda, cream of tartar and salt; mix to make a firm dough.
4. Shape dough into balls about ¾ inch in diameter; roll in sugar mixture. Arrange on baking sheets; flatten with bottom of glass dipped in sugar mixture.
5. Bake in preheated oven for 10 minutes.

Mrs. Albert Metzger, President, National Council
of Jewish Women, Mobile, Ala.

SUGAR CRINKLES

Makes About 60

2⅔ cups presifted flour
1 teaspoon cream of tartar
1 teaspoon baking soda
1 teaspoon salt
1 cup butter
Sugar
2 eggs

1 teaspoon vanilla
Water

1. Onto piece of waxed paper sift together flour, cream of tartar, baking soda and salt.

2. Cream butter and 2 cups sugar in mixing bowl until light and fluffy. Add eggs, one at a time, beating well after each addition. Add vanilla; beat until smooth.

3. Gradually work in flour mixture, beating until blended. Chill for 2 hours.

4. Preheat oven to 350° F. Grease baking sheets.

5. Roll dough into small balls, using 1 tablespoon dough for each ball. Coat in sugar; place 2 inches apart on baking sheets. Sprinkle with few drops water.

6. Bake in preheated oven for 20 minutes, or until just light brown.

Mary Wigal, South Parkersburg
Woman's Club, Parkersburg, W. Va.

Refrigerator Cookies

Like the doughs in the recipes that follow, any of the molded cooky doughs in the preceding section may be formed into bricks or rolls, wrapped in waxed paper and chilled. When cold, they may be sliced and baked.

To make neat square cookies, shape refrigerator dough in an empty waxed paper box: Line the box with waxed paper. Press the dough firmly into the box and well into the corners. Chill. When ready to use, remove the dough from the box, slice and bake.

BUTTER REFRIGERATOR COOKIES

Makes About 96

1 pound butter
1½ cups sugar
1 egg
1 teaspoon vanilla
2 teaspoons milk
4 cups presifted flour
Finely chopped blanched almonds (optional)

1. Cream butter and sugar in mixing bowl. Add egg, vanilla and milk; blend well.

2. Stir in flour and almonds, if desired.

3. Shape into rolls; wrap in waxed paper; refrigerate or freeze.

4. To bake, preheat oven to 350° F.

5. Cut rolls into thin slices. Arrange on baking sheets; bake in preheated oven for 10 to 15 minutes, or until light brown.

Lorraine Paulus, Woman's Club,
Elmwood Park, Ill.

CINNAMON CRISPS

Makes About 48

1½ cups cake flour, sifted
1 teaspoon baking powder
1 teaspoon cinnamon

¼ teaspoon salt
½ cup butter
1 cup brown sugar
1 egg
1 tablespoon grated orange rind
½ cup bran flakes
¼ cup chopped pecans

1. Onto piece of waxed paper sift together flour, baking powder, cinnamon and salt.
2. Cream butter and sugar in mixing bowl until light and fluffy. Add egg; beat well.
3. Add flour mixture and orange rind; mix well. Stir in bran flakes and pecans; mix well.
4. Shape into 2-inch-thick rolls; wrap in waxed paper. Refrigerate or freeze.
5. To bake, preheat oven to 375° F. Grease baking sheets.
6. Cut rolls into ¼-inch-thick slices; place on baking sheets.
7. Bake in preheated oven for 8 to 10 minutes.

Gay Metzel, President, Champaign-Urbana Junior Woman's Club, Champaign, Ill.

CHOCOLATE PINWHEELS

Makes 48

½ cup sugar
½ cup shortening
1 egg yolk
1½ teaspoons vanilla
1½ cups presifted flour
¼ teaspoon salt
½ teaspoon baking powder
3 tablespoons milk
1-ounce square unsweetened chocolate, melted

1. Cream sugar and shortening in mixing bowl. Stir in egg yolk and vanilla.
2. Combine flour, salt and baking powder; stir alternately with milk into egg mixture to make a soft dough.
3. Divide dough in half. Add chocolate to one half; mix thoroughly.
4. On heavy waxed paper roll out each half into rectangle ⅛ inch thick. Turn white dough onto chocolate dough, with chocolate dough extending ½ inch beyond white dough along edge toward which you will roll. Remove waxed paper; roll up like a jelly roll. Wrap in waxed paper; refrigerate or freeze.
5. To bake, preheat oven to 375° F.
6. Cut roll into thin slices; bake on baking sheet for 10 minutes.

Laura Riggins, Donald District Woman's Club, Wapato, Wash.

OVERNIGHT COCONUT COOKIES

Makes About 36

1 cup butter
1 cup shortening
1 cup sugar
1 cup flaked coconut
1 teaspoon vanilla
3 cups presifted flour
1 teaspoon baking powder
1 teaspoon baking soda

1. Day before, cream butter, shortening and sugar well. Stir in coconut and vanilla.
2. Combine flour, baking powder and baking soda; stir into creamed mixture.
3. Form into rolls; wrap in waxed paper; refrigerate overnight.
4. Next day, preheat oven to 350° F. Grease baking sheets.
5. Slice rolls ¼ inch thick. Arrange on baking sheets; bake in preheated oven for 10 to 12 minutes.

Lydia Weber, Woman's Club, Ashley, N.D.

REFRIGERATOR FRUIT NUT COOKIES

Makes 60

¾ cup butter
1 cup granulated or brown sugar
1 egg
2 cups presifted flour
½ teaspoon baking soda
½ teaspoon cream of tartar
1 teaspoon vanilla
½ cup chopped nuts
½ cup chopped candied fruits

1. Cream butter and sugar in mixing bowl. Beat in egg.
2. Combine flour, baking soda and cream of tartar; stir into creamed mixture. Stir in remaining ingredients.
3. Shape dough into rolls; wrap in waxed paper; refrigerate until ready to use.
4. To bake, preheat oven to 350° F. Grease baking sheets.
5. Cut rolls into thin slices. Arrange on baking sheets; bake in preheated oven for about 10 minutes.

Junior Woman's Club, Annawan, Ill.

ORANGE REFRIGERATOR COOKIES

Makes 60

1 cup butter or 1½ cups margarine
½ cup granulated sugar
½ cup light brown sugar
1 egg
3 cups presifted flour
½ teaspoon salt
¼ teaspoon baking soda
Grated rind of 1 orange
2 tablespoons orange juice
1 teaspoon vanilla
½ cup chopped pecans or toasted almonds

1. Cream butter or margarine and sugars in mixing bowl until light and fluffy. Beat in egg.
2. Combine flour, salt and baking soda; stir into creamed mixture. Stir in orange rind and juice, vanilla and nuts. Chill.
3. Form dough into rolls about 1½ to 2 inches in diameter. Wrap in waxed paper; freeze or refrigerate.
4. To bake, preheat oven to 375° F. Grease baking sheets.

5. Slice rolls ⅛ inch thick. Arrange on baking sheets; bake in preheated oven for 12 to 15 minutes.

Mrs. L. A. Meis, Morning Study Club, Victoria, Tex.

PASTEL COOKIES

Makes About 72

1 cup shortening
2 cups sugar
8 egg whites, lightly beaten
6 cups sifted cake flour
3 teaspoons baking powder
1 teaspoon salt
Lemon, vanilla, almond and orange extract and cinnamon oil
Green, pink, yellow and orange food coloring

1. Cream shortening and sugar in mixing bowl until light. Stir in egg whites.
2. Sift together flour, baking powder and salt; work into creamed mixture to make a soft dough.
3. Divide dough into quarters. Flavor and color three parts as follows:
Part 1: ¼ teaspoon almond extract. Color green.
Part 2: 2 drops cinnamon oil. Color pink.
Part 3: ½ teaspoon lemon or orange extract. Color yellow or orange.
Part 4: ½ teaspoon vanilla extract. Leave uncolored.
4. Chill dough thoroughly: form into a variety of cookies:
PINWHEELS: Place layer of colored dough on layer of uncolored dough; press together with rolling pin. Roll up lengthwise; wrap in waxed paper; chill.
RIBBONS: Roll out different colored doughs about ⅓ inch thick. Stack in alternate layers to height of 2 inches. Press together; wrap in waxed paper; chill.
CHECKERBOARDS: Roll out two colored doughs ⅓ inch thick; stack in alternate layers. Press lightly together with rolling pin; chill. Cut into slices about ⅓ inch thick; stack 2 inches deep with strips running at right angels to each layer. Wrap in waxed paper; chill.
5. To bake, preheat oven to 350° F. Grease baking sheets.
6. Slice various colored doughs ⅛ inch thick; arrange on baking sheets. Bake in preheated oven for 8 to 10 minutes.

Suburban Cookie Book, Mutual Improvement Club, Ronceverte, W. Va.

PEANUT BUTTER WHIRLIGIGS

Makes About 24

½ cup shortening
½ cup granulated sugar
½ cup brown sugar
½ cup peanut butter
1 egg
1¼ cups presifted flour
½ teaspoon baking soda
½ teaspoon salt

6-ounce package semi-sweet chocolate pieces, melted and slightly cooled

1. Cream shortening, sugars and peanut butter in mixing bowl. Add egg; beat until light and fluffy.
2. Combine flour, baking soda and salt; blend into creamed mixture.
3. Roll dough into rectangle ¼ inch thick. Spread with chocolate; roll up like a jelly roll. Wrap in waxed paper; chill.
4. To bake, preheat oven to 375° F.
5. Slice roll ¼ inch thick; arrange baking sheets.
6. Bake in preheated oven for 10 to 12 minutes.

Suburban Cookie Book, Mutual Improvement Club, Ronceverte, W. Va.

Pan Cookies

APPLE OATMEAL BARS

Makes About 50

2 cups unsifted flour
1 teaspoon baking soda
¼ teaspoon salt
2 cups quick-cooking oats
1 cup light brown sugar
1 cup margarine
4 apples, peeled and chopped
1 cup chopped nuts
½ cup granulated sugar
3 tablespoons butter

1. Preheat oven to 300° F. Grease 15½ x 10½ x 1-inch jelly-roll pan.
2. Into mixing bowl sift together flour, baking soda and salt. Add oats, brown sugar and margarine; blend with pastry blender until grainy.
3. Pat half the oat mixture into pan. Cover with apples; sprinkle with ½ cup of the nuts and granulated sugar. Dot with butter. Pat remaining oat mixture on top; sprinkle with remaining nuts and remaining granulated sugar.
4. Bake in preheated oven for 1 hour and 15 minutes.
5. While warm, cut into 3 x 1-inch bars.

Christmas Cookies, Woman's Club, Aldan, Pa.

APRICOT BLONDIES

Makes 16

½ cup shortening
2 cup brown sugar
2 eggs
1½ teaspoons vanilla
1¾ cups presifted flour
2 teaspoons baking powder
½ teaspoon salt
½ cup chopped nuts
½ cup chopped dried apricots

1. Preheat oven to 350° F. Grease 8-inch square baking pan.
2. Cream shortening and sugar in mixing bowl. Beat in eggs and vanilla.

3. Combine flour, baking powder and salt; stir into creamed mixture. Stir in nuts and apricots.

4. Turn batter into pan; bake in preheated oven for 30 minutes, or until golden brown. Cut into 2-inch squares.

Mrs. Theodore S. Chapman, General Federation of Women's Clubs, Hinsdale, Ill.

LIBBETT'S BROWNIES

Makes 20

½ cup butter
2 cups sugar
4 eggs
½ cup milk
2 1-ounce squares unsweetened chocolate, melted
1⅓ cups presifted flour
¼ teaspoon salt
1 cup broken nuts
2 teaspoons vanilla
Mocha Butter Frosting (p. 624)

1. Preheat oven to 350° F. Grease 15½ x 10½ x 1-inch jelly roll pan.

2. Cream butter and sugar in mixing bowl well. Add eggs; beat well. Stir in milk and chocolate.

3. Stir in flour, salt, nuts and vanilla.

4. Spread batter in pan; bake in preheated oven for 20 to 30 minutes.

5. Remove from oven; while warm, frost with Mocha Butter Frosting. Cool; cut into 3-inch squares.

Elizabeth Rife, Donald District Woman's Club, Wapato, Wash.

LAZY DAY BROWNIES

Makes 16

1 cup presifted flour
¾ cup sugar
3 tablespoons cocoa
2 eggs, lightly beaten
1 teaspoon vanilla
½ cup margarine, melted
½ cup chopped nuts

1. Preheat oven to 350° F. Grease 8-inch square baking pan.

2. Combine all ingredients. Turn batter into pan; bake in preheated oven for 20 minutes. Cool; cut into 2-inch squares.

Mrs. David Brunes, Junior Woman's Club, Elgin, Ill.

COFFEE MARSHMALLOW BROWNIES

Makes 16

½ cup shortening
2 1-ounce squares unsweetened chocolate
2 eggs
1 cup sugar
1 cup sifted cake flour
¼ teaspoon baking powder
¼ teaspoon salt
3 tablespoons black coffee
1 teaspoon vanilla
1 cup tiny marshmallows
1 cup chopped walnuts

1. Preheat oven to 350° F. Grease 8-inch square baking pan.

2. Melt shortening and chocolate in top of double saucepan.

3. In mixing bowl beat eggs; add sugar and chocolate mixture. Beat for 1 minute.

4. Onto piece of waxed paper sift together flour, baking powder and salt. Mix coffee and vanilla; add alternately with flour mixture to egg mixture, beating well after each addition.

5. Stir in marshmallows and walnuts. Spread in pan.

6. Bake in preheated oven for 50 minutes. Cool; cut into 2-inch squares.

Mrs. Richard Robinson, Semper Fidelis Study Club, Clarinda, Ia.

CONGA BARS

Makes 24

2¾ cups presifted flour
2½ teaspoons baking powder
½ teaspoon salt
⅔ cup melted butter
2 cups brown sugar
3 eggs
1 teaspoon vanilla
1 cup chopped walnuts
6-ounce package semi-sweet chocolate pieces

1. Preheat oven to 350° F. Grease 15½ x 10½ x 1-inch jelly roll pan.

2. Onto piece of waxed paper sift together flour, baking powder and salt.

3. Pour butter into mixing bowl. Add sugar; stir until dissolved. Add eggs, one at a time; beating well after each addition.

4. Beat in vanilla; add flour mixture, beating well until smooth. Stir in walnuts and chocolate; spread in pan.

5. Bake in preheated oven for 25 to 30 minutes. Cool; cut into 3½ x 2-inch bars.

Mrs. George W. Clapper, Hickory Township Women's Club, Sharon, Pa.

FUDGE SQUARES

Makes 24

Butter
3 1-ounce squares unsweetened chocolate
3 eggs, lightly beaten
¾ cup presifted flour
½ teaspoon baking powder
1 cup granulated sugar
1 cup chopped nuts
1 teaspoon vanilla
Confectioners' sugar
Cream

1. Preheat oven to 350° F. Grease 13 x 9½ x 2-inch baking pan.

2. Melt ½ cup butter and 2 of the chocolate squares in top of double saucepan over simmering water; stir occasionally until smooth.

3. Beat in eggs. Stir in flour, baking powder, granulated sugar, nuts and vanilla.

4. Turn batter into pan; bake in preheated oven for 15 to 20 minutes. Remove from oven; cool.

5. Melt 3 tablespoons butter and remaining chocolate until smooth. Stir in enough confectioners' sugar and cream to

make a smooth easy-to-spread frosting. Spread on cooled cake. Cut into 2-inch squares.

Mrs. Carl Bergendoff, Woman's Club,
Glen Ellyn, Ill.

MARSHMALLOW FUDGE BARS
Makes 16

¾ cup presifted flour
¼ teaspoon baking powder
¼ teaspoon salt
2 teaspoons cocoa
½ cup shortening
¾ cup sugar
2 eggs
1 teaspoon vanilla
½ cup chopped nuts
18 marshmallows, cut into pieces
    Easy Chocolate Frosting (p. 625)

1. Preheat oven to 350° F. Grease and flour 13 x 9½ x 2-inch baking pan.
2. Combine flour, baking powder, salt and cocoa.
3. Cream shortening and sugar in mixing bowl until light and fluffy. Add eggs, one at a time, beating well after each addition.
4. Stir in flour mixture, vanilla and nuts.
5. Spread batter in pan; bake in preheated oven for 25 to 30 minutes. Remove from oven; sprinkle with marshmallows. Return to oven for 3 minutes; remove from oven; spread marshmallows evenly over top.
6. Cool in pan; frost with Easy Chocolate Frosting. Let stand for a few hours before cutting into 3 x 2-inch bars.

Wilda Matthews, Plum Creek Valley
Woman's Club, Pittsburgh, Pa.

BUTTERSCOTCH BROWNIES
Makes 16

¼ cup shortening
1 cup brown sugar
1 egg
¾ cup presifted flour
1 teaspoon baking powder
½ teaspoon salt
½ teaspoon vanilla
½ cup chopped walnuts

1. Preheat oven to 350° F. Grease 8-inch square baking pan.
2. Melt shortening in small saucepan. Stir in sugar; pour into mixing bowl to cool. Blend in egg.
3. Add flour, baking powder and salt; blend well. Add vanilla and walnuts; mix well. Turn into pan.
4. Bake in preheated oven for 20 to 25 minutes. Cool in pan; cut into 2-inch squares.

Gladys Eberhard, Woman's Club,
Brooklawn, N.J.

PEANUT BUTTER BROWNIES
Makes 16

1 cup presifted flour
1 teaspoon baking powder
¼ teaspoon salt
⅓ cup butter or margarine
½ cup peanut butter
1 cup granulated sugar
¼ cup brown sugar
2 eggs
6-ounce package semi-sweet
    chocolate pieces
½ teaspoon vanilla

1. Preheat oven to 350° F. Grease well 9-inch square baking pan.
2. Onto piece of waxed paper sift together flour, baking powder and salt.
3. Cream butter or margarine and peanut butter in mixing bowl until smooth. Add sugars; beat until light and fluffy. Add eggs, one at a time, beating well after each addition.
4. Gradually stir in flour mixture; beat until smooth. Add chocolate and vanilla; mix well. Spread in pan.
5. Bake in preheated oven for 25 to 30 minutes. Cool in pan; cut into 16 squares.

Helen Ross, Democratic Women's Club,
West Washington County, Me.

PECAN BARS
Makes 24

½ cup butter or margarine
¼ cup granulated sugar
3 eggs
    Presifted flour
⅛ teaspoon salt
2 teaspoons vanilla
1½ cups brown sugar
½ teaspoon baking powder
½ cup flaked coconut
1 cup chopped pecans

1. Preheat oven to 350° F. Grease 13 x 9½ x 2-inch baking pan.
2. Cream butter or margarine and granulated sugar in mixing bowl until light and fluffy. Add 1 of the eggs; beat until smooth.
3. Add 1¼ cups flour, salt and 1 teaspoon of the vanilla; work into a smooth dough. Pat into pan.
4. Bake in preheated oven for 15 minutes.
5. Meanwhile, prepare Pecan Topping: In mixing bowl blend remaining eggs and brown sugar. Add 2 tablespoons flour, remaining vanilla, baking powder, coconut and pecans; mix well.
6. Spread on cake; bake for 25 minutes longer. Cool in pan; cut into 3 x 1½-inch bars.

Mrs. Forrest Williams, President,
Woman's Club, Forsyth, Mont.

HOOSIER PEANUT BARS
Makes 18

2 cups presifted flour
1 teaspoon baking soda
2 teaspoons baking powder
½ teaspoon salt
½ cup shortening
½ cup granulated sugar
1½ cups brown sugar
2 eggs, separated
1 teaspoon vanilla
3 tablespoons water

6-ounce package semi-sweet
chocolate pieces
¾ cup chopped salted peanuts

1. Preheat oven to 325° F. Grease well and flour 13 x 9½ x 2-inch baking pan.
2. Onto piece of waxed paper sift together flour, baking soda, baking powder and salt.
3. In mixing bowl cream shortening, granulated sugar and ½ cup of the brown sugar until light and fluffy. Add egg yolks and vanilla; beat well.
4. Add water and flour mixture alternately to make a very stiff dough.
5. Press dough into pan; sprinkle with chocolate.
6. In mixing bowl beat egg whites until foamy. Gradually add remaining brown sugar; beat until stiff and glossy. Spread on chocolate in pan; sprinkle with peanuts.
7. Bake in preheated oven for 35 minutes.
8. Cool; cut into 18 bars; about 3 x 2 inches.

*Mrs. Shirley Wierda, Community
Women's Club, Maurice, Ia.*

BUTTERSCOTCH BARS
Makes 24

1 cup butter or margarine
½ cup granulated sugar
1½ cup brown sugar
2 eggs, separated
1 tablespoon water
1 teaspoon vanilla
2 cups presifted flour
1 teaspoon salt
1 teaspoon baking powder
6-ounce package butterscotch pieces

1. Preheat oven to 350° F.
2. Cream butter or margarine, granulated sugar and ½ cup of the brown sugar in mixing bowl. Beat in egg yolks, water and vanilla.
3. Stir in flour, salt and baking powder.
4. Spread in 13 x 9½ x 2-inch baking pan; sprinkle with butterscotch.
5. Beat egg whites until stiff but not dry; fold in the remaining brown sugar; spread over butterscotch.
6. Bake in preheated oven for 25 minutes. Cool; cut into bars, about 3 x 2 inches.

NOTE: Semi-sweet chocolate pieces may be substituted for butterscotch in this recipe.

*Mrs. Mattie Harper, Woman's Club,
Thermopolis, Wyo.*

EASY CHOCOLATE-FROSTED BUTTERSCOTCH BARS
Makes 25

1 cup butter or margarine
1 cup brown sugar
1 egg
1 teaspoon vanilla
2 cups presifted flour
6-ounce bar sweetened chocolate
Chopped nuts

1. Preheat oven to 350° F. Grease 15½ x 10½-inch baking sheet.

2. Cream butter or margarine and brown sugar in mixing bowl. Add egg and vanilla; blend thoroughly. Blend in flour.
3. Spread batter very thinly on baking sheet; bake in preheated oven for 20 minutes.
4. Remove from oven; immediately place chocolate on top to melt; spread over entire top surface. Sprinkle with nuts; cool; cut into bars, about 2 x 3 inches.

Mrs. Theresa Pease, Women's Club, Thorp. Wis.

CHILDREN'S DELIGHT
Makes 32

2 cups presifted flour
1 teaspoon baking soda
¼ teaspoon salt
1 teaspoon cinnamon
½ teaspoon nutmeg
½ teaspoon ground cloves
1 cup shortening
1 cup granulated sugar
1 egg
¼ cup molasses
1 cup buttermilk
1 cup chopped walnuts
1 cup seedless raisins
¼ cup melted butter or margarine
¼ cup heavy cream
1 teaspoon vanilla
Sifted confectioners' sugar

1. Preheat oven to 325° F. Grease and flour 15½ x 10½ x 1-inch jelly roll pan.
2. Sift together flour, baking soda, salt and spices.
3. Cream shortening and granulated sugar in mixing bowl until light and fluffy. Add egg; beat well. Add molasses and buttermilk; beat until smooth.
4. Add flour mixture; stir until smooth. Fold in walnuts and raisins; spread in pan.
5. Bake in preheated oven for 25 minutes.
6. Meanwhile, prepare Vanilla Frosting: Blend butter or margarine, cream and vanilla. Stir in sufficient confectioners' sugar to make very thin frosting.
7. Cool in pan; spead with frosting; cut into 2-inch squares.

*Gertrude L. Richards, Woman's Club,
Chicopee Falls, Mass.*

CHINESE CHEWS
Makes 24

2 eggs
1 cup granulated sugar
½ cup presifted flour
½ teaspoon baking powder
¼ teaspoon salt
1 cup chopped dates
1 cup chopped nuts
1 teaspoon vanilla
Confectioners' sugar

1. Preheat oven to 350° F. Grease 13 x 9½ x 2-inch baking pan.
2. Beat eggs until light; add granulated sugar; blend well.

3. Sift together flour, baking powder and salt; stir into egg mixture. Add dates, nuts and vanilla; mix.

4. Turn batter into pan; bake in preheated oven for 30 minutes.

5. Cut into 2-inch squares; while still hot, roll between palms into balls.

6. When nearly cold, put in bag with confectioners' sugar; shake until coated.

Mrs. Clarke Gapen, President, Wyoming Federation of Women's Club, Basin, Wyo.

CHOCOLATE DATE BARS
Makes 30

1¼ cups chopped dates
¾ cup brown sugar
½ cup butter
½ cup water
6-ounce package chocolate pieces
1½ cups presifted flour
¾ teaspoon baking soda
½ teaspoon salt
2 eggs, lightly beaten
½ cup orange juice
½ cup milk
½ cup chopped nuts

1. In saucepan combine dates, sugar, butter and water. Cook, stirring occasionally, to a smooth paste. Remove from heat; stir in chocolate. Cool.

2. Preheat oven to 350° F. Grease 15½ x 10½ x 1-inch jelly roll pan.

3. Stir remaining ingredients into date mixture; spread in pan.

4. Bake in preheated oven for 20 to 25 minutes. Cool; cut into 3 x 2-inch bars.

Mrs. M. P. Roberts, Friday Club, Barlow, N.D.

CHERRY COCONUT BARS
Makes 18

½ cup butter or margarine
3 tablespoons confectioners' sugar
1¼ cups presifted flour
1 cup granulated sugar
2 eggs
¼ teaspoon salt
½ teaspoon baking powder
½ cup chopped walnuts
½ cup flaked coconut
½ cup quartered maraschino cherries
1 teaspoon vanilla

1. Preheat oven to 350° F. Grease 13 x 9½ x 2-inch baking pan.

2. In mixing bowl combine butter or margarine, confectioners' sugar and 1 cup of the flour. Work together with finger until mixture resembles fine crumbs.

3. Press into pan; bake in preheated oven for 15 minutes.

4. Meanwhile, in mixing bowl beat granulated sugar and eggs until light and fluffy.

5. Stir in remaining flour, salt and baking powder; blend until smooth. Add remaining ingredients; mix well. Spread on cake in pan.

6. Bake in preheated oven for 25 minutes. Cool in pan; cut into 3 x 2-inch bars.

Mrs. William Askew, L. L. G. Club, Stockport, Ia.

CINNAMON SQUARES
Makes 32

1 cup sugar
¾ cup margarine
1 egg
2 cups presifted flour
2 teaspoons cinnamon
Pinch of salt
1 teaspoon vanilla
1 cup chopped nuts

1. Preheat oven to 350° F.

2. Cream sugar and margarine. Beat in egg.

3. Combine flour, cinnamon and salt; stir into creamed mixture. Stir in vanilla; mix well. (Mixture will be stiff.)

4. Spread in two 8-inch square baking pans. Sprinkle with nuts; press in.

5. Bake in preheated oven for 30 minutes. Cool; cut into 2-inch squares.

Fran Mathis, Woman's Federated Guild, Moultrie, Ga.

PRIZEWINNING DATE SQUARES
Makes 24

3½ cups quick-cooking oats
2 cups brown sugar
1½ cups butter or margarine, melted
3 cups presifted flour
1 cup granulated sugar
1 cup water
2 cups cut-up dates
Confectioners' sugar

1. Preheat oven to 350° F. Grease 13 x 9½ x 2-inch baking pan.

2. In large bowl combine oats and brown sugar. Add butter or margarine. Mix by hand until crumbed; spread half in pan.

3. Combine granulated sugar, water and dates; pour into pan. Sprinkle with remaining crumbs.

4. Bake in preheated oven for 25 minutes. Cool; sprinkle with confectioners' sugar; cut into 2-inch squares.

D. Klauser, Woman's Club, Palisades Park, N.J.

BY CRACKY BARS
Makes 32

1¾ cups presifted flour
1 teaspoon salt
¼ teaspoon baking soda
¾ cup shortening
1 cup sugar
2 eggs
⅓ cup milk
1 teaspoon vanilla
1-ounce square unsweetened chocolate, melted
¾ cup chopped walnuts
9 double graham crackers
¾ cup semi-sweet chocolate pieces

1. Preheat oven to 375° F. Grease 8-inch square baking pan well.

2. Onto piece of waxed paper sift together flour, salt and baking soda.

3. Cream shortening and sugar in mixing bowl until light and fluffy. Add eggs, one at a time, beating well after each addition.

4. Mix milk and vanilla; add alternately with flour mixture to creamed mixture, beating well after each addition.

5. Mix melted chocolate and walnuts into one-third of batter; spread in pan. Top with crackers.

6. Mix chocolate pieces into remaining batter. Spread on crackers.

7. Bake in preheated oven for 30 minutes. Cool; cut into bars.

Mary Agnes Whitman, Junior Women's Club, Nashua, N.H.

GRIZZLE NICKEL SQUARES

Makes 16

15-ounce can sweetened condensed milk
1 cup semi-sweet chocolate pieces
2 cups graham cracker crumbs
½ cup flaked coconut
½ cup chopped nuts
Confectioners' sugar

1. Preheat oven to 350° F. Grease 9-inch square baking pan very well.

2. In mixing bowl combine milk, chocolate, crumbs, coconut and nuts; mix well. Pour into pan.

3. Bake in preheated oven for 30 minutes. Cool for 10 minutes; cut into 2-inch squares; roll in sugar.

Mrs. William Vandenburg, Town & Country League, Cheyenne, Wyo.

TRADITIONAL LEBKUCHEN

Makes About 36

Bake these about 2 weeks before you use them. Store them in a tightly covered container.

2¾ cups presifted flour
½ teaspoon baking soda
1 teaspoon cinnamon
½ teaspoon ground cloves
½ teaspoon nutmeg
½ cup finely chopped candied fruits
½ cup chopped walnuts
1 egg
1 cup light corn syrup
1 tablespoon lemon juice
1 teaspoon grated lemon rind
1 cup confectioners' sugar
(sift if lumpy)
2 tablespoons water

1. Preheat oven to 400° F. Grease and flour 2 baking sheets.

2. Into mixing bowl sift together flour, baking soda and spices. Add fruits and walnuts; mix well.

3. In another mixing bowl beat egg lightly; stir in corn syrup and lemon juice and rind. Add flour mixture; mix well.

4. Divide dough in half; with palm of hand moistened with cold water press each half ⅛ inch thick onto a baking sheet.

5. Bake in preheated oven for 12 to 15 minutes, or until light brown and firm.

6. Meanwhile, prepare Sugar Glaze: In small bowl combine sugar and water to make a smooth paste.

7. Spread glaze on cookies. While warm, cut into squares or bars. Each baking sheet will yield about 18 cookies. Remove from sheets; cool.

Mrs. R. H. Sargent, Women's Club, Richland, Wash.

LEMON LOVE NOTES

Makes 32

Butter
Presifted flour
1 cup confectioners' sugar
(sift if lumpy)
2 tablespoons lemon juice
Grated rind of 1 lemon
2 eggs, lightly beaten
1 cup granulated sugar
2 teaspoons baking powder
½ teaspoon vanilla
1 tablespoon butter
1½ teaspoons milk

1. Preheat oven to 350° F.

2. Combine ½ cup butter, 1 cup flour and ¼ cup of the confectioners' sugar. Pat into 8-inch square baking pan.

3. Bake in preheated oven for 15 minutes. Cool.

4. Combine lemon juice and rind, eggs, granulated sugar, 2 tablespoons flour and baking powder. Spread on baked crust; return to preheated oven for 25 minutes. Cool in pan.

5. Make Vanilla Frosting: Combine remaining confectioners' sugar, vanilla, 1 tablespoon butter and milk.

6. Spread on crust; cut into 2 x 1-inch bars.

Mary E. Williams, Woman's Civic Club, Roselle Park, N.J.

LEMON SOURS

Makes 30

A recipe of Mrs. John Dalton, wife of the former governor of Missouri.

¾ cup presifted flour
⅓ cup butter
2 eggs
1 cup brown sugar
¾ cup flaked coconut
½ cup chopped pecans
⅛ teaspoon baking powder
1 teaspoon vanilla
1 teaspoon grated lemon rind
1½ teaspoons lemon juice
⅔ cup confectioners' sugar

1. Preheat oven to 350° F.

2. Mix flour and butter until crumbed; spread into 11 x 7 x 1½-inch baking pan. Bake in preheated oven for 10 minutes.

3. Meanwhile, combine eggs, brown sugar, coconut, pecans, baking powder and vanilla. Spread on baked crumbs; bake for 20 minutes longer.

4. Meanwhile, combine lemon rind and juice and confectioners' sugar to make a frosting. Spread on cake as soon as pan is removed from oven.

5. Cool in pan; cut into 2 x 1-inch bars.

Mary Bunyard, Woman's Club, Brownstown, Ill.

MALTED MILK DAINTIES

Makes 24

1⅜ cups presifted flour
⅓ cup butter
¾ cup brown sugar
½ cup malted milk powder
½ teaspoon baking powder
¼ teaspoon salt
1 cup chopped nuts
2 eggs, well beaten
⅔ cup granulated sugar
½ teaspoon vanilla

1. Preheat oven to 375° F. Grease 11 x 7 x 1½-baking pan.
2. Combine 1¼ cups of the flour, butter and brown sugar until crumbed. Spread in pan; bake in preheated oven for 10 minutes.
3. Meanwhile, combine remaining flour, malted milk, baking powder, salt and nuts.
4. In mixing bowl beat eggs and granulated sugar until thickened and pale. Stir in flour mixture and vanilla; blend well.
5. Spread on crumbs; bake for 25 minutes longer. Cool; cut into 24 bars.

Mrs. J. E. Melton, Book Club, Selma, Ala.

MAPLE BARS

Makes 8

2 eggs
1 cup granulated sugar
⅔ cup cooking oil
1 cup presifted flour
½ teaspoon baking powder
½ teaspoon salt
2 teaspoons maple flavoring
1 cup chopped pecans
Confectioners' sugar

1. Preheat oven to 375° F. Grease 8-inch square baking pan.
2. Beat eggs in mixing bowl; add sugar. Beat until thickened and lemon-colored. Stir in oil; blend well.
3. Into egg mixture sift together flour, baking powder and salt; mix well. Add maple flavoring and pecans; mix well. Turn into pan.
4. Bake in preheated oven for 30 minutes. Sprinkle with confectioners' sugar; cut into 4 x 2-inch bars; cool in pan.

Mrs. J. G. Bailey, President, Women's Club, Pasco, Wash.

MINCEMEAT SQUARES

Makes 15

2 eggs
2 tablespoons molasses
1½ teaspoons vanilla
1 tablespoon butter
1½ cups brown sugar
2 cups presifted flour
½ teaspoon salt
½ teaspoon baking soda
1 teaspoon cinnamon
1 teaspoon ground cloves
¼ cup seedless raisins, chopped
1 cup mincemeat
3 tablespoons hot water
1½ cups sifted confectioners' sugar
3 tablespoons hot milk

½ teaspoon almond extract
1 cup chopped walnuts

1. Preheat oven to 375° F. Grease 15½ x 10½ x 1-inch jelly roll pan well. Line with waxed paper; grease again.
2. In mixing bowl beat eggs, molasses, 1 teaspoon of the vanilla, butter and brown sugar until smooth.
3. Onto piece of waxed paper sift together flour, salt, baking soda, cinnamon and cloves. Stir into egg mixture; beat until smooth.
4. In small bowl mix raisins, mincemeat and water. Stir into batter; mix until well blended. Spread evenly in pan.
5. Bake in preheated oven for 15 minutes.
6. Meanwhile, in bowl blend confectioners' sugar, milk, remaining vanilla and almond extract. Spread on hot cake. Sprinkle with walnuts; cool in pan; cut into 3-inch squares.

Maureen Cote, Junior Woman's Club, Cheshire, Conn.

CHEWY OATMEAL BARS

Makes 24

1 cup butter
2 cups brown sugar
2 eggs
1 teaspoon vanilla
2 cups presifted flour
1 teaspoon baking soda
½ teaspoon salt
2 cups quick-cooking oats
½ cup chopped walnuts
6-ounce package semi-sweet chocolate pieces

1. Preheat oven to 400° F. Grease 15½ x 10½ x 1-inch jelly roll pan.
2. Cream butter, sugar, eggs and vanilla in mixing bowl until fluffy. Stir in flour, baking soda and salt. Add oats; mix well.
3. Spread batter in pan; sprinkle with walnuts and chocolate.
4. Bake in preheated oven for 10 minutes. Cool in pan; cut into 3½ x 2-inch bars.

Mrs. Floyd Burnside, Sigma Sorosis Club, Woodward. Okla.

PEANUT BUTTER FINGERS

Makes 27

½ cup butter
½ cup granulated sugar
½ cup brown sugar
1 egg
⅓ cup peanut butter
½ teaspoon baking soda
¼ teaspoon salt
½ teaspoon vanilla
1 cup presifted flour
1 cup quick-cooking oats
Peanut Butter Frosting (p. 625)

1. Preheat oven to 350° F. Grease 9-inch square baking pan.
2. Cream butter and sugars in mixing bowl; add egg; mix well.
3. Add peanut butter, baking soda, salt and vanilla; mix well. Stir in flour and oats.

4. Spread batter in pan; bake in preheated oven for 20 to 30 minutes.

5. Cool in pan; frost with Peanut Butter Frosting; cut into 3 x 1-inch fingers.

Mrs. Billie Wooster, Junior Woman's Club,
Smyrna, Ga.

PUMPKIN BARS

Makes 32

1 cup shortening
1 teaspoon vanilla
2 cups brown sugar
2 eggs, lightly beaten
1 cup canned pumpkin
2 cups presifted flour
1 teaspoon baking powder
¼ teaspoon baking soda
1 teaspoon cinnamon
½ teaspoon ginger
¼ teaspoon allspice
1 cup flaked coconut
1 cup chopped nuts

1. Preheat oven to 350° F. Grease 15½ x 10½ x 1-inch jelly roll pan.

2. Cream shortening and vanilla. Add sugar; cream until light and fluffy. Add eggs and pumpkin; beat well.

3. Sift together flour, baking powder, baking soda and spices; stir into pumpkin mixture, mixing until smooth. Blend in coconut and nuts.

4. Spread batter in pan; bake in preheated oven for about 35 minutes. Cool in pan; cut into 32 bars.

Mrs. Richard W. Kapke, New Jersey State
Federation of Women's Clubs, Mountainside, N.J.

RAISIN SPICE BARS

Makes 32

1 cup seedless raisins
1 teaspoon baking soda
1 cup granulated sugar
⅝ cup butter
½ cup shortening
1 egg
½ teaspoon salt
1¾ cups presifted flour
1 teaspoon cinnamon
½ teaspoon nutmeg
½ teaspoon ground cloves
1 teaspoon vanilla
Confectioners' sugar

1. In saucepan combine raisins and 2 cups water. Bring to boil; cook for 10 minutes. Remove from heat; stir in baking soda; cool.

2. Preheat oven to 350° F. Grease 13 x 9½ x 2-inch baking pan.

3. Cream granulated sugar, ½ cup of the butter and shortening in mixing bowl; beat in egg and salt.

4. Combine flour and spices; stir alternately with raisin mixture into egg mixture.

5. Turn batter into pan; bake in preheated oven for 35 minutes.

6. Combine remaining butter, 2 tablespoons water and vanilla with enough confectioners' sugar to give good spreading

consistency. Spread on cake while still warm. Cool; cut into 3 x 1-inch bars.

Mrs. Dan Mjogdalen, Book and
Thimble Club, Portland, N.D.

CRISP TOFFEE BARS

Makes About 50

1 cup butter or margarine
1 cup brown sugar
1 teaspoon vanilla
2 cups presifted flour
Dash of salt
6-ounce package semi-sweet
chocolate pieces
1 cup chopped walnuts

1. Preheat oven to 350° F.

2. Cream butter or margarine, sugar and vanilla in mixing bowl until light and fluffy. Add flour and salt; mix well.

3. Stir in chocolate and walnuts; spread in 15½ x 10½ x 1-inch jelly roll pan.

4. Bake in preheated oven for 20 minutes, or until browned. While warm, cut into 3 x 1-inch bars; cool in pan.

Mrs. Martin Gulson, Study Club, Bottineau, N.D.

No-Bake Cookies

APRICOT COCONUT BALLS

Makes 32

1½ cups ground dried apricots
2 cups shredded coconut
⅔ cup condensed milk
Confectioners' sugar

1. Combine apricots and coconut. Add milk; mix well.

2. Shape into 1-inch balls; roll in sugar.

3. Place on waxed paper to dry for 1 hour.

VARIATION: If desired, add grated rind and juice of 1 orange. Form into balls; place on waxed paper; flatten with spoon. Let stand until firm.

Anna Fuchs, Donald District
Woman's Club, Wapato, Wash.

KENTUCKY BOURBON BALLS

Makes About 36

¼ cup butter
1 pound confectioners' sugar
(sift if lumpy)
2 teaspoons lemon juice
½ cup ground pecans
¼ teaspoon salt
¼ cup bourbon
4 1-ounce squares unsweetened
chocolate
2 tablespoons shortening

1. Line baking sheet with waxed paper.

2. In mixing bowl beat butter until fluffy. Beat in about ½ pound of the sugar. With hands work in remaining sugar, lemon juice, pecans, salt and bourbon. Chill for 30 minutes.

3. Meanwhile, melt chocolate and shortening in top of double saucepan over hot water. Stir occasionally.

4. Shape dough into 1-inch balls; dip in chocolate. Place on baking sheet; set aside until firm.

Myrna McQuillen, Buechel Woman's Club,
Louisville, Ky.

CHINESE NEW YEAR'S COOKIES
Makes 36

6-ounce package semi-sweet
  chocolate pieces
6-ounce package butterscotch pieces
7-ounce can salted peanuts
3½-ounce can Chinese noodles

1. In top of double saucepan combine chocolate and butterscotch. Heat over hot (not boiling) water until smooth, stirring occasionally.
2. Remove from heat; stir in peanuts and noodles.
3. Drop by teaspoons onto waxed paper; cool.

Mrs. J. K. Owens, Senior President,
20th Century Club, Gordo, Ala.

CHOCOLATE LOGS
Makes 48 Cookies

2 6-ounce packages semi-sweet
  chocolate pieces
⅔ cup evaporated milk
1 teaspoon vanilla
¼ teaspoon salt
4½ cups sifted confectioners' sugar
  Finely chopped nuts or flaked
  coconut

1. In saucepan combine chocolate and milk. Stir over low heat until chocolate is melted and mixture is smooth.
2. Remove from heat; stir in vanilla and salt. Beat in sugar; chill until firm.
3. Put half the mixture between sheets of waxed paper; shape into 10-inch log. Repeat with other half. Roll logs in nuts or coconut; wrap in waxed paper; chill.
4. To serve, cut each roll with sharp knife into 24 slices.

Mrs. Walt Palmer, Study and Social Club,
Richfield, Kans.

CHOCOLATE COOKIES
Makes 48

2 eggs, lightly beaten
1 cup confectioners' sugar
20 marshmallows, finely cut,
  or 220 tiny marshmallows
1 cup semi-sweet chocolate pieces,
  melted
1 cup walnuts, chopped
  Dash of salt
1 teaspoon vanilla
  Shredded coconut

1. Beat eggs and sugar until thickened and pale.
2. Stir in marshmallows, chocolate, walnuts, salt and vanilla; chill.
3. Shape into 1-inch balls; roll in coconut.

Mrs. Carrol Bauske, Fortnightly Club,
Dawson, N.D.

CONDENSED MILK COOKIES
Makes About 30

12-ounce package semi-sweet
  chocolate pieces
14-ounce can sweetened condensed
  milk
1 cup grape-nut cereal

1. Melt chocolate in top of double saucepan over hot water. Stir in milk.
2. Remove from heat; stir in cereal. Drop by teaspoons onto baking sheets lined with waxed paper. Cool until firm.

Mrs. J. Gaylord Weber, Woman's Civic
League of Cheyenne, Cheyenne, Wyo.

CHRISTMAS FRUIT BALLS
Makes 48

¾ cup brown sugar
½ cup evaporated milk
1 cup candied fruits
1 cup sliced dried apricots
1 cut chopped pecans
  Shredded coconut

1. Bring sugar and milk to boil over low heat, stirring until sugar dissolves.
2. Remove from heat. Stir in remaining ingredients; cool.
3. Shape into ½-inch balls; roll in coconut.

Mrs. T. H. Slade, Women's Club, Starke, Fla.

HOLIDAY DELIGHTS
Makes About 48

½ pound Brazil nuts, halved
½ pound pecan halves
½ pound walnuts, coarsely chopped
½ pound candied cherries, halved
½ pound candied pineapple, cut
  into ½-inch pieces
3 cups sugar
1 cup light corn syrup
1½ cups light cream
1½ teaspoons vanilla

1. Day before line 9-inch loaf pan with waxed paper.
2. Combine Brazil nuts, pecans, walnuts, cherries and pineapple.
3. In saucepan combine sugar, corn syrup and cream; bring to boil, stirring constantly. Cook over medium heat to softball stage (236° F. on candy thermometer).
4. Remove from heat; beat until syrup begins to thicken and change color. Stir in vanilla; beat until creamy. At once stir in fruits and nuts; mix well.
5. Pack mixture into pan. Refrigerate for 24 hours.
6. Next day, remove from pan; cut into 1-inch slices; cut slices into finger-thick strips. Store in refrigerator, where they will keep for months.

Mrs. R. O. White, Woman's Club, Ruidoso, N.M.

COLORADO 3-BAR COOKIES
Makes 20

¾ cup plus 1 tablespoon butter
¼ cup plus 1 tablespoon cocoa
½ cup granulated sugar
1 teaspoon vanilla

1 egg, lightly beaten
2 cups graham cracker crumbs
1 cup shredded coconut
½ cup chopped nuts
2 tablespoons milk
2 cups confectioners' sugar
2 tablespoons instant vanilla
  pudding mix
5 1-ounce squares semi-sweet
  chocolate

1. In top of double saucepan combine ½ cup of the butter, cocoa and granulated sugar. Cook over simmering water until melted and smooth.
2. Remove from heat; stir in vanilla and egg. Stir in crumbs, coconut and nuts.
3. Pack mixture into 13 x 9½ x 2-inch baking pan.
4. Combine ¼ cup of the butter, milk, confectioners' sugar and pudding mix; spread on crumbs.
5. Melt chocolate and remaining butter; spread on sugar mixture.
6. Chill; cut into 2-inch squares.

Mrs. Harland Patton, Coterie Woman's Club,
Fort Collins, Colo.

HONEY BALLS

Makes 24

½ cup honey
½ cup peanut butter
1 cup confectioners' sugar
  (sift if lumpy)
Graham cracker crumbs

1. Combine honey, peanut butter and sugar.
2. Form into ½-inch balls; roll in crumbs.

Mrs. Shirley Endress, Woman's Club,
Warner Robins, Ga.

HONEY ALMOND BALLS

Makes 36

2 cups graham cracker crumbs
½ cup honey
2 tablespoons melted butter
½ teaspoon grated lemon rind
1 tablespoon lemon juice
½ teaspoon cinnamon
Dash of salt
¼ teaspoon almond extract
½ cup chopped maraschino cherries
½ cup chopped toasted almonds
Chopped almonds or
  confectioners' sugar

1. Combine crumbs, honey, butter, lemon and juice, cinnamon, salt and almond extract.
2. Stir in cherries and toasted almonds. Form into balls ¾ inch in diameter; roll in chopped almonds or sugar, as desired.

Mrs. A. B. Alkek, Morning Study Club,
Victoria, Tex.

KRISPY KRUNCH KOOKIES

Makes 24

1 cup confectioners' sugar (sift if
  lumpy)
⅔ cup plain or crunchy peanut butter

1½ to 2 cups bite-size ready-to-eat rice
  cereal
6 ounce package semi-sweet chocolate
  pieces
1 teaspoon paraffin

1. Combine sugar, peanut butter, butter and cereal (amount of cereal depends on kind of peanut butter). Form into 1-inch balls.
2. Melt chocolate and paraffin in top of double saucepan over simmering water.
3. Dip cookies on end of fork, one at a time, in chocolate. Shake off excess chocolate; cool on waxed paper.

Mrs. A. L. Timmermeister, Director of
Junior Clubs, Wash.

MOCHA BALLS

Makes About 36

Sifted confectioners' sugar
2 cups finely ground cooky crumbs
2 tablespoons cocoa
2 tablespoons instant coffee
⅔ cup finely chopped walnuts
¼ cup heavy cream
¼ cup orange juice

1. Measure 2 cups sugar into mixing bowl. Add crumbs, cocoa, coffee, and walnuts; mix well.
2. Add cream and orange juice; mix until dry ingredients are moistened.
3. Shape into 1-inch balls; roll in sugar. Chill before serving.

Mrs. George Bardens, Colony Club, Ambler, Pa.

CHOCOLATE-DIPPED NUT BALLS

Makes About 24

1 cup sifted confectioners' sugar
¾ cup peanut butter
1 egg, lightly beaten
1 cup finely shredded coconut
½ cup finely chopped nuts
¼ teaspoon salt
1 teaspoon vanilla
1 cup semi-sweet chocolate pieces

1. In mixing bowl beat sugar and peanut butter until well blended. Beat in egg.
2. Stir in coconut, nuts, dates, salt and vanilla until well mixed. Shape into 1-inch balls.
3. Melt chocolate in top of double saucepan over hot water. Dip balls in chocolate until coated; set on wire rack until hardened.

Mildred Legacy, Woman's Club, Princeton, Me.

DAINTY PEANUT BUTTER BALLS

Makes About 30

¼ teaspoon nutmeg
½ cup confectioners' sugar (sift if
  lumpy)
½ cup peanut butter
2 tablespoons lemon juice
1 cup finely chopped dates

1. In paper bag combine nutmeg and sugar.
2. Mix peanut butter, lemon juice and dates.

3. Form date mixture into ½-inch balls; drop into paper bag; shake until balls are coated.

Mrs. George Harris, Magazine Club, Roanoke, Ala.

RUM BALLS

Makes 100

2 12-ounce boxes vanilla wafers, finely crushed
2 cups cocoa
8 tablespoons light corn syrup
1 cup dark rum
1 cup bourbon
5 cups confectioners' sugar (sift if lumpy)
1 teaspoon salt
6 cups chopped pecans or walnuts

1. Day before, combine wafers and cocoa. Stir in corn syrup, rum, bourbon, 4 cups of the sugar, salt and nuts. Roll into 1-inch balls.
2. Roll balls in remaining sugar; let stand overnight.
3. Next day, store in tightly closed container.

Mary Holton, Woman's Club, Warner Robins, Ga.

SKILLET COOKIES

Makes About 36

½ cup butter
2 cups sugar
½ cup cocoa
½ cup milk

3 cups quick-cooking oats
2 tablespoons peanut butter
1 teaspoon vanilla
1 cup salted peanuts

1. Melt butter in large skillet. Add sugar, cocoa and milk; stir until sugar is dissolved. Bring to boil over medium heat.
2. Remove from heat; stir in remaining ingredients; mix well.
3. Cool slightly; beat until stiff. Drop by tablespoons onto aluminum foil to cool completely.

Mrs. Jack Greathouse, South Parkersburg Woman's Club, Parkersburg, W. Va.

SKILLET CEREAL SNACKS

Makes 24

¼ cup honey
¼ teaspoon salt
¼ cup butter
2 cups tiny marshmallows
1 teaspoon vanilla
2 cups cereal flake crumbs

1. Grease 8-inch square baking pan.
2. In large skillet combine honey, salt, butter and marshmallows. Cook over low heat, stirring constantly, until marshmallows are melted.
3. Remove from heat; stir in vanilla and crumbs. Press into pan; let stand until firm.
4. Cut into 24 pieces.

Betty Peterson, Western Cincinnati Junior Woman's Club, Cincinnati, Ohio

22. Desserts

Favorite desserts from nearly every state in the Union are represented in this chapter. Some are elaborate; but most are easy to make, and all are sweet and delicious, as dessert should be.

WHIPPED CREAM

Be sure that heavy cream, bowl and beater are as cold as possible. Never whip cream at high speed with an electric or a rotary beater. Begin on low speed, and gradually increase to moderate, turning the bowl frequently until the cream attains the desired stiffness.

Soft whipped cream or *crème chantilly* is heavy cream whipped until it just mounds on the spoon.

Stiffly beaten cream is heavy cream beaten until it holds its shape when dropped from a spoon and is stiff enough to be pressed through a pastry bag fitted with a fluted tube to make rosettes or flutes.

TO FLAVOR WHIPPED CREAM

Just before serving, fold 2 tablespoons fine granulated sugar or confectioners' sugar and 1 teaspoon vanilla, lemon or orange extract, rum or brandy into each cup of cream whipped.

TO STORE WHIPPED CREAM

If stiffly whipped cream is spooned into a sieve and stored in the refrigerator, it will keep well for several hours. Set a small bowl under the sieve to catch the milk whey, which usually exudes.

VANILLA SUGAR

Split a vanilla bean, and bury it in a canister of sugar. Reserve the sugar for desserts. As the sugar is used, add more, and stir to mix. The bean will flavor the sugar with vanilla for several months.

ORANGE, LIME OR LEMON SUGAR

Don't discard citrus fruit rinds. Cut or grate the rind from the skins, and combine 1 tablespoon grated rind (rind of 1 lemon or lime or ½ orange) with ½ cup sugar. Store in a tightly closed container, and use as needed. If the rind is left in large pieces, sift the sugar before using.

USING FLAVORING EXTRACTS

When adding an extract to a dessert, the flavor will be stronger if the ingredients are first allowed to cool.

ALMOND MILK

Almond milk used in place of plain milk gives a delicious flavor to creams and custards. To make the milk, put ½ cup dried blanched almonds and 1 cup water or milk into the container of an electric blender. Cover; then blend on high speed for 30 seconds, or until the nuts are pulverized. Strain and squeeze them through a sieve lined with cheesecloth. Use two parts almond milk to one part milk or cream in making creams and custards.

CARAMELIZED SUGAR

Caramelized sugar is often used to flavor and color desserts and to coat dessert molds. To caramelize sugar, combine 1 cup sugar and ⅓ cup water in a saucepan. Bring to a boil over moderate heat, occasionally swirling the mixture until all the sugar is dissolved. Do not stir. Boil until the syrup turns from a light gold to a dark caramel color. Be careful not to let it burn, or it will become bitter. Remove the saucepan from heat, and set it immediately into a large pan or container of cold water to stop further cooking.

CARAMEL SYRUP

Cool caramelized sugar. Stir in ⅓ cup water, and heat to simmering, stirring constantly until the caramel is dissolved.

PRALINE POWDER

> ¾ cup sugar
> ¼ cup water
> ¼ teaspoon cream of tartar
>   or lemon juice
> ½ cup blanched almonds or
>   hazelnuts

1. In small saucepan heat sugar, water and cream of tartar or lemon juice until sugar is dissolved.
2. Add nuts; cook without stirring until syrup and nuts are color of dark molasses.
3. Immediately pour onto greased baking sheet to cool.
4. When cool and brittle, remove from sheet; crush in mortar, or blend about ½

cup at a time in electric blender for 10 seconds. Store in tightly closed moisture-proof container.

CREAMS AND CUSTARDS

When eggs or egg yolks and liquid are cooked, care must be taken not to let the mixture boil, or the eggs will curdle. The mixture may be cooked over direct heat if one is careful to stir constantly and watch carefully. At the slightest sign that the custard is starting to simmer at the side of the pan, raise the pan above the heat, and stir rapidly until the spoon is coated. A safer method is to cook a cream or custard in the top of a double saucepan over simmering water for about 8 minutes, stirring frequently. The water in the bottom of the double saucepan should not be allowed to boil, nor should the water come into direct contact with the bottom of the pan containing the custard.

AMOUNT OF EGG TO USE IN A CUSTARD

For a thin custard for a dessert sauce, use 1 egg or 2 egg yolks for each 1 cup liquid.

For a thick custard, use 2 eggs or 4 egg yolks for each 1 cup liquid.

TO BAKE A CUSTARD

When a custard is baked in the oven, the baking time depends to a great extent on the size and depth of the container used. To test for doneness, insert a knife about 2 inches from the outer edge of the custard. If the knife comes out clean, the custard is done, even though it may seem soft in the center. Remember that a delicate custard continues to cook in its own heat after it is removed from the oven.

Baked and Steamed Puddings

APPLES IN BISCUIT CRUST

Serves 12 or More

2 cups presifted flour
1 teaspoon salt
½ teaspoon baking powder
¾ cup lard or shortening
1 teaspoon lemon juice
2 egg yolks, lightly beaten
1¾ cups water
3 pounds tart cooking apples
1¼ cups sugar
1 teaspoon cinnamon
2 tablespoons cornstarch
Confectioners' Sugar Icing (p. 622)

1. In mixing bowl combine flour, ½ teaspoon of the salt and baking powder. Cut in lard or shortening until mixture resembles crumbs.
2. Add lemon juice, egg yolks and ½ cup of the water. Stir with fork until dry ingredients are moistened.
3. Divide dough in half. Roll out half on lightly floured board to rectangle large enough to line bottom and sides of 13 x 9½ x 2-inch baking pan. Line pan with dough.

4. Peel and core apples. Cut in eighths.
5. In saucepan combine 1 cup of the water, sugar, cinnamon and remaining salt. Bring to boil. Add apples; simmer for 10 minutes.
6. Combine cornstarch and remaining water; stir into apple mixture. Cook for 5 minutes longer, stirring gently. Pour apple mixture in dough-lined pan.
7. Preheat oven to 450° F.
8. Roll out remaining dough to rectangle. Place over apple filling; trim; flute edge. Cut design in center to allow steam to escape.
9. Bake in preheated oven for 20 minutes; turn temperature to 350° F.; bake for 30 minutes longer.
10. Remove from oven; spread top thinly with Confectioners' Sugar Icing.

Helen Duszynski, Austin Junior Women's Club,
Oak Park, Ill.

DEEP-DISH FRUIT COBBLER

Serves 6

½ cup melted butter or margarine
1 cup presifted flour
1¼ cups sugar
½ teaspoon salt
1 teaspoon baking powder
½ cup milk
2 cups peeled diced apples, peaches, pears or other fruit

1. Preheat oven to 350° F. Grease 2-quart casserole.
2. Pour butter or margarine into casserole.
3. Into mixing bowl sift together flour, ¾ cup of the sugar, salt and baking powder. Add milk; beat until smooth. Pour into casserole.
4. Blend remaining sugar and fruit; sprinkle over batter.
5. Bake in preheated oven for 35 minutes, or until golden and firm.

Rubye McIntyre, Senior Woman's Club,
Sturgis, Ky.

BUTTERSCOTCH APPLE CRISP

Serves 4 to 6

3 medium apples, peeled and sliced
½ cup presifted flour
¾ cup brown sugar
¾ cup instant whole wheat cereal
½ cup butter
½ cup chopped walnuts
¼ cup flaked coconut
Whipped cream (optional)

1. Preheat oven to 350° F. Grease 8-inch layer cake pan.
2. Arrange apples in pan.
3. In mixing bowl combine flour, sugar and cereal. Cut in butter until mixture resembles coarse crumbs; sprinkle on apples. Sprinkle with walnuts; top with coconut.
4. Bake in preheated oven for 35 to 40 minutes. Serve warm with whipped cream, if desired.

Mrs. Victor Richardson, Chelan Country Club,
Chelan, Wash.

HONEY APPLE CRISP

Serves 6

4 cups sliced apples
½ cup brown sugar
1 tablespoon lemon juice
½ cup honey
¼ cup butter
½ cup presifted flour
¼ teaspoon salt
    Dash of cinnamon
½ cup chopped walnuts (optional)

1. Preheat oven to 375° F. Grease 1½-quart casserole.
2. Combine apples, ¼ cup of the sugar, lemon juice and honey. Turn into casserole.
3. In mixing bowl cut butter and remaining sugar into flour until mixture resembles crumbs. Stir in salt and cinnamon; sprinkle over apples. Sprinkle with walnuts, if desired.
4. Bake in preheated oven for 30 to 40 minutes. Serve warm.

Mrs. Elizabeth Champion, Mount Washington Women's Club, Cincinnati, Ohio

APPLE OR RHUBARB CRUNCH

Serves 8

2 cups presifted flour
1 cup rolled oats
1½ cups brown sugar
¼ teaspoon salt
1 cup butter or margarine
6 cups thinly sliced unpeeled
    apples (or diced rhubarb)
1 teaspoon cinnamon
1 cup granulated sugar (add ½ cup
    for rhubarb)
3 tablespoons cornstarch
    (add 1 tablespoon for rhubarb)
½ cup water
1 teaspoon vanilla
½ teaspoon red food coloring

1. Preheat oven to 400° F. Grease 11 x 7 x 1½-inch baking pan.
2. In mixing bowl combine flour, oats, brown sugar and salt. Cut in butter or margarine until mixture resembles fine crumbs. Reserve 1 cup crumbs; press remaining crumbs into pan.
3. Arrange apples or rhubarb on crumbs.
4. In small saucepan combine cinnamon, granulated sugar and cornstarch. Stir in water; cook over medium heat, stirring constantly, until thickened and clear. Remove from heat; stir in vanilla and food coloring. Pour on apples or rhubarb. Sprinkle with reserved crumbs.
5. Bake in preheated oven for 10 minutes. Turn temperature to 325° F. Bake for 40 minutes longer.

Mrs. Leonard Garhart, Women's Club, Osage, Wyo.

APPLE OAT PUDDING

Serves 6

1 cup presifted flour
½ cup brown sugar
1 cup quick-cooking oats
    Dash of salt
½ teaspoon baking soda

½ cup butter
2 cups chopped peeled apples
½ cup granulated sugar
½ teaspoon nutmeg

1. Preheat oven to 350° F. Grease 1½-quart casserole.
2. In mixing bowl combine flour, brown sugar, oats, salt and baking soda. Cut in butter until mixture resembles coarse crumbs; spread half in casserole.
3. Combine apples, granulated sugar and nutmeg. Turn into casserole.
4. Sprinkle remaining crumbs over apples; bake in preheated oven for 40 minutes.

Jennie F. Slack, Social and Benevolent Woman's Club, Lyons, Ind.

MOTHER'S APPLE DUMPLING

Serves 8

2 cups presifted flour
1 teaspoon salt
    Sugar
⅔ cup shortening
1 teaspoon vanilla
6 tablespoons melted butter
    Cinnamon
    Nutmeg
4 large apples, peeled, cored and
    quartered

1. In mixing bowl combine flour, salt and 2 tablespoons sugar. Cut in shortening. Add 4 to 5 tablespoons water and vanilla; stir until all flour is moistened and dough holds together.
2. Roll out on lightly floured board; brush with some of the butter; fold in half. Roll out thinly to rectangle; sprinkle with a little sugar, cinnamon and nutmeg; cut into 2-inch strips.
3. Preheat oven to 450° F. Grease 13 x 9½ x 2-inch baking pan.
4. Wrap dough strips around apple quarters; place 1 inch apart in pan. Sprinkle with remaining butter, ⅔ cup sugar, 1 teaspoon nutmeg and 2 teaspoons cinnamon.
5. Pour 1⅓ cups water into pan; bake in preheated oven for 30 minutes, or until browned, basting frequently with pan liquid.

Mrs. Leonore Kirchem, Gentilly Woods Woman's Club, New Orleans, La.

APPLE PANDOWDY

Serves 6

¾ cup presifted flour
1 teaspoon baking powder
    Dash of salt
2 tablespoons butter or margarine
1 cup sugar
1 egg, lightly beaten
2 cups chopped peeled apples
1 cup chopped walnuts
1 teaspoon vanilla
½ teaspoon lemon extract
    Whipped cream or ice cream

1. Preheat oven to 350° F. Grease 9-inch pie plate well.
2. Onto piece of waxed paper sift together flour, baking powder and salt.

3. Cream butter or margarine, sugar and egg in mixing bowl until smooth. Add flour mixture; blend well.

4. Stir in apples, walnuts, vanilla and lemon extract. Pour into pie plate.

5. Bake in preheated oven for 45 minutes.

6. Serve warm with whipped cream or ice cream.

Lib Fidler, Junior Woman's Club, Augusta, Ga.

OZARK PUDDING

Serves 4 to 6

⅓ cup presifted flour
1¼ teaspoons baking powder
⅛ teaspoon salt
1 egg
¾ cup sugar
½ cup chopped apples
½ cup chopped walnuts
1 teaspoon vanilla
1 cup heavy cream, whipped
¼ cup rum

1. Preheat oven to 325° F. Grease 1-quart casserole.

2. Onto piece of waxed paper sift together flour, baking powder and salt.

3. In mixing bowl beat egg and sugar until light and creamy. Add flour mixture; blend well. Fold in apples, walnuts and vanilla. Turn into casserole.

4. Bake in preheated oven for 30 minutes.

5. Blend cream and rum; serve with pudding.

Submitted by Junior Woman's Club, Floral Park, N.Y., on behalf of Mrs. Harry S. Truman

SPICY APPLE PUDDING

Serves 6

¾ cup butter
1½ cups sugar
1 egg
1½ cups presifted flour
1½ teaspoon baking soda
1 teaspoon cinnamon
½ teaspoon allspice
½ teaspoon ground cloves
4 medium apples, peeled and chopped

1. Preheat oven to 375° F. Grease 11 x 7 x 1½-inch pan.

2. Cream butter and sugar in mixing bowl until light and fluffy. Beat in egg.

3. Combine flour, baking soda and spices; stir into creamed mixture. Stir in apples.

4. Turn into pan; bake in preheated oven for 30 minutes.

Mrs. W. C. McClellan, Wimodausis Study Club, Cameron, Mo.

APPLE ROLY-POLY

Serves 9

¾ cup sugar
2 tablespoons butter
1 cup water
1 teaspoon grated lemon rind
1 tablespoon lemon juice
1 cup presifted flour
1 teaspoon baking powder
3 tablespoons shortening
⅓ cup milk
2 cups finely chopped peeled apples
¼ teaspoon cinnamon
Whipped cream or ice cream

1. Preheat oven to 450° F.

2. Prepare syrup: In saucepan combine ½ cup of the sugar, butter, water and lemon rind and juice. Bring to boil; boil over high heat for 5 minutes. Pour into 10 x 6 x 1½-inch baking pan.

3. Into mixing bowl sift together flour and baking powder. Cut in shortening until mixture resembles fine crumbs. Add milk; mix to form a soft dough.

4. Turn onto lightly floured board; roll out to 6 x 6-inch rectangle.

5. Sprinkle dough with apples, remaining sugar and cinnamon. Roll up like a jelly roll. Cut into 1-inch slices; place, cut side down, in syrup in pan.

6. Bake in preheated oven for 35 minutes.

7. Serve warm, with whipped cream or ice cream.

Mrs. C. Armstrong, Woman's Club, Kamsville, Ill.

BANANA CASSEROLE PUDDING

Serves 4

4 ripe bananas, sliced
3 tablespoons lemon juice
½ cup brown sugar
1 bread crumbs
1 tablespoon butter or margarine

1. Preheat oven to 350° F. Grease 1-quart casserole.

2. Arrange alternate layers of bananas, lemon juice, sugar and crumbs in casserole, finishing with crumbs. Dot with butter or margarine.

3. Bake in preheated oven for 20 to 30 minutes.

Mrs. K. E. Underhill, Home Life Chairman, Washington State Federation of Women's Clubs, Centralia, Wash.

FRESH BERRY COBBLER

Serves 6

1 cup sugar
3 cups blackberries, blueberries or boysenberries
1 cup shortening
1 cup presifted flour
1 teaspoon salt
1 teaspoon baking powder
¼ cup milk
1 teaspoon vanilla
2 egg whites, stiffly beaten

1. Preheat oven to 425° F. Grease 2-quart casserole.

2. Sprinkle ½ cup of the sugar over berries; arrange in casserole.

3. Cream shortening and remaining sugar in mixing bowl.

4. On piece of waxed paper combine flour, salt and baking powder; add alternately with milk to creamed mixture, beating well after each addition. Fold in vanilla and egg whites. Spread over berries.

5. Bake in preheated oven for 30 minutes.

NOTE: If canned berries are used, reduce amount of sugar to ½ cup.

Mrs. C. H. Hatch, Cultural Club, Alto, La.

BLUEBERRY BOY BAIT

Serves 6 to 8

2 cups presifted flour
1½ cups sugar
⅔ cup butter or margarine
2 teaspoons baking powder
2 eggs, separated
1 teaspoon salt
1 cup milk
1 cup drained fresh, canned or
   defrosted blueberries
Whipped cream (optional)

1. Preheat oven to 350° F. Grease and flour 11 x 7 x 1½-inch baking pan.
2. Into mixing bowl sift together flour and sugar. Cut in butter or margarine until mixture resembles fine crumbs. Remove one-fourth of mixture; reserve.
3. Add baking powder, egg yolks, salt and milk to mixture remaining in bowl; beat until smooth.
4. In another mixing bowl beat egg whites until stiff but not dry; fold into batter. Spread in pan.
5. Sprinkle with blueberries; top with reserved crumbs.
6. Bake in preheated oven for 40 to 50 minutes.
7. Serve hot, warm or cold with whipped cream, as desired.

Mrs. Lester Seegert, Plum Lake Woman's Club,
Star Lake, Wis.

BAKED BLUEBERRY PUDDING

Serves 6 to 8

½ cup butter or margarine
1 cup sugar
1 egg
2 cups presifted flour
1 teaspoon baking powder
1 teaspoon baking soda
1 teaspoon cinnamon
¼ teaspoon salt
¼ teaspoon ground cloves
1¼ cups canned applesauce
1-pound can blueberries, drained
Lemon Sauce (p. 702)

1. Preheat oven to 350° F. Grease and flour 6-cup mold.
2. Cream butter or margarine and sugar in mixing bowl until light and fluffy. Beat in egg.
3. Combine dry ingredients; add alternately with applesauce to creamed mixture, beating well after each addition. Fold in berries.
4. Pour batter into mold; bake in preheated oven for 1 hour and 10 minutes.
5. Serve warm with Lemon Sauce.

Mrs. Dexter Otis Arnold, Honorary President,
General Federation of Women's Clubs,
Saugerties-on-Hudson, N.Y.

BREAD CUSTARD

Serves 4

1½ cups fresh bread crumbs
4 eggs
2 cups milk
½ cup sugar
Dash of salt
½ teaspoon nutmeg

1. Preheat oven to 325° F. Grease 9-inch pie plate.
2. Sprinkle crumbs in pie plate.
3. In mixing bowl combine eggs, milk, sugar and salt; beat until smooth.
4. Pour egg mixture over crumbs; sprinkle with nutmeg.
5. Bake in preheated oven for 35 minutes.

Mrs. Fenton E. Brannon, Home Life Chairman,
Vienna, W. Va.

BREAD PUDDING

Serves 4

1 cup bread crumbs
2 cups milk
2 eggs, lightly beaten
¼ cup sugar
Pinch of cinnamon
Pinch of nutmeg
Brandy Sauce (p. 700)

1. Soak crumbs in milk for 20 minutes.
2. Preheat oven to 350° F. Grease 1-quart casserole.
3. Add eggs, sugar and spices to crumb mixture; mix well. Turn into casserole; set casserole in shallow pan containing hot water; bake in preheated oven for 1 hour.
4. Serve with Brandy Sauce.

Woman's Club, Plainville, Conn.

QUEEN OF PUDDINGS

Serves 6

1½ cups fresh bread crumbs
3 eggs, separated
⅓ cup granulated sugar
4½ cups milk
Grated rind of 2 lemons
1 tablespoon butter
Dash of salt
1 teaspoon vanilla
1 cup currant jelly
½ teaspoon cream of tartar
3 tablespoons confectioners' sugar
Cream

1. Preheat oven to 325° F. Grease 1½-quart casserole.
2. Sprinkle crumbs in casserole.
3. In mixing bowl beat egg yolks and granulated sugar until light. Stir in milk, lemon rind, butter, salt and vanilla. Pour over crumbs.
4. Set casserole in pan containing 1 inch of hot water; bake in preheated oven for about 1 hour, or until set.
5. Cool for 10 minutes; place spoonfuls of jelly on top. Turn temperature to 375° F.
6. In mixing bowl beat egg whites and cream of tartar until foamy. Add confectioners' sugar; beat until stiff and glossy. Spread on jelly.

7. Bake for 15 minutes, or until light brown.

8. Serve warm with cream.

Mrs. Harold S. Goldsmith, Woman's Club, Flemington, N.J.

BROWN SUGAR PUDDING

Serves 6

2 cups boiling water
1½ cups brown sugar
½ cup milk
1 tablespoon softened butter
1 cup presifted flour
2 teaspoons baking powder
½ cup seedless raisins
1 teaspoon vanilla

1. Preheat oven to 350° F. Grease 1½-quart casserole.
2. Prepare syrup: In small saucepan combine water and 1 cup of the sugar. Bring to boil; then simmer.
3. In mixing bowl combine milk, butter, remaining ½ cup sugar, flour and baking powder; beat until smooth. Stir in raisins and vanilla.
4. Pour syrup into casserole; pour batter in center of syrup.
5. Bake in preheated oven for 25 to 30 minutes.

Mrs. Herbert Thompson, Woman's Club, Ebensburg, Pa.

BAKED CARAMEL DUMPLINGS

Serves 4

1 cup packaged biscuit mix
½ cup chopped walnuts
⅜ to 1 cup milk
¾ cup brown sugar
1 cup water
2 tablespoons butter or margarine
Whipped cream

1. Preheat oven to 375° F. Grease 10 x 6 x 1½-inch baking pan.
2. In mixing bowl combine biscuit mix and walnuts. Add sufficient milk to make stiff dough.
3. Knead lightly on lightly floured board; roll out very thinly to 6 x 10-inch rectangle. Place in pan.
4. Prepare syrup: In saucepan combine sugar, water and butter or margarine. Bring to boil; pour over dough.
5. Bake in preheated oven for 30 minutes.
6. Cut into squares; serve warm topped with whipped cream.

Study Club, Montgomery City, Mo.

CHERRY MUFFIN COBBLER

Serves 6

1-pound can sour cherries
Presifted flour
1 cup sugar
1½ teaspoons baking powder
¼ teaspoon salt
1 egg
2 tablespoons melted shortening
½ cup milk

1. Preheat oven to 425° F. Lightly grease 8- to 10-inch iron skillet.

2. Drain cherries.
3. Pour syrup into small saucepan; blend in 2 tablespoons flour. Add ½ cup of the sugar; cook over low heat, stirring constantly, until thickened and smooth. Stir in cherries; pour into skillet.
4. Into mixing bowl sift together 1 cup flour, remaining sugar, baking powder and salt. Add egg, shortening and milk; mix only until dry ingredients are moistened. Spoon on cherries.
5. Bake in preheated oven for 15 to 20 minutes.

Aggie Powers, Brook Run Junior Woman's Club, Richmond, Va.

CHERRY CRUNCH

Serves 8

1 cup quick-cooking oats
½ cup presifted flour
1 cup brown sugar
½ cup butter or margarine
1-pound can cherry pie filling
Whipped cream

1. Preheat oven to 350° F. Grease 8-inch square baking pan.
2. In mixing bowl combine oats, flour and sugar. Cut in butter or margarine until mixture resembles coarse crumbs; press half into pan.
3. Top with pie filling; sprinkle with remaining crumbs.
4. Bake in preheated oven for 45 minutes.
5. Cut into squares; serve topped with whipped cream.

Laura Mifflin, Ingram Civic Club, Junior Section, Pittsburgh, Pa.

UPSIDE-DOWN CHERRY PUDDING

Serves 6

1½ cups presifted flour
1½ teaspoons baking powder
¼ teaspoon salt
½ cup butter
2 cups sugar
1 egg
1 teaspoon vanilla
1 cup milk
2 cups fresh sour cherries, pitted, or 2 cups canned pitted sour cherries, drained (reserve syrup)
1 cup hot water or cherry syrup
Cream, ice cream or fruit sauce

1. Preheat oven to 350° F. Grease 2½-quart casserole.
2. Sift together flour, baking powder and salt.
3. Cream butter and 1 cup of the sugar in mixing bowl until light and fluffy. Beat in egg and vanilla. Stir in milk alternately with flour mixture.
4. Turn batter into casserole. Sprinkle cherries over batter; sprinkle cherries with remaining sugar. Pour water or syrup over all.
5. Bake in preheated oven for 35 to 45 minutes, or until pudding shrinks from sides of casserole.

6. Serve with cream, ice cream or sauce, as desired.

VARIATION: Substitute fresh or canned berries for cherries.

Thelma Stevens, Woman's Club,
Lavalette, W. Va.

CHERRY ROLLS

Serves 6

1½ cups plus 1 tablespoon cake flour
½ teaspoon salt
2 teaspoons baking powder
2 tablespoons shortening
½ cup evaporated milk
2 cups cooked fresh or canned pitted red cherries, drained (reserve 1 cup syrup)
1 cup water
1 cup sugar
1 tablespoon butter

1. Into mixing bowl sift 1½ cups of the flour, salt and baking powder. Cut in shortening. Stir in milk to make a soft dough.
2. Roll out dough on lightly floured board to rectangle ¼ inch thick. Cover with cherries. Roll lengthwise like a jelly roll; press edges together. Cut into 1½-inch-thick slices.
3. Preheat oven to 425° F. Grease 9-inch square baking pan.
4. Arrange dough cut side down, in pan.
5. Combine reserved syrup, water, sugar and remaining flour. Bring to boil, stirring; cook for 1 minute. Add butter; pour over rolls.
6. Bake in preheated oven for 30 minutes, basting frequently. Serve warm.

Mrs. L. E. Wilson, Women's Club,
San Bernardino, Calif.

STEAMED CHOCOLATE PUDDING

Serves 4 to 6

2 cups presifted flour
2½ teaspoons baking powder
Dash of salt
1 egg
½ cup sugar
1 cup milk
2 1-ounce squares unsweetened chocolate, melted
Whipped Cream Sauce (p. 701)

1. Grease 1½-quart mold with cover.
2. In mixing bowl sift together flour, baking powder and salt.
3. In another mixing bowl beat egg and sugar until fluffy. Stir in milk.
4. Pour egg mixture over flour mixture; add chocolate; stir until well blended. Pour into mold. Cover.
5. Place in large saucepan; add sufficient boiling water to come halfway up side of the mold. Cover saucepan; steam for 1½ hours.
6. Let stand for 5 minutes; unmold pudding onto serving dish; serve with Whipped Cream Sauce.

Mrs. Gladys S. Gonser, Women's Swope Park
Civic Club, Kansas City, Mo.

HOT FUDGE PUDDING

Serves 6 to 8

1 cup presifted flour
2 teaspoons baking powder
¼ teaspoon salt
¾ cup granulated sugar
⅜ cup cocoa
½ cup milk
2 tablespoons melted shortening
1 cup chopped nuts
1 cup brown sugar
1¾ cups boiling water

1. Preheat oven to 350° F. Grease 9-inch square baking pan.
2. Into mixing bowl sift together flour, baking powder, salt, granulated sugar and 2 tablespoons of the cocoa. Add milk and shortening; stir until smooth.
3. Stir in nuts; pour into pan. Sprinkle with remaining cocoa and brown sugar. Pour water over all.
4. Bake in preheheated oven for 45 minutes.

Lucille Woelful, Paramount Junior Woman's
Club, Bellflower, Calif.

QUICK FUDGE PUDDING

Serves 6

1½ cups packaged biscuit mix
½ cup granulated sugar
½ cup milk
½ cup brown sugar
½ to 1 cup chopped nuts
1½ cups boiling water
6-ounce package semi-sweet chocolate pieces

1. Preheat oven to 350° F. Grease 10 x 6 x 1½-inch baking pan.
2. In mixing bowl combine biscuit mix and granulated sugar. Stir in milk to make a drop batter. Drop by spoons into pan, making 6 mounds. Sprinkle with brown sugar and nuts.
3. Pour water over chocolate; let stand 2 minutes; stir until smooth. Pour over biscuit mounds.
4. Bake in preheated oven for 35 minutes. Cool for 5 minutes. Invert each biscuit on serving plate; spoon chocolate sauce from pan over biscuits.

Mrs. Dell Healy, Juniors of Eastchester
Woman's Club, Eastchester, N.Y.

CRANBERRY PUDDING

Serves 4

½ cup sugar
1 cup presifted flour
1½ teaspoons baking powder
½ cup milk
1 cup cranberries
1½ tablespoons melted butter
Vanilla Sauce (p. 703)

1. Preheat oven to 375° F. Grease 8-inch square baking pan.
2. In mixing bowl combine sugar, flour and baking powder. Add milk; beat until smooth.
3. Stir in cranberries and butter. Pour into pan.

4. Bake in preheated oven for 30 minutes.

5. Serve hot with Vanilla Sauce.

Sarah Johnson, Women's Club, Tinley Park, Ill.

STEAMED CRANBERRY MOLASSES PUDDING

Serves 6

1½ cups presifted flour
1 teaspoon baking powder
2 cups cranberries
⅓ cup hot water
2 teaspoons baking soda
1 egg
½ cup molasses
Butter Sauce (p. 700)

1. Grease 1-quart mold well.
2. Into mixing bowl sift together 1 cup of the flour and baking powder.
3. In small bowl mix remaining flour and cranberries.
4. In measuring cup mix water and baking soda.
5. Add egg, molasses and baking soda to sifted flour mixture; beat until smooth. Stir in cranberries; turn into mold. Cover.
6. Place mold in large saucepan; add boiling water to come halfway up side of mold. Cover saucepan; steam for 1 hour.
7. Unmold pudding onto serving dish; serve with Butter Sauce.

STEAMED FIG PUDDING: Substitute 2 cups diced figs for cranberries in preceding recipe. Add 1 teaspoon mixed spices if desired.

Mrs. C. K. Brainerd, Woman's Club, Durand, Wis.

FOOD FOR THE GODS

Serves 6

3 eggs
¾ cup sugar
7 tablespoons cracker crumbs
½ teaspoon baking powder
1½ cups coarsely cut nuts
1½ cups cut-up dates

1. Preheat oven to 325° F. Grease 9-inch square baking pan.
2. Beat eggs and sugar until thickened and pale. Fold in remaining ingredients.
3. Spread in pan; bake in preheated oven for 45 minutes. Serve warm or cold.

Mrs. Luther P. Kuhn, Cassadago–Lake Helen Woman's Club, Cassadaga, Fla.

DATE PUDDING

Serves 8

1 cup chopped dates
1 teaspoon baking soda
1¾ cups boiling water
2 cups sugar
1 tablespoon butter or margarine
1½ cups presifted flour
1 teaspoon baking powder
1 teaspoon vanilla
½ cup chopped walnuts
Whipped cream or ice cream

1. Preheat oven to 350° F. Grease 9-inch square baking pan.

2. In saucepan combine ½ cup of the dates, baking soda and 1 cup of the water. Bring to boil; then simmer for 5 minutes.
3. Cream 1 cup of the sugar and butter or margarine in mixing bowl. Add flour and baking powder alternately with date mixture, beating well after each additon.
4. Add vanilla; beat until smooth. Pour into pan.
5. Bake in preheated oven for 30 minutes.
6. Meanwhile, prepare topping: In saucepan combine remaining dates, remaining water, remaining sugar and walnuts. Bring to boil; then simmer for 5 minutes.
7. When pudding is removed from oven, spread topping over surface. Serve with whipped cream or ice cream.

Mrs. M. E. Beenblossom, Woman's Club, Red Cloud, Neb.

STEAMED SPICED DATE OR FIG PUDDING

Serves 8 to 10

2 cups presifted flour
1 teaspoon baking soda
¼ teaspoon nutmeg
¼ teaspoon cinnamon
¼ teaspoon salt
1 cup brown sugar
1 cup chopped suet
1 cup buttermilk
1 cup seedless raisins
1 cup chopped dates or figs
1 cup chopped walnuts

1. Grease well and flour 2-quart mold.
2. Into large mixing bowl sift together flour, baking soda, nutmeg, cinnamon and salt. Stir in sugar and suet. Gradually blend in buttermilk.
3. Stir in raisins, dates or figs and walnuts; mix well. Pour into mold. Cover.
4. Place in large saucepan; add water to come halfway up side of mold. Cover saucepan; steam for 2½ hours.

Tola W. Jenkins, 20th Century Club, Nephi, Utah

DATE PUDDING SQUARES

Serves 6 to 8

3 cups cut-up dates
½ cup granulated sugar
1½ cups water
1½ cups presifted flour
½ teaspoon baking soda
½ teaspoon salt
1½ cups rolled oats
1 cup brown sugar
¾ cup shortening
1 teaspoon vanilla
¼ teaspoon almond extract
1 cup heavy cream, whipped

1. Preheat oven to 350° F. Grease 9-inch square baking pan.
2. In saucepan combine dates, granulated sugar and water. Cook over medium heat until thickened, stirring occasionally. Set aside.
3. Into mixing bowl sift together flour, baking soda and salt. Stir in oats and

brown sugar. Cut in shortening until mixture resembles fine crumbs. Stir in vanilla and almond extract.

4. Press half the flour mixture into pan. Top with date filling. Top with remaining flour mixture.

5. Bake in preheated oven for 25 minutes.

6. Cut into squares; serve topped with whipped cream.

Mrs. G. M. Noble, Woman's Club, Paxton, Ill.

UPSIDE-DOWN DATE PUDDING

Serves 9

1 cup pitted dates, cut up
2½ cups boiling water
½ cup granulated sugar
2 cups brown sugar
1 egg
2 tablespoons melted butter
1½ cups presifted flour
1 teaspoon baking soda
½ teaspoon baking powder
½ teaspoon salt
1 cup chopped nuts
1 tablespoon butter
Whipped cream

1. Combine dates and 1 cup of the water. Cool.

2. Preheat oven to 375° F. Grease 11 x 7 x 1½-inch baking pan.

3. Combine granulated sugar and ½ cup of the brown sugar. Beat in egg and melted butter. Combine flour, baking soda, baking powder and salt; stir into egg mixture. Stir in nuts and date mixture. Turn into pan.

4. Combine remaining brown sugar, 1 tablespoon butter and remaining water. Pour over batter.

5. Bake in preheated oven for 40 minutes.

6. Invert on serving plate. Cut into squares; serve warm with whipped cream.

Mrs. James Humphries, Juniors, Saratoga, Fla.

FRUIT COCKTAIL PUDDING

Serves 6

1 cup presifted flour
1 cup granulated sugar
½ teaspoon baking soda
½ teaspoon salt
1 egg, lightly beaten
½ teaspoon vanilla
1-pound can fruit cocktail, drained
½ cup brown sugar
½ cup chopped walnuts
1 teaspoon cinnamon
1 tablespoon butter

1. Preheat oven to 350° F. Grease 1½-quart casserole.

2. In mixing bowl combine flour, granulated sugar, baking soda and salt. Add egg and vanilla; mix well.

3. Fold in fruit cocktail. Turn into casserole.

4. In small bowl mix brown sugar, walnuts and cinnamon; sprinkle over batter. Dot with butter.

5. Bake in preheated oven for 30 minutes.

Mrs. Naum James, Delphian Literary Club, Amory, Miss.

MOTHER'S BAKED FRUIT CASSEROLE

Serves 6

3 large apples, peeled and sliced
1-pound 4-ounce can sliced peaches, drained (reserve syrup)
36 almond macaroons or 24 coconut macaroons
½ teaspoon almond extract
½ cup chopped nuts

1. Put apples in saucepan; add reserved syrup. Bring to simmer; simmer for 20 minutes, or until mushy. Mash and add peaches. Set aside.

2. Preheat oven to 400° F. Grease 1½-quart casserole.

3. Crush macaroons; sprinkle with almond extract.

4. Arrange fruit mixture, macaroons and nut in layers in casserole, finishing with nuts.

5. Bake in preheated oven for 15 minutes, or until browned.

Mrs. F. B. Marks, Jrs., Athenia Study Club, Tuscaloosa, Ala.

GRAPE-NUT PUDDING

Serves 4

½ cup butter
2 cups sugar
4 eggs, separated
¼ cup presifted flour
Juice and grated rind of 2 lemons
⅜ cup grape-nut cereal
2 cups milk

1. Preheat oven to 350° F. Grease 1½-quart casserole.

2. Cream butter and sugar. Beat in egg yolks and flour. Stir in lemon juice and rind, cereal and milk.

3. Beat egg whites until stiff but not dry; fold into egg yolk mixture.

4. Turn batter into casserole; set in shallow container of hot water; bake in preheated oven for 50 to 60 minutes.

Edna L. Conrad, Cabot Club, Middleboro, Mass.

BAKED HALVA (Wheat Pudding)

Makes About 40

This is a Greek version of a traditional Turkish or Near Eastern dish, popular in many areas of southeastern Europe. It may be kept in the refrigerator for a long time.

3¾ cups farina (cream of wheat)
2 tablespoons flour
3½ teaspoons baking powder
5¼ cups sugar
2 cups melted butter
1¼ cups milk
3 teaspoons almond extract
12 eggs, separated
1 quart water
1 teaspoon vanilla

1. Preheat oven to 375° F. Grease 13 x 9½ x 2-inch baking pan.

2. Combine farina, flour and baking powder.

3. Put 1¼ cups of the sugar and butter in mixing bowl; stir until well blended. stir in milk and almond extract.

4. Beat egg yolks until fluffy; stir into sugar mixture. Add farina mixture; stir until smooth.

5. Beat egg whites until stiff but not dry; fold into farina mixture. Turn into pan.

6. Bake in preheated oven for 25 minutes. Cool for 5 minutes; cut into diamond shapes in pan.

7. Meanwhile, while halva is baking, prepare syrup: In large saucepan combine remaining sugar and water. Bring to boil, stirring occasionally; boil over medium heat for 15 minutes. Remove from heat; cool for 5 minutes. Stir in vanilla.

8. Pour syrup over halva; cover with aluminum foil. Cool.

Teddy Spanos, Rodgers Forge Woman's Club, Baltimore, Md.

INDIAN PUDDING

Serves 6 to 8

1 quart plus 1 cup (optional) milk
⅓ cup corn meal
¾ cup molasses
¼ cup butter
1 teaspoon salt
1 teaspoon ginger
3 tablespoons sugar
Vanilla ice cream

1. Preheat oven to 325° F. Grease 1½-quart casserole.

2. In top of double saucepan bring 1 quart milk to boil. Stir in cornmeal; cook over hot water, stirring occasionally, for 15 minutes.

3. Stir in molasses; cook for 5 minutes longer.

4. Remove from heat; stir in butter, salt, ginger and sugar. Turn into casserole.

5. Bake in preheated oven for 1½ to 2 hours. If softer top is desired, pour remaining milk on batter before baking.

6. Serve warm with ice cream or as desired.

Mrs. John E. Marshall, Carmichaels and Cumberland Civic Woman's Club, Carmichaels, Pa.

FRUITED INDIAN PUDDING

Serves 8 to 10

2 tablespoons corn meal
2 tablespoons pearl tapioca
Dash of salt
Dash of ginger
½ teaspoon cinnamon
½ teaspoon nutmeg
2 eggs, lightly beaten
½ cup molasses
1 quart scalded milk
1 tablespoon butter
2 apples, peeled and sliced
1 cup seedless raisins (optional)

1. Preheat oven to 350° F. Grease 2½-quart casserole.

2. In mixing bowl combine corn meal, tapioca, salt and spices. Stir in eggs, molasses and milk. Add butter, apples and raisins; mix well.

3. Pour into casserole; bake in preheated oven for 3 hours. If necessary, add a little milk during baking.

Mrs. Maude E. MacKenzie, Past President, Maine Federation of Women's Clubs, and Woman's Club, Orono, Me.

GREEN MANGO BETTY

Serves 6 to 8

⅜ cup butter or margarine
1 cup fresh bread crumbs
4 cups sliced peeled green mangoes
2 cups brown sugar
2 teaspoons cinnamon
¼ cup lime or lemon juice
¼ cup water

1. Preheat oven to 350° F. Grease 1½-quart casserole.

2. Melt butter or margarine in casserole. Add ⅓ cup of the crumbs; top with layer of 2 cups of the mangoes. Sprinkle with 1 cup of the sugar, 1 teaspoon of the cinnamon and ⅛ cup of the lime or lemon juice. Add another ⅓ cup of the crumbs, then remaining mangoes, sugar, cinnamon, lime or lemon juice and water. Top with remaining crumbs.

3. Bake in preheated oven for 1 hour, or until mangoes are tender.

APPLE BROWN BETTY: Substitute apples for mangoes in above recipe.

Wilton Manors Women's Club, Fort Lauderdale, Fla.

MULBERRY COBBLER

Serves 8

2 quarts mulberries
1 cup sugar
¼ cup water
1 package refrigerator biscuits
Whipped cream

1. Preheat oven to 375° F. Grease 10 x 6 x 1½-inch baking pan.

2. Put mulberries in saucepan; sprinkle with sugar and water. Bring to boil, stirring occasionally; then simmer for 10 minutes. Turn into pan.

3. Flatten biscuits slightly; arrange on mulberries.

4. Bake in preheated oven for 15 minutes, or until puffed and golden.

5. Serve warm with whipped cream.

Mrs. B. G. Hurt, Woman's Club, Pikeville, Ky.

NOODLE PUDDING

Serves 6

8-ounce package wide noodles
2 eggs
3 tablespoons sugar
¼ teaspoon cinnamon
⅛ teaspoon salt
¼ cup melted butter or margarine
½ cup seedless raisins
1 cup small-curd cottage cheese

1. Preheat oven to 400° F. Grease 1½-quart casserole.

2. Cook noodles in boiling salted water according to package directions. Drain well; turn into mixing bowl.

3. Beat eggs, sugar, cinnamon and salt. Stir in remaining ingredients.

4. Pour egg mixture over noodles; toss well to mix. Pour into casserole.

5. Bake in preheated oven for 45 minutes.

Floraine Weltman, Adams-Arapahoe Women's Club, Aurora, Colo.

CZECHOSLAVAKIAN-STYLE NOODLE PUDDING

Serves 8

½ cup butter
¼ cup sugar
4 eggs, separated
¼ teaspoon lemon extract
12 ounces large-curd cottage cheese
¼ cup seedless raisins
¼ cup chopped almonds
¼ cup chopped walnuts
8-ounce package wide noodles, cooked and drained
1 cup heavy cream
¼ cup fresh bread crumbs

1. Preheat oven to 325° F. Grease 10 x 6 x 1½-inch baking pan.

2. Cream butter and sugar in mixing bowl until light and fluffy. Add egg yolks; beat until smooth. Stir in lemon extract, cheese, raisins, almonds, walnuts and noodles.

3. In another mixing bowl beat egg whites until stiff but not dry; fold into noodle mixture; turn into pan. Pour cream over top; sprinkle with crumbs.

4. Bake in preheated oven for 50 minutes.

Sophia Safranek, President, Women's Club, Pawpaw, Ill.

PEACH FESTIVAL COBBLER

Serves 4 to 6

½ cup butter
2 cups sliced peeled peaches
1¼ cups sugar
1 cup presifted flour
2 teaspoons baking powder
½ teaspoon salt
½ teaspoon nutmeg
1 cup milk
½ teaspoon vanilla

1. Preheat oven to 350° F.

2. Melt butter in 1-quart casserole. Add peaches; sprinkle with ¼ cup of the sugar.

3. Combine remaining sugar, flour, baking powder, salt and nutmeg. Stir in milk and vanilla.

4. Pour batter over peaches; bake in preheated oven for 30 minutes, or until golden brown.

Mrs. S. R. Aycock, Cosmos Club, Ruston, La.

PEACH-A-BERRY COBBLER

Serves 6

1 tablespoon cornstarch
¼ cup brown sugar
½ cup water
2 cups sugared sliced fresh or frozen peaches
1 cup fresh or frozen blueberries
1 tablespoon butter
1 tablespoon lemon juice
1 cup presifted flour
½ cup granulated sugar
1½ teaspoons baking powder
½ teaspoon salt
½ cup milk
¼ cup softened butter
2 tablespoons granulated sugar, mixed with ¼ teaspoon nutmeg
Cream

1. In saucepan combine cornstarch, brown sugar and water. Add peaches and blueberries. Bring to boil; cook, stirring constantly, until thickened. Add 1 tablespoon butter and lemon juice. Pour into 1½-quart casserole.

2. Preheat oven to 350° F.

3. In mixing bowl combine flour, ½ cup granulated sugar, baking powder and salt. Add milk and softened butter; beat until smooth. Spread batter over fruits; sprinkle with granulated sugar mixture.

4. Bake in preheated oven for 30 minutes.

5. Serve warm with cream.

Barbara Hetlage, Anna Day Club, Troy, Mo.

SPEEDY PEACH DESSERT

Serves 4

½ cup presifted flour
1 cup sugar
1 teaspoon baking powder
½ cup milk
2 cups sliced peeled peaches
2 tablespoons butter or margarine

1. Preheat oven to 350° F.

2. In mixing bowl combine flour, ½ cup of the sugar and baking powder. Stir in milk.

3. Combine peaches and remaining sugar.

4. Dot bottom of 10 x 6 x 1½-inch baking pan with butter or margarine. Pour in batter; arrange peaches on top.

5. Bake in preheated oven for 30 minutes. When baked, batter will be on top and fruit underneath.

Ellen D. Rodgers, Tuesday Study Club, Aliceville, Ala.

PERSIMMON PUDDING

Serves 4

1 cup persimmon pulp
1 cup sugar
2 teaspoons baking soda
1 cup presifted flour
½ teaspoon ginger
½ teaspoon nutmeg
½ cup chopped nuts
½ cup seedless raisins
½ cup milk
1 tablespoon melted butter
1 teaspoon vanilla

1. Preheat oven to 350° F. Grease 1-quart baking dish.

2. In mixing bowl combine persimmon, sugar and baking soda. Stir in remaining ingredients.

3. Pour mixture into baking dish; bake in preheated oven for 1 hour. Serve hot.

Mrs. Sophia Emmerton, Women's Club, San Bernardino, Calif.

PINEAPPLE PUDDING

Serves 6

1 medium pineapple
½ cup sugar
2 tablespoons quick-cooking tapioca
2 eggs
½ cup light corn syrup
1 tablespoon cornstarch
2 teaspoons grated lemon rind
2 cups cornflakes
2 tablespoons butter or margarine

1. Peel and core pineapple. Dice pineapple; put in mixing bowl. Sprinkle with sugar and tapioca; let stand for 1 hour.

2. Preheat oven to 350° F. Grease 1½-quart casserole.

3. In another mixing bowl beat eggs until light. Blend in corn syrup, cornstarch and lemon rind. Add pineapple mixture; mix well.

4. Sprinkle cornflakes on bottom and sides of casserole; fill casserole with pineapple mixture. Dot with butter or margarine.

5. Bake in preheated oven for 45 minutes. Serve warm.

Submitted by Junior Woman's Club, Floral Park, N.Y., on behalf of Clare Boothe Luce

TROPICAL CRISP

Serves 9

¼ cup melted shortening
¾ cup brown sugar
1 cup presifted flour
½ teaspoon baking soda
¾ teaspoon salt
¾ cup flaked coconut
1 cup cracker crumbs
¾ cup granulated sugar
2 tablespoons cornstarch
1 cup boiling water
1 egg, lightly beaten
8-ounce can crushed pineapple, undrained
1 cup heavy cream, whipped
¼ cup toasted flaked coconut

1. Preheat oven to 350° F. Grease 8-inch square baking pan.

2. In mixing bowl beat shortening and brown sugar. Stir in flour, baking soda, ½ teaspoon of the salt, the ¾ cup coconut and crumbs; mix well.

3. Press half of mixture into pan.

4. Bake in preheated oven for 10 minutes.

5. In saucepan mix granulated sugar, remaining salt and cornstarch. Gradually stir in water; cook over low heat, stirring constantly, until thickened and clear.

6. Put egg in small bowl; stir in a little of cornstarch mixture; return to rest of

mixture; cook over low heat, stirring constantly, for 1 minute.

7. Remove from heat; stir in pineapple and lemon juice. Pour over crumbs in pan; sprinkle with remaining crumbs.

8. Bake in preheated oven for 30 minutes.

9. Cool; top with whipped cream. Sprinkle with toasted coconut; cut into squares.

Mrs. Lynn C. Bailey, Women's Swope Park Civic Club, Kansas City, Mo.

ENGLISH PLUM PUDDING

Serves 10 to 12

This pudding may be steamed, then stored in the refrigerator for 2 to 3 weeks. Just before serving, steam for 1 hour to heat.

½ cup presifted flour
1 pound seedless raisins
1 pound currants
½ cup chopped almonds
¼ pound candied lemon peel
½ pound candied mixed peel
1 teaspoon allspice
2 teaspoons baking powder
½ teaspoon salt
4 cups fresh bread crumbs
2 cups finely chopped suet
1 carrot, grated
2 cups sugar
3 eggs
¼ cup brandy
Milk
Hard Sauce (p. 702)

1. Grease 2-quart ovenproof bowl.

2. Combine flour, raisins, currants, almonds, lemon peel, mixed peel, allspice, baking powder and salt in mixing bowl; mix well to coat fruits with flour.

3. In another mixing bowl mix crumbs, suet, carrot and sugar. Stir in eggs, brandy and ½ cup milk; mix. Add fruit mixture to crumb mixture; mix well. Add milk, if necessary, to moisten all ingredients.

4. Turn into bowl. Cover with waxed paper and aluminum foil; secure with string. Place bowl in large saucepan; add boiling water to pan to come halfway up side of bowl. Cover saucepan; steam for 6 hours, adding water, if necessary.

5. Unmold pudding onto serving dish; flame, if desired; serve with Hard Sauce.

Mrs. Rodger Whittington, New Century Club, Parkside, Pa.

QUICK PUDDING

Serves 4

2½ cups water
1 cup brown sugar
2 tablespoons butter
¾ teaspoon vanilla
1 cup presifted flour
½ cup granulated sugar
2 teaspoons baking powder
¼ teaspoon ground cloves
½ teaspoon cinnamon
½ cup seedless raisins
⅓ cup milk

1. Preheat oven to 375° F.
2. In 2-quart flameproof dish combine water, brown sugar, butter and vanilla. Bring to boil.
3. In mixing bowl combine flour, granulated sugar, baking powder and spices. Stir in raisins. Stir in milk. Spoon onto boiling liquid.
4. Bake in preheated oven for 45 minutes. Serve warm or cold.

Mrs. Gray McCasland, Junior Women's Federated Club, Union Grove, Wis.

STEAMED RASPBERRY OR BLUEBERRY PUDDING

Serves 6

    1 cup presifted flour
    1 teaspoon baking soda
    1½ teaspoons baking powder
    ¼ teaspoon salt
    1 cup sugar
    2 tablespoons butter
    1 egg
    ⅔ cup milk
    2 cups fresh drained canned
        raspberries or blueberries

1. Grease well and flour 2-quart mold with tight cover.
2. Onto piece of waxed paper sift together flour, baking soda, baking powder and salt.
3. In mixing bowl beat sugar, butter, egg and milk. Stir in flour mixture; beat until smooth. Stir in berries. Pour into mold. Cover.
4. Place mold in large saucepan; add boiling water to saucepan to come half way up side of mold. Cover saucepan; steam for 1 hour.

Mrs. Eugene Murphy, St. Andrew's by the Lake Women's Club, Seal Cove, Me.

BAKED RHUBARB

Serves 4

    3 cups rhubarb, cut into 1-inch
        lengths
    2 cups toasted bread cubes
    1 cup sugar
    ¼ cup butter

1. Preheat oven to 350° F. Grease 1½-quart casserole.
2. In casserole arrange alternate layers of rhubarb, bread cubes and sugar until all ingredients are used. Dot with butter.
3. Bake in preheated oven for 30 minutes.

Mrs. O. S. Griggs, Woman's Club, Bent Mountain, Va.

RHUBARBETTES

Serves 8 to 12

    2 cups diced rhubarb
    Sugar
    2 cups packaged biscuit mix
    ¼ cup milk
    Cream

1. In mixing bowl combine rhubarb and ½ to ¾ cup sugar to taste. Let stand for 30 minutes.
2. Preheat oven to 375° F. Grease 8 large or 12 medium muffin cups.

3. Combine biscuit mix, 2 tablespoons sugar and milk; gently mix into rhubarb.
4. Spoon batter into muffin cups, filling them two-thirds full; bake in preheated oven for 25 minutes. Serve warm with cream.

Mrs. Del De Forest, Junior Woman's Club, Diamond Bar, Calif.

STRAWBERRY-RHUBARB PUFFS

Makes 9

    3 cups cut rhubarb
    1 pint strawberries, sliced
    Sugar
    ½ cup water
    2 cups presifted flour
    3 teaspoons baking powder
    1 teaspoon salt
    ⅓ cup cooking oil
    ¾ cup milk
    Butter
    Cinnamon
    Cream or whipped cream

1. Preheat oven to 450° F.
2. Mix rhubarb, strawberries, 1½ to 2 cups sugar to taste and water in 9-inch square baking pan. Cook over moderate heat for 5 minutes.
3. In mixing bowl combine flour, baking powder, salt and 2 tablespoons sugar. Stir in oil and milk until dry ingredients are moistened.
4. Drop batter by spoons onto hot fruits, making 9 biscuits. Make a hole in top of each biscuit; put in a little butter, sugar and cinnamon.
5. Bake in preheated oven for 20 to 25 minutes. Serve warm with cream or whipped cream, as desired.

VARIATIONS: 1-pound package frozen rhubarb, defrosted, and 10-ounce package frozen strawberries, defrosted, may be used in place of fresh fruits in recipe above. Reduce sugar to ½ cup; omit ½ cup water.

Mrs. Charles Hamon, Centenarian Club, Valley Falls, Kans.

PRIZE STRAWBERRY DESSERT

Serves 6

    ½ cup butter
    1 cup presifted flour
    1 cup sugar
    1 teaspoon baking powder
    ¾ cup milk
    1 quart strawberries, hulled

1. Preheat oven to 425° F. Melt butter in 1½-quart baking dish.
2. Into mixing bowl sift together flour, sugar and baking powder. Add milk; blend well. Pour over butter. Sprinkle with strawberries.
3. Bake in preheated oven for 25 to 30 minutes.
4. Serve warm.

Brenda Holt, Women's Club, Rockville, Va.

GREAT-GREAT-GRANDMOTHER'S SUET PUDDING

Serves 6 to 8

Presifted flour
1 teaspoon salt
1 teaspoon cinnamon
1 cup seedless raisins
1 cup currants
1 cup ground suet
½ teaspoon baking soda
½ cup molasses
1 cup milk
½ cup butter or margarine
2 cups sugar
2 eggs

1. Grease and flour 1½-quart mold with tight-fitting lid.
2. Into mixing bowl sift together 1¾ cups flour, salt and cinnamon. Stir in raisins, currants and suet; mix well.
3. Dissolve baking soda in molasses; stir into batter. Stir in milk; mix well.
4. Pour into mold. Cover. Place in large saucepan; add boiling water to saucepan to come halfway up side of mold. Cover saucepan; steam for 4 hours.
5. Just before pudding is ready, prepare Custard Sauce: In top of double saucepan combine butter or margarine and sugar. Cook over hot water until butter is melted. Stir in 2 tablespoons flour and eggs. Cook over hot water, stirring constantly, until thickened and smooth.
6. Serve pudding with sauce.

Mary Seidler, Woman's Club, Jamaica, Ia.

SWEET POTATO PONE PUDDING

Serves 6 to 8

4 eggs
2 cups milk
4 cups grated sweet potatoes
¼ cup melted butter
1 cup sugar
½ teaspoon salt
1 teaspoon nutmeg
1 teaspoon cinnamon
Custard Sauce (above)
or whipped cream

1. Preheat oven to 350° F. Grease 2-quart casserole well.
2. Break eggs into mixing bowl; beat until blended. Add milk; beat until smooth.
3. In another mixing bowl mix remaining ingredients; add to egg mixture; blend well. Turn into casserole.
4. Bake in preheated oven for 1 hour, stirring occasionally.
5. Serve with Custard Sauce or whipped cream, as desired.

Mrs. Warren L. Cornell, Woman's Club, Honesdale, Pa.

WOODFORD PUDDING

Serves 6 to 8

4 eggs
1¾ cups sugar
1 cup melted butter
3 cups presifted flour
¾ cup strawberry jam or preserves
1 teaspoon baking soda

1 tablespoon sour milk
or buttermilk
Cinnamon
Nutmeg
1 cup butter
1 cup heavy cream
½ teaspoon vanilla

1. Preheat oven to 300° F. Grease 1½-quart casserole.
2. Beat 3 of the eggs and ¾ cup of the sugar until light and pale. Stir in melted butter, flour and jam or preserves.
3. Mix baking soda and milk or buttermilk; stir into batter. Season with cinnamon and nutmeg.
4. Turn into casserole; bake in preheated oven for 1 hour.
5. Meanwhile, in saucepan combine 1 cup butter, cream, remaining sugar and remaining egg. Cook over moderate heat, stirring just until mixture coats spoon. Remove from heat; stir in vanilla.
6. Serve warm sauce over pudding.

Mrs. James C. Helton, Junior Woman's Club, Bristol, Tenn.-Va.

Creamy Desserts and Custards

OSLO ALMOND PUDDING

Serves 6

5 tablespoons cornstarch
¼ cup water
4 eggs, lightly beaten
1 quart milk
2 tablespoons butter or margarine
½ cup sugar
½ cup slivered blanched almonds
1 teaspoon vanilla
½ teaspoon almond extract
½ teaspon lemon extract
Raspberry Jelly Sauce (p. 703)

1. In top of double saucepan blend cornstarch and water to a smooth paste. Stir in eggs and milk. Add butter or margarine, sugar and almonds.
2. Cook over hot water, stirring constantly, until thickened and smooth.
3. Remove from heat; stir in vanilla and almond and lemon extracts. Cool for 5 minutes, stirring frequently.
4. Turn into serving dish; chill. Serve with Raspberry Jelly Sauce.

Anna Dahlstrom, Woman's Club, Sebastian, Fla.

OLD-FASHIONED "BOILED" CUSTARD

Serves 6

1 quart plus ¼ cup milk
4 eggs yolks
1 cup sugar
⅜ cup presifted flour
1½ to 2 teaspoons vanilla
Whipped cream

1. In top of double saucepan heat 1 quart of the milk to scalding.
2. Cream egg yolks and sugar thoroughly. Stir in flour. Stir in remaining

milk; gradually stir into scalding-hot milk. Cook over hot water, stirring constantly, until custard thickens and coats spoon.

3. Remove from heat; stir in vanilla.

4. Pour custard through sieve into large bowl; whip vigorously for a few minutes. Chill; serve with whipped cream, or as desired.

Mrs. Otis Barry, Maids and Matrons Club, Jackson, Miss.

FLOATING ISLAND

Serves 4

2 cups milk
1 egg white
5 tablespoons sugar
2 egg yolks
Pinch of salt
½ teaspoon vanilla

1. In top of double saucepan heat milk to scalding.

2. Beat egg white until soft peaks form. Gradually beat in 1 tablespoon of the sugar; beat until meringue is glossy and smooth.

3. Drop meringue by spoons into scalding-hot milk; cook, uncovered, for 2 minutes. Remove meringues to waxed paper.

4. Beat egg yolks, remaining sugar and salt. Stir into milk mixture; cook over simmering water, stirring constantly, until custard coats spoon. Remove from heat; stir in vanilla.

5. Pour custard into shallow serving dish; top with meringues. Refrigerate until serving time.

Mrs. Henry Hartig, Library Club, Robbinsdale, Minn.

BAKED CUSTARD

Serves 4 to 6

4 eggs
¼ cup sugar
¼ teaspoon salt
2½ cups milk
1 teaspoon vanilla
Nutmeg

1. Preheat oven to 300° F. Grease 1-quart casserole or 6 6-ounce baking cups.

2. In mixing bowl beat eggs until foamy. Add sugar and salt; beat until thickened and lemon-colored. Add milk and vanilla; beat until smooth.

3. Pour into casserole or baking cups; sprinkle with nutmeg.

4. Place casserole or baking cups in pan containing 1 inch of hot water; bake in preheated oven for 1¼ hours, for casserole; 45 minutes for baking cups.

Woman's Club, Lake Hiawatha, N.J.

CRUNCHY FRENCH CUSTARD

Serves 4

2 cups light cream
4 egg yolks
2½ tablespoons granulated sugar
Pinch of salt
1 teaspoon vanilla
2 tablespoons brown sugar

1. Preheat oven to 350° F.

2. Scald cream.

3. Beat egg yolks until thickened and pale. Gradually beat in granulated sugar and salt.

4. Pour cream into egg mixture very slowly, stirring vigorously. Stir in vanilla.

5. Pour into 1-quart casserole; set casserole in pan containing 1 inch of hot water; bake in preheated oven for 1 hour.

6. Remove from oven. Sift brown sugar over top; broil 4 to 5 inches from heat until sugar melts and turns crunchy.

7. Chill for 1 to 2 hours before serving.

Betty Stein, Modern Study Club, Mobile, Ala.

BAKED CHOCOLATE CUSTARD

Serves 6

3 eggs
2 teaspoons vanilla
½ cup chocolate syrup
⅛ teaspoon salt
2 tablespoons sugar
3 cups milk

1. Preheat oven to 325° F. Grease 6 individual baking cups.

2. In mixing bowl beat eggs until smooth. Add vanilla, chocolate syrup, salt and sugar; stir well to mix. Stir in milk; pour into cups.

3. Place cups in pan containing 1 inch of hot water; bake in preheated oven for 40 minutes.

Frances Blair, Woman's Club, Lincroft, N.J.

MOUSSE AU CHOCOLAT

Serves 8 to 10

4 1-ounce squares unsweetened chocolate
¾ cup sugar
¼ cup water
6 eggs, separated
2 tablespoons dark rum

1. In top of double saucepan combine chocolate, sugar and water. Cook over hot water, stirring occasionally, until chocolate is melted.

2. Add egg yolks, one at a time, beating well after each addition. Remove from heat; cool.

3. Meanwhile, in mixing bowl beat egg whites until stiff but not dry.

4. Stir rum into chocolate mixture; pour over egg whites. Fold gently until well blended.

5. Turn into individual dishes or large serving bowl. Refrigerate for 12 hours.

Junior Woman's Club, Teaneck, N.J.

UPSIDE-DOWN LEMON CUPS

Serves 6

1 tablespoon melted butter
2 eggs, separated
3 tablespoons lemon juice
2 teaspoons grated lemon rind
Dash of salt
1 cup sugar
3 tablespoons flour
1 cup milk

1. Preheat oven to 375° F. Grease 6 individual baking cups.

2. In mixing bowl blend butter, egg yolks and lemon juice. Stir in lemon rind, salt, sugar and flour; beat until smooth. Add milk; stir to blend.

3. Beat egg whites until stiff but not dry; fold into egg yolk mixture. Turn into cups; set in shallow pan containing 1 inch of hot water.

4. Bake in preheated oven for 30 to 35 minutes.

5. Refrigerate; invert onto serving dish.

Annabelle Hopper, Woman's Club,
East Concord, N.H.

ORANGE SPONGE CUSTARD

Serves 4 to 6

1 cup sugar
¼ cup presifted flour
2 eggs, separated
2 tablespoons melted butter
1 cup milk
¾ cup orange juice
1 tablespoon lemon juice
1 tablespoon grated orange rind

1. Preheat oven to 325° F. Grease 1-quart casserole.

2. Combine sugar and flour. Stir in egg yolks and butter. Stir in milk, orange juice, lemon juice and orange rind.

3. Beat egg whites until stiff but not dry; fold into egg yolk mixture.

4. Pour into casserole; set casserole in pan containing 1 inch of hot water.

5. Bake in preheated oven for about 45 minutes.

Edith Mattson, Marri-eds Junior Women's Club,
Santa Cruz, Calif.

ITALIAN CREAM

Serves 8 to 10

2 pounds ricotta cheese
½ cup plus 2 tablespoons
    confectioners' sugar
2 tablespoons instant coffee
1 cup heavy cream
3 tablespoons brandy

1. Combine cheese, sugar and coffee. Stir in cream and brandy; beat until smooth.

2. Chill thoroughly before serving.

Mrs. Russell Rabone, Thursday Morning Club,
Madison, N.J.

RASPBERRY CREAM

Serves 6

2 cups heavy cream
½ cup brown sugar
    Ginger to taste
2 10-ounce packages frozen
    raspberries, defrosted

1. Whip cream. Gradually beat in sugar and ginger.

2. Drain syrup from raspberries; reserve. Fold raspberries into cream; chill.

3. Just before serving, stir in enough reserved syrup to provide pretty color.

Caren Heft, Junior Woman's Club,
Racine, Wis.

CREAMY RICE PUDDING

Serves 4 to 6

2 tablespoons rice
1 quart milk
1 teaspoon vanilla
½ teaspoon salt
⅓ cup sugar

1. Preheat oven to 275° F. Grease 1½-quart casserole.

2. Put rice, 2 cups of the milk, vanilla, salt and sugar into casserole. Stir; let stand for 15 minutes. Stir in remaining milk.

3. Bake in preheated oven for 3 hours, stirring occasionally.

4. Serve hot or very cold.

Mrs. S. Wolcott Linsley, Woman's Club,
Webster, Mass.

BANANA RICE CUSTARD

Serves 8

3 ripe medium bananas
1 tablespoon lemon juice
3 cups cooked rice
¾ cup sugar
3 eggs
1½ teaspoons grated lemon rind
2 cups milk
    Nutmeg
    Whipped cream
    Sliced bananas

1. Preheat oven to 325° F. Grease 2-quart casserole.

2. In mixing bowl mash bananas; stir in lemon juice and rice.

3. Beat sugar and eggs until smooth; stir in lemon rind and milk. Add to rice mixture; mix well.

4. Pour into casserole; sprinkle with nutmeg.

5. Place casserole in pan containing 1 inch of hot water; bake in preheated oven for 1 hour.

6. Chill for at least 4 hours. Just before serving, garnish top with whipped cream and sliced bananas.

Margaret Farris, Study Club,
Hull and Daisetta, Tex.

KESARI BAATH
(Near Eastern Rice Pudding)

Serves 6

3 cups water
1 cup rice
1 cup sugar
¼ teaspoon turmeric
¼ cup unsalted cashew nuts
¼ cup seedless raisins
½ cup shortening
1 teaspoon powdered cardamom

1. In saucepan bring 2 cups of the water to boil. Add rice; cook for 15 minutes.

2. In another saucepan combine remaining water, sugar and turmeric. Bring to boil; boil until sugar is dissolved and thin syrup reaches soft-ball stage (236° F. on candy thermometer).

3. Add rice to syrup; stir in nuts, raisins and ¼ cup of the shortening. Cook over low heat for 10 to 15 minutes, or until rice

is soft. Stir in remaining shortening and cardamom. Serve hot or cold.

Mary Mudge, Woman's Club, Canterbury. N.H.

NORWEGIAN ROMMEGROT
(Cream Pudding)

Serves 8 to 10

1 quart 2- or 3-day old cream
½ cup presifted flour
5 cups scalded milk
2 tablespoons sugar
½ teaspoon salt
Sugar and cinnamon (optional)

1. Pour cream into large saucepan. Bring to boil; boil for 20 minutes.
2. Gradually add 6 tablespoons of the flour, stirring constantly. As butter fat from cream comes to surface, remove and reserve. Stir in remaining flour.
3. Add milk, a cup at a time, until all is added, boiling constantly. Add sugar and salt; remove from heat.
4. Pour half the reserved butter fat into bowl. Add pudding mixture; top with remaining butter fat.
5. If desired, serve with sugar and cinnamon.

Mrs. George Erickson, Study Club, Hatton, N.D.

OLD-FASHIONED TAPIOCA PUDDING

Serves 6

1 cup pearl tapioca
1¾ cups brown sugar
2 tablespoons softened butter
¾ teaspoon vanilla
Whipped cream

1. Day before, put tapioca in 1½ cups water. Soak overnight.
2. Next day, preheat oven to 350° F.
3. Add sugar, 2 cups water, butter and vanilla to tapioca.
4. Pour into 13 x 9½ x 2-inch baking pan; bake in preheated oven for about 1 hour, or until clear.
5. Serve with whipped cream.

Mrs. Russell Murton, Woman's Club, Lantana, Fla.

ENGLISH TOFFEE

Serves 9

½ 12-ounce package vanilla wafers, crushed
¼ cup butter or margarine
1⅓ cups confectioners' sugar
3 tablespoons cocoa
3 eggs, separated
1 teaspoon vanilla
½ teaspoon salt
1⅓ cups chopped pecans
Whipped cream

1. Day before, lightly grease 9-inch square baking pan.
2. Arrange half the wafer crumbs in pan.
3. In mixing bowl beat butter or margarine, sugar and cocoa until light and fluffy. Add egg yolks, vanilla and salt; beat.

4. In another mixing bowl beat egg whites until stiff but not dry; fold with pecans into egg yolk mixture.
5. Turn into pan. Top with remaining crumbs. Refrigerate overnight.
6. Next day, cut into squares; top with whipped cream.

Mrs. Fred Fleischbein, Women's Civic League, Cheyenne, Wyo.

ZABAGLIONE

Serves 2

3 tablespoons honey
4 egg yolks
2 tablespoons Marsala
Cinnamon

1. Blend honey and egg yolks in top of double saucepan. Beat over hot water until thickened and lemon-colored.
2. Gradually beat in Marsala; beat until mixture has consistency of thick cream.
3. Pour into tall glasses; sprinkle with cinnamon; serve at once.

Woman's Club, Wahoo, Neb.

Gelatin Desserts

BLANC MANGE

Serves 6

2 envelopes gelatin
3½ cups milk
¾ cup sugar
1 teaspoon vanilla
Light cream

1. Soften gelatin in ½ cup of the milk.
2. Put remaining milk in suacepan; heat to just below boiling point. Pour over gelatin; stir until dissolved.
3. Add sugar and vanilla; stir until sugar is dissolved.
4. Pour into 6 individual molds or custard cups. Chill until set. Unmold onto serving dish; serve with cream.

Mrs. Herbert L. Anders, President, Springfield Improvement Association and Woman's Club, Jacksonville, Fla.

CRÈME ST.-HONORÉ

Serves 6

½ cup presifted flour
¾ cup granulated sugar
1 tablespoon butter
4 eggs
2 cups milk, scalded with 1-inch stick vanilla bean
1 envelope gelatin
¼ cup water
6 egg whites
Dash of salt
2 tablespoons confectioners' sugar, sifted

1. In heavy saucepan combine flour, granulated sugar, butter and eggs. Work mixture with wooden spoon; gradually stir in milk. Cook over low heat, stirring constantly, until thickened and smooth. Cool, stirring frequently.

2. In small bowl soften gelatin in water; dissolve over hot water. Stir into custard.

3. In mixing bowl beat egg whites, salt and confectioners' sugar until stiff and glossy. Fold into custard. Turn into serving dish. Refrigerate until serving time.

Submitted by Woman's Club, Kankakee, Ill., on behalf of Mrs. John F. Kennedy

RICE AND CHERRIES IN THE SNOW
Serves 8 to 10
    3 cups water
    Dash of salt
    1½ cups rice
    3⅓ cups milk
    ½ cup sugar
    1 tablespoon butter
    1 envelope gelatin
    1 teaspoon almond extract
    1 cup heavy cream, whipped
    2 1-pound cans cherry pie filling

1. In large saucepan bring water and salt to boil. Add rice; cover; cook over medium heat for 15 minutes.

2. Stir in 3 cups of the milk, sugar and butter; cook over low heat, stirring occasionally, until thickened.

3. Meanwhile, soften gelatin in remaining milk; stir into rice mixture. Cook for 2 to 3 minutes longer.

4. Remove from heat; stir in almond extract. Cool.

5. Fold cream into rice mixture; turn into serving dish. Chill until firm.

6. Spread cherries on top; chill for 2 to 3 hours.

Mrs. Henry Ankeny, Semper Fidelis Study Club, Clarinda, Ia.

COLD CHOCOLATE SOUFFLÉ
Serves 8
    5 1-ounce squares unsweetened chocolate
    1 cup milk
    1 envelope gelatin
    ½ cup cold water
    ½ cup boiling water
    5 eggs, separated
    1¼ cups sugar
    1½ tablespoons vanilla
    1 cup heavy cream
    Maraschino cherries or chopped nuts

1. Heat chocolate and milk in top of double saucepan over simmering water, stirring occasionally, until chocolate is melted and mixture is smooth. Cool slightly.

2. Soften gelatin in cold water. Add boiling water; stir until thoroughly dissolved.

3. Beat egg yolks and 1 cup of the sugar until thickened and pale. Stir in chocolate mixture. Stir in gelatin mixture and 1 tablespoon of the vanilla.

4. Beat egg whites until stiff but not dry; fold into chocolate mixture. Pour into serving dish; chill for several hours.

5. When ready to serve, whip cream until stiff; flavor with remaining sugar and remaining vanilla; use to garnish soufflé. Decorate with cherries or nuts.

Mrs. Walter Klie, Thursday Morning Club, Madison, N.J.

COLD COFFEE SOUFFLÉ
Serves 6
    ⅔ cup sugar
    1 envelope gelatin
    1½ cups black coffee
    ½ cup milk
    3 eggs, separated
    ¼ teaspoon salt
    ½ teaspoon vanilla
    Heavy cream

1. Lightly oil 1½-quart mold.

2. In top of double saucepan blend ⅓ cup of the sugar and gelatin. Gradually stir in coffee and milk.

3. In small bowl blend egg yolks and salt; stir into gelatin mixture. Cook over hot water, stirring constantly, until custard is thickened and smooth and gelatin is dissolved.

4. Remove from heat; stir in vanilla. Cool, stirring occasionally.

5. In mixing bowl beat egg whites until foamy. Gradually beat in remaining sugar; beat until stiff and glossy. Pour custard over egg whites; carefully fold together. Pour into mold; chill until set.

6. Unmold onto serving dish; serve with cream.

Mrs. John C. Duncan, Woman's Club, Albany, N.Y.

MEXICAN CREAM
Serves 6
    ½ cup sugar
    1 envelope gelatin
    1½ teaspoons instant coffee
    ¼ teaspoon cinnamon
    ⅛ teaspoon salt
    ½ teaspoon vanilla
    2 eggs, separated
    1¼ cups milk
    1 cup heavy cream, whipped

1. In top of double saucepan combine ¼ cup of the sugar, gelatin, coffee, cinnamon, salt and vanilla.

2. Beat egg yolks and milk; stir into coffee mixture. Cook over simmering water, stirring constantly, until custard coats spoon. Set aside.

3. Beat egg whites until soft peaks form. Gradually beat in remaining sugar; beat until meringue is thickened and glossy.

4. Place bowl of meringue in pan of ice water; gradually fold in custard. Fold in cream; fold until mixture holds shape.

5. Spoon into 6-cup mold or individual molds; chill until firm.

Annie L. Chase, Woman's Club, Harwichport, Mass.

GRAPEFRUIT SNOW
    2 envelopes gelatin
    1 cup grapefruit juice
    1 cup sugar
    1½ cups water

2 egg whites
½ teaspoon salt
Custard Sauce (676)

1. In mixing bowl soften gelatin in ½ cup of the grapefruit juice.
2. In saucepan combine sugar and water. Bring to boil; boil rapidly for 3 minutes. Add to gelatin mixture; stir until thoroughly dissolved. Add remaining grapefruit juice. Cool.
3. When gelatin begins to set, beat egg whites and salt until stiff but not dry; fold into gelatin mixture. Turn into 1-quart mold; chill until set.
4. Unmold; serve with Custard Sauce.

Mrs. R. B. Sherman, Cassadaga–Lake Helen Woman's Club, Cassadaga, Fla.

GULAH MALACCA (Coconut Cream)
Serves 6

2 cups milk
2 envelopes gelatin
½ cup water
1 cup sugar
1 cup heavy cream, whipped
1½ teaspoons vanilla
1 cup flaked coconut
Caramel Nut Sauce (p. 700)

1. Day before, lightly oil 1½-quart mold or 6 individual molds.
2. In saucepan bring milk to boil.
3. Soften gelatin in water.
4. Add gelatin and sugar to milk; cook over low heat, stirring until gelatin is dissolved. Cool until slightly thickened.
5. Fold in cream, vanilla and coconut. Turn into mold or individual molds; refrigerate overnight.
6. Next day, unmold onto serving dish; serve with Caramel Nut Sauce.

Pat Haughwout, Civic Club, Belleville, Pa.

ORANGE AMBROSIA
Serves 8

6-ounce package lemon gelatin
2 cups boiling water
¼ cup sugar
Dash of salt
2 tablespoons lemon juice
½ cup orange juice
2 tablespoons grated orange rind
1 cup heavy cream, whipped
Orange sections

1. Dissolve gelatin in water.
2. Stir in sugar, salt, lemon juice and orange juice and rind. Chill until slightly thickened.
3. Fold in cream; turn into 8 individual molds. Chill until firm.
4. Unmold; decorate with orange sections.

Mrs. F. R. Summerfield, Woman's Club, Charleston, W. Va.

ORANGE OR APRICOT ICEBOX PUDDING
Serves 6

2 eggs
1 cup sugar

1½ cups orange or apricot juice
3-ounce package orange gelatin
1 cup heavy cream, whipped

1. Beat eggs thoroughly in top of double saucepan; stir in sugar and fruit juice. Cook over simmering water, stirring constantly, until custard coats spoon.
2. Remove from heat; stir in gelatin. Cool until mixture begins to thicken.
3. Fold in cream. Pour into 1-quart mold; chill until set.

Mrs. Mary E. Stafford (mother of astronaut Thomas P. Stafford), Mother's Study Club, Weatherford, Okla.

PINEAPPLE MOUSSE
Serves 6

3-ounce package pineapple gelatin
1 cup boiling water
8-ounce can crushed pineapple, undrained
Dash of salt
1 cup heavy cream, whipped

1. Add gelatin to water; stir until dissolved. Add pineapple and salt; mix well. Chill until slightly thickened.
2. Fold cream into gelatin mixture; turn into 1-quart mold. Chill until firm.
3. Unmold onto serving dish; decorate as desired.

Mrs. Theodore Ebell, New Century Club, Parkside, Pa.

SUNSHINE IN THE SNOW
Serves 6 to 8

1-pound 14-ounce can sliced pineapple
1 envelope gelatin
1 egg
¼ cup sugar
1 teaspoon lemon juice
½ teaspoon salt
1½ cups macaroon crumbs
½ cup heavy cream, whipped

1. Drain pineapple; reserve ¼ cup syrup. Cut half the pineapple slices into ½-inch pieces. Set aside remaining slices.
2. Soften gelatin in reserved syrup; stir over hot water until dissolved. Cool.
3. Beat egg and sugar until fluffy. Stir in gelatin, diced pineapple, lemon juice, salt and crumbs.
4. Fold in cream; pour into 8-inch loaf pan. Chill until set.
5. Unmold; decorate with remaining pineapple.

Mrs. Robb Gover, Woman's Club, Charleston, W. Va.

MINUTE PLUM PUDDING
Serves 6

5 tablespoons sugar
1 envelope gelatin
2 tablespoons cold water
2 cups boiling water
Juice of 1 lemon
1 teaspoon vanilla
Pinch of salt
¾ cup grape-nut cereal
¾ cup chopped seedless raisins
¼ cup chopped citron
⅓ cup chopped walnuts
½ apple, peeled and finely chopped
Flavored whipped cream

1. Combine sugar and gelatin. Add cold water; soak for 5 minutes.
2. Stir gelatin into boiling water. Add all remaining ingredients except whipped cream; mix well.
3. Pour into 1½-quart mold; chill until firm.
4. Unmold; serve with whipped cream.

Mrs. W. H. Strickland, Madison County Federation of Woman's Clubs, Athens, Ga.

RHUBARB DESSERT
Serves 6 to 8

1 quart water
2 cups sugar
¼ cup quick-cooking tapioca
8 cups rhubarb, cut into 2-inch pieces
2 3-ounce packages strawberry gelatin

1. In large saucepan combine water, sugar and tapioca. Cook over moderate heat until thickened.
2. Add rhubarb; cook until soft.
3. Add gelatin; stir until dissolved. Pour into large serving dish; chill until set.

Mrs. Charles Mininger, Women's Auxiliary to the Chiropractic Association of New York; member, New York State Federation of Women's Clubs

RIS À LA MANG
(Danish Rice Cream)
Serves 6 to 8

2½ cups milk
¼ cup rice
1 envelope gelatin
¼ cup slivered almonds
¼ cup sweet sherry
⅓ cup sugar
1 teaspoon vanilla
1 cup heavy cream, whipped
Fruit Sauce (p. 701)
or frozen berries, defrosted

1. In saucepan bring 2 cups of the milk to boil. Stir in rice; cook over low heat, stirring occasionally for 20 minutes, or until cooked.
2. In small bowl soften gelatin in remaining milk. Stir into rice; cook, stirring, until dissolved.
3. Remove from heat; stir in almonds, sherry, sugar and vanilla. Cool until almost set.
4. Fold in cream; turn into glass serving dish. Chill until serving time.

5. Serve with Fruit Sauce or berries, as desired.

Helen Nelson, Pine Ridge Woman's Club, Fairfax, Va.

STRAWBERRY BAVARIAN CREAM
Serves 6 to 8

2 envelopes gelatin
½ cup water
¾ cup sugar
1 pint strawberries, sliced
2 cups heavy cream, whipped
Whole strawberries (optional)

1. Lightly oil 2-quart mold.
2. In small bowl soften gelatin in water.
3. In saucepan combine sugar and strawberries; bring to boil.
4. Remove from heat; add gelatin; stir until dissolved. Cool until mixture starts to thicken.
5. Fold in cream; spoon into mold. Chill until firm.
6. Unmold onto serving dish; decorate with whole strawberries, if desired.

Mrs. Ralph Allen, Friendship Club, La Monte, Mo.

STRAWBERRY MOUSSE
Serves 8 to 10

1 quart strawberries, hulled
½ cup sugar
½ cup sweet white wine
2 envelopes gelatin
½ cup cold water
½ cup boiling water
2 cups heavy cream, whipped
Whole strawberries (optional)

1. Lightly oil 2-quart mold.
2. In mixing bowl crush strawberries with potato masher or fork. Add sugar and wine; mix well.
3. In saucepan combine sugar and cold water. Stir in boiling water; cook over low heat, stirring frequently, until dissolved. Mix into strawberries; cool for 15 minutes.
4. Beat until slightly thickened. Fold in cream. Turn into mold; chill until set.
5. Unmold onto serving dish; decorate with whole strawberries, if desired.

Mrs. Guy Wher, Junior Woman's Club, Steubenville, Ohio

STRAWBERRY PINEAPPLE MOLD
Serves 6 to 8

3-ounce package strawberry gelatin
1½ cups boiling water
1 pint vanilla ice cream, softened
1-pound 4-ounce can crushed pineapple, drained

1. Dissolve gelatin in water; chill until syrupy.
2. Stir in ice cream. Fold in pineapple. Pour into 1-quart ring mold; chill until set.

Mrs. Glen Pommerening, Junior Woman's Club, Wauwatosa, Wis.

CHRISTMAS DESSERT

Serves 8

3 eggs, separated
¾ cup sweet sherry
1½ envelopes gelatin
½ cup water
1 cup sugar
½ teaspoon salt
2 cups heavy cream, whipped

1. Lightly oil 2-quart mold.
2. In mixing bowl beat egg yolks until thickened. Gradually stir in sherry; set aside.
3. In top of double saucepan soften gelatin in water. Cook over hot water until dissolved. Add sugar; stir until dissolved.
4. Stir gelatin mixture and salt into egg yolk mixture.
5. In another mixing bowl beat egg whites until stiff but not dry; fold with cream into egg yolk mixture. Turn into mold; chill until set.
6. Unmold; decorate as desired.

Katherine L. Howard, Woman's Club,
Crawford, Ga.

WINE JELLY

Serves 6

2 envelopes gelatin
1 cup cold water
1 cup boiling water
Juice of 1 lemon
1 cup sugar
1 cup sweet white wine
¼ cup brandy
Whipped cream or Custard Sauce (p. 676)

1. In saucepan soften gelatin in cold water. Stir in boiling water, lemon juice and sugar. Bring to boil; then simmer until gelatin and sugar are dissolved.
2. Remove from heat; stir in wine and brandy. Pour into 1-quart mold; chill until firm.
3. Unmold; decorate as desired. Serve with whipped cream or Custard Sauce.

Mrs. Chester E. Martin, Treasurer,
General Federation of Women's Clubs,
Atlanta, Ga.

Crumb and Cake Desserts

APRICOT ICEBOX DESSERT

Serves 8

Make this a day before serving.

3 eggs
1½ cups confectioners' sugar
¾ cup butter or margarine
1-pound 13-ounce can apricots, drained and chopped
½ cup chopped walnuts
12-ounce package vanilla wafers, crushed
2 cups heavy cream, whipped

1. In top of double saucepan combine eggs, sugar and butter or margarine. Cook over hot water, stirring constantly, until thickened and smooth.

2. Remove from heat; stir in apricots and walnuts. Cool for 5 minutes.
3. In bottom of 11 x 7 x 1½-inch baking pan sprinkle half the wafer crumbs. Spread custard mixture over crumbs.
4. Top with whipped cream; sprinkle with remaining crumbs. Refrigerate overnight.

Athenaeum Club, Sapulpa, Okla.

APRICOT CRÈME CAKE DESSERT

Serves 8 to 10

1 pound vanilla wafers
3 egg yolks
¾ cup sugar
½ cup melted butter
1-pound can apricot halves
1 cup chopped walnuts
1 cup heavy cream, whipped

1. Day before crush wafers; reserve 1 cup crumbs. Sprinkle half the remaining crumbs into 10 x 6 x 1½-inch baking pan.
2. Prepare filling: In mixing bowl beat egg yolks until thickened and lemon-colored. Add ½ cup of the sugar; beat well. Add butter; beat well. Drain apricots; reserve ½ cup syrup. Chop apricots; add with walnuts to egg yolk mixture; mix well. Stir in reserved crumbs.
3. Spread filling in pan; chill for 1 hour.
4. Fold remaining sugar and reserved syrup into cream. Sprinkle half the remaining crumbs over filling; spread flavored cream on top. Sprinkle with remaining crumbs. Refrigerate overnight.
5. Next day, cut into squares to serve.

Mrs. Jim Widrig, Delphian Junior
Woman's Club, Beloit, Kans.

BLUEBERRY DESSERT

Serves 8

2 cups vanilla wafer crumbs
½ cup melted butter
½ cup milk
16 marshmallows
1 cup heavy cream, whipped
1-pound can blueberries
¼ cup sugar
2 tablespoons cornstarch
1 tablespoon lemon juice
Whipped cream (optional)

1. Day before, grease 10 x 6 x 1½-inch baking pan.
2. In mixing bowl blend crumbs and butter; spread half in pan.
3. In top of double saucepan combine milk and marshmallows. Cook over hot water, stirring occasionally, until marshmallows are melted. Remove from heat; cool.
4. Fold cream into marshmallows; spread over crumbs in pan.
5. Drain blueberries; reserve syrup.
6. In small saucepan combine sugar, cornstarch and reserved syrup. Cook over low heat, stirring constantly, until thickened and clear. Remove from heat; stir in lemon juice and blueberries. Cool.

7. Spread blueberry mixture over marshmallows in pan. Sprinkle with remaining crumbs. Refrigerate overnight.

8. Next day, cut into squares to serve; top with whipped cream, if desired.

Marian Sharp, Woman's Club, Boone, Ia.

CHOCOLATE ANGEL FOOD DESSERT

Serves 12 to 16

2 6-ounce packages semi-sweet chocolate pieces
4 eggs, separated
Dash of salt
2 cups heavy cream, whipped
10-inch angel food cake

1. Day before, oil 13 x 9½ x 2-inch baking pan.

2. In top of double saucepan cook chocolate over hot water until melted.

3. Beat in egg yolks; remove from heat. Cool.

4. In mixing bowl beat egg whites and salt until stiff but not dry; fold in cream and chocolate mixture.

5. Break cake into bite-size pieces.

6. Arrange alternate layers of cake and chocolate mixture in pan. Refrigerate overnight.

7. Next day, cut into slices to serve.

Joanne Feiter, North Shore Junior Woman's Club, Shorewood, Wis.

CHOCOLATE ICEBOX PUDDING

Serves 9

2 1-ounce squares unsweetened chocolate
2 tablespoons hot water
½ cup sugar
3 eggs, separated
1 cup heavy cream, whipped
Crushed vanilla wafers
Whipped cream and maraschino cherries (optional)

1. Day before, in top of double saucepan combine chocolate and water. Heat over simmering water, stirring occasionally, until chocolate is melted and mixture is smooth.

2. Beat egg yolks lightly; stir with sugar into chocolate. Cool.

3. Beat egg whites until stiff but not dry; fold into chocolate mixture. Fold in cream.

4. Arrange crushed wafers in 10 x 6 x 1½-inch baking dish. Cover with half the chocolate mixture. Sprinkle with crushed wafers; cover with remaining chocolate mixture; cover with more crushed wafers. Refrigerate overnight.

5. Next day, serve plain or topped with whipped cream and maraschino cherries if desired.

Mrs. Claude Hill, Young Matron's Study Club, Slater, Mo.

CHARLOTTE RUSSE

Serves 8

8 egg yolks
1 cup sugar

2 cups hot milk
2 envelopes gelatin
¼ cup water
2 teaspoons vanilla
2 cups heavy cream, whipped
12 ladyfingers, split
Fruit and whipped cream (optional)

1. In top of double saucepan combine egg yolks and sugar; beat until smooth. Gradually stir in milk; cook over boiling water, stirring constantly, until custard coats spoon.

2. Soften gelatin in water. Add to custard; stir until thoroughly dissolved. Cool custard, but do not let set. Stir in vanilla.

3. Fold cream into custard.

4. Place small circle of ladyfingers in center of 2-quart mold; radiate ladyfingers daisy-fashion, to sides to cover bottom. (Cut ladyfingers when necessary to fit neatly.) Stand ladyfingers side by side and close together around sides of mold.

5. Pour custard mixture into mold; chill until set. Unmold. If desired, garnish with fruit and whipped cream.

A. S.

CHOCOLATE CHARLOTTE RUSSE

Serves 10 to 12

4 1-ounce squares unsweetened chocolate
¾ cup granulated sugar
⅓ cup milk
6 eggs, separated
1½ cups sweet butter
1½ cups confectioners' sugar (sift if lumpy)
1½ teaspoons vanilla
36 ladyfingers, split
1 cup heavy cream, whipped
Shaved chocolate

1. Day before, melt chocolate in top of double saucepan.

2. Combine granulated sugar, milk and egg yolks. Stir into chocolate; cook over simmering water, stirring constantly, until thickened.

3. Cream butter thoroughly. Add ¾ cup of the confectioners' sugar; blend thoroughly. Add chocolate mixture; beat well.

4. Beat egg whites and salt until stiff but not dry. Gradually beat in remaining confectioners' sugar; beat until thick and glossy; fold into chocolate mixture. Stir in vanilla.

5. Line 9-inch spring-form pan with ladyfingers. Put in one-third of chocolate mixture, then layer of ladyfingers. Repeat, finishing with layer of ladyfingers. Refrigerate overnight.

6. Next day, garnish with whipped cream and shaved chocolate.

Harriet Truitt, Junior Woman's Club, Norfolk, Va.

FRENCH CREAM PUDDING

Serves 6 to 8

Refrigerate for 24 hours before serving.

8-ounce package vanilla wafers, crushed

½ cup butter or margarine
1 cup confectioners' sugar
(sift if lumpy)
2 eggs
1 teaspoon vanilla
¾ cup chopped walnuts
¾ cup chopped maraschino cherries
1 cup heavy cream, whipped

1. Grease 8-inch square baking pan.
2. Spread wafer crumbs in pan.
3. Cream butter or margarine and sugar in mixing bowl until light and fluffy. Add eggs and vanilla; beat well until smooth. Spread over crumbs in pan.
4. Fold walnuts and cherries into cream, spread over pudding.

Gerry Guenther, Progressive Arts Club,
South Bend, Ind.

JIFFY LEMON DESSERT

Serves 4

16 chocolate-covered graham crackers
3-ounce package lemon chiffon pie filling mix
1 cup heavy cream, whipped

1. Crush crackers; spread half in 13 x 9½ x 2-inch baking pan.
2. Prepare pie filling according to package directions. Pour over crackers; cool.
3. Spread cream over filling; sprinkle with remaining crackers. Refrigerate.

Mrs. James A. Holter, Woman's Club,
Casselton, N.D.

LEMON PINEAPPLE FLUFF

Serves 16

1 cup quick-cooking oats
1 cup brown sugar
½ cup presifted flour
½ cup margarine
3-ounce package lemon gelatin
1½ cups boiling water
1 cup drained crushed pineapple
3½ cups tiny marshmallows
2 cups heavy cream
½ cup granulated sugar
1 cup finely chopped nuts

1. Preheat oven to 350° F.
2. Mix oats, brown sugar, flour and margarine until crumbed. Spread in shallow baking pan; bake in preheated oven for 10 minutes.
3. Spread half the crumbs in 13 x 9½ x 2-inch baking pan.
4. Dissolve gelatin in water. Cool.
5. Mix pineapple and marshmallows; let stand until gelatin begins to thicken.
6. Whip cream until stiff. Fold in gelatin, pineapple mixture, granulated sugar and nuts. Turn into crumb-lined pan. Sprinkle remaining crumbs on top. Refrigerate until serving time.

Mrs. Gary Alstot, Junior Woman's Club,
Wauwatosa, Wis.

LEMON-LIME TREAT

Serves 4 to 6

½ 12-ounce package vanilla wafers, crushed
½ cup flaked coconut

¼ cup melted butter or margarine
3-ounce package lime gelatin
1½ cups boiling water
½ cup sugar
3 tablespoons lemon juice
1 cup evaporated milk

1. Grease 8-inch pie plate.
2. In mixing bowl combine wafer crumbs, coconut and butter or margarine. Press into pie plate. Chill for 30 minutes.
3. Stir gelatin into water. Stir in sugar and lemon juice. Chill until slightly thickened.
4. Beat milk until foamy; fold into gelatin mixture. Turn into crumb shell. Chill until set.

Mrs. Stanley Goeglein, President,
Moirae Junior Women's Club, Fort Wayne, Ind.

MACAROON SHIMMY PUDDING

Serves 8 to 10

18 almond macaroons
2 envelopes gelatin
1 cup water
4 eggs, separated
2 cups milk
1½ cups sugar
Dash of salt
1 teaspoon vanilla
Whipped cream

1. Oil 10 x 6 x 1½-inch baking pan. Line bottom with macaroons.
2. In top of double saucepan soften gelatin in water.
3. Stir in egg yolks, milk, sugar and salt. Cook over hot water, stirring constantly, until thickened and smooth. Remove from heat; cool, stirring occasionally.
4. In mixing bowl beat egg whites until stiff but not dry; fold with vanilla into gelatin mixture.
5. Pour over macaroons; refrigerate for at least 12 hours.
6. Serve topped with whipped cream.

Virginia Wince, Saturday Review Club,
Utica, Ohio

MINT DESSERT

Serves 8

12-ounce package chocolate wafers
¼ cup melted butter
2 cups heavy cream
2 cups marshmallows
1 cup after-dinner mints

1. Crush wafers; mix two-thirds with butter; spread in 13 x 9½ x 2-inch pan.
2. Whip cream. Fold in marshmallows and mints.
3. Turn into pan; sprinkle with remaining crumbs. Refrigerate for at least 8 hours before serving.

Mrs. Claude Richardson, Women's Club,
Milton Junction, Wis.

MARSHMALLOW DELIGHT
Serves 6

30 marshmallows
1 cup milk
1-pound can crushed pineapple, drained
1 cup heavy cream, whipped
14 graham crackers, crushed

1. In top of double saucepan combine marshmallows and milk. Heat over simmering water, stirring occasionally, until marshmallows are melted. Cool.
2. Stir pineapple into marshmallow mixture; fold in cream.
3. Spread half the cracker crumbs in 9-inch square baking pan. Spoon pineapple mixture over crumbs; sprinkle remaining crumbs on top. Chill until set.

Mrs. Donald Himes, Junior Woman's Club, Diamond Bar, Calif.

BERRY BAVARIAN CROWN
Serves 10 to 12

3-ounce package strawberry gelatin
½ cup boiling water
½ cup ice water
2 10-ounce packages frozen sliced strawberries, defrosted
1 cup heavy cream, whipped
10-inch angel food cake
1 tablespoon cornstarch
Few drops red food coloring
1 teaspoon butter

1. In mixing bowl add gelatin to boiling water; stir until dissolved. Stir in ice water; chill until slightly thickened.
2. Meanwhile, drain strawberries; reserve 1 cup syrup.
3. Beat gelatin until light and fluffy; fold in strawberries and cream.
4. Break angel food cake into bite-size pieces. Arrange alternate layers of cake and gelatin mixture in 10-inch tube pan, finishing with layer of cake. Chill until set.
5. Meanwhile, prepare glaze: In small saucepan blend cornstarch and reserved syrup to make a smooth paste. Cook over medium heat, stirring constantly, until thickened and clear. Remove from heat; stir in food coloring and butter.
6. Unmold cake onto serving dish; drizzle glaze over top. Refrigerate until serving time.

Mrs. Bernard Leaf, Glenbrook Woman's Club, Louisville, Ky.

STRAWBERRY SHORTCAKE
Serves 4 to 6

2 eggs
2 cups sugar
1 cup cake flour
⅛ teaspoon salt
1 teaspoon baking powder
1 tablespoon melted butter
½ cup hot milk
1 pint strawberries
1 cup heavy cream, whipped

1. Preheat oven to 375° F. Grease and flour 8-inch layer cake pan.

2. Beat eggs in mixing bowl until light. Gradually add 1 cup of the sugar; beat until thickened and lemon-colored.
3. Onto piece of waxed paper sift together flour, salt and baking powder; fold into eggs. Carefully stir in butter and milk.
4. Turn into pan; bake in preheated oven for 30 minutes.
5. Meanwhile, slice strawberries; sprinkle with remaining sugar.
6. Cool cake for 5 minutes; remove from pan; cool on wire rack.
7. Split cake. Put bottom half on serving dish; arrange half the strawberries on bottom layer; top with half the cream. Cover with other cake half; top with remaining strawberries and cream.

Mrs. Anna L. Sims, Woman's Club, Hawthorne, Fla.

STRAWBERRY BANANA DESSERT
Serves 10

2 3-ounce packages strawberry gelatin
3 cups boiling water
1 quart strawberries, sliced
3 bananas, sliced
15 graham crackers, crumbed
Whipped cream

1. Dissolve gelatin in water. Cool; chill until almost set; whip until fluffy.
2. Fold strawberries and bananas into gelatin.
3. Grease 13 x 9½ x 2-inch baking pan; sprinkle bottom with half the crumbs. Pour gelatin mixture over crumbs; top with remaining crumbs. Chill for several hours.
4. Serve with whipped cream.

Mrs. Iva Butler, Women's Club, Lusk, Wyo.

TRIFLE
Serves 6 to 8

8-inch white or yellow cake layer
½ cup raspberry or strawberry preserves
1-pound can pear halves or slices
⅓ cup sweet sherry
1 cup sliced peaches, strawberries or bananas
2 cups Custard Sauce (p. 676)
1 cup heavy cream
¼ cup confectioners' sugar (sift if lumpy)
1 teaspoon vanilla
¼ cup slivered roasted almonds

1. Split cake into 2 layers; sandwich together with preserves; cut into 2-inch cubes. Arrange in large serving bowl.
2. Drain pears. Combine ½ cup syrup with sherry; sprinkle over cake.
3. Dice pears; arrange pears and peaches, strawberries or bananas on cake. Pour Custard Sauce over fruits; chill for 1 hour.
4. Whip cream until stiff; fold in sugar and vanilla; spread on custard. Sprinkle with almonds. Chill.

Lyn Williams, Pierian Study Club, Vivian, La.

Frozen Desserts

VANILLA ICE CREAM

Makes About 1 Quart

2 eggs
⅓ cup sugar
⅔ cup light corn syrup
1 cup heavy cream
1½ cups milk
1½ teaspoons vanilla

1. Beat eggs in mixing bowl until foamy. Gradually beat in sugar and corn syrup; beat until thickened.
2. Stir in cream, milk and vanilla. Pour into refrigerator tray. Freeze for about 1 hour, or until firm.
3. Turn ice cream into mixing bowl; beat until smooth. Return to tray; freeze until firm.

CHOCOLATE ICE CREAM: Reduce vanilla to 1 teaspoon. In saucepan combine ⅓ cup cocoa, the corn syrup and ½ cup of the milk; bring to boil over medium heat, stirring constantly; cool slightly; add to eggs beaten with sugar. Then follow Steps 2 and 3 above, using remaining milk.

LEMON ICE CREAM: Increase sugar to ½ cup. Substitute ½ cup lemon juice for ½ cup of the milk and 1 teaspoon grated lemon rind for vanilla. Follow directions above.

MAPLE ICE CREAM: Reduce vanilla to 1 teaspoon and milk to 1 cup. Substitute light brown sugar for granulated sugar and maple syrup for light corn syrup. Follow directions above.

BUTTER PECAN ICE CREAM: Reduce vanilla to 1 teaspoon and milk to 1 cup. Substitute ⅓ cup light brown sugar for granulated sugar. Follow Steps 1 and 2 above. Then combine ½ cup chopped pecans, 2 tablespoons butter and ⅛ teaspoon salt; toast in moderate oven (350° F.) for about 10 minutes, stirring once or twice; fold into ice cream mixture just before freezing as in Step 3.

Carolyn Carpenter, Junior Woman's Club,
Rock Hill, S.C.

FROZEN ALMOND CREAM

Serves 8 to 12

1 cup sugar
2½ tablespoons flour
2 eggs
¼ cup water
¾ cup light corn syrup
1 tablespoon butter or margarine
¼ teaspoon vanilla
⅓ cup milk
2 cups heavy cream
1 teaspoon almond extract
½ cup slivered almonds
½ cup red and green candied
cherries, chopped

1. In small saucepan mix sugar and flour. In bowl beat eggs lightly; stir in water and corn syrup; add to saucepan.

Cook over low heat, stirring constantly, until thickened and smooth.
2. Remove from heat; beat in butter or margarine. Cool.
3. Stir in vanilla, milk, cream and almond extract. Pour into refrigerator trays; freeze until mushy.
4. Turn into mixing bowl; beat until smooth. Stir in almonds and cherries. Return to trays; freeze until firm.

Woman's Club, Sheldon, Wis.

APPLE DELIGHT

Serves 6

16 marshmallows
½ cup boiling water
3 tablespoons lemon juice
2 tablespoons orange juice
1-pound can applesauce
1 cup heavy cream, whipped

1. Cut marshmallows in fourths; put in mixing bowl. Pour water over marshmallows; stir until smooth. Cool.
2. Stir in lemon juice, orange juice and applesauce.
3. Fold in cream; turn into refrigerator tray. Freeze until firm.

Annotawo Club, Owatonna, Minn.

APRICOT SHERBET

Makes 1 Gallon

1-pound 13-ounce can apricots,
undrained
Juice of 4 lemons
Juice of 4 oranges
3 cups sugar
1 quart water
2 cups heavy cream, whipped

1. Force apricots through sieve, or purée in electric blender. Stir in fruit juices; set aside.
2. In saucepan combine sugar and water; bring to boil; boil for 5 minutes. Stir into fruit juices; cool. Turn into refrigerator trays; freeze until ice crystals form at edges.
3. Turn into mixing bowl; beat until smooth. Fold in cream. Return to trays; freeze until firm.

Mrs. E. H. Brinkman, Ladies Reading Circle,
Alma, Kans.

BISCUIT TORTONI

Serves 12

1 cup coconut macaroon crumbs
1 envelope gelatin
¼ cup water
1 cup scalded milk
2 eggs
½ cup sugar
½ teaspoon salt
2 tablespoons sweet sherry
1 cup heavy cream, whipped
12 maraschino cherries

1. Arrange paper liners in 12 muffin cups; sprinkle half the crumbs into cups; set aside.
2. In small bowl sprinkle gelatin over water; stir to soften. Pour in milk; stir until gelatin is dissolved.

3. In mixing bowl beat eggs until foamy. Gradually add sugar; beat until thickened and lemon-colored.

4. Stir in gelatin mixture, salt and sherry; chill until syrupy.

5. Fold cream into egg mixture; turn into crumb-lined cups. Sprinkle with remaining crumbs; freeze until firm.

6. Top with cherries before serving.

*Betty Gearhart, Junior Woman's Club,
Altoona, Pa.*

FROZEN COFFEE CUSTARD
Serves 6

1½ cups cold strong black coffee
½ cup milk
⅔ cup sugar
¼ teaspoon salt
1 envelope gelatin
2 tablespoons water
3 eggs, separated
1 teaspoon vanilla
Whipped cream (optional)

1. In saucepan combine coffee, milk, sugar and salt; bring to simmer.

2. Soften gelatin in water; add to coffee mixture; stir until thoroughly dissolved.

3. Beat egg yolks; gradually stir into coffee mixture. Cook over low heat stirring constantly, for 3 minutes. Remove from heat.

4. Beat egg whites until stiff but not dry; gradually beat in coffee mixture; beat until smooth. Stir in vanilla.

5. Pour into 1-quart mold rinsed in cold water; freeze until firm.

6. Unmold. Garnish with whipped cream, if desired.

*Mrs. James Kennedy, Woman's Club,
Chappaqua, N.Y.*

COFFEE MARSHMALLOW DESSERT
Serves 6

22 marshmallows
1 cup strong black coffee
1 cup heavy cream, whipped

1. In top of double saucepan combine marshmallows and coffee. Cook over hot water, stirring occasionally, until marshmallows are melted; cool.

2. Fold in cream. Turn into 6 parfait glasses; freeze until firm.

*Mrs. Richard Cotter, Mathews County
Woman's Club, Grimstead, Va.*

COFFEE MOUSSE
Serves 6

4 egg yolks
1 cup sugar
1 cup hot strong black coffee
2 cups heavy cream, whipped
Hot Fudge Sauce (p. 701)

1. Beat egg yolks until thickened and pale. Beat in sugar. Stir in coffee. Cool; then chill thoroughly.

2. Fold in cream. Turn into mold; cover; freeze for 4 to 5 hours.

3. Unmold; serve with Hot Fudge Sauce.

*Mrs. Charles Sweeney, Woman's Club,
St. Mary's, W. Va.*

CRANBERRY ICE
Serves 8 to 10

4 cups cranberries
2¼ cups water
3 cups sugar
1 envelope gelatin
1 tablespoon lemon juice

1. Put cranberries and 2 cups of the water in saucepan. Bring to boil; cook over medium heat until soft; force through sieve, or purée in electric blender until smooth.

2. Return purée to saucepan; stir in sugar. Bring to boil, stirring occasionally; boil over medium heat for 2 minutes.

3. Soften gelatin in remaining water; stir into purée; stir until dissolved. Stir in lemon juice.

4. Pour into 2-quart refrigerator tray; freeze until mushy.

5. Turn into mixing bowl; beat until smooth. Return to tray; freeze until firm.

*Ethel Henry, Mutual Improvement Club,
Sterling, Kans.*

FROZEN DATE PARFAIT
Serves 6 to 8

½ cup chopped dates
1½ cups water
½ cup sugar
¼ teaspoon salt
4 egg yolks, lightly beaten
1 cup orange juice
1 cup heavy cream, whipped
2 teaspoons vanilla

1. In saucepan combine dates, water, sugar and salt. Cook over low heat, stirring occasionally, for 30 minutes.

2. Put egg yolks in small bowl; stir in a little of date mixture; return to rest of mixture. Cook over low heat, stirring constantly, until thickened. Cool.

3. Stir in orange juice; fold in cream and vanilla. Freeze until firm.

4. Turn into mixing bowl; beat until smooth. Pour into parfait glasses; freeze until firm.

*Mrs. Wilmer Bullock, President,
Alabama Federation of Women's Clubs*

FROZEN LEMON CREAM
Serves 6

3 tablespoons lemon juice
2 teaspoons grated lemon rind
1 cup sugar
2 cups light cream
Few drops yellow food coloring

1. In mixing bowl blend lemon juice and rind and sugar. Gradually stir in cream; stir until sugar is dissolved. Add food coloring.

2. Pour into refrigerator tray; freeze until firm.

*Mrs. W. H. Frick, Woman's Club,
Mount Dora, Fla.*

LEMON VELVET

Serves 12

Grated rind and juice of 6 lemons
½ cup boiling water
4 cups sugar
1 quart milk
1 quart heavy cream, whipped

1. Put lemon rind and juice in large mixing bowl. Add water. Stir in sugar; stir until dissolved. Cool.
2. Stir in milk; fold in cream. Turn into refrigerator trays; freeze until firm.
3. Turn into large mixing bowl; beat until smooth. Return to trays; freeze until firm.

Mrs. R. O. Everson, Study Club, Washburn, N.D.

LEMON LIME SHERBET

Serves 8

3-ounce package lime gelatin
1 cup boiling water
½ cup sugar
1 cup light corn syrup
6-ounce can frozen lemonade concentrate
1 quart milk

1. In mixing bowl combine gelatin and water; stir in sugar, corn syrup and lemonade concentrate. Stir in milk. Turn into 2 refrigerator trays; freeze until almost firm.
2. Turn into mixing bowl; beat until smooth. Return to trays; freeze until firm.

Mrs. George Eller, Marquette Starlight Literary Club, McPherson, Kans.

MAPLE MOUSSE

Serves 6

1 cup maple syrup
4 eggs, separated
2 cups heavy cream, whipped

1. In top of double saucepan combine maple syrup and egg yolks. Cook over simmering water, stirring constantly, for about 10 minutes, or until thickened. Remove from heat; cool.
2. Beat egg whites until stiff but not dry. Fold in cream.
3. Beat custard until light; stir into egg white mixture.
4. Pack into 6-cup mold; freeze until firm.

Julia C. Pease, Ladies of Enosburg, Vt.

FROSTED MINT DELIGHT

Serves 10 to 12

2 1-pound cans crushed pineapple
¾ cup mint flavored apple jelly
3-ounce package lemon gelatin
2 cups heavy cream, whipped
2 teaspoons confectioners' sugar, sifted

1. Drain pineapple; reserve syrup. Put pineapple in mixing bowl.
2. Melt jelly in saucepan; stir into pineapple.
3. In saucepan bring reserved syrup to boil. Add gelatin; stir until dissolved. Add to pineapple mixture; cool slightly.

4. Sweeten whipped cream with sugar; fold into pineapple mixture. Turn into 2 refrigerator trays; freeze until firm.

Submitted to Woman's Club, Kankakee, Ill., on behalf of Mrs. Dwight D. Eisenhower

FRESH PEACH ICE CREAM

Serves 20

12 ripe medium peaches
1 tablespoon lemon juice
2¾ cups sugar
1½ quarts heavy cream, chilled
1 teaspoon vanilla
1 teaspoon almond extract
½ teaspoon salt

1. Chill 4-quart freezer container.
2. Dip peaches in boiling water; plunge into cold water. Slip off skins, cut in half; discard pits.
3. Press peaches through sieve or food mill into mixing bowl. Stir in lemon juice and sugar; let stand for 15 to 20 minutes.
4. Combine remaining ingredients; stir into peach mixture.
5. Fill freezer container two-thirds full of peach mixture; cover tightly; set in freezer tub. Freeze until firm.

Mrs. Julian Deal, Twentieth Century Club, Eudora, Ark.

PINEAPPLE BUTTERMILK SHERBET

Makes About 1 Quart

2 cups buttermilk
⅔ cup sugar
Dash of salt
1 cup drained crushed pineapple
2 teaspoons vanilla
1 egg yolk
1 egg white, stiffly beaten

1. In mixing bowl combine all ingredients except egg white. Pour into refrigerator tray; freeze until mushy.
2. Gently fold in egg white. Freeze until firm.

Mrs. Robert W. Banta, Thursday Morning Club, Madison, N.J.

SUMMER SHERBET

Makes About 1 Quart

2 cups sugar
2 cups water
1 cup fresh orange juice
⅜ cup fresh lemon juice
2 medium bananas, mashed
2 egg whites, stiffly beaten

1. In saucepan combine sugar and water. Bring slowly to boil; then simmer for 15 minutes. Remove from heat; cool.
2. Stir fruit juices into syrup. Pour into refrigerator tray; freeze until mushy.
3. Turn into mixing bowl; beat well. Fold in bananas and egg whites.
4. Return to tray; freeze until mushy. Stir well while still in tray; freeze until firm.

Mrs. Carl Bergendoff, Woman's Club, Glen Ellyn, Ill.

FRUIT CREAM

Serves 4 to 6

1 cup heavy cream
1 cup mashed peeled ripe peaches
3 tablespoon sugar
1 tablespoon lemon juice

1. In mixing bowl whip cream until stiff.
2. Fold in remaining ingredients. Turn into refrigerator tray. Freeze until firm.

Mrs. J. S. Arnow, Woman's Club,
Hawthorne, Fla.

PEANUT BUTTER MOUSSE

Makes About 1 Quart

½ cup peanut butter
½ cup milk
Dash of salt
3 tablespoons light corn syrup
1 egg white
¼ cup sugar
1 cup heavy cream, whipped

1. In mixing bowl beat peanut butter and ¼ cup of the milk until smooth. Beat in remaining milk; beat until smooth. Add salt and corn syrup; blend.
2. Beat egg white until foamy. Gradually add sugar, beating constantly; beat until smooth and glossy; fold into cream. Stir in peanut butter mixture.
3. Pour into refrigerator tray; freeze at coldest setting without stirring. When frozen, set control at normal.

Mrs. Otis Durham, Woman's Federated Guild,
Moultrie, Ga.

FROZEN STRAWBERRY DESSERT

Serves 6

1 cup strawberries, mashed
1 tablespoon orange juice
2 tablespoons sugar
16 marshmallows
¼ cup water
1 cup heavy cream, whipped
1 teaspoon vanilla
Dash of salt

1. In mixing bowl combine strawberries, orange juice and sugar. Set aside.
2. Meanwhile, cook marshmallows and water in top of double saucepan over hot water until melted. Cool slightly.
3. Stir marshmallows into strawberry mixture; mix well. Fold in cream, vanilla and salt. Spoon into refrigerator tray. Freeze until firm.

Mrs. Fred Cole, Woman's Club,
Hawthorne, Fla.

STRAWBERRY MOUSSE

Makes About 1 Quart

1 cup sugar
1 cup crushed strawberries
1 cup heavy cream, whipped
2 egg whites, stiffly beaten
Pinch of salt

1. Combine sugar and strawberries; stir until sugar is dissolved.
2. Fold strawberry mixture into cream. Fold in egg whites and salt. Pour into refrigerator tray; freeze until firm.

VARIATIONS: Raspberries, bananas or other soft fruits may be substituted for strawberries in above recipe.

Sibyl F. Robinson, Women's Club, Durham, N.H.

FROZEN FRENCH PASTRY

Serves 8

½ cup butter
2 eggs
1 cup confectioners' sugar
1 teaspoon vanilla
3 cups vanilla wafer crumbs
2 cups ground pecans
¼ cup granulated sugar
2 cups heavy cream, whipped
1-pound 13-ounce can apricot halves, well drained

1. Melt butter in top of double saucepan over hot water. Stir in eggs and confectioners' sugar. Cook over hot water, stirring constantly, until mixture is smooth and has consistency of mayonnaise. Remove from heat; stir in vanilla; cool.
2. Sprinkle 2 cups of the crumbs into 10 x 6 x 1½-inch baking pan.
3. Pour egg mixture over crumbs; sprinkle with 1 cup of the pecans.
4. Blend granulated sugar and cream; spread half over pecans in pan. Arrange apricots on top. Spread remaining cream over apricots. Sprinkle with remaining pecans. Sprinkle with remaining crumbs.
5. Cover with aluminum foil; freeze until firm.

Mrs. Mary Gambill, Junior Woman's Club,
Carlsbad, N.M.

LIME FREEZE

Serves 6

1 cup finely ground graham cracker crumbs
3 tablespoons melted butter
2 eggs, separated
12-ounce can sweetened condensed milk
½ cup lime juice
1 teaspoon grated lime rind
¼ teaspoon vanilla
¼ cup sugar
3 to 4 drops green food coloring
Lime slices

1. Lightly grease refrigerator tray.
2. Combine crumbs and butter; reserve ¼ cup. Press remaining crumbs onto bottom and sides of tray. Chill.
3. Beat egg yolks until thickened; combine with milk, lime juice and rind and vanilla. Stir until thickened.
4. Beat egg whites until soft peaks form. Gradually beat in sugar; beat until thickened and glossy; fold with food coloring into lime mixture. Pour into tray.
5. Border with reserved crumbs; decorate with lime slices. Freeze until firm.

Phyllis Bradford, El Camino Women's Club,
Ventura, Calif.

CRÈME DE MENTHE PIE
Makes 9-Inch Pie

9-inch Baked Chocolate Crumb
   Crust (p. 551)
24 marshmallows
⅔ cup milk
¼ cup crème de menthe
1 cup heavy cream, whipped
   Shaved chocolate or crushed nuts
   and whipped cream (optional)

1. Prepare Baked Chocolate Crumb Crust.
2. In saucepan combine marshmallows and milk. Stir over low heat until marshmallows are melted. Cool.
3. Fold in crème de menthe and cream. Pour into crumb crust; freeze until firm.
4. Remove from freezer 20 minutes before serving. If desired, garnish with chocolate or nuts; serve with whipped cream.

Mrs. Robert Viel, Junior Woman's Club,
Wauwatosa, Wis.

FRANGO MINT DESSERT
Serves 12 to 18

1 cup butter
2 cups confectioners' sugar
   (sift if lumpy)
4 1-ounce squares unsweetened
   chocolate, melted
4 eggs lightly beaten
¾ teaspoon peppermint extract
2 teaspoons vanilla
1 cup vanilla wafer crumbs
¾ cup toasted flaked coconut

1. Cream butter and sugar in mixing bowl until light and fluffy. Stir in chocolate. Blend in eggs, peppermint extract and vanilla.
2. Sprinkle crumbs into 12 to 18 paper cup liners (depending on size). Pour chocolate mixture over crumbs; freeze until firm.
3. Just before serving, sprinkle coconut on top.

Mrs. J. A. Fosland, Woman's Club, Scobey, Mont.

FROZEN PINEAPPLE DESSERT
Serves 6

¼ cup butter
1 cup sugar
2 eggs, separated
1 cup drained crushed pineapple
1 cup heavy cream, whipped
1 teaspoon vanilla
12 vanilla wafers, crumbed

1. Cream butter and sugar until light and fluffy. Beat in egg yolks. Fold in pineapple.
2. Beat egg whites until stiff but not dry; fold whipped cream and vanilla into pineapple mixture.
3. Sprinkle refrigerator tray with half the crumbs. Spread cream mixture over crumbs; top with remaining crumbs. Freeze until firm.

Helen Burke, Longvue Women's Club,
Pittsburgh, Pa.

FROZEN PUMPKIN PIE
Makes 9-Inch Pie

18 gingersnaps
1½ cups sugar
¼ cup melted butter or margarine
1 quart vanilla ice cream
1 cup mashed cooked pumpkin
½ teaspoon salt
½ teaspoon ground cloves
1 teaspoon ginger
1 teaspoon cinnamon
½ cup heavy cream, whipped
½ cup chopped walnuts

1. Crush gingersnaps; combine with ½ cup of the sugar and butter or margarine. Press onto bottom and sides of 9-inch pie plate; chill for 15 minutes.
2. Turn ice cream into mixing bowl; stirring until smooth. Spread on crumb crust; freeze until firm.
3. In mixing bowl blend pumpkin, remaining sugar, salt and spices. Fold in cream; spread on ice cream. Freeze until firm.
4. Just before serving, sprinkle with walnuts.

Mrs. Ellsworth B. Mink, President,
Junior Woman's Club, Fort Lauderdale, Fla.

MILE-HIGH STRAWBERRY PIE
Makes 9-Inch Pie

9-inch Graham Cracker Crumb
   Crust (p. 551)
10-ounce package frozen strawberries,
   defrosted
1 cup sugar
2 egg whites
1 tablespoon lemon juice
   Dash of salt
½ cup heavy cream, whipped
1 teaspoon vanilla

1. Prepare Graham Cracker Crumb Crust.
2. In mixing bowl combine strawberries, sugar, egg whites, lemon juice and salt. Beat for 15 minutes, or until stiff.
3. Fold in cream and vanilla; pile into crumb crust. Freeze until firm.

Elta Dorris, Tuesday Literary Club,
Bolivar, Tenn.

FROSTY STRAWBERRY SQUARES
Serves 10 to 12

1 cup presifted flour
¼ cup brown sugar
½ cup chopped walnuts
½ cup melted butter or margarine
2 egg whites
1 cup granulated sugar
2 cups sliced strawberries
2 tablespoons lemon juice
1 cup heavy cream, whipped
   Whole strawberries (optional)

1. Preheat oven to 350° F.
2. In mixing bowl combine flour, brown sugar and walnuts. Stir in butter or margarine; sprinkle onto baking sheet. Bake crumbs in preheated oven for 20 minutes, stirring occasionally.

3. Sprinkle two-thirds of crumbs into 13 x 9½ x 2-inch baking pan.

4. In mixing bowl combine egg whites, granulated sugar, sliced strawberries and lemon juice. Beat vigorously for 10 minutes, or until stiff peaks form.

5. Fold in cream; pour over crumbs in pan. Sprinkle with remaining crumbs.

6. Cover with aluminum foil; freeze for 6 hours or overnight.

7. Cut into squares; serve topped with whole strawberries, if desired.

Mrs. Thomas K. Vickers, Junior Sorosis, Orlando, Fla.

BAKED ALASKA

Serves 8 to 10

9-inch square layer cake
1 quart brick vanilla ice cream
4 egg whites
¼ teaspoon cream of tartar
½ cup sugar

1. Preheat oven to 475° F. Line baking sheet or wooden board with brown paper.

2. Place cake in center of paper; top with ice cream, spreading to within 1 inch of edges. Set aside in freezer.

3. Put egg whites in mixing bowl; add cream of tartar; beat until foamy. Gradually add sugar; beat until meringue is stiff and glossy.

4. Quickly spread meringue over ice cream and cake, sealing well.

5. Bake in preheated oven for 5 minutes, or until slightly browned. Serve at once.

Pat Deason, Paramount Junior Woman's Club, Bellflower, Calif.

RAISIN ICE CREAM ALASKA

Makes 9-Inch Pie

9-inch Graham Cracker Crumb
   Crust (p. 551)
1 pint vanilla ice cream
¼ cup butter or margarine
1 cup brown sugar
1 cup seedless raisins
½ cup light cream
3 egg whites
¾ cup granulated sugar

1. Prepare Graham Cracker Crumb Crust.

2. Soften ice cream slightly; spread on crumb crust. Freeze for 3 to 4 hours, or until firm.

3. Melt butter or margarine in saucepan. Stir in brown sugar; simmer for 5 minutes. Remove from heat; stir in raisins and cream. Cook, stirring constantly, for 1 minute. Cool.

4. Just before serving, preheat oven to 400° F.

5. In mixing bowl beat egg whites until foamy. Gradually add granulated sugar; beat until meringue is stiff and glossy.

6. Spread raisin mixture on ice cream; cover completely with meringue, sealing well.

7. Bake in preheated oven for 5 minutes. Serve at once.

Mrs. Glenn Thorne, Delphian Club, Pendleton, Ore.

CHERRIES JUBILEE

Serves 6

1-pound can Bing cherries
2 teaspoons cornstarch
2 tablespoons water
¼ cup kirschwasser
1 quart vanilla ice cream

1. Drain cherries. Pour syrup into chafing dish; bring to boil.

2. Blend cornstarch and water to make a paste; stir into syrup. Stir constantly until sauce is thickened and clear.

3. Add cherries; simmer for 2 minutes.

4. Sprinkle kirschwasser over sauce; flame. Serve at once on ice cream.

Chris Notopoulos, Junior Woman's Club, Altoona, Pa.

WASHINGTON CHERRY ICE CREAM PIE

Makes 9-Inch Pie

9-inch baked pie shell
1 quart vanilla ice cream
1-pound can red cherries
2 tablespoons cornstrach
½ teaspoon salt
½ cup sugar
1 tablespoon lemon juice
   Few drops red food coloring
1 cup heavy cream, whipped

1. Prepare pie shell.

2. Turn ice cream into mixing bowl; stir until softened and smooth. Spread in pie shell; freeze for 2 hours, or until firm.

3. Drain cherries; reserve syrup.

4. In small saucepan combine cornstarch, salt and sugar. Gradually stir in reserved syrup; cook over low heat, stirring constantly, until thickened and clear.

5. Remove from heat; stir in lemon juice, food coloring and cherries. Cool.

6. Just before serving, spoon cherry mixture onto ice cream; top with whipped cream.

Mrs. William Buchanan, Junior Women's Civic Club, Indiana, Pa.

FROZEN CHOCOLATE SUNDAES

Serves 12

12-ounce package vanilla wafers,
   crumbed
½ cup butter or margarine
2 1-ounce squares unsweetened
   chocolate
2 cups sifted confectioners' sugar
3 eggs, separated
1 teaspoon vanilla
⅛ teaspoon salt
1 cup chopped pecans
½ gallon vanilla ice cream, slightly
   softened

1. Lightly grease 10-inch loaf pan.

2. Spread half the crumbs in pan.

3. In top of double saucepan combine butter or margarine and chocolate; cook over hot water until melted.

4. Remove from heat; beat in sugar. Add egg yolks, one at a time, beating well after each addition. Stir in vanilla and salt.

5. In mixing bowl beat egg whites until stiff but not dry; fold into chocolate mixture.

6. Pour over crumbs in pan. Top with layer of pecans. Spread ice cream on pecans. Sprinkle with remaining crumbs.

7. Cover; freeze until firm. Unmold; cut into slices to serve.

Mrs. Ted Rotenberger, Woman's Club,
Canby, Minn.

SWEET CHOCOLATE ICE CREAM CUPS

Serves 12

12-ounce package semi-sweet chocolate
    pieces
¼ cup butter
    Peppermint or other preferred
    flavor ice cream

1. Cook chocolate and butter in top of double saucepan over hot water until smooth.

2. Coat insides of 12 paper cup liners with chocolate mixture; refrigerate until firm.

3. Apply second coat of chocolate; refrigerate until firm.

4. Carefully peel off liners; refrigerate until needed.

5. At serving time, fill chocolate cups with ice cream.

Mrs. George Wessendorf, Women's Club,
Nemaha, Ia.

ICE CREAM COCONUT BALLS

Serves 8

1 cup flaked coconut
1 cup slivered almonds
    Dash of salt
1 tablespoon melted butter
1 tablespoon cooking oil
1 quart vanilla ice cream
    Maple Butterscotch Sauce (p. 700)

1. Preheat oven to 325° F. Line baking sheet with aluminum foil.

2. In mixing bowl combine coconut, almonds, salt, butter and oil; mix well. Sprinkle on baking sheet; bake in preheated oven for about 10 minutes, stirring occasionally, or until golden.

3. Meanwhile, make large scoops of ice cream into balls; roll in coconut mixture; place on waxed paper. Freeze until serving time.

4. Serve topped with Maple Butterscotch Sauce.

American Home Department, Woman's Club,
Middletown, N.J.

ICE CREAM PIE

Makes 9-Inch Pie

2 1-ounce squares unsweetened
    chocolate
2 tablespoons butter or margarine

¾ cup confectioners' sugar
    (sift if lumpy)
¾ cup flaked coconut
2 tablespoons boiling water
1 quart mint-flavored or other
    preferred flavor of ice cream
1 cup heavy cream, whipped

1. Grease 9-inch pie plate well.

2. In top of double saucepan melt chocolate and butter or margarine.

3. Remove from heat; stir in sugar, coconut and water; mix well. Spread on bottom and sides of pie plate. Chill for 30 minutes.

4. Soften ice cream slightly; spread on pie shell. Freeze until firm.

5. At serving time, spread whipped cream over ice cream.

Mrs. William Waterhouse, Contemporary Club,
Salem, N.H.

PUMPKIN ICE CREAM PIE

Makes 9-Inch Pie

9-inch Graham Cracker Crumb
    Crust (p. 551)
¾ cup mashed cooked pumpkin
¼ cup brown sugar
½ teaspoon cinnamon
¼ teaspoon nutmeg
½ teaspoon ginger
¼ teaspoon ground cloves
¼ teaspoon salt
⅓ cup finely chopped pecans
1 quart vanilla ice cream, softened

1. Prepare Graham Cracker Crumb Crust.

2. In mixing bowl combine all remaining ingredients except ice cream; mix well.

3. Stir in ice cream; mix until blended and smooth.

4. Pour into crumb crust; freeze until firm.

Jo Brookman, Current Literature Club,
Burkburnett, Tex.

JEWELED SHERBET MOLD

Serves 12 to 14

1 pint lime sherbet, softened
1 pint lemon sherbet
9-ounce can crushed pineapple,
    drained
⅓ cup chopped candied fruits
2 tablespoons dark rum
    Whipped cream
    Maraschino cherries

1. Line bottom and sides of 5-cup mold with lime sherbet. Freeze for 15 minutes, or until hardened.

2. Soften lemon sherbet; mix with pineapple, fruits and rum. Pack into center of mold. Freeze until firm.

3. Turn onto chilled plate; decorate with whipped cream and cherries. Freeze until serving time.

Mrs. Don Clothier, Junior Woman's Club,
Diamond Bar, Calif.

FROZEN RAINBOW DELIGHT
Serves 10 to 12

    2 cups heavy cream
    1 teaspoon vanilla
    2 tablespoons sugar
    18 coconut macaroons, crushed
    1 pint orange sherbet
    1 pint lime sherbet
    1 pint raspberry sherbet

1. In mixing bowl whip cream until stiff. Fold in vanilla, sugar and macaroons.
2. Spoon half the mixture into 13 x 9½ x 2-inch baking pan. Cover with alternate small spoonfuls of orange, lime and raspberry sherbet, so that some of each color will be in each serving.
3. Top with remaining whipped cream mixture. Freeze until firm.

Mrs. Ruth Kittleson, Woman's Club, Canby, Minn.

STRAWBERRY ICE CREAM PIE
Makes 9-Inch Pie

    3½-ounce can flaked coconut
    1 quart vanilla ice cream
    1½ cups sliced strawberries
    ½ cup sugar

1. Preheat oven to 350° F. Grease 9-inch pie plate well. Line baking sheet with aluminum foil.
2. Spread coconut on foil; bake in preheated oven, stirring frequently, for 10 minutes, or until golden. Cool; press into bottom and sides of pie plate.
3. Stir ice cream until slightly softened; spoon into coconut-lined plate. Smooth top; freeze until firm.
4. In mixing bowl combine strawberries and sugar. Just before serving, spoon over ice cream.

Mrs. L. D. Gerlach, Library Club, Robbinsdale, Minn.

WALNUT ICE CREAM ROLL
Serves 8 to 12

    4 eggs, separated
    ½ teaspoon salt
    1 teaspoon vanilla
    ½ cup sugar
    ¼ cup sifted cake flour
    ½ cup finely chopped walnuts
    1 pint vanilla ice cream

1. Preheat oven to 375° F. Grease 15½ x 10½ x 1-inch jelly roll pan. Line bottom and sides with waxed paper; grease again.
2. In mixing bowl combine egg whites, salt and vanilla; beat until soft peaks form. Gradually add sugar; beat until stiff and glossy.
3. In small bowl beat egg yolks until thickened and lemon-colored. Fold into egg white mixture. Carefully fold in flour and walnuts. Spread evenly in pan.
4. Bake in preheated oven for 12 to 15 minutes.
5. Loosen paper; invert cake onto clean cloth; carefully remove paper from bottom. Roll up cake along with towel; cool on wire rack. Meanwhile, let ice cream soften slightly.

6. Unroll cake; remove towel; spread ice cream in center. Reroll cake; freeze.

Mrs. Bob Bryant, Jr., Woman's Club, Worland, Wyo.

Fruit Desserts

ORANGE BAKED APPLES
Serves 4

    4 large baking apples
    ½ cup seedless raisins
    2 tablespoons flour
    ⅓ cup sugar
    ½ teaspoon cinnamon
    2 tablespoons softened butter
    ⅓ cup orange juice
    ⅓ cup water

1. Preheat oven to 350° F.
2. Core but do not peel apples; put in 8-inch square baking pan. Fill centers with raisins.
3. In small bowl blend flour, sugar and cinnamon. Add butter; beat until blended; spread over apples.
4. Pour orange juice and water into pan.
5. Bake in preheated oven for 1 hour and 15 minutes, basting frequently with pan liquid.

Betty Ann Chesser, Women's Club, Yorkewood, Md.

BUTTERSCOTCH APPLES
Serves 6

    8 apples
    ¼ cup presifted flour
    ⅓ cup brown sugar
    ¼ cup granulated sugar
    ¼ cup butter
    1 teaspoon vanilla
    1 cup water

1. Preheat oven to 350° F. Grease 10 x 6 x 1½-inch baking pan.
2. Peel, core and quarter apples; arrange in pan.
3. In mixing bowl blend flour and sugars. Cut in butter until mixture resembles coarse crumbs. Add vanilla and water; mix well.
4. Spread on top of apples; cover with aluminum foil.
5. Bake in preheated oven for 1 hour.

Mrs. Noah Lehmer, County Club, Chelan, Wash.

BUTTERSCOTCH APPLE PUDDING
Serves 10

    ½ cup butter or margarine
    1½ cups brown sugar
    1⅜ cups presifted flour
    Salt
    3 cups water
    3 cups chopped peeled apples
    2 tablespoons lemon juice
    1½ teaspoons baking powder
    ½ teaspoon cinnamon
    1 egg, lightly beaten
    ¼ cup milk
    2 tablespoons melted shortening
    Cream (optional)

1. Melt butter or margarine in large skillet or kettle with cover. Stir in 1 cup of the brown sugar, ⅜ cup of the flour and ⅛ teaspoon salt. Gradually stir in water; cook, stirring constantly, until thickened and smooth.

2. Add apples and lemon juice; mix well. Remove from heat.

3. In mixing bowl combine remaining flour, baking powder, ½ teaspoon salt and cinnamon. Stir in remaining brown sugar.

4. Combine egg, milk and shortening. Add to flour mixture; stir until dry ingredients are moistened.

5. Drop batter by spoons into applesauce mixture.

6. Bring pan to boil over high heat; cover; simmer for 20 minutes. Serve warm with cream, if desired.

Geneva Masterson, El Camino Women's Club, Ventura, Calif.

BAKED GRAPEFRUIT

Serves 4

2 medium grapefruits
¾ cup brown sugar
½ teaspoon cinnamon
2 tablespoons butter or margarine

1. Preheat oven to 425° F.

2. Cut grapefruits in half. Discard seeds and membranes. Arrange, cut side up, on baking sheet.

3. In small bowl blend sugar and cinnamon; sprinkle over grapefruits. Dot with butter or margarine.

4. Bake in preheated oven for 10 minutes. Serve at once.

Mrs. Lon Rogers, Woman's Club, Greenville, Ky.

HUCKLEBERRY PUDDING

Serves 8

12 slices white bread
1 quart huckleberries, stewed
Whipped cream

1. 48 hours before, discard crusts from bread; line 2-quart glass baking dish with layer bread. Pour in layer of huckleberries. Repeat, finishing with layer of berries.

2. Refrigerate for 48 hours.

3. When ready to use, serve with whipped cream.

Submitted to Woman's Club, Kankakee, Ill., by Mrs. Franklin D. Roosevelt

STEWED GOOSEBERRIES

Serves 6 to 8

1 quart gooseberries
½ cup water
2 cups sugar
Old-Fashioned "Boiled" Custard (p. 676)

1. Discard tops and tails of gooseberries; wash.

2. In large skillet mix water and sugar; cook over low heat, stirring occasionally, until sugar is dissolved.

3. Bring syrup to boil; stir in gooseberries. Cover; simmer for 5 minutes, or until tender.

4. Serve hot or cold with Old-Fashioned "Boiled" Custard.

Mrs. J. F. Roche, Neighborly Club, Norfolk, Mass.

BAKED SPICED PEACHES

Serves 4

1-pound 13-ounce can peach halves
¼ cup brown sugar
½ teaspoon cinnamon
¼ teaspoon nutmeg
¼ cup crushed cornflakes
2 tablespoons finely chopped pecans
2 tablespoons melted butter or margarine
Whipped cream or ice cream

1. Preheat oven to 350° F. Grease 4 individual casseroles.

2. Drain peaches; reserve ¼ cup syrup.

3. Arrange peaches, cut side up, in casseroles.

4. In small bowl blend reserved syrup, sugar, cinnamon and nutmeg. Pour over peaches.

5. Bake in preheated oven for 10 minutes. Turn temperature to 400° F.

6. Blend cornflakes, pecans and butter or margarine; sprinkle on peaches. Bake for 5 minutes longer.

7. Serve warm with whipped cream or ice cream.

Bywood Junior Women's Club, Upper Darby, Pa.

PEACH MELBA

Serves 6

2 cups fresh raspberries or 10-ounce package frozen raspberries, defrosted
½ cup currant jelly
1 teaspoon cornstarch
1 tablespoon water
6 cooked fresh or canned peach halves
1 quart vanilla ice cream

1. Prepare Melba Sauce: In saucepan heat raspberries and jelly until jelly is dissolved and mixture is boiling. Put through sieve to remove seeds; return to heat. Dissolve cornstarch in water. Add to raspberry puree; cook for 2 minutes, stirring constantly. Remove from heat; cool.

2. For each serving place peach, hollow side up, on individual serving dish. Fill hollow with large scoop of ice cream. Serve with Melba Sauce.

A. S.

PEAR ORANGE BAKE

Serves 8

½ cup sugar
¼ cup orange juice
¼ cup water
4 pears, peeled, cored and halved
1½ teaspoons grated orange rind
Vanilla ice cream

1. In saucepan stir sugar, orange juice and water. Bring to boil; add pears. Cover; simmer for 15 minutes, or until tender.

2. Remove pears; set aside. Add orange rind to syrup remaining in pan; simmer for 5 minutes.

3. Arrange pears in shallow dish; cover with syrup. Chill.

4. Put ice cream in pears; top with orange syrup.

*Lorraine Hertema, Vienna and Beaman
Woman's Club, Beaman, Ia.*

PEPPERMINT PEARS

Serves 6

6 peppermint stick candies, crushed
1 cup boiling water
½ cup light corn syrup
1 tablespoon lemon juice
6 pears, peeled, cored and quartered
Ice cream

1. Put candies in large skillet. Add water; cook over low heat, stirring constantly, until dissolved.

2. Add corn syrup and lemon juice; simmer over medium heat for 3 minutes. Add pears; cover; simmer over low heat for 10 minutes, or until tender.

3. Cool; serve on ice cream or as desired.

*Mrs. Will C. Johnson, Sr., Woman's Club,
Nettleton, Miss.*

BAKED PINEAPPLE

Serves 4

1-pound 4-ounce can crushed
 pineapple, undrained
½ cup sugar
2 tablespoons cornstarch
2 eggs
1 tablespoon melted butter
½ teaspoon cinnamon

1. Preheat oven to 350° F. Grease 1-quart casserole.

2. Turn pineapple into mixing bowl. Sprinkle with sugar and cornstarch. Add remaining ingredients; mix well; turn into casserole.

3. Bake in preheated oven for 25 minutes, or until thickened.

*Mrs. Frank McNees, Hickory Township
Women's Club, Sharon, Pa.*

PINEAPPLE CHANTILLY

Serves 6

1½ cups pineapple juice
1 cup water
¼ cup quick-cooking tapioca
½ cup sugar
1 teaspoon salt
2 tablespoons lemon juice
13½-ounce can crushed pineapple,
 undrained
1 cup heavy cream, whipped
Maraschino cherries

1. In saucepan combine pineapple juice, water, tapioca, sugar and salt. Bring to boil. Stir constantly over medium heat until tapioca is cooked.

2. Stir in lemon juice and pineapple. Refrigerate.

3. 2 hours before serving, fold cream into pineapple mixture. Chill. Serve decorated with cherries.

Nancy Lilly, Woman's Club, Canterbury, N.H.

NORWEGIAN PRUNE PUDDING

Serves 6 to 8

1 pound prunes
2½ tablespoons flour
1½ tablespoons lemon juice
1 cup sugar
½ cup chopped walnuts
Whipped cream

1. Put prunes in saucepan; cover with water. Bring to boil; cover; simmer for 20 minutes, or until tender.

2. Drain prunes; add water to liquid to total 2 cups; reserve.

3. Discard prune pits; return prunes and reserved liquid to saucepan.

4. In small bowl blend flour and lemon juice to a smooth paste. Stir into saucepan. Add sugar; cook over medium heat, stirring constantly, until thickened and smooth.

5. Remove from heat; stir in walnuts. Turn into serving dish; chill.

6. Serve topped with whipped cream.

*Mrs. Walter C. Kaufmann, Vienna and Beaman
Woman's Club, Beaman, Ia.*

SEVEN-MINUTE PRUNE WHIP

Serves 4 to 6

3 egg whites
1 teaspoon grated lemon rind
2 tablespoons lemon juice
½ cup sugar
3 tablespoons prune juice
Dash of salt
½ cup chopped cooked prunes
Custard Sauce (p. 676)

1. Combine all ingredients except prunes and Custard Sauce in top of double saucepan. Place over boiling water; beat with whisk or beater, for 5 to 7 minutes, or until stiff peaks form.

2. Remove from heat; fold in prunes. Turn into serving dish; chill.

3. Serve with Custard Sauce.

*Mrs. Robert Macfarlane, Woman's Club,
Charleston, W. Va.*

Meringue Desserts

AMERICAN MERINGUE DESSERT

Serves 6

2 cups sugar
2 teaspoons water
8 eggs, separated
2 cups milk
Dash of salt
2 tablespoons vanilla

1. Preheat oven to 350° F.

2. Into top of double saucepan combine 1 cup of the sugar and water. Cook over low heat, stirring only until sugar is dissolved. Cook until golden and caramelized.

3. Pour into 2-quart fluted mold. Turn and tip mold to coat bottom and sides well.

4. Stir egg yolks into any caramel remaining in saucepan. Add milk and ½ cup

of the sugar; stir over hot water until caramel melts and is blended into milk. Add salt and 1 tablespoon of the vanilla; cook over hot water, stirring constantly, until thickened and smooth. Cool.

5. Beat egg whites until foamy. Gradually beat in remaining sugar; beat until stiff and glossy. Stir in remaining vanilla; turn into caramel-lined mold.

6. Set mold in pan of hot water; bake in preheated oven for 20 minutes, or until light brown.

7. Remove mold from pan; cool.

8. Pour custard into deep serving dish; unmold caramel-coated meringue in center.

Lilian T. de Canels, President,
Puerto Rico Federation of Women's Clubs

MERINGUE GLACÉE

Makes 12

4 egg whites
1 cup sugar
1 teaspoon vinegar
1 teaspoon vanilla
Whipped cream or ice cream

1. Preheat oven to 275° F. Line baking sheet with brown paper; grease the paper.

2. In mixing bowl beat egg whites until foamy. Gradually beat in sugar; beat until very stiff and glossy. Fold in vinegar and vanilla.

3. Drop by tablespoons onto baking sheet.

4. Bake in preheated oven for 1½ hours.

5. Carefully remove meringues from paper, using spatula; cool on wire rack.

6. Sandwich together with whipped cream or ice cream, as desired.

Mrs. Emma Zind, Woman's Fortnightly
Reading Club, Cincinnati, Ohio

KISS TORTE

Serves 6

4 egg whites
1 cup sugar
1 teaspoon vanilla
1 teaspoon vinegar
3 cups diced mixed fruits
1 cup heavy cream, whipped

1. Day before, preheat oven to 300° F. Grease 10 x 6 x 1½-inch baking pan well.

2. In mixing bowl beat egg whites until foamy. Gradually add sugar; beat until stiff and glossy. Fold in vanilla and vinegar. Spread in pan.

3. Bake in preheated oven for 1 hour.

4. Turn off heat; keep pan in oven for 15 minutes.

5. Cool overnight. It will fall as it cools.

6. Next day, just before serving, top with fruits; garnish with whipped cream.

Babs Ross, Cadmean Club, Fort Worth, Tex.

LEMON MERINGUE SHELLS

Serves 6

3 egg whites
¼ teaspoon cream of tartar
Dash of salt
½ cup sugar
½ teaspoon lemon extract
Lemon Filling (p. 631)

1. Preheat oven to 200° F. Line baking sheet with brown paper; grease the paper.

2. Put egg whites, cream of tartar and salt in mixing bowl; beat until foamy. Gradually add sugar; beat until stiff and glossy. Fold in lemon extract.

3. Spoon onto baking sheet, forming into 6 mounds; with back of spoon, round out centers to form cup in each.

4. Bake in preheated oven for 1 hour, or until shells leave paper easily.

5. Carefully remove shells from paper; cool on wire rack.

6. Just before serving, fill with Lemon Filling.

Mrs. R. T. Smith, Woman's Culture Club,
Post, Tex.

Dessert Pancakes and Fritters

FRENCH DESSERT PANCAKES (CRÊPES)

Makes 24

1⅛ cups presifted flour
¼ cup granulated sugar
Dash of salt
3 eggs, lightly beaten
1½ cups milk
1 tablespoon melted butter
Butter
Jelly
Confectioners' sugar

1. Into mixing bowl sift together flour, granulated sugar and salt.

2. Combine eggs and milk; add to flour mixture. Beat until smooth. Stir in butter. Batter should just coat spoon.

3. Put ½ teaspoon butter in 5-to 6-inch skillet. Swirl pan over high heat, to coat sides and bottom. Pour in about 2 tablespoons of the batter; swirl pan to spread evenly. Cook for about 1 minute, or until set and browned on one side. Turn pancake; cook on other side until browned. Spread with jelly; roll up; sprinkle with confectioners' sugar; put on serving dish in warm place.

4. Repeat with remaining batter.

Barbara Culberson, Junior Alpha Club,
Lompoc, Calif.

CRÊPES SUZETTE

Serves 4

4 lumps sugar
Rind and juice of 1 orange
5 tablespoons butter
1 teaspoon lemon juice
¼ cup Curaçao or Cointreau
¼ cup Benedictine or Grand Marnier
½ cup warm brandy
12 crêpes

1. Rub lumps of sugar on orange rind until covered with aromatic oil. Crush lumps with 3 tablespoons of the butter; mix until creamy.

2. Put remaining butter in flat skillet or chafing dish. Add orange and lemon juice and liqueurs. Bring to boil. Stir in sugar mixture.

3. Place crêpes, one by one, in sauce. Spoon sauce over them so that they are moistened on both sides. Fold into quarters.

4. Put crêpes in pan; pour brandy over them; ignite. Serve with sauce when flame burns out.

A. S.

APPLE DESSERT FRITTERS

Serves 4 to 6

    1 cup presifted flour
    1½ teaspoons baking powder
    ¼ teaspoon salt
    1 egg, lightly beaten
    ⅔ cup milk
    4 large apples
    2 tablespoons confectioners' sugar
    1 tablespoon lemon juice
    Fat for deep frying
    Mixed cinnamon and confectioners'
      sugar
    Maple syrup

1. Into mixing bowl sift together flour, baking powder and salt. Add egg and milk; beat until smooth.

2. Peel and slice apples. Sprinkle with sugar and lemon juice.

3. Dip apples in batter, coating completely.

4. Drop into deep fat heated to 365° F. Fry for 3 to 4 minutes, or until golden.

5. Drain on absorbent paper; sprinkle with cinnamon mixture. Serve at once with maple syrup.

Dorothy Wadman, Gardens Century Club,
Wilmington, Del.

PINEAPPLE FRITTERS

Serves 4

    8-ounce can crushed pineapple
    Presifted flour
    1 teaspoon baking powder
    Sugar
    Dash of salt
    1 egg
    ½ cup milk
    Fat for deep frying
    1 tablespoon butter

1. Drain pineapple; reserve syrup.

2. Prepare fritters: Into mixing bowl sift together 1 cup flour, baking powder, 1 tablespoon sugar and salt. Add egg and milk; beat until smooth. Stir in pineapple.

3. Drop batter by tablespoon into deep fat heated to 365° F. Fry for 4 to 5 minutes, or until golden.

4. Drain on absorbent paper.

5. Meanwhile, prepare Pineapple Sauce: In small saucepan blend 1 tablespoon flour and 1 cup sugar. Stir in reserved syrup and butter; cook over medium heat, stirring constantly, until thickened and smooth.

6. Serve at once with sauce.

Mary Ann Gilstrap, Junior Woman's Club,
Augusta, Ga.

ROSETTES

Makes 36

    3 eggs
    1 cup milk

    1 cup presifted flour
    1 teaspoon granulated sugar
    ¼ teaspoon salt
    Fat for deep frying
    Confectioners' sugar

1. Put eggs, milk, flour, granulated sugar and salt in mixing bowl; beat until smooth.

2. Heat fat to 365° F.

3. Dip rosette iron into batter; lower into fat; fry until golden brown.

4. Gently remove rosette with fork tines; drain on absorbent paper. When cool, roll in confectioners' sugar.

Mrs. Joseph Paulick, D. & L. Club,
Loretta, Wis.

Sweet Omelets and Soufflés

STRAWBERRY OMELET WITH SOUR CREAM

Serves 2

    3 eggs
    1 tablespoon light cream
    ¼ teaspoon salt
    2 tablespoons butter
    ¼ cup sour cream
    ½ cup sliced strawberries
    Confectioners' sugar

1. In mixing bowl beat eggs until frothy. Add cream and salt; beat with fork for 30 seconds.

2. Melt butter in 10-inch skillet; when butter starts to brown, pour in eggs. Stir once or twice with fork. Lift edges as eggs begin to cook. Shake back and forth to keep omelet free.

3. When eggs are cooked but soft, add ⅛ cup of the sour cream and ¼ cup of the strawberries. Fold and slide omelet onto heated serving dish.

4. Top with remaining sour cream and strawberries; sprinkle with sugar.

Mrs. T. J. Holleran, Churchill Manor
Women's Club, Penn Hills, Pa.

OMELETTE SOUFFLÉ

Serves 2

    Sugar
    2 egg yolks
    Dash of salt
    1 teaspoon vanilla
    3 egg whites

1. Preheat oven to 450° F. Grease oval ovenware omelet pan well; sprinkle with sugar.

2. In mixing bowl combine egg yolks, ⅓ cup sugar, salt and vanilla; beat until thickened and lemon-colored.

3. In another mixing bowl beat egg whites until stiff but not dry; fold into egg yolk mixture. Turn into pan.

4. Bake in preheated oven for 15 minutes, until light brown and set.

Jean Serra, Junior Woman's Club,
Scotch Plains, N.J.

CHOCOLATE SOUFFLÉ WITH SAUCE

Serves 4

¼ cup melted butter
¼ cup presifted flour
¼ teaspoon salt
2 1-ounce squares unsweetened chocolate, chopped
¾ cup milk
3 eggs, separated
½ cup sugar
1 teaspoon vanilla
¼ teaspoon cream of tartar
3-ounce package vanilla pudding mix
1 cup heavy cream, whipped

1. In saucepan combine butter and flour. Add salt and chocolate. Gradually stir in milk; cook, stirring constantly, until thickened and smooth. Remove from heat.
2. Preheat oven to 350° F.
3. Beat egg yolks, sugar and vanilla until thickened and pale. Add to chocolate mixture; mix well.
4. Beat egg whites and cream of tartar until stiff but not dry; fold into chocolate mixture.
5. Turn into 1½-quart casserole; set in shallow pan containing 1 inch of hot water.
6. Bake in preheated oven for 45 minutes.
7. Meanwhile, make pudding according to package directions; fold in cream. Serve on soufflé.

Joan Schoone, Junior Woman's Club, Racine, Wis.

SOUFFLÉ GRAND MARNIER

Serves 6

⅓ cup presifted flour
½ cup sugar
½ cup milk
1 tablespoon butter
3 egg yolks
¼ cup Grand Marnier
6 egg whites

1. Preheat oven to 350° F.
2. In saucepan combine flour and sugar. Gradually stir in milk; cook over medium heat, stirring constantly, until thickened and smooth.
3. Remove from heat; beat in butter and egg yolks. Stir in Grand Marnier.
4. In mixing bowl beat egg whites until stiff but not dry; fold into egg yolk mixture. Turn into 1-quart soufflé dish.

5. Bake in preheated oven for 20 minutes. Turn temperature to 400° F. Bake for 10 to 15 minutes longer.

Faith Allen, Pine Ridge Woman's Club, Fairfax, Va.

ORANGE MARMALADE SOUFFLÉ

Serves 6

This sauce may be made ahead of time and reheated just before serving.

4 eggs, separated
¾ cup sugar
Dash of salt
¼ cup orange marmalade
1 tablespoon cornstarch
1 cup milk
1 cup orange juice
1 tablespoon grated orange rind
1 orange, sliced

1. Grease top of double saucepan well.
2. Beat egg whites until foamy; gradually beat in ¼ cup of the sugar and salt; beat until stiff and glossy. Fold in marmalade; turn into saucepan. Cover; steam over hot water for 50 minutes.
3. Meanwhile, prepare sauce: In top of another double saucepan blend remaining sugar and cornstarch. Stir in egg yolks, milk and orange juice and rind. Cook over hot water, stirring constantly, until sauce is thickened and smooth.
4. Unmold soufflé onto serving dish; surround with orange slices; serve with sauce.

Mrs. W. M. Arnstein, Woman's Club, Albany, N.Y.

WALNUT PRUNE SOUFFLÉ

Serves 4

3 egg whites
Dash of salt
½ cup sugar
1 cup prune purée
½ teaspoon cinnamon
½ teaspoon vanilla
⅔ cup chopped walnuts
Whipped cream

1. Preheat oven to 350° F. Grease 1½-quart soufflé dish.
2. Beat egg whites and salt until stiff but not dry. Gradually beat in sugar; beat until stiff and glossy.
3. Carefully fold in prune purée, cinnamon, vanilla and walnuts.
4. Turn into soufflé dish; bake in preheated oven for 25 minutes.
5. Serve at once with whipped cream.

Jeannette Cochnower, Mount Washington Women's Club, Cincinnati, Ohio

23. Dessert Sauces

BRANDY SAUCE
Makes 2 Cups
Serve on Bread Pudding (p. 667) or as desired.

1 egg
½ cup confectioners' sugar
1 cup heavy cream
¼ cup brandy

1. Beat egg and sugar until thickened and pale.
2. Whip cream; fold in brandy. Combine egg and whipped cream mixtures.

Woman's Club, Plainville, Conn.

BUTTER SAUCE
Makes About 2 Cups
Serve with Steamed Cranberry Molasses Pudding (p. 670) or as desired.

1 cup sugar
½ cup butter
1 cup heavy cream
Dash of salt
2 egg yolks
1 teaspoon vanilla

1. In top of double saucepan blend ½ cup of the sugar, butter, cream and salt.
2. In mixing bowl beat remaining sugar and egg yolks until thickened and lemon-colored; stir into sugar mixture. Cook over hot water, stirring constantly, until thickened and smooth.
3. Remove from heat; stir in vanilla.

Mrs. C. K. Brainerd, Woman's Club,
Durand, Wis.

WHIPPED BUTTER
Makes About 2 Cups
Serve with Oven French Toast (p. 167) or pancakes, as desired.

1 cup butter
1 cup sugar
½ cup ground almonds
2 tablespoons grated orange rind
¼ cup brandy
1 tablespoon orange juice

1. Cream butter in mixing bowl until soft. Add sugar; cream until light and fluffy.
2. Add remaining ingredients; beat until smooth.

Doris Miser, Woman's Club, Sunland, Calif.

BUTTERSCOTCH SAUCE
Makes About 3 Cups
1¼ cups brown sugar
⅔ cup light corn syrup
¼ cup butter or margarine
¾ cup light cream

1. In saucepan combine all ingredients except cream. Bring to boil, stirring frequently. Boil, without stirring, to soft-ball stage (236° F. on candy thermometer).
2. Remove from heat; slowly stir in cream.

Junior Woman's Club, Pacific Beach, Calif.

MAPLE BUTTERSCOTCH SAUCE
Makes About 3 Cups
Serve on ice cream or as desired.

½ cup butter or margarine
¼ cup maple syrup
1 pound brown sugar
2 tablespoons cornstarch
¼ cup heavy cream
1 teaspoon vanilla

1. Melt butter or margarine in saucepan. Add maple syrup and sugar; cook over low heat, stirring constantly, until sugar is melted.
2. Blend cornstarch and cream; stir into syrup mixture. Cook over medium heat, stirring constantly, until thickened and smooth.
3. Remove from heat; stir in vanilla.

American Home Department, Woman's Club,
Middletown, N.J.

CARAMEL NUT SAUCE
Makes About 2½ Cups
Serve with Gulah Malacca (p. 680) or vanilla ice cream, as desired.

2 cups brown sugar
1 cup light cream
1 tablespoon butter
½ cup chopped walnuts

1. In saucepan combine sugar, cream and butter. Cook over low heat, stirring constantly, until syrupy and smooth.
2. Stir in walnuts.

Pat Haughwout, Civic Club, Belleville, Pa.

CARAMEL SAUCE DE LUXE
Makes 4 Cups
Serve on Southern Caramel Cake (p. 595) or as desired.

1⅓ cups light corn syrup
⅔ cup granulated sugar
1 pound brown sugar
8 marshmallows
½ cup butter
1½ cups evaporated milk

1. In saucepan combine corn syrup and sugars. Bring to boil, stirring occasionally. Cook over medium heat to soft-ball stage (236° F. on candy thermometer).

2. Remove from heat; stir in marshmallows and butter; stir until blended and smooth. Cool.

3. Stir in milk.

Mrs. Velton Williams, Study Club, Farber, Mo.

VELVET CHOCOLATE SAUCE
Makes About 2 Cups

1 cup sugar
½ cup cocoa
2 tablespoons flour
½ teaspoon salt
1 cup boiling water or
  scalding-hot milk
1 teaspoon vanilla
1 tablespoon butter or margarine

1. In top of double saucepan combine sugar, cocoa, flour and salt. Gradually blend in water or milk. Cook over hot water, stirring constantly, until thickened and smooth.

2. Remove from heat; stir in vanilla and butter or margarine.

*Mrs. John J. Burns, Woman's Club of
Mount Washington, Baltimore, Md.*

HOT FUDGE SAUCE
Makes About 1⅓ Cups

Serve on Coffee Mousse (p. 688) or as desired.

1 cup milk
1½ 1-ounce squares unsweetened
  chocolate
1 cup sugar
2 tablespoons light corn syrup
  Dash of salt
1 teaspoon vanilla

1. In saucepan combine milk and chocolate; cook over low heat, stirring occasionally, until chocolate is melted.

2. Stir in sugar, corn syrup and salt; bring to boil over medium heat, stirring occasionally. Simmer for 5 minutes.

3. Remove from heat; stir in vanilla.

Annotawo Club, Owatonna, Minn.

RICH DARK FUDGE SAUCE
Makes About 3 Cups

Use thick for fillings or thin with a little hot water for sauce.

½ cup butter
1 pound confectioners' sugar
  (sift if lumpy)
6-ounce can evaporated milk
6 1-ounce squares unsweetened
  chocolate
1 teaspoon vanilla

1. Cook butter and sugar in top of double saucepan over boiling water, stirring constantly, until butter is melted and mixture is smooth.

2. Add milk and chocolate. Do not stir in. Cover; cook over simmering water for 30 minutes. *Do not stir.*

3. Remove from heat; add vanilla; beat.

Flora Mears, Woman's Club, Harwich Port, Mass.

WHIPPED CREAM WITH SUGAR AND FLAVORING
Makes About 2 Cups

Pinch of salt
1 cup heavy cream
1 to 2 tablespoons confectioners'
  sugar
½ teaspoon vanilla or other extract

1. Chill cream, bowl and beater.

2. Add salt to cream; beat slowly at first until cream begins to thicken. Increase beating speed; beat only until light and fluffy.

3. Stir in sugar and vanilla or other extract; chill until serving time.

FROZEN WHIPPED CREAM: Empty whipped cream into refrigerator tray; freeze. Cut into cubes to serve.

HONEY WHIPPED CREAM: Use 1 tablespoon honey in place of sugar in recipe above.

A. S.

WHIPPED CREAM SAUCE
Makes About 2 Cups

Serve at once on Steamed Chocolate Pudding (p. 669) or as desired.

2 tablespoons butter
1 cup confectioners' sugar, sifted
1 egg
  Dash of salt
1 teaspoon vanilla
1 cup heavy cream, whipped

1. In mixing bowl beat butter, sugar, egg, salt and vanilla until smooth.

2. Fold in cream.

*Mrs. Gladys S. Gonser, Women's Swope Park
Civic Club, Kansas City, Mo.*

FRUIT SAUCE
Makes About 2 Cups

Serve with Ris à la Mang (p. 682) or as desired.

1½ tablespoons cornstarch
1 cup sugar
1½ cups red fruit juice (red currants
  or raspberries)

1. In saucepan combine cornstarch and sugar. Gradually stir in fruit juice; cook over medium heat, stirring constantly, until thickened and clear.

2. Cool.

*Helen Nelson, Pine Ridge Woman's Club,
Fairfax, Va.*

HARD SAUCE

Makes About 2½ Cups

Serve with English Plum Pudding (p. 674) or mincemeat pie, as desired.

> 1 cup butter
> Dash of salt
> 1 cup granulated sugar
> 2 cups confectioners' sugar, sifted
> ¼ cup brandy

1. Cream butter and salt in mixing bowl until soft. Gradually add sugars; cream until light and fluffy.

2. Add brandy; beat until smooth. Turn into serving dish; chill until firm.

Mrs. Rodger Whittington, New Century Club, Parkside, Pa.

ICE CREAM SAUCE

Makes 2 Cups

Serve on vanilla ice cream.

> ½ cup sugar
> ½ cup water
> ¼ cup chopped maraschino cherries
> 1 cup mincemeat
> ¼ cup chopped nuts

1. In saucepan combine sugar and water. Bring to boil; boil for 5 minutes.

2. Remove from heat. Add remaining ingredients. Cool.

TO FLAME: Dip 6 sugar cubes in lemon extract; push down lightly on top of each serving; ignite.

Eleanor Brazell, Woman's Club, Sandy Springs, Ga.

LEMON SAUCE

Makes About 3 Cups

Serve with Baked Blueberry Pudding (p. 667) or as desired.

> ¾ cup sugar
> 2 tablespoons cornstarch
> ¼ teaspoon salt
> 2 cups water
> 1 egg, lightly beaten
> 1 teaspoon grated lemon rind
> 3 tablespoons lemon juice

1. In saucepan combine sugar, cornstarch and salt. Gradually stir in water. Stir in egg.

2. Cook over moderate heat, stirring constantly, until thickened, do not boil.

3. Remove from heat; stir in lemon rind and juice.

Mrs. Dexter Otis Arnold, Honorary President, General Federation of Women's Clubs, Saugerties-on-Hudson, N.Y.

LEMON PUDDING SAUCE

Makes 2 Cups

> 1 tablespoon cornstarch
> 1 cup sugar
> 2 cups boiling water
> 1 tablespoon butter
> Dash of salt
> Grated rind of 1 lemon
> Juice of ½ lemon or to taste

1. In saucepan combine cornstarch and sugar. Gradually stir in water. Add butter

and salt; cook over medium heat for 30 minutes, stirring occasionally.

2. Remove from heat; stir in lemon rind and juice.

Saundra Herre, Junior Woman's Club, Racine, Wis.

MAHOGANY SAUCE

Makes About 2 Cups

Serve hot or cold on coffee or vanilla ice cream.

> 1 cup sugar
> 1½ cups hot water
> 2 tablespoons instant coffee
> 3 tablespoons cornstarch
> 2 tablespoons cold water
> 3 tablespoons butter
> ¼ cup rum

1. Heat sugar in large skillet over medium heat, stirring constantly, until golden brown.

2. Add hot water to coffee; pour into syrup. Remove from heat.

3. Blend cornstarch and cold water; stir into syrup mixture. Return to heat; cook over medium heat, stirring constantly, until thickened and smooth.

4. Remove from heat; beat in butter and rum.

Audley Hurlbut, Beach Woman's Club, St. Petersburg, Fla.

OLD-FASHIONED MOLASSES SAUCE

Makes About 1 Cup

Good on steamed fruit puddings.

> ¼ cup molasses
> ¼ cup sugar
> 1 tablespoon flour
> ½ teaspoon salt
> ½ cup hot water
> 1 tablespoon butter
> Dash of nutmeg

1. In saucepan combine molasses, sugar, flour and salt. Stir in water; cook, stirring constantly, until thickened and smooth.

2. Remove from heat; stir in butter and nutmeg.

Sadie M. Stewart, Woman's Club, Durham, N.H.

ORANGE SAUCE

Makes About 3 Cups

Excellent on any plain cake.

> 2 tablespoons flour
> ⅔ cup sugar
> 6-ounce can frozen orange juice concentrate, defrosted
> ¾ cup water
> 1 cup heavy cream, whipped

1. In saucepan combine flour and sugar. Stir in juice concentrate and water. Cook over medium heat, stirring constantly, until thickened and smooth.

2. Refrigerate for 2 hours, stirring occasionally. Fold in cream.

Mrs. P. F. Haynes, Woman's Club, Lake Worth, Fla.

ORANGE CUSTARD SAUCE
Makes About 2 Cups

Use this on angel food cake or pound-cake.

4 egg yolks
⅓ cup orange juice
1 tablespoon grated orange rind
1 tablespoon lemon juice
1 cup sugar
1 cup heavy cream, whipped

1. Beat egg yolks in top of double saucepan.
2. Stir in orange juice and rind, lemon juice and sugar. Cook over hot water, stirring constantly, until thickened and smooth.
3. Remove from heat; cool. Fold in cream; serve at once.

Mrs. Helen Rose, Woman's Club, Ithaca, Mich.

PINEAPPLE SAUCE
Makes About 1 Cup

1 cup pineapple juice
½ cup sugar
1 teaspoon butter

1. In small saucepan blend pineapple juice and sugar. Bring to boil, stirring constantly, until sugar is dissolved. Cook over medium heat until slightly thickened.
2. Remove from heat; beat in butter.

Mrs. P. A. Whitsett, Woman's Club,
Henderson, Ky.

MELBA SAUCE FOR ICE CREAM
Makes About 2 Cups

1-pound can black raspberries
1 tablespoon cornstarch
6-ounce currant jelly
½ cup sugar
Dash of salt

1. Mix enough syrup from raspberries and cornstarch to make a thin paste. Set aside.
2. Turn raspberries and remaining syrup into saucepan; bring to boil. Strain. Add jelly, sugar and salt.
3. Stir in cornstarch mixture; cook over moderate heat, stirring constantly, for 5 to 10 minutes, or until thickened and clear.

Eleanor Rieker, Overlook Hills Women's Club,
Abington, Pa.

RASPBERRY SAUCE
Makes About 2 Cups

Serve on ice cream or cake, as desired.

2 teaspoons cornstarch
¼ cup sugar
½ cup currant jelly
10-ounce package frozen raspberries, defrosted

1. In saucepan combine cornstarch and sugar. Stir in jelly and raspberries. Cook over medium heat, stirring constantly, until thickened and clear.

2. Remove from heat; force through sieve to remove seeds.

Jane Markuson, Women's Club, Yorkewood, Md.

RASPBERRY JELLY SAUCE
Makes 3 Cups

Serve with Oslo Almond Pudding (p. 676) or vanilla ice cream, as desired.

2 tablespoons cornstarch
2 cups water
1 cup raspberry jelly

1. In saucepan mix cornstarch and ¼ cup of the water to make a smooth paste. Gradually stir in remaining water. Add jelly.
2. Cook over medium heat, stirring constantly, until thickened and smooth.

Anna Dahlstrom, Woman's Club, Sebastian, Fla.

RUM SAUCE
Makes About 2 Cups

Serve with baked puddings or on sliced poundcake, as desired.

2 egg yolks
½ cup confectioners' sugar, sifted
1 cup heavy cream, whipped
1 tablespoon dark rum

1. In mixing bowl beat egg yolks and sugar until thickened and lemon-colored.
2. Fold in cream and rum.

Myra Shaw, Mitzger Women's Club,
Portland, Ore.

HOT RUM SAUCE
Makes About 2 Cups

Serve on ice cream or poundcake, as desired.

1 cup sugar
½ cup light cream
⅓ cup melted butter
2 tablespoons dark rum

1. In saucepan blend sugar and cream. Cook over low heat, stirring constantly, until sugar is dissolved. Simmer over very low heat for 2 minutes.
2. Remove from heat; beat in butter and rum.

Mrs. Fern Brown, Study Club, Colorado City, Tex.

VANILLA SAUCE
Makes About 1½ Cups

Serve with Cranberry Pudding (p. 669) or as desired.

¾ cup butter
1 cup sugar
½ cup heavy cream
1 teaspoon vanilla

1. In top of double saucepan combine butter, sugar and cream. Cook over boiling water, stirring occasionally, until smooth.
2. Remove from heat; stir in vanilla.

Sarah Johnson, Women's Club, Tinley Park, Ill.

24. Candy

Candy is fun to make. The majority of the recipes in this chapter are easy if a few simple rules for candy making are observed.

Rules for Candy Making

1. *Choose a good day.* The cold months are best for candy making, but most candies can be made all year if the weather is cool and dry. Don't attempt to make candy on warm humid days—especially hard brittle candies, for they quickly absorb moisture from the air and become soft and sticky.
2. *Use a large saucepan.* The most important utensil for candy making is a large heavy-bottomed saucepan. All syrups boil up in the pan and can quickly boil over unless the pan is about four times larger than the quantity of ingredients used.
3. *Use a wooden spoon.* Never beat candy with a metal spoon or a rotary beater unless it is specified.
4. *Measure accurately, and don't double ingredients.* If more candy is desired than the recipe yields, make two batches rather than increase the recipe ingredients.

Cooking Syrups

A candy thermometer is a great help in determining the accurate temperature of boiling syrups. Immerse the bulb of the thermometer in the syrup, being careful to keep it from touching the bottom of the pan. If no candy thermometer is available, cold-water tests can be used, but it takes a little experience to judge the exact stage of the syrup. Always remove the boiling syrup from the heat while testing, for syrups gain quickly in temperature and change rapidly from one stage to another.

Cold-Water Tests

Soft ball: When a little syrup is dropped into very cold water, it forms a ball that flattens on removal from water.

Firm ball: When a little syrup is dropped into very cold water, it forms a ball that does not flatten on removal from water.

Hard ball: When a little syrup is dropped into very cold water, it forms a ball that is hard, yet still pliable when pressed between thumb and finger.

Soft crack: When a little syrup is dropped into very cold water, it separates into threads that are firm but not brittle.

Hard crack: When a little syrup is dropped into very cold water, it separates into hard brittle threads.

Pulling Taffy

Don't let the syrup get too cold. It should be hot to the hands. Roll the very warm syrup into a ball, and pull the ball out into a long rope with both hands. Turn the ends over into the center so that all parts will be evenly pulled. Continue to pull until the taffy becomes light and shiny. Keep the hands well greased.

Chocolate Dipping

To dip candies in chocolate, work in a cool dry room. The ideal temperature is from 60° to 65° F. Melt dipping chocolate in top of a double saucepan over simmering water. Put one candy at a time on a long-handled two-tined fork; dip into the melted chocolate; and place it on a wire rack to dry. If the chocolate becomes too thick, add boiling water to the lower part

Degrees and Stages of Boiling Syrups

Stage	Temperature Range
Thread	230° to 234° F.
Soft ball	234° to 240° F.
Firm ball	244° to 248° F.
Hard ball	250° to 265° F.
Soft crack	270° to 290° F.
Hard crack	300° to 310° F.

General Types of Candy

Fudge, penuche, creams, fondant, pralines
Caramels
Divinities, taffies, nougat
Butterscotch, toffees
Brittles, hard candies

of the saucepan. Never add water or other liquid to the chocolate itself. When the chocolate coating is dry, pack the candies in a box lined with waxed paper; cover tightly. Exposed to air for any length of time, chocolate becomes dull and milky.

Coloring Sugar

Pour sugar onto a piece of waxed paper, and sprinkle it with a few drops of the desired food coloring. Lift up the sugar, and rub it between the hands until the color is evenly distributed. Sprinkle it onto waxed-paper-lined baking sheet, and dry it in a slow (275° F.) oven, rubbing it through the hands occasionally to separate the crystals. Store in tightly covered container; use as desired.

Candied Fruit

CANDIED FRUIT

1 lemon, orange or grapefruit rind,
  cut into strips
Sugar
½ cup water or pineapple juice
Food coloring (optional)

1. Cover rind with water, bring to boil; then simmer for 20 minutes, or until tender. Drain.
2. In large saucepan combine 2 cups sugar, water or juice and food coloring. Add rind; bring slowly to boil. Cook over low heat until rind absorbs all the syrup and becomes transparent.
3. Cool on waxed paper. Roll in sugar.

Mrs. J. O. Cramer, Monday Study Club,
Poplar Bluffs, Mo.

Fudge, Penuche, Creams, Fondant and Pralines

BUTTERSCOTCH FUDGE

Makes About 5 Pounds
3 cups sugar
14½-ounce can evaporated milk
1 cup butter
2 6-ounce packages butterscotch
  pieces
1-pint 2½-ounce jar marshmallow
  cream
1 teaspoon vanilla
1 cup coarsely chopped walnuts

1. In heavy 3-quart saucepan combine sugar, milk and butter. Bring to boil; cook over medium heat, stirring frequently, to soft-ball stage (236° F.).
2. Remove from heat. Add butterscotch, marshmallow cream, vanilla and walnuts. Beat until butterscotch is melted.

3. Spread in greased 8- or 9-inch square baking pan; cool. When firm, cut into squares.

Madelyn Clore, Woman's Club,
Blandinsville, Ill.

ONE-MINUTE FUDGE

Makes ½ Pound
1-ounce square unsweetened
  chocolate, finely cut
1 cup sugar
⅓ cup milk
¼ cup shortening
¼ teaspoon salt
1 teaspoon vanilla
1 tablespoon cream, if necessary

1. Grease shallow baking pan.
2. In large saucepan combine chocolate, sugar, milk, shortening and salt. Bring slowly to full rolling boil, stirring constantly. Boil for 1 minute.
3. Add vanilla; cool to lukewarm.
4. Beat until thick enough to spread. If fudge becomes too thick, beat in cream.
5. Spread in pan. When cool, cut into squares.

Priscilla Kschinka, Tuesday Club, Dunshore, Pa.

SMITH COLLEGE FUDGE

Makes About 1½ Pounds
¼ cup butter
2 cups sugar
¼ cup light corn syrup
½ cup evaporated milk
2 1-ounce squares unsweetened
  chocolate, cut up
1 teaspoon vanilla
½ cup chopped walnuts

1. Grease 10 x 6 x 1½-inch baking pan well.
2. Melt butter in large saucepan. Stir in sugar, corn syrup and milk; bring to boil over medium heat, stirring occasionally. Boil for 2½ minutes.
3. Add chocolate; stir until melted. Boil for 5 minutes longer.
4. Remove from heat; stir in vanilla and walnuts. Cool.
5. Beat until creamy; pour into pan. Set aside until firm; cut into 1-inch squares.

Mrs. George Clarkson, Junior Woman's Club,
New Bedford, Mass.

CREAMY CHOCOLATE FUDGE

Makes About 3 Pounds
14½-ounce can evaporated milk
4½ cups sugar
3 6-ounce packages semi-sweet
  chocolate pieces
1 cup butter
2 teaspoons vanilla
1 cup finely chopped walnuts

1. Grease 2 11 x 7 1½-inch baking pans.
2. In large saucepan combine milk and sugar. Cook over medium heat, stirring constantly, until sugar is dissolved. Bring to boil; boil for 7 minutes.

3. Remove from heat; add chocolate and butter; beat until smooth.

4. Stir in vanilla and walnuts; pour into pans.

5. Cool until firm; cut into squares.

Mrs. Philip Poats, Junior Woman's Club, Hickory, N.C.

MARSHMALLOW NUT FUDGE
Makes 36 Squares

2½ cups sugar
¼ cup butter
16 marshmallows
¼ teaspoon salt
1½ cups evaporated milk
1 teaspoon vanilla
1 6-ounce package semi-sweet chocolate pieces
1 cup coarsely chopped walnuts

1. Grease 9-inch square baking pan.

2. In large saucepan combine sugar, butter, marshmallows, salt and milk. Cook over medium heat, stirring constantly, until sugar is dissolved. Bring to boil; cook, stirring frequently for 5 minutes, or to soft-ball stage (236° F.).

3. Remove from heat; stir in vanilla and chocolate; stir until chocolate is melted.

4. Stir in walnuts; pour into pan. Cool; cut into 1½-inch squares.

Clyde E. Stockton, Woman's Club, Crawford, Ga.

MAMIE EISENHOWER'S FUDGE
Makes About 5 Pounds

4½ cups sugar
2 tablespoons butter
Dash of salt
14½-ounce can evaporated milk
12-ounce package semi-sweet chocolate pieces
12-ounce package sweetened chocolate, broken up
1 pint marshmallow cream
2 cups chopped walnuts or pecans

1. Grease 13 x 9½ x 2-inch baking pan well.

2. In large saucepan combine sugar, butter, salt and milk. Bring to boil over medium heat, stirring constantly. Boil for 6 minutes, stirring occasionally.

3. Put semi-sweet and sweetened chocolate, marshmallow cream and nuts in mixing bowl; pour in syrup; beat until chocolate is melted.

4. Pour into pan; cool for several hours, or until firm. Cut into squares. Store in airtight container.

Mrs. Bruno Peloso, Twentieth Century Club, Iron River, Mich.

COFFEE FUDGE
Makes About 1½ Pounds

2 cups sugar
1 cup strong black coffee
1 tablespoon cream
1 tablespoon butter
⅛ teaspoon salt
¼ teaspoon cream of tartar
½ teaspoon almond extract
1 cup broken pecans

1. Grease platter.

2. In large saucepan combine all ingredients except almond extract and pecans. Stir over low heat until sugar is dissolved; then boil rapidly, stirring constantly, to soft-ball stage (236° F.).

3. Remove from heat; cool slightly. Add almond extract. Beat until mixture begins to stiffen; stir in pecans.

4. Pour onto platter; cool. When firm, cut into squares.

Mary Burright, El Camino Women's Club, Ventura, Calif.

PEANUT BUTTER FUDGE
Makes 81 Squares

1½ cups milk
4 cups sugar
1 cup peanut butter
½ cup butter

1. Grease 9-inch square baking pan.

2. In large saucepan combine milk, sugar and peanut butter. Bring to boil, stirring constantly. Cook to hard-ball stage (252° F.), stirring constantly.

3. Remove from heat; stir in butter. Cool to lukewarm.

4. Beat until thickened; pour into pan; cool. When firm, cut into 1-inch squares.

Mrs. G. C. Marlette, Progressive Study Club, Bay Minette, Ala.

PEANUT BUTTER DATE FUDGE
Makes About 2 Pounds

14-ounce can sweetened condensed milk
2 tablespoons peanut butter
2 cups sugar
1 cup finely chopped dates
1 teaspoon vanilla

1. Grease 9-inch square baking pan.

2. In large saucepan blend milk, peanut butter and sugar. Cook over low heat, stirring frequently, until sugar is dissolved. Cook over low heat, stirring occasionally, to soft-ball stage (236° F.).

3. Remove from heat; stir in dates and vanilla. Beat until thickened. Pour into pan.

4. Cool; cut into squares.

Boo Olson, Woman's Culture Club, Post, Tex.

SOUR CREAM FUDGE
Makes About 1 Pound

2 cups sugar
½ teaspoon salt
1 cup sour cream
2 tablespoons butter
½ cup chopped walnuts

1. Grease 8-inch square baking pan.

2. In large saucepan combine sugar, salt and sour cream. Bring to boil over medium heat, stirring constantly. Boil to soft-ball stage (236° F.).

3. Remove from heat; stir in butter and walnuts. Cool. Beat until creamy; pour into pan.

4. Cool until firm; cut into squares.

Jane Storrer, Mid Century Study Club, Montpelier, Ohio

PENUCHE

Makes About 1 Pound

2 cups brown sugar
½ cup light cream
2 tablespoons butter
⅛ teaspoon salt
1 cup chopped nuts
1 teaspoon vanilla

1. Grease 9-inch square baking pan.
2. In large saucepan combine sugar and cream. Cook over low heat, stirring constantly, until mixture is boiling and sugar is melted. Cook to soft-ball stage (236° F.).
3. Remove from heat; stir in butter, salt and nuts. Cool. Add vanilla; beat until creamy.
4. Pour into pan; when almost cold, cut into squares.

*Anne Moucka, Progressive Woman's Club,
Fresno, Calif.*

PECAN PENUCHE

Makes About 1½ Pounds

3 cups brown sugar
1 cup milk
1 tablespoon butter
Dash of salt
1 cup chopped pecans

1. Grease 9-inch square baking pan.
2. In large saucepan combine sugar and milk; bring to boil over low heat, stirring constantly. Boil over medium heat to soft-ball stage (236° F.).
3. Remove from heat; stir in butter and salt. Cool without stirring.
4. Beat until creamy; stir in pecans. Pour into pan; cool.
5. Cut into squares.

*Mrs. G. G. Jackson, Woman's Club,
Williston, Fla.*

RICH PENUCHE

Makes 81 Squares

2 cups brown sugar
¾ cup milk
¼ cup butter or margarine
1 teaspoon vanilla
½ cup chopped nuts

1. Grease 9-inch square baking pan.
2. In large saucepan combine sugar, milk and butter or margarine. Cook over low heat, stirring frequently, until sugar is dissolved. Cook over medium heat to soft-ball stage (236° F.).
3. Remove from heat; stir in vanilla and nuts. Stir until mixture starts to thicken; pour into pan.
4. Cool until firm; cut into 1-inch squares.

Mrs. Julian McRae, Woman's Club, Starke, Fla.

BOSTON CREAMS

Makes About 2 Pounds

3 cups sugar
1 cup light corn syrup
⅓ cup milk
¼ cup butter
1 cup finely chopped walnuts

1. Grease 15½ x 10½ x 1-inch jelly roll pan well.
2. In large saucepan combine sugar, corn syrup, milk and butter. Cook over low heat, stirring occasionally, until sugar is dissolved. Cook over medium heat to soft-ball stage (236° F.).
3. Remove from heat; stir in walnuts. Beat until stiff; pour into pan.
4. Cool until firm; cut into desired shapes.

*Mrs. Freeman Lewis, Tuesday Club,
Cape Girardeau, Mo.*

CHOCOLATE BOSTON CREAMS

Makes 64

3 cups sugar
1 cup light corn syrup
1 cup light cream
1 teaspoon vanilla
1 cup chopped walnuts
2 1-ounce squares unsweetened
    chocolate, melted

1. Grease 8-inch square baking pan.
2. In large saucepan combine sugar, corn syrup and cream. Stir over low heat until sugar is dissolved. Cook to soft-ball stage (236° F.).
3. Remove from heat; stir in vanilla and walnuts; and beat until white and shiny.
4. Pour into pan. Cool.
5. Spread chocolate over surface; let stand for 6 hours. Cut into 1-inch squares.

*Mrs. William Shotwell, Study Club,
Farber, Mo.*

BUTTERSCOTCH NUT CREAMS

Makes About 72

2 cups brown sugar
1 cup granulated sugar
1 tablespoon corn syrup
1 cup light cream
2 tablespoons butter or margarine
2 teaspoons vanilla
1 cup chopped nuts

1. Grease baking sheets.
2. In large saucepan combine sugars, corn syrup and cream. Cook over very low heat, stirring constantly, until sugars are dissolved. Cook to soft-ball stage (236° F.).
3. Remove from heat; stir in butter or margarine. Cool. Add vanilla and nuts; beat for about 10 minutes or until thickened.
4. Drop by teaspoons onto baking sheets; put in cool place until firm.

*Burnita Reed, Woman's Literary Club,
Winthrop, Ia.*

DEPENDABLE FONDANT

Makes About 1½ Pounds

2 cups sugar
2 tablespoons light corn syrup
¼ teaspoon cream of tartar
1½ cups boiling water

1. Day before, combine all ingredients in heavy saucepan. Cook over low heat until sugar is dissolved. Bring to boil; cover; cook for 3 minutes. Remove cover;

cook, without stirring, to soft-ball stage (236° F.). Wipe sugar crystals from sides of pan several times while cooking with fork wrapped in damp cloth.

2. As soon as mixture reaches soft-ball stage, pour onto slab or platter rinsed with very cold water. Do not scrape pan. Cool until fondant feels only slightly warm.

3. Scrape fondant from edge of platter toward center with wooden spoon. Work with spoon until creamy and stiff; knead until smooth and free from lumps.

4. Wrap in waxed paper. Put in covered container to ripen for at least 24 hours, or store in refrigerator, where it will keep for 1 month.

NOTE: After fondant has ripened, it may be kneaded, flavored, tinted and either shaped into patties and decorated or dipped in chocolate. Fondant may be used as a filling for dried fruits, or it may be melted over warm water in top of a double saucepan and used for dipping fruits and nuts.

TO MAKE MINIATURE FRUITS:

1. Fill a dried fig with peanut butter; dip in melted yellow fondant. Add a blush of red food coloring on one cheek and tiny artificial leaf in top to make a pear.

2. Dip a nut-stuffed prune in red fondant to make an apple, and so forth. Don't melt more fondant than you can use quickly, since it soon becomes hard.

Mrs. Melvin Lynn, Woman's Club, Lovell, Wyo.

5-POUND FONDANT CANDY

Makes 5 1-Pound Loaves

3 pounds sugar
1 cup butter
2 cups light corn syrup
About 2½ cups evaporated milk
1 pound chopped mixed nuts

1. Several days before, in preserving pan or heavy saucepan combine sugar, butter, corn syrup and milk. Bring to boil, stirring occasionally.

2. Boil, without stirring, to soft-ball stage (236° F.).

3. Remove from heat; beat until creamy. Stir in nuts; cool.

4. Turn onto marble slab or large platter rinsed in cold water; knead until creamy and smooth.

5. Form into 5 loaves; wrap in waxed paper; ripen for several days in refrigerator. Slice as needed.

*Frankie Marshall, Woman's Club,
West Milford, W. Va.*

COCONUT PATTIES

Makes About 60

3 cups sugar
3 tablespoons cocoa
¼ cup sweetened condensed milk
½ cup water
2 cups flaked coconut
½ cup chopped nuts
1 tablespoon butter
1½ teaspoons vanilla

1. In large saucepan combine sugar and cocoa. Stir in milk and water; cook over low heat, stirring constantly, until sugar is dissolved.

2. Cook over medium heat to soft-ball stage (236° F.).

3. Remove from heat; cool to room temperature.

4. Add remaining ingredients; beat until mixture starts to thicken.

5. Drop by teaspoons onto waxed paper; set aside until firm.

*Mrs. George Tinsley, Jr., Younger Woman's Club,
Barbourville, Ky.*

PECAN ROLL

Makes About 2 Pounds

1 cup milk
2 cups sugar
1 cup chopped dates
½ cup chopped pecans
2 tablespoons butter

1. In large saucepan combine milk, sugar and dates. Bring to boil over medium heat, stirring frequently. Boil to soft-ball stage (236° F.).

2. Remove from heat; and beat in pecans and butter. Beat until cool.

3. Shape into long roll; roll in damp cloth. Slice when firm.

*Mrs. A. L. Shuck, President, 4th District,
Oklahoma State Federation of Women's Clubs,
Weatherford, Okla.*

BURNT SUGAR PRALINES

Makes 12

1¾ cups sugar
1 cup water
Dash of nutmeg
1 tablespoon butter
1 cup pecan halves
½ teaspoon vanilla

1. Line baking sheet with waxed paper.

2. Melt ½ cup of the sugar in heavy skillet over low heat, stirring constantly, until golden. Turn off heat; let stand for 5 minutes.

3. Add remaining sugar and water; stir carefully; melt over medium heat. Add nutmeg and butter; cook, stirring occasionally, to soft-ball stage (236° F.).

4. Remove from heat; let stand for 3 minutes. Stir until mixture looks cloudy. Add pecans and vanilla; stir until creamy.

5. Drop by tablespoons onto baking sheet; spread out slightly.

*Ernestine Brooks, Junior Woman's Club,
St. Cloud, Fla.*

SOUTHERN PRALINES

Makes About 24

1 cup brown sugar
2 cups granulated sugar
1 cup water
1 tablespoon butter or margarine
¼ teaspoon salt
1 teaspoon vanilla
3 cups pecan halves

1. Line baking sheets with waxed paper.

2. In saucepan combine sugars and

water. Stir over medium heat until sugars are melted. Bring to boil; boil to soft-ball stage (236° F.).

3. Remove from heat; stir in butter or margarine, salt and vanilla. Beat until syrup starts to become creamy. Stir in pecans.

4. Drop by teaspoons onto baking sheets.

5. If candy becomes too hard to drop from spoon, place pan over hot water; stir few drops hot water into mixture to soften.

Mrs. H. Carl Gates, President, Woman's Club, Park Ridge, Ill.

PRALINE CANDY COOKIES
Makes 48

24 double graham crackers
1 cup butter
1 cup brown sugar
1 cup finely chopped pecans

1. Preheat oven to 350° F.
2. Arrange crackers on baking sheets.
3. Combine butter and sugar in large saucepan; stir over medium heat until melted and boiling. Boil for 2 minutes, without stirring; stir in pecans.
4. Spoon over crackers. Bake in pre-heated oven for 10 minutes. While still hot, cut crackers in half.

Mrs. Erna Steinbrook, Masonic Service Association, Washington, D.C.

TURKISH PASTE
Makes 60

4 cups granulated sugar
6 envelopes gelatin
Juice and rind of 1 orange
Juice of 1 lemon
1½ cups water
Sifted confectioners' sugar

1. Grease 10 x 6 x 1½-inch baking pan.
2. In large saucepan combine granulated sugar and gelatin. Stir in orange juice and rind, lemon juice and water. Cook over low heat, stirring constantly, until sugar and gelatin are dissolved. Boil over medium heat for 20 minutes.
3. Remove from heat; pour into pan. Cool.
4. When cold and firm, cut into 1-inch squares; roll in confectioners' sugar.

Ruth Anthony Davis, Women's Club, Barrington, R.I.

MINTED WALNUTS
Makes About 2 Pounds

¼ cup light corn syrup
1 cup sugar
½ cup water
½ teaspoon peppermint extract
10 marshmallows
3 cups walnut halves

1. Line baking sheets with waxed paper.
2. In large saucepan combine corn syrup, sugar and water. Bring to boil over medium heat, stirring constantly. Cook, without stirring, to soft-ball stage (236° F.).

3. Remove from heat; stir in peppermint extract and marshmallows. Stir until marshmallows are dissolved. Add walnuts; stir until well coated.

4. Pour onto baking sheets; separate walnut halves, using two forks. Cool.

Mrs. C. W. Wagoner, Athenaeum Club, Kansas City, Mo.

ORANGE CREAM WALNUTS
Makes About 2 Pounds

1½ cups sugar
½ cup orange juice
1 tablespoon grated orange rind
3 cups walnut halves

1. Line baking sheets with waxed paper.
2. In large saucepan combine sugar and orange juice; cook over high heat to soft-ball stage (236° F.).
3. Remove from heat; stir in orange rind and walnuts. Stir until mixture starts to turn cloudy.
4. Drop each walnut half onto baking sheet. Cool until hardened.

Dorothy Lere, Mar Vista Woman's Club, Los Angeles, Calif.

Caramels

DELICIOUS CARAMELS
Makes 64

2 cups granulated sugar
1 cup brown sugar
¾ cup light corn syrup
1½ cups light cream
½ cup butter or margarine

1. Grease 8-inch square baking pan.
2. Combine all ingredients in large saucepan. Cook over low heat, stirring constantly, until sugars are dissolved. Bring to boil; boil, without stirring, to firm-ball stage (248° F.).
3. Pour into pan; cool. Cut into 1-inch squares; wrap in waxed paper.

Mrs. William McClain, Studere Club, Wellsville, Mo.

NUT CARAMELS
Makes 81

1 cup sugar
1 cup light corn syrup
2 cups heavy cream
1 teaspoon vanilla
1 cup chopped nuts

1. Grease 9-inch square baking pan.
2. In large saucepan combine sugar, corn syrup and 1 cup of the cream. Cook over medium heat, stirring constantly, until sugar is dissolved and mixture reaches soft-ball stage (236° F.).
3. Gradually stir in remaining cream; cook, stirring constantly, to firm-ball stage (248° F.).
4. Remove from heat; stir in vanilla and nuts. Pour into pan. Cool; let stand for 12 hours.

5. Cut into 1-inch squares; wrap in waxed paper.

Mrs. Vernon McMullin, Woman's Club,
La Monte, Mo.

VANILLA CARAMELS
Makes About 2 Pounds
2 cups sugar
2 cups light cream
1 cup light corn syrup
½ teaspoon salt
⅓ cup butter
1 teaspoon vanilla
½ cup chopped walnuts

1. Grease 8-inch square baking pan well.
2. In large saucepan combine sugar, 1 cup of the cream, corn syrup and salt. Cook over low heat, stirring constantly, for 10 minutes.
3. Slowly add remaining cream. Cook for 5 minutes longer. Add butter, a teaspoon at a time, stirring constantly. Cook to firm-ball stage (248° F.).
4. Remove from heat; stir in vanilla and walnuts. Pour into pan; cool.
5. Cut into ¾-inch squares. Wrap in waxed paper.

Mrs. Walden R. Peterson, Alkaid Club,
Lindsborg, Kans.

CARAMEL APPLES
Makes 8
8 firm red apples
2 cups granulated sugar
1 cup brown sugar
⅔ cup light corn syrup
⅔ cup butter
1 cup evaporated milk
1 teaspoon salt
1 teaspoon vanilla

1. Wash apples; dry well; insert wooden skewer in each. Place on waxed paper on baking sheet; set aside.
2. In heavy saucepan combine sugars, corn syrup, butter, milk and salt. Cook over low heat, stirring until sugars are dissolved. Cook, without stirring, to firm-ball stage (248° F.).
3. Remove from heat; stir in vanilla. Cool slightly.
4. Dip apples in caramel coating; cool on waxed paper.

Woman's Club, Yakima, Wash.

CARAMEL CORN
Makes 2 Quarts
1 cup brown sugar
1 cup light corn sprup
⅓ cup water
1 teaspoon vinegar
¼ teaspoon baking soda
2 quarts popcorn

1. In large saucepan combine sugar, corn syrup, water, vinegar and baking soda. Bring to boil, stirring frequently.
2. Boil, without stirring, to firm-ball stage (248° F.).

3. Remove from heat; stir in popcorn at once, coating well. Spread on waxed paper to cool.

Marjorie Sidebottom, Woman's Club,
West Milford, W. Va.

Divinities, Taffies and Nougat

DIVINITY CANDY
Makes About 2 Pounds
½ cup water
½ cup light corn syrup
2 cups granulated sugar
1 cup brown sugar
2 egg whites
1 cup chopped walnuts
1 teaspoon vanilla

1. Grease 13 x 9½ x 2-inch baking pan.
2. In large saucepan combine water, corn syrup and sugars. Cook over medium heat, stirring until sugars are dissolved. Cook over medium heat to hard-ball stage (252° F.).
3. Meanwhile, in mixing bowl beat egg whites until stiff but not dry. While continuing to beat, gradually pour in syrup. Beat until stiff.
4. Stir in walnuts and vanilla; pour into pan. Cool; cut into squares.

Progressive Study Club, Bay Minette, Ala.

DIVINITY NUT CANDY
Makes About 60
3 cups sugar
1 cup light corn syrup
½ cup water
2 egg whites
1 cup chopped pecans
1 teaspoon vanilla
60 pecan halves

1. Line baking sheets with waxed paper.
2. In large saucepan combine sugar, corn syrup and water. Cook over medium heat, stirring constantly, until sugar is dissolved. Cook, without stirring, to hard-ball stage (252° F.).
3. Meanwhile, in mixing bowl beat egg whites until stiff but not dry. While continuing to beat, gradually pour in half the syrup.
4. Return remaining syrup to heat; cook to hard-crack stage (300° F.); gradually pour into egg white mixture; beat until stiff.
5. Stir in chopped pecans and vanilla; mix well. Drop by teaspoons onto baking sheets; top each candy with pecan half. Set aside until firm.

Mrs. C. C. Grage, Woman's Club, Hugoton, Kans.

CANDIED POPCORN
Makes 3 Quarts
1½ cups sugar or maple syrup
1 tablespoon butter
3 tablespoons water
1 teaspoon vanilla
¼ teaspoon almond extract
3 quarts popcorn

1. In large saucepan combine sugar or maple syrup, butter and water. Cook over high heat to hard-ball stage (252° F.).

2. Remove from heat; stir in vanilla, almond extract and popcorn; mix well. If desired, shape into popcorn balls.

Blanche Holston, Century Gardens Club, Wilmington, Del.

PULLED MINTS

Makes About 1 Pound

3 cups granulated sugar
1 cup water
2 tablespoons light corn syrup
½ teaspoon peppermint extract
1 cup sifted confectioners' sugar
1 cup cornstarch

1. 2 days before, grease 11 x 7 x 1½-inch baking pan.

2. In large saucepan combine granulated sugar, water and corn syrup. Cook over medium heat, stirring occasionally, until sugar is dissolved. Cook, without stirring, to 265° F.

3. Cover pan to steam down crystals; remove from heat.

4. Pour syrup into baking pan (do not scrape saucepan); let stand until cool enough to handle.

5. Sprinkle peppermint extract over syrup. Fold syrup in half; begin to pull out and fold over until syrup becomes milky. Continue to pull and fold until firm.

6. Pull into long rope; cut into ½-inch pieces with scissors.

7. Onto piece of waxed paper sift together confectioners' sugar and cornstarch. Roll candy in mixture.

8. Store candy in airtight tin for 2 days to soften and become creamy.

Mrs. E. G. Ryall, Woman's Club, Jessup, Md.

WHITE TAFFY

Makes About 60

1 cup sugar
⅓ cup water
¼ cup light corn syrup
1 tablespoon vinegar
¼ teaspoon baking soda

1. Grease shallow baking pan.

2. In large saucepan combine sugar, water and corn syrup. Cook over low heat, stirring until sugar is dissolved. Cook over medium heat, without stirring, to hard-ball stage (265° F.).

3. Remove from heat; stir in vinegar and baking soda.

4. Pour into pan; let stand until cool enough to handle. Pull until snow white and porous. Grease hands, if necessary.

5. Twist into long ropes; cut into ½-inch pieces with scissors.

Mrs. Jack Wood, Jr., Modern Study Club, Wolfe City, Tex.

NOUGAT

Makes About 4 Pounds

5 cups sugar
1 cup light corn syrup
1 cup water

4 egg whites
1 pound pistachio nuts
1 teaspoon vanilla

1. Line 15½ x 10½ x 1-inch jelly roll pan with waxed paper.

2. In large saucepan combine sugar, corn syrup and water. Bring to boil, stirring occasionally. Boil over medium heat to soft-ball stage (236° F.).

3. Meanwhile, in mixing bowl beat egg whites until stiff but not dry.

4. When syrup has reached soft-ball stage, gradually beat 1 cup into egg whites; beat until meringue is stiff.

5. Cook remaining syrup in pan to hard-ball stage (252° F.). Gradually beat into meringue. Add nuts and vanilla; beat until cool.

6. Pour into pan; smooth surface. Cool until firm.

7. Cut into squares; wrap in waxed paper. Keep in airtight container.

VARIATIONS: Pecans or walnuts may be used instead of pistachios; add red and green candied cherries for Christmas candy.

Grace Johnston Parkhurst, Inter Circle, Marion, Ala.

Butterscotch and Toffees

CREAMY TOFFEE

Makes About 2½ Pounds

3 cups sugar
1 cup water
½ teaspoon salt
1 cup cream
Desired flavoring, coloring and nuts

1. Grease marble slab.

2. In large saucepan combine sugar, water and salt. Bring to boil; cook, without stirring, to soft-ball stage (236° F.).

3. While syrup continues to boil, gradually add cream. Boil, without stirring, to 272° F.

4. Pour onto slab; let stand until cool enough to handle. Put in flavoring, coloring and nuts, as desired.

5. Pull into rope; cut into pieces; pack into jars. Store in refrigerator.

Martha Whitt, 20th Century Club, Gordo, Ala.

BUTTERSCOTCH CANDY

Makes 81

1½ cups brown sugar
¼ cup butter
⅓ cup dark corn syrup
½ cup light cream
1 teaspoon vanilla

1. Grease 9-inch square baking pan.

2. In large saucepan combine sugar, butter, corn syrup and cream; cook over low heat, stirring until sugar is dissolved. Cook over medium heat, without stirring, to soft-crack stage (290° F.).

3. Remove from heat; stir in vanilla. Pour into pan; cool.

4. Mark into 1-inch squares; cut when cold and firm.

Mrs. Martin Huseman, Civic Club, Galva, Ia.

BUTTERSCOTCH DROPS

Makes About 24

½ cup sugar
¼ cup light corn syrup
¼ cup water
1 tablespoon butter
½ teaspoon vanilla

1. Grease baking sheet.
2. In large saucepan combine sugar, corn syrup and water; bring to boil; cook over low heat, stirring constantly, until sugar is dissolved. Cook without stirring, to hard-ball stage (265° F.).
3. Add butter; cook to soft-crack stage (290° F.). Remove from heat; stir in vanilla.
4. Drop by teaspoons onto baking sheet. When firm, remove with spatula.

Mrs. Paul Duchaine, Junior Women's Club, Rye, N.H.

ENGLISH CHOCOLATE TOFFEE

Makes About 2 Pounds

3 tablespoons water
1 tablespoon light corn syrup
1 cup sugar
1 cup butter or margarine
¾ cup chopped almonds
3 1-ounce squares unsweetened chocolate, grated

1. Grease 9-inch square baking pan.
2. In large saucepan combine water, corn syrup, sugar and butter or margarine. Cook over medium heat, stirring until sugar is dissolved. Cook, without stirring, to hard-crack stage (300° F.).
3. Sprinkle ½ cup of the almonds in pan; pour in syrup; sprinkle with remaining almonds and chocolate.
4. Cool; break into pieces.

Progressive Study Club, Bay Minette, Ala.

BUTTER TOFFEE

Makes About 1½ Pounds

1 cup brown sugar
¼ cup water
½ cup butter
1½ cups finely chopped walnuts
12-ounce package semi-sweet chocolate pieces

1. Grease baking sheet.
2. In large saucepan combine sugar, water and butter. Cook over low heat, stirring until sugar is dissolved. Cook over medium heat, without stirring, to soft-crack stage (290° F.).
3. Remove from heat; stir in ½ cup of the walnuts. Pour onto baking sheet; let stand until cool and hard.
4. Meanwhile, put chocolate in top of double saucepan; cook over hot water until melted and smooth.

5. Spread toffee mixture with half the chocolate; sprinkle with ½ cup of the walnuts; press into chocolate. Cool.

6. When firm, turn toffee. Spread underside with remaining chocolate; sprinkle with remaining walnuts; press into chocolate.

7. Cool. When firm, break into pieces.

Mrs. Marvan Fillerup, Woman's Club, Lovell, Wyo.

Brittles and Hard Candies

PEANUT BRITTLE

Makes About 2 Pounds

2 cups sugar
¾ cup light corn syrup
¼ cup water
2½ cups shelled peanuts
4 teaspoons baking soda

1. Grease baking sheets well.
2. In large saucepan cook sugar, corn syrup and water until sugar is dissolved. Add peanuts; boil rapidly to hard-crack stage (300° F.). Do not stir while syrup is boiling, but shake pan several times.
3. Add baking soda; stir well. Pour onto baking sheets; spread as thinly as possible.
4. When cool, break into pieces.

Mrs. G. C. Hilman, Cosmos Club, Ruston, La.

CRACKER JAX

Makes About 3 Quarts

1 cup molasses
2 cups sugar
1 tablespoon butter
2 tablespoons vinegar
½ teaspoon baking soda
3 quarts popcorn
2 cups chopped nuts

1. Grease 15½ x 10½ x 1-inch jelly roll pan.
2. In large saucepan blend molasses, sugar, butter and vinegar. Cook over low heat, stirring occasionally, until sugar is dissolved. Cook over medium heat to hard-crack stage (300° F.).
3. Remove from heat; beat in baking soda.
4. Put popcorn in mixing bowl; pour syrup on top. Add nuts; mix well. Spread in pan.
5. When cool, break into pieces.

Mrs. W. W. Kelly, Woman's Club, Bakersfield, Calif.

BUTTER CRUNCH

Makes About 2 Pounds

1 cup butter
1 cup sugar
2 tablespoons water
1 tablespoon light corn syrup
¾ cup walnuts or pecans
4 1-ounce squares unsweetened chocolate, melted

1. Grease baking sheet.
2. Melt butter in large saucepan. Remove from heat; stir in sugar. Bring to boil; add water and corn syrup.
3. Cook over medium heat for about 15 minutes, or to hard-crack stage (300° F.).
4. Remove from heat; stir in nuts. Pour at once onto baking sheet.
5. As mixture cools, carefully loosen with spatula; spread surface with half the chocolate. Cool; turn; spread underside with remaining chocolate.
6. Cool; break into pieces; store in glass jar with tight-fitting cover.

B. Claude, Totowa Junior Women's Club,
Wayne, N.J.

CLEAR RED ANISE CANDY

Makes About 3 Pounds

2 cups light corn syrup
4 cups sugar
1 cup boiling water
¾ teaspoon anise oil
¾ teaspoon red food coloring

1. Grease 13 x 9½ x 2-inch baking pan.
2. Combine corn syrup and sugar in large saucepan; pour in water; stir to mix.
3. Cover; boil over high heat for 5 minutes.
4. Remove cover; boil to hard-crack stage (300° F.).
5. Remove from heat; stir in anise oil and food coloring. Pour into pan.
6. When cool, break into pieces.

Mrs. James A. Holter, Woman's Club,
Casselton, N.D.

CHRISTMAS HARD CANDY

Makes About 3 Pounds

4 cups sugar
1 cup light corn syrup
1 cup water
1 teaspoon salt

1. Grease baking sheet.
2. In large saucepan combine all ingredients; cook over low heat, stirring until sugar is dissolved. Cook over medium heat, without stirring, to hard-crack stage (300° F.).
3. Remove from heat; pour onto baking sheet. When cool and hard, break into pieces.

Woman's Club, Lincoln, Neb.

SPONGE CANDY

Makes About 2 Pounds

1 tablespoon vinegar
1 cup sugar
1 cup dark corn syrup
1 tablespoon baking soda

1. Grease 9-inch square baking pan.
2. In large saucepan combine vinegar, sugar and corn syrup. Cook over medium heat, stirring until sugar is dissolved. Cooking, without stirring, to hard-crack stage (300° F.).
3. Remove from heat; quickly stir in baking soda. Pour into pan. When cool, break into pieces.

Mrs. Francis Hulett, Phi Lambda Club,
Slater, Mo.

Uncooked Confections

APRICOT COCONUT BALLS

Makes About 60

1½ cups ground dried apricots
2⅔ cups flaked coconut
¾ cup sweetened condensed milk
Confectioners' sugar

1. In mixing bowl combine apricots and coconut. Add milk; mix to blend.
2. Shape into 1-inch balls, using sugar to prevent sticking.
3. Roll in more sugar; place on baking sheets for 2 hours, or until firm.

Magazine Club, Union Springs, Ala.

BUTTER CREAMS

Makes About 24

1 pound confectioners' sugar (sift if lumpy)
¼ pound butter
2 tablespoons cream
Dash of salt
1 teaspoon vanilla
1-ounce square unsweetened chocolate, melted

1. Day before, blend sugar, butter, cream, salt and vanilla to a smooth paste. Chill for 24 hours.
2. Next day, mold mixture into small balls; dip in chocolate. Place on wire rack until set.

Mrs. George A. Fenton, Thursday Morning Club,
Madison, N.J.

CHOCOLATE CHERRY CREAMS

Makes About 30

½ cup evaporated milk
6-ounce package semi-sweet chocolate pieces
2½ cups confectioners' sugar (sift if lumpy)
⅓ cup chopped maraschino cherries, well drained
1¼ cups flaked coconut

1. In saucepan cook milk and chocolate over low heat, stirring frequently, until chocolate is melted.
2. Remove from heat; stir in sugar and cherries; mix well. Chill for 1 hour.
3. Shape into 1-inch balls; roll in coconut. Chill for 3 hours, or until firm. Store in refrigerator.

Colleen Kaiser, Western Cincinnati Junior
Woman's Club, Cincinnati, Ohio

EASY CHOCOLATE MINTS

Makes About 106

14-ounce can sweetened condensed milk
3½ cups sifted confectioners' sugar
1 cup flaked coconut
1 cup chopped nuts
½ teaspoon mint extract
⅛ teaspoon green food coloring
12-ounce package semi-sweet chocolate pieces
½ bar paraffin

1. In mixing bowl combine all ingredients except chocolate and paraffin; mix well; chill for 2 hours.
2. Cook chocolate and paraffin in top of double saucepan over hot water, stirring occasionally, until melted and very smooth.
3. Shape coconut mixture into ¾-inch balls; use cocktail pick to dip balls into chocolate, coating completely.
4. Set aside on waxed paper until cool and firm.

Mrs. Mark Hughes, Junior Women's Club, Bismarck, N.D.

CHOCOLATE OYSTERS

Makes About 60

1½ pounds semi-sweet chocolate
  1 cup heavy cream
  Chopped nuts

1. Melt chocolate in top of double saucepan over simmering water. Cool.
2. Whip cream until stiff; fold into chocolate. Chill.
3. Form mixture into small balls; roll in nuts.

Sally Dolam, Junior Women's Club, Libertyville, Ill.

MARTHA WASHINGTON BONBONS

Makes About 5 Pounds

½ cup butter, melted
2 pounds confectioners' sugar
  (sift if lumpy)
14-ounce can sweetened condensed milk
4 cups chopped nuts
2 cups flaked coconut
12-ounce package semi-sweet chocolate pieces
¼ bar paraffin

1. Combine butter, sugar, milk, nuts and coconut; mix well; shape into 1-inch balls. Place on baking sheets; chill until firm.
2. Meanwhile, melt chocolate in top of double saucepan.
3. In another saucepan melt paraffin; stir into chocolate. Remove from heat; cool slightly.
4. Dip balls in chocolate; place on baking sheets until firm.

Mrs. Larry Frandson, Woman's Club, Minden, Neb.

NO-COOK CHOCOLATE CREAM CHEESE FUDGE

Makes 64 Squares

8-ounce package cream cheese
2 cups sifted confectioners' sugar
2 1-ounce squares unsweetened chocolate, melted
½ teaspoon vanilla
  Dash of salt
½ cup chopped pecans

1. Grease 8-inch square baking pan.
2. In mixing bowl beat cheese until soft. Gradually beat in sugar. Then stir in chocolate, vanilla and salt. Add pecans; mix well. Turn into pan.

3. Chill until firm. Cut into 1-inch squares; store in refrigerator.

Jean Luttrell, Woman's Club, Natick, Mass.

FRENCH CHOCOLATE TRUFFLES

Makes About 36

6 1-ounce squares unsweetened chocolate
½ cup butter
1 cup confectioners' sugar
  (sift if lumpy)
1 teaspoon vanilla
1 tablespoon brandy
  Cocoa
1 tablespoon heavy cream

1. Cook chocolate and butter in top of double saucepan over hot water, stirring occasionally, until melted and smooth.
2. Remove from heat; stir in sugar, vanilla, brandy, 2 tablespoons cocoa and cream. Beat until smooth.
3. Cool until firm enough to mold.
4. Shape into ½-inch balls; roll in additional cocoa. Wrap in waxed paper.

Nell Harverty, Progressive Woman's Club, Fresno, Calif.

COBBLESTONE CANDY

Makes About 60

3 6-ounce packages semi-sweet chocolate pieces
2 cups tiny marshmallows
1 cup chopped nuts

1. Line 8-inch square baking pan with aluminum foil.
2. Melt chocolate in top of double saucepan over hot water, stirring occasionally. Stir in marshmallows; stir until melted.
3. Remove from heat; stir in nuts. Turn into pan. Cool until firm; cut into 1-inch squares.

Mary Slothower, Junior Women's Club, Renton, Wash.

COCADA (Coconut Candy)

Makes 48

¼ cup butter
2 cups confectioners' sugar
  (sift if lumpy)
¼ cup light cream
3 cups grated coconut
6-ounce package semi-sweet chocolate pieces
2 teaspoons shortening

1. Melt butter in saucepan. Gradually stir in sugar, cream and coconut.
2. Remove from heat; drop by teaspoons onto waxed paper.
3. Chill; shape each mound into peak.
4. Melt chocolate and shortening in top of double saucepan over hot water.
5. Dip each peak in chocolate; cool on waxed paper.

Mrs. Eugene Emerson, Woman's Club, Green River, Wyo.

CREAMY UNCOOKED FONDANT
Makes About 2 Pounds

¼ cup butter
5 to 6 cups confectioners' sugar
 (sift if lumpy)
1 egg white
3 tablespoons heavy cream
Flavoring extract

1. Cream butter until soft. Add 2 cups of the sugar and egg white; beat until smooth.
2. Gradually add cream; blend well.
3. Stir in remaining sugar, adding only enough to make easy to handle.
4. Turn onto board dusted with confectioners' sugar. Knead until smooth and even-textured. Knead in extract; shape according to desire.

Mrs. Joe Brandon, Senior Woman's Club,
Benton, Ky.

MASHED POTATO FONDANT
Makes About 1½ Pounds

½ cup mashed potatoes
1 teaspoon vanilla
 Sifted confectioners' sugar
½ cup chopped nuts
1 cup chopped candied fruits

1. In mixing bowl blend potatoes, vanilla and sufficient sugar to make a stiff dough.

2. Turn onto marble slab or board sprinkled with confectioners' sugar; knead until smooth.
3. Work in nuts and fruits; shape into flat patties. Place on waxed paper; set aside until firm.

Woman's Club, Yakima, Wash.

TROPICAL DATES
Makes About 3 Pounds

2 pounds fresh dates
3 tablespoons softened butter
3 cups confectioners' sugar
3 tablespoons milk
1 teaspoon vanilla
½ cup grated coconut
½ cup finely chopped dried apricots
 Granulated sugar

1. Pit dates.
2. In bowl beat butter, confectioners' sugar, milk and vanilla to a smooth soft fondant, adding a little sugar, if necessary. Knead in coconut and apricots.
3. Form into balls; press each ball into date. Cover with another date. Repeat until all fondant and dates are used.
4. Roll in granulated sugar.

Mrs. Vance V. Omohundro, President,
Crafts and Hobbies Club, St. Louis, Mo.

25. Preserves

Even with the tremendous variety of ready-made jams, jellies, pickles and bottled condiments at their fingertips, American homemakers find preserving a rewarding experience. Each year throughout the country millions of jars and bottles of home-processed foods are "put up" to add color, flavor and texture to daily menus. Every American cook has at least one canned specialty that her family enjoys. A selection of these home favorites has been compiled in this chapter.

The word "preserves" not only means a specific type of canned fruit but also encompasses the various jarred and bottled fruits and vegetables, which fall into the following categories:

Types of Preserves

Jam is a form of preserve in which the fruit is diced or mashed and cooked with sugar to a good spreading consistency.

Jellies are made from the strained juice of fruits cooked with sugar to the jellying stage (p. 717).

Preserves are whole or sectioned fruits cooked in a clear syrup until tender and plump.

Marmalade is a variety of jam in which the juice and rind of citrus fruits are used.

Fruit butters are puréed fruits cooked with sugar to a smooth glossy spread.

Conserve is a blend of several fruits, similar to jam, but usually containing nuts or raisins or both.

Chutney is a form of conserve, usually hot and spicy.

Pickles are many kinds and shapes of fruits and vegetables or a mixture of both preserved either in brine or in a spicy mixture of vinegar and sugar.

Relish is a specific pickle made from vegetables and fruits, usually finely chopped or ground and cooked in a sweet and sour sauce.

Rules for Successful Preserving

1. Use a large heavy pot, preferably a special preserving pan.
2. Never cook more than 4 quarts of fruit at a time. The smaller the quantity, the better the quality.
3. Use a wooden spoon for stirring and a metal spoon for skimming.
4. Do not overcook fruit or fruit juice, or the strength of the pectin will be reduced and both color and flavor destroyed.
5. When sealing jelly or jam, hang a short piece of string over the edge of the jar before topping with paraffin for easy removal of paraffin.
6. If a jam or jelly becomes sugary, remove lid and paraffin, and put it in a warm oven until the sugar is dissolved.
7. A tablespoon of vinegar added to strawberries when making strawberry preserves helps retain color of the berries.
8. To prevent jam from burning, rub the bottom of the pot with a little oil.
9. If a circle of tissue paper the size of the top of the jelly glass is dipped in vinegar and placed on top of the jelly or jam, it will prevent the growth of mold.
10. Wash strawberries thoroughly before stemming to keep them firm.
11. Do not peel pears or peaches with a knife; scald them as you do tomatoes, and the skins will easily slip off.
12. To keep dill pickles crisp, add a little alum to the pickling liquid, or add 1 heaping tablespoon alum to the first salted water.
13. Use pure or pickling salt for pickles and sauerkraut. Table salt contains chemicals which will soften, shrivel and discolor the vegetables.
14. For pickling, use a sparkling clear vinegar with an acid content of 4 to 6 percent.
15. Use the best quality spices, not over 1 year old, for pickling. Ground spices lose their flavor from one season to the next.

Out-of-Season Jams, Jellies and Conserves

Freeze fresh fruit, and make it into preserves as needed. Laboratory tests at the Illinois College of Agriculture indicate that this method is superior to that of making preserves when the fruit is in season and storing them.

Test for Pectin

Some fruits are lacking in pectin and do not make good jelly unless pectin, either from unripe apples or commercial pectin in powdered and bottled form, is added. To determine whether your fruit juice will jell, simply add 1 tablespoon wood alcohol to 1 tablespoon cooked juice, and stir slowly. *Do not taste,* for wood alcohol is poisonous:

Juices rich in pectin will form a large clot.

Juices moderately rich in pectin will form a few small clots.

Juices poor in pectin will form small flaky sediment.

Test for Acid

The best determination of acid content is the taste. If the juice is too bland, add lemon juice to give it tartness.

Jelly-Making Properties of Fruits

To make good jelly, you need adequate quantities of both pectin and acid. If you are using a fruit poor in either of these elements, combine it with the juice of another fruit in which the lacking pectin or acidity is abundant.

Rich in Pectin, Rich in Acid	*Rich in Pectin, Poor in Acid*
Sour apples	Sweet apples
Blackberries	Quinces
Crab apples	
Cranberries	
Red currants	
Grapefruits	
Grapes	
Sour guavas	
Lemons	
Loganberries	
Sour oranges	
Plums	

Rich in Acid, Poor in Pectin	*Poor in Acid, Poor in Pectin*
Pomegranates	Raspberries
Apricots	Elderberries
Cherries	Peaches
Pineapples	Overripe fruits
Strawberries	

How Much Sugar?

The correct amount of sugar to use in jelly making is determined by the pectin content of the juice.

To juices rich in pectin, add ¾ cup sugar for every 1 cup juice.

To juices poor in pectin, add ½ cup sugar for every 1 cup juice.

The juice should be boiling when the sugar is added, and the juice and sugar should be cooked as rapidly as possible until the jellying stage is reached.

Test for Jellying Stage

Dip a spoon into the boiling syrup. As the jellying point nears, the syrup will drop from the side of the spoon in two large drops. When the drops run together and slide off the spoon in a "sheet," the jelly is finished; it should be immediately removed from the heat.

A thermometer may be used successfully in jelly making, but the sheet test should also be used, since the jellying point of some fruits differs. The range of temperature may vary from 7° to 10° above the boiling point, or from 212° to 222° F. at sea level.

Sterilizing Jars

If jars are to be filled with boiling-hot jams or pickles, sterilization is not essential, but the jars must be thoroughly washed in hot soapy water and rinsed well. They should be filled with very hot or boiling water and drained just before the hot fruit or pickle is jarred to prevent any possibility of cracking.

For other types of canning, jars should be washed and sterilized. Put them on a rack in a large saucepan, and add water to cover. Bring the water to a boil; boil for 10 minutes. Leave the jars in the hot water until ready to fill; then remove the jars one at a time with a pair of tongs, and drain.

Sealing with Paraffin

A small metal pot is an ideal container for paraffin. Cut paraffin into small pieces, put it in the pot and set the pot in a container of hot water. Cook over low heat until the paraffin is liquid. Pour hot jam or jelly into clean hot jars, leaving ¼-inch head space. Wipe the top of the jar so it is perfectly clean. Pour a small amount of melted paraffin over the top of the jam or jelly, and rotate the jar to cover the top of the mixture completely. Let it cool; then add another layer of melted paraffin (two thin layers are better than one thick one). When the paraffin is set, cover the jar with a lid.

Jams and Jellies

APRICOT JAM
Makes About 5 Pints

1 pound dried apricots
1-pound can crushed pineapple, undrained
1 orange, peeled, seeded and chopped
6 cups sugar

1. Day before, chop apricots; add water to cover; let stand for 24 hours.

2. Next day, turn apricots and water into large pot; stir in remaining ingredients. Cook over low heat, stirring until sugar is dissolved. Cook for 1 hour longer, stirring frequently.

3. Pour into hot sterilized jars; seal at once.

Mrs. John Spellman, Woman's Club,
Barrington, R.I.

"CARORANGE" CONFITURE

Makes About 3 Pints

½ cup dried orange peel
3 cups water
3 cups mashed cooked carrots
3 lemons, ground
5 cups sugar

1. Put orange peel and water into large pot. Bring to boil; then simmer for 30 minutes.

2. Add carrots, lemons and sugar. Bring to boil, stirring until sugar is dissolved. Cook over low heat for about 1 hour, to jelly stage (220° F.).

3. Pour into hot sterilized jars; seal at once.

Mrs. Harold M. Graham, Woman's Club,
Ruidoso, N.M.

CHERRY JAM

Makes 4 Pints

1 quart sour cherries, pitted
¼ cup water
5 cups sugar
1 bottle liquid pectin

1. Put cherries and water in large pot. Bring to boil; then simmer for 15 minutes.

2. Add sugar. Bring back to boil; boil rapidly for 3 minutes, stirring constantly.

3. Stir in pectin; cook, stirring and skimming constantly, for 5 minutes.

4. Pour into hot sterilized jars; seal at once.

A. S.

GRAPE JAM

Makes About 3 Pints

4 pounds Concord grapes
1 cup water
3 oranges
4 pounds sugar
1 pound seedless raisins

1. Put grapes and water in large pot; bring to boil. Cook over medium heat for 20 minutes.

2. Force grapes and juice through sieve to remove seeds.

3. Rinse pot; return grape juice, pulp and skin to pot.

4. Meanwhile, grate oranges; squeeze juice. Add rind and juice to pot. Stir in sugar and raisins; cook over medium heat, stirring constantly, until sugar is dissolved.

5. Bring to boil; cook over medium heat for 20 minutes, or until thickened.

6. Pour into hot sterilized jars; seal at once.

Mrs. Rebecca T. Mooney, Woman's Club,
Mount Dora, Fla.

HEAVENLY JAM

Makes About 5 Pints

3 pounds ripe peaches, peeled
  and chopped
6 cups sugar
2 oranges
4-ounce jar maraschino cherries

1. Day before, combine peaches and sugar. Cover; let stand overnight.

2. Next day, quarter oranges; remove seeds. Put oranges through medium blade of meat grinder.

3. Drain cherries; reserve syrup; chop cherries.

4. Put peaches and liquid, oranges, cherries and cherry syrup in large pot. Bring to boil; cook over medium heat for 1 hour, stirring occasionally.

5. Pour into hot sterilized jars; seal at once.

Lillian Warner, Monday Club, Spencer, Mass.

MARASCHINO PEAR JAM

Makes About 3 Quarts

6 cups finely chopped peeled pears
3 tablespoons lemon juice
7½ cups sugar
1-pound 4-ounce can crushed pineapple, drained
¾ cup quartered maraschino cherries

1. Mix pears, lemon juice and sugar in large pot. Cook over low heat, stirring constantly, until sugar is dissolved. Cook over medium heat, stirring occasionally, for 15 minutes, or until pears are tender and syrup thickens.

2. Stir in pineapple and cherries; cook over medium heat for 15 minutes.

3. Pour into hot sterilized jars; seal at once.

Woman's Club, Lincoln, Neb.

PINEAPPLE ORANGE JAM

Makes About 5 Pints

3 oranges
4 large or 6 small apples
2 lemons
1-pound 4-ounce can crushed
  pineapple
Sugar

1. Cut fruits into sections; remove seeds. Do not peel. Put through medium blade of meat grinder; combine with pineapple.

2. Measure fruit mixture into large pot; add equal amount of sugar.

3. Bring slowly to boil; boil for 20 minutes.

4. Turn into hot sterilized jelly glasses; seal at once.

Mrs. Richard C. Paul, President,
Cassadaga–Lake Helen Woman's Club,
Cassadaga, Fla.

PLUM JAM

Makes About 4 Pints

36 prune plums
1 orange, quartered and seeded
Sugar

1. Pit plums; do not peel.
2. Put plums and orange through medium blade of meat grinder.
3. Measure pulp into large pot; add equal amount of sugar.
4. Cook over low heat, stirring until sugar is dissolved. Bring to boil; boil, stirring occasionally, for 10 minutes, or to jelly stage (220° F.).
5. Pour into hot sterilized jars; seal at once.

Woman's Club, Lincoln, Neb.

RASPBERRY JAM

Makes About 2 Pints

3 cups raspberries
3 cups sugar
3 tablespoons lemon juice
3 ounces liquid pectin

1. Put raspberries in large pot; bring to boil, stirring occasionally. Boil over medium heat for 2 minutes.
2. Stir in sugar and lemon juice; boil for 3 minutes.
3. Bring to full rolling boil; pour in pectin. Boil for 30 seconds; remove from heat.
4. Beat for 5 minutes; pour into hot sterilized jars; seal at once.

Mrs. Karl Bleyl, Younger Woman's Club,
Barbourville, Ky.

EASY OVERNIGHT STRAWBERRY JAM

Makes About 4 Pints

2 quarts ripe large strawberries
6 cups sugar
2 tablespoons lemon juice

1. Day before, wash and hull strawberries. Cover with boiling water; let stand for 2 minutes. Drain well; put in large pot.
2. Stir in 4 cups of the sugar and lemon juice. Bring to boil, stirring occasionally. Boil hard for 2 minutes.
3. Remove from heat; when bubbling stops, stir in remaining sugar.
4. Return to heat; bring back to boil. Boil rapidly for 5 minutes longer.
5. Remove from heat; skim carefully.
6. Pour berries onto baking sheets or into shallow baking pans, with berries not more than ½ inch deep. Let stand overnight.
7. Next day, scrape berries from sheets or pans; turn into hot sterilized jars; seal at once.

Mrs. Everett Ray Williams, President,
Glenbrook Woman's Club, Louisville, Ky.

YEAR-ROUND JAM

Makes About 3½ Pints

4 10-ounce packages frozen
  strawberries, defrosted
2 tablespoons lemon juice

5 cups sugar
3 ounces liquid pectin

1. Put strawberries in large pot. Add lemon juice and sugar; mix well. Bring to full rolling boil over high heat; boil rapidly for 1½ minutes, stirring constantly.
2. Remove from heat; stir in pectin. Stir and skim for 5 minutes to cool slightly.
3. Pour into hot sterilized jars; seal at once.

VARIATION: Raspberries or peaches may be substituted for strawberries.

Mrs. E. S. Glen, Town and Country League,
Cheyenne, Wyo.

APPLE JELLY

Makes About 2 Pints

4 pounds firm tart apples
2 cups water
Sugar

1. Wash, core and slice apples.
2. Put apples and water in large pot; bring to boil. Cook over low heat for 15 minutes, or until soft.
3. Remove from heat; pour through jelly bag or large sieve lined with several layers of cheesecloth. Allow juice to drip into container below.
4. Measure juice; return to pot. Add ¾ cup sugar for every 1 cup juice. Cook over low heat, stirring until sugar is dissolved.
5. Boil rapidly to jelly stage (220° F.).
6. Skim surface; pour into hot sterilized jars; seal at once.

Mrs. Lucille Chastain, President, Washington
State Federation of Women's Organizations,
Spokane, Wash.

CINNAMON CANDY JELL

Makes About 9 Pints

1 pound red cinnamon candies
11 cups sugar
6 cups water
6 ounces liquid pectin

1. Put candies, sugar and water in large pot. Cook over medium heat, stirring until candies and sugar are dissolved. Bring to full rolling boil; pour in pectin.
2. Bring again to full rolling boil; boil for 1 minute.
3. Pour into hot sterilized jars; seal at once.

Mrs. Ross Crowley, Civic Club, Sandpoint, Ida.

GRAPE JELLY

Makes About 2 Pints

4 pounds slightly underripe
  Concord grapes
1 cup water
Sugar

1. Day before, wash, stem and crush grapes. Put in large pot; add water. Bring to boil; boil over medium heat for 10 minutes.
2. Remove from heat; pour through jelly bag or large sieve lined with several layers of cheesecloth. Allow juice to drip through without pressing grapes against side of bag or sieve. Let stand in cool place overnight.

3. Next day, measure juice; return to pot. Add ¾ cup sugar for every 1 cup juice. Cook over low heat, stirring until sugar is dissolved.

4. Boil rapidly to jelly stage (220° F.).

5. Pour into hot sterilized jars; seal at once.

A. S.

MINT JELLY
Makes About 2 Pints
½ cup fresh mint leaves
1¼ cups boiling water
2 tablespoons lemon juice
3 cups sugar
3 ounces liquid pectin
Few drops green food coloring

1. Put leaves in bowl; cover with water. Add lemon juice; let stand for 1 hour. Strain, pouring liquid into large pot. Add sugar; cook over medium heat, stirring until dissolved. Bring to full rolling boil; pour in pectin.

2. Bring back to full rolling boil; boil for 30 seconds.

3. Pour into hot sterilized jars; seal at once.

Woman's Club, Lincoln, Neb.

TABASCO JELLY
Makes About 1½ Pints
1 cup water
⅓ cup lemon juice
2 teaspoons Tabasco
3 cups sugar
3 ounces liquid pectin
Few drops red food coloring

1. In large pot combine water, lemon juice, Tabasco and sugar. Cook over low heat, stirring until sugar is dissolved. Bring to full rolling boil over high heat.

2. Stir in pectin and food coloring; bring back to full rolling boil. Boil for 30 seconds. Pour into hot sterilized jars; seal at once.

*Mrs. Donald W. Smith, Bedford Hills
Woman's Club, Chappaqua, N.Y.*

Preserves, Conserves, Marmalades and Chutneys

PEACH PRESERVES
Makes About 3 Pints
4 pounds peaches
1 quart water
6 cups sugar

1. Peel peaches; cut in half; pit.

2. Combine water and sugar in large pot; bring to boil; boil over high heat until syrup coats spoon.

3. Add peaches; boil over medium heat until syrup is thickened or reaches jelly stage (220° F.).

4. Pour into hot sterilized jars; seal at once.

*Mrs. W. O. Cockrell, Sesame Club,
Marshall, Tex.*

BRANDIED PEACHES
Makes 4 Pints
Store for about 1 month before using.
1 quart water
3 cups sugar
12 ripe peaches
½ cup brandy

1. Combine water and sugar in large pot. Bring to boil; boil for 10 minutes.

2. Peel a few peaches at a time; drop immediately into syrup; cook for about 5 minutes, or until barely tender when tested with toothpick; pack into hot sterilized jars. Repeat until all peaches have been poached and packed.

3. Add ¼ cup of the brandy to each jar; 2 tablespoons to each jar if pint jars are used. Fill jars with syrup; seal at once.

A. S.

PEAR PRESERVES
Makes About 3 Pints
1 cup water
1½ cups sugar
12 pears

1. Combine water and sugar in large pot; cook over low heat, stirring until sugar is dissolved. Bring to boil; boil for 5 minutes.

2. Meanwhile, peel, core and quarter pears. Cut each quarter in half.

3. Add pears to syrup; cook over medium heat until pears are clear and syrup is thickened and spins a thread.

4. Pour into hot sterilized jars; seal at once.

*Martha Jo Davis, Modern Study Club,
Wolfe City, Tex.*

STRAWBERRY PRESERVES
Makes About 4 Pints
1 cup water
8 cups sugar
2 quarts strawberries, hulled

1. Combine water and sugar in large pot. Stir over low heat, stirring until sugar is dissolved. Bring to boil; add strawberries.

2. Boil over medium heat for 30 minutes, shaking pot occasionally.

3. Skim; pour into shallow trays.

4. Cool; turn into hot sterilized jars; seal at once.

*Mrs. Hilda Bogardus, Woman's Club,
Pikeville, Ky.*

APRICOT CONSERVE
Makes About 8 Pints
2 pound dried apricots
4 quarts water
5 pounds sugar
Juice of 2 lemons
1 cup chopped blanched almonds

1. Day before, combine apricots and water in mixing bowl. Cover; let stand overnight.

2. Next day, turn apricots and liquid into large pot; bring to boil. Cook over medium heat, stirring occasionally, until tender.

3. Stir in sugar. Bring to boil; cook until thickened.

4. Remove from heat; stir in lemon juice and almonds.

5. Pour into hot sterilized jars; seal at once.

E. Andrus, Woman's Club, Ashton, Ill.

MELON PEACH CONSERVE

Makes About 6 Pints

4 cups diced cantaloupe
4 cups diced peeled peaches
6 cups sugar
¼ cup lemon juice
¼ teaspoon salt
½ cup blanched almonds
½ teaspoon nutmeg

1. Put cantaloupe and peaches in large pot; cook over medium heat for 20 minutes, stirring occasionally.

2. Add sugar and lemon juice; stir until sugar is dissolved. Boil over medium heat for 20 minutes, or until thickened.

3. Remove from heat; stir in salt, almonds and nutmeg.

4. Pour into hot sterilized jars; seal at once.

Woman's Club, Lincoln, Neb.

CHRISTMAS CONSERVE

Makes About 2 Pints

3 oranges
1 large lemon
1-pound 14-ounce can crushed
  pineapple, undrained
½ cup water
6 cups sugar
8-ounce jar maraschino cherries,
  drained and chopped
½ cup chopped walnuts

1. Remove seeds from oranges and lemon; put through medium blade of meat grinder. Turn into large pot.

2. Add pineapple and water. Bring to boil; cook over medium heat for 45 minutes.

3. Stir in sugar, cherries and walnuts; bring back to boil. Boil rapidly to jelly stage (220° F.).

4. Pour into hot sterilized jars; seal at once.

*Mrs. Calvin Robertson, Garden and Bird Club,
Brewer, Me.*

HOMEMADE MINCEMEAT

Makes 8 Pints

1 pound diced cooked pork
½ pound diced cooked veal
10 medium tart apples, cored
2 cups seedless raisins
2 cups currants
1 cup cooked cranberries
2 cups sugar
1 cup sweet apple cider
1 tablespoon cinnamon
1 tablespoon ground cloves
1 tablespoon nutmeg
1 cup beef broth
2 tablespoons vinegar

1. Put pork, veal and apples through medium blade of meat grinder.

2. Turn into large pot; add remaining ingredients. Mix well. Bring to boil, stirring frequently.

3. Pack into hot sterilized jars; seal at once.

Leora Pullen, Woman's Club, West Frankfort, Ill.

PEACH NUT CONSERVE

Makes About 3 Pints

6 cups sliced peeled ripe peaches
4 cups sugar
1 orange, quartered and seeded
14-ounce can pineapple tidbits,
  drained
1 cup coarsely chopped walnuts

1. Put peaches in bowl; sprinkle with sugar. Let stand for 1 hour.

2. Meanwhile, put orange and pineapple through medium blade of meat grinder.

3. Put peaches and liquid, orange and pineapple in large pot. Bring to boil over low heat, stirring constantly. Cook over low heat, stirring occasionally, for 40 minutes, or until thickened.

4. Remove from heat; stir in walnuts.

5. Pour into hot sterilized jars; seal at once.

Mrs. Carl Ackley, Woman's Club, Barrington, R.I.

PLUM RHUBARB CONSERVE

Makes About 12 Pints

3 pounds prune plums, pitted
6 10-ounce packages frozen rhubarb
  or 10 pounds fresh rhubarb, cut up
8 pounds sugar
6 oranges, peeled, seeded and diced
1 pound seedless raisins
1 pound chopped walnuts

1. Combine plums, rhubarb, sugar, oranges and raisins in large pot. Cook over low heat, stirring occasionally, for about 4 hours, or until thickened.

2. Remove from heat; stir in walnuts.

3. Pour into hot sterilized jars; seal at once.

*Submitted to Woman's Club,
Kankakee, Ill., by Charlotte Montgomery,
Good Housekeeping magazine*

RHUBARB À CONSERVE

Makes About 7 Pints

8 cups chopped pineapple
8 cups peeled finely cut rhubarb
Juice of 1 orange
Juice of 1 lemon
6 pounds sugar

1. Combine all ingredients in large pot. Stir over medium heat until sugar is dissolved. Bring to boil; boil over medium heat for 45 minutes, or until mixture is thick and sheets from spoon.

2. Pour into hot sterilized jars; seal at once.

Julia J. Behrens, Woman's Club, Greenview, Ill.

LEMON MARMALADE
Makes About 6 Pints
4 cups thinly sliced seeded lemons
3 quarts water
9 cups sugar

1. Combine lemons and water in large pot. Bring to boil; cook rapidly for 20 minutes, or until tender.
2. Drain; add water to liquid to total 3 quarts.
3. Put liquid, lemons and sugar in pot. Cook over low heat, stirring until sugar is dissolved. Boil rapidly to jelly stage (220° F.).
4. Remove from heat; skim; cool for 5 minutes.
5. Stir to allow fruits to be suspended in syrup; pour into hot sterilized jars; seal at once.

A. S.

ENGLISH MARMALADE
Makes About 4 Pints
1 large lemon
2 pounds Seville or bitter oranges
2 quarts plus 1 cup water
8 cups sugar

1. 2 days before, cut lemon and oranges into thin slices; remove seeds. Put fruits in bowl; cover with water. Cover; let stand for 24 hours.
2. Next day, pour water and fruits into large pot; bring to boil. Cook over medium heat for 1 hour. Remove from heat; cover; and let stand for 24 hours.
3. Next day, return to heat; bring to boil. Stir in sugar; cook over low heat, stirring until sugar is dissolved. Boil rapidly for 30 minutes, or to jelly stage (220° F.).
4. Remove from heat; skim; cool for 5 minutes.
5. Stir to allow fruits to be suspended in syrup; pour into hot sterilized jars; seal at once.

A. S.

THREE FRUITS MARMALADE
Makes About 3 Pints
1 grapefruit
2 oranges
1 lemon
5 pounds sugar

1. 2 days before, cut grapefruit, oranges and lemon into very thin slices; remove seeds. Put fruits in mixing bowl. Cover with three times as much water. Cover; let stand for 24 hours.
2. Next day, turn fruits and water into large pot; bring to boil. Boil for 1 hour, or until tender. Remove from heat; cover; let stand for 24 hours.
3. Next day, add sugar. Slowly bring to boil, stirring occasionally until sugar is dissolved. Boil over medium heat for 20 minutes. Remove from heat; let stand for 5 minutes.

4. Pour into hot sterilized jars; seal at once.

Mrs. E. M. Broderick, Woman's Club,
State College, Pa.

APPLE CHUTNEY
Makes About 5 Pints
8 cups chopped peeled apples
1 clove garlic, crushed
1 cup chopped onions
2 sweet red peppers, chopped
4 cups brown sugar
2 pounds seedless raisins
2 teaspoons salt
2 teaspoons black mustard seed
2 teaspoons ground ginger
1 quart vinegar
2 hot pepper pods
2 tablespoons white mustard seed
2 teaspoons allspice

1. Mix all ingredients in large pot. Bring to boil; cook over medium heat, stirring occasionally, for 30 minutes, or until thickened.
2. Pour into hot sterilized jars; seal at once.

County Club, Chelan, Wash.

PEACH CHUTNEY
Makes About 5 Pints
8 cups cut-up peeled peaches
1 cup finely chopped onions
2 cloves garlic, crushed
1 cup seedless raisins
4 ounces crystallized ginger, chopped
1 pound brown sugar
3 cups vinegar
½ cup Worcestershire
½ cup lime juice
1 tablespoon salt
1 tablespoon crushed hot red pepper
1 tablespoon mustard seed

1. Combine all ingredients in large pot. Bring to boil, stirring occasionally. Boil over medium heat, stirring occasionally, for 45 minutes, or until thickened.
2. Pour into hot sterilized jars; seal at once.

Mathews County Woman's Club, Grimstead, Va.

FRESH PRUNE CHUTNEY
Makes About 1½ Pints
1 cup brown sugar
1 cup granulated sugar
¾ cup cider vinegar
1½ teaspoons crushed hot red peppers
2 teaspoons salt
2 teaspoons mustard seed
2 cloves garlic, crushed
1 small onion, thinly sliced
½ cup preserved ginger, thinly sliced
1 cup seedless raisins
3½ cups prune plums, halved and pitted

1. In large pot combine sugars and vinegar; bring to boil, stirring until sugars are dissolved.
2. Stir in all remaining ingredients except plums; mix well.

3. Add plums; mix well. Cook over low heat, stirring occasionally, for about 50 minutes, or until thickened.

4. Pour into hot sterilized jars; seal at once.

Mrs. Clark Burrell, Woman's Club, Lovell, Wyo.

CHUTNEY SANDWICH SPREAD
Makes About 2 Pints

4 cups ground carrots
1 cup ground onions
6 mangoes, peeled and ground
½ cup sugar
1 tablespoon prepared mustard
1 tablespoon butter
2 cups vinegar
3 tablespoons flour
2 tablespoons water
1 tablespoon salt
½ teaspoon pepper

1. In large pot combine carrots, onions, mangoes, sugar, mustard, butter and vinegar. Bring to boil; then simmer, stirring occasionally, for 15 minutes.

2. Meanwhile, in small bowl blend remaining ingredients; stir into carrot mixture; bring to boil, stirring constantly. Simmer for 15 minutes, stirring frequently.

3. Pour into hot sterilized jars; seal at once.

Bessie Ewing, Advance Club, Pandora, Ohio

PEAR HONEY
Makes About 8 Pints

16 cups ground seeded pears
1 lemon, ground
12 cups sugar

1. Mix all ingredients in large pot. Cook over low heat, stirring until sugar is dissolved. Bring to boil; cook over very low heat for 1 hour, or until transparent.

2. Pour into hot sterilized jars; seal at once.

Mrs. V. W. Francis, Woman's Club, Capron, Va.

QUINCE HONEY
Makes About 4 Pints

1 cup water
6 cups sugar
6 quinces, finely chopped
3 apples, peeled, cored and
  finely chopped

1. Combine water and sugar in large pot. Cook over low heat, stirring occasionally until sugar is dissolved. Bring to boil; boil hard for 5 minutes.

2. Stir in quinces and apples; boil for 15 minutes.

3. Pour into hot sterilized jars; seal at once.

Helen P. Wayt, Women's Literary Club, Pentwater, Mich.

AUNT MOLLIE'S APPLE BUTTER
Makes About 10 Pints

10 pounds tart cooking apples
9 cups sugar
4 cinnamon sticks
1 gallon apple cider

1. Preheat oven to 250° F.

2. Wash and core apples. Put through medium blade of meat grinder.

3. Put apples in large roasting pan; stir in sugar, cinnamon and 1 quart of the cider.

4. Put pan in preheated oven; when apples come to boil, stir well. Cook in oven for about 6 hours, adding cider as purée thickens.

5. Remove cinnamon; pour into hot sterilized jars; seal at once.

Mrs. James Dunlap, Woman's Club, Jacksonville, Ill.

Pickles, Relishes and Condiments

PICKLED BEETS
Makes About 4 Pints

Young small beets
2 cups sugar
2 cups water
2 cups cider vinegar
1 teaspoon cloves
1 teaspoon whole allspice
1 lemon, thinly sliced
1 tablespoon broken cinnamon
  sticks

1. Wash beets; simmer in water to cover for 30 minutes, or until tender. Drain; dip in cold water; trim tops; peel off skins.

2. Pack beets in hot sterilized jars.

3. Combine remaining ingredients in saucepan. Bring to boil; then simmer for 15 minutes.

4. Pour over beets; seal at once.

NOTE: A little grated horseradish may be added, if desired.

Mrs. Dorothy Stertzach, Friendly Hills Woman's Club, Rural East Canton, Ohio

CAULIFLOWER PICKLE
Makes 3 Pints

2 pounds cauliflower
2 sweet red peppers
¼ teaspoon black pepper
¼ tablespoon marjoram
¼ teaspoon garlic powder
¼ cup white vinegar
2 cups salad oil

1. Trim cauliflower; break into flowerets. Put in large pot; cover with water; bring to boil. Simmer for 5 minutes. Drain and pack into 3 hot sterilized pint jars.

2. Cut red peppers into thin rings; mix with remaining ingredients; pour into jars. Seal at once.

Dotty Risley, Junior Woman's Club, Jacksonville, Fla.

BREAD AND BUTTER PICKLES

Makes 8 Pints

20 medium cucumbers, thinly sliced
6 medium onions, thinly sliced
2 tablespoons salt
2 cups sugar
1 tablespoon turmeric
1½ tablespoons ginger
1 tablespoon mustard seed
1 tablespoon celery seed
1 sweet red pepper or pimiento,
    finely chopped
12 cassia buds
1 quart cider vinegar

1. Put cucumbers and onions in large mixing bowl; sprinkle with 1 tablespoon of the salt. Let stand for 1 hour; drain. Put in large pot.
2. Combine remaining salt and all remaining ingredients except vinegar. Stir in vinegar.
3. Pour over vegetables; bring to boil.
4. Pour into hot jars; seal at once.

Mrs. Russell Barr, President, Federated
Woman's Club, Laurel, Mont.

CRYSTAL SWEET PICKLES

Makes About 8 Pints

36 medium cucumbers
4 cups salt
1 gallon water
2 tablespoons powdered alum
1 quart vinegar
8 cups sugar
2 cinnamon sticks
1 teaspoon cloves
1 tablespoon celery seed

1. 2 weeks before, put cucumbers in large bowl or crock; cover with salt and water. Cover; let stand for 2 weeks. Weight down top to keep cucumbers under brine. Skim surface every day, if necessary.
2. At end of 2 weeks, drain and wash cucumbers. Cut into chunks; put in large bowl or crock. Cover with water; sprinkle with alum. Let stand for 24 hours; drain; rinse.
3. Next day, in large pot mix vinegar and 2 cups of the sugar. Tie cinnamon, cloves and celery seed in cheesecloth, add to vinegar mixture. Bring to boil; pour over cucumbers. Let stand for 24 hours.
4. Next day, drain cucumbers; return liquid to pot. Add 2 cups of the sugar; bring to boil; pour over cucumbers. Let stand for 24 hours.
5. Repeat process until all sugar has been added.
6. Final day, pack cucumbers into hot sterilized jars.
7. Bring liquid to boil; remove spice bag. Pour vinegar into jars; seal at once.

Mrs. Kenneth F. Scott, Woman's Club,
Clinton, Mo.

MONTANA PICKLES

Makes About 8 Pints

14 medium cucumbers
1 quart vinegar

8 cups sugar
2 tablespoons salt
15 allspice
20 cloves
3-inch cinnamon stick

1. Day before, put cucumbers in large bowl; add boiling water to cover. Let stand overnight.
2. Next day, drain; repeat same procedure for next 3 days.
3. Cut cucumbers into ¼-inch-thick slices; return to bowl. In large pot combine remaining ingredients; bring to boil. Pour liquid over cucumbers; let stand overnight.
4. Next day, drain; reserve liquid; bring back to boil. Repeat this same procedure for next 2 days.
5. Put liquid in large pot; bring to boil. Add cucumbers; bring back to boil.
6. Pour into hot sterilized jars; seal at once.

Dorothy R. Todd, Junior Woman's Club,
Coronado, Calif.

OLIVE OIL PICKLES

Makes About 6 Pints

25 medium cucumbers, thinly sliced
1 cup salt
1 teaspoon celery seed
½ cup white mustard seed
½ cup black mustard seed
½ cup olive oil
Vinegar

1. Arrange alternate layers of cucumbers and salt in mixing bowl. Let stand for 3 hours.
2. Rinse and drain; stir in celery seed, mustard seeds and olive oil. Mix well; pack into hot sterilized jars.
3. Fill each jar with vinegar. Seal at once.

Mary Hart, Woman's Club, Sioux City, Ia.

KOSHER DILL PICKLES

Makes 4 Quarts

4 quarts medium cucumbers
8 dill sprays
4 cloves garlic
4 hot red pepper pods
1 quart vinegar
1 cup salt
3 quarts water

1. Day before, wash cucumbers; cover with cold water; let stand overnight.
2. Next day, put 1 of dill sprays in bottom of each quart jar. Pack cucumbers into jars, being careful not to bruise them. Add garlic clove and red pepper pod to each jar; place 1 of remaining dill sprays on top.
3. Combine vinegar, salt and water, bring to rolling boil. Fill jars to overflowing with vinegar brine; seal; store in cool dark place for 10 days to 2 weeks. (Brine will cloud, but then clear as fermentation ceases. Then pickles are ready to eat.)

A. S.

SWEET DILL PICKLES

Makes About 2 Pints

1-quart jar dill pickles
2 cups sugar
2 tablespoons vinegar

1. Drain pickles; slice into mixing bowl. Sprinkle with sugar and vinegar.
2. Refrigerate for 2 days.

Mrs. L. Simmons, President, Woman's Club, Clinton, Ia.

PICKLED DILL OKRA

Makes About 6 Pints

3 pounds (tender baby pods) okra
or 3 10-ounce packages frozen
whole baby okra
Garlic cloves
Celery leaves
1 quart water
2 cups white vinegar
½ cup pickling salt
1 tablespoon dillweed
2 teaspoons celery seed
1 teaspoon mustard seed

1. Wash okra well; place in hot sterilized jars. Add garlic clove and a few celery leaves to each jar.
2. Combine remaining ingredients in saucepan. Bring to boil; pour over okra in jars.
3. Seal jars. Place in large pot. Add sufficient water to come to within 2 inches of top of jars. Bring to boil; boil for 25 minutes.
4. Let stand for at least 4 weeks before using.

Mrs. Henry L. Howell, 20th Century Club, Gordo, Ala.

DILLED ONION RINGS

Makes 1 Quart

4 medium onions, sliced
1 gallon water
1 cup salt
2 tablespoons powdered alum
1 cup white vinegar
12 peppercorns
1 teaspoon dill seed
1 clove garlic

1. Day or 2 before, soak onions in 2 quarts of the water with salt for 1 hour. Drain; rinse.
2. Soak onions in remaining water with alum for 2 to 3 hours. Drain; rinse thoroughly.
3. Pack onions into quart jar; add remaining ingredients. Let stand for 1 or 2 days before using.

Modern Study Club Cook Book, Mobile, Ala.

STUFFED PICKLED PEPPERS

Serves 12

12 large green or red peppers
2 tablespoons salt
4 cups shredded cabbage
1 cup sugar
2 tablespoons mustard seed
1 tablespoon celery seed
Vinegar

1. Day before, cut slice from stem end of each green or red pepper; reserve slices. Remove seeds and membranes; put peppers and slices into large bowl. Cover with water; sprinkle with 1 tablespoon of the salt; cover; let stand overnight.
2. Next day, drain well; turn peppers upside down.
3. In mixing bowl combine cabbage, remaining salt, sugar, mustard seed and celery seed; mix well; use to fill peppers; replace tops; tie in place.
4. Place peppers in large crock; cover with vinegar. May be used in about 2 weeks; if weighted down and covered, may be kept all winter in cool place.

Myrtie Blackborn, Grant County Junior Woman's Club, Williamstown, Ky.

GREEN TOMATO PICKLES (CRISP)

Makes About 9 Pints

2 gallons water
3 cups slaked lime
6 pounds small, solid green tomatoes, sliced ⅛ inch thick
5 pounds sugar
1½ quart white vinegar
1 teaspoon ground cloves
1 teaspoon ground allspice
1 teaspoon ground ginger
1 teaspoon ground celery seed
1 teaspoon ground mace
1 teaspoon ground cinnamon
½ bottle green food coloring

1. Day before, combine water and lime in enamel pan. Add tomatoes; soak for 24 hours.
2. Next day, drain, rinse and soak tomatoes in clear water for 4 hours, changing water every hour.
3. In large pot combine sugar, vinegar and spices. Bring to boil. Add food coloring.
4. Drain tomatoes; pour syrup over them. Let stand overnight.
5. Next day, bring tomatoes and syrup to boil; then simmer for 1 hour, or until tender.
6. Pack in hot sterilized jars; seal at once.

Mrs. Bennett Ellsberry, Woman's Club, Ruskin, Fla.

PICKLED FIGS

Makes About 3 Pints

3 cups sugar
2 cups vinegar
2 cinnamon sticks, broken
1 teaspoon cloves
3 pounds fresh black figs

1. Day before, combine sugar, vinegar, cinnamon and cloves in large pot. Bring to boil; boil rapidly for 8 minutes.
2. Meanwhile, wash figs. Pour boiling water over figs; let stand for 1 minute. Rinse in cold water; drain thoroughly.
3. Put figs in syrup; boil for 10 minutes. Let stand overnight.
4. Next day, bring syrup back to boil; boil for 15 minutes. Let stand overnight.

5. Next day, bring back to boil; boil for 15 minutes.

6. Pack into hot sterilized jars; seal at once.

Ruth Adams, Woman's Club, Oceanside, Calif.

PICKLED PEACHES
Makes About 6 Pints
4 pounds underripe peaches
3 cups cider vinegar
3 cups sugar
3 cinnamon sticks
1 teaspoon cloves
1 teaspoon allspice
2 teaspoons quick-cooking tapioca

1. Put peaches in large bowl; cover with boiling water. Let stand for 3 minutes; drain; remove skins.

2. In large pot combine remaining ingredients. Bring to boil, stirring occasionally; boil over high heat for 5 minutes.

3. Add a few peaches at a time; poach over low heat for 3 minutes, or until peaches are heated through and are pierced easily with fork.

4. Put peaches in hot sterilized jars; strain syrup over them; seal at once.

June Summers, Junior Woman's Club, Hickory, N.C.

PICKLED PINK PEACHES
Makes About 2 Pints
¼ cup vinegar
⅓ cup sugar
3-inch cinnamon stick
10 cloves
¼ teaspoon salt
2 tablespoons red cinnamon candies
1-pound 13-ounce can peach halves, drained
¼ cup brandy (optional)

1. In saucepan combine vinegar, sugar, cinnamon, cloves, salt and candies. Bring to boil; then simmer for 10 minutes.

2. Add peaches; bring back to boil; then simmer for 5 minutes.

3. Remove from heat; stir in brandy, if desired.

4. Cover; chill in refrigerator, where peaches will keep for several weeks.

Jessie Wyckoff, Fargo Chapter of Pioneer Daughters, Fargo, N.D.

SPICED PEACHES
Makes About 2 Pints
1-pound 4-ounce can peach halves
¾ cup cider vinegar
⅓ cup sugar
Cinnamon stick
1 teaspoon whole allspice
Cloves

1. Drain peaches; reserve ½ cup syrup.

2. In large pot combine reserved syrup, vinegar, sugar, cinnamon and allspice. Bring to boil, stirring until sugar is dissolved. Boil over medium heat for 10 minutes.

3. Meanwhile, stud peach halves with cloves; add to syrup; bring back to boil.

4. Pour into hot sterilized jars; seal at once.

Mrs. William H. Hasebroock, Honorary President, General Federation of Women's Clubs, West Point, Neb.

PINEAPPLE PICKLE
(From Maui, Hawaii)
Makes 6 Pints
12 cups pineapple cubes or 2 medium pineapples
2½ cups white vinegar
4 cups sugar
2 cups water
2 tablespoons cloves
2 cinnamon sticks

1. If fresh pineapple is used, peel and cut crosswise into 1-inch slices. Remove core; cut into sections about 1 inch wide.

2. In large pot combine vinegar, sugar and water. Bring to boil.

3. Tie spices in cheesecloth; add to vinegar mixture; simmer for 15 minutes. Add pineapple; cover; simmer for 30 minutes, or until tender.

4. Remove spice bag; pour pineapple into hot sterilized jars; seal at once.

NOTE: If desired, about 4 cloves may be added to each jar before sealing.

Mrs. Murry Snoddy, Magazine Club, Roanoke, Ala.

SWEET WATERMELON PICKLE
Makes About 4 Pints
2 pounds watermelon rind, cut into small squares
¼ cup salt
4 cups sugar
2 cups vinegar
¼ cup mixed pickling spices
4-ounce jar maraschino cherries, drained

1. Day before, put watermelon rind in large bowl; cover with 1 quart water. Add salt. Let stand overnight.

2. Next day, drain rind; put in large pot. Cover with fresh water; bring to boil; then simmer for 30 minutes, or until tender. Drain; set aside.

3. In another large pot combine sugar, vinegar, 2 cups water and pickling spices tied in cheesecloth. Bring to boil, stirring occasionally.

4. Add watermelon rind; simmer until clear and transparent. Add cherries; simmer for 5 minutes longer.

5. Remove spices; pour into hot sterilized jars; seal at once.

Mica Cowan, Woman's Club, Dundee, Ill.

SPICED BEANS
Makes 2 Quarts
1-pound can whole green beans, drained
1-pound can wax beans, drained
1-pound can kidney beans, drained and washed
½ green pepper, sliced
½ cup thinly sliced onion rings

¾ cup sugar
1 cup vinegar
Salt and pepper to taste

1. Combine beans, green pepper and onions; pack into hot sterilized quart jars.
2. In saucepan combine sugar and vinegar; heat, stirring until sugar is dissolved. Stir in salt and pepper. Pour over beans in jars; seal at once.

A. S.

BEET AND CABBAGE RELISH

Makes About 4 Pints

4 cups finely chopped cooked beets
4 cups finely chopped cabbage
½ cup grated horseradish
1 teaspoon salt
⅛ teaspoon pepper
2 cups sugar
1 cup cider vinegar
1 cup water

1. Put beets, cabbage and horseradish in mixing bowl. Sprinkle with salt and pepper; toss lightly to mix.
2. In saucepan combine sugar, vinegar and water. Cook over medium heat, stirring occasionally, until sugar is dissolved. Bring to boil; pour over vegetables; mix.
3. Turn into hot sterilized jars; seal at once.

Kathleen McClellan, Woman's Club,
Lynn, Mass.

QUICK CABBAGE CHOW-CHOW

Makes About 8 Pints

1 medium cabbage, chopped
2 cups small onions, chopped
2 green peppers, chopped
2 tablespoons salt
1 quart vinegar
1 cup brown sugar
¼ cup black mustard seed
¼ cup white mustard seed
1 teaspoon celery seed

1. In bowl or crock mix vegetables and salt; let stand for 1 hour. Turn into colander; drain for 3 hours.
2. In large pot combine remaining ingredients. Bring to boil; boil for 1 minute. Add vegetables; bring back to boil.
3. Pour into hot sterilized jars; seal at once.

Mrs. Nell Rice, Ethan Club, Dadeville, Ala.

PRESERVED HORSERADISH

Horseradish roots
Salt
White vinegar

1. Scrape horseradish roots; drop immediately into salted cold water to prevent discoloration.
2. Drain. Put through meat grinder, or cut coarsely and grate ½ cup at a time at high speed in electric blender.
3. Fill sterilized pint jars about two-thirds full. Add 1 teaspoon salt to each jar; fill with vinegar. Seal at once.

A. S.

KIM CHEE

Makes 5 or 6 Pints

5 to 6 pounds Chinese cabbage
1 cup rock salt
2½ quarts water
2 or 3 chili peppers, chopped
1 teaspoon sugar
½ teaspoon monosodium glutamate
1 teaspoon chopped ginger
1 teaspoon minced garlic
½ teaspoon salt
3 tablespoons chopped scallions

1. Cut cabbage into pieces about 1½ inches long. Put in large crock; add rock salt and water; soak for 6 to 7 hours. Drain; rinse.
2. Combine cabbage and remaining ingredients. Pack into sterilized jars; cover with cold water, leaving ½-inch head space.
3. Cover tightly; let stand at room temperature for 2 to 3 days. Then refrigerate.

Hilo Woman's Club Cook Book, Hilo, Hawaii

CORN RELISH

Makes About 4 Pints

9 ears corn
1 medium cabbage, shredded
2 medium green peppers, chopped
2 medium onions, chopped
¼ cup salt
1 cup sugar
2 quarts vinegar
2 tablespoons prepared mustard
1 tablespoon flour
1 tablespoon celery seed

1. Cut corn from cob; put in large pot.
2. Add cabbage, green peppers, onions, salt, sugar and vinegar. Bring to boil; then simmer for 30 minutes.
3. In small bowl blend mustard and flour; stir into vegetable mixture. Add celery seed; simmer for 5 minutes, stirring frequently.
4. Pour into hot sterilized jars; seal at once.

Mrs. J. W. Van Dyke, Woman's Club,
Sioux City, Ia.

SWEET AND SOUR CORN RELISH

Makes About 5 Pints

8 cups corn kernels
4 cups chopped cabbage
1 cup diced celery
1 medium sweet red pepper, diced
1 quart cider vinegar
2 cups brown sugar
¼ cup dry mustard
2 tablespoons salt
1 teaspoon turmeric

1. In large pot mix all ingredients except turmeric. Bring to boil. Then simmer for 30 minutes, stirring occasionally.
2. Add turmeric; simmer for 5 minutes.
3. Pour into hot sterilized jars; seal at once.

Mrs. James Stamper, Woman's Club,
Belle, W. Va.

HOT DOG RELISH

Makes 5 Pints

5 cups ground unpeeled 5- to
  6-inch-long cucumbers
3 cups ground onions
3 cups chopped celery
2 medium green peppers, ground
2 hot red peppers, ground
¾ cup salt
1½ quarts water
1 quart vinegar
3 cups sugar
2 teaspoons mustard seed
2 tablespoons celery seed

1. Day before, in large mixing bowl
combine cucumbers, onions, celery and
green and red peppers. Add salt and water;
let stand overnight.
2. Next day, drain vegetables.
3. In large pot combine remaining ingredients. Bring to boil; stir in vegetables.
Bring back to boil; then simmer for 10
minutes.
4. Pour into hot sterilized jars; seal at
once.

Mrs. Arthur Freeman, G. T. Club,
Huntsville, Mo.

PEAR RELISH

Makes 18 to 20 Pints

6 green peppers, cored and seeded
6 sweet red peppers, cored and seeded
½ bushel pears, cored and peeled
10 medium onions
¼ cup mixed whole spices tied
  in bag
4 pounds sugar
2 tablespoons turmeric
2 tablespoons salt
2 quarts vinegar

1. Grind green and red peppers; drain.
2. Grind pears and onions; reserve juice.
3. Combine all ingredients in large pot;
bring to boil; then simmer for 30 minutes.
4. Pour into hot sterilized jars; seal at
once.

Carol Pitman, Junior Woman's Club,
Jacksonville, Fla.

GREEN PEPPER RELISH

Makes About 8 Pints

24 medium green peppers, cored
  and seeded
12 medium onions
3 cups sugar
3 cups vinegar
2 tablespoons salt
2 tablespoons celery seed
2 tablespoons mustard seed
1 tablespoon crushed red pepper
  flakes
4-ounce can pimientos, drained
  and diced

1. Put green peppers and onions
through medium blade of meat grinder.
Place in colander. Pour boiling water over
vegetables; drain; repeat with more boiling
water.
2. Turn vegetables into large pot; add
remaining ingredients. Bring to boil; cook

over very low heat for 40 minutes, stirring
occasionally.
3. Pour into hot sterilized jars; seal at
once.

Margaret Brunson, Junior Solitic Club,
Crowley, La.

PEPPER RELISH

Makes About 6 Pints

24 red peppers, cored and seeded
24 green peppers, cored and seeded
12 medium onions
1 quart vinegar
2 cups sugar
2 teaspoons salt

1. Put red and green peppers and onions
through meat grinder. Cover with boiling
water; let stand for 20 minutes; drain.
2. Put vegetables and remaining ingredients in large pot. Bring to boil; cook over
low heat for 1 hour.
3. Pour into hot sterilized jars; seal at
once.

Mrs. D. E. Lloyd, Woman's Club, Western, Neb.

JELLIED PEPPER RELISH

Makes About 4 Pints

6 medium red peppers, cored
  and seeded
7 cups sugar
⅔ cup cider vinegar
⅓ cup water
6 ounces liquid pectin

1. Put red peppers through medium
blade of meat grinder; turn 2½ cups into
large pot. Stir in sugar, vinegar and water.
Bring to boil over low heat, stirring until
sugar is dissolved. Bring to full rolling
boil; boil on high heat for 5 minutes,
stirring frequently.
2. Stir in pectin; bring back to full
rolling boil. Boil for 1 minute.
3. Cool for 5 minutes. Skim; stir well.
4. Pour into hot sterilized jars; seal at
once.

Christina Roark, Woman's Club, Cortland, N.Y.

HOT RED PEPPER RELISH

Makes About 8 Pints

24 medium sweet green peppers,
  cored and seeded
24 medium sweet red peppers,
  cored and seeded
18 red and green hot peppers,
  cored and seeded
24 medium onions
1 quart vinegar
3½ cups sugar
¼ cup salt

1. Put peppers and onions through
medium blade of meat grinder.
2. Turn into large bowl; cover with
boiling water. Let stand for 5 minutes;
drain well; turn into large pot.
3. Add vinegar, sugar and salt; bring to
full rolling boil. Boil over medium heat for
10 minutes.

4. Turn into hot sterilized jars; seal at once.

Mrs. James K. Coleman, Modern Culture Club, Tuscaloosa, Ala.

PEPPER SLAW
Makes 14 Pints
12 large sweet green peppers, cored and seeded
12 large sweet red peppers, cored and seeded
12 large onions
2 large cabbages, cut into wedges
¼ cup pickling salt
2½ tablespoons mustard seed
2½ tablespoons celery seed
6 cups sugar
Vinegar

1. Day before, put all vegetables through coarse blade of meat grinder. Sprinkle with salt; mix; let stand overnight.
2. Next day, drain off juice from vegetables; add mustard seed, celery seed and sugar; mix well. Add vinegar just to cover. Pack in hot sterilized jars; seal at once. Will keep for 1 year if stored in cool place.

Mrs. E. A. Irby, Woman's Club, Lavalette, W. Va.

SWEET SOUR RELISH
Makes About 2 Pints
2 cups sauerkraut, drained and chopped
1 cup chopped celery
1 cup chopped onions
1 cup vinegar
1 cup sugar
1 canned pimiento, chopped

Mix all ingredients; refrigerate.

Mrs. Richard Roland, Woman's Club, Tampa, Fla.

PICCALILLI
Makes About 12 Pints
½ peck ripe tomatoes, finely chopped
½ peck green tomatoes, finely chopped
6 sweet red peppers, finely chopped
6 green peppers, finely chopped
12 small onions, finely chopped
1 cup salt
1 quart cider vinegar
6 cups brown sugar
1 teaspoon cloves
1 tablespoon mustard seed
1 tablespoon cinnamon

1. Day before, in large container mix tomatoes, peppers and onions. Sprinkle with salt. Cover; let stand overnight.
2. Next day, drain vegetables well; turn into large pot. Add remaining ingredients. Bring to boil, stirring occasionally until sugar is dissolved. Boil over medium heat for 45 minutes, stirring occasionally.
3. Pour into hot sterilized jars; seal at once.

Dagma Mason, Woman's Club, Southwick, Mass.

MRS. SAWYER'S BOSTON RELISH
Makes About 12 Pints
12 cups ground green tomatoes
12 cups ground ripe tomatoes
3 cups ground onions
1 large bunch celery, chopped
½ cup salt
1½ quarts vinegar
6 cups sugar
½ teaspoon ground cloves
½ teaspoon cinnamon

1. Day before, combine tomatoes, onions, celery and salt in large pot. Let stand overnight.
2. Next day, drain vegetables. Add remaining ingredients. Bring to boil; then simmer for 30 minutes, or until tender.
3. Spoon off excess liquid. Pour into hot sterilized jars; seal at once.

Mrs. Thomas Nickerson, Junior Women's Club, Rye, N.H.

UNCOOKED GREEN TOMATO RELISH
Makes About 6 Pints
½ peck green tomatoes
1 small cabbage
12 small onions
10 green or 2 red and 8 green peppers, cored and seeded
1 teaspoon turmeric
1 teaspoon celery seed
1 teaspoon dry mustard
1 tablespoon cinnamon
1 tablespoon allspice
1 tablespoon white mustard seed
1 quart vinegar
5 cups sugar
½ cup salt

1. Day before, grind tomatoes; drain in colander. Grind cabbage, onions and peppers. Combine all ingredients; let stand overnight.
2. Next day, pack into hot sterilized jars; seal at once.

Loreen Bliss, Woman's Club, Orem, Utah

BARBECUE SAUCE
Makes About 1½ Pints
¼ cup finely chopped onion
1 cup catsup
½ cup water
2 tablespoons brown sugar
½ teaspoon salt
Dash of pepper
Dash of cayenne
¼ cup vinegar
¼ cup lemon juice
3 tablespoons Worcestershire
1 tablespoon prepared mustard

1. Combine all ingredients in large pot. Bring to boil over low heat, stirring occasionally; then simmer for 30 minutes, stirring occasionally.
2. Pour into hot sterilized jars; seal at once.

Dot Hanson, Yorkewood Women's Club, Baltimore, Md.

CHILI SAUCE

Makes About 3 Quarts

12 ripe large tomatoes
4 large onions
3 green peppers, cored and seeded
3 bunches celery
1½ cup cider vinegar
1 tablespoon salt
2 tablespoons chili powder
Bouquet garni (see Glossary)
1 cup sugar

1. Finely chop tomatoes, onions, green peppers and celery.
2. Turn into large pot; add remaining ingredients; bring to boil. Boil over medium heat for 30 minutes, stirring occasionally.
3. Discard bouquet garni; pour into hot sterilized jars; seal at once.

Claire Kerr, Gardens Century Club,
Wilmington, Del.

GRANDMOTHER'S CHILI SAUCE

Makes About 2 Quarts

18 ripe large tomatoes
6 large onions, chopped
3 medium green peppers, chopped
1½ cups brown sugar
1 cup vinegar
2 tablespoons salt
1½ teaspoons cinnamon
½ teaspoon ground cloves
½ teaspoon nutmeg

1. Scald and peel tomatoes.
2. Put tomatoes, onions and green peppers in large pot. Bring to boil; then simmer for 1 hour.
3. Stir in remaining ingredients; simmer for 20 minutes.
4. Pour into hot sterilized jars; seal at once.

Helen Nelson, Beverly Hills Junior
Woman's Club, Chicago, Ill.

CRANBERRY APPLE SAUCE

Makes About 2 Pints

1½ cups cranberries
3 cups thinly sliced peeled
tart apples
2 teaspoons grated orange rind
½ cup water
1 cup sugar

1. In large pot combine all ingredients except sugar. Bring to boil over low heat, stirring occasionally. Cover; simmer for 15 minutes.
2. Stir in sugar; bring to full rolling boil.
3. Pour into hot sterilized jars; seal at once.

Betty Ann Chesser, Yorkewood Women's Club,
Baltimore, Md.

GRAPE CATSUP

Makes About 2 Quarts

5 pounds ripe Concord grapes
1 cup water
2 cups vinegar
6 cups sugar
1 tablespoon cinnamon

1 tablespoon black pepper
1 tablespoon ground cloves
2 teaspoons salt

1. Wash and crush grapes.
2. Put in large pot; add water. Bring to boil; simmer over medium heat for 20 minutes.
3. Strain grapes through sieve; pour liquid back into pot. Stir remaining ingredients into grape juice.
4. Bring to boil over low heat, stirring until sugar is dissolved. Boil over medium heat, stirring frequently, for about 30 minutes, or until thickened.
5. Pour into hot sterilized jars; seal at once.

Mrs. J. M. Jeffords, L.V.I.S., Enosburg, Vt.

PRUNE CATSUP

Makes About 3 Pints

2 pounds dried prunes
1 cup water
2 medium onions, finely chopped
2 medium green peppers, finely
chopped
2 cups vinegar
4 cups sugar
1 teaspoon cinnamon
1 teaspoon ground cloves
¼ teaspoon black pepper
1½ teaspoons salt

1. Pit prunes; chop finely. Turn into bowl; mix with water.
2. In large pot combine onions, green peppers and vinegar. Bring to boil; cook over medium heat for 20 minutes.
3. Stir in prunes with water and remaining ingredients. Cook over low heat, stirring until sugar is dissolved. Cook over medium heat, stirring occasionally, for 45 minutes, or until thickened.
4. Pour into hot sterilized jars; seal at once.

Mrs. L. G. Moon, Civic Club, Sandpoint, Ida.

RED SAUCE

Makes About 12 Pints

24 ripe large tomatoes
8 large onions
6 large green peppers, cored and
seeded
5 cups sugar
1½ quarts vinegar
3 tablespoons salt
2 small red pepper pods (optional)

1. Scald and skin tomatoes; cut finely.
2. Put onions and peppers through meat grinder.
3. Combine all ingredients in large pot; bring to boil; then simmer for 3 hours, stirring often.
4. Pour into hot sterilized jars; seal at once.

Mrs. A. Melvin Skellett, Thursday Morning Club,
Madison, N.J.

TOMATO CATSUP

Makes About 6 Pints

2 gallons tomatoes, diced
3 mangoes, diced
4 medium onions, sliced
6 peach leaves
3 cups sugar
1 cup plus 2 tablespoons vinegar
1 tablespoon salt
2 tablespoons catsup spices
1 tablespoon cornstarch
¼ teaspoon turmeric
¼ teaspoon cayenne

1. In large pot combine tomatoes, mangoes, onions and peach leaves. Cook over medium heat for 30 minutes, stirring occasionally.

2. Strain; reserve juice.

3. Return juice to pot; stir in sugar, 1 cup of the vinegar, salt and catsup spices. Bring to boil, stirring until sugar is dissolved. Cook over high heat, stirring occasionally, until reduced by half.

4. Meanwhile, in small bowl blend cornstarch, turmeric and cayenne. Add remaining vinegar to make a smooth paste.

5. Stir paste into juice mixture; stir over medium heat until thickened. Simmer for 10 minutes.

6. Pour into hot sterilized jars; seal at once.

Grace Steiner, Advance Club, Pandora, Ohio

SPICED TOMATO JUICE

Makes About 5 Pints

7 pounds ripe tomatoes
2 cups white vinegar
6 cups sugar
1 tablespoon each of whole cloves
    and broken cinnamon stick
    tied in cheesecloth

1. Put tomatoes in large container; cover with boiling water. Let stand for 3 minutes.

2. Skin tomatoes, remove green cores; slice.

3. Put tomatoes and vinegar in large pot. Bring to boil; then simmer for 30 minutes.

4. Drain off juice through colander; return juice to pot. Stir in sugar; add spice bag. Bring to boil, stirring occasionally until sugar is dissolved. Boil over medium heat for 30 minutes.

5. Remove spice bag; pour into hot sterilized jars; seal at once.

Mrs. Carl G. Kasperson, Woman's Club,
Northborough, Mass.

26. Beverages

❧❧❧❧❧❧❧❧❧❧❧❧❧❧❧❧❧❧

The Service of Wine

Each year, the pleasure of a glass of wine with a meal is appreciated by an ever greater number of Americans. One need not be an expert to offer wine at the table for the "right" wine is the one you enjoy most. Ideally, however, the wine should complement the dish with which it is served.

White and rosé wines should be refrigerated for several hours before serving and should be served chilled. Red wines should be served at a cool room temperature, or about 60° F., and the cork should be removed from the bottle about 30 minutes before serving to bring out the full flavor of the wine.

Remove the foil from the top of the bottle, wipe the neck and cork and extract the cork in one piece with any good bottle opener. Again wipe the neck and mouth of the bottle.

Pour a little wine into the host's glass, so that any particles of dust or cork will not be served to the guests. Then fill the remaining glasses from a third to half full, depending on the size. A general wine glass may be used for the serving of most wines; it should have a capacity of 8 to 10 ounces.

If more than one wine is served at a meal, the dry wines should be served before sweet wines; light wines before heavier ones; and white wines before the reds.

General Guide to the Service of Wines

Before the meal	Dry sherry
	Vermouth
	Dry madeira
	Dry champagne

Appetizers	Dry sherry
Hors d'oeuvres	Dry madeira
Soups	

White fish	Graves
Bland dishes of	Chablis
chicken, turkey or	Rhine
or veal	Dry champagne
	Moselle

Dark fish	Rosé
Robust-flavored dishes	Light red wine
of chicken and	Sparkling
turkey	burgundy
	White burgundy

Beef	Burgundy
Duck	Claret or Bordeaux
Lamb	Chianti or other
Game	red wine
Pork	

Dessert	Cream sherry
	Port
	Champagne
	Madeira
	Sauterne
	Tokay

Cheese	Burgundy
	Bordeaux or other
	red wine
	Port

Tea

Buy a good quality tea of the preferred type. Black tea leaves are black owing to a processing treatment which gives the tea a rich flavor. Green tea brews a light-colored beverage. Oolong tea is a cross between black and green tea, and the leaves are brown and green mixed; it has a light color when brewed.

TO MAKE TEA

1. Bring fresh cold water to a full rolling boil. Reheated water gives tea a flat taste.
2. A china or pottery pot makes the best tea. Fill it with hot water, and let it stand for a few minutes.
3. When the water is boiling rapidly, drain the teapot. Add 1 teaspoon tea leaves or 1 teabag for each cup of tea needed.
4. Pour boiling water into the teapot, and let it brew from 3 to 5 minutes, depending on the desired strength.
5. Serve plain, with lemon or milk and with sugar, if desired.

ICED TEA

Follow the same rules as for making hot tea, but use 50 percent more tea leaves or teabags. Ice cubes will dilute the tea to the correct strength. Cool the tea at room temperature to prevent cloudiness. To serve, pour over ice cubes in a tall glass. Serve with a lemon wedge and sugar, if desired.

Coffee

Use a good fresh coffee and a grind that is correct for your coffee maker. Some people like to grind the coffee beans just before making coffee, and coffee beans keep for a long time without deterioration. Ground coffee should be kept in a tightly closed container; it will retain its freshness longer if it is stored in the refrigerator.

TO MAKE COFFEE

1. Be sure that your coffee maker is sparkling clean. Merely rinsing after use is not good enough; it should be thoroughly scrubbed after each use to remove the oils from the coffee grounds which coat the inside.
2. Brew to the full capacity of your coffee maker. Use 1 Approved Coffee Measure or its equivalent—2 level measuring tablespoons of fresh coffee to each ¾ measuring cup of fresh water.
3. Serve coffee piping hot as soon as possible after it is made.

DIFFERENT METHODS OF COFFEE MAKING

Drip coffee: Bring the water to a full rolling boil. Measure the coffee into the basket. Then measure the exact amount of boiling water, allowing ¾ cup to each 2 level tablespoons ground coffee. When the water has dripped through, remove the coffee basket and water container. Stir the hot coffee to ensure a brew of even strength; serve immediately.

Vacuum coffee: Measure fresh water into the lower bowl. Place over heat, and while it is reaching a boil, insert the filter in upper bowl. Measure the coffee into the filter. When the water boils, lower the heat, and insert the upper bowl. When most of the water has risen into upper bowl, stir the water and coffee briskly. Brew for 2 to 3 minutes; then remove the maker from the heat. As soon as all the coffee has returned to the lower bowl, remove the upper section, and serve.

Percolator coffee: Measure fresh water accurately into the pot, and place it over the heat. When the water boils, remove the pot from the heat, and measure the proper amount of coffee into the basket. Cover; return to heat; percolate gently for 6 to 8 minutes.

Pot coffee: Measure the coffee and fresh water into pot. Stir, and place over medium heat. Bring just to boiling point. Stir, and remove from heat. Let stand for 5 minutes. Strain, and serve.

Espresso: A special pot is required to force steam through the coffee grounds. The steam condenses and falls into the container.

Fill the pot with fresh water. Measure the correct amount of coffee into the basket. Screw on the lid securely. Insert the cord, if using an electric espresso maker or place the pot over medium heat. Serve as soon as steam has condensed into coffee.

Iced coffee: Make coffee in the usual manner, but use twice the amount of coffee as for hot coffee. Pour into tall glasses over ice cubes.

CAFÉ AU LAIT

Hot strong black coffee
Hot milk
Sugar (optional)

For each drink use large heated cup. Pour half coffee and half milk simultaneously into cup. Add sugar, if desired.

A. S.

IRISH COFFEE

Sugar
Irish whiskey
Hot strong black coffee
Whipped cream

For each drink, use a goblet or Irish coffee glass. Put 1 teaspoon sugar and 1½ ounces Irish whiskey into each glass. Fill with coffee; top with whipped cream.

A. S.

Hot Beverages

BEEF TEA

Makes About 2 Cups

A nourishing beverage for anyone recuperating from an illness.

2-pound sirloin steak
2 teaspoons salt

1. Cut all fat and skin from steak; cut meat into small cubes.
2. Put in top of double saucepan; cover with water. Add salt; bring to boil. Cover; cook over simmering water for 4 hours, stirring occasionally. Add water to upper and lower pans as necessary.
3. Strain; pour into container. Cover; chill. Heat as required.

Mrs. J. Reid, Mother's Club, Tieton, Wash.

CHOCOLATE SYRUP FOR HOT CHOCOLATE

Makes About 1½ Cups Syrup

Use 2 tablespoons of this syrup for every glass of milk; stir well to blend. Serve hot or cold.

1 cup cocoa
⅛ teaspoon salt
1¾ cups sugar
1½ cups boiling water

1. In saucepan combine cocoa, salt and sugar. Gradually stir in water until smooth.
2. Cook over medium heat for 5 minutes, stirring frequently.

3. Cool; pour into container; cover; store in refrigerator.

Mrs. Mittie Murphy, Modern Study Club, Wolfe City, Tex.

PARTY HOT CHOCOLATE

Makes About 2 Cups Syrup

1 cup cocoa
1½ cups sugar
Dash of salt
1 cup water
1 cup heavy cream
Milk

1. In saucepan combine cocoa, sugar and salt. Stir in water to make a smooth paste. Bring to boil; cook over medium heat, stirring frequently for 5 minutes, or until thickened.
2. Cool; stir in cream.
3. Prepare hot chocolate, heat milk, Spoon 1 tablespoon chocolate mixture into mugs; pour in milk; stir.

Mrs. Ralph J. Stahle, Woman's Club, Lovell, Wyo.

REAL RICH FRENCH CHOCOLATE

Serves 16

½ cup semi-sweet chocolate pieces
½ cup light corn syrup
¼ cup water
1 teaspoon vanilla
2 cups heavy cream
2 quarts hot milk

1. One hour before serving, combine chocolate, corn syrup and water in saucepan. Heat until chocolate is melted and mixture is smooth.
2. Pour into cup; refrigerate until cool. Stir in vanilla.
3. In large bowl beat cream until stiff. Gradually beat in chocolate syrup; beat until mixture mounds in bowl.
4. Spoon chocolate mixture into an attractive serving bowl.
5. Drop spoonful of chocolate mixture into chocolate cup; fill cup with milk.

Pauline Romero, El Camino Women's Club, Ventura, Calif.

HOT PEPPERMINT CHOCOLATE

Serves 6

3 cups milk
8 chocolate peppermint patties
1 cup heavy cream
⅛ teaspoon salt

1. Heat milk in saucepan to just below boiling point.
2. Add chocolate; stir until melted and smooth.
3. Stir in cream and salt; heat to serving temperature, stirring.

Sesame Club, Fordyce, Ark.

CAFÉ BRÛLOT

Serves 8

6 lumps sugar
Rind of 1 orange
4 cloves
3 small cinnamon sticks
1½ ounces brandy
1 quart hot strong black coffee

1. Put sugar, orange rind, cloves and cinnamon in flameproof bowl. Pour brandy over sugar. Ignite; burn for 3 minutes, stirring constantly.
2. Gradually pour coffee into flaming bowl; stir until flame burns out. Serve immediately in demitasse cups.

Mrs. Lawrence Levert, Jr., Junior Woman's Club, Thibodaux, La.

SPICED PINEAPPLE TEA

Serves 5 or 6

⅓ cup sugar
3½ cups water
1 teaspoon grated lemon rind
Cinnamon stick
1 teaspoon grated orange rind
⅛ teaspoon cloves
2 tablespoons lemon juice
¼ cup orange juice
¼ cup pineapple juice
¼ cup tea leaves

1. In saucepan combine sugar, ½ cup of the water, lemon rind, cinnamon, orange rind and cloves. Bring to boil; boil for 10 minutes.
2. Remove cinnamon; stir in fruit juices. Keep warm over low heat.
3. Meanwhile, bring remaining water to boil; pour over tea. Let stand for 10 minutes. Strain; add to fruit juices.

Mrs. Lawrence Sonneman, Semper Fidelis Study Club, Clarinda, Ia.

RUSSIAN TEA

Makes About 1 Gallon

3 lemons
3 oranges
1 tablespoon cloves
2 tablespoons tea
1 gallon boiling water
2 cups sugar

1. Remove rind from lemons and oranges; reserve.
2. Squeeze juice from lemons and oranges; set aside.
3. Put lemon and orange rinds, cloves and tea in large bowl. Pour in 1 quart of the water. Cool for 10 minutes.
4. Strain; return to bowl. Stir in sugar and lemon and orange juice.
5. Chill until serving time; heat to just below boiling point; stir in remaining water.

Mrs. Ike Skelton, Sr., Woman's Club, Lexington, Mo.

SAIGON TEA

Serves 25

1 orange
3 lemons
3 tablespoons tea
½ cinnamon stick
14 allspice
14 cloves
2 quarts boiling water
1 cup sugar

1. Squeeze juice from orange and lemons; set aside.

2. Remove rind from orange and lemons; put in large container. Add tea, cinnamon, allspice and cloves. Pour water over mixture; stir; let stand for 7 minutes.

3. Strain; return to container. Stir in orange and lemon juice and sugar.

4. Serve hot or over crushed ice, as desired.

Irene G. Rice, Federation of Women's Clubs, Pandora, Ohio

HOT CIDER PUNCH

Serves 12 to 16

2 quarts apple cider
½ teaspoon cinnamon
½ teaspoon mint leaves
¼ teaspoon nutmeg
½ cup confectioners' sugar
3 oranges, sliced
  Cloves
½ cup apricot brandy or other spirits

1. In large saucepan combine cider, cinnamon, mint, nutmeg and sugar.

2. Stud orange slices with cloves; add to cider. Simmer very slowly; do not boil. The longer it simmers, the better.

3. Just before serving, add brandy or other spirits.

Junior Women's Club, Country Club Hills, Ill.

APPLE WASSAIL BOWL

Serves 12

An especially nice holiday punch; leftover punch can be stored, covered, in the refrigerator and reheated.

6 small tart apples
1 tablespoon brown sugar
1 quart apple cider
¼ teaspoon nutmeg
½ teaspoon cinnamon
¼ cup granulated sugar
2 cups dry sherry
4 thin lemon slices

1. Preheat oven to 350° F. Grease 10 x 6 x 1½-inch baking pan.

2. Core apples; cut in half; arrange, cut side up, in pan. Sprinkle with brown sugar; bake in preheated oven for 20 minutes, or until tender; set aside.

3. Just before serving, pour cider into saucepan; heat to just below boiling point. Stir in remaining ingredients; stir over low heat until sugar is dissolved. Cover; put over very low heat for 3 minutes.

4. Remove lemon slices; pour mixture into punch bowl. Garnish with apple halves.

Mary Ann Dehlin, Woman's Club, Anchorage, Alaska

SPICED ORANGE WASSAIL BOWL

Serves 10

3 oranges
  Cloves
2 quarts apple cider
  Cinnamon sticks

1. Preheat oven to 350° F.

2. Stud oranges with cloves; bake in preheated oven for 30 minutes.

3. Bring cider to boil in large saucepan. Pour into punch bowl; add oranges.

4. Serve in mugs, using cinnamon sticks as stirrers.

Mary Ballentine, Finneytown Junior Women's Club, Cincinnati, Ohio

CRANBERRY PUNCH

Serves 50

4½ pounds fresh or frozen cranberries
4½ cups water
1 tablespoon cloves
3 cups sugar
1½ cups orange juice
½ cup lemon juice

1. Put cranberries, water and cloves in saucepan. Bring to boil; then simmer for 20 minutes. Strain.

2. Add sugar to cranberry juice; stir until dissolved. Chill.

3. Stir in orange and lemon juice. Serve hot or cold.

Mrs. G. C. Hilman, Cosmos Club, Ruston, La.

HOT BUTTERED CRANBERRY PUNCH

Makes About 1¾ Quarts

⅓ cup brown sugar
½ cup water
½ teaspoon ground cloves
¼ teaspoon allspice
½ teaspoon cinnamon
⅛ teaspoon nutmeg
⅛ teaspoon salt
1 quart cranberry juice cocktail
2 cups pineapple juice
  Butter

1. In saucepan combine sugar, water, spices and salt. Bring to boil.

2. Add fruit juices; bring back to boil.

3. Serve steaming hot in mugs. Dot each serving with butter.

Nelle Montague, North Long Beach Women's Club, Long Beach, Calif.

MULLED GRAPE JUICE

Makes About 1¾ Quarts

1 quart grape juice
3 cups water
1 cup sugar
12 cloves
2 cinnamon sticks
  Juice of 2 lemons

1. In saucepan combine all ingredients except lemon juice. Bring to boil. Add lemon juice; remove from heat; let stand for 10 minutes.

2. Serve hot or chilled.

Mrs. Haskell Hewson, Thursday Morning Club, Madison, N.J.

SNOWY NIGHT PUNCH

Makes About 2 Quarts

¼ cup honey
1¼ teaspoons allspice
5 cups evaporated milk
2½ cups water
¼ teaspoon salt
2½ teaspoons vanilla
  Nutmeg

1. In saucepan combine honey, allspice, milk, water and salt. Heat to just below boiling point, stirring occasionally.

2. Remove from heat; stir in vanilla. Sprinkle nutmeg on each serving.

Barbara Kibett, Junior Woman's Club,
Tullahoma, Tenn.

AMERICAN WASSAIL

Makes 1½ Gallons

1-quart 14-ounce can pineapple juice
1 quart orange juice
½ cup lemon juice
5 teabags or 5 teaspoons tea leaves
2½ quarts boiling water
1 quart cold water
3 cups sugar
2 teaspoons cloves
½ teaspoon salt
3 cinnamon sticks

1. Combine fruit juices.

2. Steep tea in boiling water for 5 to 10 minutes. Remove bags, or strain leaves.

3. In saucepan combine remaining ingredients. Bring to boil; boil for 3 minutes. Strain.

4. Just before serving, combine fruit juices, tea, and spiced water. Bring to boil.

Mrs. R. D. Bruce, Junior Women's Club,
Coos Bay, Ore.

HOT TOMATO TODDY

Serves 3 or 4

2 cups tomato juice
¼ cup sugar
6 cloves
1-inch cinnamon stick
¼ teaspoon salt
1 cup water
⅛ teaspoon celery salt
⅛ teaspoon paprika
3 tablespoons lemon juice

1. In saucepan combine all ingredients except lemon juice. Cover; simmer for 15 minutes. Let stand until cold.

2. Strain; return to saucepan; add lemon juice. Reheat without boiling.

Frances E. Jones, Women's Club, Durham, N.H.

THE BISHOP

Serves 8

This is an old and traditional hot wine drink. Dr. Samuel Johnson was known to be exceedingly fond of it.

Whole cloves
2 large lemons
¼ teaspoon cinnamon
¼ teaspoon ground cloves
¼ teaspoon nutmeg
¼ teaspoon allspice
¼ teaspoon ginger
1 cup water
1 bottle port
Cubed sugar
Grated nutmeg

1. Stick whole cloves into rind of 1 of the lemons until it resembles pincushion.

2. Spear lemon with long fork; roast over low flame for about 15 minutes, or until rind and lemon soften.

3. In small saucepan combine cinnamon, ground cloves, nutmeg, allspice, ginger and water; bring to boil; set aside.

4. Bring port to boil in large saucepan. Ignite surface; burn for few seconds.

5. Add roasted lemon and spice mixture to port; stand in warm place for 10 minutes.

6. Meanwhile, rub rind of remaining lemon with sugar. Squeeze half the juice from this lemon; put sugar and juice in warm large serving bowl. Stir in wine mixture. Add grated nutmeg to taste.

7. Serve hot with lemon and spices floating.

Junior Women's Club, Country Club Hills, Ill.

SWEDISH GLÖGG

Serves About 25

4 ounces dried apples or apricots
3 ounces seedless raisins
3 ounces prunes
1 ounce pommerance (dried orange peel)
2 ounces almonds
1 ounce cardamom
1 ounce cloves
1 ounce cinnamon sticks
1 cup sugar
2 bottles port
1 bottle claret or dry red wine
Brandy
Almonds, raisins and cloves (optional)

1. Day before, tie fruits, almonds and spices in cheesecloth; put in large pot. Add sugar, port and claret or dry red wine. Bring to boil; then simmer over medium heat until reduced to about 2½ bottles. Pour into glass jar; cover; cool for 24 hours.

2. Next day, remove spice bag from wine.

3. Heat 1 part wine with 1 part brandy; do not boil. Serve in punch glasses. If desired, garnish each serving with a couple of almonds, raisins and cloves.

Helen Nelson, Pine Ridge Woman's Club,
Fairfax, Va.

HOT EGGNOG

Serves 12

1 quart milk
3 eggs, separated
½ cup sugar
Small strip orange rind
1 cup whiskey or as desired
Nutmeg

1. Scald milk.

2. Beat egg yolks and sugar until light and pale. Stir in milk; add orange rind; stir over low heat until steaming hot but not boiling.

3. Remove from heat; stir in whiskey. Discard rind.

4. Beat egg whites until stiff but not dry; fold into egg yolk mixture.

5. Serve piping hot, with dash of nutmeg on each serving.

Mrs. Peter J. O'Neil, Sr., Junior Woman's Club,
Thibodaux, La.

MARY'S TOM AND JERRY

Serves 12 to 18

7 eggs, separated
1 pound confectioners' sugar
(sift if lumpy)
1 teaspoon vanilla
Whiskey
Grated nutmeg

1. In mixing bowl beat egg yolks until pale. Gradually beat in ½ pound of the sugar. Stir in vanilla.
2. In another mixing bowl beat egg whites until foamy. Gradually beat in remaining sugar; beat until stiff and glossy; fold into egg yolk mixture.
3. Put tablespoon of egg mixture in serving cup; add jigger of whiskey. Add boiling water to fill cup. Sprinkle with nutmeg.

NOTE: Egg mixture may be made ahead of time and refrigerated.

Mrs. James Dunlap, Woman's Club, Jacksonville, Ill.

Cold Beverages

SUGAR SYRUP

Makes About 2 Cups

Punches and various beverages are better when sweetened with syrup rather than sugar; syrup gives a clearer brew and can be stored indefinitely in the refrigerator.

2 cups sugar
2 cups water

1. Combine sugar and water in medium saucepan. Cook over low heat, stirring until sugar is dissolved.
2. Bring to boil; boil over medium heat for 5 minutes.

Barbara Sullivan, Junior Woman's Club, Tullahoma, Tenn.

CHOCOLATE SYRUP

Makes 3 Cups

2 cups water
2 cups sugar
6 1-ounce squares unsweetened
chocolate
1 teaspoon vanilla

1. In saucepan combine water and sugar. Bring to boil.
2. Add chocolate; cook, stirring constantly, until smooth.
3. Cool; stir in vanilla.
4. Store in covered jar.

A. S.

CHOCOLATE MILK

Cold milk
Chocolate Syrup (above)

For each drink, combine ⅔ cup milk and 2 to 3 tablespoons Chocolate Syrup in glass. Stir.

A. S.

CHOCOLATE MALTED

Chocolate Syrup (opposite)
Malted milk powder
Cold milk
Vanilla or chocolate ice cream

For each drink, beat, shake or blend 2 tablespoons Chocolate Syrup, 1 tablespoon malted milk powder, ½ cup milk and 1 scoop ice cream.

A. S.

DELIGHTFUL COCKTAIL

Serves 4 to 6

2 cups unsweetened pineapple juice
1 cup tomato juice
¼ cup lemon juice

1. Combine all ingredients; mix well.
2. Chill; stir before serving.

Woman's Club, Patten, Me.

ICE CREAM SODAS

Fruit syrup or Chocolate Syrup
(opposite)
Any suitable flavor ice cream
Soda water

For each drink, put 2 to 3 tablespoons fruit syrup or Chocolate Syrup in each tall glass. Add scoop of ice cream. Fill with soda water; stir well.

A. S.

LEMONADE

Serves 1

2 tablespoons lemon juice
2 tablespoons sugar
Ice cubes

Mix lemon juice and sugar in tall glass. Add ice cubes; fill with water. Stir thoroughly.

VARIATIONS:

PINK LEMONADE: Add 1 teaspoon maraschino cherry juice to lemon juice and sugar in above recipe.

PINEAPPLE LEMONADE: Add ½ cup unsweetened pineapple juice before filling glass with water in above recipe.

A. S.

ORANGEADE

Serves 1

½ cup orange juice
1 teaspoon sugar
Ice cubes
Soda water

Combine orange juice and sugar in tall glass. Add ice cubes; fill with soda water.

A. S.

LEMON TEA

Makes About 2 Quarts

⅜ cup tea
¾ cup sugar
¾ cup lemon juice
Ice cubes

1. Bring 1 quart water to full rolling boil. Remove from heat; stir in tea. Brew for 3 to 4 minutes.
2. Strain; stir in 3 cups water.

3. Meanwhile, in saucepan combine sugar and ¾ cup water; bring to boil, stirring constantly. Boil over medium heat for 10 minutes.

4. Add syrup to tea; stir in lemon juice.

5. Fill glasses with ice cubes; pour in tea.

Doris Heater, Woman's Club,
Thompson Falls, Mont.

MINT COOLER

Makes About 2 Quarts

1¾ cups sugar
3½ cups boiling water
1 large handful fresh mint leaves
Juice of 6 lemons
Juice of 3 oranges
Shaved ice

1. Put sugar in mixing bowl; stir in water. Stir in mint and fruit juices. Cover; let stand for 2 hours.

2. Strain juices. Serve in glasses filled with shaved ice.

Elva Scott, Modern Study Club,
Wolfe City, Tex.

ORANGE LIME COCKTAIL

Serves 6

3 cups orange juice
3 teaspoons lime juice
Dash of salt
½ cup crushed ice
6 maraschino cherries or hulled
strawberries

1. Put fruit juices salt and ice in cocktail shaker or tall jar with lid. Shake well.

2. Pour into cocktail glasses; garnish each with cherry or strawberry.

Mrs. H. G. Hearnsberger, Sesame Club,
Fordyce, Ark.

ORANGE MINT JULEP

Makes 1 Quart

2½ cups water
2 cups sugar
Juice and rind of 2 oranges
Juice of 6 lemons
1 cup fresh mint leaves
Crushed ice
Ginger ale

1. Combine water and sugar in saucepan. Bring to boil; then simmer for 10 minutes.

2. Stir in orange juice and rind and lemon juice.

3. Put mint in mixing bowl; pour juice mixture over it. Cover; let stand for 2 hours.

4. Strain through sieve lined with cheesecloth. Pour into container; cover; refrigerate.

5. To serve, fill tall glasses with ice. Top each with ⅓ cup syrup; fill with ginger ale.

Mrs. Marvin Millspaugh, Woman's Club,
Heavener, Okla.

RASPBERRY COOLER

Serves 9

10-ounce package frozen raspberries, defrosted

6-ounce can frozen lemonade concentrate, defrosted
1½ cups water
1 quart chilled ginger ale

1. Press raspberries and juice through sieve until puréed.

2. Stir in lemonade concentrate and water. Chill.

3. Just before serving, stir in ginger ale.

Mrs. Glenn Haugen, Study Club,
Washburn, N.D.

RASPBERRY SHRUB

Makes About 3 Quarts

4 quarts raspberries
1 quart vinegar
Sugar
Ice cubes

1. Day before, combine raspberries and vinegar in mixing bowl. Cover; let stand in cool place for 24 hours.

2. Next day, strain and measure juice. Turn into large pot. For every 1 cup juice add 1 cup sugar.

3. Bring to boil over low heat, stirring until sugar is dissolved. Simmer for 20 minutes.

4. Pour into hot sterilized bottles; seal at once. Keep in cool place.

5. To serve, fill glass with ice cubes; pour in raspberry syrup.

Elsie Greenwood, L.V.I.S., Enosburg, Vt.

ALASKA PUNCH

Serves 50

3 cups water
3 cups sugar
1 quart cranberry juice
1 quart apricot nectar
3 cups lemon juice
2 cups orange juice
2 cups pineapple juice
2 quarts chilled ginger ale

1. Combine water and sugar in saucepan. Bring to boil over low heat stirring until sugar is dissolved. Boil over medium heat for 5 minutes.

2. Remove from heat; pour into large bowl. Add fruit juices; mix well; refrigerate until serving time.

3. Just before serving, pour mixture into punch bowl; stir in ginger ale.

Ramona Blackburn, Woman's Club,
Anchorage, Alaska

APPLE PUNCH

Serves 30

1 cup Sugar Syrup (p. 737)
2 tablespoons lemon juice
1 quart chilled apple juice
2 quarts chilled red wine
1 quart chilled ginger ale

1. Combine Sugar Syrup and lemon juice in punch bowl; mix well. Stir in apple juice; stir in wine; add ginger ale, blending well.

2. Serve at once, adding ice cubes if desired.

Lucille Chastain, President, Washington State Federation of Women's Organizations, Spokane, Wash.

APRICOT PUNCH

Makes About 5½ Quarts

5 quarts water
2 cups sugar
1-pound 4-ounce can apricots, undrained
3 bananas, mashed
Juice of 6 oranges
Juice of 6 lemons

1. In saucepan combine 1 quart of the water, sugar and apricots. Bring to boil, stirring until sugar is dissolved.
2. Force mixture through sieve, or blend in electric blender until smooth. Stir in bananas; blend until smooth. Add fruit juices; chill.
3. Just before serving, stir in remaining water.

Mrs. Sam Williams, Sesame Club, Fordyce, Ark.

CHERRY PUNCH

Makes About 3½ Quarts

6-ounce package cherry gelatin
2 cups boiling water
2 quarts chilled apple juice
½ cup chilled lemon juice
1 quart chilled lemon soda
Cracked ice

1. Dissolve gelatin in water. Stir in fruit juices and soda; mix well.
2. Fill glasses with ice; pour in punch.

Naomi Jergensen, Woman's Club, St. Anthony, Ida.

CHRISTMAS CHEER PUNCH

Serves 10 to 12

1 quart cranberry juice
1 cup sugar
2 cups orange juice
1 cup pineapple juice
¾ cup lemon juice
2 cups chilled ginger ale
1 pint pineapple sherbet

1. Blend cranberry juice, sugar and fruit juices. Refrigerate until serving time.
2. Just before serving, stir in ginger ale and sherbet.

Mrs. Harold Foree, President, Etudion Club, Great Bend, Kans.

CHRISTMAS PARTY PUNCH

Serves 50

6-ounce can frozen orange juice concentrate, defrosted
6-ounce can frozen lemonade concentrate, defrosted
2½ cups pineapple juice
1½ quarts cranberry juice
Ice cubes

Add water to orange juice and lemonade according to package directions. Pour all ingredients into punch bowl; stir to mix. Add ice cubes; serve.

Mrs. W. S. Robinson, Woman's Club, Heavener, Okla.

CRANBERRY PUNCH

Serves 25

3 pints chilled cranberry juice
1-quart 14-ounce can pineapple juice, chilled
1 quart chilled ginger ale

Mix all ingredients in punch bowl; serve.

Jean Drake, Finneytown Junior Women's Club, Cincinnati, Ohio

FLEMINGTON WOMAN'S CLUB PUNCH

Serves 24

3 pints chilled cranberry juice cocktail
½ cup chilled bottled lime juice
2 cups chilled pineapple juice
¼ to ½ cup sugar
½ teaspoon almond extract
2 quarts chilled ginger ale
Ice block or mold

1. Just before serving, combine all ingredients except ginger ale in large punch bowl. Stir until sugar is dissolved.
2. Add ginger ale; stir to combine. Add ice block or mold.

Woman's Club, Flemington, N.J.

DELICIOUS FRUIT PUNCH

Serves 50

1 gallon cold-water tea (see below)
2 1-pint 2-ounce cans grapefruit juice
Juice of 12 oranges
Juice of 12 lemons
2 1-pint 2-ounce cans pineapple juice
6 cups sugar
3 cups water
2 quarts chilled ginger ale

1. Prepare cold-water tea: Pour 1 gallon cold water over 1½ ounces tea. Let stand for 12 hours. Strain.
2. Add juices to tea.
3. Combine sugar and water in saucepan. Bring to boil; boil for 5 minutes. Stir enough syrup into fruit juice mixture to sweeten to taste. Chill or freeze. (If frozen, remove from freezer 4 to 5 hours before using.)
4. Just before serving, add ginger ale.

What's Cookin' in Hapeville?, Woman's Club, Hapeville, Ga.

PUNCH BOWL DELIGHT

Serves 35 to 40

2 quarts water
1½ cups sugar
6-ounce can frozen lemonade concentrate
6-ounce can frozen orange juice concentrate
6-ounce can frozen pineapple juice concentrate

2 1-quart 14-ounce cans red Hawaiian punch
2 quarts chilled ginger ale

1. Combine water and sugar in saucepan. Cook over low heat, stirring until sugar is dissolved. Bring to boil; then simmer for 5 minutes.

2. Remove from heat; stir in lemonade, orange juice and pineapple juice concentrates; mix well.

3. Turn into large container; stir in Hawaiian punch. Refrigerate until serving time.

4. Pour mixture into punch bowl; stir in ginger ale.

Mrs. A. W. Hafenstein, Ladies Reading Circle, Alma, Kans.

DELIGHTFUL SUMMERTIME DRINK

Makes 1 Gallon

3 cups sugar
3 cups water
1 cup fresh mint leaves
1 cup orange juice
1 cup lemon juice

1. Combine sugar and water in saucepan. Cook over medium heat, stirring until sugar is dissolved.

2. Bring to boil; add mint. Simmer for 5 minutes. Cool; strain.

3. Stir in fruit juices and water to total 1 gallon. Chill.

Mrs. Agnes Lane, Woman's Club, Lantana, Fla.

MINTED FRUIT PUNCH

Makes 8 6-Ounce Servings

3 quarts unsweetened pineapple juice
Juice of 8 lemons
Juice of 8 oranges
Juice of 3 limes
2 cups sugar
1 cup fresh mint leaves
4 quarts chilled ginger ale
2 quarts chilled soda water
1 pint strawberries, quartered
Cake of ice
Thin lemon and lime slices

1. Combine fruit juices, sugar and mint. Chill thoroughly.

2. Just before serving, add ginger ale, soda water and strawberries. Pour over cake of ice in punch bowl; garnish with lemon lime.

Mrs. S. D. Harris, Jr., Twentieth Century Club, Eudora, Ark.

GRAPEFRUIT MINT PUNCH

Serves 12

2 cups sugar
1 cup cold water
1 quart orange juice
2 cups lemon juice
1 cup grapefruit juice
1 quart ice water
Crushed fresh mint or mint sprigs

1. Combine sugar and cold water in saucepan. Bring to boil; then simmer for 3 minutes. Cool.

2. Combine fruit juices and syrup.

3. Just before serving, add ice water. Add handful of crushed mint or sprig to each glass.

Mrs. Irving Legendre, Junior Woman's Club, Thibodaux, La.

HOLIDAY PUNCH

Serves 12 to 18

1 bottle chilled champagne
2 quarts chilled ginger ale
1 cup chilled cranberry juice
Ice ring or cube

Mix all ingredients in punch bowl just before serving. Add ice ring or cubes to chill thoroughly.

NOTE: To make ice ring, freeze cold water in ring mold.

Mrs. John Ludwigsen, Palm Springs Woman's Club, Hialeah, Fla.

RHUBARB PUNCH

Makes About 3 Quarts

2 pounds rhubarb, diced
5 cups water
Sugar
Grapefruit juice
Lemon juice
Chilled ginger ale

1. Combine rhubarb and water in saucepan. Bring to boil; then simmer for 15 minutes, or until mushy.

2. Strain. Measure liquid; pour into pan; for each 1 cup liquid add ⅓ cup sugar. Bring to boil over low heat, stirring until sugar is dissolved. Simmer for 2 minutes.

3. Remove from heat; measure liquid. Pour into punch bowl; for every 1 cup mixture add ½ cup grapefruit juice and ¼ cup lemon juice.

4. Refrigerate until serving time; stir in ginger ale to taste.

Mrs. P. L. Parks, Woman's Club, Lovell, Wyo.

STRAWBERRY PUNCH

Serves 25

1-quart 14-ounce can pineapple juice, chilled
¾ cup sugar
6-ounce can frozen pink lemonade concentrate, defrosted
2¼ cups water
1 quart strawberry ice cream
2 quarts chilled ginger ale

1. In punch bowl combine pineapple juice, sugar, lemonade concentrate and water. Add ice cream; stir until blended.

2. Stir in ginger ale. Serve at once.

Virginia Leidheiser, Tri-Club, Richmond, Va.

TEA PUNCH

Serves 50

Juice of 18 oranges
Juice of 6 lemons
2 pounds sugar
1 quart grape juice
1 gallon tea
1 quart ginger ale

1. In large container combine all ingredients except ginger ale. Stir until sugar is dissolved.

2. Refrigerate until serving time. Just before serving stir in ginger ale.

Pearl Lemley, Federation of Women's Clubs,
Pandora, Ohio

WEDDING PUNCH

Serves 10 to 12

6-ounce can frozen pink lemonade
    concentrate
6-ounce can frozen orange juice
    concentrate
4½ cups water
1 pint pineapple sherbet
1 pint vanilla ice cream

1. Put lemonade and orange juice concentrates and water in punch bowl. Stir to blend.

2. Fold in sherbet and ice cream. Serve at once.

Mrs. P. F. Haynes, Woman's Club,
Lake Worth, Fla.

WHITE WEDDING PUNCH

Serves 50

1 cup water
2 pounds sugar
1 quart lemon juice
½ gallon lemon sherbet
1 bottle light rum
2 quarts chilled soda water

1. Combine water and sugar in saucepan. Bring to boil, stirring until sugar is dissolved. Boil for 5 minutes. Remove from heat; cool.

2. Stir in lemon juice; set aside until serving time.

3. Just before serving, stir in sherbet. Add rum and soda water; stir rapidly.

Mrs. Edward R. Miller, Woman's Club,
State College, Pa.

COFFEE CREAM PUNCH

Serves 20

⅓ cup instant coffee
1 cup boiling water
½ cup sugar
2 quarts milk
1 cup heavy cream, whipped
1 quart vanilla ice cream

1. In mixing bowl dissolve coffee in water. Add sugar; stir until dissolved.

2. Stir in milk; refrigerate until ready to serve.

3. Just before serving, fold whipped cream into milk mixture.

4. Put ice cream in punch bowl; pour milk mixture over ice cream; stir to blend.

Bess Koons, Cadmean Club, Fort Worth, Tex.

COFFEE VANILLA PUNCH

Serves 50 to 60

1 quart heavy cream
5 tablespoons sugar
5 teaspoons vanilla
2 quarts vanilla ice cream
1 gallon strong black coffee,
    well chilled

1. Whip cream until stiff; beat in sugar and vanilla.

2. Put ice cream and whipped cream in punch bowl. Pour chilled coffee over all. Mix.

Mrs. Reuben Pitts, Thursday Morning Club,
Madison, N.J.

COFFEE CHOCOLATE PUNCH

Serves 50

½ cup instant coffee
2 cups hot water
1 cup sugar
1 gallon milk
½ gallon chocolate ice cream
½ gallon vanilla ice cream

1. In saucepan combine coffee, water and sugar. Bring to boil over medium heat, stirring frequently. Remove from heat; cool.

2. Pour into punch bowl; stir in milk. Add ice creams; stir until smooth.

Elaine Moses, Tri-Club, Richmond, Va.

EGGNOG

Serves 18

6 eggs, separated
½ cup sugar
    Dash of salt
2 cups milk
2 cups heavy cream, whipped
2 cups brandy or rum

1. In mixing bowl combine egg yolks and sugar; beat until thickened and lemon-colored. Add salt and milk; blend well.

2. In another mixing bowl beat egg whites until stiff but not dry; fold with cream and brandy or rum into egg yolk mixture. Beat for 1 minute.

Dot Mowery, Woman's Club, Billings, Mont.

RICH EGGNOG

Serves 12 to 16

So thick it must be eaten with a spoon.

12 large eggs, separated
¾ cup sugar
1 cup whiskey
1 quart heavy cream, whipped

1. In large mixing bowl beat egg yolks until fluffy. Add sugar; beat until thickened and pale. Add whiskey; beat well.

2. In another mixing bowl beat egg whites until stiff but not dry; fold in cream. Fold in egg yolk mixture.

Mrs. J. K. Coleman, Modern Culture Club,
Tuscaloosa, Ala.

CHOCOLATE HONEY EGGNOG

Makes About 3 Quarts

6 eggs
½ cup honey
2 quarts chocolate milk
1½ cups heavy cream, whipped

1. In mixing bowl beat eggs until foamy. Add honey; beat until smooth. Stir in chocolate milk; blend well.

2. Fold in three-fourths of the cream; turn into pitchers.

3. Top with remaining cream.

Mrs. Clayton R. Schule, Woman's Club, Anchorage, Alaska

SHERRY EGGNOG

Serves 24

4 eggs, separated
1 cup sugar
2 quarts milk
1 bottle cream sherry
Grated nutmeg

1. In mixing bowl beat egg yolks and ¾ cup of the sugar until thickened and lemon-colored. Add milk and sherry; stir to blend. Refrigerate until just before serving.

2. In another mixing bowl beat egg whites until foamy. Gradually add remaining sugar; beat until stiff and glossy; spoon into punch bowl.

3. Pour in sherry mixture. Sprinkle with nutmeg.

Woman's Club, Edwin, Tenn.

STRAWBERRY MILK SHAKE

Serves 8 to 10

1 quart fresh, frozen or canned strawberries
5 cups milk
¼ teaspoon salt
1 cup heavy cream
¾ cup sugar
2 teaspoons lemon juice

1. Crush strawberries; force through strainer, or blend in electric blender until puréed.

2. Turn into mixing bowl; stir in milk, salt, ½ cup of the cream, sugar and lemon juice; blend well. Refrigerate until serving time.

3. Stir before serving. Whip remaining cream; use as topping.

Sesame Club, Fordyce, Ark.

Index

Abalone, 237
  Sautéed, 238
Acorn Squash. See Squash
Adlai's Delight Shrimp Casserole, 256
Afternoon Tea Doughnuts, 141
Alabama
  Fried Clams, 249
  Oysters, 249
Alaska
  Baked, 692
    Salmon Fillets, 230
  Punch, 738
  Raisin Ice Cream, 692
Alaskan Mixed Vegetables, 438
  Nuggets, 232
Albondigas (Beef Ball)
  Soup, 171
All
  -America Pork and Bean Casserole, 346
  -Bran Molasses Muffins, 127
  Chocolate Cake, 549
  -Day Chili and Beans, 334
  -in-One Spaghetti Casserole, 505
Almond(s)
  and Mushrooms with Fried Rice, 477
  Butter, 77
  Chicken, 284
    Salad, 520
  Currant Rice, 473
  Custard Pie, 558
  Delight Cookies, 645
  Fried Rice, 477
  Frozen Cream, 687
  Honey Balls, 661
  Lace Wafers, 641
  Lemon Fritters, 465
  Milk, 663
  Oslo Pudding, 676
  Pastry, 550
  Rice, 473
    Stuffing, 454
  Scandinavian Cooky, 635
  Soup, Cream of, 186
Amber Pecan Pie, 560
Ambrosia Cake, 585
  Orange, 681
  Pie, 571
American
  Cheese Open Face Sandwich, 91

Chop Suey, 346
Chow Mein, 346
  Meringue Dessert, 696
  Scrapple, 465
  Wassail, 736
Amish Lemon Sponge Pie, 577
Anadama Bread, 146
Anchovy
  Butter, 77
  Canapés, 80, 86
  Dip
    Cream Cheese, 71
    Sour Cream, 71
  Egg Butter, 77
  French Dressing, 541
  Radishes, 57
  -Stuffed Baked Tomatoes, 435
Angel Food
  Cake, 609
    Bits of Gold, 609
    Daffodil, 609
  Chocolate Dessert, 684
  Pie, 563
Angel Pie, Lemon Cream, 569
Anise Clear Red Candy, 667
Antelope. See Game
Antipasto, 57
Appetizer Ham Ball, 61
Appetizers, 47–90. See Canapés and Party Sandwiches; Cocktail Snacks and Wafers; Cocktails; Dips; Hors d'Oeuvres; Juices; Seafood Cocktails
Apple(s)
  and Cream Cheese Sandwich, 92
  and Turnip Casserole, 437
  Brown Betty, 672
  Butter, Aunt Mollie's, 723
  Butterscotch, 694
    Crisp, 664
  Cake, 596
    Coffee, Pan, 604
    Quickie, 596
    Upside-Down, 608
  Caramel, 710
  Chutney, 722
  Cinnamon Biscuits, 122
    Relish, 456
  Cookies, Fresh, 637
  Cranberry Sauce, 730

Crunch, 665
Delight, 687
Dumpling, Mother's, 665
Fritters, 457
  Dessert, 698
Honey Crisp, 665
in Biscuit Crust, 664
Jelly, 719
Juice Frosting, Fluffy, 626
Muffins, 126
  Pecan, 126
Oatmeal Bars, 652
Orange Baked, 694
Pancakes, 132
Pandowdy, 665
Pie
  Crumb, 555
  Crumb-Topped, 576
  Dutch, 555
  French, 555
  Little Fried, 578
  Mock, 553
  Mom's, 553
  Norwegian, 576
  Paper Bag, 556
  Refrigerator, 563
  Rich, 553
Pincushion, 57
-Potato Meat Loaf, 328
Pudding
  Butterscotch, 694
  Oat, 665
  Spicy, 666
Punch, 738
Relish, 456
Roly-Poly, 666
Salad, 522
  Bacon, 522
  Cinnamon, Stuffed, 522
    Candy, 526
  Cranberry, Frozen, 525
    Nut, 530
  Orange, 523
Slices, 577
  Red, 456
Strudel, Home Style, 577
-Stuffed Ham Steak, 353
  Tenderloins, 343
Stuffing
  for Doves, 296
  for Grouse, 296
  for Pheasant, 297
  for Spareribs, 350
  Sausage, 455
Wassail Bowl, 735

Applesauce, 419
  and Bacon Sandwich,
    Grilled, 96
  Cake, 596
  Ham Loaf, 354
  Nut Bread, 108
  Pineapple Salad, 527
  Squash Scallop, 433
Apricot(s)
  and Cream Cheese Sand-
    wich, 92
  and Sweet Potatoes, Scal-
    loped, 427
  Blondies, 652
  Bread, 108
  Coconut Balls, 659, 713
  Conserve, 674
  Dessert
    Creme Cake, 683
    Icebox, 683
  Filling for Kolachky, 162
  Glaze for Ham, 351
  -Glazed Ham, 351
  Golden Jellied, 457
  Icebox Pudding, 681
  Jam, 717
  Pie, 553
    Cream, 563
    Little Fried, 578
  Pork Roast, 341
  Punch, 739
  Salad, 527
    Nectar, 527
  Sauce, for Babas, 159
  Sherbet, 687
  Stuffing, 452
  Turnovers, 578
  Upside-Down Muffins, 126
Arabian Veal Chops, 361
Arizona Ranch-Style Frijoles,
  471
Arlette's Original "Water-
  Melon-Feed" Salad, 536
Armenian
  Cheese-Filled Boraks
    (Turnovers), 215
  Dinner in Foil, 369
  Lamb Shank Stew, 369
  Pizza, 100
  Rice, 473
    Pilaf, 475
Arroz con Pollo (Chicken
  with Yellow Rice), 483
Artichoke(s)
  al Forno (with Peas), 384
  and Seafood Casserole,
    257
  Boiled, 383
    Italian Style, 384
  Butter, 77
  Deep-Fried, 384
  Hearts with Chicken
    Breasts, 282
  in Lemon, 58
  Jerusalem
    Baked, 385
    Boiled, 384
  Marinated, 58
  Sicilian Style, 384
  To Prepare, 383

To Remove the Choke,
  383
Asparagus
  Amandine, 386
  and Eggs au Gratin, 203
  and Ham Rolls with
    Cheese Sauce, 352
  Casserole, 386
    and Egg, 395
    Macaroni, 500
  Chinese, 385
  Cup Salad, 527
  Daffodil, 385
  Escalloped, 386
  Parmesan, 385
  Soup, Cream of, 185
    Quick Tomato, 195
  Steamed, 385
Aspics, 537–39
  Basic All-Purpose, 537
  Beef, 537
  Beet, red, 537
  Broccoli Salad in, 538
  Clam Stock, 537
  Fish, 537
  Ham in, 538
  of Foie Gras, 63
  Salmon, Molded, 539
    Swedish, 538
  Tarragon, 537
  Tomato, Best, 539
    Shrimp and Potato
      Salad in, 497
    with Cheese Balls, 539
  Wine, Red, 537
    White, 537
Aubergine Provençale (Egg-
  plant and Tomatoes),
  409
Aunt
  Lydia's Macaroni and
    Cheese, 498
  Mollie's Apple Butter, 577
Austrian Green Beans, 388
Autumn Beef-Tomato Soup,
  172
Avgolemono (Greek Lemon
  Soup), 174
Avocado
  Chicken à la, 285
  Crab Burger, 105
  Cocktail, Fruit, 49
    with Shrimp, 52
  Dip, 72
    Sour Cream, 72
  Guacamole, 72
  Mold, 528
  Ring, 528
  Mousse, 540
  Purée of, 386
  Salad, 523
  Salmon Half-and-Half
    Canapés, 84
  Soup, 186
    Iced, 191
  Spread, 80
  with Shrimp, Eleanor's
    Baked, 386

Babas
  Flaming, 159

Little, 159
  Sauces for, 159
Babcock Sauce, 442
Babka, Beef-Filled, 334
Baby Submarine Sandwich,
  99
Bacon
  and Corn Chowder, Old-
    Fashioned New Eng-
    land, 184
  and Hominy, New Eng-
    land, 466
  Balls with Chutney, 65
  Biscuits, 86, 120
  Canapés
    and Egg, 86
    and Sardine, 90
  Egg and Mushroom
    Spread, 83
  -Flavored French Toast,
    167
  Muffins, 125
  Popovers, 131
  Roast Canadian, 352
  Salad
    and Green Bean, 510
    -Apple, 522
  Sandwich
    and Cottage Cheese, 91
    and Grilled Applesauce,
      96
  Stuffing, 452
  Tomato and Peanut But-
    ter Squares, 80
Baconized Sweet Potatoes,
  427
Baguettes de Berne (Swiss
  Sticks), 58
Baked
  Alaska, 692
  Apples, Orange, 694
  Bananas, 387
  Barbecue Spareribs, 348
  Beans, Bourbon Street,
    469
    Golden Topped, 469
    Old-Fashioned, 469
    Soup, 178
    Spicy, 470
    Vermont, 469
  Beef Hash, 338
  Beef Tenderloin, 307
  Blueberry Pudding, 667
  Bluefish in Sour Cream,
    224
  Brown Bread, 110
  Butterscotch Pie, 556
  Cabbage, 396
  Caramel Dumplings, 668
  Carrots, 398
  Cauliflower, Stuffed, 401
  Celery, 402
    -Stuffed Shad, 233
  Cheese Sandwich, 96
  Chicken, 264–71
    Breasts in cream, 281
    in foil, 280
    Kentucky, 280
    Frozen, 265
    Salad, 289

Baked (*Cont.*)
Chocolate Crumb Crust, 551
Custard, 677
Clams au Gratin, 239
Corn Custard, 405
Corned Beef, 315
Crab and Egg Salad, 242
Casserole, 242
Crushed Pineapple, 458
Cucumbers, 370
Custard, 677
Doves with Apple Stuffing, 296
with Rice, 296
Dried Beef and Noodles, 495
Eel, 225
Egg(s), 199
-Cheese dish, 199
Croquettes, 205
in Mushroom Sauce, 202
Stuffed, 204
Fish, 220
Fillets, 221
Florida, 220
Steaks, 224
with Green Sauce, 222
with Oyster Stuffing, 220
Flounder Supreme, 226
Grapefruit, 695
Halva, 671
Ham, 351
Ready-to-Serve, 351
Salad, 356
Slice, 352
with Sweet Potatoes, 353
Hawaiian Hash, 355
Hominy, 466
Huevos Rancheros (Eggs), 199
Jerusalem Artichokes, 385
Kasha, 468
Kibby (Syrian Lamb and Wheat Patties), 371
Leg of Lamb, 366
Liver and Onions, 374
Lobster, 245
Mushrooms, Stuffed, 413
Stuffed with Cheese, 69
Noodles
and Crab Meat, 492
Yukon, 492
Northern Pike, 228
Ocean Perch, 288
Onions, 415
Stuffed, 415
Oranges, 458
Oysters Homestead, 248
Parsnips, 416
Peach Halves, 458
Pineapple, 696
Pork and Beans, 469
Pork Chops, 343
Tenderloin, 342
Potatoes, 419, 420
Shoestring, 420

Stuffed, 420
with Chives, 420
with Russian Caviar, 420
Puddings, 664–76
Red Snapper in Wine Sauce, 229
Rhubarb, 675
Rice, 473, 478–80
Sole in Foil, 234
Spanish Mackerel, 228
Spareribs, 348
Spiced Peaches, 695
Spinach, 430
Squash, 432
Squirrel, 382
Sweetbreads, 376
Tart Shells, 550
Tomatoes, 435
Stuffed
Anchovy-, 435
with Crab Meat, 435
with Rice, 435
Tongue, 377
Trout, 235
Tuna Sandwich, 102
Turkey, 293
Wild Goose with Prune Stuffing, 299
Winter Squash with Walnuts, 395
Zucchini Casserole, 438
Baking
Chart, 38
High-Altitude, 584
Fish, 219
Hints, 15
Powder Biscuits, Basic, 119
Bambinos, 87
Banana(s), 387
Baked, 387
in Wine Hawaiian Style, 387
Bread
Cranberry, 113
Date, 109
Jelly, 113
Nut, 108
Peanut Butter, 109
Sour Cream, 109
Cake, 596
Casserole Pudding, 666
Cream Cheese Filling, 579
Doughnuts, 139
East Indian Curried, 387
Fried, 387
Fritters, Tarry-Hi, 139
Ham Rolls, 356
Mousse, 690
Muffins, 126
Nuggets, 643
Pancakes, 132
Pastry Puffs, Sweet, 578
Pie
Cream, 563
Split, 564
Platanutri (Fried Plantains), 387
Raisin Drops, 644
Rice Custard, 678

Salad
Fan Peach, 524
Marshmallow, 528
Molded Cranberry Special, 531
Pineapple, 524
Banbury Tarts, 578
Bar-B-Cue Pot Roast, 313
Bar-B-Q Flat Chuck Roast, Eileen's, 310
Sandwiches, 98
Bar-B-Que, Beef 'n' Cheese, 102
Barbecue(d). See also Barbecues
Baked Hamburgers, 326
Beef and Beans, 333
Brisket of Beef, 308
Chicken, 265
South Carolina, 266
Fish, Whole, 221
Sauce for, 221
Frankfurters, 339
Ham Burger, 105
Sandwich, 98
Lamb, Boned, 367
Leg of, 366–67
Mullet, 228
Pork and Bean Bake, 343
Burger, 105
Chinese, 346
Short Ribs, 314
Shrimp, 70
Spareribs, Western, 349
Barbecue(s). See also Barbecued
Baked Chicken, 268
Bulgur, 330
Buns, 155
Ham, 355
Kidney Beans, 333
Peach and Pork Chops, Skillet, 344
Sauce, 729
for Fish, 221
for Lamb Croquettes, 442
for Roast Pork, 342
for Spareribs, Pork Chops, and Chicken, 442
Orono, 442
Spareribs, Baked, 348
Style Meat Loaf, 329
Wafers, 56
Barley, 463
Casserole, 467
Pilaf, 467
Soup, Vegetable, 175
Basic
All-Purpose Aspic, 537
Baking Powder Biscuits, 119–20
Batter for Frying Vegetables, 383
Cheese Sticks, 55
Cream Pie and Variations, 563
Dough, Rich Sweet, 159
Doughnuts, with Buttermilk, 138

Basic (*Cont.*)
  Doughnuts (*Cont.*)
    with Sweet Milk, 138
  Pancakes, 132
  Popovers, 131
  Soufflé, Savory, 207
  White Bread, 144
Batter, Frying
  for Fish, 223
  for Vegetables, 383
Batter Rolls, 156
Bavarian Cream Pie, 564
Bayou Leftover Turkey Rice
  Dinner, 485
Bean(s)
  and Beets, 510
  and Chili, All-Day, 334
  and Pork Bake, Barbe-
    cued, 343
  and Pork Casserole, All-
    America, 346
  Baked. *See* Baked Beans
  Butter. *See* Dried Beans,
    Peas and Lentils
  Dip, Hot, 72
    Mexican, 74
  Dried. *See* Dried Beans,
    Peas and Lentils
  Frankfurter Fare, 339
  Lima. *See* Dried Beans,
    Peas and Lentils
  Rarebit, 470
  Salad, 509
    Relish, 510
  Snap, String or Wax. *See*
    Green Beans
  Soup, 177
    Baked Bean, 178
    Chowder, 178
    Lima, and Macaroni,
      178
    Pot, Hamburger, 178
    Senate Restaurant, 177
    with Potatoes, 177
  Spiced, 726
  with Enchiladas, 337
  with Venison Chili, 380
Béarnaise Sauce, 444
Beaten Biscuits, 120–21
Béchamel Sauce, 441
Beef
  à la Venison, 312
  and Cabbage Stuffing for
    Roast Pig, 341
  and Eggplant Parmesan,
    410
  Aspic, 537
  At Its Best, 312
  Bengal Curry, 321
  Boiled, 309
  Bourguignonne, 320
  Braised, 301, 317–19
  Brisket of, and Sauer-
    kraut, 309
    Barbecued, 308
  Broiled, 300
  Burgers, 102–5
    Beef 'n' Cheese Bar-B-
      Que, 102
    Beef-wiches, 103
    Irish Sweep Steak, 103

  Maid Rites, 103
  Pizza, 103
  Sarah's Hulamagusha,
    103
  Sloppy Joes, 104
  Southern, 103
  Stroganoff Buns, 104
  Super Hamburgers, 104
  Texas Bar-B-Que, 104
  Wimpies, 105
Carne con Chili Verde,
  321
Casserole
  and Rice, 486
  De Luxe Herbed, 320
  Hominy, 466
Chateaubriand, 308
Chipped, Pecan Log, 60
Corned Beef. *See* Corned
  Beef
Cornish Pasties, 323
Cuts of, 301
Dill Birds, 317
Dried Beef. *See* Dried
  Beef
Fillet of, 307
Filling for Babka, 334
Frankfurters. *See* Frank-
  furters
Goulashes, 320–24. *See*
  Goulash
Grades of, 301
Grilled, 300
Ground, 330–38. *See*
  Beef Burgers;
  Hamburgers; Meat
  Balls; Meat Loaf
Ham and Pork Loaf, 353
Hamburgers. *See* Ham-
  burgers
Hash, Baked, 338
How to Cook, 301
Large Cuts of, 307–9
Lenore's Boeuf en Daube,
  319
Meat Balls. *See* Meat Balls
Meat Loaves. See Meat
  Loaf
Olives, 317
Oriental Marinade for, 445
Oxtails, Braised, 324
Pies, 320–24
  Steak and Kidney, 323
  Steak and Potato Pie,
    Cousin Jack, 324
Pinwheels, 335
Pot Roasts, 312–15. *See*
  Pot Roast
Ragout with Onions, 321
Rib Eye, Roast Peppered,
  308
Roast, 300
  and Herring Salad, 522
  How to Carve, 301
  Onion Sauce, 448
  Pan-Browned Hash, 353
  Peking, 309
  Rolled, 307
  Roulades, 317
Sandwich
  Cheddar, 91

  Open Face, 93
  Sautéed, 300
  Smothered, 320
Soup
  Autumn Tomato-, 172
  Ball, 171
  Muriel Humphrey's,
    171
  Parisian, 193
  Vegetable, 172
Spaghetti Sauces
  Gravy, 507
  Italian, with Pork,
    507
Standing Ribs of, 307
Steak, 309–12. *See* Steak
  How to Carve, 301
  Parmigiana, 319
  Swiss, 319
Stew, 301, 320–24
  Black Walnut, 322
  English, 322
  Flemish Carbonades,
    322
  Gone-All-Afternoon,
    322
  Real Irish, 323
  Savory Baked, 322
Stock, 170
Stroganoff, 311
  Balls, 328
  Buns, 104
  Liver, 375
  with Tomato, 318
Stuffed, 308
Superb, 312
Tea, 733
Tenderloin, Baked, 307
  Broiled Whole, 307
Timetable for Cooking,
  306
Tongue, 377
  Braised, 378
  with Mushrooms, 320
  with Spanish Rice, 486
Beer Batter for Vegetables,
  383
Beer Potatoes, 421
Beet(s), 392
  and Beans, 510
  and Cabbage Relish, 727
  and Raisins, 393
  Aspic, Red, 537
  Deviled, 392
  Ginger, 392
  Greens, 392, 411
  Harvard, 393
  in Honey Sauce, 393
  in Turnip Cups, 393
  Jelly-Glazed, 393
  Pickled, 723
    Relish, 457
  Roots, Boiled, 392
  Scalloped, 393
  Yale, 393
Belgian
  Chicken Soup, 174
  Egg Casserole, 199
  Eggs, 203
  Mayonnaise, 543
Benedict, Eggs, 198

Bengal Curry, 321
Berliner Kranzer, 645
Berry Bavarian Crown, 686
Cobbler, Fresh, 666
Best Tomato Aspic, 539
Yet Corn Bread, 111
Best-Ever Stuffed Peppers, 418
Beverages, 732–42
American Wassail, 736
Apple Wassail Bowl, 735
Beef Tea, 733
Chocolate Malted, 737
Milk, 737
Party Hot, 734
Peppermint, Hot, 734
Real Rich French, 688
Syrup, 737
for Hot Chocolate, 733
Coffee. See Coffee
Cold, 737–42
Delightful Cocktail, 737
Summertime Drink, 740
Eggnog. See Eggnog
Grape Juice, Mulled, 735
Hints, 16
Hot, 733–37
Ice Cream Sodas, 691
Lemonade, 737
Pineapple, 737
Pink, 737
Mint Cooler, 738
Orange Lime Cocktail, 738
Mint Julep, 738
Spiced Wassail Bowl, 735
Orangeade, 737
Punch. See Punch
Raspberry Cooler, 738
Shrub, 738
Strawberry Milk Shake, 742
Sugar Syrup, 737
Swedish Glögg, 736
Tea. See Tea
Tom and Jerry, Mary's, 737
Tomato Toddy, Hot, 736
Wine
General Guide, 732
Service, 732
Bill's Cheesecake, 615
Bing Cherry Cola Salad, 529
Biscuit Tortoni, 687
Biscuits, 119–24. See also
Rolls and Biscuits,
Yeast
Bacon, 120
Baking Powder, Basic, 119
Variations, 120
Beaten, 120
Blue Cheese Cocktail, 87
Butter Dips, 121
Buttermilk, 121
Causes of Failure, 119
Cheese, 120, 121
Rolls, 121
Swirls, 122
Cinnamon Apple, 122

Cloud, 122
Corn Fingers, Oven-But-
tered, 122
Corn Meal, 122
Date Butterscotch Pin-
wheels, 123
Empanadas, 123
Jelly, 123
Master Mix, 120
Mile-High, 123
Onion, 123
Orange, Upside-Down, 124
Preparation of, 119
Royal Rusks, 123
Scones, Breakfast, 124
Standard, 119
Sweet Potato, 124
Tomato Cheese Whirls, 124
Turnovers, 123
Bishop, The, 736
Bishop's
Bread, 109
Sour Milk, 109
Cake, 613
Bits and Pieces Torte, 616
Bits of Gold Angel Cake, 609
Bizcochos, 634
Black
Bottom Cups, 620
Pie, 564
Currant Jam Cake, 602
-Eyed Peas and Tomatoes, 470
Forest Torte, 617
Rosebuds, 54
Walnut Stew, 322
Blanc Mange, 679
Blanquette de Veau, 362
Blender Mayonnaise, 445
Blind Date Cake, 504
Blinis (Russian Pancakes), 165
Blitz Torte, 616
Blue Cheese, 171
Cocktail Biscuits, 87
Dip
and Sour Cream, 72
Double Good, 73
Dressing
for Tossed Salad, 509
Sour Cream, 544
Fluff, 72
Sandwich, 91
Sauce for Salmon Steaks, 230
Blueberry
Boy Bait, 667
Cheesecake, 615
Dessert, 683
Muffins, 126
Maine, 127
Pancakes, 132
Pie, 553
Deep-Dish (Deep-Dish
Fresh Fruit Pie), 559
Freshy's, 565
Pudding, Baked, 667

Steamed, 675
Tarts, 578
Torte, 616
Blushing Cauliflower, 400
Bobette Sandwich, 93
Bohemian
Dumplings, Raised, 423
Sauerkraut Snacks, 56
Boiled
Artichokes, 383
Italian Style, 384
Jerusalem, 384
Beef, 309
Beet Roots, 392
Broccoli, 394
Brussels Sprouts, 395
Cabbage, Shredded, 396
Cabbage Wedges, 396
Carrots, 398
Cauliflower, 400
Celery Root, 403
Cucumbers, 407
Dressing, No-Cook, 545
Fresh Limas, 391
Kohlrabi, 411
Lobster, 244
Okra, 413
Parsnips, 416
Potatoes, 419
Snap Beans, 388
Bolichi (Stuffed Beef), 308
Bologna Sandwich, 91
Bombay Curry, 370
Bon Secour Oyster Dressing, 454
Bonbon Frosting, 622
Boned Barbecued Lamb, 367
Bonnie Bluestone Bread, 147
Borscht, 175
Cream of, 191
Boston Cream Pie, 586
Creams, 707
Bouillabaisse, 182
Bouillon. See Soups, Stocks
and Consommés
Bourbon
Balls, Kentucky, 659
Kentucky Pie, 565
Street Baked Beans, 469
Brains
Calf's, Breaded, 373
Sautéed, 373
with Scrambled Eggs, 373
Braised Beef Tongue, 378
Celery, 402
Chayote, 403
Chicken, 271–75
Duck, 295
Lettuce, 412
Liver, 375
Moose, 378
Oxtails, 324
Partridge, 297
Sirloin Tip Roast, 312
Spinach, 430
Venison, 379
Bran Muffins, 127
All-Bran Molasses, 127
by the Pailful, 127
Raisin Nut, 127
Brandied Peaches, 720

Brandy Sauce, 700
Brazil Nut Torte, 619
Brazilian Rice, 480
Bread and Butter Pickles, 724
Bread Chunks, Herbed, 195
Bread Crumb Crust for Haddock Pie, 226
Bread Custard, 667
Bread Dressing for Fish, 230
Bread Hints, 16
Bread Pudding, 667
  Chicken, 289
Bread, Spoon. *See* Spoon Bread
Bread Sticks, Cheese Garlic, 55
Bread Stuffing, 452
  for Beef Olives, 317
  for Fillets of Fish, 221
  for Pork Chops, 345
  Indian, 453
Breaded Calf's Brains, 373
Breads and Toasts, Ready-Made, 167–79
  Toasts
    Butterscotch, 167
    Cinnamon, 167
    Easy Patty Shells, 168
    French
      Bacon-Flavored, 167
      Oven, 167
      Spiced Breakfast, 167
    Garlic, 167, 168
    Herb Loaf, 168
    Melba, 167
  Breads
    Garlic, 167, 168
    Hot French, with Seasoned Butter, 168
    Peanut Sticks, 169
Breads, Quick, 108–42
  Applesauce Nut, 108
  Apricot, 108
  Banana Date, 109
    Nut, 108
    Peanut Butter, 109
    Sour Cream, 109
  Biscuits. *See* Biscuits
  Bishop's, 109
    Sour Milk, 109
  Brown, Baked, 110
    Heirloom Boston, 110
    Steamed, 110
    Sugar Nut, 110
  Butterscotch Nut, 110
  Carrot, 110
    Corn, 111
  Cheese, 111
  Coffee Cake. *See* Coffee Cake
  Corn, 111
    Best Yet, 111
    Custardy, 112
    Jalapeña Buttermilk, 112
    Meal Skillet, 112
    North Dakota Buttermilk, 111
    Prout's Neck Cake, 112

Spanish, 112
Crackling, 113
Cranberry
  Banana, 113
  Jelly, 113
  Orange, 113
Date Nut, 113
  -Brown Sugar, 114
Doughnuts and Fried Cakes. *See* Doughnuts
Gingerbread, 114
  Election Day, 114
  Small-Family, 114
  Soft, 114
Grape-Nut Quick, 115
Hobo, 115
Indian, Steamed, 115
Irish Soda, 115
Lemon, 115
Little, 116
Marmalade, 116
Muffins, 83–89. *See* Muffins
Nut
  Sour Cream, 116
  White, 116
  Whole Wheat, 116
  with Lemon Cheese Filling, 116
Onion Cheese, 117
Orange Date, 117
  -Brown Sugar, 117
Pain d'Épice, 117
Peanut Butter, 118
Pineapple Nut, 118
Popovers. *See* Popovers
Poppy Seed, 118
Pumpkin, 118
  Raisin Nut, 118
Rolls. *See* Rolls and Biscuits
Tomato, 119
Walnut Honey, 119
Breads, Yeast, 143–70
  Anadama, 146
  Bonnie Bluestone, 147
  Buttermilk, 145
  Casserole, 149
    Onion, 149
  Causes of Failure, 144
  Doughnuts, 138–42. *See* Pancakes, Waffles and Doughnuts, Yeast
  French, 145
    Crusty, 145
  Herb, 149
  Ingredients for, 143
  Irish Molly, 150
  Making of, 144
  Mixed, 146
  Oatmeal, 147
    Molasses Raisin, 147
  Pancakes, 131–38
  Pineapple, 150
  Raisin, 150
  Rye, Milwaukee, 147
  Salt-Rising, Minnesota Centennial, 146
  Shredded Wheat, 148
  Swedish Limpa, 148

Waffles, 131–38
White, Basic, 144
  How to Make Perfect, 144
  Water, 145
  Whole Wheat, 148
Breakfast
  Cookies, English, 640
  Eggs, Country, 200
    Scrambled, 198
  Fruit Soup, 192
  Perfect Muffins, 125
  Scones, 124
Breasts of Chicken Supreme, 284
Brioches, 156
Brisket of Beef and Sauerkraut, 309
Brittles, 712–13. *See* Candy
Broccoli, 394–95
  à la Polonaise, 394
  and Cheese Custard, 395
  and Chicken, 285
  Boiled, 394
  Casserole
    and Egg, 395
    Mushroom, 395
  Creole, 394
  Glazed, with Almonds, 394
  Salad in Aspic, 538
  with Green Rice, 480
  with Zesty Sauce, 394
Broiled
  Beef Liver, 374
  Bluefish, 224
  Cheese Rolls, 87
  Chicken, Calypso, 263
    Western Style, 262
  Fillets of Pompano or Mullet, 229
  Fish with Green Sauce, 222
  Flounder, 226
  Grapefruit, 49
  Lobster, 245
    Tails, 245
  Olive, Cheese and Bacon Canapés, 88
  Oysters, 249
  Scallops, 251
  Steak, 309
  Sweetbreads, 376
  Tomatoes, with French Dressing, 397
  Trout, 235
  Whole Beef Tenderloin, 307
Broth, Scotch, 172
Brown Breads
  Baked, 110
  Boston Heirloom, 110
  Buns, 160
  Steamed, 110
Brown Rice, 474
Brown Sugar
  Cookies, Crisp, 646
    Old-Time, 634
  Frosting, 627
  -Glazed Carrots, 399
  Icing, 627

Brown Sugar (*Cont.*)
  Meringue Frosting for
      Leather Cake, 595
  Nut Bread, 110
  Pudding, 668
  Topping for Queen Eliza-
      beth Cake, 597
Brownie Pie, 576
Brownies. *See* Cookies
Brunswick Stew, 277
  Alabama, 277
Brussels Sprouts, 395
  and Green Beans Napoli,
      389
  Boiled, 395
  Deviled, 395
  Tangy, 396
  with Grapes, 396
Bubble Loaf, 151
Buckwheat
  Cakes, Old-Fashioned,
      165
  Groats. *See* Kasha
  Pancakes, 132
Bulgar Barbecue, 330
Bulgarian Noodles, 495
  Salad, 512
Bulgur (Cracked Wheat),
      463, 467
  Pilaf, 468
  Stuffing, 453
  Tab Ulee (Salad with
      Wheat), 468
Bumsteads, 106
Bun-ies, 96
Burger Macaroni Casserole,
      501
Burgers, Miscellaneous
  Bumsteads, 106
  Chicken, 105
  Crab, 105
  -Avocado, 105
  Ham, Barbecued, 105
  Pork, Barbecued, 105
  Sea, 106
  Shrimp Boat, 106
  Tuna, 106
Burgundy Beans, 470
  Beef Balls, 326
Burnt Sugar Pralines, 708
Butter
  Aunt Mollie's Apple, 723
  Balls, 460
    Norwegian, 648
  Cake, Regal, 542
  Canapés. *See* Canapé
      Butters
  Chocolate Cookies, Mrs.
      Nixon's, 634
  Cream Frosting, 623
  Creams, 713
  Crumb Dumplings, 461
  Crunch, 712
    for Pie Shell and Top-
      ping, 550
  Crust Parfait Pie, 567
    Pastry, 549
  Dips, 121
  for Fish
    Cucumber, 444
    Lemon, 226, 444

Lemon Caper, 445
Lemon Parsley, 445
for French Bread
  Chive, 168
  Garlic, 168
Frostings, Creamy, 622
  for Mincemeat Coffee
      Cake, 606
Horns, 160
Icing, Never-Fail, 625
Nut Filling, 623
Pecan Cake, Toasted, 587
Pecan Frosting, 587
Pecan Ice Cream, 687
Refrigerator Cookies, 650
Sauce for Desserts, 700
  for Fish, Seafood and
      Vegetables, 442
  Onion, for Steak, 448
Semmels, 157
Tarts, 579
Toffee, 712
Whipped, 700
-Crusted Baked Chicken,
      264
Buttered Popcorn, 55, 254
Butterfly Shrimp, 70
Buttermilk Biscuits, 121
  Bread, 145
  Cake, White, 585
  Doughnuts, Basic, 138
  Fried Chicken, 263
  Glaze for Sugar Plum
      Cake, 600
  Muffins, 125
  Pancakes, Super Duper,
      132
    with Wheat Germ, 133
  Pie, 556
    Lemon, 556
  Pineapple Sherbet, 689
  Rolls, 156
  Salad Dressing, Low Cal-
      orie, 542
  Spoon Bread, Old Vir-
      ginia, 464
  Waffles, James River, 137
  Whole Wheat, 138
Butternut Squash. *See*
  Squash
Butternut Squash Soufflé,
      433
Butterscotch, 711
  Apple Crisp, 664
  Apple Pudding, 694
  Apples, 694
  Bars, 655
    Easy Chocolate-Frosted,
      655
  Brownies, 654
  Cake, 587, 594
    and Caramel, 594
  Candy, 711
  Cookies, 637
  Date Pinwheels, 123
  Drops, 712
  Filling, 630
  Fudge, 705
  Maple Sauce, 700
  Nut Bread, 110
  Nut Creams, 707

Pie, Baked, 556
  Coconut, 565
  Cream, 563
  Peach, 554
  Rolls, Dakota, 160
  Sauce, 700
  Toast, 167
By Cracky Bars, 656

Cabbage, 396
  and Beef Stuffing for
      Roast Pig, 341
  and Beet Relish, 727
  and Corned Beef, 215
  and Corned Beef Salad,
      522
  and Green Beans, Ger-
      man, 388
  Baked, 396
  Boiled Shredded, 396
  Chinese, 398
  Chow-Chow, Quick, 727
  Dilled with Sour Cream,
      397
  Dressed-Up, 397
  Fried, 396
  Leaves, Stuffed, 330
  Palm, 398
  Pigeons, 331
  Pineapple Nut Salad, 534
  Red. *See* Red Cabbage
  Salad with Sweet Oil
      Dressing, 510
    Twenty-Four-Hour, 510
  Scalloped, and Cheese,
      397
  Soup, Sweet and Sour,
      175
  Wedges, Boiled, 396
  with Onions, 396
Caesar Salad, 508
  Daleen's, 508
Café au Lait, 733
  Brûlot, 734
Cakes, 583–621
  Angel Food. *See* Angel
      Food Cakes
  Butterscotch, 594
    and Caramel, Southern,
      594
    Leather, 595
    Mardi Gras Party, 595
  Cheese. *See* Cheesecakes
  Chiffon. *See* Chiffon Cakes
  Chocolate, 590–94
    All, 593
    Beer, 591
    Blind Date, 594
    Crazy, 592
    Devil's Food, Red, 592
    Dominican, 591
    Eggless, 591
    French, 593
    Fudge, 590
      Kathryn's, 590
    Macaroon, 594
    Marble, 594
    $100, 590
    Starlight Delight, 592
    Very Fluffy, 591

Cakes (*Cont.*)
　Chocolate (*Cont.*)
　　Walnut-Filled Cocoa,
　　　593
　Coffee. *See* Coffee Cakes
　Common Causes of Fail-
　　ure, 584
　Cupcakes, 619–21. *See*
　　Cupcakes
　Desserts, 683–86
　　Apricot Crême, 683
　Fillings. *See* Fillings;
　　Frostings
　Freezing, 584
　Frostings. *See* Frostings
　Frosting the Cake, 583
　Fruit. *See* Fruitcakes
　Fruit-Flavored, 596–601
　　Apple, 596
　　　Quickie, 596
　　Applesauce, 596
　　Banana, 596
　　Cherry Meringue, 596
　　Date-Nut, 597
　　Fig with Lemon-Orange
　　　Glaze, 597
　　Fruit Cocktail, 597
　　Grand Marnier, 599
　　"I Smell Christmas,"
　　　599
　　Lemon Loaf, 598
　　　Quick, 598
　　　Treasure, 598
　　Orange Cake, Quick,
　　　599
　　　Layer Cake, Fresh,
　　　　598
　　Pineapple, Quick, 600
　　Parfait, 599
　　Prune, 600
　　Queen Elizabeth, 597
　　Rhubarb, Fresh, 600
　　Strawberry, Delicious,
　　　600
　　Sugar Plum, 600
　How to Make Good
　　Cakes, 583
　Pan Substitutes, 584
　Pineapple Cream, 610
　Pound. *See* Poundcakes
　Spice, 601–3
　　Black Currant Jam, 602
　　Carrot, 601
　　Crofts, 601
　　Hillbilly, 601
　　Oatmeal, 602
　　Orleans Meringue, 602
　　Raisin, Eggless, Milk-
　　　less, Butterless,
　　　601
　　Sour Cream, Never-
　　　Fail, 602
　Sponge. *See* Sponge
　　Cakes
　Storing, 584
　Tortes. *See* Tortes
　Types, 583
　Upside-Down. *See* Up-
　　side-Down Cakes
　Vegetable, 439

White, 585–86
　Ambrosia, 585
　Buttermilk, 585
　Cake for Two, 585
　Ice Water, 585
　Lemon and Pineapple,
　　585
　Queen of May, 586
　Vienna, 586
Yellow, 586–90
　Boston Cream Pie, 586
　Butter, Regal, 586
　Butter Pecan, Toasted,
　　587
　Butterscotch, 587
　California Sunshine,
　　589
　Coconut Layer, 587
　Danish Layer, 588
　Easy Pudding and
　　Cake, 589
　Hot Milk, 588
　Icelandic Vinartarta,
　　588
　Lazy Daisy, 588
　Mincemeat Tea Loaf,
　　589
　Rum, 589
　Tarta Baba, 590
　Vanilla Wafer Crumb,
　　588
　Walnut Wonder, 590
Calamity Jane Cream of
　Turnip Soup, 191
Calexico Rice, 479
Calf's Liver en Brochette,
　374
California Baked Chicken,
　266
　Pea Bean Soup, 177
　Sunshine Cake, 589
Calorie Chart, 26–33
Canadian Pie Pastry, 549
Canapés and Party Sand-
　wiches, 77–90
　Bases, 77
　Cocktail Pastry Boats, 77
　Cold
　　Anchovy, 80
　　Avocado, 80
　　Bacon, Tomato and
　　　Peanut Butter
　　　Squares, 80
　　Caviar and Smoked
　　　Salmon, 80
　　Cheese Nut, 81
　　　Garlic, 81
　　Cucumber, 82, 83
　　Date Nut Sandwich
　　　Filling, 83
　　Dried Beef, 83
　　French Roll, 83
　　Ham Canapés, 83
　　　Pinwheels, 83
　　Pickle, 84
　　Salmon Avocado Half-
　　　and-Half, 84
　　Shrimp, 85
　　　Carnations, 85
　　Garnishes for, 78

Hot
　Anchovy, 86
　Bacon Biscuits, 86
　Bacon 'n' Egg, 86
　Bambinos, 87
　Blue Cheese Biscuits,
　　87
　Cocktail Dreams, 86
　　Pizzas, 87
　　Teasers, 86
　　Twirlups, 86
　Cheese, 88
　　Broiled Olive, Bacon,
　　　88
　　Cheddar, Puffs, 88
　　Date Rounds, 87
　　English Rarebit, 88
　　Rolls, Broiled, 87
　　Roquefort Cream
　　　Cheese Rolls, 88
　　Turnovers, 88
　Clam Puffs, 88
　　Rolls, Hot, 89
　Crab Meat, 89
　Deviled Ham Puffs, 89
　Hawaiian Sandwiches,
　　89
　Mushroom, 89
　　Rolls, 89
　Noche Specials, 88
　Sardine and Bacon, 90
　Sausage Bites, 90
　　Rolls, 90
　Tuna Crab, 90
　　Olive Bites, 90
　How to Keep Fresh, 78
　Spreads. *See* Spreads,
　　Canapé
　Suggestions, 80
　Tray, 79
Canapé Butters
　Anchovy, 77
　　Egg, 77
　Artichoke, 77
　Caper, 77
　Cheese, 77
　　Bacon, 79
　Chive, 77
　Chutney, 77
　Crab Meat, 77
　Egg, 77
　Garlic, 77
　　and Parsley, 79
　Ham and Egg, 77
　Honey, 77
　Horseradish, 77, 79
　Jam, 77
　Lemon, 77
　Liver, 77
　Lobster, 77
　Marmalade, 77
　Mustard, 77
　Nut, 77
　Olive, 77
　Orange, 77
　Parsley, 77
　Pimiento, 77
　Sardine, 77
　Shrimp, 77, 85
　Spice, 78
　Water Cress, 78

Canapé Spreads. *See*
  Spreads, Canapé
Candied Carrots with Ap-
  ples, 399
  Fruit, 705
  Fruitcake, 612
  Parsnips, 416
  Popcorn, 710
Candies
  Candied Fruits, 659
  Hard, 712–13
Candy, 704–15
  Apricot Coconut Balls,
    713
  Boiling Syrups, 704
  Butter Creams, 713
    Crunch, 712
  Butterscotch, 711
    Drops, 712
    Fudge, 705
  Caramels, 709–10
    Apples, 710
    Corn, 710
    Delicious, 663
    Nut, 709
    Vanilla, 710
  Chocolate Dipping, 658
  Chocolate Mints, Easy,
    713
    Oysters, 714
    Truffles, French, 714
  Christmas Hard, 713
  Clear Red Anise, 713
  Cobblestone, 714
  Cocada (Coconut), 714
  Coconut Patties, 708
  Cold-Water Tests, 704
  Coloring Sugar, 705
  Cooking Syrups, 704
  Cracker Jax, 712
  Creams, Boston, 707
    Chocolate, 707
    Butterscotch Nut, 707
    Chocolate Cherry, 713
  Divinity, 710
    Nut Candy, 710
  English Chocolate Toffee,
    712
  Fondant
    Creamy Uncooked, 715
    Dependable, 707
    5-Pound, 708
    Mashed Potato, 715
  Fudge. *See also* Fudge
    Coffee, 706
    Creamy Chocolate, 705
    Mamie Eisenhower's,
      706
    Marshmallow Nut, 706
    No-Cook Chocolate
      Cream Cheese, 714
    One-Minute, 705
    Peanut Butter, 706
    Date, 706
    Smith College, 705
  Martha Washington Bon-
    bons, 714
  Miniature Fruits, 708
  Nougat, 711
  Peanut Brittle, 712
  Pecan Roll, 708

Penuche. *See* Penuche
Praline Cookies, 709
Pralines, Burnt Sugar, 708
  Sugar, 708
Pulled Mints, 711
Pulling Taffy, 704
Rules for Making, 704
Sponge, 713
Taffy, White, 711
Toffee, Butter, 712
  Creamy, 711
Tropical Dates, 715
Turkish Paste, 709
Types, 704
Uncooked, 713–15
Walnuts, Minted, 709
  Orange, Cream, 709
Canned
  Crab Meat Cocktail, 51
  Lobster Cocktail, 51
  Soup Combinations, 193
Cannelloni, 497. *See also*
  Pasta
Canning, 39–41
  Commercial Can Sizes, 34
Cantaloupe Salad, Stuffed,
  523
  Tarts, Seafoam, 579
Cantonese Ham Casserole,
  355
  Spareribs, 349
Cape Cod Lobster Pie, 247
Caper and Egg Sauce, 441
  Butter, 77
  Cream Sauce, 441
  Lemon Butter, 445
  Sour Cream Sauce for
    Shrimp, 450
Caracus (Beef Rabbit), 316
Caramel Cakes. *See* Cakes,
  Butterscotch and Cara-
  mel
Caramel Cake Filling, 627
  Corn, 710
  Dumplings, 668
  Frosting, Mrs. Kittler's,
    628
  Icing, Mrs. Sharp's, 628
  Pie, Cream, 563
    Cream Meringue, 565
    Pecan Pumpkin, 560
  Sauce, Nut, 700
  Sauce de Luxe, 700
  Syrup, 663
Caramels, 709–10
Caramelized Sugar, 663
Cardinale Sauce for Lob-
  ster, 245
Carmelita's Favorite Lemon
  Pie, 569
  Lemon Meringue Frost-
  ing, 626
Carne con Chili Verde, 321
"Carorange" Confiture, 718
Carrots, 398
  and Celery, Scalloped,
    400
  and Raisin Sandwich, 93
  Baked, 398
  Boiled, 398
  Bread, 110

Brown Sugar-Glazed, 399
Cake, 601
Candied, with Apples, 399
Cookies, Cooked, 638
Corn Bread, 111
Creamed, 399
Deviled, 399
Marinated, 511
Pancakes, 133
Peanut Sandwich Filling,
  80
Pie, 556
Shoestring, 399
Soufflé, 400
Soup, Cream of, 186
Stuffed, 399
Vitamin, 400
Zesty, 400
Carter's Special Spaghetti
  Sauce, 507
Casserole
  Adlai's Delight Shrimp,
    256
  All-America Pork and
    Bean, 346
  All-in-One Spaghetti, 505
  Artichoke and Seafood,
    257
  Asparagus, 386
    and Egg, 395
    Macaroni, 500
  Banana Sweet Potato,
    428
  Barley, 467
  Beef and Rice, 486
    Chow Mein, 331
  Bread, 149
    Onion, 149
  Broccoli and Egg, 395
    Mushroom, 395
  Cantonese Ham, 355
  Cauliflower and Egg, 395
  Cheese, 214
  Cheese-a-Roni, 500
  Cherokee, 486
  Chicken, 286
    and Wild Rice, 488
    Noodle, 493
  Chow, 485
  Company Chicken and
    Rice, 288
  Corn and Mushroom, 406
    Clam, 239
    Sausage, 357
  Corned Beef, 315
  Coronado, 202
  Country, 330
  Crab, Baked, 242
    Imperial, 243
  Easy Down East Seafood,
    257
  Egg, Belgian, 199
    Spanish, 203
  Eggplant and Mushroom,
    409
    Olive, 409
  English Pea, 417
  Favorite Green Bean, 390
  Frankfurter Crown, 339
  German, 344
  Greek, 372

Casserole (*Cont.*)
Green Bean, 389
and Mushroom, 390
Green Enchilada, 215
Ham, Potato and Onion,
356
Herbed Beef, de Luxe,
320
Hominy, 466
Beef, 466
Japanese Chicken, 273
Lamb, 369–71
Lima Bean, 392
and Mushroom, 392
Lobster with Wild Rice,
246
Macaroni Burger, 501
Chipped Beef, 502
Corn and Oyster, 500
Hamburger Upside-
Down, 501
Mother's Baked Fruit, 671
Noodle, Cottage Cheese
and Ham, 455
with Pork, 495
Oklahoma Spinach, 431
Overnight Italian, 501
Pot Chicken in, 279
Potato, 425
Egg and Salami, 425
Rice and Corn, 478
and Vegetable, 479
Ruby Mountain Special,
336
Seafood and Egg, 257
Serendipity, 432
Southern Corn, 405
Spanish Veal, 363
Spring Salmon, 231
Squash, 433
Superb Crab Meat, 242
Sweet Potato and Orange,
428
Tamale, 336
Toasted Rice, 439
Tuna, 237
Noodle, 237, 492
Turkey Cashew, 294
Turnip and Apple, 437
Venison Steaks, 379
Wild Rice, 488
with Sausage, 489
Wisconsin, 363
Zucchini and Beef, 333
Baked, 438
Casserole Cookies, 647
Casserole Pudding, Banana,
666
Catsup
Grape, 730
Prune, 730
Tomato, 731
Catsup French Dressing, 541
Salad Dressing, 541
Cauliflower, 400
and Egg Casserole, 395
au Gratin, 401
Baked Stuffed, 401
Blushing, 400
Boiled, 400
Company, 401

Pickle, 723
Salad, Turkish, 513
Soup, Cream of, 185
Timbales, 401
Caviar
and Smoked Salmon Can-
apés, 80
Cheese Mold, 58
Dip, Red, 72
Open-Face Sandwich, 94
Poor Man's, 61
Russian, with Baked Po-
tatoes, 420
with Cheese in Tomato
Cup, 59
Cebolla-Frijoles Soup,
Quick, 193
Celeriac, 403
Celery, 402
Amandine, 402
and Carrots, Scalloped,
400
and Mushroom Dressing,
453
and Peas, Tasty, 417
Baked, 402
Braised, 402
Curls, 58
Dressing, 453
Loaf, Golden Baked, 402
Rings, Stuffed, 58
Root, 403
Boiled, 403
Scalloped, 402
Stuffed with Cream
Cheese, 58
Cream Cheese and But-
ter, 58
Stuffings for, 58
Cereal(s), 463–64
Crunch Piecrust, 550
Servings and Pounds, 36
Snacks, Skillet, 662
Types, 463
Ceylon Chicken, 272
Chafing Dish Sweet and
Sour Meat Balls, 68
Chantilly Potatoes, 425
Charcoal-Grilled Swordfish
Steak, 235
Chard, 403
Charlotte Russe, 684
Chocolate, 684
Chart, Baking, 38–39. *See
also* Tables
Canning, 40–41
Oven Temperature, 38
Wine Cookery, 37–38
Chateaubriand, 308
Chayote, 403
Braised, 403
Checkerboard Cookies, 652
Sandwich, 78
Cheddar Beef Sandwich, 91
Cheese and Chutney
Spread, 81
Puffs, 88
Soufflé, 207
Cheese and Cheese Dishes,
210–16
and Egg Sandwich, 91

and Macaroni, Aunt
Lydia's, 498
Supreme, 458
with Olives, 500
and Olive, 91
and Rice, Savory, 479
and Scalloped Cabbage,
397
and Tongue Hors
d'Oeuvres, 64
Apples, 59
Armenian Cheese-Filled
Boraks, 215
Bacon Butter, 79
Balls, 59
Nippy, 56
Rosy, 59
Stuffed, 65
with Tomato Aspic,
498
Biscuits, 120–21
Blintzes, 211
Bread, 111
Butter, 77
Canapés
Bacon and Olive, 88
-Garlic Nut, 81
Hot, 87
Nut, 81
Casserole, 214
-a-Roni, 500
Caviar
in Tomato Soup, 59
Mold, 58
Chili con Queso on Tor-
tillas, 215
Crescents, Double, 56
Croquettes, 214
Custard and Broccoli, 395
Date Rounds, 87
Dips
and Hot Pepper, 74
and Green Pepper, 73
Hot, 74
Dumplings in Tomato
Sauce, 463
Egg and Liverwurst, 95
Croquettes, 204
-Egg Dish, Baked, 199
Enchilada(s), 215
Casserole, Green, 215
Filling, for Kolachky, 162
for Ravioli, 497
Garlic Bread Sticks, 55
Grits, 467
Hominy Bake, 466
Monkey, 212
Moons, 56
Muffins, 125
Omelet, 205
Soufflé, 208
Orégano Salad Dressing,
542
Overnight Bake, 213
Pancakes, 132
Pastry, 549
Pie
Easy Cherry, 565
Pineapple Icebox, 573
Strawberry, 575

Cheese and Cheese Dishes
(Cont.)
Pimiento Sauce, 443
Popovers, 131
Puffs, 56, 67, 214
Fish, 221
Pudding, 213
Quiche Lorraine, 214
Rarebit
Easy, 212
Mushroom, 212
Oyster, 213
Spanish, 212
Welsh, 212
with Beer, 211
Red Devil, 212
Rinktum Diddie, 212
Rolls, 59–60, 121
Broiled, 87
Salad
and Pineapple, 526
Frosting for Molded
Salad, 534
Pineapple Cherry, 524
Sandwich
Baked, 96
Open-Face, 96
Salmon, Grilled, 101
Sauce, 442
Cheddar, 441
for Moussaka, 332
Mornay, 441
Snacks, Evening, 88
Soufflé
and Ham, 209
and Mushroom, 208
with Bread, 208
Soup Elegant, 187
Spoon Bread, 464
Sticks, Basic, 55
Roquefort, 55
Strata, 213
Swedish Ostraka (Cus-
tard), 215
Swirls, 121
Swiss Fondue, 211
with Sauterne, 211
Tomato Whirls, 124
Tomatoes, Scalloped, 436
Turnovers, 88
Types and How to Use,
210
Winkum, 212
with Green Rice, 480
Cheesecake
Bill's, 615
Blueberry, 615
Cherry, 615
Cottage, 615
Cranberry, 615
Cherokee Casserole, 486
Cherries and Rice in the
Snow, 680
Cherry
Cake, Christmas, 614
Meringue, 596
Upside-Down, 608
Cheese Cups, 620
Cheesecake, 615
Chocolate Creams, 713

Cobbler Coffee Cake, 604
Coconut Bars, 656
Cookies, 638
Crunch, 668
Icing, 623
Jam, 718
Jubilee, 692
Muffin Cobbler, 668
Pie, 553
Cheese, Easy, 565
Deep-Dish, 559
Dutch, 557
Meringue-Topped, 566
Nut Parfait, 566
Tapioca, 554
Washington Ice Cream,
692
-Pineapple Cocktail, 49
Poundcake, 603
Pudding, Upside-Down,
668
Punch, 739
Rolls, 669
Salad, Jelly, 529
Pineapple Cheese, 524
Tarts, 579
Chef's Lamb and Mush-
rooms, 372
Chess Pie, 557
Lemon, 557
Pineapple, 560
Chesterfield Pie, 499
Chestnut and Rye Bread
Turkey Filling, 453
and Wild Rice Stuffing,
455
Dressing, 453
Drool Dish, 404
Purée, 403
Chestnuts, 403
Water, and Green Beans,
Creamed, 390
Water, Stuffing, 455. See
Water Chestnuts
Chewy Chocolate Cookies,
638
Oatmeal Bars, 658
Chicken
à la Avocado, 285
à la King, New Orleans
Style, 287
à la Maryland, 273
Alfred, 268
Almond, 284
and Broccoli, 285
and Rice in Foil, 483
Polynesian, 273
Supreme, 483
and Seafood Gumbo, 181
and Spaghetti, San Fran-
cisco, 462
and Spinach Filling for
Ravioli, 498
Baked, 264–71
Barbecue, 268
Cacciatore, 268
California, 266
Dorothy's Easy, 268
Epicure, 269
Frozen, 265
in Currant Sauce, 269

in Honey, 266
in Sour Cream, 267
with Orange, 269
with Sour Cream Wine
Sauce, 270
Barbecue, 265
South Carolina, 266
Bisque, 187
Braised, 271–75
Bread Pudding, 289
Breasts, 280–84
Baked in Cream, 281
in Foil, 280
in Sour Cream, 284
Creamed Hot Dish, 282
Delight, 280
Divan, 282
Kentucky Baked, 280
Kiev, 281
Macadamia, 281
Poulet Cintra, 284
Romano, 283
Supreme, 284
Grilled in Foil, 280
with Artichoke Hearts,
282
with Potato Stuffing,
280
with Tarragon, 283
with Thin Spaghetti,
Chinese, 283
with Wine and Mush-
room Sauce, 282
Broiled, Western Style,
262
Calypso, 263
Burgers, 105
Butter-Crusted, 264
Buttermilk Fried, 263
Cacciatore, 272
Can-Can, 286
Casserole, 286
and Rice, Company,
288
and Wild Rice, 488
Noodle, 493
Ceylon, 272
Cha-Cha-Cha, 268
Club, 285
Coq au Vin, 270
Corn-Crisped, 264
Country Captain, 270
Cranberry-Braised, 272
Croquettes, 285
Curry, 286
Dumplings, 461
Dishes, Cooked, 284–90
Dixie Deviled, 263
Élégante, 286
Enchiladas, 287
Filipino, 270
Filling for Cannelloni, 497
Georgia Fried, 263
Grace Moore's Spanish,
274
Gumbo, 180
Hash, 287
Hawaiian, 272
Henny Penny, 289
Honduras, 272

Chicken (*Cont.*)
  in Almond-Orange Sauce, 271
  Jambalaya, 484
  Japanese Casserole, 273
  Leone, 267
  Little Red Chick, 267
  Livers, 290–91
    and Mushrooms, Sautéed, 291
    Hors d'Oeuvres
      Chopped, 65
      Party, 65
      Rumaki (Oriental), 65
      with Capers in Tomato Sauce, 66
    in Sherry, 291
    in Sour Cream, 291
    Pâté, 60
    and Mushroom, 60
    Sauté, 290
  Loaf, 287
    Molded, 529
  Margo, 273
  Missouri Deep-Fried, 264
  Monte Cristo, 99
  Monterey with Pecan Pilaf, 271
  Mousse, 540
  'n' Stuffing Scallop, 290
  New Orleans, 264
  Oriental Marinade for, 445
  Oven Lemon, 266
  Paprika, 273
  Parmesan Oven-Fried, 265
  Party Perfect Glazed, 266
  Peuffle, 483
  Pie
    and Oyster, 288
    Sunday, 288
    with Sweet Potato Crust, 289
  Pilaf, 482
  Poached, 278. *See* Chicken Chop Suey
  Poppy Seed Smothered, 274
  Poule au Pot, 264
  Pressed, 538
  Rice Bake, 482
  Ring with Mushroom Velouté Sauce, 288
  Roast
    in Foil with Oyster Cracker Stuffing, 262
    Whole Boneless with Wild Rice and Foie Gras Stuffing, 262
    with Pan Gravy, 262
  Rodger, 483
  Salad, 520
    Almond, 520
    and Meat, 520–22
    and Sour Cream, 530
    Baked, 289
    Curried, 521

Egg, 529
  Elegant, 521
  Hawaiian, 521
  Macaroni, 516
  Parsnip, 521
  Sweetheart, 521
  Sandwich, 91, 92, 94, 97
  Sauce, 441
    Quick, 443
  Sauté Sec, 274
  Sesame, 265
  Sherried, 274
  Sopa de Fritos, 290
  Soufflé, 208
    Rice Loaf, 288
  Soup
    Belgian, 174
    Noodle, 173
      Easy, 173
    Sauce for de Luxe Tuna Sandwich, 102
  South Sea, 287
  Spread, 81
    Liver, 82
    Salad, 81
  Squares, 290
  Stewed, 275–80
    à la King, Excellent, 276
    Alabama, 277
    and Sweetbreads, Cream of, 279
    Brunswick, 277
    Eight-Boy Curry, 278
    Fricassee, 275
    in Milk, 279
    Kentucky Burgoo, 277
    Old-Fashioned, 276
    Pie, 276
      Grandmother's, 276
    Pollo in Umido con Polenta, 276
    Pot, in Casserole, 279
    Scalloped, 279
  Stock, 170
  Sub Gum Chow Mein, 290
  Sunday, 265
  Supreme, 270
  Tarragon, 275
  Tchakhokbelli (in Paprika Sauce), 271
  Teriyaki, 267
  Tetrazzini, 503
    Mrs. Stuart Symington's, 463
  Véronique, 275
  Vintage, 275
  with Curried Tomato Sauce, 275
  with Lobster Sauce, 283
  with Wild Rice Stuffing, 455
  with Yellow Rice, 483
Chickeroni Bake, 286
Chiffon
  Cake
    Lemon, 610
    Mahogany, 610

Pie
  Coconut Sherry, 568
  Lemon, 570
  Mint, 570
  Rum, 574
Chiffonade Dressing, 541
  French, 541
Children's Delight, 655
Chiles Rellenos con Queso (Stuffed Chili Peppers), 66
Chili and Beans, All-Day, 334
  Beef Dip, 72
  Con Carne, 334
  con Queso Dip (Cheese and Hot Peppers), 74
  on Tortillas, 215
  Enchiladas, Green, 337
  Jailhouse, 334
  Meat Balls, 69
  Pedernales River, 334
  Peppers, Stuffed, 66
  Sauce, 730
    Cocktail, 52
    Grandmother's, 730
    Red, 443
  Venison, with Beans, 380
Chinese
  Asparagus, 385
  Barbecued Pork, 346
  Beef and Beans, 331
  Cabbage, 398
  Chews, 655
  Chicken with Thin Spaghetti, 283
  Egg Petal Soup, 174
  Meat Balls, 68
  New Year's Cookies, 660
  Pepper Steak, 318
  Pork Chops, 343
  Shrimp Sub Gum. *See* Chinese Sub Gum
  String Beans, 390
  Sub Gum, 347
  Sweet and Sour Radishes, 459
Chipped Beef. *See* Dried Beef
  Pecan Log, 60
Chive Butter, 77, 168
Chocolate
  Acorns, 638
  Angel Food Dessert, 683
  Cake
    All, 593
    Beer, 591
    Crazy, 592
    Eggless, 591
    French, 593
    Fudge, 590
    Macaroon, 594
    $100, 590
    Very Fluffy, 591
  Charlotte Russe, 684
  Chippers, 638
  Coffee Punch, 741
  Cookies, 660
    Butter, Mrs. Richard Nixon's, 634
    Chewy, 638

Chocolate (*Cont.*)
Cream Cheese Frosting, 624
Fudge, No-Cook, **714**
Creams
Boston, 707
Cherry, 713
Cupcakes, 620
Custard, Baked, 677
Date Bars, 656
-Dipped Nut Balls, 661
Filling, Mary's, 630
-Frosted Butterscotch Bars, Easy, 655
Frosting, 623
Chip, 623
Easy, 625
Kathryn's, 628
Mrs. Hood's, 628
Nut, 623
Pecan, 626
Rum, 623
Sammye's, 628
Shiny, 629
Whipped Cream, 625
Fudge, Creamy, 705
Fudge Icing, 628
Glaze, 629
Honey Eggnog, 741
Hot Party, 734
Ice Cream, 687
Cups, Sweet, 693
Logs, 660
Malted, 737
Milk, 737
Mint Topping, 630
Mints, Easy, 713
Mousse au, 677
Oysters, 714
Peppermint, Hot, 734
Pie, Bar, 566
Cream, 563
Pecan, 566
Cream Cheese, 566
Crust
Crumb, 551
Wafer Crust, **551**
Pinwheels, 651
Pixies, 646
Poundcake, 603
Pudding, Icebox, 684
Steamed, 669
Real Rich French, 734
Roll, 611
Sauce, Velvet, 701
Shell, 551
Soufflé, Cold, 680
with Sauce, 699
Sundaes, Frozen, 692
Syrup, 737
for Hot Chocolate, 733
Toffee, English, 712
Torte Lili, 617
Truffles, French, 714
Waffles, 136
Spiced, 137
Chop Suey, American, 346
Chicken, 278
Chopped Chicken Livers, 65
Chow Casserole, 485
Chow Mein, American, 346

Casserole, Beef, 331
Shrimp, 256
Sub Gum, 290
Chowders
Bean, 178
Clam, 182
Corn, 185
and Crab Meat, Hearty, 185
Crab Meat, 183
Manhattan, 182
New England Fish, 183
Old-Fashioned New England Bacon and Corn, 184
Rhode Island Quahog, 182
Salmon, 184
Shrimp, 184
Christmas
Cheer Punch, 739
Cherry Cake, 614
Conserve, 721
Cookies, 641
German, 635
Dessert, 683
Fruit Balls, 660
Hard Candy, 713
Party Punch, 739
Chuck. *See* Pot Roasts
Roast, Eileen's Bar-B-Q Flat, 310
Steak with Vegetables, 311
Cider Dressing, 543
Punch, Hot, 735
Cigarettes de Bayonne (Ham and Truffles), 62
Cinnamon
Apple Biscuits, 122
Relish, 456
Salad, Stuffed, 522
Candy Apple Salad, 526
Candy Jell, 719
Cream Salad Dressing, 545
Crisps, 650
Doughnuts, 139
Honey Muffins, 128
Rolls, Quick, 160
Squares, 656
Toast, 167
Cioppino (Fish Soup), 182
Clam(s)
Alabama Fried, 211
-bake for Ten, 238
Baked au Gratin, 239
Chowder, 182
Rhode Island Quahog, 182
Corn Casserole, 239
Dip, 74
on the Half Shell, 238
Pie, Kennebunkport, 239
Puffs, 88
Rolls, Hot, 88
Sauce, Red, 506
White, 506
Steamed, 238
Stock, 537
Stuffed Quahogs, 239
To Open, 238
with Risotto, 480

Claret Sauce, 443
Soup, 194
Clear Red Anise Candy, 713
Tomato Soup, 176
Cloud Biscuits, 122
Cloverleaf Rolls, 154
Club Chicken, 285
Cobblestone Candy, 714
Cocada (Coconut Candy), 714
Cock Kebabs, 66
Cocktails
Delightful, 737
Dreams, 86
Fruit
Avocado, 49
Cherry Pineapple, 49
Cup, 49
Flower, 50
Grapefruit, 49
Broiled, 49
Hot Brandied, 49
Melon Ball, 50
Orange, 49
Mint, 50
Papaya Appetizer, 50
Strawberry Orange, 50
Suggestions, 48
To Remove Sections, 49
Watermelon, 50
with Sherry, 49
Juice
Cranberry, Fresh, 47
Pineapple, Minted, 48
Water Cress, 48
Sauerkraut, 48
Tomato, 48
-Orange, 48
Meat Balls, 68
Nibbles, 53
Orange Lime, 738
Pastry Boats, 77
Pizzas, 87
Potato Puffs, 70
Seafood, 50
Crab Meat, Canned, 51; Fresh, 51
Hawaiian Fish, 51
Lobster, Canned, 51; Fresh, 51
Mixed, 50
Oyster I, II, 51
in Tomato Cups, 51
on Half Shell, 52
Shrimp, 52
Avocado Appetizer, 52
How to Cook, 52
Seafood Sauces, 52–53
for Crab Meat, 52
for Oyster, 53
for Seafood, 52
for Shrimp, 53
Snacks and Wafers, 53–57
Barbecue Wafers, 56
Black Rosebuds, 54
Bohemian Sauerkraut, 56
Cheese Balls, Nippy, 56
Crescent, Double, 56
Sticks, Basic, 55

Cocktails (*Cont.*)
  Snacks and Wafers
    Cheese (*Cont.*)
      -Garlic Bread Sticks, 55
      Moons, 56
      Puffs, 56
      Corn Meal Crackers, 57
      Hot Nut Crackers, 54
      Kumquat Tidbits, 53
      Nuts, Curried, 53
        French-Fried Peanuts, 53
        Roquefort Pecans or Walnuts, 53
        Spiced, 53
      Olives, Curried Ripe, 54
        Curried Stuffed, 54
        Garlic Ripe, 54
        in Flaky Pastry, 54
        Puffs, 54
      Popcorn, Buttered, 55
        Herb Buttered, 55
      Roast Pumpkin Seeds, 55
    Teasers, 86
    Twirlups, 86
Cocoa
  Cake, Walnut-Filled, 593
  Cake Filling, French, 629
  Cream Pie, 567
  Frosting, French, 629
  Waffles, 136
Coconut
  Apricot Balls, 659, 713
  Candy, 714
  Cherry Bars, 656
  Cookies, 639
    Oatmeal, 648
    Overnight, 606
    Pineapple Drop, 644
  Cream, 681
  Fruitcake, 612
  Grove Thousand Island Dressing, 544
  Ice Cream Balls, 693
  Layer Cake, 587
  Macaroon Pie Shell, 551
  Macaroons, 642
  Nut Topping, 630
  Patties, 708
  Pie
    Butterscotch, 565
    Cream, 563
    No Crust, 576
    Pumpkin Chiffon, 574
    Sherry Chiffon, 568
  Tropical Dream Spread, 82
  Waffles, 137
  Yuletide Balls, 646
Coddled Egg, 197
Codfish Balls, 225
  Cakes, 224
  Pamplona, 225
  Timbales, 225
Coffee, 733
  Café au Lait, 733
  Café Brûlot, 734
  Cakes, 150–54
    Apple Pan, 604

Bubble Loaf, 151
Cherry Cobbler, 604
Coffee Kringle, 151
Cowboy, 604
Crumb, 605
Danish, 151
Favorite, 606
Jewish, 606
Kugelhopf, 152
Marble, Spicy, 607
Mincemeat, 606
Overnight German Refrigerator Kuchen, 152
Poteca (Polish Coffee Bread), 152
Radio, 606
Raisin Praline, 605
Ring, 606
Saffron Crown, 153
Snickerdoodle, 606
Sour Cream, 606
Streusel-Filled, 608
Swedish Coffee Braids, 153
Sweetheart, 153
Custard, Frozen, 688
Fudge, 706
  Irish, 733
  Kringle, 151
  Marshmallow Brownies, 653
  Dessert, 688
  Methods of Making, 733
  Mousse, 688
  Punch
    Chocolate, 741
    Cream, 741
    Vanilla, 741
  Ring, 606
  Soufflé, Cold, 680
Cola Salad, Bing Cherry, 529
Cold Chocolate Soufflé, 680
  Coffee Soufflé, 680
  -Water Tests for Candy, 704
Coleslaw, Hot, 512
  Soufflé Salad, 528
  Sour Cream, 513
  Texas, 511
Colochi, 432
Colonial Lemon Pie, 558
Colorado 3-Bar Cookies, 660
Company Cauliflower, 401
  Chicken and Rice Casserole, 288
Conches, 239
Condensed Milk Cookies, 660
Condiments. *See* Pickles, Relishes and Condiments
Confectioners' Sugar Icing, 622
  Sugar Orange Glaze, 629
Conga Bars, 653
Congealed Corned Beef Salad, 529
Conserves, 720–23. *See* Preserves

Consommés, 170–71
  Jellied, 192
  Madrilene, Hot, 171
  Wild Rice, 487
Constant Comment Pineapple-Orange Salad, 535
Cooked
  Beef Dishes, 338–40
  Carrot Cookies, 638
  Fluffy Frostings, 622
  Pineapple Salad Dressing for Fruit Salad, 546
  Topping for White Cake, 630
Cookies, 633–62
  Almond Delight, 645
    Lace Wafers, 641
  Apple Oatmeal Bars, 652
  Apricot Blondies, 652
    Coconut Balls, 659
  Banana Nuggets, 643
    Raisin Drops, 644
  Berliner Kranzer, 645
  Bizcochos, 634
  Brown Sugar, Old-Time, 634
  Brownies
    Butterscotch, 654
    Coffee Marshmallow, 653
    Lazy Day, 653
    Libbett's, 653
    Peanut Butter, 654
  Butter Refrigerator, 650
  Butterscotch Bars, 655
    Easy Chocolate-Frosted, 650
  Butterscotch Drop, 637
  By Cracky Bars, 656
  Casserole, 647
  Cereal Skillet Snacks, 663
  Checkerboard, 652
  Cherry, 638
    Coconut Bars, 656
  Chewy Chocolate, 638
  Children's Delight, 655
  Chinese Chews, 655
  Chinese New Year's, 660
  Chocolate, 614
    Acorns, 638
    Butter, Mrs. Nixon's, 589
    Chippers, 638
    Date Bars, 656
    -Dipped Nut Balls, 661
    Logs, 660
    Pinwheels, 651
    Pixies, 646
  Christmas, 641
    Fruit Balls, 660
  Cinnamon Crisps, 650
    Squares, 656
  Coconut, 639
    Macaroons, 642
    Overnight, 651
  Colorado 3-Bar Cookies, 660
  Condensed Milk, 660
  Conga Bars, 653
  Cooked Carrot, 638

Cookies (*Cont.*)
Cream Cheese, 625
Crisp
Brown Sugar, 646
Oatmeal Wafers, 643
Toffee Bars, 659
Date Hermits, 640
Drop, 633, 637–45
Egg Rings, Danish, 646
English Breakfast Cookies, 640
Fig Honey, 639
Finska Kahar (Almond Cooky), 635
Fresh Apple, 637
Frosted Ginger Creams, 641
Fudge Squares, 653
German Christmas, 635
Gobs, 639
Grizzle Nickel Squares, 657
Hazelnut Meringues, Mrs. John Kennedy's, 642
Hermits, 635
Date, 640
Holiday Delights, 660
Honey Balls, 661
Almond Balls, 661
Hoosier Peanut Bars, 654
Hot Crunchies, 640
Italian Sesame Seed, 649
Kentucky Bourbon Balls, 659
Krispy Crunch, 661
Lemon
Bonbon, 647
Love Notes, 657
Sours, 657
Lemonade, 642
Malted Milk Dainties, 658
Maple Bars, 658
Marshmallow Fudge Bars, 654
Melting Moments, 646
Mexican Wedding, 648
Mincemeat Squares, 658
Mocha Balls, 661
Molasses Crinkles, 648
Molded, 633, 645–50
Mother's Crumpets, 640
No-Bake, 659–62
Noels, 640
Norwegian Jelly, 647
Nut Crispies, 643
Nutmeg Butter Balls, 648
Oatmeal, 636
Bars, Chewy, 658
Coconut, 648
Drop, 643
Orange, 644
Crisps, 649
Refrigerator, 651
Pan, 633, 652–59
Pastel, 652
Pinwheels, 652
Peanut Blossoms, 649
Peanut Butter Balls, Dainty, 661
Peanut Butter Fingers, 658

Pecan
Bars, 654
Dainties, 643
Puffs, Dick Morrow's, 648
Pepparkakor (Swedish Ginger), 636
Pfeffernusse, 649
Pineapple Coconut, 644
Polka Dot Macaroons, 642
Praline Candy, 709
Pressed, 645–50
Prizewinning
Date Squares, 656
Kansas Rocks, 641
Prune, 644
Pumpkin, 645
Bars, 659
Raisin, 649
Spice Bars, 659
Refrigerator, 633, 650–52
Fruit Nut, 651
Ribbon, 652
Ricearoons, 642
Rolled, 633, 634–37
Wheat, 644
Rum Balls, 662
Sand Tarts, 636
Shortbread, Scottish, 636
Short'nin' Bread, 636
Skillet, 662
Snickerdoodles, 650
Snowdrops, 648
Spritz, 650
Sugar, 589, 634
Crinkles, 650
Mrs. Eisenhower's, 634
Sour Cream, 645
Stir-and-Drop, 645
Swedish Cream Wafers, 637
Surprise Meringues, 642
To Freeze, 633
To Make, 633
To Store, 633
Traditional Lebkuchen, 657
Viennese Specials, 637
Walnut Clusters, Mrs. Nixon's, 638
Woodcocks, 647
Yuletide Coconut Balls, 646
Cooking, Simple Rules for, 24
Terms, Glossary of, 42–46
with Wines and Spirits, 37
Cooky Frosting, Orange, 644
Pies, Whoopie, 639
Coq au Vin, 270
Coquilles St. Jacques, 252
Corn, 404
and Oysters, Scalloped, 250
Balls, 405
Bread, 111
Best Yet, 111
Carrot, 111
Custardy, 112
Dressing, 454

Jalapeña Buttermilk, 112
North Dakota Buttermilk, 111
Spanish, 112
Cake, Prouts Neck, 112
Caramel, 710
Casserole, 239
and Mushroom, 406
and Rice, 478
Oyster and Macaroni, 500
Sausage, 357
Southern, 405
Chip Pie, 337
Chowder, 185
and Bacon, Old-Fashioned New England, 184
and Crab Meat, Hearty, 185
Crisped Chicken, 264
Custard, Baked, 405
Dogs, 339
Dollars, Crisp, 133
Fingers, Oven Buttered, 122
Fried, 404
Fritters, 405
Fluffy, 405
Griddle Cakes, 133
Loaf, 406
Onion Gems, 129
On the Cob, 404
Oven, 404
Picnic Style, 404
Oysters, Nugen's, 405
Pie, 406
Pudding, 406
Florida, 406
Relish, 727
Sweet and Sour, 727
Scalloped, with Cheese, 406
Soup, 175
Cream of, 185
Cream of, Fresh, 187
Sticks, Kentucky, 128
Sour Cream, 128
Stuffing, 454
Waffles, 136
Corn Meal, 463
American Scrapple, 465
Biscuits, 122
Crackers, 57
Dumplings, 460
Mamaliguta cu Branza (Mush with Meat), 465
-Molasses Griddle Cakes, 133
Mush, 464
Polenta, 464
Mushroom, 464
Skillet Bread, 112
Soufflé, 465
Spoon Bread, 464
Cheese, 464
Mexican, with Cheese Topping, 465

Corn Meal (*Cont.*)
  Spoon Bread (*Cont.*)
    Old Virginia Butter-
      milk, 464
  Waffles, 137
Corned Beef
  and Cabbage, 315
  and Lima Beans, 316
  and Sauerkraut Appetizer,
    Deep Fried, 66
  Baked, 315
  Brisket, 315
  Casserole, 315
  Hash, 338
    Red Flannel, 316
    with Pineapple Top-
      ping, 316
  Patties, 316
  Salad
    and Cabbage, 522
    Congealed, 529
  Sandwich, 91, 97
  Spread, Egg, 82
  Zippy, 82
Cornets de Saumon Fumé
  (Smoked Salmon
  Cones), 63
Cornish Pasties, 323
  with Ground Beef, 335
Cottage Cheese
  Ham and Noodle Cas-
    serole, 496
  Lime Mold with Shrimp,
    535
  Pancakes, 133
  Salad
    Out of This World, 530
    Pineapple, 530
    Potato, 516
  Sandwich, 94
    and Bacon, 91
    and Nut, 92
    Tuna, 530
  with Olives and Pickles,
    80
Cottage Cheesecake, 615
Cottage Potatoes, 424
  Fried, 419
Country
  Breakfast, 200
  Captain, 270
  Casserole, 330
  Club Eggs, 202
  Fried Quail, 298
  Pea Soup, 179
Cous-Cous (Lamb Stew with
  Semolina), 370
Cousin Jack Steak and Po-
  tato Pie, 324
Cowboy Cake, 605
Crab Meat, 240–44
  à la Maryland, Imperial,
    242
  and Egg Salad, Baked,
    242
  and Mushrooms in Wine
    Sauce, 243
  and Shrimp Loaf, 258
  Baked Noodles and, 492
  Bisque, 188
    Quick, 194

Burgers, 105
  Avocado, 105
  Butter, 77
  Cakes, Maryland, 240
  Canapés, 89
    Tuna, 90
  Casserole, Imperial, 243
    Superb, 242
  Chowder, 183
    Hearty Corn and, 185
  Cocktail, Canned, 51
    Fresh, 51
    Sauce, 52
  Cream Puffs, 66
  Cutlets, Sautéed, 241
  Deviled, 241
    Florida, 240
    Maryland, 240
    Stuffing, 241
  Dip
    Favorite, 74
    Party, 74
    Roquefort, 74
    Sour Cream Caper, 75
  Filling for Baked Toma-
    toes, 435
  Fried Soft-Shell, 240
  Gumbo, 180
  Louie, 518
  Monza, 243
  Mornay, 243
  Mousse, 540
  Newburg, 243
  Pie, Easy, 244
  Potato Soufflé, 244
  Ravigote, 518
  Ring, 532
  Salad, 518
    Diablo, 518
  Sandwich, 92
    and Egg, 98
    Hot, 97
    Hot Soufflé, 208
    Open-Face King Crab,
      98
  Spread, 82
  Scalloped, 244
  Stuffed, à la Creole, 240
  Stuffing for Fried Shrimp,
    255
    for Mushrooms, 69
    for Rolled Fillets, 222
  To Clean, 240
  To Cook Live Hard-
    Shell, 240
Cracker Jax, 712
Cracker Meal Balls, 195
Cracker Pie, 576
Crackling Bread, 113
Cracklings, Preparation of,
  113
Crackly Gingersnaps, 647
Cranberries, Spiced, 458
Cranberry
  Applesauce, 730
  Banana Special, Molded,
    531
  -Braised Chicken, 272
  Cheesecake, 615
  Ham Rollups, 61
  Ice, 688

Jelly Banana Bread, 113
Juice Cocktail, Fresh, 47
  Spiced, 48
Muffins, 125
Orange Bread, 113
Pie, New England, 557
  Raisin, 554
Pork Chops, 344
Pudding, 669
  Steamed Molasses, 670
Punch, 689, 735, 739
Relish, 457
Salad
  Apple, Frozen, 525
  Nut, 530
  Orange, 523
  Grape, 523
  Juice Peach, 531
  Molded Party, 531
  Pineapple and Sour
    Cream, 531
  Nut, 523
  Prize Christmas, 531
Sauce, 458
  Hot, for Ham, 443
Crawfish Bisque, 187
Crayfish, 244
Crazy Chocolate Cake, 592
Cream
  and Peaches Salad, 533
  Apricot Cake Dessert, 683
  Cheese
    Banana Filling, 624
    Cookies, 635
    Dips, 71, 73, 75
    Frosting, 624
      Chocolate, 624
      Fudge, No-Cook Choco-
        late, 714
    Pastry, 549
      Hungarian, 580
    Pie, 568
      Chocolate, 566
      Minnesota Baked, 557
    Rolls, Roquefort, 88
    Topping, Fruity for
      Salads, 545
    Sandwich
      and Apple, 92
      and Apricot, 92
      and Cucumber, 92
      and Date, 92
      and Dried Beef, 92
      and Egg, 94
      and Green Pepper
        Filling, 79
      and Pineapple, 92
      and Raspberry, 92
    Spread(s)
      and Egg, 81
      and Olive, 79
      and Roquefort, 80
      and Shrimp, 79
    Coconut, 681
    Cupcakes, 620
    Danish Rice, 682
    Dressing, Tart, for Vege-
      tables, 449
    Filling, 630
      Pineapple, 632
    Frozen Lemon, 688

Cream (*Cont.*)
  Italian, 678
  Meringue Pie, Caramel, 565
  Mexican, 680
  Muffins, 128
Cream of
  Almond Soup, 186
  Asparagus Soup, 185
  Avocado Soup, 186
  Carrot Soup, 186
  Cauliflower Soup, 185
  Chicken and Sweetbreads, 279
  Corn Soup, 185
  Cucumber Soup, 188
  Fresh Corn Soup, 187
  Mushroom Soup, 188
  Onion Soup, 189
  Pea Soup, 185
  Potato Soup, 185
  Spinach Soup, 185
    Easy, 190
  Tomato Bisque, 190
  Tomato Soup, 185
    Garden, 190
  Turnip Soup, Calamity Jane, 191
  Wheat, 465
Cream Pies
  Angel Lemon, 569
  Apricot, 563
  Banana, 563
  Basic, 563
  Bavarian, 564
  Boston, 586
  Butterscotch, 563
  Caramel, 563
  Chocolate, 563
    Pecan with Meringue Topping, 566
  Cocoa, 567
  Coconut, 563
  Date, 563
  Neiman-Marcus, 564
  Orange, 571
  Pineapple, 563, 573
  Rhubarb, 561
  Sherry, 575
  Streusel Peach, 559
Cream Pudding, 679
  French, 684
Cream Puff Pastry, 552
Cream Puffs, 579
  Crab, 66
  Lemon-Filled, 580
Cream Punch, Coffee, 741
Cream, Raspberry, 678
Cream Sauce(s), 441–42
  Mushroom, 447
  Quick Chicken, 443
  To Add Egg Yolks, 442
Cream Strawberry Bavarian, 682
Cream Walnuts, Orange, 709
Creamed
  Carrots, 399
  Chicken Hot Dish, 282
  Green Beans and Water Chestnuts, 390
  Mushrooms, 412

Oysters, 250
  Sauerkraut, 430
  Stuffed Eggs, 204
  Sweetbreads, 376
Creams, 664, 705–9
  Boston, 707
  Butter, 713
  Butterscotch Nut, 707
  Chocolate Boston, 707
    Cherry, 713
  Creamy Chocolate Fudge, 705
Creamy Desserts, 676–79.
    See Desserts
  Nut Filling, 626
    Frosting, 626
  Rice Pudding, 678
  Roquefort Cheese Dressing, 542
  Shrimp Dip, 76
  Toffee, 711
  Uncooked Fondant, 715
Crème de Menthe Pie, 568, 691
Crème Patissière, 631
Crème St. Honoré, 679
Creole
  Broccoli, 394
  Dried Beef, 316
  Duck, 295
  Eggs, 203
  Gumbo, 181
  Halibut Steak, 227
  Jambalaya, 481
  Okra, 413
  Peas, 417
  Rice, 484
  Sauce, 443
    for Frankfurters, 106
    Quick, 443
    with Macaroni Omelet, 499
  Shrimp, 253
  Stuffed Crabs, 240
  Style Rabbit, 381
    Wild Duck, 298
  Vegetables, 439
  Wieners, 106
Crêpes Orange, 134
  Suzette, 697
Crisp
  Brown Sugar Cookies, 646
  Corn Dollars, 133
  Oatmeal Wafers, 643
  Toffee Bars, 659
Crock Salad, 512
Crofts Cake, 601
Croissants, 157
Croquettes
  Cheese, 176, 214
  Chicken, 285
  Egg and Cheese, 204
  Egg, Baked, 205
  Lamb, 372
  Oven Ham, 355
  Rice, 477
  Salmon, 231
  Sweetbread, 376
  Turkey, 294
Croutons
  Fried, 195

Garlic, 195
  Toasted, 195
Crown Roast
  of Lamb, 367
  of Pork, 342
Crumb
  Butter Dumplings, 461
  Cake, 605
    Vanilla Wafer, 588
  Crust
    Baked Chocolate, 551
    Graham Cracker, 551
    Macaroon, 551
  Desserts, 683–86
  -Topped Apple Pie, 576
Crumpets, Mother's, 640
Crunchy
  Bean Salad with Mayonnaise, 512
  French Custard, 677
  Kidney Bean Salad, 510
Crust, Bread Crumb, for
  Fish Pie, 226
  Sweet-Potato, for Chicken Pie, 289
Crusts
  for a 1-Crust Pie, 548
  for a 2-Crust Pie, 548
Crystal Sweet Pickles, 724
Cuban Spaghetti, 504
Cucumbers, 407
  and Cream Cheese Sandwich, 92
  Baked, 407
  Boiled, 370
  Butter for Fish, 444
  Canapés, 82
  Cheese Slices, 60
  Cream Cheese Dip, 75
  Fried, 407
  in Sour Cream, 513
  Mayonnaise, 445. *See*
    Whole Egg Mayonnaise
  Pennsylvania Dutch, 513
  Poulette, 407
  Salad, Molded, 532
    Relish, Tokay, 523
  Sandwiches, 83, 92, 94
  Sauce for Salmon, 444
  Soup, Cream of, 188
  Sour Cream Dip, 75
  Squares, Fresh, 532
Cupcakes, 619
  Black Bottom, 620
  Cherry Cheese, 620
  Chocolate, 620
  Cream, 620
  Rum, 620
  Snowballs, 621
Currant Almond Rice, 473
Curried
  Bananas, East Indian, 387
  Beef, Indian, 331
  Chicken Salad, 521
  Eggs in Shrimp Sauce, 204
  French Dressing, 541
  Fruits, 458
  Nuts, 53
  Oysters, 250

Curried (*Cont.*)
Pea Soup, Quick, 194
Peppers, 418
Rice, 474
and Lamb Shanks, 369
Indian, 474
Ripe Olives, 54
Smoked Salmon Spread, 85
Stuffed Olives, 54
Turkey, 294
Curry
Bengal, 321
Bombay, 370
Chicken, 286
Dumplings, 461
Eight-Boy, 278
Dip, 75
Egg Ring, 205
Indian, Bombay Style, 338
Mayonnaise, Blender, 445
Sauce, 441
Shrimp, 255
Custard(s), 664
Baked, 677
Chocolate, 677
Corn, 405
Banana Rice, 678
Broccoli and Cheese, 395
Cheese (Swedish Ostraka), 215
Cream Filling for Boston Cream Pie, 631
Crunchy French, 677
Desserts, 676–79
Dressing for Fruit Salad, 525
Filling, Quick, 631
Rich, 631
Floating Island, 677
Frozen Coffee, 688
Lemon, for Lemon Treasure Cake, 598
Old-Fashioned "Boiled," 676
Orange Sauce, 702
Orange Sponge, 678
Pie, Almond, 558
Egg, 558
No-Crust, 576
Peanut Butter, 559
Rhubarb, 574
Velvety, 558
-Pineapple Cake Filling, 586
Sauce, for Suet Pudding, 676
Custardy Corn Bread, 112
Czechoslovakian Kolachky, 162
-Style Noodle Pudding, 673

Danish
Coffee Cake, 151
Cream Vegetable Spread, 81
Egg Rings, 646
Layer Cake, 588
Meat Cakes, 325
Pastries, 161

Pie, 568
Red Cabbage, 398
Rice Cream, 682
Daffodil Cake, 609
Dainty Peanut Butter Balls, 661
Daiquiri Pie, Frosted, 570
Dakota Butterscotch Rolls, 160
Daleen's Caesar Salad, 508
Dark Mystery Dip, 72
Dasheen, 407
Date
and Cream Cheese Sandwich, 92
Butterscotch Pinwheels, 123
Cheese Rounds, 87
Chocolate Bars, 656
Hermits, 640
Muffins, Luncheon, 128
Nut Bread, 113
-Brown Bread, 114
Cake, 597
Sandwich Filling, 83
Parfait, Frozen, 688
Peanut Butter Fudge, 706
Pie
Cream, 563
Old English, 558
Pudding, 670
Squares, 670
Steamed Spiced, 670
Upside-Down, 671
Squares, Prizewinning, 656
Dates, Tropical, 715
De Luxe Tuna Sandwich, 102
Deep-Dish
Fruit Cobbler, 664
Pie
Blueberry, 559
Cherry, 559
Fresh Fruit, 559
Peach, 559
Salmon, 231
Deep-Fried Artichokes, 384
Corned Beef and Sauerkraut Appetizer, 66
Eggs, 201
Fish, 223
Deep-Sea Sauce, 444
Delicious Caramels, 709
Fruit Punch, 739
Salad Dressing for Fruit Salads, 546
Delightful Cocktail, 737
Summertime Drink, 740
Delmonico Potatoes, 425
Dependable Fondant, 707
Desserts, 663–99
Almond Milk, 663
Apple Delight, 687
Apples, Butterscotch, 694
Orange, Baked, 694
Apricot Crème Cake, 683
Icebox, 683
Baked Alaska, 692
Grapefruit, 695
Berry Bavarian Crown, 686
Biscuit Tortoni, 687

Blanc Mange, 679
Blueberry, 683
Cake, 683–86. *See* Cakes
Caramel Syrup, 663
Charlotte Russe, 684
Chocolate, 684
Cherries Jubilee, 692
Chocolate Angel Food, 684
Ice Cream Cups, Sweet, 693
Soufflé, Cold, 680
Christmas, 683
Coffee Marshmallow, 688
Mousse, 688
Soufflé, Cold, 680
Creamy, 676–79
Crème de Menthe Pie, 691
St.-Honoré, 679
Crumb, 683–86
Custards, 676–79. *See* Custards
English Toffee, 679
Flavoring Extracts, Use of, 63
Floating Island, 677
Frango Mint, 691
Fritters, 697–98
Apple, 698
Pineapple, 698
Rosettes, 698
Frozen, 687–94
Almond Cream, 687
Chocolate Sundaes, 692
Coffee Custard, 688
French Pastry, 690
Lemon Cream, 688
Pineapple, 691
Rainbow Delight, 694
Strawberry, 690
Fruit, 694–96
Fruit Cream, 690
Gelatin, 679–83
Gooseberries, Stewed, 695
Gulah Malacca (Coconut Cream), 681
Ice Cream. *See* Ice Cream
Ices. *See* Ices
Italian, 678
Kesari Baath (Near Eastern Rice Pudding), 678
Lemon Cups, Upside-Down, 677
Jiffy, 685
-Lime Treat, 685
Meringue Shells, 697
Pineapple Fluff, 685
Velvet, 689
Lime Freeze, 690
Macaroon Shimmy Pudding, 685
Marshmallow Delight, 686
Meringues, 696–97. *See* Meringues
Mexican, 680
Mint, 685
Delight, Frosted, 689
Mousses. *See* Mousses

Desserts (*Cont.*)
Norwegian Rommegrot
(Cream Pudding), 679
Omelets. *See* Omelets,
Sweet
Orange Ambrosia, 681
Sponge Custard, 678
Oslo Almond Pudding,
676
Pancakes, 697–98
Crêpes Suzette, 697
French, 697
Peach Melba, 695
Peaches, Baked Spiced,
695
Pear Orange Bake, 695
Pears, Peppermint, 696
Pies. *See* Pies
Pineapple, Baked, 696
Chantilly, 696
Mousse, 681
Praline Powder, 663
Prune Whip, Seven-Min-
ute, 696
Puddings, Baked and
Steamed. *See* Pud-
dings, Baked; Pud-
dings, Steamed
Raisin Ice Cream Alaska,
692
Raspberry Cream, 678
Rhubarb, 682
Rice and Cherries in the
Snow, 680
Pudding, Creamy, 678
Ris à la Mange (Danish
Rice Cream), 682
Sauces, 700–3
Sherbets. *See* Sherbets
Soufflés. *See* Soufflés,
Sweet
Strawberry Banana, 686
Bavarian, 682
Mousse, 682
Pineapple Mold, 682
Shortcake, 686
Squares, Frosty, 691
Sugar
Caramelized, 663
Lemon, 663
Lime, 663
Orange, 663
Vanilla, 663
Sunshine in the Snow,
681
Tapioca Pudding, Old-
Fashioned, 679
Trifle, 686
Whipped Cream, 663
Wine Jelly, 683
Zabaglione, 679
Deviled
Beets, 392
Brussels Sprouts, 395–96
Carrots, 399
Crab, 241
Florida, 241
Maryland, 241
Crab Meat or Stuffing for
Shellfish, 241
Egg Mold, 532
Eggs, 60

Ham and Easter Monday
Eggs, 202
and Egg Dip, 75
Dip, 76
Puffs, 89
Sandwich, 95
Filling, 79
Lamb Chops, 368
Macaroni, 498
Spaghetti, 504
Devil's Food Cake, Red, 592
Devonshire Sandwich, 96
Dick Morrow's Pecan Puffs,
648
Dill Green Beans, 390
Dilled Cabbage with Sour
Cream, 397
Onion Rings, 725
Dinner Lamb Chops, 368
Dipping Sauce for Crab
Meat, Lobster, Shrimp,
Vegetables, 75
Dips, 71–76, 78
Anchovy Cream Cheese,
71
Anchovy Sour Cream, 71
Avocado, 72
Sour Cream, 72
Blue Cheese and Sour
Cream, 72
Fluff, 72
Cheese and Green Pepper,
73
Chili Beef, 72
con Queso, 74
Clam, 74
Cream Cheese, 73
and Olives, 73
-Horseradish, 73
Creamy Shrimp, 76
Cucumber Cream Cheese,
75
Sour Cream, 75
Curry, 75
Dark Mystery, 72
Deviled Ham, 76
Dipping Sauce for Sea-
food and Vegetables,
75
Double Good Blue
Cheese, 73
Egg and Chive Cream
Cheese, 75
and Deviled Ham, 75
Favorite Crab, 74
for Chips, 73
Guacamole, 72
Hot Bean, 72
Cheese, 74
Shrimp, 76
Kim Chee, 76
Mexican, 74
Bean, 73
Onion, 76
Party Crab Meat, 75
Pink Devil, 75
Quick Dip 'n' Dunk, 76
Red, 75
Caviar, 72
Roquefort Crab, 74
Salsa, 74
Shrimp Cocktail, 76

Soup, 76
Smoky Cheese-Olive, 73
Sour Cream Crab Meat
Caper, 75
Horseradish, 76
Divinities, 710–11. *See*
Candy
Divinity Never-Fail Icing,
626
Dixie Deviled Chicken, 263
Dolma Armenian (Stuffed
Peppers), 371
Dominican Cake, 591
Donato Mix-Up, 357
Dorothy's Easy Baked
Chicken, 269
Double Cheese Crescents, 56
Good Blue Cheese Dip,
73
Doughnuts and Fried Cakes,
138–42
Afternoon Tea, 141
Basic, 138
Jelly, 138
Sugar, 138
Banana, 139
Buttermilk, 138
Cinnamon, 139
Cream, 139
Drop, 141
Eirohrli (Fried Squares),
140
Fiocchi or Guanti, 140
Hush Puppies, 142
Georgia, 142
Indian Fried Bread, 141
Navajo Fried Bread, 141
Orange, 139
Potato, 140
Popovers, 141
Sopapillas, 140
Tarry-Hi Banana Fritters,
139
Doves. *See* Game Birds
Dressed-Up Cabbage, 397
Dressing. *See* Salad Dress-
ings; Stuffings; Sauces
Custard for Fruit Salad,
525
Louie, for Crab Louie,
518
Russian, 545
Dried Beans, Peas and Len-
tils, 468–472. *See also*
Lima Beans
Arizona Ranch-Style Fri-
joles, 471
Baked Beans, Bourbon
Street, 469
Golden-Topped, 469
Old-Fashioned, 469
Spicy, 470
Vermont, 469
Baked Pork and Beans,
469
Bean Rarebit, 470
Black-Eyed Peas and To-
matoes, 471
Burgundy Beans, 470
Hopping John, 470
How to Cook, 469
Kidney Beans, Fancy, 470

Dried Beans, Peas and Lentils (*Cont.*)
Lentils, 472
Lima Bean Scallop, Savory, 470
Lima Beans in Sour Cream, 471
Ripe Olive Bean Bake, 470
Dried Beef
and Cream Cheese Sandwich, 92
and Noodles, Baked, 495
Canapés, 83
Caracus (Beef Rabbit), 316
Cheddar-Beef Sandwich, 91
Creole, 316–17
in Wine Sauce, Lila's, 317
Macaroni Chipped Beef Casserole, 502
Drool Dish, 404
Drop Cookies, 637–45
Doughnuts, 141
Duchess Soup, 187
Duck
à l'Orange, 295
Bigarade, 295
Braised, 295
Creole, 295
of the Four Seasons, 295–96
Wild. *See* Game Birds
Dudie's Boeuf Flambé, 312
Dumplings, 460–63
and Starch Substitutes, 460–472
Baked Caramel, 668
Butter Balls, 460
Crumb, 461
Cheese, in Tomato Sauce (Spanish Vanish), 463
Chicken Curry, 461
Corn Meal. *See* Fluffy Dumplings
Egg, 460
Fluffy, 460
German Parsley, 462
Italian, 462
Knedlich (Matzo Balls), 463
Old-Fashioned, 460
Onion, 461
Pirohi, 461
Piroshki, 462
Potato Drop, 462
Potato Puffs, 462
Raised Bohemian, 461
Swedish Potato, 462
Three-Minute Water, 461
Dupizza (Indian Curried Beef), 331–32
Dutch
Apple Pie, 555
Cherry Pie, 557
Pancake, 134
Potatoes, 426

Early Settler's Orange Pie, 554

East Indian Curried Bananas, 387
Easter Monday Eggs and Deviled Ham, 202
Easy
Cherry Cheese Pie, 565
Chocolate-Frosted Butterscotch Bars, 655
Frosting, 625
Mints, 713
Crab Pie, 244
Cream of Spinach Soup, 190
Down East Seafood Casserole, 257
Mushroom Sauce, 447
Overnight Strawberry Jam, 719
Pudding and Cake, 589
Rarebit, 212
Sukiyaki, 311
Toast Patty Shells for Creamed Foods, 168
Eclairs, 580
Economy
Meat Loaf, 329
Mints, 16
Eel, 225
Egg(s) and Egg Dishes, 197–209
à la Goldenrod, 201
à la Junkin, 200
and Asparagus au Gratin, 203
and Cheese Croquettes, 204–5
and Deviled Ham, Easter Monday, 202
and Salmon, à la Wrigley, 519
and Tomatoes, 200
Baked, 199
Cheese Dish, 199
Huevos Rancheros, 199
in Mushroom Sauce, 202
Stuffed, 204
Belgian, 203
Benedict, 198
Butter, 77
Casserole
Asparagus, 395
Belgian, 199
Broccoli, 395
Cauliflower, 395
Coronado, 202
Potato and Salami, 388
Seafood, 257
Spanish, 203
Chive Cream Cheese Dip, 75
Coddled, 197
Continental, 201
Country Breakfast, 200
Country Club, 202
Creamed Stuffed, 204
Creole, 203
Croquettes, Baked, 205
Curried, in Shrimp Sauce, 204
Curry Ring, 205
Custard Pie, 558

Deep-Fried, 201
Deviled, 60
Deviled Ham Dip, 75
Drop Soup, 174
Drops, 195–96
Dumplings, 460
Fluffy, 199
Foo Young, 200
Shrimp, 200–1
Fried Raw, 201
Fried Stuffed, 204
Hard-Cooked, 197, 201–5
Hints, 16–17
How to Separate an Egg, 197
in Nest, 199
Luncheon Dish, 204
Mayonnaise, Whole, 445
Mold, Deviled, 532
'n' Bacon Canapés, 86–87
'n' Chips, 201
Omelets. *See* Omelets
Pan-Fried, 200
Petal Soup, Chinese, 174
Pickled, 60
Poached, 197
Country Style, 197–98
Rings, Danish, 646
Rolls, 67
Pancake Skins for, 136
Salad
Chicken, 529
Crab, Baked, 242
Salmon, 519
Sandwich Filling, 79
Shrimp, 536
Sour Cream Potato, 517
Sandwich, 92–93
Cheese, 91, 94
Cheese and Liverwurst, 95
Crab, Toasted, 98
Filling, 79
Hot, 98
Olive, 92
Sauce
Caper, 441
Cream, 441
Sautéed, 200
Scalloped, 201
Scotch Woodcock, 203
Scrambled, 198
and Peppers, 198
and Zucchini, 198
Breakfast, 198
Mexican, 198
with Brains, 373
Shirred, 199
Six-Minute "Boiled," 197
Soft-Cooked, 197
Soufflés. *See* Soufflés
Spread
Bacon and Mushroom, 83
Corned Beef, 82
Stzuddla Brod, 198
Tetrazzini, 202
Eggless
Chocolate Cake, 591
Milkless, Butterless Raisin Spice Cake, 601

Eggnog, 741
Cake, 614
Chocolate Honey, 741
Hot, 736
Rich, 741
Sherry, 742
Eggplant, 407
à la Mexican Way, 408
Amandine, 408
and Beef Parmesan, 409
and Mushroom Casserole, 409
and Rice on Parade, 478
and Tomatoes, 409
Cakes, 408
Fried, 408
Marinara, 61
Olive Casserole, 409
Oven-Crisp, 408
Parmesan, 409
Pickled, 458
Pie, 410
Seafood-Stuffed, 257–58
Scalloped, 408
Southern-Style, 410
Stuffed, 410
Eight-Boy Curry, 278
Eileen's Bar-B-Q Flat Chuck Roast, 310
Eirohrli (Swiss Fried Squares), 140
Eleanor's Baked Avocado with Shrimp, 386–87
Election-Day Gingerbread, 114
Elegant Cheese Soup, 187
Chicken Salad, 521
Empanadas (Biscuit Turnovers), 123
Enchiladas, 215
Casserole, Green, 215
Chicken, 287
Green Chili, 337
with Beans, 337
Endive. See Lettuce, 411
Endives Printemps, 412
English
Beef Stew, 322
Breakfast Cookies, 640
Chocolate Toffee, 712
Marmalade, 722
Muffins, 166
Pea Casserole, 417
Plum Pudding, 674
Rarebit Canapés, 88
Soup, 186
Toffee, 679
Escalloped Asparagus, 386
Pineapple, 459
Potatoes and Ham, 424
Escalopes de Veau, 360
Excellent Chicken à la King, 276

Fairy Tart, 569
Fancy Kidney Beans, 470
Farina, 463, 465
Farina Dishes
Frettura Dolce (Lemon Almond Fritters), 465
Farmer's Pie, 331
Favorite Coffee Cake, 606

Crab Dip, 74
Green Bean Casserole, 390
Rice Salad, 517
Fennel, 411
Fettucini Alfredo, 493
Fiesta Ribbon Sandwich, 78
Fillings, 79
Fig Cake with Lemon Orange Glaze, 597
Honey Cookies, 639
Pickled, 725
Pudding, Steamed, 670
Sandwich, 94
Filé for Gumbos, 180
French, 180
Oyster Gumbo, 181
Filet Mignon Semiramis, 310
de Sole au Raisins Blancs, 233–34
of Beef, 307
Fillets. See Fish
Fillings
See also Frostings
Banana Cream Cheese, 624
Butter Nut, 623
Caramel Cake, 627
Cheese, for Ravioli, 497
Chicken and Spinach, for Ravioli, 498
Chicken, for Cannelloni, 497
Cocoa, French, 629
Cooked
Nut, Creamy, 626
Crab Meat for Baked Tomatoes, 435
for Meat Loaf, Onion, 329
Lemon Custard, 598
Meat, for Ravioli, 498
Mocha, 624
Pineapple Custard, for White Cakes, 586
Prune, for Yellow Cakes, 588
Ricotta Cheese, for Ravioli, 497
Soft-Cooked, 630–32
Butterscotch, 630
Chocolate, Mary's, 630
Cream, 630
Crème Patissière, 631
Custard Cream for Boston Cream Pie, 631
Custard, Quick, 631
Rich, 631
Lemon, 631
Lemon Butter, 631
Marshmallow, 631
Orange, 632
Orange Custard, 632
Orange Pineapple, 632
Pineapple, 632
Pineapple Cream, 632
Wine, Flavorful, 632
Walnut Apple, for Cocoa Cake, 593
Fines Herbes Omelette, 205–6
Finger Sandwich, 78
Fish, Shellfish, and Foods Prepared like Fish, 217–

59. See also Individual Names
Fish
and Shellfish Salads, 518–20
Aspic, 537
Baked, 220
Florida, 220
with Oyster Stuffing, 220
Balls, Blender Method for, 223
Sweet Sour Pineapple, 223
Bluefish
Baked in Sour Cream, 224
Broiled, 224
Broiled or Baked with Green Sauce, 222
Cheese Puff, 221
Chowders. See Chowders, 180–85
Cleaning and Dressing, 217
Cocktail, Hawaiian, 51
Codfish, Balls, 225
Cakes, 224
Pamplona, 225
Timbales, 225
Cucumber Butter for, 444
Deep-Fried, 223
Filets de Sole au Raisins Blancs, 233
Fillets, Baked, 221
Baked in Tomato Sauce, 222
of Sole Amandine, 233
of Sole Marguéry, 234
Rolled Stuffed, 222
Rolls, Fried, 223
Stuffed, 221
with Mustard Sour Cream Sauce, 222
with Shrimp Sauce, 222
Freezing Whole Fish, 217
Gefullte, 223
Herb Broiled, 224
Hints, 17–18
Horseradish Sauce for, 444
in Lime Juice (Seviche), 61
Mackerel, Baked Spanish, 228
Marinated Stuffed, 220
Methods of Cooking, 218
Baking, 219
Breading and Pan-Frying, 219
Broiling, 219
Deep-Frying, 219
Poaching, 218
Sautéing, 219
Mullet, Barbecued, 228
Ocean Perch, Baked, 228
Pan-Broiled, 223
Perch, Maître d'Hôtel, 228
Red Snapper, Baked in Wine Sauce, 229
Rice Shrimp Biloxi, 481

Fish *(Cont.)*
Rice Shrimp Biloxi *(Cont.)*
Risotto with Clams, 480
with Fish, 481
Sandwich, 92
Sauces for, 441–51
Butter, 442
Tartar, 450
Selecting Fresh Fish, 217
Servings and Pounds, 35
Smoked and Salted, 217
Sole, Baked in Foil, 234
Soufflé with Pecan Sauce, 224
Steaks, Baked, 224
Stews, 180–85
Stock, 171
Storing Fish, 217
Stuffing for, 454
Vegetable Platter Bake, Sizzling, 220
Whole Barbecued, 221
with Rice, 480
Finger Sandwiches, Fillings for, 80
Finnan Haddie à la King, 227
Finska Kahar (Scandinavian Almond Cooky), 635
Fire and Ice Tomatoes, 459
Five
-Egg-White Fruit Meringue, 552
-Minute Tomato Sauce, 450
-Pound Fondant Candy, 708
Flaky Puff Pastry, 549
Flaming Babas, 159
Flank Steak Roll, 318
Flavoring Extracts, Use of, 663
Flavorful Veal Chops, 361
Flavorful Wine Filling, 632
Flemington Woman's Club Punch, 739
Flemish Carbonades, 322
Floating Island, 677
Florida Corn Pudding, 406
Florida Deviled Crab, 241
Flounder
Baked, Supreme, 226
Broiled, 226
Flower Cocktail, 50
Fluff, 485
Fluffy Apple Juice Frosting, 626
Corn Fritters, 405
Dumplings, 460
Eggs, 199
Foie Gras and Wild Rice Stuffing, 456
Fondue, Swiss, 211
with Sauterne, 211
Food for Fifty, 23–24
Food for the Gods, 670
Fondant, 705–9
Creamy Uncooked, 715
Dependable, 707
5-Pound Candy, 708
Mashed Potato, 715

Franconia Potatoes, 419
Frango Mint Dessert, 691
Frankfurter(s) Barbecued, 339
Bean Fare, 339
Corn Dogs, 339
Crown Casserole, 339
de Luxe, 339
Italian Cartwheel, 340
Pronto-Puppy Hors d'Oeuvres, 67
Sandwich, 92
and Sauerkraut Bake, Grace's, 340
Specials
Red Hot Sandwich, 64
Creole Wieners, 106
Sauce for, 106
Hot Dog Surprise, 107
Sesame Dogs, 107
Spicy Appetizer, 67
Stuffed Hot Dogs, 340
with Noodles, 495
Freezing, Home, 41
Tips, 41
French Apple Pie, 555
French
Bread, 145
Crusty, 145–46
Hot, with Seasoned Butter, 168
Breakfast Puffs, 128–29
Cocoa Filling, 629
Frosting, 629
Chocolate Cake, 593
Chocolate Truffles, 714
Cream Pudding, 684
Custard, Crunchy, 677
Dessert Pancakes, 697
Dressing, 541
Anchovy, 541
Catsup, 541
Chiffonade, 541
Curried, 541
Garlic, 541
Herb, 541
Mint, 541
Peanut Butter, 541
Roquefort, 541
-Fried Onion Rings, 414
Peanuts, 53
Potatoes, 419
Fries, Oven-Baked, 421
Gumbo filé, 180
Omelet, 205
Fillings for, 205
Onion Soup, 176
Pastry, Frozen, 690
Peas, 417
Peasant Potato Soup, 189
Petit Déjeuner Rolls, 155
Roll Canapés, 83
Silk Pie, 567
Spaghetti Sauce, 505
Toast, 167
Bacon-Flavored, 167
Spiced Breakfast, 167
Yeast Cakes (Little Babas), 159
Fresh
Apple Cookies, 637
Berry Cobbler, 666

Crab Meat Cocktail, 51
Cucumber Squares, 532
Fruit Sandwiches, 94–95
Lobster Cocktail, 51
Orange Layer Cake, 598
Peach Ice Cream, 689
Prune Chutney, 722
Rhubarb Cake, 600
Strawberry Pie, 575
Freshy's Blueberry Pie, 565
Huckleberry Pie, 565
Frettura Dolce, (Lemon Almond Fritters), 465
Fricadeller (Danish Meat Cakes), 325
Fricassee, Chicken, 275–76
Veal, 362
Fried Bananas, 387
Cabbage, 396–97
Corn, 404
Croutons, 195
Cucumbers, 407
Eggplant, 408
Fillet Rolls, 223
Okra, 413
Onions and Green Tomatoes, 414
Peach Pies, 581
Potatoes, 421
Quail, Country, 298
Raw Eggs, 201
Rice, 476–78
with Mushrooms and Almonds, 477
with Shrimp, 477
Shrimp, 254
Soft-Shell Crabs, 240
Stuffed Eggs, 204
Tomatoes, 434
Wontons, 71
Frijoles, Arizona, Ranchstyle, 471
Frijole Pie, 336
Fiocchi, 140
Fritters, Apple, 457
Apple Dessert, 698
Batter, 383
Corn, 405
Dessert, 697–98
Rosettes, 698
Lemon Almond, 465
Mexican, 140
Pineapple, 459, 698
Tuna, 236
Water Chestnut, 437
Frog's Legs, 258
Sautés, 258
Provencale, 258
Frosted Daiquiri Pie, 570
Ginger Creams, 641
Mint Delight, 689
Pineapple Lime and Walnut Salad, 534
Frostings. *See also* Fillings; Glazes; Toppings
Frostings and Fillings, 622–32
Frosting
and Topping Hints, 17
Brown Sugar Meringue Frosting for Leather Cake, 595

Frosting (*Cont.*)
Butter, Creamy, 622
for Mincemeat Coffee
Cake, 606
Butter Pecan, 587
Cheese Salad for Molded
Salads, 534
Cooked, 625–29
Apple Juice, Fluffy, 626
Brown Sugar, 627
Butter, Never-Fail, 625
Caramel, Mrs. Kittler's,
628
Mrs. Sharp's, 628
Chocolate, Easy, 625
Fudge, 628
Kathryn's, 628
Mrs. Hood's, 628
Pecan, 626
Sammye's, 628
Shiny, for Boston
Cream Pie, 629
Cocoa, French, 629
Divinity Never-Fail,
626
Fluffy, 622
Fruit-Nut, Special, 629
Fudge, 628
German, 626
Lemon, 629
Lemon Meringue, Car-
melita's, 626
Melody, 627
Nut, Creamy, 626
Penuche, 628
Peppermint, 627
Pineapple Parfait, 627
Seafoam, 627
Three-Minute, Never-
Fail, 626
Vienna, 625
Creamy
Banana Cream Cheese,
624
Butter, 623
Butter Nut, 623
Cherry, 623
Chocolate, 623
Chocolate Chip, 623
Chocolate Nut, 623
Chocolate Rum, 623
Chocolate Whipped
Cream, 625
Cream Cheese, 624
Chocolate, 624
Mocha, 624
Mocha Butter, 624
Party, 624
Peanut Butter, 625
Pineapple, 624
Prune, 625
Raisin, 625
Strawberry, 625
Vanilla Butter, 624
Fudge, 622
Orange, for Orange
Cookies, 644
Sugar, 622
Bonbon, 622
Confectioners', 622
Miracle, 622
Orange, 622

Sweet, 622
Vanilla, for Children's De-
light, 610
Frosty Strawberry Squares,
691
Frozen
Almond Cream, 687
Chocolate Sundaes, 692
Coffee Custard, 688
Cranberry Apple Salad,
525
Date Parfait, 688
Dessert's, 687–94
French Pastry, 690
Fruit Salad, 525
Ginger Ale Salad, 525
Grape Salad, 526
Lemon Cream, 688
Peach Salad, 526
Pear Salad, 526
Pineapple Dessert, 691
Pumpkin Pie, 691
Rrainbow Delight, 694
Strawberry Dessert, 690
Whipped Cream, 701
Fruit
Balls, Christmas, 660
Candied, 705
Canning, 40
Syrups for, 40
Casserole, Mother's Baked,
671
Cobbler, Deep-Dish, 664
Cocktails, 48–50
Cocktail Cake, 597
Cocktail Pudding, 671
Cocktail Suggestions, 48
Cocktail with Sherry, 49
Cream, 689
Cup, 49
Curried, 458
Desserts, 694–96
Hints, 17
How to Remove Sections,
49
Mold, Sour Cream, 535
Nut Cookies, Refrigerator,
651
Nut Frosting Special, 629
Pie, Deep-Dish Fresh, 559
Punch, Delicious, 739
Minted, 740
Salads, 522–24
Salad Dressing, 546
Tangy, 542
Salad, Frozen, 525
Salmon, 519
Summer Fresh, 524
with Custard Dress-
ing, Twenty-
Four-Hour, 525
with Sour Cream,
Twenty-Four-
Hour, 524
Sandwiches, Fresh, 94–95
Sauce, 701
Servings and Pounds, 35–
36
Soup, Breakfast, 192
Norwegian, 192
Torte, 618
Turnovers, 580

Fruitcakes, 612–14
Bishop's, 613
Candied, 612
Cherry, Christmas, 614
Coconut, 612
Eggnog, 614
Golden, 613
Holiday, 613
King's, 614
Sausage, 614
Tropical, 612
White, 613
Fruited Ham Loaf, 354
Indian Pudding, 672
Fruity Cream Cheese Top-
ping, 545
Frying Batter for Fish, 223–
24
Fu Chu, 485
Fudge
Butterscotch, 705
Cake, Chocolate, 590
Kathryn's, 590
Coffee, 706
Chocolate, Creamy, 705
Frostings, 628
Icing, Chocolate, 628
Mamie Eisenhower's, 706
Marshmallow Bars, 654
Marshmallow Nut, 706
No-Cook Chocolate Cream
Cheese, 714
One-Minute, 705
Peanut Butter, 706
Peanut Butter Date, 706
Pie, 577
Pudding, Hot, 669
Quick, 669
Sauce, Hot, 701
Rich Dark, 701
Smith College, 705
Sour Cream, 706
Squares, 653

Game
Antelope Steak Supreme,
378
Doves, Baked with Apple
Stuffing, 296
with Rice, 296
Duck, Wild
Creole Style, 298
Pot-Roasted, 298–99
Roast, 298
with Apples, 298
with Rice, 298
Goose, Baked Wild, with
Prune Stuffing, 299
Grouse, Larded, 296
Roast, 296
Partridge, Braised, 297
Roast, 296–97
Moose, Braised, 378
Steak, 378
Rabbit
Creole Style, 381
de Luxe, 381
Hasenpfeffer, 381
Hunter's, 382
Squirrel, Baked, 382
Venison, 379
Braised, 379

Game (*Cont.*)
Venison (*Cont.*)
Chili with Beans, 383
Loaf, 381
Meat Balls in Sauce, 380
Pot Roast, 379
Roast, 379
Steak, 379
Steaks, Casserole of, 379–80
Stew, 380
Teriyaki, 380
Wine Sauce for, 451
Game Birds
Pheasant, Roast with Apple Stuffing, 297
with Rice Stuffing, 297
Quail, Country Fried, 298
Sherried, 297–98
Garden Cream of Tomato Soup, 190
Garlic
and Oil Sauce, 506
and Parsley Butter, 79
Bread, 168
Roman, 168
sticks, 168
Butter, 77, 168
Cheese Grits, 467
Cheese Nut Canapés, 81
Croutons, 195
French Dressing, 541
Green Beans, 388
Mayonnaise, Blender, 445
Ripe Olives, 54
Salad Dressing, 542
Sauce, 505
Toast, 167
Garnishes, 456–59. *See also* Stuffings and Garnishes
for Canapés, 78
for Juices, 47
Meat, 456. *See also* Relish
Gâteau St.-Honoré, 561
Gazpacho, Tropical, 192
Gefullte Fish, 223
Gelatin
Desserts, 679–83
Salad, Orange, 533
Peachy, 533
Georgia
Fried Chicken with Cream Gravy, 263
Hush Puppies, 142
Pecan Pie, 560
German
Casserole, 344
Christmas Cookies, 635
Frosting, 626
Parsley Dumplings, 462
Potato Pancakes, 422
Pot Roast, Spiced, 313
Stuffed Breast of Veal, 358–59
Gilde Salad (Roast Beef and Herring), 522
Ginger
Beets, 392
Cookies, Swedish, 636
Creams, Frosted, 641
Muffins, Refrigerator, 129

Sherried Sweet Potatoes, 428
Ginger Ale
Pineapple Nut Salad, 534
Salad, Frozen, 525
Gingerbread, 114
Election Day, 114
Small-Family, 114
Soft, 114
Waffles, 136
Gingersnap Crust, 551
Gingersnaps, Crackly, 647
Gizo, 347
Glamorous Nesselrode Pie, 570
Glaze, 629
Apricot, for Ham, 351
Buttermilk, for Sugar Plum Cake, 600
Chocolate, 629
Ham, 350
Lemon, for Lemon Loaf Cake, 598
Orange, for Fig Cake, 597
Orange,
Confectioners' Sugar, 629
for Pork Chops, 344
Sugar, for Lebkuchen, 657
Vanilla, 629
Glazed Broccoli with Almonds, 394–95
Pork Loin, 342
Glazes and Toppings, 629–30
Chocolate Mint, 630
Cooked, for White Cake, 630
Coconut Nut, 630
Meringue Crunch, 630
Nut, 630
Glossary of Cooking Terms, 42–46
Gnocchi (Italian Dumplings), 462
Gobs (Sandwich Cooky), 639
Golden Baked Celery Loaf, 402
Fruitcake, 613
Jellied Apricots, 457
Peach Pie, 554
Potato Soup, 189
Topped Baked Beans, 469
Gone-All-Afternoon Stew, 322–23
Goober Ham Spread, 83
Goose
Roast, 294
Watertown, 294–95
Wild, Wine Sauce for, 451
Gooseberries, Stewed, 695
Gougère (Cheese Puff), 67
Goulash, Hungarian, 321
Veal (Kalbs Gulyas), 363
Goulashes, 320–24
Gourmet
Meat Loaf, 329
Sauce, 444
Grace Moore's Spanish Chicken, 274

Grace's Sauerkraut and Frankfurter Bake, 340
Graham Cracker Crumb Crust, 551
Grandfather's Sausage, 356
Grandma's Red Cabbage, 398
Grand Marnier Cake, 599
Grandmother's Chicken Pie, 276
Chili Sauce, 730
Grape
and Chicken Sandwich, 91
Catsup, 730
-Cluster Salad, Individual, 524
Cranberry Salad, 523
Jam, 718
Jelly, 719
Juice, Mulled, 735
Leaves, Stuffed, 68
-Nut Pudding, 671
Quick Bread, 115
Pie,
Old-Fashioned, Concord, 554
Salad, Frozen, 526
Grapefruit
Baked, 695
Broiled, 49
Cocktail, 49
Hot Brandied, 49
Mint Punch, 740
Snow, 680
Gratin Dauphinoise 423
of Oysters and Mushrooms, 251
Gravy Hints, 18
Great-Great-Grandmother's Suet Pudding, 676
Greek
Casserole (Lamb Moussaka), 372
Lemon Soup, 174
Greek Salad
Dressing for Raw Vegetables, 543
Louis Pappas' Famous, 511
Green Beans, 388
Amandine, 389
and Bacon Salad, 510
and German Cabbage, 388
and Mushroom Casserole, 390
and Sprouts Napoli, 389
and Water Chestnuts, Creamed, 390–91
Austrian, 388
Boiled Snap, 388
Casserole, 389
Favorite, 390
Chinese String, 390
Dill, 390
Garlic, 388
Hungarian String, 388
Italian, 389
Wax, Mustard, 457
Piccadilly, 391
Savory, 391
with Potatoes in Tomato Sauce, 389

Green
  Chili Enchiladas, 337
  Enchilada Casserole, 215
  Mango Betty, 672
  Mayonnaise, blender, 445
  Noodles, 490
  Rice, 474
    Mold, 480
    with Broccoli, 480
    with Cheese, 480
  Salad with Herring Dress-
    ing, 509
  Sauce for Fish, 222
  Split Pea Soup, 179
  Tomato Pickles (Crisp),
    725
    Pie, 436
Green Goddess Salad, 514
  Salad Dressing, Mrs.
    Hasebroock's, 543
Green Pepper(s)
  and Zucchini, 438
  Best-Ever Stuffed, 418
  Curried, 418
  Italian Fried, 418
  Macaroni-Stuffed, 418
  Pork-Stuffed, 357
  Relish, 728
  Stuffed (Dolma Armeni-
    an), 371
  with Ham, 418
  Turnip Puffs in, 437
Greenest Salad in Town, 509
Greens, 411
Ground Beef Dishes. *See also*
  Hamburgers, Meat
  Balls, Meat Loaf
  All-Day Chili and Beans,
    334
  Barbecued Beef and
    Beans, 333
  Beef Bohemian, 330
  Beef Chow Mein Casse-
    role, 331
  Beef-Filled Babka, 334–
    35
  Beef Pinwheels, 335
  Bulgur Barbecue, 330
  Cabbage Pigeons, 331
  Chili con Carne, 334
  Corn Chip Pie, 337
  Cornish Pasties, 335
  Country Casserole, 330
  Dupyza (Indian Curried
    Beef), 331–32
  Enchiladas with Beans,
    337
  Farmer's Pie, 331
  Frijole Pie, 336
  Hamburger-Onion Pie,
    335
    Stroganoff, 332–33
  Jailhouse Chili, 334
  Kidney Beans Barbecue,
    333–34
  Meat-a Pie, 332
  Meat Upside-Down Pie,
    335
  Moussaka, 332
  Ok-Yok-Sung, 331
  Pedernales River Chili,
    334

Pizza Hamburger, 332
Ruby Mountain Special
  Casserole, 336
Shepherd's Pie with Beef,
  332
Stuffed Cabbage Leaves,
  330
Tacos, 337–38
Tamale Casserole, 336
  Pie, 336–37
Texas Hash, 333
Turkish Beef with Okra,
  333
Zucchini and Beef Cas-
  serole, 333
Ground Beef Parmesan,
  324–25
Grouse. *See* Game Birds
Guanti, 140
Guineas Gala, 292
Guisado de Papas (Stewed
  Potatoes), 424
Gulah Malacca (Coconut
  Cream), 681
Gumbos, 180–685
Gum Soozle, 481
Gurkensalat (Cucumbers in
  Sour Cream), 513
Grilled
  Applesauce and Bacon
    Sandwich, 96
  Heroine, 99
  Tropical Lamb Chops, 368
Grits de Luxe, 467. *See also*
  Hominy
Grizzle Nickel Squares, 657
Grostini (Chicken Livers and
  Capers in Tomato
  Sauce), 66

Hacienda Hamburg, 494
Haddock. *See also* Fish
  Crumb Pie, 226
  Fillets Provençale in To-
    mato Sauce, 226
  Finnan Haddie à la King,
    227
  Scalloped, 226
Half-Time Spoon Rolls, 156
Halibut. *See also* Fish
  Baked in Milk, 227
  Herb Broiled, 227
  Steak Creole, 227
Halva, Baked, 671
Ham
  à la King, 356
  and Asparagus Rolls with
    Cheese Sauce, 352
  and Cheese Buns, Hot,
    98–99
    Soufflé, 209
  and Egg Butter, 77
  and Macaroni, Scalloped,
    502
  and Potatoes, Escalloped,
    424
  and Sweet Potato Roll,
    354
  and Truffles (Cigarettes de
    Bayonne), 62
  and Veal Pâté, 62
  Apricot-Glazed, 351

Baby Submarine, 99
Bacon, Roast Canadian,
  352
Baked, 351
  in Milk, 352–53
Ball, Appetizer, 61
Balls, 354
Banana Rolls, 356
Barbecue, 355
  Burgers, Barbecued, 105
Canapés, 83
Casserole, Cantonese, 355
  Noodle and Cottage
    Cheese, 496
  Potato and Onion, 356
Cheese Balls, 68
Cranberry Rollups, 61
Dip, Deviled, 76
  and Egg, 75
  Pink Devil, 75
Glaze, 350
Hash, Pan-Browned, 353
How to Carve, 350
How to Cook a Country-
  Cured Ham, 350
in Aspic, 538
Loaf, Applesauce, 354
  Fruited, 354
  Pork and Beef, 353
  with Vinegar Sauce, 354
Mama's Favorite Gulyas,
  352
Mousse, 540
Oven Croquettes, 355
Pancake Omelet, 134
Pinwheels, 83
Ready-to-Serve, 351
Roast Fresh, 342
Salad, Baked, 356
  and Peas, 522
  Cheese and Rice, 518
Sandwich, 92
  Barbecued, 98
  Monte Cristo, 99–100
  Slumgullion, 99
  Soufflé, 99
Slice, Baked, 352
  with Sweet Potatoes,
    353
Soufflés, 355
Spice-Crusted, 351–52
Spread, 79
  Goober, 83
Steak, Apple-Stuffed, 353
  Stuffed, 353
Stuffed, 351
Stuffed Green Peppers,
  418
Timbales, 355
Waffles, 136
Hamburg, Hacienda, 494
Hamburger(s), 92, 324–30.
  See also Beef Burgers;
  Burgers
Barbecued Baked, 326
Bean Pot Soup, 178
Fricadeller (Danish Meat
  Cakes), 325
Ground Beef Parmesan,
  324
Just Plain, 324

Hamburger(s) (*Cont.*)
　Macaroni Upside-Down
　　Casserole, 501
　Nut Steak Patties, 325
　Onion Pie, 335
　Pizza, 332
　Potato, 325
　Salisbury Steak, 325
　Stroganoff, 332
　Wild West, 325
Hard Candies. *See* Candy
Hard-Cooked Egg, 197
Hard Sauce, 702
Harvard Beets, 393
Hasenpfeffer (Rabbit), 381
Hash
　Baked Bean, 338
　Baked Hawaiian, 355–56
　Chicken, 287
　Corned Beef, 338
　Pan-Browned Ham, 353
　Pan-Browned Roast Beef.
　　See Pan-Browned
　　Ham Hash
　Red Flannel, 316
　Texas, 333
　with Pineapple Topping,
　　316
Hazelnut Meringues, Mrs.
　John Kennedy's, 642
Hawaiian
　Chicken, 272
　Chicken Salad, 521
　Fish Cocktail, 51
　Hash, Baked, 355
　Pork, 346
　Sandwiches, 89
　Style Baked Bananas in
　　Wine, 387
He-Man Sandwiches, 93
Hearty Corn and Crab Meat
　Chowder, 185
Heavenly Jam, 718
　Lemon Pie, 569
Heirloom Boston Brown
　Bread, 110
　Pie Pastry, 548
Hello Dolly Torte, 618
Henny Penny, 289
Herb
　Bread, 149
　Broiled Fish, 224
　　Halibut, 227
　Butter Popcorn, 55
　Cream Sauce, 441
　French Dressing, 541
　Fried Potatoes, 421
　Loaf, Toasted, 168
　Mayonnaise, Blender, 445
　Popovers, 89
Herbed Beef Casserole de
　Luxe, 320
　Bread Chunks, 195
Herbs, Seeds and Spices,
　36–37
Hermits, 635
　Date, 640
Hero for Six, 93
Heroes, 93
Herring
　Marinated in Sour Cream,
　　62

Pickled Salted, 62
Salad, Swedish
　(Sillsallad), 517
High Hat Salad, 524
Hillbilly Cake, 601
Hobo Bread, 115
Holiday
　Delights, 660
　Fruitcake, 613
　Macaroon Pie, 568
　Punch, 740
Hollandaise Sauce, 444
Hollywood Pie, 567
Home Freezing, 41
Homemade
　Mincemeat, 721
　Noodles, 490
　Sausage, 356–57
Hominy, 463
　and Bacon, New England,
　　466
　Baked, 466
　Beef Casserole, 466
　Casserole, 466
　Cheese Bake, 466
　Dish, 466
　Grits de Luxe, 467
　　Garlic Cheese, 467
　Pie, 466
Honey
　Almond Balls, 661
　Apple Crisp, 665
　Balls, 661
　Bread (Pain d'Épice), 117
　Butter, 77
　Chocolate Eggnog, 741
　Fig Cookies, 639
　Pear, 723
　Quince, 723
　Raisin Poundcake, 604
　Waffles, 137
　Walnut Loaf, 119
　Whipped Cream, 701
Hoosier Peanut Bars, 654
Hopping John, 471
Hors
　Cold
　　Anchovy Radishes, 57
　　Antipasto, 57
　　Appetizer Ham Ball, 61
　　Apple Pincushion, 57
　　Artichokes, in Lemon,
　　　58
　　　Marinated, 58
　　Aspic of Foie Gras, 63
　　Baguettes de Berne, 58
　　Celery Curls, 58
　　　Rings, Stuffed, 58
　　　Stuffed with Cream
　　　　Cheese, 58
　　　Stuffed with Cream
　　　　Cheese and Pea-
　　　　nut Butter, 58
　　　Stuffings for, 58
　　Cheese Apples, 59
　　　Balls, 59
　　Caviar in Tomato
　　　Cup, 59
　　Caviar Mold, 58
　　Liver Pâté, 60
　　Rolls, 59

Chicken Liver and
　Mushroom Pâté, 60
Chipped Beef Pecan
　Log, 60
Cigarettes de Bayonne,
　62
Cornets de Saumon
　Fumé, 63
Cranberry Ham Rollups,
　61
Cucumber Cheese
　Slices, 60
Deviled Eggs, 60
Eggplant Marinara, 61
Ham and Veal Pâté, 62
Italian Raw Mushrooms,
　63
Marinated Herring in
　Sour Cream, 62
　Shrimp, 64
Mint Bouquet, 59
Molded Shrimp Pâté,
　64
Pickled Eggs, 60
　Salt Herring, 62
Poor Man's Caviar, 61
Roquefort Ball, 59
Rosy Cheese Ball, 59
Rullepolye (Spiced
　Meat), 63
Seviche (Fish in Lime
　Juice), 61
Shrimp Balls, 64
　in Beer, 64
Spiced Pineapple and
　Ham Kebabs, 61
Stuffed Lettuce, 62
Tipsy Mushrooms, 63
Tongue and Cheese, 64
Torrid Shrimp, 64
Hot
　Baked Mushrooms
　　Stuffed with
　　Cheese, 69
　Barbecued Shrimp, 20
　Butterfly Shrimp, 70
　Chafing Dish Sweet and
　　Sour Meat Balls,
　　68
　Chiles Rellenos con
　　Queso, 66
　Chili Meat Balls, 69
　Chinese Meat Balls, 68
　Chutney Bacon Balls,
　　65
　Cock Kebabs, 66
　Cocktail Meat Balls, 68
　　Potato Puffs, 70
　Crab Cream Puffs, 66
　Deep Fried Corned Beef
　　and Sauerkraut
　　Appetizers, 66
　Egg Rolls, 67
　Fried Wontons, 71
　Gougère, 67
　Grostini, 66
　Ham Cheese Balls, 68
　Mushrooms Stuffed with
　　Crab Meat, 69
　Oyster Patties, 69
　Party Chicken Livers,
　　65

Hors (*Cont.*)
Hot (*Cont.*)
Pigs in Blankets, 70
Pineapple Wrapped in
Bacon, 70
Pronto-Puppy, 67
Quiche Tartlets, 65
Rumaki, 65
Sausage Roll, 70
Shrimp Balls with Sour
Cream Caper
Sauce, 71
Spicy Appetizer Frank-
furters, 67
Stuffed Cheese Balls, 65
Grape Leaves, 68
Shrimp, 71
Wine Meat Balls, 69
Suggestions for, 57
Horseradish, 459
Butter, 77, 79
Cream Sauce, 442
Preserved, 727
Sauce for Fish, 444
Tuna Spread, 85
Hot
Bean Dip, 72
Brandied Grapefruit, 49
Buttered Cranberry
Punch, 735
Cheese Canapés, 87
Dip, 74
Cider Punch, 735
Clam Rolls, 89
Combination Party Sand-
wich, 97
Consommé Madrilène, 171
Crab Sandwich, 97
Soufflé Sandwich, 208
Cranberry Sauce for
Ham, 443
Cross Buns, 161
Crunchies, 640
Dog Relish, 728
Surprise, 107
Egg Sandwich, 98
Eggnog, 736
French Bread with Sea-
soned Butter, 168
Roll Sandwich, 99
Fudge Pudding, 669
Sauce, 701
Ham and Cheese Buns,
98–99
Milk Cake, 588
Nut Crackers, 54
Peppermint Chocolate,
734
Red Pepper Relish, 728
Rum Sauce, 703
Sandwich Loaf, 101
Shrimp Dip, 76
Slaw, 512
Swedish Mustard, 448
Tartar Sauce, 450
Tomato Toddy, 736
Tuna Crab Canapé, 90
Water Pie Pastry, 548
Huckleberry
Pie, Freshy's, 565
Pudding, 695

Huevos Rancheros, Baked,
199
Hungarian
Cream Cheese Pastry, 580
Goulash, 321
Noodles, 491
Pastries, 161
Nut Rolls, 163
String Beans, 388
Walnut Torte, 619
Hunter's Rabbit, 382
Hush Puppies, 142
Georgia, 142

Ice, Cranberry, 688
Icebox
Dessert, Apricot, 683
Pie, Pineapple Cheese,
573
Pudding, Apricot, 681
Chocolate, 684
Orange, 681
Ice Cream
Alaska, Raisin, 692
Butter Pecan, 687
Chocolate, 687
Cups, 693
Coconut Balls, 693
Lemon, 687
Maple, 687
Pastry for Fruit Tarts or
Turnovers, 552
Peach, Fresh, 689
Pie, 693
Pumpkin, 693
Strawberry, 694
Washington Cherry, 692
Roll, Walnut, 694
Sauce, 702
Melba Sauce for, 702
Sodas, 737
Vanilla, 687
Iced Avocado Soup, 191
Tomato Soup, 192
Icelandic Vinartarta, 588
Ice Water White Cake, 585
Icings. *See* Frostings;
Glazes; Toppings
Imperial
Casserole of Crab, 243
Crab à la Maryland, 242
Sauce for Crab, 243
Indian
Bread Stuffing, 453
Curried Beef, 331–32
Rice, 474
Curry Bombay Style, 338
Fried Bread, 141
Pudding, 672
Fruited, 672
Individual Grape-Cluster
Salad, 524
Indonesian Pork Chops,
344–45
Irish
Coffee, 733
Molly Bread, 150
Soda Bread, 115
Stew, Real, 323
Sweep Steak, 103
"I Smell Christmas" Cake,
599

Italian
Bread Sticks, 155–56
Cartwheel, 340
Casserole, Overnight, 501
Cream, 678
Dumplings, 462
Fried Peppers, 418
Green Beans, 389
Meat Balls, 327
with Spaghetti, 504
Meat Loaf, 329
Noodles and Zucchini, 496
Open Sandwich, 97
Raw Mushrooms, 63
Sesame Seed Cookies, 649
Shrimp (Scampi), 254
Spaghetti Sauce, 506
with Beef and Pork, 507
Sponges, 196
Style Pizza, 100
Tomato Salad, 512

Jackpot Noodle, 494
Jailhouse Chili, 334
Jam(s)
and Jellies, 717–20
Apricot, 717
Butter, 77
Jalapeña Buttermilk Corn
Bread, 112
"Carorange" Confiture,
718
Cherry, 718
Grape, 718
Heavenly, 718
Maraschino Pear Jam, 718
Pineapple Orange, 718
Plum, 719
Raspberry, 719
Strawberry, Easy Over-
night, 719
Year-Round, 719
Jambolaya, 481
à la Creole, 481
Chicken, 484
James River Buttermilk
Waffles, 137
Japanese
Chicken Casserole, 273
Steak Dish, 311
Javanese Fried Rice, 477
Jell, Cinnamon Candy, 719
Jellied
Apricots, Golden, 457
Consommé, 192
Neat's Tongue, 377
Pepper Relish, 728
Veal, 362
Waldorf Luncheon Salad,
527
Jellies and Jams, 717–20
Jelly
Apple, 719
Biscuits, 123
Cherry Salad, 529
Cookies, Norwegian, 647
Dessert Wine, 683
Doughnuts, 138
Glazed Beets, 393
Grape, 719
Mint, 720

Jelly (*Cont.*)
  Roll. *See* Sponge Cake.
    Old-Fashioned, 611
    Tabasco, 720
Jeweled Sherbet Mold, 693
Jewish Coffee Cake, 606
Jerusalem Artichokes. *See*
    Artichokes
Jiffy Lemon Dessert, 685
  Sponge Cake, 610
Johnny Cakes, Rhode Island,
    135
Juice
  Grape, Mulled, 735
  Tomato, Spiced, 731
Juices
  Chilled, 47
  Fruit, 47
  Vegetable, 47
Jumbo Pizza Sandwich, 100
Just Plain Hamburgers, 324

Kalbs Gulyas (Veal Goulash),
    363
Kale, 411
Kartoffel Puffer (German Po-
    tato Pancakes), 422
Kasha, 464, 468
  Baked, 468
Kathryn's Chocolate Frost-
    ing, 628
  Fudge Cake, 590
Kebabs, Cock, 66–67
  Spiced Pineapple and
    Ham, 61
Kennebunkport Clam Pie,
    239
Kentucky
  Baked Chicken Breasts,
    280
  Bourbon Balls, 659
  Bourbon Pie, 565
  Burgoo, 277–78
  Corn Sticks, 128
  Muffins, 128
Kesari Baath (Near Eastern
    Rice Pudding), 678
Kidney and Steak Pie, 323
Kidney Beans. *See* Dried
    Beans, Peas and Lentils
  Barbecue, 333–34
  Salad, Crunchy, 510
Kidneys, 373–74
  Flambé, Veal, 374
  Lamb, in Wine Sauce, 374
Kim Chee, 727
  Party Dip, 76
King's Cake, 614
Kiss Torte, 697
Kitchen Hints
  Baking, 15
  Beverage, 16
  Bread, 16
  Economy, 16
  Egg, 16
  Equipment, 34
  Fish, 17
  Frosting and Topping, 17
  Fruit, 17
  General, 15
  Meat, 17
  Poultry, 17

Pudding, 17
Salad, 18
Sauce and Gravy, 18
Soup and Stew, 19
Storing, 19
Vegetable, 19
Knedlich (Matzo Balls), 463
Kohlrabi, 411
  Boiled, 411
Kolachky (Turnovers), 580
Kosher Dill Pickles, 724
Krapsua (Oven Pancake), 134
Krispie Rolls, 162
Krispy Crunch Cookies, 661
Kugelhopf, 152
Kumquat Tidbits, 53

Lamaize Sauce, 544
Lamb, 364–73
  and Mushrooms, Chef's,
    372
  Armenian Dinner in Foil,
    369
  Baked Kibby (Syrian
    Lamb and Wheat
    Patties, 371
  Bombay Curry, 370
  Boned Barbecued, 367
  Casserole, 369
  Chops, Deviled, 368
    Dinner, 368
    Grilled Tropical, 368
    Polly's Baked, 368
  Cooked Dishes, 372–73
  Cous-cous (Lamb Stew
    with Semolina), 370
  Croquettes, 372
  Crown Roast of, 367
  Cuts of Lamb, 364
  Dolma Armenian (Stuffed
    Peppers), 371
  Ground Dishes, 371–72
  How to Carve, 365
  How to Cook, 364
  Kidneys in Wine Sauce,
    374
  Lamburgers with Pine
    Nuts, 371
  Lancashire Hot Pot, 370
  Leg of
    Baked, 366
    Barbecued, 366
    in Foil, 366
    Roast, 366
    Savory Roast, 366
    Texas Style, 366
  Loaf, 371
  Moussaka, 372
  Roast, Mint Sauce for, 446
  Shanks, 368
    and Curried Rice, 369
    Stew, Armenian, 369
  Shepherd's Pie, 372
  Shish Kebab, 367
  Short Cakes, 372–73
  Steak Luscious, 367
  Stew, 369
  Timetable for Cooking,
    365
Lamburgers with Pine Nuts,
    371
Lancashire Hot Pot, 370

Larded Grouse, 296
Lasagne, 496. *See also* Pasta,
    Filled
  Old-Fashioned Neapoli-
    tan, 496
Lazy Daisy Cake, 588
Lazy Day Brownies, 653
Leather Cake, 595
Lebkuchen, Sugar Glaze for,
    657
Lebkuchen, Traditional, 657
Leek(s), 411
  Soup, Potato and, 189
Leftover Turkey Rice Din-
    ner, Bayou, 485
Leg of Lamb in Foil, 366
    Texas Style, 366
Lelah's Slow-Cooked Beef
    and Vegetable Dinner,
    314
Lemon
  Almond Fritters, 465
  Bonbon Cookies, 647
  Bread, 115
  Butter, 77, 444
    Caper, 445
    Filling, 631
    for Fish, 226
    Parsley, 445
  Cake
    Chiffon, 610
    Loaf, 598
    Pineapple White, 585
    Quick, 598
    Treasure, 598
  Cream, Frozen, 688
  Cups, Upside-Down, 677
  Custard, for Lemon Trea-
    sure Cake, 598
  Dessert, Jiffy, 685
  Dressing for Fruit Salads,
    545
  Filled Cream Puffs, 580
  Filling, 631
  Frosting, 629
  Glaze, for Lemon Loaf
    Cake, 598
  Ice Cream, 687
  Lime Sherbet, 689
    Treat, 685
  Love Notes, 657
  Marmalade, 722
  Mayonnaise, Blender, 445
  Meringue Frosting,
    Carmelita's, 626
    Shells, 697
  Nut Rolls, 162
  Orange Glaze for Fig
    Cake, 597
  Pie, 558
    Angel Cream, 569
    Buttermilk, 556
    Carmelita's Favorite,
      569
    Chess, 557
    Chiffon, 569
    Colonial, 558
    Heavenly, 569
    Rhubarb, 555
    Sponge, Amish, 577
  Pineapple Fluff, 685
  Pudding Sauce, 702

Lemon (*Cont.*)
  Sauce, 702
  Soup, Greek, 174
  Sours, 657
  Sugar, 663
  Tea, 737
  Velvet, 689
Lemonade, 737
  Cookies, 642
  Pie, Mile-High, 570
  Pineapple, 737
  Pink, 737
Lenore's Boeuf en Daube, 319
Lenten Soup, Quick, 194
Lentil Soup, 179, 180
Lentils, 472. *See also* Dried Beans, Peas and Lentils
Lettuce, 411
  Braised, 412
  Endives Printemps, 412
  Stuffed, 62
  Iceberg, 514
  Wilted, 509
Libbett's Brownies, 653
Lila's Chipped Beef in Wine Sauce, 317
Lilies (Sandwiches), 78
Lima Bean(s). *See also* Dried Beans, Peas and Lentils
  and Corned Beef, 316
  and Macaroni Soup, 178
  and Mushroom Salad, 514
  Boiled Fresh, 391
  Casserole, 392
    and Mushroom, 392
  in Sour Cream, 391–92, 471
  Succotash, 391
Lime
  Cottage Cheese Mold with Shrimp, 535
  Freeze, 690
  Lemon Sherbet, 689
    Treat, 685
  Orange Cocktail, 738
  Pie, 570
  Pineapple Salad, 534
    and Walnut Salad, Frosted, 534
  Sugar, 663
Lithuanian Potato Pudding, 422
Little
  Little Babas, 159
    Variations, 159
  Breads, 116
  Fried Pies, 578
  Red Chick, 267
Live Lobster Stew, 183
Liver
  and Onions, Baked, 374
    with French Dressing, 375
  Braised, 375
  Broiled Beef, 374
  Butter, 77
  Cheese, 84
  en Brochette, Calf's, 374
  Loaf, 375
  Pâté with Truffles, 84
  Sandwiches, 95

Scalloped, 375
Stroganoff, Beef, 375
Liverwurst Sandwich, 92, 95
  Cheese and Egg, 95
Loaf
  Celery, Golden Baked, 402
  Chicken, 287
    Rice Soufflé, 288
  Chicken, Molded, 529
  Lamb, 371
  Macaroni, 499
  Seafood Mousse, 541
Lobster(s), 244–47
  Baked, 245
  Bisque, 188
  Boiled, 244
  Broiled, 245
  Butter, 77
  Cantonese, 246
  Cardinale, 245
  Casserole with Wild Rice, 246
  Cocktail, Canned, 51
    Fresh, 51
  Fra Diavolo, 247
  Mixed Seafood Cocktail, 50
  Mousse. *See* Chicken Mousse
  Newburg, 247
  Omelet, 206
  Pie, Cape Cod, 247
  Ring, 532
  Rock, Tetrazzini, 247
  Salad, 519
  Sauce for Chicken, 283
  Spread, 80
  Stew, 183
    Live, 183
  Tails, Broiled, 245
    Stuffed, 246
  Thermidor, 246
London Broil with Claret Sauce, 310
Long Johns, 166
Louie Dressing for Crab Louie, 518
Louis Pappas' Famous Greek Salad, 511
Louisiana Yam Goodies, 428
Low-Calorie
  Buttermilk Salad Dressing, 542
  Party Rolls, 155
  Salad Dressings
    Buttermilk, 542
    Tomato, Peppy, 543
Lullaby Special, 97
Luncheon
  Date Muffins, 128
  Egg Dish, 204
  Salad, Jellied Waldorf, 527
  Yum Yums, 236

Macadamia Nut Pie, 559
Macaroni, 498–502
  and Cheese, Aunt Lydia's, 498
  Supreme, 498
  with Olives, 500
  and Ham, Scalloped, 502

and Meat Balls, 501
Casserole
  Asparagus, 460
  Burger, 501
  Cheese-a-Roni, 500
  Chipped Beef, 502
  Corn and Oyster, 500
  Hamburger Upside-Down, 460
  Overnight Italian, 501
Chesterfield Pie, 999
Delight, 500
Deviled, 498
Loaf, 499
Omelet with Creole Sauce, 499
Pasticcio with Kima (Baked Macaroni with Greek Meat Sauce), 502
Rigatoni with Sausage, 502
Ring, 499
Salad, 515
  Chicken, 516
  Seafood, 515
  Tangy, 515
and Lima Bean Soup, 178
-Stuffed Peppers, 418
Macaroon(s)
  Chocolate Cake, 594
  Coconut, 642
    Pie Shell, 551
  Crumb Crust, 551
  Pie, 576
    Holiday, 568
    Polka Dot, 642
  Shimmy Pudding, 685
Macédoine of Vegetables, 439
Mackerel, Baked Spanish, 228
Magic Cake, 611
Magyar Vajas Teszta or Knifli (Hungarian Nut Rolls), 163
Mahogany Chiffon Cake, 610
  Sauce, 702
Maid Rites, 103
Maine Blueberry Muffins, 127
Maison, Sauce, for Steaks or Chops, 445
Malted, Chocolate, 737
  Milk Dainties, 658
Mamaliguta cu Branza (Mush with Meat), 465
Mama's Favorite Gulyas (Stew), 352
Mamie Eisenhower's Fudge, 706
Mandarin Tuna Salad, 520
Mango Betty, Green, 672
Manicotti, 497
Maple
  Bars, 658
  Butterscotch Sauce, 700
  Ice Cream, 687
  Mousse, 689
  Marinade, Oriental, for Beef or Chicken, 445
    Wine, 445

Marinated
  Artichokes, 58
  Carrots, 511
  Herring in Sour Cream, 62
  Shrimp, 64
  Stuffed Fish, 220
Maraschino Pear Jam, 718
Marble Cake, 594
  Coffee Cake, Spicy, 607
Mardi Gras Party Cake, 595
Marinara Sauce, 505
  for Lobster fra Diavolo, 247
Marmalade(s), 720–23
  Bread, 116
  Butter, 77
  English, 222
  Lemon, 722
  Muffins, 129
  Sandwich, 95
  Three Fruits, 722
Marshmallow
  Banana Salad, 528
  Coffee Brownies, 653
  Coffee Dessert, 688
  Delight, 686
  Filling, 631
  Fudge Bars, 654
  Nut Fudge, 706
Martha Washington Bon-
    bons, 714
Maryland
  Chicken à la, 273
  Crab Cakes, 240
  Deviled Crab, 241
  Imperial Crab à la, 242
  Oysters, 249
  Terrapin à la, 259
Mary's Chocolate Filling, 630
  Tom and Jerry, 737
Mashed Potatoes, 419
  à la Phyfe, 424
  Fondant, 715
Matzo Balls, 463
Mayonnaise
  Belgian, 543
  Blender, 445
    Cucumber, 445
    Curry, 445
    Garlic, 445
    Green, 445
    Herb, 445
    Lemon, 445
  Dressing, 543
  Sauce, Mustard, 448
  Whole Egg, 445
Mazetti, 495
Meal Planning, 25
Measure, How to, 22–23
Measurements, Before and
    After Cooking, 21
  Table of, 22
Meat, 300–82. See also Beef;
    Corned Beef; Dried
    Beef; Hamburgers; Meat
    Balls; Meat Loaf; Steaks;
    Individual Names
  Amount to Serve, 300
  and Rice Dishes, 485–87
  and Tomato Sauce, 507
  Balls, 324–30. See also

Ground Beef Dishes;
    Hamburgers; Meat
    Loaf
  and Macaroni, 501
  Beef, Stroganoff, 328
  Burgundy Beef Balls, 326
  Chafing Dish Sweet
    and Sour, 68–69
  Chili, 69
  Chinese, 68
  Cocktail, 68
  Ham, 354
  in Red Wine Sauce, 326
  Italian, 327
    with Spaghetti, 504
  Oriental, 327
  Pancakes, 327
  Sour Cream Porcupines, 326
  Spanish, 327–28
  Swedish, 328
  Sweet and Sour, 327
  Venison, in Sauce, 380
  Wine, 69
  with Spaghetti, 504
Basic Methods of Cook-
    ing, 300–11
Brains. See Brains
Care of, in Refrigerator or
    Freezer, 300
Charts for Meat Cuts
  Beef, 302
  Lamb, 305
  Pork, 303
  Veal, 304
Filling for Ravioli, 498
Game, 378–82
Garnishes, 456. See also
    Pickles, Relishes and
    Condiments
Ham. See Ham
Hints, 17–18
Kidneys. See Kidneys
Lamb. See Lamb
Liver. See Liver
Loaf, 92, 324–30, 328
  Apple-Potato, 328
  Applesauce-Ham, 354
  Barbecue Style, 329
  Economy, 329
  Gourmet, 329
  Ham and Sweet Potato
    Roll, 354
  Ham, Fruited, 354
  Ham, with Vinegar
    Sauce, 354
  Pork and Beef, 353
  Italian, 329
  Liver, 375–76
  Sausage, 357
  Stuffed, 329–30
  Swiss, 330
  Veal, 364
    with Mashed Pota-
      toes, 364
  Venison, 381
Pork. See Pork
Rules for Preparation of, 300
Sandwich, 92
Sauce, 441

for Spaghetti, 506
Sauces for, 301, 441–51
Sausage. See Sausage
Servings and Pounds, 35
Spiced (Rullepolze), 63
Sweetbreads. See Sweet-
    breads
Tongue. See Tongue
Upside-Down Pie, 335
Veal. See Veal
  with Risotto, 486
Meat-a Pie, 332
Meatless Minestrone, 176
Medium White Sauce, 441
Mélange d'Oeufs, 83
Melanzane Satt Aceto
    (Pickled Eggplant), 458
Melba
  Peach, 695
  Sauce, 695
    for Ice Cream, 702
  Toast, 167
    Canapé Bases, 77
Melody Frosting, 627
Melon Ball Cocktail, 50
  Peach Conserve, 721
Melting Moments, 646
Menudo (Mexican Tripe), 172
Meringue(s)
  Brown Sugar Frosting for
    Leather Cake, 595
  Cake, Cherry, 596
  Crunch Topping, 630
  Dessert, American, 696
  Desserts, 696–97
  Frosting, Carmelita's
    Lemon, 626
  Glacée, 697
  Hazelnut Meringues, Mrs.
    John Kennedy's, 642
  Nest, 552
  Pie, Caramel Cream, 565
    Orange, 571
    Peach, 571
  Shell, 552
    Lemon, 697
  Surprise, 642
  -Topped Cherry Pie, 566
  Toppings, 552
  2-Egg-White Cooked, 552
Mexican
  Bean Dip, 73
  Cream, 680
  Dip, 74
  Fritters (Sopapillas), 140
  Omelet, 206
  Rice, 475
  Sandwiches (Tacos), 102
  Scrambled Eggs, 198
  Spoon Bread with Cheese
    Topping, 465
  Tripe Soup, 172
  Wedding Cookies, 648
Midnight Omelet Scramble, 206
Mile-High Biscuits, 123
  Lemonade Pie, 570
  Strawberry Pie, 691
Milk
  Almond, 663
  Cake, Hot, 588

Milk (*Cont.*)
Chocolate, 737
Cookies, Condensed, 660
Shake, Strawberry, 742
Milwaukee Rye Bread, 147–48
Mincemeat
Coffee Cake, 606
Homemade, 721
Squares, 658
Tea Loaf, 589
Minestrone, 176
Meatless, 176
Minnesota Baked Cream
Cheese Pie, 557
Centennial Salt-Rising
Bread, 146
Mint
Bouquet, 59
Chiffon Pie, 570
Chocolate Topping, 630
Cooler, 738
Delight, Frosted, 689
Dessert, 685
Frango, 691
French Dressing, 541
Grapefruit Punch, 740
Jelly, 720
Julep, Orange, 738
Sauce for Roast Lamb, 446
Minted
Fruit Punch, 740
Pineapple Juice Cocktail, 48
Sugar, 49
Walnuts, 709
Mints, Chocolate, Easy, 713
Pulled, 711
Minute Plum Pudding, 682
Miracle Icing, 622
Missouri Deep-Fried
Chicken, 264
Mixed
Bread, 146
Seafood Cocktail, 50
Vegetable Dishes. See
Vegetables; also Individual Vegetables
Vegetable Salad, 515
Mocha
Balls, 661
Butter Frosting, 624
Filling, 624
Frosting, 624
Pecan Chiffon Pie, 572
Mock Apple Pie, 553
Turtle Soup, 175
Molasses
Cranberry Pudding, Steamed, 670
Crinkles, 648
Sauce, Old-Fashioned, 702
Mold, Jeweled Sherbet, 693
Strawberry Pineapple, 682
Molded
Ambrosia Salad, 526
Chicken Loaf, 529
Cookies, 645–50
Cranberry Banana Special, 531

Party Salad, 531
Cucumber Salad, 532
Salad, Bing Cherry Cola, 529
Cherry Jelly, 529
Jellied Waldorf
Luncheon, 527
Salmon, 535
Aspic, 539
Shrimp Pâté, 64
Waldorf Luncheon Salad,
Jellied, 527
Mom's Apple Pie, 553
Montana Pickles, 724
Monte Cristo Sandwich, 99–100
Moose. See Game
Mornay Sauce, 293, 441
Pat's, 446
Mosaic Sandwich, 78
Mother's Apple Dumpling, 665
Baked Fruit Casserole, 671
Crumpets, 640
Orange Roll, 611
Moules Marinière, 248
Moussaka, 332
Mousseline Sauce for Cooked
Vegetables, 446
Mousse(s)
au Chocolat, 677
Avocado, 540
Banana, 690
Chicken, 540
Coffee, 688
Crab, 540
Fruit, 690
Ham, 540
Lobster. See Chicken
Mousse
Maple, 689
Peanut Butter, 690
Pineapple, 681
Raspberry, 690
Salmon, 540
Savory, 540–41
Seafood, Loaf, 541
Strawberry, 682, 690
Mrs. Cutler's Veal Delight, 362
Mrs. Eato's Speck Salad, 530
Mrs. Eisenhower's Sugar
Cookies, 634
Mrs. Haseebroock's Green
Goddess Salad Dressing, 543
Mrs. Hood's Chocolate
Frosting, 628
Mrs. John Kennedy's Hazelnut Meringues, 642
Mrs. Kittler's Caramel Frosting, 628
Mrs. Nixon's Walnut Clusters, 638
Mrs. Richard Nixon's Chocolate Butter Cookies, 634
Mrs. Sawyer's Boston Relish, 729
Mrs. Sharp's Caramel Icing, 628
Mrs. Shepard's Swedish Hot
Cakes, 135

Mrs. Stuart Symington's
Chicken Tetrazzini, 504
Muffins, 125–31
All-Bran Molasses, 127
Apple, 126
Pecan, 126
Bacon, 125
Banana, 126
Blueberry, 126
Maine, 127
Bran, 127
by the Pailful, 127
Buttermilk, 125
Causes of Failure, 125
Cheese, 125
Cinnamon Honey, 128
Cranberry, 125
Cream, 128
English, 166
French Breakfast Puffs, 128
Kentucky, 128
Luncheon Date, 128
Marmalade, 129
Nut, 125
Oatmeal, 129
Onion Corn Gems, 129
Orange, 129
Buttermilk, 130
Pecan Sour Cream, 130
Peach Gems, 130
Perfect Breakfast, 125
Popovers. See Popovers
Prune Rye, 130
Raisin Nut Bran, 127
Refrigerator Ginger, 129
Rice, 130
Sour Cream, 128
Sweet, 125
Upside-Down Apricot, 126
Very Sweet, 125
Mulberry Cobbler, 672
Mulled Grape Juice, 735
Mullet
Barbecued, 228
Broiled Fillets, 229
Mulligatawny Soup, 188
Muriel Humphrey's Beef
Soup, 171
Mush with Meat, 465
Mushrooms, 412
and Almonds with Fried
Rice, 477
and Celery Dressing, 453
and Cheese Soufflé, 208
and Crab Meat in Wine
Sauce, 243
and Lamb, Chef's, 372
and Lima Bean Salad, 514
and Oyster Gratin, 251
and Rice Stuffing, 455
and Veal Neapolitan, 364
au Gratin, 412
Baked Stuffed, 413
Bisque, Quick Tomato, 195
Canapés, 89
Casserole
Broccoli, 395
Corn, 406
Eggplant, 409

Mushrooms (*Cont.*)
  Casserole (*Cont.*)
    Green Bean, 390
    Lima Bean, 392
  Creamed, 412
  Egg and Bacon Spread, 83
  Italian Raw, 63
  Onions, Potatoes—au
    Gratin, 423
  Piquante, 413
  Polenta, 464
  Potato Soup, 176
  Rarebit, 212
  Rolls, 89
  Salad, Raw. Susan's, 511
  Sandwich, 92
  Sauce, 446
    Baked Eggs in, 202
    Cream, 446
    Easy, 447
    for Ham, 447
    Quick Pimiento, 447
    Velouté, 447
    Wine for Chicken, 282
  Soup, Cream of, 188
    Sauce, Quick, 447
  Stuffed, 413
    with Crab Meat, 69
    with Cheese, Baked, 69
  Tipsy, 63
  with Beef, 320
  with Sautéed Chicken
    Livers, 291
  with Sour Cream, 413
Mussels, 248
  Moules Marinière, 248
Mustard
  Butter, 77
  Cream Sauce, 442
  Greens. *See* Greens
  Hot Swedish, 448
  Mayonnaise Sauce, 448
  Pineapple Sauce, 449
  Sauce, 448
  Sour Cream Sauce for
    fillets, 222
  Tomato Sauce, 448
  Wax Beans, 457
My Favorite Summer Salad,
  533

Napoleons, 580
Navajo Fried Bread, 141
Neapolitan Spaghetti Sauce,
  506
Neat's Tongue, Jellied, 377
Neiman-Marcus Cream Pie,
  564
Nesselrode Pie, Glamorous,
  570
Never-Fail
  Butter Icing, 625
  Pie Pastry, 548
  Sour Cream Spice Cake,
    602
  Three-Minute Frosting,
    626
New England
  Bacon and Hominy, 466
  and Corn Chowder, Old-
    Fashioned, 184
  Boiled Dinner, 315

Cranberry Pie, 557
Fish Chowder, 183
Salad Bowl, 511
New Peas, 416
1916 Sauce for Ham, 445
Nippy Cheese Balls, 56
No-Bake Cookies, 658
No-Beat Popovers, 131
Noche Specials (Evening
  Cheese Snacks), 88
No-Cook Boiled Dressing,
  545
  Chocolate Cream Cheese
    Fudge, 714
No-Crust Coconut Pie, 576
  Custard Pie, 576
Noels, 640
Noodle
  Casserole
    Tuna, 237, 492
    with Pork, 495
  Jackpot, 494
  Pudding, 491, 672
    Czechoslovakian-Style,
      673
    with Sour Cream, 491
  Ring, 491
  Soufflé with Creamed
    Chicken Sauce, 493
Noodles
  and Zucchini Italiano, 496
  Baked
    and Crab Meat, 492
    and Dried Beef, 495
    Yukon, 492
  Bulgarian, 495
  Chicken Casserole, 493
  Cottage Cheese and Ham
    Casserole, 496
  Fettucini Alfredo, 493
  Gratinée, 491
  Green. *See* Homemade
    Noodles
  Hacienda Hamburg, 494
  Homemade, 490
  Hungarian, 491
  Mazetti, 495
  Napoli, 493
  Romanoff, 491
  Round Steak Royale, 494
  Spanish Delight, 494
  with Frankfurters, 495
  with Water Chestnuts, 492
Normandy Dressing, 545
  Omelet, 206
North Dakota Buttermilk
  Corn Bread, 111
Norwegian
  Apple Pie, 576
  Fruit Soup, 192
  Jelly Cookies, 647
  Preene Pudding, 696
  Rommegrot (Cream Pud-
    ding), 679
Nougat, 710. *See also* Candy
Nugen's Corn Oysters, 404
Nut
  Balls, Chocolate-Dipped,
    661
  Bread
    Applesauce, 108
    Banana, 108

Brown Sugar, 110
Date, 113
Pineapple, 118
Pumpkin Raisin, 118
Sour Cream, 116
White, 116
Whole Wheat, 116
with Lemon Filling, 116
Butter, 77
Butterscotch Creams, 707
Candy, Divinity, 710
Caramel Sauce, 700
Caramels, 709
Crackers, Hot, 54
Crispies, 643
Filled Horns, 581
Filling, Creamy, 626
Frosting, Creamy, 626
-Fruit Frosting, Special,
  629
    Refrigerator Cookies,
      651
Marshmallow Fudge, 706
Muffins, 125
Peach Conserve, 721
Pie, Cherry Parfait, 566
  Macadamia, 559
  Washington, 562
Rolls, Hungarian, 163
  Pecan, 163
Salad
  Apple Cranberry, 530
  Cranberry Pineapple,
    523
  Ginger Ale Pineapple,
    534
  Pineapple Cabbage, 534
Sandwich
  Cottage Cheese, 92
  Pimiento, 95
Steak Patties, 325
Topping, 630
  Coconut, 630
  for Lazy Daisy Cake,
    589
  for Sour Cream Coffee
    Cake, 606
Waffles, 136
Nutmeg Butter Balls, 648
Nutrients of Familiar Foods,
  26
Nutrition, 25
Nuts, Curried, 53
  Spiced, 53

Oat Crumble Rhubarb Pie,
  561
Apple Pudding, 665
Oatmeal
  Apple Bars, 652
  Bars, Chewy, 658
  Bread, 147
    Molasses Raisin, 147
  Coconut Cookies, 648
  Cookies, 636
  Drop Cookies, 643
  Muffins, 129
  Pie, 559
  Spice Cake, 602
  Wafers, Crisp, 643
O'Brien Potatoes, 422
Oil and Garlic Sauce, 506

Oklahoma Spinach Casserole, 431
Okra, 413
  Boiled, 413
  Creole, 413
  Fried, 414
  Southern Browned, 414
    with Turkish Beef, 333
Ok-Yok-Sung (Chinese Beef and Beans), 331
Old-Country Kitchen Dressing, 544
Old English Date Pie, 558
Old-Fashioned
  Baked Beans, 469
  "Boiled" Custard, 676
  Buckwheat Cakes, 165
  Chicken Stew, 276
  Concord Grape Pie, 554
  Doughnuts, 166
  Dumplings, 460
  Jelly Roll, 611
  Molasses Sauce, 702
  Neapolitan Lasagne, 496
  New England Bacon and Corn Chowder, 184–85
  Peanut Soup, 189
  Poundcakes, 603
  Tapioca Pudding, 679
Old-Time Brown Sugar Cookies, 634
Old Virginia Buttermilk Spoon Bread, 464
Olive(s)
  and Cheese Sandwich, 91
  and Egg Sandwich, 92
  Bean Bake, Ripe, 470
  Butter, 77
  Cheese Sandwich Filling, 80
  Chow Yuk (Sautéed Vegetables with Olives), 438
  Creamed Potatoes, 424
  Curried Ripe, 54
    Stuffed, 54
  Eggplant Casserole, 409
  Garlic Ripe, 54
  in Flaky Pastry, 54
  Puffs, 54
  Sauce, 448
  Wreath Mold, 533
  with Macaroni and Cheese, 500
  with Sautéed Vegetables, 438
Olive Oil Pickles, 724
Olympian Rice, 486
Omelet
  Cheese, 205
  French, 205
    Fillings for, 205
  Ham Pancake, 134
  Lobster, 206
  Macaroni, with Creole Sauce, 499
  Mexican, 206
  Midnight Scramble, 206
  Normandy, 206
  Sour Cream Soufflé, 206
  Spanish, 206–7

Sweet, and Soufflé, 698–99
  Strawberry, with Sour Cream, 698
Top o' the Range, 207
Soufflé, 698
Omelette, Fines Herbes, 205–6
$100 Chocolate Cake, 590
One-Minute Fudge, 705
Onion(s), 414
  and Green Tomatoes, Fried, 414
  Baked, 415
    Stuffed, 415
  Biscuits, 123–24
  Bread
    Casserole, 149
    Cheese, 117
  Butter Sauce for Steak, 448
  Corn Gems, 129
  Dip, 76
  Dumplings, 461
  Filling, for Stuffed Meat Loaf, 329
  Ham and Potato Casserole, 356
  Hamburger Pie, 335
  'n' Spud Bake, 420
  Pie, 415
  Potatoes, Mushrooms—au gratin, 423
  Rings, Dilled, 725
    French-Fried, 414
  Salad, 514
  Sauce for Roast Beef, 448
  Scalloped, with Cheese Sauce, 415
  Soup
    Cream of, 189
    French, 176
  Spanish, 415
  Stewed, 415
Open-Face
  Beef Sandwiches, 93
  Cheese Sandwich, 96
  King Crab Sandwich, 98
  Sardine Sandwiches, 95
  Shrimp Sandwiches, 95
  Tongue Sandwich, 96
Open Pork and Bean Sandwich, 101
Orange(s)
  Ambrosia, 681
  and Sweet Potato Casserole, 428
  Baked, 458
  Baked Apples, 694
  Biscuits, 120
    Upside-Down, 124
  Bread
    Cranberry, 113
    Date-Brown Sugar, 117
  Butter, 77
  Cake, Quick, 599
  Cocktail, 49
  Cookies, 644
  Cranberry Apple Salad, 523
  Cream Pie, 571

  Walnuts, 709
  Crêpes, 134
  Crisp, 649
  Custard Filling, 632
    Sauce, 702
  Date Loaf, 117
  Doughnuts, 139
  Filling, 632
  Gelatin Mold, 533
  Glaze, Confectioners' Sugar, 629
    for Pork Chops, 344
  Glazed Pork Chops, 344
  Icebox Pudding, 681
  Icing, 622
    for Orange Cookies, 644
  Layer Cake, 598
  Lime Cocktail, 738
  Marmalade Soufflé, 699
  Meringue Pie, 571
  Mint Cocktail, 50
    Julep, 738
  Muffins, 129
    Buttermilk, 130
    Pecan Sour Cream, 130
  -Peanut Butter Sandwich, 92
  Pear Bake, 695
  Pie, Early Settlers, 554
  Pineapple Filling, 632
  Pineapple Jam, 718
  Salad, Constant Comment, 535
  Raisin Sauce, 448
  Refrigerator Cookies, 651
  Roll, Mother's, 611
  Sauce, 702
  Sponge Custard, 678
  Stuffing for Pork Chops, 345
  Sugar, 663
  Wassail Bowl, Spiced, 735
  Water Chestnut Salad, 533
  Yeast Rolls, 163
Orangeade, 737
Orégano Cheese Dressing for Green Salad, 542
Oriental
  Flank Steak, 310–11
  Marinade for Beef or Chicken, 445
  Sauce, 278
    Chicken, 278
Orleans Meringue Cake, 602
Orono Barbecue Sauce, 442
Oslo Almond Pudding, 676
Out of This World Salad, 530
Oven
  Baked French Fries, 421
  Buttered Corn Fingers, 122–23
  Canapé Bases, 77
  Chuck Roast, 315
  Corn on the Cob, 404
  -Crisp Eggplant, 408
  French Toast, 167
  Fried Chicken, 265
    Parmesan, 265
  Ham Croquettes, 355
  Hashed Brown Potatoes, 421

Oven (*Cont.*)
  Lemon Chicken, 266–67
  Spareribs, 349–50
  Temperature Chart, 38
Overnight
  Cheese Strata, 213
  Coconut Cookies, 651
  German Refrigerator Coffee Kuchen, 152
  Italian Casserole, 501
Oxtail Soup, 172–73
Oxtails, Braised, 324
Oyster(s), 248–51
  Alabama Fried, 249
  and Chicken Pie, 288–89
  and Corn, Scalloped, 250–51
  and Mushroom, Gratin of, 251
  and Rice, 482
  and Wild Rice Dressing, 456
  Baked Homestead, 248
  Bienville, 249
  Broiled, 249
  Cocktail I, II, 51
    Sauce, 53
  Cracker Stuffing for Roast Chicken, 262
  Creamed, 250
  Curried, 250
  Dip for, 248
  Dressing, Bon Secour, 454
  Gumbo Filé, 181
  in Bacon Slices (pigs in blankets), 70
  in Tomato Cups, 51
  Macaroni and Corn Casserole, 500
  Maryland, 249
  on Half Shell, Party, 52
  Patties, 69
  Pie, 251
  Plant, 416
  Rarebit, 213
  Roasted, 249
  Rockefeller, 250
  Sandwich Spread, 84
  Sauce, 53
  Scald, 248
  Scalloped, 250
  Soup, 184
  Stew, 184
  Stuffing for Baked Fish, 220
  Tetrazzini, 492
  to Open, 238
Ozark Pudding, 666
  Yeast, 165–67
    Blinis, 165
    Buckwheat Cakes, Old-Fashioned, 165
    Doughnuts, Old-Fashioned, 166
      Refrigerator, 166
    English Muffins, 166
    Long Johns, 166
    Pancakes, Raised, 165
    Sourdough, 165
    Waffles, Raised, 165

Paella con Vino, 484
Pain d'Épice (Honey Bread), 117
Pan
  -Broiled Fish, 223
  -Browned Ham Hash, 353
    Roast Beef Hash, 353
  Cookies, 652–59
  -Fried Eggs, 260
Pancakes and Waffles, 131–38
  Pancakes
    Apple, 132
    Banana, with Sweet and Sour Sauce, 132
    Basic, 132
    Blueberry, 132
    Buckwheat, 132
    Buttermilk, Super-Duper, 132
      with Wheat Germ, 133
    Carrot, 133
    Cheese, 132
    Corn Dollars, Crisp, 133
      Griddle Cakes, 133
    Corn Meal–Molasses, 133
    Cottage Cheese, 133
    de Luxe, 132
      Mix, 132
    Dessert, 697–98
      French, 697
    Dutch, 134
    Ham Omelet, 134
    Krapsua (Oven Pancake), 134
    Master Mix for, 120
    Meat Ball, 327
    Mrs. Shepard's Swedish Hot Cakes, 135
    Orange Crêpes, 134
    Paper-Thin, 134
    Plättar (Swedish Pancakes), 135
    Potato, 135, 422
    Rhode Island Johnny Cakes, 135
    Rice, 135
    Skins for Egg Rolls, 136
    Sour Milk Griddle Cakes, 135
    Tortillas, 136
    Whole-Wheat, 132
  Waffles
    Basic Velvet, 136
      Cocoa, 136
      Corn, 136
      Gingerbread, 136
      Ham, 136
      Nut, 136
      Sour Cream, 136
    Buttermilk, James River, 137
      Whole Wheat, 138
    Chocolate, 136
      Spiced, 137
    Coconut, 137
    Corn Meal, 137
    Honey, 137
    Sunday Nite, 138

Pandowdy, Apple, 665
Pantry Shelf Pie Pastry, 550
Papaya Appetizer Cocktail, 50
Paper Bag Apple Pie, 556
Paper-Thin Pancakes or Crêpes, 134–35
Paprika Wiener Schnitzel, 361
Parfait
  Cake, Pineapple, 599
  Date, Frozen, 688
  Frosting, Pineapple, 627
  Pie, Butter Crust, 567
    Cherry Nut, 566
    Peach, 572
Parisian Beef Soup, Quick, 193
Parker House Rolls, 154
Parmesan Oven-Fried Chicken, 265
Parsley
  Biscuits, 120
  Butter, 77
  Dumplings, German, 462
  Lemon Butter, 445
  Rice Ring, 480
Parsnip Chicken Salad, 521
Parsnips, 416
  Baked, 416
  Boiled, 416
  Candied, 416
Partridge. *See* Game Birds
Party
  Cake, Mardi Gras, 595
  Chicken Livers, 65
  Crab Meat Dip, 74
  Frosting, 624
  Hot Chocolate, 734
  Oysters on Half Shell, 52
  Perfect Glazed Chicken, 266
  Pink Congealed Salad, 532
  Rolls, Low-Calorie, 155
  Salad, Molded Cranberry, 531
Pasta
  Cooking Time, 490
  Dishes, 490–506
    Filled, 496–98
  How to Cook, 490
  Lasagne, 496
  Macaroni. *See* Macaroni
  Manicotti, 497
  Noodles. *See* Noodles
  Ravioli
    Chicken and Spinach Filling for, 498
    Meat Filling for, 498
    with Ricotta Cheese Filling, 497
  Rigatoni, 498
  Sauces for, 505–7
  Servings and Pounds, 36
Pastel Cookies, 652
  Pinwheels, 652
Pasticcio with Kima (Baked Macaroni with Greek Meat Sauce), 502
Pastries. *See* Tarts, Turnovers and Small Pastries

Pastries, Small. *See* Tarts,
  Turnovers and Small
  Pastries
Pastry
  Cream Puff, 552
  for Pies. *See* Piecrusts
  French, Frozen, 690
Pâté
  Aspic of Foie Gras, 63
  Chicken Liver, 60
    and Mushroom, 60
  Cigarettes de Bayonne, 62
  Ham and Veal, 62
  Liver with Truffles, 84
  Molded Shrimp, 64
  Sandwich, 92
Pat's Mornay Sauce, 446
Peach(es)
  -a-Berry Cobbler, 673
  and Pork Chops Barbecue
    Skillet, 344
  Baked Spiced, 695
  Brandied, 720
  Chutney, 722
  Dessert, Speedy, 673
  Festival Cobbler, 673
  Gems, 130
  Halves, Baked, 458
  Ice Cream, Fresh, 689
  Melba, 695
  Melon Conserve, 721
  Nut Conserve, 721
  Pickled, 726
    Pink, 726
  Pie, 559
    Butterscotch, 554
    Deep-Dish, 559
    Fried, 581
    Golden, 554
    Meringue, 571
    Parfait, 572
    Rice, 572
    Streusel Cream, 559
  Preserves, 720
  Salad
    and Cream, 533
    Banana Fan, 524
    Cranberry Juice, 531
    Frozen, 526
    Gelatin, 533
  Spiced, 726
Peachy Gelatin Salad, 533
Peanut(s)
  Bars, Hoosier, 654
  Blossoms, 649
  Brittle, 712
  Soup, Old-Fashioned, 189
  -Squash Pie, 433
  Sticks, 169
  French-Fried, 53
Peanutatoes, 426
Peanut Butter
  and Mayonnaise Sand-
    wich, 92
  and Tomato Soup, 194
  Balls, Dainty, 661
  Biscuits, 120
  Bread, 118
    Banana, 109
  Brownies, 654
  Date Fudge, 706

Fingers, 658
French Dressing, 541
Frosting, 625
Fudge, 706
Mousse, 690
Pie, 572
  Custard, 559
Sandwich
  and Pickle, 92
  and Prune, 92
  Orange, 92
Tomato and Bacon
  Squares, 80
Whirligigs, 652
Pea(s), 416
  and Celery, Tasty, 417
  Bean Soup, California, 177
  Black-Eyed. *See* Dried
    Beans, Peas and
    Lentils
  Casserole, English, 417
  Creole, 417
  Delicious, 417
  Dried. *See* Dried Beans,
    Peas and Lentils
  French, 417
  in Potato Nests, 426
  New, 416
  Salad, 514
  Soup, Cream of, 185
    Quick Curried, 194
  Split. *See* Split Pea
Pear(s)
  Honey, 723
  Maraschino Jam, 718
  Orange Bake, 695
  Peppermint, 696
  Preserves, 720
  Relish, 728
  Salad, Frozen, 526
Pecan
  and Pineapple Sandwich,
    95
  Bars, Topping for, 654
  Chocolate Frosting, 626
  Dainties, 643
  Penuche, 707
Pie
  Amber, 560
  Caramel Pumpkin, 560
  Chiffon, Mocha, 572
  Chocolate Cream, 566
  Georgia, 560
  Prize Sweet Potato, 562
  Pilaf, for Chicken, 271
  Poundcake, 604
  Puffs, Dick Morrow's, 648
  Roll, 708
  Rolls, 163–64
  Roquefort, 53
  Sauce, 449
  Sour Cream Salad Dress-
    ing, 544
Pedernales River Chili, 334
Peeket Potatoes, 422
Peking Roast, 309
Pennsylvania Pot Roast, 314
  Dutch Cucumbers, 513
Penuche, 705–9
  Icing, 628
  Pecan, 707

Rich, 707
Pepparkakor (Swedish Gin-
  ger Cookies), 636
Pepper
  Pot Soup, 173
  Relish, Jellied, 728
  Slaw, 729
  Steak, 310
Peppermint
  Bonbon Pie, 572
  Chocolate, Hot, 734
  Frosting, 627
  Pears, 696
Peppers
  and Eggs, Scrambled, 198
  Chili, Stuffed, 66
  Green. *See* Green Peppers
  Red. *See* Green Peppers
  Stuffed Pickled, 725
Peppy Low-Calorie Tomato
  Dressing, 543
  Shrimp Ring, 536
Perch, Baked Ocean, 228
  Maître d'hôtel, 228
Perfect Breakfast Muffins,
  125
Pie Pastry, 548
Persimmon Pudding, 673
Petits Millefeuilles, 580
Pfeffernüsse, 649
Pheasant. *See* Games Birds
  with Rice Stuffing, 297
Piccadilly Wax Beans, 391
Piccalilli, 729
Pickle Canapés, 84
Pickled
  Beet Relish, 457
  Beets, 723
  Dill Okra, 725
  Eggplant, 458
  Eggs, 60
  Figs, 725
  Peaches, 726
    Pink, 726
  Pig's Feet, 347
  Salted Herring, 62
  Shrimp, 253
  Spiced Salmon, 229–30
Pickles, Relishes and Con-
  diments
Catsup
  Grape, 730
  Prune, 730
  Tomato, 731
Chow-Chow, Quick Cab-
  bage, 727
Dilled Onion Rings, 725
Horseradish, 727
Kim Chee, 727
Pepper Slaw, 729
Piccalilli, 729
Pickled
  Beets, 723
  Dill Okra, 725
  Figs, 725
  Peaches, 679
    Pink, 680
Pickles
  Bread and Butter, 724
  Cauliflower, 723
  Crystal Sweet, 724

Pickles, Relishes and Con-
diments (Cont.)
Pickles (Cont.)
Green Tomato, Crisp,
725
Kosher Dill, 724
Montana, 724
Olive Oil, 724
Pineapple, 226
Sweet Dill, 725
Sweet Watermelon, 726
Relish
Cabbage and Beet, 727
Corn, 727
Corn, Sweet and Sour,
727
Green Peppers, 728
Hot Dogs, 728
Mrs. Sawyer's Boston,
729
Pear, 728
Pepper, 682
Hot Red, 728
Jellied, 728
Sweet Sour, 729
Uncooked Green To-
mato, 729
Sauce
Barbecue, 729
Chili, 730
Grandmother's, 730
Cranberry Apple, 730
Red, 730
Spiced
Beans, 726
Peaches, 726
Tomato Juice, 731
Stuffed Pickled Peppers,
725
Pie Fillings, 563–75
Pies and Pastries, 547–82
Ambrosia, 571
Angel Food, 563
Apple, Refrigerator, 563
Baking Temperatures for,
547
Banana Split, 564
Black Bottom, 564
Blueberry, Freshy's, 565
Butter Crust Parfait, 567
Cherry
Cheese, 565
Meringue-Topped, 566
Nut Parfait, 566
Chiffon
Coconut Pumpkin, 574
Sherry, 568
Lemon, 569
Mint, 570
Mocha Pecan, 572
Rum, 574
Chocolate Bar, 566
Coconut Butterscotch,
565
Cream
Angel Lemon, 569
Apricot, 563
Banana, 563
Bavarian, 564
Butterscotch, 563
Caramel, 563

Meringue, 565
Chocolate, 563
Pecan with Meringue
Topping, 566
Cocoa, 567
Coconut, 563
Date, 563
Neiman-Marcus, 564
Orange, 571
Pineapple, 573
Sherry, 575
Cream Cheese, 568
Chocolate Cream Cheese,
566
Crème de Menthe, 568,
691
Crustless, 576–77
Apple, Crumb-Topped,
576
Norwegian, 576
Brownie, 576
Cracker, 576
Coconut, 576
Custard, 576
Fudge, 577
Lemon Sponge, Amish
577
Macaroon, 576
Crusts, 548–53
Almond, 550
Butter, 549
Crunch, 550
Canadian, 549
Cereal Crunch, 550
Cheese, 549
Chocolate
Crumb, Baked, 551
Shell, 551
Wafer, 551
Coconut Macaroon, 551
Cooky, Rich, 550
Cream Cheese, 549
Gingersnap, 551
Graham Cracker, 551
Heirloom, 548
Hot Water, 548
Ice Cream, 552
Macaroon Crumb, 551
Meringue
5-Egg-White Fruit,
552
Nest, 552
Shell, 552
2-Egg-White Cooked,
552
Never-Fail, 548
Pantry Shelf, 550
for One Shell, 550
Perfect, 548
Puff, Flaky, 549
Rich, 549
Tart, 550
Vanilla Wafer, 551
Wheat, 551
Daiquiri, Frosted, 570
Danish, 568
Deep-Dish
Blueberry, 559
Cherry, 559
Peach, 559
Equipment for, 547

Failure, Causes of, 547
Fairy Tart, 569
French Silk, 567
Hollywood, 567
How to Make a Lattice-
Topped Pie, 547
How to Make a 1-Crust
Pie, 547
How to Make a Pie Shell,
547
How to Make a 2-Crust
Pie, 547
Huckleberry, Freshy's, 565
Ice Cream, 693
Washington Cherry, 692
Kentucky Bourbon, 565
Lemon, Carmelita's Fa-
vorite, 569
Heavenly, 569
Lemonade, Mile-High, 570
Lime, 570
Little Fried
Apple, 578
Apricot, 578
Macaroon, Holiday, 568
Meringue Toppings, 552
Nesselrode, Glamorous,
570
Nut, Washington, 562
1-Crust
Almond Custard, 558
Apple
Crumb, 555
Dutch, 555
French, 555
Paper Bag, 556
Buttermilk, 556
Lemon, 556
Butterscotch, Baked,
556
Caramel Pecan Pump-
kin, 560
Carrot, 556
Cherry, Dutch, 557
Chess, 557
Cranberry, New Eng-
land, 557
Cream Cheese, Minne-
sota Baked, 557
Custard, Velvety, 558
Date, Old English, 558
Egg Custard, 558
Fruit, Deep-Dish Fresh,
559
Gâteau St.-Honoré, 561
Lemon, 558
Chess, 557
Colonial, 558
Nut, Macadamia, 559
Oat Crumble Rhubarb,
561
Oatmeal, 559
Peach, Streusel Cream,
559
Peanut Butter Custard,
560
Pecan
Amber, 560
Georgia, 560
Sweet Potato, Prize,
562

Pies and Pastries (*Cont.*)
1-Crust (*Cont.*)
  Pineapple, 560
    Chess, 560
  Pumpkin, 560
  Rhubarb Cream, 516
  Shoofly, 562
  Sour Cream, Raisin, 518
    Walnut, 562
  Syrup, 562
  Orange Meringue, 571
  Parfait. *See* Parfait Pies
  Peach, 559
    Fried, 581
    Meringue, 571
    Rice, 572
  Peanut Butter, 572
  Peppermint Bonbon, 572
  Pineapple, 573
    Cheese Icebox, 573
      Sour Cream, 573
    Pumpkin, Frozen, 691
    Ice Cream, 693
  Raspberry, 575
    Minute, 575
    Pony, 574
  Strawberry
    Bavarian, 575
    Cheese, 575
    Fresh, 575
    Ice Cream, 694
    Mile-High, 691
    Minute, 575
  Tarts. *See* Tarts, Turn-
    overs and Small
    Pastries
  Turnovers. *See* Tarts,
    Turnovers and Small
    Pastries
2-Crust
  Apple
    Mock, 553
    Mom's, 553
    Rich, 553
  Apricot, 553
  Blueberry, 553
  Butterscotch Peach, 554
  Cherry, 553
  Concord Grape, Old-
    Fashioned, 554
  Cranberry Raisin, 554
  Orange, Early Set-
    tler's, 554
  Peach, Golden, 554
  Rhubarb and Lemon,
    555
    Custard, 555
  Tapioca Cherry, 554
Pies, Beef, Poultry and
  Vegetable, 320–24
  Beef, 324
  Cape Cod Lobster, 247
  Chesterfield, 499
  Chicken, 276
    and Oyster, 288
    Grandmother's, 276
    Sunday, 288
    with Sweet Potato
      Crust, 289
  Corn, 406
    Chip, 337

Deep-Dish Salmon, 231
Easy Crab, 244
Eggplant, 410
Farmer's, 331
Frijole, 336
Green Tomato, 436
Haddock Crumb, 226–27
Hominy, 466
Kennebunkport Clam, 239
Meat-a, 332
Meat Upside-Down, 335
Onion, 415
  Hamburger, 335
Oyster, 251
Shepherd, 338
  Lamb, 372
  with Beef, 332
Squash-Peanut, 433
Steak and Potato Pie,
  Cousin Jack, 324
Swiss Cheese, 214
Tamale, 336
Tamale Pork, 348
Pies, Dessert. *See* Pies and
  Pastries
Pigs' Feet, Pickled, 347
Pigs in Blankets (Oysters),
  70
Pike, Baked Northern, 228
Pilaf
  Barley, 467
  Bulgur, 468
  Chicken, 482
  Rice, 475
    Armenian, 475
  Turkish, 476
Pilau, Shrimp, 482
Pimiento
  and Nut Sandwich, 95
  Butter, 77, 80
  Cheese Sauce, 443
  Spread, 81
  Mushroom Sauce, Quick,
    447
Pineapple
  and Ham Kebabs, 61
  and Rice, 478
  Baked, 696
  Bread, 150
  Buttermilk Sherbet, 689
  Cakes
    Cream, 610
    Custard Filling for
      Lemon and Pine-
      apple White Cake,
      585
    Parfait, 599
    Quick, 608
    Upside-Down, 608
    White, and Lemon, 585
  Chantilly, 696
  Coconut Drop Cookies,
    599
  Crushed, 458
  Dessert, Frozen, 691
  Escalloped, 459
  Filling, 632
    Creamy, 632
    Orange, 632
  Fish Balls, Sweet Sour,
    223

Fritters, 459, 698
  Sauce for, 698
Frosting, 624
  Parfait, 627
Juice Cocktail, Minted, 48
Lemon Fluff, 685
Lemonade, 737
Mousse, 681
Mustard Sauce, 449
Nut Bread, 118
  Sandwich Spread, 84
Orange Jam, 718
Pickle, 726
Pie, 560, 573
Pie
  Cheese, Icebox, 573
  Chess, 560
  Cream, 563, 573
  Sour Cream, 573
Pudding, 674
Rolls, 164
Salad
  and Yellow Cheese, 526
  -Applesauce, 527
  Banana, 524
  Cabbage Nut, 534
  Cherry Cheese, 524
  Cottage Cheese, 530
  Cranberry, and Sour
    Cream, 531
  Cranberry Nut, 523
  Lime, 534
  Lime and Walnut,
    Frosted, 534
  Nut Ginger Ale, 534
  -Orange, Constant
    Comment, 535
  Sour Cream, 534
Salad Dressing, Cooked,
  for Fruit Salad, 546
Sandwich
  and Chicken, 91
  and Cream Cheese, 92
  and Pecan, 95
  Sauce, 449, 702
  Sweet Sour, 450
Strawberry Mold, 682
Tea, Spiced, 734
Torte, 618
Wrapped in Bacon, 70
Water Cress Cocktail, 48
Pink Arctic Salad, 525
  Devil Dip, 75
  Lemonade, 737
Pinto Beans. *See* Dried
  Beans, Peas and
  Lentils
Pinwheel
  Ham, 83
  Sandwich, 78
Piquant Sauce, 449
Pirohi, 461
Piroshki, 462
Pizza(s)
  Armenian, 100
  Burgers, 103
  Cocktail, 87
  Hamburger, 332
  Italian Style, 100
  Jumbo Sandwich, 100
  Quick, 101

Planked Steak, 310
Plantains, Fried, 387
Platanutri (Fried Plan-
tains), 387
Plättar (Swedish Pan-
cakes), 135
Plum
Jam, 719
Jelly Tarts, 581
English, 674
Pudding, Minute, 682
Rhubarb Conserve, 721
Torte, Vienna, 618
Poached
Chicken. See Chicken
Chop Suey
Chicken in the Pot
(Poule au Pot), 264
Egg, 197
Fish, 218
Shrimp, 253
Poinsettia Sandwich Loaf, 79
Fillings, 79
Polenta, 464
Mushroom, 464
Polish Coffee Bread, 152
Polka Dot Macaroons, 642
Rice, 475
Pollo in Umido con Polenta,
276
Polly's Baked Lamb Chops,
368
Polynesian Mingle, 475
Pompano
Broiled Fillets, 229
En Papillote, 229
Pone Pudding, Sweet Po-
tato, 676
Poor Man's Caviar, 61
Goose, 344
Popcorn
Buttered, 55
Herb Butter, 55
Candied, 710
Popovers, 131
Basic, 89
Bacon, 131
Cheese, 131
Herb, 131
No-Beat, 131
Yorkshire Pudding, 131
Poppy Seed
Bread, 118
Dressing for Fruit Salad,
542
Filling for Kolachky, 162
Smothered Chicken, 274
Pork
Pork and Bean(s)
Bake, Barbecued, 343
Baked, 469
Casserole, All-America,
346
Sandwich, 92
Open, 101
Pork and Beef Italian
Spaghetti Sauce, 507
Balls, Swedish, in Brown
Sauce, 348
Beef, and Ham Loaf, 353
Burgers, Barbecued, 105

Chinese Barbecued, 346
Chops, 343–46
à la Baudoin, 343
and Peach Barbecue
Skillet, 344
Apricot, 341
Crown, 342
Fresh Ham, 342
Glazed Loin, 342
Pig, 341
Suckling, 341
Ribs of Loin, 342
Tenderloins, Apple-
Stuffed, 343
with Rum, 342
Baked, 343
Casserole, German, 344
Chinese, 343
Cranberry, 344
Goose, Poor Man's, 344
Indonesian, 344–45
'n' Sweets, 345–46
Orange-Glazed, 344
Smothered, 345
Stuffed, 345
with Orange Stuffing,
345
with Prunes, 345
Chop Suey, American,
346
Chow Mein, 346
Cuts and How to Cook,
340
Fried Rice, 477
Gizo (Stew), 347
Ham. See Ham
Hawaiian, 346–47
Pickled Pigs' Feet, 347
Pie, Tamale, 348
Roasts, 341–43
Sarmi, 348
Sausage. See Sausage
Spareribs. See Spareribs
Stuffed Green Peppers,
357
Sub Gum, Chinese, 347
Chinese Shrimp, 347
Sweet and Sour, 347–48
Timetable for Cooking,
341
with Noodle Casserole,
495
Potage Crécy, 186
St. Germain, Quick, 194
Pot and Pan Dimensions, 34
Potato(es)
and Ham, Escalloped, 424
and Steak Pie, Cousin
Jack, 324
-Apple Meat Loaf, 328
au Gratin, 423
Baked, 419
with Russian Caviar, 420
Shoestring, 420
Stuffed, 420
with Chives, 420
Basic Ways to Cook, 419
Beer, 421
Boiled, 419
Burgers, 325
Casserole, 425

Egg and Salami, 425
Ham and Onion, 356
Chantilly, 425
Cottage, 424
-Fried, 419
Crab Meat Soufflé, 244
Delmonico, 425
Dishes
Cooked, 424
Mashed, 425–26
Raw, 222
Doughnuts, 140
Drop Dumplings, 462
Dumplings, Swedish, 462
Dutch, 426
Fondant, Mashed, 715
Franconia, 419
French-Fried, 419
Oven-Baked, 421
Gratin Dauphinoise, 423
Griddle Scones, 125
Herb Fried, 421
Latkes, 422
Lyonnaise, 419
Mashed, 419
à la Phyfe, 424
Mushrooms, Onions—au
Gratin, 423
Nests with Peas, 426
O'Brien, 422
Olive Creamed, 424
Oven Hashed Brown, 421
Pancakes, German, 422
Shallow-Fried, 422
Peanutatoes, 426
Peeket, 422
Pimiento, 423
Popovers, 141
Pudding, Lithuanian, 422
Puffs, 462
Cocktail, 70
Romanoff, 425
Salad, 516
and Shrimp in Tomato
Aspic, 539
Cottage Cheese, 516
Rich, 516
Sour Cream, 516
Egg, 517
Turkish, 517
Scalloped, 424
Sesame Spears, 421
Soufflé, 426
Soup
Bean, 117
Cream of, 185
and Leek, 189
French Peasant, 189
Golden, 189
Sour Cream, 190
Mushroom, 176
Spanish, 425
Spud 'n' Onion Bake, 420
Stewed, 424
Stuffed with Shrimp, 420
Stuffing for Chicken
Breasts, 280
Sweet. See Sweet Pota-
toes
Toasted, 421

Potato(es) (*Cont.*)
  with Green Beans in To-
    mato Sauce, 389
Pot-au-Feu, 173, 309
Pot Chicken in Casserole,
    279
Poteca (Polish Coffee
    Bread), 152
Pot Roast
  Bar-B-Cue, 313
  Beef
    à la Venison, 312
    and Vegetable Dinner,
      Lelah's Slow-
      Cooked, 314
    at Its Best, 312
    Superb, 312
    with Lemon Flavor,
      313–14
  Braised Sirloin Tip
    Roast, 312
  Dudie's Boeuf Flambé,
    312
  Oven Chuck Roast, 315
  Pennsylvania, 314
  Sauerbraten, 313
  Short Ribs of Beef, 314
    Barbecued, 314
  with Chocolate Sauce, 313
Pot-Roasted Wild Duck,
    298
Potted Rock Cornish Game
    Hens, 292
Poule au Pot (Poached
    Chicken), 264
Poulet Cintra, 284
Poultry. *See also* Chicken;
    Duck; Game Birds;
    Goose; Guinea Fowl;
    Rock Cornish Game
    Hens; Squab; Turkey
  and Rice Dishes, 482–85
  Hints, 17–18
  How to Buy, 260
  How to Carve, 261
  How to Store, 260
  How to Stuff, 452
  Partridge. *See* Game
    Birds
  Sauces for, 441–51
  Selecting, 260
  Servings and Pounds, 35
  Timetable for Roasting,
    261
  To Bone, 261
  To Draw, 260
  To Stuff and Truss, 261
  Types of, 260
Poundcake, 603
  Cherry, 603
  Chocolate, 603
  Old-Fashioned, 603
  Pecan, 604
  Raisin Honey, 604
  Sour Cream, 604
Pow-Wow Sandwiches, 101
Praline(s), 705–9
  Burnt Sugar, 708
  Candy Cookies, 709
  Powder, 663
  Raisin Coffee Cake, 605

Southern, 708
Preserved Horseradish, 727
Preserves, 716–30
  Amount of Sugar to Use,
    717
  Apple Butter, Aunt Mol-
    lie's, 723
  Apricot Conserve, 720
  Christmas Conserve, 721
  Jams. *See* Jams
  Jellies. *See* Jellies
  Jelly-Making Properties
    of Fruits, 717
  Melon Peach Conserve,
    721
  Mincemeat, Homemade,
    721
  Out-of-Season Jams, Jel-
    lies and Conserves,
    716
  Peach, 720
    Brandied, 720
    Nut Conserve, 721
  Pear, 720
    Honey, 723
  Plum Rhubarb Conserve,
    721
  Prune Chutney, Fresh,
    722
  Quince Honey, 723
  Rhubarb à la Conserve,
    721
  Rules for Successful Pre-
    serving, 716
  Sealing with Paraffin, 717
  Sterilizing Jars, 717
  Strawberry, 720
  Test for Acid, 717
  Tests for Jellying Stage,
    717
  Tests for Pectin, 716
  Types, 716
Pressed Chicken, 538
  Cookies, 645–50
Pressure Cooking, 39
Prime Short Ribs, 315
Prism Torte, 616
Prize
  Christmas Cranberry
    Salad, 531
  Strawberry Dessert, 675
  Sweet Potato Pecan Pie,
    562
  -Winning Date Squares,
    656
  -Winning Kansas Rocks,
    641
Projiteroles, 579
Pronto-Puppy Hors
    d'Oeuvres, 67
Prouts Neck Corn Coke, 112
Prune(s)
  and Peanut Butter Sand-
    wich, 92
  Cake, 600
  Catsup, 730
  Cookies, 644
  Icing, 625
  Filling for Kolachky, 162
    for Icelandic Vinartarta,
    588

Pudding, Norwegian, 696
Rye Muffins, 130
Stuffing, 454
  for Wild Goose, 299
Walnut Soufflé, 699
Whip, Seven-Minute, 696
  with Pork Chops, 345
Puddings
  Apple Butterscotch, 694
  Apricot Icebox, 681
  Baked, 664–76
    Apple Brown Betty, 672
    Crunch, 665
    Dumpling, Mother's,
      665
    in Biscuit Crust, 664
    Oat Pudding, 665
    Pandowdy, 665
    Roly-Poly, 666
    Spicy, 666
  Banana Casserole, 666
  Berry Cobbler, Fresh,
    666
  Blueberry, 667
  Boy Bait, 667
  Bread, 667
    Custard, 667
  Brown Sugar, 668
  Butterscotch Apple
    Crisp, 664
  Caramel Dumpling, 668
  Cherry Crunch, 668
    Muffin Cobbler, 668
    Rolls, 669
  Cranberry, 669
  Date, 670
    Squares, 670
    Upside-Down, 671
  Deep-Dish Fruit Cob-
    bler, 664
  Food for the Gods, 670
  Fruit Casserole,
    Mother's, 671
    Cocktail, 671
  Fudge, Hot, 669
    Quick, 669
  Grape-Nut, 671
  Green Mango Betty,
    672
  Halva (Wheat Pud-
    ding), 671
  Honey Apple Crisp, 665
  Indian, 672
    Fruited, 672
  Mulberry Cobbler, 672
  Noodle, 672
    Czechoslovakian-
    Style, 673
  Ozark, 666
  Peach Dessert, Speedy,
    673
    Festival Cobbler, 673
    -a-Berry Cobbler,
    673
  Persimmon, 373
  Pineapple, 674
  Queen of, 667
  Quick, 674
  Rhubarb, 675
    Crunch, 665
  Rhubarbettes, 675

Puddings (*Cont.*)
Baked (*Cont.*)
Strawberry Dessert,
Prize, 675
-Rhubarb Puffs, 675
Sweet Potato Pone
Pudding, 676
Tropical Crisp, 674
Upside-Down Cherry,
668
Woodford, 676
Cheese, 213
Chicken Bread, 289
Chocolate Icebox, 684
Corn, 406
Florida, 406
Cream, 679
French, 684
Hints, 18
Huckleberry, 695
Lithuanian Potato, 422
Macaroon Shimmy, 685
Noodle, 491
with Sour Cream, 491
Orange Icebox, 681
Oslo Almond, 676
Plum, Minute, 682
Norwegian, 696
Rice, Creamy, 678
Steamed, 664–76
Blueberry, 675
Chocolate, 669
Cranberry Molasses, 670
Fig, 670
Plum, English, 674
Raspberry, 675
Spiced Date, 670
Suet, Great-Great-
Grandmother's,
676
Sweet Potato, 429
Tapioca, Old-Fash-
ioned, 679
Tomato, 436
Puff, Cheese, 214
Pulled Mints, 711
Pumpkin
Bars, 659
Bread, 118
Raisin Nut, 118
Cookies, 645
Fanchonettes, 581
Pie, 560
Caramel Pecan, 560
Coconut Chiffon, 574
Frozen, 691
Ice Cream, 693
Seeds, Roast, 55
Punch
Alaska, 738
Apple, 738
Apricot, 739
Bowl Delight, 739
Cherry, 739
Christmas Cheer, 739
Party, 739
Coffee Chocolate, 741
Cream, 741
Vanilla, 741
Cranberry, 739
Hot Buttered, 735

Delicious Fruit, 739
Flemington Woman's
Club, 739
Grapefruit Mint, 740
Holiday, 740
Hot Cider, 735
Minted Fruit, 740
Rhubarb, 740
Snowy Night, 735
Strawberry, 740
Tea, 740
Wedding, 741
White, 741
Purée
Chestnut, 403
Mongole, 194
of Avocado, 386

Quail. *See* Game Birds
Queen Elizabeth Cake, 597
Queen of May Cake, 586
Queen of Puddings, 667
Quiche Lorraine, 214
Quiche Tartlets, 65
Quick
Cabbage Chow-Chow,
727
Chicken Cream Sauce,
443
Cinnamon Rolls, 160
Creole Sauce, 443
Custard Filling, 631
Dip 'n' Dunk, 76
Fudge Pudding, 669
Lemon Cake, 598
Mushroom Pimiento
Sauce, 447
Mushroom Soup Sauce,
447
Orange Cake, 599
Pineapple Cake, 600
Pizzas, 101
Pudding, 674
Shrimp Sauce, 449
Soups, 193–95
Spaghetti Sauce without
Meat, 506
Tomato Sauce, 451
Quickie Apple Cake, 596
Quince Honey, 723

Rabbit. *See also* Game
Rabbit Baked in Sour
Cream, 381
Radio Cake, 606
Radish, 429
Chinese Sweet and Sour,
459
Roses, 538. *See* Broccoli
Salad in Aspic
Ragalach (Hungarian
Cream Cheese Pastry),
580
Ragout of Beef with Onions,
321
of Veal, 363
Raised Bohemian Dum-
plings, 461
Biscuits, 158
Pancakes or Waffles, 165
Raisin

and Carrot Sandwich, 93
Banana Drops, 644
Bread, 150
Cookies, 649
Cranberry Pie, 554
Frosting, 625
Honey Poundcake, 604
Ice Cream Alaska, 692
Nut Bran Muffins, 127
Orange Sauce, 448
Pie, Sour Cream, 561
Praline Coffee Cake, 605
Rice, 475
Spice Bars, 659
Spice Cake, Eggless,
Milkless, Butterless,
601
Stuffing for Flank Steak
Roll, 318
Raisins and Beets, 393
Rancho Salad Dressing, 544
Rarebit, Bean, 470
Canapés, English, 88
Easy, 212
Mushroom, 213
Oyster, 213
Spanish, 212
Welsh, 211
with Beer, 211
Raspberry
and Cream Cheese Sand-
wich, 92
Cooler, 738
Cream, 678
Jam, 719
Jelly Sauce, 703
Mousse, 690
Pie, 574
Minute, 575
Pouf, 574
Pudding, Steamed, 675
Sauce, 702
Shrub, 738
Ratatouille (Vegetables
Stewed in Olive Oil),
439
Ravioli, with Cheese Filling,
497. *See also* Pasta
Real Irish Stew, 323
Really Roasted Corn on the
Cob Picnic Style, 404
Real Rich French Chocolate,
734
Reception Salad, 526
Red
Apple Slices, 456
Beet Aspic, 537
Cabbage, 397
Danish, 398
Grandma's, 398
Rotkraut, 397
Sweet and Sour Spiced,
398
Caviar Dip, 72
Chili Sauce, 443
Clam Sauce, 506
Devil, 212
Devil's Food, 592
Dip, 30
Fish Court Bouillon, 183
Flannel Hash, 316

Red (*Cont.*)
 Hot Sandwich, 107
 -Letter Day Torte, 617
 Pepper Relish, Jellied, 728
  Hot, 728
  See also Green Peppers
 Sauce, 730
 Snapper, Baked in Wine
  Sauce, 229
 Velvet Salad, 534
 Wine Aspic, 537
 Wine Sauce, 451
Refrigerator
 Apple Pie, 563
 Butter Cookies, 650
 Checkerboards, 652
 Chocolate Pinwheels, 651
 Cinnamon Crisps, 650
 Cookies, 650–52
 Fruit Nut Cookies, 651
 Orange Cookies, 651
 Overnight Coconut
  Cookies, 651
 Overnight German Cof-
  fee Kuchen, 152
 Ginger Muffins, 129
 Pastel Cookies, 652
 Pastel Pinwheels, 652
 Pastel Ribbons, 652
 Peanut Butter Whirli-
  gigs, 652
 Rolls, 158
  Potato, 158
 Soda Biscuits, 120
 Yeast Doughnuts, 166
Regal Butter Cake, 586
Relish
 Apple, 456
 Apple Cinnamon, 456
 Apple Fritters, 457
 Applesauce, 457
 Apricots, Golden Jellied,
  457
 Beans, Mustard Wax, 457
 Cranberries, Spiced, 458
 Cranberry, 457
 Cranberry Sauce, 458
 Fruits, Curried, 458
 Horseradish, 459
 Melanzane Satt Aceto
  (Pickled Eggplant),
  458
 Oranges, Baked, 458
 Peach Halves, Baked, 458
 Pickled Beet, 457
 Pineapple, Baked
  Crushed, 458
  Escalloped, 459
  Fritters, 459
 Radishes, Chinese Sweet
  and Sour, 459
 Red Apple Slices, 456
 Tomatoes, Fire and Ice,
  459
Relishes. *See* Pickles, Rel-
  ishes and Condiments
Rémoulade Sauce, 449
 Shrimp, 520
Ribbon Cookies, 652
 Sandwich, 78–79

Rice and Rice Dishes, 473–
  89
 Almond, 473
  Currant, 474
  Fried, 477
  Stuffing, 454
 and Cheese, Savory, 479
 and Cherries in the Snow,
  680
 and Chicken
  Chicken Bake, 482
  Peuffle, 483
  Pilaf, 482
  Rodger, 483
  in Foil, 483
  Supreme, 483
  with Chicken, Yellow,
   483
 and Eggplant on Parade,
  478
 and Mushroom Stuffing,
  455
 and Oysters, 482
 and Pineapple, 478
 Armenian, 474
 Baked, 473
 Banana Custard, 678
 Brazilian, 480
 Brown, 474
  Rhode Island Turkey
   Dressing, 455
 Calexico, 479
 Casserole
  and Beef, 486
  and Corn, 478
  and Vegetable, 479
  Cherokee, 486
  Chow, 485
  Company Chicken, 288
  Toasted, 478
 Cream, Danish, 682
 Creole, 484
 Croquettes, 477
 Curried, 474
  Indian, 474
  with Lamb Shanks, 369
 Dishes, Baked, 478–80
  with Fish or Seafood,
   480–82
  with Meat, 485–87
  with Poultry, 482–85
 Fluff, 485
 Fried, 476
  Croquettes, 478
  with Mushrooms and
   Almonds, 477
  with Shrimp, 477
 Fu Chu, 485
 Green, 474
  with Broccoli, 480
  with Cheese, 480
 Gum Soozle, 481
 How to Cook, 473
 Jambalaya, 481
 Jambalaya à la Creole,
  481
 Javanese Fried, 477
 Loaf Soufflé, Chicken,
  288
 Mexican, 475
 Milanese, 484

 Mold, Green, 480
 Muffins, 130
  Olympian, 486
 Paella con Vino, 484
 Pancakes, 135
 Pie, Peach, 572
 Pilaf, 475
  Armenian, 475
  Polka Dot, 475
  Polynesian Mingle, 475
  Pork Fried, 477
 Pudding, Creamy, 678
  New Eastern, 678
  Raisin, 475
 Ring, 476
  Pilaf, 480
 Risotto, 476
  All'erbe, 476
  with Meat, 486
 Russian Fluff, 487
 Salad, 517
  and Shrimp, 517
  Favorite, 517
  Ham and Cheese, 518
 Shrimp Pilau, 482
  Purlo, 482
 Sour Cream, 479
 Spanish, 479
  with Beef, 486
 Stuffed Baked Salmon,
  230
  Baked Tomatoes, 435
 Stuffing for Baked Salmon,
  230
  for Pheasant, 297
  Wild, for Game Hens,
   292
 Tomato Soup, 191
 Turkey Dinner, Bayou
  Leftover, 485
  Pom-Poms, 485
 Turkish Pilaf, 476
 Waikiki, 475
 Wild. *See* Wild Rice
  and Foie Gras Stuffing,
   456
 Yankee Fried, 476
Ricearoons, 642
Rich Apple Pie, 553
 Cooky Crust, 550
 Custard Filling, 631
 Dark Fudge Sauce, 701
 Eggnog, 741
 Penuche, 707
 Pie Pastry, 549
 Potato Salad, 516
Ricotta Cheese Filling for
  Ravioli, 497
Rigatoni, 498
 with Sausage, 502
 See also Pastas
Ring of Plenty, 502
Rinktum Diddie, 212
Ripe Olive Bean Bake, 470
Ris à la Mange (Danish
  Rice Cream), 682
Risotto, 476
 All'erbe, 476
 with Clams, 480
 with Meat, 486
Rivels, 196

Rhode Island Brown Rice
    Turkey Dressing, 455
    Johnny Cakes, 135
    Quahog Chowder, 182–83
Rhubarb
    à la Conserve, 721
    and Lemon Pie, 555
    Baked, 675
    Cake, Fresh, 600
    Cream Pie, 561
    Crunch, 665
    Custard Pie, 555, 574
    Dessert, 682
    Pie, Oat Crumble, 561
    Plum Conserve, 721
    Punch, 740
    -Strawberry Puffs, 675
    Salad, 536
Rhubarbettes, 675
Roast
    Beef, Rolled, 307
    Canadian Bacon, 352
    Chicken in Foil with
        Oyster Cracker Stuff-
        ing, 262
        with Pan Gravy, 262
    Fresh Ham, 342
    Goose, 294
    Grouse, 296
    Leg of Lamb, 365
    Partridge, 296–97
    Peppered Rib Eye, 308
    Pheasant with Apple
        Stuffing, 297
    Pig, 341
    Pork Tenderloin, Baked,
        342–43
    Pumpkin Seeds, 55
    Ribs of Pork Loin with
        Barbecue Sauce, 342
    Spareribs with Apple
        Stuffing, 350
    Squabs, 292–93
    Suckling Pig, 341
    Turkey, 293
    Watertown Goose, 294–95
    Whole Boneless Chicken
        with Wild Rice-Foie
        Gras Stuffing, 262
    Wild Duck, 298
        with Apples, 298
        with Rice, 298
Roasted Oysters, 249
Rock Cornish Game Hen,
    291–92
    Potted, 292
    Stuffed with Wild Rice,
        292
    with Bacon Stuffing, 291
    with Celery and Mush-
        room Dressing, 291
Rock Lobster Tetrazzini, 247
Rolled Cookies, 634–37
    Roast Beef, 307
    Stuffed Fillets, 222
    Wheat Cookies, 644
Rolls and Biscuits, Yeast,
    113–25
    See also Biscuits
    Babas, Little, 119
    Bacon, 42

Biscuits, 113
    How to Shape, 113
    Raised, 117
Buns
    Barbecue, 114
    Brown, 119
    Hot Cross, 121
    Saffron, 125
    Czechoslovakian Ko-
        lachky, 121
Rolls
    Basic Rich Sweet
        Dough, 119
    Batter, 115
    Brioches, 156
    Butter Horns, 120
    Butter Semmels, 116
    Buttermilk, 115
    Butterscotch, Dakota,
        120
    Cinnamon, Quick, 120
    Cloverleaf, 113, 114
    Croissants, 117
    Danish Pastries, 120
    French, 115
    How to Shape, 113
    Hungarian Pastries, 121
    Italian Bread Sticks, 115
    Krispie, 122
    Lemon Nut, 122
    Magyar Vajas Teszta or
        Knifli, 122
    Orange Yeast, 123
    Parkerhouse, 113, 114
    Party, Low-Calorie, 114
    Pecan, 123
    Pineapple, 124
    Refrigerator, 118
        Potato, 118
    Rum, 124
    Spoon, Half-Time, 116
    Squash, 117
    Sweet, 119
Roman Garlic Bread, 168
Ronda Jo's Salad, 520
Roquefort
    and Cream Cheese
        Spread, 80
    Ball, 59
    Cheese Dressing, Creamy,
        542
    Sandwich, 91
    Sticks, 55
    Crab Dip, 74
    Cream Cheese Rolls, 88
    Dressing, 544
    French Dressing, 541
    Pecans, 53
    Ring Salad, 535
    Walnuts, 53
Rosettes, 698
Rosy Cheese Ball, 59
Rotkraut (Red Cabbage),
    397–98
Round Steak Royale, 494
Royal Rusks, 124
Ruby Mountain Special Cas-
    serole, 336
Rules for Cooking, 24
Rullepolze (Spiced Meat),
    63

Rumaki (Oriental Chicken
    Livers), 65–66
Rum Balls, 662
    Cake, 589
    Cakes, 620
    Chiffon Pie, 574
    Rolls, 164
    Sauce, 703
        Hot, 703
    Syrup, for Rum Cake, 589
Russian Dressing, 545
    Fluff, 487
    Pancakes, Small (Blinis),
        165
    Stew, 323
    Tea, 734
Rye Bread, and Chestnut
    Filling for Turkey, 453
    Milwaukee, 147–48
    Swedish, 148

Sacher Torte, Vienna, 618
Saffron Buns, 164–65
    Crown Coffee Cake, 153
Saigon Tea, 734
Salade Verte, 509
Salads, 508–41
    Apple, 522
        Bacon, 522
    Applesauce Pineapple, 527
    Apricot, 527
        Nectar, 527
    Aspics. See Aspics
    Asparagus Cup, 527
    Avocado, 523
    Baked Ham, 356
    Banana Marshmallow, 528
    Bean, 509
        and Beets, 510
        and Vegetable, with
            Cream Mayon-
            naise, 512–15
        Crunchy, with Mayon-
            naise, 512
        Relish, 510
    Bowl, 511
    Broccoli in Aspic, 538
    Bulgarian, 512
    Cabbage, Twenty-Four-
        Hour, 510
        with Sweet Oil Dress-
            ing, 510
    Caesar, 508
        Daleen's, 508
    Canteloupe, Stuffed, 523
    Carrots, Marinated, 511
    Cauliflower, Turkish, 513
    Chicken, 520
        Almond, 520
        Baked, 289
        Curried, 521
        Elegant, 521
        Hawaiian, 521
        Macaroni, 516
        Sweetheart, 521
    Cinnamon Apple, Stuffed,
        522
    Coleslaw, Sour Cream, 513
        Texas, 511
    Corned Beef and Cabbage,
        522

Salads (*Cont.*)
Cottage Cheese Potato, 516
Crab, 518
Diablo, 518
Louie, 518
Ravigote, 518
Cranberry Apple, Frozen, 525
Nut, 530
Orange, 523
Cranberry Grape, 523
Pineapple Nut, 523
Crock, 512
Cucumbers, Pennsylvania Dutch, 513
in Sour Cream, 513
Dressings, 541–46
Blue Cheese, for Tossed Salad, 509
Sour Cream, 544
Buttermilk, Low-Calorie, 542
Catsup, 541
Cheese Frosting for Fruit Salad, 534
Orégano for Green Salad, 542
Chiffonade, 541
Cider, 543
Cinnamon Cream, 545
for Fruit Salads, 546
French. *See* French Dressings
Fruit, 546
Salad, Tangy, 542
Fruity Cream Cheese Topping, 545
Garlic, 542
Greek, for Raw Vegetables, 543
Green Goddess, 543
Green Goddess, Mrs. Hasebroock's, 543
Lemaize Sauce, 544
Lemon, for Fruit, 545
Mayonnaise, 543
Belgian, 543
No-Cook Boiled, 545
Normandy, 545
Old-Country Kitchen, 544
Pineapple, Cooked, for Fruit Salad, 546
Poppy Seed, for Fruit Salad, 542
Roquefort, 544
Cheese, Creamy, 542
Rancho, 544
Sour Cream, 544
Chili, 544
Pecan Dressing for Fruit Salads, 544
Special, for Seafood, 545
Sweet Oil, for Cabbage, 510
Thousand Island, 544
Coconut Grove, 544
Tomato, Peppy Low-Calorie, 543

Vinaigrette, with Olives, 542
Sauce Vinaigrette, 542
Frozen, 525–26
Fruit, 525
Ginger Ale, 525
Grape, 526
Peach, 526
Pear, 526
Pink Arctic, 525
Reception, 526
Fruit, 522–24
Summer Fresh, 524
Twenty-Four-Hour, 525
with Sour Cream, 524
Gilde (Roast Beef and Herring), 522
Grape-Cluster, Individual, 524
Greek, Louis Pappas' Famous, 511
Green
Tossed, 508
with Herring Dressing, 509
Green Bean and Bacon, 510
Green Goddess, 514
Greenest in Town, 509
Gurkensalat (Cucumbers in Sour Cream), 513
Ham and Peas, 522
High Hat, 524
Hints, 18
Hot Slaw, 512
Iceberg Lettuce, Stuffed, 514
Kidney Bean, Crunchy, 510
Lettuce, Wilted, 509
Lobster, 519
Macaroni, 515
Potato and Rice, 515–18
Seafood, 515
Tangy, 515
Molded, 526–37
Ambrosia, 526
Avocado, 528
Ring Mold, 528
Chicken and Sour Cream, 530
Egg, 529
Loaf, 529
Cinnamon Candy Apple, 526
Cottage Cheese Pineapple, 488
Tuna, 530
Cranberry, Prize Christmas, 531
Banana Special, 531
Juice Peach, 531
Party, 531
Pineapple and Sour Cream, 531
Coleslaw Soufflé, 528
Corned Beef, Congealed, 529
Cucumber, 532

Squares, Fresh, 532
Egg, Deviled, 532
Fruit, White, 536
Ginger Ale Pineapple Nut, 534
Lime Cottage Cheese with Shrimp, 535
Pineapple, 534
Lobster or Crab Ring, 532
Mrs. Eato's Speck, 530
My Favorite Summer, 533
Olive Wreath, 533
Orange Gelatin, 533
Water Chestnut, 533
Out of This World, 530
Party Pink Congealed, 532
Peaches and Cream, 533
Peachy Gelatin, 533
Pineapple Cabbage Nut, 534
Lime and Walnut, Frosted, 534
-Orange, Constant Comment, 535
Sour Cream, 534
Red Velvet, 534
Roquefort Ring, 535
Salmon, 535
Aspic, 539
Shrimp Egg, 536
Ring, Peppy, 536
Sour Cream Fruit, 535
Springtime, 532
Strawberries and Cream, 536
Strawberry Rhubarb, 536
Vegetable Delight, 528
"Watermelon-Feed," Arlette's Original, 536
Mousses. *See* Mousses
Mushroom, Susan's Raw, 511
and Lima Bean, 514
Onion, 514
Parsnip Chicken, 521
Pea, 514
Peach Banana Fan, 524
Pineapple Banana, 524
Cherry Cheese, 524
Potato, Rich, 516
Turkish, 517
Rice, 517
and Shrimp, 517
Favorite, 517
Ham and Cheese, 518
Roast Beef and Herring, 522
Rolls, Swiss, 514
Ronda Jo's, 520
Salmon and Eggs à la Wrigley, 519
Egg, 519
Fruit, 519
Salsa, 512
Sauerkraut, 512
Seafood Pierre, 519

Salads (*Cont.*)
Shrimp Arnaud, 519
Rémoulade, 520
Sour Cream Potato, 516
Egg, 517
Swedish Herring (Sill-salad), 517
Tokay Cucumber Relish, 523
Tomato, Italian, 512
Clowns, Stuffed, 515
Tuna Fish, 520
Mandarin, 520
Vegetable, Mixed, 515
Slaw, Triple, 513
Waldorf, 523
with Wheat, 468
Yellow Cheese and Pineapple, 526
Zucchini Tossed, 509
Salami Appetizer (Apple Pincushion), 57
Potato and Egg Casserole, 425
Salisbury Steak, 325
Salmon
Alaska Baked Fillets, 230
Alaskan Nuggets, 232
and Eggs à la Wrigley, 519
Aspic, 539
Avocado Canapés, 84–85
Biscuit Loaf, 237
Box, 230–31
Casserole, Spring, 231
Chowder, 184
Croquettes, 231
Cucumber Sauce for, 444
Egg Salad, 519
Fruit Salad, 519
Loaf, 232
Steamed, 232
with Shrimp Sauce, 232
Molded, 535
Mousse, 540
Pickled Spiced, 229
Pie, Deep-Dish, 231
Sandwich, 93
Grilled Cheese, 101
Smoked. *See* Smoked Salmon
Spread, 85
Steaks with Blue Cheese Sauce, 230
Stuffed Baked, 230
with Rice, 230
Swedish, in Aspic, 538
Tetrazzini, 231
Salsa, 512
Dip, 74
Salsify. *See* Oyster Plant
Sammye's Chocolate Frosting, 628
San Francisco Chicken and Spaghetti, 503
Sand Tarts, 636
Sandwich
Cooky, 639
Fillings
Carrot Peanut, 80

Cream Cheese and
Green Pepper, 79
Date Nut, 83
Deviled Ham, 79
Egg, 79
Egg Salad, 79
Olive Cheese, 80
Tuna, 79
Walnut Cheese, 79
Spread
Chutney, 723
Pineapple Nut, 84
Sandwiches, Hearty, 91–107
Cold
Bobette, 93
Caviar Open-Face, 94
Chicken Delight, 94
Cottage Cheese, 94
Cucumber, 94
Deviled Ham, 95
Egg and Cheese, 94
Fig, 94
Fresh Fruit, 94
He-Man, 93
Hero, 93
Heroes for Six, 93
Liver, 95
Liverwurst, 95
Cheese and Egg, 95
Marmalade, 95
Nut and Pineapple, 95
Open-Face Beef, 93
Sardine, 95
Shrimp, 95
Tongue, 95
Hot
Armenian Pizza, 100
Baby Submarine, 99
Baked Cheese, 96
Tuna, 102
Bar-B-Q, 98
Barbecued Ham, 98
Bun-ies, 96
Combination for Party, 97
Corned Beef, 97
Crab, 97
de Luxe Tuna, 102
Devonshire, 96
Egg, 98
French Rolls, 99
Grilled Applesauce and Bacon, 96
Heroine, 99
Ham and Cheese, 99
Soufflé, 99
Italian Open, 97
Jumbo Pizza, 100
Lullaby Special, 97
Monte Cristo, 99
Open-Face Cheese, 96
King Crab, 98
Open Pork and Bean, 101
Pizza Italian Style, 100
Pow-Wow, 101
Quick Pizza, 101
Salmon Grilled Cheese, 101
Sandwich Loaf, 101
Slumgullion, 99
Swedish Tamales, 102

Tacos, 102
Toasted Chicken, 97
Crab and Egg, 98
Party, 77–90
Checkerboard, 78
Cucumber, 83
Fiesta Ribbon, 78
Finger, 78
Fillings, 80
Hawaiian, 89
Lilies, 78
Mosaic, 78
Pinwheels, 78
Poinsettia Sandwich
Loaf, 79
Ribbon, 78
Suggestions
American Cheese Open Face, 91
Blue Cheese or Roquefort, 91
Bologna, 91
Cheddar Beef, 91
Cheese and Egg, 91
and Olive, 91
Chicken, 92
and Grape, 91
and Pineapple, 91
Corned Beef, 91
Cottage Cheese
and Bacon, 91
and Nuts, 91
Crab or Shrimp, 92
Cream Cheese
and Apple, 92
and Apricot, 92
and Cucumber, 92
and Date, 92
and Dried Beef, 92
and Pineapple, 92
and Raspberry, 92
Cucumber, 92
Egg, 92
and Olive, 92
Fish, 92
Frankfurter, 92
Ham, 92
Hamburger, 92. *See also* Beef Burgers; Burgers; Hamburgers
Liverwurst, 92
Meat, 92
Loaf, 92
Mushroom, 92
Orange Peanut Butter, 92
Pâté, 92
Peanut Butter
and Mayonnaise, 92
and Prune, 92
with Pickle, 92
Pork and Bean, 92
Raisin and Carrot, 93
Sardine, 93
Tomato Open Face, 93
Tuna or Salmon, 93
Sarah's Hulamagusha, 103
Sardine
Butter, 77
Canapés, 80
and Bacon, 90
Olive, 85

Sardine (*Cont.*)
Paddies, 232
Sandwich, 93
Open-Face, 95
Spread, 80
Sarmi, 348
Sauce Gribiche, 446
Sauces, Dessert, 700–3
Apricot, 159
Rum, 159
Caramel de Luxe, 700
Nut, 700
Chocolate Velvet, 701
Custard, for Suet Pudding, 676
Fudge, Hot, 701
Rich Dark, 701
Fruit, 701
Hard, 702
Ice Cream, 702
Lemon, 702
Pudding, 702
Mahogany, 702
Maple Butterscotch, 700
Melba, 695
for Ice Cream, 702
Molasses, Old-Fashioned, 702
Orange, 702
Custard, 702
Pineapple, 702
for Fritters, 698
Raspberry, 702
Jelly, 703
Rum, 703
Hot, 703
Sweet and Sour, for Banana Pancakes, 132
Vanilla, 703
Whipped Cream, 701
Frozen, 701
Honey, 701
with Sugar and Flavorings, 701
Sauces for Fish, Poultry, Meat and Vegetables, 441–51
à la Ritz, 446
and Gravy Hints, 18
Babcock, 442
Barbecue, 729
for Chicken, 268
for Fish, 221
for Lamb Croquettes, 442
for Roast Pork, 342
for Spareribs, Pork Chops and Chicken, 442
Béarnaise, 444
Blender Tomato, for Fish, 226
Blue Cheese, for Salmon, 230
Brandy, 700
Butter, 700
for Fish, Seafood and Vegetables, 442
Whipped, 700
Butterscotch, 700
Caper Cream, 441

Cardinale, for Lobster, 245
Cheese, 442
Cheddar, 441
for Moussaka, 332
Mornay, 441
Pimiento, 443
Chicken, 441
Chili, 730
Grandmother's, 730
Claret, 443
Cranberry, 458
Apple, 730
Cream, 441
Creole, 443
Cucumber, for Salmon, 444
Butter, for Fish, 444
Curry, 441
Deep-Sea, 444
Diablo, for Crab Salad, 518
Dipping, 75
Egg Cream, 441
Fish, 441
Five-Minute Tomato, 450
Gourmet, 444
Green, for Fish, 222
Gribiche, 446
Herb, 224
Cream, 441
Hollandaise, 444
Horseradish, for Fish, 444
Cream, 442
Hot Cranberry, for Ham, 443
Imperial for Crab, 243
Lemaize, 544
Lemon Butter, 444
Cuper Butter, 445
Parsley Butter, 445
Lobster, for Chicken, 283
Maison, for Steaks or Chops, 445
Marinara, for Lobster, 247
Mayonnaise
Blender, 445
Curry, 445
Garlic, 445
Herb, 445
Lemon, 445
Sauce Verte, 445
Cucumber, 445
Whole Egg, 445
Meat, 441
Mint, for Roast Lamb, 446
Mornay, 293
Pat's, 446
Mousseline for Cooked Vegetables, 446
Mushroom, 446
Easy, 447
Cream, 446
for Ham, 447
Velouté, 447
Mustard, 448
Cream, 442
Mayonnaise, 448
Sour Cream with Fish, 222
Tomato, 448
1916, for Ham, 445

Olive, 448
Onion, for Roast Beef, 448
Butter, for Steak, 448
Orange Raisin, 448
Oriental Marinade for Beef or Chicken, 445
Orono Barbecue, 442
Pecan, 449
Pineapple, 449
Mustard, 449
Piquant, 449
Quick Chicken Cream, 443
Creole, 443
Mushroom Pimiento, 447
Soup, 447
Shrimp, 449
Tomato, 451
Ravigote, 446
Red, 730
Chili, 443
Wine, 451
Rémoulade, 446, 449
Seafood Cocktail, 52–53
Sherry Cream, 442
for Glazed Broccoli, 394
Shrimp, for Salmon Loaf, 232
Skillet Tomato, for Fish, 222
Sour Cream, for Brussels Sprouts, 396
Caper for Fish, 450
No-Cook, 449
Sweet Sour, for Fried Chicken, 450
Hot, 450
Pineapple, 450
Tartar, for Fish, 450
Tartare, 446
Tart Cream Dressing for Vegetables, 449
Teriyaki, 450
for Chicken, 267
Tetrazzini, for Chicken, 503
Thermidor, for Lobster, 246
Tomato for Chicken, 268
Veronica, 451
Vinaigrette, 542
White
for Cream Soups, 185
Thick, Medium, Thin, 441
Wine
and Mushroom for Chicken, 282
for Game, 451
for Wild Goose or other Game, 451
Marinade, 445
Stock for Sauce, 229
Sauces for Pasta Dishes, 505–7
Beef Gravy for Spaghetti, 507
Clam
Red, 506
White, 506

Sauces for Pasta Dishes
(*Cont.*)
  Creole, with Macaroni
    Omelet, 499
  Garlic, 505
  Marinara, 505
  Spaghetti
    Carter's Special, 507
    French, 505
    Italian, 506
      With Beef and Pork,
        506
    Meat, 506
    Neapolitan, 506
    Oil and Garlic, 506
    Quick, Without Meat,
      506
  Tomato and Meat, 507
Sauerbraten (Spiced German
  Pot Roast), 313
  Slices, 338
Sauerkraut, 429
  and Frankfurter Bake,
    Grace's, 340
  and Split Peas, 430
  Appetizer, Deep Fried
    Corned Beef, 66
  Creamed, 430
  Juice Cocktail, 48
  Salad, 512
  Snacks, Bohemian, 56
  To Make, 430
Sausage, 356–57
  and Pea Soup with Egg
    Dumplings, 179
  Apple Stuffing, 455
  Bites, 90
  Cake, 614
  Corn Casserole, 357
  Donato Mix-Up, 357
  Grandfather's, 356
  Homemade, 356–57
  Loaf, 357
  Pork-Stuffed Green Pep-
    pers, 357
  Ring, 357
  Roll(s), 70, 90
  Toad in the Hole, 357
  with Rigatoni, 502
  with Wild Rice Casserole,
    489
Sautéed
  Abalone, 238
  Calf's Brains, 373
  Canapé Bases, 77
  Chicken Livers and Mush-
    rooms, 291
  Crab Cutlets, 241
  Eggs, 200
  Fish, 219
  Rainbow Trout, 235
  Scallops, 251
  Squid, 234
  Vegetables with Olives,
    438
Savory
  Baked Stew, 322
  Lima Bean Scallop, 470
  Rice and Cheese, 479
  Roast Leg of Lamb, 366
  Summer Squash, 432
  Wax Beans, 391

Scallop Stew, 184
Scalloped
  Beets, 393
  Cabbage and Cheese, 397
  Carrots and Celery, 400
  Celery, 402
  Cheese Tomatoes, 436
  Chicken, 279
  Corn and Oysters, 250–51
    with Cheese, 406
  Crab Meat, 244
  Eggplant, 408
  Eggs, 201
  Haddock, 226
  Ham and Macaroni, 502
  Liver, 375
  Onions with Cheese
    Sauce, 415
  Oysters, 250
  Potatoes, 424
  Squash, 432
  Sweet Potatoes and Apri-
    cots, 427
Scallops, 251–52
  Baked in Cream, 252
    in Shells, 252
  Broiled, 251
  Coquilles St. Jacques, 252
  in White Wine Sauce, 252
  Sautéed, 251
Scampi, 254
Scandinavian Almond
  Cooky, 635
Scones, Breakfast, 124–25
  Potato Griddle, 125
Scotch Broth, 172
  Woodcock, 203
Scottish Shortbread, 636
Scrapple, American, 465
Sea Burgers, 106
Seafoam Cantaloupe Tarts,
  579
  Frosting, 627
Seafood. *See also* Crab Meat;
  Fish; Lobster; Oyster;
  Shrimp
  Bisque, 190
  Butter Sauce for, 442
  Casserole
    and Artichoke, 257
    and Egg, 257
    Easy Down East, 257
  Cocktail(s), 50–53
    Mixed, 50
    Sauces, 52–53
  Dishes, Mixed, 257–58
  Gumbo with Chicken, 181
  Mousse Loaf, 541
  Pierre, 519
  Salad
    Macaroni, 515
    Spread, 85
  Shellfish Delight, 258
  Shrimp and Crab Meat
    Loaf, 258
  -Stuffed Eggplant, 257
  with Rice, 480–82
Seeds, 36–37
Semolina, 463
Senate Restaurant Bean
  Soup, 177

Senegalese Soup with Fresh
  Pineapple, 193
  Soup, Quick, 194
Serendipity Casserole, 432
Servings and Pounds, 34–36
Sesame
  Baked Chicken, 265
  Dogs, 107
  Egg Braids, 149
  Potato Spears, 421
  Seed Cookies, Italian, 649
Seven Minute Prune Whip,
  696
Seviche (Fish in Lime Juice),
  61
Shad
  Baked Celery-Stuffed, 233
  Roe, 233
    Baked in Foil, 233
    Poached in Butter, 233
Shallow-Fried Potato Pan-
  cakes, 422
Shellfish. *See also* Seafood;
  Individual Names
  Delight, 258
Shepherd Pie, 338
  Lamb, 372
  with Beef, 332
Sherbet
  Apricot, 687
  Lemon Lime, 689
  Jeweled Mold, 693
  Pineapple Buttermilk, 689
  Summer, 689
Sherried Chicken, 274
  Quail, 297–98
Sherry
  Cream Sauce, 442
  Cream Pie, 575
  Eggnog, 742
  Sauce, for Glazed Broc-
    coli, 394
Shiny Chocolate Frosting
  for Boston Cream Pie,
  629
Shirred Eggs, 199
Shish Kebab, 367
Shoestring Carrots, 399
Shoofly Pie, 562
Short Ribs of Beef, 314
Shortbread, Scottish, 636
Shortcake, Strawberry, 686
Shortcakes, Lamb, 372–73
Short'nin' Bread, 636
Shredded Wheat Bread, 148
Shredded Yams, 427
Shrimp
  and Crab Meat Loaf, 258
  and Cream Cheese
    Spread, 79
  Arnaud, 519
  Avocado Appetizer Cock-
    tail, 52
  Balls, 64
    with Sour Cream Caper
      Sauce, 71
  Barbecued, 70
  Bisque, 188
  Boat Burgers, 106
  Butter, 77, 85
  Butterfly, 70, 254
  Canapés, 85

Shrimp (*Cont.*)
Carnations, 85
Casserole, Adlai's Delight, 256
Chow Mein, 256
Chowder, 184
Cocktail, 52
Sauce, 53
Cooking for Cocktail, 52
Creole, 253
Curry, 255
de Jonghe, 255
di Sciulle, 254
Dip
Cocktail, 76
Creamy, 76
Hot, 76
Soup, 76
Eggs Foo Young, 200–1
Fiesta, 256
Fried, 254
in Beer, 64
Italiano, 254
Manhattan, 255
Marengo, 253
Marinated, 64
Newburg Style, 255
Pâté, Molded, 64
Pickled, 253
Pilau, 482
Poached, 253
Purlo, 482
Rémoulade, 520
Rice Biloxi, 481
Ring, Peppy, 536
Royale, 254
Salad
and Potato Salad in To-
mato Aspic, 539
Egg, 536
Rice and, 517
Sandwich, 92
Open-Face, 95
Sauce
for Fish Fillets, 222
for Salmon Loaf, 232
Quick, 449
with Curried Eggs, 204
Scampi, 254
Stuffed, 71
Fried, 255
-Stuffed Potatoes, 420
Sub Gum, Chinese. *See*
Chinese Sub Gum
Tempura, 254
Tetrazzini, 256
Thermidor, 256
to Butterfly, 253
to Clean, 253
Torrid, 64
with Eleanor's Baked
Avocado, 386
with Fried Rice, 477
Sillsallad (Swedish Herring
Salad), 517
Six-Minute "Boiled" Egg,
197
Sizzling Fish-Vegetable
Platter Bake, 220
Skillet Cereal Snacks, 662
Cookies, 662

Skillet Tomato Sauce for
Fish, 222
Slaw, Hot, 512
Pepper, 729
Sliced Breast of Turkey
Mornay on Toast, 293
Sloppy Joe Hamburgers, 104
Sloppy Joes, 104
Slumgullion Sandwich, 99
Small-family Gingerbread,
114
Smith College Fudge, 705
Smoked Salmon
and Caviar Canapés, 80
Cones, 63
Spread, Curried, 85
Smoky Cheese-Olive Dip, 73
Smothered Beef, 320
Pork Chops, 345
Snacks and Wafers. *See*
Cocktail Snacks and
Wafers
Snails, 258–59
Bourguignonne, 259
Snickerdoodle Coffee Cake,
606
Snickerdoodles, 650
Snowballs, 621
Snowdrops, 648
Snowy Night Punch, 735
Sodas, Ice Cream, 691
Soft Cooked Egg, 197
Gingerbread, 114
Sole. *See* Fish; Shellfish
Sopa de Fritos, 290
Sopapillas (Mexican Frit-
ters), 140
Soufflé(s)
Butternut Squash, 433
Carrot, 400
Cheese
Cheddar, 207
Omelet, 208
and Mushroom, 208
with Bread, 208
Chicken, 208
Rice Loaf, 288
Corn Meal, 465
Crab Meat Potato, 244
Sandwich, Hot, 208
Fish, with Pecan Sauce,
224
Ham, 355
Cheese, 209
How to Make Basic
Savory, 207
Noodle, with Creamed
Chicken Sauce, 493
Potato, 426
Salad, Coleslaw, 528
Sour Cream Omelet, 167
Spinach, 209
Sweet Potato, 429
Tomato, 436
Sweet Chocolate
Cold, 680
with Sauce, 699
Grand Marnier, 699
Omelette, 698
Orange Marmalade, 699
Walnut Prune, 699
Zucchini, 438

Soups, 170–96
Albondigas (Beef Ball),
171
Avgolernono (Greek
Lemon), 174
Baked Bean, 178
Bean, 177
with Chorizo, Spanish,
178
with Potatoes, 177
Beef
Muriel Humphrey's, 171
-Tomato, Autumn, 172
Vegetable, 172
Bisque
Chicken, 187
Crawfish, 187
Cream of Tomato, 190
Lobster, Shrimp or
Crab, 188
Seafood, 190
Borscht, 175
Bouillabaisse, 182
Cabbage, Sweet and Sour,
175
California Pea Bean, 177
Chicken
Noodle, 173
Easy, 173
Chowder
Bean, 178
Clam, 182
Crab Meat, 183
Manhattan, 182
New England Fish, 183
Rhode Island Quahog,
182
Cioppino, 182
Cold
Avocado, Iced, 191
Borscht, 191
Consommé, Jellied, 192
Fruit, Breakfast, 192
Norwegian, 192
Gazpacho, Tropical,
192
Senegalese, with Fresh
Pineapple, 193
Vegetable Salad, 192
Vichyssoise, 193
Consommé, 170–1
Madrilène, Hot, 171
Corn, 175
Cream
Avocado, 186
Duchess, 187
Elegant Cheese, 187
English, 186
Mulligatawny, 188
Peanut, Old-Fashioned,
189
Potage Crécy, 186
Potato and Leek, 189
French Peasant, 189
Golden, 189
Sour Cream, 190
Tomato Rice, 191
Velvet, 191
Cream of
Almond, 186
Asparagus, 185
Carrot, 186

Soups (*Cont.*)
  Cream of (*Cont.*)
    Cauliflower, 185
    Corn, 185
    Cucumber, 188
    Mushroom, 188
    Onion, 189
    Pea, 185
      Fresh, 187
    Potato, 185
    Spinach, 185
      Easy, 190
    Tomato, 185
      Bisque, 190
      Garden, 190
    Turnip, Calamity Jane, 191
  Egg Drop, 174
    Petal, Chinese, 174
  Filé for Gumbos, 180
  Fish Stew
    Lobster, 183
    Live, 183
    Oyster, 184
    Oyster Soup, 184
    Scallop, 184
  Garnishes, 195–96
  Gumbo(s)
    Chicken, 180
    Crab, 180
    Creole, 181
    French Filé, 180
    Oyster Filé, 180
    Seafood, with Chicken, 180
  Hamburger Bean Pot, 178
  Hints, 18–19
  Le Waterzoie (Belgian Chicken), 174
  Lentil, 180
  Lima Bean and Macaroni, 178
  Menudo (Mexican Tripe), 172
  Minestrone, 176
    Meatless, 176
  Mushroom Potato, 176
  of the Inner Sanctum, 177
  Onion, French, 176
  Oxtail, 172
  Pepper Pot, 173
  Pot-au-Feu, 173
  Quick
    Beef, Parisian, 193
    Canned Combinations, 193
    Cebolla-Frijoles, 193
    Claret, 194
    Crab Bisque, 194
    Curried Pea, 194
    Lenten, 194
    Peanut Butter and Tomato, 194
    Potage St. Germain, 194
    Purée Mongole, 194
    Senegalese, 194
    Tomato Asparagus, 195
    Mushroom Bisque, 195
  Red Fish Court Bouillon, 183
  Scotch Broth, 172

Split Pea
  Country, 179
  Green, 179
  or Lentil, 179
  with Egg Dumplings and Sausage, 179
Stock
  Beef, 170
  Chicken, 170
  Fish, 171
  Veal, 171
  Tomato, Clear, 176
  Turtle, 174
    Mock, 175
  Vegetable, 175
    Barley, 175
  Wonton, 174
Sour Cream
  and Chicken Salad, 530
  Bread
    Banana, 109
    Nut, 116
  Cake, Never-Fail Spice, 602
  Caper Sauce for Shrimp, 450
  Coffee Cake, 606
  Coleslaw, 513
  Corn Sticks, 128
  Crescents, 158
  Dip
    Anchovy, 71
    Avocado, 72
    Blue Cheese, 72
    Crab Meat Caper, 75
    Cucumber, 75
    Horseradish, 76
  Dressing, 544
    Blue Cheese, 544
    Chili, 544
    Pecan, for Fruit Salads, 544
  Fruit Mold, 535
  Fudge, 706
  Muffins, 128
  No-Cook Sauce, 449
  Pie
    Pineapple, 573
    Raisin, 561
    Walnut, 562
  Porcupines, 326
  Potato Soup, 190
  Poundcake, 604
  Rice, 479
  Salad
    Cranberry and Pineapple, 531
    Egg, 517
    Pineapple, 534
    Potato, 516
  Sauce for Brussels Sprouts, 396
  Soufflé Omelet, 206
  Sugar Cookies, 645
  Waffles, 136
Sour Milk
  Biscuits 120
  Bishop's Bread, 109
  Griddle Cakes, 135
Sourdough Pancakes, 165–66

South Carolina Barbecued Chicken, 266
South Sea Chicken, 287
Southern
  Browned Okra, 414
  Burgers, 103
  Caramel Cake, 594
  Corn Casserole, 405
  Pralines, 708
  -Style Eggplant, 410
Spaetzle, (German Parsley Dumplings) 462
Spaghetti, 502–5
  and Chicken, San Francisco, 503
  Casserole, All-in-One, 505
  Chicken Tetrazzini, 503
    Mrs. Stuart Symington's, 504
  Cuban, 504
  Deviled, 504
  Giovanni, 503
  Ring of Plenty, 502
  Sauces, 505–7
    Beef Gravy Sauce for, 507
    Carter's Special, 507
    French, 505
    Italian, 506
      with Beef and Pork, 507
    Meat, 506
    Neapolitan, 506
    Without Meat, Quick, 506
  With Meat Balls, 504
    Italian, 504
Spanish
  Bean Soup with Chorizo, 178–79
  Casserole
    Egg, 203
    Veal, 363
  Chicken, Grace Moore's, 274
  Corn Bread, 112
  Delight, 494
  Mackerel, Baked, 228
  Meat Balls, 327–28
  Omelet, 206–7
  Onions, 415
  Potatoes, 425
  Rarebit, 212
  Rice, 479
    with Beef, 486
  Tomatoes, 434
  Vanish Cheese Dumplings, 463
Spareribs, 348–50
  Baked, 348
    Barbecue, 348–49
    in Cherry Sauce, 349
  Cantonese, 349
  Dick Van Dyke, 349
  Oven, 349–50
  Roast, with Apple Stuffing, 350
  Western Barbecued, 349
Special Fruit-Nut Frosting, 629
  Salad Dressing for Seafood, 545

Special Fruit Nut Frosting
  (*Cont.*)
  Wild Rice, 487
Speedy Peach Dessert, 673
Spice Butter, 78
  -Crusted Ham, 351–52
  Raisin Bars, 659
Spiced
  Beans, 726
  Breakfast French Toast,
    167
  Cranberries, 458
  Cranberry Juice Cocktail,
    48
  Date Pudding, Steamed,
    670
  Nuts, 53
  Orange Wassail Bowl,
    735
  Peaches, 726
    Baked, 695
  Pineapple and Ham
    Kebabs, 61
  Pineapple Tea, 734
  Tomato Juice, 731
Spices, 36–37
Spicy Appetizer Frankfur-
    ter, 67
  Apple Pudding, 666
  Baked Beans, 470
  Marble Coffee Cake, 607
Spinach, 430
  and Chicken Filling for
    Ravioli, 498
  and Sour Cream, 430
  au Gratin, 431
  Baked, 430
  Braised, 430
  Casserole, Oklahoma, 431
  Dish, 431
  Loaf, 431
  Palo Alto, 430
  Parmesan, 431
  Soufflé, 209
  Soup, Cream of, 185
    Easy, 190
Split Pea(s)
  and Sauerkraut, 430
  Soup, 179
    and Sausage, with
      Dumplings, 179
    Country, 179
    Green, 179
Spongecake(s)
  Chocolate Roll, 611
  Jelly Roll, Old Fashioned,
    611
  Jiffy, 610
  Magic, 611
  Orange Roll, Mother's,
    611
  Pineapple Cream, 610
Sponge Candy, 713
Spoon Bread, 464
  Cheese, 464
  Mexican, with Cheese
    Topping, 465
  Old Virginia Buttermilk,
    464
Spoon Rolls, Half-Time, 156
Spreads, Canapé. *See also*
  Canapés and Party

Sandwiches, Canapé
  Butters
Avocado, 80
Cheddar Cheese and
  Chutney, 81
Chicken, 81
  Liver, 82
  Salad, 81
Coconut Tropical Dream,
  82
Corned Beef Egg, 82
Cottage Cheese with
  Olives and Pickles,
  86
Crab Meat, 82
Cream Cheese and Egg,
  81
Cream Cheese and Olive,
  79
  and Shrimp, 79
Curried Smoked Salmon,
  85
Danish Cream Vegetable,
  81
Goober Ham, 83
Ham, 79
Horseradish Tuna, 85
Liver Cheese, 84
Liver Pâté with Truffles,
  84
Lobster, 80
Mélange des Oeufs, 82
Oyster Sandwich, 84
Pimiento, 80
Pimiento Cheese, 81
Pineapple Nut Sandwich,
  84
Roquefort and Cream
  Cheese, 80
Salmon, 85
Sardine, 80
Strawberry Nut, 80
Zippy Corned Beef, 82
Spring Salmon Casserole,
  231
Springtime Salad, 532
Spritz Cookies, 650
Spud 'n' Onion Bake, 420
Squabs, Roast, 292–93
Squash
  Applesauce Scallop, 433
  Baked, 432
    Winter, with Walnuts,
    432
  Biscuits, 158
  Butternut Soufflé, 433
  Casserole, 433
    Serendipity, 432
  Colochi (Vegetable Stew),
    432
  Mexican. *See* Chayote
  -Peanut Pie, 433
  Savory Summer, 432
  Scalloped, 432
  Spice Cake, 603
  Stuffed Acorn, 434
  Timbales, 434
  Types of, 432
Squid, sautéed, 234
Standard Biscuits, 119
Standing Ribs of Beef, 307

Starlight Double Delight
  Cake, 592
Steak
  and Kidney Pie, 323–24
  and Potato Pie, Cousin
    Jack, 324
  Beef Stroganoff, 311
  Broiled, 309
  Easy Sukiyaki, 311
  Eileen's Bar-B-Q Flat
    Chuck Roast, 310
  Filet Mignon Semiramis,
    310
  Ham, Apple-Stuffed, 353
  How to Carve, 301–2
  London Broil with Claret
    Sauce, 310
  Luscious Lamb, 367
  Moose, 378
  Onion Butter Sauce for,
    448
  Oriental Flank, 310
  Pepper, 310
  Planked, 310
  Round, Royale, 494
  Sauce Maison for, 445
  Stuffed Ham, 353
  Stuffed Round, 318
  Supreme, Antelope, 378
  Tenderloin Tips in Bur-
    gundy, 311
  Vegetable-Stuffed, 319
  Venison, Casserole of, 379
Steamed
  Asparagus, 385
  Blueberry Pudding, 675
  Brown Bread, 110
  Chocolate Pudding, 669
  Clams, 238
  Cranberry Molasses Pud-
    ding, 670
  Fig Pudding, 670. *See*
    Steamed Cranberry
    Molasses Pudding
  Indian Bread, 115
  Puddings, 664–76
  Raspberry Pudding, 675
  Salmon Loaf, 232
  Spiced Date Pudding, 670
Stewed
  Chicken, 275–80
  Gooseberries, 695
  Onions, 415
  Potatoes, 424
  Tomatoes, 434
Stews, 320–24
  Armenian Lamb Shank,
    369
  Black Walnut, 322
  Chicken
    Chop Suey, 278
    Oriental, 278
    See also Chicken,
      Stewed
  English Beef, 322
  Fish. *See* Soups, Chow-
    ders, Stews
  Gizo (Pork), 347
  Hints, 18–19
  Lamb, 369–71

Stews (*Cont.*)
  Lamb (Cous-Cous), 370
    Flemish Carbonades, 322
    Gone-All Afternoon, 322
    Mama's Favorite Gulyas, 352
  Real Irish, 323
  Russian, 323
  Savory Baked, 322
  Vegetable, 432
  Venison, 380
Stir-and-Drop Sugar Cookies, 645
Stock, Clam, 537
Storing, Hints, 19
Strawberry(ies)
  and Cream Salad, 536
  Banana Dessert, 686
  Bavarian Cream, 682
  Cake Delicious, 600
  Easy Overnight Jam, 719
  Frosting, 625
  Frozen Dessert, 690
  Frozen Squares, 691
  Milk Shake, 742
  Mousse, 682, 690
  Nut Spread, 80
  Omelet with Sour Cream, 698
  Orange Cup, 50
  Pie
    Bavarian, 575
    Cheese, 575
    Fresh, 575
    Ice Cream, 694
    Mile-High, 691
    Minute, 575
  Pineapple Mold, 682
  Preserves, 720
  Prize Dessert, 675
  Punch, 740
  -Rhubarb Puffs, 675
  Rhubarb Salad, 536
  Shortcake, 686
  Tarts, 581
  Upside-Down Cake, 608
Streusel Cream Peach Pie, 559
  Filled Coffee Cake, 608
Stroganoff
  Beef Balls, 328
  Beef Liver, 375
  Beef with Tomato, 318
  Buns, 104
  Hamburger, 332–33
Strudel, Apple, Home Style, 577
Stuffed
  Acorn Squash, 434
  Baked Onions, 415
  Baked Potatoes, 420
    with Chives, 420
  Baked Salmon, 230
  Baked Tomatoes, with Anchovy, 435
  Beef, 308
  Cabbage Leaves, 330
  Cantaloupe Salad, 523
  Carrots, 399
  Celery Rings, 58

Cheese Balls, 65
Cinnamon Apple Salad, 522
Crabs à la Creole, 240
Eggplant, 410
Fillets of Fish, 221
Fried Shrimp, 255
Grape Leaves, 68
Green Peppers with Ham, 418
Ham, 351
  Steak, 353
Hot Dogs, 340
Iceberg Lettuce, 514
Lettuce, 62
Lobster Tails, 246
Meat Loaf, 329
Mushrooms, 413
  Baked, 413
Peppers, Best-Ever, 418
  Macaroni, 418
Pickled Peppers, 725
Pork Chops, 345
Potatoes with Shrimp, 420
Quahogs, 239
Round Steak, 318
Shrimp, 71
Tomato Clowns, 515
Stuffings and Garnishes for
    Fish, poultry, Meat and
    Vegetables, 452–59
  See also Dressings
  Apple, for Pheasant, 297
    for Doves, 296
    for Grouse, 296
    for Spareribs, 350
  Apricot, 452
  Bacon, 452
  Beef and Cabbage, for
    Roast Pig, 341
  Bread, 452
    for Beef, 317
    for Fish, 221
    for Pork Chops, 345
  Bulgur, 453
  Celery Dressing, 453
  Celery and Mushroom
    Dressing, 453
  Chestnut Dressing, 453
  Corn, 454
  Corn Bread Dressing, 454
  Crab Meat for Rolled Fil-
    lets, 222
    Deviled, for Shellfish, 241
    for Stuffed Fried
      Shrimp, 255
  for Celery, 58
  for Fish, 454
  Indian Bread, 453
  Orange, for Pork Chops, 345
  Oyster Cracker for Roast
    Chicken, 262
  Oyster Dressing, Bon
    Secour, 454
  Oyster, for Fish, 220
  Potato, with Chicken
    Breasts, 280
  Prune, 454
    for Wild Goose, 299

Raisin, for Flank Steak
    Roll, 318
Rice Almond, 454
Rice and Mushroom, 455
Rice, for Pheasant, 297
Rhode Island Brown Rice
    Turkey Dressing, 455
Rye Bread and Chestnut
    for Turkey, 453
Sausage Apple, 455
Tomato, 456
Water Chestnut, 455
Wild Rice, 455
  and Chestnut, 455
  and Foie Gras, 456
  and Oyster Dressing, 456
  for Chicken, 455
  for Game Hens, 292
Stzuddla Brod, 198
Sub Gum, Chinese, 347
Sub Gum Chow Mein, 290
Substitutions for Ingredients, 20
Succotash, 391
Suet Pudding, Great-Great-
    Grandmother's, 676
Sugar
  Caramelized, 663
  Cookies, 634
    Mrs. Eisenhower's, 634
    Sour Cream, 645
    Stir-and-Drop, 645
  Crinkles, 650
  Doughnuts, 138
  Frostings, 622
  Glaze for Lebkuchen, 657
  Lemon, 663
  Lime, 663
  Minted, 49
  Orange, 663
  Plum Cake, 600
  Syrup, 737
  Vanilla, 663
Sukiyaki, Easy, 311
Summer
  Fresh Fruit Salad, 524
  Sherbet, 689
  Squash. *See* Squash, 432
Sundaes, Frozen Chocolate, 692
Sunday Chicken, 265
Sunday Chicken Pie, 288
Sunday Nite Waffles, 138
Sunshine in the Snow, 681
Super Candied Sweet Pota-
    toes, 427
Super-Duper Buttermilk
    Pancakes, 132
Super Hamburgers, 104
Superb Crab Meat Casse-
    role, 242
Surprise Meringues, 642
Susan's Raw Mushroom
    Salad, 511
Swedish
  Coffee Braids, 153
  Cream Wafers, 637
  Ginger Cookies, 636
  Glögg, 736
  Herring Salad (Sillsallad), 517

Swedish (*Cont.*)
Limpa (Rye), 148
Meat Balls, 328
Ostraka (Cheese Custard), 215
Mustard, Hot, 448
Pancakes (Plättar), 135
Pastries, 582
Pork Balls in Brown Sauce, 348
Potato Dumplings, 462
Salmon in Aspic, 538
Tamales, 102
Veal Roast, 358
Sweet
Banana Pastry Puffs from India, 578
Chocolate Ice Cream Cups, 693
Dill Pickles, 725
Muffins, 125
Very, 125
Rolls, 159
Toppings, 622. *See also* Frostings
Watermelon Pickle, 726
Sweet and Sour. *See also* Sweet Sour
Cabbage Soup, 175
Corn Relish, 727
Meat Balls, 327
Pineapple Fish Balls, 223
Pork, 347–48
Radishes, Chinese, 459
Spiced Red Cabbage, 398
Sweet Potato(es)
and Apricots, Scalloped, 427
and Ham Roll, 354
and Orange Casserole, 428
Baconized, 427
Banana Casserole, 428
Biscuits, 124
Crust for Chicken Pie, 289
Ginger -Sherried, 428
How to Cook, 426
in Orange Cups, 427
on Half Shell, 426
Pecan Pie, Prize, 562
Pone, 428
Pudding, 429
Pone, 676
Ring, 429
Soufflé, 429
Super Candied, 427
Tipsy, 428
Tropical, 428
Yam Goodies, Louisiana, 428
Yams, Shredded, 427
Sweet Sour. *See also* Sweet and Sour
Pineapple Sauce, 450
Relish, 729
Sauce for Fried Chicken, 450
Sweetbreads
and Chicken, Cream of, 279
Baked, 376
Broiled, 376
Creamed, 376

Croquettes, 376
Versailles, 377
Sweetheart Chicken Salad, 521
Coffee Cake, 153
Swiss
Chard, 403
Cheese Pie, 214
Fondue, 211
with Sauterne, 211
Loaf, 330
Salad Rolls, 514
Steak, 319
Sticks (Baguettes de Berne), 58–59
Swordfish Steak, Charcoal—Grilled, 235
Syrian Lamb and Wheat Patties, 371
Syrup
Caramel, 663
Chocolate, 737
for Hot Chocolate, 733
for Canning Fruit, 40
Pie, 562
rum, for Rum Cake, 589
Sugar, 737

Tabasco Jelly, 720
Table of Calories, 26–33
of Measurements, 22
of Nutrients, 26
Tab Ulee (Salad with Wheat), 468
Tacos, 102, 337–38
Taffies, 710. *See also* Candy
Taffy Pulling, 704
White, 711
Tangy Brussels Sprouts, 396
Fruit Salad Dressing, 542
Macaroni Salad, 515
Tapioca Cherry Pie, 554
Pudding, Old-Fashioned, 679
Tarragon Aspic, 537
Tarry-Hi Banana Fritters, 139
Tart Cream Dressing for Vegetables, 449
Tarta Baba, 590
Tartar Sauce, for Fish, 450
Hot, 450
Tartare Sauce, 446
Tarts, Turnovers and Small Pastries, 577–82
Apple Pie, Little Fried, 578
Slices, 577
Strudel Home Style, 577
Apricot Pie, Little Fried, 535
Turnovers, 578
Banana Pastry Puffs, Sweet, from India, 578
Banbury, 578
Blueberry, 578
Butter, 579
Cantaloupe, Seafoam, 579
Cherry, 579
Cream Puffs, 579
Lemon-Filled, 580

Eclairs, 580
Fairy, 569
Kolachey (Fruit Turnovers), 162
Napoleons, 580
Nut-Filled Horns, 581
Pastry, 550
Peach Pies, Fried, 581
Petits Millefeuilles, 580
Plum Jelly, 581
Profiteroles, 579
Pumpkin Fanchonettes (Tartlets), 581
Ragalach, 580
Shells, Baked, 550
Strawberry, 581
Swedish Pastries, 582
Teatime Tassies, 579
Walnut, 582
Tasty Peas and Celery, 417
Tea, 732
Beef, 733
Iced, 732
Lemon, 737
Punch, 740
Russian, 734
Saigon, 734
Spiced Pineapple, 734
to Make, 732
Tea Loaf, Mincemeat, 589
Teatime Tassies, 579
Tenderloin Tips in Burgundy, 311
Teriyaki Sauce, 450
for Chicken, 267
Terrapin, 259. *See also* Turtle à la Maryland, 259
How to Prepare Diamond-Back, 259
Tetrazzini Sauce for Chicken, 503
Texas Bar-B-Que Burgers, 104
Coleslaw, 511
Hash, 333
Thermidor Sauce, 246
Thick White Sauce (Sauce Béchamel), 441
Thin White Sauce, 441
Thousand Island Dressing, 544
Coconut Grove, 544
Three Fruits Marmalade, 722
Three-Minute Water Dumplings, 461
Timbales, Cauliflower, 401
Codfish, 225
Ham, 355
Squash, 434
Tipsy Mushrooms, 63
Sweet Potatoes, 428
Toad in the Hole, 357
Toasted
Butter Pecan Cake, 587
Chicken Sandwich, 97
Crab and Egg Sandwich, 98
Croutons, 195
Herb Loaf, 168
Potatoes, 421

Toasted (*Cont.*)
  Rice Casserole, 478
Toffees, 711–12
  Bars, Crisp, 659
  Butter, 712
  Chocolate, English, 712
  Creamy, 711
  English, 679
Tokay Cucumber Relish
  Salad, 523
Tom and Jerry, Mary's, 737
Tomale Casserole, 336
  Pie, 336–37
  Pork Pie, 348
Tomato(es)
  Anchovy-Stuffed Baked,
    435
  and Black-Eyed Peas, 470
  and Eggplant, 409
  and Meat Sauce, 507
  and Onions, Fried, Green,
    414
  Asparagus Soup, Quick,
    195
  Aspic, Best, 539
    Shrimp and Potato
      Salad in, 539
  Baked, 435
    Stuffed with Rice, 435
    with Crab Meat Filling,
      435
  -Beef Soup, Autumn, 172
  Bread, 119
  Broiled with French
    Dressing, 435
  Canning, 41
  Catsup, 731
  Cheese Whirls, 124
  Clowns, Stuffed, 515
  Dressing, Peppy Low-
    Calorie, 543
  Eggs and, 200
  Fire and Ice, 459
  Fried, 434
  Juice, Canning, 41
    Cocktail, 48
    Spiced, 731
  Mushroom Bisque, Quick,
    195
  Open Face Sandwich, 93
  Orange Juice Cocktail, 48
  Peanut Butter and Bacon
    Squares, 80
  Pickles, Green, 725
  Pie, Green, 436
  Pudding, 436
  Relish, Green, Uncooked,
    729
  Rice Soup, 191
  Salad, Italian, 512
  Sauce, Five-Minute, 450
    for Dorothy's Easy
      Baked Chicken,
      268
    Mustard, 448
    Quick, 451
    Skillet, for Baked
      Fillets, 222
    with Haddock Fillets
      Provençale, 226
  Scalloped Cheese, 436

Soufflé, 436
Soup, Clear, 176–77
  Cream of, 185, 190–91
    Garden, 190
  Iced, 192
  Quick Peanut Butter
    and, 194
  Rice, 191
  Spanish, 434
  Stewed, 434
  Stuffing, 456
  Toddy, Hot, 736
  with Cheese Balls, 539
Tongue and Cheese Hors
  d'Oeuvres, 64
  Baked, 377
  Beef, 377
  Braised Beef, 378
  Jellied Neat's (Boiled,
    Smoked), 377
  Open-Face Sandwich, 96
Top o' the Range Omelet,
  207
Topping, Brown Sugar for
  Queen Elizabeth Cake,
  597
  Nut, for Lazy Daisy Cake,
  589
  Nut, for Sour Cream
    Coffee Cake, 606
  Pecan for Pecan Bars, 654
  See also Glazes and Top-
    pings; Frostings
Torrid Shrimp, 64
Torte
  Bits and Pieces, 616
  Black Forest, 617
  Blitz, 616
  Blueberry, 616
  Brazil Nut, 619
  Chocolate, Lili, 617
  Fruit, 618
  Hello Dolly, 618
  Kiss, 697
  Pineapple, 618
  Plum, Vienna, 618
  Prism, 616
  Red-Letter-Day, 617
  Vienna Sacher, 618
  Walnut, 619
  Walnut, Hungarian, 619
Tortillas, 136
  for Tacos, 337–38
Tossed Salad, 508
  Blue Cheese Dressing for,
    509
  Zucchini, 509
Traditional Lebkuchen, 657
Trifle, 686
Tripe Soup, Mexican, 172
Triple Vegetable Slaw, 513
Tropical Cake, 612
  Crisp, 674
  Dates, 715
  Gazpacho, 192
  Sweet Potatoes, 428
Trout
  Baked, 235
  Broiled, 235
  Gulf Coast, 235
  Sautéed Rainbow, 235

Tuna
  Bake with Cheese Swirls,
    236
  Biscuit Loaf, 237
  Burgers, 106
  Casserole, 237
    Noodle, 237
  Cottage Cheese Salad, 530
  Crab Canapés, Hot, 90
  Fish Salad, 520
  Fritters, 236
  Horseradish Spread, 85
  Luncheon Yum-Yums,
    236
  Noodle Casserole, 492
  Olive Bites, 90
  Polynesian, 237
  Salad, Mandarin, 520
  Sandwich, 93
    Baked, 102
    de Luxe, 102
    Filling, 79
  Terrapin, 236
Turkey
  Amandine, 293
  and Wild Rice Ring, 489
  Baked, 293
  Cashew Casserole, 294
  Cauliflower Salad, 513
  Croquettes, 294
  Curried, 294
  in Foil, 293
  Mornay on Toast, Sliced
    Breast of, 293–94
  Paste, 709
  Pilaf, 476
  Potato Salad, 517
  Rhode Island Brown Rice
    Dressing for, 455
  Rice Dinner, Bayou
    Leftover, 485
  Rice Pom-Poms, 485
  Roast, 293
  Rye Bread and Chestnut
    Filling for, 453
  See also Chicken
Turkish Beef with Okra,
  333
Turnip(s), 436
  and Apple Casserole, 437
  Balls, 437
  Cabbage, 411
  Fluff, 437
  Greens. *See* Greens
  Puffs in Green Peppers,
    437
  Soup, Calamity Jane
    Cream of, 191
Turnovers. *See* Tarts, Turn-
  overs and Small Pastries
Turtle
  See also Terrapin
  with Sauce Piquant, 259
  Soup, 174–75
    Mock, 175
Twenty-Four-Hour Cabbage
  Salad, 510
  Fruit Salad with Custard
    Dressing, 525
    with Sour Cream, 524

Two-Egg-White Cooked
    Meringue, 552

Uncooked Green Tomato
    Relish, 729
Upside-Down
    Apricot Muffins, 126
    Cake, 608–9
        Apple, 608
        Cherry, 608
        Pineapple, 608
        Strawberry, 608
    Casserole, Macaroni
        Hamburger, 501
    Cherry Pudding, 668
    Date Pudding, 671
    Lemon Cups, 677
    Orange Biscuits, 124
    Pie, Meat, 335
    Vegetable Cake, 439

Vanilla Butter Frosting, 624
    Caramels, 710
    Coffee Punch, 741
    Frosting for Children's
        Delight, 655
    Glaze, 629
    Ice Cream, 687
    Sauce, 703
    Sugar, 663
    Wafer Crumb Cake, 588
        Pie Crust, 551
Veal
    and Ham Pâté, 62
    and Mushrooms Neapoli-
        tan, 364
    au Crème Aigre (with
        Sour Cream), 359
    Birds, 359
    Blanquette de Veau, 362
    Calabrese Style, 362
    Casserole, Spanish, 363
    Chops, Arabian, 361
        Flavorful, 361
    Cutlets, 359
        Cordon Bleu, 359
    Delight, Mrs. Cutler's,
        362
    Escalopes de Veau, 360
    Fricassee, 362
    German Stuffed Breast
        of, 358
    Goulash, 363
    Jellied, 362
    Kidneys, Flambé, 374
    Loaf, 364
        with Mashed Potatoes,
        364
    Madeleine, 363
    Paprika Wiener Schnitzel,
        361
    Parmesan, 360
    Pâté, Stock for, 171
    Ragoût of 363
    Roast, Swedish, 358
    Scallops, 360
    Scaloppine, 360
    Stock, 171
    Timetable for Cooking,
        358
    Veneto, 360

Wiener Schnitzel, 361
    Holstein, 361
Wisconsin Casserole, 363
Zurich, 358
Vegetable(s), 383–40. See
    also Individual Names
    Alaskan Mixed, 438
    and Rice Casserole, 479
    Beer Batter for Frying,
        383
    Cake, Upside-Down, 439
    Creole, 439
    Delight Salad, 528
    -Fish Platter Bake,
        Sizzling, 220–21
    Frying Batter for, 383
    Hints, 19–20
    Macédoine of, 439
    Medley, 439
    Ratatouille, 439
    Salad, Mixed, 515
    Sauces for, 441–51
    Sautéed, with Olives, 438
    Servings and Pounds,
        35–36
    Slaw, Triple, 513
    Soup, 175
        Barley, 175
        Beef, 172
        Salad, 192
    Stew, 432
    Stewed in Olive Oil, 439
    -Stuffed Steak, 319
    Tart Cream Dressing, 449
Velvet Chocolate Sauce, 701
    Soup, 191
Velvety Custard Pie, 558
Venison. See Game
Vermont Baked Beans, 469
Veronica, Sauce, 451
Very Fluffy Chocolate Cake,
    591
Vichyssoise, 193
Vienna Cake, 586
    Frosting, 625
    Plum Torte, 618
    Sacher Torte, 618
Viennese Specials, 637
Vinaigrette Dressing with
    Olives, 542
    Sauce, 542
Vintage Chicken, 275
Vitamin Carrots, 400

Waffles, Master Mix for, 120
    See also Pancakes and
    Waffles
Waikiki Rice, 475
Waldorf Salad, 523
Walnut(s)
    Appetizer (Black Rose-
        buds), 54
    Apple Filling for Cocoa
        Cake, 593
    Cake
        Filled Cocoa, 593
        Wonder, 590
    Cheese Sandwich Filling,
        79
    Clusters, Mrs. Nixon's,
        638

Honey Loaf, 119
Ice Cream Roll, 694
    Minted, 709
    Orange Cream, 709
    Pie, Sour Cream, 562
Pineapple and Lime Salad,
    Frosted, 534
Prune Soufflé, 699
Roquefort, 53
Tarts, 582
Torte, 619
    Hungarian, 619
Washington Cherry Ice
    Cream Pie, 692
Water Chestnut(s), 437
    Fritters, 437
    Salad, Orange, 533
    Stuffing, 455
    with Noodles, 492
Water Cress Butter, 78
    Pineapple Cocktail, 48
Water Dumplings, Three-
    Minute, 461
Watermelon Cocktail, 50
    -Feed Salad, Arlette's
        Original, 536
    Pickle, Sweet, 726
Waterzoie, Le (Belgian
    Chicken Soup), 174
Nut Pie, 562
Wedding Punch, 741
    White, 741
Welsh Rarebit, 211
    with Beer, 211
Western Barbecued Spare-
    ribs, 349
What Makes What?, 21
Wheat
    Cookies, Rolled, 644
    Cracked. See Bulgur
    Crust, 551
    Pudding, 671
Whipped Butter, 700
Whipped Cream, 663
    Frosting, Chocolate, 625
    Frozen, 701
    Honey, 701
    Sauce, 701
    Soft, 663
    to Flavor, 663
    to Store, 663
    with Sugar and Flavor-
        ings, 701
White
    Buttermilk, 585
    Cakes, 585–86
        for Two, 585
    Clam Sauce, 506
    Fruitcake, 613
    Fruit Salad, 536
    Nut Bread, 116
    Sauce
        for Cream Soups, 185
        Medium, 441
        Thick, 441
        Thin, 441
    Taffy, 711
    Water Bread, 145
    Wedding Punch, 741
    Wine Aspic, 537
Whole Egg Mayonnaise, 445

Whole Wheat
  Bread, 148–49
    Nut, 116
  Buttermilk Waffles, 138
  Pancakes, 132
Whoopie Cooky Pies, 639
Wiener Schnitzel, 361
  Holstein, 361
  Paprika, 361
Wild Duck. *See* Game Birds
Wild Rice, 487–89
  and Oyster Dressing, 456
  and Turkey Ring, 489
  Casserole, 488
    and Chicken, 488
    with Sausage, 489
  Consommé, 487
  Hot Dish, 488
  Ring Mold, 488
  Special, 487
  Stuffing, 455
    Chestnut, 455
    Foie Gras, 456
    for Chicken, 455
    for Game Hens, 292
    See also Stuffings
  to Cook Indian Style, 487
Wild West Hamburgers, 325

Wilted Lettuce, 509
Wimpies, 105
Wine, 732
  Aspic, Red, 537
    White, 537
  Bishop, The, 736
  Cookery Chart, 37–38
  Filling, Flavorful, 632
  Jelly, 683
  Marinade, 445
  Meat Balls, 69
  Sauce for Game, 451
    for Wild Goose or
      Other Game, 451
    Mushroom for Chicken,
      282
    Red, 451
  Stock to Cook Fish. *See*
    Pickled Spiced Sal-
    mon, 229
Wines and Spirits in
  Cooking, 37
Winkum, 212
Winter Squash. *See* Squash
Wisconsin Casserole, 363
Wontons, 196
  Fried, 71
  Soup, 174

Woodchucks, 647
Woodford Pudding, 676

Yale Beets, 393
Yams, Shredded, 427
Yankee Fried Rice, 476
Year-Round Jam, 719
Yellow Cheese and Pine-
  apple Salad, 526
Yorkshire Pudding, 131
Yuletide Coconut Balls, 646

Zabaglione, 679
Zesty Carrots, 400
Zippy Corned Beef Spread,
  82
Zucchini, 437–39. *See also*
  Squash
  and Beef Casserole, 333
  and Noodles Italiano, 496
  and Peppers, 438
  Casserole, Baked, 438
  in Skillet, 437
  Roma, 438
  Scrambled Eggs and, 198
  Soufflé, 438
  Tossed Salad, 509